ABSOLUTE
JAVA™ **3**rd Edition

ABSOLUTE
JAVA™ **3**rd Edition

Walter Savitch

University of California, San Diego

PEARSON

Addison
Wesley

Boston San Francisco New York
London Toronto Sydney Tokyo Singapore Madrid
Mexico City Munich Paris Cape Town Hong Kong Montreal

Publisher	Greg Tobin
Executive Editor	Michael Hirsch
Acquisitions Editor	Matt Goldstein
Manager, Product Development	Pat Mahtani
Editorial Assistant	Maurene Goo
Associate Managing Editor	Jeffrey Holcomb
Digital Assets Manager	Marianne Groth
Senior Media Producer	Bethany Tidd
Senior Marketing Manager	Michelle Brown
Marketing Assistant	Sarah Milmore
Senior Manufacturing Buyer	Carol Melville
Media Manufacturing Buyer	Ginny Michaud
Production Coordination, Composition, and Illustrations	Argosy Publishing

If you purchased this book within the United States or Canada, you should be aware that it has been wrongfully imported without the approval of the Publisher or the Author

Many of the designations used by manufacturers and sellers to distinguish their products are claimed as trademarks. Where those designations appear in this book, and Addison-Wesley was aware of a trademark claim, the designations have been printed in initial caps or all caps.

The interior of this book was composed in Adobe FrameMaker.

ISBN-13: 978-0-321-50504-0
ISBN-10: 0-321-50504-2

1 2 3 4 5 6 7 8 9 10—CRW—11 10 09 08 07

Preface

This book is designed to serve as a textbook and reference for programming in the Java language. Although it does include programming techniques, it is organized around the features of the Java language rather than any particular curriculum of programming techniques. The main audience I had in mind when writing this book was undergraduate students who have not had extensive programming experience with the Java language. As such, it would be a suitable Java text or reference for either a first programming course or a later computer science course that uses Java. This book is designed to accommodate a wide range of users. The beginning chapters are written at a level that is accessible to beginners, while the boxed sections of those chapters serve to quickly introduce more experienced programmers to basic Java syntax. Later chapters are still designed to be accessible, but are written at a level suitable for students who have progressed to these more advanced topics.

CHANGES IN THIS EDITION

If you have not used the second edition of this text, you can skip this subsection. If you have used the second edition, this subsection will tell you how this third edition differs from the second. For instructors, the transition from the second to this third edition is easy. You can teach the same course, presenting the same topics in the same order with no changes in the material covered or the chapters assigned. The changes to this edition consist almost exclusively of supplementary material added to the chapters of the previous edition. Additional new programming projects and programming examples have been added at various places in the text. Additional material on debugging has been added to Chapter 3. The discussion of linked lists and of sets in Chapters 15 have been expanded. Material on hash tables has also been added to Chapter 15. Chapter 16 which covers the Java Collection classes has been expanded. Specifically, additional material on the HashSet<T> class has been added and a more detailed section on maps as been added. Also, a brief introduction to sockets has been added to the final chapter.

NO NONSTANDARD SOFTWARE

Only classes in the standard Java libraries are used. No nonstandard software is used anywhere in the book.

JAVA COVERAGE

All programs have been tested with both Java version 5.0 and a beta release of Java version 6.0. Moreover, Sun is not proposing any changes in Java 6.0 that would affect the approach in this book. Therefore, we expect the book to be fully compatible with Java 6.0.

v

OBJECT-ORIENTED PROGRAMMING

This book gives extensive coverage of encapsulation, inheritance, and polymorphism as realized in the Java language. The chapters on Swing GUIs provide coverage of and extensive practice with event driven programming. A chapter on UML and patterns gives additional coverage of OOP-related material.

FLEXIBILITY IN TOPIC ORDERING

This book allows instructors wide latitude in reordering the material. This is important if a book is to serve as a reference. It is also in keeping with my philosophy of writing books that accommodate themselves to an instructors style rather than tying the instructor to an authors personal preference of topic ordering. With this in mind, each chapter has a prerequisite section at the start of the chapter; it explains what material must be covered before doing each section of the chapter. Starred sections, which are explained next, further add to flexibility.

STARRED SECTIONS

Each chapter has a number of starred (✩) sections, which can be considered optional sections. These sections contain material that beginners might find difficult and that can be omitted or delayed without hurting the continuity of the text. It is hoped that eventually the reader would return and cover this material. For more advanced students, the starred sections should not be viewed as optional.

ACCESSIBLE TO STUDENTS

It is not enough for a book to present the right topics in the right order. It is not even enough for it to be clear and correct when read by an instructor or other expert. The material needs to be presented in a way that is accessible to the person who does not yet know the material. Like my other textbooks that have proven to be very popular with students, this book was written to be friendly and accessible to the student.

SUMMARY BOXES

Each major point is summarized in a short boxed section. These boxed sections are spread throughout each chapter. They serve as summaries of the material, as a quick reference source, and as a way to quickly learn the Java syntax for features the reader knows about in general but for which he or she needs to know the Java particulars.

SELF-TEST EXERCISES

Each chapter contains numerous Self-Test Exercises at strategic points in the chapter. Complete answers for all the Self-Test Exercises are given at the end of each chapter.

OTHER FEATURES

Pitfall sections, programming tip sections, and examples of complete programs with sample I/O are given throughout each chapter. Each chapter ends with a summary section and a collection of programming projects suitable to assign to students.

MYCODEMATE ONLINE TUTORIAL RESOURCE

MyCodeMate is an online resource that provides tutorial help and evaluation of student work on programming projects. The code displays and selected programming projects in this edition have been fully integrated into MyCodeMate. Using MyCodeMate, a student can get hints on programming projects, write and compile the project, and receive feedback on how to address compiler errors messages, and all this can be done over the Internet from any computer with Internet access. Instructors can track each student's progress and review submitted programming projects. A complimentary subscription is offered when an access code is bundled with a new copy of this text. Subscriptions may also be purchased online. For more information on MyCodeMate, go to

```
www.mycodemate.com
```

SUPPORT MATERIAL

The following support materials are available to all users of this book at www.aw-bc.com/cssupport:

- Source code from the book
- PowerPoint® slides

The following resources are available to qualified instructors only. Please contact your local sales representative or send e-mail to computing@aw.com for access information:

- Instructor access to Addison-Wesley's MyCodeMate
- Instructors Manual with Solutions
- PowerPoint Slides

CD

The CD that accompanies this book contains:

- The source code for all the code displays in the book
- A copy of the Java version 5.0 Software Development Kit, which includes a Java 5.0 compiler
- A copy of the Java version 6.0 Software Development Kit, which includes a Java 6.0 compiler
- Several popular Java integrated development environments (see the CD for a complete listing).
- Chapter 20, "Applets and HTML"

OBTAINING JAVA

The CD that accompanies this book contains free copies of both the Java version 5.0 Software Development Kit (which includes a Java 5.0 compiler) and the Java version 6.0 Software Development Kit (which includes a Java 6.0 compiler). You also need an IDE (integrated development environment) or at least an editor. There are a number of elaborate IDEs available. However, weve found that a simple IDE works best for beginning student since it presents fewer distractions from the task of designing programs. We recommend the TextPad environment or any similarly simple IDE. A free trial copy of TextPad for Windows is included on the CD that accompanies this book.

ACKNOWLEDGMENTS

Numerous individuals have contributed invaluable help and support in making this book happen: My former editor Susan Hartman at Addison-Wesley first conceived of the idea for this book and worked with me on the first editions; My current editor Matt Goldstein provided support and inspiration for getting the second and this third edition reviewed, revised, and out the door; Maurene Goo, Bethany Tidd, Joyce Wells, Jeff Holcomb, Michelle Brown, and the other fine people at Addison-Wesley also provided valuable support and encouragement. A special thanks to Patty Mahtani at Addison-Wesley. She was an inspiration as well as an indispensable help.

Thanks to Kathleen Kenny and Nancy Kotary at Argosy Publishing for their expert work in producing the final typeset book.

The following reviewers provided corrections and suggestions for this edition of the book. I thank them for their contributions. In alphabetical order they are:

Tom Brown	Texas A&M University, Commerce
Janet Brown-Sederberg	Massasoit Community College
Charlotte Busch	Texas A&M University, Corpus Christi
KY Daisy Fan	Cornell University
Ahmad Ghafarian	North Georgia College & State University
Edwin Kay	Lehigh University
Neil Rhodes	University of California, San Diego
Tom Smith	Skidmore College
Thomas VanDrunen	Wheaton College
Shon Vick	University of Maryland, Baltimore County

The following reviewers provided corrections and suggestions for earlier editions of this book. Their contributions were a great help. I thank them all. In alphabetical order they are:

Jim Adams	Chandler-Gilbert Community College
Gerald W. Adkins	Georgia College & State University

Dr. Bay Arinze	Drexel University
Prof. Richard G. Baldwin	Austin Community College
Kevin Bierre	Rochester Institute of Technology
Jon Bjornstad	Gavilan College
Stephen Chandler	NW Shoals Community College
Adrienne Decker	University of Buffalo
Arthur Geis	College of DuPage
Massoud Ghyam	University of Southern California
Nigel Gwee	Louisiana State University
Judy Hankins	Middle Tennessee State University
Chris Howard	DeVry University
Eliot Jacobson	University of California, Santa Barbara
Balaji Janamanchi	Texas Tech University
Suresh Kalathur	Boston University
Dr. Clifford R. Kettemborough	IT Consultant and Professor
Frank Levey	Manatee Community College
Xia Lin	Drexel University
Mark M. Meysenburg	Doane College
Sridhar P. Nerur	The University of Texas at Arlington
Hoang M. Nguyen	Deanza College
Rick Ord	University of California, San Diego
Prof. Bryson R. Payne	North Georgia College & State University
David Primeaux	VA Commonwealth University
W. Brent Seales	University of Kentucky
Riyaz Sikora	The University of Texas at Arlington
Jeff Six	University of Delaware
Xueqing (Clare) Tang	Governors State University
Ronald F. Taylor	Wright State University
Natalie S. Wear	University of South Florida
Dale Welch	University of West Florida
Wook-Sung Yoo	Gannon University

A special thanks goes to Kenrick Mock (University of Alaska) who executed the updating of this edition. He had the difficult job of satisfying me, the editor, and himself. I thank him for a truly excellent job.

Walter Savitch

Feature Walkthrough

Summary Boxes

These boxes provide a brief synopsis of major points in each chapter, both highlighting and reinforcing core concepts throughout the book. Readers will find them to be a handy, quick reference for Java syntax and features.

It sounds as though Java byte-code just adds an extra step in the process. Why not write compilers that translate directly from Java to the machine language for your particular computer? That is what is done for most other programming languages. However, Java byte-code makes your Java program very portable. After you compile your Java program into byte-code, you can use that byte-code on any computer. When you run your program on another type of computer, you do not need to recompile it. This means that you can send your byte-code over the Internet to another computer and have it easily run on that computer. This is one of the reasons Java is good for Internet applications. Of course, every kind of computer must have its own byte-code interpreter, but these interpreters are simple programs when compared to a compiler.

Byte-Code

The Java compiler translates your Java program into a language called **byte-code**, which is the machine language for a fictitious computer. It is easy to translate this byte-code into the machine language of any particular computer. Each type of computer will have its own interpreter that translates and executes byte-code instructions.

Self-Test Exercises

1. If the following statement were used in a Java program, it would cause something to be written to the screen. What would it cause to be written to the screen?

   `System.out.println("Java is not a drink.");`

2. Give a statement or statements that can be used in a Java program to write the following to the screen:

   `I like Java.`
   `You like tea.`

3. Write a complete Java program that uses `System.out.println` to output the following to the screen when run:

   `Hello World!`

   Note that you do not need to fully understand all the details of the program in order to write the program. You can simply follow the model of the program in Display 1.1.

Self-Test Exercises and Answers

Strategically placed within each chapter, Self-Test Exercises offer readers an opportunity to assess their mastery of key topics.

Answers to Self-Test Exercises

1. All the methods in Display 18.1. If there is no particular action that you want the method to perform, you can give the method an empty body.

2. The smaller window goes away but the larger window stays. This is the default action for the close-window button and we did not change it for the smaller window.

3. `dispose`

4. The import statements are the same as in Display 18.2. The rest of the definition follows. This definition is in the file `WindowListenerDemo3` on the accompanying CD.

extra code
on CD

Detailed answers are provided at the end of the chapter.

Code Displays

There are abundant code listings through-out the text. Informal comments that explain potentially confusing or difficult portions appear alongside the code. Key lines are highlighted and color-coding visually distinguishes comments and reserved words (blue).

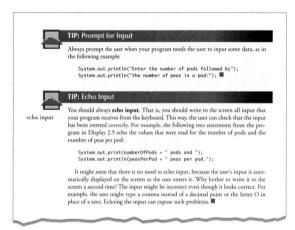

Display 2.6 Keyboard Input Demonstration

```java
1   import java.util.Scanner;                              Makes the Scanner class available to
                                                           your program.
2   public class ScannerDemo
3   {
4       public static void main(String[] args)             Creates an object of the class
5       {                                                  Scanner and names the
6           Scanner keyboard = new Scanner(System.in);     object keyboard.

7           System.out.println("Enter the number of pods followed by");
8           System.out.println("the number of peas in a pod:");
9           int numberOfPods = keyboard.nextInt();         Each reads one int
10          int peasPerPod = keyboard.nextInt();           from the keyboard

11          int totalNumberOfPeas = numberOfPods*peasPerPod;

12          System.out.print(numberOfPods + " pods and ");
13          System.out.print(peasPerPod + " peas per pod.");
14          System.out.println("The total number of peas = "
15                                      + totalNumberOfPeas);
16      }
17  }
```

TIP: Prompt for Input

Always prompt the user when your program needs the user to input some data, as in the following example:

```java
System.out.println("Enter the number of pods followed by");
System.out.println("the number of peas in a pod:"); ■
```

TIP: Echo Input

echo input

You should always **echo input**. That is, you should write to the screen all input that your program receives from the keyboard. This way, the user can check that the input has been entered correctly. For example, the following two statements from the program in Display 2.9 echo the values that were read for the number of pods and the number of peas per pod:

```java
System.out.print(numberOfPods + " pods and ");
System.out.println(peasPerPod + " peas per pod.");
```

It might seem that there is no need to echo input, because the user's input is auto-matically displayed on the screen as the user enters it. Why bother to write it to the screen a second time? The input might be incorrect even though it looks correct. For example, the user might type a comma instead of a decimal point or the letter O in place of a zero. Echoing the input can expose such problems. ■

Tips

These helpful hints instruct readers on best programming practices. The author explains the rationale behind these prac-tices and includes suggestions on how to execute them effectively.

Pitfalls

These sections warn of common mistakes that can trip up beginning programmers and offer advice on how to avoid them.

 PITFALL: Dealing with the Line Terminator, '\n'

The method nextLine of the class Scanner reads the *remainder* of a line of text *starting wherever the last keyboard reading left off.* For example, suppose you create an object of the class Scanner as follows:

```
Scanner keyboard = new Scanner(System.in);
```

and suppose you continue with the following code:

```
int n = keyboard.nextInt();
String s1 = keyboard.nextLine();
String s2 = keyboard.nextLine();
```

Now, assume that the input typed on the keyboard is:

```
2 heads are
better than
1 head.
```

This sets the value of the variable n to 2, that of the variable s1 to " heads are", and that of the variable s2 to "better than".

So far there are no problems, but suppose the input were instead

```
2
heads are better than
1 head.
```

You might expect the value of n to be set to 2, the value of the variable s1 to "heads are better than", and that of the variable s2 to "1 head.". But that is not what happens.

What actually happens is that the value of the variable n is set to 2, that of the variable s1 is set to the empty string, and that of the variable s2 to "heads are better than". The method nextInt reads the 2 but does not read the end-of-line character '\n'. So the first nextLine invocation reads the rest of the line that contains the 2. There is nothing more on that line (except for '\n'), so nextLine returns the empty string. The second invocation of nextLine begins on the next line and reads "heads are better than".

When combining different methods for reading from the keyboard, you sometimes have to include an extra invocation of nextLine to get rid of the end of a line (to get rid of a '\n'). This is illustrated in Display 2.8. ∎

Examples

These sections usually feature a complete program that solves a specific problem. The code examples are lengthier than in the standard code displays and highlight useful features of Java.

EXAMPLE: A GUI with a Label and Color

Display 17.6 shows a class for GUIs with a label and a background color. We have already discussed the use of color for this window. The label is used to display the text string "Close-window button works." The label is created as follows:

```
JLabel aLabel = new JLabel("Close-window button works.");
```

The label is added to the JFrame with the method add as shown in the following line from Display 17.6:

```
add(aLabel);
```

The GUI class ColoredWindow in Display 17.6 programs the close-window button as follows:

```
setDefaultCloseOperation(JFrame.EXIT_ON_CLOSE);
```

This way, when the user clicks the close-window button, the program ends. Note that if the program has more than one window, as it does in Display 17.6, and the user clicks the close-window button in any one window of the class ColoredWindow, then the entire program ends and all windows go away.

Note that we set the title of the JFrame by making it an argument to super rather than an argument to setTitle. This is another common way to set the title of a JFrame.

If you run the program DemoColoredWindow in Display 17.6, then the two windows will be placed one on top of the other. To see both windows, you need to use your mouse to move the top window.

Chapter Summaries

This end-of-chapter tool provides a concise overview of the fundamental concepts presented in the chapter.

Chapter Summary

* Late binding (also called dynamic binding) means that the decision of which version of a method is appropriate is decided at run time. Java uses late binding.

* Polymorphism means using the process of late binding to allow different objects to use different method actions for the same method name. *Polymorphism* is essentially another word for late binding.

* You can assign an object of a derived class to a variable of its base class (or any ancestor class), but you cannot do the reverse.

* If you add the modifier final to the definition of a method, that indicates that the method may not be redefined in a derived class. If you add the modifier final to the definition of a class, that indicates that the class may not be used as a base class to derive other classes.

* An abstract method serves as a placeholder for a method that will be fully defined in a descendent class.

* An abstract class is a class with one or more abstract methods.

* An abstract class is designed to be used as a base class to derive other classes. You cannot create an object of an abstract class type (unless it is an object of some concrete descendent class).

* An abstract class is a type. You can have variables whose type is an abstract class and you can have parameters whose type is an abstract type.

Programming Projects

Found at the end of each chapter, Programming Projects challenge readers to design and implement a Java program to solve a problem. Example solutions for all programming projects are available to instructors.

Programming Projects

 Many of these Programming Projects can be solved using AW's MyCodeMate. To access these please go to: www.mycodemate.com.

1. In Programming Project 3 from Chapter 7 the Alien class was rewritten to use inheritance. The rewritten Alien class should be made abstract since there will never be a need to create an instance of it, only its derived classes. Change this to an abstract class and also make the getDamage method an abstract method. Test the class from your main method to ensure that it still operates as expected.

MyCodeMate

MyCodeMate brings end-of-chapter programming projects to life. Working online, students can view, compile, run, and edit select programming problems as well as all code listings from the textbook. Best of all, MyCodeMate's tutorial feedback helps students work through common programming errors, improving their programming skills. An automated gradebook allows instructors to assign MyCodeMate problems and track student progress online.

 7. Define a class named MultiItemSale that represents a sale of multiple items of type Sale given in Display 8.1 (or of the types of any of its descendent classes). The class MultiItemSale will have an instance variable whose type is Sale[], which will be used as a partially filled array. There will also be another instance variable of type int that keeps track of how much of this array is currently used. The exact details on methods and other instance variables, if any, are up to you. Use this class in a program that obtains information for items of type Sale and of type DiscountSale (Display 8.2) and computes the total bill for the list of items sold.

Brief Contents

Contents

Getting Started

1

1 Getting Started

She starts—she moves—she seems to feel
The thrill of life along her keel.

HENRY WADSWORTH LONGFELLOW, *The Building of the Ship*

Introduction

This chapter introduces you to the Java language and gives you enough details to allow you to write simple programs involving expressions, assignments, and console output. The details about assignments and expressions are similar to that of most other high-level languages. Every language has its own way of handling strings and console output, so even the experienced programmer should look at that material. Even if you are already an experienced programmer in some language other than Java, you should read at least the subsection entitled "A Sample Java Application Program" in Section 1.1 and preferably all of Section 1.2, and you should read all of Section 1.3 on strings and at least skim Section 1.4 to find out about Java defined constants and comments.

Prerequisites

This book is self-contained and requires no preparation other than some simple high school algebra.

1.1 Introduction to Java

Eliminating the middle man is not necessarily a good idea.

Found in my old economics class notes

In this section we give you an overview of the Java programming language.

Origins of the Java Language ★

Java is well-known as a programming language for Internet applications. However, this book, and many other books and programmers, view Java as a general-purpose programming language that is suitable for most any application whether it involves the Internet or not. The first version of Java was neither of these things, but it evolved into both of these things.

In 1991, James Gosling led a team at Sun Microsystems that developed the first version of Java (which was not yet called *Java*). This first version of the language was designed for programming home appliances, such as washing machines and television sets. Although that may not be a very glamorous application area, it is no easy task to design such a language. Home appliances are controlled by a wide variety of computer processors (chips). The language that Gosling was designing needed to work on all these different processors. Moreover, a home appliance is typically an inexpensive item, so the manufacturer would be unwilling to invest large amounts of money into developing complicated compilers. (A compiler is a program that translates the program into a language the processor can understand.) To simplify the tasks of writing compilers (translation programs) for each class of appliances, the team used a two-step translation process. The programs are first translated into an **intermediate language** that is the same for all appliances (or all computers), then a small, easy-to-write, and hence inexpensive, program translates this intermediate language into the machine language for a particular appliance or computer. This intermediate language is called **Java byte-code** or simply **byte-code**. Since there is only one intermediate language, the hardest step of the two-step translation from program to intermediate language to machine language is the same for all appliances (or all computers), and hence, most of the cost of translating to multiple machine languages was saved. The language for programming appliances never caught on with appliance manufacturers, but the Java language into which it evolved has become a widely used programming language.

> **intermediate language**

> **byte-code**

> **code**

Why call it *byte-code*? The word **code** is commonly used to mean a program or part of a program. A byte is a small unit of storage (eight bits to be precise). Computer-readable information is typically organized into bytes. So the term *byte-code* suggests a program that is readable by a computer as opposed to a person.

In 1994, Patrick Naughton and Jonathan Payne at Sun Microsystems developed a Web browser that could run (Java) programs over the Internet. That Web browser has evolved into the browser known as HotJava. This was the start of Java's connection to the Internet. In the fall of 1995, Netscape Incorporated made its Web browser capable of running Java programs. Other companies followed suit and have developed software that accommodates Java programs.

Objects and Methods

> **OOP**

Java is an **object-oriented programming** language, abbreviated **OOP**. What is OOP? The world around us is made up of objects, such as people, automobiles, buildings, streets, adding machines, papers, and so forth. Each of these objects has the ability to perform certain actions, and each of these actions has some effect on some of the other objects in the world. OOP is a programming methodology that views a program as similarly consisting of objects that interact with each other by means of actions.

> **object**
> **method**
> **class**

Object-oriented programming has its own specialized terminology. The objects are called, appropriately enough, **objects**. The actions that an object can take are called **methods**. Objects of the same kind are said to have the same *type* or, more often, are said to be in the same **class**. For example, in an airport simulation program, all the

> ### Why Is the Language Named "Java"?
>
> The current custom is to name programming languages according to the whims of their designers. Java is no exception. There are conflicting explanations of the origin of the name "Java." Despite these conflicting stories, one thing is clear: The word "Java" does not refer to any property or serious history of the Java language. One believable story about where the name "Java" came from is that the name was thought of when, after a fruitless meeting trying to come up with a new name for the language, the development team went out for coffee, and hence the inspiration for the name "Java."

simulated airplanes might belong to the same class, probably called the `Airplane` class. All objects within a class have the same methods. Thus, in a simulation program, all airplanes have the same methods (or possible actions) such as taking off, flying to a specific location, landing, and so forth. However, all simulated airplanes are not identical. They can have different characteristics, which are indicated in the program by associating different data (that is, some different information) with each particular airplane object. For example, the data associated with an airplane object might be two numbers for its speed and altitude.

application program

If you have used some other programming language, it might help to explain Java terminology in terms of the terminology used in other languages. Things that are called *procedures, methods, functions,* or *subprograms* in other languages are all called *methods* in Java. In Java, all methods (and for that matter, any programming constructs whatsoever) are part of a class. As we will see, a Java **application program** is a class with a method named `main`, and when you run the Java program, the run-time system automatically invokes the method named `main` (that is, it automatically initiates the `main` action). An application program is a "regular" Java program; as we are about to see, there is another kind of Java program known as an applet. Other Java terminology is pretty much the same as the terminology in most other programming languages and, in any case, will be explained when each concept is introduced.

Applets ★

applet

application

There are two kinds of Java programs, **applets** and **applications**. An application or application program is just a regular program. Although the name *applet* may sound like it has something to do with apples, the name really means a *little Java application,* not a little apple. Applets and applications are almost identical. The difference is that applications are meant to be run on your computer like any other program, whereas an **applet** is meant to be run from a Web browser, and so can be sent to another location on the Internet and run there. Applets always use a windowing interface, but not all programs with a windowing interface are applets, as you will see in Chapters 16–18.

applet viewer

Although applets were designed to be run from a Web browser, they can also be run with a program known as an **applet viewer**. The applet viewer is really meant as a debugging aid and not as the final environment to allow users to run applets. Nonetheless, applets are now often run as stand-alone programs using an applet viewer.[1] We find this to be a somewhat unfortunate accident of history. Java has multiple libraries of software for designing windowing interfaces that run with no connection to a browser. We prefer to use these libraries, rather than applets, to write windowing programs that will not be run from a Web browser. In this book we show you how to do windowing interfaces as applets and as programs with no connection to a Web browser. In fact, the two approaches have a large overlap of both techniques and the Java libraries that they use. Once you know how to design and write either applets or applications, it is easy to learn to write the other of these two kinds of programs.

An applet always has a windowing interface. An application program may have a windowing interface or use simple console I/O. So as not to detract from the code being studied, most of our example programs, particularly early in the book, use simple console I/O (that is, simple text I/O).

A Sample Java Application Program

Display 1.1 contains a simple Java program and the screen displays produced when it is run. A Java program is really a class definition (whatever that is) with a method named `main`. When the program is run, the method named `main` is invoked; that is, the action specified by `main` is carried out. The body of the method `main` is enclosed in braces, {}, so that when the program is run, the statements in the braces are executed. (If you are not even vaguely familiar with the words *class* and *method,* they will be explained. Read on.)

The following line says that this program is a class called `FirstProgram`:

```
public class FirstProgram
{
```

The next two lines, shown below, begin the definition of the `main` method:

```
public static void main(String[] args)
{
```

The details of exactly what a Java class is and what words like `public`, `static`, `void`, and so forth mean will be explained in the next few chapters. Until then, you can think of these opening lines, repeated below, as being a rather wordy way of saying "Begin the program named `FirstProgram`."

```
public class FirstProgram
{
    public static void main(String[] args)
    {
```

---

[1] An applet viewer does indeed use a browser to run an applet, but the look and feel is that of a stand-alone program with no interaction with a browser.

Display 1.1 A Sample Java Program

```
 1 public class FirstProgram                    Name of class
 2 {                                            (program)              The main method
 3     public static void main(String[] args)
 4     {
 5         System.out.println("Hello reader.");
 6         System.out.println("Welcome to Java.");

 7         System.out.println("Let's demonstrate a simple calculation.");
 8         int answer;
 9         answer = 2 + 2;
10         System.out.println("2 plus 2 is " + answer);
11     }
12 }
```

Sample Dialogue

```
Hello reader.
Welcome to Java.
Let's demonstrate a simple calculation.
2 plus 2 is 4
```

The next two lines, shown in what follows, are the first actions the program performs:

println

```
System.out.println("Hello reader.");
System.out.println("Welcome to Java.");
```

Each of these lines begins with System.out.println. Each one causes the quoted string given within the parentheses to be output to the screen. For example, consider

```
System.out.println("Hello reader.");
```

This causes the line

```
Hello reader.
```

to be written to the screen. The output produced by the next line that begins with System.out.println will go on the following line. Thus, these two lines cause the following output:

```
Hello reader.
Welcome to Java.
```

**System.out.
    println**

These lines that begin with System.out.println are a way of saying "output what is shown in parentheses," and the details of why the instruction is written this way need not concern us yet. However, we can tell you a little about what is going on here.

Java programs work by having things called *objects* perform actions. The actions performed by an object are called *methods.* System.out is an object used for sending output to the screen; println is the method (that is, the action) that this object performs. The action is to send what is in parentheses to the screen. When an object performs an action using a method, that is called **invoking** the method (or **calling** the method). In a Java program, you write such a method invocation by writing the object followed by a **dot** (period), followed by the method name, and some parentheses that may or may not have something inside them. The thing (or things) inside the parentheses is called an **argument(s)** and provides information needed by the method to carry out its action. In each of these two lines and the similar line that follows them, the method is println. The method println writes something to the screen, and the argument (a string in quotes) tells it what it should write.

invoking

dot

argument

Invoking a method is also sometimes called **sending a message** to the object. With this view a message is sent to the object (by invoking a method) and in response the object performs some action (namely the action taken by the method invoked). We seldom use the terminology *sending a message,* but it is standard terminology used by some programmers and authors.

sending a message

Variable declarations in Java are similar to what they are in other programming languages. The following line from Display 1.1 declares the variable answer:

variable int

```
int answer;
```

The type int is one of the Java types for integers (whole numbers). So, this line says that answer is a variable that can hold a single integer (whole number).

The following line is the only real computing done by this first program:

equal sign

```
answer = 2 + 2;
```

assignment operator

In Java, the equal sign is used as the **assignment operator**, which is an instruction to set the value of the variable on the left-hand side of the equal sign. In the preceding program line, the equal sign does not mean that answer *is equal to* 2 + 2. Instead, the equal sign is an instruction to the computer to *make* answer *equal to* 2 + 2.

The last program action is

```
System.out.println("2 plus 2 is " + answer);
```

This is an output statement of the same kind as we discussed earlier, but there is something new in it. Note that the string "2 plus 2 is " is followed by a plus sign and the variable answer. In this case the plus sign is an operator to concatenate (connect) two strings. However, the variable answer is not a string. If one of the two operands to + is a string, Java will convert the other operand, such as the value of answer, to a string. In this program, answer has the value 4, so answer is converted to the string "4" and then concatenated to the string "2 plus 2 is ", so the output statement under discussion is equivalent to

```
System.out.println("2 plus 2 is 4");
```

The remainder of this first program consists of two closing braces. The first closing brace ends the definition of the method `main`. The last closing brace ends the definition of the class named `FirstProgram`.

Self-Test Exercises

1. If the following statement were used in a Java program, it would cause something to be written to the screen. What would it cause to be written to the screen?

   ```
   System.out.println("Java is not a drink.");
   ```

2. Give a statement or statements that can be used in a Java program to write the following to the screen:

   ```
   I like Java.
   You like tea.
   ```

3. Write a complete Java program that uses `System.out.println` to output the following to the screen when run:

   ```
   Hello World!
   ```

Note that you do not need to fully understand all the details of the program in order to write the program. You can simply follow the model of the program in Display 1.1.

Byte-Code and the Java Virtual Machine

high-level, low-level, and machine languages

Most modern programming languages are designed to be (relatively) easy for people to write and to understand. These languages that were designed for people to read are called **high-level languages**. The language that the computer can directly understand is called **machine language**. Machine language or any language similar to machine language is called a **low-level language**. A program written in a high-level language, like Java, must be translated into a program in machine language before the program can be run. The program that does the translating (or at least most of the translating) is called a **compiler** and the translation process is called **compiling**.

compiler

Compiler

A **compiler** is a program that translates a high-level-language program, such as a Java program, into an equivalent low-level-language program.

One disadvantage of most programming languages is that the compiler translates the high-level-language program directly into the machine language for your computer. Since different computers have different machine languages, this means you need a different compiler for each type of computer. Java, however, uses a slightly different and much more versatile approach to compiling.

The Java compiler does not translate your program into the machine language for your particular computer. Instead, it translates your Java program into a language **byte-code** called **byte-code**. Byte-code is not the machine language for any particular computer. **Java Virtual** Byte-code is the machine language for a fictitious computer called the **Java Virtual Machine**. The Java Virtual Machine is very similar to all typical computers. Thus, it is easy to translate a program written in byte-code into a program in the machine language for any particular computer. The program that does this translation is called an **interpreter** **interpreter**. An interpreter combines the translation of the byte-code and the execution of the corresponding machine-language instructions. The interpreter works by translating an instruction of byte-code into instructions expressed in your computer's machine language and then executing those instructions on your computer. It does this one byte-code instruction at a time. Thus, an interpreter translates and executes the instructions in the byte-code one after the other, rather than translating the entire byte-code program at once.[2]

To run a Java program, you proceed as follows. First, you use the compiler to translate the Java program into byte-code. Then, you use the byte-code interpreter for your computer to translate each byte-code instruction to machine language and to run the machine-language instructions.

It sounds as though Java byte-code just adds an extra step in the process. Why not write compilers that translate directly from Java to the machine language for your particular computer? That is what is done for most other programming languages. However, Java byte-code makes your Java program very portable. After you compile your Java program into byte-code, you can use that byte-code on any computer. When you run your program on another type of computer, you do not need to recompile it. This means that you can send your byte-code over the Internet to another computer and have it easily run on that computer. This is one of the reasons Java is good for Internet applications. Of course, every kind of computer must have its own byte-code interpreter, but these interpreters are simple programs when compared to a compiler.

Byte-Code

The Java compiler translates your Java program into a language called **byte-code**, which is the machine language for a fictitious computer. It is easy to translate this byte-code into the machine language of any particular computer. Each type of computer will have its own interpreter that translates and executes byte-code instructions.

---

[2] Sometimes people use the term *Java Virtual Machine* (JVM) to refer to the Java byte-code interpreter (as well as to refer to the underlying hypothetical machine that the interpreter is based on).

When compiling and running a Java program, you are usually not even aware of the fact that your program is translated into byte-code and not directly translated into machine-language code. You normally give two commands, one to compile your program (into byte-code) and one to run your program. The **run command** executes the Java byte-code interpreter on the byte-code.

run command

When you use a compiler, the terminology can get a bit confusing, because both the input to the compiler program and the output from the compiler program are also programs. Everything in sight is some kind of program. To make sure it is clear which program we mean, we call the input program, which in our case will be a Java program, the **source program**, or **source code**, and call the translated low-level-language program that the compiler produces the **object program**, or **object code**. The word **code** just means a program or a part of a program.

source code
object code
code

Class Loader ★

A Java program is divided into smaller parts called *classes*, and normally each class definition is in a separate file and is compiled separately. In order to run your program, the byte-code for these various classes needs to be connected together. The connecting is done by a program known as the **class loader**. This connecting is typically done automatically, so you normally need not be concerned with it. (In other programming languages, the program corresponding to the Java class loader is called a *linker*.)

Compiling a Java Program or Class

As we noted in the previous subsection, a Java program is divided into classes. Before you can run a Java program, you must compile these classes.

Before you can compile a Java program, each class definition used in the program (and written by you, the programmer) should be in a separate file. Moreover, the name of the file should be the same as the name of the class, except that the file name has .java added to the end. The program in Display 1.1 is a class called FirstProgram and so it should be in a file named FirstProgram.java. This program has only one class, but a more typical Java program would consist of several classes.

.java files

If you are using an IDE (Integrated Development Environment), there will be a simple command to compile your Java program from the editor. You will have to check your local documentation to see exactly what this command is, but it is bound to be very simple. (In the TextPad environment the command is Compile Java on the Tools menu.)

If you want or need to compile your Java program or class with a one-line command given to the operating system, then that is easy to do. We will describe the commands for the Java system distributed by Sun Microsystems (usually called "the SDK" or "the JDK" or "Java 2").

Suppose you want to compile a class named FirstProgram. It will be in a file named FirstProgram.java. To compile it, you simply give the following command:

javac

```
javac FirstProgram.java
```

You should be in the same directory (folder) as the file FirstProgram.java when you give this javac command. To compile any Java class, whether it is a full program or not, the command is javac followed by the name of the file containing the class.

.class files

When you compile a Java class, the resulting byte-code for that class is placed in a file of the same name, except that the ending is changed from .java to .class. So, when you compile a class named FirstProgram in the file FirstProgram.java, the resulting byte-code is stored in a file named FirstProgram.class.

Running a Java Program

A Java program can consist of a number of different classes, each in a different file. When you run a Java application program, you only run the class that you think of as the program; that is, the class that contains a main method. Look for the following line, which starts the main method:

```
public static void main(String[] args)
```

The critical words to look for are public static void main. The remaining portion of the line might be spelled slightly different in some cases.

If you are using an IDE, you will have a menu command that can be used to run a Java program. You will have to check your local documentation to see exactly what this command is. (In the TextPad environment the command is Run Java Application on the Tools menu.)

If you want or need to run your Java program with a one-line command given to the operating system, then (in most cases) you can run a Java program by giving the command java followed by the name of the class containing the main method. For example, for the program in Display 1.1, you would give the following one-line command:

```
java FirstProgram
```

Note that when you run a program, you use the class name, such as FirstProgram, without any .java or .class ending.

When you run a Java program, you are actually running the Java byte-code interpreter on the compiled version of your program. When you run your program, the system will automatically load in any classes you need and run the byte-code interpreter on those classes as well.

We have been assuming that the Java compiler and related software were already set up for you. We were also assuming that all the files were in one directory. (Directories are also called *folders*.) If you need to set up the Java compiler and system software, consult the manuals that came with the software. If you wish to spread your class definitions across multiple directories, that is not difficult, but we will not concern ourselves with that detail until later.

Syntax and Semantics

The description of a programming language, or any other kind of language, can be thought of as having two parts, called the *syntax* and *semantics* of the language.

The **syntax** tells what arrangement of words and punctuations are legal in the language. The syntax of the language is often called the *grammar rules* of the language. For Java, the syntax describes what arrangements of words and punctuations are allowed in a class or program definition.

The **semantics** of a language describes the meaning of things written while following the syntax rules of the language. For a Java program, the syntax describes how you write a program and the semantics describes what happens when you run the program.

When writing a program in Java, you are always using both the syntax and the semantics of the Java language.

TIP: Error Messages

bug
debugging

A mistake in a program is called a **bug**. For this reason, the process of eliminating mistakes in your program is called **debugging**. There are three commonly recognized types of bugs or errors, and they are known as *syntax errors*, *run-time errors*, and *logic errors*. Let's consider them in order.

syntax error

A **syntax error** is a grammatical mistake in your program; that is, a mistake in the allowed arrangement of words and punctuations. If you violate one of these rules, for example, by omitting a required punctuation, that is a syntax error. The compiler will catch syntax errors and output an error message telling you that it has found the error, where it thinks the error is, and what it thinks the error is. If the compiler says you have a syntax error, you undoubtedly do have an error. However, the compiler could be incorrect about where and what the error is.

run-time
error

An error that is not detected until your program is run is called a **run-time error**. If the computer detects a run-time error when your program is run, then it will output an error message. The error message may not be easy to understand, but at least it lets you know that something is wrong.

logic error

A mistake in the underlying algorithm for your program is called a **logic error**. If your program has only logic errors, it will compile and run without any error message. You have written a valid Java program, but you have not written a program that does what you want. The program runs and gives output, but gives incorrect output. For example, if you were to mistakenly use the multiplication sign in place of the addition sign, that would be a logic error. Logic errors are the hardest kind of error to locate, because the computer does not give you any error messages. ∎

Self-Test Exercises

4. What is a compiler?

5. What is a source program?

6. What is an object program?

7. What do you call a program that runs Java byte-code instructions?

8. Suppose you define a class named NiceClass in a file. What name should the file have?

9. Suppose you compile the class NiceClass. What will be the name of the file with the resulting byte-code?

1.2   Expressions and Assignment Statements

Once a person has understood the way variables are used in program-
ming, he has understood the quintessence of programming.

E. W. DIJKSTRA, Notes on Structured Programming

Variables, expressions, and assignments in Java are similar to their counterparts in most other general-purpose languages. In this section we describe the details.

Identifiers

identifier

The name of a variable (or other item you might define in a program) is called an **identifier**. A Java identifier must not start with a digit and all the characters must be letters, digits, or the underscore symbol. (The symbol $ is also allowed, but it is reserved for special purposes, and so you should not use $ in your Java identifiers.) For example, the following are all valid identifiers:

```
x x1 x_1 _abc ABC123z7 sum RATE count data2 bigBonus
```

All of the preceding names are legal and would be accepted by the compiler, but the first five are poor choices for identifiers, since they are not descriptive of the identifier's use. None of the following are legal identifiers and all would be rejected by the compiler:

```
12  3X  %change  data-1  myfirst.java  PROG.CLASS
```

The first two are not allowed because they start with a digit. The remaining four are not identifiers because they contain symbols other than letters, digits, and the underscore symbol.

case-sensitive   Java is a **case-sensitive** language; that is, it distinguishes between uppercase and lowercase letters in the spelling of identifiers. Hence, the following are three distinct identifiers and could be used to name three distinct variables:

```
rate  RATE  Rate
```

However, it is usually not a good idea to use two such variants in the same program, since that might be confusing. Although it is not required by Java, variables are usually spelled with their first letter in lowercase. The convention that has now become universal in Java programming is to spell variable names with a mix of upper- and lowercase letters (and digits), to always start a variable name with a lowercase letter, and to indicate "word" boundaries with an uppercase letter, as illustrated by the following variable names:

```
topSpeed bankRate1 bankRate2 timeOfArrival
```

A Java identifier can theoretically be of any length, and the compiler will accept even unreasonably long identifiers.

Names (Identifiers)

The name of something in a Java program, such as a variable, class, method, or object name, must not start with a digit and may only contain letters, digits (0 through 9), and the underscore character (_). Uppercase and lowercase letters are considered to be different characters. (The symbol $ is also allowed, but it is reserved for special purposes, and so you should not use $ in a Java name.)

Names in a program are called **identifiers**.

Although it is not required by the Java language, the common practice, and the one followed in this book, is to start the names of classes with uppercase letters and to start the names of variables, objects, and methods with lowercase letters. These names are usually spelled using only letters and digits.

---

keyword   There is a special class of identifiers, called **keywords** or **reserved words**, that have a predefined meaning in Java and that you cannot use as names for variables or anything else. In the code displays of this book, keywords are shown in a different color, as illustrated by the keyword public. A complete list of keywords is given in Appendix 1.

Some predefined words, such as System and println, are not keywords. These predefined words are not part of the core Java language and you are allowed to redefine them. These predefined words are not keywords. However, they are defined in libraries required by the Java language standard. Needless to say, using a predefined identifier for anything other than its standard meaning can be confusing and dangerous, and thus should be avoided. The safest and easiest practice is to treat all predefined identifiers as if they were keywords.

Variables

declare

Every variable in a Java program must be *declared* before it is used. When you **declare** a variable, you are telling the compiler—and, ultimately, the computer—what kind of data you will be storing in the variable. For example, the following are two declarations that might occur in a Java program:

```
int numberOfBeans;
double oneWeight, totalWeight;
```

floating-point number

The first declares the variable `numberOfBeans` so that it can hold a value of type `int`, that is, a whole number. The name `int` is an abbreviation for "integer." The type `int` is the default type for whole numbers. The second definition declares `oneWeight` and `totalWeight` to be variables of type `double`, which is the default type for numbers with a decimal point (known as **floating-point numbers**). As illustrated here, when there is more than one variable in a declaration, the variables are separated by commas. Also, note that each declaration ends with a semicolon.

Every variable must be declared before it is used. A variable may be declared anyplace, so long as it is declared before it is used. Of course, variables should always be declared in a location that makes the program easier to read. Typically variables are declared either just before they are used or at the start of a block (indicated by an opening brace {). Any legal identifier, other than a keyword, may be used for a variable name.

Variable Declarations

In Java, a variable must be declared before it is used. Variables are declared as follows:

SYNTAX

Type Variable_1, Variable_2,. . .;

EXAMPLES

```
int count, numberOfDragons, numberOfTrolls;
char answer;
double speed, distance;
```

Syntactic Variables

Remember that when you see something such as *Type*, *Variable_1*, or *Variable_2*, these words do not literally appear in your Java code. They are **syntactic variables**, which means they are replaced by something of the category that they describe. For example, *Type* can be replaced by `int`, `double`, `char`, or any other type name. *Variable_1* and *Variable_2* can each be replaced by any variable name.

primitive
types

Java has basic types for characters, different kinds of integers, and different kinds of floating-point numbers (numbers with a decimal point), as well as a type for the values true and false. These basic types are known as **primitive types**. Display 1.2 shows all of Java's primitive types. The preferred type for integers is int. The type char is the type for single characters. The preferred type for floating-point numbers is double. The type boolean has the two values true and false. (Unlike some other programming languages, the Java values true and false are not integers and will not be automatically converted to integers.) Objects of the predefined class String represent strings of characters. String is not a primitive type, but is often considered a basic type along with the primitive types. The class String is discussed later in this chapter.

Display 1.2 Primitive Types

TYPE NAME	KIND OF VALUE	MEMORY USED	SIZE RANGE
boolean	true or false	1 byte	not applicable
char	single character (Unicode)	2 bytes	all Unicode characters
byte	integer	1 byte	−128 to 127
short	integer	2 bytes	−32768 to 32767
int	integer	4 bytes	−2147483648 to 2147483647
long	integer	8 bytes	−9223372036854775808 to 9223372036854775807
float	floating-point number	4 bytes	$-\pm3.40282347 \times 10^{+38}$ to $-\pm1.40239846 \times 10^{-45}$
double	floating-point number	8 bytes	$\pm\pm1.76769313486231570 \times 10^{+308}$ to $\pm\pm4.94065645841246544 \times 10^{-324}$

Assignment Statements

assignment
statement

assignment
operator

The most direct way to change the value of a variable is to use an **assignment statement**. In Java the equal sign is used as the **assignment operator**. An assignment statement always consists of a variable on the left-hand side of the assignment operator (the equal sign) and an expression on the right-hand side. An assignment statement ends with a semicolon. The expression on the right-hand side of the equal sign may be a variable, a number, or a more complicated expression made up of variables, numbers, operators, and method invocations. An assignment statement instructs the computer to evaluate (that is, to compute the value of) the expression on the right-hand side of the equal sign and to set the value of the variable on the left-hand side equal to the value of that expression. The following are examples of Java assignment statements:

```
totalWeight = oneWeight * numberOfBeans;
temperature = 98.6;
count = count + 2;
```

The first assignment statement sets the value of totalWeight equal to the number in the variable oneWeight multiplied by the number in numberOfBeans. (Multiplication is expressed using the asterisk * in Java.) The second assignment statement sets the value of temperature to 98.6. The third assignment statement increases the value of the variable count by 2.

Note that a variable may occur on both sides of the assignment operator (both sides of the equal sign). The assigned statement

```
count = count + 2;
```

sets the new value of count equal to the old value of count plus 2.

The assignment operator when used with variables of a class type requires a bit more explanation, which we will give in Chapter 4.

Assignment Statements with Primitive Types

An assignment statement with a variable of a primitive type on the left-hand side of the equal sign causes the following action: First, the expression on the right-hand side of the equal sign is evaluated, and then the variable on the left-hand side of the equal sign is set equal to this value.

SYNTAX

Variable = *Expression*;

EXAMPLE

```
distance = rate * time;
count = count + 2;
```

An assigned statement may be used as an expression that evaluates to a value. When used this way, the variable on the left-hand side of the equal sign is changed as we have described, and the new value of the variable is also the value of the assignment expression. For example,

```
number = 3;
```

both changes the value of number to 3 and evaluates to the value 3. This allows you to chain assignment statements. The following changes the values of both the variables, number1 and number2, to 3:

```
number2 = (number1 = 3);
```

The assignment operator automatically is executed right-to-left if there are no parentheses, so this is normally written in the following equivalent way:

```
number2 = number1 = 3;
```

TIP: Initialize Variables

uninitialized variable

A variable that has been declared but that has not yet been given a value by some means, such as an assignment statement, is said to be **uninitialized**. In some cases an uninitialized variable may be given some default value, but this is not true in all cases. Moreover, it makes your program clearer to explicitly give the variable a value, even if you are simply reassigning it the default value. (The exact details on default values have been known to change and should not be counted on.)[3]

One easy way to ensure that you do not have an uninitialized variable is to initialize it within the declaration. Simply combine the declaration and an assignment statement, as in the following examples:

```
int count = 0;
double speed = 65.5;
char grade = 'A';
int initialCount = 50, finalCount;
```

Note that you can initialize some variables and not initialize other variables in a declaration.

Sometimes the compiler may say that you have failed to initialize a variable. In most cases, you will indeed have failed to initialize the variable. Occasionally, the compiler is mistaken in giving this advice. However, the compiler will not compile your program until you convince it that the variable in question is initialized. To make the compiler happy, initialize the variable when it is declared, even if the variable will be given a different value before the variable is used for anything. In such cases, you cannot argue with the compiler. ■

---

[3] The official rules are that the variables we are now using, which we will later call *local variables*, are not automatically initialized. Later in this book we will introduce variables called *static variables* and *instance variables* that are automatically initialized. However, we urge you to never rely on automatic initialization.

Initializing a Variable in a Declaration

You can combine the declaration of a variable with an assignment statement that gives the variable a value.

SYNTAX

Type Variable_1 = Expression__1, Variable_2 = Expression__2, ...;

Some of the variables may have no equal sign and no expression, as in the first example.

EXAMPLE

```
int numberReceived = 0, lastNumber, numberOfStations = 5;
double speed = 98.9, distance = speed * 10;
char initial = 'J';
```

More Assignment Statements ★

There is a shorthand notation that combines the assignment operator (=) and an arithmetic operator so that a given variable can have its value changed by adding, subtracting, multiplying, or dividing by a specified value. The general form is

Variable Op = Expression

which is equivalent to

Variable = Variable Op (Expression)

The *Expression* can be another variable, a constant, or a more complicated arithmetic expression. The *Op* can be any of +, −, *, /, %, as well as some operators we have not yet discussed. The operator % has not yet been discussed but is explained later in this chapter. (A full list of values for *Op* can be seen at the bottom of the precedence table in Appendix 2.) Below are examples:

EXAMPLE:	EQUIVALENT TO:
count += 2;	count = count + 2;
total -= discount;	total = total - discount;
bonus *= 2;	bonus = bonus * 2;
time /= rushFactor;	time = time / rushFactor;
change %= 100;	change = change % 100;
amount *= count1 + count2;	amount = amount * (count1 + count2);

Self-Test Exercises

10. Which of the following may be used as variable names in Java?

    ```
    rate1, 1stPlayer, myprogram.java, long,
    TimeLimit, numberOfWindows
    ```

11. Can a Java program have two different variables named number and Number?

12. Give the declaration for two variables called feet and inches. Both variables are of type int and both are to be initialized to zero in the declaration.

13. Give the declaration for two variables called count and distance. count is of type int and is initialized to zero. distance is of type double and is initialized to 1.5.

14. Write a Java assignment statement that will set the value of the variable distance to the value of the variable time multiplied by 80. All variables are of type int.

15. Write a Java assignment statement that will set the value of the variable interest to the value of the variable balance multiplied by the value of the variable rate. The variables are of type double.

16. What is the output produced by the following lines of program code?

    ```
    char a, b;
    a = 'b';
    System.out.println(a);
    b = 'c';
    System.out.println(b);
    a = b;
    System.out.println(a);
    ```

Assignment Compatibility

As a general rule, you cannot store a value of one type in a variable of another type. For example, the compilers will object to the following:

```
int intVariable;
intVariable = 2.99;
```

The problem is a type mismatch. The constant 2.99 is of type double and the variable intVariable is of type int.

assigning int values to double variables
There are some special cases where it is permitted to assign a value of one type to a variable of another type. It is acceptable to assign a value of an integer type, such as int, to a variable of a floating-point type, such as the type double. For example, the following is both legal and acceptable style:

```
double doubleVariable;
doubleVariable = 2;
```

The preceding will set the value of the variable named doubleVariable equal to 2.0.

Similarly, assignments of integer type variables to floating-point type variables are also allowed. For example, the following is allowed:

```
int intVariable;
intVariable = 42;
double doubleVariable;
doubleVariable = intVariable;
```

More generally, you can assign a value of any type in the following list to a variable of any type that appears further down in the list:

```
byte -> short -> int -> long -> float -> double
```

For example, you can assign a value of type `int` to a variable of type `long`, `float`, or `double` (or of course to a variable of type `int`), but you cannot assign a value of type `int` to a variable of type `byte` or `short`. Note that this is not an arbitrary ordering of the types. As you move down the list from left to right, the range of allowed values for the types becomes larger.

You can assign a value of type `char` to a variable of type `int` or to any of the numeric types that follow `int` in our list of types (but not to those that precede `int`). However, in most cases it is not wise to assign a character to an `int` variable, because the result could be confusing.[4]

If you want to assign a value of type `double` to a variable of type `int`, then you must change the type of the value by using a *type cast,* as explained in the subsection later in this chapter that is entitled "Type Casting."

integers and booleans

In many languages other than Java, you can assign integers to variables of type `boolean` and assign `boolean` values to integer variables. You cannot do that in Java. In Java, the `boolean` values `true` and `false` are not integers nor will they be automatically converted to integers. (In fact, it is not even legal to do an explicit type cast from the type `boolean` to the type `int` or vice versa. Explicit type casts are discussed later in this chapter.)

Constants

literals constants

Constants or **literals** are names for one specific value. For example, 2 and 3.1459 are two constants. We prefer the name *constants* because it contrasts nicely with the word *variables.* Constants do not change value; variables can change their values. Integer constants

---

[4] Readers who have used certain other languages, such as C or C++, may be surprised to learn that you cannot assign a value of type `char` to a variable of type `byte`. This is because Java uses the Unicode character set rather than the ASCII character set, and so Java reserves two bytes of memory for each value of type `char`, but naturally only reserves one byte of memory for values of type `byte`. This is one of the few cases where you might notice that Java uses the Unicode character set. Indeed, if you convert from an `int` to a `char` or vice versa, you can expect to get the usual correspondence of ASCII numbers and characters. It is also true that you cannot assign a value of type `char` to a variable of type `short`, even though they both use two bytes of memory.

Assignment Compatibilities

You can assign a value of any type on the following list to a variable of any type that appears further down on the list:

```
byte -> short -> int -> long -> float -> double
```

In particular, note that you can assign a value of any integer type to a variable of any floating-point type. You can also assign a value of type char to a variable of type int or of any type that follows int in the above list.

---

are written in the way you are used to writing numbers. Constants of type int (or any other integer type) must not contain a decimal point. Constants of floating-point types (float and double) may be written in either of two forms. The simple form for floating-point constants is like the everyday way of writing decimal fractions. When written in this form, a floating-point constant must contain a decimal point. No number constant (neither integer nor floating point) in Java may contain a comma.

e notation   A more complicated notation for floating-point constants, such as constants of type double, is called **scientific notation** or **floating-point notation** and is particularly handy for writing very large numbers and very small fractions. For instance,

3.67×10^5, which is the same as 367000.0,

is best expressed in Java by the constant 3.67e5. The number

5.89×10^{-4}, which is the same as 0.000589,

is best expressed in Java by the constant 5.89e−4. The e stands for *exponent* and means "multiply by 10 to the power that follows." The e may be either uppercase or lowercase.

Think of the number after the e as telling you the direction and number of digits to move the decimal point. For example, to change 3.49e4 to a numeral without an e, you move the decimal point 4 places to the right to obtain 34900.0, which is another way of writing the same number. If the number after the e is negative, you move the decimal point the indicated number of spaces to the left, inserting extra zeros if need be. So, 3.49e−2 is the same as 0.0349.

The number before the e may contain a decimal point, although that is not required. However, the exponent after the e definitely must *not* contain a decimal point.

Constants of type char are expressed by placing the character in single quotes, as illustrated in what follows:

```
char symbol = 'Z';
```

Note that the left and right single quote symbol are the same symbol.

What Is Doubled?

How did the floating-point type `double` get its name? Is there another type for floating-point numbers called "single" that is half as big? Something like that is true. There is a type that uses half as much storage, namely the type `float`. Many programming languages tradition-ally used two types for floating-point numbers. One type used less storage and was very imprecise (that is, it did not allow very many significant digits). The second type used *double* the amount of storage and so could be much more precise; it also allowed numbers that were larger (although programmers tend to care more about precision than about size). The kind of numbers that used twice as much storage were called *double precision* numbers; those that used less storage were called *single precision*. Following this tradition, the type that (more or less) corresponds to this double precision type in Java was named `double` in Java. The type that corresponds to single precision in Java was called `float`.

(Actually, the type name `double` was inherited from C++, but this explanation applies to why the type was named `double` in C++, and so ultimately it is the explanation of why the type is called `double` in Java.)

Constants for strings of characters are given in double quotes, as illustrated by the following line taken from Display 1.1:

```
System.out.println("Welcome to Java.");
```

quotes   Be sure to notice that string constants are placed inside of double quotes, while con-stants of type `char` are placed inside of single quotes. The two kinds of quotes mean different things. In particular, `'A'` and `"A"` mean different things. `'A'` is a value of type `char` and can be stored in a variable of type `char`. `"A"` is a string of characters. The fact that the string happens to contain only one character does *not* make the string `"A"` a value of type `char`. Also notice that, for both strings and characters, the left and right quotes are the same. We will have more to say about strings later in this chapter.

The type `boolean` has two constants, `true` and `false`. These two constants may be assigned to a variable of type `boolean` or used anyplace else an expression of type `bool-ean` is allowed. They must be spelled with all lowercase letters.

Arithmetic Operators and Expressions

As in most other languages, Java allows you to form expressions using variables, con-stants, and the arithmetic operators: + (addition), – (subtraction), * (multiplica-tion), / (division), % (modulo, remainder). These expressions can be used anyplace it is legal to use a value of the type produced by the expression.

mixing types   All of the arithmetic operators can be used with numbers of type `int`, numbers of type `double`, and even with one number of each type. However, the type of the value produced and the exact value of the result depends on the types of the numbers being combined. If both operands (that is, both numbers) are of type int, then the result of combining them with an arithmetic operator is of type int. If one, or both, of the operands is of type double, then the result is of type double. For example, if the variables baseAmount and increase are both of type int, then the number produced by the following expression is of type int:

```
baseAmount + increase
```

However, if one, or both, of the two variables is of type double, then the result is of type double. This is also true if you replace the operator + with any of the operators −, *, /, or %.

More generally, you can combine any of the arithmetic types in expressions. If all the types are integer types, the result will be the integer type. If at least one of the subexpressions is of a floating-point type, the result will be a floating-point type.

Knowing whether the value produced is of an integer type or a floating-point type is typically all that you need to know. However, if you need to know the exact type of the value produced by an arithmetic expression, it can be determined as follows: The type of the value produced is one of the types used in the expression. Of all the types used in the expression, it is, with rare exceptions, the last type (reading left to right) on the following list:

```
byte -> short -> int -> long -> float -> double
```

Here are the rare exceptions: Of all the types used in the expression, if the last type (reading left to right) is byte or short, then the type of the value produced is int. In other words, an expression never evaluates to either of the types byte or short. These exceptions have to do with an implementation detail that need not concern us, especially since we almost never use the types byte and short in this book.

Note that this sequence of types is the same sequence of types we saw when discussing assignment compatibility. As you go from left to right, the types increase in the range of values they allow.[5]

Parentheses and Precedence Rules ★

If you want to specify exactly what subexpressions are combined with each operator, you can fully parenthesize an expression. For example:

```
((base + (rate * hours))/(2 + rate))
```

If you omit some parentheses in an arithmetic expression, Java will, in effect, put in parentheses for you. When adding parentheses, Java follows rules called **precedence**

---

[5] Although we discourage the practice, you can use values and variables of type char in arithmetic expressions using operators such as +. If you do so, the char values and variables will contribute to the expression as if they were of type int.

rules that determine how the operators, such as + and *, are enclosed in parentheses. These precedence rules are similar to rules used in algebra. For example,

```
base + rate * hours
```

is evaluated by Java as if it were parenthesized as follows:

```
base + (rate * hours)
```

So, the multiplication will be done before the addition.

Except in some standard cases, such as a string of additions or a simple multiplication embedded inside an addition, it is usually best to include the parentheses, even if the intended groupings are the ones dictated by the precedence rules. The parentheses make the expression easier to read and less prone to programmer error.

A partial list of precedence rules is given in Display 1.3. A complete set of Java precedence rules is given in Appendix 2. Operators that are listed higher on the list are said to have **higher precedence**. When the computer is deciding which of two adjacent operations to group with parentheses, it groups the operation of higher precedence and its apparent arguments before the operation of lower precedence. Some operators have equal precedence, in which case the order of operations is determined by **associativity rules**. A brief summary of associativity rules is that binary operators of equal precedence are grouped in left-to-right order.[6] Unary operators of equal precedence are grouped in right-to-left order. So, for example,

```
base + rate + hours
```

is interpreted by Java to be the same as

```
(base + rate) + hours
```

And, for example,

```
+-+rate
```

is interpreted by Java to be the same as

```
+(-(+rate))
```

For now you can think of the explicit parentheses put in by the programmer and the implicit parentheses determined by precedence and associativity rules as determining the order in which operations are performed. For example, in

```
base + (rate * hours)
```

the multiplication is performed first and the addition is performed second.

---

[6] There is one exception to this rule. A string of assignment operators, like n1 = n2 = n3;, is performed right to left, as we noted earlier in this chapter.

Display 1.3 Precedence Rules

Highest Precedence

First: the unary operators: +, −, ++, −−, and !
Second: the binary arithmetic operators: *, /, and %
Third: the binary arithmetic operators: + and −

Lowest Precedence

The actual situation is a bit more complicated than what we have described for evaluating expressions, but we will not encounter any of these complications in this chapter. A complete discussion of evaluating expressions using precedence and associativity rules will be given in Chapter 3.

Integer and Floating-Point Division

integer division

When used with one or both operands of type double, the division operator, /, behaves as you might expect. However, when used with two operands of type int, the division operator yields the integer part resulting from division. In other words, integer division discards the part after the decimal point. So, 10/3 is 3 (not 3.3333...), 5/2 is 2 (not 2.5), and 11/3 is 3 (not 3.6666...). Notice that the number *is not rounded*; the part after the decimal point is discarded no matter how large it is.

the % operator

The operator % can be used with operands of type int to recover the information lost when you use / to do division with numbers of type int. When used with values of type int, the two operators / and % yield the two numbers produced when you perform the long division algorithm you learned in grade school. For example, 14 divided by 3 is 4 with a remainder of 2. The / operation yields the number of times one number "goes into" another (often called the *quotient*). The % operation gives the remainder. For example, the statements

```
System.out.println("14 divided by 3 is " + (14/3));
System.out.println("with a remainder of " + (14%3));
```

yield the following output:

```
14 divided by 3 is 4
with a remainder of 2
```

The % operator can be used to count by 2's, 3's, or any other number. For example, if you want to do something to every other integer, you need to know if the integer is even or odd. Then, you can do it to every even integer (or alternatively every odd integer). An integer n is even if n%2 is equal to 0 and the integer is odd if n%2 is equal to 1. Similarly, to do something to every third integer, your program might step through all integers n but only do the action when n%3 is equal to 0.

PITFALL: Round-Off Errors in Floating-Point Numbers

For all practical purposes, floating-point numbers are only approximate quantities. For example, in formal mathematics the floating-point number 1.0/3.0 is equal to

    0.3333333...

where the three dots indicate that the 3s go on forever. The computer stores numbers in a format somewhat like this decimal representation, but it has room for only a limited number of digits. If it can store only 10 digits after the decimal, then 1.0/3.0 is stored as

    0.3333333333

with only 10 threes. Thus, 1.0/3.0 is stored as a number that is slightly smaller than one-third. In other words, the value stored as 1.0/3.0 is only approximately equal to one-third.

In reality, the computer stores numbers in binary notation, rather than in base 10 notation, but the principles are the same and the consequences are the same. Some floating-point numbers lose accuracy when they are stored in the computer.

Floating-point numbers (like numbers of type double) and integers (like numbers of type int) are stored differently. Floating-point numbers are, in effect, stored as approximate quantities. Integers are stored as exact quantities. This difference sometimes can be subtle. For example, the numbers 42 and 42.0 are different in Java. The whole number 42 is of type int and is an exact quantity. The number 42.0 is of type double because it contains a fractional part (even though the fraction is 0), and so 42.0 is stored with only limited accuracy.

As a result of this limited accuracy, arithmetic done on floating-point numbers only gives approximate results. Moreover, one can easily get results on floating-point numbers that are very far from the true result you would obtain if the numbers could have unlimited accuracy (unlimited number of digits after the decimal point). For example, if a banking program used numbers of type double to represent amounts of money and did not do sophisticated manipulations to preserve accuracy, it would quickly bring the bank to ruin since the computed amounts of money would frequently be very incorrect. Dealing with these inaccuracies in floating-point numbers is part of the field of Numerical Analysis, a topic we will not discuss in this book. But, there is an easy way to obtain accuracy when dealing with amounts of money: use integers instead of floating-point numbers (perhaps one integer for the dollar amount and another integer for the cents amount). ■

Although the % operator is primarily used with integers, it can also be used with two floating-point numbers, such as two values of type double. However, we will not discuss nor use % with floating-point numbers.

PITFALL: Division with Whole Numbers

When you use the division operator / on two integers, the result is an integer. This can be a problem if you expect a fraction. Moreover, the problem can easily go unnoticed, resulting in a program that looks fine but is producing incorrect output without your even being aware of the problem. For example, suppose you are a landscape architect who charges $5,000 per mile to landscape a highway, and suppose you know the length in feet of the highway you are working on. The price you charge can easily be calculated by the following Java statement:

```
totalPrice = 5000 * (feet/5280.0);
```

This works because there are 5,280 feet in a mile. If the stretch of highway you are landscaping is 15,000 feet long, this formula will tell you that the total price is

```
5000 * (15000/5280.0)
```

Your Java program obtains the final value as follows: `15000/5280.0` is computed as `2.84`. Then the program multiplies `5000` by `2.84` to produce the value `14200.00`. With the aid of your Java program, you know that you should charge $14,200 for the project.

Now suppose the variable `feet` is of type `int`, and you forget to put in the decimal point and the zero, so that the assignment statement in your program reads:

```
totalPrice = 5000 * (feet/5280);
```

It still looks fine, but will cause serious problems. If you use this second form of the assignment statement, you are dividing two values of type `int`, so the result of the division `feet/5280` is `15000/5280`, which is the `int` value 2 (instead of the value `2.84`, which you think you are getting). So the value assigned to `totalPrice` is `5000*2`, or `10000.00`. If you forget the decimal point, you will charge $10,000. However, as we have already seen, the correct value is $14,200. A missing decimal point has cost you $4,200. Note that this will be true whether the type of `totalPrice` is `int` or `double`; the damage is done before the value is assigned to `totalPrice`. ∎

Self-Test Exercises

17. Convert each of the following mathematical formulas to a Java expression:

$$3x \qquad 3x+y \qquad \frac{x+y}{7} \qquad \frac{3x+y}{z+2}$$

18. What is the output of the following program lines?

```
double number = (1/3) * 3;
System.out.println("(1/3) * 3 is equal to " + number);
```

19. What is the output produced by the following lines of program code?

```java
int quotient, remainder;
quotient = 7/3;
remainder = 7%3;
System.out.println("quotient = " + quotient);
System.out.println("remainder = " + remainder);
```

20. What is the output produced by the following code?

```java
int result = 11;
result /= 2;
System.out.println("result is " + result);
```

21. Given the following fragment that purports to convert from degrees Celsius to degrees Fahrenheit, answer the following questions:

```java
double celsius = 20;
double fahrenheit;
fahrenheit = (9/5) * celsius + 32.0;
```

a. What value is assigned to `fahrenheit`?

b. Explain what is actually happening, and what the programmer likely wanted.

c. Rewrite the code as the programmer intended.

Type Casting

A type cast takes a value of one type and produces a value of another type that is Java's best guess of an equivalent value. We will motivate type casts with a simple division example.

Consider the expression 9/2. In Java this expression evaluates to 4, because when both operands are of an integer type, Java performs integer division. In some situations, you might want the answer to be the `double` value 4.5. You can get a result of 4.5 by using the "equivalent" floating-point value 2.0 in place of the integer value 2, as in the expression 9/2.0, which evaluates to 4.5. But, what if the 9 and the 2 are the values of variables of type `int` named n and m. Then, n/m yields 4. If you want floating-point division in this case, you must do a type cast from `int` to `double` (or another floating-point type), such as in the following:

```java
double ans = n/(double)m;
```

The expression

```java
(double)m
```

is a type cast. The expression takes an int (in this example the value of m) and evaluates to an "equivalent" value of type double. So, if the value of m is 2, the expression (double)m evaluates to the double value 2.0.

Note that (double)m does not change the value of the variable m. If m has the value 2 before this expression is evaluated, then m still has the value 2 after the expression is evaluated.

You may use other type names in place of double to obtain a type cast to another type. We said this produces an "equivalent" value of the target type. The word "equivalent" is in quotes because there is no clear notion of equivalent that applies between any two types. In the case of a type cast from an integer type to a floating-point type, the effect is to add a decimal point and a zero. A type cast in the other direction, from a floating-point type to an integer type, simply deletes the decimal point and all digits after the decimal point. Note that when type casting from a floating-point type to an integer type, the number is truncated not rounded: (int)2.9 is 2; it is not 3.

As we noted earlier, you can always assign a value of an integer type to a variable of a floating-point type, as in

```
double d = 5;
```

In such cases Java performs an automatic type cast, converting the 5 to 5.0 and placing 5.0 in the variable d. You cannot store the 5 as the value of d without a type cast, but sometimes Java does the type cast for you. Such an automatic type cast is sometimes called a **type coercion**.

type coercion

By contrast, you cannot place a double value in an int variable without an explicit type cast. The following is illegal:

```
int i = 5.5; //Illegal
```

Instead, you must add an explicit type cast, like so:

```
int i = (int)5.5;
```

Increment and Decrement Operators

The **increment operator** ++ adds one to the value of a variable. The **decrement operator** −− subtracts one from the value of a variable. They are usually used with variables of type int, but they can be used with any numeric type. If n is a variable of a numeric type, then n++ increases the value of n by one and n−− decreases the value of n by one. So, n++ and n−− (when followed by a semicolon) are executable statements. For example, the statements

```
int n = 1, m = 7;
n++;
System.out.println("The value of n is changed to " + n);
m--;
System.out.println("The value of m is changed to " + m);
```

yield the following output:

```
The value of n is changed to 2
The value of m is changed to 6
```

An expression like n++ also evaluates to a number as well as changing the value of the variable n, so n++ can be used in an arithmetic expression such as

```
2*(n++)
```

The expression n++ changes the value of n by adding one to it, but it evaluates to the value n had *before* it was increased. For example, consider the following code:

```
int n = 2;
int valueProduced = 2*(n++);
System.out.println(valueProduced);
System.out.println(n);
```

This code produces the following output:

```
4
3
```

Notice the expression 2*(n++). When Java evaluates this expression, it uses the value that number has *before* it is incremented, not the value that it has after it is incremented. Thus, the value produced by the expression n++ is 2, even though the increment operator changes the value of n to 3. This may seem strange, but sometimes it is just what you want. And, as you are about to see, if you want an expression that behaves differently, you can have it.

The expression ++n also increments the value of the variable n by one, but it evaluates to the value n has after it is increased. For example, consider the following code:

```
int n = 2;
int valueProduced = 2*(++n);
System.out.println(valueProduced);
System.out.println(n);
```

This code is the same as the previous piece of code except that the ++ is before the variable, so this code will produce the following output:

```
6
3
```

v++ versus ++v   Notice that the two increment operators n++ and ++n have the exact same effect on a variable n: they both increase the value of n by one. But the two expressions evaluate to different values. Remember, if the ++ is *before* the variable, then the incrementing is done *before* the value is returned; if the ++ is *after* the variable, then the incrementing is done *after* the value is returned.

decrement
operator

Everything we said about the increment operator applies to the **decrement operator** as well, except that the value of the variable is decreased by one rather than increased by one. For example, consider the following code:

```
int n = 8;
int valueProduced = n--;
System.out.println(valueProduced);
System.out.println(n);
```

This produces the output:

```
8
7
```

On the other hand, the code

```
int n = 8;
int valueProduced = --n;
System.out.println(valueProduced);
System.out.println(n);
```

produces the output:

```
7
7
```

Both n-- and --n change the value of n by subtracting one, but they evaluate to different values. n-- evaluates to the value n had before it was decremented; on the other hand, --n evaluates to the value n has after it is decremented.

You cannot apply the increment and decrement operators to anything other than a single variable. Expressions such as (x + y)++, --(x + y), 5++, and so forth are all illegal in Java.

The use of the increment and decrement operators can be confusing when used inside of more complicated expressions, and so, we prefer to not use increment or decrement operators inside of expressions, but to only use them as simple statements, such as:

```
n++;
```

Self-Test Exercises

22. What is the output produced by the following lines of program code?

```
int n = (int)3.9;
System.out.println("n == " + n);
```

23. What is the output produced by the following lines of program code?

```
int n = 3;
n++;
System.out.println("n == " + n);
n--;
System.out.println("n == " + n);
```

1.3 The Class String

Words, words, mere words, no matter from the heart.

WILLIAM SHAKESPEARE, *Troilus and Cressida*

String

There is no primitive type for strings in Java. However, there is a class called `String` that can be used to store and process strings of characters. This section introduces the class `String`.

String Constants and Variables

You have already seen constants of type `String`. The quoted string

```
"Hello reader."
```

which appears in the following statement from Display 1.1, is a string constant:

```
System.out.println("Hello reader.");
```

A quoted string is a value of type `String`, although it is normally called an *object* of type `String` rather than a value of type `String`. An object of type `String` is a sequence of characters treated as a single item. A variable of type `String` can name one of these string objects.

For example, the following declares `blessing` to be the name for a `String` variable:

```
String blessing;
```

The following assignment statement sets the value of `blessing` so that `blessing` serves as another name for the `String` object `"Live long and prosper.":`

```
blessing = "Live long and prosper.";
```

The declaration and assignment can be combined into a single statement, as follows:

```
String blessing = "Live long and prosper.";
```

You can write the object named by the `String` variable `blessing` to the screen as follows:

```
System.out.println(blessing);
```

which produces the screen output

```
Live long and prosper.
```

The String Class

The class `String` is a predefined class that is automatically made available to you when you are programming in Java. Objects of type `String` are strings of characters that are written within double quotes. For example, the following declares the variable `motto` to be of type `String` and makes `motto` a name for the `String` object `"We aim to please."`:

```
String motto = "We aim to please.";
```

Concatenation of Strings

+ operator
concatenation

When you use the **+ operator** on two strings, the result is the string obtained by connecting the two strings to get a longer string. This is called **concatenation**. So, when it is used with strings, the + is sometimes called the **concatenation operator**. For example, consider the following:

```
String noun = "Strings";
String sentence;
sentence = noun + "are cool.";
System.out.println(sentence);
```

This will set the variable `sentence` to `"Stringsare cool."` and will output the following to the screen:

```
Stringsare cool.
```

Note that no spaces are added when you concatenate two strings. If you wanted `sentence` set to `"Strings are cool."`, then you should change the assignment statement to add the extra space. For example, the following will add the desired space:

```
sentence = noun + " are cool.";
```

We added a space before the word "are".

You can concatenate any number of `Strings` using the + operator. Moreover, you can use the + operator to concatenate a `String` to almost any other type of item. The result is always a `String`. In most situations, Java will convert an item of any type to a

---

Using the + Sign with Strings

If you connect two strings with the + operator, the result is the concatenation (pasting) of the two strings.

EXAMPLE

```
String name = "Chiana";
String farewell = "Good bye " + name;
System.out.println(farewell);
```

This sets `farewell` to the string **"Good bye Chiana"**. So, it outputs the following to the screen:

```
Good bye Chiana
```

Note that we added a space at the end of **"Good bye "**.

---

string when you connect it to a string with the + operator. For numbers, it does the obvious thing. For example,

```
String solution = "The answer is " + 42;
```

will set the `String` variable `solution` to "The answer is 42". Java converts the integer constant 42 to the string "42" and then concatenates the two strings "The answer is " and "42" to obtain the longer string "The answer is 42".

Notice that a number or other value is converted to a string object only when it is connected to a string with a plus sign. If it is connected to another number with a plus sign, it is not converted to a string. For example,

```
System.out.println("100" + 42);
```

outputs

```
10042
```

but

```
System.out.println(100 + 42);
```

outputs

```
142
```

Classes

Classes are central to Java and you will soon be defining and using your own classes. The class `String`, which we discuss in this section, gives us an opportunity to introduce some class

object

method

of the notation and terminology used for classes. A **class** is the name for a type whose values are objects. **Objects** are entities that store data and can take actions. For example, objects of the class `String` store data consisting of strings of characters, such as `"Hello"`. The actions that an object can take are called **methods**. Most of the methods for the class `String` return some value—that is, produce some value. For example, the method `length()` returns the number of characters in a `String` object. So, `"Hello".length()` returns the integer 5 and this returned value can be stored in an `int` variable as follows:

```
int n = "Hello".length();
```

As indicated by the example `"Hello".length()`, a method is called into action by writing a name for the object followed by a dot followed by the method name with parentheses. When you call a method into action, you are (or your code is) said to **invoke** the method or **call** the method, and the object before the dot is known as the **calling object**.

method call
or method
invocation

calling object

Although you can call a method with a constant object, as in `"Hello".length()`, it is more common to use a variable as the calling object, as illustrated by the following:

```
String greeting = "Hello";
int n = greeting.length();
```

Information needed for the method invocation is given in the parentheses. In some cases, like the method `length`, no information is needed (other than the data in the calling object) and the parentheses are empty. In other cases, which we see soon, there is some information that must be provided inside the parentheses. The information in parentheses is known as an **argument** (or arguments).

argument

sending a
message

Invoking a method is also sometimes called **sending a message** to the object. With this view a message is sent to the object (by invoking a method) and in response the object performs some action. For example, in response to the message

```
greeting.length()
```

the object `greeting` answers with the value 5.

All objects within a class have the same methods, but each object can have different data. For example, the two `String` objects `"Hello"` and `"Good-Bye"` have different data—that is, different strings of characters. However, they have the same methods. Thus, since we know that the `String` object `"Hello"` has the method `length()`, we know that the `String` object `"Good-Bye"` must also have the method `length()`.

You now have seen two kinds of types in Java: primitive types and class types. The main difference you have seen between these two kinds of types is that classes have methods and primitive types do not have methods. We will later see more differences between classes and primitive types. A smaller difference between primitive types and class types is that all the primitive types are spelled using only lowercase letters but, by convention, class types are spelled with their first letter in uppercase, as in `String`.

Classes, Objects, and Methods

A Java program works by having things called **objects** perform actions. The actions are known as **methods** and typically involve data contained in the object. All objects of the same kind are said to be of the same class. So, a **class** is a category of objects. When the object performs the action of a given method, that is called **invoking** the method (or **calling** the method). Information provided to the method in parentheses is called the **argument** (or arguments).

For example, in Display 1.1, `System.out` is an object, `println` is a method, and the following is an invocation of the method by this object using the argument `"Hello reader."`:

```
System.out.println("Hello reader.");
```

String Methods

The class `String` has a number of useful methods that can be used for string-processing applications. A sample of these `String` methods is presented in Display 1.4. Some of the notation and terminology used in Display 1.4 is described in the box entitled "Returned Value." A more complete list of `String` methods is given in Appendix 4.

Returned Value

An expression like `numberOfGirls + numberOfBoys` produces a value. If `numberOfGirls` has the value 2 and `numberOfBoys` has the value 10, then the number produced is 12. The number 12 is the result of evaluating the expression.

Some method invocations are simple kinds of expression, and any such method invocation evaluates to some value. If a method invocation produces a value, we say that the method *returns* the value. For example, suppose your program executes

```
String greeting = "Hello!";
```

After that, if you evaluate `greeting.length()`, the value returned will be 6. So the following code outputs the integer 6:

```
String greeting = "Hello!";
System.out.println(greeting.length());
```

A method can return different values depending on what happens in your program. However, each method can return values of only one type. For example, the method `length` of the class `String` always returns an `int` value. In Display 1.4, the type given before the method name is the type of the values returned by that method. Since `length` always returns an `int` value, the entry for `length` begins

```
int length()
```

As with any method, a `String` method is called (invoked) by writing a `String` object, a dot, the name of the method, and finally a pair of parentheses that enclose any arguments to the method. Let's look at some examples.

length

As we've already noted, the method `length` can be used to find out the number of characters in a string. You can use a call to the method `length` anywhere that you can use a value of type `int`. For example, all of the following are legal Java statements:

```java
String greeting = "Hello";
int count = greeting.length();
System.out.println("Length is " + greeting.length());
```

Display 1.4 Some Methods in the Class **String** (part 1 of 4)

`int length()`

Returns the length of the calling object (which is a string) as a value of type `int`.

EXAMPLE

After program executes `String greeting = "Hello!";`
`greeting.length()` returns 6.

`boolean equals(Other_String)`

Returns **true** if the calling object string and the *Other_String* are equal. Otherwise, returns **false**.

EXAMPLE

After program executes `String greeting = "Hello";`
`greeting.equals("Hello")` returns `true`
`greeting.equals("Good-Bye")` returns `false`
`greeting.equals("hello")` returns `false`

Note that case matters. `"Hello"` and `"hello"` are not equal because one starts with an uppercase letter and the other starts with a lowercase letter.

`boolean equalsIgnoreCase(Other_String)`

Returns **true** if the calling object string and the *Other_String* are equal, considering uppercase and lowercase versions of a letter to be the same. Otherwise, returns **false**.

EXAMPLE

After program executes `String name = "mary!";`
`greeting.equalsIgnoreCase("Mary!")` returns `true`

Display 1.4 Some Methods in the Class **String** (part 2 of 4)

String toLowerCase()

Returns a string with the same characters as the calling object string, but with all letter characters converted to lowercase.

EXAMPLE

After program executes **String greeting = "Hi Mary!";**
greeting.toLowerCase() returns **"hi mary!"**.

String toUpperCase()

Returns a string with the same characters as the calling object string, but with all letter characters converted to uppercase.

EXAMPLE

After program executes **String greeting = "Hi Mary!";**
greeting.toUpperCase() returns **"HI MARY!"**.

String trim()

Returns a string with the same characters as the calling object string, but with leading and trailing white space removed. White space characters are the characters that print as white space on paper, such as the blank (space) character, the tab character, and the new-line character **'\n'**.

EXAMPLE

After program executes **String pause = "   Hmm   ";**
pause.trim() returns **"Hmm"**.

char charAt(*Position*)

Returns the character in the calling object string at the *Position*. Positions are counted 0, 1, 2, etc.

EXAMPLE

After program executes **String greeting = "Hello!";**
greeting.charAt(0) returns **'H'**, and
greeting.charAt(1) returns **'e'**.

String substring(*Start*)

Returns the substring of the calling object string starting from *Start* through to the end of the calling object. Positions are counted 0, 1, 2, etc. Be sure to notice that the character at position *Start* is included in the value returned.

EXAMPLE

After program executes **String sample = "AbcdefG";**
sample.substring(2) returns **"cdefG"**.

(continued)

Display 1.4 **Some Methods in the Class String** (part 3 of 4)

`String substring(`*Start*`, `*End*`)`

Returns the substring of the calling object string starting from position *Start* through, but not including, position *End* of the calling object. Positions are counted 0, 1, 2, etc. Be sure to notice that the character at position *Start* is included in the value returned, but the character at position *End* is not included.

EXAMPLE

After program executes `String sample = "AbcdefG";`
`sample.substring(2, 5)` returns `"cde"`.

`int indexOf(`*A_String*`)`

Returns the index (position) of the first occurrence of the string *A_String* in the calling object string. Positions are counted 0, 1, 2, etc. Returns −1 if *A_String* is not found.

EXAMPLE

After program executes `String greeting = "Hi Mary!";`
`greeting.indexOf("Mary")` returns `3`, and
`greeting.indexOf("Sally")` returns −1.

`int indexOf(`*A_String*`, `*Start*`)`

Returns the index (position) of the first occurrence of the string *A_String* in the calling object string that occurs at or after position *Start*. Positions are counted 0, 1, 2, etc. Returns −1 if *A_String* is not found.

EXAMPLE

After program executes `String name = "Mary, Mary quite contrary";`
`name.indexOf("Mary", 1)` returns `6`.
The same value is returned if `1` is replaced by any number up to and including `6`.
`name.indexOf("Mary", 0)` returns `0`.
`name.indexOf("Mary", 8)` returns −1.

`int lastIndexOf(`*A_String*`)`

Returns the index (position) of the last occurrence of the string *A_String* in the calling object string. Positions are counted 0, 1, 2, etc. Returns −1, if *A_String* is not found.

EXAMPLE

After program executes `String name = "Mary, Mary, Mary quite so";`
`greeting.indexOf("Mary")` returns `0`, and
`name.lastIndexOf("Mary")` returns `12`.

Display 1.4   Some Methods in the Class **String** (part 4 of 4)

---

int **compareTo**(*A_String*)

Compares the calling object string and the string argument to see which comes first in the lexicographic ordering. Lexicographic order is the same as alphabetical order but with the characters ordered as in Appendix 3. Note that in Appendix 3 all the uppercase letters are in regular alphabetical order and all the lowercase letters are in alphabetical order, but all the uppercase letters precede all the lowercase letters. So, lexicographic ordering is the same as alphabetical ordering provided both strings are either all uppercase letters or both strings are all lowercase letters. If the calling string is first, it returns a negative value. If the two strings are equal, it returns zero. If the argument is first, it returns a positive number.

EXAMPLE

After program executes `String entry = "adventure";`
`entry.compareTo("zoo")` returns a negative number,
`entry.compareTo("adventure")` returns 0, and
`entry.compareTo("above")` returns a positive number.

int **compareToIgnoreCase**(*A_String*)

Compares the calling object string and the string argument to see which comes first in the lexicographic ordering, treating uppercase and lowercase letters as being the same. (To be precise, all uppercase letters are treated as if they were their lowercase versions in doing the comparison.) Thus, if both strings consist entirely of letters, the comparison is for ordinary alphabetical order. If the calling string is first, it returns a negative value. If the two strings are equal ignoring case, it returns zero. If the argument is first, it returns a positive number.

EXAMPLE

After program executes `String entry = "adventure";`
`entry.compareToIgnoreCase("Zoo")` returns a negative number,
`entry.compareToIgnoreCase("Adventure")` returns 0, and
`"Zoo".compareToIgnoreCase(entry)` returns a positive number.

---

position

Some methods for the class `String` depend on counting **positions** in the string. Positions are counted starting with 0 not with 1. So, in the string `"Surf time"`, `'S'` is in position 0, `'u'` is in position 1, and so forth. A position is usually referred to as an **index**. So, it would be preferable to say: `'S'` is at index 0, `'u'` is at index 1, and so forth.

index

The method `indexOf` can be used to find the index of a substring of the calling objects. For example, consider

```
String phrase = "Java is fun.";
```

After this declaration, the invocation `phrase.indexOf("is")` will return 5 because the `'i'` of `"is"` is at index 5. (Remember, the first index is 0, not 1.) This is illustrated in Display 1.5.

Display 1.5 **String Indexes**

The 12 characters in the string "Java is fun." have indexes 0 through 11.

0	1	2	3	4	5	6	7	8	9	10	11
J	a	v	a		i	s		f	u	n	.

*Notice that the blanks and the period
count as characters in the string.*

Escape Sequences

**backslash **
escape
sequence

A backslash, \, preceding a character tells the compiler that the character following the \ does not have its usual meaning. Such a sequence is called an **escape sequence** or an **escape character**. The sequence is typed in as two characters with no space between the symbols. Several escape sequences are defined in Java.

If you want to put a backslash, \, or a quote symbol, ", into a string constant, you must escape the ability of the " to terminate a string constant by using \", or the ability of the \ to escape, by using \\. The \\ tells the compiler you mean a real backslash, \, not an escape sequence, and \" means a quote character, not the end of a string constant. A list of escape sequences is given in Display 1.6.

It is important to note that each escape sequence is a single character, even though it is spelled with two symbols. So, the string "Say \"Hi\"!" contains 9 characters ('S', 'a', 'y', the blank character, '\"', 'H', 'i', '\"', and '!'), not 11 characters.

Including a backslash in a quoted string is a little tricky. For example, the string "abc\def" is likely to produce the error message "Invalid escape character." To include a backslash in a string, you need to use two backslashes. The string "abc\\def", if output to the screen, would produce

        abc\def

Display 1.6 **Escape Sequences**

```
\" Double quote.
\' Single quote.
\\ Backslash.
\n New line. Go to the beginning of the next line.
\r Carriage return. Go to the beginning of the current line.
\t Tab. White space up to the next tab stop.
```

The escape sequence \n indicates the start of a new line. For example, the statement

```
System.out.println("To be or\nNot to be.");
```

will write the following to the screen:

```
To be or
Not to be.
```

You do not need to use the escape sequence \' to include a single quote inside a quoted string. For example, "Time's up!" is a valid quoted string. However, you do need \' if you want to indicate the constant for the single-quote character, as in

```
char singleQuote = '\'';
```

String Processing

immutable object

In Java an object of type String is an **immutable object**, meaning that the characters in the String object cannot be changed. This will eventually prove to be important to us, but at this stage of our exploration of Java, it is a misleading statement. To see that an object of type String cannot be changed, note that none of the methods in Display 1.4 changes the value of the String calling object. There are more String methods than those shown in Display 1.4, but none of them lets you write statements that say things like "Change the fifth character in the calling object string to 'x'". This was done intentionally to make the implementation of the String class more efficient and for other reasons that we will discuss later in this book. There is another string class, called StringBuffer, that has methods for altering its string object. We will not discuss the class StringBuffer in this text, but a table explaining many of the methods of the class StringBuffer is included in Appendix 4.

Although there is no method that allows you to change the value of a String object, such as "Hello", you can still write programs that change the value of a String variable, which is probably all you want anyway. To perform the change, you simply use an assignment statement, as in the following example:

```
String name = "Soprano";
name = "Anthony " + name;
```

The assignment statement in the second line changes the value of the name variable so that the string it names changes from "Soprano" to "Anthony Soprano". Display 1.7 contains a demonstration of some simple string processing.

The Unicode Character Set ★

ASCII

Until recently, most programming languages used the *ASCII* character set, which is given in Appendix 3. The **ASCII** character set is simply a list of all the characters normally used on an English-language keyboard plus a few special characters. In this list, each character has been assigned a number so that characters can be stored by storing

Display 1.7 Using the **String** Class

```
1   public class StringProcessingDemo
2   {
3     public static void main(String[] args)
4     {
5        String sentence = "I hate text processing!";
6        int position = sentence.indexOf("hate");
7        String ending =
8              sentence.substring(position + "hate".length());
9
10       System.out.println("01234567890123456789012");
11       System.out.println(sentence);
12       System.out.println("The word \"hate\" starts at index "
13                                          + position);
14       sentence = sentence.substring(0, position) + "adore"
15                                          + ending;
16       System.out.println("The changed string is:");
17       System.out.println(sentence);
18     }
19  }
```

You could just use 4 here, but if you had a String variable instead of "hate", you would have to use length as shown.

Sample Dialogue

```
01234567890123456789012
I hate text processing!
The word "hate" starts at index 2
The changed string is:
I adore text processing!
```

Unicode

the corresponding number. Java, and now many other programming languages, uses the *Unicode* character set. The **Unicode** character set includes the ASCII character set plus many of the characters used in languages with a different alphabet from English. This is not likely to be a big issue if you are using an English-language keyboard. Normally, you can just program as if Java were using the ASCII character set. The ASCII character set is a subset of the Unicode character set, and the subset you are likely to use. Thus, Appendix 3, which lists the ASCII character set, in fact lists the subset of the Unicode character set that we will use in this book. The advantage of the Unicode character set is that it makes it possible to easily handle languages other than English. For example, it is legal to spell a Java identifier using the letters of the Greek alphabet (although you may want a

Greek-language keyboard and monitor to do this). The disadvantage of the Unicode character set is that it sometimes requires more computer memory to store each character than it would if Java used only the ASCII character set.

Self-Test Exercises

24. What is the output produced by the following?

```
String verbPhrase = "is money";
System.out.println("Time" + verbPhrase);
```

25. What is the output produced by the following?

```
String test = "abcdefg";
System.out.println(test.length());
System.out.println(test.charAt(1));
```

26. What is the output produced by the following?

```
String test = "abcdefg";
System.out.println(test.substring(3));
```

27. What is the output produced by the following?

```
System.out.println("abc\ndef");
```

28. What is the output produced by the following?

```
System.out.println("abc\\ndef");
```

29. What is the output produced by the following?

```
String test = "Hello Tony";
test = test.toUpperCase();
System.out.println(test);
```

30. What is the output of the following two lines of Java code?

```
System.out.println("2 + 2 = " + (2 + 2));
System.out.println("2 + 2 = " + 2 + 2);
```

31. Suppose sam is an object of a class named Person and suppose increaseAge is a method for the class Person that takes one argument that is an integer. How do you write an invocation of the method increaseAge using sam as the calling object and using the argument 10? The method increaseAge will change the data in sam so that it simulates sam aging by 10 years.

1.4   Program Style

In matters of grave importance,
style, not sincerity, is the vital thing.

OSCAR WILDE, The Importance of Being Earnest

Java programming style is similar to that used in other languages. The goal is to make your code easy to read and easy to modify. This section gives some basic points on good programming style in general and some information on the conventions normally followed by Java programmers.

Naming Constants

There are two problems with numbers in a computer program. The first is that they carry no mnemonic value. For example, when the number 10 is encountered in a program, it gives no hint of its significance. If the program is a banking program, it might be the number of branch offices or the number of teller windows at the main office. To understand the program, you need to know the significance of each constant. The second problem is that when a program needs to have some numbers changed, the changing tends to introduce errors. Suppose that 10 occurs 12 times in a banking program, that 4 of the times it represents the number of branch offices, and that 8 of the times it represents the number of teller windows at the main office. When the bank opens a new branch and the program needs to be updated, there is a good chance that some of the 10's that should be changed to 11 will not be, or some that should not be changed will be. The way to avoid these problems is to name each number and use the name instead of the number within your program. For example, a banking program might have two constants with the names BRANCH_COUNT and WINDOW_COUNT. Both of these numbers might have a value of 10, but when the bank opens a new branch, all you need to do to update the program is to change the definition of BRANCH_COUNT.

One way to name a number is to initialize a variable to that number value, as in the following example:

```
int BRANCH_COUNT = 10;
int WINDOW_COUNT = 10;
```

There is, however, one problem with this method of naming number constants: You might inadvertently change the value of one of these variables. Java provides a way of marking an initialized variable so that it cannot be changed. The syntax is

```
public static final Type Variable = Constant;
```

For example, the names BRANCH_COUNT and WINDOW_COUNT can be given values that cannot be changed by your code as follows:

```
public static final int BRANCH_COUNT = 10;
public static final int WINDOW_COUNT = 10;
```

These constant definitions must be placed outside of the main method and, when we start having more methods, outside of any other methods. This is illustrated in Display 1.8. When we start writing programs and classes with multiple methods, you will see that the defined constants can be used in all the methods of a class.

Display 1.8 Comments and a Named Constant

```
1    /**
2     Program to show interest on a sample account balance.
3     Author: Jane Q. Programmer.
4     E-mail Address: janeq@somemachine.etc.etc.
5     Last Changed: September 21, 2004.
6    */
7    public class ShowInterest
8    {
9        public static final double INTEREST_RATE = 2.5;
10
11       public static void main(String[] args)
12       {
13           double balance = 100;
14           double interest; //as a percent
15
16           interest = balance * (INTEREST_RATE/100.0);
17           System.out.println("On a balance of $" + balance);
18           System.out.println("you will earn interest of $"
19                                              + interest);
20           System.out.println("All in just one short year.");
21       }
22
23   }
```

Although it would not be as clear, it is legal to place the definition of INTEREST_RATE *here instead.*

Sample Dialogue

```
On a balance of $100.0
you will earn interest of $2.5
All in just one short year.
```

We will fully explain the modifiers `public static final` later in this book, but we can now explain most of what they mean. The part

```
int BRANCH_COUNT = 10;
```

simply declares `BRANCH_COUNT` as a variable and initializes it to `10`. The words that precede this modify the variable `BRANCH_COUNT` in various ways. The word `public` says there are no restrictions on where you can use the name `BRANCH_COUNT`. The word `static` will have to wait until Chapter 5 for an explanation, but be sure to include it. The word `final` means that the value `10` is the *final* value assignment to `BRANCH_COUNT`, or, to phrase it another way, that the program is not allowed to change the value of `BRANCH_COUNT`.

Naming Constants

The syntax for defining a name for a constant, such as a name for a number, is as follows:

SYNTAX
```
public static final Type Variable = Constant;
```

EXAMPLE
```
public static final int MAX_SPEED = 65;
public static final double MIN_SIZE = 0.5;
public static final String GREETING = "Hello friend!";
public static final char GOAL = 'A';
```

Although it is not required, it is the normal practice of programmers to spell named constants using all uppercase letters with the underscore symbol used to separate "words."

Java Spelling Conventions

In Java, as in all programming languages, identifiers for variables, methods, and other items should always be meaningful names that are suggestive of the identifiers' meanings. Although it is not required by the Java language, the common practice of Java programmers is to start the names of classes with uppercase letters and to start the names of variables, objects, and methods with lowercase letters. Defined constants are normally spelled with all uppercase letters and underscore symbols for "punctuation," as we did in the previous subsection.

For example, `String`, `FirstProgram`, and `JOptionPane` are classes, although we have not yet discussed the last one. The identifiers `println`, `balance`, and `readLine` should each be either a variable, object, or method.

Since blanks are not allowed in Java identifiers, "word" boundaries are indicated by an uppercase letter, as in `numberOfPods`. Since defined constants are spelled with all uppercase letters, the underscore symbol is used for "word" boundaries, as in `MAX_SPEED`.

The identifier `System.out` seems to violate this convention, since it names an object but yet begins with an uppercase letter. It does not violate the convention, but the explanation hinges on a topic we have not yet covered. `System` is the name of a class. Within the class named `System` there is a definition of an object named `out`. So, the identifier `System.out` is used to indicate the object `out` (starting with a lowercase letter for an object) that is defined in the class `System` (starting with an uppercase letter for a class). This sort of dot notation will be explained later in the book.

There is one Java convention that people new to Java often find strange. Java programmers normally do not use abbreviations in identifiers, but rather spell things out in full. A Java programmer would not use `numStars`. He or she would use `number-OfStars`. A Java programmer would not use `FirstProg`. He or she would use `First-Program`. This can produce long identifiers and sometimes exceedingly long identifiers. For example, `BufferedReader` and `ArrayIndexOutOfBoundsException` are the names of two standard Java classes. The first will be used in the next chapter and the second will be used later in this book. These long names cause you to do more typing and they make program lines quickly get too long. However, there is a very good reason for using these long names: With the long names, there is seldom any confusion on how the identifiers are spelled. With abbreviations, you often cannot recall how the identifier was abbreviated. Was it `BufReader` or `BuffReader` or `BufferedR` or `BR` or something else? Since all the words are spelled out, you know it must be `Buffered-Reader`. Once they get used to using these long names, most programmers learn to prefer them.

Comments

// comments

There are two ways to insert **comments** in a Java program. In Java the symbols `//` are used to indicate the start of a comment. All of the text between the `//` and the end of the line is a comment. The compiler simply ignores anything that follows `//` on a line. If you want a comment that covers more than one line, place a `//` on each line of the comment. The symbols `//` are two slashes (without a space between them). Comments indicated with `//` are often called **line comments**.

line comments
/*comments*/

There is another way to insert comments in a Java program. Anything between the symbol pair `/*` and the symbol pair `*/` is considered a comment and is ignored by the compiler. Unlike the `//` comments, which require an additional `//` on each line, the `/*` to `*/` comments can span several lines like so:

```
/*This is a multi-line comment.
Note that there is no comment symbol
of any kind on the second line.*/
```

block comments

Comments of the `/* */` type are often called **block comments**. These block comments may be inserted anywhere in a program that a space or line break is allowed. However, they should not be inserted anywhere except where they do not distract from the layout of the program. Usually comments are only placed at the ends of lines or on separate lines by themselves.

Java comes with a program called `javadoc` that will automatically extract documentation from the classes you define. The workings of the `javadoc` program dictate when you normally use each kind of comment.

The `javadoc` program will extract a /* */ comment in certain situations, but `javadoc` will not extract a // comment. We will say more about `javadoc` and comments after we discuss defining classes. In the meantime you may notice the following conventions in our code:

> We use line comments (that is, the // kind) for comments meant only for the code writer or for a programmer who modifies the code and not for any other programmer who merely uses the code.

> For comments that would become part of the documentation for users of our code, we use block comments (that is, the /* */ kind). The `javadoc` program allows you to indicate whether or not a block comment is eligible to be extracted for documentation. If the opening /* has an extra asterisk, like so /**, then the comment is eligible to be extracted. If there is only one asterisk, `javadoc` will not extract the comment. For this reason, our block comments invariably open with /**.

when to comment
It is difficult to say just how many comments a program should contain. The only correct answer is "just enough," which of course conveys little to the novice programmer. It will take some experience to get a feel for when it is best to include a comment. Whenever something is important and not obvious, it merits a comment. However, providing too many comments is as bad as providing too few. A program that has a comment on each line is so buried in comments that the structure of the program is hidden in a sea of obvious observations. Comments like the following contribute nothing to understanding and should not appear in a program:

```
interest = balance * rate; //Computes the interest.
```

self-documenting
A well-written program is what is called **self-documenting**, which means that the structure of the program is clear from the choice of identifier names and the indenting pattern. A completely self-documenting program would need none of these // comments that are only for the programmer who reads or modifies the code. That may be an ideal that is not always realizable, but if your code is full of // comments and you follow our convention on when to use // comments, then either you simply have too many comments or your code is poorly designed.

A very simple example of the two kinds of comments is given in Display 1.8.

Indenting

We will say more about indenting as we introduce more Java. However, the general rule is easy to understand and easy to follow. When one structure is nested inside another structure, the inside structure is indented one more level. For example, in our programs, the `main` method is indented one level, and the statements inside the main method are indented two levels. We prefer to use four spaces for each level of indenting. More than four spaces eats up too much line length. It is possible to get by with indenting only two or three spaces for each level so long as you are consistent. One space for a level of indenting is not enough to be clearly visible.

Self-Test Exercises

32. What are the two kinds of comments in Java?

33. What is the output produced by the following Java code?

```java
/**
 Code for Exercise.
*/
System.out.println("Hello");
//System.out.print("Mr. or Ms. ");
System.out.println("Student");
```

34. What is the normal spelling convention for named constants?

35. Write a line of Java code that will give the name ANSWER to the int value 42. In other words, make ANSWER a named constant for 42.

Chapter Summary

- Compiling a Java class or program produces byte-code, which is the machine language for a fictitious computer. When you run the byte-code, a program called an *interpreter* translates and executes the byte-code instructions on your computer one instruction at a time.

- A variable can be used to hold values, like numbers. The type of the variable must match the type of the value stored in the variable. All variables must be declared before they are used.

- The equal sign, =, is used as the assignment operator in Java. An assignment statement is an instruction to change the value of a variable.

- Each variable should be initialized before the program uses its value.

- Parentheses in arithmetic expressions indicate which arguments are given to an operator. When parentheses are omitted, Java adds implicit parentheses using precedence rules and associativity rules.

- You can have variables and constants of type String. String is a class type, not a primitive type.

- You can use the plus sign to concatenate two strings.

- There are methods in the class String that can be used for string processing.

- Variables (and all other items in a program) should be given names that indicate how they are used.

- You should define names for number constants in a program and use these names rather than writing out the numbers within your program.

- Programs should be self-documenting to the extent possible. However, you should also insert comments to explain any unclear points.

Answers to Self-Test Exercises

1. `Java is not a drink.`

2. ```
   System.out.println("I like Java.");
   System.out.println("You like tea.");
   ```

3. ```
   public class HelloWorld
   {
       public static void main(String[] args)
       {
           System.out.println("Hello World!");
       }
   }
   ```

4. A compiler translates a program written in a programming language such as Java into a program in a low-level language. When you compile a Java program, the compiler translates your Java program into a program expressed in Java byte-code.

5. The program that is input to a compiler is called the *source program*.

6. The translated program that is produced by a compiler is called the *object program* or *object code*.

7. A program that runs Java byte-code instructions is called an *interpreter*. It is also often called the *Java Virtual Machine*.

8. `NiceClass.java`

9. `NiceClass.class`

10. `1stPlayer` may not be used because it starts with a digit; `myprogram.java` may not be used because it contains an illegal symbol, the dot; `long` may not be used because it is a keyword. All the others may be used as variable names. However, `TimeLimit`, while legal, violates the style rule that all variable names begin with a lowercase letter.

11. Yes, a Java program can have two different variables named `number` and `Number`. However, it would not be good style to do so.

12. `int feet = 0, inches = 0;`

13. `int count = 0;`
    `double distance = 1.5;`

14. `distance = time * 80;`

15. `interest = balance * rate;`

16. b
    c
    c

17. `3*x`
    `3*x + y`
    `(x + y)/7`   Note that `x + y/7` is not correct.
    `(3*x + y)/(z + 2)`

18. `(1/3) * 3 is equal to 0.0`

    Since 1 and 3 are of type `int`, the `/` operator performs integer division, which discards the remainder, so the value of 1/3 is 0, not 0.3333…. This makes the value of the entire expression 0 * 3, which of course is 0.

19. `quotient = 2`
    `remainder = 1`

20. `result is 5`

21. a. `52.0`

    b. 9/5 has `int` value 1; because the numerator and denominator are both of type `int`, integer division is done; the fractional part is discarded. The programmer probably wanted floating-point division, which does not discard the part after the decimal point.

    c. `fahrenheit = (9.0/5) * celsius + 32.0;`
       or this
       `fahrenheit = 1.8 * celsius + 32.0;`

22. `n == 3`

23. `n == 4`
    `n == 3`

24. `Time is money`

25. `7`
    `b`

26. `defg`

27. `abc`
    `def`

28. `abc\ndef`

29. `HELLO TONY`

30. The output is

```
2 + 2 = 4
2 + 2 = 22
```

In the expression `"2 + 2 = " + (2 + 2)` the integers 2 and 2 in `(2 + 2)` are added to obtain the integer 4. When 4 is connected to the string `"2 + 2"` with a plus sign, the integer 4 is converted to the string `"4"` and the result is the string `"2 + 2 = 4"`. However `"2 + 2 = " + 2 + 2` is interpreted by Java to mean

```
("2 + 2 = " + 2) + 2
```

The first integer 2 is changed to the string `"2"` because it is being combined with the string `"2 + 2"`. The result is the string `"2 + 2 = 2"`. The last integer 2 is combined with the string `"2 + 2 = 2"`. So, the last 2 is converted to the string `"2"`. So the final result is

```
"2 + 2 = 2" + "2"
```

which is `"2 + 2 = 22"`.

31. `sam.increaseAge(10);`

32. The two kinds of comments are `//` comments and `/* */` comments. Everything following a `//` on the same line is a comment. Everything between a `/*` and a matching `*/` is a comment.

33. `Hello`
    `Student`

34. The normal spelling convention is to spell named constants using all uppercase letters with the underscore symbol used to separate words.

35. `public static final int ANSWER = 42;`

Programming Projects

Many of these Programming Projects can be solved using AW's MyCodeMate. To access these please go to: www.mycodemate.com.

1. One way to measure the amount of energy that is expended during exercise is to use metabolic equivalents (MET). Here are some METS for various activities:

   Running 6 MPH: 10 METS

   Basketball: 8 METS

   Sleeping: 1 MET

The number of calories burned per minute may be estimated using the formula:

Calories/Minute = 0.0175 × MET × Weight(Kg)

Write a program that calculates and outputs the total number of calories burned for a 150-pound person who runs 6 MPH for 30 minutes, plays basketball for 30 minutes, and then sleeps for 6 hours. One kilogram is equal to 2.2 pounds.

2. The video game machines at your local arcade output coupons according to how well you play the game. You can redeem 10 coupons for a candy bar or 3 coupons for a gumball. You prefer candy bars to gumballs. Write a program that defines a variable initially assigned to the number of coupons you win. Next, the program should output how many candy bars and gumballs you can get if you spend all of your coupons on candy bars first, and any remaining coupons on gumballs.

3. Write a program that starts with the string variable `first` set to your first name and the string variable `last` set to your last name. Both names should be all lowercase. Your program should then create a new string that contains your full name in pig latin with the first letter capitalized for the first and last name. Use only the pig latin rule of moving the first letter to the end of the word and adding "ay". Output the pig latin name to the screen. Use the `substring` and `toUpperCase` methods to construct the new name.

For example, given
```
first = "walt";

last = "savitch";
```

the program should create a new string with the text "Altway Avitchsay" and print it.

4. A government research lab has concluded that an artificial sweetener commonly used in diet soda pop will cause death in laboratory mice. A friend of yours is desperate to lose weight but cannot give up soda pop. Your friend wants to know how much diet soda pop it is possible to drink without dying as a result. Write a program to supply the answer. The program has no input but does have defined constants for the following items: the amount of artificial sweetener needed to kill a mouse, the weight of the mouse, the starting weight of the dieter, and the desired weight of the dieter. To ensure the safety of your friend, be sure the program uses the weight at which the dieter will stop dieting, rather than the dieter's current weight, to calculate how much soda pop the dieter can safely drink. You may use any reasonable values for these defined constants. Assume that diet soda contains 1/10th of one percent artificial sweetener. Use another named constant for this fraction. You may want to express the percent as the `double` value `0.001`. (If your program turns out not to use a defined constant, you may remove that defined constant from your program.)

5. Write a program that starts with a line of text and then outputs that line of text with the first occurrence of "hate" changed to "love". For example, a possible sample output might be

```
The line of text to be changed is:
I hate you.
I have rephrased that line to read:
I love you.
```

You can assume that the word "hate" occurs in the input. If the word "hate" occurs more than once in the line, your program will replace only the first occurrence of "hate". Since we will not discuss input until Chapter 2, use a defined constant for the string to be changed. To make your program work for another string, you should only need to change the definition of this defined constant.

Console Input and Output

2

2 Console Input and Output

*Don't imagine you know what a computer terminal is. A computer termi-
nal is not some clunky old television with a typewriter in front of it. It is
an interface where the mind and the body can connect with the universe and move bits of it about.*

DOUGLAS ADAMS, Mostly Harmless
(*the fifth volume in* The Hitchhiker's Trilogy)

Introduction

console I/O

This chapter covers simple output to the screen and input from the keyboard, often
called **console I/O**. We have already been using console output, but this chapter covers it in more detail. In particular, this chapter shows you how to format numerical
output so that you control such details as the number of digits shown after the decimal
point. This chapter also covers the Scanner class, which is new in version 5.0 of Java
and which can be used for console input.

Prerequisites

This chapter uses material from Chapter 1.

2.1   Screen Output

Let me tell the world.

WILLIAM SHAKESPEARE, *Henry IV*

In this section, we review System.out.println and present some material on formatting numeric output. As part of that material, we give a brief introduction to *packages*
and *import statements*. Packages are Java libraries of classes. Import statements make
classes from a package available to your program.

System.out.println

System.out.
println

We have already been using System.out.println for screen output. In Display 1.7, we
used statements such as the following to send output to the display screen:

```
System.out.println("The changed string is:");
System.out.println(sentence);
```

System.out is an object that is part of the Java language, and println is a method invoked by that object. It may seem strange to spell an object name with a dot in it, but that need not concern us for now.

When you use System.out.println for output, the data to be output is given as an argument in parentheses, and the statement ends with a semicolon. The things you can output are strings of text in double quotes, such as "The changed string is:"; String variables such as sentence; variables of other types such as variables of type int; numbers such as 5 or 7.3; and almost any other object or value. If you want to output more than one thing, simply place an addition sign between the things you want to output. For example:

```
System.out.println("Answer is = " + 42
                    + " Accuracy is = " + precision);
```

If the value of precision is 0.01, the output will be

```
Answer is = 42 Accuracy is = 0.01
```

Notice the space at the start of " Accuracy is = ". No space is added automatically.

The + operator used here is the concatenation operator that we discussed earlier. So the above output statement converts the number 42 to the string "42" and then forms the following string using concatenation:

```
"Answer is = 42 Accuracy is = 0.01"
```

System.out.println then outputs this longer string.

Every invocation of println ends a line of output. For example, consider the following statements:

```
System.out.println("A wet bird");
System.out.println("never flies at night.");
```

These two statements cause the following output to appear on the screen:

```
A wet bird
never flies at night.
```

print versus println

If you want the output from two or more output statements to place all their output on a single line, then use print instead of println. For example, the statements

```
System.out.print("A ");
System.out.print("wet ");
System.out.println("bird");
System.out.println("never flies at night.");
```

---

println Output

You can output one line to the screen using **System.out.println**. The items that are output can be quoted strings, variables, numbers, or almost any object you can define in Java. To output more than one item, place a plus sign between the items.

SYNTAX

```
System.out.println(Item_1 + Item_2 + ... + Last_Item);
```

EXAMPLE

```
System.out.println("Welcome to Java.");
System.out.println("Elapsed time = " + time + " seconds");
```

---

produce the same output as our previous example:

```
A wet bird
never flies at night.
```

Notice that a new line is not started until you use println, rather than print. Also notice that the new line starts *after* outputting the items specified in the println. This is the only difference between print and println.

---

println versus print

The only difference between **System.out.println** and **System.out.print** is that with **println**, the *next* output goes on a *new line*, whereas with **print**, the next output is placed on the *same line*.

EXAMPLE

```
System.out.print("Tom ");
System.out.print("Dick ");
System.out.println("and ");
System.out.print("Harry ");
```

produces the following output:

```
Tom Dick and
Harry
```

(The output would look the same whether the last line read **print** or **println**.)

Another way to describe the difference between print and println is to note that

```
System.out.println(SomeThing);
```

is equivalent to

```
System.out.print(SomeThing + "\n");
```

Self-Test Exercises

1. What output is produced by the following lines?

```
String s = "Hello" + "Joe";
System.out.println(s);
```

2. Write Java statements that will cause the following to be written to the screen:

```
One two buckle your shoe.
Three four shut the door.
```

3. What is the difference between System.out.println and System.out.print?

4. What is the output produced by the following lines?

```
System.out.println(2 + " " + 2);
System.out.println(2 + 2);
```

TIP: Different Approaches to Formatting Output

If you have a variable of type double that stores some amount of money, you would like your programs to output the amount in a nice format. However, if you just use System.out. println, you are likely to get output that looks like the following:

```
Your cost, including tax, is $19.98327634144
```

You would like the output to look like this:

```
Your cost, including tax, is $19.98
```

To obtain this nicer form of output, you need some formatting tools.

We will present three approaches to formatting numeric (and other) output. We will discuss the method printf and the two formatting classes NumberFormat and DecimalFormat. The printf method is often the simplest way to format output. However, printf uses an older methodology and so some authorities prefer to use NumberFormat, DecimalFormat, or similar formatting classes because these classes use a programming methodology that is perhaps more in the spirit of modern (object-oriented) programming. We will let you (or your instructor if you are in a class) decide which methodology to use. After this chapter, this book seldom uses any of these formatting details. ∎

Formatting Output with printf

System.out.
printf

Starting with version 5.0, Java includes a method named printf that can be used to give output in a specific format. The method printf is used the same way as the method `print` but allows you to add formatting instructions that specify such things as the number of digits to include after a decimal point. For example, consider the following:

```
double price = 19.8;
System.out.print("$");
System.out.printf("%6.2f", price);
System.out.println(" each");
```

This code outputs the following line:

```
$ 19.80 each
```

The line

```
System.out.printf("%6.2f", price);
```

outputs the string " 19.80" (one blank followed by 19.80), which is the value of the variable `price` written in the format `%6.2f`. In these simple examples, the first argument to `printf` is a string known as the **format specifier**, and the second argument is the number or other value to be output in that format. Let's explain this first sample format specifier.

The format specifier `%6.2f` says to output a floating-point number in a **field** (number of spaces) of width 6 (room for `six` characters) and to show exactly two digits after the decimal point. So, `19.8` is expressed as "19.80" in a field of width 6. Because "19.80" has only `five` characters, a blank character is added to obtain the 6-character string " 19.80". Any extra blank space is added to the front (left-hand end) of the value output. That explains the `6.2` in the format specifier `%6.2f`. The `f` means the output is a floating-point number, that is, a number with a decimal point. We will have more to say about the character `%` shortly, but among other things, it indicates that a format specification (in this case, `6.2f`) follows.

Before we go on, let's note a few details about the method `printf`. Note that the first argument is a string that gives a format specifier. Also, note that `printf`, like `print`, does not advance the output to the next line. The method `printf` is like `print`, not like `println`, in this regard.

The first argument to `printf` can include text as well as a format specifier. For example, consider the following variant on our example:

```
double price = 19.8;
System.out.printf("$%6.2f each", price);
System.out.println();
```

This code also outputs the following line:

```
$ 19.80 each
```

The text before and after the format specifier `%6.2f` is output along with the formatted number. The character `%` signals the end of text to output and the start of the

format specifier (margin note, beside paragraph)

field width (margin note, beside paragraph)

conversion character — format specifier. The end of a format specifier is indicated by a **conversion character** (f in our example).

Other possible format specifiers are described in Display 2.1. (A more complete list of specifiers is given in Appendix 4.) The conversion character specifies the type of value that is output in the specified format. Note that the first number specifies the total number of spaces used to output the value. If that number is larger than the number of spaces needed for the output, extra blanks are added to the beginning of the value output. If that number is smaller than the number of spaces needed for the output, enough extra space is added to allow the value to be output; no matter what field width is specified, printf uses enough space to fit in the entire value output. Both of the numbers in a format specifier such as %6.2f are optional. You may omit either or both numbers, in which case Java chooses an appropriate default value or values. For example, %6f and %.2f. Note that the dot goes with the second number. You can use a format specifier that is just a % followed by a conversion character, such as %f or %g, in which case Java decides on the format details for you. For example, the format specifier %f is equivalent to %.6f, meaning six spaces after the decimal point and no extra space around the output.

e and g — The e and g format specifiers are partially explained in Display 2.1. We still need to explain the meaning of the number after the decimal point in e and g format specifiers, such as %8.3e and %8.3g. The first number, 8 in the examples, is the total field width for the value output. The second number (the one after the decimal point) specifies the number of digits after the decimal point of the output. So the numbers, such as 8.3, have the same meaning in the f, e, and g formats.

s and c — The s and c formats, for strings and characters, may include one number that specifies the field width for outputting the value, such as %15s and %2c. If no number is given, the value is output with no leading or trailing blank space.

right justified — When the value output does not fill the field width specified, blanks are added in front of the value output. The output is then said to be **right justified**. If you add a hyphen after the %, any extra blank space is placed after the value output, and the output is said to be **left justified**. For example, the lines

left justified

```
double value = 12.123;
System.out.printf("Start%8.2fEnd", value);
System.out.println();
System.out.printf("Start%-8.2fEnd", value);
System.out.println();
```

produce the following output. The first line has three spaces before the 12.12 and the second has three spaces after the 12.12.

```
Start   12.12End
Start12.12   End
```

more arguments — So far we have used printf to output only one value. However, printf can output any number of values. The first argument always is a string known as the

format string   **format string**, which can be followed with any number of additional arguments, each of which is a value to output. The format string should include one format specifier, such as `%6.2f` or `%s`, for each value output, and they should be in the same order as the values to be output. For example:

```
double price = 19.8;
String name = "magic apple";
System.out.printf("$%6.2f for each %s.", price, name);
System.out.println();
System.out.println("Wow");
```

Display 2.1   Format Specifiers for `System.out.printf`

CONVERSION CHARACTER	TYPE OF OUTPUT	EXAMPLES
d	Decimal (ordinary) integer	`%5d` `%d`
f	Fixed-point (everyday notation) floating point	`%6.2f` `%f`
e	E-notation floating point	`%8.3e` `%e`
g	General floating point (Java decides whether to use E-notation or not)	`%8.3g` `%g`
s	String	`%12s` `%s`
c	Character	`%2c` `%c`

This code outputs the following:

```
$ 19.80 for each magic apple.
Wow
```

new lines   Note that the format string may contain text as well as format specifiers, and this text is output along with the values of the other arguments to `printf`.

You can include line breaks in a format string. For example, the two lines

```
System.out.printf("$%6.2f for each %s.", price, name);
System.out.println();
```

can be replaced by the single line below, which uses the escape sequence \n:

```
System.out.printf("$%6.2f for each %s.\n", price, name);
```

%n   Although it is legal to use the escape sequence \n to indicate a line break in a format string, it is preferable to use %n. Exactly what happens when a \n is output can be system dependent, whereas %n should always mean a simple new line on any system. So our last line of code would be a little more robust if rewritten using %n as follows:

```
System.out.printf("$%6.2f for each %s.%n", price, name);
```

Many of the details we have discussed about printf are illustrated in the program given in Display 2.2.

TIP: Formatting Money Amounts with printf

A good format specifier for outputting an amount of money stored as a value of type double (or other floating-point value) is %.2f. It says to include exactly two digits after the decimal point and to use the smallest field width that the value will fit into. For example,

```
double price = 19.99;
System.out.printf("The price is $%.2f each.", price);
```

produces the output:

```
The price is $19.99 each.  ■
```

Display 2.2 The **printf** Method (part 1 of 2)

```
1   public class PrintfDemo
2   {
3       public static void main(String[] args)
4       {
5           String aString = "abc";

6           System.out.println("String output:");
7           System.out.println("START1234567890");
8           System.out.printf("START%sEND %n", aString);
9           System.out.printf("START%4sEND %n", aString);
10          System.out.printf("START%2sEND %n", aString);
11          System.out.println();

12          char oneChracter = 'Z';

13          System.out.println("Character output:");
14          System.out.println("START1234567890");
15          System.out.printf("START%cEND %n", oneCharacter);
16          System.out.printf("START%4cEND %n", oneCharacter);
17          System.out.println();
```

(continued)

Display 2.2   **The printf Method** (part 2 of 2)

```
18              double d = 12345.123456789;

19              System.out.println("Floating-point output:");
20              System.out.println("START1234567890");
21              System.out.printf("START%fEND %n", d);
22              System.out.printf("START%.4fEND %n", d);
23              System.out.printf("START%.2fEND %n", d);
24              System.out.printf("START%12.4fEND %n", d);
25              System.out.printf("START%eEND %n", d);
26              System.out.printf("START%12.5eEND %n", d);
27      }
28  }
```

Sample Dialogue

```
String output:
START1234567890
STARTabcEnd
START abcEnd
STARTabcEnd
```
The value is always output. If the specified field width is too small, extra space is taken.

```
Character output:
START1234567890
STARTZEND
START    ZEND
```

```
Floating-point output:
START1234567890
START12345.123457END
START12345.1235END
START12345.12END
START   12345.1235END
START1.234512e+04END
START 1.23451e+04END
```
Note that the output is rounded, not truncated, when digits are discarded.

TIP: Legacy Code

legacy code   Some code is so expensive to replace that it is used even if it is "old fashioned" or otherwise less than ideal. This sort of code is called **legacy code**. One approach to legacy code is to translate it into a more modern language. The Java method printf is essentially the same as a function[1] in the C language that is also named printf. This was done intentionally so that it would be easier to translate C code into Java code. ■

---

[1] Methods are called *functions* in the C language.

System.out.printf

System.out.printf is used for formatted screen output. System.out.printf can have any number of arguments. The first argument is always a format string for the remaining arguments. All the arguments except the first are values to be output to the screen, and these values are output in the formats specified by the format string. The format string can contain text as well as format specifiers, and this text is output along with the values.

Self-Test Exercises

5. What output is produced by the following code?

```
String aString = "Jelly beans";

System.out.println("START1234567890");
System.out.printf("START%sEND %n", aString);
System.out.printf("START%4sEND %n", aString);
System.out.printf("START%13sEND %n", aString);
System.out.println();
```

6. What output is produced by the following code? For each output line, describe whether the line begins or ends with a blank or blanks.

```
String aString = "Jelly beans";
double d = 123.1234567890;

System.out.println("START1234567890");
System.out.printf("START%sEND %n %9.4f %n", aString, d);
```

7. Write a Java statement to output the value in variable d of type double to the screen. The output should be in e-notation with three digits after the decimal point. The output should be in a field of width 15.

Money Formats Using NumberFormat ★

NumberFormat

Using the class NumberFormat, you can tell Java to use the appropriate format when outputting amounts of money. The technique is illustrated in Display 2.3. Let's look at the code in the main method that does the formatting. First consider the following:

```
NumberFormat moneyFormatter =
                NumberFormat.getCurrencyInstance();
```

The method invocation NumberFormat.getCurrencyInstance() produces an object of the class NumberFormat and names the object moneyFormatter. You can use any valid identifier

Display 2.3 **Currency Format** (part 1 of 2)

```
1  import java.text.NumberFormat;
2  import java.util.Locale;
3  public class CurrencyFormatDemo
4  {
5      public static void main(String[] args)
6      {
7          System.out.println("Without formatting:");

8          System.out.println(19.8);
9          System.out.println(19.81111);
10         System.out.println(19.89999);
11         System.out.println(19);
12         System.out.println();

13         System.out.println("Default location:");
14         NumberFormat moneyFormatter =
15                         NumberFormat.getCurrencyInstance();

16         System.out.println(moneyFormatter.format(19.8));
17         System.out.println(moneyFormatter.format(19.81111));
18         System.out.println(moneyFormatter.format(19.89999));
19         System.out.println(moneyFormatter.format(19));
20         System.out.println();

21         System.out.println("US as location:");
22         NumberFormat moneyFormatter2 =
23                         NumberFormat.getCurrencyInstance(Locale.US);

24         System.out.println(moneyFormatter2.format(19.8));
25         System.out.println(moneyFormatter2.format(19.81111));
26         System.out.println(moneyFormatter2.format(19.89999));
27         System.out.println(moneyFormatter2.format(19));
28     }

29  }
```

If you use only the default location, you do not need to import **Locale**.

Notice that this number is rounded to 19.90.

(other than a keyword) in place of moneyFormatter. This object moneyFormatter has a method named format that takes a floating-point number as an argument and returns a String value representing that number in the local currency (the default currency). For example, the invocation

```
moneyFormatter.format(19.8)
```

Display 2.3   **Currency Format** (part 2 of 2)

Sample Dialogue

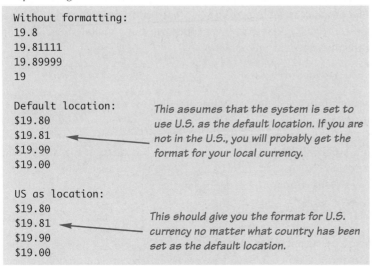

```
Without formatting:
19.8
19.81111
19.89999
19

Default location:
$19.80
$19.81
$19.90
$19.00

US as location:
$19.80
$19.81
$19.90
$19.00
```

This assumes that the system is set to use U.S. as the default location. If you are not in the U.S., you will probably get the format for your local currency.

This should give you the format for U.S. currency no matter what country has been set as the default location.

returns the `String` value `"$19.80"`, assuming the default currency is the U.S. dollar. In Display 2.3, this method invocation occurs inside a `System.out.println` statement, but it is legal anyplace a `String` value is legal. For example, the following would be legal:

```
String moneyString = moneyFormatter.format(19.8);
```

In order to make the class `NumberFormat` available to your code, you must include the following near the start of the file with your program:

```
import java.text.NumberFormat;
```

This is illustrated in Display 2.3.

The method invocation `NumberFormat.getCurrencyInstance()` produces an object that formats numbers according to the default location. In Display 2.3, we are assuming the default location is the United States, and so the numbers are output as U.S. dollars. On other systems, the default should be set to the local currency. If you wish, you can specify the location, and hence the local currency, by giving an argument to `NumberFormat.getCurrencyInstance`. For example, in Display 2.3 we used the constant `Locale.US` to specify that the location is the United States. The relevant line from Display 2.3 is repeated in what follows:

```
NumberFormat moneyFormatter2 =
            NumberFormat.getCurrencyInstance(Locale.US);
```

Some constants for other countries (and hence other currencies) are given in Display 2.4. However, unless your screen is capable of displaying the currency symbol for the country whose constant you use, the output might not be as desired.

These location constants are objects of the class `Locale`. In order to make the class `Locale` and these constants available to your code, you must include the following near the start of the file with your program:

```
import java.util.Locale;
```

If you do not use any of these location constants and only use the default location, you do not need this `import` statement.

The notation `Locale.US` may seem a bit strange, but it follows a convention that is frequently used in Java code. The constant is named `US`, but we want specifically that constant named `US` that is defined in the class `Locale`. So we use `Locale.US`. The notation `Locale.US` means the constant `US` as defined in the class `Locale`.

Importing Packages and Classes

package   Libraries in Java are called **packages**. A package is simply a collection of classes that has been given a name and stored in such a way as to make it easily accessible to your Java programs. Java has a large number of standard packages that automatically come with Java. Two such packages are named `java.text` and `java.util`. In Display 2.3 we used the class `NumberFormat`, which is a member of the package `java.text`. In order to use `NumberFormat`, you must import the class, which we did as follows:

java.text
```
import java.text.NumberFormat;
```

Display 2.4   **Locale Constants for Currencies of Different Countries**

`Locale.CANADA`	Canada (for currency, the format is the same as US)
`Locale.CHINA`	China
`Locale.FRANCE`	France
`Locale.GERMANY`	Germany
`Locale.ITALY`	Italy
`Locale.JAPAN`	Japan
`Locale.KOREA`	Korea
`Locale.TAIWAN`	Taiwan
`Locale.UK`	United Kingdom (English pound)
`Locale.US`	United States

Outputting Amounts of Money

Using the class `MoneyFormat,` you can output an amount of money correctly formatted. To do so, proceed as follows:

Place the following near the start of the file containing your program:

```
import java.text.NumberFormat;
```

In your program code, create an object of the class `NumberFormat` as follows:

```
NumberFormat FormatterObject =
                NumberFormat.getCurrencyInstance();
```

When outputting numbers for amounts of money, change the number to a value of type `String` using the method `FormatterObject.format`, as illustrated in what follows:

```
double moneyAmount = 9.99;
System.out.println(FormatterObject.format(moneyAmount));
```

The string produced by invocations such as `FormatterObject.format(moneyAmount)` adds the dollar sign and ensures that there are exactly two digits after the decimal point. (This is assuming the U.S. dollar is the default currency.)

The numbers formatted in this way may be of type `double`, `int`, or `long`. You may use any (nonkeyword) identifier in place of `FormatterObject`. A complete example is given in Display 2.3.

The above always outputs the money amount in the default currency, which is typically the local currency. You can specify the country whose currency you want. See the text for details.

---

import statement   This kind of statement is called an **import statement**. In this example, the import statement tells Java to look in the package `java.text` to find the definition of the class `NumberFormat`.

If you wanted to import all the classes in the `java.text` package, you would use

```
import java.text .*;
```

Then you can use any class in the `java.text` package.

You don't lose any efficiency in importing the entire package instead of importing only the classes you use. However, many programmers find that it is an aid to documentation if they import only the classes they use, which is what we will do in this book.

java.util   In Display 2.3, we also used the class `Locale`, which is in the `java.util` package. So we also included the following import statement:

```
import java.util.Locale;
```

java.lang

One package requires no import statement. The package java.lang contains classes that are fundamental to Java programming. These classes are so basic that the package is always imported automatically. Any class in java.lang does not need an import statement to make it available to your code. So, when we say that a class is in the package java.lang, you can simply use that class in your program without needing any import statement. For example, the class String is in the java.lang package, so you can use it without any import statement.

More material on packages is covered in Chapter 5.

Self-Test Exercises

8. What output is produced by the following code? (Assume a proper import statement has been given.)

```
NumberFormat exerciseFormatter =
              NumberFormat.getCurrencyInstance(Locale.US);
double d1 = 1.2345, d2 = 15.67890;
System.out.println(exerciseFormatter.format(d1));
System.out.println(exerciseFormatter.format(d2));
```

9. Suppose the class Robot is a part of the standard Java libraries and is in the package named java.awt. What import statement do you need to make the class Robot available to your program or other class?

The DecimalFormat Class ★

System.out.println will let you output numbers but has no facilities to format the numbers. If you want to output a number in a specific format, such as having a specified number of digits after the decimal point, then you must convert the number to a string that shows the number in the desired format and then use System.out.println to output the string. We have seen one way to accomplish this for amounts of money. The class DecimalFormat provides a versatile facility to format numbers in a variety of ways.

The class DecimalFormat is in the Java package named java.text. So you must add the following (or something similar) to the beginning of the file with your program or other class that uses the class DecimalFormat:

import

```
import java.text.DecimalFormat;
```

An object of the class DecimalFormat has a number of different methods that can be used to produce numeral strings in various formats. In this subsection, we discuss one of these methods, which is named format. The general approach to using the format method is discussed in the following pages.

patterns

Create an object of the class DecimalFormat, using a String *Pattern* as follows:

```
DecimalFormat Variable_Name = new DecimalFormat(Pattern);
```

For example,

```java
DecimalFormat formattingObject = new DecimalFormat("000.000");
```

The method `format` of the class `DecimalFormat` can then be used to convert a floating-point number, such as one of type `double`, to a corresponding numeral `String` following the *Pattern* used to create the `DecimalFormat` object. Specifically, an invocation of `format` takes the form

Decimal_Format_Object.`format`(*Double_Expression*)

which returns a `String` value for a string representation of the value of *Double_Expression*. *Double_Expression* can be any expression, such as a variable or sum of variables, that evaluates to a value of type `double`.

For example, consider the following code:

```java
DecimalFormat formattingObject = new DecimalFormat("000.0000");
String numeral = formattingObject.format(12.3456789);
System.out.println(numeral);
```

This produces the output

```
012.3457
```

Of course, you can use an invocation of `format`, such as `formattingObject.format` `(12.3456789)`, directly in `System.out.println`. So, the following code produces the same output:

```java
System.out.println(formattingObject.format(12.3456789));
```

The format of the string produced is determined by the *Pattern* string that was used as the argument to the constructor that created the object of the class `DecimalFormat`. For example, the pattern `"000.0000"` means that there will be three digits before the decimal point and four digits after the decimal point. Note that the result is rounded when the number of digits is less than the number of digits available in the number being formatted. If the format pattern is not consistent with the value of the number, such as a pattern that asks for two digits before the decimal point for a number like `123.456`, then the format rules are violated so that no digits are lost.

A pattern can specify the exact number of digits before and after the decimal, or it can specify minimum numbers of digits. The character `'0'` is used to represent a required digit, and the character `'#'` is used to indicate an optional digit. For example, the pattern `"#0.0##"` indicates one or two digits before the decimal point and one, two, or three digits after the decimal point. The optional digit `'#'` is shown if it is a nonzero digit and is not shown if it is a zero digit. The `'#'` optional digits should go where zero placeholders would appear in a numeral string; in other words, any `'#'` optional digits precede the zero digits `'0'` before the decimal point in the pattern, and any '#' optional digits follow the zero digits '0' after the decimal point in the pattern. Use "#0.0##"; do not use "0#.0##" or "#0.##0".

For example, consider the following code:

```
DecimalFormat formattingObject = new DecimalFormat("#0.0##");
System.out.println(formattingObject.format(12.3456789));
System.out.println(formattingObject.format(1.23456789));
```

This produces the output

```
12.346
1.235
```

percentages   The character '%' placed at the end of a pattern indicates that the number is to be expressed as a percentage. The '%' causes the number to be multiplied by 100 and appends a percent sign, '%'. Examples of this and other formatting patterns are given in Display 2.5.

E-notation   E-notation is specified by including an 'E' in the pattern string. For example, the pattern "00.###E0" approximates specifying two digits before the decimal point, three or fewer digits after the decimal point, and at least one digit after the 'E', as in 12.346E1. As you can see by the examples of E-notation in Display 2.5, the exact details of which E-notation string is produced can be a bit more involved than our explanation so far. Here are a couple more details:

The number of digits indicated after the 'E' is the minimum number of digits used for the exponent. As many more digits as are needed will be used.

mantissa   The **mantissa** is the decimal number before the 'E'. The minimum number of significant digits in the mantissa (that is, the sum of the number of digits before and after the decimal point) is the *minimum* of the number of digits indicated before the decimal point plus the *maximum* of the number of digits indicated after the decimal point. For example, 12345 formatted with "##0.##E0" is "12.3E3".

To get a feel for how E-notation patterns work, it would pay to play with a few cases. In any event, do not count on a very precisely specified number of significant digits.

DecimalFormat Class

Objects of the class DecimalFormat are used to produce strings of a specified format from numbers. As such, these objects can be used to format numeric output. The object is associated with a pattern when it is created using **new**. The object can then be used with the method **format** to create strings that satisfy the format. See Display 2.5 for examples of the DecimalFormat class in use.

Display 2.5 The **DecimalFormat** Class (part 1 of 2)

```
1    import java.text.DecimalFormat;

2    public class DecimalFormatDemo
3    {
4        public static void main(String[] args)
5        {
6            DecimalFormat pattern00dot000 = new DecimalFormat("00.000");
7            DecimalFormat pattern0dot00 = new DecimalFormat("0.00");

8            double d = 12.3456789;
9            System.out.println("Pattern 00.000");
10           System.out.println(pattern00dot000.format(d));
11           System.out.println("Pattern 0.00");
12           System.out.println(pattern0dot00.format(d));

13           double money = 19.8;
14           System.out.println("Pattern 0.00");
15           System.out.println("$" + pattern0dot00.format(money));
16
17           DecimalFormat percent = new DecimalFormat("0.00%");

18           System.out.println("Pattern 0.00%");
19           System.out.println(percent.format(0.308));

20           DecimalFormat eNotation1 =
21               new DecimalFormat("#0.###E0");//1 or 2 digits before point
22           DecimalFormat eNotation2 =
23               new DecimalFormat("00.###E0");//2 digits before point

24           System.out.println("Pattern #0.###E0");
25           System.out.println(eNotation1.format(123.456));
26           System.out.println("Pattern 00.###E0");
27           System.out.println(eNotation2.format(123.456));

28           double smallNumber = 0.0000123456;
29           System.out.println("Pattern #0.###E0");
30           System.out.println(eNotation1.format(smallNumber));
31           System.out.println("Pattern 00.###E0");
32           System.out.println(eNotation2.format(smallNumber));
33       }
34   }
```

(continued)

Display 2.5   **The DecimalFormat Class** (part 2 of 2)

Sample Dialogue

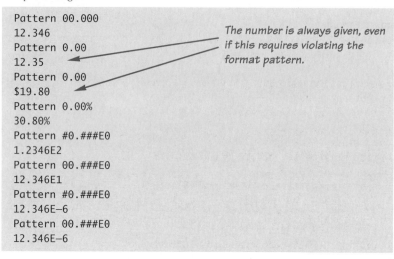

```
Pattern 00.000
12.346
Pattern 0.00
12.35
Pattern 0.00
$19.80
Pattern 0.00%
30.80%
Pattern #0.###E0
1.2346E2
Pattern 00.###E0
12.346E1
Pattern #0.###E0
12.346E-6
Pattern 00.###E0
12.346E-6
```

The number is always given, even if this requires violating the format pattern.

2.2   Console Input Using the Scanner Class

Let the world tell me.

FRANK SHAKESPEARE, *Franky I*

Starting with version 5.0, Java includes a class for doing simple keyboard input. In this section, we show you how to do keyboard input using this class, which is named Scanner.

The Scanner Class

Display 2.6 contains a simple program that uses the Scanner class to read two int values typed in on the keyboard. The numbers entered on the keyboard are shown in color. Let's go over the Scanner-related details line by line. The following line, which should be placed near the start of the file, tells Java where to find the definition of the Scanner class:

import

```
import java.util.Scanner;
```

This line says the Scanner class is in the java.util package; util is short for *utility*, but in Java code, you always use the abbreviated spelling util. A package is simply a library of classes. This import statement makes the Scanner class available to your program.

Display 2.6 **Keyboard Input Demonstration**

```
1    import java.util.Scanner;                          Makes the Scanner class available to
                                                        your program.
2    public class ScannerDemo
3    {
4        public static void main(String[] args)         Creates an object of the class
5        {                                              Scanner and names the
6            Scanner keyboard = new Scanner(System.in); object keyboard.

7            System.out.println("Enter the number of pods followed by");
8            System.out.println("the number of peas in a pod:");
9            int numberOfPods = keyboard.nextInt();      Each reads one int
10           int peasPerPod = keyboard.nextInt();        from the keyboard

11           int totalNumberOfPeas = numberOfPods*peasPerPod;

12           System.out.print(numberOfPods + " pods and ");
13           System.out.println(peasPerPod + " peas per pod.");
14           System.out.println("The total number of peas = "
15                                            + totalNumberOfPeas);
16       }
17   }
```

Sample Dialogue **1**

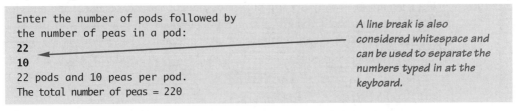

```
Enter the number of pods followed by       The numbers that
the number of peas in a pod:               are input must be
22 10                                      separated by
22 pods and 10 peas per pod.               whitespace, such as
The total number of peas = 220             one or more blanks.
```

Sample Dialogue **2**

```
Enter the number of pods followed by       A line break is also
the number of peas in a pod:               considered whitespace and
22                                         can be used to separate the
10                                         numbers typed in at the
22 pods and 10 peas per pod.               keyboard.
The total number of peas = 220
```

The following line creates an object of the class Scanner and names the object keyboard:

```
Scanner keyboard = new Scanner(System.in);
```

nextInt

After this line appears, you can use methods of the Scanner class with the object keyboard to read data that the user types on the keyboard. For example, the method nextInt reads one int value typed on the keyboard. So, the following line from Display 2.6 reads one value of type int and makes that the value of the variable numberOfPods:

```
int numberOfPods = keyboard.nextInt();
```

In Display 2.6, two such statements each read one int value that the user types in at the keyboard:

```
int numberOfPods = keyboard.nextInt();
int peasPerPod = keyboard.nextInt();
```

whitespace

The numbers typed in must be separated by **whitespace**, such as one or more spaces, a line break, or other whitespace. Whitespace is any string of characters, such as blank spaces, tabs, and line breaks, that prints as whitespace when written on (white) paper.

We often use the identifier keyboard for our Scanner object because the Object is being used for keyboard input. However, you may use other names. If you instead want your object of the class Scanner to be named scannerObject, you would use

```
Scanner scannerObject = new Scanner(System.in);
```

To read a single int value from the keyboard and save it in the int variable n1, you would then use:

```
n1 = scannerObject.nextInt();
```

This is illustrated in the program in Display 2.7.

nextDouble

The program in Display 2.7 also illustrates some of the other Scanner methods for reading values from the keyboard. The method nextDouble works in exactly the same way as nextInt, except that it reads a value of type double. The following example is from Display 2.7:

```
double d1, d2;
d1 = scannerObject.nextDouble();
d2 = scannerObject.nextDouble();
System.out.println("You entered " + d1 + " and " + d2);
```

Display 2.7   **Another Keyboard Input Demonstration** (part 1 of 2)

```
1    import java.util.Scanner;

2    public class ScannerDemo2
3    {
4        public static void main(String[] args)
5        {
6            int n1, n2;
7            Scanner scannerObject = new Scanner(System.in);

8            System.out.println("Enter two whole numbers");
9            System.out.println("separated by one or more spaces:");

10           n1 = scannerObject.nextInt();
11           n2 = scannerObject.nextInt();
12           System.out.println("You entered " + n1 + " and " + n2);

13           System.out.println("Next enter two numbers.");
14           System.out.println("Decimal points are allowed.");

15           double d1, d2;
16           d1 = scannerObject.nextDouble();
17           d2 = scannerObject.nextDouble();
18           System.out.println("You entered " + d1 + " and " + d2);

19           System.out.println("Next enter two words:");

20           String word1 = scannerObject.next();
21           String word2 = scannerObject.next();
22           System.out.println("You entered \"" +
23                                   word1 + "\" and \"" + word2 + "\"");

24           String junk = scannerObject.nextLine(); //To get rid of '\n'

25           System.out.println("Next enter a line of text:");
26           String line = scannerObject.nextLine();
27           System.out.println("You entered: \"" + line + "\"");
28       }
29   }
```

Creates an object of the class **Scanner** *and names the object* **scannerObject**.

Reads one **int** *from the keyboard.*

Reads one **double** *from the keyboard.*

Reads one word from the keyboard.

This line is explained in the Pitfall section "Dealing with the Line Terminator, '\n'"

Reads an entire line.

(continued)

Display 2.7 **Keyboard Input Demonstration** (part 2 of 2)

Sample Dialogue

```
Enter two whole numbers
separated by one or more spaces:
  42    43
You entered 42 and 43
Next enter two numbers.
A decimal point is OK.
 9.99  57
You entered 9.99 and 57.0
Next enter two words:
jelly beans
You entered "jelly" and "beans"
Next enter a line of text:
Java flavored jelly beans are my favorite.
You entered "Java flavored jelly beans are my favorite."
```

The method next reads in a word, as illustrated by the following lines from Display 2.7:

```
String word1 = scannerObject.next();
String word2 = scannerObject.next();
```

If the input line is

```
jelly beans
```

then this will assign w1 the string "jelly" and w2 the string "beans".

word   For the method next, a **word** is any string of nonwhitespace characters delimited by whitespace characters such as blanks or the beginning or ending of a line.

If you want to read in an entire line, you would use the method nextLine. For example,

```
String line = scannerObject.nextLine();
```

reads in one line of input and places the string that is read into the variable line.

The end of an input line is indicted by the escape sequence '\n'. This '\n' character is what you input when you press the Enter (Return) key on the keyboard. On the screen, it is indicated by the ending of one line and the beginning of the next line. When nextLine reads a line of text, it reads this '\n' character, so the next reading of input begins on the next line. However, the '\n' does not become part of the string value returned. So, in the previous code, the string named by the variable line does not end with the '\n' character.

These and other methods for reading in values from the keyboard are given in Display 2.8.

Display 2.8　**Methods of the Scanner Class**　(part 1 of 2)

The Scanner class can be used to obtain input from files as well as from the keyboard. However, here we are assuming it is being used only for input from the keyboard.

To set things up for keyboard input, you need the following at the beginning of the file with the keyboard input code:

import java.util.Scanner;

You also need the following before the first keyboard input statement:

Scanner *Scannner_Object_Name* = new Scanner(System.in);

The *Scannner_Object_Name* can then be used with the following methods to read and return various types of data typed on the keyboard.

Values to be read should be separated by whitespace characters, such as blanks and/or new lines. When reading values, these whitespace characters are skipped. (It is possible to change the separators from whitespace to something else, but whitespace is the default and is what we will use.)

Scannner_Object_Name.nextInt()

Returns the next value of type **int** that is typed on the keyboard.

Scannner_Object_Name.nextLong()

Returns the next value of type **long** that is typed on the keyboard.

Scannner_Object_Name.nextByte()

Returns the next value of type **byte** that is typed on the keyboard.

Scannner_Object_Name.nextShort()

Returns the next value of type **short** that is typed on the keyboard.

Scannner_Object_Name.nextDouble()

Returns the next value of type **double** that is typed on the keyboard.

Scannner_Object_Name.nextFloat()

Returns the next value of type **float** that is typed on the keyboard.

Scannner_Object_Name.next()

Returns the **String** value consisting of the next keyboard characters up to, but not including, the first delimiter character. The default delimiters are whitespace characters.

(continued)

Display 2.8 Methods of the **Scanner** Class (part 2 of 2)

Scannner_Object_Name.`nextBoolean()`

Returns the next value of type **boolean** that is typed on the keyboard. The values of **true** and **false** are entered as the strings **"true"** and **"false"**. Any combination of upper- and/or lowercase letters is allowed in spelling **"true"** and **"false"**.

Scanner_Object_Name.`nextLine()`

Reads the rest of the current keyboard input line and returns the characters read as a value of type **String**. Note that the line terminator **'\n'** is read and discarded; it is not included in the string returned.

Scanner_Object_Name.`useDelimiter(`*New_Delimiter*`);`

Changes the delimiter for keyboard input with *Scanner_Object_Name*. The *New_Delimiter* is a value of type String. After this statement is executed, *New_Delimiter* is the only delimiter that separates words or numbers. See the subsection "Other Input Delimiters" for details.

Keyboard Input Using the Scanner Class

You can use an object of the class **Scanner** to read input from the keyboard. To make the **Scanner** class available for use in your code, you should include the following at the start of the file that contains your program (or other code that does keyboard input):

```
import java.util.Scanner;
```

Before you do any keyboard input, you must create an object of the class **Scanner** as follows:

```
Scanner Object_Name = new Scanner(System.in);
```

where *Object_Name* is any (nonkeyword) Java identifier. For example,

```
Scanner keyboard = new Scanner(System.in);
```

The methods **nextInt**, **nextDouble**, and **next** read a value of type **int**, a value of type **double**, and a word, respectively. The method **nextLine** reads the remainder of the current input line including the terminating **'\n'**. However, the **'\n'** is not included in the string value returned. Other input methods are given in Display 2.8.

SYNTAX

```
Int_Variable = Object_Name.nextInt()
Double_Variable = Object_Name.nextDouble();
String_Variable = Object_Name.next();
String_Variable = Object_Name.nextLine();
```

EXAMPLE

```
int number;
number = keyboard.nextInt();
double cost;
cost = keyboard.nextDouble();
String word;
word = keyboard.next();
String line;
line = keyboard.nextLine();
```

 PITFALL: Dealing with the Line Terminator, '\n'

The method nextLine of the class Scanner reads the *remainder* of a line of text *starting wherever the last keyboard reading left off.* For example, suppose you create an object of the class Scanner as follows:

```
Scanner keyboard = new Scanner(System.in);
```

and suppose you continue with the following code:

```
int n = keyboard.nextInt();
String s1 = keyboard.nextLine();
String s2 = keyboard.nextLine();
```

Now, assume that the input typed on the keyboard is:

```
2 heads are
better than
1 head.
```

This sets the value of the variable n to 2, that of the variable s1 to " heads are", and that of the variable s2 to "better than".

So far there are no problems, but suppose the input were instead

```
2
heads are better than
1 head.
```

You might expect the value of n to be set to 2, the value of the variable s1 to "heads are better than", and that of the variable s2 to "1 head.". But that is not what happens.

What actually happens is that the value of the variable n is set to 2, that of the variable s1 is set to the empty string, and that of the variable s2 to "heads are better than". The method nextInt reads the 2 but does not read the end-of-line character '\n'. So the first nextLine invocation reads the rest of the line that contains the 2.

(continued)

PITFALL: (continued)

There is nothing more on that line (except for `'\n'`), so nextLine returns the empty string. The second invocation of nextLine begins on the next line and reads "heads are better than".

When combining different methods for reading from the keyboard, you sometimes have to include an extra invocation of nextLine to get rid of the end of a line (to get rid of a `'\n'`). This is illustrated in Display 2.8. ■

The Empty String

empty string

A string can have any number of characters. For example, "Hello" has five characters. There is a string with zero characters, which is called the **empty string**. The empty string is written by giving a pair of double quotes with nothing in between the quotes, like so "". The empty string is encountered more often than you might think. If your code is executing the nextLine method to read a line of text, and the user types nothing on the line other than pressing the Enter (Return) key, then the nextLine method reads the empty string.

TIP: Prompt for Input

Always prompt the user when your program needs the user to input some data, as in the following example:

```
System.out.println("Enter the number of pods followed by");
System.out.println("the number of peas in a pod:"); ■
```

TIP: Echo Input

echo input

You should always **echo input**. That is, you should write to the screen all input that your program receives from the keyboard. This way, the user can check that the input has been entered correctly. For example, the following two statements from the program in Display 2.9 echo the values that were read for the number of pods and the number of peas per pod:

```
System.out.print(numberOfPods + " pods and ");
System.out.println(peasPerPod + " peas per pod.");
```

It might seem that there is no need to echo input, because the user's input is automatically displayed on the screen as the user enters it. Why bother to write it to the screen a second time? The input might be incorrect even though it looks correct. For example, the user might type a comma instead of a decimal point or the letter O in place of a zero. Echoing the input can expose such problems. ■

Display 2.9 Self-Service Check Out Line

```java
1    import java.util.Scanner;

2    public class SelfService
3    {
4        public static void main(String[] args)
5        {
6            Scanner keyboard = new Scanner(System.in);

7            System.out.println("Enter number of items purchased");
8            System.out.println("followed by the cost of one item.");
9            System.out.println("Do not use a dollar sign.");

10           int count = keyboard.nextInt();
11           double price = keyboard.nextDouble();
12           double total = count*price;

13           System.out.printf("%d items at $%.2f each.%n", count, price);
14           System.out.printf("Total amount due $%.2f.%n", total);

15           System.out.println("Please take your merchandise.");
16           System.out.printf("Place $%.2f in an envelope %n", total);
17           System.out.println("and slide it under the office door.");
18           System.out.println("Thank you for using the self-service line.");
19       }
20   }
21
```

The dot after %.2f is a period in the text, not part of the format specifier.

Sample Dialogue

```
Enter number of items purchased
followed by the cost of one item.
Do not use a dollar sign.
   10    19.99
10 items at $19.99 each.
Total amount due $199.90.
Please take your merchandise.
Place $199.90 in an envelope
and slide it under the office door.
Thank you for using the self-service line.
```

Self-Test Exercises

10. Write an import statement that makes the `Scanner` class available to your program or other class.

11. Write a line of code that creates a `Scanner` object named `frank` to be used for obtaining keyboard input.

12. Write a line of code that uses the object `frank` from the previous exercise to read in a word from the keyboard and store the word in the `String` variable named `w`.

13. Write a complete Java program that reads in a line of keyboard input containing two values of type `int` (separated by one or more spaces) and outputs the two numbers as well as the sum of the two numbers.

14. Write a complete Java program that reads in a line of text containing exactly three words (separated by any kind or amount of whitespace) and outputs the line with spacing corrected; that is, the output has no space before the first word and exactly one space between each pair of adjacent words.

EXAMPLE: Self-Service Check Out

Display 2.9 contains a first draft of a program to use in the self-service line of a hardware store. It still needs some more details and even some more hardware for accepting payment. However, it does illustrate the use of the `Scanner` class for keyboard input and the `printf` method for formatted output.

Note that in `printf`, we used the format specifier `%.2f` for amounts of money. This specifies a floating-point number with exactly two digits after the decimal point, but gives no field width. Because no field width is given, the number output is placed in the fewest number of spaces that still allows the full value to be shown.

Other Input Delimiters

When using the `Scanner` class for keyboard input, you can change the delimiters that separate keyboard input to almost any combination of characters, but the details are a bit involved. In this book, we will describe only one simple kind of delimiter change. We will tell you how to change the delimiters from whitespace to one specific delimiter string.

For example, suppose you create a Scanner object as follows:

```
Scanner keyboard2 = new Scanner(System.in);
```

You can change the delimiter for the object keyboard2 to "##" as follows:

```
keyboard2.useDelimiter("##");
```

After this invocation of the useDelimiter method, "##" will be the only input delimiter for the input object keyboard2. Note that whitespace will no longer be a delimiter for keyboard input done with keyboard2. For example, suppose the user enters the following keyboard input:

```
one two##three##
```

The following code would read the two strings "one two" and "three" and make them the values of the variables word1 and word2:

```
String word1, word2;
word1 = keyboard2.next();
word2 = keyboard2.next();
```

This is illustrated in Display 2.10. Note that you can have two different objects of the class Scanner with different delimiters in the same program.

Note that no whitespace characters, not even line breaks, serve as an input delimiter for keyboard2 once this change is made to keyboard2.

Self-Test Exercises

15. Suppose your code creates an object of the class Scanner named keyboard (as described in this chapter). Write code to change the delimiter for keyboard to a comma followed by a blank.

16. Continue with the object keyboard from Self-Test Exercise 15. Consider the following input:

```
one,two three, four, five
```

What values will the following code assign to the variables word1 and word2?

```
String word1 = keyboard.next();
String word2 = keyboard.next();
```

Display 2.10 Changing the Input Delimiter

```
1    import java.util.Scanner;

2    public class DelimiterDemo
3    {
4        public static void main(String[] args)
5        {
6            Scanner keyboard1 = new Scanner(System.in);
7            Scanner keyboard2 = new Scanner(System.in);
8            keyboard2.useDelimiter("##");
9            //Delimiter for keyboard1 is whitespace.
10           //Delimiter for keyboard2 is ##.


11           String word1, word2;
12           System.out.println("Enter a line of text:");
13           word1 = keyboard1.next();
14           word2 = keyboard1.next();
15           System.out.println("For keyboard1 the two words read are:");
16           System.out.println(word1);
17           System.out.println(word2);
18           String junk = keyboard1.nextLine(); //To get rid of rest of line.
19
20           System.out.println("Reenter the same line of text:");
21           word1 = keyboard2.next();
22           word2 = keyboard2.next();
23           System.out.println("For keyboard2 the two words read are:");
24           System.out.println(word1);
25           System.out.println(word2);
26       }
27   }
```

Sample Dialogue

```
Enter a line of text:
one two##three##
For keyboard1 the two words read are:
one
two##three##
Reenter the same line of text:
one two##three##
For keyboard2 the two words read are:
one two
three
```

Chapter Summary

- You can use `System.out.println` for simple console output.

- You can use `System.out.printf` for formatted console output.

- You can use `NumberFormat.getCurrencyInstance()` to produce an object that can convert numbers to strings that show the number as a correctly formatted currency amount, for example, by adding a dollar sign and having exactly two digits after the decimal point.

- You can use the class `DecimalFormat` to output numbers using almost any format you desire.

- You can use an object of the class `Scanner` for reading keyboard input.

Answers to Self-Test Exercises

1. `HelloJoe`

2. ```
System.out.println("One two buckle your shoe.");
System.out.println("Three four shut the door.");
```

3. `System.out.println` ends a line of input, so the next output goes on the next line. With `System.out.print`, the next output goes on the same line.

4. 2 2
   4

   Note that

   `2 + " " + 2`

   contains a string, namely " ". So, Java knows it is supposed to produce a string. On the other hand, 2 + 2 contains only integers. So Java thinks + denotes addition in this second case and produces the value 4 to be output.

5. ```
START1234567890
STARTJelly beansEND
STARTJelly beansEND
START  Jelly beansEND
```

6. The last two of the following lines end with a blank. The last line begins with two blanks, one that follows %n in the format string and one because the field width is 9 but the number to be output fills only eight spaces.

   ```
START1234567890
STARTJelly beansEND
   123.1235
```

7. `System.out.printf("%15.3e", d);`

8. $1.23
   $15.68

9. Either

```
import java.awt.Robot;
```

or

```
import java.awt.*;
```

10. `import java.util.Scanner;`

11. `Scanner frank = new Scanner(System.in);`

12. `w = frank.next();`

13. `import java.util.Scanner;`

```
public class Exercise
{
    public static void main(String[] args)
    {
        Scanner keyboard = new Scanner(System.in);

        System.out.println("Enter two numbers.");
        int n1 = keyboard.nextInt();
        int n2 = keyboard.nextInt();

        int sum = n1 + n2;

        System.out.println(n1 + " plus " + n2 + " is " + sum);
    }
}
```

14. `import java.util.Scanner;`

```
public class Exercise2
{
    public static void main(String[] args)
    {
        Scanner keyboard = new Scanner(System.in);

        System.out.println("Enter a line with three words:");
        String w1 = keyboard.next();
        String w2 = keyboard.next();
        String w3 = keyboard.next();

        System.out.println(w1 + " " + w2 + " " + w3);
    }
}
```

15. `keyboard.useDelimiter(", ");`

16. w1 is assigned "one,two three"; w2 is assigned "four".

Programming Projects

 Many of these Programming Projects can be solved using AW's MyCodeMate.
To access these please go to: www.mycodemate.com.

 1. The Babylonian algorithm to compute the square root of a number **n** is as follows:

   1. Make a **guess** at the answer (you can pick **n**/2 as your initial guess).
   2. Compute **r = n / guess**
   3. Set **guess = (guess +r) / 2**
   4. Go back to step 2 for as many iterations as necessary. The more you repeat steps 2 and 3, the closer **guess** will become to the square root of **n**.

   Write a program that inputs an integer for **n**, iterates through the Babylonian algorithm five times, and outputs the answer as a `double` to two decimal places. Your answer will be most accurate for small values of **n**.

2. (This is a version with input of an exercise from Chapter 1.) Write a program that inputs two string variables, `first` and `last`, which the user should enter with their name. First, convert both strings to all lowercase. Your program should then create a new string that contains the full name in pig latin with the first letter capitalized for the first and last name. Use only the pig latin rule of moving the first letter to the end of the word and adding "ay". Output the pig latin name to the screen. Use the `substring` and `toUpperCase` methods to construct the new name.

   For example, if the user inputs "Walt" for the first name and "Savitch" for the last name, then the program should create a new string with the text "Altway Avitchsay" and print it.

 3. Write a program that reads in two integers typed on the keyboard and outputs their sum, difference, and product.

4. An automobile is used for commuting purposes. Write a program that takes as input the distance of the commute in miles, the automobile's fuel consumption rate in miles per gallon, and the price of a gallon of gas. The program should then output the cost of the commute.

 5. The straight-line method for computing the yearly depreciation in value D for an item is given by the formula

$$D = \frac{P - S}{Y}$$

   where P is the purchase price, S is the salvage value, and Y is the number of years the item is used. Write a program that takes as input the purchase price of an item, the expected number of years of service, and the expected salvage value. The program should then output the yearly depreciation for the item.

6. (This is a better version of an exercise from Chapter 1.) A government research lab has concluded that an artificial sweetener commonly used in diet soda pop

causes death in laboratory mice. A friend of yours is desperate to lose weight but cannot give up soda pop. Your friend wants to know how much diet soda pop it is possible to drink without dying as a result. Write a program to supply the answer. The input to the program is the amount of artificial sweetener needed to kill a mouse, the weight of the mouse, and the desired weight of the dieter. Assume that diet soda contains 1/10th of one percent artificial sweetener. Use a named constant for this fraction. You may want to express the percent as the double value 0.001.

7. Write a program that determines the change to be dispensed from a vending machine. An item in the machine can cost between 25 cents and a dollar, in 5-cent increments (25, 30, 35, . . . 90, 95, or 100), and the machine accepts only a single dollar bill to pay for the item. For example, a possible sample dialog might be

```
Enter price of item
(from 25 cents to a dollar, in 5-cent increments): 45

You bought an item for 45 cents and gave me a dollar,
so your change is
2 quarters,
0 dimes, and
1 nickels.
```

8. Write a program that reads in a line of text and then outputs that line of text first in all uppercase letters and then in all lowercase letters.

9. (This is a better version of an exercise from Chapter 1.) Write a program that reads in a line of text and then outputs that line of text with the first occurrence of "hate" changed to "love". For example, a possible sample dialog might be

```
Enter a line of text.
I hate you.
I have rephrased that line to read:
I love you.
```

You can assume that the word "hate" occurs in the input. If the word "hate" occurs more than once in the line, your program should replace only the first occurrence of "hate".

3

Flow of Control

If you think we're wax-works," he said, "you ought to pay, you know.
Wax-works weren't made to be looked at for nothing. Nohow!"
"Contrariwise," added the one marked "DEE," "if you think we're alive,
you ought to speak."

LEWIS CARROLL, *Through the Looking-Glass*

Introduction

As in most programming languages, Java handles flow of control with branching and looping statements. Java branching and looping statements are the same as in the C and C++ languages and are very similar to those in other programming languages. (However, the Boolean expressions that control Java branches and loops are a bit different in Java from what they are in C and C++.)

Most branching and looping statements are controlled by Boolean expressions. A Boolean expression is any expression that is either true or false. In Java, the primitive type `boolean` has only the two values `true` and `false`, and Boolean expressions evaluate to one of these two values. Before we discuss Boolean expressions and the type `boolean`, we will introduce the Java branching statements using only Boolean expressions whose meaning is intuitively obvious. This will serve to motivate our discussion of Boolean expressions.

Prerequisites

This chapter uses material from Chapters 1 and 2.

3.1   Branching Mechanism

When you come to a fork in the road, take it.

Attributed to Yogi Berra

`if-else` Statements

An `if-else` statement chooses between two alternative statements based on the value of a Boolean expression. For example, suppose you want to design a program to compute a week's salary for an hourly employee. Assume the firm pays an overtime rate of one and one half times the regular rate for all hours after the first 40 hours worked. When the employee works 40 or more hours, the pay is then equal to

```
rate*40 + 1.5*rate*(hours - 40)
```

However, if the employee works less than 40 hours, the correct pay formula is simply

```
rate*hours
```

The following `if-else` statement computes the correct pay for an employee whether the employee works less than 40 hours or works 40 or more hours:

```
if (hours > 40)
    grossPay = rate*40 + 1.5*rate*(hours - 40);
else
    grossPay = rate*hours;
```

The syntax for an `if-else` statement is given in the box entitled "`if-else` Statement." If the Boolean expression in parentheses (after the `if`) evaluates to `true`, then the statement before the `else` is executed. If the Boolean expression evaluates to `false`, then the statement after the `else` is executed.

    Remember that when you use a Boolean expression in an `if-else` statement, the

parentheses   Boolean expression must be enclosed in **parentheses**.

    Notice that an `if-else` statement has smaller statements embedded in it. Most of the statement forms in Java allow you to make larger statements out of smaller ones by combining the smaller statements in certain ways.

Omitting the `else`

Sometimes you want one of the two alternatives in an `if-else` statement to do nothing at all. In Java, this can be accomplished by omitting the `else` part. These sorts of

if statement   statements are referred to as **if statements** to distinguish them from if-else statements. For example, the first of the following two statements is an `if` statement:

```
if (sales > minimum)
    salary = salary + bonus;
System.out.println("salary = $" + salary);
```

If the value of `sales` is greater than the value of `minimum`, the assignment statement is executed and then the following `System.out.println` statement is executed. On the other hand, if the value of `sales` is less than or equal to `minimum`, then the embedded assignment statement is not executed, so the `if` statement causes no change (that is, no bonus is added to the base salary), and the program proceeds directly to the `System.out.println` statement.

Compound Statements

You will often want the branches of an if-else statement to execute more than one statement each. To accomplish this, enclose the statements for each branch between a pair of braces, { and }. A list of statements enclosed in a pair of braces is called a **compound statement**. A compound statement is treated as a single statement by Java and may be used anywhere that a single statement may be used. Thus, the "Multiple Statement Alternatives" version described in the box entitled "if-else Statement" is really just a special case of the "simple" case with one statement in each branch.

---

if-else Statement

The if-else statement chooses between two alternative actions based on the value of a *Boolean_Expression*; that is, an expression that is either true or false, such as balance < 0.

SYNTAX

```
if (Boolean_Expression)
    Yes_Statement
else
    No_Statement
```

Be sure to note that the Boolean_Expression must be enclosed in parentheses.

If *Boolean_Expression* is true, then *Yes_Statement* is executed. If *Boolean_Expression* is false, then *No_Statement* is executed.

EXAMPLE

```
if (time < limit)
    System.out.println("You made it.");
else
    System.out.println("You missed the deadline.");
```

Omitting the else Part

You may omit the else part to obtain what is often called an **if statement**.

Syntax

```
if (Boolean_Expression)
    Action_Statement
```

If *Boolean_Expression* is true, then *Action_Statement* is executed; otherwise, nothing happens and the program goes on to the next statement.

EXAMPLE

```
if (weight > ideal)
    calorieAllotment = calorieAllotment - 500;
```

Multiple Statement Alternatives

In an `if-else` statement, you can have one or both alternatives contain several statements. To accomplish this, group the statements using braces, as in the following example:

```java
if (myScore > yourScore)
  {
    System.out.println("I win!");
    wager = wager + 100;
  }
  else
  {
    System.out.println("I wish these were golf scores.");
    wager = 0;
  }
```

TIP: Placing of Braces

There are two commonly used ways of indenting and placing braces in `if-else` statements. They are illustrated below:

```java
if (myScore > yourScore)
{
    System.out.println("I win!");
    wager = wager + 100;
}
else
{
    System.out.println("I wish these were golf scores.");
    wager = 0;
}
```

and

```java
if (myScore > yourScore) {
    System.out.println("I win!");
    wager = wager + 100;
} else {
    System.out.println("I wish these were golf scores.");
    wager = 0;
}
```

The only difference is the placement of braces. We find the first form easier to read and so prefer the first form. The second form saves lines, so some programmers prefer the second form or some minor variant of it.

Be sure to note the indenting pattern in these examples. ■

Nested Statements

As you have seen, if-else statements and if statements contain smaller statements within them. Thus far, we have used compound statements and simple statements, such as assignment statements, as these smaller substatements, but there are other possibilities. In fact, any statement at all can be used as a subpart of an if-else statement or other statement that has one or more statements within it.

indenting

When nesting statements, you normally indent each level of nested substatements, although there are some special situations (such as a multiway if-else statement) where this rule is not followed.

Self-Test Exercises

1. Write an if-else statement that outputs the word "High" if the value of the variable score is greater than 100 and outputs "Low" if the value of score is at most 100. The variable score is of type int.

2. Suppose savings and expenses are variables of type double that have been given values. Write an if-else statement that outputs the word "Solvent", decreases the value of savings by the value of expenses, and sets the value of expenses to zero, provided that savings is larger than expenses. If, however, savings is less than or equal to expenses, the if-else statement should simply output the word "Bankrupt" without changing the value of any variables.

3. Suppose number is a variable of type int. Write an if-else statement that outputs the word "Positive" if the value of the variable number is greater than 0 and outputs the words "Not positive" if the value of number is less than or equal to 0.

4. Suppose salary and deductions are variables of type double that have been given values. Write an if-else statement that outputs the word "Crazy" if salary is less than deductions; otherwise, it should output "OK" and set the variable net equal to salary minus deductions.

Multiway if-else Statement

multiway if-else statement

The **multiway if-else statement** is not really a different kind of Java statement. It is simply ordinary if-else statements nested inside of if-else statements, but it is thought of as a different kind of statement and is indented differently from other nested statements so as to reflect this thinking.

The syntax for a multiway if-else statement and a simple example are given in the box entitled "Multiway if-else Statement." Note that the Boolean expressions are aligned with one another, and their corresponding actions are also aligned with one another. This makes it easy to see the correspondence between Boolean expressions and actions. The Boolean expressions are evaluated in order until a true Boolean expression is found. At that point, the evaluation of Boolean expressions stops, and the action corresponding to the first true Boolean expression is executed. The final else is optional. If there is a final else and all the Boolean expressions are false, the final action is executed. If there is no final else and all the Boolean expressions are false, then no action is taken. An example of a multiway if-else statement is given in the following Programming Example.

Multiway if-else Statement

SYNTAX

```
if (Boolean_Expression_1)
     Statement_1
 else if (Boolean_Expression_2)
     Statement_2
           .
           .
           .
 else if (Boolean_Expression_n)
     Statement_n
 else
     Statement_For_All_Other_Possibilities
```

EXAMPLE

```
if (numberOfPeople < 50)
    System.out.println("Less than 50 people");
 else if (numberOfPeople < 100)
    System.out.println("At least 50 and less than 100 people");
 else if (numberOfPeople < 200)
    System.out.println("At least 100 and less than 200 people");
 else
    System.out.println("At least 200 people");
```

The Boolean expressions are checked in order until the first true Boolean expression is encountered, and then the corresponding statement is executed. If none of the Boolean expressions is true, then the *Statement_For_All_Other_Possibilities* is executed.

EXAMPLE: State Income Tax

Display 3.1 contains a program that uses a multiway if-else statement to compute state income tax. This state computes tax according to the rate schedule below:

1. No tax is paid on the first $15,000 of net income.
2. A tax of 5% is assessed on each dollar of net income from $15,001 to $30,000.
3. A tax of 10% is assessed on each dollar of net income over $30,000.

(continued)

EXAMPLE: (continued)

The program uses a multiway `if-else` statement with one action for each of the above three cases. The condition for the second case is actually more complicated than it needs to be. The computer will not get to the second condition unless it has already tried the first condition and found it to be `false`. Thus, you know that whenever the computer tries the second condition, it knows that `netIncome` is greater than `15000`. Hence, you can replace the line

```
else if ((netIncome > 15000) && (netIncome <= 30000))
```

with the following, and the program will perform exactly the same:

```
else if (netIncome <= 30000)
```

Self-Test Exercises

5. What output will be produced by the following code?

```
int extra = 2;
if (extra < 0)
    System.out.println("small");
else if (extra == 0)
    System.out.println("medium");
else
    System.out.println("large");
```

6. What would be the output in Exercise 5 if the assignment were changed to the following?

```
int extra = -37;
```

7. What would be the output in Exercise 5 if the assignment were changed to the following?

```
int extra = 0;
```

8. Write a multiway `if-else` statement that classifies the value of an `int` variable n into one of the following categories and writes out an appropriate message:

```
n < 0 or 0 ≤ n < 100 or n ≥ 100
```

Hint: Remember that the Boolean expressions are checked in order.

Display 3.1 Tax Program

```
1    import java.util.Scanner;

2    public class IncomeTax
3    {
4        public static void main(String[] args)
5        {
6            Scanner keyboard = new Scanner(System.in);
7            double netIncome, tax, fivePercentTax, tenPercentTax;

8            System.out.println("Enter net income.\n"
9                        + "Do not include a dollar sign or any commas.");
10           netIncome = keyboard.nextDouble( );

11           if (netIncome <= 15000)
12               tax = 0;
13           else if ((netIncome > 15000) && (netIncome <= 30000))
14               //tax = 5% of amount over $15,000
15               tax = (0.05*(netIncome – 15000));
16           else //netIncome > $30,000
17           {
18               //fivePercentTax = 5% of income from $15,000 to $30,000.
19               fivePercentTax = 0.05*15000;
20               //tenPercentTax = 10% of income over $30,000.
21               tenPercentTax = 0.10*(netIncome – 30000);
22               tax = (fivePercentTax + tenPercentTax);
23           }

24           System.out.printf("Tax due = $%.2f", tax);
25       }
26   }
27
```

Sample Dialogue

```
Enter net income.
Do not include a dollar sign or any commas.
40000
Tax due = $1750.00
```

The switch Statement

switch statement

The **switch statement** is the only other kind of Java statement that implements multi-way branches. The syntax for a switch statement and a simple example are shown in the box entitled "The switch Statement."

controlling
expression

case labels

When a switch statement is executed, one of a number of different branches is executed. The choice of which branch to execute is determined by a **controlling expression** given in parentheses after the keyword switch. Following this are a number of occurrences of the reserved word case followed by a constant and a colon. These constants are called **case labels**. The controlling expression for a switch statement must be one of the types char, int, short, or byte.[1] The case labels must all be of the same type as the controlling expression. No case label can occur more than once, because that would be an ambiguous instruction. There may also be a section labeled default:, which is usually last.

When the switch statement is executed, the controlling expression is evaluated and the computer looks at the case labels. If it finds a case label that equals the value of the controlling expression, it executes the code for that case label.

break
statement

The switch statement ends when either a break statement is executed or the end of the switch statement is reached. A **break statement** consists of the keyword break followed by a semicolon. When the computer executes the statements after a case label, it continues until it reaches a break statement. When the computer encounters a break statement, the switch statement ends. If you omit the break statements, then after executing the code for one case, the computer will go on to execute the code for the next case.

Note that you can have two case labels for the same section of code, as in the following portion of a switch statement:

```
case 'A':
case 'a':
    System.out.println("Excellent. You need not take the final.");
    break;
```

Because the first case has no break statement (in fact, no statements at all), the effect is the same as having two labels for one case, but Java syntax requires one keyword case for each label, such as 'A' and 'a'.

default

If no case label has a constant that matches the value of the controlling expression, then the statements following the **default** label are executed. You need not have a default section. If there is no default section and no match is found for the value of the controlling expression, then nothing happens when the switch statement is executed. However, it is safest to always have a default section. If you think your case labels list all possible outcomes, you can put an error message in the default section.

The default case need not be the last case in a switch statement, but making it the last case, as we have always done, makes the code clearer.

A sample switch statement is shown in Display 3.2. Notice that the case labels do not need to be listed in order and need not span a complete interval.

---

[1] As we will see in Chapter 6, the type may also be an enumerated type, but we do not cover enumerated types until Chapter 6.

The switch Statement

SYNTAX

```
switch (Controlling_Expression)
  {
      case Case_Label_1:
          Statement_Sequence_1
          break;
      case Case_Label_2:
              Statement_Sequence_2
          break;
                  .
                  .
                  .
      case Case_Label_n:
          Statement_Sequence_n
          break;
      default:
          Default_Statement_Sequence
          break;
  }
```

Each *Case_Label* *is a constant of the same type as the Controlling_Expression. The Controllng_Expression must be of type* **char**, **int**, **short**, *or* **byte**.

A **break** *may be omitted. If there is no* **break**, *execution just continues to the next case.*

The **default** *case is optional.*

EXAMPLE

```
int vehicleClass;
  double toll;
        .
        .
        .
  switch (vehicleClass)
  {
      case 1:
          System.out.println("Passenger car.");
          toll = 0.50;
          break;
      case 2:
          System.out.println("Bus.");
          toll = 1.50;
          break;
      case 3:
          System.out.println("Truck.");
          toll = 2.00;
          break;
      default:
          System.out.println("Unknown vehicle class!");
          break;
  }
```

Display 3.2 **A switch Statement** (part 1 of 2)

```
1   import java.util.Scanner;
2
3   public class SwitchDemo
4   {
5       public static void main(String[] args)
6       {
7           Scanner keyboard = new Scanner(System.in);
8
8           System.out.println("Enter number of ice cream flavors:");
9           int numberOfFlavors = keyboard.nextInt( );
10          switch (numberOfFlavors)
11          {
12              case 32:
13                  System.out.println("Nice selection.");
14                  break;
15              case 1:
16                  System.out.println("I bet it's vanilla.");
17                  break;
18              case 2:
19              case 3:
20              case 4:
21                  System.out.println(numberOfFlavors + " flavors");
22                  System.out.println("is acceptable.");
23                  break;
24              default:
25                  System.out.println("I didn't plan for");
26                  System.out.println(numberOfFlavors + " flavors.");
27                  break;
28          }
29      }
30  }
```

Controlling expression (arrow pointing to line 10 `(numberOfFlavors)`)

case labels (arrow pointing to lines 12–14)

break statement (arrow pointing to line 17 `break;`)

Sample Dialogue 1

```
Enter number of ice cream flavors:
1
I bet it's vanilla.
```

Sample Dialogue 2

```
Enter number of ice cream flavors:
32
Nice selection.
```

Display 3.2 **A switch Statement** (part 2 of 2)

Sample Dialogue 3

```
Enter number of ice cream flavors:
3
3 flavors
is acceptable.
```

Sample Dialogue 4

```
Enter number of ice cream flavors:
9
I didn't plan for
9 flavors.
```

PITFALL: Forgetting a break in a switch Statement

If you forget a break in a switch statement, the compiler does not issue an error message. You will have written a syntactically correct switch statement, but it will not do what you intended it to do. Notice the annotation in the example in the box entitled "The switch Statement."

The last case in a switch statement does not need a break, but it is a good idea to include it nonetheless. That way, if a new case is added after the last case, you will not forget to add a break (because it is already there). This advice about break statements also applies to the default case when it is last. It is best to place the default case last, but that is not required by the Java language, so there is always a possibility of somebody adding a case after the default case. ■

Self-Test Exercises

9. What is the output produced by the following code?

```java
char letter = 'B';
switch (letter)
{
    case 'A':
    case 'a':
        System.out.println("Some kind of A.");
    case 'B':
    case 'b':
        System.out.println("Some kind of B.");
        break;
    default:
        System.out.println("Something else.");
        break;
}
```

(continued)

Self-Test Exercises (continued)

10. What is the output produced by the following code?

```java
int key = 1;
switch (key + 1)
{
    case 1:
        System.out.println("Apples");
        break;
    case 2:
        System.out.println("Oranges");
        break;
    case 3:
        System.out.println("Peaches");
    case 4:
        System.out.println("Plums");
        break;
    default:
        System.out.println("Fruitless");
}
```

11. What would be the output in Exercise 10 if the first line were changed to the following?

```java
int key = 3;
```

12. What would be the output in Exercise 10 if the first line were changed to the following?

```java
int key = 5;
```

The Conditional Operator ★

conditional
operator
ternary
operator
arithmetic if

You can embed a branch inside of an expression by using a ternary operator known as the **conditional operator** (also called the **ternary operator** or **arithmetic if**). Its use is reminiscent of an older programming style, and we do not advise using it. It is included here for the sake of completeness (and in case you disagree with our programming style).

The conditional operator is a notational variant on certain forms of the if-else statement. The following example illustrates the conditional operator. Consider the following if-else statement:

```java
if (n1 > n2)
    max = n1;
else
    max = n2;
```

This can be expressed using the *conditional operator* as follows:

```
max = (n1 > n2) ? n1 : n2;
```

The expression on the right-hand side of the assignment statement is the conditional operator expression:

```
(n1 > n2) ? n1 : n2
```

The ? and : together form a ternary operator known as the conditional operator. A conditional operator expression starts with a Boolean expression followed by a ? and then followed by two expressions separated with a colon. If the Boolean expression is true, then the value of the first of the two expressions is returned as the value of the entire expression; otherwise, the value of the second of the two expressions is returned as the value of the entire expression.

3.2 Boolean Expressions

"Contrariwise," continued Tweedledee, "if it was so, it might be; and if it were so, it would be; but as it isn't, it ain't. That's logic."

LEWIS CARROLL, *Through the Looking-Glass*

Boolean expression

Now that we have motivated Boolean expressions by using them in if–else statements, we will discuss them and the type boolean in more detail. A **Boolean expression** is simply an expression that is either true or false. The name *Boolean* is derived from George Boole, a 19th-century English logician and mathematician whose work was related to these kinds of expressions.

Simple Boolean Expressions

We have already been using simple Boolean expressions in if–else statements. The simplest Boolean expressions are comparisons of two expressions, such as

```
time < limit
```

and

```
balance <= 0
```

A Boolean expression does not need to be enclosed in parentheses to qualify as a Boolean expression, although it does need to be enclosed in parentheses when it is used in an if–else statement.

Display 3.3 shows the various Java comparison operators you can use to compare two expressions.

PITFALL: Using = in Place of ==

Because the equal sign, =, is used for assignment in Java, something else is needed to indicate equality. In Java, equality is indicated with two equal signs with no space between them, as in

```
if (yourScore == myScore)
    System.out.println("A tie.");
```

Fortunately, if you do use = in place of ==, Java will probably give you a compiler error message. (The only case that does not give an error message is when the expression in parentheses happens to form a correct assignment to a boolean variable.) ■

Display 3.3 Java Comparison Operators

MATH NOTATION	NAME	JAVA NOTATION	JAVA EXAMPLES
=	Equal to	==	`x + 7 == 2*y` `answer == 'y'`
≠	Not equal to	!=	`score != 0` `answer != 'y'`
>	Greater than	>	`time > limit`
≥	Greater than or equal to	>=	`age >= 21`
<	Less than	<	`pressure < max`
≤	Less than or equal to	<=	`time <= limit`

The Methods equals and equalsIgnoreCase

When testing strings for equality, do not use ==. Instead, use either `equals` or `equalsIgnoreCase`.

SYNTAX

String.`equals`(*Other_String*)
String.`equalsIgnoreCase`(*Other_String*)

EXAMPLE

```
String s1;
    .
    .
    .
if ( s1.equals("Hello") )
    System.out.println("The string is Hello.");
else
    System.out.println("The string is not Hello.");
```

 PITFALL: Using == with Strings

Although == correctly tests two values of a primitive type, such as two numbers, to see whether they are equal, it has a different meaning when applied to objects, such as objects of the class String.[2] Recall that an object is something whose type is a class, such as a string. All strings are in the class String (that is, are of type String), so == applied to two strings does not test to see whether the strings are equal. Instead, this tests whether two strings refer to the same object. We'll discuss references in Chapter 15. To test two strings (or any two objects) to see if they have equal values, you should use the method equals rather than ==. For example, suppose s1 and s2 are String variables that have been given values, and consider the statement

```
if (s1.equals(s2))
    System.out.println("They are equal strings.");
else
    System.out.println("They are not equal strings.");
```

If s1 and s2 name strings that contain the same characters in the same order, then the output will be

```
They are equal strings.
```

The notation may seem a bit awkward at first, because it is not symmetric between the two things being tested for equality. The two expressions

```
s1.equals(s2)
s2.equals(s1)
```

are equivalent.

(continued)

---

[2] When applied to two strings (or any two objects), == tests to see if they are stored in the same memory location, but we will not discuss that until Chapter 4. For now, we need only note that == does something other than test for the equality of two strings.

PITFALL: (continued)

The method `equalsIgnoreCase` behaves similarly to `equals`, except that with `equalsIgnoreCase`, the upper- and lowercase versions of the same letter are considered the same. For example, `"Hello"` and `"hello"` are not equal because their first characters, `'H'` and `'h'`, are different characters. But they would be considered equal by the method `equalsIgnoreCase`. For example, the following will output `Equal ignoring case.`:

```
if ("Hello".equalsIgnoreCase("hello"))
    System.out.println("Equal ignoring case.");
```

Notice that it is perfectly legal to use a quoted string with a `String` method, as in the preceding use of `equalsIgnoreCase`. A quoted string is an object of type `String` and has all the methods that any other object of type `String` has.

For the kinds of applications we are looking at in this chapter, you could also use `==` to test for equality of objects of type `String`, and it would deliver the correct answer. However, there are situations in which `==` does not correctly test strings for equality, so you should get in the habit of using `equals` rather than `==` to test strings. ∎

Lexicographic and Alphabetical Order

lexicographic ordering

The method `compareTo` tests two strings to determine their lexicographic order. **Lexicographic ordering** is similar to alphabetic ordering and is sometimes, but not always, the same as alphabetic ordering. The easiest way to think about lexicographic ordering is to think of it as being the same as alphabetic ordering *but with the alphabet ordered differently.* Specifically, in lexicographic ordering, the letters and other characters are ordered as in the ASCII ordering, which is shown in Appendix 3.

compareTo

If `s1` and `s2` are two variables of type `String` that have been given `String` values, then

```
s1.compareTo(s2)
```

returns a negative number if `s1` comes before `s2` in lexicographic ordering, returns zero if the two strings are equal, and returns a positive number if `s2` comes before `s1`. Thus,

```
s1.compareTo(s2) < 0
```

returns true if `s1` comes before `s2` in lexicographic order and returns false otherwise. For example, the following will produce correct output:

```
if (s1.compareTo(s2) < 0)
    System.out.println(
        s1 + " precedes " + s2 + " in lexicographic ordering");
else if (s1.compareTo(s2) > 0)
    System.out.println(
        s1 + " follows " + s2 + " in lexicographic ordering");
else //s1.compareTo(s2) == 0
    System.out.println(s1 + " equals " + s2);
```

If you look at the ordering of characters in Appendix 3, you will see that *all* uppercase letters come before *all* lowercase letters. For example, 'Z' comes before 'a' in lexicographic order. So when comparing two strings consisting of a mix of lowercase and uppercase letters, lexicographic and alphabetic ordering are not the same. However, as shown in Appendix 3, all the lowercase letters are in alphabetic order. So for any two strings of all lowercase letters, lexicographic order is the same as ordinary alphabetic order. Similarly, in the ordering of Appendix 3, all the uppercase letters are in alphabetic order. So for any two strings of all uppercase letters, lexicographic order is the same as ordinary alphabetic order. Thus, if you treat all uppercase letters as if they were lowercase, then lexicographic ordering becomes the same as alphabetic ordering. This is exactly what the method `compareToIgnoreCase` does. Thus, the following produces correct output:

compareTo
IgnoreCase

```java
if (s1.compareToIgnoreCase(s2) < 0)
    System.out.println(
        s1 + " precedes " + s2 + " in ALPHABETIC ordering");
else if (s1.compareToIgnoreCase(s2) > 0)
    System.out.println(
        s1 + " follows " + s2 + " in ALPHABETIC ordering");
else //s1.compareToIgnoreCase(s2) == 0
    System.out.println(s1 + " equals " + s2 + " IGNORING CASE");
```

The above code will compile and produce results no matter what characters are in the strings s1 and s2. However, alphabetic order and the output only make sense if the two strings consist entirely of letters.

The program in Display 3.4 illustrates some of the string comparisons we have just discussed.

Self-Test Exercises

13. Suppose n1 and n2 are two int variables that have been given values. Write a Boolean expression that returns true if the value of n1 is greater than or equal to the value of n2; otherwise, it should return false.

14. Suppose n1 and n2 are two int variables that have been given values. Write an if-else statement that outputs "n1" if n1 is greater than or equal to n2 and outputs "n2" otherwise.

15. Suppose variable1 and variable2 are two variables that have been given values. How do you test whether they are equal when the variables are of type int? How do you test whether they are equal when the variables are of type String?

16. Assume that nextWord is a String variable that has been given a String value consisting entirely of letters. Write some Java code that outputs the message "First half of the alphabet", provided nextWord precedes "N" in alphabetic ordering. If nextWord does not precede "N" in alphabetic ordering, the code should output "Second half of the alphabet". (Note that "N" uses double quotes to produce a String value, as opposed to using single quotes to produce a char value.)

Display 3.4 **Comparing Strings**

```
1    public class StringComparisonDemo
2    {
3        public static void main(String[] args)
4        {
5            String s1 = "Java isn't just for breakfast.";
6            String s2 = "JAVA isn't just for breakfast.";

7            if (s1.equals(s2))
8                System.out.println("The two lines are equal.");
9            else
10               System.out.println("The two lines are not equal.");

11           if (s2.equals(s1))
12               System.out.println("The two lines are equal.");
13           else
14               System.out.println("The two lines are not equal.");

15           if (s1.equalsIgnoreCase(s2))
16               System.out.println("But the lines are equal, ignoring case.");
17           else
18               System.out.println("Lines are not equal, even ignoring case.");

19           String s3 = "A cup of java is a joy forever.";
20           if (s3.compareToIgnoreCase(s1) < 0)
21           {
22               System.out.println("\"" + s3 + "\"");
23               System.out.println("precedes");
24               System.out.println("\"" + s1 + "\"");
25               System.out.println("in alphabetic ordering");
26           }
27           else
28               System.out.println("s3 does not precede s1.");
29       }
30   }
```

Sample Dialogue

```
The two lines are not equal.
The two lines are not equal.
But the lines are equal, ignoring case.
"A cup of java is a joy forever."
precedes
"Java isn't just for breakfast."
in alphabetic ordering
```

Building Boolean Expressions

&& means "and"

You can combine two Boolean expressions using the "and" operator, which is spelled && in Java. For example, the following Boolean expression is true provided number is greater than 2 and number is less than 7:

```
(number > 2) && (number < 7)
```

When two Boolean expressions are connected using &&, the entire expression is true, provided both of the smaller Boolean expressions are true; otherwise, the entire expression is false.

The "and" Operator &&

You can form a more elaborate Boolean expression by combining two simpler Boolean expressions using the "and" operator &&.

SYNTAX (FOR A BOOLEAN EXPRESSION USING &&)

(Boolean_Exp_1) && *(Boolean_Exp_2)*

EXAMPLE (WITHIN AN if–else STATEMENT)

```
if ( (score > 0) && (score < 10) )
    System.out.println("score is between 0 and 10.");
else
    System.out.println("score is not between 0 and 10.");
```

If the value of **score** is greater than 0 and the value of **score** is also less than 10, then the first System.out.println statement is executed; otherwise, the second System.out.println statement is executed.

|| means "or"

You can also combine two Boolean expressions using the "or" operator, which is spelled || in Java. For example, the following is true provided count is less than 3 or count is greater than 12:

```
(count < 3) || (count > 12)
```

When two Boolean expressions are connected using ||, the entire expression is true, provided that one or both of the smaller Boolean expressions are true; otherwise, the entire expression is false.

You can negate any Boolean expression using the ! operator. If you want to negate a Boolean expression, place the expression in parentheses and place the ! operator in front of it. For example, !(savings < debt) means "savings is not less than debt." The ! operator can usually be avoided. For example,

```
!(savings < debt)
```

is equivalent to savings >= debt. In some cases, you can safely omit the parentheses, but the parentheses never do any harm. The exact details on omitting parentheses are given in the subsection entitled "Precedence and Associativity Rules."

The "or" Operator ||

You can form a more elaborate Boolean expression by combining two simpler Boolean expressions using the "or" operator ||.

SYNTAX (FOR A BOOLEAN EXPRESSION USING ||)

(*Boolean_Exp_1*) || (*Boolean_Exp_2*)

EXAMPLE (WITHIN AN if-else STATEMENT)

```
if ((salary > expenses) || (savings > expenses))
    System.out.println("Solvent");
else
    System.out.println("Bankrupt");
```

If `salary` is greater than `expenses` or `savings` is greater than `expenses` (or both), then the first `System.out.println` statement is executed; otherwise, the second `System.out.println` statement is executed.

PITFALL: Strings of Inequalities

Do not use a string of inequalities such as `min < result < max`. If you do, your program will produce a compiler error message. Instead, you must use two inequalities connected with an &&, as follows:

```
(min < result) && (result < max)
```

Self-Test Exercises

17. Write an `if-else` statement that outputs the word "Passed" provided the value of the variable `exam` is greater than or equal to 60 and also the value of the variable `programsDone` is greater than or equal to 10. Otherwise, the `if-else` statement should output the word "Failed". The variables `exam` and `programsDone` are both of type `int`.

18. Write an `if-else` statement that outputs the word "Emergency" provided the value of the variable `pressure` is greater than 100 or the value of the variable `temperature` is greater than or equal to 212. Otherwise, the `if-else` statement should output the word "OK". The variables `pressure` and `temperature` are both of type `int`.

Evaluating Boolean Expressions

Boolean expressions are used to control branch and loop statements. However, a Boolean expression has an independent identity apart from any branch statement or loop statement you might use it in. A Boolean expression returns either `true` or `false`. A variable of type `boolean` can store the values `true` and `false`. Thus, you can set a variable of type `boolean` equal to a Boolean expression. For example:

```
boolean madeIt = (time < limit) && (limit < max);
```

A Boolean expression can be evaluated in the same way that an arithmetic expression is evaluated. The only difference is that an arithmetic expression uses operations such as +, *, and / and produces a number as the final result, whereas a Boolean expression uses relational operations such as == and < and Boolean operations such as &&, ||, and !, and produces one of the two values true and false as the final result.

First, let's review evaluating an arithmetic expression. The same technique will work in the same way to evaluate Boolean expressions. Consider the following arithmetic expression:

```
(number + 1) * (number + 3)
```

Assume that the variable number has the value 2. To evaluate this arithmetic expression, you evaluate the two sums to obtain the numbers 3 and 5, and then you combine these two numbers 3 and 5 using the * operator to obtain 15 as the final value. Notice that in performing this evaluation, you do not multiply the expressions (number + 1) and (number + 3). Instead, you multiply the values of these expressions. You use 3; you do not use (number + 1). You use 5; you do not use (number + 3).

The computer evaluates Boolean expressions the same way. Subexpressions are evaluated to obtain values, each of which is either true or false. In particular, ==, !=, <, <=, and so forth operate on pairs of any primitive type to produce a Boolean value of true or false. These individual values of true or false are then combined according to the rules **truth tables** in the **truth tables** shown in Display 3.5. For example, consider the Boolean expression

```
!( ( count < 3) || (count > 7) )
```

which might be the controlling expression for an if–else statement. Suppose the value of count is 8. In this case, (count < 3) evaluates to false and (count > 7) evaluates to true, so the preceding Boolean expression is equivalent to

```
!( false || true )
```

Consulting the tables for || (which is labeled "OR"), the computer sees that the expression inside the parentheses evaluates to true. Thus, the computer sees that the entire expression is equivalent to

```
!(true)
```

Consulting the tables again, the computer sees that !(true) evaluates to false, and so it concludes that false is the value of the original Boolean expression.

The boolean Values Are true and false

true and false are predefined constants of type boolean. (They must be written in lower-case.) In Java, a Boolean expression evaluates to the boolean value true when it is satisfied and evaluates to the boolean value false when it is not satisfied.

Display 3.5   Truth Tables

AND

Exp_1	Exp_2	Exp_1 && Exp_2
true	true	true
true	false	false
false	true	false
false	false	false

NOT

Exp	! (Exp)
true	false
false	true

OR

Exp_1	Exp_2	Exp_1 || Exp_2
true	true	true
true	false	true
false	true	true
false	false	false

boolean variables in assignments

A `boolean` variable, that is, one of type `boolean`, can be given the value of a Boolean expression by using an assignment statement, in the same way that you use an assignment statement to set the value of an `int` variable or any other type of variable. For example, the following sets the value of the `boolean` variable `isPositive` to `false`:

```
int number = -5;
boolean isPositive;
isPositive = (number > 0);
```

If you prefer, you can combine the last two lines as follows:

```
boolean isPositive = (number > 0);
```

The parentheses are not needed, but they do make it a bit easier to read.

Once a `boolean` variable has a value, you can use the `boolean` variable just as you would use any other Boolean expression. For example, the following code

```
boolean isPositive = (number > 0);
if (isPositive)
    System.out.println("The number is positive.");
else
    System.out.println("The number is negative or zero.");
```

is equivalent to

```
if (number > 0)
    System.out.println("The number is positive.");
else
    System.out.println("The number is negative or zero.");
```

Of course, this is just a toy example. It is unlikely that anybody would use the first of the preceding two examples, but you might use something like it if the value of number, and therefore the value of the Boolean expression, might change. For example, the following code could (by some stretch of the imagination) be part of a program to evaluate lottery tickets:

```
boolean isPositive = (number > 0);
while (number > 0);
{
    System.out.println("Wow!");
    number = number - 1000;
}
if (isPositive)
    System.out.println("Your number is positive.");
else
    System.out.println("Sorry, number is not positive.");
System.out.println("Only positive numbers can win.");
```

---

true and false Are Not Numbers

Many programming languages traditionally use 1 and 0 for **true** and **false**. The latest versions of most languages have changed things so that now most languages have a type like **boolean** with values for **true** and **false**. However, even in these newer language versions, values of type **boolean** are automatically converted to integers and vice versa when context requires it. In particular, C++ automatically makes such conversions.

In Java, the values **true** and **false** are not numbers, nor can they be type cast to any numeric type. Similarly, values of type **int** cannot be type cast to **boolean** values.

 TIP: Naming Boolean Variables

Name a boolean variable with a statement that will be true when the value of the boolean variable is true, such as isPositive, pressureOK, and so forth. That way you can easily understand the meaning of the boolean variable when it is used in an if-else statement or other control statement. Avoid names that do not unambiguously describe the meaning of the variable's value. Do not use names like numberSign, pressureStatus, and so forth. ∎

Short-Circuit and Complete Evaluation

Java takes an occasional shortcut when evaluating a Boolean expression. Notice that in many cases, you need to evaluate only the first of two or more subexpressions in a Boolean expression. For example, consider the following:

```
(savings >= 0) && (dependents > 1)
```

If `savings` is negative, then `(savings >= 0)` is `false`, and, as you can see in the tables in Display 3.5, when one subexpression in an `&&` expression is `false`, then the whole expression is `false`, no matter whether the other expression is `true` or `false`. Thus, if we know that the first expression is `false`, there is no need to evaluate the second expression. A similar thing happens with `||` expressions. If the first of two expressions joined with the `||` operator is `true`, then you know the entire expression is `true`, whether the second expression is `true` or `false`. In some situations, the Java language can and does use these facts to save itself the trouble of evaluating the second subexpression in a logical expression connected with an `&&` or an `||`. Java first evaluates the leftmost of the two expressions joined by an `&&` or an `||`. If that gives it enough information to determine the final value of the expression (independent of the value of the second expression), then Java does not bother to evaluate the second expression. This method of evaluation is called **short-circuit evaluation** or **lazy evaluation**.

short-circuit evaluation
lazy evaluation

Now let's look at an example using `&&` that illustrates the advantage of short-circuit evaluation, and let's give the Boolean expression some context by placing it in an `if` statement:

```
if ( (kids != 0) && ((pieces/kids) >= 2) )
    System.out.println("Each child may have two pieces!");
```

If the value of `kids` is not zero, this statement involves no subtleties. However, suppose the value of `kids` is zero and consider how short-circuit evaluation handles this case. The expression `(kids != 0)` evaluates to `false`, so there would be no need to evaluate the second expression. Using short-circuit evaluation, Java says that the entire expression is `false`, without bothering to evaluate the second expression. This prevents a run-time error, since evaluating the second expression would involve dividing by zero.

complete evaluation

Java also allows you to ask for **complete evaluation**. In complete evaluation, when two expressions are joined by an "and" or an "or," both subexpressions are always evaluated, and then the truth tables are used to obtain the value of the final expression. To obtain complete evaluation in Java, you use `&` rather than `&&` for "and" and use `|` in place of `||` for "or."

In most situations, short-circuit evaluation and complete evaluation give the same result, but, as you have just seen, there are times when short-circuit evaluation can avoid a run-time error. There are also some situations in which complete evaluation is preferred, but we will not use those techniques in this book. We will always use `&&` and `||` to obtain short-circuit evaluation.

Precedence and Associativity Rules

precedence rules

associativity rules

Boolean expressions (and arithmetic expressions) need not be fully parenthesized. If you omit parentheses, Java follows **precedence rules** and **associativity rules** in place of the missing parentheses. One easy way to think of the process is to think of the computer adding parentheses according to these precedence and associativity rules. Some of the Java precedence and associativity rules are given in Display 3.6. (A complete set of precedence and associativity rules is given in Appendix 2.) The computer uses precedence rules to decide where to insert parentheses, but the precedence rules do not differentiate between two operators at the same precedence level, in which case the computer uses the associativity rules to "break the tie."

higher precedence

If one operator occurs higher on the list than another in the precedence table (Display 3.6), the higher-up one is said to have **higher precedence**. If one operator has higher precedence than another, the operator of higher precedence is grouped with its operands (its arguments) before the operator of lower precedence. For example, if the computer is faced with the expression

```
balance * rate + bonus
```

it notices that * has a higher precedence than +, so it first groups * and its operands, as follows:

```
( balance * rate) + bonus
```

Next it groups + with its operands to obtain the fully parenthesized expression

```
(( balance * rate) + bonus)
```

Sometimes two operators have the same precedence, in which case the parentheses are added using the associativity rules. To illustrate this, let's consider another example:

```
bonus + balance * rate / correctionFactor - penalty
```

The operators * and / have higher precedence than either + or –, so * and / are grouped first. But * and / have equal precedence, so the computer consults the associativity rule for * and /, which says they associate from left to right. This means that the *, which is the leftmost of * and /, is grouped first. So the computer interprets the expression as

```
bonus + (balance * rate) / correctionFactor - penalty
```

which in turn is interpreted as

```
bonus + ((balance * rate) / correctionFactor) - penalty
```

because / has higher precedence than either + or –.

This expression is still not fully parenthesized, however. The computer still must choose to group + first or – first. According to the table, + and – have equal prece-

Display 3.6 **Precedence and Associativity Rules**

	Precedence	Associativity
Highest Precedence (Grouped First)	From highest at top to lowest at bottom. Operators in the same group have equal precedence.	
	Dot operator, array indexing, and method invocation ., [ ], ( )	Left to right
	++ (postfix, as in x++), –– (postfix)	Right to left
	The unary operators: +, –, ++ (prefix, as in ++x), –– (prefix), and !	Right to left
	Type casts (Type)	Right to left
	The binary operators *, /, %	Left to right
	The binary operators +, –	Left to right
	The binary operators <, >, <=, >=	Left to right
	The binary operators ==, !=	Left to right
	The binary operator &	Left to right
	The binary operator		Left to right
	The binary operator &&	Left to right
	The binary operator ||	Left to right
Lowest Precedence (Grouped Last)	The ternary operator (conditional operator) ?:	Right to left
	The assignment operators =, *=, /=, %=, +=, –=, &=, |=	Right to left

dence, so the computer must use the associativity rules, which say that + and – are associated left to right. So, it interprets the expression as

```
(bonus + ((balance * rate) / correctionFactor)) - penalty
```

which in turn is interpreted as the following fully parenthesized expression:

```
((bonus + ((balance * rate) / correctionFactor)) - penalty)
```

As you can see from studying the table in Display 3.6, most binary operators associate from left to right. But the assignment operators associate from right to left. So the expression

```
number1 = number2 = number3
```

means

```
number1 = (number2 = number3)
```

which in turn is interpreted as the following fully parenthesized expression:

```
(number1 = (number2 = number3))
```

However, this fully parenthesized expression may not look like it means anything until we explain a bit more about the assignment operator.

Although we do not advocate using the assignment operator = as part of a complex expression, it is an operator that returns a value, just as + and * do. When an assignment operator = is used in an expression, it changes the value of the variable on the left-hand side of the assignment operator and also returns a value—namely, the new value of the variable on the left-hand side of the expression. So (number2 = number3) sets number2 equal to the value of number3 and returns the value of number3. Thus,

```
number1 = number2 = number3
```

which is equivalent to

```
(number1 = (number2 = number3))
```

sets both number2 and number1 equal to the value of number3. It is best to not use assignment statements inside of expressions, although simple chains of assignment operators such as the following are clear and acceptable:

```
number1 = number2 = number3;
```

Although we discourage using expressions that combine the assignment operator and other operators in complicated ways, let's try to parenthesize one just for practice. Consider the following:

```
number1 = number2 = number3 + 7 * factor
```

The operator of highest precedence is *, and the operator of next-highest precedence is +, so this expression is equivalent to

```
number1 = number2 = (number3 + (7 * factor))
```

which leaves only the assignment operators to group. They associate right to left, so the fully parenthesized equivalent version of our expression is

```
(number1 = (number2 = (number3 + (7 * factor))))
```

(Note that there is no case where two operators have equal precedence but one associates from left to right while the other associates from right to left. That must be true or else there would be cases with conflicting instructions for inserting parentheses.)

binding
The association of operands with operators is called **binding**. For example, when parentheses determine which two expressions (two operands) are being added by a particular + sign, that is called binding the two operands to the + sign. A fully parenthesized expression accomplishes binding for all the operators in an expression.

These examples should make it clear that it can be risky to depend too heavily on the precedence and associativity rules. It is best to include most parentheses and only omit parentheses in situations where the intended meaning is very obvious, such as a simple combination of * and +, or a simple chain of &&'s or a simple chain of ||'s. The following examples have some omitted parentheses, but their meaning should be clear:

```
rate * time + lead
(time < limit) && (yourScore > theirScore) && (yourScore > 0)
(expenses < income) || (expenses < savings) || (creditRating > 0)
```

Notice that the precedence rules include both arithmetic operators such as + and * as well as Boolean operators such as && and ||. This is because many expressions combine arithmetic and Boolean operations, as in the following simple example:

```
(number + 1) > 2 || (number + 5) < -3
```

If you check the precedence rules given in Display 3.6, you will see that this expression is equivalent to

```
(((number + 1) > 2) || ((number + 5) < (-3)))
```

because > and < have higher precedence than ||. In fact, you could omit all the parentheses in the above expression and it would have the same meaning (but would be less clear).

It might seem that once an expression is fully parenthesized, the meaning of the expression is then determined. It would seem that to evaluate the expression, you (or the computer) simply evaluate the inner expressions before the outer ones. So, in

```
((number + 1) > 2) || ((number + 5) < (-3))
```

first the expressions (number + 1), (number + 5), and (-3) are evaluated (in any order), then the > and < are evaluated, and then the || is applied. That happens to work in this simple case. In this case, it does not matter which of (number + 1), (number + 5), and (-3) is evaluated first, but in certain other expressions it will be necessary to specify which subexpression is evaluated first. The rules for evaluating a fully parenthesized expression are (and indeed must be) more complicated than just evaluating inner expressions before outer expressions.

For an expression with no side effects, the rule of performing inner parenthesized expressions before outer ones is all you need. That rule will get you through most simple expressions, but for expressions with side effects, you need to learn the rest of the story, which is what we will do next.

side effects

The complications come from the fact that some expressions have *side effects*. When we say an expression has **side effects**, we mean that in addition to returning a value, the expression also changes something, such as the value of a variable. Expressions with the assignment operator have side effects; pay = bonus, for example, changes the value of pay. Increment and decrement operators have side effects; ++n changes the value of n. In expressions that include operators with side effects, you need more rules.

For example, consider

    ((result = (++n)) + (other = (2*(++n))))

The parentheses seem to say that you or the computer should first evaluate the two increment operators, ++n and ++n, but the parentheses do not say which of the two ++n's to do first. If n has the value 2 and we evaluate the leftmost ++n first, then the variable result is set to 3 and the variable other is set to 8 (and the entire expression evaluates to 11). But if we evaluate the rightmost ++n first, then other is set to 6 and result is set to 4 (and the entire expression evaluates to 10). We need a rule to determine the order of evaluation when we have a tie like this. However, rather than simply adding a rule to break such ties, Java instead takes a completely different approach.

To evaluate an expression, Java uses the following three rules:

1. Java first does binding; that is, it first fully parenthesizes the expression using precedence and associativity rules, just as we have outlined.
2. Then it simply evaluates expressions left to right.
3. If an operator is waiting for its two (or one or three) operands to be evaluated, then that operator is evaluated as soon as its operands have been evaluated.

We'll first do an example with no side effects and then an example of an expression with side effects. First the simple example. Consider the expression

    6 + 7 * n - 12

and assume the value of n is 2. Using the precedence and associativity rules, we add parentheses one pair at a time as follows:

    6 + (7 * n) - 12

then

    (6 + (7 * n)) - 12

and finally the fully parenthesized version

    ((6 + (7 * n)) - 12)

Next, we evaluate subexpressions left to right. (6 evaluates to 6 and 7 evaluates to 7, but that's so obvious we will not make a big deal of it.) The variable n evaluates to 2. (Remember, we assumed the value of n was 2.) So, we can rewrite the expression as

```
((6 + (7 * 2)) - 12)
```

The * is the only operator that has both of its operands evaluated, so it evaluates to 14 to produce

```
((6 + 14) - 12)
```

Now + has both of its operands evaluated, so (6 + 14) evaluates to 20 to yield

```
(20 - 12)
```

which in turn evaluates to 8. So 8 is the value for the entire expression.

This may seem like more work than it should be, but remember, the computer is following an algorithm and proceeds step by step; it does not get inspired to make simplifying assumptions.

Next, let's consider an expression with side effects. In fact, let's consider the one we fully parenthesized earlier. Consider the following fully parenthesized expression and assume the value of n is 2:

```
((result = (++n)) + (other = (2*(++n))))
```

Subexpressions are evaluated left to right. So, result is evaluated first. When used with the assignment operator =, a variable simply evaluates to itself. So, result is evaluated and waiting. Next, ++n is evaluated, and it returns the value 3. The expression is now known to be equivalent to

```
((result = 3) + (other = (2*(++n))))
```

Now the assignment operator = has its two operands evaluated, so (result = 3) is evaluated. Evaluating (result = 3) sets the value of result equal to 3 and returns the value 3. Thus, the expression is now known to be equivalent to

```
(3 + (other = (2*(++n))))
```

(and the side effect of setting result equal to 3 has happened). Proceeding left to right, the next thing to evaluate is the variable other, which simply evaluates to itself, so you need not rewrite anything.

Proceeding left to right, the next subexpression that can be evaluated is n, which evaluates to 3. (Remember, n has already been incremented once, so n now has the value 3.) Then ++ has its only argument evaluated, so it is ready to be evaluated. The evaluation of (++n) has the side effect of setting n equal to 4 and evaluates to 4. So, the entire expression is equivalent to

```
(3 + (other = (2*4)))
```

The only subexpression that has its operands evaluated is (2*4), so it is evaluated to 8 to produce

```
(3 + (other = 8))
```

Now the assignment operator = has both of its operands evaluated, so it evaluates to 8 and has the side effect of setting other equal to 8. Thus, we know the value of the expression is

```
(3 + 8)
```

which evaluates to 11. So, the entire expression evaluates to 11 (and has the side effects of setting result equal to 3, setting n equal to 4, and setting other equal to 8).

These rules also allow for method invocations in expressions. For example, in

```
(++n > 0) && (s.length( ) > n)
```

the variable n is incremented before n is compared to s.length( ). When we start defining and using more methods, you will see less-contrived examples of expressions that include method invocations.

All of these rules for evaluating expressions are summarized in the box entitled "Rules for Evaluating Expressions."

Rules for Evaluating Expressions

Expressions are evaluated as follows:

1. Binding: Determine the equivalent fully parenthesized expression using the precedence and associativity rules.
2. Proceeding left to right, evaluate whatever subexpressions you can evaluate. (These subexpressions will be operands or method arguments. For example, in simple cases they may be numeric constants or variables.)
3. Evaluate each outer operation (and method invocation) as soon as all of its operands (all its arguments) have been evaluated.

Self-Test Exercises

19. Determine the value, true or false, of each of the following Boolean expressions, assuming that the value of the variable count is 0 and the value of the variable limit is 10. (Give your answer as one of the values true or false.)

    a. (count == 0) && (limit < 20)

    b. count == 0 && limit < 20

    c. (limit > 20) || (count < 5)

(continued)

d. `!(count == 12)`

e. `(count == 1) && (x < y)`

f. `(count < 10) || (x < y)`

g. `!( ((count < 10) || (x < y)) && (count >= 0) )`

h. `((limit/count) > 7) || (limit < 20)`

i. `(limit < 20) || ((limit/count) > 7)`

j. `((limit/count) > 7) && (limit < 0)`

k. `(limit < 0) && ((limit/count) > 7)`

20. Does the following sequence produce a division by zero?

```
int j = -1;
if ((j > 0) && (1/(j+1) > 10))
    System.out.println(i);
```

21. Convert the following expression to an equivalent fully parenthesized expression:

```
bonus + day * rate / correctionFactor * newGuy - penalty
```

3.3 Loops

It is not true that life is one damn thing after another—
It's one damn thing over and over.

EDNA ST. VINCENT MILLAY,
Letter to Arthur Darison Ficke, October 24, 1930

Looping mechanisms in Java are similar to those in other high-level languages. The three Java loop statements are the `while` statement, the `do-while` statement, and the `for` statement. The same terminology is used with Java as with other languages. The code that is repeated in a loop is called the **body of the loop**. Each repetition of the loop body is called an **iteration** of the loop.

body of the loop
iteration

`while` Statement and `do-while` Statement

while and do-while compared

The syntax for the `while` statement and its variant, the `do-while` statement, is given in the box entitled "Syntax for `while` and `do-while` Statements." In both cases, the multistatement body is a special case of the loop with a single-statement body. The multistatement body is a single compound statement. Examples of `while` and `do-while` statements are given in Display 3.7.

The important difference between the while and do–while loops involves when the controlling Boolean expression is checked. With a while statement, the Boolean expression is checked *before* the loop body is executed. If the Boolean expression evaluates to false, then the body is not executed at all. With a do–while statement, the body of the

Display 3.7   Demonstration of while Loops and do–while Loops (part 1 of 2)

```
1    public class WhileDemo
2    {
3        public static void main(String[] args)
4        {
5            int countDown;

6            System.out.println("First while loop:");
7            countDown = 3;
8            while (countDown > 0)
9            {
10                System.out.println("Hello");
11                countDown = countDown - 1;
12            }

13            System.out.println("Second while loop:");
14            countDown = 0;
15            while (countDown > 0)
16            {
17                System.out.println("Hello");
18                countDown = countDown - 1;
19            }

20            System.out.println("First do-while loop:");
21            countDown = 3;
22            do
23            {
24                System.out.println("Hello");
25                countDown = countDown - 1;
26            } while (countDown > 0);

27            System.out.println("Second do-while loop:");
28            countDown = 0;
29            do
30            {
31                System.out.println("Hello");
32                countDown = countDown - 1;
33            } while (countDown > 0);
34        }
35    }
```

(continued)

Display 3.7 Demonstration of `while` Loops and `do-while` Loops (part 2 of 2)

Sample Dialogue

```
First while loop:
Hello                          A while loop can iterate its
Hello                          body zero times.
Hello
Second while loop:
First do-while loop:
Hello
Hello
Hello
Second do-while loop:
Hello                          A do-while loop always iterates
                               its body at least one time.
```

loop is executed first and the Boolean expression is checked *after* the loop body is executed. Thus, the `do-while` statement always executes the loop body at least once. After this start-up, the `while` loop and the `do-while` loop behave the same. After each iteration of the loop body, the Boolean expression is again checked, and if it is true, the loop is iterated again. If it has changed from `true` to `false`, then the loop statement ends.

executing the body zero times

The first thing that happens when a `while` loop is executed is that the controlling Boolean expression is evaluated. If the Boolean expression evaluates to `false` at that point, the body of the loop is never executed. It might seem pointless to execute the body of a loop zero times, but that is sometimes the desired action. For example, a `while` loop is often used to sum a list of numbers, but the list could be empty. To be more specific, a checkbook-balancing program might use a `while` loop to sum the values of all the checks you have written in a month, but you might take a month's vacation and write no checks at all. In that case, there are zero numbers to sum, so the loop is iterated zero times.

Algorithms and Pseudocode

Dealing with the syntax rules of a programming language is not the hard part of solving a problem with a computer program. The hard part is coming up with the underlying method of solution. This method of solution is called an algorithm. An **algorithm** is a set of precise instructions that leads to a solution. Some approximately equivalent words to *algorithm* are *recipe*, *method*, *directions*, *procedure*, and *routine*.

algorithm

An algorithm is normally written in a mixture of a programming language, in our case Java, and English (or other human language). This mixture of programming language and human language is known as **pseudocode**. Using pseudocode frees you from worrying about fine details of Java syntax so that you can concentrate on the method of solution. Underlying the program in Display 3.8 is an algorithm that can be expressed as the following pseudocode:

pseudocode

Syntax for while and do–while Statements

A while STATEMENT WITH A SINGLE-STATEMENT BODY

```
while (Boolean_Expression)
    Statement
```

A while STATEMENT WITH A MULTISTATEMENT BODY

```
while (Boolean_Expression)
{
    Statement_1
    Statement_2
      .
      .
      .
    Statement_Last
}
```

A do–while STATEMENT WITH A SINGLE-STATEMENT BODY

```
do
    Statement
while (Boolean_Expression);
```

*Do not forget the
final semicolon.*

A do–while STATEMENT WITH A MULTISTATEMENT BODY

```
do
{
    Statement_1
    Statement_2
      .
      .
      .
    Statement_Last
} while (Boolean_Expression);
```

```
Give the user instructions.
count = 0;
sum = 0;
Read a number and store it in a variable named next.
while(next >= 0)
{
    sum = sum + next;
    count++;
    Read a number and store it in next.
}
The average is sum/count provided count is not zero.
Output the results.
```

Display 3.8 Averaging a List of Scores

```java
1   import java.util.Scanner;

2   public class Averager
3   {
4       public static void main(String[] args)
5       {
6           Scanner keyboard = new Scanner(System.in);

7               System.out.println("Enter a list of nonnegative scores.");
8               System.out.println("Mark the end with a negative number.");
9               System.out.println("I will compute their average.");

10              double next, sum = 0;
11              int count = 0;

12              next = keyboard.nextDouble( );
13              while(next >= 0)
14              {
15                  sum = sum + next;
16                  count++;
17                  next = keyboard.nextDouble( );
18              }

19              if (count == 0)
20                  System.out.println("No scores entered.");
21              else
22              {
23                  double average = sum/count;
24                  System.out.println(count + " scores read.");
25                  System.out.println("The average is " + average);
26              }
27      }
28  }
```

Sample Dialogue

```
Enter a list of nonnegative scores.
Mark the end with a negative number.
I will compute their average.
87.5  0  89  99.9  -1
4 scores read.
The average is 69.1.
```

Note that when using pseudocode, we do not necessarily declare variables or worry about the fine syntax details of Java. The only rule is that the pseudocode be precise and clear enough for a good programmer to convert the pseudocode to syntactically correct Java code.

As you will see, significant programs are written not as a single algorithm, but as a set of interacting algorithms; however, each of these algorithms is normally designed in pseudocode unless the algorithm is exceedingly simple.

EXAMPLE: Averaging a List of Scores

Display 3.8 shows a program that reads in a list of scores and computes their average. It illustrates a number of techniques that are commonly used with loops.

The scores are all nonnegative. This allows the program to use a negative number as an end marker. Note that the negative number is not one of the numbers being averaged in. This sort of end marker is known as a **sentinel value**. A sentinel value need not be a negative number, but it must be some value that cannot occur as a "real" input value. For example, if the input list were a list of even integers, then you could use an odd integer as a sentinel value.

sentinel values

To get the loop to end properly, we want the Boolean expression

```
next >= 0
```

checked before adding in the number read. This way we avoid adding in the sentinel value. So, we want the loop body to end with

```
next = keyboard.nextDouble( );
```

To make things work out, this in turn requires that we also place this line before the loop. A loop often needs some preliminary statements to set things up before the loop is executed.

Self-Test Exercises

22. What is the output produced by the following?

```
int n = 10;
while (n > 0)
{
    System.out.println(n);
    n = n - 3;
}
```

23. What output would be produced in Exercise 22 if the > sign were replaced with < ?

(continued)

24. What is the output produced by the following?

```
int n = 10;
do
{
    System.out.println(n);
    n = n - 3;
} while (n > 0);
```

25. What output would be produced in Exercise 24 if the > sign were replaced with < ?

26. What is the output produced by the following?

```
int n = -42;
do
{
    System.out.println(n);
    n = n - 3;
} while (n > 0);
```

27. What is the most important difference between a while statement and a do–while statement?

The for Statement

for statement

The third and final loop statement in Java is the **for statement**. The for statement is most commonly used to step through some integer variable in equal increments. The for statement is, however, a completely general looping mechanism that can do anything that a while loop can do.

For example, the following for statement sums the integers 1 through 10:

```
sum = 0;
for (n = 1; n <= 10; n++)
    sum = sum + n;
```

A for statement begins with the keyword for followed by three expressions in parentheses that tell the computer what to do with the controlling variable(s). The beginning of a for statement looks like the following:

for (*Initialization*; *Boolean_Expression*; *Update*)

The first expression tells how the variable, variables, or other things are initialized, the second expression gives a Boolean expression that is used to check for when the loop should end, and the last expression tells how the loop control variable or variables are updated after each iteration of the loop body. The loop body is a single statement (typically a compound statement) that follows the heading we just described.

The three expressions at the start of a `for` statement are separated by two, and only two, semicolons. Do not succumb to the temptation to place a semicolon after the third expression. (The technical explanation is that these three things are expressions, not statements, and so do not require a semicolon at the end.)

A `for` statement often uses a single `int` variable to control loop iteration and loop ending. However, the three expressions at the start of a `for` statement may be any Java expressions and therefore may involve more (or even fewer) than one variable, and the variables can be of any type.

The semantics of the `for` statement are given in Display 3.9. The syntax for a `for` statement is given in Display 3.10. Display 3.10 also explains how the `for` statement can be viewed as a notational variant of the `while` loop.

The for Statement

SYNTAX

```
for (Initialization; Boolean_Expression; Update)
        Body
```

The *Body* may be any Java statement—either a simple statement or, more likely, a compound statement consisting of a list of statements enclosed in braces, {}. Notice that the three things in parentheses are separated by two, not three, semicolons.

You are allowed to use any Java expression for the *Initializing* and the *Update* expressions. Therefore, you may use more, or fewer, than one variable in the expressions; moreover, the variables may be of any type.

EXAMPLE

```
int next, sum = 0;
for (next = 0; next <= 10; next++)
{
    sum = sum + next;
    System.out.println("sum up to " + next + " is " + sum);
}
```

A variable can be declared in the heading of a `for` statement at the same time that it is initialized. For example:

```
for (int n = 1; n < 10; n++)
    System.out.println(n);
```

There are some subtleties to worry about when you declare a variable in the heading of a `for` statement. These subtleties are discussed in Chapter 4 in the Programming Tip subsection entitled "Declaring Variables in a `for` Statement." It might be wise to avoid such declarations within a `for` statement until you reach Chapter 4, but we mention it here for reference value.

Display 3.9 Semantics of the **for** Statement

```
for (Initialization; Boolean_Expression; Update)
        Body
```

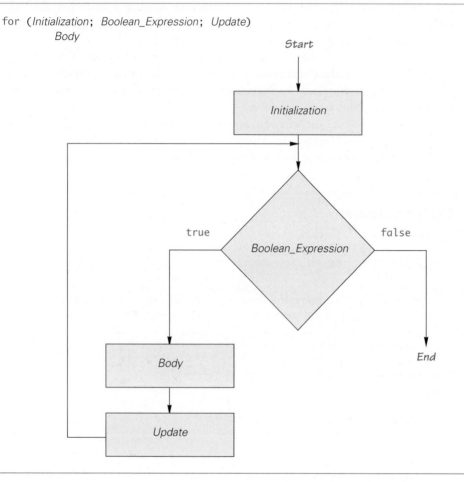

Display 3.10 **for** Statement Syntax and Alternate Semantics (part 1 of 2)

for Statement Syntax

```
for (Initialization; Boolean_Expression; Update)
        Body
```

EXAMPLE

```
for (number = 100; number >= 0; number- -)
    System.out.println(number + " bottles of beer on the shelf.");
```

Equivalent while Loop Syntax

```
Initialization;
while (Boolean_Expression)
{
    Body
    Update;
}
```

EQUIVALENT EXAMPLE

```
number = 100;
while (number >= 0)
{
    System.out.println(number + " bottles of beer on the shelf.");
    number--;
}
```

Sample Dialogue

```
100 bottles of beer on the shelf.
99 bottles of beer on the shelf.
              .
              .
              .
0 bottles of beer on the shelf.
```

The Comma in for Statements

A for loop can contain multiple initialization actions. Simply separate the actions with commas, as in the following:

```
for (term = 1, sum = 0; term <= 10; term++)
    sum = sum + term;
```

This for loop has two initializing actions. The variable term is initialized to 1, and the variable sum is also initialized to 0. Note that you use a comma, not a semicolon, to separate the initialization actions.

You can also use commas to place multiple update actions in a for loop. This can lead to a situation in which the for loop has an empty body but still does something useful. For example, the previous for loop can be rewritten to the following equivalent version:

```
for (term = 1, sum = 0; term <= 10; sum = sum + term, term++)
    //Empty body;
```

This, in effect, makes the loop body part of the update action. We find that it makes for a more readable style if you use the update action only for variables that control the loop, as in the previous version of this for loop. We do not advocate using for loops with no body, but if you do use a for loop with no body, annotate it with a comment such as we did in the preceding for loop. As indicated in the upcoming Pitfall, "Extra Semicolon in a for Statement," a for loop with no body can also occur as the result of a programmer error.

The comma used in a for statement, as we just illustrated, is quite limited in how it can be used. You can use it with assignment statements and with incremented and decremented variables (such as term++ or term--), but not with just any arbitrary statements. In particular, both declaring variables and using the comma in for statements can be troublesome. For example, the following is illegal:

```
for (int term = 1, double sum = 0; term <= 10;  term++)
    sum = sum + term;
```

Even the following is illegal:

```
double sum;
for (int term = 1, sum = 0; term <= 10; term++)
    sum = sum + term;
```

Java will interpret

```
int term = 1, sum = 0;
```

as declaring both term and sum to be int variables and complain that sum is already declared.

If you do not declare sum anyplace else (and it is acceptable to make sum an int variable instead of a double variable), then the following, although we discourage it, is legal:

```
for (int term = 1, sum = 0; term <= 10; term++)
    sum = sum + term;
```

The first part in parentheses (up to the semicolon) declares both term and sum to be int variables and initializes both of them.

It is best to simply avoid these possibly confusing examples. When using the comma in a for statement, it is safest to simply declare all variables outside the for statement. If you declare all variables outside the for loop, the rules are no longer complicated.

A for loop can have only one Boolean expression to test for ending the for loop. However, you can perform multiple tests by connecting the tests using && or || operators to form one larger Boolean expression.

(C, C++, and some other programming languages have a general-purpose comma operator. Readers who have programmed in one of these languages need to be warned that, in Java, there is no comma operator. In Java, the comma is a separator, not an operator, and its use is very restricted compared with the comma operator in C and C++.)

TIP: Repeat *N* Times Loops

The simplest way to produce a loop that repeats the loop body a predetermined number of times is with a `for` statement. For example, the following is a loop that repeats its loop body three times:

```
for (int count = 1; count <= 3; count++)
    System.out.println("Hip, Hip, Hurray");
```

The body of a `for` statement need not make any reference to a loop control variable, such as the variable `count`. ■

PITFALL: Extra Semicolon in a for Statement

You normally do not place a semicolon after the closing parenthesis at the beginning of a `for` loop. To see what can happen, consider the following `for` loop:

```
for (int count = 1; count <= 10; count++);    ◄————————    Problem
    System.out.println("Hello");                            semicolon
```

If you did not notice the extra semicolon, you might expect this `for` loop to write `Hello` to the screen 10 times. If you do notice the semicolon, you might expect the compiler to issue an error message. Neither of those things happens. If you embed this `for` loop in a complete program, the compiler will not complain. If you run the program, only one `Hello` will be output instead of 10 `Hello`s. What is happening? To answer that question, we need a little background.

One way to create a statement in Java is to put a semicolon after something. If you put a semicolon after `number++`, you change the expression

```
number++
```

into the statement

```
number++;
```

empty
statement
null
statement

If you place a semicolon after nothing, you still create a statement. Thus, the semicolon by itself is a statement, which is called the **empty statement** or the **null statement**. The empty statement performs no action, but still is a statement. Therefore, the following is a complete and legitimate `for` loop, whose body is the empty statement:

```
for (int count = 1; count <= 10; count++);
```

(continued)

PITFALL: (continued)

This for loop is indeed iterated 10 times, but since the body is the empty statement, nothing happens when the body is iterated. This loop does nothing, and it does nothing 10 times! After completing this for loop, the computer goes on to execute the following, which writes Hello to the screen one time:

```
System.out.println("Hello");
```

This same sort of problem can arise with a while loop. Be careful to not place a semicolon after the closing parenthesis that encloses the Boolean expression at the start of a while loop. A do-while loop has just the opposite problem. You must remember to always end a do-while loop with a semicolon. ■

PITFALL: Infinite Loops

A while loop, do-while loop, or for loop does not terminate as long as the controlling Boolean expression evaluates to true. This Boolean expression normally contains a variable that will be changed by the loop body, and usually the value of this variable eventually is changed in a way that makes the Boolean expression false and therefore terminates the loop. However, if you make a mistake and write your program so that the Boolean expression is always true, then the loop will run forever. A loop that runs forever is called an **infinite loop**.

infinite loop

Unfortunately, examples of infinite loops are not hard to come by. First, let's describe a loop that *does* terminate. The following Java code writes out the positive even numbers less than 12. That is, it outputs the numbers 2, 4, 6, 8, and 10, one per line, and then the loop ends.

```
number = 2;
while (number != 12)
{
    System.out.println(number);
    number = number + 2;
}
```

The value of number is increased by 2 on each loop iteration until it reaches 12. At that point, the Boolean expression after the word while is no longer true, so the loop ends.

Now suppose you want to write out the odd numbers less than 12, rather than the even numbers. You might mistakenly think that all you need to do is change the initializing statement to

```
number = 1;
```

But this mistake will create an infinite loop. Because the value of number goes from 11 to 13, the value of number is never equal to 12, so the loop never terminates.

PITFALL: (continued)

This sort of problem is common when loops are terminated by checking a numeric quantity using == or !=. When dealing with numbers, it is always safer to test for passing a value. For example, the following will work fine as the first line of our `while` loop:

```
while (number < 12)
```

With this change, `number` can be initialized to any number and the loop will still terminate.

There is one subtlety about infinite loops that you need to keep in mind. A loop might terminate for some input values but be an infinite loop for other values. Just because you tested your loop for some program input values and found that the loop ended does not mean that it will not be an infinite loop for some other input values.

A program that is in an infinite loop might run forever unless some external force stops it, so it is a good idea to learn how to force a program to terminate. The method for forcing a program to stop varies from operating system to operating system. The keystrokes Control-C will terminate a program on many operating systems. (To type Control-C, hold down the Control key while pressing the C key.)

In simple programs, an infinite loop is almost always an error. However, some programs are intentionally written to run forever, such as the main outer loop in an airline reservation program that just keeps asking for more reservations until you shut down the computer (or otherwise terminate the program in an atypical way). ■

Nested Loops

nested loops

It is perfectly legal to nest one loop statement inside another loop statement. For example, the following nests one `for` loop inside another `for` loop:

```
int rowNum, columnNum;
for (rowNum = 1; rowNum <= 3; rowNum++)
{
    for (columnNum = 1; columnNum <= 2; columnNum++)
        System.out.print(" row " + rowNum + " column " + columnNum);
    System.out.println( );
}
```

This produces the following output:

```
row 1 column 1 row 1 column 2
row 2 column 1 row 2 column 2
row 3 column 1 row 3 column 2
```

For each iteration of the outer loop, the inner loop is iterated from beginning to end and then one `println` statement is executed to end the line.

(It is best to avoid nested loops by placing the inner loop inside a method definition and placing a method invocation inside the outer loop. Method definitions are covered in Chapters 4 and 5.)

Self-Test Exercises

28. What is the output of the following?

```java
for (int count = 1; count < 5; count++)
    System.out.print((2 * count) + " ");
```

29. What is the output of the following?

```java
for (int n = 10; n > 0; n = n - 2)
    System.out.println("Hello " + n);
```

30. What is the output of the following?

```java
for (double sample = 2; sample > 0; sample = sample - 0.5)
    System.out.print(sample + " ");
```

31. Rewrite the following `for` statement as a `while` loop (and possibly some additional statements):

```java
int n;
for (n = 10; n > 0; n = n - 2)
    System.out.println("Hello " + n);
```

32. What is the output of the following loop? Identify the connection between the value of n and the value of the variable `log`.

```java
int n = 1024;
int log = 0;
for (int i = 1; i < n; i = i * 2)
    log++;
System.out.println(n + " " + log);
```

33. What is the output of the following loop? Comment on the code. (This is not the same as the previous exercise.)

```java
int n = 1024;
int log = 0;
for (int i = 1; i < n; i = i * 2);
    log++;
System.out.println(n + " " + log);
```

34. Predict the output of the following nested loops:

```java
int n, m;
for (n = 1; n <= 10; n++)
    for (m = 10; m >= 1; m- -)
        System.out.println(n + " times " + m
                            + " = " + n*m);
```

Self-Test Exercises (continued)

35. For each of the following situations, tell which type of loop (`while`, `do–while`, or `for`) would work best:

    a. Summing a series, such as 1/2 + 1/3 + 1/4 + 1/5 + . . . 1/10.

    b. Reading in the list of exam scores for one student.

    c. Reading in the number of days of sick leave taken by employees in a department.

36. What is the output of the following?

```java
int number = 10;
while (number > 0)
{
    System.out.println(number);
    number = number + 3;
}
```

37. What is the output of the following?

```java
int n, limit = 10;
for (n = 1; n < limit; n++)
{
    System.out.println("n == " + n);
    System.out.println("limit == " + limit);
    limit = n + 2;
}
```

38. What is the output produced by the following?

```java
int number = 10;
while (number > 0)
{
    number = number - 2;
    if (number == 4)
        break;
    System.out.println(number);
}
System.out.println("The end.");
```

39. What is the output produced by the following?

```java
int number = 10;
while (number > 0)
{
    number = number - 2;
    if (number == 4)
        continue;
    System.out.println(number);
}
System.out.println("The end.");
```

The break and continue Statements ★

In previous subsections, we described the basic flow of control for the while, do–while, and for loops. This is how the loops should normally be used and is the way they are usually used. However, you can alter the flow of control in two additional ways. The two ways of altering the flow of control are to insert either a break or a continue statement. The break statement ends the loop. The continue statement ends the current iteration of the loop body. The break and continue statements can be used with any of the Java loop statements.

break statement

We described the break statement earlier when we discussed the switch statement. The **break statement** consists of the keyword break followed by a semicolon. When executed, the break statement ends the nearest enclosing switch or loop statement.

continue statement

The **continue statement** consists of the keyword continue followed by a semicolon. When executed, the continue statement ends the current loop body iteration of the nearest enclosing loop statement.

One point that you should note when using the continue statement in a for loop is that the continue statement transfers control to the update expression. Thus, any loop control variable will be updated immediately after the continue statement is executed.

Note that a break statement completely ends the loop. In contrast, a continue statement merely ends one loop iteration, and the next iteration (if any) continues the loop.

You never absolutely need a break or continue statement. Any code that uses a break or continue statement can be rewritten to do the same thing without a break or continue statement. The continue statement can be particularly tricky and can make your code hard to read. It may be best to avoid the continue statement completely or at least use it only on very rare occasions. The use of the break and continue statements in loops is controversial, with many experts saying they should never be used. You will need to make your own decision on whether you will use either or both of these statements.

You can nest one loop statement inside another loop statement. When doing so, remember that any break or continue statement applies to the innermost loop statement containing the break or continue statement. If there is a switch statement inside a loop, any break statement applies to the innermost loop or switch statement.

There is a type of break statement that, when used in nested loops, can end any containing loop, not just the innermost loop. If you label an enclosing loop statement with an *Identifier*, then the following version of the break statement will exit the labeled loop, even if it is not the innermost enclosing loop:

```
break Identifier;
```

label

To **label** a loop statement, simply precede it with an *Identifier* and a colon. The following is an outline of some sample code that uses a labeled break statement:

```
outerLoop:
do
```

```
    {
        ...
        while (next >= 0)
        {
            next = keyboard.nextInt( );
            if (next < –100)
                break outerLoop;
            ...
        }
        ...
        answer = ...
    } while (answer.equalsIgnoreCase("yes"));
```

The identifier outerLoop labels the outer loop, which is a do loop. If the number read into the variable next is negative but not less than –100, then the inner while loop ends normally. If, however, the number read is less than –100, then the labeled break statement is executed, and that ends the enclosing do loop.

You can actually label any statement, not just loop statements and switch statements. A labeled break will always end the enclosing statement with the matching label, no matter what kind of statement is labeled.

The labeled break can be handy when you have a switch statement in the body of a loop and you want a break statement that ends the loop rather than just ending the switch statement.

The exit Statement

The break statement ends a loop (or switch statement), but does not end the program. The following statement immediately ends the program:

```
System.exit(0);
```

System is a predefined Java class that is automatically provided by Java, and exit is a method in the class System. The method exit ends the program as soon as it is invoked. In the programs that we will write, the integer argument 0 can be any integer, but by tradition we use 0, because 0 is used to indicate a normal ending of the program.

The following is a bit of code that uses the exit statement:

```
System.out.println("Enter a negative number:");
int negNumber = keyboard.nextInt( );
if (negNumber >= 0)
{
    System.out.println(negNumber + " is not a negative number.");
    System.out.println("Program aborting.");
    System.exit(0);
}
```

There are more examples of the use of System.exit in Chapter 4.

3.4 Debugging

The road to wisdom? — Well, it's plain and simple to express: Err, and err, and err again, but less, and less, and less.

PIET HEIN

Loop Bugs

There is a pattern to the kinds of mistakes you are most likely to make when programming with loops. Moreover, there are some standard techniques you can use to locate and fix bugs in your loops.

The two most common kinds of loop errors are unintended infinite loops and *off-by-one* errors. We have already discussed infinite loops, but we still need to consider off-by-one errors.

If your loop has an **off-by-one error**, that means the loop repeats the loop body one too many or one too few times. These sorts of errors can result from carelessness in designing a controlling Boolean expression. For example, if you use less-than when you should use less-than-or-equal, this can easily make your loop iterate the body the wrong number of times.

Use of == to test for equality in the controlling Boolean expression of a loop can often lead to an off-by-one error or an infinite loop. This sort of equality testing can work satisfactorily for integers and characters, but is not reliable for floating-point numbers. This is because the floating-point numbers are approximate quantities, and == tests for exact equality. The result of such a test is unpredictable. When comparing floating-point numbers, always use something involving less-than or greater-than, such as <=; do not use == or !=. Using == or != to test floating-point numbers can produce an off-by-one error or an unintended infinite loop or even some other type of error. Even when using integer variables, it is best to avoid using == and != and to instead use something involving less-than or greater-than.

Off-by-one errors can easily go unnoticed. If a loop is iterated one too many times or one too few times, the results might still look reasonable but be off by enough to cause trouble later on. Always make a specific check for off-by-one errors by comparing your loop results to results you know to be true by some other means, such as a pencil-and-paper calculation.

off-by-one error

Tracing Variables

One good way to discover errors in a loop or any kind of code is to trace some key variables. **Tracing variables** means watching the variables change value while the program is running. Most programs do not output each variable's value every time the variable changes, but being able to see all of these variable changes can help you to debug your program.

Many IDEs (Integrated Development Environments) have a built-in utility that lets you easily trace variables without making any changes to your program. These debugging systems vary from one IDE to another. If you have such a debugging facility, it is worth learning how to use it.

tracing variables

If you do not want to use such a debugging facility, you can trace variables by inserting some temporary output statements in your program. For example, the following code compiles but still contains an error:

```
int n = 10;
int sum = 10;
while (n > 1)
{
    sum = sum + n;
    n--;
}
System.out.println("The sum of the integers 1 to 10 is " + sum);
```

To find out what is wrong, you can trace the variables n and sum by inserting output statements as follows:

```
int n = 10;
int sum = 10;
while (n > 1)
{
    System.out.println("At the beginning of the loop: n = " + n); //trace
    System.out.println("At the beginning of the loop: sum = " + sum); //trace
    sum = sum + n;
    n--;
    System.out.println("At the end of the loop: n = " + n); //trace
    System.out.println("At the end of the loop: sum = " + sum); //trace
}
System.out.println("The sum of the integers 1 to 10 is "  + sum);
```

The first four lines of the execution are as follows:

```
At the beginning of the loop: n = 10
At the beginning of the loop: sum = 10
At the end of the loop: n = 9
At the end of the loop: sum = 20
```

We can immediately see that something is wrong. The variable sum has been set to 20. Since it was initialized to 10, it is set to 10 + 10, which is incorrect if we want to sum the numbers from 1 to 10. There are several ways to correct the problem. One solution is given as the answer to Self-Test Exercise 40.

General Debugging Techniques

Tracing errors can sometimes be a difficult and time-consuming task. It is not uncommon to spend more time debugging a piece of code than it took to write the code in the first place. If you are having difficulties finding the source of your errors then there are some general debugging techniques to consider.

Examine the system as a whole and don't assume that the bug occurs in one particular place. If the program is giving incorrect output values, then you should examine the source code, different test cases using a range of input and output values, and the logic behind the algorithm itself. For example, consider the tax program in Display 3.1. If the wrong tax is displayed, you might spend a lot of time trying to find an error in the code that calculates the tax. However, the error might simply be that the input values were different from those you were expecting, leading to an apparently incorrect program output. For example, in German the decimal point and comma are reversed from the English usage. Thus, an income of 25,000.50 becomes 25.000,50. A German programmer might make this type of error if the code was written assuming input in the English format. Although this scenario might seem like a stretch, consider the $125 million Mars Climate Orbiter launched by NASA in 1998. In 1999 it was lost approaching the planet because one team used metric units while another used English units to control the spacecraft's thrusters.

Determining the precise cause and location of a bug is one of the first steps in fixing the error. Examine the input and output behavior for different test cases to try to localize the error. A related technique is to trace variables to show what code the program is executing and what values are contained in key variables. You might also focus on code that has recently changed or code that has had errors before. Finally, you can also try removing code. If you comment out blocks of code and the error still remains, then the culprit is in the uncommented code. The process can be repeated until the location of the error can be pinpointed. The /* and */ notation is particularly useful to comment out large blocks of code. After the error has been fixed, it is easy to remove the comments and reactivate the code.

The first mistakes you should look for are common errors that are easy to make. These are described throughout this textbook in the Pitfall sections. Examples of common errors include off-by-one errors, comparing floating-point types with ==, adding extra semicolons that terminate a loop early, or using == to compare strings for equality.

Some novice programmers may become frustrated if they can't find the bug and may resort to guessing. This technique involves changing the code without really understanding the effect of the change but hoping that it will fix the error. Avoid such slipshod hackery at all costs! Sometimes this method will work for the first few simple programs that you write. However, it will almost certainly fail for larger programs and will most likely introduce new errors to the program. Make sure that you understand the logical impact a change to the code will make before committing the modification.

Finally, if allowed by your instructor, you could show the program to someone else. A fresh set of eyes can sometimes quickly pinpoint an error that you have been missing. Taking a break and returning to the problem a few hours later or the next day can also sometimes help in discovering an error.

EXAMPLE: Debugging an Input Validation Loop

Let's illustrate both good and bad debugging techniques with an example. Suppose our program is presenting a menu where the user can select 'A' or 'B'. The purpose of the following code is to validate user input from the keyboard and to make the user type a choice again if something other than 'A' or 'B' is entered. To be more user-friendly, the program should allow users to make their selections in either uppercase or lowercase.

EXAMPLE: (continued)

```
String s = "";
char c = ' ';
Scanner keyboard = new Scanner(System.in);

do
{
  System.out.println("Enter 'A' for option A or 'B' for option B.");
  s = keyboard.next( );
  s.toLowerCase( );
  c = s.substring(0,1);
}
while ((c != 'a') || (c != 'b'));
```

This program generates a syntax error when compiled:

```
c = s.substring(0,1);  :  incompatible types
found    : java.lang.String
required: char
```

The intent was to extract the first character from the string entered by the user and check to see whether it is 'a' or 'b'. The substring(0,1) call returns a String containing the first character of s, but c is of type char and the types need to match on both sides of the assignment. If we employ the "guessing" debugging technique, then we might make the types match by changing the data type of c to String. Such a change will "fix" this error, but it will cause new errors because the rest of the code treats c like a char. As a result, we have added even more errors! Before making any change, consider the larger context and what the effect of the change will be. In this case, the simplest and best fix is to use

```
c = s.charAt(0)
```

to retrieve the first character from s instead of retrieving a substring.

At this point we have corrected the syntax error and our program will compile, but it will still not run correctly. A sample execution is shown below:

```
Enter 'A' for option A or 'B' for option B.
C
Enter 'A' for option A or 'B' for option B.
B
Enter 'A' for option A or 'B' for option B.
A
Enter 'A' for option A or 'B' for option B.
(Control-C)
```

The program is stuck in an infinite loop even when we type in a valid choice. The only way to stop it is to break out of the program (in the sample output by hitting Control-C, but you may have to use a different method depending on your computing environment).

(continued)

EXAMPLE: (continued)

At this point we could employ tracing to try to locate the source of the error. Here is the code with output statements inserted:

```
do
{
    System.out.println("Enter 'A' for option A or 'B' for option B.");
    s = keyboard.next( );
    System.out.println("String s = " + s);
    s.toLowerCase( );
    System.out.println("Lowercase s = " + s);
    c = s.charAt(0);
    System.out.println("c = " + c);
}
while ((c != 'a') || (c != 'b'));
```

Sample output is as follows:

```
Enter 'A' for option A or 'B' for option B.
A
String s = A
Lowercase s = A
c = A
Enter 'A' for option A or 'B' for option B.
```

The println statements make it clear what is wrong—the string s does not change to lowercase. A review of the toLowerCase( ) documentation reveals that this method does not change the calling string, but instead returns a new string converted to lowercase. The calling string remains unchanged. To fix the error, we can assign the lowercase string back to the original string with

```
s = s.toLowerCase( );
```

However, we're not done yet. Even after fixing the lowercase error, the program is still stuck in an infinite loop, even when we enter 'A' or 'B'. A novice programmer might "patch" the program like so to exit the loop:

```
do
{
    System.out.println("Enter 'A' for option A or 'B' for option B.");
    s = keyboard.next( );
    s = s.toLowerCase( );
    c = s.charAt(0);
    if ( c == 'a')
      break;
    if (c == 'b')
      break;
}
while ((c != 'a') || (c != 'b'));
```

EXAMPLE: (continued)

This forces the loop to exit if 'a' or 'b' is entered, and it will make the program work. Unfortunately, the result is a coding atrocity that should be avoided at all costs. This "quick fix" does not address the root cause of the error—only the symptoms. Moreover, such patches usually won't work for new cases. This particular fix also results in inconsistent code because the expression((c!='a') || (c!='b')) becomes meaningless when we already handle the 'a' and 'b' with the if and break statements.

To really find the bug, we can turn again to tracing, this time focusing on the Boolean values that control the do-while loop:

```
do
{
    System.out.println("Enter 'A' for option A or 'B' for option B.");
    s = keyboard.next( );
    s = s.toLowerCase( );
    c = s.charAt(0);
    System.out.println("c != 'a' is " + (c != 'a'));
    System.out.println("c != 'b' is " + (c != 'b'));
    System.out.println("(c != 'a') || (c != 'b')) is "
            + ((c != 'a') || (c != 'b')));
}
while ((c != 'a') || (c != 'b'));
```

The sample output is now as follows:

```
Enter 'A' for option A or 'B' for option B.
A
c != 'a' is false
c != 'b' is true
(c != 'a') || (c != 'b')) is true
```

Since c equals 'a', the statement (c != 'a') evaluates to false and the statement (c != 'b') evaluates to true. When combined, (false || true) is true, which makes the loop repeat. In spoken English it sounds like "c not equal to 'a' or "c not equal to 'b'" is a correct condition to repeat the loop. After all, if the character typed in is not 'a' or the character typed in is not 'b', then the user should be prompted to try again. Logically however, if (c != 'a') is false (i.e., the character is 'a'), then (c != 'b') must be true. A character cannot make both expressions false, so the final Boolean condition will always be true. The solution is to replace the "or" with an "and" so that the loop repeats only if (c != 'a') && (c != 'b')). This makes the loop repeat as long as the input character is not 'a' and it is not 'b'.

(continued)

EXAMPLE: (continued)

An even better solution is to declare a `boolean` variable to control the `do-while` loop. Inside the body of the loop we can set this variable to `false` when the loop should exit. This technique has the benefit of making the code logic easier to follow, especially if we pick a meaningful name for the variable. In the following example it is easy to see that the loop repeats if `invalidKey` is true:

```
boolean invalidKey;
do
{
    System.out.println("Enter 'A' for option A or 'B' for option B.");
    s = keyboard.next( );
    s = s.toLowerCase( );
    c = s.charAt(0);
    if (c == 'a')
      invalidKey = false;
    else if (c == 'b')
      invalidKey = false;
    else
      invalidKey = true;
}
while (invalidKey);
```

Preventive Coding

The best way to make debugging easier is to make no mistakes in the first place. Although this is unrealistic for programs of any complexity, there are some techniques we can use to eliminate or reduce the number of bugs in a program.

incremental development — **Incremental development** is the technique of writing a small amount of code and testing it before moving on and writing more code. The test may require some new code, or a "test harness," that won't be part of your final program but exercises your code in some way to see if it is working. This technique makes debugging easier because if the test fails then the error is likely in the small section of the new code that was just written.

When an error is made, be sure to learn from your mistake so you don't make it again in the future. Did the mistake occur because of sloppy programming? Was there some aspect of the program's design that you didn't understand or left off before writing the code? Was there something you could have done to find the error more quickly or prevent it from happening at all? Are there other errors in your program similar to the one you just fixed? A critical review of your coding and debugging techniques should become a learning experience so you don't repeat your mistakes.

code review — Finally, show your code to other programmers. Another developer might be able to immediately spot an error in your code and eliminate a lengthy debugging process. Many software development organizations have a formal process called **code review** that involves the inspection of code by other programmers. Such reviews have the additional benefit that

pair
programming programmers end up sharing coding techniques and learning best practices in the process of reviewing each other's code. A related technique is called **pair programming**, in which two programmers work together at the same computer. The programmers take turns, one typing while the other watches and looks for errors and thinks about the task at hand.

Assertion Checks ★

assertion An **assertion** is a sentence that says (asserts) something about the state of your program. An assertion must be a sentence that is either true or false and should be true if there are no mistakes in your program. You can place assertions in your code by making them comments. For example, all the comments in the following code are assertions:

```
int n = 0;
int sum = 0;
//n == 0 and sum == 0
while (n < 100)
{
    n++;
    sum = sum + n;
    //sum == 1 + 2 + 3 + ... + n
}
//sum == 1 + 2 + 3 + ... + 100
```

Note that each of these assertions can be either true or false, depending on the values of n and sum, and they all should be true if the program is performing correctly.

Java has a special statement to check whether an assertion is true. An assertion check statement has the following form:

assert
```
assert Boolean_Expression;
```

If you run your program in the proper way, the assertion check behaves as follows: If the *Boolean_Expression* evaluates to true, nothing happens, but if the *Boolean_Expression* evaluates to false, the program ends and outputs an error message saying that an assertion failed.

For example, the previously displayed code can be written as follows, with the first comment replaced by an assertion check:

```
int n = 0;
int sum = 0;
assert (n == 0) && (sum == 0);
while (n < 100)
{
    n++;
    sum = sum + n;
    //sum == 1 + 2 + 3 + ...+ n
}
//sum == 1 + 2 + 3 + ...+ 100
```

Note that we translated only one of the three comments into an assertion check. Not all assertion comments lend themselves to becoming assertion checks. For example, there is no simple way to convert the other two comments into Boolean expressions. Doing so would not be impossible, but you would need to use code that would itself be more complicated than what you would be checking.

---

assertion
check

Assertion Checking

An **assertion check** is a Java statement consisting of the keyword `assert` followed by a Boolean expression and a semicolon. If assertion checking is turned on and the Boolean expression in the assertion check evaluates to `false` when the assertion check is executed, the program will end and output a suitable error message. If assertion checking is not turned on, the assertion check is treated as a comment.

SYNTAX

```
assert Boolean_Expression;
```

EXAMPLE

```
assert (n == 0) && (sum == 0);
```

You can turn assertion checking on and off. When debugging code, you can turn assertion checking on so that a failed assertion will produce an error message. Once your code is debugged, you can turn assertion checking off and your code will run more efficiently.

A program or other class containing assertions is compiled in the usual way. After all classes used in a program are compiled, you can run the program with assertion checking either turned on or turned off.

If you compile your classes using a one-line command, you would compile a class with assertion in the usual way:

```
javac YourProgram.java
```

You can then run your program with assertion checking turned on or off. The normal way of running a program has assertion checking turned off. To run your program with assertion checking turned on, use the following command:

```
java –enableassertions YourProgram
```

If you are using an IDE, check the documentation for your IDE to see how to handle assertion checking. If you do not find an entry for "assertion checking," which is likely, check to see how you set run options. (With TextPad, you can set things up for assertion checking as follows: On the Configure menu, choose Preferences, and then choose the Run Java Application command and set the "Prompt for parameters" option for it.[3] After you set this preference, when you run a program, a window will appear in which you can enter options for the java run command—for example, -enableassertions.)

Self-Test Exercises

40. Fix the bug in the code in the subsection "Tracing Variables."

41. Add some suitable output statements to the following code so that all variables are traced:

```java
int n, sum = 0;
for (n = 1; n < 10; n++)
    sum = sum + n;
System.out.println("1 + 2 + ...+ 9 + 10 == " + sum);
```

42. What is the bug in the following code? What do you call this kind of loop bug?

```java
int n, sum = 0;
for (n = 1; n < 10; n++)
    sum = sum + n;
System.out.println("1 + 2 + ...+ 9 + 10 == " + sum);
```

43. Write an assertion check that checks to see that the value of the variable time is less than or equal to the value of the variable limit. Both variables are of type int.

---

[3] If you are running applets, you also need to select the "Prompt for parameters" option for the Run Java Applet command on the Tools submenu.

Chapter Summary

- The Java branching statements are the if-else statement and the switch statement.
- A switch statement is a multiway branching statement. You can also form multiway branching statements by nesting if-else statements to form a multiway if-else statement.
- Boolean expressions are evaluated similar to the way arithmetic expressions are evaluated. The value of a Boolean expression can be saved in a variable of type boolean.
- The Java loop statements are the while, do-while, and for statements.
- A do-while statement always iterates its loop body at least one time. Both a while statement and a for statement might iterate its loop body zero times.

- A for loop can be used to obtain the equivalent of the instruction "repeat the loop body *n* times."

- Tracing variables is a good method for debugging loops.

- An assertion check can be added to your Java code so that if the assertion is false, your program halts with an error message.

Answers to Self-Test Exercises

1.
```java
if (score > 100)
        System.out.println("High")
else
        System.out.println("Low");
```

2.
```java
if (savings > expenses)
{
    System.out.println("Solvent");
    savings = savings - expenses;
    expenses = 0;
}
else
{
    System.out.println("Bankrupt");
}
```

3.
```java
if (number > 0)
        System.out.println("Positive");
else
        System.out.println("Not positive");
```

4.
```java
if (salary < deductions)
{
    System.out.println("Crazy");
}
else
{
    System.out.println("OK");
    net = salary - deductions;
}
```

5. large

6. small

7. medium

8.
```
if (n < 0)
    System.out.println(n + " is less than zero.");
else if (n < 100)
    System.out.println(
            n + " is between 0 and 99 (inclusive).");
else
    System.out.println(n + " is 100 or larger.");
```

9. Some kind of B.

10. Oranges

11. Plums

12. Fruitless

13. n1 >= n2

14.
```
if (n1 >= n2)
    System.out.println("n1");
else
    System.out.println("n2");
```

15. When the variables are of type int, you test for equality using ==, as follows:

```
variable1 == variable2
```

When the variables are of type String, you test for equality using the method equals, as follows:

```
variable1.equals(variable2)
```

In some cases, you might want to use equalsIgnoreCase instead of equals.

16.
```
if (nextWord.compareToIgnoreCase("N") < 0)
    System.out.println( "First half of the alphabet");
else
    System.out.println("Second half of the alphabet");
```

17.
```
if ( (exam >= 60) && (programsDone >= 10) )
    System.out.println("Passed");
else
    System.out.println("Failed");
```

18.
```
if ( (pressure > 100) || (temperature >= 212) )
    System.out.println("Emergency");
else
    System.out.println("OK");
```

19. a. true.

b. `true`. Note that expressions a and b mean exactly the same thing. Because the operators `==` and `<` have higher precedence than `&&`, you do not need to include the parentheses. The parentheses do, however, make it easier to read. Most people find the expression in a easier to read than the expression in b, even though they mean the same thing.

c. `true`.

d. `true`.

e. `false`. Because the value of the first subexpression, (`count == 1`), is `false`, you know that the entire expression is `false` without bothering to evaluate the second subexpression. Thus, it does not matter what the values of x and y are. This is called short-circuit evaluation, which is what Java does.

f. `true`. Since the value of the first subexpression, (`count < 10`), is `true`, you know that the entire expression is `true` without bothering to evaluate the second subexpression. Thus, it does not matter what the values of x and y are. This is called short-circuit evaluation, which is what Java does.

g. `false`. Notice that the expression in g includes the expression in f as a subexpression. This subexpression is evaluated using short-circuit evaluation as we described for f. The entire expression in g is equivalent to

```
!( (true || (x < y)) && true )
```

which in turn is equivalent to `!( true && true )`, and that is equivalent to `!(true)`, which is equivalent to the final value of `false`.

h. This expression produces an error when it is evaluated because the first subexpression, (`(limit/count) > 7`), involves a division by zero.

i. `true`. Since the value of the first subexpression, (`limit < 20`), is `true`, you know that the entire expression is `true` without bothering to evaluate the second subexpression. Thus, the second subexpression, (`(limit/count) > 7`), is never evaluated, so the fact that it involves a division by zero is never noticed by the computer. This is short-circuit evaluation, which is what Java does.

j. This expression produces an error when it is evaluated because the first subexpression, (`(limit/count) > 7`), involves a division by zero.

k. `false`. Since the value of the first subexpression, (`limit < 0`), is `false`, you know that the entire expression is `false` without bothering to evaluate the second subexpression. Thus, the second subexpression, (`(limit/count) > 7`), is never evaluated, so the fact that it involves a division by zero is never noticed by the computer. This is short-circuit evaluation, which is what Java does.

20. No. Since (j > 0) is false and Java uses short-circuit evaluation for &&, the expression (1/(j+1) > 10) is never evaluated.

21. ((bonus + (((day * rate) / correctionFactor) * newGuy)) - penalty)

22. 10
    7
    4
    1

23. There will be no output. Because n > 0 is false, the loop body is executed zero times.

24. 10
    7
    4
    1

25. 10

    A do-while loop always executes its body at least one time.

26. -42

    A do-while loop always executes its body at least one time.

27. With a do-while statement, the loop body is always executed at least once. With a while statement, there can be conditions under which the loop body is not executed at all.

28. 2 4 6 8

29. Hello 10
    Hello 8
    Hello 6
    Hello 4
    Hello 2

30. 2.0 1.5 1.0 0.5

31. ```
    n = 10;
    while (n > 0)
    {
        System.out.println("Hello " + n);
        n = n - 2;
    }
    ```

32. The output is 1024 10. The second number is the log to the base 2 of the first number. (If the first number is not a power of 2, then only an approximation to the log base 2 is produced.)

33. The output is 1024 1. The semicolon after the first line of the for loop is probably a pitfall error.
    ```

34. The output is too long to reproduce here. The pattern is as follows:

```
1 times 10 = 10
1 times 9 = 9

     .

     .

     .

1 times 1 = 1
2 times 10 = 20
2 times 9 = 18

     .

     .

     .

2 times 1 = 2
3 times 10 = 30

     .

     .

     .
```

35. a. A for loop

   b. and c.   Both require a `while` loop because the input list might be empty. (A `for` loop also might work, but a `do-while` loop definitely would not work.)

36. This is an infinite loop. The first few lines of output are

```
10
13
16
19
21
```

37. This is an infinite loop. The first few lines of output are

```
n == 1
limit == 10;
n == 2
limit == 3
n == 3
limit == 4
n == 4
limit == 5
```

38.
```
8
6
The end.
```

39.
```
8
6
2
0
The end.
```

40. If you look at the trace, you will see that after one iteration, the value of sum is 20. But the value should be 10 + 9, or 19. This should lead you to think that the variable n is not decremented at the correct time. Indeed, the bug is that the two statements

```
sum = sum + n;
n--;
```

should be reversed to

```
n--;
sum = sum + n;
```

41.
```
int n, sum = 0;
for (n = 1; n < 10; n++)
{
    System.out.println("n == " + n + " sum == " + sum);
        //Above line is a trace.
    sum = sum + n;
}
System.out.println("After loop");//trace
System.out.println("n == " + n + " sum == " + sum);//trace
System.out.println("1 + 2 + ...+ 9 + 10 == " + sum);
```

If you study the output of this trace, you will see that 10 is never added in. This is a bug in the loop.

42. This is the code you traced in the previous exercise. If you study the output of this trace, you will see that 10 is never added in. This is an off-by-one error.

43. `assert (time <= limit);`

Programming Projects

Many of these Programming Projects can be solved using AW's MyCodeMate. To access these please go to: www.mycodemate.com.

1. (This is a version of an exercise from Chapter 2). The Babylonian algorithm to compute the square root of a number n is as follows:

   1. Make a guess at the answer (you can pick n/2 as your initial guess).
   2. Compute r = n / guess.
   3. Set guess = (guess +r) / 2.
   4. Go back to step 2 until the last two guess values are the same.

   Write a program that inputs an integer for n, iterates through the Babylonian algorithm until the guess is within 1% of the previous guess, and outputs the answer as a double to two decimal places. Your answer should be accurate even for large values of n.

2. In the game of craps, a pass line bet proceeds as follows. Two six-sided dice are rolled; the first roll of the dice in a craps round is called the "come out roll." A come out roll of 7 or 11 automatically wins, and a come out roll of 2, 3, or 12 automatically loses. If 4, 5, 6, 8, 9, or 10 is rolled on the come out roll, that number becomes "the point." The player keeps rolling the dice until either 7 or the point is rolled. If the point is rolled first, then the player wins the bet. If a 7 is rolled first, then the player loses.

    Write a program that simulates a game of craps using these rules without human input. Instead of asking for a wager, the program should calculate whether the player would win or lose. The program should simulate rolling the two dice and calculate the sum. Add a loop so that the program plays 10,000 games. Add counters that count how many times the player wins, and how many times the player loses. At the end of the 10,000 games, compute the probability of winning [i.e., Wins / (Wins + Losses)] and output this value. Over the long run, who is going to win the most games, you or the house?

    Note: To generate a random number x, where 0 < x <= 1, use x = Math.random( );. For example, multiplying Math.random( ) by 6 and converting to an integer results in a random integer that is between 0 and 5.

3. One way to estimate the adult height of a child is to use the following formula, which uses the height of the parents:

    $$H_{male\_child} = ((H_{mother} \times 13/12) + H_{father})/2$$
    $$H_{female\_child} = ((H_{father} \times 12/13) + H_{mother})/2$$

    All heights are in inches. Write a program that takes as input the gender of the child, the height of the mother in inches, and the height of the father in inches, and outputs the estimated adult height of the child in inches. The program should allow the user to enter a new set of values and output the predicted height until the user decides to exit. The user should be able to input the heights in feet and inches, and the program should output the estimated height of the child in feet and inches. Use the int data type to store the heights.

4. It is difficult to make a budget that spans several years, because prices are not stable. If your company needs 200 pencils per year, you cannot simply use this year's price as the cost of pencils two years from now. Because of inflation, the cost is likely to be higher than it is today. Write a program to gauge the expected cost of an item in a specified number of years. The program asks for the cost of the item, the number of years from now that the item will be purchased, and the rate of inflation. The program then outputs the estimated cost of the item after the specified period. Have the user enter the inflation rate as a percentage, such as 5.6 (percent). Your program should then convert the percent to a fraction, such as 0.056, and should use a loop to estimate the price adjusted for inflation.

5. You have just purchased a stereo system that cost $1,000 on the following credit plan: no down payment, an interest rate of 18% per year (and hence 1.5% per month), and monthly payments of $50. The monthly payment of $50 is used to pay the interest, and whatever is left is used to pay part of the remaining debt. Hence, the first month you pay 1.5% of $1,000 in interest. That is $15 in interest. So, the remaining $35 is deducted from your debt, which leaves you with a debt of $965.00. The next month, you pay interest of 1.5% of $965.00, which is $14.48. Hence, you can deduct $35.52 (which is $50 – $14.48) from the amount you owe. Write a program that tells you how many months it will take you to pay off the loan, as well as the total amount of interest paid over the life of the loan. Use a loop to calculate the amount of interest and the size of the debt after each month. (Your final program need not output the monthly amount of interest paid and remaining debt, but you may want to write a preliminary version of the program that does output these values.) Use a variable to count the number of loop iterations and hence the number of months until the debt is zero. You may want to use other variables as well. The last payment may be less than $50 if the debt is small, but do not forget the interest. If you owe $50, your monthly payment of $50 will not pay off your debt, although it will come close. One month's interest on $50 is only 75 cents.

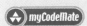

6. The Fibonacci numbers F_n are defined as follows: F_0 is 1, F_1 is 1, and

$$F_{i+2} = F_i + F_{i+1}$$

$i = 0, 1, 2, \ldots$. In other words, each number is the sum of the previous two numbers. The first few Fibonacci numbers are 1, 1, 2, 3, 5, and 8. One place where these numbers occur is as certain population growth rates. If a population has no deaths, then the series shows the size of the population after each time period. It takes an organism two time periods to mature to reproducing age, and then the organism reproduces once every time period. The formula applies most straightforwardly to asexual reproduction at a rate of one offspring per time period. In any event, the green crud population grows at this rate and has a time period of 5 days. Hence, if a green crud population starts out as 10 pounds of crud, then in 5 days, there is still 10 pounds of crud; in 10 days, there is 20 pounds of crud; in 15 days, 30 pounds; in 20 days, 50 pounds; and so forth. Write a program that takes both the initial size of a green crud population (in pounds) and a number of days as input and outputs the number of pounds of green crud after that many days. Assume that the population size is the same for 4 days and then increases every fifth day. Your program should allow the user to repeat this calculation as often as desired.

7. The value e^x can be approximated by the sum:

$$1 + x + x^2/2! + x^3/3! + \ldots + x^n/n!$$

Write a program that takes a value x as input and outputs this sum for n taken to be each of the values 1 to 10, 50, and 100. Your program should repeat the calculation for new values of x until the user says she or he is through. The expression n! is called the *factorial* of n and is defined as

$$n! = 1 * 2 * 3 * \ldots * n$$

Use variables of type double to store the factorials (or arrange your calculation to avoid any direct calculation of factorials); otherwise, you are likely to produce integer overflow, that is, integers larger than Java allows.

8. In cryptarithmetic puzzles, mathematical equations are written using letters. Each letter can be a digit from 0 to 9, but no two letters can be the same. Here is a sample problem:

SEND + MORE = MONEY

A solution to the puzzle is S = 9, R = 8, O = 0, M = 1, Y = 2, E = 5, N = 6, D = 7

Write a program that finds a solution to the cryptarithmetic puzzle of:

TOO + TOO + TOO + TOO = GOOD

The simplest technique is to use a nested loop for each unique letter (in this case T, O, G, D). The loops would systematically assign the digits from 0 to 9 to each letter. For example, it might first try T = 0, O = 0, G = 0, D = 0, then T = 0, O = 0, G =0, D = 1, then T = 0, O = 0, G = 0, D = 2, etc., up to T = 9, O = 9, G = 9, D = 9. In the loop body, test that each variable is unique and that the equation is satisfied. Output the values for the letters that satisfy the equation.

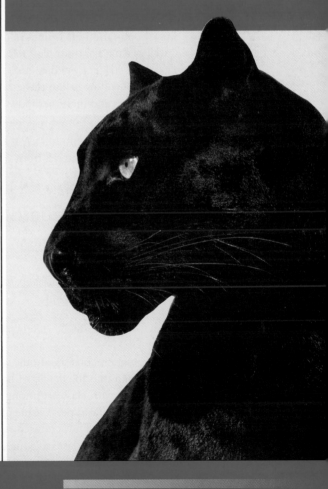

4

Defining Classes I

This is the exciting part.
This is like the Supremes.
See the way it builds up?

Attributed to FRANK ZAPPA

Introduction

Classes are the single most important language feature that facilitates object-oriented programming (OOP), the dominant programming methodology in use today. You have already been using predefined classes. String and Scanner are two of the classes we have used. An object is a value of a class type and is referred to as an *instance of the class.* An object differs from a value of a primitive type in that it has methods (actions) as well as data. For example, "Hello" is an object of the class String. It has the characters in the string as its data and also has a number of methods, such as length. You already know how to use classes, objects, and methods. This chapter tells you how to define classes and their methods.

Prerequisites

This chapter uses material from Chapters 1, 2, and 3.

4.1 Class Definitions

"The Time has come," the Walrus said,
"to talk of many things:
of shoes and ships and sealing wax
of cabbages and kings."

LEWIS CARROLL, *Through the Looking-Glass*

A Java program consists of objects from various classes interacting with one another. Before we go into the details of how you define classes, let's review some of the terminology used with classes. Among other things, a class is a type and you can declare variables of a class type. A value of a class type is called an **object**. An object has both data and actions. The actions are called **methods**. Each object can have different data, but all objects of a class have the same types of data and all objects in a class have the same methods. An object is usually referred to as an object of the class or as an

object
method

instance   **instance of the class** rather than as a value of the class, but it is a value of the class type. To make this abstract discussion come alive, we need a sample definition.

A Class Is a Type

If A is a class, then the phrases "bla is of type A," "bla is an instance of the class A," and "bla is an object of the class A" all mean the same thing.

Display 4.1 contains a definition for a class named `DateFirstTry` and a program that demonstrates using the class. Objects of this class represent dates such as December 31, 2007 and July 4, 1776. This class is unrealistically simple, but it will serve to introduce you to the syntax for a class definition. Each object of this class has three pieces of data: a string for the month name, an integer for the day of the month, and another integer for the year. The objects have only one method, which is named `writeOutput`. Both the data items and the methods are sometimes called

member   **members** of the object, because they belong to the object. The data items are also

field   sometimes called **fields**. We will call the data items **instance variables** and call the

instance   methods *methods*.

variable   The following three lines from the start of the class definition define three instance variables (three data members):

```
public String month;
public int day;
public int year; //a four digit number.
```

The word `public` simply means that there are no restrictions on how these instance variables are used. Each of these lines declares one instance variable name. You can think of an object of the class as a complex item with instance variables inside of it. So, an instance variable can be thought of as a smaller variable inside each object of the class. In this case, the instance variables are called `month`, `day`, and `year`.

An object of a class is typically named by a variable of the class type. For example, the program `DateFirstTryDemo` in Display 4.1 declares the two variables `date1` and `date2` to be of type `DateFirstTry`, as follows:

```
DateFirstTry date1, date2;
```

This gives us variables of the class `DateFirstTry`, but so far there are no objects of the class. Objects are class values that are named by the variables. To obtain an object, you

new   must use the `new` operator to create a "new" object. For example, the following creates an object of the class `DateFirstTry` and names it with the variable `date1`:

```
date1 = new DateFirstTry();
```

Display 4.1 A Simple Class

```
1    public class DateFirstTry                    This class definition goes in a file named
2    {                                            DateFirstTry.java.
3        public String month;
4        public int day;        ◄──────           Later in this chapter, we will
5        public int year; //a four digit number.  see that these three public
                                                   modifiers should be replaced
6        public void writeOutput()                 with private.
7        {
8            System.out.println(month + " " + day + ", " + year);
9        }
10   }
```

```
1    public class DateFirstTryDemo               This class definition (program) goes in a file named
2    {                                           DateFirstTryDemo.java.
3        public static void main(String[] args)
4        {
5            DateFirstTry date1, date2;
6            date1 = new DateFirstTry();
7            date2 = new DateFirstTry();
8            date1.month = "December";
9            date1.day = 31;
10           date1.year = 2007;
11           System.out.println("date1:");
12           date1.writeOutput();

13           date2.month = "July";
14           date2.day = 4;
15           date2.year = 1776;
16           System.out.println("date2:");
17           date2.writeOutput();
18       }
19   }
```

Sample Dialogue

```
date1:
December 31, 2007
date2:
July 4, 1776
```

We will discuss this kind of statement in more detail later in this chapter when we discuss something called a *constructor*. For now simply note that

```
Class_Variable = new Class_Name();
```

creates a new object of the specified class and associates it with the class variable.[1] Because the class variable now names an object of the class, we will often refer to the class variable as an object of the class. (This is really the same usage as when we refer to an int variable n as "the integer n," even though the integer is, strictly speaking, not n but the value of n.)

Unlike what we did in Display 4.1, the declaration of a class variable and the creation of the object are more typically combined into one statement, as follows:

```
DateFirstTry date1 = new DateFirstTry();
```

The new Operator

The **new** operator is used to create an object of a class and associate the object with a variable that names it.

SYNTAX

Class_Variable = new *Class_Name*();

EXAMPLE

```
DateFirstTry date;
date = new DateFirstTry();
```

which is usually written in the following equivalent form:

```
DateFirstTry date = new DateFirstTry();
```

Instance Variables and Methods

We will illustrate the details about instance variables using the class and program in Display 4.1. Each object of the class DateFirstTry has three instance variables, which can be named by giving the object name followed by a dot and the name of the instance variable. For example, the object date1 in the program DateFirstTryDemo has the following three instance variables:

```
date1.month
date1.day
date1.year
```

Similarly, if you replace date1 with date2, you obtain the three instance variables for the object date2. Note that date1 and date2 together have a total of six instance variables. The instance variables date1.month and date2.month, for example, are two different (instance) variables.

---

[1] For many, the word "new" suggests a memory allocation. As we will see, the new operator does indeed produce a memory allocation.

The instance variables in Display 4.1 can be used just like any other variables. For example, `date1.month` can be used just like any other variable of type `String`. The instance variables `date1.day` and `date1.year` can be used just like any other variables of type `int`. Thus, although the following is not in the spirit of the class definition, it is legal and would compile:

```
date1.month = "Hello friend.";
```

More likely assignments to instance variables are given in the program `DateFirstTry-Demo`.

The class `DateFirstTry` has only one method, which is named `writeOutput`. We reproduce the definition of the method here:

```
public void writeOutput()  ◄─────── Heading
{
    System.out.println(month + " " + day + ", " + year);  ──► Body
}
```

All method definitions belong to some class, and all method definitions are given inside the definition of the class to which they belong. A method definition is divided into two parts, a **heading** and a **method body**, as illustrated by the annotation on the method definition. The word `void` means this is a method for performing an action as opposed to producing a value. We will say more about method definitions later in this chapter (including some indication of why the word `void` was chosen to indicate an action). You have already been using methods from predefined classes. The way you invoke a method from a class definition you write is the same as the way you do it for a predefined class. For example, the following from the program `DateFirstTryDemo` is an invocation of the method `writeOutput` with `date1` as the calling object:

heading
method body

```
date1.writeOutput();
```

This invocation is equivalent to execution of the method body. So, this invocation is equivalent to

```
System.out.println(month + " " + day + ", " + year);
```

However, we need to say more about exactly how this is equivalent. If you simply replace the method invocation with this `System.out.println` statement, you will get a compiler error message. Note that within the definition for the method `writeOutput`, the names of the instance variables are used without any calling object. This is because the method will be invoked with different calling objects at different times. When an instance variable is used in a method definition, it is understood to be the instance variable of the calling object. So in the program `DateFirstTryDemo`,

```
date1.writeOutput();
```

Class Definition

The following shows the form of a class definition that is most commonly used; however, it is legal to intermix the method definitions and the instance variable declarations.

SYNTAX

```
public class Class_Name
{
        Instance_Variable_Declaration_1
        Instance_Variable_Declaration_2
            . . .
        Instance_Variable_Declaration_Last

        Method_Definition_1
        Method_Definition_2
            . . .
        Method_Definition_Last
}
```

EXAMPLES

See Displays 4.1 and 4.2.

---

is equivalent to

```
System.out.println(date1.month + " " + date1.day
                                  + ", " + date1.year);
```

Similarly,

```
date2.writeOutput();
```

is equivalent to

```
System.out.println(date2.month + " " + date2.day
                                  + ", " + date2.year);
```

File Names and Locations

Remember that a file must be named the same as the class it contains with an added `.java` at the end. For example, a class named `MyClass` must be in a file named `MyClass.java`.

We will eventually see other ways to arrange files, but at this point, your program and all the classes it uses should be in the same directory (same folder).

Self-Test Exercises

1. Write a method called `makeItNewYears` that could be added to the class `DateFirstTry` in Display 4.1. The method `makeItNewYears` has no parameters and sets the `month` instance variable to `"January"` and the `day` instance variable to 1. It does not change the `year` instance variable.

2. Write a method called `yellIfNewYear` that could be added to the class `DateFirstTry` in Display 4.1. The method `yellIfNewYear` has no parameters and outputs the string `"Hurrah!"` provided the `month` instance variable has the value `"January"` and the `day` instance variable has the value 1. Otherwise, it outputs the string `"Not New Year's Day."`

More about Methods

As we noted for predefined methods, methods of the classes you define are of two kinds: methods that return (compute) some value and methods that perform an action other than returning a value. For example, the method `println` of the object `System.out` is an example of a method that performs an action other than returning a value; in this case, the action is to write something to the screen. The method `nextInt` of the class `Scanner`, introduced in Chapter 2, is a method that returns a value; in this case, the value returned is a number typed in by the user. A method that performs some action other than returning a value is called a `void` method. This same distinction between `void` methods and methods that return a value applies to methods in the classes you define. The two kinds of methods require slight differences in how they are defined.

Both kinds of methods have a method heading and a method body, which are similar but not identical for the two kinds of methods. The method heading for a void method is of the form

```
public void Method_Name(Parameter_List)
```

The method heading for a method that returns a value is

```
public Type_Returned Method_Name(Parameter_List)
```

Later in the chapter we will see that `public` may sometimes be replaced by a more restricted modifier and that it is possible to add additional modifiers, but these templates will do for now. For now, our examples will have an empty *Parameter_List*.

If a method returns a value, then it can return different values in different situations, but all values returned must be of the same type, which is specified as the type returned. For example, if a method has the heading

```
public double myMethod()
```

then the method always returns a value of type `double`, and the heading

```
public String yourMethod()
```

indicates a method that always returns a value of type `String`.

The following is a `void` method heading:

```
public void ourMethod()
```

Notice that when the method returns no value at all, we use the keyword `void` in place of a type. If you think of `void` as meaning "no returned type," the word `void` begins to make sense.

invocation　　An **invocation** of a method that returns a value can be used as an expression anyplace that a value of the *Type_Returned* can be used. For example, suppose `anObject` is an object of a class with methods having our sample heading; in that case, the following are legal:

```
double d = anObject.myMethod();
String aStringVariable = anObject.yourMethod();
```

A `void` method does not return a value, but simply performs an action, so an invocation of a `void` method is a statement. A `void` method is invoked as in the following example:

```
anObject.ourMethod();
```

Note the ending semicolon.

So far, we have avoided the topic of parameter lists by only giving examples with empty parameter lists, but note that parentheses are required even for an empty parameter list. Parameter lists are discussed later in this chapter.

body　　The **body** of a `void` method definition is simply a list of declarations and statements enclosed in a pair of braces, {}. For example, the following is a complete `void` method definition:

```
public void ourMethod()
{
    System.out.println("Hello");
    System.out.println("from our method.");
}
```

The body of a method that returns a value is the same as the body of a `void` method but with one additional requirement. The body of a method that returns a value must
return statement　　contain at least one `return` statement. A **return statement** is of the form

```
return Expression;
```

where *Expression* can be any expression that evaluates to something of the *Type_Returned* that is listed in the method heading. For example, the following is a complete definition of a method that returns a value:

```java
public String yourMethod()
{
    Scanner keyboard = new Scanner(System.in);
    System.out.println("Enter a line of text");
    String result = keyboard.nextLine();
    return result + " was entered.";
}
```

Notice that a method that returns a value can do other things besides returning a value, but style rules dictate that whatever else it does should be related to the value returned.

A return statement always ends a method invocation. Once the `return` statement is executed, the method ends, and any remaining statements in the method definition are not executed.

return in a void method

If you want to end a void method before it runs out of statements, you can use a return statement without any expression, as follows:

```java
return;
```

A void method need not have any `return` statements, but you can place a `return` statement in a `void` method if there are situations that require the method to end before all the code is executed.

Method Definitions

There are two kinds of methods: methods that return a value and methods, known as `void` methods, that perform some action other than returning a value.

Definition of a Method That Returns a Value

SYNTAX

```java
public Type_Returned Method_Name(Parameter_List)
{
    <List of statements, at least one of which
        must contain a return statement.>
}
```

If there are no *Parameters*, then the parentheses are empty.

EXAMPLE

```java
public int getDay()
{
    return day;
}
```

void Method Definition

SYNTAX

```java
public void Method_Name(Parameter_List)
{
   <List of statements>
}
```

If there are no *Parameters*, then the parentheses are empty.

EXAMPLE

```java
public void writeOutput()
{
    System.out.println(month + " " + day + ", " + year);
}
```

All method definitions are inside of some class definition. See Display 4.2 to see these example method definitions in the context of a class.

When an instance variable name is used in a method definition, it refers to an instance variable of the calling object.

return Statements

The definition of a method that returns a value must have one or more **return** statements. A **return** statement specifies the value returned by the method and ends the method invocation.

SYNTAX

```java
return Expression;
```

EXAMPLE

```java
public int getYear()
{
    return year;
}
```

A **void** method definition need not have a **return** statement. However, a **return** statement can be used in a **void** method to cause the method to immediately end. The form for a **return** statement in a **void** method is

```java
return;
```

Although it may seem that we have lost sight of the fact, all these method definitions must be inside of some class definition. Java does not have any stand-alone methods that are not in any class. Display 4.2 rewrites the class given in Display 4.1 but this time we have added a more diverse set of methods. Display 4.3 contains a sample program that illustrates how the methods of the class in Display 4.2 are used.

TIP: Any Method Can Be Used as a `void` Method

A method that returns a value can also perform some action besides returning a value. If you want that action, but do not need the returned value, you can invoke the method as if it were a `void` method and the returned value will simply be discarded. For example, the following contains two invocations of the method `nextLine()`, which returns a value of type `String`. Both are legal.

```
Scanner keyboard = new Scanner(System.in);
    . . .
String inputString = keyboard.nextLine();
    . . .
System.out.println("Press Enter to continue with program.");
keyboard.nextLine(); //Reads a line and discards it. ■
```

Display 4.2   A Class with More Methods (part 1 of 2)

```
1    import java.util.Scanner;

2    public class DateSecondTry
3    {
4        private String month;
5        private int day;
6        private int year; //a four digit number.

7        public void writeOutput()
8        {
9            System.out.println(month + " " + day + ", " + year);
10       }

11       public void readInput()
12       {
13           Scanner keyboard = new Scanner(System.in);
14           System.out.println("Enter month, day, and year.");
15           System.out.println("Do not use a comma.");
16           month = keyboard.next();
17           day = keyboard.nextInt();
```

The significance of the modifier `private` is discussed in the subsection "`public` and `private` Modifiers" in Section 4.2 a bit later in this chapter.

Display 4.2   **A Class with More Methods** (part 2 of 2)

```java
18              year = keyboard.nextInt();
19          }

20          public int getDay()
21          {
22              return day;
23          }
24          public int getYear()
25          {
26              return year;
27          }

28          public int getMonth()
29          {
30              if (month.equalsIgnoreCase("January"))
31                  return 1;
32              else if (month.equalsIgnoreCase("February"))
33                  return 2;
34              else if (month.equalsIgnoreCase("March"))
35                  return 3;
36              else if (month.equalsIgnoreCase("April"))
37                  return 4;
38              else if (month.equalsIgnoreCase("May"))
39                  return 5;
40              else if (month.equals("June"))
41                  return 6;
42              else if (month.equalsIgnoreCase("July"))
43                  return 7;
44              else if (month.equalsIgnoreCase("August"))
45                  return 8;
46              else if (month.equalsIgnoreCase("September"))
47                  return 9;
48              else if (month.equalsIgnoreCase("October"))
49                  return 10;
50              else if (month.equalsIgnoreCase("November"))
51                  return 11;
52              else if (month.equalsIgnoreCase("December"))
53                  return 12;
54              else
55              {
56                  System.out.println("Fatal Error");
57                  System.exit(0);
58                  return 0; //Needed to keep the compiler happy
59              }
60          }
61      }
```

Self-Test Exercises

3. Write a method called getNextYear that could be added to the class DateSecondTry in Display 4.2. The method getNextYear returns an int value equal to the value of the year instance variable plus one.

Display 4.3 Using the Class in Display 4.2

```
1    public class DemoOfDateSecondTry
2    {
3        public static void main(String[] args)          An invocation of a void method is a
4        {                                                 statement.
5            DateSecondTry date = new DateSecondTry();
6            date.readInput();

7            int dayNumber = date.getDay();
8            System.out.println("That is the " + dayNumber
9                                    + "th day of the month.");
10       }
11   }
```

An invocation of a method that returns a value is an expression that can be used anyplace that a value of the type returned by the method can be used.

Sample Dialogue

```
Enter month, day, and year.
Do not use a comma.
July 4 1776
That is the 4th day of the month.
```

Local Variables

local variable

Look at the definition of the method readInput() given in Display 4.2. That method definition includes the declaration of a variable called keyboard. A variable declared within a method is called a **local variable**. It is called *local* because its meaning is local to—that is, confined to—the method definition. If you have two methods and each of them declares a variable of the same name—for example, if both were named keyboard—they would be two different variables that just happen to have the same name. Any change that is made to the variable named keyboard within one method would have no effect upon the variable named keyboard in the other method.

As we noted in Chapter 1, the main part of a program is itself a method. All variables declared in main are variables local to the method main. If a variable declared in main happens to have the same name as a variable declared in some other method, they are two different variables that just happen to have the same name. Thus, all the variables we have seen so far are either local variables or instance variables. There is only one more kind of variable in Java, which is known as a *static variable*. Static variables will be discussed in Chapter 5.

Local Variable

A variable declared within a method definition is called a **local variable**. If two methods each have a local variable of the same name, they are two different variables that just happen to have the same name.

Global Variables

Thus far, we have discussed two kinds of variables: instance variables, whose meaning is confined to an object of a class, and local variables, whose meaning is confined to a method definition. Some other programming languages have another kind of variable called a **global variable**, whose meaning is confined only to the program. Java does not have these global variables.

Blocks

block
compound
statement

The terms **block** and **compound statement** mean the same thing, namely, a set of Java statements enclosed in braces, {}. However, programmers tend to use the two terms in different contexts. When you declare a variable within a compound statement, the compound statement is usually called a *block*.

Blocks

A **block** is another name for a compound statement—that is, a list of statements enclosed in braces. However, programmers tend to use the two terms in different contexts. When you declare a variable within a compound statement, the compound statement is usually called a *block*. The variables declared in a block are local to the block, so these variables disappear when the execution of the block is completed. However, even though the variables are local to the block, their names cannot be used for anything else within the same method definition.

If you declare a variable within a block, that variable is local to the block. This means that when the block ends, all variables declared within the block disappear. In many programming languages, you can even use that variable's name to name some other variable outside the block. However, *in Java, you cannot have two variables with the same name inside a single method definition*. Local variables within blocks can sometimes create problems in Java. It is sometimes easier to declare the variables outside the block. If you declare a variable outside a block, you can use it both inside and outside the block, and it will have the same meaning both inside the block and outside the block.

TIP: Declaring Variables in a for Statement

You can declare a variable (or variables) within the initialization portion of a for statement, as in the following:

```
int sum = 0;
for (int n = 1; n < 10; n++)
    sum = sum + n;
```

If you declare n in this way, the variable n will be *local to the* for *loop.* This means that n cannot be used outside the for loop. For example, the following use of n in the System.out.println statement is illegal:

```
for (int n = 1; n < 10; n++)
    sum = sum + n;
System.out.println(n);//Illegal
```

Declaring variables inside a for loop can sometimes be more of a nuisance than a helpful feature. We tend to avoid declaring variables inside a for loop except for very simple cases that have no potential for confusion. ■

Self-Test Exercises

4. Write a method called happyGreeting that could be added to the class DateSecondTry in Display 4.2. The method happyGreeting writes the string "Happy Days!" to the screen a number of times equal to the value of the instance variable day. For example, if the value of day is 3, then it should write the following to the screen:

```
Happy Days!
Happy Days!
Happy Days!
```

Use a local variable.

Parameters of a Primitive Type

parameter

All the method definitions we have seen thus far had no parameters, which was indicated by an empty set of parentheses in the method heading. A **parameter** is like a blank that is filled in with a particular value when the method is invoked. (What we are calling *parameters* are

argument

also called *formal parameters*.) The value that is plugged in for the parameter is called an **argument**.[2] We have already used arguments with predefined methods. For example, the string `"Hello"` is the argument to the method `println` in the following method invocation:

```
System.out.println("Hello");
```

Display 4.4 contains the definition of a method named `setDate` that has the three parameters `newMonth`, `newDay`, and `newYear`. It also contains the definition of a method named `monthString` that has one parameter of type `int`.

The items plugged in for the parameters are called *arguments* and are given in parentheses at the end of the method invocation. For example, in the following call from Display 4.4, the integers `6` and `17` and the variable `year` are the arguments plugged in for `newMonth`, `newDay`, and `newYear`, respectively:

```
date.setDate(6, 17, year);
```

When you have a method invocation like the preceding, the argument (such as `6`) is plugged in for the corresponding formal parameter (such as `newMonth`) *everywhere that the parameter occurs in the method definition*. After all the arguments have been plugged in for their corresponding parameters, the code in the body of the method definition is executed.

The following invocation of the method `monthString` occurs within the definition of the method `setDate` in Display 4.4:

```
month = monthString(newMonth);
```

The argument is `newMonth`, which is plugged in for the parameter `monthNumber` in the definition of the method `monthString`.

Note that each of the formal parameters must be preceded by a type name, even if there is more than one parameter of the same type. Corresponding arguments must match the type of their corresponding formal parameter, although in some simple cases, an automatic type cast might be performed by Java. For example, if you plug in an argument of type `int` for a parameter of type `double`, Java automatically type casts the `int` value to a value of type `double`. The following list shows the type casts that Java automatically performs for you. An argument in a method invocation that is of any of these types is automatically type cast to any of the types that appear to its right if that is needed to match a formal parameter.[3]

```
byte -> short -> int -> long -> float -> double
```

---

[2] Some programmers use the term *actual parameters* for what we are calling *arguments*.

[3] An argument of type `char` is also converted to a matching number type, if the formal parameter is of type `int` or any type to the right of `int` in our list of types.

Display 4.4 **Methods with Parameters** (part 1 of 2)

```
1    import java.util.Scanner;

2    public class DateThirdTry
3    {
4        private String month;
5        private int day;
6        private int year; //a four digit number.

7        public void setDate(int newMonth, int newDay, int newYear)
8        {
9            month = monthString(newMonth);
10           day = newDay;
11           year = newYear;
12       }

13       public String monthString(int monthNumber)
14       {
15           switch (monthNumber)
16           {
17           case 1:
18               return "January";
19           case 2:
20               return "February";
21           case 3:
22               return "March";
23           case 4:
24               return "April";
25           case 5:
26               return "May";
27           case 6:
28               return "June";
29           case 7:
30               return "July";
31           case 8:
32               return "August";
33           case 9:
34               return "September";
35           case 10:
36               return "October";
37           case 11:
38               return "November";
39           case 12:
40               return "December";
```

The significance of the modifier **private** *is discussed in the subsection* "**public and private** *Modifiers" in Section 4.2.*

The method **setDate** *has an* int *parameter for the month, even though the month instance variable is of type* **String**. *The method* **setDate** *converts the month* int *value to a string with a call to the method* **monthString**.

This is the file **DateThirdTry.java**.

Display 4.4   **Methods with Parameters** (part 2 of 2)

```
41            default:
42                System.out.println("Fatal Error");
43                System.exit(0);
44                return "Error"; //to keep the compiler happy
45            }
46        }
```

<The rest of the method definitions are identical to the ones given in Display 4.2.>

```
47    }
```
                                                This is the file **DateThirdTry.java**.

```
1    public class DateThirdTryDemo                      This is the file
2    {                                                   DateThirdTryDemo.java.
3        public static void main(String[] args)
4        {
5            DateThirdTry date = new DateThirdTry( );
6            int year = 1882;                  The variable year is NOT plugged in for the
7            date.setDate(6, 17, year);        parameter newYear in the definition of the
8            date.writeOutput( );              method setDate. Only the value of year,
9        }                                     namely 1882, is plugged in for the parameter
10    }                                        newYear.
```

Sample Dialogue

```
June 17, 1882
```

Note that this is exactly the same as the automatic type casting we discussed in Chapter 1 for storing values of one type in a variable of another type. The more general rule is that you can use a value of any of the listed types anywhere that Java expects a value of a type further down on the list.

Note that the correspondence of the parameters and arguments is determined by their order in the lists in parentheses. In a method invocation, there must be exactly the same number of arguments in parentheses as there are formal parameters in the method definition heading. The first argument in the method invocation is plugged in for the first parameter in the method definition heading, the second argument in the method invocation is plugged in for the second parameter in the heading of the method definition, and so forth. This is diagrammed in Display 4.5.

It is important to note that only the value of the argument is used in this substitution process. If an argument in a method invocation is a variable (such as year in Display 4.4), it is the

Display 4.5   Correspondence between Formal Parameters and Arguments

```
public class DateThirdTry
{
    private String month;
    private int day;
    private int year; //a four digit number.

    public void setDate(int newMonth, int newDay, int newYear)
    {
        month = monthString(newMonth);
        day = newDay;
        year = newYear;
    }
    ...
```

This is in the file
`DateThirdTry.java`.

Only the value of year,
namely 1882, is plugged in
for the parameter newYear.

```
public class DateThirdTryDemo
{
    public static void main(String[] args)
    {
        DateThirdTry date = new DateThirdTry( );
        int year = 1882;
        date.setDate(6, 17, year);
        date.writeOutput( );
    }
}
```

This is in the file
`DateThirdTryDemo.java`.
This is the file for a program that
uses the class DateThirdTry.

The arrows show which argument is
plugged in for which formal
parameter.

Parameters of a Primitive Type

Parameters are given in parentheses after the method name in the heading of a method definition. A parameter of a primitive type, such as `int`, `double`, or `char`, is a local variable. When the method is invoked, the parameter is initialized to the value of the corresponding argument in the method invocation. This mechanism is known as the **call-by-value** parameter mechanism. The argument in a method invocation can be a literal constant, such as 2 or 'A'; a variable; or any expression that yields a value of the appropriate type. This is the only kind of parameter that Java has for parameters of a primitive type. (Parameters of a class type are discussed in Chapter 5.)

> ### main Is a void Method
>
> The `main` part of a program is a **void** method, as indicated by its heading:
>
> ```
> public static void main(String[] args)
> ```
>
> The word **static** will be explained in Chapter 5. The identifier `args` is a parameter of type `String[]`, which is the type for an array of strings. Arrays are discussed in Chapter 6, and you need not be concerned about them until then. In the examples in this book, we never use the parameter `args`. Because `args` is a parameter, you may replace it with any other non-keyword identifier and your program will have the same meaning. Aside from possibly changing the name of the parameter `args`, the heading of the `main` method must be exactly as shown above. Although we will not be using the parameter `args`, we will tell you how to use it in Chapter 6.
>
> A program in Java is just a class that has a `main` method. When you give a command to run a Java program, the run-time system invokes the method `main`.

value of the variable that is plugged in for its corresponding parameter; it is not the variable name that is plugged in. For example, in Display 4.4, the value of the variable `year` (that is, 1882) is plugged in for the parameter `newYear`. The variable `year` is not plugged in to the body of the method `setDate`. Because only the value of the argument is used, this method **call-by-value** of plugging in arguments for formal parameters is known as the **call-by-value** mechanism. In Java, this is the only method of substitution that is used with parameters of a primitive type, such as `int`, `double`, and `char`. As you will eventually see, this is, strictly speaking, also the only method of substitution that is used with parameters of a class type. However, there are other differences that make parameters of a class type appear to use a different substitution mechanism. For now, we are concerned only with parameters and arguments of primitive types, such as `int`, `double`, and `char`. (Although the type `String` is a class type, you will not go wrong if you consider it to behave like a primitive type when an argument of type `String` is plugged in for its corresponding parameter. However, for most class types, you need to think a bit differently about how arguments are plugged in for parameters. We discuss parameters of a class type in Chapter 5.)

parameters as local variables   In most cases, you can think of a parameter as a kind of blank, or placeholder, that is filled in by the value of its corresponding argument in the method invocation. However, parameters are more than just blanks; a parameter is actually a local variable. When the method is invoked, the value of an argument is computed, and the corresponding parameter, which is a local variable, is initialized to this value. Occasionally, it is useful to use a parameter as a local variable. An example of a parameter used as local variable is given in Display 4.6. In that display, notice the parameter `minutesWorked` in the method `computeFee`. The value of `minutesWorked` is changed within the body of the method definition. This is allowed because a parameter is a local variable.

Display 4.6 A Formal Parameter Used as a Local Variable (part 1 of 2)

```java
1    import java.util.Scanner;
                                              This is the file Bill.java.
2    public class Bill
3    {
4        public static double RATE = 150.00; //Dollars per quarter hour

5        private int hours;
6        private int minutes;
7        private double fee;

8        public void inputTimeWorked()
9        {
10           System.out.println("Enter number of full hours worked");
11           System.out.println("followed by number of minutes:");
12           Scanner keyboard = new Scanner(System.in);       computeFee uses the
13           hours = keyboard.nextInt();                      parameter minutesWorked
14           minutes = keyboard.nextInt();                    as a local variable.
15       }

16       public double computeFee(int hoursWorked, int minutesWorked)
17       {
18           minutesWorked = hoursWorked*60 + minutesWorked;
19           int quarterHours = minutesWorked/15; //Any remaining fraction of a
20                                       // quarter hour is not charged for.
21           return quarterHours*RATE;
22       }                                       Although minutes is plugged in
                                                 for minutesWorked and
23       public void updateFee()                 minutesWorked is changed, the
24       {                                        value of minutes is not changed.
25           fee = computeFee(hours, minutes);
26       }

27       public void outputBill()
28       {
29           System.out.println("Time worked: ");
30           System.out.println(hours + " hours and " + minutes + " minutes");
31           System.out.println("Rate: $" + RATE + " per quarter hour.");
32           System.out.println("Amount due: $" + fee);
33       }
34   }
```

Display 4.6   A Formal Parameter Used as a Local Variable (part 2 of 2)

```
1   public class BillingDialog
2   {                                                This is the file BillingDialog.java.
3       public static void main(String[] args)
4       {
5           System.out.println("Welcome to the law offices of");
6           System.out.println("Dewey, Cheatham, and Howe.");
7           Bill yourBill = new Bill();
8           yourBill.inputTimeWorked();
9           yourBill.updateFee();
10          yourBill.outputBill();
11          System.out.println("We have placed a lien on your house.");
12          System.out.println("It has been our pleasure to serve you.");
13      }
14  }
```

Sample Dialogue

```
Welcome to the law offices of
Dewey, Cheatham, and Howe.
Enter number of full hours worked
followed by number of minutes:
3 48
Time worked:
2 hours and 48 minutes
Rate: $150.0 per quarter hour.
Amount due: $2250.0
We have placed a lien on your house.
It has been our pleasure to serve you.
```

PITFALL: Use of the Terms "Parameter" and "Argument"

The use of the terms *parameter* and *argument* that we follow in this book is consistent with common usage, but people also often use the terms *parameter* and *argument* interchangeably. When you see these terms, you must determine their exact meaning from context. Many people use the term *parameter* for both what we call *parameters* and what we call *arguments*. Other people use the term *argument* both for what we call *parameters* and what we call *arguments*. Do not expect consistency in how people use these two terms.

formal parameter

actual parameter

The term **formal parameter** is often used for what we describe as a *parameter*. We will sometimes use the term *formal parameter* for emphasis. The term **actual parameter** is often used for what we call an *argument*. We do not use the term *actual parameter* in this book, but you will encounter it in other books. ■

Self-Test Exercises

5. Write a method called `fractionDone` that could be added to the class `DateThirdTry` in Display 4.4. The method `fractionDone` has a parameter `targetDay` of type `int` (for a day of the month) and returns a value of type `double`. The value returned is the value of the `day` instance variable divided by the `int` parameter `targetDay`. (So it returns the fraction of the time passed so far this month where the goal is reaching the `targetDay`.) Do floating-point division, not integer division. To get floating-point division, copy the value of the `day` instance variable into a local variable of type `double` and use this local variable in place of the `day` instance variable in the division. (You may assume the parameter `targetDay` is a valid day of the month that is greater than the value of the `day` instance variable.)

6. Write a method called `advanceYear` that could be added to the class `DateThirdTry` in Display 4.4. The method `advanceYear` has one parameter of type `int`. The method `advanceYear` increases the value of the `year` instance variable by the amount of this one parameter.

7. Suppose we redefine the method `setDate` in Display 4.4 to the following:

```
public void setDate(int newMonth, int newDay, int newYear)
{
    month = monthString(newMonth);
    day = newDay;
    year = newYear;
    System.out.println("Date changed to "
                        + newMonth + " " + newDay + ", " + newYear);
}
```

Indicate all instances of `newMonth` that have their value changed to 6 in the following invocation (also from Display 4.4):

```
date.setDate(6, 17, year);
```

8. Is the following a legal method definition that could be added to the class `DateThirdTry` in Display 4.4?

```
public void multiWriteOutput(int count)
{
    while (count > 0)
    {
        writeOutput();
        count--;
    }
}
```

9. Consider the definition of the method `monthString` in Display 4.4. Why are there no `break` statements in the `switch` statement?

Simple Cases with Class Parameters

Methods can have parameters of a class type. Parameters of a class type are more subtle and more powerful than parameters of a primitive type. We will discuss parameters of class types in detail in Chapter 5. In the meantime, we will occasionally use a class type parameter in very simple situations. For these simple cases, you do not need to know any details about class type parameters except that, in some sense or other, the class argument is plugged in for the class parameter.

The `this` Parameter

As we noted earlier, if `today` is of type `DateSecondTry` (Display 4.2), then

```java
today.writeOutput();
```

is equivalent to

```java
System.out.println(today.month + " " + today.day
                                  + ", " + today.year);
```

This is because, although the definition of `writeOutput` reads

```java
public void writeOutput()
{
    System.out.println(month + " " + day + ", " + year);
}
```

it really means

```java
public void writeOutput()
{
    System.out.println(<the calling object>.month + " "
        + <the calling object>.day + ", " + <the calling object>.year);
}
```

The instance variables are understood to have `<the calling object>.` in front of them. Sometimes it is handy, and on rare occasions even necessary, to have an explicit name for the calling object. Inside a Java method definition, you can use the keyword `this` as a name for the calling object. So, the following is a valid Java method definition that is equivalent to the one we are discussing:

```java
public void writeOutput()
{
    System.out.println(this.month + " " + this.day
                                  + ", " + this.year);
}
```

The definition of `writeOutput` in Display 4.2 could be replaced by this completely equivalent version. Moreover, this version is in some sense the true version. The version

this
parameter

without the this and a dot in front of each instance variable is just an abbreviation for this version. However, the abbreviation of omitting the this is used frequently.

The keyword this is known as the **this parameter**. The this parameter is a kind of hidden parameter. It does not appear on the parameter list of a method, but is still a parameter. When a method is invoked, the calling object is automatically plugged in for this.

The this Parameter

Within a method definition, you can use the keyword this as a name for the calling object. If an instance variable or another method in the class is used without any calling object, then this is understood to be the calling object.

There is one common situation that requires the use of the this parameter. You often want to have the parameters in a method such as setDate be the same as the instance variables. A first, although incorrect, try at doing this is the following rewriting of the method setDate from Display 4.4:

```
public void setDate(int month, int day, int year) //Not correct
{
    month = monthString(month);
    day = day;
    year = year;
}
```

This rewritten version does not do what we want. When you declare a local variable in a method definition, then within the method definition, that name always refers to the local variable. A parameter is a local variable, so this rule applies to parameters. Consider the following assignment statement in our rewritten method definition:

```
day = day;
```

mask a
variable

Both the identifiers day refer to the parameter named day. The identifier day does not refer to the instance variable day. All occurrences of the identifier day refer to the parameter day. This is often described by saying the parameter day **masks** or hides the instance variable day. Similar remarks apply to the parameters month and year.

This rewritten method definition of the method setDate will produce a compiler error message because the following attempts to assign a String value to the int variable (the parameter) month:

```
month = monthString(month);
```

However, in many situations, this sort of rewriting will produce a method definition that will compile but that will not do what it is supposed to do.

To correctly rewrite the method `setDate`, we need some way to say "the instance variable `month`" as opposed to the parameter `month`. The way to say "the instance variable `month`" is `this.month`. Similar remarks apply to the other two parameters. So, the correct rewriting of the method `setDate` is as follows:

```java
public void setDate(int month, int day, int year)
{
    this.month = monthString(month);
    this.day = day;
    this.year = year;
}
```

This version is completely equivalent to the version in Display 4.4.

Self-Test Exercises

10. The method `writeOutput` in Display 4.2 uses the instance variables `month`, `day`, and `year`, but gives no object name for these instance variables. Every instance variable must belong to some object. To what object or objects do these instance variables in the definition of `writeOutput` belong?

11. Rewrite the definitions of the methods `getDay` and `getYear` in Display 4.2 using the `this` parameter.

12. Rewrite the method `getMonth` in Display 4.2 using the `this` parameter.

Methods That Return a Boolean Value

There is nothing special about methods that return a value of type `boolean`. The type `boolean` is a primitive type, just like the types `int` and `double`. A method that returns a value of type `boolean` must have a `return` statement of the form

```java
return Boolean_Expression;
```

So, an invocation of a method that returns a value of type `boolean` returns either `true` or `false`. It thus makes sense to use an invocation of such a method to control an `if-else` statement, to control a `while` loop, or anyplace else that a Boolean expression is allowed. Although there is nothing new here, people who have not used `boolean` valued methods before sometimes find them to be uncomfortable. So we will go through one small example.

The following is a method definition that could be added to the class `DateThirdTry` in Display 4.4:

```java
public boolean isBetween(int lowYear, int highYear)
{
    return ( (year > lowYear) && (year < highYear) );
}
```

Consider the following lines of code:

```
DateThirdTry date = new DateThirdTry();
date.setDate(1, 2, 3001);
if (date.isBetween(2000, 4000))
    System.out.println(
                    "The date is between the years 2000 and 4000");
else
    System.out.println(
                    "The date is not between the years 2000 and 4000");
```

The expression date.isBetween(2000, 4000) is an invocation of a method that returns a boolean value—that is, returns one of the two values true and false. So, it makes perfectly good sense to use it as the controlling Boolean expression in an if-else statement. The expression year in the definition of isBetween really means this.year, and this stands for the calling object. In date.isBetween(2000, 4000) the calling object is date. So, this returns the value

```
(date.year > lowYear) && (date.year < highYear)
```

But, 2000 and 4000 are plugged in for the parameters lowYear and highYear, respectively. So, this expression is equivalent to

```
(date.year > 2000) && (date.year < 4000)
```

Thus, the if-else statement is equivalent to[4]

```
if ((date.year > 2000) && (date.year < 4000))
    System.out.println(
                    "The date is between the years 2000 and 4000.");
else
    System.out.println(
                    "The date is not between the years 2000 and 4000.");
```

Thus, the output produced is

```
The date is between the years 2000 and 4000.
```

Another example of a boolean valued method, which we will, in fact, add to our date class, is shown below:

```
public boolean precedes(DateFourthTry otherDate)
{
    return ( (year < otherDate.year) ||
```

---

[4] Later in this chapter, we will see that because year is marked private, it is not legal to write date.year in a program, but the meaning of such an expression is clear even if you cannot include it in a program.

```
        (year == otherDate.year && getMonth() < otherDate.getMonth()) ||
        (year == otherDate.year && month.equals(otherDate.month)
                                    && day < otherDate.day) );

}
```

The version of our date class with this method is given in Display 4.7. The other new methods in that class will be discussed shortly in the subsection entitled "The Methods equals and toString." Right now, let's discuss this new method named precedes.

An invocation of the method precedes has the following form, where date1 and date2 are two objects of our date class:

```
date1.precedes(date2)
```

This is a Boolean expression that returns true if date1 comes before date2. Because it is a Boolean expression, it can be used anyplace a Boolean expression is allowed, such as to control an if-else or while statement. For example:

```
if (date1.precedes(date2))
    System.out.println("date1 comes before date2.");
else
    System.out.println("date2 comes before or is equal to date1.");
```

Display 4.7   A Class with Methods **equals** and **toString** (part 1 of 2)

```
1    import java.util.Scanner;

2    public class DateFourthTry
3    {
4        private String month;
5        private int day;
6        private int year; //a four digit number.

7        public String toString()
8        {
9            return (month + " " + day + ", " + year);
10       }

11       public void writeOutput()
12       {
13           System.out.println(month + " " + day + ", " + year);
14       }
```

This is the method equals in the class DateFourthTry.

This is the method equals in the class String.

```
15       public boolean equals(DateFourthTry otherDate)
16       {
17           return ( (month.equals(otherDate.month))
18                   && (day == otherDate.day) && (year == otherDate.year) );
19       }
```

(continued)

Display 4.7   A Class with Methods **equals** and **toString** (part 2 of 2)

```
20        public boolean precedes(DateFourthTry otherDate)
21        {
22            return ( (year < otherDate.year) ||
23                (year == otherDate.year && getMonth() < otherDate.getMonth()) ||
24                (year == otherDate.year && month.equals(otherDate.month)
25                                    && day < otherDate.day) );
26        }
```

<The rest of the method definitions are identical to the ones in `DateThirdTry` *in Display 4.4.>*

```
27    }
```

The return statement in the definition of the method `precedes` may look intimidating, but it is really straightforward. It says that `date1.precedes(date2)` returns true, provided one of the following three conditions is satisfied:

```
date1.year < date2.year
date1.year equals date2.year and date1.month comes before date2.month
date1 and date2 have the same year and month and
        date1.day < date2.day.
```

If you give it a bit of thought, you will realize that `date1` precedes `date2` in time precisely when one of these three conditions is satisfied.

The Methods **equals** and **toString**

Java expects certain methods to be in all, or almost all, classes. This is because some of the standard Java libraries have software that assumes such methods are defined. Two of these methods are `equals` and `toString`. Therefore, you should include such methods and be certain to spell their names exactly as we have done. Use `equals`, not `same` or `areEqual`. Do not even use `equal` without the s. Similar remarks apply to the `toString` method. After we have developed more material, we will explain this in more detail. In particular, we will then explain how to give a better method definition for `equals`. For now, just get in the habit of including these methods.

equals   The method `equals` is a `boolean` valued method to compare two objects of the class to see if they satisfy the intuitive notion of "being equal." So, the heading should be

```
public boolean equals(Class_Name Parameter_Name)
```

Display 4.7 contains definitions of the methods `equals` and `toString` that we might add to our date class, which is now named `DateFourthTry`. The heading of that `equals` method is

```
public boolean equals(DateFourthTry otherDate)
```

When you use the method `equals` to compare two objects of the class `DateFourth-Try`, one object is the calling object and the other object is the argument, like so:

    date1.equals(date2)

or equivalently

    date2.equals(date1)

Because the method `equals` returns a value of type `boolean`, you can use an invocation of `equals` as the Boolean expression in an `if-else` statement, as shown in Display 4.8. Similarly, you can also use it anyplace else that a Boolean expression is allowed.

There is no absolute notion of "equality" that you must follow in your definition of `equals`. You can define the method `equals` any way you wish, but to be useful, it should reflect some notion of "equality" that is useful for the software you are

---

Display 4.8 Using the Methods `equals` and `toString`

```
1    public class EqualsAndToStringDemo
2    {
3        public static void main(String[] args)
4        {
5            DateFourthTry date1 = new DateFourthTry(),
6                          date2 = new DateFourthTry();
7            date1.setDate(6, 17, 1882);
8            date2.setDate(6, 17, 1882);

9            if (date1.equals(date2))
10               System.out.println(date1 + " equals " + date2);
11           else
12               System.out.println(date1 + " does not equal " + date2);

13           date1.setDate(7, 28, 1750);

14           if (date1.precedes(date2))
15               System.out.println(date1 + " comes before " + date2);
16           else
17               System.out.println(date2 + " comes before or is equal to "
18                                     + date1);
19       }
20   }
```

These are equivalent to
date1.toString().

These are equivalent to
date2.toString().

Sample Dialogue

```
June 17, 1882 equals June 17, 1882
July 28, 1750 comes before June 17, 1882
```

designing. A common way to define equals for simple classes of the kind we are looking at now is to say equals returns true if each instance variable of one object equals the corresponding instance variable of the other object. This is how we defined equals in Display 4.7.

If the definition of equals in Display 4.7 seems less than clear, it may help to rewrite it as follows using the this parameter:

```
public boolean equals(DateFourthTry otherDate)
{
    return ( ((this.month).equals(otherDate.month))
        && (this.day == otherDate.day) && (this.year == otherDate.year) );
}
```

So if date1 and date2 are objects of the class DateFourthTry, then date1.equals (date2) returns true provided the three instance variables in date1 have values that are equal to the three instance variables in date2.

Also, note that the method in the definition of equals that is used to compare months is not the equals for the class DateFourthTry but the equals for the class String. You know this because the calling object, which is this.month, is of type String.

(Remember that we use the equals method of the class String because == does not work correctly for comparing String values. This was discussed in the Pitfall section of Chapter 3 entitled "Using == with Strings.")

In Chapter 7, you will see that there are reasons to make the definition of the equals method a bit more involved. But the spirit of what an equals method should be is very much like what we are now doing, and it is the best we can do with what we know so far.

toString The method toString should be defined so that it returns a String value that represents the data in the object. One nice thing about the method toString is that it makes it easy to output an object to the screen. If date is of type DateFourthTry, then you can output the date to the screen as follows:

```
System.out.println(date.toString());
```

println used with objects In fact, System.out.println was written so that it automatically invokes toString() if you do not include it. So, the object date can also be output by the following simpler and equivalent statement:

```
System.out.println(date);
```

This means that the method writeOutput in Display 4.7 is superfluous and could safely be omitted from the class definition.

If you look at Display 4.8, you will see that toString is also called automatically when the object is connected to some other string with a +, as in

```
System.out.println(date1 + " equals " + date2);
```

+ used with objects

In this case, it is really the plus operator that causes the automatic invocation of `toString()`. So, the following is also legal:

```
String s = date1 + " equals " + date2;
```

The preceding is equivalent to

```
String s = date1.toString() + " equals " + date2.toString();
```

Recursive Methods

recursive method

Java does allow **recursive method** definitions. Recursive methods are covered in Chapter 11. If you do not know what recursive methods are, do not be concerned until you reach that chapter. If you want to read about recursive methods early, you can read Sections 11.1 and 11.2 of Chapter 11 after you complete Chapter 5.

The Methods equals and toString

Usually, your class definitions should contain an **equals** method and a **toString** method.

An **equals** method compares the calling object to another object and should return **true** when the two objects are intuitively equal. When comparing objects of a class type, you normally use the method **equals**, not ==.

The **toString** method should return a string representation of the data in the calling object. If a class has a **toString** method, you can use an object of the class as an argument to the methods **System.out.println** and **System.out.print**.

See Display 4.7 for an example of a class with **equals** and **toString** methods.

 TIP: Testing Methods

driver program

Each method should be tested in a program in which it is the only untested program. If you test methods this way, then when you find an error, you will know which method contains the error. A program that does nothing but test a method is called a **driver program**.

bottom-up testing

If one method contains an invocation of another method in the same class, this can complicate the testing task. One way to test a method is to first test all the methods invoked by that method and then test the method itself. This is called **bottom-up testing**.

(continued)

It is sometimes impossible or inconvenient to test a method without using some other method that has not yet been written or has not yet been tested. In this case, you can use a simplified version of the missing or untested method. These simplified methods are called **stubs**. These stubs will not necessarily perform the correct calculation, but they will deliver values that suffice for testing, and they are simple enough that you can have confidence in their performance. For example, the following is a possible stub:

stub

```
/**
 Computes the probability of rain based on temperature, barometric pressure,
 and relative humidity. Returns the probability as a fraction between
 0 and 1.
*/
public double rainChance(double temperature,
                          double pressure, double humidity)
{
    return 0.5;//Not correct but good enough for a stub.
}
```

The Fundamental Rule for Testing Methods

Every method should be tested in a program in which every other method in the testing program has already been fully tested and debugged.

Self-Test Exercises

13. In the definition of `precedes` in Display 4.7, we used

    `month.equals(otherDate.month)`

    to test whether two months are equal; but we used

    `getMonth() < otherDate.getMonth()`

    to test whether one month comes before another. Why did we use `month` in one case and `getMonth` in another case?

14. What is the fundamental rule for testing methods?

4.2   Information Hiding and Encapsulation

We all know—the Times *knows—but we pretend we don't.*

VIRGINIA WOOLF, *Monday or Tuesday*

information hiding

Information hiding means that you separate the description of how to use a class from the implementation details, such as how the class methods are defined. You do this so that a programmer who uses the class does not need to know the implementation details of the class definition. The programmer who uses the class can consider the implementation details as hidden, since he or she does not need to look at them. Information hiding is a way of avoiding information overloading. It keeps the information needed by a programmer using the class within reasonable bounds. Another term for information hiding is **abstraction**. The use of the term *abstraction* for information hiding makes sense if you think about it a bit. When you abstract something you are discarding some of the details.

abstraction

encapsulation

Encapsulation means grouping software into a unit in such a way that it is easy to use because there is a well-defined simple interface. So, encapsulation and information hiding are two sides of the same coin.

Java has a way of officially hiding details of a class definition. To hide details, you mark them as private, a concept we discuss next.

Encapsulation

Encapsulation means that the data and the actions are combined into a single item (in our case, a class object) and the details of the implementation are hidden. The terms *information hiding* and *encapsulation* deal with the same general principle: If a class is well designed, a programmer who uses a class need not know all the details of the implementation of the class but need only know a much simpler description of how to use the class.

API

The term **API** stands for *application programming interface.* The API for a class is a description of how to use the class. If your class is well designed, using the encapsulation techniques we discuss in this book, then a programmer who uses your class need only read the API and need not look at the details of your code for the class definition.

ADT

The term **ADT** is short for *abstract data type.* An ADT is a data type that is written using good information-hiding techniques.

public and private Modifiers

public
private

Compare the instance variables in Displays 4.1 and 4.2. In Display 4.1, each instance variable is prefaced with the modifier public. In Display 4.2, each instance variable is prefaced with the modifier private. The modifier public means that there are no restrictions on where the instance variable can be used. The modifier private means that the instance variable cannot be accessed by name outside of the class definition.

For example, the following would produce a compiler error message if used in a program:

```
DateSecondTry date = new DateSecondTry();
date.month = "January";
date.day = 1;
date.year = 2006;
```

In fact, any one of the three assignments would be enough to trigger a compiler error. This is because, as shown in Display 4.2, each of the instance variables month, day, and year is labeled private.

If, on the other hand, we had used the class DateFirstTry from Display 4.1 instead of the class DateSecondTry in the preceding code, the code would be legal and would compile and run with no error messages. This is because, in the definition of Date-FirstTry (Display 4.1), each of the instance variables month, day, and year is labeled public.

It is considered good programming practice to make all instance variables private. As we will explain a little later in this chapter, this is intended to simplify the task of any programmer using the class. But before we say anything about how, on balance, this simplifies the job of a programmer who uses the class, let's see how it complicates the job of a programmer who uses the class.

Once you label an instance variable as private, there is then no way to change its value (nor to reference the instance variable in any other way) except by using one of the methods belonging to the class. Note that even when an instance variable is private, you can still access it through methods of the class. For the class DateSecondTry, you can change the values of the instance variables with the method readInput, and you can obtain the values of the instance variables with the methods whose names start with get. So, the qualifier private does not make it impossible to access the instance variables. It just makes it illegal to use their names, which can be a minor nuisance.

The modifiers public and private before a method definition have a similar meaning. If the method is labeled public, there are no restrictions on its usage. If the method is labeled private, the method can only be used in the definition of another method of the same class.

Any instance variable can be labeled either public or private. Any method can be public or private. However, normal good programming practices require that *all* instance variables be private and typically most methods be public. Normally, a method is private only if it is being used solely as a helping method in the definition of other methods.

EXAMPLE: Yet Another Date Class

Display 4.9 contains another, much improved, definition of a class for a date. Note that all instance variables are private and that two methods are private. We made the methods `dateOK` and `monthString` private because they are just helping methods used in the definitions of other methods. A user of the class `DateFifthTry` would not (in fact, cannot) use either of the methods `dateOK` or `monthString`. This is all hidden information that need not concern a programmer using the class. The method `monthString` was public in previous versions of our date classes because we had not yet discussed the `private` modifier. It is now marked `private` because it is just a helping method.

Note that the class `DateFifthTry` uses the method `dateOK` to make sure that any changes to instance variables make sense. Because the methods of the class `DateFifthTry` use the method `dateOK` to check for impossible dates, you cannot use any methods, such as `readInput` or `setDate`, to set the instance variables so that they represent an impossible date like January 63, 2005. If you try to do so, your program would end with an error message. (To make our definition of the method `dateOK` simple, we did not check for certain impossible dates, such as February 31, but it would be easy to exclude these dates as well.)

The methods `dateOK` and `equals` each return a value of type `boolean`. That means they return a value that is either `true` or `false` and so can be used as the Boolean expression in an `if-else` statement, `while` statement, or other loop statement. This is illustrated by the following, which is taken from the definition of the method `setDate` in Display 4.9:

```
if (dateOK(month, day, year))
{
    this.month = monthString(month);
    this.day = day;
    this.year = year;
}
else
{
    System.out.println("Fatal Error");
    System.exit(0);
}
```

Note that, although all the instance variables are private, a programmer using the class can still change or access the value of an instance variable using the methods that start with `set` or `get`. This is discussed more fully in the next subsection, "Accessor and Mutator Methods."

(continued)

EXAMPLE: (continued)

Note that there is a difference between what we might call the *inside view* and the *outside view* of the class DateFifthTry. A date like July 4, 1776, is represented inside the class object as the string value "July" and the two int values 4 and 1776. But if a programmer using the same class object asks for the date using getMonth, getDay, and getYear, he or she will get the three int values 7, 4, and 1776. From inside the class, a month is a string value, but from outside the class, a month is an integer. The description of the data in a class object need not be a simple direct description of the instance variables. (To further emphasize the fact that the month has an inside view as a string but an outside view as a number, we have written the method readInput for the class DateFifthTry so that the user enters the month as an integer rather than a string.)

Note that the method definitions in a class need not be given in any particular order. In particular, it is perfectly acceptable to give the definition the method dateOK after the definitions of methods that use dateOK. Indeed, any ordering of the method definitions is acceptable. Use whatever order seems to make the class easiest to read. (Those who come to Java from certain other programming languages should note that there is no kind of forward reference needed when a method is used before it is defined.)

Self-Test Exercises

15. Following the style guidelines given in this book, when should an instance variable be marked private?

16. Following the style guidelines given in this book, when should a method be marked private?

Accessor and Mutator Methods

You should always make all instance variables in a class private. However, you may sometimes need to do something with the data in a class object. The special-purpose methods, such as toString, equals, and any input methods, will allow you to do many things with the data in an object. But sooner or later you will want to do something with the data for which there are no special-purpose methods. How can you do anything new with the data in an object? The answer is that you can do anything that you might reasonably want (and that the class design specifications consider to be legitimate), provided you equip your classes with suitable *accessor* and *mutator* methods. These are methods that allow you to access and change the data in an object, **accessor** usually in a very general way. **Accessor methods** allow you to obtain the data. In Dis**methods** play 4.9, the methods getMonth, getDay, and getYear are accessor methods. The accessor methods need not literally return the values of each instance variable, but they must return something equivalent to those values. For example, the method getMonth returns the number of the month, even though the month is stored in a String instance variable. Although it is not required by the Java language, it is a generally accepted good programming practice to spell the names of accessor methods starting with get.

mutator methods

Mutator methods allow you to change the data in a class object. In Display 4.9, the methods whose names begin with the word set are mutator methods. It is a generally accepted good programming practice to use names that begin with the word set for mutator methods. Your class definitions will typically provide a complete set of public accessor methods and typically at least some public mutator methods. There are, however, important classes, such as the class String, that have no public mutator methods.

At first glance, it may look as if accessor and mutator methods defeat the purpose of making instance variables private, but if you look carefully at the mutator methods in Display 4.9, you will see that the mutator and accessor methods are not equivalent to making the instance variables public. Notice the mutator methods, that is, the ones that begin with set. They all test for an illegal date and end the program with an error message if there is an attempt to set the instance variables to any illegal values. If the variables were public, you could set the data to values that do not make sense for a date, such as January 42, 1930. With mutator methods, you can control and filter changes to the data. (As it is, you can still set the data to values that do not represent a real date, such as February 31, but as we already noted, it would be easy to exclude these dates as well. We did not exclude these dates to keep the example simple. See Self-Test Exercise 19 for a more complete date check method.)

Display 4.9 Yet Another Date Class (part 1 of 4)

```
1   import java.util.Scanner;

2   public class DateFifthTry
3   {
4       private String month;
5       private int day;
6       private int year; //a four digit number.


7       public void writeOutput()
8       {
9           System.out.println(month + " " + day + ", " + year);
10      }
11      public void readInput()
12      {
```

*Note that this version of **readInput** has the user enter the month as an integer rather than as a string. In this class, a month is an integer to the user, but is a string inside the class.*

(continued)

Display 4.9   Yet Another Date Class (part 2 of 4)

```
13            boolean tryAgain = true;
14            Scanner keyboard = new Scanner(System.in);
15            while (tryAgain)
16            {
17                System.out.println("Enter month, day, and year");
18                System.out.println("as three integers:");
19                System.out.println("do not use commas or other punctuations.");
20                int monthInput = keyboard.nextInt();
21                int dayInput = keyboard.nextInt();              Note that this
22                int yearInput = keyboard.nextInt();             version of
23                if (dateOK(monthInput, dayInput, yearInput) )   readInput checks
24                {                                               to see that the
25                    setDate(monthInput, dayInput, yearInput);   input is reasonable.
26                    tryAgain = false;
27                }
28                else
29                    System.out.println("Illegal date. Reenter input.");
30            }
31        }

32    public void setDate(int month, int day, int year)
33    {
34        if (dateOK(month, day, year))
35        {
36            this.month = monthString(month);
37            this.day = day;
38            this.year = year;
39        }
40        else
41        {
42            System.out.println("Fatal Error");
43            System.exit(0);
44        }
45    }

46    public void setMonth(int monthNumber)
47    {
48        if ((monthNumber <= 0) || (monthNumber > 12))
49        {
50            System.out.println("Fatal Error");
51            System.exit(0);
52        }
53        else
54            month = monthString(monthNumber);
55    }
```

Display 4.9   **Yet Another Date Class** (part 3 of 4)

```
56        public void setDay(int day)
57        {
58            if ((day <= 0) || (day > 31))
59            {
60                System.out.println("Fatal Error");
61                System.exit(0);
62            }
63            else
64                this.day = day;
65        }

66        public void setYear(int year)
67        {
68            if ( (year < 1000) || (year > 9999) )
69            {
70                System.out.println("Fatal Error");
71                System.exit(0);
72            }
73            else
74                this.year = year;
75        }

76        public boolean equals(DateFifthTry otherDate)
77        {
78            return ( (month.equalsIgnoreCase(otherDate.month))
79                    && (day == otherDate.day) && (year == otherDate.year) );
80        }
```

Within the definition of DateFifthTry, *you can directly access private instance variables of any object of type* DateFifthTry.

```
81        public boolean precedes(DateFifthTry otherDate)
82        {
83            return ( (year < otherDate.year) ||
84               (year == otherDate.year && getMonth() < otherDate.getMonth()) ||
85               (year == otherDate.year && month.equals(otherDate.month)
86                                    && day < otherDate.day) );
87        }
```

Within the definition of **DateFifthTry,** *you can directly access private instance variables of any object of type* **DateFifthTry.**

<The definitions of the following methods are the same as in Display 4.2 and Display 4.7:
  getMonth, getDay, getYear, *and* toString.*>*

```
88        private boolean dateOK(int monthInt, int dayInt, int yearInt)
89        {
```

(continued)

Display 4.9 **Yet Another Date Class** (part 4 of 4)

```
90             return ( (monthInt >= 1) && (monthInt <= 12) &&
91                     (dayInt >= 1) && (dayInt <= 31) &&
92                     (yearInt >= 1000) && (yearInt <= 9999) );
93         }

94      private String monthString(int monthNumber)
95      {
96          switch (monthNumber)
97          {
98          case 1:
99              return "January";
100         case 2:
101             return "February";
102         case 3:
103             return "March";
104         case 4:
105             return "April";
106         case 5:
107             return "May";
108         case 6:
109             return "June";
110         case 7:
111             return "July";
112         case 8:
113             return "August";
114         case 9:
115             return "September";
116         case 10:
117             return "October";
118         case 11:
119             return "November";
120         case 12:
121             return "December";
122         default:
123             System.out.println("Fatal Error");
124             System.exit(0);
125             return "Error"; //to keep the compiler happy
126         }
127     }
128 }
```

The way that a well-designed class definition uses private instance variables and public accessor and mutator methods to implement the principle of encapsulation is diagrammed in Display 4.10.

Display 4.10   Encapsulation

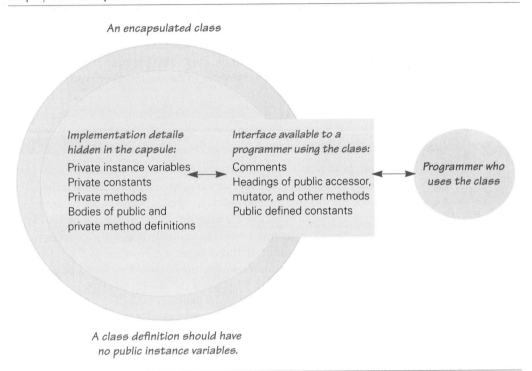

An encapsulated class

Implementation details
hidden in the capsule:

Private instance variables
Private constants
Private methods
Bodies of public and
private method definitions

Interface available to a
programmer using the class:

Comments
Headings of public accessor,
mutator, and other methods
Public defined constants

Programmer who
uses the class

A class definition should have
no public instance variables.

TIP: A Class Has Access to Private Members of All Objects of the Class

Consider the definition of the method `equals` for the class `DateFifthTry`, given in Display 4.9 and repeated below:

```
public boolean equals(DateFifthTry otherDate)
{
    return ( (month.equalsIgnoreCase(otherDate.month))
            && (day == otherDate.day) && (year == otherDate.year) );
}
```

You might object that `otherDate.month`, `otherDate.day`, and `otherDate.year` are illegal because `month`, `day`, and `year` are private instance variables of some object other than the calling object. Normally, that objection would be correct. However, the object `otherDate` is of the same type as the class being defined, so this is legal. In the definition of a class, you can access private members of any object of the class, not just private members of the calling object.

(continued)

TIP: (continued)

Similar remarks apply to the method `precedes` in the same class. In one place in the definition of `precedes`, we used `otherDate.getMonth()` rather than `otherDate.month` only because we wanted the month as an integer instead of a string. We did, in fact, use `otherDate.month` elsewhere in the definition of `precedes`. ■

TIP: Mutator Methods Can Return a Boolean Value ★

In the definition of the class `DateFifthTry` (Display 4.9), the mutator methods tested to see if the new values for instance variables were sensible values. If they were not sensible values, the mutator method ended the program and issued an error message. An alternative approach is to have the mutator do the test, but to never have it end the program. Instead, it returns a `boolean` value. It makes the changes to the instance variables and returns `true` if the changes are sensible. If the attempted changes are not sensible, the mutator method returns `false`. That way a programmer can program in an alterative action to be taken if the attempted changes to instance variables do not make sense.

For example, an alternative definition of the method `setMonth` of the class `DateFifthTry` (Display 4.9) is the following:

```
public boolean setMonth(int monthNumber)
{
    if ((monthNumber <= 0) || (monthNumber > 12))
        return false;
    else
    {
        month = monthString(monthNumber);
        return true;
    }
}
```

A sample use of this `boolean` valued version of `setMonth` could be the following:

```
DateFifthTry date = new DateFifthTry();
...
System.out.println("Enter month as a number:");
int number = keyboard.nextInt();
while (!date.setMonth(number))
{
    System.out.println("Not a legal month number. Try again.");
    System.out.println("Enter month as a number:");
    number = keyboard.nextInt();
}
```

■

Preconditions and Postconditions

precondition

postcondition

One good way to write a method comment is to break it down into two kinds of information, called the *precondition* and the *postcondition*. The **precondition** states what is assumed to be true when the method is called. The method should not be used and cannot be expected to perform correctly unless the precondition holds. The **postcondition** describes the effect of the method call; that is, the postcondition tells what will be true after the method is executed in a situation in which the precondition holds. For a method that returns a value, the postcondition describes the value returned by the method.

For example, the following is an example of a method heading from Display 4.9 with a precondition and postcondition added:

```
/**
 Precondition: All instance variables of the calling object have values.
 Postcondition: The data in the calling object has been written to the screen.
*/
public void writeOutput()
```

You do not need to know the definition of the method writeOutput to use this method. All that you need to know to use this method is given by the precondition and postcondition. (The importance of this is more dramatic when the definition of the method is longer than that of writeOutput.)

When the only postcondition is a description of the value returned, programmers usually omit the word Postcondition, as in the following example:

```
/**
 Precondition: All instance variables of the calling object have
 values.
 Returns a string describing the data in the calling object.
*/
public String toString()
```

Some programmers choose not to use the words *precondition* and *postcondition* in their method comments. However, whether you use the words or not, you should always think in terms of precondition and postcondition when designing a method and when deciding what to include in the method comment.

Self-Test Exercises

17. List all the accessor methods in the class DateFifthTry in Display 4.9.

18. List all the mutator methods in the class DateFifthTry in Display 4.9.

(continued)

Self-Test Exercises (continued)

19. Write a better version of the method dateOK with three int parameters (Display 4.9). This better version should check for the correct number of days in each month and should not just allow 31 days in any month. It will help to define another helping method named leapYear, which takes an int argument for a year and returns true if the year is a leap year. February has 29 days in leap years and only 28 days in other years. Use the following rule for determining if the year is a leap year: A year is a leap year if it is divisible by 4 but is not divisible by 100 or if it is divisible by 400.

4.3 Overloading

A good name is better than precious ointment.

Ecclesiastes 7:1

Two (or more) different classes can have methods with the same name. For example, many classes have a method named toString. It is easy to see why this is acceptable. The type of the calling object allows Java to decide which definition of the method toString to use. It uses the definition of toString given in the definition of the class for the calling object. You may be more surprised to learn that two or more methods *in the same class* can have **overloading** the same method name. This is called **overloading** and is the topic of this section.

Rules for Overloading

In Display 4.11, we have added two methods named setDate to our date class so that there is a total of three methods named setDate. This is an example of overloading the method name setDate. On the following three lines, we display the headings of these three methods:

```
public void setDate(int month, int day, int year)
public void setDate(String month, int day, int year)
public void setDate(int year)
```

Notice that each method has a different parameter list. The first two differ in the type of their first parameter. The last one differs from the other two by having a different number of parameters.

method signature   The name of a method and the list of parameter types in the heading of the method definition is called the **method signature**. The signatures for these three method definitions are

```
setDate(int, int, int)
setDate(String, int, int)
setDate(int)
```

Display 4.11 Overloading Method Names (part 1 of 2)

```
1    import java.util.Scanner;

2    public class DateSixthTry
3    {
4        private String month;
5        private int day;
6        private int year; //a four digit number.

7        public void setDate(int monthInt, int day, int year)
8        {
9            if (dateOK(monthInt, day, year))
10           {
11               this.month = monthString(monthInt);
12               this.day = day;
13               this.year = year;
14           }
15           else
16           {
17               System.out.println("Fatal Error");
18               System.exit(0);
19           }
20       }

21       public void setDate(String monthString, int day, int year)
22       {
23           if (dateOK(monthString, day, year))
24           {
25               this.month = monthString;
26               this.day = day;
27               this.year = year;
28           }
29           else
30           {
31               System.out.println("Fatal Error");
32               System.exit(0);
33           }
34       }

35       public void setDate(int year)
36       {
37           setDate(1, 1, year);
38       }
```

There are three different methods named setDate.

Two different methods named setDate.

(continued)

Display 4.11 Overloading Method Names (part 2 of 2)

```
39      private boolean dateOK(int monthInt, int dayInt, int yearInt)
40      {
41          return ( (monthInt >= 1) && (monthInt <= 12) &&
42                   (dayInt >= 1) && (dayInt <= 31) &&
43                   (yearInt >= 1000) && (yearInt <= 9999) );
44      }

45      private boolean dateOK(String monthString, int dayInt, int yearInt)
46      {
47          return ( monthOK(monthString) &&
48                   (dayInt >= 1) && (dayInt <= 31) &&
49                   (yearInt >= 1000) && (yearInt <= 9999) );
50      }

51      private boolean monthOK(String month)
52      {
53          return (month.equals("January") || month.equals("February") ||
54                  month.equals("March") || month.equals("April") ||
55                  month.equals("May") || month.equals("June") ||
56                  month.equals("July") || month.equals("August") ||
57                  month.equals("September") || month.equals("October") ||
58                  month.equals("November") || month.equals("December") );
59      }

60      public void readInput()
61      {
62          boolean tryAgain = true;
63          Scanner keyboard = new Scanner(System.in);
64          while (tryAgain)
65          {
66              System.out.println("Enter month, day, and year.");
67                System.out.println("Do not use a comma.");
68              String monthInput = keyboard.next();
69              int dayInput = keyboard.nextInt();
70              int yearInput = keyboard.nextInt();
71              if (dateOK(monthInput, dayInput, yearInput) )
72              {
73                  setDate(monthInput, dayInput, yearInput);
74                  tryAgain = false;
75              }
76              else
77                  System.out.println("Illegal date. Reenter input.");
78          }
79      }
```

Two different methods named dateOK.

*<The rest of the methods are the same as in Display 4.9, except that the parameter to **equals** and **precedes** is, of course, of type **DateSixthTry**.>*

```
80  }
```

When you overload a method name, each of the method definitions in the class must have a different signature.

Signature

The **signature** of a method consists of the method name and the list of types for parameters that are listed in the heading of the method name.

EXAMPLE

If a method has the heading

```
public int computeSomething(int n1, double x1,
                                      double x2, String name);
```

then the signature is

```
computeSomething(int, double, double, String)
```

Note that the return type is not part of the method signature.

In Display 4.11, we also overloaded the method name dateOK so that there are two different methods named dateOK. The two signatures for the two methods named dateOK are

```
dateOK(int, int, int)
dateOK(String, int, int)
```

Display 4.12 gives a simple example of a program using the overloaded method name setDate. Note that for each invocation of a method named setDate, only one of the definitions of setDate has a signature that matches the types of the arguments.

Overloading

Within one class, you can have two (or more) definitions of a single method name. This is called **overloading** the method name. When you overload a method name, any two definitions of the method name must have different signatures; that is, any two definitions of the method name either must have different numbers of parameters or some parameter position must be of differing types in the two definitions.

PITFALL: Overloading and Automatic Type Conversion

Automatic type conversion of arguments (such as converting an int to a double when the parameter is of type double) and overloading can sometimes interact in unfortunate ways. So, you need to know how these two things interact.

For example, consider the following method that might be added to the class DateSixthTry in Display 4.11:

```
public void increase(double factor)
{
    year = (int)(year + factor*year);
}
```

If you add this method to the class DateSixthTry, then the following presents no problems, where date is an object of type DateSixthTry that has been set to some date:

```
date.increase(2);
```

The int value of 2 is type cast to the double value 2.0, and the value of date.year is changed as follows:

```
date.year = (int)(date.year + 2.0*date.year);
```

(Because year is private in the class DateSixthTry, you cannot write this in a program that uses the class DateSixthTry, but the meaning of this expression is clear.)

So far, so good. But now suppose we also add the following method definition to the class DateSixthTry:

```
public void increase(int term)
{
    year = year + term;
}
```

This is a valid overloading because the two methods named increase take parameters of different types. With both of these methods named increase added to the class, the following now behaves differently:

```
date.increase(2);
```

If Java can find an exact match of types, it uses the method definition with an exact match before it tries to do any automatic type casts. So now the displayed invocation of date.increase is equivalent to

```
date.year = date.year + 2;
```

However, if you meant to use an argument of 2.0 for date.increase and instead used 2, counting on an automatic type cast, then this is not what you want. It is best to avoid overloading where there is a potential for interacting dangerously with automatic type casting, as in the examples discussed in this Pitfall section.

PITFALL: (continued)

In some cases of overloading, a single method invocation can be resolved in two different ways, depending on how overloading and type conversion interact. Such ambiguous method invocations are not allowed in Java and will produce an error message. For example, you can overload a method named doSomething by giving two definitions that have the following two method headings in a SampleClass:

```
public class SampleClass
{
    public void doSomething(double n1, int n2)
        .
        .
        .
    public void doSomething(int n1, double n2)
        .
        .
        .
```

Such overloading is legal, but there is a problem. Suppose aSampleObject is an object of type SampleClass. An invocation such as the following will produce an error message, because Java cannot decide which overloaded definition of doSomething to use:

```
aSampleObject.doSomething(5, 10);
```

Java cannot decide whether it should convert the int value 5 to a double value and use the first definition of doSomething, or convert the int value 10 to a double value and use the second definition. In this situation, the Java compiler issues an error message indicating that the method invocation is ambiguous.

The following two method invocations are allowed:

```
aSampleObject.doSomething(5.0, 10);
aSampleObject.doSomething(5, 10.0);
```

However, such situations, while legal, are confusing and should be avoided. ■

Display 4.12 **Using an Overloaded Method Name** (part 1 of 2)

```
1   public class OverloadingDemo
2   {

3       public static void main(String[] args)
4       {
5           DateSixthTry date1 = new DateSixthTry(),
6                       date2 = new DateSixthTry(),
7                       date3 = new DateSixthTry();
```

(continued)

Display 4.12   Using an Overloaded Method Name (part 2 of 2)

```
 8          date1.setDate(1, 2, 2008);
 9          date2.setDate("February", 2, 2008);
10          date3.setDate(2008);

11          System.out.println(date1);
12          System.out.println(date2);
13          System.out.println(date3);
14      }
15   }
```

Sample Dialogue

```
January 2, 2008
February 2, 2008
January 1, 2008
```

Overloading and Automatic Type Conversion

Java always looks for a method signature that exactly matches the method invocation before it tries to use automatic type conversion. If Java can find a definition of a method that exactly matches the types of the arguments, it uses that definition. Only after it fails to find an exact match does Java try automatic type conversions to find a method definition that matches the (type cast) types of the method invocation.

 ## PITFALL: You Cannot Overload Based on the Type Returned

Note that the signature of a method lists only the method name and the types of the parameters and does not include the type returned. When you overload a method name, any two methods must have different signatures. The type returned has nothing to do with the signature of a method. For example, a class could not have two method definitions with the following headings:

```
public class SampleClass2
{
public int computeSomething(int n)
        .
        .
        .
    public double computeSomething(int n)
        .
        .
        .
```

> ### PITFALL: You Cannot Overload Based on the Type Returned
>
> If you think about it, there is no way that Java could allow this sort of overloading. Suppose anObject is an object of the class SampleClass2. Then in the following assignment, Java could not decide which of the above two method definitions to use:
>
> ```
> double answer = anObject.computeSomething(10);
> ```
>
> Either a value of type int or a value of type double can legally be assigned to the variable answer. So, either method definition could be used. Because of such problems, Java says it is illegal to have both of these method headings in the same class. ■

You Cannot Overload Operators in Java

Many programming languages, such as C++, allow you to overload operators, such as +, so that the operator can be used with objects of some class you define, as well as being used for such things as numbers. You cannot do this in Java. If you want to have an "addition" in your class, you must use a method name, such as **add**, and ordinary method syntax; you cannot define operators, such as the + operator, to work with objects of a class you define.

Self-Test Exercises

20. What is the signature of each of the following method headings?

    ```
    public void doSomething(int p1, char p2, int p3)
    public void setMonth(int newMonth)
    public void setMonth(String newMonth)
    public int amount(int balance, double duration)
    public double amount(int balance, double duration)
    ```

21. Consider the class DateSixthTry in Display 4.11. Would it be legal to add two method definitions with the following two method headings to the class DateSixthTry?

    ```
    public void setMonth(int newMonth)
    public void setMonth(String newMonth)
    ```

22. Consider the class DateSixthTry in Display 4.11. Would it be legal to add two method definitions with the following two method headings to the class DateSixthTry?

    ```
    public void setMonth(int newMonth)
    private void setMonth(int newMonth)
    ```

23. Consider the class DateSixthTry in Display 4.11. Would it be legal to add two method definitions with the following two method headings to the class DateSixthTry?

```
public int getMonth()
public String getMonth()
```

4.4 Constructors

Well begun is half done.

Proverb

You often want to initialize the instance variables for an object when you create the object. As you will see later in this book, there are other initializing actions you might also want to take, but initializing instance variables is the most common sort of initialization. A *constructor* is a special variety of method that is designed to perform such initialization. In this section, we tell you how to define and use constructors.

Constructor Definitions

Although you may not have realized it, you have already been using constructors every time you used the new operator to create an object, as in the following example:

```
DateSixthTry date1 = new DateSixthTry();
```

constructor

The expression new DateSixthTry() is an invocation of a constructor. A **constructor** is a special variety of method that, among other things, must have the same name as the class. So, the first occurrence of DateSixthTry in the previous code is a class name, and the second occurrence of DateSixthTry is the name of a constructor. If you add no constructor definitions to your class, then Java automatically creates a constructor that takes no arguments. We have been using this automatically provided constructor up until now. The automatically provided constructor creates the object but does little else. It is preferable to define your own constructors so that you can have the constructor initialize instance variables, or do whatever other initialization actions you want.

In Display 4.13, we have rewritten our date class one last time by adding five constructors. Since this is our final date class, we have included all method definitions in the display so you can see the entire class definition. (We have omitted writeOutput because it would be superfluous, as noted in the earlier subsection entitled "The Methods equals and toString.")

Display 4.13   **A Class with Constructors** (part 1 of 5)

```
1    import java.util.Scanner;
```
This is our final definition of a class whose objects are dates.

```
2    public class Date
3    {
4        private String month;
5        private int day;
6        private int year; //a four digit number.

7        public Date()
8        {
9            month = "January";
10           day = 1;
11           year = 1000;
12       }
```
No-argument constructor

```
13       public Date(int monthInt, int day, int year)
14       {
15           setDate(monthInt, day, year);
16       }
```
You can invoke another method inside a constructor definition.

```
17       public Date(String monthString, int day, int year)
18       {
19           setDate(monthString, day, year);
20       }

21       public Date(int year)
22       {
23           setDate(1, 1, year);
24       }
```
A constructor usually initializes all instance variables, even if there is not a corresponding parameter.

```
25       public Date(Date aDate)
26       {
27           if (aDate == null)//Not a real date.
28           {
29               System.out.println("Fatal Error.");
30               System.exit(0);
31           }

32           month = aDate.month;
33           day = aDate.day;
34           year = aDate.year;
35       }
```
We will have more to say about this constructor in Chapter 5. Although you have had enough material to use this constructor, you need not worry about it until Section 5.3 of Chapter 5.

(continued)

Display 4.13   A Class with Constructors (part 2 of 5)

```
36      public void setDate(int monthInt, int day, int year)
37      {
38          if (dateOK(monthInt, day, year))
39          {
40              this.month = monthString(monthInt);
41              this.day = day;
42              this.year = year;
43          }
44          else
45          {
46              System.out.println("Fatal Error");
47              System.exit(0);
48          }
49      }

50      public void setDate(String monthString, int day, int year)
51      {
52          if (dateOK(monthString, day, year))
53          {
54              this.month = monthString;
55              this.day = day;
56              this.year = year;
57          }
58          else
59          {
60              System.out.println("Fatal Error");
61              System.exit(0);
62          }
63      }

64      public void setDate(int year)
65      {
66          setDate(1, 1, year);
67      }

68      public void setYear(int year)
69      {
70          if ( (year < 1000) || (year > 9999) )
71          {
72              System.out.println("Fatal Error");
73              System.exit(0);
74          }
75          else
76              this.year = year;
77      }
```

The mutator methods, whose names begin with set, are used to reset the data in an object after the object has been created using new and a constructor.

Display 4.13   **A Class with Constructors** (part 3 of 5)

```
78      public void setMonth(int monthNumber)
79      {
80          if ((monthNumber <= 0) || (monthNumber > 12))
81          {
82              System.out.println("Fatal Error");
83              System.exit(0);
84          }
85          else
86              month = monthString(monthNumber);
87      }

88      public void setDay(int day)
89      {
90          if ((day <= 0) || (day > 31))
91          {
92              System.out.println("Fatal Error");
93              System.exit(0);
94          }
95          else
96              this.day = day;
97      }

98      public int getMonth()
99      {
100        if (month.equals("January"))
101            return 1;
102        else if (month.equals("February"))
103            return 2;
104        else if (month.equals("March"))
105            return 3;
                . . .
```

<The omitted cases are obvious, but if need be, you can see all the cases in Display 4.2.>

```
                . . .
106        else if (month.equals("November"))
107            return 11;
108        else if (month.equals("December"))
109            return 12;
110        else
111        {
112            System.out.println("Fatal Error");
113            System.exit(0);
114            return 0; //Needed to keep the compiler happy
115        }
116     }
```

(continued)

Display 4.13 A Class with Constructors (part 4 of 5)

```
117     public int getDay()
118     {
119         return day;
120     }
```

We have omitted the method writeOutput because it would be superfluous, as noted in the subsection entitled "The Methods equals and toString."

```
121     public int getYear()
122     {
123         return year;
124     }

125     public String toString()
126     {
127         return (month + " " + day + ", " + year);
128     }
```

The method equals of the class String

```
129     public boolean equals(Date otherDate)
130     {
131         return ( (month.equals(otherDate.month))
132                 && (day == otherDate.day) && (year == otherDate.year) );
133     }

134     public boolean precedes(Date otherDate)
135     {
136         return ( (year < otherDate.year) ||
137             (year == otherDate.year && getMonth() < otherDate.getMonth()) ||
138             (year == otherDate.year && month.equals(otherDate.month)
139                                 && day < otherDate.day) );
140     }

141     public void readInput()
142     {
143         boolean tryAgain = true;
144         Scanner keyboard = new Scanner(System.in);
145         while (tryAgain)
146         {
147             System.out.println("Enter month, day, and year.");
148             System.out.println("Do not use a comma.");
149             String monthInput = keyboard.next();
150             int dayInput = keyboard.nextInt();
151             int yearInput = keyboard.nextInt();
152             if (dateOK(monthInput, dayInput, yearInput) )
153             {
154                 setDate(monthInput, dayInput, yearInput);
155                 tryAgain = false;
156             }
```

Display 4.13   **A Class with Constructors** (part 5 of 5)

```
157              else
158                  System.out.println("Illegal date. Reenter input.");
159          }
160      }

161      private boolean dateOK(int monthInt, int dayInt, int yearInt)
162      {
163          return ( (monthInt >= 1) && (monthInt <= 12) &&
164                   (dayInt >= 1) && (dayInt <= 31) &&
165                   (yearInt >= 1000) && (yearInt <= 9999) );
166      }

167      private boolean dateOK(String monthString, int dayInt, int yearInt)
168      {
169          return ( monthOK(monthString) &&
170                   (dayInt >= 1) && (dayInt <= 31) &&
171                   (yearInt >= 1000) && (yearInt <= 9999) );
172      }

173      private boolean monthOK(String month)
174      {
175          return (month.equals("January") || month.equals("February") ||
176                  month.equals("March") || month.equals("April") ||
177                  month.equals("May") || month.equals("June") ||
178                  month.equals("July") || month.equals("August") ||
179                  month.equals("September") || month.equals("October") ||
180                  month.equals("November") || month.equals("December") );
181      }

182      private String monthString(int monthNumber)
183      {
184          switch (monthNumber)
185          {
186          case 1:
187              return "January";
```

The private methods need not be last, but that's as good a place as any.

            . . .

<The omitted cases are obvious, but if need be, you can see all the cases in Display 4.9.>

            . . .

```
188          default:
189              System.out.println("Fatal Error");
190              System.exit(0);
191              return "Error"; //to keep the compiler happy
192          }
193      }
194 }
```

In Display 4.13, we have used overloading to create five constructors for the class Date. It is normal to have more than one constructor. Since every constructor must have the same name as the class, all the constructors in a class must have the same name. So, when you define multiple constructors, you must use overloading.

Note that when you define a constructor, you do not give any return type for the constructor; you do not even use void in place of a return type. Also notice that constructors are normally public.

All the constructor definitions in Display 4.13 initialize all the instance variables, even if there is no parameter corresponding to that instance variable. This is normal.

In a constructor definition, you can do pretty much anything that you can do in any ordinary method definition, but normally you only perform initialization tasks such as initialization of instance variables.

constructor arguments

When you create a new object with the operator new, you must always include the name of a constructor after the operator new. This is the way you invoke a constructor. As with any method invocation, you list any arguments in parentheses after the constructor name (which is the same as the class name). For example, suppose you want to use new to create a new object of the class Date defined in Display 4.13. You might do so as follows:

```
Date birthday = new Date("December", 16, 1770);
```

This is a call to the constructor for the class Date that takes three arguments: one of type String and two of type int. This creates a new object to represent the date December 16, 1770, and sets the variable birthday so that it names this new object. Another example is the following:

```
Date newYearsDay = new Date(3000);
```

This creates a new object to represent the date January 1, 3000, and sets the variable newYearsDay so that it names this new object.

Constructor

A **constructor** is a variety of method that is called when an object of the class is created using **new**. Constructors are used to initialize objects. A constructor must have the same name as the class to which it belongs. Arguments for a constructor are given in parentheses after the class name, as in the following examples.

EXAMPLES
```
Date birthday = new Date("December", 16, 1770),
    theDate = new Date(2008);
```

A constructor is defined very much like any ordinary method except that it does not have a type returned and does not even include a **void** in the constructor heading. See Display 4.13 for examples of constructor definitions.

A constructor is called when you create a new object, such as with the operator new. An attempt to call a constructor in any other way, such as the following, is illegal:

```
birthday.Date("January", 27, 1756); //Illegal!
```

Because you cannot call a constructor for an object after it is created, you need some other way to change the values of the instance variables of an object. That is the purpose of the setDate methods and other methods that begin with set in Display 4.13. If birthday already names an object that was created with new, you can change the values of the instance variables as follows:

```
birthday.setDate("January", 27, 1756);
```

Although it is not required, such methods that reset instance variables normally are given names that start with set.

Although you cannot use a constructor to reset the instance variables of an already created object, you can do something that looks very similar. The following is legal:

```
Date birthday = new Date("December", 16, 1770);
                        .
                        .
                        .
      birthday = new Date("January", 27, 1756);
```

However, the second invocation of the constructor does not simply change the values of instance variables for the object. Instead, it discards the old object and allocates storage for a new object before setting the instance variables. So, for efficiency (and occasionally for other reasons we have not yet discussed), it is preferable to use a method such as setDate to change the data in the instance variables of an already created object.

Display 4.14 contains a demonstration program for the constructors defined in Display 4.13.

Display 4.14 Use of Constructors

```
1   public class ConstructorsDemo
2   {
3       public static void main(String[] args)
4       {
5           Date date1 = new Date("December", 16, 1770),
6                date2 = new Date(1, 27, 1756),
7                date3 = new Date(1882),
8                date4 = new Date();

9           System.out.println("Whose birthday is " + date1 + "?");
10          System.out.println("Whose birthday is " + date2 + "?");
11          System.out.println("Whose birthday is " + date3 + "?");
12          System.out.println("The default date is " + date4 + ".");
13      }
14  }
```

(continued)

Display 4.15 Use of Constructors

Sample Dialogue

```
Whose birthday is December 16, 1770?
Whose birthday is January 27, 1756?
Whose birthday is January 1, 1882?
The default date is January 1, 1000.
```

Is a Constructor Really a Method?

There are differing opinions on whether or not a constructor should be called a *method*. Most authorities call a constructor a method but emphasize that it is a special kind of method with many properties not shared with other kinds of methods. Some authorities say a constructor is a method-like entity but not, strictly speaking, a method. All authorities agree about what a constructor is; the only disagreement is over whether or not it should be referred to as *a method*. Thus, this is not a major issue. However, whenever you hear a phrase like "all methods," you should make sure you know whether it does or does not include constructors. To avoid confusion, we try to use the phrase "constructors and methods" when we want to include constructors.

TIP: You Can Invoke Another Method in a Constructor

It is perfectly legal to invoke another method within the definition of a constructor. For example, several of the constructors in Display 4.13 invoke a mutator method to set the values of the instance variables. This is legal because the first action taken by a constructor is to automatically create an object with instance variables. You do not write any code to create this object. Java creates it automatically when the constructor is invoked. Any method invocation in the body of the constructor definition has this object as its calling object.

You can even include an invocation of one constructor within the definition of another constructor. However, we will not discuss the syntax for doing that in this chapter. It will be covered in Chapter 7. ∎

TIP: A Constructor Has a this Parameter

Just like the ordinary methods we discussed before we introduced constructors, every constructor has a this parameter. The this parameter can be used explicitly, but it is more often understood to be present although not written down. Whenever an instance variable of the class is used in a constructor (without an object name and a dot before it), it is understood to have an implicit this and dot before it. Similarly, when-

TIP: (continued)

ever a method is used in a constructor and the method has no explicit calling object, the method is understood to have this and a dot before it; that is, it is understood to have this as its calling object.

As noted in the previous Programming Tip, the first action taken by a constructor is to automatically create an object with instance variables. This object is automatically plugged in for the this parameter. So, within the definition of a constructor, the this parameter refers to the object created by the constructor. ■

TIP: Include a No-Argument Constructor

no-argument
constructor

A constructor that takes no arguments is called a **no-argument constructor** or **no-arg constructor**. If you define a class and include absolutely no constructors of any kind, then a no-argument constructor is automatically created. This no-argument constructor does not do much, but it does give you an object of the class type. So, if the definition of the class MyClass contains absolutely no constructor definitions, then the following is legal:

```
MyClass myObject = new MyClass();
```

If your class definition includes one or more constructors of any kind, then no constructor is generated automatically. So, for example, suppose you define a class called YourClass. If you include one or more constructors that each take one or more arguments, but you do not include a no-argument constructor in your class definition, then there is not a no-argument constructor and the following is illegal:

```
YourClass yourObject = new YourClass();
```

The problem with the above declaration is that it asks the compiler to invoke the no-argument constructor, but there is no no-argument constructor in this case.

To avoid problems, you should normally include a no-argument constructor in any class you define. If you do not want the no-argument constructor to initialize any instance variables, you can simply give it an empty body when you implement it. The following constructor definition is perfectly legal. It does nothing but create an object (and, as we will see later in this chapter, set the instance variables equal to default values):

```
public MyClass()
{/*Do nothing.*/}
```

default constructor

A no-argument constructor is also known as a **default constructor**. However, the term *default constructor* is misleading since, as we have explained, a no-argument constructor is not always provided by default. There is now a movement to replace the term *default constructor* with the term *no-argument constructor,* but you will frequently encounter the term *default constructor.* ■

No-Argument Constructor

A constructor with no parameters is called a **no-argument constructor**. If your class definition contains absolutely no constructor definitions, then Java automatically creates a no-argument constructor. If your class definition contains one or more constructor definitions, then Java does not automatically generate any constructor; in this case, what you define is what you get. Most of the classes you define should include a definition of a no-argument constructor.

EXAMPLE: The Final Date Class

The final version of our class for a date is given in Display 4.13. We will be using this class `Date` again in Chapter 5.

Self-Test Exercises

24. If a class is named `CoolClass`, what names are allowed as names for constructors in the class `CoolClass`?

25. Suppose you have defined a class like the following for use in a program:

```java
public class YourClass
{
    private int information;
    private char moreInformation;

    public YourClass(int newInfo, char moreNewInfo)
    {
        <Details not shown.>
    }
    public YourClass()
    {
```

```
                <Details not shown.>
        }
        public void doStuff()
        {
                <Details not shown.>
        }
}
```

Which of the following are legal in a program that uses this class?

```
YourClass anObject = new YourClass(42, 'A');
YourClass anotherObject = new YourClass(41.99, 'A');
YourClass yetAnotherObject = new YourClass();
yetAnotherObject.doStuff();
YourClass oneMoreObject;
oneMoreObject.doStuff();
oneMoreObject.YourClass(99, 'B');
```

26. What is a no-argument constructor? Does every class have a no-argument constructor? What is a default constructor?

Default Variable Initializations

Local variables are not automatically initialized in Java, so you must explicitly initialize a local variable before using it. Instance variables, on the other hand, are automatically initialized. Instance variables of type `boolean` are automatically initialized to `false`. Instance variables of other primitive types are automatically initialized to the zero of their type. Instance variables of a class type are automatically initialized to `null`, which is a kind of placeholder for an object that will be filled in later. We will discuss `null` in Chapter 5. Although instance variables are automatically initialized, we prefer to always explicitly initialize them in a constructor, even if the initializing value is the same as the default initialization. That makes the code clearer.

An Alternative Way to Initialize Instance Variables

Instance variables are normally initialized in constructors, and that is where we prefer to initialize them. However, there is an alternative. You can initialize instance variables when you declare them in a class definition, as illustrated by the following:

```
public class Date
{
    private String month = "January";
    private int day = 1;
    private int year = 1000;
```

If you initialize instance variables in this way, you may or may not want to define constructors. But if you do define any constructors, it is usually best to define a no-argument constructor even if the body of the no-argument constructor is empty.

EXAMPLE: A Pet Record Class

Display 4.15 contains another example of a class definition. In this case, the objects of the class represent pet records consisting of the pet's name, age, and weight. Notice the similarities and differences between the constructors and the mutator methods (the ones whose names begin with set). They both set instance variables, but they are used differently. The constructors are used to create and initialize new objects of the class. However, after the object is created using a constructor and new, any changes to the object are performed by the mutator methods such as set or setAge. This is illustrated by the program in Display 4.16.

It would be possible to use constructors in place of the mutators, such as the method set. For example, the program in Display 4.16 would produce the same dialogue if you replace the line

```
usersPet.set(name, age, weight);
```

with

```
usersPet = new Pet(name, age, weight);
```

However, this use of constructors is a bad idea.

The following mutator method invocation simply changes the values of the instance variables of the object named by usersPet:

```
usersPet.set(name, age, weight);
```

However, the following use of a constructor creates a completely new object, which is a much less efficient process than just changing the values of some instance variables:

```
usersPet = new Pet(name, age, weight);
```

Display 4.16 A Class for Pet Records (part 1 of 4)

```
1   /**
2    Class for basic pet records: name, age, and weight.
3   */
4   public class Pet
5   {
6       private String name;
7       private int age;//in years
8       private double weight;//in pounds
9
```

Display 4.16 **A Class for Pet Records** (part 1 of 4)

```
10      public String toString()
11      {
12          return ("Name: " + name + " Age: " + age + " years"
13                          + "\nWeight: " + weight + " pounds");
14      }
15
16      public Pet(String initialName, int initialAge,
17                                      double initialWeight)
18      {
19          name = initialName;
20          if ((initialAge < 0) || (initialWeight < 0))
21          {
22              System.out.println("Error: Negative age or weight.");
23              System.exit(0);
24          }
25          else
26          {
27              age = initialAge;
28              weight = initialWeight;
29          }
30      }
31
32      public void set(String newName, int newAge, double newWeight)
33      {
34          name = newName;
35          if ((newAge < 0) || (newWeight < 0))
36          {
37              System.out.println("Error: Negative age or weight.");
38              System.exit(0);
39          }
40          else
41          {
42              age = newAge;
43              weight = newWeight;
44          }
45      }
46      public Pet(String initialName)
47      {
48          name = initialName;
49          age = 0;
50          weight = 0;
51      }
52
53      public void setName(String newName)
54      {
55          name = newName;
56      }
57
```

Constructors are only called when you create an object, such as with new. To change an already existing object, you use one or more methods like these set methods.

Constructors normally set all instance variables, even if there is not a full set of parameters.

Age and weight are unchanged.

(continued)

Display 4.15 **A Class for Pet Records** (part 2 of 4)

```
58      public Pet(int initialAge)
59      {
60          name = "No name yet.";
61          weight = 0;
62          if (initialAge < 0)
63          {
64              System.out.println("Error: Negative age.");
65              System.exit(0);
66          }
67          else
68              age = initialAge;
69      }
70
71      public void setAge(int newAge)
72      {
73          if (newAge < 0)
74          {
75              System.out.println("Error: Negative age.");
76              System.exit(0);
77          }
78          else                    Name and weight are unchanged.
79              age = newAge;
80      }
81
82
83
84
85
86      public Pet(double initialWeight)
87      {
88          name = "No name yet";
89          age = 0;
90          if (initialWeight < 0)
91          {
92              System.out.println("Error: Negative weight.");
93              System.exit(0);
94          }
95          else
96              weight = initialWeight;
97      }
98
98      public void setWeight(double newWeight)
99      {
```

Display 4.15   A Class for Pet Records (part 3 of 4)

```
100            if (newWeight < 0)
101            {
102                System.out.println("Error: Negative weight.");
103                System.exit(0);
104            }
105            else
106                weight = newWeight;
107        }
108        public Pet()
109        {
110            name = "No name yet.";
111            age = 0;
112            weight = 0;
113        }

114        public String getName()
115        {
116            return name;
117        }

118        public int getAge()
119        {
120            return age;
121        }

122        public double getWeight()
123        {
124            return weight;
125        }
126 }
```

Name and age are unchanged.

Display 4.16   Using Constructors and Set Methods (part 1 of 2)

```
1    import java.util.Scanner;

2    public class PetDemo
3    {
4        public static void main(String[] args)
5        {
```

(continued)

Display 4.17   Using Constructors and Set Methods (part 2 of 2)

```
6          Pet usersPet = new Pet("Jane Doe");
7          System.out.println("My records on your pet are incomplete.");
8          System.out.println("Here is what they currently say:");
9          System.out.println(usersPet);

10         Scanner keyboard = new Scanner(System.in);
11         System.out.println("Please enter the pet's name:");
12         String name = keyboard.nextLine();
13         System.out.println("Please enter the pet's age:");
14         int age = keyboard.nextInt();
15         System.out.println("Please enter the pet's weight:");
16         double weight = keyboard.nextDouble();
17         usersPet.set(name, age, weight);
18         System.out.println("My records now say:");
19         System.out.println(usersPet);
20     }
21 }
```

This is equivalent to
`System.out.println(usersPet.toString());`

Sample Dialogue

```
My records on your pet are incomplete.
Here is what they currently say:
Name: Jane Doe Age: 0 years
Weight: 0.0 pounds
Please enter the pet's name:
Fang Junior
Please enter the pet's age:
5
Please enter the pet's weight:
87.5
My records now say:
Name: Fang Junior Age: 5 years
Weight: 87.5 pounds
```

The StringTokenizer Class ★

The StringTokenizer class is used to recover the words in a multiword string. It is often used when reading input. However, when we covered input in Chapter 2, we could not cover the StringTokenizer class because use of the StringTokenizer class normally involves knowledge of loops and constructors, two topics that we had not yet covered. We now have covered enough material to explain the StringTokenizer class.

One approach to reading keyboard input is to read an entire line of input into a variable of type String—for example, with the method nextLine of the Scanner class—and then to use the StringTokenizer class to decompose the string in the variable into words.

The class StringTokenizer is in the standard Java package (library) java.util. To tell Java where to find the class StringTokenizer, any class or program that uses the class StringTokenizer must contain the following (or something similar) at the start of the file:

import

```
import java.util.StringTokenizer;
```

Perhaps the most common use of the StringTokenizer class is to decompose a line of input. However, the StringTokenizer class can be used to decompose any string. The following example illustrates a typical way that the class StringTokenizer is used:

```
StringTokenizer wordFactory =
            new StringTokenizer("A single word can be critical.");
while(wordFactory.hasMoreTokens())
{
    System.out.println(wordFactory.nextToken());
}
```

This will produce the following output:

```
A
single
word
can
be
critical.
```

The constructor invocation

```
new StringTokenizer("A single word can be critical.")
```

produces a new object of the class StringTokenizer. The assignment statement

```
StringTokenizer wordFactory =
            new StringTokenizer("A single word can be critical.");
```

gives this StringTokenizer object the name wordFactory. You may use any string in place of "A single word can be critical." and any variable name in place of word-Factory. The StringTokenizer object created in this way can be used to produce the individual words in the string used as the argument to the StringTokenizer construc-

tokens

tor. These individual words are called **tokens**.

nextToken   The method nextToken returns the first token (word) when it is invoked for the first time, returns the second token when it is invoked the second time, and so forth. If your code invokes nextToken after it has returned all the tokens in its string, then your program will halt and issue an error message.

hasMore–
Tokens   The method hasMoreTokens is a method that returns a value of type boolean; that is, it returns either true or false. Thus an invocation of hasMoreTokens, such as the following:

```
wordFactory.hasMoreTokens()
```

is a Boolean expression, and so it can be used to control a while loop. The method hasMoreTokens returns true as long as nextToken has not yet returned all the tokens in the string, and it returns false after the method nextToken has returned all the tokens in the string.

choosing
delimiters   When the constructor for StringTokenizer is used with a single argument, as in the preceding example, the tokens are substrings of non-whitespace characters, and the whitespace characters are used as the separators for the tokens. Any string of one or more whitespace characters is considered a separator. Thus, in the preceding example, the last token produced by the method nextToken is "critical." including the period. This is because the period is not a whitespace character and so is not a separator.

You can specify your own set of separator characters. When you create your own set of separator characters, you give a second argument to the constructor for StringTokenizer. The second argument is a string consisting of all the separator characters. Thus, if you want your separators to consist of the blank, the new-line character, the period, and the comma, you could proceed as in the following example:

```
StringTokenizer wordfactory2 =
        new StringTokenizer("Give me the word, my friend.", " \n.,");
while(wordfactory2.hasMoreTokens())
{
    System.out.println(wordfactory2.nextToken());
}
```

This will produce the output

```
Give
me
the
word
my
friend
```

Notice that the period and comma are not part of the tokens produced, because they are now token separators. Also note that the string of token separators is the second argument to the constructor.

Some of the methods for the class `StringTokenizer` are summarized in Display 4.17. A sample use of `StringTokenizer` is given in Display 4.18.

Display 4.18   Some Methods in the Class `StringTokenizer`

The class `StringTokenizer` is in the `java.util package`.

public `StringTokenizer(String theString)`

Constructor for a tokenizer that will use whitespace characters as separators when finding tokens in `theString`.

public `StringTokenizer(String theString, String delimiters)`

Constructor for a tokenizer that will use the characters in the string `delimiters` as separators when finding tokens in `theString`.

public boolean `hasMoreTokens()`

Tests whether there are more tokens available from this tokenizer's string. When used in conjunction with `nextToken`, it returns `true` as long as `nextToken` has not yet returned all the tokens in the string; returns `false` otherwise.

public `String nextToken()`

Returns the next token from this tokenizer's string. (Throws `NoSuchElementException` if there are no more tokens to return.)[5]

public `String nextToken(String delimiters)`

First changes the delimiter characters to those in the string `delimiters`. Then returns the next token from this tokenizer's string. After the invocation is completed, the delimiter characters are those in the string `delimiters`. (Throws `NoSuchElementException` if there are no more tokens to return. Throws `NullPointerException` if `delimiters` is `null`.)[5]

public int `countTokens()`

Returns the number of tokens remaining to be returned by `nextToken`.

---

[5] Exceptions are covered in Chapter 9. You can ignore any reference to `NoSuchElementException` until you reach Chapter 9. We include it here for reference value only.

Display 4.19 Use of the **StringTokenizer** Class

```
1   import java.util.Scanner;
2   import java.util.StringTokenizer;
```

```
1   public class StringTokenizerDemo
2   {
3       public static void main(String[] args)
4       {
5           Scanner keyboard = new Scanner(System.in);

6           System.out.println("Enter your last name");
7           System.out.println("followed by your first and middle names.");
8           System.out.println("If you have no middle name,");
9           System.out.println("enter \"None\".");
10          String inputLine = keyboard.nextLine();

11          String delimiters = ", "; //Comma and blank space
12          StringTokenizer nameFactory =
13                  new StringTokenizer(inputLine, delimiters);

14          String lastName = nameFactory.nextToken();
15          String firstName = nameFactory.nextToken();
16          String middleName = nameFactory.nextToken();
17          if (middleName.equalsIgnoreCase("None"))
18              middleName = ""; //Empty string
19          System.out.println("Hello " + firstName
20                              + " " + middleName + " " + lastName);
21      }
22  }
```

Sample Dialogue

```
Enter your last name
followed by your first and middle names.      Note that the comma is not
If you have no middle name,                   read because it is a
enter None.                                   delimiter.
Savitch, Walter None
Hello Walter Savitch
```

Self-Test Exercises

27. What would be the last line in the dialog in Display 4.18 if the user entered the following input line instead of the one shown in Display 4.18? (The comma is omitted.)

    ```
    Savitch Walter None
    ```

28. What would be the last line in the dialog in Display 4.18 if the user entered the following input line instead of the one shown in Display 4.18?

    ```
    Tom, Dick, and Harry
    ```

Chapter Summary

- Objects have both instance variables and methods. A class is a type whose values are objects. All objects in a class have the same methods and the same types of instance variables.

- There are two main kinds of methods: methods that return a value and void methods. (Some specialized methods, such as constructors, are neither void methods nor methods that return a value.)

- When defining a method, the this parameter is a name used for the calling object.

- Normally, your classes should have both an equals method and a toString method.

- If an instance variable or method is marked private, then it cannot be directly referenced anyplace except in the definition of a method of the same class.

- Outside of the class in which it is defined, a private instance variable can be accessed via accessor methods and changed via mutator methods.

- A variable declared in a method is said to be a *local variable*. The meaning of a local variable is confined to the method in which it is declared. The local variable goes away when a method invocation ends. The name of a local variable can be reused for something else outside of the method in which it is declared.

- A parameter is like a blank in a method definition that is filled in with an argument when the method is invoked. A parameter is actually a local variable that is initialized to the value of the corresponding argument. This is known as the *call-by-value* parameter-passing mechanism.

- If a variable is used as an argument to a method, then only the value of the variable, not the variable itself, is plugged in to the corresponding parameter.

- *Encapsulation* means that the data and the actions are combined into a single item (in our case, a class object) and that the *details of the implementation are hidden.* Making all instance variables private is part of the encapsulation process.

- A class can have two (or more) different definitions for the same method name, provided the two definitions have different numbers of parameters or some parameters of differing types. This is called *overloading* the method name.

- A constructor is a variety of method that is called when you create an object of the class using new. A constructor is intended to be used to perform initialization tasks such as initializing instance variables. A constructor must have the same name as the class to which it belongs.

- A constructor with no parameters is called a *no-argument constructor*. If your class definition includes no constructor definitions at all, then Java automatically provides a no-argument constructor. If your class definition contains any constructor definitions at all, then no additional constructors are provided by Java. Your class definitions should usually include a no-argument constructor.

Answers to Self-Test Exercises

1.
```java
public void makeItNewYears()
{
    month = "January";
    day = 1;
}
```

2.
```java
public void yellIfNewYear()
{
    if ( (month.equalsIgnorewCase("January")) && (day == 1) )
        System.out.println("Hurrah!");
    else
        System.out.println("Not New Year's Day.");
}
```

3.
```java
public int getNextYear()
{
    int nextYear = year + 1;
    return nextYear;
}
```

4.
```java
public void happyGreeting()
{
    int count;
    for (count = 1; count <= day; count++)
        System.out.println("Happy Days!");
}
```

5.  ```
    public double fractionDone(int targetDay)
    {
        double doubleDay = day;
        return doubleDay/targetDay;
    }
    ```

6.  ```
    public void advanceYear(int increase)
    {
        year = year + increase;
    }
    ```

7. The instances of newMonth that have their values changed to 6 are indicated in color below:

    ```
    public void setDate(int newMonth, int newDay, int newYear)
    {
        month = monthString(newMonth);
        day = newDay;
        year = newYear;
        System.out.println("Date changed to "
                        + newMonth + " " + newDay + ", " + newYear);
    }
    ```

    The point being emphasized here is that all instances of newMonth have their values changed to 6. Technically speaking, the parameter newMonth is a local variable. So, there is only one local variable named newMonth whose value is changed to 6, but the net effect, in this case, is the same as replacing all occurrences of newMonth with 6.

8. Yes, it is legal. The point being emphasized here is that the parameter count is a local variable and so can have its value changed, in this case by the decrement operator.

9. Each case has a return statement. A return statement always ends the method invocation, and hence ends the execution of the switch statement. So, a break statement would be redundant.

10. They are assumed to be instance variables of the calling object.

11. ```
    public int getDay()
    {
        return this.day;
    }
    ```

    ```
    public int getYear()
    {
        return this.year;
    }
    ```
    ```

12.
```java
public int getMonth()
{
    if (this.month.equals("January"))
        return 1;
    else if (this.month.equals("February"))
        return 2;
    else if (this.month.equals("March"))
        return 3;
    else if (this.month.equals("April"))
        return 4;
    else if (this.month.equals("May"))
        return 5;
    else if (this.month.equals("June"))
        return 6;
    else if (this.month.equals("July"))
        return 7;
    else if (this.month.equals("August"))
        return 8;
    else if (this.month.equals("September"))
        return 9;
    else if (this.month.equals("October"))
        return 10;
    else if (this.month.equals("November"))
        return 11;
    else if (this.month.equals("December"))
        return 12;
    else
    {
        System.out.println("Fatal Error");
        System.exit(0);
        return 0; //Needed to keep the compiler happy
    }
}
```

13. The instance variable `month` contains a string, so we used `month` with `equals`. It would have been just as good to use

```java
getMonth() == otherDate.getMonth()
```

We used `getMonth()` with the less-than sign because it is of type `int` and so works with the less-than sign. The instance variable `month` is of type `String` and does not work with the less-than sign.

14. Every method should be tested in a program in which every other method in the testing program has already been fully tested and debugged.

15. All instance variables should be marked `private`.

16. Normally, a method is private only if it is being used solely as a helping method in the definition of other methods.

17. getMonth, getDay, and getYear.

18. setDate, setMonth, setDay, and setYear.

19.
```java
private boolean dateOK(int monthInt, int dayInt, int yearInt)
{
    if ((yearInt < 1000) || (yearInt > 999))
        return false;

    switch (monthInt)
    {
    case 1:
        return (dayInt >= 1) && (dayInt <= 31);
    case 2:
        if (leapYear(yearInt))
            return (dayInt >= 1) && (dayInt <= 29);
        else
            return (dayInt >= 1) && (dayInt <= 28);
    case 3:
        return (dayInt >= 1) && (dayInt <= 31);
    case 4:
        return (dayInt >= 1) && (dayInt <= 30);
    case 5:
        return (dayInt >= 1) && (dayInt <= 31);
    case 6:
        return (dayInt >= 1) && (dayInt <= 30);
    case 7:
        return (dayInt >= 1) && (dayInt <= 31);
    case 8:
        return (dayInt >= 1) && (dayInt <= 31);
    case 9:
        return (dayInt >= 1) && (dayInt <= 30);
    case 10:
        return (dayInt >= 1) && (dayInt <= 31);
    case 11:
        return (dayInt >= 1) && (dayInt <= 30);
    case 12:
        return (dayInt >= 1) && (dayInt <= 31);
    default:
        return false;
    }
}
```

```
/**
   Returns true if yearInt is a leap year.
*/
private boolean leapYear(int yearInt)
{
    return ((yearInt % 4 == 0) && (yearInt % 100 != 0))
            || (yearInt % 400 == 0);
}
```

20. `doSomething(int, char, int)`
    `setMonth(int)`
    `setMonth(String)`
    `amount(int, double)`
    `amount(int, double)`

21. Yes, it is legal because they have different signatures. This is a valid example of overloading.

22. No, it would be illegal because they have the same signature.

23. No, it would be illegal. You cannot overload on the basis of the type of the returned value.

24. If a class is named `CoolClass`, then all constructors must be named `CoolClass`.

25. `YourClass anObject = new YourClass(42, 'A');//Legal`
    `YourClass anotherObject = new YourClass(41.99, 'A');//Not legal`
    `YourClass yetAnotherObject = new YourClass();//Legal`
    `yetAnotherObject.doStuff();//Legal`
    `YourClass oneMoreObject;//Legal`
    `oneMoreObject.doStuff();//Not legal`
    `oneMoreObject.YourClass(99, 'B');//Not legal`

26. A no-argument constructor is a constructor with no parameters. If you define a class and define some constructors but do not define a no-argument constructor, then the class will have no no-argument constructor. *Default constructor* is another name for a no-argument constructor.

27. The last line would be the same. Because the blank space is a delimiter, a blank space is enough to separate the tokens.

28. `Hello Dick and Tom`

    The other token in the input line is just not used.

Programming Projects

 Many of these Programming Projects can be solved using AW's MyCodeMate.
To access these please go to: www.mycodemate.com.

1. Write a program that outputs the lyrics for "Ninety-nine Bottles of Beer on the Wall." Your program should print the number of bottles in English, not as a number. For example:

   Ninety-nine bottles of beer on the wall,

   Ninety-nine bottles of beer,

   Take one down, pass it around,

   Ninety-eight bottles of beer on the wall.

   ...

   One bottle of beer on the wall,

   One bottle of beer,

   Take one down, pass it around,

   Zero bottles of beer on the wall.

   Your program should not use ninety-nine output statements!

   Design your program with a class named `BeerSong` whose constructor takes an integer parameter that is the number of bottles of beer initially on the wall. If the parameter is less than zero, set the number of bottles to zero. Similarly, if the parameter is greater than 99, set the number of beer bottles to 99. Then make a public method called `printSong` that outputs all stanzas from the number of bottles of beer down to zero. Add any additional private methods you find helpful.

2. Define a class called `Fraction`. This class is used to represent a ratio of two integers. Include mutator functions that allow the user to set the numerator and the denominator. Also include a member function that returns the value of numerator or denominator as a double. Include an additional member function that outputs the value of the fraction reduced to lowest terms (e.g., instead of outputting 20/60 the method should output 1/3). This will require finding the greatest common divisor for the numerator and denominator, then dividing both by that number. Embed your class in a test program.

3. Define a class called `Odometer` that will be used to track fuel and mileage for an automobile. The class should have member variables to track the miles driven and the fuel efficiency of the vehicle in miles per gallon. Include a mutator function to reset the odometer to zero miles, a mutator function to set the fuel efficiency, a mutator function that accepts miles driven for a trip and adds it to the odometer's total, and an accessor method that returns the number of gallons of gasoline that the vehicle has consumed since the odometer was last reset.

   Use your class with a test program that creates several trips with different fuel efficiencies. You should decide which variables should be public, if any.

4. Define a class called `BlogEntry` that could be used to store an entry for a Web log. The class should have member variables to store the poster's username, text of the entry, and the date of the entry using the `Date` class from Chapter 4. Add a constructor that allows the user of the class to set all member variables. Also add a method, `DisplayEntry`, that outputs all of the member variables, and another method called `getSummary` that returns the first 10 words from the text (or the entire text if it is less than 10 words). Test your class from your main method.

 5. Define a class called `Counter` whose objects count things. An object of this class records a count that is a nonnegative integer. Include methods to set the counter to 0, to increase the count by 1, and to decrease the count by 1. Be sure that no method allows the value of the counter to become negative. Include an accessor method that returns the current count value and a method that outputs the count to the screen. There should be no input method or other mutator methods. The only method that can set the counter is the one that sets it to zero. Also, include a `toString` method and an `equals` method. Write a program (or programs) to test all the methods in your class definition.

6. Write a grading program for a class with the following grading policies:

   a. There are three quizzes, each graded on the basis of 10 points.

   b. There is one midterm exam, graded on the basis of 100 points.

   c. There is one final exam, graded on the basis of 100 points.

   The final exam counts for 40 percent of the grade. The midterm counts for 35 percent of the grade. The three quizzes together count for a total of 25 percent of the grade. (Do not forget to convert the quiz scores to percentages before they are averaged in.)

   Any grade of 90 or more is an A, any grade of 80 or more (but less than 90) is a B, any grade of 70 or more (but less than 80) is a C, any grade of 60 or more (but less than 70) is a D, and any grade below 60 is an F. The program should read in the student's scores and output the student's record, which consists of three quiz scores and two exam scores as well as the student's overall numeric score for the entire course and final letter grade.

   Define and use a class for the student record. The class should have instance variables for the quizzes, midterm, final, overall numeric score for the course, and final letter grade. The overall numeric score is a number in the range 0 to 100, which represents the weighted average of the student's work. The class should have methods to compute the overall numeric grade and the final letter grade. These last methods should be `void` methods that set the appropriate instance variables. Your class should have a reasonable set of accessor and mutator methods, an `equals` method, and a `toString` method, whether or not your program uses them. You may add other methods if you wish.

 7. Write a `Temperature` class that has two instance variables: a temperature value (a floating-point number) and a character for the scale, either `C` for Celsius or `F` for Fahrenheit. The class should have four constructor methods: one for each

instance variable (assume zero degrees if no value is specified and Celsius if no scale is specified), one with two parameters for the two instance variables, and a no-argument constructor (set to zero degrees Celsius). Include the following: (1) two accessor methods to return the temperature—one to return the degrees Celsius, the other to return the degrees Fahrenheit—use the following formulas to write the two methods, and round to the nearest tenth of a degree:

$degreesC$ = 5($degreesF$ – 32)/9
$degreesF$ = (9($degreesC$)/5) + 32;

(2) three mutator methods: one to set the value, one to set the scale (F or C), and one to set both; (3) three comparison methods: an `equals` method to test whether two temperatures are equal, one method to test whether one temperature is greater than another, and one method to test whether one temperature is less than another (note that a Celsius temperature can be equal to a Fahrenheit temperature as indicated by the above formulas); and (4) a suitable `toString` method. Then write a driver program (or programs) that tests all the methods. Be sure to use each of the constructors, to include at least one true and one false case for each of the comparison methods, and to test at least the following temperature equalities: 0.0 degrees C = 32.0 degrees F, –40.0 degrees C = –40.0 degrees F, and 100.0 degrees C = 212.0 degrees F.

8. Redefine the class `Date` in Display 4.13 so that the instance variable for the month is of type `int` instead of type `String`. None of the method headings should change in any way. In particular, no `String` type parameters should change to `int` type parameters. You must redefine the methods to make things work out. Any program that uses the `Date` class from Display 4.13 should be able to use your `Date` class without any changes in the program. In particular, the program in Display 4.14 should work the same whether the `Date` class is defined as in Display 4.13 or is defined as you do it for this project. Write a test program (or programs) that tests each method in your class definition.

9. Define a class whose objects are records on animal species. The class should have instance variables for the species name, population, and growth rate. The growth rate is a percentage that can be positive or negative and can exceed 100 percent. Include a suitable collection of constructors, mutator methods, and accessor methods. Include a `toString` method and an `equals` method. Include a `boolean` valued method named `endangered` that returns `true` when the growth rate is negative and returns `false` otherwise. Write a test program (or programs) that tests each method in your class definition.

5

Defining Classes II

5 Defining Classes II

*After a certain high level of technical skill is achieved, science and art
tend to coalesce in esthetics, plasticity, and form. The greatest scientists
are always artists as well.*

ALBERT EINSTEIN, Quoted in Alice Calaprice, *The Quotable Einstein*

Introduction

This chapter is a continuation of Chapter 4. It covers the rest of the core material on
defining classes. We start by discussing *static methods* and *static variables*, which are
methods and variables that belong to the class as a whole and not to particular
objects. We then go on to discuss how class type variables name objects of their class
and how class type parameters are handled in Java.

This chapter also discusses *packages*, which are Java's way of grouping classes into
libraries. We end this chapter with a discussion of javadoc, a program that automatically extracts documentation from classes and packages.

Prerequisites

This chapter uses material from Chapters 1 through 4.

Sections 5.3 and 5.4 are independent of each other and may be covered in any
order. Section 5.3 covers some subtle points about references, and Section 5.4 covers
packages and javadoc. The material on javadoc is not used in the rest of this book.
The other material in Sections 5.3 and 5.4 is not heavily used in the next few chapters
and can be digested as needed if the material seems difficult on first reading.

The material on packages in Section 5.4 assumes that you know about directories
(which are called folders in some operating systems), that you know about path names
for directories (folders), and that you know about PATH (environment) variables.
These are not Java topics. They are part of your operating system, and the details
depend on your particular operating system. If you can find out how to set the PATH
variable on your operating system, then you will know enough about these topics to
understand the material on packages in Section 5.4.

5.1   Static Methods and Static Variables

All for one, one for all, that is our device.

ALEXANDRE DUMAS, *The Three Musketeers*

Static Methods

Some methods do not require a calling object. Methods to perform simple numeric calculations are good examples. For example, a method to compute the maximum of two
integers has no obvious candidate for a calling object. In Java, you can define a method
so that it requires no calling object. Such methods are known as **static methods**. You
define a static method in the same way as any other method, but you add the keyword
`static` to the method definition heading, as in the following example:

**static
methods**

```
public static int maximum(int n1, int n2)
{
    if (n1 > n2)
        return n1;
    else
        return n2;
}
```

Although a static method requires no calling object, it still belongs to some class,
and its definition is given inside the class definition. When you invoke a static
method, you normally use the class name in place of a calling object. So if the above
definition of the method `maximum` were in a class named `SomeClass`, then the following
is a sample invocation of `maximum`:

```
int budget = SomeClass.maximum(yourMoney, myMoney);
```

where `yourMoney` and `myMoney` are variables of type `int` that contain some values.

A sample of some static method definitions, as well as a program that uses the
methods, are given in Display 5.1.

We have already been using one static method. The method `exit` in the class `Sys-`
`tem` is a static method. To end a program immediately, we have used the following
invocation of the static method `exit`:

```
System.exit(0);
```

Note that with a static method, the class name serves the same purpose as a calling
object. (It would be legal to create an object of the class `System` and use it to invoke the
method `exit`, but that is confusing style; we usually use the class name when invoking
a static method.)

Display 5.1   Static Methods (part 1 of 2)

```
1   /**
2   Class with static methods for circles and spheres.
3   */
4   public class RoundStuff
5   {
6       public static final double PI = 3.14159;
7
8       /**
9        Return the area of a circle of the given radius.
10      */
11      public static double area(double radius)
12      {
13          return (PI*radius*radius);
14      }                                            This is the file
15                                                   RoundStuff.java.
16      /**
17       Return the volume of a sphere of the given radius.
18      */
19      public static double volume(double radius)
20      {
21          return ((4.0/3.0)*PI*radius*radius*radius);
22      }
23  }
```

```
1   import java.util.Scanner;
                                                     This is the file
2   public class RoundStuffDemo                       RoundStuffDemo.java.
3   {
4       public static void main(String[] args)
5       {
6           Scanner keyboard = new Scanner(System.in);
7           System.out.println("Enter radius:");
8           double radius = keyboard.nextDouble();

9           System.out.println("A circle of radius "
10                                      + radius + " inches");
11          System.out.println("has an area of " +
12              RoundStuff.area(radius) + " square inches.");
13          System.out.println("A sphere of radius "
14                                      + radius + " inches");
15          System.out.println("has an volume of " +
16              RoundStuff.volume(radius) + " cubic inches.");
17      }
18  }
```

Sample Dialogue

```
Enter radius:
2
A circle of radius 2.0 inches
has an area of 12.56636 square inches.
A sphere of radius 2.0 inches
has a volume of 33.51029333333333 cubic inches.
```

Within the definition of a static method, you cannot do anything that refers to a calling object, such as accessing an instance variable. This makes perfectly good sense, because a static method can be invoked without using any calling object and so can be invoked when there are no instance variables. (Remember instance variables belong to the calling object.) The best way to think about this restriction is in terms of the this parameter. In a static method, you cannot use the this parameter, either explicitly or implicitly. For example, the name of an instance variable by itself has an implicit this and a dot before it. So you cannot use an instance variable in the definition of a static method.

Static Methods

A **static method** is one that can be used without a calling object. With a static method, you normally use the class name in place of a calling object.

When you define a static method, you place the keyword **static** in the heading of the definition.

Since it does not need a calling object, a static method cannot refer to an instance variable of the class, nor can it invoke a nonstatic method of the class (unless it creates a new object of the class and uses that object as the calling object). Another way to phrase it is that, in the definition of a static method, you cannot use an instance variable or method that has an implicit or explicit **this** for a calling object.

PITFALL: Invoking a Nonstatic Method Within a Static Method

If myMethod() is a nonstatic (that is, ordinary) method in a class, then within the definition of any method of this class, an invocation of the form

```
myMethod();
```

means

```
this.myMethod();
```

(continued)

and so it is illegal within the definition of a static method. (A static method has no `this`.)

However, it is legal to invoke a static method within the definition of another static method.

There is one way that you can invoke a nonstatic method within a static method: if you create an object of the class and use that object (rather than `this`) as the calling object. For example, suppose myMethod() is a nonstatic method in the class MyClass. Then, as we already discussed, the following is illegal within the definition of a static method in the class MyClass:

```
myMethod();
```

However, the following is perfectly legal in a static method or any method definition:

```
MyClass anObject = new MyClass();
anObject.myMethod();
```

The method main is a static method, and you will often see code similar to this in the main method of a class. This point is discussed in the subsection "You Can Put a main in Any Class." ■

TIP: You Can Put a main in Any Class

So far, whenever we have used a class in the main part of a program, that main method was by itself in a different class definition within another file. However, sometimes it makes sense to have a main method within a regular class definition. The class can then be used for two purposes: It can be used to create objects in other classes, or it can be run as a program. For example, you can combine the class definition RoundStuff and the program RoundStuffDemo (both in Display 5.1) by placing the main method inside the definition of the class RoundStuff, to obtain the class definition shown in Display 5.2.

Another example of a class with a main added is given in Display 5.3. Note that in addition to the static method main, the class has another static method named toCelsius. The class has both static and nonstatic methods. Note that the static method toCelsius can be invoked without the class name or a calling object because it is in another static method (namely main) in the same class. However, the nonstatic method toString requires an explicit calling object (temperatureObject). Java requires that a program's main method be static. Thus, within a main method, you cannot invoke a nonstatic method of the same class (such as toString) unless you create an object of the class and use it as a calling object for the nonstatic method.

You do not want to place just any main method in a class definition that is to be used as a regular class to create objects. One handy trick is to place a small diagnostic program in a main method that is inside of your class definition. ■

Display 5.2   Class Definition with a **main** Added

```java
1    import java.util.Scanner;

2    /**
3    Class with static methods for circles and spheres.
4    */
5    public class RoundStuff2
6    {
7        public static final double PI = 3.14159;

8        /**
9         Return the area of a circle of the given radius.
10        */
11        public static double area(double radius)
12        {
13            return (PI*radius*radius);
14        }

15

16        /**
17         Return the volume of a sphere of the given radius.
18        */
19        public static double volume(double radius)
20        {
21            return ((4.0/3.0)*PI*radius*radius*radius);
22        }

23        public static void main(String[] args)
24        {
25            Scanner keyboard = new Scanner(System.in);
26            System.out.println("Enter radius:");
27            double radius = keyboard.nextDouble();

28
29            System.out.println("A circle of radius "
30                                         + radius + " inches");
31            System.out.println("has an area of " +
32                RoundStuff.area(radius) + " square inches.");
33            System.out.println("A sphere of radius "
34                                         + radius + " inches");
35            System.out.println("has an volume of " +
36                RoundStuff.volume(radius) + " cubic inches.");
37        }
38    }
```

The dialogue is the same as in Display 5.1.

Display 5.3   **Another Class with a main Added** (part 1 of 2)

```
1    import java.util.Scanner;

2    /**
3    Class for a temperature (expressed in degrees Celsius).
4    */
5    public class Temperature
6    {
7        private double degrees; //Celsius

8        public Temperature()
9        {
10           degrees = 0;
11       }

12       public Temperature(double initialDegrees)
13       {
14           degrees = initialDegrees;
15       }

16       public void setDegrees(double newDegrees)
17       {
18           degrees = newDegrees;
19       }

20       public double getDegrees()
21       {
22           return degrees;
23       }

24       public String toString()
25       {
26           return (degrees + " C");
27       }
28
29       public boolean equals(Temperature otherTemperature)
30       {
31           return (degrees == otherTemperature.degrees);
32       }
33       /**
34        Returns number of Celsius degrees equal to
35        degreesF Fahrenheit degrees.
36        */
```

Note that this class has a main method and both static and nonstatic methods.

Display 5.3 **Another Class with a main Added** (part 2 of 2)

```
37        public static double toCelsius(double degreesF)
38        {
39
40            return 5*(degreesF - 32)/9;
41        }
42        public static void main(String[] args)
43        {
44            double degreesF, degreesC;
45
46            Scanner keyboard = new Scanner(System.in);
47            System.out.println("Enter degrees Fahrenheit:");
48            degreesF = keyboard.nextDouble();
49
50            degreesC = toCelsius(degreesF);
51
52            Temperature temperatureObject = new Temperature(degreesC);
53            System.out.println("Equivalent Celsius temperature is "
54                            + temperatureObject.toString());
55        }
56    }
```

Because this is in the definition of the class Temperature, *this is equivalent to* Temperature.toCelsius(degreesF).

Because main *is a static method,* toString *must have a specified calling object like* temperatureObject.

Sample Dialogue

```
Enter degrees Fahrenheit:
212
Equivalent Celsius temperature is 100.0 C
```

Self-Test Exercises

1. Is the following legal? The class RoundStuff is defined in Display 5.1.

    ```
    RoundStuff roundObject = new RoundStuff();
    System.out.println("A circle of radius 5.5 has area"
                    + roundObject.area(5.5);
    ```

2. In Display 5.1, we did not define any constructors for the class RoundStuff. Is this poor programming style?

3. Can a class contain both static and nonstatic (that is, regular) methods?

4. Can you invoke a nonstatic method within a static method?

5. Can you invoke a static method within a nonstatic method?

6. Can you reference an instance variable within a static method? Why or why not?

Static Variables

static variable

A class can have static variables as well as static methods. A **static variable** is a variable that belongs to the class as a whole and not just to one object. Each object has its own copies of the instance variables. However, with a static variable there is only one copy of the variable, and all the objects can use this one variable. Thus, a static variable can be used by objects to communicate between the objects. One object can change the static variable, and another object can read that change. To make a variable static, you declare it like an instance variable but add the modifier `static` as follows:

```
private static int turn;
```

Or if you wish to initialize the static variable, which is typical, you might declare it as follows instead:

```
private static int turn = 0;
```

default
initialization

If you do not initialize a static variable, it is automatically initialized to a default value: Static variables of type `boolean` are automatically initialized to `false`. Static variables of other primitive types are automatically initialized to the zero of their type. Static variables of a class type are automatically initialized to `null`, which is a kind of placeholder for an object that we will discuss later in this chapter. However, we prefer to explicitly initialize static variables, either as just shown or in a constructor.

Display 5.4 shows an example of a class with a static variable along with a demonstration program. Notice that the two objects, `lover1` and `lover2`, access the same static variable `turn`.

As we already noted, you cannot directly access an instance variable within the definition of a static method. However, it is perfectly legal to access a static variable within a static method, because a static variable belongs to the class as a whole. This is illustrated by the method `getTurn` in Display 5.4. When we write `turn` in the definition of the static method `getTurn`, it does not mean `this.turn`; it means `TurnTaker.turn`. If the static variable `turn` were marked `public` instead of `private`, it would even be legal to use `TurnTaker.turn` outside of the definition of the class `TurnTaker`.

Defined constants that we have already been using, such as the following, are a special kind of static variable:

```
public static final double PI = 3.14159;
```

The modifier `final` in the above means that the static variable `PI` cannot be changed. Such defined constants are normally public and can be used outside the class. This defined constant appears in the class `RoundStuff` in Display 5.1. To use this constant outside of the class `RoundStuff`, you write the constant in the form `RoundStuff.PI`.

Good programming style dictates that static variables should normally be marked `private` unless they are marked `final`, that is, unless they are defined constants. The reason is the same as the reason for making instance variables `private`.

Display 5.4   **A Static Variable** (part 1 of 2)

```
1   public class TurnTaker
2   {
3       private static int turn = 0;

4       private int myTurn;
5       private String name;

6       public TurnTaker(String theName, int theTurn)
7       {
8           name = theName;
9           if (theTurn >= 0)
10              myTurn = theTurn;
11          else
12          {
13              System.out.println("Fatal Error.");
14              System.exit(0);
15          }
16      }

17      public TurnTaker()
18      {
19          name = "No name yet";
20          myTurn = 0;//Indicating no turn.
21      }

22      public String getName()
23      {
24          return name;
25      }

26      public static int getTurn()
27      {
28          turn++;
29          return turn;
30      }

31      public boolean isMyTurn()
32      {
33          return (turn == myTurn);
34      }
35  }
```

*This is the file
TurnTaker.java.*

*You cannot access an instance
variable in a static method, but you
can access a static variable in a
static method.*

(continued)

Display 5.4 **A Static Variable** (part 2 of 2)

```
36   public class StaticDemo
37   {                                          This is the file
38       public static void main(String[] args)    StaticDemo.java.
39       {
40           TurnTaker lover1 = new TurnTaker("Romeo", 1);
41           TurnTaker lover2 = new TurnTaker("Juliet", 3);
42           for (int i = 1; i < 5; i++)
43           {
44               System.out.println("Turn = " + TurnTaker.getTurn());
45               if (lover1.isMyTurn())
46                   System.out.println("Love from " + lover1.getName());
47               if (lover2.isMyTurn())
48                   System.out.println("Love from " + lover2.getName());
49           }
50       }
51   }
```

Sample Dialogue

```
Turn = 1
Love from Romeo
Turn = 2
Turn = 3
Love from Juliet
Turn = 4
```

Another example of a static variable is given in Display 5.5. The static variable numberOfInvocations is used to keep track of how many invocations have been made by all objects of the class StaticDemo. The program counts all invocations of the methods defined in Display 5.4, except for the method main.

Display 5.5 **A Static Variable** (part 1 of 2)

```
1   public class InvocationCounter
2   {
3       private static int numberOfInvocations = 0;

4       public void demoMethod()
5       {                                          object1 and object2 use
6           numberOfInvocations++;                 the same static variable
7           //In a real example, more code would go here.   numberOfInvocations.
8       }
```

Display 5.5 **A Static Variable** (part 2 of 2)

```
 9        public void outPutCount()
10        {
11            numberOfInvocations++;
12            System.out.println("Number of invocations so far = "
13                                              + numberOfInvocations);
14        }

15        public static int numberSoFar()
16        {
17            numberOfInvocations++;
18            return numberOfInvocations;
19        }

20        public static void main(String[] args)
21        {
22            int i;
23            InvocationCounter object1 = new InvocationCounter();
24            for (i = 1; i <= 5 ; i++)
25                object1.demoMethod();
26            object1.outPutCount();
27
28            InvocationCounter object2 = new InvocationCounter();
29            for (i = 1; i <= 5 ; i++)
30            {
31                object2.demoMethod();
32                object2.outPutCount();
33            }

34            System.out.println("Total number of invocations = "
35                                          + numberSoFar());
36        }
37    }
```

Outputs 6 *for five invocations of* demoMethod *and one invocation of* outputCount.

Sample Dialogue

```
Number of invocations so far = 6
Number of invocations so far = 8
Number of invocations so far = 10
Number of invocations so far = 12
Number of invocations so far = 14
Number of invocations so far = 16
Total number of invocations = 17
```

Static Variables

A **static variable** belongs to the class as a whole. All objects of the class can read and change the static variable. Static variables should normally be private, unless they happen to be defined constants.

SYNTAX

```
private static Type Variable_Name;
private static Type Variable_Name = Initial_Value;
public static final Type Variable_Name = Constant_Value;
```

EXAMPLES

```
private static String lastUser;
private static int turn = 0;
public static final double PI = 3.14159;
```

Self-Test Exercises

7. What is the difference between a static variable and an instance variable?

8. Can you use an *instance variable* (without an object name and dot) in the definition of a *static method* of the same class? Can you use an *instance variable* (without an object name and dot) in the definition of a *nonstatic (ordinary) method* of the same class?

9. Can you use a *static variable* in the definition of a *static method* of the same class? Can you use a *static variable* in the definition of a *nonstatic (ordinary) method* of the same class?

10. Can you use the this parameter in the definition of a static method?

11. When we defined the class Date in Display 4.11 in Chapter 4, we had not yet discussed static methods, so we did not mark any of the methods static. However, some of the methods could have been marked static (and should have been marked static, if only we'd known what that meant). Which of the methods can be marked static? (If you omit the modifier static when it is appropriate, then the method cannot be invoked with the class name; it must be invoked with a calling object.)

12. Following the style guidelines given in this book, when should a static variable be marked private?

13. What do static methods and static variables have in common? After all, they are both called *static*, so it sounds like they have something in common.

The Math Class

Math methods

The class Math provides a number of standard mathematical methods. The class Math is provided automatically and requires no import statement. Some of the methods in the class Math are described in Display 5.6. A more complete list of methods is given in Appendix 4. All of these methods are static, which means that you normally use the class name Math in place of a calling object.

Display 5.6 Some Methods in the Class Math (part 1 of 2)

The Math class is in the java.lang package, so it requires no import statement.

```
public static double pow(double base, double exponent)
```

Returns base to the power exponent.

EXAMPLE

Math.pow(2.0,3.0) returns 8.0.

```
public static double abs(double argument)
public static float abs(float argument)
public static long abs(long argument)
public static int abs(int argument)
```

Returns the absolute value of the argument. (The method name abs is overloaded to produce four similar methods.)

EXAMPLE

Math.abs(−6) and Math.abs(6) both return 6. Math.abs(−5.5) and Math.abs(5.5) both return 5.5.

```
public static double min(double n1, double n2)
public static float min(float n1, float n2)
public static long min(long n1, long n2)
public static int min(int n1, int n2)
```

Returns the minimum of the arguments n1 and n2. (The method name min is overloaded to produce four similar methods.)

EXAMPLE

Math.min(3, 2) returns 2.

```
public static double max(double n1, double n2)
public static float max(float n1, float n2)
public static long max(long n1, long n2)
public static int max(int n1, int n2)
```

Returns the maximum of the arguments n1 and n2. (The method name max is overloaded to produce four similar methods.)

EXAMPLE

Math.max(3, 2) returns 3.

(continued)

Display 5.6 **Some Methods in the Class Math** (part 2 of 2)

```
public static long round(double argument)
public static int round(float argument)
```

Rounds its argument.

EXAMPLE

Math.round(3.2) returns 3; Math.round(3.6) returns 4.

```
public static double ceil(double argument)
```

Returns the smallest whole number greater than or equal to the argument.

EXAMPLE

Math.ceil(3.2) and Math.ceil(3.9) both return 4.0.

```
public static double floor(double argument)
```

Returns the largest whole number less than or equal to the argument.

EXAMPLE

Math.floor(3.2) and Math.floor(3.9) both return 3.0.

```
public static double sqrt(double argument)
```

Returns the square root of its argument.

EXAMPLE

Math.sqrt(4) returns 2.0.

The class Math has three similar methods named round, floor, and ceil. Some of these return a value of type double, but they all return a value that is intuitively a whole number that is close to the value of their arguments. The method round rounds a number to the nearest whole number, and (if the argument is a double) it returns that whole number as a value of type long. If you want that whole number as a value of type int, you must use a type cast as in the following:

```
double exact = 7.56;
int roundedValue = (int)Math.round(exact);
```

You cannot assign a long value to a variable of type int, even if it is a value such as 8, which could just as well have been an int. A value such as 8 can be of type either int or long (or even of type short or byte) depending on how it was created.

**floor and
ceil**

The methods `floor` and `ceil` are similar to, but not identical to, `round`. Neither one rounds, although they both yield a whole number that is close to their argument. They both return a whole number as a value of type `double` (not of type `int` or `long`). The method `floor` returns the nearest whole number that is less than or equal to its argument. So `Math.floor(5.9)` returns `5.0`, not `6.0`. `Math.floor(5.2)` also returns `5.0`.

The method `ceil` returns the nearest whole number that is greater than or equal to its argument. The word `ceil` is short for "ceiling." `Math.ceil(5.1)` returns `6.0`, not `5.0`. `Math.ceil(5.9)` also returns `6.0`.

If you want to store the value returned by either `floor` or `ceil` in a variable of type `int`, you must use a type cast as in the following example:

```
double exact = 7.56;
int lowEstimate = (int)Math.floor(exact);
int highEstimate = (int)Math.ceil(exact);
```

`Math.floor(exact)` returns the `double` value `7.0`, and the variable `lowEstimate` receives the `int` value `7`. `Math.ceil(exact)` returns the `double` value `8.0`, and the variable `highEstimate` receives the `int` value `8`.

Because values of type `double` are effectively approximate values, a safer way to compute the floor or ceiling as an `int` value is the following:

```
double exact = 7.56;
int lowEstimate = (int)Math.round(Math.floor(exact));
int highEstimate = (int)Math.round(Math.ceil(exact));
```

This way, if `Math.floor(exact)` returns slightly less than `7.0`, the final result will still be 7 not 6, and if `Math.ceil(exact)` returns slightly less than `8.0`, the final result will still be 8 not 7.

**Math
constants**

The class `Math` also has the two predefined constants `E` and `PI`. The constant `PI` (often written π in mathematical formulas) is used in calculations involving circles, spheres, and other geometric figures based on circles. `PI` is approximately `3.14159`. The constant `E` is the base of the natural logarithm system (often written *e* in mathematical formulas) and is approximately `2.72`. (We do not use the predefined constant `E` in this text.) The constants `PI` and `E` are defined constants, as described in Chapter 1. For example, the following computes the area of a circle, given its radius:

```
area = Math.PI * radius * radius;
```

Notice that because the constants `PI` and `E` are defined in the class `Math`, they must have the class name `Math` and a dot before them. For example, in Display 5.7, we have redone the program in Display 5.2, but this time we used the constant `Math.PI` instead of including our own definition of `PI`.

Display 5.7   Using `Math.PI`

```
 1   import java.util.Scanner;

 2   /**
 3   Class with static methods for circles and spheres.
 4   */
 5   public class RoundStuff3
 6   {

 7       /**
 8        Return the area of a circle of the given radius.
 9       */
10      public static double area(double radius)
11      {
12          return (Math.PI*radius*radius);
13      }

15      /**
16       Return the volume of a sphere of the given radius.
17      */
18      public static double volume(double radius)
19      {
20          return ((4.0/3.0)*Math.PI*radius*radius*radius);
21      }

22      public static void main(String[] args)
23      {
24          Scanner keyboard = new Scanner(System.in);
25          System.out.println("Enter radius:");
26          double radius = keyboard.nextDouble();

28          System.out.println("A circle of radius "
29                                          + radius + " inches");
30          System.out.println("has an area of " +
31              RoundStuff.area(radius) + " square inches.");
32          System.out.println("A sphere of radius "
33                                          + radius + " inches");
34          System.out.println("has a volume of " +
35              RoundStuff.volume(radius) + " cubic inches.");
36      }
37  }
38
39
```

The dialogue is the same as in Display 5.1.

Self-Test Exercises

14. What values are returned by each of the following?

    ```
    Math.round(3.2), Math.round(3.6),
    Math.floor(3.2), Math.floor(3.6),
    Math.ceil(3.2), and Math.ceil(3.6).
    ```

15. Suppose answer is a variable of type double. Write an assignment statement to assign Math.round(answer) to the int variable roundedAnswer.

16. Suppose n is of type int and m is of type long. What is the type of the value returned by Math.min(n, m)? Is it int or long?

Wrapper Classes

wrapper class

Integer class

Java treats the primitive types, such as int and double, differently from the class types, such as the class String and the programmer-defined classes. For example, later in this chapter you will see that an argument to a method is treated differently depending on whether the argument is of a primitive or class type. At times, you may find yourself in a situation where you want to use a value of a primitive type but you want or need the value to be an object of a class type. **Wrapper classes** provide a class type corresponding to each of the primitive types so that you can have an object of a class type that behaves somewhat like its corresponding value of a primitive type.

To convert a value of a primitive type to an "equivalent" value of a class type, you create an object of the corresponding wrapper class using the primitive type value as an argument to the wrapper class constructor. The wrapper class for the primitive type int is the predefined class Integer. If you want to convert an int value, such as 42, to an object of type Integer, you can do so as follows:

```
Integer integerObject = new Integer(42);
```

The variable integerObject now names an object of the class Integer that corresponds to the int value 42. (The object integerObject does, in fact, have the int value 42 stored in an instance variable of the object integerObject.) This process of going from a value of a primitive type to an object of its wrapper class is sometimes called **boxing**, and as you will see in the next subsection, you can let Java automatically do all the work of boxing for you.

boxing

To go in the reverse direction, from an object of type Integer to the corresponding int value, you can do the following:

```
int i = integerObject.intValue();
```

The method `intValue()` recovers the corresponding `int` value from an object of type `Integer`. This process of going from an object of a wrapper class to the corresponding value of a primitive type is sometimes called **unboxing**, and as you will see in the next subsection, you can let Java automatically do all the work of unboxing for you.

The wrapper classes for the primitive types `byte`, `short`, `long`, `float`, `double`, and `char` are `Byte`, `Short`, `Long`, `Float`, `Double`, and `Character`, respectively. The methods for converting from the wrapper class object to the corresponding primitive type are `intValue` for the class `Integer`, as we have already seen, `byteValue` for the class `Byte`, `shortValue` for the class `Short`, `longValue` for the class `Long`, `floatValue` for the class `Float`, `doubleValue` for the class `Double`, and `charValue` for the class `Character`.

Wrapper Classes

Every primitive type has a corresponding wrapper class. A wrapper class allows you to have a class object that corresponds to a value of a primitive type. Wrapper classes also contain a number of useful predefined constants and static methods.

Automatic Boxing and Unboxing

Converting from a value of a primitive type, such as `int`, to a corresponding object of its associated wrapper class, such as `Integer`, is called boxing. You can think of the object as a "box" that contains the value of the primitive type. In fact, the wrapper object does contain the value of the primitive type as the value of a private instance variable. The following are examples of boxing:

```
Integer numberOfSamuri = new Integer(47);
Double price = new Double(499.99);
Character grade = new Character('A');
```

Starting with version 5.0, Java will automatically do this boxing and so the previous three assignments can be written in the following equivalent, but simpler, forms:

```
Integer numberOfSamuri = 47;
Double price = 499.99;
Character grade = 'A';
```

This is an automatic type cast. What is actually done by Java is what we showed in the forms using the `new`, but it is handy to be able to write the assignments in the simpler form.

automatic
unboxing

The reverse conversion from an object of a wrapper class to a value of its associated primitive type is called unboxing. Unboxing is also done automatically in Java (starting in version 5.0). The following are examples of automatic unboxing:

```
Integer numberOfSamuri = new Integer(47);
int n = numberOfSamuri;
Double price = new Double(499.99);
double d = price;
Character grade = new Character('A');
char c = grade;
```

Java automatically applies the appropriate accessor method (intValue, doubleValue, or charValue in these cases) to obtain the value of the primitive type that is assigned to the variable. So the previous examples of automatic unboxing are equivalent to the following code, which is what you had to write in older versions of Java that did not do automatic unboxing:

```
Integer numberOfSamuri = new Integer(47);
int n = numberOfSamuri.intValue();
Double price = new Double(499.99);
double d = price.doubleValue();
Character grade = new Character('A');
char c = grade.charValue();
```

Our previous examples involved either only automatic boxing or only automatic unboxing. That was done to simplify the discussion by allowing you to see each of automatic boxing and automatic unboxing in isolation. However, code can often involve a combination of automatic boxing and unboxing. For example, consider the following code, which uses both automatic boxing and automatic unboxing:

```
Double price = 19.90;
price = price + 5.12;
```

This code is equivalent to the following, which is what you had to write in older versions of Java that did not do automatic boxing and unboxing:

```
Double price = new Double(19.90);
price = new Double(price.doubleValue() + 5.12);
```

Automatic boxing and unboxing applies to parameters as well as the simple assignment statements we just discussed. You can plug in a value of a primitive type, such as a value of type int, for a parameter of the associated wrapper class, such as Integer. Similarly, you can plug a wrapper class argument, such as an argument of type Integer, for a parameter of the associated primitive type, such as int.

Self-Test Exercises

17. Which of the following are legal?

```java
Integer n = new Integer(42);
int m = 42;
n = m;
m = n;
```

If any are illegal, explain how to write a valid Java statement that does what the illegal statement is trying to do.

18. In the following, is the value of the variable `price` after the assignment statement an object of the class `Double` or a value of the primitive type `double`?

```java
Double price = 1.99;
```

19. In the following, is the value of the variable `count` after the assignment statement an object of the class `Integer` or a value of the primitive type `int`?

```java
int count = new Integer(12);
```

Static Methods in Wrapper Classes

The material on wrapper classes that we have seen thus far explains why they are called *wrapper classes*. However, possibly more importantly, the wrapper classes contain a number of useful constants and static methods. So, wrapper classes have two distinct personalities: one is their ability to produce class objects corresponding to values of primitive types, and the other is as a repository of useful constants and methods. It was not necessary to combine these two personalities into one kind of class. Java could have had two sets of classes, one for each personality, but the designers of the Java libraries chose to have only one set of classes for both personalities.

largest and smallest values You can use the associated wrapper class to find the value of the **largest and smallest values** of any of the primitive number types. For example, the largest and smallest values of type `int` are

```java
Integer.MAX_VALUE and Integer.MIN_VALUE
```

The largest and smallest values of type `double` are

```java
Double.MAX_VALUE and Double.MIN_VALUE
```

parse-Double Wrapper classes have static methods that can be used to convert back and forth between string representations of numbers and the corresponding number of type `int`, `double`, `long`, or `float`. For example, the static method `parseDouble` of the wrapper class `Double` converts a string to a value of type `double`. So, the code

```java
Double.parseDouble("199.98")
```

returns the double value 199.98. If there is any possibility that the string named by theString has extra leading or trailing blanks, you should instead use

```
Double.parseDouble(theString.trim())
```

The method trim is a method in the class String that trims off leading and trailing whitespace, such as blanks.

If the string is not a correctly formed numeral, then the invocation of Double.parseDouble will cause your program to end. The use of trim helps somewhat in avoiding this problem.

parseInt   Similarly, the static methods Integer.parseInt, Long.parseLong, and Float.parseFloat convert from string representations to numbers of the corresponding primitive types int, long, and float, respectively.

Each of the numeric wrapper classes also has a static method called toString that converts in the other direction, from a numeric value to a string representation of the numeric value. For example,

```
Double.toString(123.99)
```

returns the string value "123.99".

Character   Character, the wrapper class for the primitive type char, contains a number of static methods that are useful for string processing. Some of these methods are shown in Display 5.8. A simple example of using the static method toUpperCase of the class Character is given in Display 5.9. As is typical, this program combines the string-processing methods of the class String with the character-processing methods in the class Character.

Boolean   There is also a wrapper class Boolean corresponding to the primitive type boolean. It has names for two constants of type Boolean: Boolean.TRUE and Boolean.FALSE, which are the Boolean objects corresponding to the values true and false of the primitive type boolean.

Display 5.8 Some Methods in the Class **Character** (part 1 of 2)

The class **Character** is in the java.lang package, so it requires no import statement.

public static char **toUpperCase**(char argument)

Returns the uppercase version of its argument. If the argument is not a letter, it is returned unchanged.

EXAMPLE

Character.toUpperCase('a') and Character.toUpperCase('A') both return 'A'.

public static char **toLowerCase**(char argument)

Returns the lowercase version of its argument. If the argument is not a letter, it is returned unchanged.

EXAMPLE

Character.toLowerCase('a') and Character.toLowerCase('A') both return 'a'.

(continued)

Display 5.8 Some Methods in the Class **Character** (part 2 of 2)

```
public static boolean isUpperCase(char argument)
```

Returns **true** if its **argument** is an uppercase letter; otherwise returns **false**.

EXAMPLE

Character.isUpperCase('A') returns true. Character.isUpperCase('a') and
Character.isUpperCase('%') both return **false**.

```
public static boolean isLowerCase(char argument)
```

Returns **true** if its **argument** is a lowercase letter; otherwise returns **false**.

EXAMPLE

Character.isLowerCase('a') returns true. Character.isLowerCase('A') and
Character.isLowerCase('%') both return **false**.

```
public static boolean isWhitespace(char argument)
```

Returns **true** if its **argument** is a whitespace character; otherwise returns **false.** Whitespace characters are those that print as white space, such as the space character (blank character), the tab character ('\t'), and the line break character ('\n').

EXAMPLE

Character.isWhitespace(' ') returns true. Character.isWhitespace('A') returns **false**.

```
public static boolean isLetter(char argument)
```

Returns **true** if its **argument** is a letter; otherwise returns **false**.

EXAMPLE

Character.isLetter('A') returns true. Character.isLetter('%') and Character.
isLetter ('5') both return **false**.

```
public static boolean isDigit(char argument)
```

Returns **true** if its **argument** is a digit; otherwise returns **false**.

EXAMPLE

Character.isDigit('5') returns true. Character.isDigit('A') and Character.
is Digit('%') both return **false**.

```
public static boolean isLetterOrDigit(char argument)
```

Returns **true** if its **argument** is a letter or a digit; otherwise returns **false**.

EXAMPLE

Character.isLetterOrDigit('A') and Character.isLetterOrDigit('5') both return **true**.
Character.isLetterOrDigit('&') returns **false**.

PITFALL: A Wrapper Class Does Not Have a No-Argument Constructor

Normally, it is good programming practice to define a no-argument constructor for any class you define. However, on rare occasions, a no-argument constructor simply does not make sense. The wrapper classes discussed in the previous subsection do not have a no-argument constructor. This makes sense if you think about it. To use the static methods in a wrapper class, you need no calling object and hence need no constructor at all. The other function of a wrapper class is to provide a class object corresponding to a value of a primitive type. For example,

```
new Integer(42)
```

creates an object of the class `Integer` that corresponds to the `int` value 42. There is no no-argument constructor for the class `Integer`, because it makes no sense to have an object of the class `Integer` unless it corresponds to an `int` value, and if it does correspond to an `int` value, that `int` value is naturally an argument to the constructor. ■

Display 5.9 String Processing with a Method from the Class Character (part 1 of 2)

```java
1   import java.util.Scanner;

2   /**
3   Illustrate the use of a static method from the class Character.
4   */

5
6   public class StringProcessor
7   {
8       public static void main(String[] args)
9       {
10          System.out.println("Enter a one line sentence:");
11          Scanner keyboard = new Scanner(System.in);
12          String sentence = keyboard.nextLine();

13
14          sentence = sentence.toLowerCase();
15          char firstCharacter = sentence.charAt(0);
16          sentence = Character.toUpperCase(firstCharacter)
17                          + sentence.substring(1);

18
19          System.out.println("The revised sentence is:");
20          System.out.println(sentence);
21      }
22  }
```

(continued)

Display 5.9 **String Processing with a Method from the Class Character** (part 2 of 2)

Sample Dialogue

```
Enter a one line sentence:
is you is OR is you ain't my BABY?
The revised sentence is:
Is you is or is you ain't my baby?
```

Self-Test Exercises

20. What is the output produced by the following code?

    ```
    Character characterObject1 = new Character('a');
    Character characterObject2 = new Character('A');
    if (characterObject1.equals(characterObject2))
        System.out.println("Objects are equal.");
    else
        System.out.println("Objects are Not equal.");
    ```

21. Suppose `result` is a variable of type `double` that has a value. Write a Java expression that returns a string that is the normal way of writing the value in `result`.

22. Suppose `stringForm` is a variable of type `String` that names a `String` that is the normal way of writing some `double`, such as `"41.99"`. Write a Java expression that returns the `double` value named by `stringForm`.

23. How would you do Exercise 22 if the string might contain leading and/or trailing blanks, such as `"   41.99   "`?

24. Write Java code to output the largest and smallest values of type `long` allowed in Java.

25. How do you create an object of the class `Character` that corresponds to the letter `'Z'`?

26. Does the class `Character` have a no-argument constructor?

5.2 References and Class Parameters

Do not mistake the pointing finger for the moon.

Zen Saying

Variables of a class type and variables of a primitive type behave quite differently in Java. Variables of a primitive type name their values in a straightforward way. For example, if n is an int variable, then n can contain a value of type int, such as 42. If v is a variable of a class type, then v does not directly contain an object of its class. Instead, v names an object by containing the memory address of where the object is located in memory. In this section, we discuss how a variable of a class type names objects, and we also discuss the related topic of how method parameters of a class type behave in Java.

Variables and Memory

secondary and main memory

A computer has two forms of memory called *secondary memory* and *main memory* . The **secondary memory** is used to hold files for more or less permanent storage. The **main memory** is used by the computer when it is running a program. Values stored in a program's variables are kept in this main memory. It will help our understanding of class type variables to learn a few details about how program variables are represented in main memory. For now, assume that each variable in a program is of some primitive type, such as int, double, or char. Once you understand how variables of a primitive type are stored in memory, it will be easier to describe how variables of a class type behave.

byte

address

Main memory consists of a long list of numbered locations called **bytes**, each containing eight bits; that is, eight 0/1 digits. The number that identifies a byte is called its **address**. A data item, such as a number or a letter, can be stored in one of these bytes, and the address of the byte is then used to find the data item when it is needed.

memory location

Most data types have values that require more than one byte of storage. When a data type requires more than one byte of storage, several adjacent bytes are used to hold the data item. In this case, the entire chunk of memory that holds the data item is still called a **memory location**. The address of the first of the bytes that make up this memory location is used as the address for this larger memory location. Thus, as a practical matter, you can think of the computer's main memory as a long list of memory locations of *varying sizes*. The size of each of these locations is expressed in bytes, and the address of the first byte is used as the address (name) of that memory location. Display 5.10 shows a picture of a hypothetical computer's main memory. Each primitive type variable in a program is assigned one of these memory locations, and the value of the variable is stored in this memory location.

variables of a primitive type

Bytes and Addresses

Main memory is divided into numbered locations called **bytes**. The number associated with a byte is called its **address**. A group of consecutive bytes is used as the location for the value of a variable. The address of the first byte in the group is used as the address of this larger memory location.

Why Eight Bits?

A **byte** is a memory location that can hold eight bits. What is so special about eight? Why not ten bits? There are two reasons why eight is special. First, eight is a power of 2 (8 is 2^3). Since computers use bits, which have only two possible values, powers of 2 are more convenient than powers of 10. Second, it turns out that seven bits are required to code a single character of the ASCII character set. So eight bits (one byte) is the smallest power of 2 that will hold a single ASCII character.

Display 5.10 Variables in Memory

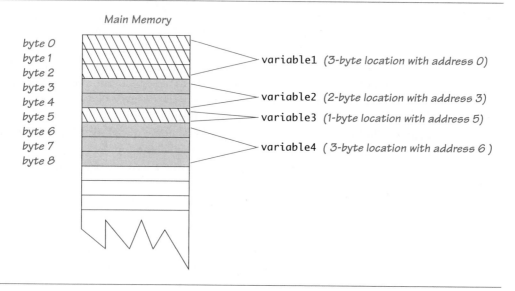

References

In order to have a simple example to help explain *references*, we will use the class ToyClass defined in Display 5.11.

Variables of a class type name objects of their class differently than how variables of primitive types, such as int or char, store their values. Every variable, whether of a primitive type or a class type, is implemented as a location in the computer memory. For a variable of a primitive type, the value of the variable is stored in the memory location assigned to the variable. However, a variable of a class type stores only the memory address of where an object is located. The object named by the variable is stored in some other location in memory, and the variable contains only the memory

Display 5.11   A Simple Class

```
1    public class ToyClass
2    {
3        private String name;
4        private int number;

5        public ToyClass(String initialName, int initialNumber)
6        {
7            name = initialName;
8            number = initialNumber;
9        }

10       public ToyClass()
11       {
12           name = "No name yet.";
13           number = 0;
14       }

15       public void set(String newName, int newNumber)
16       {
17           name = newName;
18           number = newNumber;
19       }

20       public String toString()
21       {
22           return (name + " " + number);
23       }

24       public static void changer(ToyClass aParameter)
25       {
26           aParameter.name = "Hot Shot";
27           aParameter.number = 42;
28       }

29       public boolean equals(ToyClass otherObject)
30       {
31           return ( (name.equals(otherObject.name))
32                       && (number == otherObject.number) );
33       }
34   }
```

references address of where the object is stored. This memory address is called a **reference** (to the object).[1] This is diagrammed in Display 5.12.

Variables of a primitive type and variables of a class type are different for a reason. A value of a primitive type, such as the type int, always requires the same amount of memory to store one value. There is a maximum value of type int, so values of type int have a limit on their size. However, an object of a class type, such as an object of the class String, might be of any size. The memory location for a variable of type String is of a fixed size, so it cannot store an arbitrarily long string. It can, however, store the address of any string because there is a limit to the size of an address.

Because variables of a class type contain a reference (memory address), two variables may contain the same reference, and in such a situation, both variables name the same object. Any change to the object named by one of these variables will produce a change to the object named by the other variable, because they are the same object. For example, consider the following code. (The class ToyClass is defined in Display 5.11, but the meaning of the code should be obvious and you should not need to look up the definition.)

```
ToyClass variable1 = new ToyClass("Joe", 42);
ToyClass variable2;
variable2 = variable1; //Now both variables name the same object.
variable2.set("Josephine", 1);
System.out.println(variable1);
```

The output is

```
Josephine 1
```

The object named by variable1 has been changed without ever using the name variable1. This is diagrammed in Display 5.13.

Variables of a Class Type Hold References

A variable of a primitive type stores a value of that type. However, a variable of a class type does not store an object of that class. A variable of a class type stores the reference (memory address) of where the object is located in the computer's memory. This causes some operations, such as = and ==, to behave quite differently for variables of a class type than they do for variables of a primitive type.

Reference Types

A type whose variables contain references are called **reference types**. In Java, class types are reference types, but primitive types are not reference types.

---

[1] Readers familiar with languages that use pointers will recognize a reference as another name for a pointer. However, Java does not use the term *pointer*, but instead uses the term *reference*. Moreover, these references are handled automatically. There are no programmer-accessible pointer (reference) operations for de-referencing or other pointer operations. The details are all handled automatically in Java.

Display 5.12 **Class Type Variables Store a Reference**

```
public class ToyClass
{
        private String name;
        private int number;
```
The complete definition of the class
ToyClass is given in Display 5.11.

ToyClass sampleVariable;
Creates the variable **sampleVariable** *in*
memory but assigns it no value.

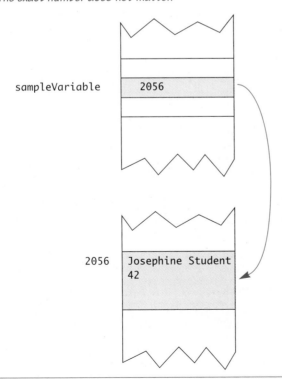

sampleVariable =
new ToyClass("Josephine Student", 42);
Creates an object, places the object someplace in memory, and then
places the address of the object in the variable **sampleVariable**. *We*
do not know what the address of the object is, but let's assume it is
2056. The exact number does not matter.

sampleVariable   2056

For emphasis, we made the
arrow point to the memory
location referenced.

2056   Josephine Student
        42

Display 5.13 **Assignment Operator with Class Type Variables** (part 1 of 2)

```
ToyClass variable1 = new ToyClass("Joe", 42);
ToyClass variable2;
```

variable1 | 4068

variable2 | ?

We do not know what memory address (reference) is stored in the variable **variable1.** *Let's say it is* **4068.** *The exact number does not matter.*

Someplace else in memory:

Note that you can think of

`new ToyClass("Joe", 42)`

as returning a reference.

4068 | Joe
       42

```
variable2 = variable1;
```

variable1 | 4068

variable2 | 4068

Someplace else in memory:

4068 | Joe
       42

Display 5.13 **Assignment Operator with Class Type Variables** (part 2 of 2)

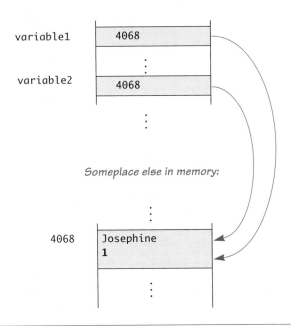

```
variable2.set("Josephine", 1);
```

Note that when you use the assignment operator with variables of a class type, you are assigning a reference (memory address), so the result of the following is to make variable1 and variable2 two names for the same object:

```
variable2 = variable1;
```

A variable of a class type stores a memory address, and a memory address is a number. However, a variable of a class type cannot be used like a variable of a number type, such as int or double. This is intentional. The important property of a memory address is that it identifies a memory location. The fact that the implementors used numbers, rather than letters or strings or something else, to name memory locations is an accidental property. Java prevents you from using this accidental property to prevent you from doing things such as obtaining access to restricted memory or otherwise screwing up the computer.

Class Parameters

Strictly speaking, all parameters in Java are call-by-value parameters. This means that when an argument is plugged in for a parameter (of any type), the argument is evaluated and the value obtained is used to initialize the value of the parameter. (Recall that a parameter is really a local variable.) However, in the case of a parameter of a class type, the value plugged in is a reference (memory address), and that makes class parameters behave quite differently from parameters of a primitive type.

Recall that the following makes variable1 and variable2 two names for the same object:

```
ToyClass variable1 = new ToyClass("Joe", 42);
ToyClass variable2;
variable2 = variable1;
```

So, any change made to variable2 is, in fact, made to variable1. The same thing happens with parameters of a class type. The parameter is a local variable that is set equal to the value of its argument. But if its argument is a variable of a class type, this copies a reference into the parameter. So, the parameter becomes another name for the argument, and any change made to the object named by the parameter is made to the object named by the argument, because they are the same object. Thus, a method can change the instance variables of an object given as an argument. A simple program to illustrate this is given in Display 5.14. Display 5.15 contains a diagram of the computer's memory as the program in Display 5.14 is executed.

Many programming languages have a parameter passing mechanism known as *call-by-reference*. If you are familiar with call-by-reference parameters, we should note that the Java parameter passing mechanism is similar to, but is not exactly the same as, call-by-reference.

Display 5.14 Parameters of a Class Type

```
1   public class ClassParameterDemo              ToyClass is defined in Display 5.11.
2   {
3       public static void main(String[] args)
4       {
5           ToyClass anObject = new ToyClass("Mr. Cellophane", 0);
6           System.out.println(anObject);
7           System.out.println(
8                   "Now we call changer with anObject as argument.");
9           ToyClass.changer(anObject);
10          System.out.println(anObject);
11      }
12  }
```

Notice that the method changer changed the instance variables in the object anObject.

Sample Dialogue

```
Mr. Cellophane 0
Now we call changer with anObject as argument.
Hot Shot 42
```

Differences Between Primitive and Class-Type Parameters

A method cannot change the value of a variable of a primitive type that is an argument to the method. On the other hand, a method can change the values of the instance variables of an argument of a class type. This is illustrated in Display 5.16.

Display 5.15   Memory Picture for Display 5.14 (part 1 of 2)

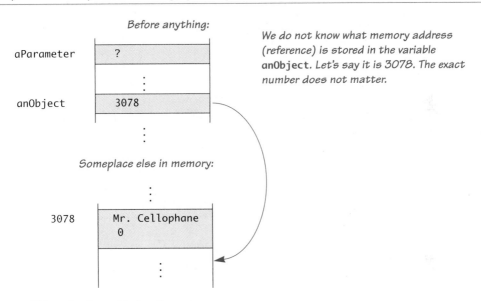

Before anything:

aParameter   ?

anObject   3078

We do not know what memory address (reference) is stored in the variable anObject. Let's say it is 3078. The exact number does not matter.

Someplace else in memory:

3078   Mr. Cellophane
       0

anObject *is plugged in for* **aParamter.**
anObject *and* **aParameter** *become two names for the same object.*

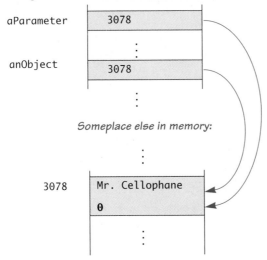

aParameter   3078

anObject   3078

Someplace else in memory:

3078   Mr. Cellophane

       0

Display 5.15 Memory Picture for Display 5.14 (part 2 of 2)

ToyClass.changer(anObject); *is executed*
and so the following are executed:
aParameter.name = "Hot Shot";
aParameter.number = 42;
As a result, **anObject** *is changed.*

aParameter

3078

anObject

3078

Someplace else in memory:

3078

Hot Shot
42

Display 5.16 Comparing Parameters of a Class Type and a Primitive Type (part 1 of 2)

```
1   public class ParametersDemo
2   {
3       public static void main(String[] args)
4       {
5           ToyClass2 object1 = new ToyClass2(),
6                     object2 = new ToyClass2();
7           object1.set("Scorpius", 1);
8           object2.set("John Crichton", 2);
9           System.out.println("Value of object2 before call to method:");
10          System.out.println(object2);
11          object1.makeEqual(object2);
12          System.out.println("Value of object2 after call to method:");
13          System.out.println(object2);
14
```

ToyClass2 is defined in
Display 5.17.

Display 5.16   Comparing Parameters of a Class Type and a Primitive Type (part 2 of 2)

```
15              int aNumber = 42;
16              System.out.println("Value of aNumber before call to method: "
17                          + aNumber);
18              object1.tryToMakeEqual(aNumber);
19              System.out.println("Value of aNumber after call to method: "
20                          + aNumber);
21          }
22    }
```

Sample Dialogue

An argument of a class type can change.

```
Value of object2 before call to method:
John Crichton 2
Value of object2 after call to method:
Scorpius 1
Value of aNumber before call to method: 42
Value of aNumber after call to method: 42
```

An argument of a primitive type cannot change.

PITFALL: Use of = and == with Variables of a Class Type

You have already seen that the assignment operator used with variables of a class type produces two variables that name the same object, which is very different from how assignment behaves with variables of a primitive type.

== with variables of a class type

The test for equality using == with variables of a class type also behaves in what may seem like a peculiar way. The operator == does not check that the objects have the same values for their instance variables. It merely checks for equality of memory addresses, so two objects in two different locations in memory would test as being "not equal" when compared using ==, even if their instance variables contain equivalent data. For example, consider the following code. (The class ToyClass2 is defined in Display 5.17.)

```
ToyClass2 variable1 = new ToyClass2("Chiana", 3),
          variable2 = new ToyClass2("Chiana", 3);
if (variable1 == variable2)
    System.out.println("Equal using ==");
else
    System.out.println("Not equal using ==");
```

This code will produce the output

```
Not equal using ==
```

PITFALL: (continued)

Even though these two variables name objects that are intuitively equal, they are stored in two different locations in the computer's memory. This is why you usually use an `equals` method to compare objects of a class type. The variables `variable1` and `variable2` would be considered "equal" if compared using the `equals` method as defined for the class `ToyClass2` (Display 5.17). ■

Display 5.17 A Toy Class to Use in Display 5.16

```
1   public class ToyClass2
2   {
3       private String name;
4       private int number;

5       public void set(String newName, int newNumber)
6       {
7           name = newName;
8           number = newNumber;
9       }

10      public String toString()
11      {
12          return (name + " " + number);
13      }

14      public void makeEqual(ToyClass2 anObject)
15      {
16          anObject.name = this.name;
17          anObject.number = this.number;
18      }

19      public void tryToMakeEqual(int aNumber)
20      {
21          aNumber = this.number;
22      }

23      public boolean equals(ToyClass2 otherObject)
24      {
25          return ( (name.equals(otherObject.name))
26                      && (number == otherObject.number) );
27      }
```

Read the text for a discussion of the problem with this method.

<Other methods can be the same as in Display 5.11, although no other methods are needed or used in the current discussion.>

```
28  }
```

Self-Test Exercises

27. What is a reference type? Are class types reference types? Are primitive types (such as int) reference types?

28. When comparing two objects of a class type to see if they are "equal" or not, should you use == or the method equals?

29. When comparing two objects of a primitive type (such as int) to see if they are "equal" or not, should you use == or the method equals?

30. Can a method with an argument of a class type change the values of the instance variables in the object named by the argument? For example, if the argument is of type ToyClass defined in Display 5.11, can the method change the name of its argument?

31. Suppose a method has a parameter of type int and the method is given an int variable as an argument. Could the method have been defined so that it changes the value of the variable given as an argument?

The Constant null

null   The constant null is a special constant that may be assigned to a variable of any class type. It is used to indicate that the variable has no "real value." If the compiler insists that you initialize a variable of a class type and there is no suitable object to initialize it with, you can use the value null, as in the following example:

```
YourClass yourObject = null;
```

It is also common to use null in constructors to initialize instance variables of a class type when there is no obvious object to use. We will eventually see other uses for the constant null.

Note that null is not an object. It is like a reference (memory address) that does not refer to any object (does not name any memory location). So if you want to test whether a class variable contains null, you use == or !=; you do not use an equals method. For example, the following correctly tests for null:

```
if (yourObject == null)
    System.out.println("No real object here.");
```

---

null

null is a special constant that can be used to give a value to any variable of any class type. The constant null is not an object but a sort of placeholder for a reference to an object. Because it is like a reference (memory address), you use == and != rather than the method equals when you test to see whether a variable contains null.

PITFALL: Null Pointer Exception

If the compiler asks you to initialize a class variable, you can always initialize the variable to null. However, null is not an object, so you cannot invoke a method using a variable that is initialized to null. If you try, you will get an error message that says "Null Pointer Exception." For example, the following code would produce a "Null Pointer Exception" if it were included in a program:

```
ToyClass2 aVariable = null;
String representation = aVariable.toString();
```

The problem is that you are trying to invoke the method toString() using null as a calling object. But null is not an object; it is just a placeholder. So null has no methods. Because you are using null incorrectly, the error message reads "Null Pointer Exception." You get this error message any time a class variable has not been assigned a (reference to an) object, even if you have not assigned null to the variable. Any time you get a "Null Pointer Exception," look for an uninitialized class variable.

The way to correct the problem is to use new to create a class object, as follows:

```
ToyClass2 aVariable = new ToyClass2("Chiana", 3);
String representation = aVariable.toString();
```

■

The new Operator and Anonymous Objects

Consider an expression such as the following, where ToyClass is defined in Display 5.11:

```
ToyClass variable1 = new ToyClass("Joe", 42);
```

As illustrated in Display 5.13, the portion new ToyClass("Joe", 42) is an invocation of a constructor. You can think of the constructor as returning a reference to the location in memory of the object created by the constructor. If you take this view, the equal sign in this line of code is just an ordinary assignment operator.

There are times when you create an object using new and use the object as an argument to a method, but then never again use the object. In such cases, you need not give the object a variable name. You can instead use the expression with the new operator and the constructor directly as the argument. For example, suppose you wanted to test to see whether the object in variable1 (in the earlier line of code) is equal to an object with the same number and with the name spelled in all uppercase letters. You can do so as follows:

```
if (variable1.equals(new ToyClass("JOE", 42)))
    System.out.println("Equal");
else
    System.out.println("Not equal");
```

This is equivalent to the following:

```
ToyClass temp = new ToyClass("JOE", 42);
if (variable1.equals(temp))
    System.out.println("Equal");
else
    System.out.println("Not equal");
```

In the second version, the object is created, and its reference is placed in the variable `temp`. Then `temp` is plugged in for the parameter in the `equals` method. But all the parameter passing mechanism does is to take the reference stored in `temp` and plug it into the parameter for `equals`. The first version simplifies the process. It creates the reference to the object and directly plugs it into the parameter in `equals`. It bypasses the variable `temp` but ends up plugging in the same reference as the argument to `equals`.

An expression such as

```
new ToyClass("JOE", 42)
```

anonymous object

when not assigned to a variable is known as an **anonymous object**. It evaluates a reference to an object of the class. It is called *anonymous* because the object is not assigned a variable to serve as its name. We will eventually encounter situations where the use of such anonymous objects is common.

Anonymous Objects

An expression with a **new** operator and a constructor creates a new object and returns a reference to the object. If this reference is not assigned to a variable, but instead the expression with **new** and the constructor is used as an argument to some method, then the object produced is called an **anonymous object**.

EXAMPLE
```
if (variable1.equals(new ToyClass("JOE", 42)))
    System.out.println("Equal");
else
    System.out.println("Not equal");
```

The expression new `ToyClass("JOE", 42)` (or more exactly, the object it creates) is an example of an anonymous object.

EXAMPLE: Another Approach to Keyboard Input ⋆

This example uses the class `StringTokenizer`, which was covered in a starred section of Chapter 4. If you have not yet covered the `StringTokenizer` class, you may omit this example until you have covered the `StringTokenizer` class.

The program in Display 5.18 is an example of the use of both the `StringTokenizer` class and the method `Double.parseDouble` to read multiple values of type `double` entered on a single line and separated with something other than whitespace.

(continued)

EXAMPLE: Another Approach to Keyboard Input ⋆

The entire line is read as a single long string using the method nextLine of the Scanner class. The long string is decomposed into tokens using the class StingTokenizer. The tokens are the numbers that were input, but they are in the form of string values, not values of type double. Finally, the tokens are converted to values of type double using the method Double.parseDouble.

Note that the String variables are initialized to null. If you omit the nulls, the compiler will complain that the variables string1 and string2 might not be initialized before they are used. The compiler is incorrect. However, it does no good to argue with the compiler. Including null as initial values for the variables string1 and string2 will keep the compiler happy and allow you to run the program.

Display 5.18   Use of the Method **Double.parseDouble** (part 1 of 2)

```
1   import java.util.Scanner;
2   import java.util.StringTokenizer;

3   public class InputExample
4   {
5       public static void main(String[] args)
6       {
7           Scanner keyboard = new Scanner(System.in);

8           System.out.println("Enter two numbers on a line.");
9           System.out.println("Place a comma between the numbers.");
10          System.out.println("Extra blank space is OK.");
11          String inputLine = keyboard.nextLine();

12          String delimiters = ", "; //Comma and blank space
13          StringTokenizer numberFactory =
14              new StringTokenizer(inputLine, delimiters);

15          String string1 = null;
16          String string2 = null;
17          if (numberFactory.countTokens() >= 2)
18          {
19              string1 = numberFactory.nextToken();
20              string2 = numberFactory.nextToken();
21          }
22          else
23          {
24              System.out.println("Fatal Error.");
25              System.exit(0);
26          }
```

Display 5.18   Use of the Method **Double.parseDouble** (part 1 of 2)

```
27            double number1 = Double.parseDouble(string1);
28            double number2 = Double.parseDouble(string2);

29            System.out.print("You input ");
30            System.out.println(number1 + " and " + number2);
31        }
32    }
```

Sample Dialogue

```
Enter two numbers on a line.
Place a comma between the numbers.
Extra blank space is OK.
    41.98,  42
You input is 41.98 and 42.0
```

Self-Test Exercises

32. What is wrong with a program that starts as follows? The class `ToyClass` is defined in Display 5.11.

    ```
    ToyClass anObject = null;
    anObject.set("Josephine", 42);
    ```

33. What is the type of the constant `null`?

34. Suppose `aVariable` is a variable of a class type. Which of the following correctly tests to see whether `aVariable` contains `null`?

    ```
    aVariable.equals(null)
    aVariable == null
    ```

35. Is the following legal in Java? The class `ToyClass` is defined in Display 5.11.

    ```
    System.out.println(new ToyClass("Mr. Cellophane", 0));
    ```

TIP: Use Static Imports ★

You have already seen `import` statements, such as the following from Display 5.9:

```
import java.util.Scanner;
```

static import statement

There is another form of `import` statement which, while not essential, can be a convenience. These are called **static import statements** and are best explained with an example.

(continued)

It would be convenient to be able to write static method invocations in the following simple form:

```
toUpperCase(firstCharacter)
```

instead of having to write the following longer version (taken from Display 5.9):

```
Character.toUpperCase(firstCharacter)
```

If you add the following static `import` statement to the start of your program, you can then write the invocation of `toUpperCase` in the desired shorter way:

```
import static java.lang.Character.toUpperCase;
```

The class `Character` is in the Java package `java.lang`. Note that you need to give the package name as well as the class name, just as you did with ordinary `import` statements, such as the above `import` statement for the class `Scanner` in the `java.util` package.

The package `java.lang` is imported automatically. So you can, for example, use the method `Character.toUpperCase` without any `import` statement of any kind. But note that there is nothing special about the package `java.lang` when it comes to static `import` statements. If you want to use the abbreviated form `toUpperCase`, you must give a static `import` statement.

If you use the following form of the static `import` statement, then your code can use the name of any static method in the class `Character` without the preface of `Character` and a dot.

```
import static java.lang.Character.*;
```

For example, consider the program in Display 5.9. If you replace

```
import java.util.Scanner;
```

with either

```
import java.util.Scanner;
import static java.lang.Character.toUpperCase;
```

or

```
import java.util.Scanner;
import static java.lang.Character.*;
```

then you can change the statement

```
sentence = Character.toUpperCase(firstCharacter)
                        + sentence.substring(1);
```

One word of warning: This only works for static methods. This does not in any way apply to ordinary nonstatic methods.

to

```
sentence = toUpperCase(firstCharacter)
                        + sentence.substring(1);
```

extra code on CD

The program `StaticImportDemo.java` on the accompanying CD redoes the program in Display 5.9 using a static `import` statement in this way.

You can, of course, do this with `Character` replaced by any other class, and then you can use static methods in that class without the need to preface the method name with the class name and a dot.

static import of constants

You can use static `import` statements for constants as well as methods. If you want to use `PI` instead of `Math.PI` in the program in Display 5.7 just include one of the following `import` statements at the beginning of the program file:

```
import static java.lang.Math.PI;
```

or

```
import static java.lang.Math.*;
```

extra code on CD

The program `StaticImportDemo2.java` on the accompanying CD redoes the program in Display 5.7 using a static `import` statement in this way. ∎

5.3   Using and Misusing References

Loose lips sink ships.

Military slogan

Just as a military campaign requires constant vigilance to ensure that its plans are kept secret, so your programming requires constant vigilance to ensure that private instance variables remain truly private. As we will see, adding the `private` modifier before instance variable declarations is not always all that you need to do. There can be privacy leaks in a poorly designed class just as there can be privacy leaks in a military campaign.

The material in this section is important but more subtle and harder to digest than the material we have seen before now. If you want, you may postpone reading this section until you have had more practice defining and using classes. You do not need the material in this section before doing Section 5.4.

EXAMPLE: A Person Class

It is common to have instance variables of a class type. The class Person defined in Display 5.19 has two instance variables of type Date. So, the class Person has instance variables of a class type. (The class Date was defined in Chapter 4, Display 4.11. We have reproduced the relevant portions of the date class definition in Display 5.20.) In fact, all the instance variables for the class Person are of class types. An object of the class Person has the basic data about people that is found in such places as on tombstones and in author listings in library catalogues. It describes a person by giving the person's name, date of birth, and date of death. If the person is still alive, then the value null is used as the date of death. (So null is good.) A simple program illustrating the class Person is given in Display 5.21. We will discuss a few details about the class Person here, but most of the various methods in the class Person will be discussed as we cover the corresponding topic in the following subsections.

Normally, a class definition should include a no-argument constructor. However, there are cases where a no-argument constructor makes little sense. For example, the wrapper classes such as Integer and Double have no no-argument constructors, as we explained in the Pitfall subsection "A Wrapper Class Does Not Have a No-Argument Constructor," which appeared earlier in this chapter. The class Person also has no no-argument constructor for a reason. A person may have no date of death, but a person always has a date of birth. A no-argument constructor should initialize all instance variables, but there is no suitable value to initialize the instance variable born unless it is provided as an argument to the constructor. In particular, it makes no sense to initialize the instance variable born to null; that would indicate that the person was never born. It makes little sense to have a person who was never born, so it makes little sense to have a no-argument constructor for the class Person. Note that because we defined some constructors for the class Person but did not define a no-argument constructor, it follows that the class Person has no no-argument constructor.

Since we are assuming that an object of the class Person always has a birth date (which is not null), the following should always be true of an object of the class Person:

An object of the class Person has a date of birth (which is not null), and if the object has a date of death, then the date of death is equal to or later than the date of birth.

If you check the definition of the class Person, you will see that this statement is always true. It is true of every object created by a constructor, and all the other methods preserve the truth of this statement. In fact, the private method consistent was designed to provide a check for this property. A statement, such as the above, that is always true for every object of the class is called a **class invariant**.

Note that the definition of equals for the class Person includes an invocation of equals for the class String and an invocation of the method equals for the class Date. Java determines which equals method is being invoked from the type of its calling object. Because the instance variable name is of type String, the invocation name.equals(...) is an invocation of the method equals for the class String. Because the instance variable born is of type Date, the invocation born.equals(...) is an invocation of the method equals for the class Date.

Similarly, the definition of the method toString for the class Person includes invocations of the method toString for the class Date.

Display 5.19   **A Person Class** (part 1 of 5)

```
1    /**
2     Class for a person with a name and dates for birth and death.
3     Class invariant: A Person always has a date of birth, and if the Person
4     has a date of death, then the date of death is equal to or later than the
5     date of birth.
6    */
7    public class Person
8    {
9        private String name;
10       private Date born;
11       private Date died;//null indicates still alive.

12       public Person(String initialName, Date birthDate, Date deathDate)
13       {
14           if (consistent(birthDate, deathDate))
15           {
16               name = initialName;
17               born = new Date(birthDate);
18               if (deathDate == null)
19                   died = null;
20               else
21                   died = new Date(deathDate);
22           }
23           else
24           {
25               System.out.println("Inconsistent dates. Aborting.");
26               System.exit(0);
27           }
28       }

29       public Person(Person original)
30       {
31           if (original == null)
32           {
33               System.out.println("Fatal error.");
34               System.exit(0);
35           }

36           name = original.name;
37           born = new Date(original.born);

38           if (original.died == null)
39               died = null;
40           else
41               died = new Date(original.died);
42       }
```

The class **Date** *was defined in Display 4.11 and many of the details are repeated in Display 5.20.*

We will discuss **Date** *and the significance of these constructor invocations in the subsection entitled "Copy Constructors."*

Copy constructor

(continued)

Display 5.19 **A Person Class** (part 2 of 5)

```
43        public void set(String newName, Date birthDate, Date deathDate)
          <Definition of this method is Self Test Exercise 41.>

44        public String toString()
45        {
46            String diedString;
47            if (died == null)
48                diedString = ""; //Empty string
49            else
50                diedString = died.toString();
51            return (name + ", " + born + "-" + diedString);
52        }
53        public boolean equals(Person otherPerson)
54        {
55            if (otherPerson == null)
56                return false;
57            else
58                return (name.equals(otherPerson.name)
59                        && born.equals(otherPerson.born)
60                        && datesMatch(died, otherPerson.died) );
61        }
62        /**
63         To match date1 and date2 must either be the same date or both be null.
64        */
65        private static boolean datesMatch(Date date1, Date date2)
66        {
67            if (date1 == null)
68                return (date2 == null);
69            else if (date2 == null) //&& date1 != null
70                return false;
71            else // both dates are not null.
72                return(date1.equals(date2));
73        }

74        /**
75         Precondition: newDate is a consistent date of birth.
76         Postcondition: Date of birth of the calling object is newDate.
77        */
78        public void setBirthDate(Date newDate)
79        {
80            if (consistent(newDate, died))
81                born = new Date(newDate);
82            else
83            {
```

This is the toString method of the class Date.

This is equivalent to born.toString().

This is the equals method for the class String.

This is the equals method for the class Date.

Display 5.19   **A Person Class** (part 3 of 5)

```
84                      System.out.println("Inconsistent dates. Aborting.");
85                      System.exit(0);
86              }
87      }

88      /**
89       Precondition: newDate is a consistent date of death.
90       Postcondition: Date of death of the calling object is newDate.
91      */
92      public void setDeathDate(Date newDate)
93      {
94
95          if (!consistent(born, newDate))
96          {
97              System.out.println("Inconsistent dates. Aborting.");
98              System.exit(0);
99          }
100
101         if (newDate == null)
102             died = null;
103         else
104             died = new Date(newDate);
105     }
```

The date of death can be **null**. However, there is no corresponding code in **setBirthDate** because the method **consistent** ensures that the date of birth is never **null**.

```
106     public void setName(String newName)
107     {
108         name = newName;
109     }

110     /**
111      Precondition: The date of birth has been set, and changing the year
112      part of the date of birth will give a consistent date of birth.
113      Postcondition: The year of birth is (changed to) newYear.
114     */
115     public void setBirthYear(int newYear)
116     {
117         if (born == null) //Precondition is violated
118         {
119             System.out.println("Fatal Error. Aborting.");
120             System.exit(0);
121         }
122         born.setYear(newYear);
123         if (!consistent(born, died))
124         {
125             System.out.println("Inconsistent dates. Aborting.");
126              System.exit(0);
127         }
128     }
```

(continued)

Display 5.19 **A Person Class** (part 4 of 5)

```
129      /**
130       Precondition: The date of death has been set, and changing the year
131       part of the date of death will give a consistent date of death.
132       Postcondition: The year of death is (changed to) newYear.
133      */
134      public void setDeathYear(int newYear)
135      {
136          if (died == null) //Precondition is violated
137          {
138              System.out.println("Fatal Error. Aborting.");
139              System.exit(0);
140          }
141          died.setYear(newYear);
142          if (!consistent(born, died))
143          {
144              System.out.println("Inconsistent dates. Aborting.");
145              System.exit(0);
146          }
147      }

148      public String getName()
149      {
150          return name;
151      }

152      public Date getBirthDate()
153      {
154          return new Date(born);
155      }

156      public Date getDeathDate()
157      {
158          if (died == null)
159              return null;
160          else
161              return new Date(died);
162      }

163      /**
164       To be consistent, birthDate must not be null. If there is no date of
165       death (deathDate == null), that is consistent with any birthDate.
166       Otherwise, the birthDate must come before or be equal to the deathDate.
167      */
```

Display 5.19   **A Person Class** (part 5 of 5)

```
168        private static boolean consistent(Date birthDate, Date deathDate)
169        {
170            if (birthDate == null)
171                return false;
172            else if (deathDate == null)
173                return true;
174            else
175                return (birthDate.precedes(deathDate)
176                        || birthDate.equals(deathDate));
177        }
178  }
```

Class Invariant

A statement that is always true for every object of the class is called a **class invariant**. A class invariant can help to define a class in a consistent and organized way.

PITFALL: `null` Can Be an Argument to a Method

If a method has a parameter of a class type, then `null` can be used as the corresponding argument when the method is invoked. Sometimes using `null` as an argument can be the result of an error, but it can sometimes be an intentional argument. For example, the class `Person` (Display 5.19) uses `null` for a date of death to indicate that the person is still alive. So `null` is sometimes a perfectly normal argument for methods such as `consistent`. Method definitions should account for `null` as a possible argument and not assume the method always receives a true object to plug in for a class parameter.

Notice the definition of the method `equals` for the class `Person`. A test for equality has the form

```
object1.equals(object2)
```

The calling object `object1` must be a true object of the class `Person`; a calling object cannot be `null`. However, the argument `object2` can be either a true object or `null`. If the argument is `null`, then `equals` should return `false`, because a true object cannot reasonably be considered to be equal to `null`. In fact, the Java documentation specifies that when the argument to an `equals` method is `null`, the `equals` method should return `false`. Notice that our definition does return `false` when the argument is `null`. ∎

Display 5.20 **The Class Date** (Partial Definition) (part 1 of 2)

```
1    public class Date
2    {
3        private String month;
4        private int day;
5        private int year; //a four digit number.

6        public Date(String monthString, int day, int year)
7        {
8            setDate(monthString, day, year);
9        }

10       public Date(Date aDate)
11       {
12           if (aDate == null)//Not a real date.
13           {
14               System.out.println("Fatal Error.");
15               System.exit(0);
16           }

17           month = aDate.month;
18           day = aDate.day;
19           year = aDate.year;
20       }

21       public void setDate(String monthString, int day, int year)
22       {
23           if (dateOK(monthString, day, year))
24           {
25               this.month = monthString;
26               this.day = day;
27               this.year = year;
28           }
29           else
30           {
31               System.out.println("Fatal Error");
32               System.exit(0);
33           }
34       }
35       public void setYear(int year)
36       {
37           if ( (year < 1000) || (year > 9999) )
38           {
```

This is not a complete definition of the class Date. The complete definition of the class Date is in Display 4.11, but this has the details that are important to what we are discussing in this chapter.

Copy constructor

The method dateOK checks that the date is a legitimate date, such as not having more than 31 days.

Display 5.20   **The Class Date** (Partial Definition) (part 2 of 2)

```
39                System.out.println("Fatal Error");
40                System.exit(0);
41            }
42        else
43            this.year = year;
44    }
45
46    public String toString()
47            ...
48    public boolean equals(Date otherDate)
49            ....

       /**
50      Returns true if the calling object date is before otherDate (in time).
51      */
52    public boolean precedes(Date otherDate)
53            ...
54    private boolean dateOK(String monthString, int dayInt, int yearInt)
55            ...
56    }
```

The complete definition of equals *is given in the answer to Self-Test Exercise 37, and is a better version than the one given in Chapter 4.*

These methods have the obvious meanings. If you need to see a full definition, see Display 4.11 in Chapter 4 and Self-Test Exercise 37 in this chapter.

Self-Test Exercises

36. What is the difference between the following two pieces of code? The first piece appears in Display 5.21.

```
Person adams =
        new Person("John Adams",
            new Date("February", 15, 1947), null);
//Second piece is below:

Date theDate = new Date("February", 15, 1947);
Person adams = new Person("John Adams", theDate, null);
```

37. When we defined the class Date in Chapter 4 (Display 4.11), we had not yet discussed null. So, the definition of equals given there did not account for the possibility that the argument could be null. Rewrite the definition of equals for the class Date to account for the possibility that the argument might be null.

Display 5.21 Demonstrating the Class **Person**

```
1    public class PersonDemo
2    {
3        public static void main(String[] args)
4        {
5            Person bach =
6                new Person("Johann Sebastian Bach",
7                    new Date("March", 21, 1685), new Date("July", 28, 1750));
8            Person stravinsky =
9                new Person("Igor Stravinsky",
10                   new Date("June", 17, 1882), new Date("April", 6, 1971));
11           Person adams =
12               new Person("John Adams",
13                   new Date("February", 15, 1947), null);

14           System.out.println("A Short List of Composers:");
15           System.out.println(bach);
16           System.out.println(stravinsky);
17           System.out.println(adams);

18           Person bachTwin = new Person(bach);
19           System.out.println("Comparing bach and bachTwin:");
20           if (bachTwin == bach)
21               System.out.println("Same reference for both.");
22           else
23               System.out.println("Distinct copies.");

24           if (bachTwin.equals(bach))
25               System.out.println("Same data.");
26           else
27               System.out.println("Not same data.");
28       }
29   }
```

Sample Dialogue

```
A Short List of Composers:
Johann Sebastian Bach, March 21, 1685-July 28, 1750
Igor Stravinsky, June 17, 1882-April 6, 1971
John Adams, February 15, 1947-
Comparing bach and bachTwin:
Distinct copies.
Same data.
```

Copy Constructors

copy
constructor

A **copy constructor** is a constructor with a single argument of the same type as the class. The copy constructor should create an object that is a separate, independent object but with the instance variables set so that it is an exact copy of the argument object.

For example, Display 5.20 reproduces the copy constructor for the class Date defined in Display 4.11. The copy constructor, or any other constructor, creates a new object of the class Date. That part happens automatically and is not shown in the code for the copy constructor. The code for the copy constructor then goes on to set the instance variables to the values equal to those of its one parameter, aDate. But the new date created is a separate object even though it represents the same date. Consider the following code:

```
Date date1 = new Date("January", 1, 2006);
Date date2 = new Date(date1);
```

After this code is executed, both date1 and date2 represent the date January 1, 2006, but they are two different objects. So, if we change one of these objects, it will not change the other. For example, consider

```
date2.setDate("July", 4, 1776);
System.out.println(date1);
```

The output produced is

```
January 1, 2006
```

When we changed date2, we did not change date1. This may not be a difficult or even subtle point, but it is critically important to much of what we discuss in this section of the chapter. (See Self-Test Exercise 39 in this chapter to see the copy constructor contrasted with the assignment operator.)

Now let's consider the copy constructor for the class Person (Display 5.19), which is a bit more complicated. It is reproduced in what follows:

```
public Person(Person original)
{
    if (original == null)
    {
        System.out.println("Fatal error.");
        System.exit(0);
    }
    name = original.name;
    born = new Date(original.born);
    if (original.died == null)
        died = null;
    else
        died = new Date(original.died);
}
```

We want the object created to be an independent copy of `original`. That would not happen if we had used the following instead:

```
public Person(Person original) //Unsafe
{
    if (original == null)
    {
        System.out.println("Fatal error.");
        System.exit(0);
    }
    name = original.name;
    born = original.born; //Not good.
    died = original.died; //Not good.
}
```

Although this alternate definition looks innocent enough and may work fine in many situations, it does have serious problems.

Assume we had used the unsafe version of the copy constructor instead of the one in Display 5.19. The "Not good." code simply copies references from `original.born` and `original.died` to the corresponding arguments of the object being created by the constructor. So, the object created is not an independent copy of the `original` object. For example, consider the code

```
Person original =
        new Person("Natalie Dressed", new Date("April", 1, 1984), null);
Person copy = new Person(original);
copy.setBirthYear(1800);
System.out.println(original);
```

The output would be

```
Natalie Dressed, April 1, 1800-
```

When we changed the birth year in the object `copy`, we also changed the birth year in the object `original`. This is because we are using our unsafe version of the copy constructor. Both `original.born` and `copy.born` contain the same reference to the same `Date` object.

All this assumed that, contrary to fact, we have used the unsafe version of the copy constructor. Fortunately, we used a safer version of the copy constructor that sets the `born` instance variables as follows:

```
born = new Date(original.born);
```

which is equivalent to

```
this.born = new Date(original.born);
```

This version, which we did use, makes the instance variable `this.born` an independent `Date` object that represents the same date as `original.born`. So if you change a date in the `Person` object created by the copy constructor, you will not change that date in the `original` `Person` object.

Note that if a class, such as `Person`, has instance variables of a class type, such as the instance variables `born` and `died`, then to define a correct copy constructor for the class `Person`, you must already have copy constructors for the class `Date` of the instance variables. The easiest way to ensure this for all your classes is to always include a copy constructor in every class you define.

Copy Constructor

A **copy constructor** is a constructor with one parameter of the same type as the class. A copy constructor should be designed so the object it creates is intuitively an exact copy of its parameter, but a completely independent copy. See Displays 5.19 and 5.20 for examples of copy constructors.

---

clone
The Java documentation says to use a method named `clone` instead of a copy constructor, and, as you will see later in this book, there are situations where the copy constructor will not work as desired and you need the `clone` method. However, we do not yet have enough background to discuss the `clone` method. The `clone` method is discussed later in this book (Chapters 8 and 13). Despite the Java documentation, many excellent programmers prefer to sometimes use copy constructors. In this book, we will use both copy constructors and the `clone` method.

 PITFALL: Privacy Leaks

leaking accessor methods
Consider the accessor method `getBirthDate` for the class `Person` (Display 5.19), which we reproduce in what follows:

```java
public Date getBirthDate()
{
    return new Date(born);
}
```

Do not make the mistake of defining the accessor method as follows:

```java
public Date getBirthDate() //Unsafe
{
    return born; //Not good
}
```

(continued)

PITFALL: (continued)

Assume we had used the unsafe version of getBirthDate instead of the one in Display 5.19. It would then be possible for a program that uses the class Person to change the private instance variable born to any date whatsoever and bypass the checks in constructor and mutator methods of the class Person. For example, consider the following code, which might appear in some program that uses the class Person:

```
Person citizen = new Person(
  "Joe Citizen", new Date("January", 1, 1900), new Date("January", 1,
      1990));
Date dateName = citizen.getBirthDate();

dateName.setDate("April", 1, 3000);
```

privacy leak

This code changes the date of birth so it is after the date of death (an impossibility in the universe as we know it). This citizen was not born until after he or she died! This sort of situation is known as a **privacy leak**, because it allows a programmer to circumvent the private modifier before an instance variable such as born and change the private instance variable to anything whatsoever.

The following code would be illegal in our program:

```
citizen.born.setDate("April", 1, 3000); //Illegal
```

This is illegal because born is a private instance variable. However, with the unsafe version of getBirthDate (and we are now assuming that we did use the unsafe version), the variable dateName contains the same reference as citizen.born and so the following is legal and equivalent to the illegal statement:

```
dateName.setDate("April", 1, 3000);//Legal and equivalent to illegal
    one.
```

It is as if you have a friend named Robert who is also known as Bob. Some bully wants to beat up Robert, so you say "You cannot beat up Robert." The bully says "OK, I will not beat up Robert, but I will beat up Bob." Bob and Robert are two names for the same person. So, if you protect Robert but do not protect Bob, you have really accomplished nothing.

All this assumes that, contrary to fact, we have used the unsafe version of getBirthDate, which simply returns the reference in the private instance variable born. Fortunately, we used a safer version of getBirthDate, which has the following return statement:

```
return new Date(born);
```

This `return` statement does not return the reference in the private instance variable `born`. Instead, it uses the copy constructor to return a reference to a new object that is an exact copy of the object named by `born`. If the copy is changed, that has no effect on the date whose reference is in the instance variable `born`. Thus, a privacy leak is avoided.

leaking mutator methods

Note that returning a reference is not the only possible source of privacy leaks. A privacy leak can also arise from an incorrectly defined constructor or mutator method. Notice the definition for the method `setBirthDate` in Display 5.19 and reproduced below:

```
public void setBirthDate(Date newDate)
{
    if (consistent(newDate, died))
        born = new Date(newDate);
    else
    {
        System.out.println("Inconsistent dates. Aborting.");
        System.exit(0);
    }
}
```

Note that the instance variable `born` is set to a copy of the parameter `newDate`. Suppose that instead of

```
born = new Date(newDate);
```

we had simply used

```
born = newDate;
```

And suppose we use the following code in some program:

```
Person personObject = new Person(
    "Josephine", new Date("January", 1, 2000), null);
Date dateName = new Date("February", 2, 2002);
personObject.setBirthDate(dateName);
```

where `personObject` names an object of the class `Person`. The following will change the year part of the `Date` object named by the `born` instance variable of the object `personObject` and will do so without going through the checks in the mutator methods for `Person`:

```
dateName.setYear(1000);
```

(continued)

PITFALL: (continued)

Because `dateName` contains the same reference as the private instance variable `born` of the object `personObject`, changing the year part of `dateName` changes the year part of the private instance variable `born` of `personObject`. Not only does this bypass the consistency checks in the mutator method `setBirthDate`, but it also is a likely source of an inadvertent change to the `born` instance variable.

If we define `setBirthDate` as we did in Display 5.19 and as shown below, this problem does not happen. (If you do not see this, go through the code step by step and trace what happens.)

```
public void setBirthDate(Date newDate)
{
    if (consistent(newDate, died))
        born = new Date(newDate);
    . . .
```

clone

One final word of warning: Using copy constructors as we have been doing is not the officially sanctioned way to make copies of an object in Java. The officially sanctioned way to create copies of an object is to define a method named `clone`. We will discuss `clone` methods in Chapters 8 and 13. In Chapter 8 we show you that, in some situations, there are advantages to using a `clone` method instead of a copy constructor. In Chapter 13 we describe the officially sanctioned way to define the `clone` method. For what we will be doing until then, a copy constructor will be a very adequate way of creating copies of an object. ■

Self-Test Exercises

38. What is a copy constructor?

39. What output is produced by the following code?

```
Date date1 = new Date("January", 1, 2006);
Date date2;
date2 = date1;
date2.setDate("July", 4, 1776);
System.out.println(date1);
```

What output is produced by the following code? Only the third line is different from the previous case.

```
Date date1 = new Date("January", 1, 2006);
Date date2;
date2 = new Date(date1);
date2.setDate("July", 4, 1776);
System.out.println(date1);
```

---

40. What output is produced by the following code?

```
Person original =
            new Person("Natalie Dressed",
                             new Date("April", 1, 1984), null);
Person copy = new Person(original);
copy.setBirthDate( new Date("April", 1, 1800));
System.out.println(original)
```

Mutable and Immutable Classes

Contrast the accessor methods getName and getBirthDate of the class Person (Display 5.19). We reproduce the two methods in what follows:

```
public String getName()
{
    return name;
}
```

```
public Date getBirthDate()
{
    return new Date(born);
}
```

Notice that the method getBirthDate does not simply return the reference in the instance variable born, but instead uses the copy constructor to return a reference to a copy of the birth date object. We have already explained why we do this. If we return the reference in the instance variable born, then we can place this reference in a variable of type Date, and that variable could serve as another name for the private instance variable born, which would allow us to violate the privacy of the instance variable born by changing it using a mutator method of the class Date. This is exactly what we discussed in the previous subsection. So why didn't we do something similar in the method getName?

The method getName simply returns the reference in the private instance variable name. So, if we do the following in a program, then the variable nameAlias will be another name for the String object of the private instance variable name:

```
Person citizen = new Person(
"Joe Citizen", new Date("January", 1, 1900), new Date("January", 1, 1990));
String nameAlias = citizen.getName();
```

It looks as though we could use a mutator method from the class `String` to change the name referenced by `nameAlias` and so violate the privacy of the instance variable `name`. Is something wrong? Do we have to rewrite the method `getName` to use the copy constructor for the class `String`? No, everything is fine. We cannot use a mutator method with `nameAlias` because the class `String` has no mutator methods! The class `String` contains no methods that change any of the data in a `String` object.

At first, it may seem as though you can change the data in an object of the class `String`. What about the string processing we have seen, such as the following?

```
String greeting = "Hello";
greeting = greeting + " friend.";
```

Have we not changed the data in the `String` object from `"Hello"` to `"Hello friend."`? No, we have not. The expression `greeting + " friend."` does not change the object `"Hello"`; it creates a new object, so the assignment statement

```
greeting = greeting + " friend.";
```

replaces the reference to `"Hello"` with a reference to the different `String` object `"Hello friend."`. The object `"Hello"` is unchanged. To see that this is true, consider the following code:

```
String greeting = "Hello";
String helloVariable = greeting;
greeting = greeting + " friend.";
System.out.println(helloVariable);
```

This produces the output `"Hello"`. If the object `"Hello"` had been changed, the output would have been `"Hello friend."`

immutable

A class that contains no methods (other than constructors) that change any of the data in an object of the class is called an **immutable class**, and objects of the class are called **immutable objects**. The class `String` is an immutable class. It is perfectly safe to return a reference to an immutable object, because the object cannot be changed in any undesirable way; in fact, it cannot be changed in any way whatsoever.

mutable

A class that contains public mutator methods or other public methods, such as input methods, that can change the data in an object of the class is called a **mutable class**, and objects of the class are called **mutable objects**. The class `Date` is an example of a mutable class; many, perhaps most, of the classes you define will be mutable classes. As we noted in the subsection entitled "Privacy Leaks" (but using other words): You should never write a method that returns a mutable object, but should instead use a copy constructor (or other means) to return a reference to a completely independent copy of the mutable object.

TIP: Deep Copy versus Shallow Copy

In the previous two subsections, we contrasted the following two ways of defining the method `getBirthDate` (Display 5.19):

```
public Date getBirthDate()
{
    return new Date(born);
}
public Date getBirthDate() //Unsafe
{
    return born; //Not good
}
```

As we noted, the first definition is the better one (and the one used in Display 5.19). The first definition returns what is known as a *deep copy* of the object born. The second definition returns what is known as a *shallow copy* of the object born.

deep copy

A **deep copy** of an object is a copy that, with one exception, has no references in common with the original. The one exception is that references to immutable objects are allowed to be shared (because immutable objects cannot change in any way and so cannot be changed in any undesirable way). For example, the first definition of `getBirthDate` returns a deep copy of the date stored by the instance variable born. So, if you change the object returned by `getBirthDate`, that does not change the `Date` object named by the instance variable born. The reason is that we defined the copy constructor for the class `Date` to create a deep copy (Display 5.20). Normally, copy constructors and accessor methods should return a deep copy.

shallow copy

Any copy that is not a deep copy is called a **shallow copy**. For example, the second definition of `getBirthDate` returns a shallow copy of the date stored by the instance variable born.

We will have more to say about deep and shallow copies in later chapters. ∎

Never Return a Reference to a Mutable Private Object

A class that contains mutator methods or other methods, such as input methods, that can change the data in an object of the class is called a *mutable class*, and objects of the class are called *mutable objects*. When defining accessor methods (or almost any methods), your method should not return a reference to a mutable object. Instead, use a copy constructor (or other means) to return a reference to a completely independent copy of the mutable object.

TIP: Assume Your Coworkers Are Malicious

Our discussion of privacy leaks in the previous subsections was concerned with the effect of somebody trying to defeat the privacy of an instance variable. You might object that your coworkers are nice people and would not knowingly sabotage your software. That is probably true, and we do not mean to accuse your coworkers of malicious intent. However, the same action that can be performed intentionally by a malicious enemy can also be performed inadvertently by your friends or even by you yourself. The best way to guard against such honest mistakes is to pretend that you are defending against a malicious enemy. ■

Self-Test Exercises

41. Complete the definition of the method set for the class Person (Display 5.19).

42. Classify each of the following classes as either mutable or immutable: Date (Display 4.11), Person (Display 5.19), and String.

43. Normally, it is dangerous to return a reference to a private instance variable of a class type, but it is OK if the class type is String. What's special about the class String that makes this OK?

5.4 Packages and javadoc

...he furnished me,

From mine own library with volumes that

I prize above my dukedom.

WILLIAM SHAKESPEARE, *The Tempest*

In this section, we cover packages, which are Java libraries, and then cover the javadoc program, which automatically extracts documentation from packages and classes. Although these are important topics, they are not used in the rest of this book. You can cover this section at any time you wish; you need not cover this section before going on in this book.

This section does not use any of the material in Section 5.3, and so can be covered before Section 5.3.

This section assumes that you know about directories (which are called folders in some operating systems), that you know about path names for directories (folders), and that you know about PATH (environment) variables. These are not Java topics. They are part of your operating system, and the details depend on your particular operating system. If you can find out how to set the PATH variable on your operating system, you will know enough about these topics to understand this section.

Packages and `import` Statements

package

A **package** is Java's way of forming a library of classes. You can make a package from a group of classes and then use the package of classes in any other class or program you write without the need to move the classes to the directory (folder) in which you are working. All you need to do is include an `import` **statement** that names the package. We have already used `import` statements with some predefined standard Java packages. For example, the following, which we have used before, makes available the classes Scanner of the package `java.util`:

import statement

```
import java.util.Scanner;
```

You can make all the classes in the package available by using the following instead:

```
import java.util.*;
```

There is no overhead cost for importing the entire package as opposed to just a few classes.

The `import` statements should be at the beginning of the file. Only blank lines, comments, and `package` statements may precede the list of `import` statements. We discuss `package` statements next.

`import` Statement

You can use a class from a package in any program or class definition by placing an `import` statement that names the package and the class from the package at the start of the file containing the program (or class definition). The program (or class definition) need not be in the same directory as the classes in the package.

SYNTAX

```
import Package_Name.Class_Name;
```

EXAMPLE

```
import java.util.Scanner;
```

You can import all the classes in a package by using an asterisk in place of the class's name.

SYNTAX

```
import Package_Name.*;
```

EXAMPLE

```
import java.util.*;
```

To make a package, you group all the classes together into a single directory (folder) and add the following package statement to beginning of each class file:

```
package Package_Name;
```

This `package` statement should be at the beginning of the file. Only blank lines and comments may precede the `package` statement. If there are both `import` statements and `package` statements, any `package` statements come before the `import` statements. Aside from the addition of the `package` statement, class files are just as we have already described them. (It is technically only the `.class` files that must be in the package directory.)

The Package `java.lang`

The package `java.lang` contains classes that are fundamental to Java programming. These classes are so basic that the package is always imported automatically. Any class in `java.lang` does not need an `import` statement to make it available to your code. For example, the classes `Math` and `String` and the wrapper classes introduced earlier in this chapter are all in the package `java.lang`.

Package

A **package** is a collection of classes that have been grouped together into a directory and given a package name. The classes in the package are each placed in a separate file, and the file is given the same name as the class, just as we have been doing all along. Each file in the package must have the following at the beginning of the file. Only comments and blank lines may precede this package statement.

SYNTAX

```
package Package_Name;
```

EXAMPLES

```
package utilities.numericstuff;
package java.util;
```

Package Names and Directories

A package name is not an arbitrary identifier. It is a form of path name to the directory containing the classes in the package.

In order to find the directory for a package, Java needs two things: the name of the package and the value of your *CLASSPATH variable.*

CLASSPATH variable

You should already be familiar with the environment variable of your operating system that is known as the *PATH variable.* The **CLASSPATH variable** is a similar environment variable used to help locate Java packages. The value of your CLASSPATH variable tells Java where to begin its search for a package. The CLASSPATH variable is not a Java variable. It is an environment variable that is part of your operating system. The value of your CLASSPATH variable is a list of directories. The exact syntax for this list varies from one operating system to another, but it should be the same syntax as that used for the (ordinary) PATH variable. When Java is looking for a package, it begins its search in the directories listed in the CLASSPATH variable.

The name of a package specifies the relative path name for the directory that contains the package classes. It is a relative path name because it assumes that you start in one of the directories listed in the value of your CLASSPATH variable. For example, suppose the following is a directory listed in your CLASSPATH variable (your operating system might use / instead of \):

```
\libraries\newlibraries
```

And suppose your package classes are in the directory

```
\libraries\newlibraries\utilities\numericstuff
```

In this case, the package *should* be named

```
utilities.numericstuff
```

and all the classes in the file must start with the package statement

```
package utilities.numericstuff;
```

The dot in the package name means essentially the same thing as the \ or /, whichever symbol your operating system uses for directory paths. The package name tells you (and Java) what subdirectories to go through to find the package classes, starting from a directory on the class path. This is depicted in Display 5.22. (If there happen to be two directories in the CLASSPATH variable that can be used, then of all the ones that can be used, Java always uses the first one listed in the CLASSPATH variable.)

Any class that uses the class in this utilities.numericstuff package must contain either the import statement

```
import utilities.numericstuff.*;
```

or an import statement for each class in the package that is used.

The way you set the value of your CLASSPATH variable depends on your operating system, but we can give you some suggestions that may work. The CLASSPATH variable is usually spelled as one word with all uppercase letters, as in CLASSPATH. You will probably have a plain old PATH variable that tells the operating system where to find the code for commands such as javac and other commands that you can give as single-line commands. If you can find out how to set the PATH variable, you should be able to set the CLASSPATH variable in the same way.

Display 5.22 A Package Name

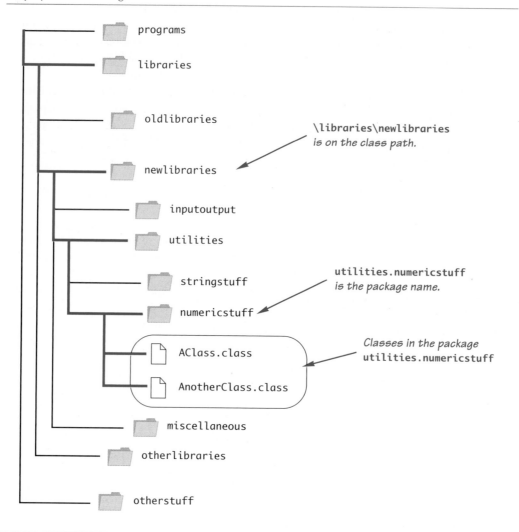

If you are on a UNIX system, you are likely to be able to set the CLASSPATH with some command similar to the following :

```
set CLASSPATH=/libraries/newlibraries;/otherstuff/specialjava;.
export CLASSPATH
```

If this does not work, you might try omitting the word set or replacing set with setenv. You might also try placing the list of directories in quotes. There are many versions of UNIX, all with their own minor variations. You may need to consult a local expert or check the documentation for your operating system.

If you are using a Windows machine, you can set the CLASSPATH variable by setting or creating an environment variable named CLASSPATH using the Control Panel.

In this book, we are assuming that class path directories are separated by a semicolon. That is common, but some operating systems use some other separator, such as a colon. Check your documentation if a semicolon does not work as a separator.

Package Names and the CLASSPATH Variable

A package name must be a path name for the directory that contains the classes in the package, but the package name uses dots in place of \ or / (whichever your operating system uses). When naming the package, you use a relative path name that starts from any directory listed in the value of the CLASSPATH (environment) variable.

EXAMPLES
```
utilities.numericstuff
java.util
```

 PITFALL: Subdirectories Are Not Automatically Imported

Suppose you have two packages, `utilities.numericstuff` and `utilities.numericstuff.statistical`. In this case, you know that `utilities.numericstuff.statistical` is in a subdirectory (subfolder) of the directory (folder) containing `utilities.numericstuff`. This leads some programmers to assume that the following `import` statement imports both packages:

```
import utilities.numericstuff.*;
```

This is not true. When you import an entire package, you do not import subdirectory packages.

To import all classes in both of these packages, you need

```
import utilities.numericstuff.*;
```

```
import utilities.numericstuff.statistical.*;
```                                                                          ■

The Default Package

default package
All the classes in your current directory (that do not belong to some other package) belong to an unnamed package called the **default package**. As long as the current directory is on your CLASSPATH, all the classes in the default package are automatically available to your code. This is why we have always assumed that all the classes we defined are in the same directory. That way, we need not clutter our discussion with concern about `import` statements.

PITFALL: Not Including the Current Directory in Your Class Path

current directory

Your CLASSPATH variable allows you to list more than one directory. Most operating systems use the dot to indicate the current directory. The **current directory** is not any one specific directory; it is the directory in which you are currently "located." If you do not know what your current directory is, then it is probably the directory that contains the class you are writing. For example, the following value for a CLASSPATH variable lists two ordinary directories and the current directory:

```
\libraries\newlibraries;\otherstuff\specialjava;.
```

Whenever you set or change the CLASSPATH variable, be sure to include the current directory as one of the alternatives. With the above displayed CLASSPATH value, if the package is not found by starting in either of the previous two directories, Java will look in the subdirectories of the current directory. If you want Java to check the current directory before the other directories on the CLASSPATH variable, list the current directory (the dot) first, as follows:

```
.;\libraries\newlibraries;\otherstuff\specialjava
```

When looking for a package, Java tries the directories in the class path in order and uses the first one that works.

Omitting the current directory from the CLASSPATH variable can interfere with running Java programs, regardless of whether or not the programs use packages. If the current directory is omitted, then Java may not even be able to find the .class file for the program itself, so you may not be able to run any programs at all. Thus, if you do set the CLASSPATH variable, it is critical that you include the current directory in the CLASSPATH. No such problems will occur if you have not set the CLASSPATH variable at all; it arises only if you decide to set the CLASSPATH variable.

If you are having problems setting the CLASSPATH variable, one interim solution is to delete the CLASSPATH variable completely and to keep all the class files for one program in the same directory. This will allow you to still do some work while you seek advice on setting the CLASSPATH variable. ∎

Specifying a Class Path When You Compile ★

You can specify a class path when you compile a class. To do so, add –classpath followed by the class path as illustrated below:

```
javac –classpath .;C:\libraries\nemeric;C:\otherstuff YourClass.java
```

This will compile YourClass.java, overriding any CLASSPATH setting, and use the class path given after –classpath. Note that the directories are separated by semicolons. If you want classes in the current directory to be available to your class, then be sure the class path includes the current directory, which is indicated by a dot.

When you run the class compiled as just shown, you should again use the −classpath option as indicated below:

```
java −classpath .;C:\libraries\nemeric;C:\otherstuff YourClass
```

It is important to include the current directory on the class path when you run the program. If your program is in the default package, it will not be found unless you include the current directory. It is best to get in the habit of always including the current directory in all class paths.

Because the class path specified in compiling and running your classes is input to a program (javac or java) that is part of the Java environment and is not a command to the operating system, you can use either / or \ in the class path, no matter which of these two your operating system uses.

Name Clashes ★

name clash

In addition to being a way of organizing libraries, packages also provide a way to deal with *name clashes*. A **name clash** is a situation in which two classes have the same name. If different programmers writing different packages have used the same name for a class, the ambiguity can be resolved by using the package name.

Suppose a package named sallyspack contains a class called HighClass, and another package named joespack also contains a class named HighClass. You can use both classes named HighClass in the same program by using the more complete names sallyspack.HighClass and joespack.HighClass. For example:

```
sallyspack.HighClass object1 = new sallyspack.HighClass();
joespack.HighClass object2 = new joespack.HighClass();
```

fully
qualified
class name

These names that include the package name, such as sallyspack.HighClass and joespack.HighClass, are called **fully qualified class names**.

If you use fully qualified class names, you do not need to import the class, since this longer class name includes the package name.

Self-Test Exercises

44. Suppose you want to use the class CoolClass in the package mypackages.library1 in a program you write. What do you need to do to make this class available to your program? What do you need to do to make all the classes in the package available to your program?

45. What do you need to do to make a class a member of the package named mypackages.library1?

46. Can a package have any name you want, or are there restrictions on what you can use for a package name? Explain any restrictions.

Introduction to javadoc ★

The principles of encapsulation using information hiding say that you should separate the interface of a class (the instructions on how to use the class) from the implementation (the detailed code that tells the computer how the class does its work). In some other programming languages, such as C⁺⁺, you normally define a class in two files. One file contains something like the interface or API that tells a programmer all that he or she needs to know to use the class. The other file contains the implementation details that are needed for the class code to run. This system is an obvious way to separate interface from implementation, but it is not what Java does.

Java does not divide a class definition into two files. Instead, Java has the interface and implementation of a class mixed together into a single file. If this were the end of the story, Java would not do a good job of encapsulation using information hiding. However, Java has a very good way of separating the interface from the implementation of a class. Java comes with a program named javadoc that automatically extracts the interface from a class definition. If your class definition is correctly commented, a programmer using your class need only look at this API (documentation) produced by javadoc. The documentation produced by javadoc is identical in format to the documentation for the standard Java library classes.

javadoc

The result of running javadoc on a class is to produce an HTML file with the API (interface) documentation for the class. HTML is the basic language used to produce documents to view with a Web browser, so the documentation produced by javadoc is viewed on a Web browser. A brief introduction to HTML is given in Chapter 18. However, you need not know any HTML to run javadoc or to read the documentation it produces.

javadoc can be used to obtain documentation for a single class. However, it is primarily intended to obtain documentation for an entire package.

We will first discuss how you should comment your classes so that you can get the most value out of javadoc. We will then describe how you run the javadoc program.

Commenting Classes for javadoc ★

To get a more useful javadoc document, you must write your comments in a particular way. All the classes in this book have been commented for use with javadoc. However, to save space, the comments in this book are briefer than what would be ideal for javadoc.

The javadoc program extracts the heading for your class (or classes) as well as the headings for all public methods, public instance variables, public static variables, and certain comments. No method bodies and no private items are extracted when javadoc is run in the normal default mode.

For javadoc (in default mode) to extract a comment, the comment must satisfy two conditions:

1. The comment must *immediately precede* a public class definition, a public method definition, or other public item.

2. The comment must be a block comment (that is, the /* and */ style of comment), and the opening /* must contain an extra *. So the comment must be marked by /** at the beginning and */ at the end.

Unless you explicitly set an extra option to javadoc, line comments (that is, // style comments) are not extracted, and comments preceding any private items also are not extracted.

The comment that precedes a public method definition can include any general information you wish it to. There is also special syntax for inserting descriptions of parameters, any value returned, and any exceptions that might be thrown. We have not yet discussed exceptions. That is done in Chapter 9, but we include mention of them here so this section will serve as a more complete reference on javadoc. You need not worry about exceptions or the details about "throws" discussed here until you reach Chapter 9.

@ tag   The special information about parameters and so forth are preceded by the @ symbol and are called **@ tags**. Below is an example of a method comment for use with javadoc:

```
/**
 Tests for equality of two objects of type Person. To be equal the two
 objects must have the same name, same birth date, and same death date.

 @param otherPerson The person being compared to the calling object.
 @return Returns true if the calling object equals otherPerson.
*/
public boolean equals(Person otherPerson)
```

(The method equals is from the class Person defined in Display 5.19. If you need more context, look at that display.)

Note that the @ tags all come after any general comment and that each @ tag is on a line by itself. The following are some of the @ tags allowed:

@param *Parameter_Name Parameter_Description*

@return *Description_Of_Value_Returned*

@throws *Exception_Type Explanation*

@deprecated

@see *Package_Name.Class_Name*

@author *Author*

@version *Version_Information*

The @ tags should appear in the above order, first @param, then @return, then @throws, and so forth. If there are multiple parameters, they should each have their own @param and appear on a separate line. The parameters and their @param description should be listed in their left-to-right order in the parameter list. If there are multiple authors, they should each have their own @author and appear on a separate line. The author and version information is not extracted unless suitable option flags have been set, as described in the next subsection.

deprecated

If @deprecated is included in a method comment, then the documentation notes that the method is *deprecated.* A **deprecated** method is one that is being phased out. To allow for backward compatibility, the method still works, but it should not be used in new code.

If an @ tag is included for an item, javadoc extracts the explanation for that item and includes it in the documentation. You should always include a more or less complete set of @ tags in the comment for each of your methods. In this book, we omit the @ tags to save space, but we encourage you to always include them. The comments that are not part of an @ tag appear as a general comment for the method, along with the method heading.

You can also insert HTML commands in your comments so that you gain more control over javadoc, but that is not necessary and may not even be desirable. HTML commands can clutter the comments, making them harder to read when you look at the source code.

Running javadoc ★

To run javadoc on a package, all you need to do is give the following command:

```
javadoc –d Documentation_Directory Package_Name
```

It would be normal to run this command from the directory containing the classes in the package, but it can be run from any directory, provided you have correctly set the CLASSPATH environment variable. The *Documentation_Directory* is the name of the directory in which you want javadoc to place the HTML documents it produces. For example, the following might be used to obtain documentation on the package mylibraries.numericstuff:

```
javadoc –d documentation/mypackages mylibraries.numericstuff
```

The HTML documents produced will be in the subdirectory documentation/mypackages of where this command is run. If you prefer, you may use a complete path name in place of the relative path name documentation/mypackages. If you omit the –d and *Documentation_Directory*, javadoc will create suitable directories for the documentation.

You can link to standard Java documents so that your HTML documents include live links to standard classes and methods. The syntax is as follows:

```
javadoc –link Link_To_Standard_Docs –d Documentation_Directory
Package_Name
```

Link_To_Standard_Docs is either a path to a local version of the Java documentation or the URL of the Sun Web site with standard Java documentation. As of this writing, that URL is

```
http://java.sun.com/j2se/1.5/docs/api/
```

You need not run `javadoc` on an entire package. You can run `javadoc` on a single class file. For example, the following should be run from the directory containing `Date.java` and will produce documentation for the class `Date`:

```
javadoc Date.java
```

You can run `javadoc` on all classes in a directory with

```
javadoc *.java
```

You can add the `-d` and/or `-link` options to any of these commands. For example:

```
javadoc -link http://java.sun.com/j2se/1.5/docs/api/ -d mydocs *.java
```

These and other options for `javadoc` are summarized in Display 5.23.

When running `javadoc`, you typically get more directories and many more HTML files than you might expect. To get a better understanding of `javadoc`, you should try running `javadoc` in various settings and observe the files it produces.

Display 5.23   Options for **java.doc**

`-link` *Link_To_Other_Docs*	Provides a link to another set of documentation. Normally, this is used with either a path name to a local version of the Java documentation or the URL of the Sun Web site with standard Java documentation.
`-d` *Documentation_Directory*	Specifies a directory to hold the documentation generated. *Documentation_Directory* may be a relative or absolute path name.
`-author`	Includes author information (from **@author** tags). This information is omitted unless this option is set.
`-version`	Includes version information (from **@version** tags). This information is omitted unless this option is set.
`-classpath` *List_of_Directories*	Overrides the CLASSPATH environment variable and makes *List_of_Directories* the CLASSPATH for the execution of this invocation of **javadoc**. Does not permanently change the CLASSPATH variable.
`-private`	Includes private members as well as public members in the documentation.

Self-Test Exercises

47. When run in default mode, does javadoc ever extract the body of a method definition? When run in default mode, does javadoc ever extract anything marked private in a class definition?

48. When run in default mode, what comments does javadoc extract and what comments does it not extract?

Chapter Summary

- A static method is one that does not require a calling object, but can use the class name in place of the calling object.

- A static variable is similar to an instance variable except that there is only one copy of the static variable that is used by all objects of the class.

- A wrapper class allows you to have a class object that corresponds to a value of a primitive type. Wrapper classes also contain a number of useful predefined constants and static methods.

- A variable of a class type stores the reference (memory address) of where the object is located in the computer's memory. This causes some operations, such as = and ==, to behave quite differently for variables of a class type than they do for variables of a primitive type.

- When you use the assignment operator with two variables of a class type, the two variables become two names for the same object.

- A method cannot change the value of a variable of a primitive type that is an argument to the method. On the other hand, a method can change the values of the instance variables of an argument of a class type. This is because with class parameters, it is a reference that is plugged in to the parameter.

- null is a special constant that can be used to give a value to any variable of any class type.

- An expression with a new operator and a constructor can be used as an argument to a method. Such an argument is called an *anonymous object*.

- A copy constructor is a constructor with one parameter of the same type as the class. A copy constructor should be designed so the object it creates is intuitively an exact copy of its parameter, but a completely independent copy, that is, a deep copy.

- A class that contains mutator methods or any methods that can change the data in an object of the class is called a *mutable class*, and objects of the class are called *mutable objects*. When defining accessor methods (or almost any methods), your method should not return a reference to a mutable object. Instead, use a copy constructor (or other means) to return a reference to a deep copy of the mutable object.

- Packages are Java's version of class libraries.

- Java comes with a program named `javadoc` that automatically extracts the interface from all the classes in a package or from a single class definition.

Answers to Self-Test Exercises

1. Yes, it is legal, although it would be preferable style to use the class name `RoundStuff` in place of `roundObject`.

2. No, all methods in the class are static, so there is no need to create objects. If we follow our style rules, no constructors would ever be used, so there is no need for constructors.

3. Yes, a class can contain both static and nonstatic (that is, regular) methods.

4. You cannot invoke a nonstatic method within a static method (unless you create an object to serve as the calling object of the nonstatic method).

5. You can invoke a static method within a nonstatic method.

6. You cannot reference an instance variable within a static method, because a static method can be used without a calling object and hence without any instance variables.

7. Each object of a class has its own copy of each instance variable, but a single copy of each static variable is shared by all objects.

8. No, you cannot use an *instance variable* (without an object name and dot) in the definition of a *static method* of the same class. Yes, you can use an *instance variable* (without an object name and dot) in the definition of a *nonstatic method* of the same class.

9. Yes, you can use a *static variable* in the definition of a *static method* of the same class. Yes, you can use a *static variable* in the definition of a *nonstatic method* of the same class. So, you can use a static variable in any method.

10. No, you cannot use either an explicit or an implicit occurrence of the `this` parameter in the definition of a static method.

11. All methods with the following names could and should be marked `static`: `dateOK`, `monthOK`, and `monthString`.

12. All static variables should be marked `private` with the exception of one case: If the static variable is used as a named constant (that is, if it is marked `final`), then it can be marked either `public` or `private` depending on the particular situation.

13. They can both be named by using the class name and a dot, rather than an object name and a dot.

14. `3, 4,`
    `3.0, 3.0,`
    `4.0, and 4.0`

15. `roundedAnswer = (int)Math.round(answer);`

16. `long`. Since one argument is of type `long`, the `int` argument is automatically type cast to `long`.

17. They are all legal.

18. An object of the class `Double`; the assignment is equivalent to

    `Double price = new Double(1.99);`

19. A value of the primitive type int; the assignment is equivalent to

    `int count = (new Integer(12)).intValue();`

20. `Objects are Not equal.`

21. `Double.toString(result)`

22. `Double.parseDouble(stringForm)`

23. `Double.parseDouble(stringForm.trim())`

24. `System.out.println("Largest long is " + Long.MAX_VALUE +`
    `                    " Smallest long is " + Long.MIN_VALUE);`

25. `Character zeeObject = new Character('Z');`

26. No, none of the wrapper classes discussed in this chapter have no-argument constructors.

27. A reference type is a type whose variables contain references, that is, memory addresses. Class types are reference types. Primitive types are not reference types.

28. When comparing two objects of a class type, you should use the method `equals`.

29. When comparing two objects of a primitive type, you should you use `==`.

30. Yes, a method with an argument of a class type can change the values of the instance variables in the object named by the argument.

31. No, a method cannot change the value of an `int` variable given as an argument to the method.

32. The variable `anObject` names no object and so the invocation of the `set` method is an error. One way to fix things is as follows:

    ```
    ToyClass anObject = new ToyClass();
    anObject.set("Josephine", 42);
    ```

33. The constant `null` can be assigned to a variable of any class type. It does not really have a type, but you can think of its type as being the type of a memory address. You can also think of `null` as being of every class type.

34. `aVariable == null`

35. It is unlikely but it is legal. This is an example of an anonymous object, as described in the text.

36. The only difference is that the object of type `Date` is given the name `theDate` in the second version. It makes no difference to the object `adams`.

37. The following of `equals` is used in the file `Date.java` in the Chapter 5 directory of the source code on the CD:

extra code on CD

```java
public boolean equals(Date otherDate)
{
    if (otherDate == null)
        return false;
    else
        return ( (month.equals(otherDate.month)) &&
            (day == otherDate.day) && (year == otherDate.year) );
}
```

38. A copy constructor is a constructor with one parameter of the same type as the class. A copy constructor should be designed so that the object it creates is intuitively an exact copy of its parameter, but a completely independent copy, that is, a deep copy.

39. The first piece of code produces the output:

```
July 4, 1776
```

The second piece of code produces the output:

```
January 1, 2006
```

40. `Natalie Dressed, April 1, 1984-`

41.
```java
public void set(String newName, Date birthDate, Date deathDate)
{
    if (consistent(birthDate, deathDate))
    {
            name = newName;
            born = new Date(birthDate);
            if (deathDate == null)
                died = null;
            else
                died = new Date(deathDate);
    }
    else
    {
        System.out.println("Inconsistent dates. Aborting.");
        System.exit(0);
    }
}
```

Note that the following is not a good definition since it could lead to a privacy leak:

```java
public void set(String newName, Date birthDate, Date deathDate)
{//Not good
    name = newName;
    born = birthDate;
    died = deathDate;
}
```

42. The class `String` is an immutable class. The classes `Date` and `Person` are mutable classes.

43. The class `String` is an immutable class.

44. To make the class available to your program, you need to insert the following at the start of the file containing your class:

```java
import mypackages.library1.CoolClass;
```

To make all the classes in the package available to your program, insert the following instead:

```java
import mypackages.library1.*;
```

45. To make a class a member of the package named `mypackages.library1`, you must insert the following at the start of the file with the class definition and place the file in the directory corresponding to the package (as described in the text):

```java
package mypackages.library1;
```

(Only the `.class` file is required to be in the directory corresponding to the package, but it may be cleaner and easier to place both the `.java` file and the `.class` file there.)

46. A package name must be a path name for the directory that contains the classes in the package, but the package name uses dots in place of \ or / (whichever your operating system uses). When naming the package, you use a relative path name that starts from any directory named in the value of the CLASSPATH (environment) variable.

47. `javadoc` never extracts the body of a method definition, nor (when run in default mode) does `javadoc` ever extract anything marked `private` in a class definition.

48. When run in default mode, `javadoc` only extracts comments that satisfy the following two conditions:

1. The comment must immediately precede a public class definition, a public method definition, or other public item.

2. The comment must use the /* and */ style, and the opening /* must contain an extra *. So the comment must be marked by /** at the beginning and */ at the end. In particular, `javadoc` does not extract any // style comments.

Programming Projects

 Many of these Programming Projects can be solved using AW's MyCodeMate.
To access these please go to: www.mycodemate.com.

1. You operate several hot dog stands distributed throughout town. Define a class named `HotDogStand` that has a member variable for the hot dog stand's ID number and a member variable for how many hot dogs the stand has sold that day. Create a constructor that allows a user of the class to initialize both values.

    Also create a method named `justSold` that increments the number of hot dogs the stand has sold by one. The idea is that this method will be invoked each time the stand sells a hot dog so that you can track the total number of hot dogs sold by the stand. Add another method that returns the number of hot dogs sold.

    Finally, add a static variable that tracks the total number of hot dogs sold by all hot dog stands and a static method that returns the value in this variable.

    Write a main method to test your class with at least three hot dog stands that each sell a variety of hot dogs.

2. Define a class called `Fraction`. This class is used to represent a ratio of two integers. Include mutator functions that allow the user to set the numerator and the denominator. Also include a method that displays the fraction on the screen as a ratio (e.g., 5/9). This method does not need to reduce the fraction to lowest terms.

    Include an additional method, `equals`, that takes as input another `Fraction` and returns `true` if the two fractions are identical and `false` if they are not. This method should treat the fractions reduced to lowest terms; that is, if one fraction is 20/60 and the other is 1/3, then the method should return `true`.

    Embed your class in a test program that allows the user to create a fraction. Then the program should loop repeatedly until the user decides to quit. Inside the body of the loop, the program should allow the user to enter a target fraction into an anonymous object and learn whether the fractions are identical.

3. In the land of Puzzlevania, Aaron, Bob, and Charlie had an argument over which one of them was the greatest puzzler of all time. To end the argument once and for all, they agreed on a duel to the death. Aaron was a poor shooter and only hit his target with a probability of 1/3. Bob was a bit better and hit his target with a probability of 1/2. Charlie was an expert marksman and never missed. A hit means a kill and the person hit drops out of the duel.

    To compensate for the inequities in their marksmanship skills, the three decided that they would fire in turns, starting with Aaron, followed by Bob, and then by Charlie. The cycle would repeat until there was one man standing, and that man would be the Greatest Puzzler of All Time.

    An obvious and reasonable strategy is for each man to shoot at the most accurate shooter still alive, on the grounds that this shooter is the deadliest and has the best chance of hitting back.

Write a program to simulate the duel using this strategy. Your program should use random numbers and the probabilities given in the problem to determine whether a shooter hits the target. Create a class named `Duelist` that contains the dueler's name and shooting accuracy, a Boolean indicating whether the dueler is still alive, and a method `ShootAtTarget(Duelist target)` that sets the target to dead if the dueler hits his target (using a random number and the shooting accuracy) and does nothing otherwise.

Once you can simulate a single duel, add a loop to your program that simulates 10,000 duels. Count the number of times that each contestant wins and print the probability of winning for each contestant (e.g., for Aaron your program might output "Aaron won 3,595/10,000 duels or 35.95%").

An alternate strategy is for Aaron to intentionally miss on his first shot. Modify the program to accommodate this new strategy and output the probability of winning for each contestant. What strategy is better for Aaron, to intentionally miss on the first shot or to try and hit the best shooter? Who has the best chance of winning, the best shooter or the worst shooter?

Note: To generate a random number x, where $0 <= x \le 1$, use $x = $ `Math.random();` . This generates a random number between 0 and 1.

4. You are interested in keeping track of the team members and competition information for your school's annual entries in computer science programming competitions. Each team consists of exactly four team members. Every year your team competes in two competitions. As an initial start for your database, create a class named `Team` that has the following data members:

```
// Name for the team
String teamName;
// Names for each team members.
String name1, name2, name3, name4;
// Info on each competition
Competition competition1, competition2;
```

Note that there is a much better way to represent the team members and competitions using arrays; this is covered in a subsequent chapter. The class should also have a method that outputs all the names of all team members and the competition information to the console.

The `Competition` class contains variables to track the following:

String: Name of the competition, Name of the winning team, Name of the runner-up

Integer: Year of the competition

Implement the `Team` and `Competition` classes with appropriate constructor, accessor, and mutator methods. In entering data for past competitions, you note that an entry is usually very similar to the previous year's entry. To help with the data entry, create a deep copy constructor for the Team class. Test your copy constructor by creating a copy of an existing team object, changing the competition information for the copy, and outputting the data for the original and the copy. The original object should be unchanged if your deep copy constructor is working properly.

5. Define a class named Money whose objects represent amounts of U.S. money. The class should have two instance variables of type int for the dollars and cents in the amount of money. Include a constructor with two parameters of type int for the dollars and cents, one with one constructor of type int for an amount of dollars with zero cents, and a no-argument constructor. Include the methods add for addition and minus for subtraction of amounts of money. These methods should be static methods and should each have two parameters of type Money and return a value of type Money. Include a reasonable set of accessor and mutator methods as well as the methods equals and toString. Write a test program for your class.

Part Two: Add a second version of the methods for addition and subtraction. These methods should have the same names as the static version but should use a calling object and a single argument. For example, this version of the add method (for addition) has a calling object and one argument. So m1.add(m2) returns the result of adding the Money objects m1 and m2. Note that your class should have all these methods; for example, there should be two methods named add.

Alternate Part Two (If you want to do both Part Two and Alternate Part Two, they must be two classes. You cannot include the methods from both Part Two and Alternate Part Two in a single class. Do you know why?): Add a second version of the methods for addition and subtraction. These methods should have the same names as the static version but should use a calling object and a single argument. The methods should be void methods. The result should be given as the changed value of the calling object. For example, this version of the add method (for addition) has a calling object and one argument. Therefore,

```
m1.add(m2);
```

changes the values of the instance variables of m1 so they represent the result of adding m2 to the original version of m1. Note that your class should have all these methods; for example, there should be two methods named add.

6. Define a class for rational numbers. A rational number is a number that can be represented as the quotient of two integers. For example, 1/2, 3/4, 64/2, and so forth are all rational numbers. (By 1/2 and so forth, we mean the everyday meaning of the fraction, not the integer division this expression would produce in a Java program.) Represent rational numbers as two values of type int, one for the numerator and one for the denominator. Your class should have two instance variables of type int. Call the class Rational. Include a constructor with two

arguments that can be used to set the instance variables of an object to any values. Also include a constructor that has only a single parameter of type int; call this single parameter wholeNumber and define the constructor so that the object will be initialized to the rational number wholeNumber/1. Also include a no-argument constructor that initializes an object to 0 (that is, to 0/1). Note that the numerator, the denominator, or both may contain a minus sign. Define methods for addition, subtraction, multiplication, and division of objects of your class Rational. These methods should be static methods that each have two parameters of type Rational and return a value of type Rational. For example, Rational.add(r1, r2) will return the result of adding the two rational numbers (two objects of the class Rational, r1 and r2). Define accessor and mutator methods as well as the methods equals and toString. You should include a method to normalize the sign of the rational number so that the denominator is positive and the numerator is either positive or negative. For example, after normalization, 4/–8 would be represented the same as –4/8. Also write a test program to test your class.

Hints: Two rational numbers *a*/*b* and *c*/*d* are equal if *a**d equals *c**b.

Part Two: Add a second version of the methods for addition, subtraction, multiplication, and division. These methods should have the same names as the static version but should use a calling object and a single argument. For example, this version of the add method (for addition) has a calling object and one argument. So r1.add(r2) returns the result of adding the rationals r1 and r2. Note that your class should have all these methods; for example, there should be two methods named add.

Alternate Part Two (If you want to do both Part Two and Alternate Part Two, they must be two classes. You cannot include the methods from both Part Two and Alternate Part Two in a single class. Do you know why?): Add a second version of the methods for addition, subtraction, multiplication, and division. These methods should have the same names as the static version but should use a calling object and a single argument. The methods should be void methods. The result is given as the changed value of the calling object. For example, this version of the add method (for addition) has a calling object and one argument. Therefore,

```
r1.add(r2);
```

changes the values of the instance variables of r1 so they represent the result of adding r2 to the original version of r1. Note that your class should have all these methods; for example, there should be two methods named add.

 7. Define a class for complex numbers. A complex number is a number of the form

```
a + b*i
```

where, for our purposes, *a* and *b* are numbers of type double, and *i* is a number that represents the quantity $\sqrt{-1}$. Represent a complex number as two values of type double. Name the instance variables real and imaginary. (The instance variable for the number that is multiplied by *i* is the one called imaginary.) Call the class Complex. Include a constructor with two parameters of type double that can be used to set the instance variables of an object to any values. Also include a constructor that has only a single parameter of type double; call this parameter realPart and define the constructor so that the object will be initialized to realPart + 0*i. Also include a no-argument constructor that initializes an object to 0 (that is, to 0 + 0*i). Define accessor and mutator methods as well as the methods equals and toString. Define static methods for addition, subtraction, and multiplication of objects of your class Complex. These methods should be static and should each have two parameters of type Complex and return a value of type Complex. For example, Complex.add(c1, c2) will return the result of adding the two complex numbers (two objects of the class Complex) c1 and c2. Also write a test program to test your class.

Hints: To add or subtract two complex numbers, you add or subtract the two instance variables of type double. The product of two complex numbers is given by the following formula:

$$(a + b*i)*(c + d*i) = (a*c - b*d) + (a*d + b*c)*i$$

Part Two: Add a second version of the methods for addition, subtraction, and multiplication. These methods should have the same names as the static version but should use a calling object and a single argument. For example, this version of the add method (for addition) has a calling object and one argument. So c1.add(c2) returns the result of adding the complex numbers c1 and c2. Note that your class should have all these methods; for example, there should be two methods named add.

Alternate Part Two (If you want to do both Part Two and Alternate Part Two, they must be two classes. You cannot include the methods from both Part Two and Alternate Part Two in a single class. Do you know why?): Add a second version of the methods for addition, subtraction, and multiplication. These methods should have the same names as the static version but should use a calling object and a single argument. The methods will be void methods. The result is given as the changed value of the calling object. For example, this version of the add method (for addition) has a calling object and one argument. Therefore,

```
c1.add(c2);
```

changes the values of the instance variables of c1 so they represent the result of adding c2 to the original version of c1. Note that your class should have all these methods; for example, there should be two methods named add.

6

Arrays

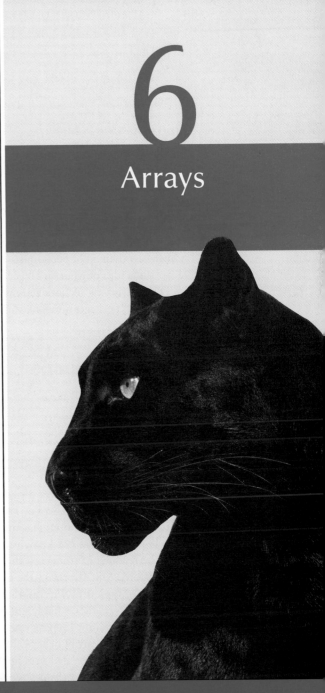

6 Arrays

Memory is necessary for all the operations of reason.

BLAISE PASCAL, *Pensées*

Introduction

An *array* is a data structure used to process a collection of data that is all of the same type, such as a list of numbers of type `double` or a list of strings. In this chapter we introduce you to the basics of defining and using arrays in Java.

Prerequisites

Section 6.1 requires only Chapters 1 through 3 and Section 4.1 of Chapter 4. Indeed, much less than all of Section 4.1 is needed. All you really need from Section 4.1 is to have some idea of what an object is and what an instance variable is.

The remaining sections require Chapters 1 through 5 with the exception that Section 5.4 on packages and `javadoc` is not required.

6.1   Introduction to Arrays

It is a capital mistake to theorize before one has data.

SIR ARTHUR CONAN DOYLE,
Scandal in Bohemia (SHERLOCK HOLMES)

Suppose we wish to write a program that reads in five test scores and performs some manipulations on these scores. For instance, the program might compute the highest test score and then output the amount by which each score falls short of the highest. The highest score is not known until all five scores are read in. Hence, all five scores must be retained in storage so that after the highest score is computed each score can be compared to it. To retain the five scores, we will need something equivalent to five variables of type `int`. We could use five individual variables of type `int`, but keeping track of five variables is hard, and we may later want to change our program to handle 100 scores; certainly, keeping track of 100 variables is impractical. An array is the per-
array   fect solution. An **array** behaves like a list of variables with a uniform naming mechanism that can be declared in a single line of simple code. For example, the names for the five individual variables we need might be `score[0]`, `score[1]`, `score[2]`, `score[3]`, and `score[4]`. The part that does not change, in this case `score`, is the name of the array. The part that can change is the integer in the square brackets `[]`.

Creating and Accessing Arrays

In Java, an array is a special kind of object, but it is often more useful to think of an array as a collection of variables all of the same type. For example, an array that behaves like a collection of five variables of type `double` can be created as follows:

```
double[] score = new double[5];
```

This is like declaring the following to be five variables of type `double`:

```
score[0], score[1], score[2], score[3], score[4]
```

indexed
variable
subscripted
variable
element
index,
subscript
length, size

These individual variables that together make up the array are referred to in a variety of different ways. We will call them **indexed variables**, though they are also sometimes called **subscripted variables** or **elements** of the array. The number in square brackets is called an **index** or a **subscript**. In Java, *indices are numbered starting with* 0, *not starting with* 1 *or any number other than* 0. The number of indexed variables in an array is called the **length** or **size** of the array. When an array is created, the length of the array is given in square brackets after the array name. The indexed variables are then numbered (also using square brackets) starting with 0 and ending with the integer that is *one less than the length of the array*.

The following

```
double[] score = new double[5];
```

is really shorthand for the following two statements:

```
double[] score;
score = new double[5];
```

The first statement declares the variable `score` to be of the array type `double[]`. The second statement creates an array with five indexed variables of type `double` and makes the variable `score` a name for the array. You may use any expression that evaluates to a nonnegative `int` value in place of the 5 in square brackets. In particular you can fill a variable with a value read from the keyboard and use the variable in place of the 5. In this way the size of the array can be determined when the program is run.

base type

An array can have indexed variables of any type, but they must all be of the same type. This type is called the **base type** of the array. In our example, the base type of the array `score` is `double`. To declare an array with base type `int`, simply use the type name `int` instead of `double` when the array is declared and created. The base type of an array can be any type. In particular it can be a class type.

Each of the five indexed variables of our example array `score` can be used just like any other variable of type `double`. For example, all of the following are allowed in Java:

```
score[3] = 32;
score[0] = score[3] + 10;
System.out.println(score[0]);
```

The five indexed variables of our sample array `score` are more than just five plain old variables of type `double`. That number in square brackets is part of the indexed variable's name. So your program can compute the name of one of these variables.

Declaring and Creating an Array

You declare an array name and create an array in almost the same way that you create and name objects of classes. There is only a slight difference in the syntax.

SYNTAX

Base_Type[] *Array_Name* = new *Base_Type*[*Length*];

The *Length* may be given as any expression that evaluates to a nonnegative integer. In particular *Length* can be an `int` variable.

EXAMPLES

```
char[] line = new char[80];
double[] reading = new double[300];
Person[] specimen = new Person[100];
```

`Person` is a class.

Instead of writing an integer constant in the square brackets, you can use any expression that evaluates to an integer that is at least 0 and at most 4. So, the following is allowed:

```
System.out.println(score[index] + " is at position " + index);
```

where `index` is a variable of type `int` that has been given one of the values 0, 1, 2, 3, or 4.

When we refer to these indexed variables grouped together into one collective item, we will call them an *array*. So, we can refer to the array named `score` (without using any square brackets).

The program in Display 6.1 shows an example of using our sample array `score` as five indexed variables, all of type `double`.

Note that the program can compute the name of an indexed variable by using a variable as the index, as in the following for loop:

```
for (index = 0; index < 5; index++)
    System.out.println(score[index] + " differs from max by "
                                    + (max - score[index]));
```

square brackets []

Do not confuse the three ways to use the **square brackets []** with an array name. First, the square brackets can be used to create a type name, such as the `double[]` in the following:

```
double[] score;
```

Second, the square brackets can be used with an integer value as part of the special syntax Java uses to create a new array, as in

```
score = new double[5];
```

Display 6.1   An Array Used in a Program (part 1 of 2)

```
1   import java.util.Scanner;

2   public class ArrayOfScores
3   {
4       /**
5        Reads in 5 scores and shows how much each
6        score differs from the highest score.
7       */
8       public static void main(String[] args)
9       {
10          Scanner keyboard = new Scanner(System.in);
11          double[] score = new double[5];
12          int index;
13          double max;

14          System.out.println("Enter 5 scores:");
15          score[0] = keyboard.nextDouble();
16          max = score[0];
17          for (index = 1; index < 5; index++)
18          {
19              score[index] = keyboard.nextDouble();
20              if (score[index] > max)
21                  max = score[index];
22          //max is the largest of the values score[0],..., score[index].
23          }

24          System.out.println("The highest score is " + max);
25          System.out.println("The scores are:");
26          for (index = 0; index < 5; index++)
27              System.out.println(score[index] + " differs from max by "
28                                  + (max - score[index]));
29      }
30  }
```

Sample Dialogue

```
Enter 5 scores:
80  99.9  75  100  85.5
The highest score is 100
The scores are:
80.0 differs from max by 20
99.9 differs from max by 0.1
75.0 differs from max by 25
100.0 differs from max by 0.0
85.5 differs from max by 14.5
```

Due to imprecision in floating-point arithmetic, this value will probably only be a close approximation to 0.1.

Display 6.1   An Array Used in a Program (part 2 of 2)

A Common Way to Visualize an Array:

The third use of square brackets is to name an indexed variable of the array, such as `score[0]` or `score[3]`, as illustrated by the following line:

```
max = score[0];
```

As we mentioned previously, the integer inside the square brackets can be any expression that evaluates to a suitable integer, as illustrated by the following:

```
int next = 1;
score[next + 3] = 100;
System.out.println(
            "Score at position 4 is " + score[next + 3]);
```

Note that, in the preceding code, `score[next + 3]` and `score[4]` are the same indexed variable, because `next + 3` evaluates to 4.

The `length` Instance Variable

In Java an array is considered to be an object, and, like other objects, it might have instance variables. As it turns out, an array has only one public instance variable, which is named `length`. The instance variable `length` is automatically set to the size of the array when the array is created. For example, if you create an array as follows,

```
double[] score = new double[5];
```

then `score.length` has a value of 5.

The `length` instance variable can be used to make your program clearer by replacing an unnamed constant, such as 5, whose meaning may not be obvious, with a meaningful name like `score.length`. In Display 6.2 we have rewritten the program in Display 6.1 using the `length` instance variable.

Display 6.2 The **length** Instance Variable

```
1    import java.util.Scanner;                              The sample dialogue is the same as in
                                                            Display 6.1.
2    public class ArrayOfScores2
3    {
4        /**
5         Reads in 5 scores and shows how much each
6         score differs from the highest score.
7        */
8        public static void main(String[] args)
9        {
10           Scanner keyboard = new Scanner(System.in);
11           double[] score = new double[5];
12           int index;
13           double max;

14           System.out.println("Enter " + score.length + " scores:");
15           score[0] = keyboard.nextDouble();
16           max = score[0];
17           for (index = 1; index < score.length; index++)
18           {
19               score[index] = keyboard.nextDouble();
20               if (score[index] > max)
21                   max = score[index];
22           //max is the largest of the values score[0],..., score[index].
23           }

24           System.out.println("The highest score is " + max);
25           System.out.println("The scores are:");
26           for (index = 0; index < score.length; index++)
27               System.out.println(score[index] + " differs from max by "
28                                       + (max - score[index]));
29       }
30   }
```

The `length` instance variable cannot be changed by your program (other than by creating a new array with another use of new).[1] For example, the following is illegal:

```
score.length = 10; //Illegal
```

---

[1] The technical details are as follows: The instance variable `length` is created when the array is created and is declared to be `public final int`.

TIP: Use for Loops with Arrays

The second for loop in Display 6.2 illustrates a common way to step through an entire array using a for loop:

```
for (index = 0; index < score.length; index++)
    System.out.println(score[index] + " differs from max by "
                                    + (max - score[index]));
```

The for loop is ideally suited for performing array manipulations. ∎

PITFALL: Array Indices Always Start with Zero

The indices of an array always start with 0 and end with the integer that is one less than the size of the array. ∎

PITFALL: Array Index Out of Bounds

The most common programming error made when using arrays is attempting to use a nonexistent array index. For example, consider the following:

```
int[] a = new int[6];
```

illegal array index

When using the array a, every index expression must evaluate to one of the integers 0 through 5. For example, if your program contains the indexed variable a[i], the i must evaluate to one of the six integers 0, 1, 2, 3, 4, or 5. If i evaluates to anything else, that is an error. When an index expression evaluates to some value other than those allowed by the array declaration, the index is said to be **out of bounds**. If your program attempts to use an array index that is out of bounds, then your program will end with an error message.[2] Note that this is a run-time error message, not a compiler error message.

Array indices get out of bounds most commonly at the first or last iteration of a loop that processes the array. So, it pays to carefully check all array processing loops to be certain that they begin and end with legal array indices. ∎

---

[2] Technically speaking, an ArrayIndexOutOfBoundsException is thrown. We will discuss exceptions in Chapter 9. Until you learn about handling exceptions, exceptions will simply appear as error conditions to you.

Initializing Arrays

An array can be initialized when it is declared. When initializing the array, the values for the various indexed variables are enclosed in braces and separated with commas. The expression with the braces is placed on the right-hand side of an assignment operator. For example:

```
int[] age = {2, 12, 1};
```

The array length (size) is automatically set to the number of values in the braces. So, this initializing declaration is equivalent to the following statements:

```
int[] age = new int[3];
age[0] = 2;
age[1] = 12;
age[2] = 1;
```

You can also initialize array elements using a for loop. For example:

```
double[] reading = new double[100];
int index;
for (index = 0; index < reading.length; index++)
    reading[index] = 42.0;
```

automatic
initialization

If you do not initialize the elements of an array, they will automatically be initialized to a default value for the base type. The default values are the usual ones. For numeric types the default value is the zero of the type. (For base type char the default value is the nonprintable zeroth character (char)0, not the space character.) For the type boolean the default value is false. For class types, the default value is null. For example, if you do not initialize an array of doubles, each element of the array will be initialized to 0.0.

Self-Test Exercises

1. In the array declaration

   ```
   String[] word = new String[5];
   ```

   what is

   a. the array name?

   b. the base type?

   c. the length of the array?

   d. the range of values an index accessing this array can have?

   e. one of the indexed variables (or elements) of this array?

(continued)

Self-Test Exercises (continued)

2. In the array:

```
double[] score = new double[10];
```

what is

a. the value of score.length?

b. the first index of score?

c. the last index of score?

3. What is the output of the following code?

```
char[] letter = {'a', 'b', 'c'};
for (int index = 0; index < letter.length; index++)
    System.out.print(letter[index] + ", ");
```

4. What is the output of the following code?

```
double[] a = {1.1, 2.2, 3.3};
System.out.println(a[0] + " " + a[1] + " " + a[2]);
a[1] = a[2];
System.out.println(a[0] + " " + a[1] + " " + a[2]);
```

5. What is wrong with the following piece of code?

```
int[] sampleArray = new int[10];
for (int index = 1; index <= sampleArray.length; index++)
    sampleArray[index] = 3*index;
```

6. Suppose we expect the elements of the array a to be ordered so that

a[0] ≤ a[1] ≤ a[2] ≤...

However, to be safe we want our program to test the array and issue a warning in case it turns out that some elements are out of order. The following code is supposed to output such a warning, but it contains a bug; what is the bug?

```
double[] a = new double[10];
    <Some code to fill the array a goes here.>
for (int index = 0; index < a.length; index++)
    if (a[index] > a[index + 1])
        System.out.println("Array elements " + index +
            " and " + (index + 1) + " are out of order.");
```

PITFALL: An Array of Characters Is Not a String

An array of characters, such as the array a created below, is conceptually a list of characters and so is conceptually like a string:

```
char[] a = {'A', ' ', 'B', 'i', 'g', ' ', 'H', 'i', '!'};
```

However, an array of characters, like a, is not an object of the class String. In particular, the following is illegal in Java:

```
String s = a;
```

Similarly, you cannot normally use an array of characters, like a, as an argument for a parameter of type String.

It is, however, easy to convert an array of characters to an object of type String. The class String has a constructor that has a single parameter of type char[]. So, you can obtain a String value corresponding to an array of characters, like a, as follows:

```
String s = new String(a);
```

The object s will have the same sequence of characters as the array a. The object s is an independent copy; any changes made to a will have no effect on s. Note that this always uses the entire array a.

There is also a String constructor that allows you to specify a subrange of an array of characters a. For example,

```
String s2 = new String(a, 2, 3);
```

produces a String object with 3 characters from the array a starting at index 2. So, if a is as above, then

```
System.out.println(s2);
```

outputs

```
Big
```

Although an array of characters is not an object of the class String, it does have some things in common with String objects. For example, you can output an array of characters using println, as follows,

```
System.out.println(a);
```

which produces the output

```
A Big Hi!
```

provided a is as given above. ∎

6.2 Arrays and References

A little more than kin, and less than kind.

WILLIAM SHAKESPEARE, *Hamlet*

Just like a variable of one of the class types you've seen, a variable of an array type holds a reference. In this section we explore the consequences of this fact, including a discussion of array parameters. We will see that arrays are objects and that array types can be considered class types, but somewhat different kinds of class types. Arrays and the kinds of classes we've seen before this chapter are *a little more than kin, and less than kind.*

Arrays Are Objects

There are two ways to view an array: as a collection of indexed variables, and as a single item whose value is a collection of values of the base type. In Section 6.1 we discussed using arrays as a collection of indexed variables. We will now discuss arrays from the second point of view.

An array can be viewed as a single item whose value is a collection of values of the base type. An array variable (as opposed to an array indexed variable) names the array as a single item. For example, the following declares a variable of an array type:

```
double[] a;
```

This variable a can and will contain a single value. The expression

```
new double[10]
```

creates an array object and stores the object in memory. The following assignment statement places a reference to (the memory address of) this array object in the variable a:

```
a = new double[10];
```

Typically we combine all this into a single statement as follows:

```
double[] a = new double[10];
```

Notice that this is almost exactly the same as the way that we view objects of a class type. In Java, an array is considered an *object*. Whenever Java documentation says that something applies to objects, that means that it applies to arrays as well as objects of the class types we've seen up to now. You will eventually see examples of methods that can take arguments that may be objects of any kind. These methods will accept array objects as arguments as well as objects of an ordinary class type. Arrays are somewhat peculiar in how they relate to classes. Some authorities say array types are not classes and some authorities say they are classes. But, all authorities agree that the arrays themselves are objects. Given that arrays are objects, it seems that one should view array types as classes, and we will do so. However, although an array type `double[]` is a class, the syntax for creating an array object is a bit different. To create an array, you use the following syntax:

```
double[] a = new double[10];
```

You can view the expression `new double[10]` as an invocation of a constructor that uses a nonstandard syntax. (The nonstandard syntax was used to be consistent with the syntax used for arrays in older programming languages.)

As we have already seen, every array has an instance variable named `length`, which is a good example of viewing an array as an object. As with any other class type, array variables contain memory addresses, or, as they are usually called in Java, *references*. So array types are reference types.[3]

Since an array is an object, you might be tempted to think of the indexed variables of an array, such as `a[0]`, `a[1]`, and so forth, as being instance variables of the object. This is actually a pretty good analogy, but it is not literally true. Indexed variables are not instance variables of the array. Indexed variables are a special kind of variable peculiar to arrays. The only instance variable in an array is the `length` instance variable.

An array object is a collection of items of the base type. Viewed as such, an array is an object that can be assigned with the assignment operator and plugged in for a parameter of an array type. Because an array type is a reference type, the behaviors of arrays with respect to assignment =, ==, and parameter passing mechanisms are the same as what we have already described for classes. In the next few subsections we discuss these details about arrays.

Arrays Are Objects

In Java, arrays are considered to be objects, and, although there is some disagreement on this point, you can safely view an array type as a class type.

Array Types Are Reference Types

A variable of an array type holds the address of where the array object is stored in memory. This memory address is called a **reference** to the array object.

---

[3] In many programming languages, such as C++, arrays are also reference types just as they are in Java. So, this detail about arrays is not peculiar to Java.

PITFALL: Arrays with a Class Base Type

The base type of an array can be of any type, including a class type. For example, suppose Date is a class and consider the following:

```
Date[] holidayList = new Date[20];
```

This creates the 20 indexed variables holidayList[0], holidayList[1], ..., holidayList[19]. It is important to note that this creates 20 indexed variables of type Date. This does not create 20 objects of type Date. (The index variables are automatically initialized to null, not to an object of the class Date.) Like any other variable of type Date, the indexed variables require an invocation of a constructor using new to create an object. One way to complete the initialization of the array holidayList is as follows:

```
Date[] holidayList = new Date[20];
for (int i = 0; i < holidayList.length; i++)
    holidayList[i] = new Date();
```

If you omit the for loop (and do not do something else more or less equivalent), then when you run your code, you will undoubtedly get an error message indicating a "null pointer exception." If you do not use new to create an object, an indexed variable like holidayList[i] is just a variable that names no object and hence cannot be used as the calling object for any method. Whenever you are using an array with a class base type and you get an error message referring to a "null pointer exception," it is likely that your indexed variables do not name any objects and you need to add something like the above for loop. ■

Array Parameters

You can use both array indexed variables and entire arrays as arguments to methods, although they are different types of parameters. We first discuss array indexed variables as arguments to methods.

indexed variable arguments An indexed variable can be an argument to a method in exactly the same way that any variable of the array base type can be an argument. For example, suppose a program contains the following declarations:

```
double n = 0;
double[] a = new double[10];
int i;
```

If myMethod takes one argument of type double, then the following is legal:

```
myMethod(n);
```

Since an indexed variable of the array a is also a variable of type double, just like n, the following is equally legal:

```
myMethod(a[3]);
```

There is one subtlety that does apply to indexed variables used as arguments. For example, consider the following method call:

```
myMethod(a[i]);
```

If the value of i is 3, then the argument is a[3]. On the other hand, if the value of i is 0, then this call is equivalent to the following:

```
myMethod(a[0]);
```

The indexed expression is evaluated to determine exactly which indexed variable is given as the argument.

Array Indexed Variables as Arguments

An array indexed variable can be used as an argument anyplace that a variable of the array's base type can be used. For example, suppose you have the following:

```
double[] a = new double[10];
```

Indexed variables such as a[3] and a[index] can then be used as arguments to any method that accepts a **double** as an argument.

---

entire array parameters

You can also define a method that has a formal parameter for an entire array so that when the method is called, the argument that is plugged in for this formal parameter is an entire array. Whenever you need to specify an array type, the type name has the form *Base_Type*[], so this is how you specify a parameter type for an entire array. For example, the method doubleArrayElements, given in what follows, will accept any array of double as its single argument:

```
public class SampleClass
{
    public static void doubleArrayElements(double[] a)
    {
        int i;
        for (i = 0; i < a.length; i++)
            a[i] = a[i]*2;
    }
    <The rest of the class definition goes here.>
}
```

To illustrate this, suppose you have the following in some method definition,

```
double[] a = new double[10];
double[] b = new double[30];
```

and suppose that the elements of the arrays a and b have been given values. Both of the following are then legal method invocations:

```
SampleClass.doubleArrayElements(a);
SampleClass.doubleArrayElements(b);
```

Note that no square brackets are used when you give an entire array as an argument to a method.

An array type is a reference type just as a class type is, so, as with a class type argument, a method can change the data in an array argument. To phrase it more precisely, a method can change the values stored in the indexed variables of an array argument. This is illustrated by the preceding method doubleArrayElements.

An array type parameter does not specify the length of the array argument that may be plugged in for the parameter. An array knows its length and stores it in the length instance variable. The same array parameter can be replaced with array arguments of different lengths. Note that the preceding method doubleArrayElements can take an array of any length as an argument.

length of array arguments

 PITFALL: Use of = and == with Arrays

assignment with arrays

Array types are reference types; that is, an array variable contains the memory address of the array it names. The assignment operator copies this memory address. For example, consider the following code:

```
double[] a = new double[10];
double[] b = new double[10];
int i;
for (i = 0; i < a.length; i++)
    a[i] = i;
b = a;
System.out.println("a[2] = " + a[2] + " b[2] = " + b[2]);
a[2] = 42;
System.out.println("a[2] = " + a[2] + " b[2] = " + b[2]);
```

This will produce the following output:

```
a[2] = 2.0 b[2] = 2.0
a[2] = 42.0 b[2] = 42.0
```

PITFALL: (continued)

Array types are reference types; that is, an array variable contains the memory address of the array it names. The assignment operator copies this memory address. For example, consider the following code:

```
double[] a = new double[10];
double[] b = new double[10];
int i;
for (i = 0; i < a.length; i++)
    a[i] = i;
b = a;
System.out.println("a[2] = " + a[2] + " b[2] = " + b[2]);
a[2] = 42;
System.out.println("a[2] = " + a[2] + " b[2] = " + b[2]);
```

This will produce the following output:

```
a[2] = 2.0 b[2] = 2.0
a[2] = 42.0 b[2] = 42.0
```

The assignment statement b = a; copies the memory address from a to b so that the array variable b contains the same memory address as the array variable a. After the assignment statement, a and b are two different names for the same array. Thus, when we change the value of a[2], we are also changing the value of b[2].

Unless you want two array variables to be two names for the same array (and on rare occasions you do want this), you should not use the assignment operator with arrays. If you want the arrays a and b in the preceding code to be different arrays with the same values in each index position, then instead of the assignment statement

```
b = a;
```

you need to use something like the following:

```
int i;
for (i = 0; (i < a.length) && (i < b.length); i++)
    b[i] = a[i];
```

Note that the above code will not make b an exact copy of a, unless a and b have the same length.

(continued)

PITFALL: (continued)

== with arrays

The equality operator == does not test two arrays to see if they contain the same values. It tests two arrays to see if they are stored in the same location in the computer's memory. For example, consider the following code:

```
int[] c = new int[10];
int[] d = new int[10];
int i;
for (i = 0; i < c.length; i++)
    c[i] = i;
for (i = 0; i < d.length; i++)
    d[i] = i;

if (c == d)
    System.out.println("c and d are equal by ==.");
else
    System.out.println("c and d are not equal by ==.");
```

This produces the output

```
c and d are not equal by ==
```

even though c and d contain the same integers in the same indexed variables. A comparison using == will say they are not equal because == only checks the contents of the array variables c and d, which are memory addresses, and c and d contain different memory addresses.

If you want to test two arrays to see if they contain the same elements, then you can define an equalArrays method for the arrays, just as you defined an equals method for a class. Display 6.3 contains one possible definition of equalArrays for arrays in a small demonstration class. ∎

Self-Test Exercises

7. Consider the following class definition:

```
public class SomeClass
{
    public static void doSomething(int n)
    {
        <Some code goes in here.>
    }
    <The rest of the definition is irrelevant to this question.>
```

Which of the following are acceptable method calls?

```
int[] a = {4, 5, 6};
int number = 2;
SomeClass.doSomething(number);
SomeClass.doSomething(a[2]);
SomeClass.doSomething(a[3]);
SomeClass.doSomething(a[number]);
SomeClass.doSomething(a);
```

8. Write a method definition for a static `void` method called `oneMore`, which has a formal parameter for an array of integers and increases the value of each array element by one. (The definition will go in some class, but you need only give the method definition.)

9. Write a method named `outOfOrder` that takes as a parameter an array of `double` and returns a value of type `int`. This method will test the array for being out of order, meaning that the array violates the condition:

```
a[0] <= a[1] <= a[2] <= ...
```

The method returns −1 if the elements are not out of order; otherwise, it returns the index of the first element of the array that is out of order. For example, consider the declaration

```
double[] a = {1.2, 2.1, 3.3, 2.5, 4.5,
              7.9, 5.4, 8.7, 9.9, 1.0};
```

In the array above, `a[2]` and `a[3]` are the first pair out of order, and `a[3]` is the first element out of order, so the method returns 3. If the array were sorted, the method would return −1.

10. What is wrong with the following method definition? It will compile but does not work as you might hope.

```
public static void doubleSize(int[] a)
{
    a = new int[a.length * 2];
}
```

Array Parameters and Array Arguments

An argument to a method may be an entire array. Array arguments are like objects of a class, in that the method can change the data in an array argument; that is, a method can change the values stored in the indexed variables of an array argument. A method with an array parameter is defined and invoked as illustrated by the following examples. Note that the array parameter specifies the base type of the array, but not the length of the array.

EXAMPLES (OF ARRAY PARAMETERS)

```java
public class AClass
{
    public static void listChars(char[] a)
    {
        int i;
        for (i = 0; i < a.length; i++)
            System.out.println(a[i] + " ");
    }
    public static void zeroAll(int[] anArray)
    {
        int i;
        for (i = 0; i < anArray.length; i++)
            anArray[i] = 0;
    }
        ...
}
```

EXAMPLES (OF ARRAY ARGUMENTS)

```java
char[] c = new char[10];
int[] a = new int[10];
int[] b = new int[20];
```

Note that arrays a and b have different lengths. Also note that no square brackets are used with array arguments.

```
<Some code to fill the arrays goes here.>
```

```java
AClass.listChars(c);
AClass.zeroAll(a);
AClass.zeroAll(b);
```

Display 6.3　**Testing Arrays for Equality** (part 1 of 2)

```java
1    public class DifferentEquals
2    {
3        /**
4         A demonstration to see how == and an equalArrays method are different.
5        */
6        public static void main(String[] args)
7        {
8            int[] c = new int[10];
9            int[] d = new int[10];

10           int i;
11           for (i = 0; i < c.length; i++)
12               c[i] = i;
```

The arrays c and d contain the same integers in each index position.

Display 6.3   Testing Arrays for Equality (part 2 of 2)

```
13            for (i = 0; i < d.length; i++)
14                d[i] = i;
15            if (c == d)
16                System.out.println("c and d are equal by ==.");
17            else
18                System.out.println("c and d are not equal by ==.");

19            System.out.println("== only tests memory addresses.");

20            if (equalArrays(c, d))
21                System.out.println(
22                        "c and d are equal by the equalArrays method.");
23            else
24                System.out.println(
25                        "c and d are not equal by the equalArrays method.");

26            System.out.println(
27                    "An equalArrays method is usually a more useful test.");
28        }

29    public static boolean equalArrays(int[] a, int[] b)
30    {
31        if (a.length != b.length)
32            return false;
33        else
34        {
35            int i = 0;
36            while (i < a.length)
37            {
38                if (a[i] != b[i])
39                    return false;
40                i++;
41            }
42        }

43        return true;
44    }

45  }
```

Sample Dialogue

```
c and d are not equal by ==.
== only tests memory addresses.
c and d are equal by the equalArrays method.
An equalArrays method is usually a more useful test.
```

Arguments for the Method `main` ★

The heading for the `main` method of a program looks as if it has a parameter for an array of base type of `String`:

```
public static void main(String[] args)
```

The identifier `args` is in fact a parameter of type `String[]`. Since `args` is a parameter, it could be replaced by any other non-keyword identifier. The identifier `args` is traditional, but it is perfectly legal to use some other identifier.

We have never given `main` an array argument, or any other kind of argument, when we ran any of our programs. So, what did Java use as an argument to plug in for `args`? If no argument is given when you run your program, then a default empty array of strings is automatically provided as a default argument to `main` when you run your program.

It is possible to run a Java program in a way that provides an argument to plug in for this array of `String` parameters. You do not provide it as an array. You provide any number of string arguments when you run the program, and those string arguments will automatically be made elements of the array argument that is plugged in for `args` (or whatever name you use for the parameter to `main`). This is normally done by running the program from the command line of the operating system, like so:

```
java YourProgram Do Be Do
```

This will set `args[0]` to `"Do"`, `args[1]` to `"Be"`, `args[2]` to `"Do"`, and `args.length` to 3. These three indexed variables can be used in the method `main`, as in the following sample program:

```java
public class YourProgram
{
    public static void main(String[] args)
    {
        System.out.println(args[1] + " " + args[0]
                                    + " " + args[1]);
    }
}
```

If the above program is run from the command line as follows,

```
java YourProgram Do Be Do
```

the output produced by the program will be

```
Be Do Be
```

Be sure to note that the argument to `main` is an array of *strings*. If you want numbers, you must convert the string representations of the numbers to values of a number type or types.

The Method `main` Has an Array Parameter

The heading for the `main` method of a program is as follows:

```
public static void main(String[] args)
```

The identifier `args` is a parameter for an array of base type `String`. The details are explained in the text.

Methods that Return an Array

In Java, a method may return an array. You specify the return type for a method that returns an array in the same way that you specify a type for an array parameter. For example, the following is an example of a method that returns an array:

```java
public static char[] upperCaseVersion(char[] a)
{
    char[] temp = new char[a.length];
    char i;
    for (i = 0; i < a.length; i++)
        temp[i] = Character.toUpperCase(a[i]);
    return temp;
}
```

Returning an Array

A method can return an array. The details are basically the same as for a method that returns an object of a class type.

SYNTAX (FOR A TYPICAL WAY OF RETURNING AN ARRAY)

```java
public static Base_Type[] Method_Name(Parameter_List)
{
    Base_Type[] temp = new Base_Type[Array_Size]
    <Some code to fill temp goes here.>
    return temp;
}
```

The method need not be static and need not be public. You do not necessarily need to use a local array variable like `temp`.

EXAMPLE (ASSUMED TO BE IN A CLASS DEFINITION)

```java
public static int[] incrementedArray(int[] a, int increment)
{
    int[] temp = new int[a.length];
    int i;
    for (i = 0; i < a.length; i++)
        temp[i] = a[i] + increment;
    return temp;
}
```

Array Type Names

Whenever you need an array type name, whether for the type of an array variable declaration, the type of an array parameter, or the type for a method that returns an array, you specify the type name in the same way.

SYNTAX

Base_Type[]

EXAMPLES

```
double[] a = new double[10];
int[] giveIntArray(char[] arrayParameter)
{ ... }
```

Self-Test Exercises

11. Give the definition of a method called `halfArray` that has a single parameter for an array of base type `double` and that returns another array of base type `double` that has the same length and in which each element has been divided by 2.0. Make it a static method. To test it, you can add it to any class or, better yet, write a class with a test program in the method `main`.

12. What is wrong with the following method definition? It is an alternate definition of the method by the same name defined in the previous subsection. It will compile.

```
public static char[] upperCaseVersion(char[] a)
{
    char i;
    for (i = 0; i < a.length; i++)
        a[i] = Character.toUpperCase(a[i]);
    return a;
}
```

6.3   Programming with Arrays

Never trust to general impressions, my boy,
but concentrate yourself upon details.

SIR ARTHUR CONAN DOYLE,
A Case of Identity (SHERLOCK HOLMES)

In this section, we discuss partially filled arrays and discuss how to use arrays as class instance variables.

Partially Filled Arrays

Often the exact size needed for an array is not known when a program is written or the size may vary from one run of the program to another. One common and easy way to handle this situation is to declare the array to be of the largest size the program could possibly need. The program is then free to use as much or as little of the array as is needed.

partially filled array   **Partially filled arrays** require some care. The program must keep track of how much of the array is used and must not reference any indexed variable that has not been given a meaningful value. The program in Display 6.4 illustrates this point. The program reads in a list of golf scores and shows how much each score differs from the average. This program will work for lists as short as 1 score, as long as 10 scores, and of any length in between. The scores are stored in the array score, which has 10 indexed variables, but the program uses only as much of the array as it needs. The variable numberUsed keeps track of how many elements are stored in the array. The elements (that is, the scores) are stored in positions score[0] through score[numberUsed – 1]. The details are very similar to what they would be if numberUsed were score.length and the entire array were used. Note that the variable numberUsed usually must be an argument to any method that manipulates the partially filled array. For example, the methods showDifference and computeAverage use the argument numberUsed to ensure that only meaningful array indices are used.

Display 6.4 **Partially Filled Array** (part 1 of 3)

```
1    import java.util.Scanner;

2    public class GolfScores
3    {
4        public static final int MAX_NUMBER_SCORES = 10;

5        /**
6         Shows differences between each of a list of golf scores and their average.
7        */
8        public static void main(String[] args)
9        {
10           double[] score = new double[MAX_NUMBER_SCORES];
11           int numberUsed = 0;

12           System.out.println("This program reads golf scores and shows");
13           System.out.println("how much each differs from the average.");
14           System.out.println("Enter golf scores:");
15           numberUsed = fillArray(score);
16           showDifference(score, numberUsed);
17       }
```

Contrary to normal practice, this allows fractional scores, such as 71.5. However, this makes it a better example for our purposes. (Anyway, when I play golf, losing a ball is only half a stroke penalty. Try it sometime.)

(continued)

Display 6.4   Partially Filled Array (part 2 of 3)

```
18      /**
19       Reads values into the array a. Returns the number of values placed in the array a.
20      */
21      public static int fillArray(double[] a)
22      {
23          System.out.println("Enter up to " + a.length
24                              + " nonnegative numbers.");
25          System.out.println("Mark the end of the list with a negative number.");
26          Scanner keyboard = new Scanner(System.in);
27
28          double next;
29          int index = 0;
30          next = keyboard.nextDouble();
31          while ((next >= 0) && (index < a.length))
32          {
33              a[index] = next;
34              index++;
35              next = keyboard.nextDouble();
36              //index is the number of array indexed variables used so far.
37          }
38          //index is the total number of array indexed variables used.
39          if (next >= 0)
40              System.out.println("Could only read in "
41                              + a.length + " input values.");
42
42          return index;
43      }
```

The value of **index** is the number of values stored in the array.

```
44      /**
45       Precondition: numberUsed <= a.length.
46                    a[0] through a[numberUsed-1] have values.
47       Returns the average of numbers a[0] through a[numberUsed-1].
48      */
49      public static double computeAverage(double[] a, int numberUsed)
50      {
51          double total = 0;
52          for (int index = 0; index < numberUsed; index++)
53              total = total + a[index];
54          if (numberUsed > 0)
55          {
56              return (total/numberUsed);
57          }
58          else
59          {
60              System.out.println("ERROR: Trying to average 0 numbers.");
61              System.out.println("computeAverage returns 0.");
62              return 0;
63          }
64      }
```

(continued)

Display 6.4   **Partially Filled Array** (part 3 of 3)

```
65        /**
66          Precondition: numberUsed <= a.length.
67                          The first numberUsed indexed variables of a have values.
68           Postcondition: Gives screen output showing how much each of the first
69           numberUsed elements of the array a differ from their average.
70        */
71        public static void showDifference(double[] a, int numberUsed)
72        {
73            double average = computeAverage(a, numberUsed);
74            System.out.println("Average of the " + numberUsed
75                                        + " scores = " + average);
76            System.out.println("The scores are:");
77            for (int index = 0; index < numberUsed; index++)
78                System.out.println(a[index] + " differs from average by "
79                                        + (a[index] - average));
80        }
81    }
```

Sample Dialogue

```
This program reads golf scores and shows
how much each differs from the average.
Enter golf scores:
Enter up to 10 nonnegative numbers.
Mark the end of the list with a negative number.
69  74  68  -1
Average of the 3 scores = 70.3333
The scores are:
69.0 differs from average by -1.33333
74.0 differs from average by 3.66667
68.0 differs from average by -2.33333
```

Self-Test Exercises

13. Complete the definition of the following method that could be added to the class GolfScores in Display 6.4:

```
/**
  Precondition: numberUsed <= argumentArray.length;
  the first numberUsed indexed variables of argumentArray
  have values.
  Returns an array of length numberUsed whose ith element
  is argumentArray[i] - adjustment.
*/
public static double[] differenceArray(
  double[] argumentArray, int numberUsed, double adjustment)
```

(continued)

Self-Test Exercises (continued)

14. Rewrite the class `GolfScores` from Display 6.4 using the method `differenceArray` from Exercise 13.

15. Rewrite the class `GolfScores` from Display 6.4 making the array of scores a static variable. Also, make the `int` variable `numberUsed` a static variable. Start with Display 6.4, not with the answer to Exercise 14. *Hint:* All, or at least most, methods will have no parameters.

EXAMPLE: A Class for Partially Filled Arrays

If you are going to use some array in a disciplined way, such as using the array as a partially filled array, then it is often best to create a class that has the array as an instance variable and to have the constructors and methods of the class provide the needed operations as methods. For example, in Display 6.5 we have written a class for a partially filled array of doubles. In Display 6.6 we have rewritten the program in Display 6.4 using this class.

In Display 6.6 we have written the code to be exactly analogous to that of Display 6.4 so that you could see how one program mirrors the other. However, this resulted in occasionally recomputing a value several times. For example, the method `computeAverage` contains the following expression three times:

```
a.getNumberOfElements()
```

Since the `PartiallyFilledArray` a is not changed in this method, these each return the same value. Some programmers advocate computing this value only once and saving the value in a variable. These programmers would use something like the following for the definition of `computeAverage` rather than what we used in Display 6.6. The variable `numberOfElementsIna` is used to save a value so it need not be recomputed.

```
public static double computeAverage(PartiallyFilledArray a)
{
    double total = 0;
    double numberOfElementsIna = a.getNumberOfElements();
    for (int index = 0; index < numberOfElementsIna; index++)
        total = total + a.getElement(index);
    if (numberOfElementsIna > 0)
    {
        return (total/numberOfElementsIna);
    }
    else
    {
```

EXAMPLE: (continued)

```
                System.out.println(
                        "ERROR: Trying to average 0 numbers.");
                System.out.println("computeAverage returns 0.");
                return 0;
        }
    }
```

This is not likely to produce a noticeable difference in the efficiency of the program
in Display 6.6, but if the number of elements in the PartiallyFilledArray were
large so that the for loop would be executed many times, it might make a difference
in a situation where efficiency is critical.

Display 6.5 **Partially Filled Array Class** (part 1 of 4)

```
1    /**
2     Class for a partially filled array of doubles. The class enforces the
3     following invariant: All elements are at the beginning of the array in
4     locations 0, 1, 2, and so forth up to a highest index with no gaps.
5    */
6    public class PartiallyFilledArray
7    {
8        private int maxNumberElements; //Same as a.length
9        private double[] a;
10       private int numberUsed; //Number of indices currently in use

11       /**
12         Sets the maximum number of allowable elements to 10.
13       */
14       PartiallyFilledArray()
15       {
16           maxNumberElements = 10;
17           a = new double[maxNumberElements];
18           numberUsed = 0;
19       }

20       /**
21         Precondition arraySize > 0.
22       */
23       PartiallyFilledArray(int arraySize)
24       {
25           if (arraySize <= 0)
26           {
27               System.out.println("Error Array size zero or negative.");
28               System.exit(0);
29           }
```

(continued)

Display 6.5   Partially Filled Array Class (part 2 of 4)

```
30              maxNumberElements = arraySize;
31              a = new double[maxNumberElements];
32              numberUsed = 0;
33          }
34      PartiallyFilledArray(PartiallyFilledArray original)
35          {
36              if (original == null)
37              {
38                  System.out.println("Fatal Error: aborting program.");
39                  System.exit(0);
40              }
41              maxNumberElements =
42                      original.maxNumberElements;
43              numberUsed = original.numberUsed;
44              a = new double[maxNumberElements];
45              for (int i = 0; i < numberUsed; i++)
46                  a[i] = original.a[i];
47          }
```

Note that the instance variable a *is a copy of* original.a. *The following would not be correct:* a = original.a; *This point is discussed in the subsection entitled "Privacy Leaks with Array Instance Variables."*

```
48      /**
49       Adds newElement to the first unused array position.
50       */
51      public void add(double newElement)
52          {
53              if (numberUsed >= a.length)
54              {
55                  System.out.println("Error: Adding to a full array.");
56                  System.exit(0);
57              }
58              else
59              {
60                  a[numberUsed] = newElement;
61                  numberUsed++;
62              }
63          }

64      public double getElement(int index)
65          {
66              if (index < 0 || index >= numberUsed)
67              {
68                  System.out.println("Error:Illegal or unused index.");
69                  System.exit(0);
70              }
71              return a[index];
72          }
```

Display 6.5   Partially Filled Array Class (part 3 of 4)

```
73      /**
74       index must be an index in use or the first unused index.
75      */
76      public void resetElement(int index, double newValue)
77      {
78          if (index < 0 || index >= maxNumberElements)
79          {
80              System.out.println("Error:Illegal index.");
81              System.exit(0);
82          }
83          else if (index > numberUsed)
84          {
85              System.out.println(
86                      "Error: Changing an index that is too large.");
87              System.exit(0);
88          }
89          else
90              a[index] = newValue;
91      }

92      public void deleteLast()
93      {
94          if (empty())
95          {
96              System.out.println("Error:Deleting from an empty array.");
97              System.exit(0);
98          }
99          else
100             numberUsed--;
101     }

102     /**
103      Deletes the element in position index. Moves down all elements with
104      indices higher than the deleted element.
105     */
106     public void delete(int index)
107     {
108         if (index < 0 || index >= numberUsed)
109         {
110             System.out.println("Error:Illegal or unused index.");
111             System.exit(0);
112         }

113         for (int i = index; i < numberUsed; i++)
114             a[i] = a[i + 1];
115         numberUsed--;
116     }
```

(continued)

Display 6.5 **Partially Filled Array Class** (part 4 of 4)

```
117      public boolean empty()
118      {
119          return (numberUsed == 0);
120      }

121      public boolean full()
122      {
123          return (numberUsed == maxNumberElements);
124      }

125      public int getMaxCapacity()
126      {
127          return maxNumberElements;
128      }
129
130      public int getNumberOfElements()
131      {
132          return numberUsed;
133      }
134  }
```

TIP: Accessor Methods Need Not Simply Return Instance Variables

Note that in the class `PartiallyFilledArray` in Display 6.5, there is no accessor method that returns a copy of the entire instance variable *a*. The reason that was not done is that, when the class is used as intended, a user of the class `PartiallyFilledArray` would have no need for the entire array *a*. That is an implementation detail. The other methods that start with get allow a programmer using the class to obtain all the data that he or she needs. ∎

The "for-each" Loop ★

As you have already seen, you can use a for loop to cycle through all the elements in an array. For example:

```
double[] a = new double[10];
<Some code to fill the array a>
for (int i = 0; i < a.length; i++)
    System.out.println(a[i]);
```

The standard Java libraries contain definitions of a number of so-called *collection classes*. A collection class is a class whose objects store a collection of values. You cannot

Display 6.6   Display 6.4 Redone Using the Class **PartiallyFilledArray** (part 1 of 2)

```
1    import java.util.Scanner;
                                              Sample dialog is the same as in Display 6.4.
2    /**
3     Demonstrates Using the class PartiallyFilledArray,
4    */
5    public class GolfScoresVersion2
6    {

7        public static final int MAX_NUMBER_SCORES = 10;

8        /**
9         Shows the differences between each of a list of golf scores and their average.
10       */
11       public static void main(String[] args)
12       {
13           PartiallyFilledArray score =
14                           new PartiallyFilledArray(MAX_NUMBER_SCORES);

15           System.out.println("This program reads golf scores and shows");
16           System.out.println("how much each differs from the average.");

17           System.out.println("Enter golf scores:");
18           fillArray(score);
19           showDifference(score);
20       }

21       /**
22        Reads values into the PartiallyFilledArray a.
23       */
24       public static void fillArray(PartiallyFilledArray a)
25       {
26           System.out.println("Enter up to " + a.getMaxCapacity()
27                                   + " nonnegative numbers, one per line.");
28           System.out.println("Mark the end of the list with a negative number");
29           Scanner keyboard = new Scanner(System.in);
30
31           double next = keyboard.nextDouble();
32           while ((next >= 0) && (!a.full()))
33           {
34               a.add(next);
35               next = keyboard.nextDouble();
36           }

37           if (next >= 0)
38                   System.out.println("Could only read in "
39                                   + a.getMaxCapacity() + " input values.");
40       }
```

(continued)

Display 6.6   Display 6.4 Redone Using the Class **PartiallyFilledArray** (part 2 of 2)

```
41      /**
42       Returns the average of numbers in the PartiallyFilledArray a.
43       */
44      public static double computeAverage(PartiallyFilledArray a)
45      {
46          double total = 0;
47          for (int index = 0; index < a.getNumberOfElements(); index++)
48              total = total + a.getElement(index);

49          if (a.getNumberOfElements() > 0)
50          {
51              return (total/a.getNumberOfElements());
52          }
53          else
54          {
55              System.out.println("ERROR: Trying to average 0 numbers.");
56              System.out.println("computeAverage returns 0.");
57              return 0;
58          }
59      }

60      /**
61       Gives screen output showing how much each of the
62       elements in the PartiallyFilledArray a differ from the average.
63       */
64      public static void showDifference(PartiallyFilledArray a)
65      {
66          double average = computeAverage(a);
67          System.out.println("Average of the " + a.getNumberOfElements()
68                              + " scores = " + average);
69          System.out.println("The scores are:");
70          for (int index = 0; index < a.getNumberOfElements(); index++)
71              System.out.println(a.getElement(index) + " differs from average by "
72                              + (a.getElement(index) - average));
73      }

74  }
```

cycle through all the elements of a collection object with this kind of for loop, because these collection classes normally do not have indices associated with their elements, as an array does.[4] However, starting with version 5.0, Java has added a new kind of for loop that can cycle through all the elements in a collection even though there are no

---

[4] You can construct a similar for loop using something called an *iterator* in place of the array index, but we will not go into that until later in this book.

for-each loop

indices for the elements, as there are with an array. This new kind of `for` loop is called a **for-each loop** or **enhanced for loop**. We will discuss these for-each loops in detail when we cover collections (Chapter 15). However, these new for-each loops can be used with arrays as well as with objects of these collection classes. In this subsection, we tell you how to use for-each loops with arrays in case you want to get started using them. However, we do not use the for-each loop in this book until we discuss collection classes in Chapter 15.

The following code ends with a for-each loop that is equivalent to the regular `for` loop that we gave at the start of this subsection:

```
double[] a = new double[10];
<Some code to fill the array a>
for (double element : a)
    System.out.println(element);
```

You can read the line beginning with `for` as "for each `element` in `a`, do the following." Note that the variable, `element`, has the same type as the elements in the array. The variable, like `element`, must be declared in the for-each loop as we have done. If you attempt to declare `element` before the for-each loop, you will get a compiler error message.

The general syntax for a for-each loop statement used with an array is

```
for (Array_Base_Type Variable : Array_Name)
    Statement
```

Be sure to notice that you use a colon (not a semicolon) after the *Variable*. You may use any legal variable name for the *Variable*; you do not have to use `element`. Although it is not required, the *Statement* typically contains the *Variable*. When the for-each loop is executed, the *Statement* is executed once for each element of the array. More specifically, for each `element` of the array, the *Variable* is set to the array element and then the *Statement* is executed.

The for-each loop can make your code a lot cleaner and a lot less error prone. If you are not using the indexed variable in a `for` loop for anything other than as a way to cycle through all the array elements, then a for-each loop is preferable. For example,

```
for (double element : a)
    element = 0.0;
```

is preferable to

```
for (int i = 0; i < a.length; i++)
    a[i]= 0.0;
```

The two loops do the same thing, but the second one mentions an index `i` that is not used for anything other than enumerating the array elements. Also, the syntax for the for-each loop is simpler than that of the regular `for` loop.

On the other hand, you should leave the following for loop as is and not attempt to convert it to a for-each loop:

```
for (int i = 0; i < a.length; i++)
    a[i]= 2*i;
```

Because this for loop uses the index i in the body of the for loop and uses it in an essential way, it does not make sense to convert this for loop to a for-each loop.

For-Each Loop for Arrays

SYNTAX

```
for (Array_Base_Type Variable : Array_Name)
    Statement
```

EXAMPLE

```
for (double element : a)
    element = 0.0;
```

The array a has base type **double**. This for-each loop sets each element of the array a to 0.0.

A good way to read the first line of the example is "For each **element** in a, do the following."

Methods with a Variable Number of Parameters ★

Because of overloading, you can have a method named max that returns the largest of two int values and have another method named max that takes three int arguments and returns the largest of the three. If you decide you need a method that returns the largest of four int values, you can define a version of the method max that takes four arguments. However, with this approach, there is no way to cover all cases of computing the maximum of some number of int values. Covering all cases in this way would require an infinite number of definitions for the method name max, and no programmer has enough time to write an infinite number of definitions. What we would like is a single method definition for a method named max that can take any number of int arguments. Starting with version 5.0, Java lets you define methods that take any number of arguments. For example, the following is the definition of a method named max that takes any number of int arguments and returns the largest of its arguments:

```
public static int max(int... arg)
{
    if (arg.length == 0)
    {
        System.out.println("Fatal Error: maximum of zero values.");
        System.exit(0);
    }
```

```
        int largest = arg[0];
        for (int i = 1; i < arg.length; i++)
            if (arg[i] > largest)
                largest = arg[i];
        return largest;
    }
```

This method max works by taking its int arguments and placing them in an array named arg whose base type is int. For example, suppose this definition of the method max is in a class named UtilityClass, and consider the following method call:

```
    int highestScore = UtilityClass.max(3, 2, 5, 1);
```

The array arg is automatically declared and initialized as follows:

```
    int[] arg = {3, 2, 5, 1};
```

So arg[0] == 3, arg[1] == 2, arg[2] == 5, and arg[3] == 1. After this, the code in the body of the method definition is executed. Display 6.7 shows a sample program that uses this method max.

Note that a method, such as max, that takes any number of arguments is basically a method that takes an array as an argument, except that the job of placing values in the array is done automatically for the programmer. The values for the array are

---

Display 6.7   Method with a Variable Number of Parameters (part 1 of 2)

```
1    public class UtilityClass
2    {
3        /**
4         Returns the largest of any number of int values.
5        */
6        public static int max(int... arg)
7        {
8            if (arg.length == 0)
9            {
10               System.out.println("Fatal Error: maximum of zero values.");
11               System.exit(0);
12           }
13
14           int largest = arg[0];
15           for (int i = 1; i < arg.length; i++)
16               if (arg[i] > largest)
17                   largest = arg[i];                    This is the file UtilityClass.java.
18           return largest;
19       }
20   }
```

(continued)

Display 6.7   Method with a Variable Number of Parameters (part 2 of 2)

```
1    import java.util.Scanner;

2    public class VariableParameterDemo
3    {
4        public static void main(String[] args)
5        {
6            System.out.println("Enter scores for Tom, Dick, and Harriet:");
7            Scanner keyboard = new Scanner(System.in);
8            int tomsScore = keyboard.nextInt();
9            int dicksScore = keyboard.nextInt();
10           int harrietsScore = keyboard.nextInt();

11           int highestScore = UtilityClass.max(tomsScore, dicksScore, harrietsScore);

12           System.out.println("Highest score = " + highestScore);
13       }
14   }
```

This is the file
VariableParameterDemo.java.

Sample Dialogue

```
Enter scores for Tom, Dick, and Harriet:
55  100  99
Highest score = 100
```

given as arguments and Java automatically creates an array and places the arguments in the array.

A parameter specification that specifies any number of parameters, such as `int...` **vararg** `arg`, is called a **vararg specification**. (It would make more sense to call it a "varparam-**specification** eter" specification, but the word "vararg" is too well entrenched, so we will go along **ellipsis** with common usage.) The three dots in a vararg specification are called an **ellipsis**. Note that the ellipsis is part of the Java syntax and not an abbreviation used in this book. You type in the three dots.

You can have only one variable parameter specification, such as `int... arg`, in a method definition. However, you may also have any number of ordinary parameters, in which case the vararg specification must be the last item on the parameter list. This is illustrated in Display 6.8, which we discuss in the next subsection.

In Chapter 2, you saw one example of a method that accepts a variable number of arguments, namely the method `System.out.printf`. However, we could not tell you how to define such methods yourself until we covered the basics about arrays.

Method with a Variable Number of Parameters

A method with a variable number of parameters has a vararg specification as the last item on its parameter list. A vararg specification has the form:

Type... *Array_Name*

Some examples of vararg specifications are

```
int... arg
double... a
String... unwanted
```

Displays 6.7 and 6.8 show two of these vararg specifications in complete method definitions.

In any invocation of a method with a vararg specification, you handle arguments corresponding to regular parameters in the usual way. Following the arguments for regular parameters, you can have any number of arguments of the type given in the vararg specification. These arguments are automatically placed in an array, and the array can be used in the method definition. See the text for a full description of the details.

Self-Test Exercises

16. Redo the definition of the method max in Display 6.7 using a for-each loop in place of the regular for loop.

17. What would be the dialogue in Display 6.8 if we omitted the following line from the program?

```
sentence = Utility2.censor(sentence, " ,"); //Deletes extra commas
```

EXAMPLE: A String Processing Example ☆

This example uses material from the starred subsection "Methods with a Variable Number of Parameters." If you have not read that subsection, you should skip this example.

Display 6.8 contains a utility class with the string processing method named censor and an example of a program that uses that method. The method censor takes a single String parameter followed by any number of additional parameters of type String. The first parameter will be a sentence or other string that may contain substrings you want to delete. The method returns its first parameter with all occurrences of the remaining string parameters removed.

(continued)

EXAMPLE: (continued)

Note that the method censor has one regular parameter followed by a specification for any number of additional string parameters. In this case, all parameters are of type String. However, that first regular parameter (or parameters) in a method heading can be of any type (or types); they need not match the type of the vararg specification. We just happen to want the type String here.

Because the first parameter is of type String and the vararg specification in this case says the remaining arguments are of type String, you might wonder why we did not omit the first String parameter sentence, have only a vararg specification, and then use unwanted[0] to serve the same role as sentence. If we had done so, then the method censor could be called with no arguments at all. A vararg specification allows any number of arguments, including the possibility of zero arguments. However, we wanted to insist that the method censor have at least one argument, and the parameter sentence ensures that censor will always have at least one argument.

Privacy Leaks with Array Instance Variables

In Chapter 5, we explained why it is a compromise of privacy for a class to have an accessor (or other method) that returns a reference to a private mutable object. As we noted there, an accessor method should instead return a reference to a *deep copy* of the private object. (See the Pitfall subsection of Chapter 5 entitled "Privacy Leaks.") At the time, we had in mind returning the contents of a private instance variable of a class type. However, the lesson applies equally well to private instance variables of an array type.

For example, suppose that you decide that you want an accessor method for the array instance variable in the class PartiallyFilledArray in Display 6.5. You might be tempted to define the accessor method as follows:

```
public double[] getInsideArray()// Problematic version
{
    return a;
}
```

As indicated in the comment, this definition has a problem. The problem is that this accessor method allows a programmer to change the array object named by the private instance variable a in ways that bypass the checks built into the mutator methods of the class PartiallyFilledArray. To see why this is true *suppose we had added this definition of the method* getInsideArray *to the class* PartiallyFilledArray, and consider the following code:

```
PartiallyFilledArray leakyArray =
                    new PartiallyFilledArray(10);
double[] arrayName = leakyArray.getInsideArray();
```

Display 6.8   String Processing Method with a Variable Number of Parameters (part 1 of 2)

```
1    public class Utility2
2    {
3        /**
4         Returns the first argument with all occurrences of other arguments deleted;
5         */
6        public static String censor(String sentence, String...  unwanted)
7        {
8            for (int i = 0; i < unwanted.length; i++)
9                sentence = deleteOne(sentence, unwanted[i]);
10           return sentence;
11       }
12       /**
13        Returns sentence with all occurrences of oneUnwanted removed.
14        */
15       private static String deleteOne(String sentence, String oneUnwanted)
16       {
17           String ending;
18           int position = sentence.indexOf(oneUnwanted);
19           while (position >= 0) //While word was found in sentence
20           {
21               ending = sentence.substring(position + oneUnwanted.length());
22               sentence = sentence.substring(0, position) + ending;
23               position = sentence.indexOf(oneUnwanted);
24           }
25           return sentence;
26       }
27   }
```

Both methods use the parameter **sentence** *as a local variable. If this puzzles you, review the material on parameters in Chapters 4 and 5, particularly Display 4.5 in Chapter 4.*

If you have trouble following this string processing, review the subsection entitled "String Processing" in Chapter 1.

This is the file **Utility2.java**.

```
1    import java.util.Scanner;
2    public class StringProcessingDemo
3    {
4        public static void main(String[] args)
5        {
6            System.out.println("What did you eat for dinner?");
7            Scanner keyboard = new Scanner(System.in);
8            String sentence = keyboard.nextLine();
9            sentence = Utility2.censor(sentence,
10                            "candy", "french fries", "salt", "beer");
11           sentence = Utility2.censor(sentence, " ,"); //Deletes extra commas
12           System.out.println("You would be healthier if you could answer:");
13           System.out.println(sentence);
14       }
15   }
```

This is the file **StringProcessingDemo.java**.

(continued)

Display 6.8   String Processing Method with a Variable Number of Parameters (part 2 of 2)

Sample Dialogue

```
What did you eat for dinner?
I ate salt cod, broccoli, french fries, salt peanuts, and apples.
You would be healthier if you could answer:
I ate cod, broccoli, peanuts, and apples.
```

The variable arrayName and the private instance variable a now contain the same reference, so both arrayName and the private instance variable a name the same array. Using arrayName as a name for the array named by the private instance variable a, we can now fill the indexed variables of a in any order and need not fill the array starting at the first element. This violates the spirit of the private modifier for the array instance variable a. For this reason, the accessor method getInsideArray should return a deep copy of the array named by the private instance variable a. A safe definition of getInsideArray is the following:

```
public double[] getInsideArray()// Good version
{
    //Recall that maxNumberElements == a.length.
    double[] temp = new double[maxNumberElements];
    for (int i = 0; i < maxNumberElements; i++)
        temp[i] = a[i];
    return temp;
}
```

If a private instance variable is an array type that has a class as its base type, then you need to be sure to make copies of the class objects in the array when you make a copy of the array. This is illustrated by the toy class in Display 6.9.

Display 6.9 also includes a copy constructor. As illustrated in that display, the copy constructor should make a completely independent copy of the array instance variable (that is, a deep copy) in the same way that the accessor method does. This same point is also illustrated by the copy constructor in Display 6.5.

Display 6.9   Accessor Method for an Array Instance Variable

```
1   /**
2     Demonstrates the correct way to define an accessor
3     method to a private array of class objects.
4   */
5   public class ToyExample
6   {
7       private Date[] a;
```

The class Date is defined in Display 4.11, but you do not need to know the details of the definition to understand the point of this example.

Display 6.9   Accessor Method for an Array Instance Variable

```
 8        public ToyExample(int arraySize)
 9        {
10            a = new Date[arraySize];
11            for (int i = 0; i < arraySize; i++)
12                a[i] = new Date();
13        }

14        public ToyExample(ToyExample object)          ←——— Copy constructor for ToyExample
15        {
16            int lengthOfArrays = object.a.length;
17            this.a = new Date[lengthOfArrays];
18            for (int i = 0; i < lengthOfArrays; i++)        ——— Copy constructor for Date
19                this.a[i] = new Date(object.a[i]);     ←
20        }

21        public Date[] getDateArray()          ←——————— Accessor method
22        {
23            Date[] temp = new Date[a.length];
24            for (int i = 0; i < a.length; i++)
25                temp[i] = new Date(a[i]);    ←
26            return temp;                          —— Copy constructor for Date
27        }
```

<There presumably are other methods that are not shown,
but they are irrelevant to the point at hand.>

```
28    }
```

Self-Test Exercises

18. Define a method named removeAll that can be added to the class
    PartiallyFilledArray. The method removeAll has no parameters. When
    invoked, the method removeAll deletes all the elements in its calling object.

19. Define a method named increaseCapacity that can be added to the class
    PartiallyFilledArray in Display 6.5. The method has one int parameter
    named newCapacity that increases the capacity of the PartiallyFilledArray so
    that it can hold up to newCapacity numbers. If newCapacity is less than or equal
    to maxNumberOfElements, then the method does nothing. If newCapacity is
    greater than maxNumberOfElements, then maxNumberElements is set equal to
    newCapacity and a new array of length newCapacity is created for the array
    instance variable a. The old values of the array instance variable are copied to the
    newly created array.

EXAMPLE: Sorting an Array

In this example, we define a method called sort that will sort a partially filled array of numbers so that they are ordered from smallest to largest.

The procedure sort has one array parameter, a. The array a will be partially filled, so there is an additional formal parameter called numberUsed, which tells how many array positions are used. Thus, the heading for the method sort will be

```
public static void sort(double[] a, int numberUsed)
```

The method sort rearranges the elements in array a so that after the method call is completed, the elements are sorted as follows:

```
a[0] ≤ a[1] ≤ a[2] ≤ ... ≤ a[numberUsed - 1]
```

The algorithm we use to do the sorting is called **selection sort**. It is one of the easiest of the sorting algorithms to understand.

One way to design an algorithm is to rely on the definition of the problem. In this case, the problem is to sort an array a from smallest to largest. That means rearranging the values so that a[0] is the smallest, a[1] the next smallest, and so forth. That definition yields an outline for the selection sort algorithm:

```
for (int index = 0; index < numberUsed; index++)
    Place the indexth smallest element in a[index]
```

There are many ways to realize this general approach. The details could be developed by using two arrays and copying the elements from one array to the other in sorted order, but using one array should be both adequate and economical. Therefore, the method sort uses only the one array containing the values to be sorted. The method sort rearranges the values in the array a by interchanging pairs of values. Let us go through a concrete example so that you can see how the algorithm works.

Consider the array shown in Display 6.10. The selection sort algorithm will place the smallest value in a[0]. The smallest value is the value in a[4]. So the algorithm interchanges the values of a[0] and a[4]. The algorithm then looks for the next smallest element. The value in a[0] is now the smallest element, so the next smallest element is the smallest of the remaining elements a[1], a[2], a[3],..., a[9]. In the example in Display 6.10, the next smallest element is in a[6], so the algorithm interchanges the values of a[1] and a[6]. This positioning of the second smallest element is illustrated in the fourth and fifth array pictures in Display 6.10. The algorithm then positions the third smallest element, and so forth. As the sorting proceeds, the beginning array elements are set equal to the correct sorted values. The sorted portion of the array grows by adding elements one after the other from the elements in the unsorted end of the array. Notice that the algorithm need not do anything with the value in the last indexed variable, a[9], because once the other elements are positioned correctly, a[9] must also have the correct value. After all, the correct value for a[9] is the smallest value left to be moved, and the only value left to be moved is the value that is already in a[9].

EXAMPLE: (continued)

The definition of the method sort, included in a class, is given in Display 6.11. sort uses the method indexOfSmallest to find the index of the smallest element in the unsorted end of the array, then it does an interchange to move this next smallest element down into the sorted part of the array.

The method interchange, shown in Display 6.11, is used to interchange the values of indexed variables. For example, the following call will interchange the values of a[0] and a[4]:

```
interchange(0, 4, a);
```

A sample use of the sort method is given in Display 6.12.

Display 6.10 Selection Sort

Unsorted array

a[0]	a[1]	a[2]	a[3]	a[4]	a[5]	a[6]	a[7]	a[8]	a[9]
8	6	11	17	3	15	5	19	28	12

a[0]	a[1]	a[2]	a[3]	a[4]	a[5]	a[6]	a[7]	a[8]	a[9]
8	6	11	17	3	15	5	19	28	12

a[0]	a[1]	a[2]	a[3]	a[4]	a[5]	a[6]	a[7]	a[8]	a[9]
3	6	11	17	8	15	5	19	28	12

a[0]	a[1]	a[2]	a[3]	a[4]	a[5]	a[6]	a[7]	a[8]	a[9]
3	6	11	17	8	15	5	19	28	12

a[0]	a[1]	a[2]	a[3]	a[4]	a[5]	a[6]	a[7]	a[8]	a[9]
3	5	11	17	8	15	6	19	28	12

.
.
.

a[0]	a[1]	a[2]	a[3]	a[4]	a[5]	a[6]	a[7]	a[8]	a[9]
3	5	6	8	11	12	15	17	19	28

Self-Test Exercises

20. How would you need to change the method sort in Display 6.11 so that it can sort an array of values of type double into decreasing order, instead of increasing order?

21. If an array of int values has a value that occurs twice (like b[0] == 42 and b[7] == 42) and you sort the array using the method SelectionSort.sort, will there be one or two copies of the repeated value after the array is sorted?

Display 6.11　Selection Sort Class (part 1 of 2)

```
1   public class SelectionSort
2   {
3       /**
4        Precondition: numberUsed <= a.length;
5                      The first numberUsed indexed variables have values.
6        Action: Sorts a so that a[0] <= a[1] <= ... <= a[numberUsed - 1].
7       */
8       public static void sort(double[] a, int numberUsed)
9       {
10          int index, indexOfNextSmallest;
11          for (index = 0; index < numberUsed - 1; index++)
12          {//Place the correct value in a[index]:
13              indexOfNextSmallest = indexOfSmallest(index, a, numberUsed);
14              interchange(index,indexOfNextSmallest, a);
15              //a[0] <= a[1] <=...<= a[index] and these are the smallest
16              //of the original array elements. The remaining positions
17              //contain the rest of the original array elements.
18          }
19      }
20      /**
21       Returns the index of the smallest value among
22       a[startIndex], a[startIndex+1], ... a[numberUsed - 1]
23      */
24      private static int indexOfSmallest(int startIndex,
25                                        double[] a, int numberUsed)
26      {
27          double min = a[startIndex];
28          int indexOfMin = startIndex;
29          int index;
30          for (index = startIndex + 1; index < numberUsed; index++)
31              if (a[index] < min)
32              {
33                  min = a[index];
34                  indexOfMin = index;
35                  //min is smallest of a[startIndex] through a[index]
36              }
```

Display 6.11   **Selection Sort Class** (part 2 of 2)

```
37              return indexOfMin;
38          }

        /**
         Precondition: i and j are legal indices for the array a.
         Postcondition: Values of a[i] and a[j] have been interchanged.
        */
        private static void interchange(int i, int j, double[] a)
        {
            double temp;
            temp = a[i];
            a[i] = a[j];
            a[j] = temp; //original value of a[i]
        }
```

Display 6.12   **Demonstration of the SelectionSort Class**

```
1   public class SelectionSortDemo
2   {
3       public static void main(String[] args)
4       {
5           double[] b = {7.7, 5.5, 11, 3, 16, 4.4, 20, 14, 13, 42};

6           System.out.println("Array contents before sorting:");
7           int i;
8           for (i = 0; i < b.length; i++)
9               System.out.print(b[i] + " ");
10          System.out.println();
11
12          SelectionSort.sort(b, b.length);

13          System.out.println("Sorted array values:");
14          for (i = 0; i < b.length; i++)
15              System.out.print(b[i] + " ");
16          System.out.println();
17      }
18  }
```

Sample Dialogue

```
Array contents before sorting:
7.7 5.5 11.0 3.0 16.0 4.4 20.0 14.0 13.0 42.0
Sorted array values:
3.0 4.4 5.5 7.7 11.0 13.0 14.0 16.0 20.0 42.0
```

Enumerated Types ★

Sometimes you need a simple type consisting of a short list of named values. For example, the values might be clothing sizes, the days of the week, or some other short list of values. Starting with version 5.0, Java allows you to have such an **enumerated type**. For example, the following is an enumerated type for the days of a five-day work week:

enumerated type

```
enum WorkDay {MONDAY, TUESDAY, WEDNESDAY, THURSDAY, FRIDAY};
```

A value of an enumerated type is a kind of named constant and so, by convention, is spelled with all uppercase letters. So, we used, for example, MONDAY, not Monday, in the above definition of the enumerated type WorkDay. Using Monday would have been legal, but poor style.

As with any other type, you can have variables of an enumerated type, for example:

```
WorkDay meetingDay, availableDay;
```

A variable of an enumerated type can have a value that must be either one of the values listed in the definition of the type or else the special value null, which serves as a placeholder indicating that the variable has no "real" value. For example, you can set the value of a variable of an enumerated type with an assignment statement:

```
meetingDay = WorkDay.THURSDAY;
```

Note that when you write the value of an enumerated type, you need to preface the name of the value, such as THURSDAY, with the name of the type. For example, you use WorkDay.THURSDAY, not THURSDAY.

As with any other type, you can combine the declaration of a variable with the assignment of a value to the variable, as in

```
WorkDay meetingDay = WorkDay.THURSDAY;
```

A program that demonstrates the syntax for using enumerated types is given in Display 6.13. Be sure to notice that we placed the definition of the enumerated type outside of the main method in the same place that you would give named constants.

Display 6.13 **An Enumerated Type** (part 1 of 2)

```
1   public class EnumDemo
2   {
3       enum WorkDay {MONDAY, TUESDAY, WEDNESDAY, THURSDAY, FRIDAY};

4       public static void main(String[] args)
5       {
6           WorkDay startDay = WorkDay.MONDAY;
7           WorkDay endDay = WorkDay.FRIDAY;
```

Display 6.13   An Enumerated Type (part 2 of 2)

```
 8              System.out.println("Work starts on " + startDay);
 9              System.out.println("Work ends on " + endDay);
10      }
11  }
```

Sample Dialogue

```
Work starts on MONDAY
Work ends on FRIDAY
```

Enumerated Type

An **enumerated type** is a type for which you give all the values of the type in a typically short list. A value of an enumerated type is a kind of named constant and so, by convention, is spelled with all uppercase letters.

SYNTAX

    enum *Type_Name* {*FIRST_VALUE*, *SECOND_VALUE*, ..., *LAST_VALUE*};

Starting with version 5.0, **enum** is a keyword in Java.

EXAMPLE

    enum Flavor {VANILLA, CHOCOLATE, STRAWBERRY};

The definition of an enumerated type is normally placed outside of all methods in the same place that you give named constants. The location for an enumerated type definition is illustrated in Display 6.13. (The definition can be placed in other locations, but we will not need to place them anywhere else.)

You can output the value of a variable of an enumerated type using `println`. For example,

    System.out.println(WorkDay.THURSDAY);

will produce the following screen output:

    THURSDAY

Note that the type name `WorkDay` is not output. Other examples of outputting an enumerated type value are given in Display 6.13.

The values of an enumerated type, such as WorkDay.THURSDAY, are not String values. In fact, you should not care what kind of values they are. How they are implemented is not relevant to being able to use the values of an enumerated type. All you really need to know is that, for example, WorkDay.THURSDAY and WorkDay.FRIDAY are different values and will test as being different if you compare them with ==.

Although values of an enumerated type are not String values, they are used for tasks that could be done by String values; but enumerated types work better than String values for some tasks. You could use a String variable in place of a variable of an enumerated type. For example, you could use

```
String meetingDay = "THURSDAY";
```

instead of

```
WorkDay meetingDay = WorkDay.THURSDAY;
```

However, using a String variable allows for the possibility of setting the variable equal to a nonsense value, such as "SUNDAY" or "GaGa" for a work day, and to do so without the computer issuing any warning statement. With an enumerated type, you know the only possible values for a variable of that type are the values given in the enumerated type definition; if you try to give the variable a different value, you will get an error message.

An enumerated type is actually a class, and its values are objects of the class. Some methods that are automatically provided with every enumerated type are given in Display 6.14.

Display 6.14 Some Methods Included with Every Enumerated Type (part 1 of 2)

```
public boolean equals(Any_Value_Of_An_Enumerated_Type)
```

Returns **true** if its argument is the same value as the calling value. While it is perfectly legal to use equals, it is easier and more common to use ==.

EXAMPLE

For enumerated types, (*Value1*.equals(*Value2*)) is equivalent to (*Value1* == *Value2*).

```
public String toString()
```

Returns the calling value as a string. This is often invoked automatically. For example, this method is invoked automatically when you output a value of the enumerated type using System.out.println or when you concatenate a value of the enumerated type to a string. See Display 6.15 for an example of this automatic invocation.

EXAMPLE

WorkDay.MONDAY.toString() returns "MONDAY".
The enumerated type WorkDay is defined in Display 6.13.

Display 6.14 **Some Methods Included with Every Enumerated Type** (part 2 of 2)

`public int ordinal()`

Returns the position of the calling value in the list of enumerated type values. The first position is `0`.

EXAMPLE

`WorkDay.MONDAY.ordinal()` returns `0`, `WorkDay.TUESDAY.ordinal()` returns `1`, and so forth. The enumerated type `WorkDay` is defined in Display 6.13.

`public int compareTo(`*Any_Value_Of_The_Enumerated_Type*`)`

Returns a negative value if the calling object precedes the argument in the list of values, returns `0` if the calling object equals the argument, and returns a positive value if the argument precedes the calling object.

EXAMPLE

`WorkDay.TUESDAY.compareTo(WorkDay.THURSDAY)` returns a negative value. The type `WorkDay` is defined in Display 6.13.

`public` *EnumeratedType*`[] values()`

Returns an array whose elements are the values of the enumerated type in the order in which they are listed in the definition of the enumerated type.

EXAMPLE

See Display 6.15.

`public static` *EnumeratedType* `valueOf(String name)`

Returns the enumerated type value with the specified name. The string `name` must be an exact match.

EXAMPLE

`WorkDay.valueOf("THURSDAY")` returns `WorkDay.THURSDAY`. The type `WorkDay` is defined in Display 6.13.

When comparing two variables (or constants) of an enumerated type, you can use the `equals` method, but it is more common to instead use the `==` operator. For example,

```
if (meetingDay == availableDay)
    System.out.println("Meeting will be on schedule.");
if (meetingDay == WorkDay.THURSDAY)
    System.out.println("Long weekend!");
```

With enumerated types, the `equals` method and the `==` operator are equivalent, but the `==` operator has nicer syntax.

To get the full potential from an enumerated type, you need some way to cycle through all the values of an enumerated type. The static method `values()` provides you with that ability. The static method `values()` returns an array whose elements are the values of the enumerated type. The static method `values()` is provided automatically for every enumerated type. Display 6.15 gives a simple example of using the method `values()` to cycle through all the values in an enumerated type. (This is one situation where it is much cleaner to use a for-each loop instead of an ordinary for loop. If you have read the starred section on the for-each loop, be sure to do Self-Test Exercise 22, which redoes Display 6.15 using a for-each loop.)

The values Method

Every enumerated type has a static method named **values()**, which returns an array whose elements are the values of the enumerated type in the order in which they are listed in the definition of the enumerated type. The base type for the array returned is the enumerated type. See Display 6.15 for an example.

Display 6.15 The Method **values** (part 1 of 2)

```
1   import java.util.Scanner;
2
3   public class EnumValuesDemo
4   {
5       enum WorkDay {MONDAY, TUESDAY, WEDNESDAY, THURSDAY, FRIDAY};
6       public static void main(String[] args)
7       {
8           WorkDay[] day = WorkDay.values();
9           Scanner keyboard = new Scanner(System.in);
10          double hours = 0, sum = 0;          This is equivalent to day[i].toString().
11          for (int i = 0; i < day.length; i++)
12          {
13              System.out.println("Enter hours worked for " + day[i]);
14              hours = keyboard.nextDouble();
15              sum = sum + hours;
16          }
17          System.out.println("Total hours work = " + sum);
18      }
19  }
```

Display 6.15   **The Method values** (part 2 of 2)

Sample Dialogue

```
Enter hours worked for MONDAY
8
Enter hours worked for TUESDAY
8
Enter hours worked for WEDNESDAY
8
Enter hours worked for THURSDAY
8
Enter hours worked for FRIDAY
7,5
Total hours worked = 39.5
```

TIP: Enumerated Types in `switch` Statements ★

You can use an enumerated type to control a `switch` statement. In other words, the type of the controlling expression in a `switch` statement can be an enumerated type. This is illustrated in Display 6.16. Note that the case labels must be unqualified names; you use `VANILLA`, not `Flavor.VANILLA`.

This program uses the static method `valueOf` to convert an input string to a value of the enumerated type. For example,

```
Flavor.valueOf("STRAWBERRY")
```

returns `Flavor.STRAWBERRY`. Note that the program changes the input to all uppercase letters before giving it as an argument to the method `valueOf`. The method `valueOf` requires an exact match. An invocation of `Flavor.valueOf("Vanilla")` will end your program with an error message;[5] you must use `"VANILLA"` to match the exact spelling (including upper- versus lowercase) of the value in `Flavor`.

At this point, you may wonder what the difference is between `STRAWBERRY` and `Flavor.STRAWBERRY` and how to tell which one to use in a given situation. The value of the enumerated type is `STRAWBERRY`. We write `Flavor.STRAWBERRY` to say we mean `STRAWBERRY` as defined in `Flavor`, as opposed to `STRAWBERRY` as defined in some other type, such as

```
enum Berry {STRAWBERRY. BLUEBERRY, RASPBERRY};
```

---

[5] After you cover exceptions in Chapter 9, you will be able to cope with answers like `PISTACHIO` which do not correspond to any value of type `Flavor`. An invocation of `Flavor.valueOf("PISTACHIO")`, will *throw an IlllegalArgumentException*, something explained in Chapter 9. Until then, your program will simply give an error message when `valueOf` cannot cope with its argument.

TIP: Enumerated Types in `switch` Statements ★

A single program with both type definitions (`Flavor` and `Berry`) could use both `Flavor.STRAWBERRY` and `Berry.STRAWBERRY`.

So, when can you use `STRAWBERRY` instead of `Flavor.STRAWBERRY`? The approximate answer is that you use `STRAWBERRY` instead of `Flavor.STRAWBERRY` when there is enough context for the compiler to know `STRAWBERRY` means `STRAWBERRY` as defined in the type `Flavor`. For example, in a `switch` statement, if the type of the controlling expression is `Flavor`, then `STRAWBERRY` can only mean `Flavor.STRAWBERRY`. This rule will help in remembering when to use `STRAWBERRY` and when to use `Flavor.STRAWBERRY`. But, sometimes you may simply have to check a reference or try the two possibilities out and see which one (or ones) the compiler accepts. ■

Display 6.16 Enumerated Type in a **switch** Statement

```
1    import java.util.Scanner;
2
3    public class EnumSwitchDemo
4    {
5        enum Flavor {VANILLA, CHOCOLATE, STRAWBERRY};
6
7        public static void main(String[] args)
8        {
9            Flavor favorite = null;
             Scanner keyboard = new Scanner(System.in);
10
11           System.out.println("What is your favorite flavor?");
12           String answer = keyboard.next();
13           answer = answer.toUpperCase();
             favorite = Flavor.valueOf(answer);
14
15           switch (favorite)        The case labels must have just the name of
16           {                        the value without the type name and dot.
17               case VANILLA:
18                   System.out.println("Classic");
19                   break;
20               case CHOCOLATE:
21                   System.out.println("Rich");
22                   break;
23               default:
24                   System.out.println("I bet you said STRAWBERRY.");
25                   break;
26           }
27       }
     }
```

Display 6.16   Enumerated Type in a `switch` Statement

Sample Dialogue

```
What is your favorite flavor?
Vanilla
Classic
```

Sample Dialogue

```
What is your favorite flavor?
STRAWBERRY
I bet you said STRAWBERRY.
```

Sample Dialogue

```
What is your favorite flavor?
PISTACHIO
```
This input causes the program to end and issue an error message.

Self-Test Exercise

22. Rewrite the program in Display 6.15 using a for-each loop.

6.4   Multidimensional Arrays

Two indices are better than one.

ANONYMOUS

Java allows you to declare arrays with more than one index. In this section, we describe these multidimensional arrays.

Multidimensional Array Basics

array declarations

It is sometimes useful to have an array with more than one index, and this is allowed in Java. The following creates an array of characters called `page`. The array `page` has two indices, the first index ranging from 0 to 29 and the second from 0 to 99.

```
char[][] page = new char[30][100];
```

This is equivalent to the following two steps:

```
char[][] page;
page = new char[30][100];
```

indexed
variables

The **indexed variables** for this array each have two indices. For example, page[0][0], page[15][32], and page[29][99] are three of the indexed variables for this array. Note that each index must be enclosed in its own set of square brackets. As was true of the one-dimensional arrays we have already seen, each indexed variable for a multidimensional array is a variable of the base type, in this case the type char.

An array may have any number of indices, but perhaps the most common number of indices is two. A two-dimensional array can be visualized as a two-dimensional display with the first index giving the row and the second index giving the column. For example, the array indexed variables of the two-dimensional array a, declared and created as

```
char[][] a = new char[5][12];
```

can be visualized as follows:

```
a[0][0], a[0][1], a[0][2], ..., a[0][11]
a[1][0], a[1][1], a[1][2], ..., a[1][11]
a[2][0], a[2][1], a[2][2], ..., a[2][11]
a[3][0], a[3][1], a[3][2], ..., a[3][11]
a[4][0], a[4][1], a[4][2], ..., a[4][11]
```

You might use the array a to store all the characters on a (very small) page of text that has five lines (numbered 0 through 4) and 12 characters on each line (numbered 0 through 11).

Declaring and Creating a Multidimensional Array

You declare a multidimensional array variable and create a multidimensional array object in basically the same way that you create and name a one-dimensional array. You simply use as many square brackets as there are indices.

SYNTAX

Base_Type[]...[] *Variable_Name* = new *Base_Type*[*Length_l*]...[*Length_n*];

EXAMPLES

```
char[][] a = new char[5][12];
char[][] page = new char[30][100];
double[][] table = new double[100][10];
int[][][] figure = new int[10][20][30];
Person[][] entry = new Person[10][10];
```

Person is a class.

A multi-
dimensional
array is an
array of
arrays

In Java, a two-dimensional array, such as a, is actually an array of arrays. The above array a is actually a one-dimensional array of size 5, whose base type is a one-dimensional array of characters of size 12. This is diagrammed in Display 6.17. As shown in that display, the array variable a contains a reference to a one-dimensional array of length 5 with a base type of char[]; that is, the base type of a is the type for an entire one-dimensional array of characters. Each indexed variable a[0], a[1], and so forth contains a reference to a one-dimensional array of characters.

Display 6.17   Two-Dimensional Array as an Array of Arrays

```
char[][] a = new char[5][12];
```

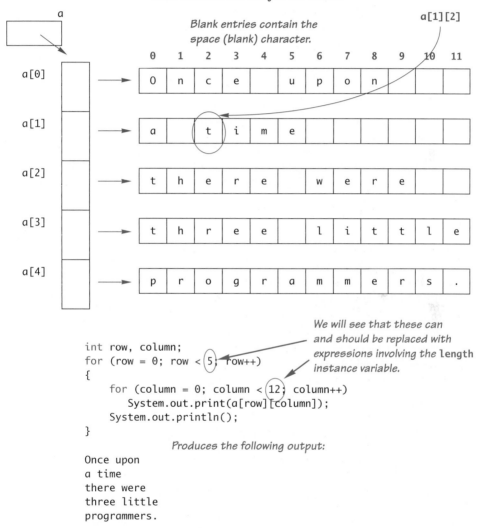

```
int row, column;
for (row = 0; row < 5; row++)
{
    for (column = 0; column < 12; column++)
        System.out.print(a[row][column]);
    System.out.println();
}
```

Produces the following output:

```
Once upon
a time
there were
three little
programmers.
```

A three-dimensional array is an array of arrays of arrays, and so forth for higher dimensions.

Normally, the fact that a two-dimensional array is an array of arrays need not concern you, and you can usually act as if the array *a* is actually an array with two indices (rather than an array of arrays, which is harder to keep track of). There are, however, some situations where a two-dimensional array looks very much like an array of arrays. For example, you will see that when using the instance variable `length`, you must think of a two-dimensional array as an array of arrays.

Using the `length` Instance Variable

Suppose you want to fill all the elements in the following two-dimensional array with `'Z'`:

```
char[][] page = new char[30][100];
```

You can use a nested `for` loop such as the following:

```
int row, column;
for (row = 0; row < page.length; row++)
    for (column = 0; column < page[row].length; column++)
        page[row][column] = 'Z';
```

Let's analyze this nested `for` loop in a bit more detail. The array `page` is actually a one-dimensional array of length 30, and each of the 30 indexed variables `page[0]` through `page[29]` is a one-dimensional array with base type `char` and with a length of 100. That is why the first `for` loop is terminated using `page.length`. For a two-dimensional array like `page`, the value of `length` is the number of first indices or, equivalently, the number of rows—in this case, 30. Now let's consider the inside `for` loop.

The 0th row in the two-dimensional array `page` is the one-dimensional array `page[0]`, and it has `page[0].length` entries. More generally, `page[row]` is a one-dimensional array of chars, and it has `page[row].length` entries. That is why the inner `for` loop is terminated using `page[row].length`. Of course, in this case, `page[0].length`, `page[1].length`, and so forth through to `page[29].length` are all equal and all equal to 100. (If you read the optional section entitled "Ragged Arrays," you will see that these need not all be equal.)

Self-Test Exercise

23. What is the output produced by the following code?

```
int[][] myArray = new int[4][4];
int index1, index2;
for (index1 = 0; index1 < myArray.length; index1++)
    for (index2 = 0;
                index2 < myArray[index1].length; index2++)
        myArray[index1][index2] = index2;
for (index1 = 0; index1 < myArray.length; index1++)
{
    for (index2 = 0;
                index2 < myArray[index1].length; index2++)
        System.out.print(myArray[index1][index2] + " ");
    System.out.println();
}
```

Ragged Arrays ★

There is no need for each row in a two-dimensional array to have the same number of entries. Different rows can have different numbers of columns. These sorts of arrays are called **ragged arrays**.

ragged arrays

To help explain the details, let's start with an ordinary, nonragged two-dimensional array, created as follows:

```
double[][] a = new double[3][5];
```

This is equivalent to the following:

```
double[][] a;
a = new double[3][];
a[0] = new double[5];
a[1] = new double[5];
a[2] = new double[5];
```

The line

```
a = new double[3][];
```

makes a the name of an array with room for three entries, each of which can be an array of doubles that can be of any length. The next three lines each create an array of doubles of length 5 to be named by a[0], a[1], and a[2]. The net result is a two-dimensional array of base type double with three rows and five columns.

If you want, you can make each of a[0], a[1], and a[2] a different length. The following code makes a ragged array b in which each row has a different length:

```
double[][] b;
b = new double[3][];
b[0] = new double[5];
b[1] = new double[10];
b[2] = new double[4];
```

There are situations in which you can profitably use ragged arrays, but most applications do not require them. However, if you understand ragged arrays, you will have a better understanding of how all multidimensional arrays work in Java.

Multidimensional Array Parameters and Returned Values

array arguments

Methods may have multidimensional array parameters and may have a multidimensional array type as the type for the value returned. The situation is similar to that of the one-dimensional case, except that you use more square brackets when specifying the type name. For example, the following method will display a two-dimensional array in the usual way as rows and columns:[6]

```java
public static void showMatrix(int[][] a)
{
    int row, column;
    for (row = 0; row < a.length; row++)
    {
        for (column = 0; column < a[row].length; column++)
            System.out.print(a[row][column] + " ");
        System.out.println();
    }
}
```

returning an array If you want to return a multidimensional array, you use the same kind of type specification as you use for a multidimensional array parameter. For example, the following method returns a two-dimensional array with base type `double`:

```java
/**
 Precondition: Each dimension of a is at least
 the value of size.
 The array returned is the same as the size-by-size
 upper-left corner of the array a.
*/
public static double[][] corner(double[][] a, int size)
{
    double[][] temp = new double[size][size];
    int row, column;
    for (row = 0; row < size; row++)
        for (column = 0; column < size; column++)
            temp[row][column] = a[row][column];
    return temp;
}
```

EXAMPLE: A Grade Book Class

Display 6.18 contains a class for grade records in a class whose only recorded scores are quiz scores. An object of this class has three array instance variables. One is a two-dimensional array named `grade` that records the grade of each student on each quiz. For example, the score that student number 4 received on quiz number 1 is recorded in `grade[3][0]`. Because the student numbers and quiz numbers start with 1 and the array indices start with 0, we subtract one from the student number or quiz number to obtain the corresponding array index.

---

[6] It is worth noting that this method works fine for ragged arrays.

EXAMPLE: (continued)

All the raw data is in the array grade, but two other arrays hold computed data. The array studentAverage is used to record the average quiz score for each of the students. For example, the program sets studentAverage[0] equal to the average of the quiz scores received by student 1, studentAverage[1] equal to the average of the quiz scores received by student 2, and so forth. The array quizAverage is used to record the average score for each quiz. For example, the program sets quizAverage[0] equal to the average of all the student scores for quiz 1, quizAverage[1] records the average score for quiz 2, and so forth. Display 6.19 illustrates the relationship between the arrays grade, studentAverage, and quizAverage. In that display, we have shown some sample data for the array grade. The data in grade, in turn, determines the values that are stored in studentAverage and in quizAverage. Display 6.19 also shows these computed values for studentAverage and quizAverage. The two arrays studentAverage and quizAverage are created and filled by the constructor that creates the GradeBook object. (The constructors do this by calling private helping methods.)

The no-argument constructor for the class GradeBook obtains the data for the array instance variable grade via a dialog with the user. Although this is not my favorite way to define a no-argument constructor, some programmers like it and you should see an example of it. Another alternative would be to have a no-argument constructor that essentially does nothing and then have an input method that sets all the instance variables, including creating the array objects.

A very simple demonstration program along with the dialog it produces is given in Display 6.20.

Display 6.18 **A Grade Book Class** (part 1 of 4)

```
1    import java.util.Scanner;

2    public class GradeBook
3    {

4        private int numberOfStudents; // Same as studentAverage.length.
5        private int numberOfQuizzes; // Same as quizAverage.length.

6        private int[][] grade; //numberOfStudents rows and numberOfQuizzes columns.
7        private double[] studentAverage;
8        private double[] quizAverage;

9        public GradeBook(int[][] a)
10       {
11           if (a.length == 0 || a[0].length == 0)
12           {
13               System.out.println("Empty grade records. Aborting.");
14               System.exit(0);
15           }
```
(continued)

Display 6.18 A Grade Book Class (part 2 of 4)

```
16          numberOfStudents = a.length;
17          numberOfQuizzes = a[0].length;
18          fillGrade(a);
19          fillStudentAverage();
20          fillQuizAverage();
21      }

22      public GradeBook(GradeBook book)
23      {
24          numberOfStudents = book.numberOfStudents;
25          numberOfQuizzes = book.numberOfQuizzes;
26          fillGrade(book.grade);
27          fillStudentAverage();
28          fillQuizAverage();
29      }

30      public GradeBook()
31      {
32          Scanner keyboard = new Scanner(System.in);

33          System.out.println("Enter number of students:");
34          numberOfStudents = keyboard.nextInt();

35          System.out.println("Enter number of quizzes:");
36          numberOfQuizzes = keyboard.nextInt();

37          grade = new int[numberOfStudents][numberOfQuizzes];
38          for (int studentNumber = 1;
39                      studentNumber <= numberOfStudents; studentNumber++)
40              for (int quizNumber = 1;
41                          quizNumber <= numberOfQuizzes; quizNumber++)
42              {
43                  System.out.println("Enter score for student number "
44                                          + studentNumber);
45                  System.out.println("on quiz number " + quizNumber);
46                  grade[studentNumber – 1][quizNumber – 1] =
47                                          keyboard.nextInt();
48              }

49          fillStudentAverage();
50          fillQuizAverage();
51      }
```

This class should have more accessor and mutator methods, but we have omitted them to save space. See Self-Test Exercises 24 through 27.

```
52      private void fillGrade(int[][] a)
53      {
54          grade = new int[numberOfStudents][numberOfQuizzes];
```

Display 6.18   **A Grade Book Class** (part 3 of 4)

```
55          for (int studentNumber = 1;
56                      studentNumber <= numberOfStudents; studentNumber++)
57          {
58              for (int quizNumber = 1;
59                          quizNumber <= numberOfQuizzes; quizNumber++)
60                  grade[studentNumber][quizNumber] =
61                                      a[studentNumber][quizNumber];
62          }
63      }

64      /**
65        Fills the array studentAverage using the data from the array grade.
66      */
67      private void fillStudentAverage()
68      {
69          studentAverage = new double[numberOfStudents];

70          for (int studentNumber = 1;
71                      studentNumber <= numberOfStudents; studentNumber++)
72          {//Process one studentNumber:
73              double sum = 0;
74              for (int quizNumber = 1;
75                          quizNumber <= numberOfQuizzes; quizNumber++)
76                  sum = sum + grade[studentNumber - 1][quizNumber - 1];
77              //sum contains the sum of the quiz scores for student number studentNumber.
78              studentAverage[studentNumber - 1] = sum/numberOfQuizzes;
79              //Average for student studentNumber is studentAverage[studentNumber - 1]
80          }
81      }
82      /**
83        Fills the array quizAverage using the data from the array grade.
84      */
85      private void fillQuizAverage()
86      {
87          quizAverage = new double[numberOfQuizzes];

88          for (int quizNumber = 1; quizNumber <= numberOfQuizzes; quizNumber++)
89          {//Process one quiz (for all students):
90              double sum = 0;
91              for (int studentNumber = 1;
92                          studentNumber <= numberOfStudents; studentNumber++)
93                  sum = sum + grade[studentNumber - 1][quizNumber - 1];
94              //sum contains the sum of all student scores on quiz number quizNumber.
95              quizAverage[quizNumber - 1] = sum/numberOfStudents;
96              //Average for quiz quizNumber is the value of quizAverage[quizNumber - 1]
97          }
98      }
```

(continued)

Display 6.18 **A Grade Book Class** (part 4 of 4)

```
 99    public void display()
100    {
101       for (int studentNumber = 1;
102                    studentNumber <= numberOfStudents; studentNumber++)

103       {//Display for one studentNumber:
104          System.out.print("Student " + studentNumber + " Quizzes: ");
105          for (int quizNumber = 1;
106                       quizNumber <= numberOfQuizzes; quizNumber++)
107            System.out.print(grade[studentNumber - 1][quizNumber - 1] + " ");
108          System.out.println(" Ave = " + studentAverage[studentNumber - 1] );
109       }

110       System.out.println("Quiz averages: ");
111       for (int quizNumber = 1; quizNumber <= numberOfQuizzes; quizNumber++)
112          System.out.print("Quiz " + quizNumber
113                             + " Ave = " + quizAverage[quizNumber - 1] + " ");
114       System.out.println();
115    }
116
```

Display 6.19 **The Two-Dimensional Array grade**

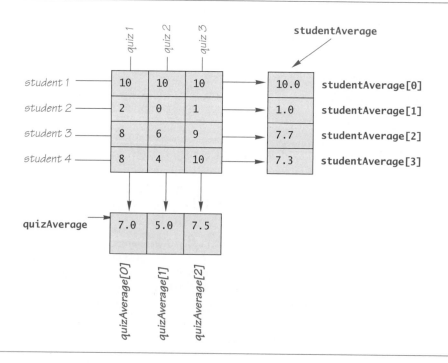

Display 6.20 Demonstration of the Class **GradeBook**

```
1    public class GradeBookDemo
2    {
3        public static void main(String[] args)
4        {
5            GradeBook book = new GradeBook();
6            book.display();
7        }
8    }
```

Sample Dialogue

```
Enter number of students:
4
Enter number of quizzes:
3
Enter score for student number 1
on quiz number 1
10
Enter score for student number 1
on quiz number 2
10

    <The rest of the input dialog is omitted to save space.>

Student 1 Quizzes: 10 10 10 Ave = 10.0
Student 2 Quizzes: 2 0 1 Ave = 1.0
Student 3 Quizzes: 8 6 9 Ave = 7.66666666667
Student 4 Quizzes: 8 4 10 Ave = 7.33333333333
Quiz averages:
Quiz 1 Ave = 7.0 Quiz 2 Ave = 5.0 Quiz 3 Ave = 7.5
```

Self-Test Exercises

24. Write a method definition for a method with the following heading. The method is to be added to the class GradeBook in Display 6.18.

```
/**
 Returns the grade that student numbered studentNumber
 received on quiz number quizNumber.
*/
public int getGrade(int studentNumber, int quizNumber)
```

(continued)

Self-Test Exercises (continued)

25. Write a method definition for a method with the following heading. The method is to be added to the class `GradeBook` in Display 6.18.

```
/**
 Changes the grade for student number studentNumber
 on quiz number quizNumber to newGrade.
*/
public void changeGrade(int studentNumber,
                   int quizNumber, int newGrade))
```

26. Write a method definition for a method with the following heading. The method is to be added to the class `GradeBook` in Display 6.18.

```
/**
 Returns an array with the average quiz score for each student.
*/
public double[] getStudentAverages()
```

27. Write a method definition for a method with the following heading. The method is to be added to the class `GradeBook` in Display 6.18.

```
/**
 Returns an array with the average score for each quiz.
*/
public double[] getQuizAverages()
```

Chapter Summary

- An array can be used to store and manipulate a collection of data that is all of the same type.

- The indexed variables of an array can be used just like any other variables of the base type of the array.

- Arrays are objects that are created with new just like the class objects we discussed before this chapter (although there is a slight difference in the syntax used).

- A for loop is a good way to step through the elements of an array and perform some program action on each indexed variable.

- The most common programming error made when using arrays is to attempt to access a nonexistent array index. Always check the first and last iterations of a loop that manipulates an array to make sure it does not use an index that is illegally small or illegally large.

- The indexed variables of an array can be used as an argument to be plugged in for a parameter of the array's base type.

- A method can have parameters of an array type. When the method is invoked, an entire array is plugged in for the array parameter.

- A method may return an array as the value returned by the method.

- When using a partially filled array, your program needs an additional variable of type int to keep track of how much of the array is being used.

- An instance variable of a class can be of an array type.

- If you need an array with more than one index, you can use a multidimensional array, which is actually an array of arrays.

Answers to Self-Test Exercises

1. a. word

   b. String

   c. 5

   d. 0 through 4 inclusive

   e. Any of the following would be correct:
      word[0], word[1], word[2], word[3], word[4]

2. a. 10

   b. 0

   c. 9

3. a, b, c,

4. 1.1 2.2 3.3
   1.1 3.3 3.3

5. The for loop uses indices 1 through sampleArray.length, but the correct indices are 0 through sampleArray.length − 1. The last index, sampleArray.length, is out of bounds. What was probably intended is the following:

   ```
   int[] sampleArray = new int[10];
   for (int index = 0; index < sampleArray.length; index++)
       sampleArray[index] = 3*index;
   ```

6. The last value of index is a.length − 1, which is the last index of the array. However, when index has the value a.length − 1, a[index + 1] has an index that is out of bounds because index + 1 is one more than the largest array index. The for loop ending condition should instead be index < a.length − 1.

7. ```
SomeClass.doSomething(number); //Legal.
SomeClass.doSomething(a[2]); //Legal.
SomeClass.doSomething(a[3]); //Illegal. Index out of bounds.
SomeClass.doSomething(a[number]); //Legal.
SomeClass.doSomething(a); //Illegal.
```

8. ```
public static void oneMore(int[] a)
{
    for (int i = 0; i < a.length; i++)
        a[i] = a[i] + 1;
}
```

9. ```
public static int outOfOrder(double[] a)
{
    for (int index = 0; index < a.length - 1; index++)
    if (a[index] > a[index + 1])
        return (index + 1);
    return - 1;
}
```

10. This method is legal but pointless. When invoked, it has no effect on its argument. The parameter *a* is a local variable that contains a reference. The reference does indeed get changed to a reference to an array of double the size of the argument, but that reference goes away when the method ends. A method can change the values of the indexed variables of its argument, but it cannot change the reference in the array variable used as an argument.

11. ```
public static double[] halfArray(double[] a)
{
    double[] temp = new double[a.length];
    for (int i = 0; i < a.length; i++)
        temp[i] = a[i]/2.0;
    return temp;
}
```

12. The method will compile and run. The array returned has the correct values for its elements. However, the method will change the values of its array argument. If you want to change the values in the array argument, a void method would make more sense. If you want to return an array, you should probably return a new array (as in the version in the previous subsection), not return a changed version of the argument array.

13. ```
/**
 Precondition: numberUsed <= argumentArray.length;
 the first numberUsed indexed variables of argumentArray
 have values.
 Returns an array of length numberUsed whose ith element
 is argumentArray[i] - adjustment.
*/
```
```

```java
public static double[] differenceArray(
 double[] argumentArray, int numberUsed, double adjustment)
{
    double[] temp = new double[numberUsed];
    for (int i = 0; i < numberUsed; i++)
        temp[i] = argumentArray[i] - adjustment;
    return temp;
}
```

14. The only changes are to add the method differenceArray and to rewrite the method showDifference as follows (the complete class definition is in the file GolfScoresExercise.java on the accompanying CD):

extra code on CD

```java
public static void showDifference(double[] a,
                                          int numberUsed)
{
    double average = computeAverage(a, numberUsed);
    System.out.println("Average of the " + numberUsed
                            + " scores = " + average);
    double[] difference =
                differenceArray(a, numberUsed, average);
    System.out.println("The scores are:");
    for (int index = 0; index < numberUsed; index++)
        System.out.println(a[index] +
                        " differs from average by "
                            + difference[index]);
}
```

15. The main differences are to remove parameters, replace the array name a by score, and make the method fillArray a void method. This code is in the file GolfScoresStaticExercise.java on the accompanying CD.

extra code on CD

```java
import java.util.Scanner;

public class GolfScoresStaticExercise
{
    public static final int MAX_NUMBER_SCORES = 10;
    private static double[] score =
                        new double[MAX_NUMBER_SCORES];
    private static int numberUsed = 0;

    /**
     Shows differences between each of a list of golf scores
     and their average.
    */
    public static void main(String[] args)
    {
```

```java
        System.out.println(
                "This program reads golf scores and shows");
        System.out.println(
                "how much each differs from the average.");

        System.out.println("Enter golf scores:");
        fillArray();
        showDifference();
    }

    /**
     Reads values into the array score.
    */
    public static void fillArray()
    {
        System.out.println("Enter up to " + score.length
                    + " nonnegative numbers:");
        System.out.println(
            "Mark the end of the list with a negative number.");
        Scanner keyboard = new Scanner(System.in);

        double next;
        int index = 0;
        next = keyboard.nextDouble();
        while ((next >= 0) && (index < score.length))
        {
            score[index] = next;
            index++;
            next = keyboard.nextDouble();
            //index is the number of
            //array indexed variables used so far.
        }
        //index is the total number of array indexed variables used.

        if (next >= 0)
            System.out.println("Could only read in "
                        + score.length + " input values.");

        numberUsed = index;
    }

    /**
     Precondition: numberUsed <= score.length.
                score[0] through score[numberUsed-1] have values.
     Returns the average of numbers ascore[0] through
     score[numberUsed-1].
    */
    public static double computeAverage()
    {
```

```
    double total = 0;
    for (int index = 0; index < numberUsed; index++)
        total = total + score[index];
    if (numberUsed > 0)
    {
        return (total/numberUsed);
    }
    else
    {
        System.out.println(
                "ERROR: Trying to average 0 numbers.");
        System.out.println("computeAverage returns 0.");
        return 0;
    }
}


/**
 Precondition: numberUsed <= score.length.
 The first numberUsed indexed variables of score have values.
 Postcondition: Gives screen output showing how much each of the
 first numberUsed elements of the array a differ from the average.
*/
public static void showDifference()
{
    double average = computeAverage();
    System.out.println("Average of the " + numberUsed
                                + " scores = " + average);
    System.out.println("The scores are:");
    for (int index = 0; index < numberUsed; index++)
    System.out.println(score[index] +
                            " differs from average by "
                            + (score[index] - average));
}
}
```

16.
```
    public static int max(int... arg)
    {
        if (arg.length == 0)
        {
            System.out.println(
                    "Fatal Error: maximum of zero values.");
            System.exit(0);
        }

        int largest = Integer.MIN_VALUE;
        for (int element : arg)
            if (element > largest)
                largest = element;
        return largest;
    }
```

17. The last line would change to the following:

```
I ate  cod, broccoli, ,  peanuts, and apples.
```

18.
```java
public void removeAll()
{
    numberUsed = 0;
}
```

19.
```java
public void increaseCapacity(int newCapacity)
{
    if (newCapacity > numberUsed)
    {
        maxNumberElements = newCapacity;
        double[] temp = new double[newCapacity];
        for (int i = 0; i < a.length; i++)
            temp[i] = a[i];
        a = temp;
    }//else do nothing.
}
```

20. All you need to do to make your code work for sorting into decreasing order is to replace the < with > in the following line of the definition of `indexOfSmallest`:

```java
if (a[index] < min)
```

However, to make your code easy to read, you should also rename the method `indexOfSmallest` to `indexOfLargest`, rename the variable `min` to `max`, and rename the variable `indexOfMin` to `indexOfMax`. You should also rewrite some of the comments to reflect these changes.

21. If an array has a value that occurs more than once and you sort the array using the method `SelectionSort.sort`, then there will be as many copies of the repeated value after the array is sorted as there originally were in the array.

extra code on CD

22. We give two slightly different versions. Both versions are on the accompanying CD.

```java
import java.util.Scanner;

public class ForEachEnumDemo
{
    enum WorkDay {MONDAY, TUESDAY, WEDNESDAY, THURSDAY, FRIDAY};

    public static void main(String[] args)
    {
        WorkDay[] day = WorkDay.values();

        Scanner keyboard = new Scanner(System.in);
        double hours = 0, sum = 0;

        for (WorkDay oneDay : day)
```

```
        {
            System.out.println("Enter hours worked for " + oneDay);
            hours = keyboard.nextDouble();
            sum = sum + hours;
        }

        System.out.println("Total hours work = " + sum);
    }
}

import java.util.Scanner;

public class ForEachEnumDemo2
{
    enum WorkDay {MONDAY, TUESDAY, WEDNESDAY, THURSDAY, FRIDAY};

    public static void main(String[] args)
    {
        Scanner keyboard = new Scanner(System.in);
        double hours = 0, sum = 0;

        for (WorkDay oneDay : WorkDay.values())
        {
            System.out.println("Enter hours worked for " + oneDay);
            hours = keyboard.nextDouble();
            sum = sum + hours;
        }

        System.out.println("Total hours work = " + sum);
    }
}
```

23. ```
    0 1 2 3
    0 1 2 3
    0 1 2 3
    0 1 2 3
    ```

24. If the array indices are out of bounds, then Java will halt the program with an error message, so no other checks on the parameters are needed.

```
/**
 Returns the grade that student number studentNumber
 received on quiz number quizNumber.
*/
public int getGrade(int studentNumber, int quizNumber)
{
    return grade[studentNumber][quizNumber];
}
```
```

25. If the array indices are out of bounds, then Java will halt the program with an error message, so no other checks on the parameters are needed.

```java
/**
 Changes the grade for student number studentNumber
 on quiz number quizNumber to newGrade.
*/
public void changeGrade(int studentNumber,
                int quizNumber, int newGrade)
{
    grade[studentNumber][quizNumber] = newGrade;
}
```

26.
```java
/**
 Returns an array with the average quiz score for each student.
*/
public double[] getStudentAverages()
{
    int arraySize = studentAverage.length;
    double[] temp = new double[arraySize];
    for (int i = 0; i < arraySize; i++)
        temp[i] = studentAverage[i];
    return temp;
}
```

27.
```java
/**
 Returns an array with the average score for each quiz.
*/
public double[] getQuizAverages()
{
    int arraySize = quizAverage.length;
    double[] temp = new double[arraySize];
    for (int i = 0; i < arraySize; i++)
        temp[i] = quizAverage[i];
    return temp;
}
```

Programming Projects

 Many of these Programming Projects can be solved using AW's MyCodeMate. To access these please go to: www.mycodemate.com.

 1. In the sport of diving, seven judges award a score between 0 and 10, where each score may be a floating-point value. The highest and lowest scores are thrown out and the remaining scores are added together. The sum is then multiplied by the degree of difficulty for that dive. The degree of difficulty ranges from 1.2 to 3.8 points. The total is then multiplied by 0.6 to determine the diver's score.

Write a computer program that inputs a degree of difficulty and seven judges' scores and outputs the overall score for that dive. The program should ensure that all inputs are within the allowable data ranges.

2. A common memory matching game played by young children is to start with a deck of cards that contain identical pairs. For example, given six cards in the deck, two might be labeled 1, two labeled 2, and two labeled 3. The cards are shuffled and placed face down on the table. A player then selects two cards that are face down, turns them face up, and if the cards match they are left face up. If the two cards do not match they are returned to their original face down position. The game continues until all cards are face up.

   Write a program that plays the memory matching game. Use sixteen cards that are laid out in a 4×4 square and are labeled with pairs of numbers from 1 to 8. Your program should allow the player to specify the cards that she would like to select through a coordinate system.

   For example, in the following layout:

   ```
        1   2   3   4

   1 |  8   *   *   *
   2 |  *   *   *   *
   3 |  *   8   *   *
   4 |  *   *   *   *
   ```

   All of the cards are face down indicated by *. The pairs of 8 which are face up are at coordinates (1,1) and (2,3). To hide the cards that have been temporarily placed face up, output a large number of newlines to force the old board off the screen.

   Hint: Use a 2D array for the arrangement of cards and another 2D array that indicates if a card is face up or face down. Or, a more elegant solution is to create a single 2D array where each element is an object that stores both the card's value and face. Write a function that "shuffles" the cards in the array by repeatedly selecting two cards at random and swapping them.

   Note: To generate a random number *x*, where 0 *x* < 1, use x = Math.random(); . For example, multiplying by six and converting to an integer results in an integer that is from 0 to 5.

 3. Write a program that reads in the average monthly rainfall for a city for each month of the year and then reads in the actual monthly rainfall for each of the previous 12 months. The program should then print out a nicely formatted table showing the rainfall for each of the previous 12 months as well as how much above or below average the rainfall was for each month. The average monthly rainfall is given for the months January, February, and so forth, in order. To obtain the actual rainfall for the previous 12 months, the program should first

ask what the current month is and then ask for the rainfall figures for the previous 12 months. The output should correctly label the months. There are a variety of ways to deal with the month names. One straightforward method is to code the months as integers and then do a conversion to a string for the month name before doing the output. A large `switch` statement is acceptable in an output method. The month input can be handled in any manner you wish so long as it is relatively easy and pleasant for the user. Include a loop that allows the user to repeat this entire calculation until the user requests that the program end.

4. Write a static method called `deleteRepeats` that has a partially filled array of characters as a formal parameter and that deletes all repeated letters from the array. Because a partially filled array requires two arguments, the method should actually have two formal parameters: an array parameter and a formal parameter of type int that gives the number of array positions used. When a letter is deleted, the remaining letters are moved one position to fill in the gap. This creates empty positions at the end of the array so that less of the array is used. Because the formal parameter is a partially filled array, a second formal parameter of type int should tell how many array positions are filled. This second formal parameter cannot be changed by a Java method, so have the method return the new value for this parameter. For example, consider the following code:

```
char a[10];
a[0] = 'a';
a[1] = 'b';
a[2] = 'a';
a[3] = 'c';
int size = 4;
size = deleteRepeats(a, size);
```

After this code is executed, the value of `a[0]` is `'a'`, the value of `a[1]` is `'b'`, the value of `a[2]` is `'c'`, and the value of `size` is 3. (The value of `a[3]` is no longer of any concern, because the partially filled array no longer uses this indexed variable.) You may assume that the partially filled array contains only lowercase letters. Write a suitable test program for your method.

5. The standard deviation of a list of numbers is a measure of how much the numbers deviate from the average. If the standard deviation is small, the numbers are clustered close to the average. If the standard deviation is large, the numbers are scattered far from the average. The standard deviation of a list of numbers n_1, n_2, n_3, and so forth is defined as the square root of the average of the following numbers:

$(n_1 - a)^2$, $(n_2 - a)^2$, $(n_3 - a)^2$, and so forth.

The number a is the average of the numbers n_1, n_2, n_3, and so forth.

Define a static method that takes a partially filled array of numbers as its argument and returns the standard deviation of the numbers in the partially filled array. Because a partially filled array requires two arguments, the method should actually have two formal parameters, an array parameter and a formal parameter of type int that gives the number of array positions used. The numbers in the array should be of type double. Write a suitable test program for your method.

6. Write a program that reads numbers from the keyboard into an array of type int[]. You may assume that there will be 50 or fewer entries in the array. Your program allows any number of numbers to be entered, up to 50 numbers. The output is to be a two-column list. The first column is a list of the distinct array elements; the second column is the count of the number of occurrences of each element. The list should be sorted on entries in the first column, largest to smallest.

For the array

−12 3 −12 4 1 1 −12 1 −1 1 2 3 4 2 3 −12

the output should be

```
N    Count
4    2
3    3
2    2
1    4
−1   1
−12  4
```

7. An array can be used to store large integers one digit at a time. For example, the integer 1234 could be stored in the array a by setting a[0] to 1, a[1] to 2, a[2] to 3, and a[3] to 4. However, for this exercise you might find it more useful to store the digits backward; that is, place 4 in a[0], 3 in a[1], 2 in a[2], and 1 in a[3]. In this exercise, write a program that reads in two positive integers that are 20 or fewer digits in length and then outputs the sum of the two numbers. Your program will read the digits as values of type char so that the number 1234 is read as the four characters '1', '2', '3', and '4'. After they are read into the program, the characters are changed to values of type int. The digits should be read into a partially filled array, and you might find it useful to reverse the order of the elements in the array after the array is filled with data from the keyboard. (Whether or not you reverse the order of the elements in the array is up to you. It can be done either way, and each way has its advantages and disadvantages.) Your program should perform the addition by implementing the usual paper-and-pencil addition algorithm. The result of the addition should be stored in an array of size 20, and the result should then be written to the screen. If the result of the addition is an integer with more than the maximum number of digits (that is, more than 20 digits), then your program should issue a message saying that it has encountered "integer overflow." You should be able to change the maximum length of the integers by changing only one named constant. Include a loop that allows the user to continue to do more additions until the user says the program should end.

8. Design a class called `BubbleSort` that is similar to the class `SelectionSort` given in Display 6.11. The class `BubbleSort` will be used in the same way as the class `SelectionSort`, but it will use the bubble sort algorithm.

The bubble sort algorithm checks all adjacent pairs of elements in the array from the beginning to the end and interchanges any two elements that are out of order. This process is repeated until the array is sorted. The algorithm is as follows:

Bubble Sort Algorithm to Sort an Array *a*

Repeat the following until the array *a* is sorted:

```
for (index = 0; index < a.length − 1; index++)
    if (a[index] > a[index + 1])
        Interchange the values of a[index] and a[index + 1].
```

The bubble sort algorithm is good for sorting an array that is "almost sorted." It is not competitive with other sorting methods for most other situations.

9. Enhance the definition of the class `PartiallyFilledArray` (Display 6.5) in the following way: When the user attempts to add one additional element and there is no room in the array instance variable *a*, the user is allowed to add the element. The object creates a second array that is twice the size of the array *a*, copies values from the array *a* to the user's new array, makes this array (or more precisely its reference) the new value of *a*, and then adds the element to this new larger array *a*. Hence, this new class should have no limit (other than the physical size of the computer) to how many numbers it can hold. The instance variable `maxNumberOfElements` remains and the method `getMaxCapacity` is unchanged, but these now refer to the currently allocated memory and not to an absolute upper bound. Write a suitable test program.

10. Write a program that will allow two users to play tic-tac-toe. The program should ask for moves alternately from player X and player O. The program displays the game positions as follows:

```
1  2  3
4  5  6
7  8  9
```

The players enter their moves by entering the position number they wish to mark. After each move, the program displays the changed board. A sample board configuration is

```
X  X  O
4  5  6
O  8  9
```

11. Write a program to assign passengers seats in an airplane. Assume a small airplane with seat numberings as follows:

```
1   A B   C D
2   A B   C D
3   A B   C D
4   A B   C D
5   A B   C D
6   A B   C D
7   A B   C D
```

The program should display the seat pattern, with an 'X' marking the seats already assigned. For example, after seats 1A, 2B, and 4C are taken, the display should look like:

```
1   X B   C D
2   A X   C D
3   A B   C D
4   A B   X D
5   A B   C D
6   A B   C D
7   A B   C D
```

After displaying the seats available, the program should prompt for the seat desired, the user can type in a seat, and then the display of available seats should be updated. This continues until all seats are filled or until the user signals that the program should end. If the user types in a seat that is already assigned, the program should say that that seat is occupied and ask for another choice.

7

Inheritance

7 Inheritance

Like mother, like daughter.

COMMON SAYING

Introduction

Object-oriented programming (OOP) is a popular and powerful programming philosophy. One of the main techniques of OOP is known as *inheritance*. **Inheritance** means that a very general form of a class can be defined and compiled. Later, more specialized versions of that class may be defined by starting with the already defined class and adding more specialized instance variables and methods. The specialized classes are said to *inherit* the methods and instance variables of the previously defined general class. In this chapter we cover inheritance in general and more specifically how it is realized in Java.

Prerequisites

This chapter does not use any material on arrays from Chapter 6. It does require Chapters 1 through 5 with the exception that most of the chapter does not require Section 5.4 on packages and javadoc. The subsection "Protected and Package Access" is the only part of this chapter that requires anything from Section 5.4 and it requires only the material on packages and not any material on javadoc. The subsection "Protected and Package Access" can be omitted without any loss of continuity in reading this chapter.

7.1 Inheritance Basics

If there is anything that we wish to change in the child, we should first examine it and see whether it is not something that could better be changed in ourselves.

CARL GUSTAV JUNG, *The Integration of the Personality*

Inheritance is the process by which a new class—known as a *derived class*—is created from another class, called the *base class*. A derived class automatically has all the instance variables and all the methods that the base class has, and can have additional methods and/or additional instance variables.

Derived Classes

Suppose we are designing a record-keeping program that has records for salaried employees and hourly employees. There is a natural hierarchy for grouping these classes. These are all classes of people who share the property of being employees.

Employees who are paid an hourly wage are one subset of employees. Another subset consists of salaried employees who are paid a fixed wage each month. Although the program may not need any type corresponding to the set of all employees, thinking in terms of the more general concept of employees can be useful. For example, all employees have a name and a hire date (when they started working for the company), and the methods for setting and changing names and hire dates will be the same for salaried and hourly employees. The classes for hourly employees and salaried employees may be further subdivided as diagrammed in Display 7.1.

Within Java you can define a class called Employee that includes all employees, whether salaried or hourly, and then use this class to define classes for hourly employees and salaried employees. You can then, in turn, use classes like HourlyEmployee to define classes like PartTimeHourlyEmployee, and so forth.

Display 7.2 shows our definition for the class Employee. The class Employee is a pretty ordinary class much like earlier classes we have seen. What will be interesting about the class Employee is how we use it to create a class for hourly employees and a class for salaried employees. It is legal to create an object of the class Employee, but our reason for defining the class Employee is so that we can define derived classes for different kinds of employees.

Display 7.1 **A Class Hierarchy**

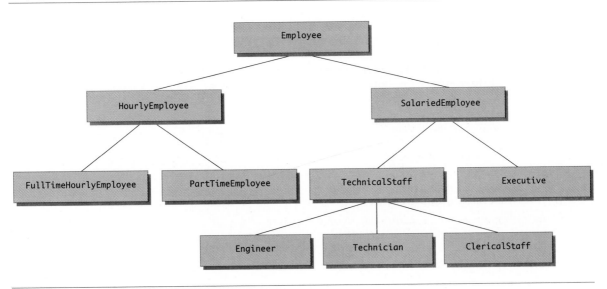

Display 7.2 **The Base Class Employee** (part 1 of 2)

```
1    /**
2     Class Invariant: All objects have a name string and hire date.
3     A name string of "No name" indicates no real name specified yet.
4     A hire date of January 1, 1000 indicates no real hire date specified yet.
5    */
6    public class Employee
7    {
8        private String name;
9        private Date hireDate;              The class Date is defined in
                                             Display 4.13.
10       public Employee()
11       {
12           name = "No name";
13           hireDate = new Date("January", 1, 1000); //Just a placeholder.
14       }

15       /**
16        Precondition: Neither theName nor theDate is null.
17       */
18       public Employee(String theName, Date theDate)
19       {
20           if (theName == null || theDate == null)
21           {
22               System.out.println("Fatal Error creating employee.");
23               System.exit(0);
24           }
25           name = theName;
26           hireDate = new Date(theDate);
27       }

28       public Employee(Employee originalObject)
29       {
30           name = originalObject.name;
31           hireDate = new Date(originalObject.hireDate);
32       }

33       public String getName()
34       {
35           return name;
36       }

37       public Date getHireDate()
38       {
39           return new Date(hireDate);
40       }
```

Display 7.2 **The Base Class Employee** (part 2 of 2)

```
41        /**
42         Precondition newName is not null.
43        */
44        public void setName(String newName)
45        {
46            if (newName == null)
47            {
48                  System.out.println("Fatal Error setting employee name.");
49                  System.exit(0);
50            }
51            else
52                  name = newName;
53        }

54        /**
55         Precondition newDate is not null.
56        */
57        public void setHireDate(Date newDate)
58        {
59            if (newDate == null)
60            {
61                  System.out.println("Fatal Error setting employee hire date.");
62                  System.exit(0);
63            }
64            else
65                  hireDate = new Date(newDate);
66        }


67        public String toString()
68        {
69            return (name + " " + hireDate.toString());
70        }

71        public boolean equals(Employee otherEmployee)
72        {
73            return (name.equals(otherEmployee.name)
74                          && hireDate.equals(otherEmployee.hireDate));
75        }
76    }
```

Display 7.3 contains the definition of a class for hourly employees. An hourly employee is an employee, so we define the class `HourlyEmployee` to be a *derived* class of the class `Employee`. A **derived class** is a class defined by adding instance variables and methods to an existing class. The existing class that the derived class is built upon is called the **base class**. In our example, `Employee` is the base class and `HourlyEmployee` is the derived class. As you can see in Display 7.3, the way we indicate that `Hourly-Employee` is a derived class of `Employee` is by including the phrase `extends Employee` on the first line of the class definition, like so:

derived class

base class

extends

```
public class HourlyEmployee extends Employee
```

subclass and superclass

A derived class is also called a **subclass**, in which case the base class is usually called a **superclass**. However, we prefer to use the terms *derived class* and *base class.*

When you define a derived class, you give only the added instance variables and the added methods. For example, the class `HourlyEmployee` has all the instance variables and all the methods of the class `Employee`, but you do not mention them in the definition of `HourlyEmployee`. Every object of the class `HourlyEmployee` has instance variables called `name` and `hireDate`, but you do not specify the instance variable `name` or the instance variable `hireDate` in the definition of the class `HourlyEmployee`. The class `HourlyEmployee` (or any other derived class) is said to **inherit** the instance variables and methods of the base class that it extends. For this reason, the topic of derived classes is called **inheritance**.

inheritance

Just as it inherits the instance variables of the class `Employee`, the class `Hourly-Employee` inherits all the methods from the class `Employee`. So, the class `Hourly-Employee` inherits the methods `getName`, `getHireDate`, `setName`, and `setHireDate`, from the class `Employee`.

For example, suppose you create a new object of the class `HourlyEmployee` as follows:

```
HourlyEmployee joe = new HourlyEmployee();
```

Then, the name of the object `joe` can be changed using the method `setName`, which the class `HourlyEmployee` inherited from the class `Employee`. The inherited method `setName` is used just like any other method; for example:

```
joe.setName("Josephine");
```

A small demonstration of this is given in Display 7.4.

Display 7.5 contains the definition of the class `SalariedEmployee`, which is also derived from the class `Employee`. The class `SalariedEmployee` inherits all the instance variables and methods of the class `Employee`. Inheritance allows you to reuse code, such as the code in the class `Employee`, without needing to literally copy the code into the definitions of the derived classes, such as `HourlyEmployee` and `SalariedEmployee`.

Display 7.3 The Derived Class HourlyEmployee (part 1 of 3)

```
1   /**
2    Class Invariant: All objects have a name string, hire date, nonnegative
3    wage rate, and nonnegative number of hours worked. A name string of
4    "No name" indicates no real name specified yet. A hire date of January 1, 1000
5    indicates no real hire date specified yet.
6   */
7   public class HourlyEmployee extends Employee
8   {
9       private double wageRate;
10      private double hours; //for the month

11      public HourlyEmployee()
12      {
13          super();
14          wageRate = 0;
15          hours = 0;
16      }

17      /**
18       Precondition: Neither theName nor theDate is null;
19       theWageRate and theHours are nonnegative.
20      */
21      public HourlyEmployee(String theName, Date theDate,
22                      double theWageRate, double theHours)
23      {
24          super(theName, theDate);
25          if ((theWageRate >= 0) && (theHours >= 0))
26          {
27              wageRate = theWageRate;
28              hours = theHours;
29          }
30          else
31          {
32              System.out.println(
33                      "Fatal Error: creating an illegal hourly employee.");
34              System.exit(0);
35          }
36      }

37      public HourlyEmployee(HourlyEmployee originalObject)
38      {
39          super(originalObject);
40          wageRate = originalObject.wageRate;
41          hours = originalObject.hours;
42      }
```

It will take the rest of Section 7.1 to explain this class definition.

If this line is omitted, Java will still invoke the no-argument constructor for the base class.

An object of the class HourlyEmployee is also an instance of the class Employee.

(continued)

Display 7.3 The Derived Class **HourlyEmployee** (part 2 of 3)

```
43        public double getRate()
44        {
45            return wageRate;
46        }

47        public double getHours()
48        {
49            return hours;
50        }

51        /**
52         Returns the pay for the month.
53        */
54        public double getPay()
55        {
56            return wageRate*hours;
57        }

58        /**
59         Precondition: hoursWorked is nonnegative.
60        */
61        public void setHours(double hoursWorked)
62        {
63            if (hoursWorked >= 0)
64                hours = hoursWorked;
65            else
66            {
67                System.out.println("Fatal Error: Negative hours worked.");
68                System.exit(0);
69            }
70        }

71        /**
72         Precondition: newWageRate is nonnegative.
73        */
74        public void setRate(double newWageRate)
75        {
76            if (newWageRate >= 0)
77                wageRate = newWageRate;
78            else
79            {
80                System.out.println("Fatal Error: Negative wage rate.");
81                System.exit(0);
82            }
83        }
```

Display 7.3 The Derived Class **HourlyEmployee** (part 3 of 3)

*The method **toString** is overridden so it is different in the derived class **HourlyEmployee** than it is in the base class **Employee**.*

```
84      public String toString()
85      {
86          return (getName() + " " + getHireDate().toString()
87                  + "\n$" + wageRate + " per hour for " + hours + " hours");
88      }

89      public boolean equals(HourlyEmployee other)
90      {
91          return (getName().equals(other.getName())
92                  && getHireDate().equals(other.getHireDate())
93                  && wageRate == other.wageRate
94                  && hours == other.hours);
95      }
96  }
```

*We will show you a better way to define **equals** later in this chapter.*

Derived Class (Subclass)

You define a **derived class** by starting with another already defined class and adding (or changing) methods, instance variables, and static variables. The class you start with is called the **base class**. The derived class inherits all the public methods, all the public and private instance variables, and all the public and private static variables from the base class and can add more instance variables, more static variables, and more methods. So, of the things we have seen thus far, the only members not inherited are private methods. (As discussed a little later in this chapter, the derived class definition can also change the definition of an inherited method.) A derived class is also called a **subclass**, in which case the base class is usually called a **superclass**.

SYNTAX

```
public class Derived_Class_Name extends Base_Class_Name
{
        Declarations_of_Added_Static_Variables
        Declarations_of_Added_Instance_Variables
        Definitions_of_Added__And_Overridden_Methods
}
```

EXAMPLE

See Displays 7.3 and 7.5.

Display 7.4 Inheritance Demonstration

```
1   public class InheritanceDemo              The methods getName and setName are
2   {                                         inherited from the base class Employee.
3       public static void main(String[] args)
4       {
5           HourlyEmployee joe = new HourlyEmployee("Joe Worker",
6                               new Date("January", 1, 2004), 50.50, 160);

7           System.out.println("joe's longer name is " + joe.getName());

8           System.out.println("Changing joe's name to Josephine.");
9           joe.setName("Josephine");

10          System.out.println("joe's record is as follows:");
11          System.out.println(joe);
12      }
13  }
```

Sample Dialogue

```
joe's longer name is Joe Worker
Changing joe's name to Josephine.
joe's record is as follows:
Josephine January 1, 2004
$50.5 per hour for 160 hours
```

Inherited Members

A derived class automatically has all the instance variables, all the static variables, and all the public methods of the base class. These members from the base class are said to be **inherited**. These inherited methods and inherited instance and static variables are, with one exception, not mentioned in the definition of the derived class, but they are automatically members of the derived class. The one exception is follows: As explained later in this chapter, you can give a definition for an inherited method in the definition of the derived class; this will redefine the meaning of the method for the derived class.

Display 7.5   The Derived Class **SalariedEmployee** (part 1 of 2)

```
1   /**
2    Class Invariant: All objects have a name string, hire date,
3    and nonnegative salary. A name string of "No name" indicates
4    no real name specified yet. A hire date of January 1, 1000 indicates
5    no real hire date specified yet.
6   */
7   public class SalariedEmployee extends Employee
8   {
9       private double salary; //annual

10      public SalariedEmployee()
11      {
12          super();
13          salary = 0;
14      }

15      /**
16       Precondition: Neither theName nor theDate are null;
17       theSalary is nonnegative.
18      */
19      public SalariedEmployee(String theName, Date theDate, double theSalary)
20      {
21          super(theName, theDate);
22          if (theSalary >= 0)
23              salary = theSalary;
24          else
25          {
26              System.out.println("Fatal Error: Negative salary.");
27              System.exit(0);
28          }
29      }

30      public SalariedEmployee(SalariedEmployee originalObject )
31      {
32          super(originalObject);
33          salary = originalObject.salary;
34      }

35      public double getSalary()
36      {
37          return salary;
38      }
```

It will take the rest of Section 7.1 to fully explain this class definition.

If this line is omitted, Java will still invoke the no-argument constructor for the base class.

An object of the class SalariedEmployee is also an object of the class Employee.

(continued)

Display 7.5   The Derived Class **SalariedEmployee** (part 2 of 2)

```
39    /**
40     Returns the pay for the month.
41    */
42    public double getPay()
43    {
44        return salary/12;
45    }

46    /**
47     Precondition: newSalary is nonnegative.
48    */
49    public void setSalary(double newSalary)
50    {
51        if (newSalary >= 0)
52            salary = newSalary;
53        else
54        {
55            System.out.println("Fatal Error: Negative salary.");
56            System.exit(0);
57        }
58    }

59    public String toString()
60    {
61        return (getName() + " " + getHireDate().toString()
62                            + "\n$" + salary + " per year");
63    }

64    public boolean equals(SalariedEmployee other)
65    {
66        return (getName().equals(other.getName())
67                && getHireDate().equals(other.getHireDate())
68                && salary == other.salary);
69    }
70 }
```

We will show you a better way to define equals later in this chapter.

parent class
child class
ancestor class
descendent
class

Parent and Child Classes

A base class is often called the **parent class**. A derived class is then called a **child class**. This analogy is often carried one step further. A class that is a parent of a parent of a parent of another class (or some other number of "parent of" iterations) is often called an **ancestor class**. If class A is an ancestor of class B, then class B is often called a **descendent** of class A.

Overriding a Method Definition

overriding

The definition of an inherited method can be changed in the definition of a derived class so that it has a meaning in the derived class that is different from what it is in the base class. This is called **overriding** the definition of the inherited method. For example, the methods `toString` and `equals` are overridden (redefined) in the definition of the derived class `HourlyEmployee`. They are also overridden in the class `Salaried-Employee`. To override a method definition, simply give the new definition of the method in the class definition, just as you would with a method that is added in the derived class.

Overriding a Method Definition

A derived class inherits methods that belong to the base class. However, if a derived class requires a different definition for an inherited method, the method may be redefined in the derived class. This is called **overriding** the method definition.

The `final` Modifier

If you add the modifier `final` to the definition of a method, that indicates that the method may not be redefined in a derived class. If you add the modifier `final` to the definition of a class, that indicates that the class may not be used as a base class to derive other classes. We will say more about the `final` modifier in Chapter 8.

Changing the Return Type of an Overridden Method

**covariant
return type**

In a derived class, you can override (change) the definition of a method from the base class. As a general rule, when overriding a method definition, you may *not* change the type returned by the method, and you may not change a `void` method to a method that returns a value, nor a method that returns a value to a `void` method. The one exception to this rule is: If the returned type is a class type, then you may change the returned type to that of any descendent class of the returned type. For example, if a function returns the type `Employee` (Display 7.2), when you override the function definition in a derived class, you may change the returned type to `HourlyEmployee` (Display 7.3), `SalariedEmployee` (Display 7.5), or any other descendent class of the class `Employee`. This sort of changed return type is known as a **covariant return type** and is new in Java version 5.0; it was not allowed in earlier versions of Java. Earlier versions of Java allowed absolutely no changes to the returned type. We will give complete examples of changing the returned type of an overridden method in Chapter 8. Here we will just outline an example.

For example, suppose one class definition includes the following details:

```
public class BaseClass
{
    ...
    public Employee getSomeone(int someKey)
    ...
```

In this case, the following details would be allowed in a derived class:

```
public class DerivedClass extends BaseClass
{
    ...
    public HourlyEmployee getSomeone(int someKey)
    ...
```

When the method definition for getSomeone is overridden in DerivedClass, the returned type is changed from Employee to HourlyEmployee.

It is worth noting that when you change the returned type of an overridden method in this way, such as from Employee to HourlyEmployee, you are not really changing the returned type so much as placing additional restrictions on the returned type. Every HourlyEmployee is an Employee with some additional properties that, while they are properties of every HourlyEmployee, are not properties of every Employee. Any code that was written for a method of the base class and that assumed the value returned by the method is Employee will be legal for an overridden version of the method that returns an HourlyEmployee. This is true because every HourlyEmployee is an Employee.

Changing the Access Permission of an Overridden Method

You can change the access permission of an overridden method from private in the base class to public in the derived class (or in any other way that makes access permissions more permissive). For example, if the following is a method heading in a base case

```
private void doSomething()
```

then you can use the following heading when overriding the method definition in a derived class:

```
public void doSomething()
```

Note that you cannot change permission to make them more restricted in the derived class. You can change private to public, but you cannot change public to private.

This makes sense, because you want code written for the base class method to work for the derived class method. You can use a public method anyplace that you can use a private method, but it is not true that you can use a private method anyplace that you can use a public method.

PITFALL: Overriding versus Overloading

Do not confuse *overriding* (that is, redefining) a method definition in a derived class with *overloading* a method name. When you override a method definition, the new method definition given in the derived class has the exact same number and types of parameters. On the other hand, if the method in the derived class were to have a different number of parameters or a parameter of a different type from the method in the base class, then the derived class would have both methods. That would be overloading. For example, suppose we added the following method to the definition of the class Hourly-Employee (Display 7.3):

```java
public void setName(String firstName, String lastName)
{
    if ( (firstName == null) || (lastName == null) )
    {
        System.out.println("Fatal Error setting employee name.");
        System.exit(0);
    }
    else
        name = firstName + " " + lastName;
}
```

The class HourlyEmployee would then have this two-argument method setName and it would also inherit the following one-argument method setName from the base class Employee:

```java
public void setName(String newName)
{
    if (newName == null)
    {
        System.out.println("Fatal Error setting employee name.");
        System.exit(0);
    }
    else
        name = newName;
}
```

The class HourlyEmployee would have two methods named setName. This would be *overloading* the method name setName.

(continued)

PITFALL: (continued)

On the other hand, both the class `Employee` and the class `HourlyEmployee` define a method with the following method heading:

```
public String toString()
```

In this case, the class `HourlyEmployee` has only one method named `toString()`, but the definition of the method `toString()` in the class `HourlyEmployee` is different from the definition of `toString()` in the class `Employee`; the method `toString()` has been *overridden* (that is, redefined).

If you get overriding and overloading confused, you do have one consolation. They are both legal. ■

The super Constructor

You can invoke a constructor of the base class within the definition of a derived class constructor. A constructor for a derived class uses a constructor from the base class in a special way. A constructor for the base class normally initializes all the data inherited from the base class. So a constructor for a derived class begins with an invocation of a constructor for the base class. The details are as follows:

There is a special syntax for invoking the base class constructor that is illustrated by the constructor definitions for the class `HourlyEmployee` given in Display 7.3. In what follows we have reproduced the beginning of one of the constructor definitions for the class `HourlyEmployee` taken from that display:

```
public HourlyEmployee(String theName, Date theDate,
                      double theWageRate, double theHours)
{
    super(theName, theDate);
    if ((theWageRate >= 0) && (theHours >= 0))
    {
        wageRate = theWageRate;
        hours = theHours;
    }
    else
    ...
```

The line

super
```
super(theName, theDate);
```

is a call to a constructor for the base class, which in this case is a call to a constructor for the class `Employee`.

Self-Test Exercises

1. Suppose the class named `DiscountSale` is a derived class of a class called `Sale`. Suppose the class `Sale` has instance variables named `price` and `numberOfItems`. Will an object of the class `DiscountSale` also have instance variables named `price` and `numberOfItems`?

2. Suppose the class named `DiscountSale` is a derived class of a class called `Sale`, and suppose the class `Sale` has public methods named `getTotal` and `getTax`. Will an object of the class `DiscountSale` have methods named `getTotal` and `getTax`? If so, do these methods have to perform the exact same actions in the class `DiscountSale` as in the class `Sale`?

3. Suppose the class named `DiscountSale` is a derived class of a class called `Sale`, and suppose the class `Sale` has a method with the following heading and no other methods named `getTax`:

```
public double getTax()
```

And suppose the definition of the class `DiscountSale` has a method definition with the following heading and no other method definitions for methods named `getTax`:

```
public double getTax(double rate)
```

How many methods named `getTax` will the class `DiscountSale` have and what are their headings?

4. The class `HourlyEmployee` (Display 7.3) has methods named `getName` and `getRate` (among others). Why does the definition of the class `HourlyEmployee` contain a definition of the method `getRate` but no definition of the methods `getName`?

There are some restrictions on how you can use the base class constructor call super. You cannot use an instance variable as an argument to super. Also, the call to the base class constructor (super) must always be the first action taken in a constructor definition. You cannot use it later in the definition of a constructor.

Notice that you use the keyword super to call the constructor of the base class. You do not use the name of the constructor; you do *not* use

```
Employee(theName, theDate); //ILLEGAL
```

If a constructor definition for a derived class does not include an invocation of a constructor for the base class, then the no-argument constructor of the base class is invoked automatically as the first action of the derived class constructor. So, the following definition of the no-argument constructor for the class `HourlyEmployee` (with `super` omitted) is equivalent to the version we gave in Display 7.3:

```
public HourlyEmployee()
{
    wageRate = 0;
    hours = 0;
}
```

A derived class object has all the instance variables of the base class. These inherited instance variables should be initialized, and the base class constructor is the most convenient place to initialize these inherited instance variables. That is why you should always include a call to one of the base class constructors when you define a constructor for a derived class. As already noted, if you do not include a call to a base class constructor (using `super`), then the no-argument constructor of the base class is called automatically. (If there is no no-argument constructor for the base class, that is an error condition.)

Call to a Base Class Constructor

Within the definition of a constructor for a class, you can use **super** as a name for a constructor of the base class. Any invocation of **super** must be the first action taken by the constructor.

EXAMPLE

```
public SalariedEmployee(SalariedEmployee originalObject)
{
    super(originalObject); //Invocation of base class constructor.
    salary = originalObject.salary;
}
```

The `this` Constructor

When defining a constructor, it is sometimes convenient to be able to call one of the other constructors in the same class. You can use the keyword `this` as a method name to

`this`

invoke a constructor in the same class. This use of `this` is similar to the use of `super`, but with `this`, the call is to a constructor of the same class, not to a constructor for the base class. For example, consider the following alternate, and equivalent, definition of the no-argument constructor for the class `HourlyEmployee` (from Display 7.3):

```
public HourlyEmployee()
{
    this("No name", new Date("January", 1, 1000), 0, 0);
}
```

The line with this is an invocation of the constructor with the following heading:

```
public HourlyEmployee(String theName, Date theDate,
                      double theWageRate, double theHours)
```

The restrictions on how you can use the base class constructor call super also apply to the this constructor. You cannot use an instance variable as an argument to this. Also, any call to the constructor this must always be the first action taken in a constructor definition. Thus, a constructor definition cannot contain both an invocation of super and an invocation of this. If you want to include both a call to super and a call to this, use a call with this, and have the constructor that is called with this have super as its first action.

Call to Another Constructor in the Same Class

Within the definition of a constructor for a class, you can use this as a name for another constructor in the same class. Any invocation of this must be the first action taken by the constructor.

EXAMPLE
```
public HourlyEmployee()
{
    this("No name", new Date("January", 1, 1000), 0, 0);
}
```

 TIP: An Object of a Derived Class Has More than One Type

An object of a derived class has the type of the derived class, and it also has the type of the base class, and more generally, has the type of every one of its ancestor classes. For example, consider the following copy constructor definition from the class HourlyEmployee (Display 7.3):

```
public HourlyEmployee(HourlyEmployee originalObject)
{
    super(originalObject);
    wageRate = originalObject.wageRate;
    hours = originalObject.hours;
}
```

(continued)

TIP: (continued)

The line

```
super(originalObject);
```

is an invocation of a constructor for the base class `Employee`. The class `Employee` has no constructor with a parameter of type `HourlyEmployee`, but `originalObject` is of type `HourlyEmployee`. Fortunately, every object of type `HourlyEmployee` is also of type `Employee`. So, this invocation of `super` is an invocation of the copy constructor for the class `Employee`.

"is a" relationship

The fact that every object not only is of its own type but is also of the type of its ancestor classes simply reflects what happens in the everyday world. An hourly employee is an employee as well as an hourly employee. This sometimes is referred to as the **"is a" relationship**: For example, an `HourlyEmployee` is an `Employee`.

Display 7.6 contains a program demonstrating that an `HourlyEmployee` and a `SalariedEmployee` are also `Employee` objects. The method `showEmployee` requires an argument of type `Employee`. The objects `joe` and `sam` are of type `Employee` because they are instances of classes derived from the class `Employee` and so they are suitable arguments for `showEmployee`. ■

An Object of a Derived Class Has More than One Type

An object of a derived class has the type of the derived class, and it also has the type of the base class. More generally, a derived class has the type of every one of its ancestor classes. So, you can assign an object of a derived class to a variable of any ancestor type (but not the other way around). You can plug in a derived class object for a parameter of any of its ancestor types. More generally, you can use a derived class object anyplace you can use an object of any of its ancestor types.

Display 7.6   An Object Belongs to Multiple Classes

```
1   public class IsADemo
2   {
3       public static void main(String[] args)
4       {
5           SalariedEmployee joe = new SalariedEmployee("Josephine",
6                               new Date("January", 1, 2004), 100000);
7           HourlyEmployee sam = new HourlyEmployee("Sam",
8                               new Date("February", 1, 2003), 50.50, 40);

9           System.out.println("joe's longer name is " + joe.getName());

10          System.out.println("showEmployee(joe) invoked:");
11          showEmployee(joe);                              A SalariedEmployee
                                                            is an Employee.
12          System.out.println("showEmployee(sam) invoked:");
13          showEmployee(sam);
                                  An HourlyEmployee is an Employee.
14      }

15      public static void showEmployee(Employee employeeObject)
16      {
17              System.out.println(employeeObject.getName());
18              System.out.println(employeeObject.getHireDate());
19      }
20  }
```

Sample Dialogue

```
joe's longer name is Josephine
showEmployee(joe) invoked:
Josephine
January 1, 2004
showEmployee(sam) invoked:
Sam
February 1, 2003
```

PITFALL: The Terms *Subclass* and *Superclass*

subclass and superclass

Many programmers and authors use the term **subclass** for a derived class and **superclass** for its base class (or any of its ancestor classes). This is logical. For example, the collection of all hourly employees in the world is a subclass of all employees. Similarly, the collection of all objects of type `HourlyEmployee` is a subcollection of the collection of all objects of the class `Employee`. As you add more instance variables and methods, you restrict the number of objects that can satisfy the class definition. Despite this logic, people often reverse the terms *subclass* and *superclass*. Remember that these terms refer to the collections of objects of the derived class and the base class and not to the number of instance variables or methods. A derived class is a **subclass** (**not a superclass**) of its base class. Another way to remember which is a superclass is as follows: Recall that the `super` constructor invocation is an invocation of the base class and so the base class is the **superclass.** ∎

Self-Test Exercises

5. Is the following program legal? The relevant classes are defined in Displays 7.2, 7.3, and 7.5.

```java
public class EmployeeDemo
{
    public static void main( String[] args)
    {
        HourlyEmployee joe =
            new HourlyEmployee("Joe Young",
                    new Date("February", 1, 2004), 10.50, 40);
        SalariedEmployee boss =
            new SalariedEmployee("Mr. Big Shot",
                        new Date("January", 1, 1999), 100000);
        printName(joe);
        printName(boss);
    }

    public void printName(Employee object)
    {
        System.out.println(object.getName());
    }
}
```

6. Give a definition for a class `TitledEmployee` that is a derived class of the base class `SalariedEmployee` given in Display 7.5. The class `TitledEmployee` has one additional instance variable of type `String` called `title`. It also has two additional methods: `getTitle`, which takes no arguments and returns a `String`, and `setTitle`, which is a `void` method that takes one argument of type `String`. It also overrides (redefines) the method definition for `getName`, so that the string returned includes the title as well as the name of the employee.

EXAMPLE: An Enhanced `StringTokenizer` Class ⭐

Inheritance allows you to reuse all the code written for a base class in a derived class and to reuse it without copying it or even seeing the code in the base class. This means that, among other things, if one of the standard Java library classes does not have all the methods you want it to have, you can, in most cases, define a derived class that has the desired additional methods. In this subsection, we give a simple example of this process. This example requires that you have already covered the basics about arrays given in Section 6.1 of Chapter 6 and that you have read the starred section on the `StringTokenizer` class in Chapter 4. If you have not covered this material, you will have to skip this example until you cover it.

The `StringTokenizer` class allows you to generate all the tokens in a string one time, but sometimes you want to cycle through the tokens a second or third time. There are lots of ways to accomplish this. For example, you can use the `StringTokenizer` constructor two (or more) times to create two (or more) `StringTokenizer` objects. However, it would be cleaner and more efficient if you could do it with just one `StringTokenizer` object. Display 7.7 shows a derived class of the `StringTokenizer` class that allows you to cycle through the tokens in a string any number of times. This class is called `EnhancedStringTokenizer`. The class `EnhancedStringTokenizer` behaves exactly the same as the `StringTokenizer` class, except that the class `EnhancedStringTokenizer` has one additional method named `tokensSoFar`. The method `tokensSoFar` has no parameters and returns an array of strings containing all the tokens that have so far been returned by the methods named `nextToken`. After an object of the class `EnhancedStringTokenizer` has gone through all the tokens with the methods `nextToken`, it can invoke the method `tokensSoFar` to produce an array containing all the tokens. This array can be used to cycle through the tokens any number of additional times. A simple example of this is given in the program in Display 7.8.

The class `EnhancedStringTokenizer` has methods, such as `countTokens`, which it inherits unchanged from the class `StringTokenizer`. The class EnhancedStringTokenizer has two methods, namely the two methods named `nextToken`, whose definitions are overridden. From the outside, the methods named `nextToken` of the class `EnhancedStringTokenizer` behaves exactly the same as the methods named `nextToken` in the class `StringTokenizer`. However, each of the two methods named `nextToken` of the class `EnhancedStringTokenizer` also saves the tokens in an array instance variable, *a*, so that an array of tokens can be returned by the method `tokensSoFar`. The method `tokensSoFar` is the only completely new method in the derived class `EnhancedStringTokenizer`.

Notice that the definitions of the methods named `nextToken` in the class `EnhancedString-Tokenizer` each includes an invocation of `super.nextToken`, which is the version of the corresponding method `nextToken` in the base class `StringTokenizer`. Each overridden version of the method `nextToken` uses the method `super.nextToken` to produce the token it returns, but before returning the token, it stores the token in the array instance variable *a*. The instance variable `count` contains a count of the number of tokens stored in the array instance variable *a*.[1]

---

[1] The class `StringTokenizer` also has a method named `nextElement` with a return type of `Object`. This method should also be overridden, but we have not yet even mentioned this method because we have not yet discussed the class `Object`. For now, you can simply pretend `StringTokenizer` has no such method `nextElement`. We will discuss this point in Self-Test Exercise 23 later in this chapter after we introduce the class `Object`.

Display 7.7 **EnhancedStringTokenizer** (part 1 of 2)

```
1   import java.util.StringTokenizer;
2
3   public class EnhancedStringTokenizer extends StringTokenizer
4   {
5       private String[] a;
6       private int count;
7
8       public EnhancedStringTokenizer(String theString)
9       {
10          super(theString);
11          a = new String[countTokens()];
12          count = 0;
13      }
14
15      public EnhancedStringTokenizer(String theString, String delimiters)
16      {
17          super(theString, delimiters);
18          a = new String[countTokens()];
19          count = 0;
20      }
```

The method **countTokens** is inherited and is not overridden.

```
19      /**
20       Returns the same value as the same method in the StringTokenizer class,
21       but it also stores data for the method tokensSoFar to use.
22      */
23      public String nextToken()
24      {
25          String token = super.nextToken();
26          a[count] = token;
27          count++;
28          return token;
29      }
```

This method **nextToken** has its definition overridden.

super.nextTokens is the version of **nextToken** defined in the base class **StringTokenizer**. This is explained more fully in Section 7.3.

```
30      /**
31       Returns the same value as the same method in the StringTokenizer class,
32       changes the delimiter set in the same way as does the same method in the
33       StringTokenizer class, but it also stores data for the method tokensSoFar to use.
34      */
35      public String nextToken(String delimiters)
36      {
37          String token = super.nextToken(delimiters);
38          a[count] = token;
39          count++;
40          return token;
41      }
```

This method **nextToken** also has its definition overridden.

super.nextTokens is the version of **nextToken** defined in the base class **StringTokenizer**.

Display 7.7   **EnhancedStringTokenizer** (part 2 of 2)

```
42        /**
43         Returns an array of all tokens produced so far.
44         Array returned has length equal to the number of tokens produced so far.
45        */
46      public String[] tokensSoFar()
47      {
48          String[] arrayToReturn = new String[count];
49          for (int i = 0; i < count; i++)
50              arrayToReturn[i] = a[i];
51          return arrayToReturn;
52      }
53  }
```

tokensSoFar *is a new method.*

Display 7.8   Use of the **EnhancedStringTokenizer** Class (part 1 of 2)

```
1   import java.util.Scanner;

2   public class EnhancedStringTokenizerDemo
3   {
4       public static void main(String[] args)
5       {
6           Scanner keyboard = new Scanner(System.in);

7           System.out.println("Enter a sentence:");
8           String sentence = keyboard.nextLine();

9           EnhancedStringTokenizer wordFactory =
10                  new EnhancedStringTokenizer(sentence);

11          System.out.println("Your sentence with extra blanks deleted:");
12          while (wordFactory.hasMoreTokens())
13              System.out.print(wordFactory.nextToken() + " ");
14          System.out.println();
15          //All tokens have been dispensed.

16          System.out.println("Sentence with each word on a separate line:");
17          String[] token = wordFactory.tokensSoFar();
18          for (int i = 0; i < token.length; i++)
19              System.out.println(token[i]);
20      }
21  }
```

(continued)

Display 7.8 Use of the `EnhancedStringTokenizer` Class (part 2 of 2)

Sample Dialogue

```
Enter a sentence:
    I    love    you,    madly.
Your sentence with extra blanks deleted:
I love you, madly.
Sentence with each word on a separate line:
I
love
you,
madly.
```

7.2   Encapsulation and Inheritance

Ignorance is bliss.

PROVERB

This section is a continuation of Section 7.1 and uses the same example classes we used in Section 7.1. In this section, we consider how the information-hiding facilities of Java, primarily the `private` modifier, interact with inheritance.

 PITFALL: Use of Private Instance Variables from the Base Class

An object of the class `HourlyEmployee` (Display 7.3) inherits, among other things, an instance variable called name from the class `Employee` (Display 7.2). For example, the following would set the value of the instance variable name of the `HourlyEmployee` object joe to "Josephine":

```
joe.setName("Josephine");
```

But you must be a bit careful about how you manipulate inherited instance variables such as name. The instance variable name of the class `HourlyEmployee` was inherited from the class `Employee`, but the instance variable name is a private instance variable in the definition of the class `Employee`. That means that name can only be accessed by name within the definition of a method in the class `Employee`. An instance variable (or method) that is private in a base class is not accessible *by name* in the definition of a method in *any other class, not even in a method definition of a derived class.*

For example, notice the following method definition taken from the definition of the class `HourlyEmployee` in Display 7.3:

```java
public String toString()
{
    return (getName() + " " + getHireDate().toString()
    + "\n$" + wageRate + " per hour for " + hours + " hours");
}
```

You might wonder why we needed to use the methods `getName` and `getHireDate`. You might be tempted to rewrite the method definition as follows:

```java
public String toString()    //Illegal version
{
    return (name + " " + hireDate.toString()
    + "\n$" + wageRate + " per hour for " + hours + " hours");
}
```

As the comment indicates, this will not work. The instance variables `name` and `hireDate` are private instance variables in the class `Employee`, and although a derived class like `HourlyEmployee` inherits these instance variables, it cannot access them directly. You must instead use some public methods to access the instance variable `name` or `hireDate`, as we did in Display 7.3.

In the definition of a derived class, you cannot mention a private inherited instance variable by name. You must instead use public accessor and mutator methods (such as `getName` and `setName`) that were defined in the base class.

The fact that a private instance variable of a base class cannot be accessed in the definition of a method of a derived class often seems wrong to people. After all, if you are an hourly employee and you want to change your name, nobody says, "Sorry, `name` is a private instance variable of the class `Employee`." After all, if you are an hourly employee, you are also an employee. In Java, this is also true; an object of the class `HourlyEmployee` is also an object of the class `Employee`. However, the laws on the use of private instance variables and methods must be as we described, or else they would be compromised. If private instance variables of a class were accessible in method definitions of a derived class, then anytime you wanted to access a private instance variable, you could simply create a derived class and access it in a method of that class, and that would mean that all private instance variables would be accessible to anybody who wants to put in a little extra effort. This scenario illustrates the problem, but the big problem is unintentional errors, not intentional subversion. If private instance variables of a class were accessible in method definitions of a derived class, then the instance variables might be changed by mistake or in inappropriate ways. (Remember, accessor and mutator methods can guard against inappropriate changes to instance variables.)

We will discuss one possible way to get around this restriction on private instance variables of the base class in the upcoming subsection entitled "Protected and Package Access." ■

Self-Test Exercises

7. Would the following be legal for the definition of a method to add to the class Employee (Display 7.2)? (Remember, the question is whether it is legal, not whether it is sensible.)

```
public void crazyMethod()
{
    Employee object = new Employee("Joe",
                            new Date("January", 1, 2005));
    System.out.println("Hello " + object.name);
}
```

Would it be legal to add this crazyMethod to the class HourlyEmployee?

8. Suppose you change the modifier before the instance variable name from private to public in the class Employee. Would it then be legal to add the method crazyMethod (from Exercise 7) to the class HourlyEmployee?

PITFALL: Private Methods Are Effectively Not Inherited

As we noted in the previous Pitfall section: An instance variable (or method) that is private in a base class is not directly accessible outside of the definition of the base class, *not even in a method definition for a derived class.* The private methods of the base class are just like private variables in terms of not being directly available. But in the case of methods, the restriction is more dramatic. A private variable can be accessed indirectly via an accessor or mutator method. A private method is simply not available. It is just as if the private method were not inherited. (In one sense, private methods in the base class may be indirectly available in the derived class. If a private method is used in the definition of a public method of the base class, then that public method can be invoked in the derived class, or any other class, so the private method can be indirectly invoked.)

This should not be a problem. Private methods should just be used as helping methods, so their use should be limited to the class in which they are defined. If you want a method to be used as a helping method in a number of inherited classes, then it is not *just* a helping method, and you should make the method public.

Protected and Package Access

As you have seen, you cannot access (by name) a private instance variable or private method of the base class within the definition of a derived class. There are two classifications of instance variables and methods that allow them to be accessed by name in a derived class. The two classifications are *protected access,* which always gives access, and *package access,* which gives access if the derived class is in the same package as the base class.

If a method or instance variable is modified by protected (rather than public or private), then it can be accessed by name inside its own class definition, it can be accessed by name inside any class derived from it, and it can also be accessed by name in the definition of any class in the same package (even if the class in the same package is not derived from it). However, the protected method or instance variable cannot be accessed by name in any other classes. Thus, if an instance variable is marked protected in the class Parent and the class Child is derived from the class Parent, then the instance variable can be accessed by name inside any method definition in the class Child. However, in a class that is not in the same package as Parent and is not derived from Parent, it is as if the protected instance variable were private.

For example, consider the class HourlyEmployee that was derived from the base class Employee. We were required to use accessor and mutator methods to manipulate the inherited instance variables in the definition of HourlyEmployee. For example, consider the definition of the toString method of the class HourlyEmployee, which we repeat here:

```
public String toString()
{
    return (getName() + " " + getHireDate().toString()
        + "\n$" + wageRate + " per hour for " + hours + " hours");
}
```

If the private instance variables name and hireDate had been marked protected in the class Employee, the definition of toString in the derived class HourlyEmployee could be simplified to the following:

```
public String toString() //Legal if instance variables in
                         // Employee are marked protected
{
    return (name + " " + hireDate.toString()
        + "\n$" + wageRate + " per hour for " + hours + " hours");
}
```

The protected Modifier

If a method or instance variable is modified by **protected** (rather than **public** or **private**), then it can be accessed by name inside its own class definition, by name inside any class derived from it, and by name in the definition of any class in the same package.

The protected modifier provides very weak protection compared to the private modifier, since it allows direct access to any programmer who is willing to go through the bother of defining a suitable derived class. Many programming authorities discourage the use of the protected modifier. Instance variables should normally not be marked protected. On rare occasions, you may want to have a method marked protected. If you want an access intermediate between public and private, then the access described in the next paragraph is often a preferable alternative to protected.

You may have noticed that if you forget to place one of the modifiers public, private, or protected before an instance variable or method definition, then your class definition will still compile. If you do not place any of the modifiers public, private, or protected before an instance variable or method definition, then the instance variable or method can be accessed by name inside the definition of any class in the same package, but not outside of the package. This is called **package access**, **default access**, or **friendly access**. You use package access in situations where you have a package of cooperating classes that act as a single encapsulated unit. Note that package access is more restricted than protected, and that package access gives more control to the programmer defining the classes. If you control the package directory (folder), then you control who is allowed package access.

The diagram in Display 7.9 may help you to understand who has access to members with public, private, protected, and package access. The diagram tells who can directly access, by name, variables that have public, private, protected, and package access. The same access rules apply to methods that have public, private, protected, and package access.

Package Access

If you do not place any of the modifiers public, private, or protected before an instance variable or method definition, then the instance variable or method is said to have **package access**. Package access is also known as **default access** and as **friendly access**. If an instance variable or method has package access, it can be accessed by name inside the definition of any class in the same package, but not outside of the package.

 PITFALL: Forgetting about the Default Package

When considering package access, do not forget the default package. Recall that all the classes in your current directory (that do not belong to some other package) belong to an unnamed package called the *default package*. So, if a class in your current directory is not in any other package, then it is in the default package. So if an instance variable or method has package access, then that instance variable or method can be accessed by name in the definition of any other class in the default package. ∎

Display 7.9 Access Modifiers

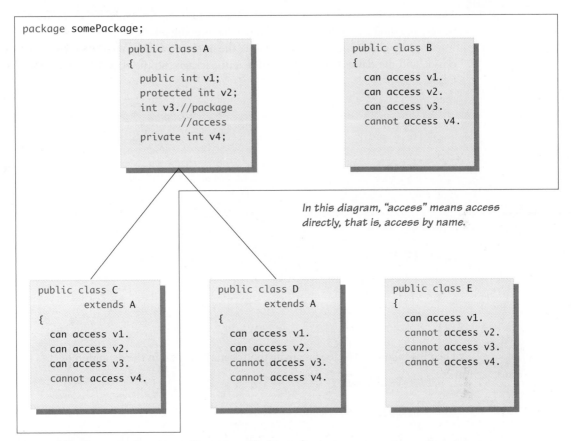

```
package somePackage;
```

public class A
{
    public int v1;
    protected int v2;
    int v3.//package
            //access
    private int v4;

public class B
{
    can access v1.
    can access v2.
    can access v3.
    cannot access v4.

In this diagram, "access" means access directly, that is, access by name.

public class C
        extends A
{
    can access v1.
    can access v2.
    can access v3.
    cannot access v4.

public class D
        extends A
{
    can access v1.
    can access v2.
    cannot access v3.
    cannot access v4.

public class E
{
    can access v1.
    cannot access v2.
    cannot access v3.
    cannot access v4.

A line from one class to another means the lower class is a derived class of the higher class.

If the instance variables are replaced by methods, the same access rules apply.

PITFALL: A Restriction on Protected Access ★

The situation described in this pitfall does not occur often, but when it does occur, it can be very puzzling if you do not understand what is going on.

Suppose class D is derived from class B, the instance variable n has protected access in class B, and the classes D and B are in different packages, so the class definitions begin as follows:

```
package one;

public class B
{
    protected int n;
        . . .
}

package two;

import one.B;

public class D extends B
{
        . . .
}
```

Then the following is a legitimate method that can appear in the definition of class D:

```
public void demo()
{
    n = 42;//n is inherited from B.
}
```

The following is also a legitimate method definition for the derived class D:

```
public void demo2()
{
    D object = new D();
    object.n = 42;//n is inherited from B.
}
```

However, the following is not allowed as a method of D:

```
public void demo3()
{
    B object = new B();
    object.n = 42; //Error
}
```

The compiler will give an error message saying n is protected in B.

PITFALL: (continued)

Similar remarks apply to protected methods.

A class can access its own classes' inherited variables and methods that are marked protected in the base class, but cannot directly access any such instance variables or methods of an object of the base class (or of any other derived class of the base class). In the above example, n is an instance variable of the base class B and an instance variable of the derived class D. D can access n whenever n is used as an instance variable of D, but D cannot access n when n is used as an instance variable of B.

If the classes B and D are in the same package, you will not get the error message because, in Java, protected access implies package access. In particular, if the classes B and D are both in the default package, you will not get the error message. ■

Self-Test Exercises

9. Suppose you change the modifier before the instance variable name from `private` to `protected` in the class `Employee` (Display 7.2). Would it then be legal to add the method `crazyMethod` (from Self-Test Exercise 7) to the class `HourlyEmployee` (Display 7.3)?

10. Which is more restricted, protected access or package access?

11. Suppose class D is derived from class B, the method `doStuff()` has protected access in class B, and the classes D and B are in different packages, so the class definitions begin as follows:

```
package one;
public class B
{
    protected void doStuff()
    {
      ...
    }
}

package two;
import one.B;
public class D extends B
{
    ...
}
```

Is the following a legitimate method that can appear in the definition of the class D?

```
public void demo()
{
    doStuff();//doStuff is inherited from B.
}
```

(continued)

Self-Test Exercises (continued)

12. Suppose B and D are as described in Self-Test Exercise 11. Is the following a legitimate method that can appear in the definition of the class D?

```java
public void demo2()
{
    D object = new D();
    object.doStuff();//doStuff is inherited from B.
}
```

13. Suppose B and D are as described in Self-Test Exercise 11. Is the following a legitimate method that can appear in the definition of the class D?

```java
public void demo3()
{
    B object = new B();
    object.doStuff();
}
```

7.3 Programming with Inheritance

The devil is in the details.

COMMON SAYING

In the previous section, we described the basic idea and basic details about derived classes. In this section, we continue that discussion and go on to discuss some more subtle points about derived classes. In the process, we also discuss the class Object, which is an ancestor class of all Java classes, and we describe a better way to define an equals method.

TIP: Static Variables Are Inherited

Static variables in a base class are inherited by any derived classes. The modifiers public, private, and protected, and package access have the same meaning for static variables as they do for instance variables. ■

TIP: "is a" Versus "has a"

Early in this chapter, we defined a derived class called `HourlyEmployee` using the class `Employee` as the base class. In such a case, an object of the derived class `HourlyEmployee` is also an instance of the class `Employee`, or, stated more simply, an `HourlyEmployee` *is an* `Employee`. This is an example of the "is a" relationship between classes. It is one way to make a more complex class out of a simpler class.

"is a" relationship

Another way to make a more complex class out of a simpler class is known as the "has a" relationship. For example, the class `Employee` defined earlier has an instance variable of the class type `Date`. We express this relationship by saying an `Employee` "has a" `Date`. Using the "has a" relationship to build a class (such as building the class `Employee` by using `Date` as an instance variable) is often called **composition**.

"has a" relationship

composition

Because the class `HourlyEmployee` inherits the instance variable of type `Date` from the class `Employee`, it is also correct to say an `HourlyEmployee` "has a" `Date`. Thus, an `HourlyEmployee` *is an* `Employee` and *has a* `Date`. ■

Access to a Redefined Base Method

Suppose you redefine a method so that it has a different definition in the derived class from what it has in the base class. The definition that was given in the base class is not completely lost to the derived class objects. However, if you want to invoke the version of the method given in the base class with an object in the derived class, you need some way to say, "use the definition of this method as given in the base class (even though I am an object of the derived class)." The way you say this is to use the keyword `super` as if it were a calling object.

super relationship

For example, the method `toString` of the class `HourlyEmployee` (Display 7.3) was defined as follows:

```
public String toString() //in the derived class HourlyEmployee
{
    return (getName() + " " + getHireDate().toString()
        + "\n$" + wageRate + " per hour for " + hours + " hours");
}
```

This overrides the following definition of `toString()` that was given in the definition of the base class `Employee`:

```
public String toString() //in the base class Employee
{
    return (name + " " + hireDate.toString());
}
```

We can use the version of the method `toString()` defined in the base class `Employee` to simplify the definition of the method `toString()` in the derived class `HourlyEmployee`. The following is an equivalent way to define `toString()` in the derived class `HourlyEmployee`:

```
public String toString() //in the derived class HourlyEmployee
{
    return (super.toString()
        + "\n$" + wageRate + " per hour for " + hours + " hours");
}
```

The expression `super.toString()` is an invocation of the method `toString()` using the definition of `toString()` given in the base class `Employee`.

You can only use `super` in this way within the definition of a method in a derived class. Outside of the definition of the derived class you cannot invoke an overridden method of the base class using an object of the derived class.

Invoking the Old Version of an Overridden Method?

Within the definition of a method of a derived class, you can invoke the base class version of an overridden method of the base class by prefacing the method name with **super** and a dot. Outside of the derived class definition, there is no way to invoke the base class version of an overridden method using an object of the derived class.

EXAMPLE
```
public String toString()
{
    return (super.toString()
        + "\n$" + wageRate + " per hour for " + hours + " hours");
}
```

 PITFALL: You Cannot Use Multiple supers

As we already noted, within the definition of a method of a derived class, you can call an overridden method of the base class by prefacing the method name with `super` and a dot. However, you cannot repeat the use of `super` to invoke a method from some ancestor class other than a direct parent. For example, suppose that the class `Employee` were derived from the class `Person`, and the class `HourlyEmployee` is derived from the class `Employee`. You might think that you can invoke a method of the class `Person` within the definition of the class `HourlyEmployee`, by using `super.super`, as in

```
super.super.toString()//ILLEGAL!
```

However, as the comment indicates, it is illegal to have such multiple supers in Java. ■

Self-Test Exercises

14. Redefine the `toString` method of the class `SalariedEmployee` (Display 7.5) so that it uses `super.toString()`. This new definition of `toString` will be equivalent to the one given in Display 7.5.

15. Redefine the `equals` method for the class `HourlyEmployee` (Display 7.3) using `super.equals` to invoke the `equals` method of the base class `Employee`.

16. Is the following program legal? The relevant classes are defined in Displays 7.2 and 7.3.

```java
public class EmployeeDemo
{
    public static void main( String[] args)
    {
        HourlyEmployee joe =
            new HourlyEmployee("Joe Young",
                    new Date("Feb", 1, 2004), 10.50, 40);
        String nameNDate = joe.super.toString();
        System.out.println(nameNDate);
    }
}
```

17. Suppose you add the following defined constant to the class `Employee` (Display 7.2):

```java
public static final int STANDARD_HOURS = 160;//per month
```

Would it then be legal to add the following method to the class `HourlyEmployee` (Display 7.3)?

```java
public void setHoursToStandard()
{
    hours = STANDARD_HOURS;
}
```

The Class `Object`

Object class

Java has a class that is an ancestor of every class. In Java, every class is a derived class of a derived class of . . . (for some number of iterations of "a derived class of") of the class `Object`. So, every object of every class is of type `Object`, as well as being of the type of its class (and also of the types of all its ancestor classes). Even classes that you define yourself are descendent classes of the class `Object`. If you do not make your class a derived class of some class, then Java will automatically make it a derived class of the class `Object`.

The class `Object` allows you to write Java code for methods with a parameter of type `Object` that can be replaced by an object of any class whatsoever. You will eventually encounter library methods that accept an argument of type `Object` and hence can be used with an argument that is an object of absolutely any class.

> ### The Class Object
>
> In Java, every class is a descendent of the class `Object`. So, every object of every class is of type `Object`, as well as being of the type of its class.

The class `Object` is in the package `java.lang`, which is always imported automatically. So, you do not need any `import` statement to make the class `Object` available to your code.

The class `Object` does have some methods that every Java class inherits. For example, every object inherits the methods `equals` and `toString` from some ancestor class, which either is the class `Object` or a class that itself inherited the methods ultimately from the class `Object`. However, the inherited methods `equals` and `toString` will not work correctly for (almost) any class you define. You need to override the inherited method definitions with new, more appropriate definitions.

toString

It is important to include definitions of the methods `toString` and `equals` in the classes you define, since some Java library classes assume your class has such methods. There are no subtleties involved in defining (actually redefining or overriding) the method `toString`. We have seen good examples of the method `toString` in many of our class definitions. The definition of the overridden method `equals` does have some subtleties and we will discuss them in the next subsection.

equals

clone

Another method inherited from the class `Object` is the method `clone`, which is intended to return a copy of the calling object. We discuss the method `clone` in Chapters 8 and 13.

The Right Way to Define equals

Earlier we said that the class `Object` has an `equals` method, and that when you define a class with an `equals` method you should override the definition of the method `equals` given in the class `Object`. However, we did not, strictly speaking, follow our own advice. The heading for the method `equals` in our definition of the class `Employee` (Display 7.2) is as follows:

```
public boolean equals(Employee otherEmployee)
```

On the other hand, the heading for the method `equals` in the class `Object` is as follows:

```
public boolean equals(Object otherObject)
```

The two `equals` methods have different parameter types, so we have not overridden the definition of `equals`. We have merely overloaded the method `equals`. The class `Employee` has both of these methods named `equals`.

In most situations, this will not matter. However, there are situations in which it does matter. Some library methods assume your class's definition of `equals` has the following heading, the same as in the class `Object`:

```
public boolean equals(Object otherObject)
```

We need to change the type of the parameter for the `equals` method in the class `Employee` from type `Employee` to type `Object`. A first try might produce the following:

```
public boolean equals(Object otherObject)
{
    Employee otherEmployee = (Employee)otherObject;
    return (name.equals(otherEmployee.name)
            && hireDate.equals(otherEmployee.hireDate));
}
```

We needed to type cast the parameter `otherObject` from type `Object` to type `Employee`. If we omit the type cast and simply proceed with `otherObject`, the compiler will give an error message when it sees

```
otherObject.name
```

The class `Object` does not have an instance variable named `name`.

This first try at an improved `equals` method does override the definition of `equals` given in the class `Object` and will work well in many cases. However, it still has a shortcoming.

Our definition of `equals` now allows an argument that can be any kind of object whatsoever. What happens if the method `equals` is used with an argument that is not an `Employee`? The answer is that a run-time error will occur when the type cast to `Employee` is executed.

We need to make our definition work for any kind of object. If the object is not an `Employee`, we simply return `false`. The calling object is an `Employee`, so if the argument is not an `Employee`, they should not be considered equal. But how can we tell whether the parameter is or is not of type `Employee`?

Every object inherits the method `getClass()` from the class `Object`. The method `getClass()` is marked `final` in the class `Object`, so it cannot be overridden. For any object o, o.getClass() returns a representation of the class used to create o. For example, after the following is executed:

```
o = new Employee();
```

o.getClass() returns a representation `Employee`.

We will not describe the details of this representation except to say that two such representations should be compared with `==` or `!=` if you want to know if two representations are the same. Thus,

```
    if (object1.getClass() == object2.getClass())
        System.out.println("Same class.");
    else
        System.out.println("Not the same class.");
```

will output Same class if object1 and object2 were created with the same class when they were created using new, and output Not same class otherwise.

Our final version of the method equals is shown in Display 7.10. Note that we have also taken care of one more possible case. The predefined constant null can be plugged in for a parameter of type Object. The Java documentation says that an equals method should return false when comparing an object and the value null. So that is what we have done.

extra code on CD On the accompanying CD, the subdirectory improvedEquals (of the directory for this chapter) has a definition of the class Employee that includes this definition of equals.

Display 7.10 A Better **equals** Method for the Class **Employee**

```
1       public boolean equals(Object otherObject)
2       {
3           if (otherObject == null)
4               return false;
5           else if (getClass() != otherObject.getClass())
6               return false;
7           else
8           {
9               Employee otherEmployee = (Employee)otherObject;
10              return (name.equals(otherEmployee.name)
11                  && hireDate.equals(otherEmployee.hireDate));
12          }
13      }
```

TIP: getClass Versus `instanceof` ★

Many authors suggest that in the definition of `equals` for a class such as `Employee`, given in Display 7.10, you should not use

```
else if (getClass() != otherObject.getClass())
    return false;
```

but should instead use

```
else if (!(otherObject instanceof Employee))
    return false;
```

instanceof   What is the difference and which should you use? At first glance it seems like you should use `instanceof` in the definition of `equals`. The `instanceof` operator checks to see if an object is of the type given as its second argument. The syntax is

Object `instanceof` *Class_Name*

which returns `true` if *Object* is of type *Class_Name*; otherwise it returns `false`. So, the following will return `true` if `otherObject` is of type `Employee`:

```
(otherObject instanceof Employee)
```

Suppose that (contrary to what we really did) we instead used `instanceof` in our definition of `equals` for the class `Employee` and we also used `instanceof` in our definition for the class `HourlyEmployee`, so that the definition of `equals` for `HourlyEmployee` is as follows:

```
public boolean equals(Object otherObject)
//This is NOT the right way to define equals.
{
    if (otherObject == null)
        return false;
    else if (!(otherObject instanceof HourlyEmployee))
        return false;
    else
    {
        HourlyEmployee otherHourlyEmployee =
                            (HourlyEmployee)otherObject;
          return (super.equals(otherHourlyEmployee)
              && (wageRate == otherHourlyEmployee.wageRate)
              && (hours == otherHourlyEmployee.hours));
    }
}
```

(continued)

TIP: (continued)

Assuming that the equals method for both Employee and HourlyEmployee are defined using instanceof (as above), consider the following situation:

```
Employee e =
        new Employee("Joe Worker", new Date("January", 1, 2004));
HourlyEmployee hourlyE = new HourlyEmployee("Joe Worker",
                        new Date("January", 1, 2004), 50.50, 160);
```

Then, with the definition of equals that uses instanceof, we get that

```
e.equals(hourlyE)
```

returns true, because hourlyE is an Employee with the same name and hire date as e. So far, it sounds reasonable.

However, since we are assuming that we also used instanceof in the definition of equals for the class HourlyEmployee, we also get that

```
hourlyE.equals(e)
```

returns false because e instanceof HourlyEmployee returns false. (e is an Employee but e is not an HourlyEmployee.)

So, if we define equals in both classes using instanceof, then e equals hourlyE, but hourlyE does not equal e. And, that's no way for equals to behave.

Since instanceof does not yield a suitable definition of equals, you should instead use getClass() as we did in Display 7.10. If we use getClass() in a similar way in the definition of equals for the class HourlyEmployee (see Self-Test Exercise 19), then

```
e.equals(hourlyE)
```

and

```
hourlyE.equals(e)
```

both return false. ∎

instanceof and getClass() ★

Both the `instanceof` operator and the `getClass()` method can be used to check the class of an object. The `instanceof` operator simply tests an object for type. The `getClass()` method, used in a test with `==` or `!=`, tests if two objects were created with the same class. The details follow.

THE `instanceof` OPERATOR

The `instanceof` operator checks if an object is of the type given as its second argument. The syntax is

Object `instanceof` *Class_Name*

which returns **true** if *Object* is of type *Class_Name*; otherwise it returns **false**. So, the following will return **true** if `otherObject` is of type `Employee`:

```
(otherObject instanceof Employee)
```

Note that this means it returns **true** if `otherObject` is of the type of any descendent class of `Employee`, because in that case `otherObject` is also of type `Employee`.

THE `getClass()` METHOD

Every object inherits the method `getClass()` from the class `Object`. The method `getClass()` is marked **final** in the class `Object`, so it cannot be overridden. For any **object** of any class,

```
object.getClass()
```

returns a representation of the class that was used with **new** to create **object**. Any two such representations can be compared with `==` or `!=` to determine whether or not they represent the same class. Thus,

```
if (object1.getClass() == object2.getClass())
    System.out.println("Same class.");
else
    System.out.println("Not the same class.");
```

will output **Same class** if `object1` and `object2` were created with the same class when they were created using **new**, and output **Not same class** otherwise.

(continued)

EXAMPLES

Suppose that `HourlyEmployee` is a derived class of `Employee` and that `employeeObject` and `hourlyEmployeeObject` are created as follows:

```
Employee employeeObject = new Employee();
HourlyEmployee hourlyEmployeeObject = new HourlyEmployee();
```

Then:

```
employeeObject.getClass() == hourlyEmployeeObject.getClass()
```

returns `false`.

```
employeeObject instanceof Employee
```

returns `true`.

```
hourlyEmployeeObject instanceof Employee
```

returns `true`.

```
employeeObject instanceof HourlyEmployee
```

returns `false`.

```
hourlyEmployeeObject instanceof HourlyEmployee
```

returns `true`.

Self-Test Exercises

18. Redefine the method `equals` given in Display 7.10 using `instanceof` instead of `getClass()`. Give the complete definition. Remember, we do not want you to define `equals` this way in your class definitions; this is just an exercise.

19. Redefine the `equals` method of the class `HourlyEmployee` (Display 7.3) so that it has a parameter of type `Object` and follows the other guidelines we gave for an `equals` method. Assume the definition of the method `equals` for the class `Employee` has been changed to be as in Display 7.10. (Remember, you should use `getClass()`, not `instanceof`.)

Self-Test Exercises (continued)

20. Redefine the `equals` method of the class `SalariedEmployee` (Display 7.5) so that it has a parameter of type `Object` and follows the other guidelines we gave for an `equals` method. Assume the definition of the method `equals` for the class `Employee` has been changed to be as in Display 7.10. (Remember, you should use `getClass()`, not `instanceof`.)

21. Redefine the `equals` method of the class `Date` (Display 4.13) so that it has a parameter of type `Object` and follows the other guidelines we gave for an `equals` method. (Remember, you should use `getClass()`, not `instanceof`.)

22. What is the output produced by the following program? (The classes `Employee` and `HourlyEmployee` were defined in this chapter.)

```
public class Test
{
    public static void main(String[] args)
    {
        Employee object1 = new Employee();
        Employee object2 = new HourlyEmployee();

        if (object1.getClass( ) == object2.getClass( ))
            System.out.println("Same class.");
        else
            System.out.println("Not the same class.");
    }
}
```

23. (This exercise requires that you have covered the starred subsection "An Enhanced StringTokenizer Class *.")

Although we did not cover it when we covered the class `StringTokenizer`, the class `StringTokenizer` has a method with the following heading:

```
public Object nextElement()
```

The method `nextElement()` returns the same string as the method `nextToken()`, but `nextElement()` returns it as something of type `Object`, as opposed to type `String`. Give a suitable definition of `nextElement` to add to the definition of `EnhancedStringTokenizer`. This definition will override the definition of `nextElement` in the class `StringTokenizer`. (*Hint*: the definition is just like the definition of `nextToken` except for fixing the type of the string returned.)

Chapter Summary

- Inheritance provides a tool for code reuse by deriving one class from another. The derived class automatically inherits the features of the old (base) class and may add features as well.

- A derived class object inherits the instance variables, static variables, and public methods of the base class, and may add additional instance variables, static variables, and methods.

- An object of a derived class has the type of the derived class, and it also has the type of the base class, and more generally, has the type of every one of its ancestor classes.

- If an instance variable is marked private in a base class, then it cannot be accessed by name in a derived class.

- Private methods are effectively not inherited.

- A method may be redefined in a derived class so that it performs differently from how it performs in the base class. This is called *overriding* the method definition. The definition for an overridden method is given in the class definition of the derived class, in the same way as the definitions of any added methods.

- A constructor of a base class can be used in the definition of a constructor for a derived class. The keyword super is used as the name for a constructor of the base class.

- A constructor definition can use the keyword this, as if it were a method name, to invoke a constructor of the same class.

- If a constructor does not contain an invocation of either super or this, then Java automatically inserts an invocation of super() as the first action in the body of the constructor definition.

- A protected instance variable or method in the base class can be accessed by name in the definition of a method of a derived class and in the definition of any method in the same package.

- If an instance variable or method has none of the modifiers public, private, or protected, then it is said to have *package access*. An instance variable or method with package access can be accessed by name in the definition of any method in the same package.

- The class Object is an ancestor class of every class in Java.

- The equals method for a class should have Object as the type of its one parameter.

Answers to Self-Test Exercises

1. Yes, it will have the instance variables. A derived class has all the instance variables that the base class has and can add more instance variables besides.

2. Yes, it will have the methods. A derived class has all the public methods that the base class has and can also add more methods. If the derived class does not override (re–define) a method definition, then it performs exactly the same action in the derived class as it does in the base class. However, the base class can contain an overriding definition of (a new definition of) a method and the new definition will replace the old definition (provided it has the same number and types of parameters).

3. The class `DiscountSale` will have two methods named `getTax` and they will have the following two headings. This is an example of overloading.

```
public double getTax()
public double getTax(double rate)
```

4. The method `getName` is inherited from the class `Employee` and so needs no definition. The method `getRate` is a new method added in the class `HourlyEmployee` and so needs to be defined.

5. Yes. You can plug in an object of a derived class for a parameter of the base class type. An `HourlyEmployee` is an `Employee`. A `SalariedEmployee` is an `Employee`.

6.
```
public class TitledEmployee extends SalariedEmployee
{
    private String title;

    public TitledEmployee()
    {
        super("no name", newDate("January," 1, 1000), 0);
        title = "No title";
    }

    public TitledEmployee(String theName, String theTitle,
                          Date theDate, double theSalary)
    {
        super(theName, theDate, theSalary);
        title = theTitle;
    }

    public String getTitle()
    {
        return title;
    }
```

```
        public void setTitle(String theTitle)
        {
            title = theTitle;
        }

        public String getName()
        {
            return (title + super.getName());
        }
    }
```

7. It would be legal to add `crazyMethod` to the class `Employee`. It would not be legal to add `crazyMethod` to the class `HourlyEmployee` because, although the class `HourlyEmployee` has an instance variable `name`, `name` is private in the base class `Employee` and so cannot be accessed by name in `HourlyEmployee`.

8. Yes, it would be legal as long as `name` is marked `public` in the base class `Employee`.

9. Yes, it would be legal as long as `name` is marked `protected` in the base class `Employee`.

10. Package access is more restricted. Anything allowed by package access is also allowed by protected access, but protected access allows even more.

11. Yes, it is legitimate.

12. Yes, it is legitimate.

13. No, it is not legitimate. The compiler will give an error message saying `doStuff()` is protected in B.

14.
```
    public String toString()
    {
            return (super.toString()
                            + "\n$" + salary + " per year");
    }
```

15.
```
    public boolean equals(HourlyEmployee other)
    {
        return (super.equals(other)
                && wageRate == other.wageRate
                && hours == other.hours);
    }
```

We will give an even better definition of `equals` for the class `HourlyEmployee` later in this chapter.

16. It is not legal. You cannot use `super` in this way. `super.toString()` as used here refers to `toString()` in the class `Employee` and can only be used in definitions of classes derived from `Employee`. Moreover, you cannot have a calling object, such as `joe`, before `super`, so this is even illegal if you add `extends Employee` to the first line of the class definition.

17. Yes, all static variables are inherited. Because a defined constant is a form of static variable, it is inherited. So, the class `HourlyEmployee` inherits the constant `STANDARD_HOURS` from the class `Employee`.

18.
```java
public boolean equals(Object otherObject)
//This is NOT the right way to define equals.
{
    if (otherObject == null)
        return false;
    else if (!(otherObject instanceof Employee))
        return false;
    else
    {
        Employee otherEmployee = (Employee)otherObject;
        return (name.equals(otherEmployee.name)
            && hireDate.equals(otherEmployee.hireDate));
    }
}
```

extra code on CD

19. A version of the `HourlyEmployee` class with this definition of `equals` is in the subdirectory `improvedEquals` of the `ch07` directory on the accompanying CD.

```java
public boolean equals(Object otherObject)
{
    if (otherObject == null)
        return false;
    else if (getClass() != otherObject.getClass())
        return false;
    else
    {
        HourlyEmployee otherHourlyEmployee =
                            (HourlyEmployee)otherObject;
        return (super.equals(otherHourlyEmployee)
            && (wageRate == otherHourlyEmployee.wageRate)
            && (hours == otherHourlyEmployee.hours));
    }
}
```

extra code on CD

20. A version of the `SalariedEmployee` class with this definition of `equals` is in the subdirectory `improvedEquals` of the `ch07` directory on the accompanying CD.

```java
public boolean equals(Object otherObject)
{
    if (otherObject == null)
        return false;
    else if (getClass() != otherObject.getClass())
        return false;
    else
    {
```

```
            SalariedEmployee otherSalariedEmployee =
                            (SalariedEmployee)otherObject;
            return (super.equals(otherSalariedEmployee)
                    && (salary == otherSalariedEmployee.salary));
        }
    }
```

extra code
on CD

21. A version of the Date class with this definition of equals is in the subdirectory improvedEquals of the ch07 directory on the accompanying CD.

```
public boolean equals(Object otherObject)
{
    if (otherObject == null)
        return false;
    else if (getClass() != otherObject.getClass())
        return false;
    else
    {
        Date otherDate =
                    (Date)otherObject;
        return ( month.equals(otherDate.month)
                && (day == otherDate.day)
                && (year == otherDate.year) );
    }
}
```

22. Not the same class.

extra code
on CD

23. The following is included in the definition of EnhancedStringTokenizer on the accompanying CD.

```
public Object nextElement()
{
    String token = super.nextToken();
    a[count] = token;
    count++;
    return (Object)token;
}
```

Programming Projects

 Many of these Programming Projects can be solved using AW's MyCodeMate. To access these please go to: www.mycodemate.com.

 1. Define a class named Payment that contains a member variable of type double that stores the amount of the payment and appropriate accessor and mutator methods. Also create a method named paymentDetails that outputs an English sentence to describe the amount of the payment.

Next, define a class named `CashPayment` that is derived from `Payment`. This class should redefine the `paymentDetails` method to indicate that the payment is in cash. Include appropriate constructor(s).

Define a class named `CreditCardPayment` that is derived from `Payment`. This class should contain member variables for the name on the card, expiration date, and credit card number. Include appropriate constructor(s). Finally, redefine the `paymentDetails` method to include all credit card information in the printout.

Create a `main` method that creates at least two `CashPayment` and two `CreditCard-Payment` objects with different values and calls `paymentDetails` for each.

2. Define a class named `Document` that contains a member variable of type `String` named `text` that stores any textual content for the document. Create a method named `toString` that returns the `text` field and also include a method to set this value.

Next, define a class for `Email` that is derived from `Document` and includes member variables for the `sender`, `recipient`, and `title` of an email message. Implement appropriate accessor and mutator methods. The body of the email message should be stored in the inherited variable `text`. Redefine the `toString` method to concatenate all text fields.

Similarly, define a class for `File` that is derived from `Document` and includes a member variable for the `pathname`. The textual contents of the file should be stored in the inherited variable `text`. Redefine the `toString` method to concatenate all text fields.

Finally, create several sample objects of type `Email` and `File` in your `main` method. Test your objects by passing them to the following subroutine that returns true if the object contains the specified keyword in the text property.

```
public static boolean ContainsKeyword(Document docObject,
                                      String keyword)
{
        if (docObject.toString().indexOf(keyword,0) >= 0)
  return true;
        return false;
}
```

3. The following is some code designed by J. Hacker for a video game. There is an `Alien` class to represent a monster and an `AlienPack` class that represents a band of aliens and how much damage they can inflict:

```
class Alien
{
    public static final int SNAKE_ALIEN = 0;
    public static final int OGRE_ALIEN = 1;
    public static final int MARSHMALLOW_MAN_ALIEN = 2;

    public int type;   // Stores one of the three above types
    public int health; // 0=dead, 100=full strength
    public String name;
```

```java
        public Alien(int type, int health, String name)
        {
            this.type = type;
            this.health = health;
            this.name = name;
        }
}

public class AlienPack
{
        private Alien[] aliens;

        public AlienPack(int numAliens)
        {
            aliens = new Alien[numAliens];
        }

        public void addAlien(Alien newAlien, int index)
        {
            aliens[index] = newAlien;
        }

        public Alien[] getAliens()
        {
            return aliens;
        }

        public int calculateDamage()
        {
            int damage = 0;
            for (int i=0; i < aliens.length; i++)
            {
                if (aliens[i].type==Alien.SNAKE_ALIEN)
                {
                    damage +=10;// Snake does 10 damage
                }
                else if (aliens[i].type==Alien.OGRE_ALIEN)
                {
                    damage +=6;// Ogre does 6 damage
                }
                 else if (aliens[i].type==Alien.MARSHMALLOW_MAN_ALIEN)
                {
                    damage +=1;
                // Marshmallow Man does 1 damage
                }
            }
            return damage;
        }
}
```

The code is not very object-oriented and does not support information hiding in the Alien class. Rewrite the code so that inheritance is used to represent the different types of aliens instead of the "type" parameter. This should result in deletion of the "type" parameter. Also rewrite the Alien class to hide the member variables and create a "getDamage" method for each derived class that returns the amount of damage the alien inflicts. Finally, rewrite the calculateDamage method to use getDamage and write a main method that tests the code.

4. Define a class called Administrator, which is a derived class of the class SalariedEmployee in Display 7.5. You are to supply the following additional instance variables and methods:

An instance variable of type String that contains the administrator's title (such as "Director" or "Vice President").

An instance variable of type String that contains the administrator's area of responsibility (such as "Production", "Accounting", or "Personnel").

An instance variable of type String that contains the name of this administrator's immediate supervisor.

Suitable constructors, and suitable accessor and mutator methods.

A method for reading in an administrator's data from the keyboard.

Override the definitions for the methods equals and toString so they are appropriate to the class Administrator.

Also, write a suitable test program.

5. Give the definition of a class named Doctor whose objects are records for a clinic's doctors. This class will be a derived class of the class SalariedEmployee given in Display 7.5. A Doctor record has the doctor's specialty (such as "Pediatrician", "Obstetrician", "General Practitioner", and so forth; so use the type String) and office visit fee (use type double). Be sure your class has a reasonable complement of constructors, accessor and mutator methods, and suitably defined equals and toString methods. Write a program to test all your methods.

6. Create a class called Vehicle that has the manufacturer's name (type String), number of cylinders in the engine (type int), and owner (type Person given below). Then, create a class called Truck that is derived from Vehicle and has the following additional properties: the load capacity in tons (type double since it may contain a fractional part) and towing capacity in pounds (type int). Be sure your class has a reasonable complement of constructors, accessor and mutator methods, and suitably defined equals and toString methods. Write a program to test all your methods.

The definition of the class Person is below. Completing the definitions of the methods is part of this programming project.

```
public class Person
{
    private String name;
```

```
            public Person()
            {...}
            public Person(String theName)
            {...}
            public Person(Person theObject)
            {...}
            public String getName()
            {...}
            public void setName(String theName)
            {...}
            public String toString()
            {...}
            public boolean equals(Object other)
            {...}
        }
```

7. Give the definition of two classes, Patient and Billing, whose objects are records for a clinic. Patient will be derived from the class Person given in Programming Project 6. A Patient record has the patient's name (inherited from the class Person) and primary physician, of type Doctor defined in Programming Project 5. A Billing object will contain a Patient object and a Doctor object, and an amount due of type double. Be sure your classes have a reasonable complement of constructors, accessor and mutator methods, and suitably defined equals and toString methods. First write a driver program to test all your methods, then write a test program that creates at least two patients, at least two doctors, and at least two Billing records, and then prints out the total income from the Billing records.

8

Polymorphism and Abstract Classes

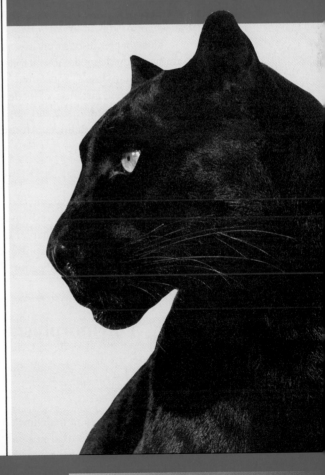

8 Polymorphism and Abstract Classes

Don't make any commitments until you have to.

ANONYMOUS

Introduction

The three main programming mechanisms that constitute object-oriented programming (OOP) are encapsulation, inheritance, and polymorphism. We have already discussed the first two. In this chapter we discuss polymorphism. *Polymorphism* refers to the ability to associate many meanings to one method name by means of a special mechanism known as *late binding* or *dynamic binding*.

This chapter also covers *abstract classes,* which are classes in which some methods are not fully defined. Abstract classes are designed to be used only as base classes for defining new classes. You cannot create instances of (objects of) an abstract class; you can only create instances of its descendent classes.

Both polymorphism and abstract classes deal with code in which a method is used before it is defined. Although this may sound paradoxical, it all works out smoothly in Java.

Prerequisites

This chapter requires Chapters 1 through 5 and Chapter 7 with the exception that Section 5.4 on packages and javadoc is not required. This chapter does not use any material on arrays from Chapter 6.

Sections 8.1 on polymorphism and 8.2 on abstract classes are independent of each other, and you may cover Section 8.2 before Section 8.1 if you wish.

8.1   Polymorphism

I did it my way.

FRANK SINATRA

Inheritance allows you to define a base class and define software for the base class. That software can then be used not only for objects of the base class but also for objects of any class derived from the base class. *Polymorphism* allows you to make changes in the method definition for the derived classes and have those changes apply to the software written *in the base class.* This all happens automatically in Java but it is important to understand the process, and to understand polymorphism we need a concrete example. The next subsection begins with such an example.

Late Binding

Suppose you are designing software for a graphics package that has classes for several kinds of figures, such as rectangles, circles, ovals, and so forth. Each figure might be an object of a different class. For example, the `Rectangle` class might have instance variables for a height, width, and center point, while the `Circle` class might have instance variables for a center point and a radius. In a well-designed programming project, all of these classes would be descendents of a single parent class called, for example, `Figure`. Now, suppose you want a method to draw a figure on the screen. To draw a circle, you need different instructions from those you need to draw a rectangle. So, each class needs to have a different method to draw its kind of figure. However, because the methods belong to the classes, they can all be called `draw`. If `r` is a `Rectangle` object and `c` is a `Circle` object, then `r.draw()` and `c.draw()` can be methods implemented with different code. All this is not new, but now we move on to something new.

Now, the parent class `Figure` may have methods that apply to all figures. For example, it might have a method called `center` that moves a figure to the center of the screen by erasing it and then redrawing it in the center of the screen. The method `center` of the class `Figure` might use the method `draw` to redraw the figure in the center of the screen. When you think of using the inherited method `center` with figures of the classes `Rectangle` and `Circle`, you begin to see that there are complications here.

To make the point clear and more dramatic, let's suppose the class `Figure` is already written and in use and at some later time you add a class for a brand-new kind of figure, say the class `Triangle`. Now `Triangle` can be a derived class of the class `Figure`, so the method `center` will be inherited from the class `Figure` and thus should apply to (and perform correctly for!) all `Triangle`s. But there is a complication. The method `center` uses `draw`, and the method `draw` is different for each type of figure. But, the method `center` is defined in the class `Figure` and so the method `center` was compiled before we wrote the code for the method `draw` of the class `Triangle`. When we invoke the method `center` with an object of the class `Triangle`, we want the code for the method `center` to use a method that was not even defined when we compiled the method `center`, namely the method `draw` for the class `Triangle`. Can this be made to happen in Java? Yes, it can, and moreover, it happens automatically. You need not do anything special when you define either the base class `Figure` or the derived class `Triangle`.

The situation we discussed for the method `center` in the derived class `Triangle` works out as we want because Java uses a mechanism known as **late binding** or **dynamic binding**. Let's see how late binding works in this case involving figure classes.

Binding refers to the process of associating a method definition with a method invocation. If the method definition is associated with the method invocation when the code is compiled, that is called **early binding**. If the method invocation is associated with the method invocation when the method is invoked (at run time), that is called **late binding** or **dynamic binding**. Java uses late binding for all methods except

late binding

binding

early binding

for a few cases discussed later in this chapter. Let's see how late binding works in the case of our method center.

Recall that the method center was defined in the class Figure and that the definition of the method center included an invocation of the method draw. If, contrary to fact, Java used early binding, then when the code for the method center was compiled the invocation of the method draw would be bound to the currently available definition of draw, which is the one given in the definition of Figure. If early binding were used, the method center would behave exactly the same for all derived classes of the class Figure as it does for objects created using the class Figure. But, fortunately, Java uses late binding, so when center is invoked by an object of the class Triangle, the invocation of draw (inside the method center) is not bound to a definition of draw until the invocation actually takes place. At that point in time, the run-time system knows the calling object is an instance of the class Triangle and so uses the definition of draw given in the definition of the class Triangle (even if the invocation of draw is inside the definition of the method center). So, the method center behaves differently for an object of the class Triangle than it would for an object that is just a plain old Figure. With late binding, as in Java, things automatically work out the way you normally want them to.

Note that in order for late binding to work, each object must somehow know which definition of each method applies to that object. So, when an object is created in a system using late binding, the description of the object must include (either directly or indirectly) a description of where the appropriate definition of each method is located. This additional overhead is the penalty you pay for the convenience of late binding.

Late Binding

With **late binding** the definition of a method is not bound to an invocation of the method until run time, in fact, not until the time at which the particular invocation takes place. Java uses late binding (for all methods except those discussed in the Pitfall section entitled "No Late Binding for Static Methods").

---

polymorphism   The terms **polymorphism** and *late binding* are essentially just different words for the same concept. The term *polymorphism* refers to the processes of assigning multiple meanings to the same method name using late binding.

Polymorphism

Polymorphism refers to the ability to associate many meanings to one method name by means of the late binding mechanism. Thus, polymorphism and late binding are really the same topic.

The `final` Modifier

You can mark a method to indicate that it cannot be overridden with a new definition in a derived class. You do this by adding the `final` modifier to the method heading, as in the following sample heading:

```
public final void someMethod()
{
    .
    .
    .
```

An entire class can be declared final, in which case you cannot use it as a base class to derive any other class from it. The syntax for declaring a class to be final is illustrated in what follows:

```
public final class SomeClass
{
    .
    .
    .
```

If a method is marked as `final`, that means the compiler can use early binding with that particular method, which enables the compiler to be more efficient. However, the added efficiency is normally not great and we suggest not using the `final` modifier solely for reasons of efficiency. (Also, it can sometimes aid security to mark certain methods as `final`.)

You can view the `final` modifier as a way of turning off late binding for a method (or an entire class). Of course, it does more than just turn off late binding—it turns off the ability to redefine the method in any descendent class.

The `final` Modifier

If you add the modifier **final** to the definition of a method, that indicates that the method may not be redefined in a derived class. If you add the modifier **final** to the definition of a class, that indicates that the class may not be used as a base class to derive other classes.

---

final

EXAMPLE: Sales Records

Suppose you are designing a record-keeping program for an automobile parts store. You want to make the program versatile, but you are not sure you can account for all possible situations. For example, you want to keep track of sales, but you cannot anticipate all types of sales. At first, there will only be regular sales to retail customers who go to the store to buy one particular part. However, later you may want to add sales with discounts or mail order sales with a shipping charge. All of these sales will be for an item with a basic price and ultimately will produce some bill. For a simple sale, the bill is just the basic price, but if you later add discounts, then some kinds of bills will also depend on the size of the discount. Now your program needs to compute daily gross sales, which intuitively should just be the sum of all the individual sales bills. You may also want to calculate the largest and smallest sales of the day or the average sale for the day. All of these can be calculated from the individual bills, but many of the methods for computing the bills will not be added until later, when you decide what types of sales you will be dealing with. Because Java uses late binding, you can write a program to total all bills even though you will not determine the code for some of the bills until later. (For simplicity in this first example, we assume that each sale is for just one item, although we could, but will not here, account for sales of multiple items.)

Display 8.1 contains the definition for a class named `Sale`. All types of sales will be derived classes of the class `Sale`. The class `Sale` corresponds to simple sales of a single item with no added discounts and no added charges. Note that the methods `lessThan` and `equalDeals` both include invocations of the method `bill`. We can later define derived classes of the class `Sale` and define their versions of the method `bill`, and the definitions of the methods `lessThan` and `equalDeals`, which we gave with the class `Sale`, will use the version of the method `bill` that corresponds to the object of the derived class.

For example, Display 8.2 shows the derived class `DiscountSale`. Notice that the class `DiscountSale` requires a different definition for its version of the method `bill`. Now the methods `lessThan` and `equalDeals`, which use the method `bill`, are inherited from the base class `Sale`. But, when the methods `lessThan` and `equalDeals` are used with an object of the class `DiscountSale`, they will use the version of the method definition for `bill` that was given with the class `DiscountSale`. This is indeed a pretty fancy trick for Java to pull off. Consider the method call `d1.lessThan(d2)` for objects `d1` and `d2` of the class `DiscountSale`. The definition of the method `lessThan` (even for an object of the class `DiscountSale`) is given in the definition of the base class `Sale`, which was compiled before we ever even thought of the class `DiscountSale`. Yet, in the method call `d1.lessThan(d2)`, the line that calls the method `bill` knows enough to use the definition of the method `bill` given for the class `DiscountSale`. This all works out because Java uses late binding.

Display 8.3 gives a sample program that illustrates how the late binding of the method `bill` and the methods that use `bill` work in a complete program.

Display 8.1   **The Base Class Sale** (part 1 of 3)

```
1    /**
2     Class for a simple sale of one item with no tax, discount, or other adjustments.
3     Class invariant: The price is always nonnegative; the name is a nonempty string.
4    */
5    public class Sale
6    {
7        private String name; //A nonempty string
8        private double price; //nonnegative

9        public Sale()
10       {
11           name = "No name yet";
12           price = 0;
13       }

14       /**
15        Precondition: theName is a nonempty string; thePrice is nonnegative.
16       */
17       public Sale(String theName, double thePrice)
18       {
19           setName(theName);
20           setPrice(thePrice);
21       }

22       public Sale(Sale originalObject)
23       {
24           if (originalObject == null)
25           {
26               System.out.println("Error: null Sale object.");
27               System.exit(0);
28           }
29           //else
30           name = originalObject.name;
31           price = originalObject.price;
32       }

33       public static void announcement()
34       {
35           System.out.println("This is the Sale class.");
36       }

37       public double getPrice()
38       {
39           return price;
40       }
```

(continued)

Display 8.1   **The Base Class Sale** (part 2 of 3)

```
41      /**
42       Precondition: newPrice is nonnegative.
43      */
44      public void setPrice(double newPrice)
45      {
46          if (newPrice >= 0)
47              price = newPrice;
48          else
49          {
50              System.out.println("Error: Negative price.");
51              System.exit(0);
52          }
53      }

54      public String getName()
55      {
56          return name;
57      }

58      /**
59       Precondition: newName is a nonempty string.
60      */
61      public void setName(String newName)
62      {
63          if (newName != null && newName != "")
64              name = newName;
65          else
66          {
67              System.out.println("Error: Improper name value.");
68              System.exit(0);
69          }
70      }

71      public String toString()
72      {
73          return (name + " Price and total cost = $" + price);
74      }

75      public double bill()
76      {
77          return price;
78      }
```

Display 8.1   **The Base Class Sale** (part 3 of 3)

```
79       /*
80        Returns true if the names are the same and the bill for the calling
81        object is equal to the bill for otherSale; otherwise returns false.
82        Also returns false if otherObject is null.
83       */
84       public boolean equalDeals(Sale otherSale)
85       {
86           if (otherSale == null)
87               return false;
88           else
89               return (name.equals(otherSale.name)
90                   && bill() == otherSale.bill());
91       }
92       /*
93        Returns true if the bill for the calling object is less
94        than the bill for otherSale; otherwise returns false.
95       */
96       public boolean lessThan (Sale otherSale)
97       {
98           if (otherSale == null)
99           {
100              System.out.println("Error: null Sale object.");
101              System.exit(0);
102          }
103          //else
104          return (bill() < otherSale.bill());
105      }

106      public boolean equals(Object otherObject)
107      {
108          if (otherObject == null)
109              return false;
110          else if (getClass() != otherObject.getClass())
111              return false;
112          else
113          {
114              Sale otherSale = (Sale)otherObject;
115              return (name.equals(otherSale.name)
116                  && (price == otherSale.price));
117          }
118      }
119  }
```

When invoked, these methods will use the definition of the method bill that is appropriate for each of the objects.

Display 8.2   The Derived Class **DiscountSale** (part 1 of 2)

```
1   /**
2   Class for a sale of one item with discount expressed as a percent of the price,
3   but no other adjustments.
4   Class invariant: The price is always nonnegative; the name is a
5   nonempty string; the discount is always nonnegative.
6   */

7   public class DiscountSale extends Sale
8   {
9       private double discount; //A percent of the price. Cannot be negative.

10      public DiscountSale()
11      {
12          super();
13          discount = 0;
14      }

15      /**
16       Precondition: theName is a nonempty string; thePrice is nonnegative;
17       theDiscount is expressed as a percent of the price and is nonnegative.
18      */
19      public DiscountSale(String theName,
20                                      double thePrice, double theDiscount)
21      {
22          super(theName, thePrice);
23          setDiscount(theDiscount);
24      }

25      public DiscountSale(DiscountSale originalObject)
26      {
27          super(originalObject);
28          discount = originalObject.discount;
29      }

30      public static void announcement()
31      {
32          System.out.println("This is the DiscountSale class.");
33      }

34      public double bill()
35      {
36          double fraction = discount/100;
37          return (1 - fraction)*getPrice();
38      }
```

The meaning would be unchanged if this line were omitted. (pointing to line 12: `super();`)

Display 8.2 The Derived Class **DiscountSale** (part 2 of 2)

```
39        public double getDiscount()
40        {
41            return discount;
42        }

43        /**
44         Precondition: Discount is nonnegative.
45        */
46        public void setDiscount(double newDiscount)
47        {
48            if (newDiscount >= 0)
49                discount = newDiscount;
50            else
51            {
52                System.out.println("Error: Negative discount.");
53                System.exit(0);
54            }
55        }

56        public String toString()
57        {
58            return (getName() + " Price = $" + getPrice()
59                    + " Discount = " + discount + "%\n"
60                    + "   Total cost = $" + bill());
61        }

62        public boolean equals(Object otherObject)
          <The rest of the definition of equals is Self-Test Exercise 4.>

63    }
```

Display 8.3   Late Binding Demonstration

```
 1   /**
 2    Demonstrates late binding.
 3    */
 4   public class LateBindingDemo
 5   {
 6       public static void main(String[] args)
 7       {
 8           Sale simple = new Sale("floor mat", 10.00);//One item at $10.00.
 9           DiscountSale discount = new DiscountSale("floor mat", 11.00, 10);
10                               //One item at $11.00 with a 10% discount.
11           System.out.println(simple);
12           System.out.println(discount);
13           if (discount.lessThan(simple))
14               System.out.println("Discounted item is cheaper.");
15           else
16               System.out.println("Discounted item is not cheaper.");

17           Sale regularPrice = new Sale("cup holder", 9.90);//One item at $9.90.
18           DiscountSale specialPrice = new DiscountSale("cup holder", 11.00, 10);
19                               //One item at $11.00 with a 10% discount.
20           System.out.println(regularPrice);
21           System.out.println(specialPrice);

22           if (specialPrice.equalDeals(regularPrice))
23               System.out.println("Deals are equal.");
24           else
25               System.out.println("Deals are not equal.");
26       }
27   }
```

The method **lessThan** *uses different definitions for* **discount.bill()** *and* **simple.bill()**.

The method **equalDeals** *uses different definitions for* **specialPrice.bill()** *and* **regularPrice.bill()**.

The **equalDeals** *method says that two items are equal provided they have the same name and the same bill (same total cost). It does not matter how the bill (the total cost) is calculated.*

Sample Dialogue

```
floor mat Price and total cost = $10.0
floor mat Price = $11.0 Discount = 10.0%
   Total cost = $9.9
Discounted item is cheaper.
cup holder Price and total cost = $9.9
cup holder Price = $11.0 Discount = 10.0%
   Total cost = $9.9
Deals are equal.
```

Self-Test Exercises

1. Explain the difference between the terms *late binding* and *polymorphism*.

2. Suppose you modify the definitions of the class `Sale` (Display 8.1) by adding the modifier `final` to the definition of the method `bill`. How would that change the output of the program in Display 8.3?

3. Would it be legal to add the following method definition to the class `Discount-Sale`?

```
public static boolean isAGoodBuy(Sale theSale)
{
    return (theSale.getDiscount() > 20);
}
```

4. Complete the definition of the method `equals` for the class `DiscountSale` (Display 8.2).

Late Binding with `toString`

In the subsection "The Methods `equals` and `toString`" in Chapter 4, we noted that if you include an appropriate `toString` method in the definition of a class, then you can output an object of the class using `System.out.println`. For example, the following works because `Sale` has a suitable `toString` method:

```
Sale aSale = new Sale("tire gauge", 9.95);
System.out.println(aSale);
```

This produces the screen output

```
tire gauge Price and total cost = $9.95
```

This happens because Java uses late binding. Here are the details.

The method invocation `System.out.println(aSale)` is an invocation of the method `println` with the calling object `System.out`. One definition of the method `println` has a single argument of type `Object`. The definition is equivalent to the following:

```
public void println(Object theObject)
{
    System.out.println(theObject.toString());
}
```

(The invocation of the method `println` inside the braces is a different, overloaded definition of the method `println`. That invocation inside the braces uses a method `println` that has a parameter of type `String`, not a parameter of type `Object`.)

This definition of println was given before the class Sale was defined. Yet in the invocation

```
System.out.println(aSale);
```

with an argument aSale of type Sale (and hence also of type Object), it is the definition of toString in the class Sale that is used, not the definition of toString in the class Object. Late binding is what makes this work.

PITFALL: No Late Binding for Static Methods ★

Java does not use late binding with private methods, methods marked final, or static methods. With private methods and final methods, this is not an issue since dynamic binding would serve no purpose anyway. However, with static methods it can make a difference when the static method is invoked using a calling object, and such cases arise more often than you might think.

static binding When Java (or any language) does not use late binding, it uses **static binding**. With static binding, the decision of which definition of a method to use with a calling object is made at compile time based on the type of the variable naming the object.

Display 8.4 illustrates the effect of static binding on a static method with a calling object. Note that the static method announcement() in the class Sale has its definition overridden in the derived class DiscountSale. However, when an object of type DiscountSale is named by a variable of type Sale, it is the definition announcement() in the class Sale that is used, not the definition of announcement in the class DiscountSale.

"So, what's the big deal?" you may ask. A static method is normally called with a class name and not a calling object. It may look that way, but there are cases where a static method has a calling object in an inconspicuous way. If you invoke a static method within the definition of a nonstatic method but without any class name or calling object, then the calling object is an implicit this, which is a calling object.

For example, suppose you add the following method to the class Sale:

```
public void showAdvertisement()
{
    announcement();
    System.out.println(toString( ));
}
```

Suppose further that the method showAdvertisement is not overridden in the class DiscountSale, then the method showAdvertisement is inherited unchanged from Sale.

PITFALL: (continued)

Now consider the following code:

```
Sale s = new Sale("floor mat", 10.00);
DiscountSale discount = new DiscountSale("floor mat", 11.00, 10);
s.showAdertisement();
discount.showAdertisement();
```

You might expect the following output:

```
This is the Sale class.
floor mat Price and total cost = $10.0
This is the DiscountSale class.
floor mat Price = $11.0 Discount = 10.0%
   Total cost = $9.9
```

However, because the definition used for the static method announcement, inside of showAdvertisement, is determined at compile time (based on the type of the variable holding the calling object), the output actually is the following, where the change is shown in red:

```
This is the Sale class.
floor mat Price and total cost = $10.0
This is the Sale class.
floor mat Price = $11.0 Discount = 10.0%
   Total cost = $9.9
```

Java uses late binding with the nonstatic method toString but static binding with the static method announcement. ■

Downcasting and Upcasting

The following is perfectly legal (given the class definitions in Displays 8.1 and 8.2):

```
Sale saleVariable;
DiscountSale discountVariable =
                new DiscountSale("paint", 15, 10);
saleVariable = discountVariable;
System.out.println(saleVariable.toString());
```

An object of a derived class, in this case the derived class DiscountSale, also has the type of its base class, in this case Sale, and so can be assigned to a variable of the base class type. Now let's consider the invocation of the method toString() on the last line of this code.

Display 8.4 No Late Binding with Static Methods ★

```
1    /**
2     Demonstrates that static methods use static binding.
3    */
4    public class StaticMethodsDemo
5    {
6        public static void main(String[] args)
7        {
8            Sale.announcement();
9            DiscountSale.announcement();
10           System.out.println(
11               "That showed that you can override a static method definition.");

12           Sale s = new Sale();
13           DiscountSale discount = new DiscountSale();
14           s.announcement();
15           discount.announcement();
16           System.out.println("No surprises so far, but wait.");

17           Sale discount2 = discount;
18           System.out.println(
19               "discount2 is a DiscountSale object in a Sale variable.");
20           System.out.println( "Which definition of announcement() will it use?");
21           discount2.announcement();
22           System.out.println(
23               "It used the Sale version of announcement()!");
24       }
25   }
```

Java uses static binding with static methods so the choice of which definition of a static method to use is determined by the type of the variable, not by the object.

discount and discount2 name the same object, but one is a variable of type Sale and one is a variable of type DiscountSale.

Sample Dialogue

```
This is the Sale class.
This is the DiscountSale class.
That showed that you can override a static method definition.
This is the Sale class.
This is the DiscountSale class.
No surprises so far, but wait.
discount2 is a DiscountSale object in a Sale variable.
Which definition of announcement() will it use?
This is the Sale class.
It used the Sale version of announcement()!
```

If Java had used late binding with static methods, then this would have been the other announcement.

Because Java uses late binding, the invocation

```
saleVariable.toString()
```

uses the definition of the method `toString` given in the class `DiscountSale`. So the output is

```
paint Price = $15.0 Discount = 10.0%
   Total cost = $13.5
```

Because of late binding, the meaning of the method `toString` is determined by the object, not by the type of the variable `saleVariable`.

You may well respond, "Who cares? Why would I ever want to assign an object of type `DiscountSale` to a variable of type `Sale`?"[1] You make such assignments more often than you might think, but you tend to not notice them because they happen behind the scenes. Recall that a parameter is really a local variable, so every time you use an argument of type `DiscountSale` for a parameter of type `Sale`, you are assigning an object of type `DiscountSale` to a variable of type `Sale`. For example, consider the following invocation taken from the definition of the copy constructor for `Discount-Sale` (Display 8.2):

```
super(originalObject);
```

In this invocation `originalObject` is of type `DiscountSale`, but `super` is the copy constructor for the base class `Sale` and so `super` has a parameter of type `Sale`, which is a local variable of type `Sale` that is set equal to the argument `originalObject` of type `DiscountSale`.

Note that the type of the variable naming an object determines which method names can be used in an invocation with that calling object. (Self-Test Exercise 3 may help you to understand this point.) However, the object itself always determines the meaning of a method invocation performed by an object; this is simply what we mean by late binding.

An Object Knows the Definitions of Its Methods

The type of a class variable determines which method names can be used with the variable, but the object named by the variable determines which definition of the method name is used. A special case of this rule is the following: The type of a class parameter determines which method names can be used with the parameter, but the argument determines which definition of the method name is used.

---

[1] It is actually the references to the object that are assigned, not the objects themselves, but that subtlety is not relevant to what we are discussing here, and the language is already complicated enough.

upcasting

downcasting

Assigning an object of a derived class to a variable of a base class (or any ancestor class) is often called **upcasting** because it is like a type cast to the type of the base class and, in the normal way of writing inheritance diagrams base classes are drawn above derived classes.[2]

When you do a type cast from a base case to a derived class (or from any ancestor class to any descendent class), that is called a **downcast**. Upcasting is pretty straightforward; there are no funny cases to worry about, and in Java things always work out the way you want them to. Downcasting is more troublesome. First of all, downcasting does not always make sense. For example, the downcast

```
Sale saleVariable = new Sale("paint", 15);
DiscountSale discountVariable;
discountVariable = (DiscountSale)saleVariable;//Error
```

does not make sense because the object named by `saleVariable` has no instance variable named `discount` and so cannot be an object of type `DiscountSale`. Every `DiscountSale` is a `Sale`, but not every `Sale` is a `DiscountSale`, as indicated by this example. It is your responsibility to use downcasting only in situations where it makes sense.

It is instructive to note that

```
discountVariable = (DiscountSale)saleVariable;
```

produces a run-time error but will compile with no error. However, the following, which is also illegal, produces a compile-time error:

```
discountVariable = saleVariable;
```

Java catches these downcasting errors as soon as it can, which may be at compile time or at run time depending on the case.

Although downcasting can be dangerous, it is sometimes necessary. For example, we inevitably use downcasting when we define an `equals` method for a class. For example, note the following line from the definition of `equals` in the class `Sale` (Display 8.1):

```
Sale otherSale = (Sale)otherObject;
```

---

[2] We prefer to think of an object of the derived class as actually having the type of its base class as well as its own type. So this is not, strictly speaking, a type cast, but it does no harm to follow standard usage and call it a type cast in this case.

This is a downcast from the type `Object` to the type `Sale`. Without this downcast, the instance variables `name` and `price` in the `return` statement, reproduced below, would be illegal, since the class `Object` has no such instance variables:

```
return (name.equals(otherSale.name)
        && (price == otherSale.price));
```

PITFALL: Downcasting

It is the responsibility of the programmer to use downcasting only in situations where it makes sense. The compiler makes no checks to see if downcasting is reasonable. However, if you use downcasting in a situation in which it does not make sense, you will usually get a run-time error message. ■

TIP: Checking to See Whether Downcasting Is Legitimate ★

You can use the `instanceof` operator to test whether or not downcasting is sensible. Downcasting to a specific type is sensible if the object being cast is an instance of that type, and that is exactly what the `instanceof` operator tests for.

instanceof   The `instanceof` operator checks whether an object is of the type given as its second argument. The syntax is

Object `instanceof` *Class_Name*

which returns `true` if *Object* is of type *Class_Name*; otherwise it returns `false`. So, the following will return `true` if `someObject` is of type `DiscountSale`:

`someObject` `instanceof` `DiscountSale`

Note that since every object of every descendent class of `DiscountSale` is also of type `DiscountSale`, this expression will return `true` if `someObject` is an instance of any descendent class of `DiscountSale`.

(continued)

TIP: (continued)

So, if you want to type cast to `DiscountSale`, then you can make the casts safer as follows:

```
DiscountSale ds = new DiscountSale();
if (someObject instanceof DiscountSale)
{
    ds = (DiscountSale)someObject;
    System.out.println("ds was changed to " + someObject);
}
else
    System.out.println("ds was not changed.");
```

`someObject` might be, for example, a variable of type `Sale` or of type `Object`. ■

Self-Test Exercises

5. Consider the following code, which is identical to the code discussed in the opening of the subsection, "Downcasting and Upcasting," except that we have added the type cast shown in color:

```
Sale saleVariable;
DiscountSale discountVariable =
            new DiscountSale("paint", 15, 10);
saleVariable = (Sale)discountVariable;
System.out.println(saleVariable.toString());
```

We saw that without the type cast, the definition of the `toString` method used is the one given in the definition of the class `DiscountSale`. With this added type cast, will the definition of the `toString` method used still be the one given in `DiscountSale` or will it be the one given in the definition of `Sale`?

6. Would it be legal to add the following method definition to the class `Discount-Sale`?

What about adding it to the class `Sale`?

```
public static void showDiscount(Sale object)
{
    System.out.println("Discount = "
                    + object.getDiscount());
}
```

Self-Test Exercises (continued)

7. ★ What output is produced by the following code?

```
Sale someObject = new DiscountSale("map", 5, 0);
DiscountSale ds = new DiscountSale();
if (someObject instanceof DiscountSale)
{
    ds = (DiscountSale)someObject;
    System.out.println("ds was changed to " + someObject);
}
else
    System.out.println("ds was not changed.");
```

8. ★ What output is produced by the following code?

```
Sale someObject = new Sale("map", 5);
DiscountSale ds = new DiscountSale();
if (someObject instanceof DiscountSale)
{
    ds = (DiscountSale)someObject;
    System.out.println("ds was changed to " + someObject);
}
else
    System.out.println("ds was not changed.");
```

9. ★ Suppose we removed the qualifier static from the method announcement() in both Sale (Display 8.1) and DiscountSale (Display 8.2). What would be the output produced by the following code (which is similar to the end of Display 8.4)?

```
Sale s = new Sale( );
DiscountSale discount = new DiscountSale();
s.announcement( );
discount.announcement( );
System.out.println("No surprises so far, but wait.");

Sale discount2 = discount;
System.out.println(
   "discount2 is a DiscountSale object in a Sale variable.");
System.out.println(
    "Which definition of announcement( ) will it use?");
discount2.announcement( );
System.out.println(
      "Did it use the Sale version of announcement( )?");
```

A First Look at the `clone` Method

clone

Every object inherits a method named `clone` from the class `Object`. The method `clone` has no parameters and is supposed to return a copy of the calling object. However, the inherited version of `clone` was not designed to be used as is. Instead, you are expected to override the definition of `clone` with a version appropriate for the class you are defining. In Chapter 13, we will describe the officially sanctioned way to define the method `clone`. The officially sanctioned way turns out to be a bit complicated and requires material we do not cover until Chapter 13. In this section, we will describe a simple way to define `clone` that will work in most situations and will allow us to discuss how polymorphism interacts with the `clone` method. If you are in a hurry to see the officially sanctioned way to define `clone`, you can read Chapter 13 immediately after this section (Section 8.1) with no loss of continuity in your reading.

The method `clone` has no parameters and should return a copy of the calling object. The returned object should have identical data to that of the calling object, but it normally should be a different object (an identical twin or "a clone"). You usually want the `clone` method to return the same kind of copy as what we have been defining for copy constructors, which is what is known as a *deep copy*. (You many want to review the subsection entitled "Copy Constructors" in Chapter 5.)

A `clone` method serves very much the same purpose as a copy constructor but, as you will see in an upcoming subsection, there are situations where a `clone` method works as you want, whereas a copy constructor does not perform as desired.

As with other methods inherited from the class `Object`, the method `clone` needs to be redefined (overridden) before it performs properly. The heading for the method `clone` in the class `Object` is as follows:

```
protected Object clone()
```

If a class has a copy constructor, you can define the `clone` method for that class by using the copy constructor to create the copy returned by the `clone` method. For example, consider the class `Sale` defined in Display 8.1. The following definition of the `clone` method can be added to the definition of `Sale` given in Display 8.1:

```
public Sale clone()
{
    return new Sale(this);
}
```

Using a copy constructor is not the officially sanctioned way to define a `clone` method, and in fact, the Java documentation says you should not define it this way. However, it does work correctly and some authorities say it is acceptable. In Chapter 13, we will discuss the officially sanctioned way of defining the method `clone` when we introduce the `Cloneable` interface.

Note that, as we defined the method `clone` for the class `Sale`, the method `clone` has `Sale` as its return type and is given `public` rather than `protected` access. Despite these changes in the method heading, this definition overrides the method `clone` inherited from the class `Object`. As we noted in Chapter 7, a change to a more permissive access, such as from `protected` to `public`, is always allowed when overriding a method definition. Changing the return type from `Object` to `Sale` is allowed because `Sale` (and every other class, for that matter) is a descendent class of the class `Object`. This is an example of a covariant return type, as discussed in the subsection of Chapter 7 entitled "Changing the Return Type of an Overridden Method."

The `clone` method for the `DiscountSale` class can be defined similarly:

```java
public DiscountSale clone()
{
    return new DiscountSale(this );
}
```

**extra code
on CD**

The definitions of the classes `Sale` and `DiscountSale` on the CD that accompanies this book each include the method `clone` defined as we just described.

PITFALL: Sometimes the `clone` Method Return Type Is `Object`

Prior to version 5.0, Java did not allow covariant return types, and so did not allow any changes whatsoever in the return type of an overridden method. In those earlier versions of Java, the `clone` method for all classes had `Object` as its return type. This is because the `clone` method for a class overrides the `clone` method of the class `Object`, and the `clone` method of the class `Object` has a return type of `Object`. If you encounter a `clone` method for a class that was designed and coded before version 5.0 of Java, the `clone` method will have a return type of `Object`. When using such older `clone` methods, you will need to use a type cast on the value returned by `clone`.

For example, suppose the class `OldClass` was defined before Java 5.0, and `original` is an object of the class `OldClass`, then the following will produce a compiler error message:

```java
OldClass copy = original.clone();
```

The problem is that `original.clone()` returns a value of type `Object`, while the variable `copy` is of type `OldClass`. To correct the situation you must add a type cast as follows:

```java
OldClass copy = (OldClass)original.clone();
```

(continued)

PITFALL: (continued)

You may encounter this problem even with classes defined after Java version 5.0. In Java version 5.0 and later, it is perfectly legal to use Object as a return type for a clone method (even if that is not the preferred return type). When in doubt, it causes no harm to include the type cast. For example, the following is legal for the clone method of the class Sale defined in the previous section:

```
Sale copySale = originalSale.clone();
```

However, adding the following type cast produces no problems:

```
Sale copySale = (Sale)originalSale.clone();
```

When in doubt about the clone method of a class, include the type cast. ∎

PITFALL: Limitations of Copy Constructors ★

Copy constructors work well in most simple cases. However, there are situations where they do not, indeed cannot, do their job. That is why Java favors using the method clone in place of using a copy constructor. Here's a simple example of where the copy constructor does not do its job, but the clone method does.

For this discussion, assume that the classes Sale and DiscountSale each have a clone method added. The definitions of these clone methods are given in the previous subsection.

Suppose you have a method with the following heading (the methods Sale and DiscountSale were defined in Displays 8.1 and 8.2):

```
/**
 Supposedly returns a safe copy of a. That is, if b is the
 array returned, then b[i] is supposedly an independent copy of a[i].
*/
public static Sale[] badCopy(Sale[] a)
{
    Sale[] b = new Sale[a.length];
    for (int i = 0; i < a.length; i++)
        b[i] = new Sale(a[i]);//Problem here!
    return b;
}
```

Now if your array a contains objects from derived classes of Sale, such as objects of type DscountSale, then badCopy(a) will not return a true copy of a. Every element of the array badCopy(a) will be a plain old Sale, since the Sale copy constructor only produces plain old Sale objects; no element in badCopy(a) will be an instance of the class DiscountSale.

If we instead use the method clone, things work out as they should; the following is the correct way to define our copy method:

```
public static Sale[] goodCopy(Sale[] a)
{
    Sale[] b = new Sale[a.length];
    for (int i = 0; i < a.length; i++)
        b[i] = a[i].clone( );
    return b;
}
```

Because of late binding (polymorphism), a[i].clone() always means the correct version of the clone method. If a[i] is an object created with a constructor of the class DiscountSale, a[i].clone() will invoke the definition of clone() given in the definition of the class DiscountSale. If a[i] is an object created with a constructor of the class Sale, a[i].clone() will invoke the definition of clone() given in the definition of the class Sale. This is illustrated in Display 8.5.

This may seem like a sleight of hand. After all, in the classes Sale and DiscountSale we defined the method clone in terms of copy constructors. We reproduce the definitions of clone from the class Sale and DiscountSale below:

```
//For Sale class
public Sale clone()
{
    return new Sale(this);
}
//For DiscountSale class
public DiscountSale clone()
{
    return new DiscountSale(this);
}
```

So, why is using the method clone any different than using a copy constructor? The difference is simply that the method creating the copy of an element a[i] has the same name clone in all the classes, and polymorphism works with method names. The copy constructors named Sale and DiscountSale have different names, and polymorphism has nothing to do with methods of different names.

We will have more to say about the clone method in Chapter 13 when we discuss the Cloneable interface. ■

Display 8.5 Copy Constructor Versus **clone** Method (part 1 of 2)

```
1   /**
2    Demonstrates where the clone method works,
3    but copy constructors do not.
4   */
5   public class CopyingDemo
6   {

7       public static void main(String[] args)
8       {
9           Sale[] a = new Sale[2];
10          a[0] = new Sale("atomic coffee mug", 130.00);
11          a[1] = new DiscountSale("invisible paint", 5.00, 10);
12          int i;

13          Sale[] b = badCopy(a);

14          System.out.println("With copy constructors:");
15          for (i = 0; i < a.length; i++)
16          {
17              System.out.println("a[" + i + "] = " + a[i]);
18              System.out.println("b[" + i + "] = " + b[i]);
19              System.out.println();
20          }
21          System.out.println();

22          b = goodCopy(a);

23          System.out.println("With clone method:");
24          for (i = 0; i < a.length; i++)
25          {
26              System.out.println("a[" + i + "] = " + a[i]);
27              System.out.println("b[" + i + "] = " + b[i]);
28              System.out.println();
29          }

30      }

31      /**
32       Supposedly returns a safe copy of a. That is, if b is the
33       array returned, then b[i] is supposedly an independent copy of a[i].
34      */
```

This program assumes that a clone method has been added to the class Sale and to the class DiscountSale.

Display 8.5   Copy Constructor Versus **clone** Method (part 2 of 2)

```
35      public static Sale[] badCopy(Sale[] a)
36      {
37          Sale[] b = new Sale[a.length];
38          for (int i = 0; i < a.length; i++)
39              b[i] = new Sale(a[i]);//Problem here!
40          return b;
41      }
42
43      /**
44       Returns a safe copy of a.That is, if b is the
45       array returned, then b[i] is an independent copy of a[i].
46      */
47      public static Sale[] goodCopy(Sale[] a)
48      {
49          Sale[] b = new Sale[a.length];
50          for (int i = 0; i < a.length; i++)
51              b[i] = a[i].clone( );
52          return b;
53      }
54  }
```

Sample Dialogue

```
With copy constructors:
a[0] = atomic coffee mug Price and total cost = $130.0
b[0] = atomic coffee mug Price and total cost = $130.0

a[1] = invisible paint Price = $5.0 Discount 10.0%
    Total cost = $4.5
b[1] = invisible paint Price and total cost = $5.0

With clone method:
a[0] = atomic coffee mug Price and total cost = $130.0
b[0] = atomic coffee mug Price and total cost = $130.0

a[1] = invisible paint Price = $5.0 Discount 10.0%
    Total cost = $4.5
b[1] = invisible paint Price = $5.0 Discount 10.0%
    Total cost = $4.5
```

The copy constructor lost the discount.

The **clone** *method did not lose the discount.*

8.2 Abstract Classes

It is for us, the living, rather to be dedicated here to the unfinished work which they who fought here have thus far so nobly advanced.

ABRAHAM LINCOLN, *Gettysburg Address*

An abstract class is a class that has some methods without complete definitions. You cannot create an object using an abstract class constructor, but you can use an abstract class as a base class to define a derived class.

Abstract Classes

In Chapter 7, we defined a class named `Employee` and two of its derived classes, `HourlyEmployee` and `SalariedEmployee`. Display 8.6 repeats the details of these class definitions, which we will use in this discussion.

Suppose that when we defined the class `Employee` we knew that we were going to frequently compare employees to see if they have the same pay. We might have added the following method to the class `Employee`:

```
public boolean samePay(Employee other)
{
    return (this.getPay() == other.getPay());
}
```

There is, however, one problem with adding the method `samePay` to the class `Employee`: The method `samePay` includes an invocation of the method `getPay`, and the class `Employee` has no `getPay` method. Moreover, there is no reasonable definition we might give for a `getPay` method so that we could add it to the class `Employee`. The only instance variables in the class `Employee` give an employee's name and hire date, but give no information about pay. To see how we should proceed, let's compare objects of the class `Employee` to employees in the real world.

Every real-world employee does have some pay because every real-world employee is either an hourly employee or a salaried employee, and the two derived classes `HourlyEmployee` and `SalariedEmployee` do each have a `getPay` method. The problem is that we do not know how to define the `getPay` method until we know if the employee is an hourly employee or a salaried employee. We would like to postpone the definition of the `getPay` method and only give it in each derived class of the `Employee` class. We would like to simply add a note to the `Employee` class that says: "There will be a method `getPay` for each `Employee` but we do not yet know how it is defined." Java lets us do exactly what we want. The official Java equivalent of our promissory note about the method `getPay` is to make `getPay` an **abstract method**. An abstract method has a

abstract method

Display 8.6 **Employee** Class and Its Derived Classes (part 1 of 2)

These show the details needed for the current discussion. You should not need to review the entire class definitions from Chapter 7. Complete definitions of all these classes are given in the subdirectory for this chapter on the CD that comes with this text.

```
1   public class Employee
2   {
3       private String name;
4       private Date hireDate;

5       public Employee()
```

*The class **Date** is defined in Display 4.13, but the details are not important to the current discussion. There is no need to review the definition of the class **Date**.*

<The body of the constructor is given in Display 7.2,
                        but the details are not needed for this discussion.>

```
6       public boolean equals(Object otherObject)
```

<The body of the method **equals** is the same as in Display 7.10
of Chapter 7, but the details of the definition are not important to the current discussion.>

<All other constructor and other method definitions are exactly the same as in Display 7.2.>

*The class **Employee** has no method named **getPay**.*

```
7   }
```

```
1   public class SalariedEmployee extends Employee
2   {
3       private double salary; //annual

4       /**
5        Returns the pay for the month.
6       */
7       public double getPay()
8       {
9           return salary/12;
10      }

11      public boolean equals(Object otherObject)
```

<The rest of the definition of **equals** is the same as in the answer to Self-Test Exercise 20
of Chapter 7, but the details of the definition are not important to the current discussion.>

<All constructor and other method definitions are exactly the same as in Display 7.5.>

```
12  }
```

(continued)

Display 8.6 **Employee** Class and Its Derived Classes (part 2 of 2)

```java
1   public class HourlyEmployee extends Employee
2   {
3       private double wageRate;
4       private double hours; //for the month

5       /**
6        Returns the pay for the month.
7        */
8       public double getPay()
9       {
10          return wageRate*hours;
11      }

12      public boolean equals(Object otherObject)
13      {
14          if (otherObject == null)
15              return false;
16          else if (getClass() != otherObject.getClass())
17              return false;
18          else
19          {
20              HourlyEmployee otherHourlyEmployee =
21                                  (HourlyEmployee)otherObject;
22              return (super.equals(otherHourlyEmployee)
23                  && (wageRate == otherHourlyEmployee.wageRate)
24                  && (hours == otherHourlyEmployee.hours));
25          }
26      }
```

<All constructor and other method definitions are exactly the same as in Display 7.3.>

```java
27  }
```

heading just like an ordinary method, but no method body. The syntax rules of Java require the modifier abstract and require a semicolon in place of the missing method body, as illustrated by the following:

```java
public abstract double getPay();
```

If we add this abstract method `getPay` to the class `Employee`, then we are free to add the method `samePay` to the class `Employee`.

abstract cannot be private

An abstract method can be thought of as the interface part of a method with the implementation details omitted. Because a private method is normally only a helping method and so not part of the interface for a programmer using the class, it follows that it does not make sense to have a private abstract method. Java enforces this reasoning. In Java, an abstract method cannot be private. Normally an abstract method is public, but protected and package (default) access are allowed.

An abstract method serves a purpose, even though it is not given a full definition. It serves as a placeholder for a method that must be defined in all (nonabstract) derived classes. Note that in Display 8.7 the method `samePay` includes invocations of the method `getPay`. If the abstract method `getPay` were omitted, this invocation of `getPay` would be illegal.

Abstract Method

An abstract method serves as a placeholder for a method that will be fully defined in a descendent class. An abstract method has a complete method heading with the addition of the modifier `abstract`. It has no method body but does end with a semicolon in place of a method body. An abstract method cannot be private.

EXAMPLES
```
public abstract double getPay();
public abstract void doSomething(int count);
```

---

abstract class

A class that has at least one abstract method is called an **abstract class** and, in Java, must have the modifier `abstract` added to the class heading. The redefined, now abstract, class `Employee` is shown in Display 8.7.

An abstract class can have any number of abstract methods. In addition it can have, and typically does have, other regular (fully defined) methods. If a derived class of an abstract class does not give full definitions to all the abstract methods or if the derived class adds an abstract method, then the derived class is also an abstract class and must include the modifier `abstract` in its heading.

concrete class

In contrast with the term abstract class, a class with no abstract methods is called a **concrete class**.

Display 8.7 **Employee Class as an Abstract Class**

```
1   /**
2    Class Invariant: All objects have a name string and hire date.
3    A name string of "No name" indicates no real name specified yet.
4    A hire date of January 1, 1000 indicates no real hire date specified yet.
5   */
6   public abstract class Employee
7   {
8       private String name;
9       private Date hireDate;

10      public abstract double getPay();

11      public Employee()
12      {
13          name = "No name";
14          hireDate = new Date("January", 1, 1000); //Just a placeholder.
15      }

16      public boolean samePay(Employee other)
17      {
18          if (other == null)
19          {
20              System.out.println("Error: null Employee object.");
21              System.exit(0);
22          }
23          //else
24          return (this.getPay() == other.getPay());
25      }
```

*The class **Date** is defined in Display 4.13, but the details are not relevant to the current discussion of abstract methods and classes. There is no need to review the definition of the class **Date**.*

<All other constructor and other method definitions are exactly the same as in Display 7.2. In particular, they are not abstract methods.>

```
26  }
```

Abstract Class

An **abstract class** is a class with one or more abstract methods. An abstract class must have the modifier `abstract` included in the class heading, as illustrated by the example.

EXAMPLE
```
public abstract class Employee
{
    private String name;
    private Date hireDate;

    public abstract double getPay();
        ...
```

PITFALL: You Cannot Create Instances of an Abstract Class

You cannot use an abstract class constructor to create an object of the abstract class. You can only create objects of the derived classes of the abstract class. For example, with the class `Employee` defined as in Display 8.7, the following would be illegal:

```
Employee joe = new Employee(); //Illegal because
                    //Employee is an abstract class.
```

But, this is no problem. The object `joe` could not correspond to any real-world employee. Any real-world employee is either an hourly employee or a salaried employee. In the real world, one cannot be just an employee. One must be either an hourly employee or a salaried employee. Still, it is useful to discuss employees in general. In particular, we can compare employees to see if they have the same pay, even though the way of calculating the pay might be different for the two employees. ■

TIP: An Abstract Class Is a Type

You cannot create an object of an abstract class (unless it is actually an object of some concrete descendent class). Nonetheless, it makes perfectly good sense to have a parameter of an abstract class type such as `Employee` (as defined in Display 8.7). Then, an object of any of the descendent classes of `Employee` can be plugged in for the parameter. It even makes sense to have a variable of an abstract class type such as `Employee`, although it can only name objects of its concrete descendent classes. ■

An Abstract Class Is a Type

You can have a parameter of an abstract class type such as the abstract class `Employee` defined in Display 8.7. Then, an object of any of the concrete descendent classes of `Employee` can be plugged in for the parameter. You can also have variables of an abstract class type such as `Employee`, although it can only name objects of its concrete descendent classes.

Self-Test Exercises

10. Can a method definition include an invocation of an abstract method?

11. Can you have a variable whose type is an abstract class?

12. Can you have a parameter whose type is an abstract class?

13. Is it legal to have an abstract class in which all methods are abstract?

14. The abstract class `Employee` (Display 8.7) uses the method definitions from Display 7.2. After we did Display 7.2, we later gave the following improved version of `equals`:

```
public boolean equals(Object otherObject)
{
    if (otherObject == null)
        return false;
    else if (getClass() != otherObject.getClass())
        return false;
    else
    {
        Employee otherEmployee =
                    (Employee)otherObject;
        return (name.equals(otherEmployee.name)
         && hireDate.equals(otherEmployee.hireDate));
    }
}
```

Would it be legal to replace the version of `equals` for the abstract class `Employee` with this improved version?

15. The abstract class `Employee` given in Display 8.7 has a constructor (in fact, it has more than one, although only one is shown in Display 8.7). But using a constructor to create an instance of an abstract class, as in the following, is illegal:

```
Employee joe = new Employee(); //Illegal
```

So why bother to have any constructors in an abstract class? Aren't they useless?

Chapter Summary

- Late binding (also called dynamic binding) means that the decision of which version of a method is appropriate is decided at run time. Java uses late binding.

- Polymorphism means using the process of late binding to allow different objects to use different method actions for the same method name. *Polymorphism* is essentially another word for late binding.

- You can assign an object of a derived class to a variable of its base class (or any ancestor class), but you cannot do the reverse.

- If you add the modifier final to the definition of a method, that indicates that the method may not be redefined in a derived class. If you add the modifier final to the definition of a class, that indicates that the class may not be used as a base class to derive other classes.

- An abstract method serves as a placeholder for a method that will be fully defined in a descendent class.

- An abstract class is a class with one or more abstract methods.

- An abstract class is designed to be used as a base class to derive other classes. You cannot create an object of an abstract class type (unless it is an object of some concrete descendent class).

- An abstract class is a type. You can have variables whose type is an abstract class and you can have parameters whose type is an abstract type.

Answers to Self-Test Exercises

1. In essence, there is no difference between the two terms. There is only a slight difference in their usage. Late binding refers to the mechanism used to decide which method definition to use when a method is invoked, and polymorphism refers to the fact that the same method name can have different meanings because of late binding.

2. There would be problems well before you wrote the program in Display 8.3. Since final means you cannot change the definition of the method bill in a derived class, the definition of the method DiscountSale would not compile. If you omit the definition of the method bill from the class DiscountSale, the output would change to

```
floor mat Price and total cost = $10.0
floor mat Price = $11.0 Discount = 10.0%
   Total cost = $11.0
Discounted item is not cheaper.
cup holder Price and total cost = $9.9
cup holder Price = $11.0 Discount = 10.0%
   Total cost = $11.0
Items are not equal.
```

Note that all objects use the definition of bill given in the definition of Sale.

3. It would not be legal to add it to any class definition because the class `Sale` has no method named `getDiscount` and so the invocation

```
theSale.getDiscount()
```

is not allowed. If the type of the parameter were changed from `Sale` to `DiscountSale`, it would then be legal.

4.
```
public boolean equals(Object otherObject)
{
    if (otherObject == null)
        return false;
    else if (getClass() != otherObject.getClass())
        return false;
    else
    {
        DiscountSale otherDiscountSale =
                        (DiscountSale)otherObject;
        return (super.equals(otherDiscountSale)
            && discount == otherDiscountSale.discount);
    }
}
```

5. The definition of `toString` used always depends on the object and not on any type cast. So, the definition used is the same as without the added type cast; that is, the definition of `toString` that is used is the one given in `DiscountSale`.

6. It would not be legal to add it to any class definition because the parameter is of type `Sale` and `Sale` has no method named `getDiscount`. If the parameter type were changed to `DiscountSale`, it would then be legal to add it to any class definition.

7.
```
ds was changed to map Price $ 5.0 discount 0.0%
Total cost $5.0
```

8. `ds was not changed.`

9. The output would be the following (the main change from Display 8.4 is shown in blue):

```
This is the Sale class.
This is the DiscountSale class.
No surprises so far, but wait.
discount2 is a DiscountSale object in a Sale variable.
Which definition of announcement() will it use?
This is the DiscountSale class.
Did it use the Sale version of announcement()?
```

10. Yes. See Display 8.7.

11. Yes, you can have a variable whose type is an abstract class.

12. Yes, you can have a parameter whose type is an abstract class.

13. Yes, it is legal to have an abstract class in which all methods are abstract.

14. Yes, it would be legal to replace the version of equals for the abstract class Employee with this improved version. In fact, the version of Employee on the accompanying CD does use the improved version of equals.

15. No, you can still use constructors to hold code that might be useful in derived classes. The constructors in the derived classes can, in fact must, include invocations of constructors in the base (abstract) class. (Recall the use of super as a name for the base class constructor.)

Programming Projects

 Many of these Programming Projects can be solved using AW's MyCodeMate. To access these please go to: www.mycodemate.com.

1. In Programming Project 3 from Chapter 7 the Alien class was rewritten to use inheritance. The rewritten Alien class should be made abstract since there will never be a need to create an instance of it, only its derived classes. Change this to an abstract class and also make the getDamage method an abstract method. Test the class from your main method to ensure that it still operates as expected.

2. Create a class named Movie that can be used with your video rental business. The Movie class should track the Motion Picture Association of America (MPAA) rating (e.g., Rated G, PG-13, R), ID Number, and movie title with appropriate accessor and mutator methods. Also create an equals() method that overrides Object's equals() method, where two movies are equal if their ID number is identical. Next, create three additional classes named Action, Comedy, and Drama that are derived from Movie. Finally, create an overridden method named calcLateFees that takes as input the number of days a movie is late and returns the late fee for that movie. The default late fee is $2/day. Action movies have a late fee of $3/day, comedies are $2.50/day, and dramas are $2/day. Test your classes from a main method.

3. Extend the previous problem with a Rental class. This class should store a Movie that is rented, an integer representing the ID of the customer that rented the movie, and an integer indicating how many days late the movie is. Add a method that calculates the late fees for the rental. In your main method create an array of type Rental filled with sample data of all types of movies. Then, create a method named lateFeesOwed that iterates through the array and returns the total amount of late fees that are outstanding.

 4. The goal for this programming project is to create a simple 2D predator-prey simulation. In this simulation, the prey are ants and the predators are doodlebugs. These critters live in a world composed of a 20×20 grid of cells. Only one critter may occupy a cell at a time. The grid is enclosed, so a critter is not allowed to move off the edges of the grid. Time is simulated in time steps. Each critter performs some action every time step.

The ants behave according to the following model:

- Move. Every time step, randomly try to move up, down, left, or right. If the cell in the selected direction is occupied or would move the ant off the grid, then the ant stays in the current cell.

- Breed. If an ant survives for three time steps, then at the end of the third time step (i.e., after moving) the ant will breed. This is simulated by creating a new ant in an adjacent (up, down, left, or right) cell that is empty. If there is no empty cell available, no breeding occurs. Once an offspring is produced, the ant cannot produce an offspring until three more time steps have elapsed.

The doodlebugs behave according to the following model:

- Move. Every time step, if there is an adjacent cell (up, down, left, or right) occupied by an ant then the doodlebug will move to that cell and eat the ant. Otherwise, the doodlebug moves according to the same rules as the ant. Note that a doodlebug cannot eat other doodlebugs.

- Breed. If a doodlebug survives for eight time steps, then at the end of the time step it will spawn off a new doodlebug in the same manner as the ant.

- Starve. If a doodlebug has not eaten an ant within the last three time steps, then at the end of the third time step it will starve and die. The doodlebug should then be removed from the grid of cells.

During one turn, all the doodlebugs should move before the ants.

Write a program to implement this simulation and draw the world using ASCII characters of "o" for an ant and "X" for a doodlebug. Create a class named Organism that encapsulates basic data common to both ants and doodlebugs. This class should have an overridden method named move that is defined in the derived classes of Ant and Doodlebug. You may need additional data structures to keep track of which critters have moved.

Initialize the world with 5 doodlebugs and 100 ants. After each time step, prompt the user to press enter to move to the next time step. You should see a cyclical pattern between the population of predators and prey, although random perturbations may lead to the elimination of one or both species.

Note: To generate a random number x, where $0 \leq x < 1$, use $x = $ Math.random(); . For example, multiplying by six and converting to an integer results in an integer that is in the range from 0 to 5.

 5. Consider a graphics system that has classes for various figures, say rectangles, boxes, triangles, circles, and so on. For example, a rectangle might have data members height, width, and center point, while a box and circle might have only a center point and an edge length or radius, respectively. In a well-designed system these would be derived from a common class, Figure. You are to implement such a system.

The class Figure is the base class. You should add only Rectangle and Triangle classes derived from Figure. Each class has stubs for methods erase and draw. Each of these methods outputs a message telling the name of the class and what method has been called. Since these are just stubs, they do nothing more than output this message. The method center calls the erase and draw methods to erase and redraw the figure at the center. Since you have only stubs for erase and draw, center will not do any "centering" but will call the methods erase and draw, which will allow you to see which versions of draw and center it calls. Also, add an output message in the method center that announces that center is being called. The methods should take no arguments. Also, define a demonstration program for your classes.

For a real example, you would have to replace the definition of each of these methods with code to do the actual drawing. You will be asked to do this in Programming Project 6.

6. Flesh out Programming Project 5. Give new definitions for the various constructors and methods center, draw, and erase of the class Figure; draw and erase of the class Triangle; and draw and erase of the class Rectangle. Use character graphics; that is, the various draw methods will place regular keyboard characters on the screen in the desired shape. Use the character '*' for all the character graphics. That way the draw methods actually draw figures on the screen by placing the character '*' at suitable locations on the screen. For the erase methods, you can simply clear the screen (by outputting blank lines or by doing something more sophisticated). There are a lot of details in this project and you will have to decide on some of them on your own.

7. Define a class named MultiItemSale that represents a sale of multiple items of type Sale given in Display 8.1 (or of the types of any of its descendent classes). The class MultiItemSale will have an instance variable whose type is Sale[], which will be used as a partially filled array. There will also be another instance variable of type int that keeps track of how much of this array is currently used. The exact details on methods and other instance variables, if any, are up to you. Use this class in a program that obtains information for items of type Sale and of type DiscountSale (Display 8.2) and computes the total bill for the list of items sold.

9

Exception Handling

9 Exception Handling

It's the exception that proves the rule.

COMMON SAYING

Introduction

One way to divide the task of designing and coding a method is to code two main cases separately: the case where nothing unusual happens and the case where exceptional things happen. Once you have the program working for the case where things always go smoothly, you can then code the second case where exceptional things can happen. In Java, there is a way to mirror this approach in your code. You write your code more or less as if nothing very unusual happens. After that, you use the Java exception handling facilities to add code for those exceptional cases.

The most important use of exceptions is to deal with methods that have some special case that is handled differently depending on how the method is used. For example, if there is a division by zero in the method, then it may turn out that for some invocations of the method the program should end, but for other invocations of the method something else should happen. Such a method can be defined to throw an exception if the special case occurs, and that exception will allow the special case to be handled outside of the method. This allows the special case to be handled differently for different invocations of the method.

In Java, exception handling proceeds as follows: Either some library software or your code provides a mechanism that signals when something unusual happens. This is called **throwing an exception**. At another place in your program you place the code that deals with the exceptional case. This is called **handling the exception**. This method of programming makes for cleaner code. Of course, we still need to explain the details of how you do this in Java.

throw
exception

handle
exception

Prerequisites

Almost all of this chapter only uses material from Chapters 1 through 5 and Chapter 7. The only exception is the subsection "ArrayIndexOutOfBoundsException," which also uses material from Chapter 6. However, that subsection may be omitted if you have not yet covered Chapter 6. Chapter 8 is not needed for this chapter.

9.1   Exception Handling Basics

Well the program works for most cases. I didn't know it had to work for
that case.

COMPUTER SCIENCE STUDENT, *appealing a grade*

Exception handling is meant to be used sparingly and in situations that are more
involved than what is reasonable to include in an introductory example. So, we will
teach you the exception handling details of Java by means of simple examples that
would not normally use exception handling. This makes a lot of sense for learning
about the exception handling details of Java, but do not forget that these first examples
are toy examples and, in practice, you would not use exception handling for anything
that simple.

EXAMPLE: A Toy Example of Exception Handling

Display 9.1 contains a simple program that might, by some stretch of the imagination,
be used at a dance studio. This program does not use exception handling, and you
would not normally use exception handling for anything this simple. The setting for use
of the program is a dance lesson. The program simply checks to see if there are more
men than women or more women than men and then announces how many partners
each man or woman will have. The exceptional case is when there are no men or no
women or both. In that exceptional case, the dance lesson is canceled.

In Display 9.2 we have redone the program using exception handling. The keyword
try labels a block known as the `try` **block**, which is indicated in the display. Inside the
try block goes the non-exceptional cases and checks for the exceptional cases. The
exceptional cases are not handled in the `try` block, but if detected they are signaled by
"throwing an exception." The following three lines taken from inside the multiway
`if–else` statement are the code for throwing the exception:

```
throw new Exception("Lesson is canceled. No students.");
throw new Exception("Lesson is canceled. No men.");
throw new Exception("Lesson is canceled. No women.");
```

If the program does not encounter an exceptional case, then none of these statements
that "throw an exception" is executed. So, in that case we need not even know what happens when an exception is "thrown." If no exception is "thrown," then the code in the
section labeled "catch block" is skipped and the program proceeds to the last statement,
which happens to output "Begin the lesson." Now, let's see what happens in an
exceptional case.

(continued)

Display 9.1 Handling a Special Case without Exception Handling (part 1 of 2)

```java
1   import java.util.Scanner;

2   public class DanceLesson
3   {
4       public static void main(String[] args)
5       {
6           Scanner keyboard = new Scanner(System.in);

8           System.out.println("Enter number of male dancers:");
9           int men = keyboard.nextInt();

10          System.out.println("Enter number of female dancers:");
11          int women = keyboard.nextInt();

12          if (men == 0 && women == 0)
13          {
14              System.out.println("Lesson is canceled. No students.");
15              System.exit(0);
16          }
17          else if (men == 0)
18          {
19              System.out.println("Lesson is canceled. No men.");
20              System.exit(0);
21          }
22          else if (women == 0)
23          {
24              System.out.println("Lesson is canceled. No women.");
25              System.exit(0);
26          }

27          // women >= 0 && men >= 0
28          if (women >= men)
29              System.out.println("Each man must dance with " +
30                                  women/(double)men + " women.");
31          else
32              System.out.println("Each woman must dance with " +
33                                  men/(double)women + " men.");
34          System.out.println("Begin the lesson.");
35      }
36  }
```

Display 9.1 Handling a Special Case without Exception Handling (part 2 of 2)

Sample Dialogue 1

```
Enter number of male dancers:
4
Enter number of female dancers:
6
Each man must dance with 1.5 women.
Begin the lesson.
```

Sample Dialogue 2

```
Enter number of male dancers:
0
Enter number of female dancers:
0
Lesson is canceled. No students.
```

Sample Dialogue 3

```
Enter number of male dancers:
0
Enter number of female dancers:
5
Lesson is canceled. No men.
```

Sample Dialogue 4

```
Enter number of male dancers:
4
Enter number of female dancers:
0
Lesson is canceled. No women.
```

Display 9.2 Same Thing Using Exception Handling (part 1 of 3)

```
1   import java.util.Scanner;

2   public class DanceLesson2
3   {
4       public static void main(String[] args)
5       {
6           Scanner keyboard = new Scanner(System.in);

7           System.out.println("Enter number of male dancers:");
8           int men = keyboard.nextInt();
```

(continued)

Display 9.3   Same Thing Using Exception Handling (part 2 of 3)

```
 9            System.out.println("Enter number of female dancers:");
10            int women = keyboard.nextInt();
```

This is just a toy example to learn Java syntax. Do not take it
as an example of good typical use of exception handling.

```
11            try
12            {
13                if (men == 0 && women == 0)
14                    throw new Exception("Lesson is canceled. No students.");
15                else if (men == 0)
16                    throw new Exception("Lesson is canceled. No men.");
17                else if (women == 0)
18                    throw new Exception("Lesson is canceled. No women.");
```
try block
```
19                // women >= 0 && men >= 0
20                if (women >= men)
21                    System.out.println("Each man must dance with " +
22                                        women/(double)men + " women.");
23                else
24                    System.out.println("Each woman must dance with " +
25                                        men/(double)women + " men.");
26            }
27            catch(Exception e)
28            {
```
catch block
```
29                String message = e.getMessage();
30                System.out.println(message);
31                System.exit(0);
32            }
33            System.out.println("Begin the lesson.");
34        }
35   }
```

Sample Dialogue 1

```
Enter number of male dancers:
4
Enter number of female dancers:
6
Each man must dance with 1.5 women.
Begin the lesson.
```

Sample Dialogue 2

```
Enter number of male dancers:
0
Enter number of female dancers:
0
Lesson is canceled. No students.
```

Note that this dialogue and
the dialogues below do not
say "Begin the lesson".

Display 9.2 Same Thing Using Exception Handling (part 3 of 3)

Sample Dialogue 3

```
Enter number of male dancers:
0
Enter number of female dancers:
5
Lesson is canceled. No men.
```

Sample Dialogue 4

```
Enter number of male dancers:
4
Enter number of female dancers:
0
Lesson is canceled. No women.
```

EXAMPLE: (continued)

If the number of men or the number of women is zero (or both), that is an exceptional case in this program and results in an exception being **thrown**. To make things concrete, let's say that the number of men is zero, but the number of women is not zero. In that case the following statement is executed, which is how Java throws an exception:

```
throw new Exception("Lesson is canceled. No men.");
```

Let's analyze this statement. The following is the invocation of a constructor for the class Exception, which is the standard Java package java.lang.

```
new Exception("Lesson is canceled. No men.");
```

The created Exception object is not assigned to a variable, but rather is used as an (anonymous) argument to the throw operator. (Anonymous arguments were discussed in Chapter 5.) The keyword throw is an operator with syntax similar to the unary + or unary − operators. To make it look more like an operator, you can write it with parentheses around the argument, as follows:

```
throw (new Exception("Lesson is canceled. No men."));
```

Although it is perfectly legal and sensible to include these extra parentheses, nobody does include them.

To understand this process of throwing, you need to know two things: What is this Exception class? And what does the throw operator do with the Exception object? The class Exception is another class from the standard Java package java.lang. As you have already seen, the class Exception has a constructor that takes a single String argument. The Exception object created stores this String argument (in a private instance variable). As you will see, this String argument can later be retrieved from the Exception object.

(continued)

EXAMPLE: (continued)

The throw operator causes a change in the flow of control and it delivers the Exception object to a suitable place, as we are about to explain. When the throw operator is executed, the try block ends immediately and control passes to the following catch block. (If it helps, you can draw an analogy between the execution of the throw operator in a try block and the execution of a break statement in a loop or switch statement.) When control is transferred to the catch block, the Exception object that is thrown is plugged in for the catch block parameter e. So, the expression e.getMessage() returns the string "Lesson is canceled. No men." The method getMessage() of the class Exception is an accessor method that retrieves the String in the private instance variable of the Exception object—that is, the String used as an argument to the Exception constructor.

To see if you get the basic idea of how this exception throwing mechanism works, study the sample dialogues. The next few sections explain this mechanism in more detail.

try–throw–catch Mechanism

The basic way of handling exceptions in Java consists of the try–throw–catch trio. The general setup consists of a try block followed by one or more catch blocks. First let's describe what a try block is. A **try block** has the syntax

try block

```
try
{
    Some_Code
}
```

This try block contains the code for the basic algorithm that tells what to do when everything goes smoothly. It is called a try block because it "tries" to execute the case where all goes smoothly.

Now, if something exceptional does happen, you want to throw an exception, which is a way of indicating that something unusual happened. So the basic outline, when we add a throw, is as follows:

```
try
{
    Code_That_May_Throw_An_Exception
}
```

The following is an example of a try block with throw statements included (copied from Display 9.2):

```
try
{
    if (men == 0 && women == 0)
        throw new Exception("Lesson is canceled. No students.");
    else if (men == 0)
        throw new Exception("Lesson is canceled. No men.");
    else if (women == 0)
        throw new Exception("Lesson is canceled. No women.");
```

```
                         // women >= 0 && men >= 0
                         if (women >= men)
                             System.out.println("Each man must dance with " +
                                                 women/(double)men + " women.");
                         else
                             System.out.println("Each woman must dance with " +
                                                 men/(double)women + " men.");
                     }
```

throw
statement

This `try` block contains the following three `throw` statements:

```
throw new Exception("Lesson is canceled. No students.");
throw new Exception("Lesson is canceled. No men.");
throw new Exception("Lesson is canceled. No women.");
```

throwing an
exception

The value thrown is an argument to the `throw` operator and is always an object of some exception class. The execution of a `throw` statement is called **throwing an exception**.

---

throw Statement

SYNTAX

```
throw new Exception_Class_Name(Possibly_Some_Arguments);
```

When the **throw** statement is executed, the execution of the surrounding **try** block is stopped and (normally) control is transferred to a **catch** block. The code in the **catch** block is executed next. See the box entitled "**try-throw-catch**" later in this chapter for more details.

EXAMPLE

```
throw new Exception("Division by zero.");
```

---

catch block

handling an
exception

As the name suggests, when something is "thrown," something goes from one place to another place. In Java, what goes from one place to another is the flow of control as well as the exception object that is thrown. When an exception is thrown, the code in the surrounding `try` block stops executing and (normally) another portion of code, known as a `catch` **block**, begins execution. The `catch` block has a parameter, and the exception object thrown is plugged in for this `catch` block parameter. This executing of the catch block is called **catching the exception** or **handling the exception**. When an exception is thrown, it should ultimately be handled by (caught by) some `catch` block. In Display 9.2, the appropriate `catch` block immediately follows the `try` block. We repeat the `catch` block in what follows:

```
catch(Exception e)
{
    String message = e.getMessage();
    System.out.println(message);
    System.exit(0);
}
```

This catch block looks very much like a method definition that has a parameter of a type Exception. It is not a method definition, but in some ways, a catch block is like a method. It is a separate piece of code that is executed when your program encounters (and executes) the following (within the preceding try block):

```
throw new Exception(Some_String);
```

So, this throw statement is similar to a method call, but instead of calling a method, it calls the catch block and says to execute the code in the catch block. A catch block is often referred to as an **exception handler**.

Let's focus on the identifier e in the following line from a catch block:

exception handler

```
catch(Exception e)
```

catch block parameter

That identifier e in the catch block heading is called the catch **block parameter**. Each catch block can have at most one catch block parameter. The catch block parameter does two things:

1. The catch block parameter is preceded by an exception class name that specifies what type of thrown exception object the catch block can catch.

2. The catch block parameter gives you a name for the thrown object that is caught, so you can write code in the catch block that does things with the thrown object that is caught.

Although the identifier e is often used for the catch block parameter, this is not required. You may use any non-keyword identifier for the catch block parameter just as you can for a method parameter.

---

catch Block Parameter

The catch block parameter is an identifier in the heading of a catch block that serves as a placeholder for an exception that might be thrown. When a (suitable) exception is thrown in the preceding try block, that exception is plugged in for the catch block parameter. The identifier e is often used for catch block parameters, but this is not required. You can use any legal (non-keyword) identifier for a catch block parameter.

SYNTAX

```
catch(Exception_Class_Name Catch_Block_Parameter)
{
    <Code to be performed if an exception of the named exception class
        is thrown in the try block.>
}
```

You may use any legal identifier for the *Catch_Block_Parameter*.

EXAMPLE

In the following, **e** is the **catch** block parameter.

```
catch(Exception e)
{
    System.out.println(e.getMessage());
    System.out.println("Aborting program.");
    System.exit(0);
}
```

Let's consider two possible cases of what can happen when a try block is executed: (1) no exception is thrown in the try block, and (2) an exception is thrown in the try block and caught in the catch block. (Later we will describe a third case where the catch block does not catch the exception.)

1. If no exception is thrown, the code in the try block is executed to the end of the try block, the catch block is skipped, and execution continues with the code placed after the catch block.

2. If an exception is thrown in the try block, the rest of the code in the try block is skipped and (in simple cases) control is transferred to a following catch block. The thrown object is plugged in for the catch block parameter, and the code in the catch block is executed. And then (provided the catch block code does not end the program or do something else to end the catch block code prematurely), the code that follows that catch block is executed.

The getMessage Method

Every exception has a **String** instance variable that contains some message, which typically identifies the reason for the exception. For example, if the exception is thrown as follows:

```
throw new Exception(String_Argument);
```

then the string given as an argument to the constructor **Exception** is used as the value of this **String** instance variable. If the object is called **e**, then the method call **e.getMessage()** returns this string.

EXAMPLE

Suppose the following **throw** statement is executed in a **try** block:

```
throw new Exception("Input must be positive.");
```

(continued)

And suppose the following is a `catch` block immediately following the `try` block:

```
catch(Exception e)
{
    System.out.println(e.getMessage());
    System.out.println("Program aborted.");
    System.exit(0);
}
```

In this case, the method call `e.getMessage()` returns the string `"Input must be positive."`

Exception Classes

There are more exception classes than just the single class `Exception`. There are more exception classes in the standard Java libraries and you can define your own exception classes. All the exception classes in the Java libraries have—and the exception classes you define should have—the following properties:

1. There is a constructor that takes a single argument of type `String`.

2. The class has an accessor method `getMessage()` that can recover the string given as an argument to the constructor when the exception object was created.

---

try–throw–catch

When used together, the **try**, **throw**, and **catch** statements are the basic mechanism for throwing and catching exceptions. The **throw** statement throws the exception. The **catch** block catches the exception. The **throw** statement is normally included in a **try** block. When the exception is thrown, the **try** block ends and then the code in the **catch** block is executed. After the **catch** block is completed, the code after the **catch** block(s) is executed (provided the **catch** block has not ended the program or performed some other special action).

If no exception is thrown in the **try** block, then after the **try** block is completed, program execution continues with the code after the **catch** block(s). (In other words, if no exception is thrown, the **catch** block(s) are ignored.)

SYNTAX

```
try
{
    Some_Statements
    <Either a throw statement or
                a method invocation that might throw an exception
                or other statement that might throw an exception.>
    Some_More_Statements
}
```

```
    catch(Exception_Class_Name  Catch_Block_Parameter)
    {
        <Code to be performed if an exception of the named exception
                                    class is thrown in the try block.>
    }
```

You may use any legal identifier for the *Catch_Block_Parameter*; a common choice is **e**. The code in the **catch** block may refer to the *Catch_Block_Parameter*. If there is an explicit **throw** statement, it is usually embedded in an **if** statement or an **if–else** statement. There may be any number of **throw** statements and/or any number of method invocations that may throw exceptions. Each **catch** block can list only one exception, but there can be more than one **catch** block.

EXAMPLE

See Display 9.2.

Exception Classes from Standard Packages

Numerous predefined exception classes are included in the standard packages that come with Java. The names of predefined exceptions are designed to be self-explanatory. Some sample predefined exceptions are

```
    IOException
    NoSuchMethodException
    FileNotFoundException
```

Exception   The predefined exception class Exception is the root class for all exceptions. Every exception class is a descendent of the class Exception (that is, it is derived directly from the class Exception or from a class that is derived from the class Exception, or it arises from some longer chain of derivations ultimately starting with the class Exception). You can use the class Exception itself, just as we did in Display 9.2, but you are even more likely to use it to define a derived class of the class Exception. The class Exception is in the java.lang package and so requires no import statement.

The Class Exception

Every exception class is a descendent class of the class Exception. You can use the class Exception itself in a class or program, but you are even more likely to use it to define a derived class of the class Exception. The class Exception is in the java.lang package and so requires no import statement.

Self-Test Exercises

1. What output is produced by the following code?

```java
int waitTime = 46;

try
{
    System.out.println("Try block entered.");
    if (waitTime > 30)
        throw new Exception("Over 30.");
    else if (waitTime < 30)
        throw new Exception("Under 30.");
    else
        System.out.println("No exception.");
    System.out.println("Leaving try block.");
}
catch(Exception thrownObject)
{
    System.out.println(thrownObject.getMessage());
}
System.out.println("After catch block");
```

2. Suppose that in exercise 1, the line

```java
int waitTime = 46;
```

is changed to

```java
int waitTime = 12;
```

How would this affect the output?

3. In the code given in exercise 1, what are the `throw` statements?

4. What happens when a `throw` statement is executed? This is a general question. Tell what happens in general, not simply what happens in the code in exercise 1 or some other sample code.

5. In the code given in exercise 1, what is the `try` block?

6. In the code given in exercise 1, what is the `catch` block?

7. In the code given in exercise 1, what is the `catch` block parameter?

8. Is the following legal?

```java
Exception exceptionObject =
                    new Exception("Oops!");
```

9. Is the following legal?

```java
Exception exceptionObject =
                    new Exception("Oops!");
throw exceptionObject;
```

Defining Exception Classes

A throw statement can throw an exception object of any exception class. A common thing to do is to define an exception class whose objects can carry the precise kinds of information you want thrown to the catch block. An even more important reason for defining a specialized exception class is so that you can have a different type to identify each possible kind of exceptional situation.

Every exception class you define must be a derived class of some already defined exception class. An exception class can be a derived class of any exception class in the standard Java libraries or of any exception class that you have already successfully defined. Our examples will be derived classes of the class Exception.

constructors   When defining an exception class, the constructors are the most important members. Often there are no other members, other than those inherited from the base class. For example, in Display 9.3, we've defined an exception class called DivisionBy-ZeroException whose only members are a no-argument constructor and a constructor with one String parameter. In most cases, these two constructors are all the exception class definition contains. However, the class does inherit all the methods of the class Exception.[1] In particular, the class DivisionByZeroException inherits the method getMessage, which returns a string message. In the no-argument constructor, this string message is set with the following, which is the first line in the no-argument constructor definition:

```
super("Division by Zero!");
```

This is a call to a constructor of the base class Exception. As we have already noted, when you pass a string to the constructor for the class Exception, it sets the value of a

Display 9.3   A Programmer-Defined Exception Class

```
 1    public class DivisionByZeroException extends Exception
 2    {
 3        public DivisionByZeroException()
 4        {                                          You can do more in an exception
 5            super("Division by Zero!");            constructor, but this form is
 6        }                                          common.

 7        public DivisionByZeroException(String message)
 8        {
 9            super(message);          super is an invocation of the constructor
10        }                           for the base class Exception.
11    }
```

_____

[1] Some programmers would prefer to derive the DivisionByZeroException class from the predefined class ArithmeticException, but that would make it a kind of exception that you are not required to catch in your code, so you would lose the help of the compiler in keeping track of uncaught exceptions. For more details, see the subsection "Exceptions to the Catch or Declare Rule" later in this chapter. If this footnote does not make sense to you, you can safely ignore it.

String instance variable that can later be recovered with a call to getMessage. The
method getMessage is an ordinary accessor method of the class Exception. The class
DivisionByZeroException inherits this String instance variable as well as the accessor
method getMessage.

For example, in Display 9.4, we give a sample program that uses this exception
class. The exception is thrown using the no-argument constructor, as follows:

```
throw new DivisionByZeroException();
```

Display 9.4 Using a Programmer-Defined Exception Class (part 1 of 3)

```
1    import java.util.Scanner;

2    public class DivisionDemoFirstVersion
3    {

4        public static void main(String[] args)
5        {
6            try
7            {
8                Scanner keyboard = new Scanner(System.in);

9                System.out.println("Enter numerator:");
10               int numerator = keyboard.nextInt();
11               System.out.println("Enter denominator:");
12               int denominator = keyboard.nextInt();

13               if (denominator == 0)
14                   throw new DivisionByZeroException();

15               double quotient = numerator/(double)denominator;
16               System.out.println(numerator + "/"
17                                       + denominator
18                                       + " = " + quotient);
19           }
20           catch(DivisionByZeroException e)
21           {
22               System.out.println(e.getMessage());
23               secondChance();
24           }

25           System.out.println("End of program.");
26       }

27       public static void secondChance()
28       {
29           Scanner keyboard = new Scanner(System.in);
```

*We will present an improved version of
this program later in this chapter.*

Display 9.5 **Using a Programmer-Defined Exception Class** (part 2 of 3)

```
30          System.out.println("Try again:");
31          System.out.println("Enter numerator:");
32          int numerator = keyboard.nextInt();
33          System.out.println("Enter denominator:");
34          System.out.println("Be sure the denominator is not zero.");
35          int denominator = keyboard.nextInt();
36
37          if (denominator == 0)
38          {
39              System.out.println("I cannot do division by zero.");
40              System.out.println("Aborting program.");
41              System.exit(0);
42          }
43
44          double quotient = ((double)numerator)/denominator;
45          System.out.println(numerator + "/"
46                                      + denominator
47                                      + " = " + quotient);
48      }
49  }
```

Sometimes it is better to handle an exceptional case without throwing an exception.

Sample Dialogue 1

```
Enter numerator:
11
Enter denominator:
5
11/5 = 2.2
End of program.
```

Sample Dialogue 2

```
Enter numerator:
11
Enter denominator:
0
Division by Zero!
Try again.
Enter numerator:
11
Enter denominator:
Be sure the denominator is not zero.
5
11/5 = 2.2
End of program.
```

(continued)

Display 9.4 Using a Programmer-Defined Exception Class (part 3 of 3)

Sample Dialogue 3

```
Enter numerator:
11
Enter denominator:
0
Division by Zero!
Try again.
Enter numerator:
11
Enter denominator:
Be sure the denominator is not zero.
0
I cannot do division by zero.
Aborting program.
```

This exception is caught in the catch block shown in Display 9.4. Consider the following line from that catch block:

```
System.out.println(e.getMessage());
```

This line produces the following output to the screen in Sample Dialogues 2 and 3:

```
Division by Zero!
```

The definition of the class DivisionByZeroException in Display 9.3 has a second constructor with one parameter of type String. This constructor allows you to choose any message you like when you throw an exception. If the throw statement in Display 9.4 had instead used the string argument

```
throw new DivisionByZeroException(
                      "Oops. Shouldn't divide by zero.");
```

then in Sample Dialogues 2 and 3, the statement

```
System.out.println(e.getMessage());
```

would have produced the following output to the screen:

```
Oops. Shouldn't divide by zero.
```

Notice that in Display 9.4, the try block is the normal part of the program. If all goes normally, that is the only code that will be executed, and the dialogue will be like the one shown in Sample Dialogue 1. In the exceptional case, when the user enters a zero for a denominator, the exception is thrown and then is caught in the catch block. The catch block outputs the message of the exception and then calls the method secondChance. The method secondChance gives the user a second chance to enter the input correctly and then carries out the calculation. If the user tries a second time to divide by zero, the method ends the program. The method secondChance is there only for this exceptional case. So, we have separated the code for the exceptional case of a division by zero into a separate method, where it will not clutter the code for the normal case.

TIP: Preserve `getMessage`

For all predefined exception classes, getMessage will return the string that is passed as an argument to the constructor (or will return a default string if no argument is used with the constructor). For example, if the exception is thrown as follows:

```
throw new Exception("Wow, this is exceptional!");
```

then "Wow, this is exceptional!" is used as the value of the String instance variable of the object created. If the object is called e, the method invocation e.getMessage() returns "Wow, this is exceptional!" You want to preserve this behavior in the exception classes you define.

For example, suppose you are defining an exception class named NegativeNumber- Exception. Be sure to include a constructor with a string parameter that begins with a call to super, as illustrated by the following constructor:

```
public NegativeNumberException(String message)
{
    super(message);
}
```

The call to super is a call to a constructor of the base class. If the base class constructor handles the message correctly, then so will a class defined in this way.

You should also include a no-argument constructor in each exception class. This no-argument constructor should set a default value to be retrieved by getMessage. The constructor should begin with a call to super, as illustrated by the following constructor:

```
public NegativeNumberException()
{
    super("Negative Number Exception!");
}
```

If getMessage works as we described for the base class, then this sort of no-argument constructor will work correctly for the new exception class being defined. A full definition of the class NegativeNumberException is given in Display 9.8. ■

Exception Object Characteristics

The two most important things about an exception object are its type (the exception class) and a message that it carries in an instance variable of type **String**. This string can be recovered with the accessor method **getMessage**. This string allows your code to send a message along with an exception object, so that the **catch** block can use the message.

Programmer-Defined Exception Classes

You may define your own exception classes, but every such class must be a derived class of an already existing exception class (either from one of the standard Java libraries or programmer defined).

GUIDELINES

- If you have no compelling reason to use any other class as the base class, use the class **Exception** as the base class.
- You should define two (or more) constructors, as described later in this list.
- Your exception class inherits the method **getMessage**. Normally, you do not need to add any other methods, but it is legal to do so.
- You should start each constructor definition with a call to the constructor of the base class, such as the following:

```
super("Sample Exception thrown!");
```

- You should include a no-argument constructor, in which case the call to **super** should have a string argument that indicates what kind of exception it is. This string can then be recovered by using the **getMessage** method.
- You should also include a constructor that takes a single string argument. In this case, the string should be an argument in a call to **super**. That way, the string can be recovered with a call to **getMessage**.

EXAMPLE

```
public class SampleException extends Exception
{
    public SampleException()
    {
        super("Sample Exception thrown!");
    }

    public SampleException(String message)
    {
        super(message);
    }
}
```

extra code on CD

The class **SampleException** is on the CD that comes with this text.

TIP: An Exception Class Can Carry a Message of Any Type

It is possible to define your exception classes so they have constructors that take arguments of other types that are stored in instance variables. In such cases, you would define accessor methods for the value stored in the instance variable. For example, if that is desired, you can have an exception class that carries an int as a message. In that case, you would need a new accessor method name, perhaps getBadNumber(). An example of one such exception class is given in Display 9.5. Display 9.6 is a demonstration of how to use the accessor method getBadNumber(). This is just a toy program, but it does illustrate the details of how an exception object can carry a numeric message. ■

Display 9.5 An Exception Class with an **int** Message

```
1   public class BadNumberException extends Exception
2   {
3       private int badNumber;

4       public BadNumberException(int number)
5       {
6           super("BadNumberException");
7           badNumber = number;
8       }

9       public BadNumberException()
10      {
11          super("BadNumberException");
12      }

13      public BadNumberException(String message)
14      {
15          super(message);
16      }

17      public int getBadNumber()
18      {
19          return badNumber;
20      }
21  }
```

Display 9.6 Demonstration of How to Use **BadNumberException**

```java
1    import java.util.Scanner;

2    public class BadNumberExceptionDemo
3    {

4        public static void main(String[] args)
5        {
6            try
7            {
8                Scanner keyboard = new Scanner(System.in);

9                System.out.println("Enter one of the numbers 42 and 24:");
10               int inputNumber = keyboard.nextInt();

11               if ((inputNumber != 42) && (inputNumber != 24))
12                   throw new BadNumberException(inputNumber);

13               System.out.println("Thank you for entering " + inputNumber);
14           }
15           catch(BadNumberException e)
16           {
17               System.out.println(e.getBadNumber() +
18                                              " is not what I asked for.");
19           }

20           System.out.println("End of program.");
21       }
22   }
23
```

Sample Dialogue 1

```
Enter one of the numbers 42 and 24:
42
Thank you for entering 42
End of program.
```

Sample Dialogue 2

```
Enter one of the numbers 42 and 24:
44
44 is not what I asked for.
End of program.
```

Self-Test Exercises

10. Define an exception class called `PowerFailureException`. The class should have a constructor with no parameters. If an exception is thrown with this zero-argument constructor, `getMessage` should return `"Power Failure!"` The class should also have a constructor with a single parameter of type `String`. If an exception is thrown with this constructor, then `getMessage` returns the value that was used as an argument to the constructor.

11. Define an exception class called `TooMuchStuffException`. The class should have a constructor with no parameters. If an exception is thrown with this zero-argument constructor, `getMessage` should return `"Too much stuff!"`. The class should also have a constructor with a single parameter of type `String`. If an exception is thrown with this constructor, then `getMessage` returns the value that was used as an argument to the constructor.

12. Suppose the exception class `ExerciseException` is defined as follows:

```
public class ExerciseException extends Exception
{
    public ExerciseException()
    {
        super("Exercise Exception thrown!");
        System.out.println("Exception thrown.");
    }

    public ExerciseException(String message)
    {
        super(message);
        System.out.println(
          "ExerciseException invoked with an argument.");
    }
}
```

What output would be produced by the following code (which is just an exercise and not likely to occur in a program)?

```
ExerciseException e =
              new ExerciseException("Do Be Do");
System.out.println(e.getMessage());
```

extra code on CD

The class `ExerciseException` is on the CD that comes with this text.

13. Suppose the exception class `TestException` is defined as follows:

```
public class TestException extends Exception
{
    public TestException()
    {
```

(continued)

```
            super("Test Exception thrown!");
            System.out.println(
                        "Test exception thrown!!");
        }

        public TestException(String message)
        {
            super(message);
            System.out.println(
              "Test exception thrown with an argument!");
        }

        public void testMethod()
        {
            System.out.println("Message is " + getMessage());
        }
    }
```

What output would be produced by the following code (which is just an exercise and not likely to occur in a program)?

```
TestException exceptionObject = new TestException();
System.out.println(exceptionObject.getMessage());
exceptionObject.testMethod();
```

extra code on CD The class `TestException` is on the CD that comes with this text.

14. Suppose the exception class `MyException` is defined as follows:

```
public class MyException extends Exception
{
    public MyException()
    {
        super("My Exception thrown!");
    }

    public MyException(String message)
    {
        super("MyException: " + message);
    }
}
```

What output would be produced by the following code (which is just an exercise and not likely to occur in a program)?

```
int number;
    try
    {
```

```
        System.out.println("try block entered:");
        number = 42;
        if (number > 0)
            throw new MyException("Hi Mom!");
        System.out.println("Leaving try block.");
    }

    catch(MyException exceptionObject)
    {
        System.out.println(exceptionObject.getMessage());
    }
    System.out.println("End of example.");
```

**extra code
on CD**

The class `MyException` is on the CD that comes with this text.

15. Suppose that in Self-Test Exercise 14 the `catch` block were changed to the following. (The type `MyException` is replaced with `Exception`.) How would this affect the output?

```
catch(Exception exceptionObject)
{
    System.out.println(exceptionObject.getMessage());
}
```

16. Suppose that in Self-Test Exercise 14 the line

    ```
    number = 42;
    ```

    were changed to

    ```
    number = -58;
    ```

    How would this affect the output?

17. Although an exception class normally carries only a string message, you can define exception classes to carry a message of any type. For example, objects of the following type can also carry a `double` "message" (as well as a string message):

```
public class DoubleException extends Exception
{
    private double doubleMessage;

    public DoubleException()
    {
        super("DoubleException thrown!");
    }

    public DoubleException(String message)
    {
        super(message);
    }
```

(continued)

```
    public DoubleException(double number)
    {
        super("DoubleException thrown!");
        doubleMessage = number;
    }

    public double getNumber()
    {
        return doubleMessage;
    }
}
```

What output would be produced by the following code (which is just an exercise and not likely to occur in a program)?

```
DoubleException e =
            new DoubleException(41.9);

System.out.println(e.getNumber());
System.out.println(e.getMessage());
```

extra code on CD   The class `DoubleException` is on the CD that comes with this text.

18. There is an exception class named `IOException` that is defined in the standard Java libraries. Can you define an exception class as a derived class of the predefined class `IOException`, or must a defined exception class be derived from the class `Exception`?

Multiple catch Blocks

A try block can potentially throw any number of exception values, and they can be of differing types. In any one execution of the `try` block, at most one exception will be thrown (since a `throw` statement ends the execution of the `try` block), but different types of exception values can be thrown on different occasions when the `try` block is executed. Each `catch` block can only catch values of the exception class type given in the `catch` block heading. However, you can catch exception values of differing types by placing more than one `catch` block after a `try` block. For example, the program in Display 9.7 has two `catch` blocks after its `try` block. The class `NegativeNumberException`, which is used in that program, is given in Display 9.8.

Display 9.7   Catching Multiple Exceptions (part 1 of 3)

```
1   import java.util.Scanner;

2   public class MoreCatchBlocksDemo
3   {
4       public static void main(String[] args)
5       {
6           Scanner keyboard = new Scanner(System.in);
7
```

Display 9.8   Catching Multiple Exceptions (part 2 of 3)

```
 8          try
 9          {
10              System.out.println("How many pencils do you have?");
11              int pencils = keyboard.nextInt();

12              if (pencils < 0)
13                  throw new NegativeNumberException("pencils");

14              System.out.println("How many erasers do you have?");
15              int erasers = keyboard.nextInt();
16              double pencilsPerEraser;

17              if (erasers < 0)
18                  throw new NegativeNumberException("erasers");
19              else if (erasers != 0)
20                  pencilsPerEraser = pencils/(double)erasers;
21              else
22                  throw new DivisionByZeroException();

23              System.out.println("Each eraser must last through "
24                      + pencilsPerEraser + " pencils.");
25          }
26          catch(NegativeNumberException e)
27          {
28              System.out.println("Cannot have a negative number of "
29                      + e.getMessage());
30          }
31          catch(DivisionByZeroException e)
32          {
33              System.out.println("Do not make any mistakes.");
34          }

35          System.out.println("End of program.");
36      }
37  }
```

Sample Dialogue 1

```
How many pencils do you have?
5
How many erasers do you have?
2
Each eraser must last through 2.5 pencils
End of program.
```

(continued)

Display 9.7   Catching Multiple Exceptions (part 3 of 3)

Sample Dialogue 2

```
How many pencils do you have?
-2
Cannot have a negative number of pencils
End of program.
```

Sample Dialogue 3

```
How many pencils do you have?
5
How many erasers do you have?
0
Do not make any mistakes.
End of program.
```

PITFALL: Catch the More Specific Exception First

When catching multiple exceptions, the order of the catch blocks can be important. When an exception is thrown in a try block, the catch blocks are examined in order, and the first one that matches the type of the exception thrown is the one that is executed. Thus, the following ordering of catch blocks would not be good:

```
catch (Exception e)
{
     .
     .
     .
}

catch(NegativeNumberException e)
{                           The second catch block can
     .                      never be reached.
     .
     .
}
```

With this ordering, the catch block for NegativeNumberException would never be used, because all exceptions are caught by the first catch block. Fortunately, the compiler will warn you about this. The correct ordering is to reverse the catch blocks so that the more specific exception comes before its parent exception class, as shown in the following:

PITFALL: (continued)

```
catch(NegativeNumberException e)
{
    .
    .
    .
}

catch(Exception e)
{
    .
    .
    .
}
```

■

Display 9.8   The Class `NegativeNumberException`

```
1    public class NegativeNumberException extends Exception
2    {
3        public NegativeNumberException()
4        {
5            super("Negative Number Exception!");
6        }
7        public NegativeNumberException(String message)
8        {
9            super(message);
10       }
11   }
```

Self-Test Exercises

19. What output will be produced by the following code? (The definition of the class
    `NegativeNumberException` is given in Display 9.8.)

```
int n;
try
{
    n = 42;
    if (n > 0)
        throw new Exception();
    else if (n < 0)
        throw new NegativeNumberException();
    else
        System.out.println("Bingo!");
}
```

(continued)

Self-Test Exercises (continued)

```
catch(NegativeNumberException e)
{
    System.out.println("First catch.");
}
catch(Exception e)
{
    System.out.println("Second catch.");
}
System.out.println("End of exercise.");
```

20. Suppose that in Self-Test Exercise 19 the line

    ```
    n = 42;
    ```

    is changed to

    ```
    n = -42;
    ```

    How would this affect the output?

21. Suppose that in Self-Test Exercise 19 the line

    ```
    n = 42;
    ```

    is changed to

    ```
    n = 0;
    ```

    How would this affect the output?

9.2 Throwing Exceptions in Methods

buck n. Games. A counter or marker formerly passed from one poker player to another to indicate an obligation, especially one's turn to deal.

THE AMERICAN HERITAGE DICTIONARY OF THE ENGLISH LANGUAGE, THIRD EDITION

The buck stops here.

HARRY S TRUMAN (sign on Truman's desk while he was president)

So far our examples of exception handling have been toy examples. We have not yet shown any examples of a program that makes good and realistic use of exception handling. However, now you know enough about exception handling to discuss more realistic uses of exception handling. This section explains the single most important exception handling technique, namely throwing an exception in a method and catching it outside the method.

Throwing an Exception in a Method

Sometimes it makes sense to throw an exception in a method but not catch it in the method. For example, you might have a method with code that throws an exception if there is an attempt to divide by zero, but you may not want to catch the exception in that method. Perhaps some programs that use that method should simply end if the exception is thrown, and other programs that use the method should do something else. So, you would not know what to do with the exception if you caught it inside the method. In such cases, it makes sense to not catch the exception in the method definition, but instead to have any program (or other code) that uses the method place the method invocation in a `try` block and catch the exception in a `catch` block that follows that `try` block.

Look at the program in Display 9.9. It has a `try` block, but there is no `throw` statement visible in the `try` block. The statement that does the throwing in that program is

```
if (bottom == 0)
    throw new DivisionByZeroException();
```

This statement is not visible in the `try` block. However, it is in the `try` block in terms of program execution, because it is in the definition of the method `safeDivide`, and there is an invocation of `safeDivide` in the `try` block.

The meaning of `throws DivisionByZero` in the heading of `safeDivide` is discussed in the next subsection.

Display 9.9   Use of a **throws** Clause (part 1 of 2)

```
1    import java.util.Scanner;

2    public class DivisionDemoSecondVersion
3    {
4        public static void main(String[] args)
5        {
6            Scanner keyboard = new Scanner(System.in);

7            try
8            {
9                System.out.println("Enter numerator:");
10               int numerator = keyboard.nextInt();
11               System.out.println("Enter denominator:");
12               int denominator = keyboard.nextInt();
```

We will present an even better version of this program later in this chapter.

(continued)

Display 9.9 Use of a **throws** Clause (part 2 of 2)

```
13              double quotient = safeDivide(numerator, denominator);
14              System.out.println(numerator + "/"
15                                      + denominator
16                                      + " = " + quotient);
17          }
18          catch(DivisionByZeroException e)
19          {
20              System.out.println(e.getMessage());
21              secondChance();
22          }
23
24          System.out.println("End of program.");
25      }
26

27      public static double safeDivide(int top, int bottom)
28                              throws DivisionByZeroException
29      {
30          if (bottom == 0)
31              throw new DivisionByZeroException();
32
32          return top/(double)bottom;
33      }
34      public static void secondChance()
35      {
36          Scanner keyboard = new Scanner(System.in);
37
38          try
39          {
40              System.out.println("Enter numerator:");
41              int numerator = keyboard.nextInt();
42              System.out.println("Enter denominator:");
43              int denominator = keyboard.nextInt();
44
44              double quotient = safeDivide(numerator, denominator);
45              System.out.println(numerator + "/"
46                                      + denominator
47                                      + " = " + quotient);
48          }
49          catch(DivisionByZeroException e)
50          {
51              System.out.println("I cannot do division by zero.");
52              System.out.println("Aborting program.");
53              System.exit(0);
54          }
55      }
56  }
```

*The input/output dialogues are
identical to those for the program in
Display 9.4.*

Declaring Exceptions in a `throws` Clause

throws clause declaring an exception

If a method does not catch an exception, then (in most cases) it must at least warn programmers that any invocation of the method might possibly throw an exception. This warning is called a *throws clause,* and including an exception class in a `throws` clause is called **declaring the exception**. For example, a method that might possibly throw a `DivisionByZeroException` and that does not catch the exception would have a heading similar to the following:

```
public void sampleMethod() throws DivisionByZeroException
```

throws clause

The part `throws DivisionByZeroException` is a **throws clause** stating that an invocation of the method `sampleMethod` might throw a `DivisionByZeroException`.

If there is more than one possible exception that can be thrown in the method definition, then the exception types are separated by commas, as illustrated in what follows:

```
public void sampleMethod()
            throws DivisionByZeroException, SomeOtherException
```

Most "ordinary" exceptions that might be thrown when a method is invoked must be accounted for in one of two ways:

1. The possible exception can be caught in a `catch` block within the method definition.
2. The possible exception can be declared at the start of the method definition by placing the exception class name in a `throws` clause (and letting whoever uses the method worry about how to handle the exception).

Catch or Declare Rule

This is often called the **Catch or Declare Rule**. In any one method, you can mix the two alternatives, catching some exceptions and declaring others in a `throws` clause.

You already know about technique 1, handling exceptions in a `catch` block. Technique 2 is a form of shifting responsibility ("passing the buck"). For example, suppose `yourMethod` has a `throws` clause as follows:

```
public void yourMethod() throws DivisionByZeroException
```

In this case, `yourMethod` is absolved of the responsibility of catching any exceptions of type `DivisionByZeroException` that might occur when `yourMethod` is executed. If, however, there is another method, `myMethod`, that includes an invocation of `yourMethod`, then `myMethod` must handle the exception. When you add a `throws` clause to `yourMethod`, you are saying to `myMethod`, "If you invoke `yourMethod`, you must handle any `DivisionByZeroException` that is thrown." In effect, `yourMethod` has passed the responsibility for any exceptions of type `DivisionByZeroException` from itself to any method that calls it.

Of course, if `yourMethod` passes responsibility to `myMethod` by including `DivisionByZeroException` in a `throws` clause, then `myMethod` may also pass the responsibility to whoever calls it by including the same `throws` clause in its definition. But in a well-written program, every exception that is thrown should eventually be caught by a `catch` block in some method that does not just declare the exception class in a `throws` clause.

---

throws Clause

If you define a method that might throw exceptions of some particular class, then normally either your method definition must include a `catch` block that will catch the exception or you must declare (that is, list) the exception class within a `throws` clause, as described in what follows.

SYNTAX (COVERS MOST COMMON CASES)

```
public Type_Or_void Method(Parameter_List) throws List_Of_Exceptions
Body_Of_Method
```

EXAMPLE

```
public void yourMethod(int n) throws MyException, YourException
{
         .
         .
         .
}
```

When an exception is thrown in a method but not caught in that method, that immediately ends the method invocation.

Be sure to note that the `throws` clause for a method is for exceptions that "get outside" the method. If they do not get outside the method, they do not belong in the `throws` clause. If they get outside the method, they belong in the `throws` clause no matter where they originate. If an exception is thrown in a try block that is inside a method definition and is caught in a `catch` block inside the method definition, then its exception class need not be listed in the `throws` clause. If a method definition includes an invocation of another method and that other method can throw an exception that is not caught, then the exception class of that exception should be placed in the `throws` clause.

Throwing an Exception Can End a Method

If a method throws an exception, and the exception is not caught inside the method, then the method invocation ends immediately after the exception is thrown.

In Display 9.9, we have rewritten the program from Display 9.4 so that the exception is thrown in the method `safeDivide`. The method `main` includes a call to the method `safeDivide` and puts the call in a `try` block. Because the method `safeDivide` can throw a `DivisionByZeroException` that is not caught in the method `safeDivide`, we needed to declare this in a `throws` clause at the start of the definition of `safeDivide`. If we set up

> ### Catch or Declare Rule
>
> Most "ordinary" exceptions that might be thrown when a method is invoked must be accounted for in one of two ways:
>
> 1. The possible exception can be caught in a `catch` block within the method definition.
> 2. The possible exception can be declared at the start of the method definition by placing the exception class name in a `throws` clause (and letting whoever uses the method worry about how to handle the exception).
>
> This is known as the **Catch or Declare Rule**. In any one method, you can mix the two alternatives, catching some exceptions and declaring others in a `throws` clause.
>
> If you use a class that is subject to the Catch or Declare Rule and you do not follow the rule, you will get a compiler error message. The box entitled "Checked and Unchecked Exceptions" explains exactly which exception classes are subject to the Catch or Declare Rule.

our program in this way, the case in which nothing goes wrong is completely isolated and easy to read. It is not even cluttered by `try` blocks and `catch` blocks.

The subsection entitled "Exceptions to the Catch or Declare Rule" explains exactly which exception classes are subject to the Catch or Declare Rule. However, the compiler will ensure that you follow the Catch or Declare Rule when it is required. So if you do not know whether a class is subject to the Catch or Declare Rule, you can rely on the compiler to tell you. If you use a class that is subject to the Catch or Declare Rule and you do not follow the rule, you will get a compiler error message.

Exceptions to the Catch or Declare Rule

As we already noted, in most "ordinary" cases, an exception must either be caught in a `catch` block or declared in a `throws` clause. That is the Catch or Declare Rule, but there are exceptions to this rule. There are some classes whose exceptions you do not need to account for in this way (although you can catch them in a `catch` block if you want to). These are typically exceptions that result from errors of some sort. They usually indicate that your code should be fixed, not that you need to add a `catch` block. They are often thrown by methods in standard library classes, but it would be legal to throw one of these exceptions in the code you write.

Exceptions that are descendents of the class `RuntimeException` do not need to be accounted for in a `catch` block or `throws` clause. Another category of classes called `Error` classes behave like exception classes in that they can be thrown and caught in a `catch` block. However, you are not required to account for `Error` objects in a `catch` block or `throws` clause. The situation is diagrammed as a class hierarchy in Display 9.10. All the classes shown in blue follow the Catch or Declare Rule, which says that if their objects are thrown, then they must either be caught in a `catch` block or declared in a `throws` clause. All the classes shown in yellow are exempt from the Catch or Declare Rule.

What Happens if an Exception Is Never Caught?

If every method up to and including the **main** method simply includes a **throws** clause for a particular class of exceptions, then it may turn out that an exception of that class is thrown but never caught. In such cases, when an exception is thrown but never caught, then for the kinds of programs we have seen so far, the program ends with an error message giving the name of the exception class. (In Chapter 17 we will discuss programs with windowing interfaces that are known as *GUI programs*. For GUI programs, if an exception is thrown but never caught, then nothing happens, but if your code does not somehow account for the thrown exception, then the user may be left in an unexplained situation.)

In a well-written program, every exception that is thrown should eventually be caught by a **catch** block in some method.

Display 9.10 **Hierarchy of Throwable Objects**

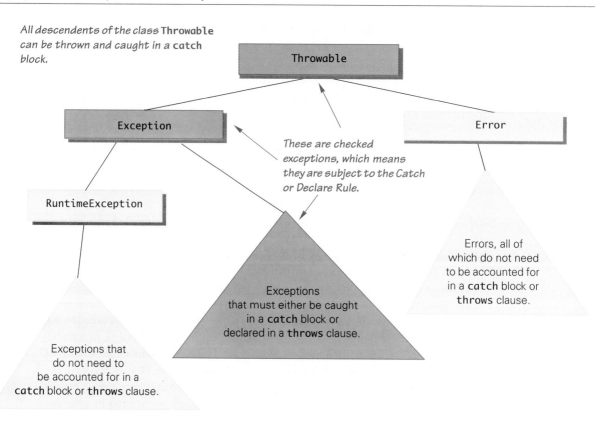

All descendents of the class **Throwable** *can be thrown and caught in a* **catch** *block.*

Throwable

Exception

Error

RuntimeException

These are checked exceptions, which means they are subject to the Catch or Declare Rule.

Exceptions that must either be caught in a **catch** block or declared in a **throws** clause.

Errors, all of which do not need to be accounted for in a **catch** block or **throws** clause.

Exceptions that do not need to be accounted for in a **catch** block or **throws** clause.

Exception classes that follow the Catch or Declare Rule are often called **checked exceptions**. Exceptions that are exempt from the Catch or Declare Rule are often called **unchecked exceptions**.

Checked and Unchecked Exceptions

Exceptions that are subject to the Catch or Declare Rule are called **checked exceptions** because the compiler *checks* to see if they are accounted for with a `catch` block or `throws` clause. Exceptions that are *not* subject to the Catch or Declare Rule are called **unchecked exceptions**. The classes `Throwable`, `Exception`, and all descendents of the class `Exception` are checked exceptions. All other exceptions are unchecked exceptions. The class `Error` and all its descendent classes are called **error classes** and are *not* subject to the Catch or Declare Rule. Although they are, strictly speaking, not exceptions, you can safely consider these error classes to be unchecked exceptions. (Strictly speaking, the class `Throwable` is neither an exception nor an error class, but it is seldom used and can be treated as a checked exception if it is used.)

You need not worry too much about which exceptions you do and do not need to declare in a `throws` clause. If you fail to account for some exception that Java requires you to account for, the compiler will tell you about it, and you can then either catch it or declare it in a `throws` clause.

`throws` Clause in Derived Classes

When you override a method definition in a derived class, it should have the same exception classes listed in its `throws` clause that it had in the base class, or it should have a `throws` clause whose exceptions are a subset of those in the base class `throws` clause. Put another way, when you override a method definition, you cannot add any exceptions to the `throws` clause (but you can delete some exceptions if you want. You also can replace an exception class by any descendent exception class). This makes sense, since an object of the derived class might be used anyplace an object of the base class can be used, and so an overridden method must fit into any code written for an object of the base class.

When to Use Exceptions

So far, most of our examples of exception handling have been unrealistically simple. A better guideline for how you should use exceptions is to separate throwing an exception and catching the exception into separate methods. In most cases, you should include any `throw` statement within a method definition, list the exception class in a `throws` clause for that method, and place the `try` and `catch` blocks in *a different method*. In outline form, the technique is as follows:

```
public void yourMethod() throws YourException
{
    ...
    throw new YourException(<Maybe an argument.>);
    ...
}
```

Then, when yourMethod is used by some otherMethod, the otherMethod must account for the exception. For example:

```
public void otherMethod()
{
        ...
    try
    {
            ...
        yourMethod();
            ...
    }
    catch(YourException e)
    {
        <Handle exception.>
    }
        ...
}
```

Even this kind of use of a throw statement should be reserved for cases where it is unavoidable. *If you can easily handle a problem in some other way, do not throw an exception. Reserve* throw *statements for situations in which the way the exceptional condition is handled depends on how and where the method is used.* If the way that the exceptional condition is handled depends on how and where the method is invoked, then the best thing to do is to let the programmer who invokes the method handle the exception. In all other situations, it is preferable to avoid throwing exceptions. Let's outline a sample scenario of this kind of situation.

Suppose you are writing a library of methods to deal with patient monitoring systems for hospitals. One method might compute the patient's average daily temperature by accessing the patient's record in some file and dividing the sum of the temperatures by the number of times the temperature was taken. Now suppose these methods are used for creating different systems to be used in different situations. What should happen if the patient's temperature was never taken and so the averaging would involve a division by zero? In an intensive-care unit, this would indicate something is very wrong. So for that system, when this potential division by zero would occur, an emergency message should be sent out. However, for a system that is to be used in a less urgent setting, such as outpatient care or even in some noncritical wards, it might have no significance, and so a simple note in the patient's record would suffice. In this scenario, the method for doing the averaging of the temperatures should throw an exception when this division by zero occurs, list the exception in the throws clause, and let each system handle the exception case in the way that is appropriate to that system.

When to Throw an Exception

Exceptions should be reserved for situations where a method has an exceptional case and different invocations of the method would handle the exceptional case differently. In this situation, you would throw an exception in the method definition, not catch the exception in the method, but list the exception in the **throws** clause for the method. That way the programmers who invoke the method can handle the exception differently in different situations,

Event-Driven Programming ★

event-driven programming

firing an event

Exception handling is our first example of a programming methodology known as **event-driven programming**. With event-driven programming, objects are defined so that they send **events**, which are themselves objects, to other objects that handle the events. Sending the event is called **firing the event**. In exception handing, the event objects are the exception objects. They are fired (thrown) by an object when the object invokes a method that throws the exception. An exception event is sent to a catch block, where it is handled. Of course, a catch block is not exactly an object, but the idea is the same. Also, our programs have mixed event-driven programming (exception handling) with more traditional programming techniques. When we study how you construct windowing systems using the Swing libraries (Chapter 17), you will see examples of programming where the dominant technique is event-driven programming.

Self-Test Exercises

22. What is the output produced by the following program?

```java
public class Exercise
{
    public static void main(String[] args)
    {
        try
        {
            System.out.println("Trying");
            sampleMethod(98.6);
            System.out.println("Trying after call.");
        }
        catch(Exception e)
        {
            System.out.println("Catching.");
        }

        System.out.println("End program.");
    }

    public static void sampleMethod(double test)
                                        throws Exception
    {
```

(continued)

```
                System.out.println("Starting sampleMethod.");
                if (test < 100)
                        throw new Exception();
        }
}
```

extra code
on CD

The class `Exercise` is on the CD that comes with this text.

23. Suppose that in Self-Test Exercise 22, the line

    ```
    sampleMethod(98.6);
    ```

    in the try block is changed to

    ```
    sampleMethod(212);
    ```

    How would this affect the output?

24. Correct the following method definition by adding a suitable `throws` clause:

    ```
    public static void doStuff(int n)
    {
        if (n < 0)
            throw new Exception("Negative number.");
    }
    ```

25. What happens if an exception is thrown inside a method invocation but the exception is not caught inside the method?

26. Suppose there is an invocation of method A inside of method B, and an invocation of method B inside of method C. When method C is invoked, this leads to an invocation of method B, and that in turn leads to an invocation of method A. Now, suppose that method A throws an exception but does not catch it within A. Where might the exception be caught? In B? In C? Outside of C?

9.3   More Programming Techniques for Exception Handling

Only use this in exceptional circumstances.

WARREN PEACE, *The Lieutenant's Tool*

In this section, we present a number of the finer points about programming with exception handling in Java.

PITFALL: Nested try–catch Blocks

You can place a try block and its following catch blocks inside a larger try block or inside a larger catch block. On rare occasions this may be useful, but it is almost always better to place the inner try catch blocks inside a method definition and place an invocation of the method in the outer try or catch block (or maybe just eliminate one or more try blocks completely).

If you place a try block and its following catch blocks inside a larger catch block, you will need to use different names for the catch block parameters in the inner and outer blocks. This has to do with how Java handles nested blocks of any kind. Remember, try blocks and catch blocks are blocks.

If you place a try block and its following catch blocks inside a larger try block, and an exception is thrown in the inner try block but is not caught in the inner catch blocks, then the exception is thrown to the outer try block for processing and might be caught in one of its catch blocks. ■

The finally Block ★

The finally block contains code to be executed whether or not an exception is thrown in a try block. The finally block, if used, is placed after a try block and its following catch blocks. The general syntax is as follows:

```
try
{
    ...
}
catch(ExceptionClass1 e)
{
    ...
}
.
.
.
catch(ExceptionClassLast e)
{
    ...
}
finally
{
    < Code to be executed whether or not an exception is thrown or caught.>
}
```

Now, suppose that the try-catch-finally blocks are inside a method definition. (After all, every set of try-catch-finally blocks is inside of some method, even if it is only the method `main`.) There are three possibilities when the code in the try–catch–finally blocks is run:

1. The `try` block runs to the end and no exception is thrown. In this case, the `finally` block is executed after the `try` block.

2. An exception is thrown in the `try` block and is caught in one of the `catch` blocks positioned after the `try` block. In this case, the `finally` block is executed after the `catch` block is executed.

3. An exception is thrown in the `try` block and there is no matching `catch` block in the method to catch the exception. In this case, the method invocation ends and the exception object is thrown to the enclosing method. However, the `finally` block is executed before the method ends. Note that you cannot account for this last case simply by placing code after the `catch` blocks.

Self-Test Exercises

27. Can you have a `try` block and corresponding `catch` blocks inside another larger `try` block?

28. Can you have a `try` block and corresponding `catch` blocks inside another larger `catch` block?

29. What is the output produced by the following program? What would the output be if the argument to `exerciseMethod` were –42 instead of 42? (The class `NegativeNumberException` is defined in Display 9.8, but you need not review that definition to do this exercise.)

```
public class FinallyDemo
{
    public static void main(String[] args)
    {
        try
        {
            exerciseMethod(42);
        }
        catch(Exception e)
        {
            System.out.println("Caught in main.");
        }
    }
    public static void exerciseMethod(int n) throws Exception
    {
        try
        {
            if (n > 0)
                throw new Exception();
            else if (n < 0)
                throw new NegativeNumberException();
```

```
            else
                System.out.println("No Exception.");
            System.out.println("Still in sampleMethod.");
        }
        catch(NegativeNumberException e)
        {
            System.out.println("Caught in sampleMethod.");
        }
        finally
        {
            System.out.println("In finally block.");
        }
        System.out.println("After finally block.");
    }
}
```

**extra code
on CD**

The class `FinallyDemo` is on the CD that comes with this text.

Rethrowing an Exception ★

A `catch` block can contain code that throws an exception. In rare cases you may find it useful to catch an exception and then, depending on the string produced by `getMessage` or depending on something else, decide to throw the same or a different exception for handling further up the chain of exception handling blocks.

The `AssertionError` Class ★

When we discussed the `assert` operator and assertion checking in Chapter 3, we said that if your program contains an assertion check and the assertion check fails, your program will end with an error message. That statement is more or less true, but it is incomplete. What happens is that an object of the class `AssertionError` is thrown. If it is not caught in a `catch` block, your program ends with an error message. However, if you wish, you can catch it in a `catch` block, although that is not a very common thing to do. The `AssertionError` class is in the `java.lang` package and so requires no import statement.

As the name suggests, the class `AssertionError` is derived from the class `Error`, so you are not required to either catch it in a `catch` block or declare it in a `throws` clause.

Exception Handling with the `Scanner` Class

When reading `int` values from the keyboard, we have been using the `nextInt` method of the `Scanner` class. We said that if the user enters something other than a well-formed `int` value, then your program will end with an error message. That's true as far as it goes, but the full detail is that if the user enters something other than a well-formed `int` value, an exception of type `InputMismatchException` will be thrown. If the exception is not caught, your program ends with an error message. However, you can catch the exception, and in the catch block, give code for some alternative action, such as asking the user to reenter the input. InputMismatchException is a descendent class of RuntimeException, so you are not required to account for an InputMismatchException by catching it in a catch block or declaring it in a throws clause. However, you are allowed to catch an InputMismatchException in a catch block, which can sometimes be useful.

InputMismatchException is in the standard Java package java.util and so if your program mentions InputMismatchException, then it needs an import statement, such as the following:

```java
import java.util.InputMismatchException;
```

Display 9.11 contains a sample of how you might usefully catch an Input-MismatchException. This program gets an input int value from the keyboard and then does nothing with it other than echo the input value. However, you can use code like this to give robust input to any program that uses keyboard input. The following Tip explains the general technique we used for the loop in Display 9.11.

 TIP: Exception Controlled Loops

Sometimes when an exception is thrown, such as an InputMismatchException for an ill-formed input, you want your code to simply repeat some code so that the user (or whatever) can get things right on a second or subsequent try. One way to set up your code to repeat a loop every time a particular exception is thrown is as follows:

```java
boolean done = false;

while (! done)
{
    try
    {
        <Code that may throw an exception in the class Exception_Class.>
        done = true; //Will end the loop.
        <Possibly more code.>
    }
    catch(Exception_Class e)
    {
        <Some code.>
    }
}
```

Note that if an exception is thrown in the first piece of code in the try block, then the try block ends before the line that sets done to true is executed and so the loop body is repeated. If no exception is thrown, then done is set to true and the loop body is not repeated.

Display 9.11 contains an example of such a loop. Minor variations on this outline can accommodate a range of different situations for which you want to repeat code on throwing an exception. ■

Display 9.11 An Exception Controlled Loop

```
1   import java.util.Scanner;
2   import java.util.InputMismatchException;

3   public class InputMismatchExceptionDemo
4   {
5       public static void main(String[] args)
6       {
7           Scanner keyboard = new Scanner(System.in);
8           int number = 0; //to keep compiler happy
9           boolean done = false;

10          while (! done)
11          {
12              try
13              {
14                  System.out.println("Enter a whole number:");
15                  number = keyboard.nextInt();
16                  done = true;
17              }
18              catch(InputMismatchException e)
19              {
20                  keyboard.nextLine();
21                  System.out.println("Not a correctly written whole number.");
22                  System.out.println("Try again.");
23              }
24          }

25          System.out.println("You entered " + number);
26      }
27  }
```

If nextInt *throws an exception, the* try *block ends and so the* boolean *variable* done *is not set to* true.

Sample Dialogue

```
Enter a whole number:
forty two
Not a correctly written whole number.
Try again.
Enter a whole number:
fortytwo
Not a correctly written whole number.
Try again.
Enter a whole number:
42
You entered 42
```

Self-Test Exercises

30. How would the dialogue in Display 9.11 change if you were to omit the following line from the catch block? (Try it and see.)

```
keyboard.nextLine();
```

31. Give the definition for the following method. Use the techniques given in Display 9.11.

```
/**
 Precondition: keyboard is an object of the class Scanner that
 has been set up for keyboard input (as we have been doing
 right along). Returns: An int value entered at the keyboard.
 If the user enters an incorrectly formed input she or he is
 prompted to reenter the value,
*/
public static int getInt(Scanner keyboard)
```

ArrayIndexOutOfBoundsException

You should read Section 6.1 of Chapter 6, which covers array basics, before reading this short subsection. If you have not yet covered some of Chapter 6, you can omit this section and return to it at a later time.

If your program attempts to use an array index that is out of bounds, an Array-IndexOutOfBoundsException is thrown and your program ends, unless the exception is caught in a catch block. ArrayIndexOutOfBoundsException is a descendent of the class RuntimeException and so need not be caught or accounted for in a throws clause. This sort of exception normally indicates that there is something wrong with your code and means that you need to fix your code, not catch an exception. Thus, an ArrayIndexOutOfBoundsException normally functions more like a run-time error message than a regular exception.

ArrayIndexOutOfBoundsException is in the standard Java package java.lang and so requires no import statement should you decide to use it by name.

Chapter Summary

- Exception handling allows you to design and code the normal case for your program separately from the code that handles exceptional situations.

- An exception can be thrown in a try block. Alternatively, an exception can be thrown in a method definition that does not include a try block (or does not include a catch block to catch that type of exception). In this case, an invocation of the method can be placed in a try block.

- An exception is caught in a catch block.

- A try block must be followed by at least one catch block and can be followed by more than one catch block. If there are multiple catch blocks, always list the catch block for a more specific exception class before the catch block for a more general exception class.

- The best use of exceptions is to throw an exception in a method (but not catch it in the method), but to only do this when the way the exception is handled will vary from one invocation of the method to another. There is seldom any other situation that can profitably benefit from throwing an exception.

- If an exception is thrown in a method but not caught in that method, then if the exception is not a descendent of the class RuntimeException (and is not a descendent of the class Error), the exception type must be listed in the throws clause for that method.

Answers to Self-Test Exercises

1. ```
   Try block entered.
   Over 30.
   After catch block
   ```

2. The output would then be

   ```
   Try block entered.
   Under 30.
   After catch block
   ```

3. There are two throw statements:

   ```
   throw new Exception("Over 30.");
   throw new Exception("Under 30.");
   ```

4. When a throw statement is executed, that is the end of the enclosing try block. No other statements in the try block are executed, and control passes to the following catch block(s). When we say that control passes to the following catch block, we mean that the exception object that is thrown is plugged in for the catch block parameter and the code in the catch block is executed.

5. ```
   try
   {
       System.out.println("Try block entered.");
       if (waitTime > 30)
           throw new Exception("Over 30.");
       else if (waitTime < 30)
           throw new Exception("Under 30.");
       else
           System.out.println("No exception.");
       System.out.println("Leaving try block.");
   }
   ```

6.
```
catch(Exception thrownObject)
{
    System.out.println(thrownObject.getMessage());
}
```

7. `thrownObject`

8. Yes, it is legal.

9. Yes, it is legal.

10.
```
public class PowerFailureException extends Exception
{
    public PowerFailureException()
    {
        super("Power Failure!");
    }

    public PowerFailureException(String message)
    {
        super(message);
    }
}
```

11.
```
public class TooMuchStuffException extends Exception
{
    public TooMuchStuffException()
    {
        super("Too much stuff!");
    }

    public TooMuchStuffException(String message)
    {
        super(message);
    }
}
```

12.
```
ExerciseException invoked with an argument.
Do Be Do
```

13.
```
Test exception thrown!!
Test Exception thrown!
Message is Test Exception thrown!
```

14.
```
try block entered:
MyException: Hi Mom!
End of example.
```

15. The output would be the same.

16. The output would then be

    ```
    try block entered:
    Leaving try block.
    End of example.
    ```

17. ```
    41.9
    DoubleException thrown!
    ```

18. Yes, you can define an exception class as a derived class of the class `IOException`.

19. ```
    Second catch.
    End of exercise.
    ```

20. The output would then be

    ```
    First catch.
    End of exercise.
    ```

21. The output would then be

    ```
    Bingo!
    End of exercise.
    ```

22. ```
    Trying
    Starting sampleMethod.
    Catching.
    End program.
    ```

23. The output would then be

    ```
    Trying
    Starting sampleMethod.
    Trying after call.
    End program.
    ```

24. ```java
    public static void doStuff(int n) throws Exception
    {
        if (n < 0)
            throw new Exception("Negative number.");
    }
    ```

25. If a method throws an exception and the exception is not caught inside the method, then the method invocation ends immediately after the exception is thrown. If the method invocation is inside a `try` block, then the exception is thrown to a matching `catch` block, if there is one. If there is no `catch` block matching the exception, then the method invocation ends as soon as that exception is thrown.

26. It might be caught in method B. If it is not caught in method B, it might be caught in method C. If it is not caught in method C, it might be caught outside of method C.

27. Yes, you can have a try block and corresponding catch blocks inside another larger try block.

28. Yes, you can have a try block and corresponding catch blocks inside another larger catch block.

29. `In finally block.`
    `Caught in main.`

    If the argument to `sampleMethod` were −42 instead of 42, the output would be

    `Caught in sampleMethod.`
    `In finally block.`
    `After finally block.`

30. Assuming the first item input is not a correctly formed `int` value, the program will go into an infinite loop after reading the first item input. The screen will continually output a prompt for an input number. The problem is that unless the new-line symbol '\n' is read, the program will continue to try to read on the first input line and so continually reads in the empty string.

31. The following is the method definition embedded in a test program. This program would give the same dialogue as the one in Display 9.11. The program is included on the CD that accompanies this book.

extra code on CD

```
import java.util.Scanner;
import java.util.InputMismatchException;

public class getIntDemo
{
    /**
    Precondition: keyboard is an object of the class Scanner that has
    been set up for keyboard input (as we have been doing right
    along).

    Returns: An int value entered at the keyboard.
    If the user enters an incorrectly formed input, she or he is
    prompted to reenter the value,
    */
    public static int getInt(Scanner keyboard)
    {
        int number = 0; //to keep compiler happy
        boolean done = false;

        while (! done)
        {
```

```
        try
        {
            System.out.println("Enter a whole number:");
            number = keyboard.nextInt();
            done = true;
        }
        catch(InputMismatchException e)
        {
            keyboard.nextLine();
            System.out.println(
                    "Not a correctly written whole number.");
            System.out.println("Try again.");
        }
    }

    return number;
}

public static void main(String[] args)
{
    Scanner keyboardArg = new Scanner(System.in);
    int number = getInt(keyboardArg);
    System.out.println("You entered " + number);
}
}
```

Programming Projects

 Many of these Programming Projects can be solved using AW's MyCodeMate.
To access these please go to: www.mycodemate.com.

   1. Write a program that calculates the average of *N* integers. The program should prompt the user to enter the value for *N* and then afterward must enter all *N* numbers. If the user enters a non-positive value for *N*, then an exception should be thrown (and caught) with the message "*N* must be positive." If there is any exception as the user is entering the *N* numbers, an error message should be displayed and the user prompted to enter the number again.

2. Here is a snippet of code that inputs two integers and divides them:

```
Scanner scan = new Scanner(System.in);
int n1, n2;
double r;

n1 = scan.nextInt();
n2 = scan.nextInt();
r = (double) n1 / n2;
```

Place this code into a try-catch block with multiple catches so that different error messages are printed if we attempt to divide by zero or if the user enters textual data instead of integers (java.util.InputMismatchException). If either of these conditions occurs then the program should loop back and let the user enter new data.

3. Modify the previous exercise so that the snippet of code is placed inside a method. The method should be named ReturnRatio and read the input from the keyboard and throw different exceptions for divide by zero or input mismatch between text and an integer. Create your own exception class for divide by zero. Invoke ReturnRatio from your main method and catch the exceptions in main. The main method should invoke the ReturnRatio method again if any exception occurs.

4. (This is a version of an exercise from Chapter 5.) Programming Project 2 from Chapter 5 asked you to create a class named Fraction. This class is used to represent a ratio of two integers. It should include mutator functions that allow the user to set the numerator and the denominator along with a method that displays the fraction on the screen as a ratio (e.g., 5/9). Modify the class so that it throws the exception DenominatorIs-ZeroException if the denominator is set to zero. Don't forget to account for the constructors! You will have to create the DenominatorIsZeroException class and it should be derived from Exception.

Write a main method that tests the new Fraction class, attempts to set the denominator to zero, and catches the DenominatorIsZeroException exception.

 5. Write a program that converts dates from numerical month/day/year format to normal "month day, year" format (for example, 12/25/2000 corresponds to December 25, 2000). You will define three exception classes, one called Month-Exception, another called DayException, and a third called YearException. If the user enters anything other than a legal month number (integers from 1 to 12), your program will throw and catch a MonthException and ask the user to reenter the month. Similarly, if the user enters anything other than a valid day number (integers from 1 to either 28, 29, 30, or 31, depending on the month and year), then your program will throw and catch a DayException and ask the user to reenter the day. If the user enters a year that is not in the range 1000 to 3000 (inclusive), then your program will throw and catch a Year-Exception and ask the user to reenter the year. (There is nothing very special about the numbers 1000 and 3000 other than giving a good range of likely dates.) See Self-Test Exercise 19 in Chapter 4 for details on leap years.

 6. Write a program that can serve as a simple calculator. This calculator keeps track of a single number (of type double) that is called result and that starts out as 0.0. Each cycle allows the user to repeatedly add, subtract, multiply, or divide by a second number. The result of one of these operations becomes the new value of result. The calculation ends when the user enters the letter R for "result" (either in uppercase or lowercase). The user is allowed to do another calculation from the beginning as often as desired.

The input format is shown in the following sample dialogue. If the user enters any operator symbol other than +, −, *, or /, then an UnknownOperatorException is thrown and the user is asked to reenter that line of input. Defining the class UnknownOperatorException is part of this project.

```
Calculator is on.
result = 0.0
+5
result + 5.0 = 5.0
new result = 5.0
*2.2
result * 2.2 = 11.0
updated result = 11.0
% 10
% is an unknown operation.
Reenter, your last line:
* 0.1
result * 0.1 = 1.1
updated result = 1.1
r
Final result = 1.1
Again? (y/n)
yes
result = 0.0
+10
result + 10.0 = 10.0
new result = 10.0
/2
result / 2.0 = 5.0
updated result = 5.0
r
Final result = 5.0
Again? (y/n)
N
End of Program
```

10

File I/O

10 File I/O

As a leaf is carried by a stream, whether the stream ends in a lake or in the sea, so too is the output of your program carried by a stream, not knowing if the stream goes to the screen or to a file.

WASHROOM WALL OF A
COMPUTER SCIENCE DEPARTMENT (1995)

Introduction

In this chapter, we explain how you can write your programs to take input from a file and send output to a file. This chapter covers the most common ways of doing file I/O in Java. However, it is not an exhaustive study of Java I/O classes. The Java I/O class library contains bewilderingly many classes and an exhaustive treatment of all of them would be a book by itself.

Prerequisites

You need only some of Chapter 9 on exception handling to read this chapter. You do not need Chapters 6, 7, or 8 on arrays, inheritance, and polymorphism, except in the final subsection, which covers writing and reading of arrays to binary files. If you have not yet covered some basic material on one-dimensional arrays, you can, of course, simply omit this last subsection.

You may postpone all or part of this chapter if you wish. Nothing in the rest of this book requires any of this chapter.

10.1 Introduction to File I/O

Good Heavens! For more than forty years I have been speaking prose without knowing it.

MOLIÈRE, *Le Bourgeois Gentilhomme*

In this section we go over some basic concepts about file I/O before we go into any Java details.

Streams

stream
input stream
output stream

A **stream** is an object that allows for the flow of data between your program and some I/O device or some file. If the flow is into your program, the stream is called an **input stream**. If the flow is out of your program, the stream is called an **output stream**. If the input stream flows from the keyboard, then your program will take input from the keyboard. If the input stream flows from a file, then your program will take its input from that file. Similarly, an output stream can go to the screen or to a file.

System.out
System.in

Although you may not realize it, you have already been using streams in your programs. The System.out that you have already used (in such things as System.out.println) is an output stream connected to the screen. System.in is an input stream connected to the keyboard. You used System.in in expressions like the following:

```
Scanner keyboard = new Scanner(System.in);
```

These two streams are automatically available to your program. You can define other streams that come from or go to files. Once you have defined them, you can use them in your program in ways that are similar to how you use System.out and System.in.

Streams

A **stream** is a flow of data. If the data flows *into your program*, then the stream is called an **input stream**. If the data flows *out of your program*, the stream is called an **output stream**.

Streams are used for both console I/O, which you have been using already, and file I/O.

Text Files and Binary Files

Text files are files that appear to contain sequences of characters when viewed in a text editor or read by a program. For example, the files that contain your Java programs are text files. **Text files** are sometimes also called **ASCII files** because they contain data encoded using a scheme known as ASCII coding. Files whose contents must be handled as sequences of binary digits are called **binary files**.

text file
ASCII file
binary file

Although it is not strictly speaking correct, you can safely think of a text file as containing a sequence of characters, and think of a binary file as containing a sequence of binary digits. Another way to distinguish between binary files and text files is to note that text files are designed to be read by human beings, whereas binary files are designed to be read only by programs.

One advantage of text files is that they are usually the same on all computers, so you can move your text files from one computer to another with few or no problems. The implementation of binary files usually differs from one computer to another, so your binary data files ordinarily must be read only on the same type of computer, and with the same programming language, as the computer that created that file.

The advantage of binary files is that they are more efficient to process than text files. Unlike other programming languages, Java also gives its binary files some of the advantages of text files. In particular, Java binary files are platform-independent; that is, with Java, you can move your binary files from one type of computer to another and your Java programs will still be able to read the binary files. This combines the portability of text files with the efficiency of binary files.

The one big advantage of text files is that you can read and write to them using a text editor. With binary files, all the reading and writing must normally be done by a program.

Text Files Versus Binary Files

Files that you write and read using an editor are called *text files*. Binary files represent data in a way that is not convenient to read with a text editor, but that can be written to and read from a program very efficiently.

Self-Test Exercises

1. A stream is a flow of data. From where and to where does the data flow in an input stream? From where and to where does the data flow in an output stream?

2. What is the difference between a binary file and a text file?

10.2 Text Files

Polonius: What do you read, my lord?
Hamlet: Words, words, words.

WILLIAM SHAKESPEARE, *Hamlet*

In this section, we describe the most common ways to do text file I/O in Java.

Writing to a Text File

PrintWriter The class PrintWriter is the preferred stream class for writing to a text file. An object of the class PrintWriter has the methods print and println, which are like the methods System.out.print and System.out.println that you have been using for screen output, but with an object of the class PrintWriter, the output goes to a text file. Display 10.1

contains a simple program that uses `PrintWriter` to send output to a text file. Let's look at the details of that program.

java.io

All the file I/O related classes we introduce in this chapter are in the package `java.io`, so all our program files begin with import statements similar to the ones in Display 10.1.

The program in Display 10.1 creates a text file named `stuff.txt` that a person can read using an editor or that another Java program can read. The program creates an object of the class `PrintWriter` as follows:

```
outputStream =
           new PrintWriter(new FileOutputStream("stuff.txt"));
```

The variable `outputStream` is of type `PrintWriter` and is declared outside the `try` block. The preceding two lines of code connect the stream named `outputStream` to

opening a file
the file named `stuff.txt`. This is called **opening the file**. When you connect a file to a stream in this way, your program always starts with an empty file. If the file `stuff.txt` already exists, the old contents of `stuff.txt` will be lost. If the file `stuff.txt` does not exist, then a new, empty file named `stuff.txt` will be created.

We want to associate the output stream `outputStream` with the file named `stuff.txt`. However, the class `PrintWriter` has no constructor that takes a file name

FileOutput-
Stream
as its argument. So we use the class `FileOutputStream` to create a stream that can be used as an argument to a `PrintWriter` constructor. The expression

```
new FileOutputStream("stuff.txt")
```

takes a file name as an argument and creates an anonymous object of the class `FileOutputStream`, which is then used as an argument to a constructor for the class `PrintWriter` as follows:

```
new PrintWriter(new FileOutputStream("stuff.txt"))
```

This produces an object of the class `PrintWriter` that is connected to the file

file name
`stuff.txt`. Note that the name of the file, in this case `stuff.txt`, is given as a `String` value and so is given in quotes.

reading the
file name
If you want to read the file name from the keyboard, you could read the name to a variable of type `String` and use the `String` variable as the argument to the `FileOutputStream` constructor.

FileNot-
Found-
Exception
When you open a text file in the way just discussed, a `FileNotFoundException` can be thrown, and any such possible exception should be caught in a `catch` block. (Actually, it is the `FileOutputStream` constructor that might throw the `FileNotFoundException`, but the net effect is the same.)

Notice that the `try` block in Display 10.1 encloses only the opening of the file. That is the only place that an exception might be thrown. Also note that the variable `outputStream` is declared outside of the `try` block. This is so that the variable `outputStream` can be used outside of the `try` block. Remember, anything declared in a block (even in a `try` block) is local to the block.

Display 10.1 Sending Output to a Text File

```
1   import java.io.PrintWriter;
2   import java.io.FileOutputStream;
3   import java.io.FileNotFoundException;

4   public class TextFileOutputDemo
5   {
6       public static void main(String[] args)
7       {
8           PrintWriter outputStream = null;
9           try
10          {
11              outputStream =
12                  new PrintWriter(new FileOutputStream("stuff.txt"));
13          }
14          catch(FileNotFoundException e)
15          {
16              System.out.println("Error opening the file stuff.txt.");
17              System.exit(0);
18          }

19          System.out.println("Writing to file.");

20          outputStream.println("The quick brown fox");
21          outputStream.println("jumped over the lazy dog.");

22          outputStream.close();

23          System.out.println("End of program.");
24      }
25  }
```

Sample Dialogue

```
Writing to file.
End of program.
```

FILE File **stuff.txt** (after the program is run.)

```
The quick brown fox
jumped over the lazy dog.
```

*You can read this file
using a text editor.*

Opening a Text File for Writing Output

You create a stream of the class `PrintWriter` and connect it to a text file for writing as follows.

SYNTAX

```
PrintWriter Output_Stream_Name;
Output_Stream_Name =
        new PrintWriter(new FileOutputStream(File_Name));
```

EXAMPLE

```
PrintWriter outputStream = null;
outputStream =
        new PrintWriter(new FileOutputStream("stuff.txt"));
```

After this, you can use the methods `println` and `print` to write to the file.

When used in this way, the `FileOutputStream` constructor, and thus the `PrintWriter` constructor invocation, can throw a `FileNotFoundException`, which is a kind of `IOException`.

File Names

The rules for how you spell file names depend on your operating system, not on Java. When you give a file name to a Java constructor for a stream, you are not giving the constructor a Java identifier. You are giving the constructor a string corresponding to the file name. A suffix, such as `.txt` in `stuff.txt`, has no special meaning to a Java program. We are using the suffix `.txt` to indicate a text file, but that is just a common convention. You can use any file names that are allowed by your operating system.

A File Has Two Names

Every input file and every output file used by your program has two names: (1) the real file name that is used by the operating system and (2) the name of the stream that is connected to the file.

The stream name serves as a temporary name for the file and is the name that is primarily used within your program. After you connect the file to the stream, your program always refers to the file by using the stream name.

We said that when you open a text file for writing output to the file, the constructor might throw a `FileNotFoundException`. But in this situation you want to create a new file for output, so why would you care that the file was not found? The answer is simply that the exception is poorly named. A `FileNotFoundException` does not mean that the file was not found. In this case, it actually means that the file could not be created.

IOException

When dealing with file I/O, there are many situations in which your code might throw an exception of some class, such as **FileNotFoundException**. Many of these various exception classes are descended classes of the class **IOException**. The class **IOException** is the root class for various exception classes having to do with input and output.

A FileNotFoundException is thrown if it is impossible to create the file—for example, because the file name is already used for a directory (folder) name.

A FileNotFoundException is a kind of IOException, so a catch block for an IOException would also work and would look more sensible. However, it is best to catch the most specific exception that you can, since that can give more information.

println
print
printf

As illustrated in Display 10.1, the method println of the class PrintWriter works the same for writing to a text file as the method System.out.println works for writing to the screen. The class PrintWriter also has the method print and printf, which behaves just like System.out.print and System.out.printf except that the output goes to a text file. Display 10.2 describes some of the methods in the class PrintWriter.

Display 10.2 Some Methods of the Class **PrintWriter** (part 1 of 2)

PrintWriter and **FileOutputStream** are in the **java.io** package.

```
public PrintWriter(OutputStream streamObject)
```

This is the only constructor you are likely to need. There is no constructor that accepts a file name as an argument. If you want to create a stream using a file name, you use

```
new PrintWriter(new FileOutputStream(File_Name))
```

When the constructor is used in this way, a blank file is created. If there already was a file named *File_Name*, then the old contents of the file are lost. If you want instead to append new text to the end of the old file contents, use

```
new PrintWriter(new FileOutputStream(File_Name, true))
```

(For an explanation of the argument **true**, read the subsection "Appending to a Text File.")

When used in either of these ways, the **FileOutputStream** constructor, and so the **PrintWriter** constructor invocation, can throw a **FileNotFoundException**, which is a kind of **IOException**.

If you want to create a stream using an object of the class **File**, you can use a **File** object in place of the *File_Name*. (The **File** class will be covered in Section 10.3. We discuss it here so that you will have a more complete reference in this display, but you can ignore the reference to the class **File** until after you've read that section.)

Display 10.2   Some Methods of the Class `PrintWriter` (part 2 of 2)

`public void println(`*Argument*`)`

The *Argument* can be a string, character, integer, floating-point number, **boolean** value, or any combination of these, connected with + signs. The *Argument* can also be any object, although it will not work as desired unless the object has a properly defined **toString()** method. The *Argument* is output to the file connected to the stream. After the *Argument* has been output, the line ends, and so the next output is sent to the next line.

`public void print(`*Argument*`)`

This is the same as `println`, except that this method does not end the line, so the next output will be on the same line.

`public PrintWriter printf(`*Arguments*`)`

This is the same as `System.out.printf`, except that this method sends output to a text file rather than to the screen. It returns the calling object. However, we have always used `printf` as a **void** method.

`public void close()`

Closes the stream's connection to a file. This method calls `flush` before closing the file.

`public void flush()`

Flushes the output stream. This forces an actual physical write to the file of any data that has been buffered and not yet physically written to the file. Normally, you should not need to invoke `flush`.

When your program is finished writing to a file, it should **close** the stream connected to that file. In Display 10.1, the stream connected to the file stuff.txt is closed with the statement

```
outputStream.close();
```

The class `PrintWriter`, and every other class for file output or file input streams, has a method named `close`. When this method is invoked, the system releases any resources used to connect the stream to the file and does any other housekeeping that is needed. If your program does not close a file before the program ends, Java will close it for you when the program ends, but it is safest to close the file with an explicit call to `close`.

buffered
Output streams connected to files are often **buffered**, which means that, rather than physically writing every instance of output data as soon as possible, the data is

buffer
saved in a temporary location, known as a **buffer**; when enough data is accumulated in this temporary location, it is physically written to the file. This can add to efficiency, since physical writes to a file can be slow. The method `flush` causes a physical write to

---

Closing a File

When your program is finished writing to a file or reading from a file, it should close the stream connected to that file by invoking the method named `close`.

SYNTAX

Stream_Object.close();

EXAMPLES:

```
outputStream.close();
inputStream.close();
```

---

the file of any buffered data. The method `close` includes an invocation of the method `flush`.

It may seem like there is no reason to use the method `close` to close a file. If your program ends normally but without closing a file, the system will automatically close it for you. So why should you bother to close files with an explicit call to the method `close`? There are at least two reasons. First, if your program ends abnormally, then Java may not be able to close the file for you. This could damage the file. In particular, if it is an output file, any buffered output will not have been physically written to the file. So the file will be incomplete. The sooner you close a file, the less likely it is that this will happen. Second, if your program writes to a file and later reads from the same file, it must close the file after it is through writing to the file and then reopen the file for reading. (Java does have a class that allows a file to be opened for both reading and writing, which we will discuss in Section 10.5.)

PITFALL: A try Block Is a Block

Notice that in Display 10.1 we declare the variable `outputStream` outside of the `try` block. If you were to move that declaration inside the `try` block, you would get a compiler error message. Let's see why.

Suppose you replace

```
PrintWriter outputStream = null;
try
{
    outputStream =
        new PrintWriter(new FileOutputStream("stuff.txt"));
}
```

in Display 10.1 with the following:

```
try
{
    PrintWriter outputStream =
        new PrintWriter(new FileOutputStream("stuff.txt"));
}
```

This replacement looks innocent enough, but it makes the variable outputStream a local variable for the try block, which would mean that you could not use output-Stream outside of the try block. If you make this change and try to compile the changed program, you will get an error message saying that outputStream when used outside the try block is an undefined identifier. ■

PITFALL: Overwriting an Output File

When you connect a stream to a text file for writing to the text file, as illustrated by what follows, you always produce an empty file:

```
outputStream =
        new PrintWriter(new FileOutputStream("stuff.txt"));
```

If there is no file named stuff.txt, this will create an empty file named stuff.txt. If a file named stuff.txt already exists, then this will eliminate that file and create a new, empty file named stuff.txt. So if there is a file named stuff.txt before this file opening, then all the data in that file will be lost. The section "The File Class" tells you how to test to see whether a file already exists so that you can avoid accidentally overwriting a file. The following subsection shows you how to add data to a text file without losing the data that is already in the file. ■

Appending to a Text File

appending

When you open a text file for writing in the way we did it in Display 10.1 and a file with the given name already exists, the old contents are lost. However, sometimes you instead want to add the program output to the end of the file. This is called **appending to a file**. If you wanted to append program output to the file stuff.txt, you would connect the file to the stream outputStream in the following manner:

```
outputStream =
    new PrintWriter(new FileOutputStream("stuff.txt", true));
```

If the file stuff.txt does not already exist, Java will create an empty file of that name and append the output to the end of this empty file. So if there is no file named stuff.txt, the effect of opening the file is the same as in Display 10.1. However, if the file stuff.txt already exists, then the old contents will remain, and the program's output will be placed after the old contents of the file.

When appending to a text file in this way, you would still use the same try and catch blocks as in Display 10.1.

That second argument of true deserves a bit of explanation. Why did the designers use true to signal appending? Why not something like the string "append"? The reason is that this version of the constructor for the class FileOutputStream was designed to also allow you to use a Boolean variable (or expression) to decide whether you append to an existing file or create a new file. For example, the following might be used:

```
System.out.println(
            "Enter A for append or N for a new file:");
char answer;
<Use your favorite way to read a single character into the variable answer.>
boolean append = (answer == 'A' || answer == 'a');
outputStream =
        new PrintWriter(new FileOutputStream("stuff.txt", append));
```

From this point on, your program writes to the file in exactly the same way that the program in Display 10.1 does. If the user answered with upper- or lowercase A, then any input will be added after the old file contents. If the user answered with upper- or lowercase N (or with anything other than an A), then any old contents of the file are lost.

TIP: toString Helps with Text File Output

In Chapter 4 we noted that if a class has a suitable toString() method and anObject is an object of that class, then anObject can be used as an argument to System.out.println and that will produce sensible output.[1] The same thing applies to the methods println and print of the class PrintWriter. Both println and print of the class PrintWriter can take any object as an argument and will produce reasonable output so long as the object has a sensible toString() method. ∎

---

[1] There is a more detailed discussion of this in Chapter 8, but you need not read Chapter 8 to use this fact.

Opening a Text File for Appending

To create an object of the class **PrintWriter** and connect it to a text file for appending to the end of the text already in the file, proceed as follows.

SYNTAX

```
Output_Stream_Name =
    new PrintWriter(
        new FileOutputStream(File_Name, True_Boolean_Expression));
```

EXAMPLE

```
PrintWriter outputStream;
outputStream =
    new PrintWriter(new FileOutputStream("stuff.txt", true));
```

After this statement, you can use the methods **println** and **print** to write to the file, and the new text will be written after the old text in the file.

(If you want to create a stream using an object of the class **File**, you can use a **File** object in place of the *File_Name*. The **File** class is discussed in the section entitled "The **File** Class.")

When used in this way, the **FileOutputStream** constructor, and so the **PrintWriter** constructor invocation, can throw a **FileNotFoundException**, which is a kind of **IOException**.

Self-Test Exercises

3. What kind of exception might be thrown by the following, and what would it indicate if this exception were thrown?

```
PrintWriter outputStream =
    new PrintWriter(new FileOutputStream("stuff.txt"));
```

4. Does the class **PrintWriter** have a constructor that accepts a string (for a file name) as an argument, so that the following code would be legal?

```
PrintWriter outputStream =
    new PrintWriter("stuff.txt");
```

(continued)

Self-Test Exercises (continued)

5. Write some code that will create a stream named `outStream` that is a member of the class `PrintWriter`, and that connects this stream to a text file named `sam` so that your program can send output to the file. Do this in a way such that the file `sam` always starts out empty. So, if there already is a file named `sam`, the old contents of `sam` are lost.

6. As in Self-Test Exercise 5, write some code that will create a stream named `outStream` that is a member of the class `PrintWriter`, and that connects this stream to a text file named `sam` so that your program can send output to the file. This time, however, do it in such a way that, if the file `sam` already exists, the old contents of `sam` will not be lost and the program output will be written after the old contents of the file.

7. The class `Person` was defined in Display 5.19 of Chapter 5. Suppose `mary` is an object of the class `Person`, and suppose `outputStream` is connected to a text file as in Display 10.1. Will the following send sensible output to the file connected to `outputStream`?

```
outputStream.println(mary);
```

Reading from a Text File

The two most common stream classes used for reading from a text file are the `Scanner` class and the `BufferedReader` class. We will discuss both of these approaches to reading from a text file. The `Scanner` class offers a richer group of methods for reading from a text file and is our preferred class to use when reading from a text file. However, the `BufferedReader` class is also widely used and is a reasonable choice. You, or your instructor, will need to decide which class you will use.

Reading a Text File Using Scanner

The same `Scanner` class that we used for reading from the keyboard can also be used for reading from a text file. To do so, you replace the argument `System.in` (in the `Scanner` constructor) with a suitable stream that is connected to the text file. This is a good illustration of the notion of a *stream*. The class `Scanner` does not care if its stream argument comes from the keyboard or from a text file.

The use of `Scanner` for reading from a text file is illustrated in Display 10.3, which contains a program that reads three numbers and a line of text from a text file named `morestuff.txt` and writes them back to the screen. The file `morestuff.txt` is a text file that a person could have created with a text editor or that a Java program could have created using `PrintWriter`.

opening a file

The program opens the `Scanner` stream and connects it to the text file `morestuff.txt` as follows:

```
Scanner inputStream = null;
    ...
inputStream =
            new Scanner(new FileInputStream("stuff.txt"));
```

The class `Scanner`, like the classes `PrintWriter`, has no constructor that takes a file name as its argument, so we need to use another class—in this case, the class `FileInputStream`—to convert the file name to an object that can be a suitable argument to the `Scanner` constructor.

Note that the methods `nextInt` and `nextLine` read from the text files in exactly the same way as they read from the keyboard. The other `Scanner` methods for reading input (given in Display 2.6 and repeated in Display 10.6) also behave the same when reading from a text file as they do when used to read from the keyboard.

Opening a Text File for Reading with Scanner

You create a stream of the class **Scanner** and connect it to a text file for reading as follows:

SYNTAX

```
Scanner Stream_Object =
            new Scanner(new FileInputStream(File_Name));
```

EXAMPLE

```
Scanner inputStream =
        new Scanner(new FileInputStream("morestuff.txt"));
```

After this statement, you can use the methods **nextInt**, **nextDouble**, **nextLine**, and so forth to read from the named text files just as you have used these methods to read from the keyboard.

When used in this way, the **FileInputStream** constructor, and hence the **Scanner** constructor invocation, can throw a **FileNotFoundException**, which is a kind of **IOException**.

FileNotFoundException

If your program attempts to open a file for reading and there is no such file, then a **FileNotFoundException** is thrown. As you saw earlier in this chapter, a **FileNotFoundException** is also thrown in some other situations. A **FileNotFoundException** is a kind of **IOException**.

Display 10.3 Reading Input from a Text File Using **Scanner** (part 1 of 2)

```java
1   import java.util.Scanner;
2   import java.io.FileInputStream;
3   import java.io.FileNotFoundException;
4
5   public class TextFileScannerDemo
6   {
7       public static void main(String[] args)
8       {
9           System.out.println("I will read three numbers and a line");
10          System.out.println("of text from the file morestuff.txt.");
11
12          Scanner inputStream = null;
13
14          try
15          {
16              inputStream =
17                  new Scanner(new FileInputStream("morestuff.txt"));
18          }
19          catch(FileNotFoundException e)
20          {
21              System.out.println("File morestuff.txt was not found");
22              System.out.println("or could not be opened.");
23              System.exit(0);
24          }
25          int n1 = inputStream.nextInt( );
26          int n2 = inputStream.nextInt( );
27          int n3 = inputStream.nextInt( );
28
29          inputStream.nextLine(); //To go to the next line
30
31          String line = inputStream.nextLine( );
32
33          System.out.println("The three numbers read from the file are:");
34          System.out.println(n1 + ", " + n2 + ", and " +  n3);
35
36          System.out.println("The line read from the file is:");
37          System.out.println(line);
38
39          inputStream.close( );
40      }
41  }
```

FILE morestuff.txt

```
1 2
3 4
Eat my shorts.
```

This file could have been made with a text editor or by another Java program.

Display 10.3   Reading Input from a Text File Using **Scanner**   (part 2 of 2)

SCREEN OUTPUT

```
I will read three numbers and a line
of text from the file morestuff.txt.
The three numbers read from the file are:
1, 2, and 3
The line read from the file is:
Eat my shorts.
```

Testing for the End of a Text File with Scanner

When using the class Scanner, if your program tries to read beyond the end of the file with any of the input methods, such as nextInt or nextLine, then the method throws an exception. If all goes well and there are no problems, such as using nextInt when the input is not a correctly formed int, then the exception thrown will be NoSuchElement-Exception. This throwing of a NoSuchElementException can be used to signal the end of input. However, there is a more robust way of testing for the end of input from a text file. Each of the input methods, such as nextInt and nextLine, has a corresponding method, such hasNextInt and hasNextLine, that checks to see if there is any more well-formed input of the appropriate type. The nice thing about these methods is that they report when there is not a suitable next token for any reason; they do not check only for the end of a file. For example, hasNextInt returns false if there is no more file input of any kind or if the next token is not a well-formed int value. It returns true if there is a well-formed int as the next token.

A sample program that illustrates the use of hasNextLine to test for the end of input is given in Display 10.4. A sample program that illustrates the use of hasNextInt to test for the end of input is given in Display 10.5. A summary of some of the methods in the Scanner class is given in Display 10.6.

Checking for the End of a Text File with Scanner

You can check for the end of input with methods such as hasNextInt, hasNextLine, and so forth.

Display 10.4   **Checking for the End of a Text File with hasNextLine** (part 1 of 2)

```java
1    import java.util.Scanner;
2    import java.io.FileInputStream;
3    import java.io.FileNotFoundException;
4    import java.io.PrintWriter;
5    import java.io.FileOutputStream;
6
7    public class HasNextLineDemo
8    {
9        public static void main(String[] args)
10       {
11           Scanner inputStream = null;
12           PrintWriter outputStream = null;
13
14           try
15           {
16               inputStream =
17                   new Scanner(new FileInputStream("original.txt"));
18               outputStream = new PrintWriter(
19                               new FileOutputStream("numbered.txt"));
20           }
21           catch(FileNotFoundException e)
22           {
23               System.out.println("Problem opening files.");
24               System.exit(0);
25           }
26
27           String line = null;
28           int count = 0;
29           while (inputStream.hasNextLine( ))
30           {
31               line = inputStream.nextLine( );
32               count++;
33               outputStream.println(count + " " + line);
34           }
35
36           inputStream.close( );
37           outputStream.close( );
38       }
39
40   }
```

```java
1    import java.util.Scanner;
2    import java.io.FileInputStream;
3    import java.io.FileNotFoundException;
4    import java.io.PrintWriter;
5    import java.io.FileOutputStream;
6
7    public class HasNextLineDemo
8    {
9        public static void main(String[] args)
10       {
11           Scanner inputStream = null;
12           PrintWriter outputStream = null;
13
14           try
15           {
16               inputStream =
17                   new Scanner(new FileInputStream("original.txt"));
18               outputStream = new PrintWriter(
19                               new FileOutputStream("numbered.txt"));
20           }
21           catch(FileNotFoundException e)
22           {
23               System.out.println("Problem opening files.");
24               System.exit(0);
25           }
26
27           String line = null;
28           int count = 0;
29           while (inputStream.hasNextLine( ))
30           {
31               line = inputStream.nextLine( );
32               count++;
33               outputStream.println(count + " " + line);
34           }
35
36           inputStream.close( );
37           outputStream.close( );
38       }
39
40   }
```

File original.txt

Little Miss Muffet
sat on a tuffet
eating her curves away.
Along came a spider
who sat down beside her
and said "Will you marry me?"

Display 10.4   Checking for the End of a Text File with **hasNextLine** (part 2 of 2)

```
File numbered.txt  (after the program is run)

    1 Little Miss Muffet
    2 sat on a tuffet
    3 eating her curves away.
    4 Along came a spider
    5 who sat down beside her
    6 and said "Will you marry me?"
```

Display 10.5   Checking for the End of a Text File with **hasNextInt**

```java
1    import java.util.Scanner;
2    import java.io.FileInputStream;
3    import java.io.FileNotFoundException;

4    public class HasNextIntDemo
5    {
6        public static void main(String[] args)
7        {
8            Scanner inputStream = null;

9            try
10           {
11               inputStream =
12                   new Scanner(new FileInputStream("data.txt"));
13           }
14           catch(FileNotFoundException e)
15           {
16               System.out.println("File data.txt was not found");
17               System.out.println("or could not be opened.");
18               System.exit(0);
19           }

20           int next, sum = 0;
21           while (inputStream.hasNextInt( ))
22           {
23               next = inputStream.nextInt( );
24               sum = sum + next;
25           }

26           inputStream.close( );

27           System.out.println("The sum of the numbers is " + sum);
28       }
29   }
```

```
File data.txt

    1  2
    3  4 hi 5
```

Reading ends when either the end of the file is reach or a token that is not an int is reached. So, the 5 is never read.

SCREEN OUTPUT

```
The sum of the numbers is 10
```

Display 10.6 Methods in the Class **Scanner** (part 1 of 4)

Scanner is in the **java.util** package.

public **Scanner(InputStream streamObject)**

There is no constructor that accepts a file name as an argument. If you want to create a stream using a file name, you can use

new **Scanner(new FileInputStream(**_File_Name_**))**

When used in this way, the **FileInputStream** constructor, and thus the **Scanner** constructor invocation, can throw a **FileNotFoundException**, which is a kind of **IOException**.

To create a stream connected to the keyboard, use

new **Scanner(System.in)**

public **Scanner(File fileObject)**

The **File** class will be covered in the section entitled "The **File** Class," later in this chapter. We discuss it here so that you will have a more complete reference in this display, but you can ignore this entry until after you've read that section.

If you want to create a stream using a file name, you can use

new **Scanner(new File(**_File_Name_**))**

public int **nextInt()**

Returns the next token as an **int**, provided the next token is a well-formed string representation of an **int**.

Throws a **NoSuchElementException** if there are no more tokens.

Throws an **InputMismatchException** if the next token is not a well-formed string representation of an **int**.

Throws an **IllegalStateException** if the **Scanner** stream is closed.

public boolean **hasNextInt()**

Returns **true** if the next token is a well-formed string representation of an **int**; otherwise returns **false**.

Throws an **IllegalStateException** if the **Scanner** stream is closed.

public long **nextLong()**

Returns the next token as a **long**, provided the next token is a well-formed string representation of a **long**.

Throws a **NoSuchElementException** if there are no more tokens.

Throws an **InputMismatchException** if the next token is not a well-formed string representation of a **long**.

Throws an **IllegalStateException** if the **Scanner** stream is closed.

Display 10.6   **Methods in the Class Scanner** (part 2 of 4)

```
public boolean hasNextLong()
```

Returns **true** if the next token is a well-formed string representation of a **long**; otherwise returns **false**.

Throws an **IllegalStateException** if the **Scanner** stream is closed.

```
public byte nextByte()
```

Returns the next token as a **byte**, provided the next token is a well-formed string representation of a **byte**.

Throws a **NoSuchElementException** if there are no more tokens.

Throws an **InputMismatchException** if the next token is not a well-formed string representation of a **byte**.

Throws an **IllegalStateException** if the **Scanner** stream is closed.

```
public boolean hasNextByte()
```

Returns **true** if the next token is a well-formed string representation of a **byte**; otherwise returns **false**.

Throws an **IllegalStateException** if the **Scanner** stream is closed.

```
public short nextShort()
```

Returns the next token as a **short**, provided the next token is a well-formed string representation of a **short**.

Throws a **NoSuchElementException** if there are no more tokens.

Throws an **InputMismatchException** if the next token is not a well-formed string representation of a **short**.

Throws an **IllegalStateException** if the **Scanner** stream is closed.

```
public boolean hasNextShort()
```

Returns **true** if the next token is a well-formed string representation of a **short**; otherwise returns **false**.

Throws an **IllegalStateException** if the **Scanner** stream is closed.

```
public double nextDouble()
```

Returns the next token as a **double**, provided the next token is a well-formed string representation of a **double**.

Throws a **NoSuchElementException** if there are no more tokens.

Throws an **InputMismatchException** if the next token is not a well-formed string representation of a **double**.

Throws an **IllegalStateException** if the **Scanner** stream is closed.

(continued)

Display 10.6 Methods in the Class **Scanner** (part 3 of 4)

public boolean **hasNextDouble()**

Returns **true** if the next token is a well-formed string representation of a **double**; otherwise returns **false**.

Throws an **IllegalStateException** if the **Scanner** stream is closed.

public float **nextFloat()**

Returns the next token as a **float**, provided the next token is a well-formed string representation of a **float**.

Throws a **NoSuchElementException** if there are no more tokens.

Throws an **InputMismatchException** if the next token is not a well-formed string representation of a **float**.

Throws an **IllegalStateException** if the **Scanner** stream is closed.

public boolean **hasNextFloat()**

Returns **true** if the next token is a well-formed string representation of a **float**; otherwise returns **false**.

Throws an **IllegalStateException** if the **Scanner** stream is closed.

public String **next()**

Returns the next token.

Throws a **NoSuchElementException** if there are no more tokens.

Throws an **IllegalStateException** if the **Scanner** stream is closed.

public boolean **hasNext()**

Returns **true** if there is another token. May wait for a next token to enter the stream.

Throws an **IllegalStateException** if the **Scanner** stream is closed.

public boolean **nextBoolean()**

Returns the next token as a **boolean** value, provided the next token is a well-formed string representation of a **boolean**.

Throws a **NoSuchElementException** if there are no more tokens.

Throws an **InputMismatchException** if the next token is not a well-formed string representation of a **boolean** value.

Throws an **IllegalStateException** if the **Scanner** stream is closed.

Display 10.6 **Methods in the Class Scanner** (part 4 of 4)

public boolean **hasNextBoolean()**

Returns **true** if the next token is a well-formed string representation of a **boolean** value; otherwise returns **false**.

Throws an **IllegalStateException** if the **Scanner** stream is closed.

public String **nextLine()**

Returns the rest of the current input line. Note that the line terminator '**\n**' is read and discarded; it is not included in the string returned.

Throws a **NoSuchElementException** if there are no more lines.

Throws an **IllegalStateException** if the **Scanner** stream is closed.

public boolean **hasNextLine()**

Returns **true** if there is a next line. May wait for a next line to enter the stream.

Throws an **IllegalStateException** if the **Scanner** stream is closed.

public Scanner **useDelimiter(String newDelimiter);**

Changes the delimiter for input so that **newDelimiter** will be the only delimiter that separates words or numbers. See the subsection "Other Input Delimiters" in Chapter 2 for the details. (You can use this method to set the delimiters to a more complex pattern than just a single string, but we are not covering that.)

Returns the calling object, but we have always used it as a **void** method.

Unchecked Exceptions

The exception classes **NoSuchElementException**, **InputMismatchException**, and **IllegalStateException** are all unchecked exceptions, which means that an exception of any of these classes is not required to be caught or declared in a throws clause.

Self-Test Exercises

8. Write some code that will create a stream named **fileIn** that is a member of the class **Scanner**. It should connect the stream to a text file named **sally** so that your program can read input from the text file **sally**.

9. Might the method **nextInt** in the class **Scanner** throw an exception? If so, what type of exception?

10. If the method **hasNextInt** returns **false**, does that mean that reading has reached the end of the file?

(continued)

Self-Test Exercises

11. Might the following throw an exception that needs to be caught or declared in a throws clause?

```java
Scanner inputStream =
        new Scanner(new FileInputStream("morestuff.txt"));
```

(The stream `inputStream` would be used to read from the text file `morestuff.txt`.)

Reading a Text File Using `BufferedReader`

Buffered-Reader

Until the `Scanner` class was introduced with version 5.0 of Java, the class `Buffered-Reader` was the preferred stream class to use for reading from a text file. It is still a commonly used class for reading from a text file. The use of `BufferedReader` is illustrated in Display 10.7, which contains a program that reads two lines from a text file named `morestuff2.txt` and writes them back to the screen. The file `morestuff2.txt` is a text file that a person could have created with a text editor or that a Java program could have created using `PrintWriter`.

opening a file

The program opens the text file `morestuff2.txt` as follows:

```java
BufferedReader inputStream =
        new BufferedReader(new FileReader("morestuff2.txt"));
```

The class `BufferedReader`, like the classes `PrintWriter` and `Scanner`, has no constructor that takes a file name as its argument, so we need to use another class—in this case, the class `FileReader`—to convert the file name to an object that can be an argument to `BufferedReader`.

readLine

An object of the class `BufferedReader` that is connected to a text file, as in Display 10.7, has a method named `readLine` that is like the method `nextLine` of the `Scanner` class. This use of `readLine` to read from a text file is illustrated in Display 10.7.

Display 10.8 describes some of the methods in the class `BufferedReader`. Notice that there are only two methods for reading from a text file, `readLine` and `read`. We have already discussed `readLine`.

Display 10.7 Reading Input from a Text File Using **BufferedReader** (part 1 of 2)

```java
1   import java.io.BufferedReader;
2   import java.io.FileReader;
3   import java.io.FileNotFoundException;
4   import java.io.IOException;

5   public class TextFileInputDemo
6   {
7       public static void main(String[] args)
8       {
```

Display 10.7   Reading Input from a Text File Using **BufferedReader** (part 2 of 2)

```
 9          try
10          {
11              BufferedReader inputStream =
12                  new BufferedReader(new FileReader("morestuff2.txt"));

13              String line = inputStream.readLine();
14              System.out.println(
15                          "The first line read from the file is:");
16              System.out.println(line);

18              line = inputStream.readLine();
19              System.out.println(
20                          "The second line read from the file is:");
21              System.out.println(line);
22              inputStream.close();
23          }
24          catch(FileNotFoundException e)
25          {
26              System.out.println("File morestuff2.txt was not found");
27              System.out.println("or could not be opened.");
28          }
29          catch(IOException e)
30          {
31              System.out.println("Error reading from morestuff2.txt.");
32          }
33      }
34  }
```

FILE morestuff2.txt

```
1 2 3
Jack jump over
the candle stick.
```

This file could have been made with a text editor or by another Java program.

SCREEN OUTPUT

```
The first line read from the file is:
1 2 3
The second line read from the file is:
Jack jump over
```

Opening a Text File for Reading with `BufferedReader`

You create a stream of the class `BufferedReader` and connect it to a text file for reading as follows:

SYNTAX

```
BufferedReader Stream_Object =
            new BufferedReader(new FileReader(File_Name));
```

EXAMPLE

```
BufferedReader inputStream =
        new BufferedReader(new FileReader("morestuff2.txt"));
```

After this statement, you can use the methods `readLine` and `read` to read from the file.

When used in this way, the `FileReader` constructor, and hence the `BufferedReader` constructor invocation, can throw a `FileNotFoundException`, which is a kind of `IOException`.

Display 10.8 **Some Methods of the Class `BufferedReader`** (part 1 of 2)

`BufferedReader` and `FileReader` are in the `java.io` package.

```
public BufferedReader(Reader readerObject)
```

This is the only constructor you are likely to need. There is no constructor that accepts a file name as an argument. If you want to create a stream using a file name, you use

```
new BufferedReader(new FileReader(File_Name))
```

When used in this way, the `FileReader` constructor, and thus the `BufferedReader` constructor invocation, can throw a `FileNotFoundException`, which is a kind of `IOException`.

The `File` class will be covered in the section entitled "The `File` Class." We discuss it here so that you will have a more complete reference in this display, but you can ignore the following reference to the class `File` until after you've read that section.

If you want to create a stream using an object of the class `File`, you use

```
new BufferedReader(new FileReader(File_Object))
```

When used in this way, the `FileReader` constructor, and thus the `BufferedReader` constructor invocation, can throw a `FileNotFoundException`, which is a kind of `IOException`.

```
public String readLine() throws IOException
```

Reads a line of input from the input stream and returns that line. If the read goes beyond the end of the file, `null` is returned. (Note that an `EOFException` is not thrown at the end of a file. The end of a file is signaled by returning `null`.)

Display 10.8   Some Methods of the Class **BufferedReader** (part 2 of 2)

```
public int read() throws IOException
```

Reads a single character from the input stream and returns that character as an `int` value. If the read goes beyond the end of the file, then −1 is returned. Note that the value is returned as an `int`. To obtain a `char`, you must perform a type cast on the value returned. The end of a file is signaled by returning −1. (All of the "real" characters return a positive integer.)

```
public long skip(long n) throws IOException
```

Skips **n** characters.

```
public void close() throws IOException
```

Closes the stream's connection to a file.

read method   The method `read` reads a single character. But note that `read` returns a value of type `int` that corresponds to the character read; it does not return the character itself. Thus, to get the character, you must use a type cast, as in

```
char next = (char)(inputStream.read());
```

If `inputStream` is in the class `BufferedReader` and is connected to a text file, this will set `next` equal to the first character in the file that has not yet been read.

Notice that the program in Display 10.7 catches two kinds of exceptions: `FileNot-FoundException` and `IOException`. An attempt to open the file may throw a `FileNot-FoundException`, and any of the invocations of `inputStream.readLine()` may throw an `IOException`. Because `FileNotFoundException` is a kind of `IOException`, you could use only the `catch` block for `IOException`. However, if you were to do this, then you would get less information if an exception were thrown. If you use only one `catch` block and an exception is thrown, you will not know if the problem occurred when opening the file or when reading from the file after it was opened.

Self-Test Exercises

12. Write some code that will create a stream named `fileIn` that is a member of the class `BufferedReader` and that connects the stream to a text file named `joe` so that your program can read input from the text file `joe`.

13. What is the type of a value returned by the method `readLine` in the class `BufferedReader`? What is the type of a value returned by the method `read` in the class `BufferedReader`?

14. Might the methods `read` and `readLine` in the class `BufferedReader` throw an exception? If so, what type of exception?

(continued)

Self-Test Exercises

15. One difference between the `try` blocks in Display 10.1 and Display 10.7 is that the `try` block in Display 10.1 encloses only the opening of the file, while the `try` block in Display 10.7 encloses most of the action in the program. Why is the `try` block in Display 10.7 larger than the one in Display 10.1?

16. Might the following throw an exception that needs to be caught or declared in a `throws` clause?

```
BufferedReader inputStream =
    new BufferedReader(new FileReader("morestuff2.txt"));
```

(The stream `inputStream` would be used to read from the text file `morestuff2.txt`.)

TIP: Reading Numbers with `BufferedReader`

Unlike the `Scanner` class, the class `BufferedReader` has no methods to read a number from a text file. You must write your code to read the number as a string and convert the string to a value of a numeric type, such as `int` or `double`. To read a single number on a line by itself, read it using the method `readLine` and then use `Integer.parseInt`, `Double.parseDouble`, or some similar method to convert the string read to a number. If there are multiple numbers on a single line, read the line using `readLine` and then use the `StringTokenizer` class to decompose the string into tokens. Then use `Integer.parseInt` or a similar method to convert each token to a number.

`Integer.parseInt`, `Double.parseDouble`, and similar methods to convert strings to numbers are explained in Chapter 5 in the subsection entitled "Wrapper Classes." The `StringTokenizer` class is discussed in Chapter 4 in the starred subsection entitled "The `StringTokenizer` Class." ∎

Testing for the End of a Text File with `BufferedReader`

When using the class `BufferedReader`, if your program tries to read beyond the end of the file with either of the methods `readLine` or `read`, then the method returns a special value to signal that the end of the file has been reached. When `readLine` tries to read beyond the end of a file, it returns the value `null`. Thus, your program can test for the end of the file by testing to see if `readLine` returns `null`. This technique is illustrated in Display 10.9. When the method `read` tries to read beyond the end of a file, it returns the value −1. Because the `int` value corresponding to each ordinary character is positive, this can be used to test for the end of a file.

Checking for the End of a Text File with BufferedReader

The method **readLine** of the class **BufferedReader** returns **null** when it tries to read beyond the end of a text file. The method **read** of the class **BufferedReader** returns −1 when it tries to read beyond the end of a text file.

Display 10.9   Checking for the End of a Text File with **BufferedReader** (part 1 of 2)

```
1   import java.io.BufferedReader;
2   import java.io.FileReader;
3   import java.io.PrintWriter;
4   import java.io.FileOutputStream;
5   import java.io.FileNotFoundException;
6   import java.io.IOException;

7   /**
8    Makes numbered.txt the same as original.txt, but with each line numbered.
9   */
10  public class TextEOFDemo
11  {
12      public static void main(String[] args)
13      {
14          try
15          {
16              BufferedReader inputStream =
17                      new BufferedReader(new FileReader("original.txt"));
18              PrintWriter outputStream =
19                      new PrintWriter(new FileOutputStream("numbered.txt"));

20              int count = 0;
21              String line = inputStream.readLine();
22              while (line != null)
23              {
24                  count++;
25                  outputStream.println(count + " " + line);
26                  line = inputStream.readLine();
27               }
28              inputStream.close();
29              outputStream.close();
30          }
31          catch(FileNotFoundException e)
32          {
```

(continued)

Display 10.9 Checking for the End of a Text File with **BufferedReader** (part 2 of 2)

```
33                  System.out.println("Problem opening files.");
34          }
35          catch(IOException e)
36          {
37                  System.out.println("Error reading from original.txt.");
38          }
39      }
40  }
```

FILE original.txt

```
Little Miss Muffet
sat on a tuffet
eating her curves away.
Along came a spider
who sat down beside her
and said "Will you marry me?"
```

FILE numbered.txt (after the program is run)

```
1 Little Miss Muffet
2 sat on a tuffet
3 eating her curves away.
4 Along came a spider
5 who sat down beside her
6 and said "Will you marry me?"
```

If your version of numbered.txt *has numbered blank lines after 6, that means you had blank lines at the end of* original.txt.

Self-Test Exercises

17. Does the class BufferedReader have a method to read an int value from a text file?

18. What happens when the method readLine in the class BufferedReader attempts to read beyond the end of a file? How can you use this to test for the end of a file?

19. What is the type of the value returned by the method read in the class Buffered-Reader?

20. What happens when the method read in the class BufferedReader attempts to read beyond the end of a file? How can you use this to test for the end of a file?

21. Does the program in Display 10.9 work correctly if original.txt is an empty file?

Path Names

When giving a file name as an argument to a constructor for opening a file in any of the ways we have discussed, you may use a simple file name, in which case it is assumed that the file is in the same directory (folder) as the one in which the program is run. You can also use a full or relative path name.

path names
A **path name** not only gives the name of the file, but also tells what directory (folder) the file is in. A **full path name**, as the name suggests, gives a complete path name, starting from the root directory. A **relative path name** gives the path to the file, starting with the directory that your program is in. The way that you specify path names depends on your particular operating system.

A typical UNIX path name is

```
/user/sallyz/data/data.txt
```

To create a BufferedReader input stream connected to this file, you use

```
BufferedReader inputStream =
        new BufferedReader(new FileReader("/user/sallyz/data/data.txt"));
```

Windows uses \ instead of / in path names. A typical Windows path name is

```
C:\dataFiles\goodData\data.txt
```

To create a BufferedReader input stream connected to this file, you use

```
BufferedReader inputStream =
    new BufferedReader(
        new FileReader("C:\\dataFiles\\goodData\\data.txt"));
```

using \,
\\, or /
Note that you need to use \\ in place of \, since otherwise Java will interpret a backslash paired with a character, such as \d, as an escape character. Although you must worry about using a backslash (\) in a quoted string, this problem does not occur with path names read in from the keyboard.

One way to avoid these escape-character problems altogether is to always use UNIX conventions when writing path names. A Java program will accept a path name written in either Windows or UNIX format, even if it is run on a computer with an operating system that does not match the syntax. Thus, an alternate way to create a BufferedReader input stream connected to the Windows file

```
C:\dataFiles\goodData\data.txt
```

is the following:

```
BufferedReader inputStream =
    new BufferedReader(
        new FileReader("C:/dataFiles/goodData/data.txt"));
```

Nested Constructor Invocations

Expressions with two constructors, such as the following, are common when dealing with Java's library of I/O classes:

```
new BufferedReader(new FileReader("original.txt"))
```

This is a manifestation of the general approach to how Java I/O libraries work. Each I/O class serves one or a small number of functions. To obtain full functionality you normally need to combine two (or more) class constructors. For example, in the above example, the object `new FileReader("original.txt")` establishes a connection with the file `original.txt` but provides only very primitive methods for input. The constructor for `BufferedReader` takes this file reader object and adds a richer collection of input methods. In these cases the inner object, such as `new FileReader("original.txt")`, is transformed into an instance variable of the outer object, such as `BufferedReader`.

Self-Test Exercises

22. Of the classes `PrintWriter`, `Scanner`, `BufferedReader`, `FileReader`, and `FileOutputStream`, which have a constructor that accepts a file name as an argument so that the stream created by the constructor invocation is connected to the named file?

23. Is the following legal?

```
FileReader readerObject =
            new FileReader("myFile.txt");
BufferedReader inputStream =
            new BufferedReader(readerObject);
```

`System.in`, `System.out`, and `System.err`

The streams `System.in`, `System.out`, and `System.err` are three streams that are automatically available to your Java code. You have already been using `System.in` and `System.out`. `System.err` is just like `System.out`, except that it has a different name. For example, both of the following statements will send the string `"Hello"` to the screen so the screen receives two lines each containing `"Hello"`:

```
System.out.println("Hello");
System.err.println("Hello");
```

The output stream `System.out` is intended to be used for normal output from code that is not in trouble. `System.err` is meant to be used for error messages.

redirecting output
Having two different standard output streams can be handy when you redirect output. For example, you can redirect the regular output to one file and redirect the error messages to a different file. Java allows you to redirect any of these three standard streams to or from a file (or other I/O device). This is done with the static methods `setIn`, `setOut`, and `setErr` of the class `System`.

For example, suppose your code connects the output stream `errStream` (of a type to be specified later) to a text file. You can then redirect the stream `System.err` to this text file as follows:

```
System.setErr(errStream);
```

If the following appears later in your code:

```
System.out.println("Hello from System.out.");
System.err.println("Hello from System.err.");
```

then "Hello from System.out." will be written to the screen, but "Hello from System.err." will be written to the file connected to the output stream errStream. A simple program illustrating this is given in Display 10.10.

Note that the arguments to the redirecting methods must be of the types shown in the following headings, and these are classes we do not discuss in this book:

```
public static void setIn(InputStream inStream)
public static void setOut(PrintStream outStream)
public static void setErr(PrintStream outStream)
```

None of the input or output streams we constructed in our previous programs are of a type suitable to be an argument to any of these redirection methods. Space constraints keep us from giving any more details on the stream classes that are suitable for producing arguments for these redirection methods. However, you can use Display 10.10 as a model to allow you to redirect either System.err or System.out to a text file of your choice.

Self-Test Exercises

24. Suppose you want the program in Display 10.10 to send an error message to the screen and regular (System.out) output to the file errormessages.txt. (Just the reverse of what the program in Display 10.10 does.) How would you change the program in Display 10.10?

25. Suppose you want the program in Display 10.10 to send all output (both System.out and System.err) to the file errormessages.txt. How would you change the program in Display 10.10?

Display 10.10 **Redirecting Error Messages** (part 1 of 2)

```
1   import java.io.PrintStream;
2   import java.io.FileOutputStream;
3   import java.io.FileNotFoundException;

4   public class RedirectionDemo
5   {
6       public static void main(String[] args)
7       {
8           PrintStream errStream = null;
9           try
10          {
```

(continued)

Display 10.10 Redirecting Error Messages (part 2 of 2)

```
11          errStream =
12              new PrintStream(
13                      new FileOutputStream("errormessages.txt"));
14      }
15      catch(FileNotFoundException e)
16      {
17          System.out.println(
18                  "Error opening file with FileOutputStream.");
19          System.exit(0);
20      }

21      System.setErr(errStream);

22      System.err.println("Hello from System.err.");
23      System.out.println("Hello from System.out.");
24      System.err.println("Hello again from System.err.");

25      errStream.close();
26  }
27 }
```

Note the stream classes used.

None of System.in, System.out, *or* System.err *needs to be closed, but the streams you create should be explicitly closed.*

FILE errormessages.txt

```
Hello from System.err.
Hello again from System.err.
```

SCREEN OUTPUT

```
Hello from System.out.
```

10.3 The File Class

The scars of others should teach us caution.

SAINT JEROME

In this section we describe the class File, which is not really an I/O stream class but is often used in conjunction with file I/O. The class File is so important to file I/O programming that it was even placed in the java.io package.

Programming with the File Class

The File class contains methods that allow you to check various properties of a file, such whether there is a file with a specified name, whether the file can be written to, and so forth. Display 10.11 gives a sample program that uses the class `File` with text files. (The class `File` works the same with binary files as it does with text files.)

abstract name   Note that the `File` class constructor takes a name, known as the **abstract name**, as an (string) argument. So the `File` class really checks properties of names. For example, the method `exists` tests whether there is a file with the abstract name. Moreover, the abstract name may be a potential directory (folder) name. For example, the method `isDirectory` tests whether the abstract name is the name of a directory (folder). The abstract name may be either a relative path name (which includes the case of a simple file name) or a full path name.

Display 10.12 lists some of the methods in the class `File`.

The File Class

The `File` class is like a wrapper class for file names. The constructor for the class `File` takes a string as an argument and produces an object that can be thought of as the file with that name. You can use the `File` object and methods of the class `File` to answer questions, such as: Does the file exist? Does your program have permission to read the file? Does your program have permission to write to the file? Display 10.14 has a summary of some of the methods for the class `File`.

EXAMPLE

```
File fileObject = new File("data.txt");
if ( ! fileObject.canRead())
    System.out.println("File data.txt is not readable.");
```

Display 10.11   Using the **File** Class (part 1 of 2)

```
1   import java.util.Scanner;
2   import java.io.File;
3   import java.io.PrintWriter;
4   import java.io.FileOutputStream;
5   import java.io.FileNotFoundException;

6   public class FileClassDemo
7   {
8       public static void main(String[] args)
9       {
10          Scanner keyboard = new Scanner(System.in);
11          String line = null;
12          String fileName = null;

13          System.out.println("I will store a line of text for you.");
14          System.out.println("Enter the line of text:");
15          line = keyboard.nextLine();
```

(continued)

Display 10.11   Using the **File** Class (part 2 of 2)

```
16              System.out.println("Enter a file name to hold the line:");
17              fileName = keyboard.nextLine();
18              File fileObject = new File(fileName);
19
20              while (fileObject.exists())
21              {
22                  System.out.println("There already is a file named "
23                                                  + fileName);
24                  System.out.println("Enter a different file name:");
25                  fileName = keyboard.nextLine();
26                  fileObject = new File(fileName);
27              }
28               PrintWriter outputStream = null;      If you wish, you can use fileObject
29              try                                    instead of fileName as the argument to
30              {                                      FileOutputStream.
31                  outputStream =
32                      new PrintWriter(new FileOutputStream(fileName));
33              }
34              catch(FileNotFoundException e)
35              {
36                  System.out.println("Error opening the file " + fileName);
37                  System.exit(0);
38              }
39
40              System.out.println("Writing \""  + line + "\"");
41              System.out.println("to the file "  + fileName);
                outputStream.println(line);
42
43              outputStream.close();
44              System.out.println("Writing completed.");
45          }
    }
```

Sample Dialogue

The dialogue assumes that there already is a file named myLine.txt but that there is no file named mySaying.txt.

```
I will store a line of text for you.
Enter the line of text:
May the hair on your toes grow long and curly.
Enter a file name to hold the line:
myLine.txt
There already is a file named myLine.txt
Enter a different file name:
mySaying.txt
Writing "May the hair on your toes grow long and curly."
to the file mySaying.txt
Writing completed.
```

Display 10.12   **Some Methods in the Class File** (part 1 of 2)

File is in the `java.io` package.

    `public File(String` *File_Name*`)`

Constructor. *File_Name* can be either a full or a relative path name (which includes the case of a simple file name). *File_Name* is referred to as the **abstract path name**.

    `public boolean exists()`

Tests whether there is a file with the abstract path name.

    `public boolean canRead()`

Tests whether the program can read from the file. Returns **true** if the file named by the abstract path name exists and is readable by the program; otherwise returns **false**.

    `public boolean setReadOnly()`

Sets the file represented by the abstract path name to be read only. Returns **true** if successful; otherwise returns **false**.

    `public boolean canWrite()`

Tests whether the program can write to the file. Returns **true** if the file named by the abstract path name exists and is writable by the program; otherwise returns **false**.

    `public boolean delete()`

Tries to delete the file or directory named by the abstract path name. A directory must be empty to be removed. Returns **true** if it was able to delete the file or directory. Returns **false** if it was unable to delete the file or directory.

    `public boolean createNewFile() throws IOException`

Creates a new empty file named by the abstract path name, provided that a file of that name does not already exist. Returns **true** if successful, and returns **false** otherwise.

    `public String getName()`

Returns the last name in the abstract path name (that is, the simple file name). Returns the empty string if the abstract path name is the empty string.

    `public String getPath()`

Returns the abstract path name as a `String` value.

    `public boolean renameTo(File` *New_Name*`)`

Renames the file represented by the abstract path name to *New_Name*. Returns **true** if successful; otherwise returns **false**. *New_Name* can be a relative or absolute path name. This may require moving the file. Whether or not the file can be moved is system dependent.

Display 10.12 **Some Methods in the Class File** (part 2 of 2)

`public boolean isFile()`

Returns **true** if a file exists that is named by the abstract path name and the file is a normal file; otherwise returns **false**. The meaning of *normal* is system dependent. Any file created by a Java program is guaranteed to be normal.

`public boolean isDirectory()`

Returns **true** if a directory (folder) exists that is named by the abstract path name; otherwise returns **false**.

`public boolean mkdir()`

Makes a directory named by the abstract path name. Will not create parent directories. See **mkdirs**. Returns **true** if successful; otherwise returns **false**.

`public boolean mkdirs()`

Makes a directory named by the abstract path name. Will create any necessary but nonexistent parent directories. Returns **true** if successful; otherwise returns **false**. Note that if it fails, then some of the parent directories may have been created.

`public long length()`

Returns the length in bytes of the file named by the abstract path name. If the file does not exist or the abstract path name names a directory, then the value returned is not specified and may be anything.

Self-Test Exercises

26. Write a complete (although simple) Java program that tests whether or not the directory (folder) containing the program also contains a file named `Sally.txt`. The program has no input and the only output tells whether or not there is a file named `Sally.txt`.

27. Write a complete Java program that asks the user for a file name, tests whether the file exists, and, if the file exists, asks the user whether or not it should be deleted. It then either deletes or does not delete the file as the user requests.

10.4 Binary Files ★

A little more than kin, and less than kind.

WILLIAM SHAKESPEARE, *Hamlet*

Binary files store data in the same format that is used in the computer's memory to store the values of variables. For example, a value of type int is stored as the same sequence of bytes (same sequence of zeros and ones) whether it is stored in an `int` variable in memory or in a binary file. So, no conversion of any kind needs to be performed when you store or retrieve a value in a binary file. This is why binary files can be handled more efficiently than text files.

Java binary files are unlike binary files in other programming languages in that they are portable. A binary file created by a Java program can be moved from one computer to another and still be read by a Java program—but only by a Java program. They cannot normally be read with a text editor or with a program written in any programming language other than Java.

The preferred stream classes for processing binary files are `ObjectInputStream` and `ObjectOutputStream`. Each has methods to read or write data one byte at a time. These streams can also automatically convert numbers and characters to bytes that can be stored in a binary file. They allow your program to be written as if the data placed in the file, or read from the file, were not just bytes but were strings or items of any of Java's primitive data types, such as `int`, `char`, and `double`, or even objects of classes you define. If you do not need to access your files using an editor, then the easiest and most efficient way to read data from and write data to files is to use binary files in the way we describe here.

We conclude this section with a discussion of how you can use `ObjectOutput-Stream` and `ObjectInputStream` to write and later read objects of any class you define. This will let you store objects of the classes you define in binary files and later read them back, all with the same convenience and efficiency that you get when storing strings and primitive type data in binary files.

Writing Simple Data to a Binary File

The class `ObjectOutputStream` is the preferred stream class for writing to a binary file.[2] An object of the class `ObjectOutputStream` has methods to write strings and values of any of the primitive types to a binary file. Display 10.13 shows a sample program that writes values of type `int` to a binary file. Display 10.14 describes the methods used for writing data of other types to a binary file.

Display 10.13 **Writing to a Binary File** (part 1 of 2)

```
1   import java.io.ObjectOutputStream;
2   import java.io.FileOutputStream;
3   import java.io.IOException;

4   public class BinaryOutputDemo
5   {
6       public static void main(String[] args)
7       {                                                    (continued)
```

---

[2] `DataOutputStream` is also widely used and behaves exactly as we describe for `ObjectOutputStream` in this section. However, the techniques given in the subsections "Binary I/O of Objects" and "Array Objects in Binary Files" only work for `ObjectOutputStream`; they do not work for `DataOutputStream`.

Display 10.13 **Writing to a Binary File** (part 2 of 2)

```
 8          try
 9          {
10              ObjectOutputStream outputStream =
11                  new ObjectOutputStream(new FileOutputStream("numbers.dat"));

12              int i;
13              for (i = 0; i < 5; i++)
14                  outputStream.writeInt(i);

15              System.out.println("Numbers written to the file numbers.dat.");
16              outputStream.close();
17          }
18          catch(IOException e)
19          {
20              System.out.println("Problem with file output.");
21          }
22      }
23  }
```

FILE REPRESENTATION (after program is run)

0
1
2
3
4

This is a binary file. It really contains representations of each number as bytes, that is, zeros and ones, and is read as bytes. You cannot read this file with your text editor.

Display 10.14 **Some Methods in the Class ObjectOutputStream** (part 1 of 2)

ObjectOutputStream and **FileOutputStream** are in the **java.io** package.

    public ObjectOutputStream(OutputStream streamObject)

There is no constructor that takes a file name as an argument. If you want to create a stream using a file name, you use

    new ObjectOutputStream(new FileOutputStream(*File_Name*))

This creates a blank file. If there already is a file named *File_Name*, then the old contents of the file are lost.

If you want to create a stream using an object of the class **File**, you use

    new ObjectOutputStream(new FileOutputStream(*File_Object*))

The constructor for **FileOutputStream** may throw a **FileNotFoundException**, which is a kind of **IOException**. If the **FileOutputStream** constructor succeeds, then the constructor for **ObjectOutputStream** may throw a different **IOException**.

Display 10.14 Some Methods in the Class `ObjectOutputStream` (part 2 of 2)

public void **writeInt**(int n) throws IOException

Writes the **int** value n to the output stream.

public void **writeShort**(short n) throws IOException

Writes the **short** value n to the output stream.

public void **writeLong**(long n) throws IOException

Writes the **long** value n to the output stream.

public void **writeDouble**(double x) throws IOException

Writes the **double** value x to the output stream.

public void **writeFloat**(float x) throws IOException

Writes the **float** value x to the output stream.

public void **writeChar**(int n) throws IOException

Writes the **char** value n to the output stream. Note that it expects its argument to be an **int** value. However, if you simply use the **char** value, then Java will automatically type cast it to an **int** value. The following are equivalent:

```
outputStream.writeChar((int)'A');
```

and

```
outputStream.writeChar('A');
```

public void **writeBoolean**(boolean b) throws IOException

Writes the **boolean** value b to the output stream.

public void **writeUTF**(String aString) throws IOException

Writes the **String** value aString to the output stream. UTF refers to a particular method of encoding the string. To read the string back from the file, you should use the method **readUTF** of the class `ObjectInputStream`.

public void **writeObject**(Object anObject) throws IOException

Writes its argument to the output stream. The object argument should be an object of a serializable class, a concept discussed later in this chapter. Throws various `IOException`s.

public void **close**() throws IOException

Closes the stream's connection to a file. This method calls **flush** before closing the file.

public void **flush**() throws IOException

Flushes the output stream. This forces an actual physical write to the file of any data that has been buffered and not yet physically written to the file. Normally, you should not need to invoke **flush**.

Notice that almost all the code in the sample program in Display 10.13 is in a try block. Any part of the code that does binary file I/O in the ways we are describing can throw an IOException.

The output stream for writing to the binary file numbers.dat is created and named with the following:

```
ObjectOutputStream outputStream =
    new ObjectOutputStream(new FileOutputStream("numbers.dat"));
```

opening a file

As with text files, this is called **opening the file**. If the file numbers.dat does not already exist, this statement will create an empty file named numbers.dat. If the file numbers.dat already exists, this statement will erase the contents of the file so that the file starts out empty. The situation is basically the same as what you learned for text files, except that we're using a different class.

As is typical of Java I/O classes, the constructor for the class ObjectOutputStream takes another I/O class object as an argument, in this case an anonymous argument of the class FileOutputStream.

Opening a Binary File for Output

You create a stream of the class ObjectOutputStream and connect it to a binary file as follows:

SYNTAX

```
ObjectOutputStream Output_Stream_Name =
    new ObjectOutputStream(new FileOutputStream(File_Name));
```

The constructor for FileOutputStream may throw a FileNotFoundException, which is a kind of IOException. If the FileOutputStream constructor succeeds, then the constructor for ObjectOutputStream may throw a different IOException. A single catch block for IOException would cover all cases.

EXAMPLES

```
ObjectOutputStream myOutputStream =
        new ObjectOutputStream(new FileOutputStream("mydata.dat"));
```

After opening the file, you can use the methods of the class ObjectOutputStream (Display 10.14) to write to the file.

The class ObjectOutputStream does not have a method named println, as we had with text file output and screen output. However, as shown in Display 10.13, an object of the class ObjectOutputStream does have a method named writeInt that can write a single int value to a file, and it also has the other output methods described in Display 10.14.

writeInt

In Display 10.13, we made it look as though the numbers in the file numbers.dat were written one per line in a human-readable form. That is not what happens, however. There are no lines or other separators between the numbers. Instead, the numbers are written in the file one immediately after the other, and they are encoded as a sequence of bytes in the same way that the numbers would be encoded in the computer's main memory. These coded int values cannot be read using your editor. Realistically, they can be read only by another Java program.

You can use a stream from the class ObjectOutputStream to output values of any primitive type and also to write data of the type String. Each primitive data type has a corresponding write method in the class ObjectOutputStream. We have already mentioned the write methods for outputting int values. The methods for the other primitive types are completely analogous to writeInt. For example, the following would write a double value, a boolean value, and a char value to the binary file connected to the ObjectOutputStream object outputStream:

```
outputStream.writeDouble(9.99);
outputStream.writeBoolean(false);
outputStream.writeChar((int)'A');
```

writeChar   The method writeChar has one possibly surprising property: It expects its argument to be of type int. So if you start with a value of type char, the char value can be type cast to an int before it is given to the method writeChar. For example, to output the contents of a char variable named symbol, you can use

```
outputStream.writeChar((int)symbol);
```

In actual fact, you do not need to write in the type cast to an int, because Java automatically performs a type cast from a char value to an int value for you. So, the following is equivalent to the above invocation of writeChar:

```
outputStream.writeChar(symbol);
```

writeUTF
for strings   To output a value of type String, you use the method writeUTF. For example, if outputStream is a stream of type ObjectOutputStream, the following will write the string "Hello friend." to the file connected to that stream:

```
outputStream.writeUTF("Hello friend.");
```

You may write output of different types to the same file. So, you may write a combination of, for example, int, double, and String values. However, mixing types in a file does require special care to make it possible to read them back out of the file. To read them back, you need to know the order in which the various types appear in the file, because, as you will see, a program that reads from the file will use a different method to read data of each different type.

closing a
binary file   Note that, as illustrated in Display 10.13 and as you will see shortly, you close a binary output or input stream in the same way that you close a stream connected to a text file.

UTF and writeUTF

Recall that Java uses the Unicode character set, a set of characters that includes many characters used in languages whose character sets are different from English. Readers of this book are undoubtedly using editors and operating systems that use the ASCII character set, which is the character set normally used for English and for our Java programs. The ASCII character set is a subset of the Unicode character set, so the Unicode character set has a lot of characters you probably do not need. There is a standard way of encoding all the Unicode characters, but for English-speaking countries, it is not a very efficient coding scheme. The UTF coding scheme is an alternative scheme that still codes all Unicode characters but that favors the ASCII character set. The UTF coding method gives short, efficient codes for the ASCII characters. The price is that it gives long, inefficient codes to the other Unicode characters. However, because you probably do not use the other Unicode characters, this is a very favorable trade-off. The method `writeUTF` uses the UTF coding method to write strings to a binary file.

The method `writeInt` writes integers into a file using the same number of bytes—that is, the same number of zeros and ones—to store any integer. Similarly, the method `writeLong` uses the same number of bytes to store each value of type `long`. (But the methods `writeInt` and `writeLong` use a different number of bytes from each other.) The situation is the same for all the other write methods that write primitive types to binary files. However, the method `writeUTF` uses differing numbers of bytes to store different strings in a file. Longer strings require more bytes than shorter strings. This can present a problem to Java, because there are no separators between data items in a binary file. The way that Java manages to make this work is by writing some extra information at the start of each string. This extra information tells how many bytes are used to write the string, so `readUTF` knows how many bytes to read and convert. (The method `readUTF` will be discussed a little later in this chapter, but, as you may have already guessed, it reads a `String` value that was written using the UTF coding method.)

The situation with `writeUTF` is even a little more complicated than what we discussed in the previous paragraph. Notice that we said that the information at the start of the string code in the file tells how many *bytes* to read, *not how many characters are in the string*. These two figures are not the same. With the UTF way of encoding, different characters are encoded in different numbers of bytes. However, all the ASCII characters are stored in just one byte, and you are undoubtedly using only ASCII characters, so this difference is more theoretical than real to you now.

Reading Simple Data from a Binary File

The stream class `ObjectInputStream` is used to read from a file that has been written to using `ObjectOutputStream`. Display 10.15 gives some of the most commonly used methods for this class. If you compare that table with the methods for `ObjectOutputStream` given in Display 10.14, you will see that each output method in `ObjectOutputStream` has a corresponding input method in `ObjectInputStream`. For example, if you write an integer to a file using the method `writeInt` of `ObjectOutputStream`, then you can read that integer back with the method `readInt` of `ObjectInputStream`. If you write a number to a file using the method `writeDouble` of `ObjectOutputStream`,

Self-Test Exercises

28. How do you open the binary file `bindata.dat` so that it is connected to an output stream of type `ObjectOutputStream` that is named `outputThisWay`?

29. Give two statements that will write the values of the two `double` variables `v1` and `v2` to the file `bindata.dat`. Use the stream `outputThisWay` that you created as the answer to Self-Test Exercise 28.

30. Give a statement that will write the string value `"Hello"` to the file `bindata.dat`. Use the stream `outputThisWay` that you created as the answer to Self-Test Exercise 28.

31. Give a statement that will close the stream `outputThisWay` created as the answer to Self-Test Exercise 28.

then you can read that number back with the method `readDouble` of `ObjectInput-Stream`, and so forth. Display 10.16 gives an example of using `readInt` in this way.

Display 10.15 Some Methods in the Class `ObjectInputStream` (part 1 of 3)

The classes `ObjectInputStream` and `FileInputStream` are in the `java.io` package.

`public ObjectInputStream(InputStream streamObject)`

There is no constructor that takes a file name as an argument. If you want to create a stream using a file name, you use

`new ObjectInputStream(new FileInputStream(File_Name))`

Alternatively, you can use an object of the class `File` in place of the *File_Name*, as follows:

`new ObjectInputStream(new FileInputStream(File_Object))`

The constructor for `FileInputStream` may throw a `FileNotFoundException`, which is a kind of `IOException`. If the `FileInputStream` constructor succeeds, then the constructor for `ObjectInputStream` may throw a different `IOException`.

`public int readInt() throws IOException`

Reads an `int` value from the input stream and returns that `int` value. If `readInt` tries to read a value from the file and that value was not written using the method `writeInt` of the class `ObjectOutputStream` (or written in some equivalent way), then problems will occur. If an attempt is made to read beyond the end of the file, an `EOFException` is thrown.

`public int readShort() throws IOException`

Reads a `short` value from the input stream and returns that `short` value. If `readShort` tries to read a value from the file and that value was not written using the method `writeShort` of the class `ObjectOutputStream` (or written in some equivalent way), then problems will occur. If an attempt is made to read beyond the end of the file, an `EOFException` is thrown.

(continued)

Display 10.15   Some Methods in the Class `ObjectInputStream` (part 2 of 3)

`public long readLong() throws IOException`

Reads a **long** value from the input stream and returns that **long** value. If **readLong** tries to read a value from the file and that value was not written using the method **writeLong** of the class **ObjectOutputStream** (or written in some equivalent way), then problems will occur. If an attempt is made to read beyond the end of the file, an **EOFException** is thrown.

`public double readDouble() throws IOException`

Reads a **double** value from the input stream and returns that **double** value. If **readDouble** tries to read a value from the file and that value was not written using the method **writeDouble** of the class **ObjectOutputStream** (or written in some equivalent way), then problems will occur. If an attempt is made to read beyond the end of the file, an **EOFException** is thrown.

`public float readFloat() throws IOException`

Reads a **float** value from the input stream and returns that **float** value. If **readFloat** tries to read a value from the file and that value was not written using the method **writeFloat** of the class **ObjectOutputStream** (or written in some equivalent way), then problems will occur. If an attempt is made to read beyond the end of the file, an **EOFException** is thrown.

`public char readChar() throws IOException`

Reads a **char** value from the input stream and returns that **char** value. If **readChar** tries to read a value from the file and that value was not written using the method **writeChar** of the class **ObjectOutputStream** (or written in some equivalent way), then problems will occur. If an attempt is made to read beyond the end of the file, an **EOFException** is thrown.

`public boolean readBoolean() throws IOException`

Reads a **boolean** value from the input stream and returns that **boolean** value. If **readBoolean** tries to read a value from the file and that value was not written using the method **writeBoolean** of the class **ObjectOutputStream** (or written in some equivalent way), then problems will occur. If an attempt is made to read beyond the end of the file, an **EOFException** is thrown.

`public String readUTF() throws IOException`

Reads a **String** value from the input stream and returns that **String** value. If **readUTF** tries to read a value from the file and that value was not written using the method **writeUTF** of the class **ObjectOutputStream** (or written in some equivalent way), then problems will occur. If an attempt is made to read beyond the end of the file, an **EOFException** is thrown.

`Object readObject() throws ClassNotFoundException, IOException`

Reads an object from the input stream. The object read should have been written using **write-Object** of the class **ObjectOutputStream**. Throws a **ClassNotFoundException** if a serialized object cannot be found. If an attempt is made to read beyond the end of the file, an **EOFException** is thrown. May throw various other **IOException**s.

Display 10.15 Some Methods in the Class `ObjectInputStream` (part 3 of 3)

```
public int skipBytes(int n) throws IOException
```
Skips **n** bytes.

```
public void close() throws IOException
```
Closes the stream's connection to a file.

The input stream for reading from the binary file `numbers.dat` is opened as follows:

```
ObjectInputStream inputStream =
            new ObjectInputStream(new FileInputStream("numbers.dat"));
```

Note that this is identical to how we opened a file using `ObjectOutputStream` in Display 10.13, except that here we've used the classes `ObjectInputStream` and `FileInputStream` instead of `ObjectOutputStream` and `FileOutputStream`.

Opening a Binary File for Reading

You create a stream of the class `ObjectInputStream` and connect it to a binary file as follows:

SYNTAX
```
ObjectInputStream Input_Stream_Name =
        new ObjectInputStream(new FileInputStream(File_Name));
```

The constructor for **FileInputStream** may throw a **FileNotFoundException**, which is a kind of **IOException**. If the **FileInputStream** constructor succeeds, then the constructor for **ObjectInputStream** may throw a different **IOException**.

EXAMPLES
```
ObjectInputStream inputFile =
        new ObjectInputStream(new FileInputStream("somefile.dat"));
```

After this, you can use the methods in Display 10.15 to read from the file.

---

reading multiple types

`ObjectInputStream` allows you to read input values of different types from the same file. So, you may read a combination of, for example, `int` values, `double` values, and `String` values. However, if the next data item in the file is not of the type expected by the reading method, the result is likely to be a mess. For example, if your program writes an integer using `writeInt`, then any program that reads that integer should read it using `readInt`. If you instead use `readLong` or `readDouble`, your program will misbehave.

closing a binary file

Note that, as illustrated in Display 10.16, you close a binary input stream in the same way that you close all the other I/O streams we have seen.

Self-Test Exercises

32. Write code to open the binary file named someStuff and connect it to an ObjectInputStream object named inputThing so it is ready for reading.

33. Give a statement that will read a number of type double from the file someStuff and place the value in a variable named number. Use the stream inputThing that you created in Self-Test Exercise 32. (Assume the first thing written to the file was written using the method writeDouble of the class ObjectOutputStream and assume number is of type double.)

34. Give a statement that will close the stream inputThing created in Self-Test Exercise 32.

35. Can one program write a number to a file using writeInt and then have another program read that number using readLong? Can a program read that number using readDouble?

36. Can you use readUTF to read a string from a text file?

Display 10.16 **Reading from a Binary File** (part 1 of 2)

```
1   import java.io.ObjectInputStream;
2   import java.io.FileInputStream;
3   import java.io.IOException;
4   import java.io.FileNotFoundException;

5   public class BinaryInputDemo
6   {
7     public static void main(String[] args)
8     {
9       try
10      {
11          ObjectInputStream inputStream =
12            new ObjectInputStream(new FileInputStream("numbers.dat"));

13          System.out.println("Reading the file numbers.dat.");
14          int n1 = inputStream.readInt();
15          int n2 = inputStream.readInt();

16          System.out.println("Numbers read from file:");
17          System.out.println(n1);
18          System.out.println(n2);
19          inputStream.close();
20      }
```

Display 10.16   **Reading from a Binary File** (part 2 of 2)

```
21          catch(FileNotFoundException e)
22          {
23              System.out.println("Cannot find file numbers.dat.");
24          }
25          catch(IOException e)
26          {
27              System.out.println("Problems with input from numbers.dat.");
28          }
29          System.out.println("End of program.");
30      }
31  }
```

Sample Dialogue

```
Reading the file numbers.dat.
Numbers read from file:          Assumes the program in
0                                Display 10.13 was run to create
1                                the file numbers.dat.
End of program.
```

Checking for the End of a Binary File

EOF-
Exception

All of the `ObjectInputStream` methods that read from a binary file will throw an `EOFException` when they try to read beyond the end of a file. So your code can test for the end of a binary file by catching an `EOFException` as illustrated in Display 10.17.

In Display 10.17, the reading is placed in an "infinite loop" through the use of `true` as the Boolean expression in the `while` loop. The loop is not really infinite, because when the end of the file is reached, an exception is thrown, and that ends the entire `try` block and passes control to the `catch` block.

EOFException

If your program is reading from a binary file using any of the methods listed in Display 10.15 for the class `ObjectInputStream`, and your program attempts to read beyond the end of the file, then an `EOFException` is thrown. This can be used to end a loop that reads all the data in a file.

The class `EOFException` is a derived class of the class `IOException`. So, every exception of type `EOFException` is also of type `IOException`.

PITFALL: Checking for the End of a File in the Wrong Way

Different file-reading methods check for the end of a file in different ways. If you test for the end of a file in the wrong way, one of two things will probably happen: Your program will either go into an unintended infinite loop or terminate abnormally.

For the classes discussed in this book, the following rules apply: If your program is reading from a binary file, then an EOFException will be thrown when the reading goes beyond the end of the file. If your program is reading from a text file, then no EOFException will be thrown when reading goes beyond the end of the file. ■

Self-Test Exercises

37. When opening a binary file for output in the ways discussed in this chapter, might an exception be thrown? What kind of exception? When opening a binary file for input in the ways discussed in this chapter, might an exception be thrown? What kind of exception?

38. Suppose a binary file contains three numbers written to the file with the method writeDouble of the class ObjectOutputStream. Suppose further that your program reads all three numbers with three invocations of the method readDouble of the class ObjectInputStream. When will an EOFException be thrown? Right after reading the third number? When your program tries to read a fourth number? Some other time?

39. The following appears in the program in Display 10.17:

```
try
{
    while (true)
    {
        number = inputStream.readInt();
        System.out.println(number);
    }
}
catch(EOFException e)
{
    System.out.println("No more numbers in the file.");
}
```

Why isn't this an infinite loop?

Binary I/O of Objects

You can output objects of classes you define as easily as you output int values using writeInt, and you can later read the objects back into your program as easily as you read int values with the method readInt. For you to be able to do this, the class of objects that your code is writing and reading must implement the Serializable interface.

Display 10.17   Using **EOFException** (part 1 of 2)

```
1   import java.io.ObjectInputStream;
2   import java.io.FileInputStream;
3   import java.io.EOFException;
4   import java.io.IOException;
5   import java.io.FileNotFoundException;

6   public class EOFDemo
7   {
8       public static void main(String[] args)
9       {
10          try
11          {
12              ObjectInputStream inputStream =
13                new ObjectInputStream(new FileInputStream("numbers.dat"));
14              int number;
15              System.out.println("Reading numbers in numbers.dat");
16              try
17              {
18                  while (true)
19                  {
20                      number = inputStream.readInt();
21                      System.out.println(number);
22                  }
23              }
24              catch(EOFException e)
25              {
26                  System.out.println("No more numbers in the file.");
27              }
28              inputStream.close();
29          }
30          catch(FileNotFoundException e)
31          {
32              System.out.println("Cannot find file numbers.dat.");
33          }
34          catch(IOException e)
35          {
36              System.out.println("Problem with input from file numbers.dat.");
37          }
38      }
39  }
```

(continued)

Display 10.17   Using **EOFException** (part 2 of 2)

Sample Dialogue

```
Reading numbers in numbers.dat
0                                    Assumes the program in
1                                    Display 10.13 was run to
2                                    create the file numbers.dat.
3
4
No more numbers in the file.
```

Serializable
interface

We will discuss interfaces in general in Chapter 13. However, the Serializable interface is particularly easy to use and requires no knowledge of interfaces. All you need to do to make a class implement the Serializable interface is add the two words implements Serializable to the heading of the class definition, as in the following example:

```
public class Person implements Serializable
{
```

The Serializable interface is in the same java.io package that contains all the I/O classes we have discussed in this chapter. For example, in Display 10.18 we define a toy class named SomeClass that implements the Serializable interface. We will explain the effect of the Serializable interface a bit later in this chapter, but first let's see how you do binary file I/O with a serializable class such as this class SomeClass in Display 10.18.

Display 10.19 illustrates how class objects can be written to and read from a binary file. To write an object of a class such as SomeClass to a binary file, you simply use the method writeObject of the class ObjectOutputStream. You use writeObject in the same way that you use the other methods of the class ObjectOutputStream, such as writeInt, but you use an object as the argument.

writeObject

readObject

If an object is written to a file with writeObject, then it can be read back out of the file with readObject of the stream class ObjectInputStream, as also illustrated in Display 10.19. The method readObject returns its value as an object of type Object. If you want to use the values retuned by readObject as an object of a class like Some-Class, you must do a type cast, as shown in Display 10.19.

The Serializable Interface

serializable

A class that implements the Serializable interface is said to be a **serializable** class. To use objects of a class with writeObject and readObject, that class must be serializable. But to make the class serializable, we change nothing in the class. All we do is add the phrase implements Serializable. This phrase tells the run-time system that it is OK to treat objects of the class in a particular way when doing file I/O. If a class is serializable, Java assigns a serial number to each object of the class that it writes to a stream of

Display 10.18   **A Serializable Class**

```
1   import java.io.Serializable;

2   public class SomeClass implements Serializable
3   {
4       private int number;
5       private char letter;

6       public SomeClass()
7       {
8           number = 0;
9           letter = 'A';
10      }

11      public SomeClass(int theNumber, char theLetter)
12      {
13          number = theNumber;
14          letter = theLetter;
15      }

16      public String toString()
17      {
18          return "Number = " + number
19                          + " Letter = " + letter;
20      }

21  }
```

Display 10.19   **Binary File I/O of Objects** (part 1 of 3)

```
1    import java.io.ObjectOutputStream;
2    import java.io.FileOutputStream;
3    import java.io.ObjectInputStream;
4    import java.io.FileInputStream;
5    import java.io.IOException;
6    import java.io.FileNotFoundException;

7    /**
8     Demonstrates binary file I/O of serializable class objects.
9    */
10   public class ObjectIODemo
11   {
12       public static void main(String[] args)
13       {
```

(continued)

Display 10.19 Binary File I/O of Objects (part 2 of 3)

```
14        try
15        {
16            ObjectOutputStream outputStream =
17                new ObjectOutputStream(new FileOutputStream("datafile"));

18            SomeClass oneObject = new SomeClass(1, 'A');
19            SomeClass anotherObject = new SomeClass(42, 'Z');

20            outputStream.writeObject(oneObject);
21            outputStream.writeObject(anotherObject);

22            outputStream.close();

23            System.out.println("Data sent to file.");
24        }
25        catch(IOException e)
26        {
27            System.out.println("Problem with file output.");
28        }

29        System.out.println(
30                "Now let's reopen the file and display the data.");
31        try
32        {
33            ObjectInputStream inputStream =
34                new ObjectInputStream(new FileInputStream("datafile"));
```

Notice the type casts.

```
35            SomeClass readOne = (SomeClass)inputStream.readObject();
36            SomeClass readTwo = (SomeClass)inputStream.readObject();

37            System.out.println("The following were read from the file:");
38            System.out.println(readOne);
39            System.out.println(readTwo);
40        }
41        catch(FileNotFoundException e)
42        {
43            System.out.println("Cannot find datafile.");
44        }
45        catch(ClassNotFoundException e)
46        {
47            System.out.println("Problems with file input.");
48        }
49        catch(IOException e)
50        {
51            System.out.println("Problems with file input.");
52        }
```

Display 10.19   Binary File I/O of Objects (part 3 of 3)

```
53          System.out.println("End of program.");
54      }
55  }
```

Sample Dialogue

```
Data sent to file.
Now let's reopen the file and display the data.
The following were read from the file:
Number = 1 Letter = A
Number = 42 Letter = Z
End of program.
```

type `ObjectOutputStream`. If the same object is written to the stream more than once, then after the first time, Java writes only the serial number for the object and not a full description of the object's data. This makes file I/O more efficient and makes the files smaller. When read back out with a stream of type `ObjectInputStream`, duplicate serial numbers are returned as references to the same object. Note that this means that if two variables contain references to the same object and you write the objects to the file and later read them from the file, then the two objects that are read will again be references to the same object. So nothing in the structure of your object data is lost when you write the objects to the file and later read them back.

class instance variables   When a serializable class has instance variables of a class type, then the classes for the instance variables must also be serializable, and so on for all levels of **class instance variables** within classes. So, a class is not serializable unless the classes for all instance variables are also serializable.

Why aren't all classes made serializable? For security reasons. The serial number system makes it easier for programmers to get access to the object data written to secondary storage. Also, for some classes it may not make sense to write objects to secondary storage, since they would be meaningless when read out again later. For example, if the object contains system-dependent data, the data may be meaningless when later read out.

PITFALL: Mixing Class Types in the Same File

The best way to write and read objects using `ObjectOutputStream` and `ObjectInput-Stream` is to store only data of one class type in any one file. If you store objects of multiple class types or even objects of only one class type mixed in with primitive type data, it has been our experience that the system can get confused and you could lose data. ∎

Array Objects in Binary Files

An array is an object and hence a suitable argument for writeObject. An entire array can be saved to a binary file using writeObject and later read using readObject. When doing so, if the array has a base type that is a class, then the class must be serializable. This means that if you store all your data for one serializable class in a single array, then you can output all your data to a binary file with one invocation of writeObject.

This way of storing an array in a binary file is illustrated in Display 10.20. Note that the base class type, SomeClass, is serializable. Also, notice the type cast that uses the array type SomeClass[]. Since readObject returns its value as an object of type Object, it must be type cast to the correct array type.

Self-Test Exercises

40. How do you make a class implement the Serializable interface?

41. What import statement do you need to be able to use the Serializable interface?

42. What is the return type for the method readObject of the class ObjectInputStream?

43. Is an array of type Object?

Display 10.20 File I/O of an Array Object (part 1 of 3)

```
1    import java.io.ObjectOutputStream;
2    import java.io.FileOutputStream;
3    import java.io.ObjectInputStream;
4    import java.io.FileInputStream;
5    import java.io.IOException;
6    import java.io.FileNotFoundException;

7    public class ArrayIODemo
8    {

9        public static void main(String[] args)
10       {
11           SomeClass[] a = new SomeClass[2];
12           a[0] = new SomeClass(1, 'A');
13           a[1] = new SomeClass(2, 'B');

14           try
15           {
16               ObjectOutputStream outputStream =
17                   new ObjectOutputStream(new FileOutputStream("arrayfile"));
18               outputStream.writeObject(a);
19               outputStream.close();
20           }
```

Display 10.20   **File I/O of an Array Object** (part 2 of 3)

```
21              catch(IOException e)
22              {
23                  System.out.println("Error writing to file.");
24                  System.exit(0);
25              }

26               System.out.println(
27                          "Array written to file arrayfile.");

28              System.out.println(
29                     "Now let's reopen the file and display the array.");

30              SomeClass[] b = null;

31              try
32              {
33                  ObjectInputStream inputStream =
34                         new ObjectInputStream(new FileInputStream("arrayfile"));
35                  b = (SomeClass[])inputStream.readObject();
36                  inputStream.close();
37              }
38              catch(FileNotFoundException e)                Notice the type cast.
39              {
40                  System.out.println("Cannot find file arrayfile.");
41                  System.exit(0);
42              }
43              catch(ClassNotFoundException e)
44              {
45                  System.out.println("Problems with file input.");
46                  System.exit(0);
47              }
48              catch(IOException e)
49              {
50                  System.out.println("Problems with file input.");
51                  System.exit(0);
52              }

53              System.out.println(
54                     "The following array elements were read from the file:");
55              int i;
56              for (i = 0; i < b.length; i++)
57                  System.out.println(b[i]);
58              System.out.println("End of program.");
59          }
60      }
```

(continued)

Display 10.20 File I/O of an Array Object (part 3 of 3)

Sample Dialogue

```
Array written to file arrayfile.
Now let's reopen the file and display the array.
The following array elements were read from the file:
Number = 1 Letter = A
Number = 2 Letter = B
End of program.
```

10.5 Random Access to Binary Files ★

Any time, any where.

Common response to a challenge for a confrontation

The streams for sequential access to files, which we discussed in the previous sections of this chapter, are the ones most often used for file access in Java. However, some applications that require very rapid access to records in very large databases require some sort of random access to particular parts of a file. Such applications might best be done with specialized database software. But perhaps you are given the job of writing such a package in Java, or perhaps you are just curious about how such things are done in Java. Java does provide for random access to files so that your program can both read from and write to random locations in a file. In this section we will describe simple uses of random access to files.

Reading and Writing to the Same File

If you want random access to both read and write to a file in Java, you use the stream class `RandomAccessFile`, which is in the `java.io` package like all other file I/O classes.

file pointer

A random access file consists of a sequence of numbered bytes. There is a kind of marker called the **file pointer** that is always positioned at one of these bytes. All reads and writes take place starting at the location of the file pointer. You can move the file pointer to a new location with the method `seek`.

Although a random access file is byte oriented, there are methods to allow for reading or writing values of the primitive types and of string values to a random access file. In fact, these are the same methods as those we already used for sequential access files, as previously discussed. A `RandomAccessFile` stream has methods `writeInt`, `writeDouble`, `writeUTF`, and so forth as well as methods `readInt`, `readDouble`, `readUTF`, and so forth. However, the class `RandomAccessFile` does not have the methods `writeObject` or `readObject`. The most important methods of the class `RandomAccessFile` are given in Display 10.21. A demonstration program for random access files is given in Display 10.22.

Display 10.21   Some Methods of the Class `RandomAccessFile` (part 1 of 3)

The class `RandomAccessFile` is in the `java.io` package.

> `public RandomAccessFile(String fileName, String mode)`
>
> `public RandomAccessFile(File fileObject, String mode)`

Opens the file, does not delete data already in the file, but does position the file pointer at the first (zeroth) location.

The **mode** must be one of the following:
   "**r**" Open for reading only.
   "**rw**" Open for reading and writing.
   "**rws**" Same as "**rw**", and also requires that every update to the file's content or metadata be written synchronously to the underlying storage device.
   "**rwd**" Same as "**rw**", and also requires that every update to the file's content be written synchronously to the underlying storage device.
   "**rws**" and "**rwd**" are not covered in this book.

> `public long getFilePointer() throws IOException`

Returns the current location of the file pointer. Locations are numbered starting with **0**.

> `public void seek(long location) throws IOException`

Moves the file pointer to the specified **location**.

> `public long length() throws IOException`

Returns the length of the file.

> `public void setLength(long newLength) throws IOException`

Sets the length of this file.

If the present length of the file as returned by the **length** method is greater than the **newLength** argument, then the file will be truncated. In this case, if the file pointer location as returned by the **getFilePointer** method is greater than **newLength**, then after this method returns, the file pointer location will be equal to **newLength**.

If the present length of the file as returned by the **length** method is smaller than **newLength**, then the file will be extended. In this case, the contents of the extended portion of the file are not defined.

> `public void close() throws IOException`

Closes the stream's connection to a file.

> `public void write(int b) throws IOException`

Writes the specified byte to the file.

> `public void write(byte[] a) throws IOException`

Writes *a*.**length** bytes from the specified byte array to the file.

Display 10.21 Some Methods of the Class **RandomAccessFile** (part 2 of 3)

`public final void writeByte(byte b) throws IOException`

Writes the **byte b** to the file.

`public final void writeShort(short n) throws IOException`

Writes the **short n** to the file.

`public final void writeInt(int n) throws IOException`

Writes the **int n** to the file.

`public final void writeLong(long n) throws IOException`

Writes the **long n** to the file.

`public final void writeDouble(double d) throws IOException`

Writes the **double d** to the file.

`public final void writeFloat(float f) throws IOException`

Writes the **float f** to the file.

`public final void writeChar(char c) throws IOException`

Writes the **char c** to the file.

`public final void writeBoolean(boolean b) throws IOException`

Writes the **boolean b** to the file.

`public final void writeUTF(String s) throws IOException`

Writes the **String s** to the file.

`public int read() throws IOException`

Reads a byte of data from the file and returns it as an integer in the range 0 to 255.

`public int read(byte[] a) throws IOException`

Reads **a.length** bytes of data from the file into the array of bytes **a**. Returns the number of bytes read or −1 if the end of the file is encountered.

`public final byte readByte() throws IOException`

Reads a **byte** value from the file and returns that value. If an attempt is made to read beyond the end of the file, an **EOFException** is thrown.

`public final short readShort() throws IOException`

Reads a **short** value from the file and returns that value. If an attempt is made to read beyond the end of the file, an **EOFException** is thrown.

Display 10.21   Some Methods of the Class `RandomAccessFile` (part 3 of 3)

```
public final int readInt() throws IOException
```

Reads an `int` value from the file and returns that value. If an attempt is made to read beyond the end of the file, an `EOFException` is thrown.

```
public final long readLong() throws IOException
```

Reads a `long` value from the file and returns that value. If an attempt is made to read beyond the end of the file, an `EOFException` is thrown.

```
public final double readDouble() throws IOException
```

Reads a `double` value from the file and returns that value. If an attempt is made to read beyond the end of the file, an `EOFException` is thrown.

```
public final float readFloat() throws IOException
```

Reads a `float` value from the file and returns that value. If an attempt is made to read beyond the end of the file, an `EOFException` is thrown.

```
public final char readChar() throws IOException
```

Reads a `char` value from the file and returns that value. If an attempt is made to read beyond the end of the file, an `EOFException` is thrown.

```
public final boolean readBoolean() throws IOException
```

Reads a `boolean` value from the file and returns that value. If an attempt is made to read beyond the end of the file, an `EOFException` is thrown.

```
public final String readUTF() throws IOException
```

Reads a `String` value from the file and returns that value. If an attempt is made to read beyond the end of the file, an `EOFException` is thrown.

opening a file   The constructor for `RandomAccessFile` takes either a string name for the file or an object of the class `File` as its first argument. The second argument must be one of the four strings "rw", "r", and two modes we will not discuss, "rws" and "rwd". The string "rw" means your code can both read and write to the file after it is open. The string "r" means your code can read from the file but cannot write to the file.

If the file already exists, then when it is opened, the length is not reset to 0, but the file pointer will be positioned at the start of the file, which is what you would expect at least for "r". If the length of the file is not what you want, you can change it with the method `setLength`. In particular, you can use `setLength` to empty the file.

Display 10.22 **Random Access to a File** (part 1 of 2)

```
1    import java.io.RandomAccessFile;
2    import java.io.IOException;
3    import java.io.FileNotFoundException;

4    public class RandomAccessDemo
5    {
6        public static void main(String[] args)
7        {
8            try
9            {
10               RandomAccessFile ioStream =
11                   new RandomAccessFile("bytedata", "rw");

12               System.out.println("Writing 3 bytes to the file bytedata.");
13               ioStream.writeByte(1);
14               ioStream.writeByte(2);
15               ioStream.writeByte(3);
16               System.out.println("The length of the file is now = "
17                                       + ioStream.length());
18               System.out.println("The file pointer location is "
19                                       + ioStream.getFilePointer());

20               System.out.println("Moving the file pointer to location 1.");
21               ioStream.seek(1);
22               byte oneByte = ioStream.readByte();
23               System.out.println("The value at location 1 is " + oneByte);
24               oneByte = ioStream.readByte();
25               System.out.println("The value at the next location is "
26                                       + oneByte);

27               System.out.println("Now we move the file pointer back to");
28               System.out.println("location 1, and change the byte.");
29               ioStream.seek(1);
30               ioStream.writeByte(9);
31               ioStream.seek(1);
32               oneByte = ioStream.readByte();
33               System.out.println("The value at location 1 is now " + oneByte);

34               System.out.println("Now we go to the end of the file");
35               System.out.println("and write a double.");
36               ioStream.seek(ioStream.length());
37               ioStream.writeDouble(41.99);
38               System.out.println("The length of the file is now = "
39                                       + ioStream.length());
```

Display 10.22   **Random Access to a File** (part 2 of 2)

```
40          System.out.println("Returning to location 3,");
41          System.out.println("where we wrote the double.");
42          ioStream.seek(3);
43          double oneDouble = ioStream.readDouble();
44          System.out.println("The double value at location 3 is "
45                                      + oneDouble);

46          ioStream.close();
47      }
48      catch(FileNotFoundException e)
49      {
50          System.out.println("Problem opening file.");
51      }
52      catch(IOException e)
53      {
54          System.out.println("Problems with file I/O.");
55      }
56      System.out.println("End of program.");
57  }
58 }
```

The location of **readDouble** *must be a location where* **writeDouble** *wrote to the file.*

The dialog assumes the file **bytedata** *did not exist before the program was run.*

Sample Dialogue

```
Writing 3 bytes to the file bytedata.
The length of the file is now = 3
The file pointer location is 3
Moving the file pointer to location 1.
The value at location 1 is 2
The value at the next location is 3
Now we move the file pointer back to
location 1, and change the byte.
The value at location 1 is now 9
Now we go to the end of the file
and write a double.
The length of the file is now = 11
Returning to location 3,
where we wrote the double.
The double value at location 3 is 41.99
End of program.
```

Byte locations are numbered starting with zero.

Three 1-byte values and one **double** *value that uses 8 bytes = 11 bytes total.*

PITFALL: A RandomAccessFile Need Not Start Empty

If a file already exists, then when it is opened with RandomAccessFile, the length is not reset to 0, but the file pointer will be positioned at the start of the file. So, old data in the file is not lost and the file pointer is set for the most likely position for reading, not the most likely position for writing.

Self-Test Exercises

44. If you run the program in Display 10.22 a second time, will the output be the same?

45. How can you modify the program in Display 10.22 so the file always starts out empty?

Chapter Summary

- Files that are considered to be strings of characters and that look like characters to your program and your editor are called text files. Files whose contents must be handled as strings of binary digits are called binary files.

- You can use the class PrintWriter to write to a text file and can use the class Scanner or BufferedReader to read from a text file.

- The class File can be used to check whether there is a file with a given name. It can also check whether your program is allowed to read the file and/or allowed to write to the file.

- Your program can use the class ObjectOutputStream to write to a binary file and can use the class ObjectInputStream to read from a binary file.

- Your program can use the method writeObject of the class ObjectOutputStream to write class objects to a binary file. The objects can be read back with the method readObject of the class ObjectInputStream.

- To use the method writeObject of the class ObjectOutputStream or the method readObject of the class ObjectInputStream, the class whose objects are written to a file must implement the Serializable interface.

- The way that you test for the end of a file depends on whether your program is reading from a text file or a binary file.

- You can use the class RandomAccessFile to create a stream that gives random access to the bytes in a file.

Answers to Self-Test Exercises

1. With an input stream, data flows from a file or input device to your program. With an output stream, data flows from your program to a file or output device.

2. A binary file contains data that is processed as binary data. A text file allows your program and editor to view the file as if it contained a sequence of characters. A text file can be viewed with an editor, whereas a binary file cannot.

3. A `FileNotFoundException` would be thrown if the file cannot be opened because, for example, there is already a directory (folder) named `stuff.txt`. Note that if the file does not exist but can be created, then no exception is thrown. If you answered `IOException`, you are not wrong, because a `FileNotFoundException` is an `IOException`. However, the better answer is the more specific exception class, namely `FileNotFoundException`.

4. No. That is why we use an object of the class `FileOutputStream` as an argument. The correct way to express the code displayed in the question is as follows:

```
PrintWriter outputStream =
    new PrintWriter(new FileOutputStream("stuff.txt"));
```

5.
```
PrintWriter outputStream =
    new PrintWriter(new FileOutputStream("sam");
```

6.
```
PrintWriter outStream =
    new PrintWriter(new FileOutputStream("sam", true));
```

7. Yes, it will send suitable output to the text file because the class `Person` has a well-defined `toString()` method.

8.
```
Scanner fileIn =
        new Scanner(new FileInputStream("sally"));
```

9. It throws a `NoSuchElementException` if there are no more tokens. It throws an `InputMismatchException` if the next token is not a well-formed string representation of an `int`. It throws an `IllegalStateException` if the `Scanner` stream is closed.

10. No. Reading may have reached the end of the file, but another possibility is that the next token may not be a well-formed string representation of an `int` value.

11. The `FileInputStream` constructor, and thus the `Scanner` constructor invocation, can throw a `FileNotFoundException`, and this exception needs to be caught or declared in a `throws` clause.

12.
```
BufferedReader fileIn =
                new BufferedReader(new FileReader("joe"));
```

13. The method `readLine` returns a value of type `String`. The method `read` reads a single *character*, but it returns it as a value of type int. To get the value to be of type char, you need to do a type cast.

14. Both read and readLine in the class BufferedReader might throw an IOException.

15. The try block in Display 10.7 is larger so that it includes the invocations of the method readLine, which might throw an IOException. The method println in Display 10.1 does not throw any exceptions that must be caught.

16. Yes.

17. No, you must read the number as a string and then convert the string to a number with Integer.parseInt (or in some other way).

18. When the method readLine tries to read beyond the end of a file, it returns the value null. Thus, you can test for the end of a file by testing for null.

19. The method read reads a single *character*, but it returns it as a value of type int. To get the value to be of type char, you need to do a type cast.

20. When the method read tries to read beyond the end of a file, it returns the value –1. Thus, you can test for the end of a file by testing for the value –1. This works because all "real" characters return a positive int value.

21. Yes, if original.txt is an empty file, then the file numbered.txt produced by the program will also be empty.

22. Only the classes FileReader and FileOutputStream have a constructor that accepts a file name as an argument. (Although we have not discussed it, the class Scanner has a constructor that takes a String argument, but the argument is not a file name.)

23. Yes, it is legal.

24. Replace

```
System.setErr(errStream);
```

with

```
System.setOut(errStream);
```

25. Add

```
System.setOut(errStream);
```

to get

```
System.setErr(errStream);
System.setOut(errStream);
```

26.
```
import java.io.File;

public class FileExercise
{
    public static void main(String[] args)
    {
        File fileObject = new File("Sally.txt");
```

```
                if (fileObject.exists())
                System.out.println(
                            "There is a file named Sally.txt.");
            else
                System.out.println(
                            "There is no file named Sally.txt.");
        }
    }

27.   import java.io.IOException;
      import java.io.File;
      import java.util.Scanner;

      public class FileExercise2
      {
          public static void main(String[] args)
          {
              Scanner keyboard = new Scanner(System.in);
              String fileName = null;
              File fileObject = null;

              try
              {
                  System.out.print("Enter a file name and I will");
                  System.out.println(" tell you if it exists.");
                  fileName = keyboard.next();
                  fileObject = new File(fileName);


                  if (fileObject.exists())
                  {
                      System.out.println("There is a file named  "
                                                    + fileName);
                      System.out.println("Delete the file? (y/n)");
                      char answer = (char)System.in.read();

                      if ((answer == 'y') || (answer == 'Y'))
                      {
                          if (fileObject.delete())
                              System.out.println("File deleted.");
                          else
                              System.out.println(
                                          "Cannot delete file.");
                      }
                  }
                  else
                      System.out.println(
                                  "No file named " + fileName);
              }
```

```
            catch(IOException e)
            {
                System.out.println(
                            "Error reading from keyboard.");
            }
        }
    }
```

28.
```
ObjectOutputStream outputThisWay =
                new ObjectOutputStream(
                    new FileOutputStream("bindata.dat"));
```

29.
```
outputThisWay.writeDouble(v1);
outputThisWay.writeDouble(v2);
```

30.
```
outputThisWay.writeUTF("Hello");
```

31.
```
outputThisWay.close();
```

32.
```
ObjectInputStream inputThing =
                new ObjectInputStream(
                    new FileInputStream("someStuff"));
```

33.
```
number = inputThing.readDouble();
```

34.
```
inputThing.close();
```

35. If a number is written to a file with `writeInt`, it should be read only with `readInt`. If you use `readLong` or `readDouble` to read the number, something will go wrong.

36. You should not use `readUTF` to read a string from a text file. You should use `readUTF` only to read a string from a binary file. Moreover, the string should have been written to that file using `writeUTF`.

37. When opening a binary file for either output or input in the ways discussed in this chapter, a `FileNotFoundException` might be thrown and other `IOExceptions` may be thrown.

38. An `EOFException` is thrown when your program tries to read the (nonexisting) fourth number.

39. It is not an infinite loop because when the end of the file is reached, an exception will be thrown, and that will end the entire `try` block.

40. You add the two words `implements Serializable` to the beginning of the class definition. You also must do this for the classes for the instance variables and so on for all levels of class instance variables within classes.

41. `import java.io.Serializable;` or `import java.io.*;`

42. The return type is `Object`, which means the returned value usually needs to be type cast.

43. Yes. That is why it is a legitimate argument for `writeObject`.

44. No. Each time the program is run, the file will get longer.

45. Add the following near the start of `main`:

```
ioStream.setLength(0);
```

Programming Projects

 Many of these Programming Projects can be solved using AW's MyCodeMate.
To access these please go to: www.mycodemate.com.

PROJECTS INVOLVING ONLY TEXT FILES

1. The textfiles `boynames.txt` and `girlnames.txt`, which are included in the source code for this book, contain a list of the 1,000 most popular boy and girl names in the United States for the year 2003 as compiled by the Social Security Administration.

   These are blank-delimited files where the most popular name is listed first, the second most popular name is listed second, and so on, to the 1,000[th] most popular name, which is listed last. Each line consists of the first name followed by a blank space and then the number of registered births using that name in the year. For example the `girlnames.txt` file begins with:

   > Emily 25494
   >
   > Emma 22532
   >
   > Madison 19986

   This indicates that Emily was the most popular name with 25,494 registered namings, Emma was the second most popular with 22,532, and Madison was the third most popular with 19,986.

   Write a program that reads both the girl's and boy's files into memory using arrays. Then, allow the user to input a name. The program should search through both arrays. If there is a match, then it should output the popularity ranking and the number of namings. The program should also indicate if there is no match.

   For example, if the user enters the name "Justice," then the program should output:

   ```
   Justice is ranked 456 in popularity among girls with 655 namings.
   Justice is ranked 401 in popularity among boys with 653 namings.
   ```

   If the user enters the name "Walter," then the program should output:

   ```
   Walter is not ranked among the top 1000 girl names.
   Walter is ranked 356 in popularity among boys with 775 namings.
   ```

 2. Write a program that will search a text file of strings representing numbers of type `int` and will write the largest and the smallest numbers to the screen. The file contains nothing but strings representing numbers of type `int`, one per line.

3. Write a program that takes its input from a text file of strings representing numbers of type `double` and outputs the average of the numbers in the file to the screen. The file contains nothing but strings representing numbers of type `double`, one per line.

4. Write a program that takes its input from a text file of strings representing numbers of type `double`. The program outputs to the screen the average and standard deviation of the numbers in the file. The file contains nothing but strings representing numbers of type `double`, one per line. The standard deviation of a list of numbers n_1, n_2, n_3, and so forth is defined as the square root of the average of the following numbers:

$$(n_1 - a)^2, (n_2 - a)^2, (n_3 - a)^2, \text{ and so forth.}$$

The number a is the average of the numbers n_1, n_2, n_3, and so forth. *Hint:* Write your program so that it first reads the entire file and computes the average of all the numbers, then closes the file, then reopens the file and computes the standard deviation. You will find it helpful to first do Programming Project 3 and then modify that program to obtain the program for this project.

5. Write a program to edit text files for extra blanks. The program will replace any string of two or more blanks with a single blank. Your program should work as follows: Create a temporary file. Copy from the file to the temporary file but do not copy extra blanks. Copy the contents of the temporary file back into the original file. Use a method (or methods) in the class `File` to remove the temporary file. You will also want to use the class `File` for other things in your program. The temporary file should have a name different from all existing files so that the existing files are not affected (except for the file being edited). Your program will ask the user for the name of the file to be edited. However, it will not ask the user for the name of the temporary file but instead will generate the name within the program. You can generate the name any way that is clear and efficient. One possible way to generate the temporary file is to start with an unlikely name, such as `"TempX"`, and to append a character, such as `'X'`, until a name is found that does not name an existing file.

6. Write a program that gives and takes advice on program writing. The program starts by writing a piece of advice to the screen and asking the user to type in a different piece of advice. The program then ends. The next person to run the program receives the advice given by the person who last ran the program. The advice is kept in a text file and the content of the file changes after each run of the program. You can use your editor to enter the initial piece of advice in the file so that the first person who runs the program receives some advice. Allow the user to type in advice of any length so that it can be any number of lines long. The user is told to end his or her advice by pressing the Return key two times. Your program can then test to see that it has reached the end of the input by checking to see when it reads two consecutive occurrences of the character `'\n'`.

PROJECTS INVOLVING BINARY FILES

7. Write a program that will search a binary file of numbers of type int and write the largest and the smallest numbers to the screen. The file contains nothing but numbers of type int written to the file with writeInt.

8. Write a program that takes its input from a binary file of numbers of type double and outputs the average of the numbers in the file to the screen. The file contains nothing but numbers of type double written to the file with writeDouble.

9. Write a program that takes its input from a binary file of numbers of type double. The file contains nothing but numbers of type double written to the file with writeDouble. The program outputs to the screen the average and standard deviation of the numbers in the file. The standard deviation of a list of numbers n_1, n_2, n_3, and so forth is defined as the square root of the average of the following numbers:

$$(n_1 - a)^2, (n_2 - a)^2, (n_3 - a)^2, \text{ and so forth.}$$

The number a is the average of the numbers n_1, n_2, n_3, and so forth. *Hint:* Write your program so that it first reads the entire file and computes the average of all the numbers, then closes the file, then reopens the file and computes the standard deviation. You will find it helpful to first do Programming Project 8 and then modify that program to obtain the program for this project.

10. Change the definition of the class Person in Display 5.19 to be serializable. Note that this requires that you also change the class Date. Then write a program to maintain a binary file of records of people (records of type Person). Allow commands to delete a record specified by the person's name, to add a record, to retrieve and display a record, and to obtain all records of people within a specified age range. To obtain the age of a person, you need the current date. Your program will ask the user for the current date when the program begins. You can do this with random access files, but for this exercise do not use random access files. Use a file or files that record records with the method writeObject of the class ObjectOutputStream.

11

Recursion

11 Recursion

After a lecture on cosmology and the structure of the solar system, William
James was accosted by a little old lady.

"Your theory that the sun is the center of the solar system, and the earth is a
ball which rotates around it has a very convincing ring to it, Mr. James, but
it's wrong. I've got a better theory," said the little old lady.

"And what is that, madam?" inquired James politely.

"That we live on a crust of earth which is on the back of a giant turtle."

Not wishing to demolish this absurd little theory by bringing to bear the
masses of scientific evidence he had at his command, James decided to
gently dissuade his opponent by making her see some of the inadequa-
cies of her position.

"If your theory is correct, madam," he asked, "what does this turtle stand on?"

"You're a very clever man, Mr. James, and that's a very good question" replied
the little old lady, "but I have an answer to it. And it is this: the first turtle
stands on the back of a second, far larger, turtle, who stands directly
under him."

"But what does this second turtle stand on?" persisted James patiently.

To this the little old lady crowed triumphantly. "It's no use, Mr. James — it's
turtles all the way down."

> J. R. ROSS, *Constraints on Variables in Syntax*

Introduction

recursive
method

A method definition that includes a call to itself is said to be **recursive**. Like most modern programming languages, Java allows methods to be recursive, and if used with a little care, this can be a useful programming technique. In this chapter we introduce the basic techniques needed for defining successful recursive methods. There is nothing in this chapter that is truly unique to Java. If you are already familiar with recursion you can safely skip this chapter. No new Java elements are introduced in this chapter.

Prerequisites

Except for the last subsection on binary search, this chapter uses material only from Chapters 1–5. The last subsection entitled "Binary Search" also uses the basic material on one-dimensional arrays from Chapter 6.

You may postpone all or part of this chapter if you wish. Nothing in the rest of this book requires any of this chapter.

11.1 Recursive void Methods

I remembered too that night which is at the middle of the Thousand
and One Nights when Scheherazade (through a magical oversight of the
copyist) begins to relate word for word the story of the Thousand and
One Nights, establishing the risk of coming once again to the night
when she must repeat it, and thus to infinity.

JORGE LUIS BORGES, *The Garden of Forking Paths*

When you are writing a method to solve a task, one basic design technique is to break the task into subtasks. Sometimes it turns out that at least one of the subtasks is a smaller example of the same task. For example, if the task is to search a list for a particular value, you might divide this into the subtask of searching the first half of the list and the subtask of searching the second half of the list. The subtasks of searching the halves of the list are "smaller" versions of the original task. Whenever one subtask is a smaller version of the original task to be accomplished, you can solve the original task by using a recursive method. We begin with a simple example to illustrate this technique. (For simplicity our examples are static methods; however, recursive methods need not be static.)

Recursion

In Java, a method definition may contain an invocation of the method being defined. In such cases the method is said to be **recursive**.

EXAMPLE: Vertical Numbers

Display 11.1 contains a demonstration program for a recursive method named writeVertical, which takes one (nonnegative) int argument and writes that int to the screen with the digits going down the screen one per line. For example, the invocation

```
writeVertical(1234);
```

would produce the output

```
1
2
3
4
```

(continued)

Display 11.1 A Recursive **void** Method

```
1    public class RecursionDemo1
2    {
3        public static void main(String[] args)
4        {
5            System.out.println("writeVertical(3):");
6            writeVertical(3);

7            System.out.println("writeVertical(12):");
8            writeVertical(12);

9            System.out.println("writeVertical(123):");
10           writeVertical(123);
11       }

12       public static void writeVertical(int n)
13       {
14           if (n < 10)
15           {
16               System.out.println(n);
17           }
18           else //n is two or more digits long:
19           {
20               writeVertical(n/10);
21               System.out.println(n%10);
22           }
23       }
24   }
```

Sample Dialogue

```
writeVertical(3):
3
writeVertical(12):
1
2
writeVertical(123):
1
2
3
```

EXAMPLE: (continued)

The task to be performed by writeVertical may be broken down into the following two subtasks:

Simple Case: If n < 10, then write the number n to the screen.

After all, if the number is only one digit long, the task is trivial.

Recursive Case: If n >= 10, then do two subtasks:

1. Output all the digits except the last digit.

2. Output the last digit.

For example, if the argument were 1234, the first part would output

```
1
2
3
```

and the second part would output 4. This decomposition of tasks into subtasks can be used to derive the method definition.

Subtask 1 is a smaller version of the original task, so we can implement this subtask with a recursive call. Subtask 2 is just the simple case we listed above. Thus, an outline of our algorithm for the method writeVertical with parameter n is given by the following pseudocode:

```
if (n < 10)
{
    System.out.println(n);
}
else //n is two or more digits long:
{
    writeVertical(the number n with the last digit removed);
    System.out.println(the last digit of n);
}
```

recursive subtask

If you observe the following identities, it is easy to convert this pseudocode to a complete Java method definition:

n/10 is the number n with the last digit removed.
n%10 is the last digit of n.

For example, 1234/10 evaluates to 123 and 1234%10 evaluates to 4.

(continued)

EXAMPLE: (continued)

The following is the complete code for the method:

```java
public static void writeVertical(int n)
{
    if (n < 10)
    {
        System.out.println(n);
    }
    else //n is two or more digits long:
    {
        writeVertical(n/10);
        System.out.println(n%10);
    }
}
```

Tracing a Recursive Call

Let's see exactly what happens when the following method call is made (as in Display 11.1):

```java
writeVertical(123);
```

When this method call is executed, the computer proceeds just as it would with any method call. The argument 123 is substituted for the parameter n and the body of the method is executed. After the substitution of 123 for n, the code to be executed is equivalent to

```java
if (123 < 10)
{
    System.out.println(123);
}
else //n is two or more digits long:
{
    writeVertical(123/10); ◄─────── Computation will stop here
    System.out.println(123%10);       until the recursive call
}                                     returns.
```

Since 123 is not less than 10, the else part is executed. However, the else part begins with the method call

```java
writeVertical(n/10);
```

which (since n is equal to 123) is the call

```
writeVertical(123/10);
```

which is equivalent to

```
writeVertical(12);
```

When execution reaches this recursive call, the current method computation is placed in suspended animation and this recursive call is executed. When this recursive call is finished, the execution of the suspended computation will return to this point and the suspended computation will continue from this point.

The recursive call

```
writeVertical(12);
```

is handled just like any other method call. The argument 12 is substituted for the parameter n and the body of the method is executed. After substituting 12 for n, there are two computations, one suspended and one active, as follows:

```
if (123 < 10)
{
    System      if (12 < 10)
}               {
else //n i          System.out.println(12);
{               }
    writeV      else //n is two or more digits long:
    System      {
}                   writeVertical(12/10);  ◄──────  Computation will stop here
                    System.out.println(12%10);        until the recursive call
                }                                      returns.
```

Since 12 is not less than 10, the else part is executed. However, as you already saw, the else part begins with a recursive call. The argument for the recursive call is n/10, which in this case is equivalent to 12/10. So, this second computation of the method writeVertical is suspended and the following recursive call is executed:

```
writeVertical(12/10);
```

which is equivalent to

```
writeVertical(1);
```

At this point, there are two suspended computations waiting to resume and the computer begins to execute this new recursive call, which is handled just like all the previous recursive calls. The argument 1 is substituted for the parameter n and the body of the method is executed. At this point, the computation looks like the following:

```
if (123 < 10)
{
    S   if (12 < 10)
}       {
else        if (1 < 10)
{       }   {
    W   else     System.out.println(1);          No recursive
    S   {       }                                 call this time.
}           else //n is two or more digits long:
            {
                writeVertical(1/10);
                System.out.println(1%10);
            }
```

When the body of the method is executed this time, something different happens. Since 1 is less than 10, the Boolean expression in the if-else statement is true, so the statement before the else is executed. That statement is simply an output statement that writes the argument 1 to the screen, so the call writeVertical(1) writes 1 to the screen and ends without any recursive call.

output the digit 1

When the call writeVertical(1) ends, the suspended computation that is waiting for it to end resumes where that suspended computation left off, as shown by the following:

```
if (123 < 10)
{
    S   if (12 < 10)
}       {
else        System.out.println(12);
{       }
    W   else //n is two or more digits long:
    S   {
}           writeVertical(12/10);    ←——— Computation resumes
            System.out.println(12%10);    here.
        }
```

output the
digit 2

When this suspended computation resumes, it executes an output statement that outputs the value 12%10, which is 2. That ends that computation, but there is yet another suspended computation waiting to resume. When this last suspended computation resumes, the situation is

```
if (123 < 10)
{
    System.out.println(123);
}
else //n is two or more digits long:
{
    writeVertical(123/10);
    System.out.println(123%10);
}
```

Computation resumes here.

output the
digit 3

When this last suspended computation resumes, it outputs the value 123%10, which is 3, and the execution of the original method call ends. And, sure enough, the digits 1, 2, and 3 have been written to the screen one per line, in that order.

A Closer Look at Recursion

The definition of the method writeVertical uses recursion. Yet, we did nothing new or different in evaluating the method call writeVertical(123). We treated it just like any of the method calls we saw in previous chapters. We simply substituted the argument 123 for the parameter n and then executed the code in the body of the method definition. When we reached the recursive call

```
writeVertical(123/10);
```

we simply repeated this process one more time.

how
recursion
works

The computer keeps track of recursive calls in the following way. When a method is called, the computer plugs in the arguments for the parameter(s) and begins to execute the code. If it should encounter a recursive call, then it temporarily stops its computation, because it must know the result of the recursive call before it can proceed. It saves all the information it needs to continue the computation later on, and proceeds to evaluate the recursive call. When the recursive call is completed, the computer returns to finish the outer computation.

how
recursion
ends

The Java language places no restrictions on how recursive calls are used in method definitions. However, in order for a recursive method definition to be useful, it must be designed so that any call of the method must ultimately terminate with some piece of code that does not depend on recursion. The method may call itself, and that recursive call may call the method again. The process may be repeated any number of times.

However, the process will not terminate unless eventually one of the recursive calls does not depend on recursion to return a value. The general outline of a successful recursive method definition is as follows:

- One or more cases in which the method accomplishes its task by using recursive call(s) to accomplish one or more smaller versions of the task.

base case
stopping
case

- One or more cases in which the method accomplishes its task without the use of any recursive calls. These cases without any recursive calls are called **base cases** or **stopping cases**.

Often an `if-else` statement determines which of the cases will be executed. A typical scenario is for the original method call to execute a case that includes a recursive call. That recursive call may in turn execute a case that requires another recursive call. For some number of times, each recursive call produces another recursive call, but eventually one of the stopping cases should apply. *Every call of the method must eventually lead to a stopping case, or else the method call will never end because of an infinite chain of recursive calls.* (In practice, a call that includes an infinite chain of recursive calls will usually terminate abnormally rather than actually running forever.)

The most common way to ensure that a stopping case is eventually reached is to write the method so that some (positive) numeric quantity is decreased on each recursive call and to provide a stopping case for some "small" value. This is how we designed the method `writeVertical` in Display 11.1. When the method `write-Vertical` is called, that call produces a recursive call with a smaller argument. This continues with each recursive call producing another recursive call until the argument is less than 10. When the argument is less than 10, the method call ends without producing any more recursive calls and the process works its way back to the original call and the process ends.

General Form of a Recursive Method Definition

The general outline of a successful recursive method definition is as follows:

- One or more cases that include one or more recursive calls to the method being defined. These recursive calls should solve "smaller" versions of the task performed by the method being defined.

- One or more cases that include no recursive calls. These cases without any recursive calls are called **base cases** or **stopping cases**.

PITFALL: Infinite Recursion

In the example of the method writeVertical discussed in the previous subsections, the series of recursive calls eventually reached a call of the method that did not involve recursion (that is, a stopping case was reached). If, on the other hand, every recursive call produces another recursive call, then a call to the method will, in theory, run forever. This is called **infinite recursion**. In practice, such a method will typically run until the computer runs out of resources and the program terminates abnormally.

Examples of infinite recursion are not hard to come by. The following is a syntactically correct Java method definition, which might result from an attempt to define an alternative version of the method writeVertical:

```java
public static void newWriteVertical(int n)
{
        newWriteVertical(n/10);
        System.out.println(n%10);
}
```

If you embed this definition in a program that calls this method, the program will compile with no error messages and you can run the program. Moreover, the definition even has a certain reasonableness to it. It says that to output the argument to new-WriteVertical, first output all but the last digit and then output the last digit. However, when called, this method will produce an infinite sequence of recursive calls. If you call newWriteVertical(12), that execution will stop to execute the recursive call newWriteVertical(12/10), which is equivalent to newWriteVertical(1). The execution of that recursive call will, in turn, stop to execute the recursive call

```java
newWriteVertical(1/10);
```

which is equivalent to

```java
newWriteVertical(0);
```

That, in turn, will stop to execute the recursive call newWriteVertical(0/10); which is also equivalent to

```java
newWriteVertical(0);
```

and that will produce another recursive call to again execute the same recursive method call newWriteVertical(0); and so on, forever. Since the definition of newWriteVertical has no stopping case, the process will proceed forever (or until the computer runs out of resources). ■

Self-Test Exercises

1. What is the output of the following program?

```
public class Exercise1
{
    public static void main(String[] args)
    {
        cheers(3);
    }
    public static void cheers(int n)
    {
        if (n == 1)
        {
            System.out.println("Hurray");
        }
        else
        {
            System.out.println("Hip ");
            cheers(n - 1);
        }
    }
}
```

2. Write a recursive void method that has one parameter which is a integer and that writes to the screen the number of asterisks '*' given by the argument. The output should be all on one line. You can assume the argument is positive.

3. Write a recursive void method that has one parameter, which is a positive integer. When called, the method writes its argument to the screen backward. That is, if the argument is 1234, it outputs the following to the screen:

   4321

4. Write a recursive void method that takes a single (positive) int argument n and writes the integers 1, 2, . . . , n to the screen.

5. Write a recursive void method that takes a single (positive) int argument n and writes integers n, n–1, . . . , 3, 2, 1 to the screen. *Hint:* Notice that you can get from the code for Self-Test Exercise 4 to that for this exercise (or vice versa) by an exchange of as little as two lines.

Stacks for Recursion ★

stack

To keep track of recursion, and a number of other things, most computer systems use a structure called a *stack*. A **stack** is a very specialized kind of memory structure that is analogous to a stack of paper. In this analogy, there is an inexhaustible supply of extra blank sheets of paper. To place some information in the stack, it is written on one of these sheets of paper and placed on top of the stack of papers. To place more information in the stack, a clean sheet of paper is taken, the information is written on it, and this new sheet of paper is placed on top of the stack. In this straightforward way, more and more information may be placed on the stack.

Getting information out of the stack is also accomplished by a very simple procedure. The top sheet of paper can be read, and when it is no longer needed, it is thrown away. There is one complication: Only the top sheet of paper is accessible. In order to read, say, the third sheet from the top, the top two sheets must be thrown away. Since the last sheet that is put on the stack is the first sheet taken off the stack, a stack is often called a **last-in/first-out** memory structure, abbreviated **LIFO**.

last-in/ first-out recursion

Using a stack, the computer can easily keep track of recursion. Whenever a method is called, a new sheet of paper is taken. The method definition is copied onto this sheet of paper, and the arguments are plugged for the method parameters. Then the computer starts to execute the body of the method definition. When it encounters a recursive call, it stops the computation it is doing on that sheet in order to compute the value returned by the recursive call. But, before computing the recursive call, it saves enough information so that, when it does finally determine the value returned by the recursive call, it can continue the stopped computation. This saved information is written on a sheet of paper and placed on the stack. A new sheet of paper is used for the recursive call. The computer writes a second copy of the method definition on this new sheet of paper, plugs in the arguments for the method parameters, and starts to execute the recursive call. When it gets to a recursive call within the recursively called copy, it repeats the process of saving information on the stack and using a new sheet of paper for the new recursive call. This process is illustrated in the subsection entitled "Tracing a Recursive Call." Even though we did not call it a stack at the time, the illustrations of computations placed one on top of the other illustrate the actions of the stack.

This process continues until some recursive call to the method completes its computation without producing any more recursive calls. When that happens, the computer turns its attention to the top sheet of paper on the stack. This sheet contains the partially completed computation that is waiting for the recursive computation that just ended. So, it is possible to proceed with that suspended computation. When that suspended computation ends, the computer discards that sheet of paper and the suspended computation that is below it on the stack becomes the computation on top of the stack. The computer turns its attention to the suspended computation that is now on the top of the stack, and so forth. The process continues until the computation on the bottom sheet is completed. Depending on how many recursive calls are made and how the method definition is written, the stack may grow and shrink in any fashion. Notice that the sheets in the stack can only be accessed in a last-in/first-out fashion, but that is exactly what is needed to keep track of recursive calls. Each suspended version is waiting for the completion of the version directly above it on the stack.

Of course, computers do not have stacks of paper. This is just an analogy. The computer uses portions of memory rather than pieces of paper. The contents of one of these portions of memory ("sheets of paper") is called a **stack frame** or **activation record**. These stack frames are handled in the last-in/first-out manner we just

stack frame

discussed. (These stack frames do not contain a complete copy of the method definition, but merely reference a single copy of the method definition. However, a stack frame contains enough information to allow the computer to act as if the stack frame contains a complete copy of the method definition.)

Stack ★

A **stack** is a last-in/first-out memory structure. The first item referenced or removed from a stack is always the last item entered into the stack. Stacks are used by computers to keep track of recursion (and for other purposes).

PITFALL: Stack Overflow ★

There is always some limit to the size of the stack. If there is a long chain in which a method makes a recursive call to itself, and that call results in another recursive call, and that call produces yet another recursive call, and so forth, then each recursive call in this chain will cause another suspended computation to be placed on the stack. If this chain is too long, then the stack will attempt to grow beyond its limit. This is an error condition known as a **stack overflow**. If you receive an error message that says *stack overflow*, it is likely that some method call has produced an excessively long chain of recursive calls. One common cause of stack overflow is infinite recursion. If a method is recursing infinitely, then it will eventually try to make the stack exceed any stack size limit.

Recursion versus Iteration

Recursion is not absolutely necessary. In fact, some programming languages do not allow it. Any task that can be accomplished using recursion can also be done in some other way without using recursion. For example, Display 11.2 contains a nonrecursive version of the method given in Display 11.1. The nonrecursive version of a method typically uses a loop (or loops) of some sort in place of recursion. For that reason, the

iterative version

nonrecursive version is usually referred to as an **iterative version**. If the definition of the method writeVertical given in Display 11.1 is replaced by the version given in Display 11.2, then the output will be the same. As is true in this case, a recursive version of a method can sometimes be much simpler than an iterative version. The full

extra code on CD

program with the iterative version of the method is given in the file IterativeDemo1 on the accompanying CD.

efficiency

A recursively written method will usually run slower and use more storage than an equivalent iterative version. The computer must do extra work manipulating the stack to keep track of the recursion. However, since the system does all this for you automatically, using recursion can sometimes make your job as a programmer easier, and can sometimes produce code that is easier to understand.

Display 11.2   Iterative Version of the Method in Display 11.1

```
1    public static void writeVertical(int n)
2    {
3        int nsTens = 1;
4        int leftEndPiece = n;
5        while (leftEndPiece > 9)
6        {
7            leftEndPiece = leftEndPiece/10;
8            nsTens = nsTens*10;
9        }
10       //nsTens is a power of ten that has the same number
11       //of digits as n. For example, if n is 2345, then
12       //nsTens is 1000.

13       for (int powerOf10 = nsTens;
14               powerOf10 > 0; powerOf10 = powerOf10/10)
15       {
16           System.out.println(n/powerOf10);
17           n = n%powerOf10;
18       }
19   }
```

Self-Test Exercises

6. If your program produces an error message that says *stack overflow,* what is a likely source of the error?

7. Write an iterative version of the method cheers defined in Self-Test Exercise 1.

8. Write an iterative version of the method defined in Self-Test Exercise 2.

9. Write an iterative version of the method defined in Self-Test Exercise 3.

10. Trace the recursive solution you made to Self-Test Exercise 4.

11. Trace the recursive solution you made to Self-Test Exercise 5.

11.2 Recursive Methods That Return a Value

To iterate is human, to recurse divine.

ANONYMOUS

General Form for a Recursive Method That Returns a Value

The recursive methods you have seen thus far are all void methods, but recursion is not limited to void methods. A recursive method can return a value of any type. The technique for designing recursive methods that return a value is basically the same as what you learned for void methods. An outline for a successful recursive method definition that returns a value is as follows:

- One or more cases in which the value returned is computed in terms of calls to the same method (that is, using recursive calls). As was the case with void methods, the arguments for the recursive calls should intuitively be "smaller."

- One or more cases in which the value returned is computed without the use of any recursive calls. These cases without any recursive calls are called **base cases** or **stopping cases** (just as they were with void methods).

This technique is illustrated in the next Programming Example.

EXAMPLE: Another Powers Method

In Chapter 5 we introduced the static method pow of the class Math. This method pow computes powers. For example, Math.pow(2.0,3.0) returns $2.0^{3.0}$, so the following sets the variable result equal to 8.0:

```
double result = Math.pow(2.0, 3.0);
```

The method pow takes two arguments of type double and returns a value of type double. Display 11.3 contains a recursive definition for a static method that is similar but that works with the type int rather than double. This new method is called power. For example, the following will set the value of result2 equal to 8, since 2^3 is 8:

```
int result2 = power(2, 3);
```

Outside the defining class, this would be written

```
int result2 = RecursionDemo2.power(2, 3);
```

Our main reason for defining the method power is to have a simple example of a recursive method, but there are situations in which the method power would be preferable to the method pow. The method pow returns a value of type double, which is only an approximate quantity. The method power returns a value of type int, which is an exact quantity. In some situations, you might need the additional accuracy provided by the method power.

The definition of the method power is based on the following formula:

x^n is equal to $x^{n-1} * x$

Translating this formula into Java says that the value returned by power(x, n) should be the same as the value of the expression

```
power(x, n - 1)*x
```

EXAMPLE: (continued)

The definition of the method `power` given in Display 11.3 does return this value for `power(x, n)`, provided n > 0.

The case where n is equal to 0 is the stopping case. If n is 0, then `power(x, n)` simply returns 1 (since x^0 is 1).

Let's see what happens when the method `power` is called with some sample values. First consider the simple expression:

```
power(2, 0)
```

When the method is called, the value of x is set equal to 2, the value of n is set equal to 0, and the code in the body of the method definition is executed. Since the value of n is a legal value, the `if-else` statement is executed. Since this value of n is not greater than 0, the `return` statement after the `else` is used, so the method call returns 1. Thus, the following would set the value of `result3` equal to 1:

```
int result3 = power(2, 0);
```

Now let's look at an example that involves a recursive call. Consider the expression

```
power(2, 1)
```

When the method is called, the value of x is set equal to 2, the value of n is set equal to 1, and the code in the body of the method definition is executed. Since this value of n is greater than 0, the following `return` statement is used to determine the value returned:

```
return ( power(x, n − 1)*x );
```

which in this case is equivalent to

```
return ( power(2, 0)*2 );
```

At this point, the computation of `power(2, 1)` is suspended, a copy of this suspended computation is placed on the stack, and the computer then starts a new method call to compute the value of `power(2, 0)`. As you have already seen, the value of `power(2, 0)` is 1. After determining the value of `power(2, 0)`, the computer replaces the expression `power(2, 0)` with its value of 1 and resumes the suspended computation. The resumed computation determines the final value for `power(2, 1)` from the above `return` statement as

```
power(2, 0)*2 is 1*2 which is 2
```

(continued)

EXAMPLE: (continued)

so the final value returned for power(2, 1) is 2. So, the following would set the value of result4 equal to 2:

```
int result4 = power(2, 1);
```

Larger numbers for the second argument will produce longer chains of recursive calls. For example, consider the statement

```
System.out.println(power(2, 3));
```

The value of power(2, 3) is calculated as follows:

```
power(2, 3) is power(2, 2)*2
  power(2, 2) is power(2, 1)*2
    power(2, 1) is power(2, 0)*2
      power(2, 0) is 1 (stopping case)
```

When the computer reaches the stopping case, power(2, 0), there are three suspended computations. After calculating the value returned for the stopping case, it resumes the most recently suspended computations to determine the value of power(2, 1). After that, the computer completes each of the other suspended computations, using each value computed as a value to plug into another suspended computation, until it reaches and completes the computation for the original call power(2, 3). The details of the entire computation are illustrated in Display 11.4.

Display 11.3 The Recursive Method power (part 1 of 2)

```
1   public class RecursionDemo2
2   {
3       public static void main(String[] args)
4       {
5           for (int n = 0; n < 4; n++)
6               System.out.println("3 to the power " + n
7                   + " is " + power(3, n));
8       }

9       public static int power(int x, int n)
10      {
11          if (n < 0)
12          {
13              System.out.println("Illegal argument to power.");
14              System.exit(0);
15          }
```

Display 11.3   **The Recursive Method power** (part 2 of 2)

```
16          if (n > 0)
17              return ( power(x, n - 1)*x );
18          else // n == 0
19              return (1);
20      }
21  }
```

Sample Dialogue

```
3 to the power 0 is 1
3 to the power 1 is 3
3 to the power 2 is 9
3 to the power 3 is 27
```

Display 11.4   Evaluating the Recursive Method Call **power(2,3)**

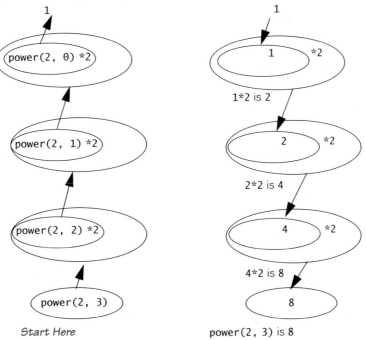

Self-Test Exercises

12. What is the output of the following program?

```java
public class Exercise12
{
    public static void main(String[] args)
    {
        System.out.println(mystery(3));
    }

    public static int mystery(int n)
    {
        if (n <= 1)
            return 1;
        else
            return ( mystery(n - 1) + n );
    }
}
```

13. What is the output of the following program? What well-known mathematical method is rose?

```java
public class Exercise13
{
    public static void main(String[] args)
    {
        System.out.println(rose(4));
    }

    public static int rose(int n)
    {
        if (n <= 0)
            return 1;
        else
            return ( rose(n - 1) * n );
    }
}
```

14. Redefine the method power (Display 11.3) so that it also works for negative exponents. To do this, you also have to change the type of the value returned to double. The method heading for the redefined version of power is as follows:

```java
/**
 Precondition: If n < 0, then x is not 0.
 Returns x to the power n.
*/
public static double power(int x, int n)
```

Hint: x^{-n} is equal to $1/(x^n)$.

11.3 Thinking Recursively

There are two kinds of people in the world, those who divide the world into two kinds of people and those who do not.

ANONYMOUS

Recursive Design Techniques

When defining and using recursive methods, you do not want to be continually aware of the stack and the suspended computations. The power of recursion comes from the fact that you can ignore that detail and let the computer do the bookkeeping for you. Consider the example of the method power in Display 11.3. The way to think of the definition of power is as follows:

```
power(x, n) returns power(x, n - 1)*x
```

Since x^n is equal to $x^{n-1}*x$, this is the correct value to return, provided that the computation will always reach a stopping case and will correctly compute the stopping case. So, after checking that the recursive part of the definition is correct, all you need to check is that the chain of recursive calls will always reach a stopping case and that the stopping case will always return the correct value. In other words, all that you need to do is check that the following three properties are satisfied:

criteria for methods that return a value

1. There is no infinite recursion. (A recursive call may lead to another recursive call, and that may lead to another, and so forth, but every such chain of recursive calls eventually reaches a stopping case.)

2. Each stopping case returns the correct value for that case.

3. For the cases that involve recursion: *if* all recursive calls return the correct value, *then* the final value returned by the method is the correct value.

For example, consider the method power in Display 11.3:

1. **There is no infinite recursion:** The second argument to power(x, n) is decreased by one in each recursive call, so any chain of recursive calls must eventually reach the case power(x, 0), which is the stopping case. Thus, there is no infinite recursion.

2. **Each stopping case returns the correct value for that case:** The only stopping case is power(x, 0). A call of the form power(x, 0) always returns 1, and the correct value for x^0 is 1. So the stopping case returns the correct value.

3. **For the cases that involve recursion: if all recursive calls return the correct value, then the final value returned by the method is the correct value:** The only case that involves recursion is when n > 1. When n > 1, power(x, n) returns

```
power(x, n - 1)*x.
```

To see that this is the correct value to return, note that: *if* power(x, n − 1) returns the correct value, *then* power(x, n − 1) returns x^{n-1} and so power(x, n) returns

$$x^{n-1} \ * \ x, \text{ which is } x^n$$

and that is the correct value for power(x, n).

That's all you need to check to be sure that the definition of power is correct. (The above technique is known as *mathematical induction,* a concept that you may have heard about in a mathematics class. However, you do not need to be familiar with the term *mathematical induction* to use this technique.)

We gave you three criteria to use in checking the correctness of a recursive method that returns a value. Basically the same rules can be applied to a recursive void method. If you show that your recursive void method definition satisfies the following three criteria, then you will know that your void method performs correctly:

criteria for void methods

1. There is no infinite recursion.

2. Each stopping case performs the correct action for that case.

3. For each of the cases that involve recursion: *if* all recursive calls perform their actions correctly, *then* the entire case performs correctly.

Binary Search ★

In this subsection we will develop a recursive method that searches an array to find out whether it contains a specified value. For example, the array may contain a list of the numbers for credit cards that are no longer valid. A store clerk needs to search the list to see if a customer's card is valid or invalid.

The indices of the array *a* are the integers 0 through finalIndex. To make the task of searching the array easier, we will assume that the array is sorted. Hence, we know the following:

$$a[0] \leq a[1] \leq a[2] \leq \ldots \leq a[\text{finalIndex}]$$

In fact, the binary search algorithm we will use requires that the array be sorted like this.

When searching an array, you are likely to want to know both whether the value is in the array and, if it is, where it is in the array. For example, if you are searching for a credit card number, then the array index may serve as a record number. Another array indexed by these same indices may hold a phone number or other information to use for reporting the suspicious card. Hence, if the sought-after value is in the array, we will have our method return an index of where the sought-after value is located. If the value is not in the array, our method will return –1. (The array may contain repeats, which is why we say "an index" and not "the index.")

Now let us proceed to produce an algorithm to solve this task. It will help to visualize the problem in very concrete terms. Suppose the list of numbers is so long that it takes a book to list them all. This is in fact how invalid credit card numbers are distributed to stores that do not have access to computers. If you are a clerk and are handed a credit card, you must check to see if it is on the list and hence invalid. How would you proceed? Open the book to the middle and see if the number is there. If it is not and it is smaller than the middle number, then work backward toward the beginning of the book. If the number is larger than the middle number, you work your way toward the end of the book. This idea produces our first draft of an algorithm:

algorithm first version

```
mid = approximate midpoint between 0 and finalIndex;
if (key == a[mid])
    return mid;
else if (key < a[mid])
    search a[0] through a[mid - 1];
else if (key > a[mid])
    search a[mid + 1] through a[finalIndex];
```

Since the searchings of the shorter lists are smaller versions of the very task we are designing the algorithm to perform, this algorithm naturally lends itself to the use of recursion. The smaller lists can be searched with recursive calls to the algorithm itself.

Our pseudocode is a bit too imprecise to be easily translated into Java code. The problem has to do with the recursive calls. There are two recursive calls shown:

```
search a[0] through a[mid - 1];
            and
search a[mid + 1] through a[finalIndex];
```

more parameters

To implement these recursive calls, we need two more parameters. A recursive call specifies that a subrange of the array is to be searched. In one case it is the elements indexed by 0 through mid − 1. In the other case it is the elements indexed by mid + 1 through finalIndex. The two extra parameters will specify the first and last indices of the search, so we will call them first and last. Using these parameters for the lowest and highest indices, instead of 0 and finalIndex, we can express the pseudocode more precisely as follows:

algorithm first refinement

```
To search a[first] through a[last] do the following:
mid = approximate midpoint between first and last;
if (key == a[mid])
    return mid;
else if (key < a[mid])
    return the result of searching a[first] through a[mid - 1];
else if (key > a[mid])
    return the result of searching a[mid + 1] through a[last];
```

To search the entire array, the algorithm would be executed with first set equal to 0 and last set equal to finalIndex. The recursive calls will use other values for first and last. For example, the first recursive call would set first equal to 0 and last equal to the calculated value mid − 1.

stopping case   As with any recursive algorithm, we must ensure that our algorithm ends rather than producing infinite recursion. If the sought-after number is found on the list, then there is no recursive call and the process terminates, but we need some way to detect when the number is not on the list. On each recursive call, the value of `first` is increased or the value of `last` is decreased. If they ever pass each other and `first` actually becomes larger than `last`, then we will know that there are no more indices left to check and that the number `key` is not in the array. If we add this test to our pseudocode, we obtain a complete solution, as shown in Display 11.5.

algorithm final version   Now we can routinely translate the pseudocode into Java code. The result is shown in Display 11.6. The method `search` is an implementation of the recursive algorithm given in Display 11.5. A diagram of how the method performs on a sample array is given in Display 11.7. Display 11.8 illustrates how the method `search` is used.

Notice that the method `search` solves a more general problem than the original task. Our goal was to design a method to search an entire array. Yet the method will let us search any interval of the array by specifying the indices `first` and `last`. This is common when designing recursive methods. Frequently, it is necessary to solve a more general problem in order to be able to express the recursive algorithm. In this case, we only wanted the answer in the case where `first` and `last` are set equal to 0 and `finalIndex`. However, the recursive calls will set them to values other than 0 and `finalIndex`.

Display 11.5   Pseudocode for Binary Search ★

ALGORITHM TO SEARCH a[**first**] THROUGH a[**last**]

```
/**
 Precondition:
 a[first]<= a[first + 1] <= a[first + 2] <= ... <= a[last]
*/
```

TO LOCATE THE VALUE KEY

```
if (first > last) //A stopping case
    return −1;
else
{
    mid = approximate midpoint between first and last;
    if (key == a[mid]) //A stopping case
        return mid;
    else if key < a[mid] //A case with recursion
        return the result of searching a[first] through a[mid − 1];
    else if key > a[mid] //A case with recursion
        return the result of searching a[mid + 1] through a[last];
}
```

Display 11.6   Recursive Method for Binary Search ★

```
1    public class BinarySearch
2    {
3        /**
4         Searches the array a for key. If key is not in the array segment, then −1 is
5         returned. Otherwise returns an index in the segment such that key == a[index].
6         Precondition: a[first] <= a[first + 1]<= ... <= a[last]
7        */
8        public static int search(int[] a, int first, int last, int key)
9        {
10           int result = 0; //to keep the compiler happy.

11           if (first > last)
12               result = −1;
13           else
14           {
15               int mid = (first + last)/2;

16               if (key == a[mid])
17                   result = mid;
18               else if (key < a[mid])
19                   result = search(a, first, mid − 1, key);
20               else if (key > a[mid])
21                   result = search(a, mid + 1, last, key);
22           }
23           return result;
24       }
25   }
```

In the subsection entitled "Tracing a Recursive Call," we gave three criteria that you should check to ensure that a recursive void method definition is correct. Let's check these three things for the method search given in Display 11.6:

1. **There is no infinite recursion:** On each recursive call the value of first is increased or the value of last is decreased. If the chain of recursive calls does not end in some other way, then eventually the method will be called with first larger than last, and that is a stopping case.

2. **Each stopping case performs the correct action for that case:** There are two stopping cases, when first > last and when key == a[mid]. Let's consider each case.

   If first > last, there are no array elements between a[first] and a[last] and so key is not in this segment of the array. (Nothing is in this segment of the array!) So, if first > last, the method search correctly returns −1, indicating that key is not in the specified range of the array.

   If key == a[mid], the algorithm correctly sets location equal to mid. Thus, both stopping cases are correct.

Display 11.7 Execution of the Method **search** ★

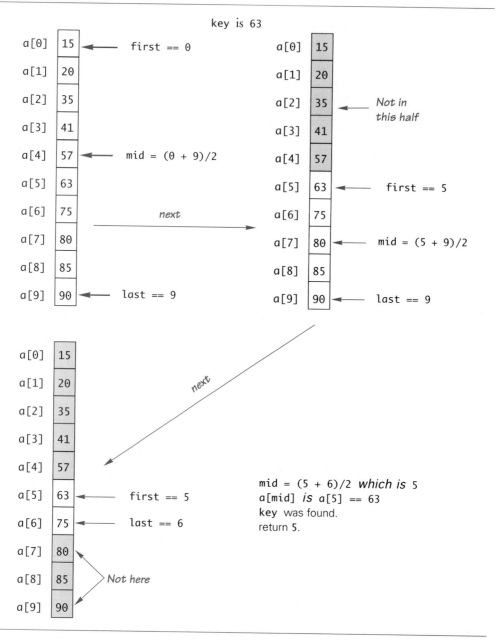

Display 11.8   Using the **search** Method ★

```
1   public class BinarySearchDemo
2   {
3       public static void main(String[] args)
4       {
5           int[] a = {-2, 0, 2, 4, 6, 8, 10, 12, 14, 16};
6           int finalIndex = 9;

7           System.out.println("Array contains:");
8           for (int i = 0; i < a.length; i++)
9               System.out.print(a[i] + " ");
10          System.out.println();
11          System.out.println();

12          int result;
13          for (int key = -3; key < 5; key++)
14          {
15              result = BinarySearch.search(a, 0, finalIndex, key);
16              if (result >= 0)
17                  System.out.println(key + " is at index " + result);
18              else
19                  System.out.println(key + " is not in the array.");
20          }
21      }
22  }
```

Sample Dialogue

```
Array contains:
-2 0 2 4 6 8 10 12 14 16

-3 is not in the array.
-2 is at index 0
-1 is not in the array.
0 is at index 1
1 is not in the array.
2 is at index 2
3 is not in the array.
4 is at index 3
```

3. **For each of the cases that involve recursion, if all recursive calls perform their actions correctly, then the entire case performs correctly:** There are two cases in which there are recursive calls, when key < a[mid] and when key > a[mid]. We need to check each of these two cases.

First suppose key < a[mid]. In this case, since the array is sorted, we know that if key is anywhere in the array, then key is one of the elements a[first] through a[mid – 1]. Thus, the method need only search these elements, which is exactly what the recursive call

```
search(a, first, mid − 1, key)
```

does. So if the recursive call is correct, then the entire action is correct.

Next, suppose key > a[mid]. In this case, since the array is sorted, we know that if key is anywhere in the array, then key is one of the elements a[mid + 1] through a[last]. Thus, the method need only search these elements, which is exactly what the recursive call

```
search(a, mid + 1, last, key)
```

does. So if the recursive call is correct, then the entire action is correct. Thus, in both cases the method performs the correct action (assuming that the recursive calls perform the correct action).

The method search passes all three of our tests, so it is a good recursive method definition.

Efficiency of Binary Search ★

The binary search algorithm is extremely fast compared to an algorithm that simply tries all array elements in order. In the binary search, you eliminate about half the array from consideration right at the start. You then eliminate a quarter, then an eighth of the array, and so forth. These savings add up to a dramatically fast algorithm. For an array of 100 elements, the binary search will never need to compare more than seven array elements to the key. A serial search could compare as many as 100 array elements to the key and on the average will compare about 50 array elements to the key. Moreover, the larger the array is, the more dramatic the savings will be. On an array with 1,000 elements, the binary search will only need to compare about 10 array elements to the key value, as compared to an average of 500 for the serial search algorithm.[1]

iterative version

An iterative version of the method search is given in Display 11.9. On some systems the iterative version will run more efficiently than the recursive version. The algorithm for the iterative version was derived by mirroring the recursive version. In the iterative version, the local variables first and last mirror the roles of the parameters in the recursive version, which are also named first and last. As this example illustrates, it

---

[1] The binary search algorithm has worst-case running time that is logarithmic, that is $O(\log n)$. The serial search algorithm is linear, that is $O(n)$. If the terms used in this footnote are not familiar to you, you can safely ignore this footnote.

Display 11.9   Iterative Version of Binary Search ★

```
1   /**
2     Searches the array a for key. If key is not in the array segment, then −1 is
3     returned. Otherwise returns an index in the segment such that key == a[index].
4     Precondition: a[lowEnd] <= a[lowEnd + 1]<= ... <= a[highEnd]
5   */
6   public static int search(int[] a, int lowEnd, int highEnd, int key)
7   {
8       int first = lowEnd;
9       int last = highEnd;
10      int mid;

11      boolean found = false; //so far
12      int result = 0; //to keep compiler happy

13      while ( (first <= last) && !(found) )
14      {
15          mid = (first + last)/2;

16          if (key == a[mid])
17          {
18              found = true;
19              result = mid;
20          }
21          else if (key < a[mid])
22          {
23              last = mid − 1;
24          }
25          else if (key > a[mid])
26          {
27              first = mid + 1;
28          }
29      }

30      if (first > last)
31          result = −1;

32      return result;
33  }
```

**extra code
on CD**

often makes sense to derive a recursive algorithm even if you expect to later convert it to an iterative algorithm. You can see the iterative method from Display 11.9 embedded in a full demonstration in the files IterativeBinarySearch.java and IterativeBinary-SearchDemo.java on the accompanying CD.

Most modern compilers will convert certain simple recursive method definitions to iterative ones before translating the code. In such cases there is no loss of efficiency for using the recursive version in place of an iterative version.

Self-Test Exercise

15. Write a recursive method definition for the following method:

```
/**
 Precondition: n >= 1
 Returns the sum of the squares of the numbers 1 through n.
*/
public static int squares(int n)
```

For example, squares(3) returns 14 because $1^2 + 2^2 + 3^2$ is 14.

Chapter Summary

- If a problem can be reduced to smaller instances of the same problem, then a recursive solution is likely to be easy to find and implement.

- A recursive algorithm for a method definition normally contains two kinds of cases: one or more cases that include at least one recursive call and one or more stopping cases in which the problem is solved without any recursive calls.

- When writing a recursive method definition, always check to see that the method will not produce infinite recursion.

- When you define a recursive method, use the three criteria given in the subsection "Recursive Design Techniques" to check that the method is correct.

- When you design a recursive method to solve a task, it is often necessary to solve a more general problem than the given task. This may be required to allow for the proper recursive calls, since the smaller problems may not be exactly the same problem as the given task. For example, in the binary search problem, the task was to search an entire array, but the recursive solution is an algorithm to search any portion of the array (either all of it or a part of it).

Answers to Self-Test Exercises

1. `Hip Hip Hurray`

2.
```java
public static void stars(int n)
{
    System.out.print('*');
    if (n > 1)
        stars(n - 1);
}
```

The following is also correct, but is more complicated:

3.
```java
public static void stars(int n)
{
    if (n <= 1)
    {
        System.out.print('*');
    }
    else
    {
        stars(n - 1);
        System.out.print('*');
    }
}

public static void backward(int n)
{
    if (n < 10)
    {
        System.out.print(n);
    }
    else
    {
        System.out.print(n%10);//write last digit
        backward(n/10);//write the other digits backward
    }
}
```

4.
```java
public static void writeUp(int n)
{
    if (n >= 1)
    {
        writeUp(n - 1);
        System.out.print(n + " "); //write while the
                            //recursion unwinds
    }
}
```

5.
```java
public static void writeDown(int n)
{
    if (n >= 1)
    {
        System.out.print(n + " "); //write while the
                                   //recursion winds
        writeDown(n - 1);
    }
}
```

6. An error message that says *stack overflow* is telling you that the computer has attempted to place more stack frames on the stack than are allowed on your system. A likely cause of this error message is infinite recursion.

7.
```java
public static void cheers(int n)
{
    while (n > 1)
    {
        System.out.print("Hip ");
        n--;
    }
    System.out.println("Hurray");
}
```

8.
```java
public static void stars(int n)
{
    for (int count = 1; count <= n; count++)
        System.out.print('*');
}
```

9.
```java
public static void backward(int n)
{
    while (n >= 10)
    {
        System.out.print(n%10);//write last digit
        n = n/10;//discard the last digit
    }
    System.out.print(n);
}
```

10. Trace for Self-Test Exercise 4: If n = 3, the code to be executed is

```java
if (3 >= 1)
{
    writeUp(2);
    System.out.print(3 + " ");
}
```

The execution is suspended before the `System.out.println`. On the next recursion, n = 2; the code to be executed is

```
if (2 >= 1)
{
    writeUp(1);
    System.out.print(2 + " ");
}
```

The execution is suspended before the `System.out.println`. On the next recursion, n = 1 and the code to be executed is

```
if (1 >= 1)
{
    writeUp(0);
    System.out.print(1 + " ");
}
```

The execution is suspended before the `System.out.println`. On the final recursion, n = 0 and the code to be executed is

```
if (0 >= 1) // condition false, body skipped
{
    // skipped
}
```

The suspended computations are completed from the most recent to the least recent. The output is 1 2 3.

11. Trace for Self-Test Exercise 5: If n = 3, the code to be executed is

```
if (3 >= 1)
{
    System.out.print(3 + " ");
    writeDown(2);
}
```

Next recursion, n = 2, the code to be executed is

```
if (2 >= 1)
{
    System.out.print(2 + " ");
    writeDown(1)
}
```

Next recursion, n = 1, the code to be executed is

```
if (1 >= 1)
{
    System.out.print(1 + " ");
    writeDown(0)
}
```

Final recursion, n = 0, and the `if` statement does nothing, ending the recursive calls:

```
if (0 >= 1) // condition false
{
    // this clause is skipped
}
```

The output is 3 2 1.

12. 6

13. The output is 24. The method rose is the factorial method, usually written *n!* and defined as follows:

n! is equal to $n*(n-1)*(n-2)*...*1$

14.
```
public static double power(int x, int n)
{
    if (n < 0 && x == 0)
    {
        System.out.println(
                "Illegal argument to power.");
        System.exit(0);
    }

    if (n < 0)
        return ( 1/power(x, -n));
    else if (n > 0)
        return ( power(x, n - 1)*x );
    else // n == 0
        return (1.0);
}
```

15.
```
public static int squares(int n)
{
    if (n <= 1)
        return 1;
    else
        return ( squares(n - 1) + n*n );
}
```

Programming Projects

 Many of these Programming Projects can be solved using AW's MyCodeMate. To access these please go to: www.mycodemate.com.

1. A savings account typically accrues savings using compound interest. If you deposit $1,000 with a 10% interest rate per year, then after one year you have a total of $1,100. If you leave this money in the account for another year at 10% interest, then after two years the total will be $1,210. After three years you would have $1,331, and so on.

Write a program that inputs the amount of money to deposit, an interest rate per year, and the number of years the money will accrue compound interest. Write a recursive function that calculates the amount of money that will be in the savings account using the input information.

To verify your function, the amount should be equal to $P(1+i)^n$, where P is the amount initially saved, i is the interest rate per year, and n is the number of years.

2. There are n people in a room, where n is an integer greater than or equal to 1. Each person shakes hands once with every other person. What is the total number, $h(n)$ of handshakes? Write a recursive function to solve this problem. To get you started, if there are only one or two people in the room, then:

```
handshake(1) = 0
handshake(2) = 1
```

If a third person enters the room, she must shake hands with each of the two people already there. This is two handshakes in addition to the number of handshakes that would be made in a room of two people, or a total of three handshakes.

If a fourth person enters the room, she must shake hands with each of the three people already present. This is three handshakes in addition to the number of handshakes that would be made in a room of three people, or six handshakes.

If you can generalize this to n handshakes then it should help you write the recursive solution.

3. Consider a frame of bowling pins shown below, where each * represents a pin:

```
    *
   * *
  * * *
 * * * *
* * * * *
```

There are five rows and a total of fifteen pins.

If we had only the top four rows then there would be a total of 10 pins.

If we had only the top three rows then there would be a total of 6 pins.

If we had only the top two rows then there would be a total of 3 pins.

If we had only the top row then there would be a total of 1 pin.

Write a recursive function that takes as input the number of rows n and outputs the total number of pins that would exist in a pyramid with n rows. Your program should allow for values of n that are larger than 5.

4. The game of "Jump It" consists of a board with n positive integers in a row except for the first column, which always contains zero. These numbers represent the cost to enter each column. Here is a sample game board where n is 6:

0	3	80	6	57	10

The object of the game is to move from the first column to the last column in the lowest total cost. The number in each column represents the cost to enter that column. You always start the game in the first column and have two types of moves. You can either move to the adjacent column or jump over the adjacent column to land two columns over. The cost of a game is the sum of the costs of the visited columns.

In the board shown above, there are several ways to get to the end. Starting in the first column, our cost so far is 0. We could jump to 80, then jump to 57, then move to 10 for a total cost of 80+57+10 = 147. However, a cheaper path would be to move to 3, jump to 6, then jump to 10, for a total cost of 3+6+10 = 19.

Write a recursive solution to this problem that computes the cheapest cost of the game and outputs this value for an arbitrarily large game board represented as an array. Your program doesn't have to output the actual sequence of jumps, only the cheapest cost of this sequence. After making sure that your solution works on small arrays, test your solution on boards of larger and larger values of n to get a feel for how efficient and scalable your solution is.

5. Write a recursive method definition for a static method that has one parameter n of type int and that returns the nth Fibonacci number. The Fibonacci numbers are F_0 is 1, F_1 is 1, F_2 is 2, F_3 is 3, F_4 is 5, and in general

$$F_{i+2} = F_i + F_{i+1} \text{ for } i = 0, 1, 2, \ldots$$

Place the method in a class that has a main that tests the method.

6. The formula for computing the number of ways of choosing r different things from a set of n things is the following:

$$C(n, r) = n!/(r!*(n-r)!)$$

The factorial method $n!$ is defined by

$$n! = n*(n-1)*(n-2)*\ldots*1.$$

Discover a recursive version of the formula for $C(n, r)$ and write a recursive method that computes the value of the formula. Place the method in a class that has a main that tests the method.

7. *Towers of Hanoi.* There is a story about Buddhist monks who are playing this puzzle with 64 stone disks. The story claims that when the monks finish moving the disks from one post to a second via the third post, time will end.

A stack of n disks of decreasing size (from bottom to top) is placed on one of three posts. The task is to move the disks one at a time from the first post to the second. To do this, any disk can be moved from any post to any other post, subject to the rule that you can never place a larger disk over a smaller disk. The (spare) third post is provided to make the solution possible. Your task is to write a recursive static method that gives instructions for a solution to this problem. We don't want to bother with graphics, so you should output a sequence of instructions that will solve the problem. The number of disks is a parameter to the method.

Hint: If you could move up n–1 of the disks from the first post to the third post using the second post as a spare, the last disk could be moved from the first post to the second post. Then, by using the same technique (whatever that may be), you can move the n–1 disks from the third post to the second post, using the first disk as a spare. There! You have the puzzle solved. You only have to decide what the nonrecursive case is, what the recursive case is, and when to output instructions to move the disks.

12

UML and Patterns

12 UML and Patterns

Einstein argued that there must be simplified explanations of nature, because God is not capricious or arbitrary. No such faith comforts the software engineer. Much of the complexity that he must master is arbitrary complexity.

F. BROOKS, "No Silver Bullet: Essence and Accidents of Software Engineering," *IEEE Computer*, April 1987

Introduction

UML and patterns are two software design tools that apply no matter what programming language you are using, as long as the language provides for classes and related facilities for object-oriented programming (OOP). This chapter presents a very brief introduction to these two topics. This chapter contains no new details about the Java language.

UML is a graphical language that is used for designing and documenting software created within the OOP framework.

A pattern in programming is very similar to a pattern in any other context. It is a kind of template or outline of a software task that can be realized as different code in different, but similar, applications.

Prerequisites

Section 12.1 on UML and Section 12.2 on patterns can be read in either order. None of this chapter is needed for the rest of the chapters in this book.

Section 12.1 on UML uses material from Chapters 1–5 and Chapter 7 on inheritance.
Section 12.2 on patterns uses material from Chapters 1–7 and Chapter 11.

12.1 UML

One picture is worth a thousand words.

Chinese proverb

Most people do not think in Java or in any other programming language. As a result, computer scientists have always sought to produce more human-oriented ways of representing programs. One widely used representation is pseudocode, which is a mixture of a programming language like Java and a natural language like English. To think about a programming problem without needing to worry about the syntax details of a language like Java, you can simply relax the syntax rules and write in pseudocode. Pseudocode has become a standard tool used by programmers, but pseudocode is a linear and algebraic representation of programming. Computer scientists have long sought to give software design a graphical representation. To this end, a number of graphical representation systems for program design have been proposed, used, and ultimately found to be wanting. Terms like *flowchart, structure diagram,* and many more names of graphical program representations are today only recognized by those of the older generation. Today's candidate for a graphical representation formalism is the **Unified Modeling Language** (or **UML**). UML was designed to reflect and be used with the OOP philosophy. It is too early to say whether or not UML will stand the test of time, but it is off to a good start. A number of companies have adopted the UML formalism to use in their software design projects.

UML

History of UML

UML developed along with OOP. As the OOP philosophy became more and more commonly used, different groups developed their own graphical or other representations for OOP design. In 1996, Grady Booch, Ivar Jacobson, and James Rumbaugh released an early version of UML. UML was intended to bring together the various different graphical representation methods to produce a standardized graphical representation language for object-oriented design and documentation. Since that time, UML has been developed and revised in response to feedback from the OOP community. Today the UML standard is maintained and certified by the Object Management Group (OMG), a nonprofit organization that promotes the use of object-oriented techniques.

UML Class Diagrams

class diagram

Classes are central to OOP and the **class diagram** is the easiest of the UML graphical representations to understand and use. Display 12.1 shows the class diagram for a class to represent a square. The diagram consists of a box divided into three sections. (The colors are optional and not standardized.) The top section has the class name, Square. The next section has the data specification for the class. In this example there are three pieces of data (three instance variables), a value of type double giving the length of a side, and two more values of type double giving the x and y coordinates of the center of the square. The third section gives the actions (class methods). The notation for method entries is not identical to that of a Java method heading but it contains the same information. A minus sign indicates a private member. So, for the class Square, all data is private. A plus sign indicates a public member. A sharp (#) indicates a protected member. A tilde (~) indicates package access. So, for the class Square, the class diagram shows two public methods and one protected method. A class diagram need not give a complete description of the class. When you do not need all the members in a class for the analysis at hand, you do not list all the members in the class diagram. Missing members are indicated with an ellipsis (three dots).

Display 12.1 A UML Class Diagram

Square
− side: double − xCoordinate: double − yCoordinate: double
+ resize(double newSide): void + move(double newX, double newY): void # erase(): void ...

Class Interactions

Class diagrams by themselves are of little value, since they simply repeat the class interface, possibly with ellipses. To understand a design, you need to indicate how objects of the various classes interact. UML has various ways to indicate class interactions; for example, various sorts of annotated arrows indicate the information flow from one class object to another. UML also has annotations for class groupings into packages, annotations for inheritance, and annotations for other interactions. Moreover, UML is extensible. If what you want and need is not in UML, you can add it to UML. Of course, this all takes place inside a prescribed framework so that different software developers can understand each other's UML. One of the most fundamental of class interactions is inheritance, which is discussed in the next subsection.

Inheritance Diagrams

inheritance diagram

arrows

Display 12.2 shows a possible **inheritance diagram** for some classes used in a university's record-keeping software. Note that the class diagrams are incomplete. You normally show only as much of the class diagram as you need for the design task at hand. Note that the arrow heads point up from a derived class to its base class.

The arrows also help in locating method definitions. If you are looking for a method definition for some class, the arrows show the path you (or the computer) should follow. If you are looking for the definition of a method used by an object of the class Undergraduate, you first look in the definition of the class Undergraduate; if it is not there, you look in the definition of Student; if it is not there, you look in the definition of the class Person.

Display 12.3 shows some possible additional details of the inheritance hierarchy for the two classes Person and one of its derived classes, Student. Suppose s is an

Display 12.2   A Class Hierarchy in UML Notation

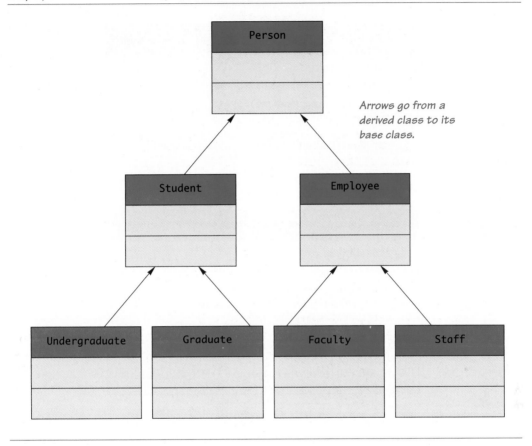

object of the class Student. The diagram in Display 12.3 tells you that you can find the definition of

        s.toString();

and

        s.set("Joe Student", 4242);

in the class Student, but the definition of

        s.setName("Josephine Student");

is found in the definition of the class Person.

Display 12.3   Some Details of a UML Class Hierarchy

More UML

This is just a hint of what UML is all about. If you are interested in learning more, consult one of the many available references on UML.

Self-Test Exercises

1. Draw a class diagram for a class whose objects represent circles. Use Display 12.1 as a model.

2. Suppose aStudent is an object of the class Student. Based on the inheritance diagram in Display 12.3, where will you find the definition of the method sameName used in the following invocation, which compares aStudent and another object named someStudent? Explain your answer.

```
Student someStudent =
            new Student("Joe Student", 7777);
if (aStudent.sameName(someStudent))
    System.out.println("wow");
```

3. Suppose aStudent is an object of the class Student. Based on the inheritance diagram in Display 12.3, where will you find the definition of the method used in the following invocation? Explain your answer.

```
aStudent.setNumber(4242);
```

12.2 Patterns

*I bid him look into the lives of men as though into a mirror, and from
others to take an example for himself.*

TERENCE (Publius Terentius Afer) 190-159 B.C., *Adelphoe*

pattern

Container-
Iterator

container

iterator

Patterns are design outlines that apply across a variety of software applications. To be useful, the pattern must apply across a variety of situations. To be substantive, the pattern must make some assumptions about the domain of applications to which it applies. For example, one well-known pattern is the **Container-Iterator** pattern. A **container** is a class (or other construct) whose objects hold multiple pieces of data. One example of a container is an array. Other examples, which will be discussed later in this book, are vectors and linked lists. Any class or other construct designed to hold multiple values can be viewed as a container. For example, a String value can be viewed as a container that contains the characters in the string. Any construct that allows you to cycle through all the items in a container is an **iterator**. For example, an array index is an iterator for an array. It can cycle through the array as follows:

```
for (int i; i < a.length; i++)
    Do something with a[i]
```

The index variable i is the iterator. The Container-Iterator pattern describes how an iterator is used on a container.

In this brief chapter we can give you only a taste of what patterns are all about. In this section we will discuss a few sample patterns to let you see what patterns look like. There are many more known and used patterns and many more yet to be explicated. This is a new and still developing field of software engineering.

Adaptor Pattern ★

Adaptor

The **Adaptor** pattern transforms one class into a different class without changing the underlying class but merely by adding a new interface. (The new interface replaces the old interface of the underlying class.) For example, in Chapter 11 we mentioned the stack data structure, which is used to, among other things, keep track of recursion. One way to create a stack data structure is to start with an array and add the stack interface. The Adaptor pattern says start with a container, like an array, and add an interface, like the stack interface.

The Model-View-Controller Pattern ★

Model-View-Controller

The **Model-View-Controller** pattern is a way of separating the I/O task of an application from the rest of the application. The Model part of the pattern performs the heart of the application. The View part is the output part; it displays a picture of the Model's state. The Controller is the input part; it relays commands from the user to the Model. Normally, each of the three interacting parts is realized as an object with responsibilities for its own tasks. The Model-View-Controller pattern is an example of a divide-and-conquer strategy. One big task is divided into three smaller tasks with well-defined responsibilities. Display 12.4 gives a diagram of the Model-View-Controller pattern.

As a very simple example, the Model might be a container class, such as an array. The View might display one element of the array. The Controller gives commands to display the element at a specified index. The Model (the array) notifies the View to display a new element whenever the array contents change or a different index location is given.

Any application can be made to fit the Model-View-Controller pattern, but it is particularly well suited to GUI (Graphical User Interface) design projects where the View can indeed be a visualization of the state of the Model. (A GUI interface is simply a windowing interface of the form you find in most modern software applications, as opposed to the simple text I/O we have used so far in this book.) For example, the Model might be an object to represent your list of computer desktop object names. The View could then be a GUI object that produces a screen display of your desktop icons. The Controller relays commands to the Model (which is a desktop object) to add or delete names. The Model object notifies the View object when the screen needs to be updated.

Display 12.4 Model-View-Controller Pattern

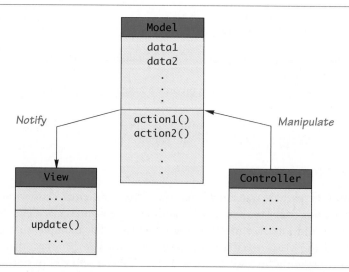

We have presented the Model-View-Controller pattern as if the user were the Controller. That was done primarily to simplify the examples. The Controller need not be under the direct control of the user, but could be some other kind of software or hardware component.

EXAMPLE: A Sorting Pattern

The most efficient sorting algorithms all seem to follow a similar pattern. Expressed recursively, they divide the list of elements to be sorted into two smaller lists, recursively sort the two smaller lists, and then recombine the two sorted lists to obtain the final sorted list. In Display 12.5 this pattern is expressed as pseudocode (in fact, almost correct Java code) for a method to sort an array into increasing order using the < operator.

Our sorting pattern uses a divide-and-conquer strategy. It divides the entire collection of elements to be sorted into two smaller collections, sorts the smaller collections by recursive calls, and then combines the two sorted collections to obtain the final sorted array. The following is the heart of our sorting pattern:

```
int splitPoint = split(a, begin, end);
sort(a, begin, splitPoint);
sort(a, splitPoint + 1, end);
join(a, begin, splitPoint, end);
```

Although the pattern does impose some minimum requirements on the methods split and join, the pattern does not say exactly how the methods split and join are defined. Different definitions of split and join will yield different sorting algorithms.

The method split rearranges the elements in the interval a[begin] through a[end] and divides the rearranged interval at a split point, splitPoint. The two smaller intervals a[begin] through a[splitPoint] and [splitPoint + 1] through a[end] are then sorted by a recursive call to the method sort. Note that the split method both rearranges the elements in the array interval a[begin] through a[end] and returns the index splitPoint that divides the interval. After the two smaller intervals are sorted, the method join then combines the two sorted intervals to obtain the final sorted version of the entire larger interval.

The pattern says nothing about how the method split rearranges and divides the interval a[begin] through a[end]. In a simple case, split might simply choose a value splitPoint between begin and end and divide the interval into the points before splitPoint and the points after splitPoint, with no rearranging. We will see an example that realizes the sorting pattern by defining split this way. On the other hand, the method split could do something more elaborate like move all the "small" elements to the front of the array and all the "large" elements toward the end of the array. This would be a step on the way to fully sorting the values. We will also see an example that realizes the sorting pattern in this second way.

(continued)

Display 12.5   **Divide-and-Conquer Sorting Pattern**

```
1    /**
2     Precondition: Interval a[begin] through a[end] of a have elements.
3     Postcondition: The values in the interval have
4     been rearranged so that a[begin] <= a[begin+1] <= ... <= a[end].
5    */
6    public static void sort(Type[] a, int begin, int end)
7    {
8        if ((end - begin) >= 1)
9        {
10           int splitPoint = split(a, begin, end);
11           sort(a, begin, splitPoint);
12           sort(a, splitPoint + 1, end);
13           join(a, begin, splitPoint, end);
14       }//else sorting one (or fewer) elements so do nothing.
15   }
```

To get a correct Java method definition Type must be replaced with a suitable type name.

Different definitions for the methods split *and* join *will give different realizations of this pattern.*

EXAMPLE: (continued)

The simplest realization of this sorting pattern is the **merge sort** realization given in Display 12.6. In this realization the array base type, *Type*, is specialized to the type double. The merge sort is an example where the definition of split is very simple. It simply divides the array into two intervals with no rearranging of elements. The join method is more complicated. After the two subintervals are sorted, the method join merges the two sorted subintervals, copying elements from the array to a temporary array. The merging starts by comparing the smallest elements in each smaller sorted interval. The smaller of these two elements is the smallest of all the elements in either subinterval and so it is moved to the first position in the temporary array. The process is then repeated with the remaining elements in the two smaller sorted intervals to find the next smallest element, and so forth. A demonstration of using the merge sort version of sort is given in Display 12.7.

There is a trade-off between the complexity of the methods split and join. You can make either of them simple at the expense of making the other more complicated. For merge sort, split was simple and join was complicated. We next give a realization where split is complicated and join is simple.

Display 12.8 gives the **quick sort** realization of our sorting pattern for the type double.

In the quick sort realization, the definition of split is quite sophisticated. An arbitrary value in the array is chosen; this value is called the **splitting value**. In our realization, we chose a[begin] as the splitting value, but any value will do equally well. The elements in the array are rearranged so that all those elements that are less than or equal to the splitting value are at the front of the array, all the values that are greater than the

Display 12.6   Merge Sort Realization of Sorting Pattern (part 1 of 2)

```
1   /**
2    Class that realizes the divide–and–conquer sorting pattern and
3    uses the merge sort algorithm.
4   */
5   public class MergeSort
6   {

7       /**
8        Precondition: Interval a[begin] through a[end] of a have elements.
9        Postcondition: The values in the interval have
10       been rearranged so that a[begin] <= a[begin+1] <= ... <= a[end].
11      */
12      public static void sort(double[] a, int begin, int end)
13      {                              The method sort is identical to the version in the
14          if ((end – begin) >= 1)    pattern (Display 12.5) except that Type is replaced
15          {                          with double.
16              int splitPoint = split(a, begin, end);
17              sort(a, begin, splitPoint);
18              sort(a, splitPoint + 1, end);
19              join(a, begin, splitPoint, end);
20          }//else sorting one (or fewer) elements so do nothing.
21      }

22      private static int split(double[] a, int begin, int end)
23      {
24          return ((begin + end)/2);
25      }

26      private static void join(double[] a, int begin, int splitPoint, int end)
27      {
28          double[] temp;
29          int intervalSize = (end – begin + 1);
30          temp = new double[intervalSize];
31          int nextLeft = begin; //index for first chunk
32          int nextRight = splitPoint + 1; //index for second chunk
33          int i = 0; //index for temp

34          //Merge till one side is exhausted:
35          while ((nextLeft <= splitPoint) && (nextRight <= end))
36          {
37              if (a[nextLeft] < a[nextRight])
38              {
39                  temp[i] = a[nextLeft];
40                  i++; nextLeft++;
41              }
```

(continued)

Display 12.6 **Merge Sort Realization of Sorting Pattern** (part 2 of 2)

```
42                  else
43                  {
44                      temp[i] = a[nextRight];
45                      i++; nextRight++;
46                  }
47              }

48          while (nextLeft <= splitPoint)//Copy rest of left chunk, if any.
49          {
50              temp[i] = a[nextLeft];
51              i++; nextLeft++;
52          }

53          while (nextRight <= end) //Copy rest of right chunk, if any.
54          {
55              temp[i] = a[nextRight];
56              i++; nextRight++;
57          }

58          for (i = 0; i < intervalSize; i++)
59              a[begin + i] = temp[i];
60      }

61  }
```

EXAMPLE: (continued)

splitting value are at the other end of the array, and the splitting value is placed so that it divides the entire array into these smaller and larger elements. Note that the smaller elements are not sorted and the larger elements are not sorted, but all the elements before the splitting value are smaller than any of the elements after the splitting value. The smaller elements are sorted by a recursive call, the larger elements are sorted by another recursive call, and then these two sorted segments are combined with the join method. In this case, the join method is as simple as it could be. It does nothing. Since the sorted smaller elements all precede the sorted larger elements, the entire array is sorted.

A demonstration program for the quick sort method sort in Display 12.8 is given in the file QuickSortDemo.java on the accompanying CD.

(Both the merge sort and the quick sort realizations can be done without the use of a second temporary array, temp. However, that detail would only distract from the message of this example. In a real application, you may or may not, depending on details, want to consider the possibility of doing a sort realization without the use of the temporary array.)

Display 12.7 Using the `MergeSort` Class

```
1   public class MergeSortDemo
2   {
3       public static void main(String[] args)
4       {
5           double[] b = {7.7, 5.5, 11, 3, 16, 4.4, 20, 14, 13, 42};

6           System.out.println("Array contents before sorting:");
7           int i;
8           for (i = 0; i < b.length; i++)
9               System.out.print(b[i] + " ");
10          System.out.println();

11          MergeSort.sort(b, 0, b.length-1);
12          System.out.println("Sorted array values:");
13          for (i = 0; i < b.length; i++)
14              System.out.print(b[i] + " ");
15          System.out.println();
16      }
17  }
```

Sample Dialogue

```
Array contents before sorting:
7.7 5.5 11.0 3.0 16.0 4.4 20.0 14.0 13.0 42.0
Sorted array values:
3.0 4.4 5.5 7.7 11.0 13.0 14.0 16.0 20.0 42.0
```

Display 12.8 Quick Sort Realization of Sorting Pattern (part 1 of 3)

```
1   /**
2    Class that realizes the divide-and-conquer sorting pattern and
3    uses the quick sort algorithm.
4   */
5   public class QuickSort
6   {

7       /**
8        Precondition: Interval a[begin] through a[end] of a have elements.
9        Postcondition: The values in the interval have
10       been rearranged so that a[begin] <= a[begin+1] <= ... <= a[end].
11      */
```

(continued)

Display 12.8 **Quick Sort Realization of Sorting Pattern** (part 2 of 3)

```
12      public static void sort(double[] a, int begin, int end)
13      {                                    The method sort is identical to the version in the
14          if ((end − begin) >= 1)          pattern (Display 12.5) except that Type is replaced
15          {                                with double.
16              int splitPoint = split(a, begin, end);
17              sort(a, begin, splitPoint);
18              sort(a, splitPoint + 1, end);
19              join(a, begin, splitPoint, end);
20          }//else sorting one (or fewer) elements so do nothing.
21      }

22      private static int split(double[] a, int begin, int end)
23      {
24          double[] temp;
25          int size = (end − begin + 1);
26          temp = new double[size];

27          double splitValue = a[begin];
28          int up = 0;
29          int down = size − 1;

30          //Note that a[begin] = splitValue is skipped.
31          for (int i = begin + 1; i <= end; i++)
32          {
33              if (a[i] <= splitValue)
34              {
35                  temp[up] = a[i];
36                  up++;
37              }
38              else
39              {
40                  temp[down] = a[i];
41                  down--;
42              }
43          }

44          //0 <= up = down < size

45          temp[up] = a[begin]; //Positions the split value, spliV.

46          //temp[i] <= splitValue for i < up
47          // temp[up] = splitValue
48          // temp[i] > splitValue for i > up

49          for (int i = 0; i < size; i++)
50              a[begin + i] = temp[i];
```

Display 12.8 **Quick Sort Realization of Sorting Pattern** (part 3 of 3)

```
51              return (begin + up);
52          }

53          private static void join(double[] a, int begin,
54                                          int splitPoint, int end)
55          {
56              //Nothing to do.
57          }

58      }
```

Restrictions on the Sorting Pattern

The sorting pattern, like all patterns, has some restrictions on where it applies. As we formulated the sorting pattern, it applies only to types for which the < operator is defined and it applies only to sorting into increasing order; it does not apply to sorting into decreasing order. However, this is a result of our simplifying details to make the presentation clearer. You can make the pattern more general by replacing the < operator with a boolean valued method called compare that has two arguments of the base type of the array and that returns true or false depending on whether the first "comes before" the second. Then, the only restriction is that the compare method must have a reasonable definition.[1] This sort of generalization is discussed in Chapter 13 in the subsection entitled "The Comparable Interface."

Efficiency of the Sorting Pattern ★

Essentially any sorting algorithm can be realized using this sorting pattern. However, the most efficient implementations are those for which the split method divides the array into two substantial size chunks, such as half and half, or one-forth and three-fourths. A realization of split that divides the array into one or a very few elements and the rest of the array will not be very efficient.

For example, the merge sort realization of split divides the array into two roughly equal parts, and merge sort is indeed very efficient. It can be shown (although we will not do so here) that merge sort has a worst-case running time that is the best possible "up to an order of magnitude."

---

[1] The technical requirement is that the compare method be a *total ordering*, a concept discussed in Chapter 13. Essentially, all common orderings that you might want to sort by are total orderings.

The Comparable interface has a method compareTo, which is slightly different from compare. However, the method we described as compare can easily be defined using the method compareTo as a helping method.

The quick sort realization of split divides the array into two portions that might be almost equal or might be very different in size depending on the choice of a splitting value. Since in extremely unfortunate cases the split might be very uneven for most cases, the worst-case running time for quick sort is not as fast as that of merge sort. However, in practice, quick sort turns out to be a very good sorting algorithm and usually preferable to merge sort.

Section sort, which we discussed in Chapter 5, divides the array into two pieces, one with a single element and one with the rest of the array interval. (See Self-Test Exercise 4.) Because of this uneven division, selection sort has a poor running time, although it does have the virtue of simplicity.

TIP: Pragmatics and Patterns

You should not feel compelled to follow all the fine details of a pattern. Patterns are guides, not requirements. For example, we did the quick sort implementation by exactly following the pattern. We did this to have a clean example. In practice we would have taken some liberties. Notice that, with quick sort, the join method does nothing. In practice we would simply eliminate the calls to join. These calls incur overhead and accomplish nothing. Other optimizations can also be done once the general pattern of the algorithm is clear. ■

Pattern Formalism

There is a well-developed body of techniques for using patterns. We will not go into the details here. The UML discussed in Section 12.1 is one formalism used to express patterns. The place within the software design process of patterns and any specific formalisms for patterns is not yet clear. However, it is clear that the basic idea of patterns, as well as certain pattern names, such as *Model-View-Controller,* have become standard and useful tools for software design.

Self-Test Exercises

4. Give an implementation of the divide-and-conquer sorting pattern (Display 12.5) that will realize the selection sort algorithm (Display 6.11) for an array with base type double.

5. Which of the following would give the fastest run time when an array is sorted using the quick sort algorithm: a fully sorted array, an array of random values, or an array sorted from largest to smallest (that is, sorted backward)? Assume all arrays are of the same size and have the same base type.

Chapter Summary

- The Unified Modeling Language (UML) is a graphical representation language for object-oriented software design.

- Patterns are design principles that apply across a variety of software applications.

- The patterns discussed in this chapter are the Container-Iterator, Adaptor, Model-View-Controller, and Divide-and-Conquer Sorting patterns.

- UML is one formalism that can and is used to express patterns.

Answers to Self-Test Exercises

1. There are many correct answers. Below is one:

Circle
− radius: double − centerX: double − centerY: double
+ resize(double newRadius): void + move(double newX, double newY): void # erase(): void ...

2. The method sameName is not listed in the class diagram for Student. So, you follow the arrow to the class diagram for Person. The method sameName with a single parameter of type Person is in the class diagram for Person. Since you know a Student is a Person, you know that this definition works for the method sameName with a single parameter of type Student. So, the definition used for the method sameName is in the class definition of Person.

3. You start at the class diagram for Student. The method setStudentNumber with a single parameter of type int is in the class diagram for Student, so you need look no further. The definition used for the method setStudentNumber is in the class definition of Student.

extra code on CD

4. The code for this is also on the CD that comes with this book. This code is in the file SelectionSort.java. A demonstration program is in the file SelectionSortDemo.java.

```java
public class SelectionSort
{
    public static void sort(double[] a,
                                        int begin, int end)
    {
        if ((end - begin) >= 1)
        {
            int splitPoint = split(a, begin, end);
            sort(a, begin, splitPoint);
            sort(a, splitPoint + 1, end);
            join(a, begin, splitPoint, end);
        }//else sorting one (or fewer) elements
         //so do nothing.
    }

    private static int split(double[] a,
                                        int begin, int end)
    {
        int index = indexOfSmallest(begin, a, end);
        interchange(begin,index, a);

        return begin;
    }

    private static void join(double[] a, int begin,
                                    int splitPoint, int end)
    {
      //Nothing to do.
    }

    private static int indexOfSmallest(int startIndex,
                                double[] a, int endIndex)
    {
        double min = a[startIndex];
        int indexOfMin = startIndex;
        int index;
        for (index = startIndex + 1;
                        index < endIndex; index++)
            if (a[index] < min)
            {
                min = a[index];
                indexOfMin = index;
                //min is smallest of a[startIndex]
                //through a[index]
            }
        return indexOfMin;
    }
```

```
private static void interchange(int i, int j, double[] a)
{
        double temp;
        temp = a[i];
        a[i] = a[j];
        a[j] = temp; //original value of a[i]
}
}
```

5. An array of random values would have the fastest run time, since it would divide the array segments into approximately equal subarrays most of the time. The other two cases would give approximately the same running time and would be significantly slower, because the algorithms would always divide an array segment into very unequal size pieces, one piece with only one element and one piece with the rest of the elements. It is ironic but true that our version of the quick sort algorithms has its worst behavior on an already sorted array. There are variations on the quick sort algorithms that perform well on a sorted array. For example, choosing the middle element as the splitting value will give good performance on an already sorted array. But, whatever splitting value you choose, there will always be a few cases with slow running time.

Programming Projects

 Many of these Programming Projects can be solved using AW's MyCodeMate. To access these please go to: www.mycodemate.com.

 1. The UML diagram below describes a class named Movie. Implement this class in Java and test it from a main method that creates several Movie objects. The printDescription() method should output all member variables for the class.

Movie
−title: String
−minutes: int
-year: int
#price: double
+Movie(in String title, in int year, in double price)
+getTitle( ): String
+setTitle(in String newTitle)
+printDescription( )

The word "in" means the parameter is used to deliver data to the method.

2. The UML diagram below shows the relationship between a class called
   `PizzaOrder` and a class called `Pizza`:

The word "in" means the parameter is used to deliver data to the method.

The `Pizza` class contains information about a specific pizza. The variables of
pepperoni, sausage, and mushrooms are booleans that indicate whether or not
these toppings are present on the pizza. The size variable is a character of value
'`s`', '`m`', or '`l`' to indicate small, medium, or large. There is also a `Pizza`
constructor that initializes all of these values. The `getSize()` method returns the
size of the pizza and the `getNumToppings()` method returns a number from 0–3
depending on what toppings are present (e.g., if the pizza has pepperoni and
mushrooms, it would be 2).

The `PizzaOrder` class contains an array of `Pizza`'s. There is a method to add a
new pizza to the array (which increments `numPizzas`) and also a method to
calculate the cost of the entire order. A small pizza costs $8, a medium pizza is
$10, and a large pizza costs $12. Each topping adds $1 to the pizza.

The arrow connecting `PizzaOrder` to `Pizza` indicates that the `PizzaOrder` class
has a reference to the `Pizza` class, but not vice versa. The solid diamond on the
`PizzaOrder` class is a UML construct that indicates that the `PizzaOrder` class has
a collection of the `Pizza` class. There may be many (*) `Pizza`'s for a single (1)
`PizzaOrder`.

Given this information, write Java code that implements the `Pizza` and
`PizzaOrder` classes. Also, write a test main function that creates a pizza order,
adds several pizzas to it, and outputs the cost of the order.

3. The UML diagram below shows the relationship between four classes. Implement the classes in a test program that creates instances of CreditCard, Cash, and Check. Output the string description of each. Note that the italicized *Payment* class indicates that this is an abstract class. The word "in" means the parameter is used to deliver data to the method.

4. Use the Model-View-Controller pattern to implement a simple timer-based counter. The counter should start at a user-specified initial value and increment by one every second until it reaches a user-specified final value. A UML diagram depicting the three classes for the pattern is shown below. The word "in" means the parameter is used to deliver data to the method.

The CounterView class should simply take an input counter value and print it on the console screen.

The CounterModel class should have a variable that represents the counter's value. The Increment method increments the counter by one and calls CounterView's Display method.

The CounterController class takes a start and end value that is specified by the user. CounterModel is then initialized with the start value. When the Start method is invoked it calls CounterModel's increment method once per second until endValue - startValue seconds have elapsed.

You will need to implement additional variables or methods in addition to those shown above in order to create the linkages between classes.

You can use the method call Thread.sleep(1000) to make the CounterController wait for one second. The call must be placed inside a try/catch block.

Test your program with a main method that counts several different ranges of values.

5. It is possible to purchase "geek" watches that output the time of day in binary. To illustrate the flexibility of the Model-View-Controller pattern, modify the view class (CounterView) of the previous problem so that the display outputs the counter's value in binary.

   Test your new program by counting values in binary. You should not have to change the model or controller classes.

6. Recode the QuickSort class implementation by adding two efficiency improvements to the method sort: (1) Eliminate the calls to join, since it accomplishes nothing. (2) Add code for the special case of an array of exactly two elements and make the general case apply to arrays of three or more elements.

7. Redo the QuickSort class so that it chooses the splitting point as follows: The splitting point is the middle (in size) of the first element, the last element, and an element at approximately the middle of the array. This will make a very uneven split less likely.

8. Redo the QuickSort class to have the modifications given for projects 6 and 7.

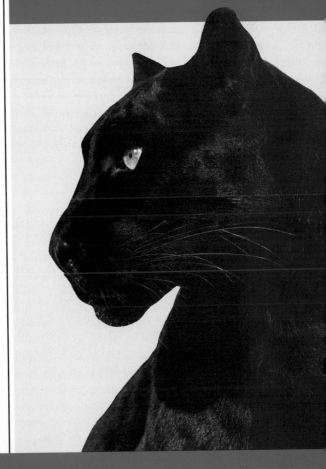

13

Interfaces and Inner Classes

13 Interfaces and Inner Classes

Art, it seems to me, should simplify. That, indeed, is very nearly the whole of the higher artistic process; finding what conventions of form and what details one can do without and yet preserve the spirit of the whole....

WILLA SIBERT CATHER, *On the Art of Fiction*

Introduction

A Java *interface* specifies a set of methods that any class that implements the interface must have. An interface is itself a type, which allows you to define methods with parameters of an interface type and then have the code apply to all classes that implement the interface. One way to view an interface is as an extreme form of an abstract class. However, as you will see, an interface allows you to do more than an abstract class allows you to do. Interfaces are Java's way of approximating multiple inheritance. You cannot have multiple base classes in Java, but interfaces allow you to approximate the power of multiple base classes.

The second major topic of this chapter is *inner classes*. An inner class is simply a class defined within another class. Since inner classes are local to the class that contains them, they can help make a class self-contained by allowing you to make helping classes inner classes.

Prerequisites

Section 13.1 on interfaces and Section 13.2 on simple uses of inner classes are independent of each other and can be covered in any order. Section 13.3 on more subtle details of inner classes requires both Sections 13.1 and 13.2.

Section 13.1 on interfaces requires Chapters 1 through 9. No material from Chapters 10 through 12 is used anywhere in this chapter.

Section 13.2 on simple uses of inner classes requires Chapters 1 through 5. It does not use any material from Chapters 6 through 12.

Section 13.3 on more advanced inner class material requires both Sections 13.1 and 13.2 (and of course their prerequisites). The material in Section 13.3 is not used elsewhere in this book.

13.1 Interfaces

Autonomy of Syntax

A linguistic concept attributed to Noam Chomsky

In this section we describe *interfaces*. An interface is a type that groups together a number of different classes that all include method definitions for a common set of method headings.

Interfaces

interface

An **interface** is something like the extreme case of an abstract class. *An interface is not a class. It is, however, a type that can be satisfied by any class that implements the interface.* An interface is a property of a class that says what methods it must have.

An interface specifies the headings for methods that must be defined in any class that implements the interface. For example, Display 13.1 shows an interface named Ordered. Note that an interface contains only method headings. It contains no instance variables nor any complete method definitions. (Although, as we will see, it can contain defined constants.)

implementing an interface

To **implement an interface**, a concrete class (that is, a class other than an abstract class) must do two things:

1. It must include the phrase

   implements *Interface_Name*

   at the start of the class definition. To implement more than one interface, you list all the interface names, separated by commas, as in

   implements SomeInterface, AnotherInterface

Display 13.1 The **Ordered** Interface

```
1    public interface Ordered                Do not forget the semicolons at
2    {                                       the end of the method headings.
3        public boolean precedes(Object other);

4        /**
5         For objects of the class o1 and o2,
6         o1.follows(o2) == o2.preceded(o1).
7        */
8        public boolean follows(Object other);
9    }
```

Neither the compiler nor the run-time system will do anything to ensure that this comment is satisfied. It is only advisory to the programmer implementing the interface.

---

2. The class must implement *all* the method headings listed in the definitions of the interfaces.

For example, to implement the Ordered interface, a class definition must contain the phrase implements Ordered at the start of the class definition, as shown in the following:

```
public class OrderedHourlyEmployee
            extends HourlyEmployee implements Ordered
    {
```

The class must also implement the two methods precedes and follows. The full definition of OrderedHourlyEmployee is given in Display 13.2.

Display 13.2 Implementation of an Interface

```
1   public class OrderedHourlyEmployee
2               extends HourlyEmployee implements Ordered
3   {
4       public boolean precedes(Object other)
5       {
6           if (other == null)
7               return false;
8           else if (!(other instanceof HourlyEmployee))
9               return false;
10          else
11          {
12              OrderedHourlyEmployee otherOrderedHourlyEmployee =
13                          (OrderedHourlyEmployee)other;
14              return (getPay() < otherOrderedHourlyEmployee.getPay());
15          }
16      }

17      public boolean follows(Object other)
18      {
19          if (other == null)
20              return false;
21          else if (!(other instanceof OrderedHourlyEmployee))
22              return false;
23          else
24          {
25              OrderedHourlyEmployee otherOrderedHourlyEmployee =
26                          (OrderedHourlyEmployee)other;
27              return (otherOrderedHourlyEmployee.precedes(this));
28          }
29      }
30  }
```

Although getClass works better than instanceof for defining equals, instanceof works better here. However, either will do for the points being made here.

An interface and all of its method headings are normally declared to be public. They cannot be given private, protected, or package access. (The modifier public may be omitted, but all the methods will still be treated as if they are public.) When a class implements an interface, it must make all the methods in the interface public.

An interface is a type. This allows you to write a method with a parameter of an interface type, such as a parameter of type Ordered, and that parameter will accept as an argument any class you later define that implements the interface.

An interface serves a function similar to a base class, but it is important to note that it is not a base class. (In fact, it is not a class of any kind.) Some programming languages (such as C++) allow one class to be a derived class of two or more different base classes. This is not allowed in Java. In Java, a derived class can have only one base class. However, in addition to any base class that a Java class may have, it can also implement any number of interfaces. This allows Java programs to approximate the power of multiple base classes without the complications that can arise with multiple base classes.

You might want to say the argument to precedes in the Ordered interface (Display 13.2) is the same as the class doing the implementation (for example, OrderedHourlyEmployee). There is no way to say this in Java, so we normally make such parameters of type Object. It would be legal to make the argument to precedes of type Ordered, but that is not normally preferable to using Object as the parameter type. If you make the argument of type Ordered, you would still have to handle the case of null and the case of an argument that (while Ordered) is not of type OrderedHourlyEmployee.

An interface definition is stored in a .java file and compiled just as a class definition is compiled.

Abstract Classes Implementing Interfaces

As you saw in the previous subsection, a concrete class (that is, a regular class) must give definitions for all the method headings given in an interface in order to implement the interface. However, you can define an abstract class that implements an interface but only gives definitions for some of the method headings given in the interface. The method headings given in the interface that are not given definitions are made into abstract methods. A simple example is given in Display 13.3.

Derived Interfaces

**extending an
interface**

You can derive an interface from a base interface. This is often called **extending** the interface. The details are similar to deriving a class. An example is given in Display 13.4.

Display 13.3 An Abstract Class Implementing an Interface ★

```
1    public abstract class MyAbstractClass implements Ordered
2    {
3        private int number;
4        private char grade;
5
6        public boolean precedes(Object other)
7        {
8            if (other == null)
9                return false;
10           else if (!(other instanceof HourlyEmployee))
11               return false;
12           else
13           {
14               MyAbstractClass otherOfMyAbstractClass =
15                                           (MyAbstractClass)other;
16               return (this.number < otherOfMyAbstractClass.number);
17           }
18       }
19       public abstract boolean follows(Object other);
20   }
```

Display 13.4 Extending an Interface

```
1    public interface ShowablyOrdered extends Ordered
2    {
3        /**
4          Outputs an object of the class that precedes the calling object.
5         */
6        public void showOneWhoPrecedes();
7    }
```

Neither the compiler nor the run-time system will do anything to ensure that this comment is satisfied.

A (concrete) class that implements the ShowablyOrdered interface must have a definition for the method showOneWhoPrecedes and also have definitions for the methods precedes and follows given in the Ordered interface.

Interfaces

An interface is a type that specifies method headings (and, as we will see, possibly defined constants as well). The syntax for defining an interface is similar to the syntax of defining a class, except that the word **interface** is used in place of **class** and only the method headings without any method body (but followed by a semicolon) are given.

Note that an interface has no instance variables and no method definitions.

A class can implement any number of interfaces. To implement an interface the class must include

```
implements Interface_Name
```

at the end of the class heading and must supply definitions for the method headings given in the interface. If the class does not supply definitions for all the method headings given in the interface, then the class must be an abstract class and the method headings without definitions must be abstract methods.

EXAMPLE

See Displays 13.1, 13.2, and 13.3.

Self-Test Exercises

1. Can you have a variable of an interface type? Can you have a parameter of an interface type?

2. Can an abstract class ever implement an interface?

3. Can a derived class have two base classes? Can it implement two interfaces?

4. Can an interface implement another interface?

PITFALL: Interface Semantics Are Not Enforced

As far as the Java compiler is concerned, an interface has syntax but no semantics. For example, the definition of the Ordered interface (Display 13.1) says the following in a comment:

```
/**
 For objects of the class o1 and o2,
 o1.follows(o2) == o2.preceded(o1).
*/
```

You might have assumed that this is true even if there were no comment in the interface. After all, in the real world, if I precede you, then you follow me. However, that is giving your intuitive interpretation to the word "precedes."

(continued)

PITFALL: (continued)

As far as the compiler and run-time systems are concerned, the Ordered interface merely says that the methods precedes and follows each take one argument of type Object and return a boolean value. The interface does not really require that the boolean value be computed in any particular way. For example, the compiler would be satisfied if both precedes and follows always return true or if they always return false. It would even allow the methods to use a random number generator to generate a random choice between true and false.

It would be nice if we could safely give an interface some simple semantics, such as saying that o1.follows(o2) means the same as o2.preceded(o1). However, if Java did allow that, there would be problems with having a class implement two interfaces or even with having a class derived from one base class and implementing an interface. Either of these situations could produce two semantic conditions both of which must be implemented for the same method, and the two semantics may not be consistent. For example, suppose that (contrary to fact) you could require that o1.follows(o2) means the same as o2.preceded(o1). You could also define another interface with an inconsistent semantics, such as saying that precedes always returns true and that follows always returns false. As long as a class can have two objects, there is no way a class could implement both of these semantics. Interfaces in Java are very well behaved, the price of which is that you cannot count on Java to enforce any semantics in an interface.

If you want to require semantics for an interface, you can add it to the documentation, as illustrated by the comment in Display 13.1 and the comment in Display 13.4, but always remember that these are just comments; they are not enforced by either the compiler or the run-time system, so you cannot necessarily rely on such semantics being followed. However, we live in an imperfect world, and sometimes you will find that you must specify a semantics for an interface; you do so in the interface's documentation. It then becomes the responsibility of the programmers implementing the interface to follow the semantics.

Having made our point about interface semantics not being enforced by the compiler or run-time system, we want to nevertheless urge you to follow the specified semantics for an interface. Software written for classes that implement an interface will assume that any class that implements the interface does satisfy the specified semantics. So, if you define a class that implements an interface but does not satisfy the semantics for the interface, then software written for classes that implement that interface will probably not work correctly for your class. ■

Interface Semantics Are Not Enforced

When you define a class that implements an interface, the compiler and run-time system will let you define the body of an interface method any way you want, provided you keep the method heading as it is given in the interface. However, you should follow the specified semantics for an interface whenever you define a class that implements that interface; otherwise, software written for that interface may not work for your class.

The `Comparable` Interface

This subsection requires material on arrays from Chapter 6. If you have not yet covered Chapter 6, you can skip this section and the following Programming Example without any loss of continuity. If you have read Chapter 6, you should not consider this section to be optional.

In Chapter 6 (Display 6.11), we introduced a method for sorting a partially filled array of base type `double` into increasing order. It is very easy to transform the code into a method to sort into decreasing order instead of increasing order. (See Self-Test Exercise 20 of Chapter 6 and its answer if this is not clear to you.) It is also easy to modify the code to obtain methods for sorting integers instead of `doubles` or sorting strings into alphabetical order. Although these changes are easy, they seem to be, and in fact are, a useless nuisance. All these sorting methods are essentially the same. The only differences are the types of the values being sorted and the definition of the ordering. It would seem that we should be able to give a single sorting method that covers all these cases. The `Comparable` interface lets us do this.

The `Comparable` interface is in the `java.lang` package and so is automatically available to your program. The `Comparable` interface has only the following method heading that must be implemented for a class to implement the `Comparable` interface:

`compareTo`
```
public int compareTo(Object other);
```

The `Comparable` interface has a semantics, and it is the programmer's responsibility to follow this semantics when implementing the `Comparable` interface. The semantics says that `compareTo` returns

a negative number if the calling object "comes before" the parameter `other`,

a zero if the calling object "equals" the parameter `other`,

and a positive number if the calling object "comes after" the parameter `other`.[1]

Almost any reasonable notions of "comes before" should be acceptable. In particular, all of the standard less-than relations on numbers and lexicographic ordering on strings are suitable ordering for `compareTo`. (The relationship "comes after" is just the reverse of "comes before.") If you need to consider other ordering, the precise rule is that the ordering must be a total ordering, which means the following rules must be satisfied:

(Irreflexive) For no object o does o come before o.

(Trichotomy) For any two objects o1 and o2, one and only one of the following holds true: o1 comes before o2, o1 comes after o2, or o1 equals o2.

(Transitivity) If o1 comes before o2 and o2 comes before o3, then o1 comes before o3.

The "equals" of the `compareTo` method semantics should coincide with the `equals` methods if that is possible, but this is not absolutely required by the semantics.

---

[1] Because the parameter to `CompareTo` is of type `Object`, an argument to `CompareTo` might not be an object of the class being defined. If the parameter `other` is not of the same type as the class being defined, then the semantics specifies that a `ClassCastException` should be thrown.

The Comparable Interface

The Comparable interface is in the `java.lang` package and so is automatically available to your program. The Comparable interface has only the following method heading that must be given a definition for a class to implement the Comparable interface:

```
public int compareTo(Object other);
```

The method **compareTo** should return

a negative number if the calling object "comes before" the parameter **other**,
a zero if the calling object "equals" the parameter **other**,
and a positive number if the calling object "comes after" the parameter **other**.

The "comes before" ordering that underlies **compareTo** should be a total ordering. Most normal ordering, such as less-than ordering on numbers and lexicographic ordering on strings, are total ordering.

If you define a class that implements the Comparable interface but that does not satisfy these conditions, then code written for Comparable objects will not work properly. It is the responsibility of you the programmer to ensure that the semantics is satisfied. Neither the compiler nor the run-time system enforces any semantics on the Comparable interface.

If you have read this subsection, you should also read the following Programming Example.

EXAMPLE: Using the Comparable Interface

Display 13.5 shows a class with a method that can sort any partially filled array whose base type implements the Comparable interface (including implementing the semantics we discussed in the previous subsection). To obtain the code in Display 13.5, we started with the sorting code in Display 6.11 and mechanically replaced all occurrences of the array type `double[]` with the type `Comparable[]`. We replaced all Boolean expressions of the form

Expression_1 < *Expression_2*

with

Expression_1.compareTo(*Expression_2*) < 0

We also changed the comments a bit to make them consistent with the compareTo notation. The changes are highlighted in Display 13.5. Only four small changes to the code were needed.

(continued on page 704)

Display 13.5 Sorting Method for Array of **Comparable** (part 1 of 2)

```java
1   public class GeneralizedSelectionSort
2   {
3       /**
4        Precondition: numberUsed <= a.length;
5                     The first numberUsed indexed variables have values.
6        Action: Sorts a so that a[0], a[1], ... , a[numberUsed – 1] are in
7        increasing order by the compareTo method.
8       */
9       public static void sort(Comparable[] a, int numberUsed)
10      {
11          int index, indexOfNextSmallest;
12          for (index = 0; index < numberUsed – 1; index++)
13          {//Place the correct value in a[index]:
14              indexOfNextSmallest = indexOfSmallest(index, a, numberUsed);
15              interchange(index,indexOfNextSmallest, a);
16              //a[0], a[1],..., a[index] are correctly ordered and these are
17              //the smallest of the original array elements. The remaining
18              //positions contain the rest of the original array elements.
19          }
20      }
21
22      /**
23       Returns the index of the smallest value among
24       a[startIndex], a[startIndex+1], ... a[numberUsed – 1]
25      */
26      private static int indexOfSmallest(int startIndex,
27                                      Comparable[] a, int numberUsed)
28      {
29          Comparable min = a[startIndex];
30          int indexOfMin = startIndex;
31          int index;
32          for (index = startIndex + 1; index < numberUsed; index++)
33              if (a[index].compareTo(min) < 0)//if a[index] is less than min
34              {
35                  min = a[index];
36                  indexOfMin = index;
37                  //min is smallest of a[startIndex] through a[index]
38              }
39          return indexOfMin;
40      }
```

(continued)

Display 13.5 **Sorting Method for Array of Comparable** (part 2 of 2)

```
40      /**
41       Precondition: i and j are legal indices for the array a.
42       Postcondition: Values of a[i] and a[j] have been interchanged.
43      */
44      private static void interchange(int i, int j, Comparable[] a)
45      {
46          Comparable temp;
47          temp = a[i];
48          a[i] = a[j];
49          a[j] = temp; //original value of a[i]
50      }

51  }
```

EXAMPLE: (continued)

Display 13.6 shows a demonstration of using the sorting method given in Display 13.5. To understand why the demonstration works, you need to be aware of the fact that both of the classes Double and String implement the Comparable interface.

If you were to check the full documentation for the class Double you would see that Double implements the Comparable interface and so has a compareTo method. Moreover, for objects o1 and o2 of Double,

```
o1.compareTo(o2) < 0 //o1 "comes before" o2
```

means the same thing as

```
o1.doubleValue() < o2.doubleValue()
```

So, the implementation of the Comparable interface for the class Double is really just the ordinary less-than relationship on the double values corresponding to the Double objects.

Similarly, if you were to check the full documentation for the class String, you would see that String implements the Comparable interface and so has a compareTo method. Moreover, the implementation of the compareTo method for the class String is really just the ordinary lexicographic relationship on the strings.

This Programming Example used the standard library classes Double and String for the base type of the array. You can do the same thing with arrays whose base class is a class you defined, so long as the class implements the Comparable interface (including the standard semantics, which we discussed earlier).

This Programming Example does point out one restriction on interfaces. They can only apply to classes. A primitive type cannot implement an interface. So, in Display 13.6 we could not sort an array with base type double using the sorting method for an array of Comparable. We had to settle for sorting an array with base type Double. This is a good example of using a wrapper class with its "wrapper class personality."

Display 13.6   **Sorting Arrays of Comparable** (part 1 of 2)

```
1   /**
2    Demonstrates sorting arrays for classes that
3    implement the Comparable interface.
4   */
5   public class ComparableDemo          The classes Double and String do
6   {                                    implement the Comparable interface.
7       public static void main(String[] args)
8       {
9           Double[] d = new Double[10];
10          for (int i = 0; i < d.length; i++)
11              d[i] = new Double(d.length - i);

12          System.out.println("Before sorting:");
13          int i;
14          for (i = 0; i < d.length; i++)
15              System.out.print(d[i].doubleValue() + ", ");
16          System.out.println();

17          GeneralizedSelectionSort.sort(d, d.length);

18          System.out.println("After sorting:");
19          for (i = 0; i < d.length; i++)
20              System.out.print(d[i].doubleValue() + ", ");
21          System.out.println();

22          String[] a = new String[10];
23          a[0] = "dog";
24          a[1] = "cat";
25          a[2] = "cornish game hen";
26          int numberUsed = 3;

27          System.out.println("Before sorting:");
28          for (i = 0; i < numberUsed; i++)
29              System.out.print(a[i] + ", ");
30          System.out.println();
31
32          GeneralizedSelectionSort.sort(a, numberUsed);

33          System.out.println("After sorting:");
34          for (i = 0; i < numberUsed; i++)
35              System.out.print(a[i] + ", ");
36          System.out.println();
37      }
38  }
```

(continued)

Display 13.6 Sorting Arrays of **Comparable** (part 2 of 2)

Sample Dialogue

```
Before Sorting
10.0, 9.0, 8.0, 7.0, 6.0, 5.0, 4.0, 3.0, 2.0, 1.0,
After sorting:
1.0, 2.0, 3.0, 4.0, 5.0, 6.0, 7.0, 8.0, 9.0, 10.0,
Before sorting;
dog, cat, cornish game hen,
After sorting:
cat, cornish game hen, dog,
```

Self-Test Exercises

These exercises are for the material on the Comparable interface.

5. The method interchange in Display 13.5 makes no use of the fact that its second argument is an array with base type Comparable. Suppose we change the parameter type Comparable[] to Object[] and change the type of the variable temp to Object. Would the program in Display 13.6 produce the same dialogue?

6. Is the following a suitable implementation of the Comparable interface?

```java
public class Double2 implements Comparable
{
    private double value;
    public Double2(double theValue)
    {
        value = theValue;
    }
    public int compareTo(Object other)
    {
        return -1;
    }
    public double doubleValue()
    {
        return value;
    }
}
```

You can think of the underlying "comes before" relationship as saying that for any objects d1 and d2, d1 comes before d2.

7. Suppose you have a class `Circle` that represents circles all of whose centers are at the same point. (To make it concrete you can take the circles to be in the usual x,y plain and to all have their centers at the origin.) Suppose there is a `boolean` valued method `inside` of the class `Circle` such that, for circles c1 and c2,

```
c1.inside(c2)
```

returns `true` if c1 is completely inside of c2 (and c2 is not the same as c1). Is the following a total ordering?

c1 comes before c2 if c1 is inside of c2
(that is, if `c1.inside(c2)` returns `true`).

You could represent objects of the class `Circle` by a single value of type `double` that gives the radius of the circle, but the answer does not depend on such details.

Defined Constants in Interfaces

The designers of Java often used the interface mechanism to take care of a number of miscellaneous details that do not really fit the spirit of what an interface is supposed to be. One example of this is the use of an interface as a way to name a group of defined constants.

An interface can contain defined constants as well as method headings or instead of method headings. When a method implements the interface, it automatically gets the defined constants. For example, the following interface defines constants for months:

```
public interface MonthNumbers
{
    public static final int JANUARY = 1,
        FEBRUARY = 2, MARCH = 3, APRIL = 4, MAY = 5,
        JUNE = 6, JULY = 7, AUGUST = 8, SEPTEMBER = 9,
        OCTOBER = 10, NOVERMBER = 11, DECEMBER = 12;
}
```

Any class that implements the `MonthNumbers` interface will automatically have the 12 constants defined in the `MonthNumbers` interface. For example, consider the following toy class:

```
public class DemoMonthNumbers implements MonthNumbers
{
    public static void main(String[] args)
    {
        System.out.println(
            "The number for January is " + JANUARY);
    }
}
```

Note that the constant JANUARY is used in the class DemoMonthNumbers but is not defined there. The class DemoMonthNumbers automatically gets the month constants because it implements the MonthNumbers interface.

no instance variables

An interface cannot have instance variables, although it can use the syntax for instance variables as a way to define constants. Any variables defined in an interface must be public, static, and final, so Java allows you to omit those modifiers. The following is an equivalent definition of the interface MonthNumbers:

```
public interface MonthNumbers
{
    int JANUARY = 1,
        FEBRUARY = 2, MARCH = 3, APRIL = 4, MAY = 5,
        JUNE = 6, JULY = 7, AUGUST = 8, SEPTEMBER = 9,
        OCTOBER = 10, NOVERMBER = 11, DECEMBER = 12;
}
```

Thus, an interface can be used to give a name for a group of defined constants, so that you can easily add the needed constants to any class by implementing the interface. This is really a different use for interfaces than what we have seen before, which was to use interfaces to specify method headings. It is legal to mix these two uses by including both defined constants and method headings in a single interface.

 PITFALL: Inconsistent Interfaces

Java allows a class to have only one base class but also allows it to implement any number of interfaces. The reason that a class can have only one base class is that if Java allowed two base classes, the two base classes could provide different and inconsistent definitions of a single method heading. Since interfaces have no method bodies at all, this problem cannot arise when a class implements two interfaces. The ideal that the designers of Java apparently hoped to realize was that any two interfaces will always be consistent. However, this ideal was not fully realized. Although it is a rare phenomenon, two interfaces can be inconsistent. In fact, there is more than one kind of inconsistency that can be exhibited. If you write a class definition that implements two inconsistent interfaces, that is an error and the class definition is illegal. Let's see how two interfaces can be inconsistent.

inconsistent constants

The most obvious way that two interfaces can be inconsistent is by defining two constants with the same name but with different values. For example:

```
public interface Interface1
{
    int ANSWER = 42;
}

public interface Interface2
{
    int ANSWER = 0;
}
```

PITFALL: (continued)

Suppose a class definition begins with

```
public class MyClass
    implements Interface1, Interface2
{ ...
```

Clearly this has to be, and is, illegal. The defined constant ANSWER cannot be simultaneously 42 and 0.[2]

inconsistent method headings

Even two method headings can be inconsistent. For example, consider the following two interfaces:

```
public interface InterfaceA
{
    public int getStuff();
}
public interface InterfaceB
{
    public String getStuff();
}
```

Suppose a class definition begins with

```
public class YourClass
                implements InterfaceA, InterfaceB
{ ...
```

Clearly this has to be, and is, illegal. The method getStuff in the class YourClass cannot be simultaneously a method that returns an int and a method that returns a value of type String. (Remember that you cannot overload a method based on the type returned; so, overloading cannot be used to get around this problem.) ■

Self-Test Exercises

8. Will the following program compile? If it does compile will it run? Interface1 and Interface2 were defined in the previous subsection.

```
public class MyClass
                implements Interface1, Interface2
{
    public static void main(String[] args)
    {
        System.out.println(ANSWER);
    }
}
```

(continued)

---

[2] If the class never uses the constant ANSWER, then there is no inconsistency and the class will compile and run with no error messages.

9. Will the following program compile? If it does compile will it run? `Interface1` and `Interface2` were defined in the previous subsection.

```java
public class MyClass
            implements Interface1, Interface2
{
    public static void main(String[] args)
    {
        System.out.println("Hello");
    }
}
```

10. Will the following program compile? If it does compile will it run? `InterfaceA` and `InterfaceB` were defined in the previous subsection.

```java
public class YourClass
            implements InterfaceA, InterfaceB
{
    public String getStuff()
    {
        return "one";
    }
}
```

11. Will the following two interfaces and the following program class compile? If they compile will the program run with no error messages?

```java
public interface InterfaceA
{
    public int getStuff();
}
public interface InterfaceOtherB
{
    public String getStuff(String someStuff);
}
public class OurClass
            implements InterfaceA, InterfaceOtherB
{
    private int intStuff = 42;

    public static void main(String[] args)
    {
        OurClass object = new OurClass();
        System.out.println(object.getStuff()
                    + object.getStuff(" Hello"));
    }
```

```
    public int getStuff()
    {
        return intStuff;

    }
    public String getStuff(String someStuff)
    {
        return someStuff;
    }
}
```

The `Serializable` Interface ★

As we have already noted, the designers of Java often used the interface mechanism
to take care of miscellaneous details that do not really fit the spirit of what an inter-

Serializable   face is supposed to be. An extreme example of this is the `Serializable` interface.
The `Serializable` interface has no method headings and no defined constants. As a
traditional interface it is pointless. However, Java uses it as a type tag that means the
programmer gives permission to the system to implement file I/O in a particular
way. If you want to know what that way of implementing file I/O is, see Chapter 10,
in which the `Serializable` interface is discussed in detail.

The `Cloneable` Interface

Cloneable   The `Cloneable` interface is another example where Java uses the interface mechanism
for something other than its traditional role. The `Cloneable` interface has no method
headings that must be implemented (and has no defined constants). However, it is
used to say something about how the method `clone`, which is inherited from the class
`Object`, should be used and how it should be redefined.

So, what is the purpose of the `Cloneable` interface? When you define a class to
implement the `Cloneable` interface, you are agreeing to redefine the `clone` method
(inherited from `Object`) in a particular way. The primary motivation for this appears
to be security issues. Cloning can potentially copy private data if not done correctly.
Also, some software may depend on your redefining the `clone` method in a certain
way. Programmers have strong and differing views on how to handle cloning and the
`Cloneable` interface. What follows is the official Java line on how to do it.

The method `Object.clone()` does a bit-by-bit copy of the object's data in storage.
If the data is all primitive type data or data of immutable class types, such as `String`,
then this works fine and has no unintended side effects. However, if the data in the
object includes instance variables whose type is a mutable class, then this would cause
what we refer to as *privacy leaks*. (See the Pitfall section entitled "Privacy Leaks" in
Chapter 5.) To avoid these privacy leaks when you define the `clone` method in a

derived class, you should invoke the clone method of the base class Object (or whatever the base class is) and then reset the values of any new instance variables whose types are mutable class types. You reset these instance variables to copies of the instance variables in the calling object. There are also issues of exception handling to deal with. An example may be clearer than an abstract discussion.

Let's start with the simple case. Suppose your class has no instance variables of a mutable class type, or to phrase it differently, suppose your class has instance variables all of whose types are either a primitive type or an immutable class type, like String. And to make it even simpler, suppose your class has no specified base class, so the base class is Object. If you want to implement the Cloneable interface, you should define the clone method as in Display 13.7.

The try-catch blocks are required because the inherited method clone can throw the exception CloneNotSupportedException if the class does not correctly implement the Cloneable interface. Of course, in this case the exception will never be thrown, but the compiler will still insist on the try-catch blocks.

Now let's suppose your class has one instance variable of a mutable class type named DataClass. Then, the definition of the clone method should be as in Display 13.8. First a bit-by-bit copy of the object is made by the invocation of super.clone(). The dangerous part of copy is the reference to the mutable object in the instance

Display 13.7   Implementation of the Method clone (Simple Case)

```
 1   public class YourCloneableClass implements Cloneable
 2   {                                    Works correctly if each instance variable is of a
 3           .                            primitive type or of an immutable type like
 4           .                            String.
 5           .
 6       public Object clone()
 7       {
 8          try
 9          {
10             return super.clone();//Invocation of clone
11                                  //in the base class Object
12          }
13          catch(CloneNotSupportedException e)
14          {//This should not happen.
15             return null; //To keep the compiler happy.
16          }
17       }
18       .
19       .
20       .
21   }
```

Display 13.8   Implementation of the Method **clone** (Harder Case)

```
1  public class YourCloneableClass2 implements Cloneable
2  {
3      private DataClass someVariable;
4          .
5          .
6          .
7      public Object clone()
8      {
9          try
10         {
11             YourCloneableClass2 copy =
12                         (YourCloneableClass2)super.clone();
13             copy.someVariable = (DataClass)someVariable.clone();
14             return copy;
15         }
16         catch(CloneNotSupportedException e)
17         {//This should not happen.
18             return null; //To keep the compiler happy.
19         }
20     }
21         .
22         .
23         .
24 }
```

DataClass is a mutable class. Any other instance variables are each of a primitive type or of an immutable type like String.

If the clone method return type is DataClass rather than Object, then this type cast is not needed.

The class DataClass must also properly implement the Cloneable interface including defining the clone method as we are describing.

variable someVariable. So, the reference is replaced by a reference to a copy of the object named by someVariable. This is done with the following line:[3]

```
copy.someVariable = (DataClass)someVariable.clone();
```

The object named by copy is now safe and so can be returned by the clone method.

If there are more instance variables that have a mutable class type, then you repeat what we did for someVariable for each of the mutable instance variables.

This requires that the class type DataClass has a correctly working clone method that is marked public, but that will be true if the class type DataClass implements the Cloneable interface in the way we are now describing. That is, DataClass should implement the Cloneable interface following the model of Display 13.7 or Display 13.8,

---

[3] Depending on how the clone method was defined in the class DataClass, the type cast may or may not be needed, but causes no harm in any case.

whichever is appropriate; similarly: all classes for instance variables in DataClass should follow the model of Display 13.7 or Display 13.8, and so forth for classes for instance variables inside of classes all the way down. You want every class in sight and every class used in every class in sight to follow the model of Display 13.7 or Display 13.8.

The same basic technique applies if your class is derived from some class other than Object, except that, in this case, there normally is no required exception handling. To implement the Cloneable interface in a derived class with a base class other than Object, the details are as follows: The base class must properly implement the Cloneable interface, and the derived class must take care of any mutable class instance variable added in the definition of the derived class. These new mutable class instance variables are handled by the technique shown in Display 13.8 for the instance variable someVariable. As long as the base class properly implements the Cloneable interface, including defining the clone method as we are describing, then the derived class's clone method need not worry about any inherited instance variables. Also, usually, you do not need to have try and catch blocks for CloneNotSupportedException because the base class clone method, super.clone(), normally catches all its CloneNotSupportedExceptions, so super.clone() will never throw a CloneNotSupportedException. (See Self-Test Exercise 14 for an example.)

Self-Test Exercises

12. Modify the following class definition so it correctly implements the Cloneable interface (all the instance variables are shown):

```
public class StockItem
{
    private int number;
    private String name;
    public void setNumber(int newNumber)
    {
        number = newNumber;
    }
        . . .
}
```

13. Modify the following class definition so it correctly implements the Cloneable interface (all the new instance variables are shown):

```
public class PricedItem extends StockItem
{
    private double price;

        . . .
}
```

14. Modify the following class definition so it correctly implements the `Cloneable` interface (all the new instance variables are shown):

```
public class PricedItem extends StockItem
{
    private double price;

        ...

}
```

15. Modify the following class definition so it correctly implements the `Cloneable` interface (all the instance variables are shown):

```
public class Record
{
    private StockItem item1;
    private StockItem item2;
    private String description;

        ...

}
```

16. Modify the following class definition so it correctly implements the `Cloneable` interface (all the new instance variables are shown):

```
public class BigRecord extends Record
{
    private StockItem item3;

        ...

}
```

17. Modify the definition of the class `Date` (Display 4.13) so it implements the `Cloneable` interface. Be sure to define the method `clone` in the style of Display 13.7.

18. Modify the definition of the class `Employee` (Display 7.2) so it implements the `Cloneable` interface. Be sure to define the method `clone` in the style of Display 13.8.

19. Modify the definition of the class `HourlyEmployee` (Display 7.3) so it implements the `Cloneable` interface. Be sure to define the method `clone` in the style of Display 13.8.

13.2 Simple Uses of Inner Classes

*The ruling ideas of each age have ever been the ideas of
its ruling class.*

KARL MARX and FRIEDRICH ENGELS, *The Communist Manifesto*

Inner classes are classes defined within other classes. In this section, we will describe one
of the most useful applications of inner classes, namely, inner classes used as helping
classes.

Helping Classes

inner class   Defining an **inner class** is straightforward; simply include the definition of the inner
class within another class, as follows:

```
public class OuterClass
{
    private class InnerClass
    {
        Declarations_of_InnerClass_Instance_Variables
        Definitions_of_InnerClass_Methods
    }

    Declarations_of_OuterClass_Instance_Variables
    Definitions_of_OuterClass_Methods
}
```

outer class   As this outline suggests, the class that includes the inner class is called an **outer class**.
The definition of the inner class (or classes) need not be the first item(s) of the outer
class, but it is good to place it either first or last so that it is easy to find. The inner class
need not be private, but that is the only case we will consider in this section. We will
consider other modifiers besides `private` in Section 13.3.

An inner class definition is a member of the outer class in the same way that the
instance variables of the outer class and the methods of the outer class are members
of the outer class. Thus, an inner class definition is local to the outer class definition.
So you may reuse the name of the inner class for something else outside the definition of the outer class. If the inner class is private, as ours will always be in this section, then the inner class cannot be accessed by name outside the definition of the
outer class.

There are two big advantages to inner classes. First, because they are defined
within a class, they can be used to make the outer class self-contained or more self-
contained than it would otherwise be. The second advantage is that the inner and
outer classes' methods have access to each other's private methods and private
instance variables.

TIP: Inner and Outer Classes Have Access to Each Other's Private Members

Within the definition of a method of an inner class, it is legal to reference a private instance variable of the outer class and to invoke a private method of the outer class. To facilitate this, Java follows this convention: If a method is invoked in an inner class and the inner class has no such method, then it is assumed to be an invocation of the method by that name in the outer class. (If the outer class also has no method by that name, that is, of course, an error.) Similarly, an inner class can use the name of an instance variable of the outer class.

The reverse situation, invoking a method of the inner class from the outer class, is not so simple. To invoke a (nonstatic) method of the inner class from within a method of the outer class, you need an object of the inner class to use as a calling object, as we did in Display 13.9 (Part 2).

As long as you are within the definition of the inner or outer classes, the modifiers `public` and `private` (used within the inner or outer classes) are equivalent.

These sorts of invocations and variable references that cross between inner and outer classes can get confusing. So, it is best to confine such invocations and variable references to cases that are clear and straightforward. It is easy to tie your code in knots if you get carried away with this sort of thing. ∎

Access Privileges between Inner and Outer Classes

Inner and outer classes have access to each other's private members.

EXAMPLE: A Bank Account Class

Display 13.9 contains a simplified bank account program with an inner class for amounts of money. The bank account class uses values of type `String` to obtain or return amounts of money, such as the amount of a deposit or the answer to a query for the account balance. However, inside the class it stores amounts of money as values of type `Money`, which is an inner class. Values of type `Money` are not stored as `String`s, which would be difficult to do arithmetic on, nor are they stored as values of type `double`, which would allow round-off errors that would not be acceptable in banking transactions. Instead, the class `Money` stores amounts of money as two integers, one for the dollars and one for the cents. In a real banking program, the class `Money` might have a larger collection of methods, such as methods to do addition, subtraction, and compute percentages, but in this simple example we have only included the method for adding an amount of money to the calling object. The outer class `BankAccount` would also have more methods in a real class, but here we have only included methods to deposit an amount of money to the account and to obtain the account balance. Display 13.10 contains a simple demonstration program using the class `BankAccount`.

(continued)

EXAMPLE: (continued)

The class Money is a private inner class of the class BankAccount. So, the class Money cannot be used outside of the class BankAccount. (Public inner classes are discussed in Section 13.3 and have some subtleties involved in their use.) Since the class Money is local to the class BankAccount, the name Money can be used for the name of another class outside of the class BankAccount. (This would be true even if Money were a public inner class.)

We have made the instance variables in the class Money private following our usual conventions for class members. When we discuss public inner classes, this will be important. However, for use within the outer class (and a private inner class cannot be used anyplace else), there is no difference between public and private or other member modifiers. All instance variables and all methods of the inner class are public to the outer class no matter whether they are marked public or private or anything else. Notice the method closeAccount of the outer class. It uses the private instance variables dollars and cents of the inner class.

This is still very much a toy example, but we will have occasion to make serious use of private inner classes when we discuss linked lists in Chapter 15 and when we study Swing GUIs starting in Chapter 17.

Display 13.9 Class with an Inner Class (part 1 of 2)

```
1    public class BankAccount
2    {
3        private class Money
4        {
5            private long dollars;
6            private int cents;
7
8            public Money(String stringAmount)
9            {
10               abortOnNull(stringAmount);
11               int length = stringAmount.length();
12               dollars = Long.parseLong(
13                       stringAmount.substring(0, length - 3));
14               cents = Integer.parseInt(
15                       stringAmount.substring(length - 2, length));
16           }
17
18           public String getAmount()
19           {
20               if (cents > 9)
```

The modifier private in this line should not be changed to public. However, the modifiers public and private inside the inner class Money can be changed to anything else and it would have no effect on the class BankAccount.

Display 13.9 **Class with an Inner Class** (part 2 of 2)

```
19                       return (dollars + "." + cents);
20                  else
21                       return (dollars + ".0" + cents);
22              }

23          public void addIn(Money secondAmount)
24          {
25              abortOnNull(secondAmount);
26              int newCents = (cents + secondAmount.cents)%100;
27              long carry = (cents + secondAmount.cents)/100;
28              cents = newCents;
29              dollars = dollars + secondAmount.dollars + carry;
30          }
31          private void abortOnNull(Object o)
32          {
33              if (o == null)
34              {
35                  System.out.println("Unexpected null argument.");
36                  System.exit(0);
37              }
38          }
39      }
40      private Money balance;

41      public BankAccount()
42      {
43          balance = new Money("0.00");
44      }

45      public String getBalance()
46      {
47          return balance.getAmount();
48      }

49      public void makeDeposit(String depositAmount)
50      {
51          balance.addIn(new Money(depositAmount));
52      }

53      public void closeAccount()
54      {
55          balance.dollars = 0;
56          balance.cents = 0;
57      }
58  }
```

The definition of the inner class ends here, but the definition of the outer class continues in Part 2 of this display.

To invoke a nonstatic method of the inner class outside of the inner class, you need to create an object of the inner class.

This invocation of the inner class method getAmount() would be allowed even if the method getAmount() were marked as private.

Notice that the outer class has access to the private instance variables of the inner class.

This class would normally have more methods, but we have only included the methods we need to illustrate the points covered here.

Display 13.10 Demonstration Program for the Class BankAccount

```
1    public class BankAccountDemo
2    {
3        public static void main(String[] args)
4        {
5            System.out.println("Creating a new account.");
6            BankAccount account = new BankAccount();
7            System.out.println("Account balance now = $"
8                                            + account.getBalance());

9            System.out.println("Depositing $100.00");
10           account.makeDeposit("100.00");
11           System.out.println("Account balance now = $"
12                                           + account.getBalance());
13           System.out.println("Depositing $99.99");
14           account.makeDeposit("99.99");
15           System.out.println("Account balance now = $"
16                                           + account.getBalance());

17           System.out.println("Depositing $0.01");
18           account.makeDeposit("0.01");
19           System.out.println("Account balance now = $"
20                                           + account.getBalance());

21           System.out.println("Closing account.");
22           account.closeAccount();
23           System.out.println("Account balance now = $"
24                                           + account.getBalance());
25       }
26   }
```

Sample Dialogue

```
Creating a new account.
Account balance now = $0.00
Depositing $100.00
Account balance now = $100.00
Depositing $99.99
Account balance now = $199.99
Depositing $0.01
Account balance now = $200.00
Closing account.
Account balance now = $0.00
```

> ### Helping Inner Classes
>
> You may define a class within another class. The inside class is called an **inner class**. A common and simple use of an inner class is to use it as a helping class for the outer class, in which case the inner class should be marked `private`.

Self-Test Exercises

20. Would the following invocation of `getAmount` in the method `getBalance` of the outer class `BankAccount` still be legal if we change the method `getAmount` of the inner class `Money` from `public` to `private`?

    ```
    public String getBalance()
    {
        return balance.getAmount();
    }
    ```

21. Since it does not matter if we make the members of a private inner class public or private, can we simply omit the `public` or `private` modifiers from the instance variables and methods of a private inner class?

22. Would it be legal to add the following method to the inner class `Money` in Display 13.9? Remember, the question is would it be legal, not would it be sensible.

    ```
    public void doubleBalance()
    {
        balance.addIn(balance);
    }
    ```

23. Would it be legal to add the following method to the inner class `Money` in Display 13.9? Remember, the question is would it be legal, not would it be sensible.

    ```
    public void doubleBalance2()
    {
        makeDeposit(balance.getAmount());
    }
    ```

The `.class` File for an Inner Class

When you compile any class in Java, that produces a `.class` file. When you compile a class with an inner class, that compiles both the outer class and the inner class and produces two `.class` files. For example, when you compile the class `BankAccount` in Display 13.9, that produces the following two `.class` files:

    BankAccount.class and BankAccount$Money.class

If `BankAccount` had two inner classes, then three `.class` files would be produced.

PITFALL: Other Uses of Inner Classes

In this section we have shown you how to use an inner class in only one way, namely to create and use objects of the inner class from within the outer class method definitions. There are other ways to use inner classes, but they can involve subtleties. If you intend to use inner classes in any of these other ways, you should consult Section 13.3. ■

13.3 More about Inner Classes

Something deeply hidden had to be behind things.

ALBERT EINSTEIN, Note quoted in *New York Times Magazine* (August 2, 1964)

In this section we cover some of the more subtle details about using inner classes. It might be best to treat this section as a reference section and look up the relevant cases as you need them. None of the material in this section is used in the rest of this book.

Static Inner Classes

A normal (nonstatic) inner class, which is the kind of inner class we have discussed so far, has a connection between each of its objects and the object of the outer class that created the inner class object. Among other things, this allows an inner class definition to reference an instance variable or invoke a method of the outer class. If you do not need this connec-

static tion, you can make your inner class **static** by adding the `static` modifier to your inner class definition, as illustrated by the following sample beginning of a class definition:

```
public class OuterClass
{
    private static class InnerClass
    {
```

A static inner class can have nonstatic instance variables and methods, but an object of a static inner class has no connection to an object of the outer class.

You may encounter situations where you need an inner class to be static. For example, if you create an object of the inner class within a static method of the outer class, then the inner class must be static. This follows from the fact that a nonstatic inner class object must arise from an outer class object.

Also, if you want your inner class to itself have static members, then the inner class must be static.

Since a static inner class has no connection to an object of the outer class, you cannot reference an instance variable or invoke a nonstatic method of the outer class within the static inner class.

To invoke a static method of a static inner class within the outer class, simply preface the method name with the name of the inner class and a dot. Similarly, to name a static variable of a static inner class within the outer class, simply preface the static variable name with the name of the inner class and a dot.

Static Inner Class

A static inner class is one that is not associated with an object of the outer class. It is indicated by including the modifier **static** in its class heading.

Self-Test Exercises

24. Can you have a static method in a nonstatic inner class?

25. Can you have a nonstatic method in a static inner class?

Public Inner Classes

public inner class

If an inner class is marked with the public modifier instead of the private modifier, then it can be used in all the ways we discussed so far, but it can also be used outside of the outer class.

The way that you create an object of the inner class outside of the outer class is a bit different for static and nonstatic inner classes. We consider the case of a nonstatic inner class first. When creating an object of a nonstatic inner class, you need to keep in mind that every object of the nonstatic inner class is associated with some object of the outer class. To put it another way, to create an object of the inner class, you must start with an object of the outer class. This has to be true, since an object of the inner class may invoke a method of the outer class or reference an instance variable of the outer class, and you cannot have an instance variable of the outer class unless you have an object of the outer class.

For example, *if you change the class* Money *in Display 13.9 from private to public*, so the class definition begins

```
public class BankAccount
{
    public class Money
```

then you can use an object of the nonstatic inner class Money outside of the class BankAccount as illustrated by the following:

```
BankAccount account = new BankAccount();
BankAccount.Money amount =
            account.new Money("41.99");
System.out.println(amount.getAmount());
```

This code produces the output

```
41.99
```

Note that the object amount of the inner class Money is created starting with an object, account, of the outer class BankAccount, as follows:

```
BankAccount.Money amount =
                account.new Money("41.99");
```

Also, note that the syntax of the second line is *not*

```
new account.Money("41.99"); //Incorrect syntax
```

Within the definition of the inner class Money, an object of the inner class can invoke a method of the outer class. However, this is not true outside of the inner class. Outside of the inner class an object of the inner class can only invoke methods of the inner class. So, we could *not* have continued the previous sample code (which is outside the class BankAccount and so outside the inner class Money) with the following:

```
System.out.println(amount.getBalance()); //Illegal
```

The meaning of amount.getBalance() is clear, but it is still not allowed. If you want something equivalent to amount.getBalance(), you should use the corresponding object of the class BankAccount; in this case, you would use account.getBalance(). (Recall that account is the BankAccount object used to create the inner class object amount.)

Now let's consider the case of a static inner class. You can create objects of a public *static* inner class and do so outside of the inner class, in fact even outside of the outer class. To do so outside of the outer class, the situation is similar to, but not exactly the same as, what we outlined for nonstatic inner classes. Consider the following outline:

```
public class OuterClass
{
    public static class InnerClass
    {
        public void nonstaticMethod()
        { ... }

        public static void staticMethod()
        { ... }

        Other_Members_of_InnerClass
    }

    Other_Members_of_OuterClass
}
```

You can create an object of the inner class outside of the outer class as in the following example:

```
OuterClass.InnerClass innerObject =
                new OuterClass.InnerClass();
```

Note that the syntax is *not*

```
OuterClass.new InnerClass();
```

This may seem like an apparent inconsistency with the syntax for creating the object of a nonstatic inner class. It may help to keep in mind that for a static inner class, `OuterClass.InnerClass` is a well-specified class name and all the information for the object is in that class name. To remember the syntax for a nonstatic inner class, remember that for that case, the object of the outer class modifies how the new operator works to create an object of the inner class.

Once you have created an object of the inner class, the object can invoke a non-static method in the usual way. For example:

```
innerObject.nonstaticMethod();
```

You can also use the object of the inner class to invoke a static method in the same way. For example:

```
innerObject.staticMethod();
```

However, it is more common, and clearer, to use class names when invoking a static method. For example:

```
OuterClass.InnerClass.staticMethod();
```

TIP: Referring to a Method of the Outer Class

As we've already noted, if a method is invoked in an inner class and the inner class has no such method, then it is assumed to be an invocation of the method by that name in the outer class. For example, we could add a method `showBalance` to the inner class `Money` in Display 13.9, as outlined in what follows:

```
public class BankAccount
{
    private class Money
    {
        private long dollars;
        private int cents;

        public void showBalance()
        {
            System.out.println(getBalance());
        }
        ...
    }//End of Money
```

(continued)

TIP: (continued)

```
        public String getBalance()
        {...}
            ...
}//End of BankAccount
```

This invocation of `getBalance` is within the definition of the inner class `Money`. But the inner class `Money` has no method named `getBalance`, so it is presumed to be the method `getBalance` of the outer class `BankAccount`.

But suppose the inner class did have a method named `getBalance`; then this invocation of `getBalance` would be an invocation of the method `getBalance` defined in the inner class.

If both the inner and outer classes have a method named `getBalance`, then you can specify that you mean the method of the outer class as follows:

```
public void showBalance()
{
    System.out.println(
                BankAccount.this.getBalance());
}
```

The syntax

Outer_Class_Name`.this.`*Method_Name*

always refers to a method of the outer class. In the example, `BankAccount.this` means the `this` of `BankAccount`, as opposed to the `this` of the inner class `Money`. ∎

Self-Test Exercises

26. Consider the following class definition:

```
public class OuterClass
{
    public static class InnerClass
    {
        public static void someMethod()
        {
            System.out.println("From inside.");
        }
    }

    Other_Members_of_OuterClass
}
```

Write an invocation of the static method `someMethod` that you could use in some class you define.

Self-Test Exercises (continued)

27. Consider the following class definition:

```
public class Outs
{
    private int outerInt = 100;

    public class Ins
    {
        private int innerInt = 25;
        public void specialMethod()
        {
            System.out.println(outerInt);
            System.out.println(innerInt);
        }
    }
    Other_Members_of_OuterClass
}
```

Write an invocation of the method `specialMethod` with an object of the class `Ins`. Part of this exercise is to create the object of the class `Ins`. This should be code that you could use in some class you define.

Nesting Inner Classes

It is legal to nest inner classes within inner classes. The rules are the same as what we have already discussed except that names can get longer. For example, if A has a public inner class B, and B has a public inner class C, then the following is valid code:

```
A aObject = new A();
A.B bObject =
            aObject.new B();
A.B.C cObject =
            bObject.new C();
```

Inner Classes and Inheritance

Suppose `OuterClass` has an inner class named `InnerClass`. If you derive `Derived-Class` from `OuterClass`, then `DerivedClass` automatically has `InnerClass` as an inner class just as if it were defined within `DerivedClass`.

Just as with any other kind of class in Java, you can make an inner class a derived class of some other class. You can also make the outer class a derived class of a different (or the same) base class.

It is not possible to override the definition of an inner class when you define a derived class of the outer class.

It is also possible to use an inner class as a base class to derive classes, but we will not go into those details in this book; there are some subtleties to worry about.

Anonymous Classes

If you wish to create an object but have no need to name the object's class, then you can embed the class definition inside the expression with the new operator. These sorts of class definitions are called **anonymous classes** because they have no class name. An expression with an anonymous class definition is, like everything in Java, inside of some class definition. Thus, an anonymous class is an inner class. Before we go into the details of the syntax for anonymous classes, let's say a little about where one might use them.

anonymous class

The most straightforward way to create an object is the following:

```
YourClass anObject = new YourClass();
```

If new YourClass() is replaced by some expression that defines the class but does not give the class any name, then there is no name YourClass to use to declare the variable anObject. So, it does not make sense to use an anonymous class in this situation. However, it can make sense in the following situation:

```
SomeOtherType anObject = new YourClass();
```

Here SomeOtherType must be a type such that an object of the class YourClass is also an object of SomeOtherType. In this situation you can replace new YourClass() with an expression including an anonymous class instead of YourClass. The type SomeOtherType is usually a Java interface.

Here's an example of an anonymous class. Suppose you define the following interface:

```
public interface NumberCarrier
{
    public void setNumber(int value);
    public int getNumber();
}
```

Then the following creates an object using an anonymous class definition:

```
NumberCarrier anObject = new NumberCarrier()
                {
                        private int number;
                        public void setNumber(int value)
                        {
                            number = value;
                        }
                        public int getNumber()
                        {
                            return number;
                        }
                };
```

The part in the braces is the same as the part inside the main braces of a class definition. The closing brace is followed by a semicolon, unlike a class definition. (This is because the entire expression will be used as a Java statement.) The beginning part, repeated below, may seem strange:

```
new NumberCarrier()
```

The new is sensible enough but what's the point of NumberCarrier()? It looks like this is an invocation of a constructor for NumberCarrier. But, NumberCarrier is an interface and has no constructors. The meaning of new NumberCarrier() is simply

```
implements NumberCarrier
```

So what is being said is that the anonymous class implements the NumberCarrier interface and is defined as shown between the main braces.

Display 13.11 shows a simple demonstration with two anonymous class definitions. For completeness we have also repeated the definition of the NumberCarrier interface in that display.

Display 13.1 **Anonymous Classes** (part 1 of 2)

```
 1   public class AnonymousClassDemo
 2   {
 3       public static void main(String[] args)
 4       {
 5           NumberCarrier anObject =
 6                   new NumberCarrier()
 7                   {
 8                       private int number;
 9                       public void setNumber(int value)
10                       {
11                           number = value;
12                       }
13                       public int getNumber()
14                       {
15                           return number;
16                       }
17                   };
18
19           NumberCarrier anotherObject =
20                   new NumberCarrier()
21                   {
22                       private int number;
23                       public void setNumber(int value)
24                       {
25                           number = 2*value;
26                       }
```

This is just a toy example to demonstrate the Java syntax for anonymous classes.

(continued)

Display 13.11 **Anonymous Classes** (part 2 of 2)

```
26                      public int getNumber()
27                      {
28                          return number;
29                      }
30                  };

31          anObject.setNumber(42);
32          anotherObject.setNumber(42);
33          showNumber(anObject);
34          showNumber(anotherObject);
35          System.out.println("End of program.");
36      }

37      public static void showNumber(NumberCarrier o)
38      {
39          System.out.println(o.getNumber());
40      }
```
This is the file **AnonymousClassDemo.java.**
```
41  }
```

Sample Dialogue

```
42
84
End of program.
```

```
1   public interface NumberCarrier          This is the file NumberCarrier.java.
2   {
3       public void setNumber(int value);
4       public int getNumber();
5   }
```

TIP: Why Use Inner Classes?

Most simple situations do not need inner classes. However, there are situations for which inner classes are a good solution. For example, suppose you want to have a class with two base classes. That is not allowed in Java. However, you can have an outer class derived from one base class with an inner class derived from the other base class. Since the inner and outer classes have access to each other's instance variables and methods, this can often serve as if it were a class with two base classes.

TIP: (continued)

As another example, if you only need one object of a class and the class definition is very short, many programmers like to use an anonymous class (but I must admit I am not one of them).

When we study *linked lists* in Chapter 15, you will see cases where using an inner class as a helping class makes the linked list class self-contained in a very natural way. We will also use inner classes when defining Graphical User Interfaces (GUIs) starting in Chapter 17. But until you learn what linked lists and GUIs are, these are not likely to be compelling examples. ■

Self-Test Exercise

28. Suppose we replace

    NumberCarrier anObject

    with

    Object anObject

    in Display 13.11. What would be the first statement in the program to cause an error message? Would it be a compiler error message or a run-time error message?

Chapter Summary

- An interface is a property of a class that says what methods a class that implements the interface must have.

- An interface is defined the same way as a class is defined except that the keyword interface is used in place of the keyword class and method bodies are replaced by semicolons.

- An interface may not have any instance variables, with one exception: An interface may have defined constants. If you use the syntax for an instance variable in an inner class, the variable is automatically a constant, not a real instance variable.

- An inner class is a class defined within another class.

- One simple use of an inner class is as a helping class to be used in the definition of the outer class methods and/or instance variables.

- A static inner class is one that is not associated with an object of the outer class. It must include the modifier static in its class heading.

- To create an object of a nonstatic inner class outside the definition of the outer class, you must first create an object of the outer class and use it to create an object of the inner class.

Answers to Self-Test Exercises

1. Yes to both. An interface is a type and can be used like any other type.

2. Yes. Any of the interface methods that it does not fully define must be made abstract methods.

3. A derived class can have only one base class, but it can implement any number of interfaces.

4. No, but the way to accomplish the same thing is to have one interface extend the other.

    These exercises are for the material on the Comparable interface.

5. Yes, the dialogue would be the same. The change from the parameter type Comparable[] to Object[] in the method interchange is in fact a good idea.

6. No. This will compile without any error messages. However, the less-than ordering does not satisfy the semantics of the Comparable interface. For example, the trichotomy law does not hold.

7. Yes. The three required conditions are true for objects of the class Circle:

    (Irreflexive) By definition, no circle is inside itself.

    (Trichotomy) For any two circles c1 and c2 with centers at the origin, one and only one of the following holds true: c1 is inside of c2 , c2 is inside of c1, or c1 equals c2.

    (Transitivity) If c1 is inside of c2 and c2 is inside of c3, then c1 is inside of c3.

8. The class will produce a compiler error message saying that there is an inconsistency in the definitions of ANSWER.

9. The class will compile and run with no error messages. Since the named constant ANSWER is never used, there is no inconsistency.

10. The class will produce a compiler error message saying that you have not implemented the heading for getStuff in InterfaceA.

11. They will all compile and the program will run. The two definitions of getStuff have different numbers of parameters and so this is overloading. There is no inconsistency.

12.
```java
public class StockItem implements Cloneable
{
    private int number;
    private String name;
    public void setNumber(int newNumber)
    {
        number = newNumber;
    }
        ...
    public Object clone()
    {
        try
        {
```

```
            return super.clone();
        }
        catch(CloneNotSupportedException e)
        {//This should not happen.
            return null; //To keep compiler happy.
        }
    }
}
```

13. Note that you do not catch a `CloneNotSupportedException` because any such thrown exception in `super.clone` is caught inside the base class method `super.clone`.

```
public class PricedItem extends StockItem
                        implements Cloneable
{
    private double price;

    ...
    public Object clone()
    {
        return super.clone();
    }
}
```

14.
```
public class Record implements Cloneable
{
    private StockItem item1;
    private StockItem item2;
    private String description;

    ...
    public Object clone()
    {
        try
        {
            Record copy =
                    (Record)super.clone();
            copy.item1 =
                    (StockItem)item1.clone();
            copy.item2 =
                    (StockItem)item2.clone();
            return copy;
        }
        catch(CloneNotSupportedException e)
        {//This should not happen.
            return null; //To keep compiler happy.
        }
    }
}
```

15. Note that you do not catch a `CloneNotSupportedException` because any such thrown exception in `super.clone` is caught inside the base class method `super.clone`.

```java
public class BigRecord extends Record
                         implements Cloneable
{
    private StockItem item3;

        ...
    public Object clone()
    {
        BigRecord copy =
                (BigRecord)super.clone();
        copy.item3 =
                (StockItem)item3.clone();
        return copy;
    }
}
```

16. The heading of the class definition changes to what is shown in the following and the method `clone` shown there is added. The version of `Date` for this chapter on the accompanying CD includes this definition of `clone`.

extra code on CD

```java
public class Date implements Cloneable
{
    private String month;
    private int day;
    private int year;

        ...
    public Object clone()
    {
        try
        {
            return super.clone();//Invocation of
                    //clone in the base class Object
        }
        catch(CloneNotSupportedException e)
        {//This should not happen.
            return null; //To keep compiler happy.
        }
    }
}
```

17. The heading of the class definition changes to what is shown in the following and the method `clone` shown there is added. The version of `Employee` for this chapter on the accompanying CD includes this definition of `clone`.

extra code on CD

```
public class Employee implements Cloneable
{
    private String name;
    private Date hireDate;


        ...
    public Object clone()
    {
        try
        {
            Employee copy =
                    (Employee)super.clone();
            copy.hireDate =
                    (Date)hireDate.clone();
            return copy;
        }
        catch(CloneNotSupportedException e)
        {//This should not happen.
            return null; //To keep compiler happy.
        }
    }
}
```

18. The heading of the class definition changes to what is shown in the following and the method `clone` shown there is added. Note that you do not catch a `CloneNotSupportedException` because any such thrown exception in `super.clone` is caught inside the base class method `super.clone`. The version of `HourlyEmployee` for this chapter on the accompanying CD includes this definition of `clone`.

**extra code
on CD**

```
public class HourlyEmployee extends Employee
                            implements Cloneable
{
    private double wageRate ;
    private double hours;


        ...
    public Object clone()
    {
        HourlyEmployee copy =
                    (HourlyEmployee)super.clone();
        return copy;
    }
}
```

19. It would still be legal. An outer class has access to all the private members of an inner class.

20. Yes, they can be omitted, but the reason is that it indicates package access, and in a private inner class, all privacy modifiers, including package access, are equivalent to public. (Note that the situation for public inner classes will be different.)

21. Yes, it is legal to add the method `doubleBalance` to the inner class `Money` because an inner class has access to the instance variables, like `balance` of the outer class. To test this out, add the following as a method of the outer class:

```java
public void test()
{
    balance.doubleBalance();
}
```

22. It would be legal. The method `makeDeposit` is assumed to be the method `makeDeposit` of the outer class. The calling object `balance` is assumed to be the instance variable of the outer class. These sorts of tricks can lead to confusing code. So, use them sparingly. This is just an exercise.

23. No, a nonstatic inner class cannot have any static methods.

24. Yes, you can have a nonstatic method in a static inner class.

25. `OuterClass.InnerClass.someMethod();`

26.
```java
Outs outerObject = new Outs();
Outs.Ins innerObject =
                outerObject.new Ins();
innerObject.specialMethod();
```

27. You would get your first error on the following statement and it would be a complier error:

```java
anObject.setNumber(42);
```

With the change described in the exercise, `anObject` is of type `Object` and `Object` has no method named `setNumber`.

Programming Projects

 Many of these Programming Projects can be solved using AW's MyCodeMate. To access these please go to: www.mycodemate.com.

1. Modify the recursive implementation of binary search from Chapter 11 so that the search method works on any array of type `Comparable[]`. Test the implementation with arrays of different types to see if it works.

2. Listed below is the skeleton for a class named `InventoryItem`. Each inventory item has a name and a unique ID number:

```java
class InventoryItem
{
 private String name;
 private int uniqueItemID;
}
```

Flesh out the class with appropriate accessors, constructors, and mutatators. The uniqueItemID's are assigned by your store and can be set from outside the InventoryItem class—your code does not have to ensure that they are unique. Next, modify the class so that it implements the Comparable interface. The compareTo() method should compare the uniqueItemID's; e.g., the InventoryItem with item ID 5 is less than the InventoryItem with ID 10. Test your class by creating an array of sample InventoryItem's and sort them using a sorting method that takes as input an array of type Comparable.

3. Listed below is a code skeleton for an interface called Enumeration and a class called NameCollection. Enumeration provides an interface to sequentially iterate through some type of collection. In this case, the collection will be the class NameCollection that simply stores a collection of names using an array of strings.

```
interface Enumeration
{
 // Returns true if another element in the collection exists
 public boolean hasNext();

 // Returns the next element in the collection as an Object
 public Object getNext();
}

/**
 * NameCollection implements a collection of names using
 * a simple array.
 */
class NameCollection
{
 String[] names;

 /**
  * The list of names is initialized from outside
  * and passed in as an array of strings
  */
 NameCollection(String[] names)
 {
   this.names = names;
 }

 /**
  * getEnumeration should return an instance of a class that implements
  * the Enumeration interface where hasNext() and getNext()
  * correspond to data stored within the names array.
  */
 Enumeration getEnumeration ()
 {
  // Complete code here using an inner class
 }
}
```

Complete the method getEnumeration() so that it returns an anonymous inner class that corresponds to the Enumeration interface for the names array in NamesCollection. Then write a main method that creates a NamesCollection object with a sample array of strings, retrieves the Enumeration for this class via getEnumeration(), and then iterates through the enumeration outputting each name using the getNext() method.

 4. In Display 13.5, we described a sorting method to sort an array of type Comparable[]. In Display 12.6, we described a sorting method that used the merge sort algorithm to sort an array of type double[] into increasing order. Redo the method in Display 12.6 so it applies to an array of type Comparable[]. Also, do a suitable test program.

 5. In Display 13.5, we described a sorting method to sort an array of type Comparable[]. In Display 12.8, we described a sorting method that used the quick sort algorithm to sort an array of type double[] into increasing order. Redo the method in Display 12.8 so it applies to an array of type Comparable[]. Also, do a suitable test program.

 6. Redo the class Person in Display 5.19 so that it implements the Cloneable interface. This may require that you also redo the class Date so it implements the Cloneable interface. Also, do a suitable test program.

7. Redo the class Person in Display 5.19 so that the class Date is a private inner class of the class Person. Also, do a suitable test program. (You need not start from the version produced in Programming Project 6. You can ignore Programming Project 6 when you do this project.)

8. This is a combination of Programming Projects 6 and 7. Redo the class Person in Display 5.19 so that the class Date is a private inner class of the class Person and so that the class Person implements the Cloneable interface. Also, do a suitable test program.

 9. Redo the class Employee and the class HourlyEmployee in Displays 7.2 and 7.3 so that the class Date is an inner class of the class Employee and an inherited inner class of the class HourlyEmployee. Also, do a suitable test program.

14

Generics and the ArrayList Class

14 Generics and the `ArrayList` Class

Hamlet: Do you see yonder cloud that's almost in shape of a camel?

Polonius: By the mass, and 'tis like a camel, indeed.

Hamlet: Me think it is like a weasel.

Polonius: It is backed like a weasel.

Hamlet: Or like a whale.

Polonius: Very like a whale.

WILLIAM SHAKESPEARE, *Hamlet*

Introduction

generics

Beginning with version 5.0, Java allows class and method definitions that include parameters for types. Such definitions are called **generics**. Generic programming with a type parameter allows you to write code that applies to any class. For example, you can define a class for a list of items of type T, where T is a type parameter. You can then use this class with the class `String` plugged in for T to automatically get a class for a list of `String` objects. Similarly, you can plug in the class `Double` for T to obtain a class for a list of `Double`s, and you can do a similar thing for any other class. The class `ArrayList` in the standard Java libraries is, in fact, just such a class for a list of items of type T, where T is a type parameter. We will first show you how to use classes with a type parameter by using the `ArrayList` class as an example. We will then tell you how you can define other classes with a type parameter.

Prerequisites

Section 14.1 covering the `ArrayList` class requires only Chapters 1 through 6 and Chapter 9. It can reasonably be read without first reading Chapter 9 if you ignore all references to "exceptions."

Section 14.2 on generics requires Chapters 1 through 7 and Chapter 9. (There is one very short Pitfall section entitled "Generic Interfaces" that requires Section 13.1 on interfaces, but that Pitfall section can easily be skipped if you have not yet read Section 13.1.) You need not read Section 14.1 before Section 14.2, but you are encouraged to do so; Section 14.1 can serve as a motivation for Section 14.2.

14.1 **The ArrayList Class**

*"Well, I'll eat it," said Alice, "and if it makes me grow larger, I can reach
the key; and if it makes me grow smaller, I can creep under the door; so
either way I'll get into the garden...."*

LEWIS CARROLL, *Alice's Adventures in Wonderland*

ArrayList

ArrayList is a class in the standard Java libraries. You can think of an ArrayList
object as an array that can grow (and shrink) in length while your program is running.
In Java, you can read in the length of an array when the program is running, but once
your program creates an array of that length, it cannot change the length of the array.
For example, suppose you write a program to record customer orders for a mail-order
house, and suppose you store all the orders for one customer in an array of objects of
some class called Item. You could ask the user how many items she or he will order,
store the number in a variable called numberOfItems, and then create the array item
with the following statement:

```
Item[] item = new Item[numberOfItems];
```

But suppose the customer enters numberOfItems and then decides to order another
item? There is no way to increase the size of the array item. There are ways around this
problem with arrays, but they are all rather complicated. ArrayLists serve the same purpose as arrays, except that an ArrayList can change length while the program is running. So an ArrayList could handle the customer's extra order without any problems.

The class ArrayList is implemented using an array as a private instance variable.
When this hidden array is full, a new larger hidden array is created and the data is
transferred to this new array. However, you need not concern yourself with this implementation detail. All you need to know is how to use the ArrayList class, and we are
about to tell you that.

If ArrayLists are like arrays but have the nice added feature of being able to change
length, then why don't we just always use ArrayLists instead of arrays? It often seems
that every silver lining has a cloud, and that is true of ArrayLists as well. There are
three main disadvantages of ArrayLists: (1) They are less efficient than arrays; (2) they
do not have the square bracket notation, and so using an ArrayList is sometimes
notationally more awkward than using ordinary arrays; and (3) the base type of an
ArrayList must be class type (or other reference type); it cannot be a primitive type,
such as int, double, or char. For example, if you want an ArrayList of int values, you
must simulate this structure with an ArrayList of Integer values, where Integer is
the wrapper class whose objects simulate int values. Automatic boxing and unboxing
(as discussed in Chapter 5) makes (3) less of a problem, since an ArrayList with base
type, for example, Integer can, in effect, store values of type int.

Using the ArrayList Class

import statement

ArrayLists are used in much the same way as arrays, but there are some important differences. First, the definition of the class ArrayList is not provided automatically. The definition is in the package java.util, and any code that uses the class ArrayList must contain the following, normally at the start of the file:

```
import java.util.ArrayList;
```

An ArrayList is created and named in the same way as objects of any class, except that you specify the base type using a new notation. For example,

```
ArrayList<String> list = new ArrayList<String>(20);
```

capacity

This statement makes list the name of an ArrayList that stores objects of the class String and that has an *initial* **capacity** of 20 items. When we say that an ArrayList has a certain capacity, we mean that it has been allocated memory for that many items, but if it needs to hold more items, the system will automatically allocate more memory. By carefully choosing the initial capacity of an ArrayList, you can often make your code more efficient, but this capacity has no effect on how many items the ArrayList can hold. If you choose your capacity to be large enough, then the system will not need to reallocate memory too often, and as a result, your program should run faster. On the other hand, if you make your capacity too large, you will waste storage space. However, no matter what capacity you choose, you can still do anything you want with the ArrayList.

base type

The type String in the previous ArrayList example is the **base type** of the ArrayList class. An ArrayList, that is, an object of the ArrayList class, stores objects of its base type. You can use any reference type as the base type of an ArrayList class. In particular, you can use any class or interface type. However, you cannot use a primitive type, such as int or double, as the base type of an ArrayList class. This is an example of a type parameter. The ArrayList class is defined as having a type parameter for the type of the elements in the list. You create a concrete class by specifying, in angular brackets, a class type to be substituted for this type parameter. For example, the following code, which we saw earlier, substitutes the type String for the type parameter to create the class ArrayList<String> and an object of this class named list:

```
ArrayList<String> list = new ArrayList<String>(20);
```

ArrayList objects can be used like arrays, but they do not have the array square-bracket notation. If you would use

```
a[index] = "Hi Mom!";
```

set

for an array of strings a, then the analogous statement for a suitable ArrayList named list would be

```
list.set(index, "Hi Mom!");
```

Creating and Naming an `ArrayList` Object

An object of the class `ArrayList` is created and named in the same way as any other object, except that you specify the base type of the `ArrayList`.

SYNTAX

```
ArrayList<Base_Type> Object_Name = new ArrayList<Base_Type>();
ArrayList<Base_Type> Object_Name =
                    new ArrayList<Base_Type>(Initial_Capacity);
```

The *Base_Type* must be a reference type, usually a class type; it cannot be a primitive type such as **int** or **double**. When a number is given as an argument to the constructor, that number determines the initial capacity of the `ArrayList`.

EXAMPLES

```
ArrayList<String> list = new ArrayList<String>();
ArrayList<Double> list2 = new ArrayList<Double>(30);
```

If you would use

```
String temp = a[index];
```

for an array of strings *a*, then the analogous statement for a suitable `ArrayList` named `list` would be

```
String temp = list.get(index);
```

Accessing at an Index

If `list` is an `ArrayList`, its elements can be accessed as follows:

EXAMPLES

```
ArrayList<String> list = new ArrayList<String>();
int index;
   ...
list.set(index, "Here"); //Sets the element
                              //at index to "Here".
String temp = list.get(index); //The expression
   //list.get(index) returns the element at position index.
ArrayList<Integer> list2 = new ArrayList<Integer>();
   ...
```

(continued)

```
list2.set(42, index); //Sets the element at index to
    //new Integer(42). This example relies on automatic boxing.
int temp2 = list2.get(index); //The expression
    //v.get(index) returns the element at position index.
    // This example relies on automatic unboxing.
```

The **index** must be greater than or equal to **0** and less than the current size of the **ArrayList list**.

The two methods set and get give ArrayLists approximately the same functionality that square brackets give to arrays. However, you need to be aware of one important point: The method invocation

```
list.set(index, "Hi Mom!");
```

is *not* always completely analogous to

```
a[index] = "Hi Mom!";
```

add

The method set can replace any existing element, but you cannot use set to put an element at just any index, as you could with an array. The method set is used to change the value of elements, not to set them for the first time. To set an element for the first time, you usually use the method add. The basic form of the method add adds elements at index position 0, position 1, position 2, and so forth in that order. This means that ArrayLists must always be filled in this order. But your code can then go back and change any individual element, just as it can in an array.

For example, suppose list is an ArrayList with base type String, which has not yet had any elements added to it; that is, list is empty. The following statements will add the strings "One", "Two", and "Three" to positions 0, 1, and 2:

```
list.add("One");
list.add("Two");
list.add("Three");
```

The method name add is overloaded. There is also a two-argument method named add that allows you to add an element at any currently used index position or at the first unused position. When inserting into an ArrayList with this version of add, elements at the specified index and higher (if any) are moved up one position to make room for the new element. For example,

```
list.add(0, "Zero");
```

adds the string "Zero" at position 0 and moves elements originally at positions 0, 1, 2, and so forth up one position to positions 1, 2, 3, and so forth.

Suppose list starts out empty and your code executes our four add invocations, which we repeat below:

```
list.add("One");
list.add("Two");
list.add("Three");
list.add(0, "Zero");
```

After these four invocations of add, list would contain the strings "Zero", "One", "Two", and "Three" in positions 0, 1, 2, and 3, respectively.

Note that the two-argument version of add cannot add an element at just any position. It can only insert an element at some already used position or at the first unused position. The elements in an ArrayList always occupy a contiguous set of positions starting at 0; that is, they are always at positions 0, 1, 2, and so forth up to some last position. This is just like a partially filled array (as discussed in Chapter 6), but unlike a partially filled array, you do not need to do anything to keep track of how many elements are on the list. The method size automatically takes care of this for any ArrayList.

The add Methods

Elements can be added to an ArrayList by using the methods named add. The elements are added to index position 0, then 1, then 2, and so forth so there are no gaps in the indices of elements.

The most straightforward method to use for adding to an ArrayList is the method named add that has only one parameter.

EXAMPLES
```
list.add("Salud");
list.add("Dinero");
list.add("Java");
```

The object list is an ArrayList with base type String.

A second method named add allows you to add an element at any currently used index position or at the first unused position. When inserting into an ArrayList with this version of add, elements at the specified index and higher (if any) are moved up one position to make room for the new element.

```
list.add(1, "Amor");
```

If list starts out empty and all four statements in the two sets of examples are executed, then list would contain the following strings in the order given: "Salud", "Amor", "Dinero", and "Java".

size You can find out how many indices already have elements by using the method size. If list is an ArrayList, list.size() returns the **size** of the ArrayList, which is the number of elements stored in it. The indices of these elements go from 0 to one less than list.size().

The size Method

The method size returns the number of elements in an ArrayList.

EXAMPLE

```
for (int index = 0; index < list.size(); index++)
    System.out.println(list.get(index));
```

list is an ArrayList object.

TIP: Summary of Adding to an ArrayList

add To place an element in an ArrayList position (at an ArrayList index) for the first time, you usually use the method add. The simplest method named add has a single parameter for the element to be added and adds elements at index positions 0, 1, 2, and so forth, in that order.

You can add an element at an already occupied list position by using the two-parameter version of add. When inserting into an ArrayList with this version of add, elements at the specified index and higher are moved up one position to make room for the new element. For example, suppose list is an ArrayList object with base type String that has three elements already on its list. Consider the following method invocation:

```
list.add(1, "Amor");
```

Before there were elements at index positions 0, 1, and 2. When this invocation of add is executed, the element "Amor" is inserted at index 1, and the elements at index positions 1 and 2 are moved to positions 2 and 3.

You can also use the two-argument version of add to add an element at the first unused position. If list has elements at index positions 0, 1, 2, and 3, then the following is legal:

```
list.add(4, "Mucho Amor");
```

Your code can then go back and change any individual element, using set. However, set can reset only the element at an index that already has an element.

The method size can be used to determine how many elements are stored in an ArrayList. ∎

Self-Test Exercises

1. Suppose `list` is an object of the class `ArrayList<String>`. How do you add the string "Hello" to the `ArrayList list`?

2. Suppose `instruction` is an object of the class `ArrayList<String>` that contains the string "Stop" at index position 5. How do you change the string at index position 5 to "Go" (without changing any of the elements at other positions)?

3. Suppose `instruction` is an object of the class `ArrayList<String>` that contains strings at index positions 0 through 10. How do you insert the string "Go" at index position 5 so that no strings are removed from the list `instruction`?

4. Can you use the method `set` to place an element in an `ArrayList` at any index you want?

5. Can you use the two-argument version of the method `add` to add an element in an `ArrayList` at any index you want?

6. Consider the following two method invocations. Are there values of `index1` that are allowed but that are not allowed for `index2`? Are there values of `index2` that are allowed but that are not allowed for `index1`? `list` is an object of the class `Array–List<String>`.

```
list.set(index1, "Hello");
list.add(index2, "Hello");
```

7. If you create an `ArrayList` with the following statement, can the `ArrayList` contain more than 20 elements?

```
ArrayList<Double> myList = new ArrayList<Double>(20);
```

Methods in the Class `ArrayList`

With arrays, the square brackets and the instance variable `length` are the only tools automatically provided for you, the programmer. If you want to use arrays for other things, you must write code to manipulate the arrays. `ArrayList`s, on the other hand, come with a selection of powerful methods that can do many of the things for which you would need to write code in order to do with arrays. For example, the class `Array–List` has a version of the method `add` that inserts a new element between two elements in the `ArrayList`. Most of these methods are described in Display 14.1.

Display 14.1 Some Methods in the Class `ArrayList` (part 1 of 4)

CONSTRUCTORS

```
public ArrayList<Base_Type>(int initialCapacity)
```

Creates an empty `ArrayList` with the specified *Base_Type* and initial capacity.

(continued)

Display 14.1 Some Methods in the Class ArrayList (part 2 of 4)

```
public ArrayList<Base_Type>()
```

Creates an empty ArrayList with the specified *Base_Type* and an initial capacity of 10.

ARRAYLIKE METHODS

```
public Base_Type set( int index, Base_Type newElement)
```

Sets the element at the specified index to newElement. Returns the element previously at that position, but the method is often used as if it were a void method. If you draw an analogy between the ArrayList and an array *a*, this statement is analogous to setting *a*[index] to the value newElement. The index must be a value greater than or equal to 0 and less than the current size of the ArrayList. Throws an IndexOutOfBoundsException if the index is not in this range.

```
public Base_Type get(int index)
```

Returns the element at the specified index. This statement is analogous to returning *a*[index] for an array *a*. The index must be a value greater than or equal to 0 and less than the current size of the ArrayList. Throws IndexOutOfBoundsException if the index is not in this range.

METHODS TO ADD ELEMENTS

```
public boolean add(Base_Type newElement)
```

Adds the specified element to the end of the calling ArrayList and increases the ArrayList's size by one. The capacity of the ArrayList is increased if that is required. Returns true if the add was successful. (The return type is boolean, but the method is typically used as if it were a void method.)

```
public void add( int index, Base_Type newElement)
```

Inserts newElement as an element in the calling ArrayList at the specified index. Each element in the ArrayList with an index greater or equal to index is shifted upward to have an index that is one greater than the value it had previously. The index must be a value greater than or equal to 0 and less than or equal to the current size of the ArrayList. Throws IndexOutOfBoundsException if the index is not in this range. Note that you can use this method to add an element after the last element. The capacity of the ArrayList is increased if that is required.

METHODS TO REMOVE ELEMENTS

```
public Base_Type remove(int index)
```

Deletes and returns the element at the specified index. Each element in the ArrayList with an index greater than index is decreased to have an index that is one less than the value it had previously. The index must be a value greater than or equal to 0 and less than the current size of the ArrayList. Throws IndexOutOfBoundsException if the index is not in this range. Often used as if it were a void method.

```
protected void removeRange(int fromIndex, int toIndex)
```

Deletes all the element with indices *i* such that fromIndex $\leq i <$ toIndex. Element with indices greater than or equal to toIndex are decreased appropriately.

Display 14.1   Some Methods in the Class `ArrayList` (part 3 of 4)

```
public boolean remove(Object theElement)
```

Removes one occurrence of **theElement** from the calling **ArrayList**. If **theElement** is found in the **ArrayList**, then each element in the **ArrayList** with an index greater than the removed element's index is decreased to have an index that is one less than the value it had previously. Returns **true** if **theElement** was found (and removed). Returns **false** if **theElement** was not found in the calling **ArrayList**.

```
public void clear()
```

Removes all elements from the calling **ArrayList** and sets the **ArrayList**'s size to zero.

SEARCH METHODS

```
public boolean contains(Object target)
```

Returns **true** if the calling **ArrayList** contains **target**; otherwise, returns **false**. Uses the method **equals** of the object **target** to test for equality with any element in the calling **ArrayList**.

```
public int indexOf(Object target)
```

Returns the index of the first element that is equal to **target**. Uses the method **equals** of the object **target** to test for equality. Returns −1 if **target** is not found.

```
public int lastIndexOf(Object target)
```

Returns the index of the last element that is equal to **target**. Uses the method **equals** of the object **target** to test for equality. Returns −1 if **target** is not found.

MEMORY MANAGEMENT (SIZE AND CAPACITY)

```
public boolean isEmpty()
```

Returns **true** if the calling **ArrayList** is empty (that is, has size **0**); otherwise, returns **false**.

```
public int size()
```

Returns the number of elements in the calling **ArrayList**.

```
public void ensureCapacity(int newCapacity)
```

Increases the capacity of the calling **ArrayList**, if necessary, in order to ensure that the **ArrayList** can hold at least **newCapacity** elements. Using **ensureCapacity** can sometimes increase efficiency, but its use is not needed for any other reason.

```
public void trimToSize()
```

Trims the capacity of the calling **ArrayList** to the **ArrayList**'s current size. This method is used to save storage space.

(continued)

Display 14.1 Some Methods in the Class `ArrayList` (part 4 of 4)

MAKE A COPY

```
public Object[] toArray()
```

Returns an array containing all the elements on the list. Preserves the order of the elements.

```
public Type[] toArray(Type[] a)
```

Returns an array containing all the elements on the list. Preserves the order of the elements. *Type* can be any class types. If the list will fit in *a*, the elements are copied to *a* and *a* is returned. Any elements of *a* not needed for list elements are set to `null`. If the list will not fit in *a*, a new array is created.

(As we will discuss in Section 14.2, the correct Java syntax for this method heading is

```
public <Type> Type[] toArray(Type[] a)
```

However, at this point we have not yet explained this kind of type parameter syntax.)

```
public Object clone()
```

Returns a shallow copy of the calling `ArrayList`. *Warning*: The clone is not an independent copy. Subsequent changes to the clone may affect the calling object and vice versa. (See Chapter 5 for a discussion of shallow copy.)

EQUALITY

```
public boolean equals(Object other)
```

If `other` is another `ArrayList` (of any base type), then `equals` returns `true` if and only if both `ArrayList`s are of the same size and contain the same list of elements in the same order. (In fact, if `other` is any kind of *list*, then `equals` returns `true` if and only if both the calling `ArrayList` and `other` are of the same size and contain the same list of elements in the same order. *Lists* are discussed in Chapter 16.)

Why Are Some Parameters of Type *Base_Type* and Others of Type `Object`?

Look at the table of methods in Display 14.1. In some cases, when a parameter is naturally an object of the base type, the parameter type is the base type, but in other cases, it is the type `Object`.

For example, look at the **add** methods and the second **remove** method in the table. The **add** methods have a parameter of the base type; the **remove** method has a parameter of type `Object`. Why the difference in parameter types? The class `ArrayList` implements a number of interfaces and inherits methods from various ancestor classes. These interfaces and ancestor classes specify that certain parameters have type `Object`.

For example, in Chapter 7 we explained that the parameter for the **equals** method is always of type `Object` because the method heading is inherited from the class `Object`. In other cases, the designers of the `ArrayList` class were free to specify the parameter types for the method.

The "for-each" Loop

In Chapter 16, we will cover a family of classes known as *collections*. The ArrayList classes are our first examples of collection classes. Starting with version 5.0, Java has added a new kind of for loop that can cycle through all the elements in a collection and can, in particular, cycle through all the elements in an ArrayList. This new kind of for loop is called a **for-each loop** or **enhanced for loop**. A for-each loop can also be used to cycle through all the elements in an array. The for-each loop was introduced for use with arrays in a starred section of Chapter 6, but you need not go back and read that subsection. The presentation of for-each loops here is complete.

For example, the following code ends with a for-each loop that outputs all the elements in the ArrayList named myList:

```java
ArrayList<String> myList = new ArrayList<String>(20);
<Some code to fill myList>
for (String element : myList)
    System.out.println(element);
```

You can read the line beginning with for as "for each element in myList do the following." Note that the variable, element, has the same type as the elements in the Array-List. The variable, in this case element, must be declared in the for-each loop as we have done. If you attempt to declare element before the for-each loop, you will get a compiler error message.

The general syntax for a for-each loop statement is

```java
for (Base_Type Variable : Collection_Object)
    Statement
```

Be sure to notice that you use a colon (not a semicolon) after the *Variable*. You may use any legal variable name for the *Variable*; you do not have to use element. The only *Collection_Object*s we have seen so far are arrays and ArrayList objects. Although it is not required, the *Statement* typically contains the *Variable*. When the for-each loop is executed, the *Statement* is executed once for each element of the *Collection_Object*. More specifically, for each element of the *Collection_Object*, the *Variable* is set to the collection element and then the *Statement* is executed.

The program in Display 14.2 includes an example of a for-each loop as well as examples of some of the other ArrayList details we have presented.

For-each Loop for ArrayList Objects

SYNTAX

```java
for (Array_Base_Type Variable : ArrayList_Object)
    Statement
```

(continued)

EXAMPLE

```
for (Integer element : numberList)
              element = 42;
```

numberList is an **ArrayList** with base type **Integer**. This for-each loop changes the value of each element of **numberList** to 42. (This example uses automatic boxing. So, 42 really means **new Integer(42)**.)

A good way to read the first line of the example is "For each **element** in **numberList**, do the following."

Display 14.2   A for-each Loop Used with an **ArrayList**   (part 1 of 2)

```
1   import java.util.ArrayList;
2   import java.util.Scanner;

3   public class ArrayListDemo
4   {
5       public static void main(String[] args)
6       {
7           ArrayList<String> toDoList = new ArrayList<String>(20);
8           System.out.println(
9                       "Enter list entries, when prompted.");
10          boolean done = false;
11          String next = null;
12          String answer;
13          Scanner keyboard = new Scanner(System.in);

14          while (! done)
15          {
16              System.out.println("Input an entry:");
17              next = keyboard.nextLine();
18              toDoList.add(next);

19              System.out.print("More items for the list? ");
20              answer = keyboard.nextLine();
21              if (!(answer.equalsIgnoreCase("yes")))
22                      done = true;
23          }

24          System.out.println("The list contains:");
25          for (String entry : toDoList)
26              System.out.println(entry);
27      }
28  }
29
```

Display 14.2   A for-each Loop Used with an **ArrayList** (part 2 of 2)

Sample Dialogue

```
Enter list entries, when prompted.
Input an entry:
Practice Dancing.
More items for the list? yes
Input an entry:
Buy tickets.
More items for the list? yes
Input an entry:
Pack clothes.
More items for the list? no
The list contains:
Practice Dancing.
Buy tickets.
Pack clothes.
```

Self-Test Exercises

8. Suppose numberList is an object of the class ArrayList<Double>. Give code that will output all the elements in numberList to the screen.

9. Write a class for sorting strings into lexicographic order that follows the outline of the class SelectionSort in Display 6.11 of Chapter 6. Your definition, however, will use an ArrayList of the class ArrayList<String>, rather than an array of elements of type double. For words, lexicographic order reduces to alphabetic order if all the words are in either all lowercase or all uppercase letters. You can compare two strings to see which is lexicographically first by using the String method compareTo. For strings s1 and s2, s1.compareTo(s2) returns a negative number if s1 is lexicographically before s2, returns 0 if s1 equals s2, and returns a positive number if s1 is lexicographically after s2. Call your class StringSelectionSort. A test program you can use to test your class follows. (The program is included with the source code provided on the CD that accompanies this book.)

extra code on CD

```java
import java.util.ArrayList;

public class StringSelectionSortDemo
{
    public static void main(String[] args)
    {
        ArrayList<String> b = new ArrayList<String>();
        b.add("time");
        b.add("tide");
        b.add("clouds");
        b.add("rain");
```

```
        System.out.println("ArrayList values before sorting:");
        for (String e : b)
            System.out.print(e + " ");
        System.out.println();
        StringSelectionSort.sort(b);
        System.out.println("ArrayList values after sorting:");
        for (String e : b)
            System.out.print(e + " ");
        System.out.println();
    }
}
```

EXAMPLE: Golf Scores

The program in Display 14.3 reads in a list of golf scores and then outputs the average of the scores and how much each differs from the average. The scores are read and stored in an `ArrayList` so that they will be available later in the program to be output along with how much each differs from the average. This is the kind of thing that is well suited to being done with an ordinary array. However, it is much easier and cleaner to use an `ArrayList` as we did in Display 14.3.

Our program deals with a list of values of type `double`. But we use an `ArrayList` with base type `Double` to store these values. We did not use an `ArrayList` with base type `double` because there is no such thing. The base type for an `ArrayList` must be a class type (or other reference type). However, thanks to Java's automatic boxing we can program as if an object of type `ArrayList<Double>` can store values of type `double`.

The `ArrayList` automatically keeps track of how many elements are stored in the `ArrayList`. If we had used an ordinary partially filled array in our program instead of an `ArrayList`, we would need an extra `int` variable to keep track of how much of the array is used. When we use an `ArrayList`, we are spared all the overhead associated with partially filled arrays. Those details are taken care of for us automatically. The code for those details is in the definition of the `ArrayList` class, but there is no need to look at that code. That code is all implementation detail that we need not worry about when using an `ArrayList`.

Notice the use of for-each loops in our program. The cleanest and easiest way to cycle through all the elements in an `ArrayList` is to use a for-each loop.

It is instructive to compare the program in Display 14.3, which uses an `ArrayList`, with the program in Display 6.4, which does the same thing but uses an ordinary array. The version that uses an `ArrayList` is much cleaner and even much shorter than the one that uses an ordinary array. This is because an `ArrayList` does so many things for you automatically, which you would have to explicitly code for if you used an ordinary array. This is a good example of information hiding and code reuse. The programmers who defined the `ArrayList` class did a lot of programming for you so that your programming task is simpler than it would otherwise be.

Display 14.3   **Golf Score Program** (part 1 of 2)

```
1   import java.util.ArrayList;
2   import java.util.Scanner;

3   public class GolfScores
4   {
5       /**
6        Shows differences between each of a list of golf scores and their average.
7       */
8       public static void main(String[] args)
9       {
10          ArrayList<Double> score = new ArrayList<Double>();

11          System.out.println("This program reads golf scores and shows");
12          System.out.println("how much each differs from the average.");

13          System.out.println("Enter golf scores:");
14          fillArrayList(score);
15          showDifference(score);
16      }

17      /**
18       Reads values into the array a.
19      */
20      public static void fillArrayList(ArrayList<Double> a)
21      {
22          System.out.println("Enter a list of nonnegative numbers.");
23          System.out.println("Mark the end of the list with a negative number.");
24          Scanner keyboard = new Scanner(System.in);

25          double next;
26          int index = 0;
27          next = keyboard.nextDouble();
28          while (next >= 0)
29          {
30              a.add(next);
31              next = keyboard.nextDouble();
32          }
33      }
34      /**
35       Returns the average of numbers in a.
36      */
37      public static double computeAverage(ArrayList<Double> a)
38      {
39          double total = 0;
40          for (Double element : a)
41              total = total + element;
```

Parameters of type `ArrayList<Double>()` *are handled just like any other class parameter.*

Because of automatic boxing, we can treat values of type **double** *as if their type were* **Double**.

A for-each loop is the nicest way to cycle through all the elements in an ArrayList.

(continued)

Display 14.3   Golf Score Program (part 2 of 2)

```
42            int numberOfScores = a.size();
43            if (numberOfScores > 0)
44            {
45                return (total/numberOfScores);
46            }
47            else
48            {
49                System.out.println("ERROR: Trying to average 0 numbers.");
50                System.out.println("computeAverage returns 0.");
51                return 0;
52            }
53        }

54        /**
55          Gives screen output showing how much each of the elements
56          in a differ from their average.
57        */
58        public static void showDifference(ArrayList<Double> a)
59        {
60            double average = computeAverage(a);
61            System.out.println("Average of the " + a.size()
62                                + " scores = " + average);
63            System.out.println("The scores are:");
64            for (Double element : a)
65                System.out.println(element + " differs from average by "
66                                + (element - average));
67        }
68    }
```

Sample Dialogue

```
This program reads golf scores and shows
how much each differs from the average.
Enter golf scores:
Enter a list of nonnegative numbers.
Mark the end of the list with a negative number.
69  74  68  -1
Average of the 3 scores = 70.3333
The scores are:
69.0 differs from average by -1.33333
74.0 differs from average by 3.66667
68.0 differs from average by -2.33333
```

TIP: Use `trimToSize` to Save Memory

`ArrayLists` automatically increase their capacity when your program needs them to have additional capacity. However, the capacity may increase beyond what your program requires. Also, when your program needs less capacity in an `ArrayList`, the `ArrayList` does not automatically shrink. If your `ArrayList` has a large amount of excess capacity, you can save memory by using the method `trimToSize` to shrink the capacity of an `ArrayList`. If `list` is an `ArrayList`, an invocation of `list.trimToSize()` will shrink the capacity of the `ArrayList` `list` down to the size of `list`, so that there is no unused capacity in `list`. Normally, you should use `trimToSize` only when you know that the `ArrayList` will not later need its extra capacity. ■

trimToSize

PITFALL: The `clone` Method Makes a Shallow Copy ★

There are situations in which you would like to make an independent copy of an `ArrayList` object; that is, you would like to make a deep copy of the `ArrayList` object. (Deep copying and shallow copying were discussed in Chapter 5; you may want to review that material.) For example, if you define a class with a private instance variable of an `ArrayList` type, then you would like an accessor method to return a deep copy of the `ArrayList` stored in the private instance variable. The reason you want a deep copy is the same as the reason that you want a deep copy of an array instance variables and that was discussed in Chapter 6 in the subsection entitled "Privacy Leaks with Array Instance Variables." It would be a good idea to review that subsection before going on with reading this subsection.

As we have often observed, the assignment operator merely copies a reference so that you have another name for the object being copied. So, you do not have an independent copy. You have what's known as a *shallow copy.* For example, assume that `Pet` is a class with the usual kinds of accessor methods and consider the following code:

```
ArrayList<Pet> petList1 = new ArrayList<Pet>();
<Some code to set the instance variables of elements of petList1.>
ArrayList<Pet> petList2 = petList1;
```

`petList2` and `petList1` are just two names for the same `ArrayList` object. Making a change to `petList1` or to an element of `petList1` will also change `petList2` because they are the same list.

If you want an independent copy (deep copy) of `petList1`, you might think the following would give you your independent copy:

```
ArrayList<Pet> petList2 = petList1.clone();
```

PITFALL: (continued)

Unfortunately, the clone method also makes a shallow copy. There is no built-in method to give you a deep copy (independent copy) of an ArrayList.

When you need a deep copy of an ArrayList, you will have to resort to some ad hoc tricks. If you have a way to make a deep copy of objects of the base type, then you can create a deep copy of each element in the ArrayList and place them into a new ArrayList object. This is the exact same approach as the one we discussed for making a deep copy of an ordinary array in the subsection of Chapter 6 entitled "Privacy Leaks with Array Instance Variables." The situation with respect to deep copying of an ArrayList is exactly the same as the situation with respect to deep copying of an ordinary array. Although the details of this subsection may seem subtle and difficult, they are not new. You have already faced the exact same problem with ordinary arrays. ∎

Self-Test Exercises

10. Can you have an ArrayList of ints?

11. The following for-each loop was used in the method showDiffernce in Display 14.3. Rewrite it as an ordinary for loop. This should help you to see how much cleaner it is to use a for-each loop.

```
for (Double element : a)
    System.out.println(element + " differs from average by "
                                  + (element − average));
```

The Vector Class

Vector   The Java standard libraries have a class named Vector that behaves almost exactly the same as the class ArrayList. In fact, everything we have said about the class ArrayList holds true for the Vector class. Although in almost all situations, you could use either the class ArrayList or the class Vector, a clear preference seems to be developing among programmers for the class ArrayList. There are some differences between the classes Vector and ArrayList, but the differences involve material we have not covered. If you encounter the class Vector in somebody's code, chances are the class Vector could be replaced by the class ArrayList and that would require at most cosmetic changes in the code.[1]

---

[1] The biggest difference between the Vector and ArrayList classes is that Vectors are *synchronized* whereas ArrayLists are not. However, synchronization is a topic that we do not cover and is not relevant to the kinds of programming we are doing.

Parameterized Classes and Generics

parameterized class

The class `ArrayList` is a **parameterized class**. It has a parameter, which we have been denoting *Base_Type*, that can be replaced by any reference type to obtain a class for `ArrayLists` with the specified base type. `ArrayList` is just a class that somebody defined (and placed in the standard Java library package `java.util`), so you should also be able to define these kinds of classes. Starting with version 5.0, Java allows class definitions with parameters for types. These classes that have type parameters are called parameterized class or **generic definitions** or, more simply, **generics**. You already know how to use classes with a type parameter, because we have been using the parameterized class `ArrayList`. In Section 14.2, we will show you how to write your own parameterized classes.

generics

PITFALL: Nonparameterized `ArrayList` and `Vector` Classes

The `ArrayList` and `Vector` classes we discussed in this section have a type parameter for the base type. There are also `ArrayList` and `Vector` classes with no parameter for the base type. (They have base type `Object`.) These `ArrayList` and `Vector` classes without type parameters are left over from earlier versions of Java. When checking details in the Java documentation, be sure you get the documentation for the `ArrayList` and `Vector` classes that have a type parameter. Using notation we introduce in Section 14.2, the versions with type parameters are usually written as `ArrayList<E>` and `Vector<E>` or as `ArrayList<T>` and `Vector<T>` in the Java documentation. ■

14.2 Generics

You can have this dish prepared with any type of meat or fish.

Entry on a restaurant menu

Starting with version 5.0, Java allows class definitions that contain a parameter (or parameters) for a type (or types). In this section, we teach you how to write class definitions that contain a type parameter.

Generic Basics

type parameter

Classes and methods can have a type parameter. The type parameter may then have any reference type, and hence any class type, plugged in for the type parameter. This plugging in produces a specific class type or method. For example, Display 14.4 shows a very simple class definition with a **type parameter** T. You may use any nonkeyword identifier for the type parameter; you need not use T. However, by convention, type parameters start with an uppercase letter, and there is some tradition of using a single letter for a type parameter. Starting with an uppercase letter makes sense because typically a class type is plugged in for the type parameter. The tradition of using a single letter is not so compelling.

A class definition with a type parameter is stored in a file and compiled just like any other class. For example, the parameterized class shown in Display 14.4 would be stored in a file named `Sample.java`. Once the parameterized class is compiled, it can be used like any other class, except that when used in your code, you must specify a class type to be plugged in for the type parameter. For example, the class `Sample` from Display 14.4 could be used as follows:

```
Sample<String> object1 = new Sample<String>();
object1.setData("Hello");
System.out.println(object1.getData());
Sample<Pet> object2 = new Sample<Pet>();
Pet p = new Pet();
<Some code to set the data for the object p>
object2.setData(p);
```

The class `Pet` can be as defined in Chapter 4, but the details do not matter; it could be any class.

instantiate   A class, such as `Sample<String>`, that you obtain from a generic class by plugging in a type for the type parameter is said to **instantiate** the generic class. So, we would say "`Sample<String>` instantiates the generic class `Sample`."

Notice the angular bracket notation for the type parameter and also for the class type that is plugged in for the type parameter.

Display 14.4   A Class Definition with a Type Parameter

```
1    public class Sample<T>
2    {
3        private T data;

4        public void setData(T newData)
5        {
6            data = newData;                          T is a parameter for a type.
7        }

8        public T getData()
9        {
10           return data;
11       }
12   }
```

Class Definition with a Type Parameter

You can define classes with a parameter for a type. Such a class is called a **generic class** or a **parameterized class**. The type parameter is included in angular brackets after the class name in the class definition heading. You may use any nonkeyword identifier for the type parameter, but by convention, the type parameter starts with an uppercase letter. The type parameter may be used like any other type in the definition of the class. (There are some restrictions on where the type parameter can be used. These are discussed in the Pitfall section entitled "Type Parameters Cannot Be Used Everywhere a Type Name Can Be Used.") For an example, see Display 14.4.

A generic class is used like any other class, except that you specify a reference type, typically a class type, to be plugged in for the type parameter. This class type (or other reference type) is given in angular brackets after the name of the generic class, as shown in the following example:

EXAMPLE

```
Sample<String> object1 = new Sample<String>();
object1.setData("Hello");
```

`Sample<String>` is said to **instantiate** the generic class `Sample`.

TIP: Compile with the –Xlint Option

There are many pitfalls that you can encounter when using type parameters. If you compile with the –Xlint option, you will receive more informative diagnostics of any problems or potential problems in your code. For example, the class `Sample` in Display 14.4 should be compiled as follows:

```
javac –Xlint Sample.java
```

If you are using an IDE to compile your programs, check your documentation to see how to set compiler options. (For the TextPad environment, you can set compiler options in the `Preferences` box under the `Configure` menu.)

When compiling with the –Xlint option, you will get more warnings than you would otherwise get. A warning is not an error, and if the compiler gives only warnings and no error message, then the class has compiled and can be used. However, in most cases, be sure you understand the warning and feel confident that it does not indicate a problem, or else change your code to eliminate the warning. One warning that you may get on some programs in this text is "no definition of serialVersionUID." Discussion of this warning is beyond the scope of this book, but you can safely ignore the warning. ∎

EXAMPLE: A Generic Class for Ordered Pairs

In Display 14.5, we have given a parameterized class for ordered pairs of values.

Notice that the constructor heading does not include the type parameter T. This is counter to many peoples' intuition, but that is the way it is done. A constructor can use the type parameter, such as T, as the type for a parameter for the constructor, but the constructor heading does not include the type parameter in angular brackets, such as <T>.

By using this parameterized class with the type String plugged in for the type parameter T, as shown below, you get a class whose objects are pairs of String values:

```
Pair<String> secretPair =
            new Pair<String>("Happy", "Day");
```

By using this parameterized class with the type Integer plugged in for the type parameter T, as shown below, you get a class whose objects are pairs of Integer objects:

```
Pair<Integer> rollOfDice =
            new Pair<Integer>(new Integer(2), new Integer(3));
```

If Pet is some class you defined, you can plug in Pet for the type parameter T, as shown below, to get a class whose objects are pairs of objects of type Pet:

```
Pet male = new Pet();
Pet female = new Pet();
<Some code to set the data for the objects male and female.>
Pair<Pet> breedingPair =
            new Pair<Pet>(male, female);
```

Display 14.6 contains a simple example of using our generic class Pair.

Display 14.5 A Generic Ordered Pair Class (part 1 of 2)

```
1   public class Pair<T>
2   {
3       private T first;
4       private T second;

5       public Pair()
6       {
7           first = null;
8           second = null;
9       }

10      public Pair(T firstItem, T secondItem)
11      {
```

Constructor headings do not include the type parameter in angular brackets.

Display 14.5   A Generic Ordered Pair Class (part 2 of 2)

```
12              first = firstItem;
13              second = secondItem;
14          }

15      public void setFirst(T newFirst)
16      {
17              first = newFirst;
18      }

19      public void setSecond(T newSecond)
20      {
21              second = newSecond;
22      }

23      public T getFirst()
24      {
25              return first;
26      }

27      public T getSecond()
28      {
29              return second;
30      }

31      public String toString()
32      {
33              return ( "first: " + first.toString() + "\n"
34                      + "second: " + second.toString() );
35      }
36

37      public boolean equals(Object otherObject)
38      {
39          if (otherObject == null)
40              return false;
41          else if (getClass() != otherObject.getClass())
42              return false;
43          else
44          {
45              Pair<T> otherPair = (Pair<T>)otherObject;
46              return (first.equals(otherPair.first)
47                  && second.equals(otherPair.second));
48          }
49      }
50  }
```

> ### Terminology
>
> The terms *generic class* and *parameterized class* mean the same thing, namely a class with one or more type parameters.

Display 14.6 **Using Our Ordered Pair Class** (part 1 of 2)

```
1    import java.util.Scanner;

2    public class GenericPairDemo
3    {
4        public static void main(String[] args)
5        {
6            Pair<String> secretPair =
7                new Pair<String>("Happy", "Day");

9            Scanner keyboard = new Scanner(System.in);
10           System.out.println("Enter two words:");
11           String word1 = keyboard.next();
12           String word2 = keyboard.next();
13           Pair<String> inputPair =
14               new Pair<String>(word1, word2);
15           if (inputPair.equals(secretPair))
16           {
17               System.out.println("You guessed the secret words");
18               System.out.println("in the correct order!");

19           }
20           else
21           {
22               System.out.println("You guessed incorrectly.");
23               System.out.println("You guessed");
24               System.out.println(inputPair);
25               System.out.println("The secret words are");
26               System.out.println(secretPair);
27           }
28       }
29   }
```

Sample Dialogue

```
Enter two words:
two words
You guessed incorrectly.
You guessed
first: two
```

Display 14.6   **Using Our Ordered Pair Class** (part 2 of 2)

```
second: words
The secret words are
first: Happy
second: Day
```

PITFALL: A Generic Constructor Name Has No Type Parameter

The class name in a parameterized class definition has a type parameter attached, such as Pair<T> in Display 14.5. This can mislead you into thinking you need to use the type parameter in the heading of the constructor definition, but you do not repeat the type parameter specification <T> in the heading of the constructor definition. For example, you use

```
public Pair()
```

You do not use

```
public Pair<T>()
```

A constructor can use the type parameter, such as T, as the type for a parameter for the constructor, as in the following, but the constructor heading does not include the type parameter in angular brackets, such as <T>:

```
public Pair(T firstItem, T secondItem)
```

For a complete example, see Display 14.5.

Sometimes it seems that people stay up late at night thinking of ways to make things confusing. As we just noted, in the definition of a parameterized class, a constructor has no type parameter in angular brackets. So, you see the following in Display 14.5:

```
public Pair(T firstItem, T secondItem)
```

But as shown in Display 14.6, when you instantiate a generic class by specifying a type for the type parameter, you do specify the type in angular brackets when writing the constructor name, as in the following from Display 14.6:

```
Pair<String> secretPair =
            new Pair<String>("Happy", "Day");
```

However, this second case is not hard to remember. If you left out the <String>, Java would not know which Pair class you meant. If you left out the <String>, the compiler could not tell if you meant Pair<String>, Pair<Double>, or some other Pair class. ■

PITFALL: You Cannot Plug in a Primitive Type for a Type Parameter

The type plugged in for a type parameter must be a reference type. It cannot be a primitive type such as `int`, `double`, or `char`. However, now that Java has automatic boxing, this is not a big restriction in practice. For example, if you want `Pair<int>`, you cannot have it, but you can have `Pair<Integer>`, and thanks to automatic boxing, you can use `Pair<Integer>` with `int` values. This is illustrated by the program in Display 14.7.

The most typical type to plug in for a type parameter is a class type. However, you can plug in any reference type. So, in particular, you can plug in an array type for a type parameter. ∎

PITFALL: A Type Parameter Cannot Be Used Everywhere a Type Name Can Be Used

Within the definition of a parameterized class definition, there are places where an ordinary class name would be allowed but a type parameter is not allowed. In particular, you cannot use the type parameter in simple expressions using `new` to create a new object. For example, the following are all illegal within the definition of a parameterized class definition with type parameter `T`:

```
T object = new T(); //The first T is legal,
                    //the second one is illegal.
T[] a = new T[10]; //The first T is legal,
                    //the second one is illegal.
```

This restriction is not as arbitrary as it might at first appear. In the first case, `T` is not being used as a type name; it is being used as a constructor name. In the second case, `T` is being used as something like a constructor, although it is not officially a constructor. ∎

PITFALL: An Instantiation of a Generic Class Cannot be an Array Base Type

Arrays such as the following are illegal (the generic class `Pair` is the one defined in Display 14.5):

```
Pair<String>[] a = new Pair<String>[10]; //Illegal
```

This is a reasonable thing to want to do, but it is not allowed because of technical details having to do with how Java implements generic classes. The full explanation for this restriction is beyond the scope of this book. ∎

Display 14.7   Using Our Ordered Pair Class and Automatic Boxing (part 1 of 2)

```
1    import java.util.Scanner;

2    public class GenericPairDemo2
3    {
4        public static void main(String[] args)
5        {
6            Pair<Integer> secretPair =
7                new Pair<Integer>(42, 24);
8
9            Scanner keyboard = new Scanner(System.in);
10           System.out.println("Enter two numbers:");
11           int n1 = keyboard.nextInt();
12           int n2 = keyboard.nextInt();
13           Pair<Integer> inputPair =
14               new Pair<Integer>(n1, n2);
15           if (inputPair.equals(secretPair))
16           {
17               System.out.println("You guessed the secret numbers");
18               System.out.println("in the correct order!");
19           }
20           else
21           {
22               System.out.println("You guessed incorrectly.");
23               System.out.println("You guessed");
24               System.out.println(inputPair);
25               System.out.println("The secret numbers are");
26               System.out.println(secretPair);
27           }
28       }
29   }
```

Automatic boxing allows you to use an int *argument for an* Integer *parameter.*

Sample Dialogue

```
Enter two numbers:
42 24
You guessed the secret numbers
in the correct order!
```

TIP: A Class Definition Can Have More Than One Type Parameter

A generic class definition can have any number of type parameters. The multiple type parameters are listed in angular brackets just as in the single type parameter case, but are separated by commas. For example, in Display 14.8, we have rewritten the class Pair so the first and second items of a pair can be of different types. In Display 14.9, we give a simple example of using our generic class with two type parameters. ∎

Display 14.8 **Multiple Type Parameters** (part 1 of 2)

```
1    public class TwoTypePair<T1, T2>
2    {
3        private T1 first;
4        private T2 second;

5        public TwoTypePair()
6        {
7            first = null;
8            second = null;
9        }

10       public TwoTypePair(T1 firstItem, T2 secondItem)
11       {
12           first = firstItem;
13           second = secondItem;
14       }

15       public void setFirst(T1 newFirst)
16       {
17           first = newFirst;
18       }
19       public void setSecond(T2 newSecond)
20       {
21           second = newSecond;
22       }
23       public T1 getFirst()
24       {
25           return first;
26       }

27       public T2 getSecond()
28       {
29           return second;
30       }

31       public String toString()
32       {
33           return ( "first: " + first.toString() + "\n"
34                   + "second: " + second.toString() );
35       }

36
37       public boolean equals(Object otherObject)
38       {
```

Display 14.8   Multiple Type Parameters (part 2 of 2)

```
39              if (otherObject == null)
40                  return false;
41              else if (getClass() != otherObject.getClass())
42                  return false;
43              else
44              {
45                  TwoTypePair<T1, T2> otherPair =
46                          (TwoTypePair<T1, T2>)otherObject;
47                  return (first.equals(otherPair.first)
48                      && second.equals(otherPair.second));
49              }
50      }
51  }
```

The first equals *is the* equals *of the type* T1. *The second* equals *is the* equals *of the type* T2.

PITFALL: A Generic Class Cannot Be an Exception Class

If you begin an exception class definition as follows, you will get a compiler error message:

```
public class MyException<T> extends Exception //Illegal
```

It is still illegal if you replace Exception with Error, Throwable, or any descendent class of Throwable. You cannot create a generic class whose objects are throwable. ■

Display 14.9   Using a Generic Class with Two Type Parameters (part 1 of 2)

```
1   import java.util.Scanner;

2   public class TwoTypePairDemo
3   {
4       public static void main(String[] args)
5       {
6           TwoTypePair<String, Integer> rating =
7               new TwoTypePair<String, Integer>("The Car Guys", 8);

8           Scanner keyboard = new Scanner(System.in);
9           System.out.println(
10                  "Our current rating for " + rating.getFirst());
11          System.out.println(" is " + rating.getSecond());

12          System.out.println("How would you rate them?");
13          int score = keyboard.nextInt();
14          rating.setSecond(score);
```

(continued)

Display 14.9   Using a Generic Class with Two Type Parameters (part 2 of 2)

```
15              System.out.println(
16                      "Our new rating for " + rating.getFirst());
17              System.out.println(" is " + rating.getSecond());
18       }
19    }
```

Sample Dialogue

```
Our current rating for The Car Guys
is 8
How would you rate them?
10
Our new rating for The Car Guys
is 10
```

Bounds for Type Parameters

Sometimes it does not make sense to plug in just any reference type for the type parameter in a generic class definition. For example, consider the generic class Pair defined in Display 14.5. Suppose we want to add a method that returns the maximum of the two elements in an ordered pair. We could add the following method definition to the class Pair in Display 14.5:

max
```
public T max()
{
    if (first.compareTo(second) <= 0)
        return first;
    else
        return second;
}
```

compareTo   Recall that the method compareTo is required to be a member of any class that implements the Comparable interface. The Comparable interface is a standard Java interface that was discussed in Chapter 13. As a reminder, recall that the Comparable interface has only the following method heading that must be implemented:

```
public int compareTo(Object other);
```

When defining a class that implements the Comparable interface, the programmer is expected to define compareTo so that it returns

a negative number if the calling object "comes before" the parameter other,

a zero if the calling object "equals" the parameter other,

and a positive number if the calling object "comes after" the parameter other.

This all works fine, except for one problem: This only makes sense if the type plugged in for the type parameter T satisfies the Comparable interface, but Java allows you to plug in any type for the type parameter T.

You can have Java enforce this restriction on the possible types that can be plugged in for T. To ensure that only classes that implement the Comparable interface are plugged in for T, you begin the class definition as follows:

```
public class Pair<T extends Comparable>
```

extends   The part extends Comparable is called a **bound** on the type parameter T. If you
bound   attempt to plug in a type for T which does not implement the Comparable interface, you will get a compiler error message. Note that you use the keyword extends, not the keyword implements as you would naturally expect.

Note that the bound extends Comparable is not just an optional little nicety. If you omit it, you will get an error message from the compiler saying it does not know about the method compareTo.

This version of the generic class Pair with the method max is summarized in Display 14.10. On the accompanying CD, this version of Pair is in a subdirectory named Bounded Pair.

A bound on a type may be a class name (rather than an interface name) in which case only descendent classes of the bounding class may be plugged in for the type parameters. For example, the following says that only descendent classes of the class Employee may be plugged in for T, where Employee is some class:

```
public class SameGenericClass<T extends Employee>
```

Display 14.10 **A Bounded Type Parameter**

```
1    public class Pair<T extends Comparable>
2    {
3        private T first;
4        private T second;

5        public T max()
6        {
7            if (first.compareTo(second) <= 0)
8                return first;
9            else
10                return second;
11        }
```

    <All the constructors and methods given in Display 14.5
                are also included as part of this generic class definition>

```
12    }
```

This explains why the keyword `extends` is used in the bounds expression rather than `implements`.

multiple bounds

You can have multiple interfaces and possibly one class in a bounds expression. Just separate the entries with the ampersand sign, &, as in the following example:

```
public class AnotherGenericClass<T extends Employee & Comparable>
```

If you have more than one type parameter, the syntax follows the following example:

```
public class YetAnotherGeneric
        <T1 extends Employee & Comparable, T2 extends Comparable>
```

You can list any number of interfaces in a bounds expression, but you may list only one class in a bounds expression. Moreover, if you do list a class and some interfaces, the class must be first in the list.

Type Parameter Bounds

You can specify that the class plugged in for a type parameter must be a descendent class of a specified class, must implement specified interfaces, or both.

SYNTAX (FOR CLASS DEFINITION HEADINGS)

```
public class Class_Name
  <Type extends Ancestor_Class & Interface_1 & Interface_2 & ...
                                      ... & Last_Interface>
```

If there are multiple type parameters, they are separated by commas. There can be any number of interfaces but only one ancestor class for each type parameter.

EXAMPLES

```
public class Pair<T extends Comparable>
public class MyClass<T extends Employee & Comparable>
public class YourClass <T1 extends Employee & Comparable
                                & Cloneable, T2 extends Comparable>
```

`Employee` is a class. `Comparable` and `Cloneable` are interfaces.

TIP: Generic Interfaces

An interface can have one or more type parameters. The details and notation are the same as they are for classes with type parameters. ■

Generic Methods ★

(This is a starred subsection because it is needed only for Chapter 16, which covers the Java collection classes. If you choose to read Chapter 16, you will need to read this subsection first.)

When you define a generic class, you can use the type parameter in the definitions of the methods for that generic class. You also can define a generic method that has its own type parameter that is not the type parameter of any class. This generic method can be a member of an ordinary (nongeneric) class or a member of some generic class with some other type parameter. For example,

```java
public class Utility
{
    . . .
    public static <T> T getMidpoint(T[] a)
    {
        return a[a.length/2];
    }

    public static <T> T getFirst(T[] a)
    {
        return a[0];
    }
    . . .
}
```

In this case, the class (Utility) has no type parameters, but the methods getMidpoint and getFirst each have a type parameter. Note that the type parameter in angular brackets, <T>, is placed after all the modifiers, in this case public static, and before the returned type.

When you invoke one of these generic methods, you preface the method name with the type to be plugged in, given in angular brackets, as in the following examples:

```java
String midString = Utility.<String>getMidpoint(b);

double firstNumber = Utility.<Double>getFirst(c);
```

Note that the dot is before the type in angular brackets; the type is part of the method name, not part of the class name. Also note that the methods getMidpoint and getFirst use different types plugged in for their type parameter. The type parameter is local to the method, not to the class. (The argument b is an array with base type String. The argument c is an array with base type Double.)

You can also define such generic methods inside of generic classes, as in the following example:

```java
public class Sample<T>
{
    private T data;

    public Sample(T forData)
    {
        data = forData;
    }
```

```
        public <ViewerType> void showTo(ViewerType viewer)
        {
            System.out.println("Hello " + viewer);
            System.out.println("Data is " + data);
        }
          ...
    }
```

Note that T and ViewerType are different type parameters. T is a type parameter for the entire class, but ViewerType is a type parameter only for the method showTo. Below is a sample use of these generic methods:

```
Sample<Integer> object = new Sample<Integer>(42);
object.<String>showTo("Friend");
```

This produces the output:

```
Hello Friend
Data is 42
```

Inheritance with Generic Classes ★

You can define a generic class to be a derived class of an ordinary class or a derived class of another generic class. Display 14.11 contains the definition of a generic class called UnorderedPair, which is a derived class of the generic class Pair (which we gave in Display 14.5). The class UnorderedPair overrides the definition of equals that it inherits from Pair. To a programmer using the class, UnorderedPair is just like the class Pair with one exception. In UnorderedPair, the two components do not have to be in the same order for two pairs to be equal. Less formally, in the Pair<String> world, "beer" and "peanuts" is not the same as "peanuts" and "beer". In the UnorderedPair<String> world, they are the same. This is illustrated by the demonstration program in Display 14.12.

Just as you would expect, an object of type UnorderedPair<String> is also of type Pair<String>. As we have seen so far, inheritance with generic classes is straightforward in most cases. However, there are some situations with subtle pitfalls. We discuss those next.

Display 14.11 **A Derived Generic Class** (part 1 of 2)

```
1   public class UnorderedPair<T> extends Pair<T>
2   {
3       public UnorderedPair()
4       {
5           setFirst(null);
6           setSecond(null);
7       }

8       public UnorderedPair(T firstItem, T secondItem)
9       {
```

```
10              setFirst(firstItem);
11              setSecond(secondItem);
12          }

13      public boolean equals(Object otherObject)
14      {
15          if (otherObject == null)
16              return false;
17          else if (getClass() != otherObject.getClass())
18              return false;
19          else
20          {
21              UnorderedPair<T> otherPair =
22                              (UnorderedPair<T>)otherObject;
23              return (getFirst().equals(otherPair.getFirst())
24                  && getSecond().equals(otherPair.getSecond()))
25                  ||
26                      (getFirst().equals(otherPair.getSecond())
27                  && getSecond().equals(otherPair.getFirst()));
28          }
29      }
30  }
```

Suppose HourlyEmployee is a derived class of the class Employee. You might think that an object of type Pair<HourlyEmployee> is also of type Pair<Employee>. You might think that, but you would be wrong. If G is a generic class, there is no relationship between G<A> and G<B>, no matter what the relationship is between the classes A and B.

Display 14.12   Using **UnorderedPair** (part 1 of 2)

```
1   public class UnorderedPairDemo
2   {
3       public static void main(String[] args)
4       {
5           UnorderedPair<String> p1 =
6               new UnorderedPair<String>("peanuts", "beer");
7           UnorderedPair<String> p2 =
8               new UnorderedPair<String>("beer", "peanuts");

9           if (p1.equals(p2))
10          {
```

(continued)

Display 14.12 Using **UnorderedPair** (part 2 of 2)

```
11              {
12                  System.out.println(p1.getFirst() + " and " +
13                          p1.getSecond() + " is the same as");
14                  System.out.println(p2.getFirst() + " and "
15                          + p2.getSecond());
16              }
17          }
18      }
```

Sample Dialogue[2]

```
peanuts and beer is the same as
beer and peanuts
```

Self-Test Exercises

12. (This question refers to the starred section "Generic Methods." You should skip this question if you have not yet read that subsection.) Define a generic method named `getMidindex`, which is like `getMidpoint`, but returns the index of the array midpoint as opposed to the element at the midpoint.

13. (This question refers to the starred section "Inheritance with Generic Classes." You should skip this question if you have not yet read that subsection.) Is an array of type `UnorderedPair<String>[]` also of type `Pair<String>[]`?

_____

[2]A note to the grammar police: I intentionally used "is" instead of "are." If you read and understand the text, you will realize that "peanuts and beer" is a single item. Starting the sentence with a low-

Chapter Summary

- `ArrayList` is a parameterized class that is like an array that can grow (and shrink) while the program is running.

- An `ArrayList` has a number of methods that allow you to use it as a kind of automated partially filled array.

- You can cycle through all the elements in an `ArrayList` using a for-each loop.

- You can define classes with one or more type parameters. Such classes are known as _generic classes_.

Answers to Self-Test Exercises

1. `list.add("Hello");`

2. `instruction.set(5, "Go");`

3. `instruction.add(5, "Go");`

4. No. The index for `set` must be greater than or equal to 0 and less than the size of the `ArrayList`. Thus, you can replace any existing element, but you cannot place the element at any higher index. This situation is unlike that of an array. If an array is partially filled to index 10, you can add an element at index 20, as long as the array is that large. With an `ArrayList`, you cannot add an element beyond the last-used index.

5. No. The index for `add` must be greater than or equal to 0 and less than or equal to the size of the `ArrayList`. Thus, you can replace any existing element or add an element to the end of the list, but you cannot place the element at any higher index. This situation is unlike that of an array. If an array is partially filled to index 10, you can add an element at index 20, as long as the array is that large. With an `ArrayList`, you cannot add an element beyond one more than the last-used index.

6. The index for `add` (that is, `index2`) is allowed to be one larger than the index for `set` (that is, `index1`). The index for `set` must be strictly less than the size of the `ArrayList`. The index for `add` can also be equal to the size of the `ArrayList`.

7. Yes. The `ArrayList` can contain more than 20 elements. The number 20 used as an argument to the constructor merely gives the initial memory allocation for the `ArrayList`. More memory is automatically allocated when it is needed.

8.
```
for (Double element : numberList)
    System.out.println(element);
```

9.
```
import java.util.ArrayList;
/**
 Class for sorting an ArrayList of Strings lexicographically
 (approximately alphabetically).
*/
public class StringSelectionSort
{

    /**
     Sorts the ArrayList a so that a.get(0), a.get(1),...,
     a.get(a.size() − 1) are in lexicographic order.
    */
    public static void sort(ArrayList<String> a)
    {
        int index, indexOfNextSmallest;
        for (index = 0; index < a.size() − 1; index++)
        {//Place the correct value in position index:
```

```
                    indexOfNextSmallest =
                            indexOfSmallest(index, a);
            interchange(index,indexOfNextSmallest, a);
            //a.get(0), a.get(1),...,a.get(index)
            //are sorted. The rest of the
            //elements are in the remaining positions.
        }
    }

    /**
     Precondition: i and j are legal indices for the ArrayList a.
     Postcondition: The values of a.get(i) and
     a.get(j) have been interchanged.
    */
    private static void interchange(
                        int i, int j, ArrayList<String> a)
    {
        String temp;
        temp = a.get(i);
        a.set(i, a.get(j));
        a.set(j, temp);
    }

    /**
     Returns the index of the lexicographically first value among
     a.get(startIndex), a.get(startIndex+1),...,a.get(a.size() − 1)
    */
    private static int indexOfSmallest(
                        int startIndex, ArrayList<String> a)
    {
        String min = a.get(startIndex);
        int indexOfMin = startIndex;
        int index;
        for (index = startIndex + 1; index < a.size(); index++)
        if ((a.get(index)).compareTo(min) < 0)
        {
            min = a.get(index);
            indexOfMin = index;
        }
        return indexOfMin;
    }
}
```

10. No the base type of an ArrayList cannot be a primitive type, such as int, double, or char. You can, however, have an ArrayList with base type Integer that
can be used to store integers.

11. Notice that the following, while correct, is not as easy to understand as the for-each loop.

```
for (int i; i < a.size(); i++)
    System.out.println(a.get(i) + " differs from average by "
                            + (a.get(i) - average));
```

12.
```
public static <T> int getMidindex(T[] a)
{
    return a.length/2;
}
```

13. This is a trick question. As we explained in the text, you cannot have an array of type UnorderedPair<String>[] or of type Pair<String>[].

Programming Projects

 *Many of these Programming Projects can be solved using AW's MyCodeMate.
To access these please go to:* www.mycodemate.com.

 1. In the sport of diving, seven judges award a score between 0 and 10, where each score may be a floating-point value. The highest and lowest scores are thrown out and the remaining scores are added together. The sum is then multiplied by the degree of difficulty for that dive. The degree of difficulty ranges from 1.2 to 3.8 points. The total is then multiplied by 0.6 to determine the diver's score.

Write a computer program that inputs a degree of difficulty and seven judges' scores and outputs the overall score for that dive. The program should use an ArrayList of type Double to store the scores.

2. Write a program that uses an ArrayList of parameter type Contact to store a database of contacts. The Contact class should store the contact's first and last name, phone number, and email address. Add appropriate accessor and mutator methods. Your database program should present a menu that allows the user to add a contact, display all contacts, search for a specific contact and display it, or search for a specific contact and give the user the option to delete it. The searches should find any contact where any member variable contains a target search string. For example, if "elmore" is the search target then any contact where the first name, last name, phone number, or email address contains "elmore" should be returned for display or deletion. Use the "for each" loop to iterate through the ArrayList.

3. Many Global Positioning Satellite (GPS) units can record waypoints. The waypoint marks the coordinates of a location on a map along with a timestamp. Consider a GPS unit that stores waypoints in terms of an (X,Y) coordinate on a map together with a timestamp t that records the number of seconds that have

elapsed since the unit was turned on. Write a program that allows the user to enter as many waypoints as desired, storing each waypoint in an `ArrayList`, where each waypoint is represented by a class that you design. Each waypoint represents a successive sample point during a hike along some route. The coordinates should be input as `doubles`, and the timestamp as an integer. Have your program compute the total distance traveled and the average speed in miles per hour. Use the map scaling factor of 1 = 0.1 miles. For example, if the only two waypoints are (X=1,Y=1,T=0) and (X=2,Y=1,T=3600) then the hiker traveled a distance of 0.1 miles in 3600 seconds, or 0.1 miles per hour.

4. Write a generic class, `MyMathClass`, with a type parameter `T` where `T` is a numeric object type (e.g., `Integer`, `Double`, or any class that extends `java.lang.Number`). Add a method named `standardDeviation` that takes an `ArrayList` of type `T` and returns as a `double` the standard deviation of the values in the `ArrayList`. Use the `doubleValue()` method in the `Number` class to retrieve the value of each number as a double. Refer to Programming Project 6.2 for a definition of computing the standard deviation. Test your method with suitable data. Your program should generate a compile-time error if your standard deviation method is invoked on an `ArrayList` that is defined for non-numeric elements (e.g., `Strings`).

5. Create a generic class with a type parameter that simulates drawing an item at random out of a box. This class could be used for simulating a random drawing. For example, the box might contain `Strings` representing names written on a slip of paper, or the box might contain `Integers` representing a random drawing for a lottery based on numeric lottery picks. Create an `add` method that allows the user of the class to add an object of the specified type along with an `isEmpty` method that determines whether or not the box is empty. Finally, your class should have a `drawItem` method that randomly selects an object from the box and returns it. If the user attempts to drawn an item out of an empty box, return `null`. Write a `main` method that tests your class. To generate a random number x, where $0 \leq x \leq 1$, use x = `Math.random();`.

6. Implement a priority queue capable of holding objects of an arbitrary type, `T`, by defining a `PriorityQueue` class that implements the queue with an `ArrayList`. A priority queue is a type of list where every item added to the queue also has an associated priority. Define priority in your application so that those items with the largest numerical value have the highest priority. Your class should support the following methods:

   - `Add(item, priority)`—Adds a new item to the queue with the associated priority.

   - `Remove()`—Returns the item with the highest priority and removes it from the queue. If the user attempts to remove from an empty queue return `null`.

For example, if q is a priority queue defined to take strings:

```
q.add("X", 10);
q.add("Y", 1);
q.add("Z", 3);

System.out.println(q.remove());// Returns X
System.out.println(q.remove());// Returns Z
System.out.println(q.remove());// Returns Y
```

Test your queue on data with priorities in various orders (e.g., ascending, descending, mixed). You can implement the priority queue by performing a linear search through the ArrayList. In future courses you may study a data structure called a heap that is a more efficient way to implement a priority queue.

15

Linked Data Structures

15 Linked Data Structures

If somebody there chanced to be
Who loved me in a manner true
My heart would point him out to me
And I would point him out to you.

GILBERT AND SULLIVAN, *Ruddigore*

Introduction

node and link

linked list

head node

A linked data structure consists of capsules of data, known as **nodes**, that are connected via things called **links**. These links can be viewed as arrows and thought of as one-way passages from one node to another. The simplest kind of linked data structure consists of a single chain of nodes, each connected to the next by a link; this is known as a **linked list**. A sample linked list can be depicted as shown in Display 15.1. In Display 15.1 the nodes are represented by boxes that can each hold two kinds of data, a string and an integer, as in a shopping list. The links are depicted as arrows, which reflects the fact that your code must traverse the linked list in one direction without backing up. So there is a first node, a second node, and so on up to the last node. The first node is called the **head node**.

That information is all very vague but provides the general picture of what is going on in a linked list. It becomes concrete when you realize a linked list in some programming language. In Java, the nodes are realized as objects of a node class. The data in a node is stored via instance variables. The links are realized as references. Recall that a reference is simply a memory address. A reference is what is stored in a variable of a class type. So the link is realized as an instance variable of the type of the node class itself. In Java, a node in a linked list is connected to the next node by having an instance variable of the node type contain a reference (that is, a memory address) of where in memory the next node is stored.

Java comes with a LinkedList library class as part of the java.util package. It makes sense to use this library class, since it is well designed, well tested, and will save you a lot of work. However, using the library class will not teach you how to implement linked data structures in Java. To do that, you need to see an implementation of a simple linked data structure, such as a linked list. So to let you see how this sort of thing is done in Java, we will construct our own simplified example of a linked list.

After discussing linked lists we then go on to discuss more elaborate linked data structures, including sets, hash tables, and trees.

Display 15.1   Nodes and Links in a Linked List

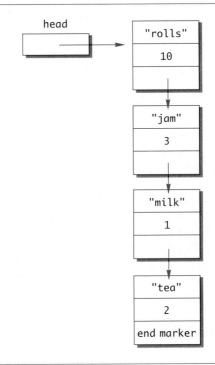

Prerequisites

If you prefer, you may skip this chapter and go directly to Chapter 16 on collection classes or to Chapter 17 to begin your study of windowing interfaces using the Swing library. You have a good deal of flexibility in how you order the later chapters of this book.

This chapter requires material from Chapters 1 through 5, Chapter 14, and simple uses of inner classes (Section 13.2 of Chapter 13). Section 15.7 on trees additionally requires Chapter 11 on recursion.

Sections 15.2 through 15.7 do not depend on each other in any essential way. In particular, you may omit Section 15.2 on cloning and still read the following sections. Sections 15.2 through 15.7 do not depend in any essential way on the material on generic linked lists in subsections of Section 15.1.

15.1 Java Linked Lists

A chain is only as strong as its weakest link.

PROVERB

A linked list is a linked data structure consisting of a single chain of nodes, each connected to the next by a link. This is the simplest kind of linked data structure, but it is nevertheless widely used. In this section, we give examples of linked lists and develop techniques for defining and working with linked lists in Java.

EXAMPLE: A Simple Linked List Class

Display 15.1 is a diagram of a linked list. In the display the nodes are the boxes. In your Java code, a node is an object of some node class, such as the class Node1 given in Display 15.2. Each node has a place (or places) for some data and a place to hold a link to another node. The links are shown as arrows that point to the node they "link" to. In Java, the links will be implemented as references to a node stored in an instance variable of the node type.

The Node1 class is defined by specifying, among other things, an instance variable of type Node1 that is named link. This allows each node to store a reference to another node of the same type. There is a kind of circularity in such definitions, but this circularity is allowed in Java. (One way to see that this definition is not logically inconsistent is to note that we can draw pictures, or even build physical models, of our linked nodes.)

The first node, or start node, in a linked list is called the head node. If you start at the head node, you can traverse the entire linked list, visiting each node exactly once. As you will see in Java code shortly, your code must intuitively "follow the link arrows." In Display 15.1 the box labeled head is not itself the head node; it is not even a node. The box labeled head is a variable of type Node1 that contains a reference to the first node in the linked list—that is, a reference to the head node. The function of the variable head is that it allows your code to find that first or head node. The variable head is declared in the obvious way:

```
Node1 head;
```

In Java, a linked list is an object that in some sense contains all the nodes of the linked list. Display 15.3 contains a definition of a linked list class for a linked list like the one in Display 15.1. Notice that a linked list object does not directly contain all the nodes in the linked list. It only contains the instance variable head that contains a reference to the first or head node. However, every node can be reached from this first or head node. The link instance variable of the first and every Node1 of the linked list contains a reference to the next Node1 in the linked list. Thus, the arrows shown in the diagram in Display 15.1 are realized as references in Java. Each node object of a linked list contains (in its link instance variable) a reference to another object of the class Node1, and this other object contains a reference to another object of the class Node1, and so on until the end of the linked list. Thus, a linked list object, indirectly at least, contains all the nodes in the linked list.

Display 15.2   A Node Class

```java
public class Node1
{
    private String item;
    private int count;
    private Node1 link;

    public Node1( )
    {
        link = null;
        item = null;
        count = 0;
    }
    public Node1(String newItem, int newCount, Node1 linkValue)
    {
        setData(newItem, newCount);
        link = linkValue;
    }

    public void setData(String newItem, int newCount)
    {
        item = newItem;
        count = newCount;
    }
    public void setLink(Node1 newLink)
    {
        link = newLink;
    }

    public String getItem( )
    {
        return item;
    }

    public int getCount( )
    {
        return count;
    }

    public Node1 getLink( )
    {
        return link;
    }
}
```

A node contains a reference to another node. That reference is the link to the next node.

We will define a number of node classes so we numbered the names as in **Node1**.

We will give a better definition of a node class later in this chapter.

Display 15.3 **A Linked List Class** (part 1 of 2)

```
1    public class LinkedList1
2    {
3        private Node1 head;
4
5        public LinkedList1( )
6        {
7            head = null;
8        }
9
10       /**
11        Adds a node at the start of the list with the specified data.
12        The added node will be the first node in the list.
13       */
14       public void addToStart(String itemName, int itemCount)
15       {
16           head = new Node1(itemName, itemCount, head);
17       }
18
19       /**
20        Removes the head node and returns true if the list contained at least
21        one node. Returns false if the list was empty.
22       */
23       public boolean deleteHeadNode( )
24       {
25           if (head != null)
26           {
27               head = head.getLink( );
28               return true;
29           }
30           else
31               return false;
32       }
33
34       /**
35        Returns the number of nodes in the list.
36       */
37       public int size( )
38       {
39           int count = 0;
40           Node1 position = head;
```

We will define a letter linked list class later in this chapter.

Display 15.3 A Linked List Class (part 2 of 2)

```
39          while (position != null)          This last node is indicated
40          {                                 by the link field being equal
41              count++;                      to null.
42              position = position.getLink( );
43          }
44          return count;
45      }

46      public boolean contains(String item)
47      {
48          return (find(item) != null);
49      }

50      /**
51       Finds the first node containing the target item, and returns a
52       reference to that node. If target is not in the list, null is returned.
53       */
54      private Node1 find(String target)
55      {
56          Node1 position = head;
57          String itemAtPosition;
58          while (position != null)
59          {
60              itemAtPosition = position.getItem( );
61              if (itemAtPosition.equals(target))        This is the way you
62                  return position;                      traverse an entire
63              position = position.getLink( );           linked list.
64          }
65          return null; //target was not found
66      }
67      public void outputList( )
68      {
69          Node1 position = head;
70          while (position != null)
71          {
72              System.out.println(position.getItem( ) + " "
73                                      + position.getCount( ));
74              position = position.getLink( );
75          }
76      }
77  }
78
```

Working with Linked Lists

When dealing with a linked list, your code needs to be able to "get to" that first or head node, and you need some way to detect when the last node is reached. To get your code to the first node, you use a variable of type Node1 that always contains a reference to the first node. In Display 15.3, the variable with a reference to the first node is named head. From that first or head node your code can follow the links through the linked list. But how does your code know when it is at the last node in a linked list?

In Java, you indicate the end of a linked list by setting the link instance variable of the last node in the linked list to null, as shown in Display 15.4. That way your code can test whether or not a node is the last node in a linked list by testing whether its link instance variable contains null. Remember that you check for a link being "equal" to null by using ==, not any equals method.

You also use null to indicate an empty linked list. The head instance variable contains a reference to the first node in the linked list, or it contains null if the linked list
empty list   is empty (that is, if the linked list contains no nodes). The only constructor sets this head instance variable to null, indicating that a newly created linked list is empty.

Display 15.4   Traversing a Linked List

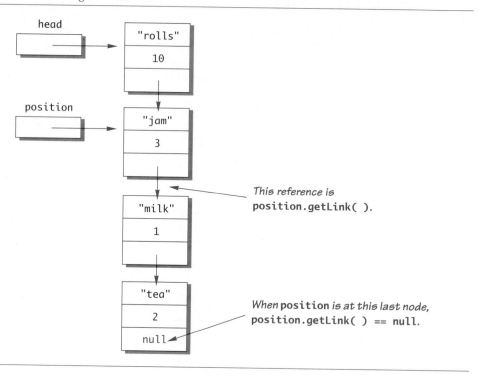

Indicating the End of a Linked List

The last node in a linked list should have its `link` instance variable set to `null`. That way, your code can check whether a node is the last node by checking whether its `link` instance variable is equal to `null`.

An Empty List Is Indicated by `null`

Suppose the variable **head** is supposed to contain a reference to the first node in a linked list. Linked lists usually start out empty. To indicate an empty linked list, you give the variable **head** the value `null`. This is traditional and works out nicely for many linked list manipulation algorithms.

---

traversing a linked list

Before we go on to discuss how nodes are added and removed from a linked list, let's suppose that the linked list already has a few nodes and that you want to write out the contents of all the nodes to the screen. You can do this with the method output-List (Display 15.3), whose body is reproduced here:

```
Node1 position = head;
while (position != null)
{
    System.out.println(position.getItem( ) + " "
                            + position.getCount( ));
    position = position.getLink( );
}
```

The method uses a local variable named `position` that contains a reference to one node. The variable `position` starts out with the same reference as the `head` instance variable, so it starts out positioned at the first node. The `position` variable then has its position moved from one node to the next with the assignment

```
position = position.getLink( );
```

This is illustrated in Display 15.4. To see that this assignment "moves" the `position` variable to the next node, note that the `position` variable contains a reference to the node pointed to by the position arrow in Display 15.4. So, `position` is a name for that node, and `position.link` is a name for the link to the next node. The value of `link` is produced with the accessor method `getLink`. Thus, a reference to the next node in the linked list is `position.getLink( )`. You "move" the position variable by giving it the value of `position.getLink( )`.

The method `outputList` continues to move the `position` variable down the linked list and outputs the data in each node as it goes along. When `position` reaches the last node, it outputs the data in that node and then again executes

```
position = position.getLink( );
```

If you study Display 15.4, you will see that when `position` leaves the last node, its value is set to `null`. At that point, we want to stop the loop, so we iterate the loop

```
while (position != null)
```

A similar technique is used to traverse the linked list in the methods `size` and `find`.

Next let's consider how the method `addToStart` adds a node to the start of the linked list so that the new node becomes the first node in the list. It does this with the single statement

adding a node

```
head = new Node1(itemName, itemCount, head);
```

The new node is created with

```
new Node1(itemName, itemCount, head)
```

which returns a reference to this new node. The assignment statement sets the variable `head` equal to a reference to this new node, making the new node the first node in the linked list. To link this new node to the rest of the list, we need only set the `link` instance variable of the new node equal to a reference to the *old first node*. But we have already done that: `head` used to point to the old first node, so if we use the name `head` on *the right-hand side of the assignment operator*, `head` will denote a reference to the old first node. Therefore, the new node produced by

```
new Node1(itemName, itemCount, head)
```

points to the old first node, which is just what we wanted. This is illustrated in Display 15.5.

Later, we will discuss adding nodes at other places in a linked list, but the easiest place to add a node is at the start of the list. Similarly, the easiest place to delete a node is at the start of the linked list.

removing a node

The method `deleteHeadNode` removes the first node from the linked list and leaves the `head` variable pointing to (that is, containing a reference to) the old second node (which is now the first node) in the linked list. This is done with the following assignment:

```
head = head.getLink( );
```

Display 15.5 Adding a Node at the Start

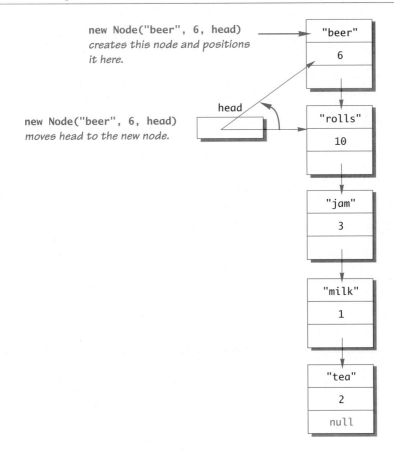

new Node("beer", 6, head)
creates this node and positions
it here.

new Node("beer", 6, head)
moves head to the new node.

This removes the first node from the linked list and leaves the linked list one node shorter. But what happens to the deleted node? At some point, Java will automatically collect it, along with any other nodes that are no longer accessible, and recycle the memory they occupy. This is known as **automatic garbage collection**.

Display 15.6 contains a simple program that demonstrates how some of the methods in the class LinkedList1 behave.

automatic garbage collection

Display 15.6 A Linked List Demonstration

```
1    public class LinkedList1Demo
2    {
3        public static void main(String[] args)
4        {
5            LinkedList1 list = new LinkedList1( );
6            list.addToStart("Apples", 1);
7            list.addToStart("Bananas", 2);
8            list.addToStart("Cantaloupe", 3);
9            System.out.println("List has " + list.size( )
10                                 + " nodes.");
11           list.outputList( );
12           if (list.contains("Cantaloupe"))
13               System.out.println("Cantaloupe is on list.");
14           else
15               System.out.println("Cantaloupe is NOT on list.");

16           list.deleteHeadNode( );

17           if (list.contains("Cantaloupe"))
18               System.out.println("Cantaloupe is on list.");
19           else
20               System.out.println("Cantaloupe is NOT on list.");

21           while (list.deleteHeadNode( ))
22               ; //Empty loop body
23           System.out.println("Start of list:");
24           list.outputList( );
25           System.out.println("End of list.");
26       }
27   }
```

Cantaloupe is now in the head node. (line 8)

*Empties the list. There is no loop body because the method **deleteHeadNode** both performs an action on the list and returns a Boolean value.* (lines 21–22)

Sample Dialogue

```
List has 3 entries.
Cantaloupe 3
Bananas 2
Apples 1
Cantaloupe is on list.
Cantaloupe is NOT on list.
Start of list:
End of list.
```

Self-Test Exercises

1. What output is produced by the following code?

   ```
   LinkedList1 list = new LinkedList1( );
   list.addToStart("apple pie", 1);
   list.addToStart("hot dogs", 12);
   list.addToStart("mustard", 1);
   list.outputList( );
   ```

2. Define a `boolean` valued method named `is Empty` that can be added to the class `LinkedList1` (Display 15.3). The method returns `true` if the list is empty and `false` if the list has at least one node in it.

3. Define a `void` method named `clear` that can be added to the class `LinkedList1` (Display 15.3). The method has no parameters and it empties the list.

PITFALL: Privacy Leaks

It may help you to understand this section if you first review the Pitfall section of the same name in Chapter 5.

Consider the method `getLink` in the class `Node1` (Display 15.2). It returns a value of type `Node1`. That is, it returns a reference to a `Node1`. In Chapter 5, we said that if a method (such as `getLink`) returns a reference to an instance variable of a (mutable) class type, then the `private` restriction on the instance variable can easily be defeated because getting a reference to an object may allow a programmer to change the private instance variables of the object. There are a number of ways to fix this, the most straightforward of which is to make the class `Node1` a private inner class in the method `Node1`, as discussed in the next subsection.

There is no danger of a privacy leak with the class `Node1` when it is used in the class definition for `LinkedList1`. However, there is no way to guarantee that the class `Node1` will be used only in this way unless you take some precaution, such as making the class `Node1` a private inner class in the class `LinkedList1 Node1`.

An alternate solution is to place both of the classes `Node1` and `LinkedList1` into a package, and change the `private` instance variable restriction to the `package` restriction as discussed in Chapter 7.

Note that this privacy problem can arise in any situation in which a method returns a reference to a private instance variable of a class type. The method `getItem( )` of the class `Node1` comes very close to having this problem. In this case, the method `getItem` causes no privacy leak, but only because the class `String` is not a mutable class (that is, it has no methods that will allow the user to change the value of the string without changing the reference). If instead of storing data of type `String` in our list we had stored data of some mutable class type, then defining an accessor method similarly to `getItem` would produce a privacy leak. ∎

Node Inner Classes

You can make a linked list, or any similar data structures, self-contained by making the node class an inner class. In particular, you can make the class `LinkedList1` more self-contained by making `Node1` an inner class, as follows:

```
public class LinkedList1
{
    private class Node1
    {
      <The rest of the definition of Node1 can be
                            the same as in Display 15.2.>
    }

    private Node1 head;
    <The constructor and methods in Display 15.3 are inserted here.>
}
```

Note that we've made the class `Node1` a private inner class. If an inner class is not intended to be used elsewhere, it should be made private. Making `Node1` a private inner class hides all objects of the inner class and avoids a privacy leak.

If you are going to make the class `Node1` a private inner class in the definition of `LinkedList1`, then you can safely simplify the definition of `Node1` by eliminating the accessor and mutator methods (the `set` and `get` methods) and just allowing direct access to the instance variables (`item`, `count`, and `link`) from methods of the outer class. In Display 15.7, we have written a class similar to `LinkedList1` in this way. The rewritten version, named `LinkedList2`, is like the class `LinkedList1` in Display 15.3 in that it has the same methods that perform basically the same actions. To keep the discussion simple, `LinkedList2` has only one data field instead of two. We could easily have retained the two data fields, but we wanted a notationally simple example without any distracting details. (See Self-Test Exercise 8 for a version that has the same kind of data in each node as in the nodes of `LinkedList1`.)

Display 15.7 **A Linked List Class with a Node Inner Class** (part 1 of 3)

```
1   public class LinkedList2
2   {
3       private class Node
4       {
5           private String item;
6           private Node link;

7           public Node( )
8           {
9               item = null;
10              link = null;
11          }
```

Display 15.7   A Linked List Class with a Node Inner Class (part 2 of 3)

```
12          public Node(String newItem, Node linkValue)
13          {
14              item = newItem;
15              link = linkValue;
16          }
17      }//End of Node inner class

18      private Node head;

19      public LinkedList2( )
20      {
21          head = null;
22      }
23      /**
24       Adds a node at the start of the list with the specified data.
25       The added node will be the first node in the list.
26      */
27      public void addToStart(String itemName)
28      {
29          head = new Node(itemName, head);
30      }

31      /**
32       Removes the head node and returns true if the list contained at least
33       one node. Returns false if the list was empty.
34      */
35      public boolean deleteHeadNode( )
36      {
37          if (head != null)
38          {
39              head = head.link;
40              return true;
41          }
42          else
43              return false;
44      }

45      /**
46       Returns the number of nodes in the list.
47      */
48      public int size( )
49      {
50          int count = 0;
51          Node position = head;
52          while (position != null)
53          {
54              count++;
```

(continued)

Display 15.7 A Linked List Class with a Node Inner Class (part 3 of 3)

```
55                    position = position.link;
56              }
57          return count;
58      }

59      public boolean contains(String item)
60      {
61          return (find(item) != null);
62      }

63      /**
64       Finds the first node containing the target item, and returns a
65       reference to that node. If target is not in the list, null is returned.
66      */
67      private Node find(String target)
68      {
69          Node position = head;
70          String itemAtPosition;
71          while (position != null)
72          {
73              itemAtPosition = position.item;
74              if (itemAtPosition.equals(target))
75                  return position;
76              position = position.link;
77          }
78          return null; //target was not found
79      }
80      public void outputList( )
81      {
82          Node position = head;
83          while (position != null)
84          {
85              System.out.println(position.item );
86              position = position.link;
87          }
88      }

89      public boolean isEmpty( )
90      {
91          return (head == null);
92      }

93      public void clear( )
94      {
95          head = null;
96      }
97  }
```

Note that the outer class has direct access to the inner class's instance variables, such as `link`.

Self-Test Exercises

4. Would it make any difference if we changed the Node inner class in Display 15.7 from a private inner class to a public inner class?

5. Keeping the inner class Node in Display 15.7 as private, what difference would it make if any of the instance variables or methods in the class Node had its access modifiers changed from private to public or package access?

6. Why does the definition of the inner class Node in Display 15.7 not have the accessor and mutator methods getLink, setLink, or other get and set methods for the link fields similar to those in the class definition of Node1 in Display 15.2?

7. Would it be legal to add the following method to the class LinkedList2 in Display 15.7?

```java
public Node startNode( )
{
    return head;
}
```

8. Rewrite the definition of the class LinkedList2 in Display 15.7 so that it has data of a type named Entry, which is a public inner class. Objects of type Entry have two instance variables defined as follows:

```java
private String item;
private int count;
```

This rewritten version of LinkedList2 will be equivalent to LinkedList1 in that it has the same methods doing the same things and it will hold equivalent data in its nodes.

EXAMPLE: A Generic Linked List

Display 15.8 shows a generic linked list with a type parameter T for the type of data stored in a node. This generic linked list has the same methods, coded in basically the same way, as our previous linked list (Display 15.7), but we have used a type parameter for the type of data in the nodes.

Display 15.10 contains a demonstration program for our generic linked list. The demonstration program uses the class Entry, defined in Display 15.9, as the type plugged in for the type parameter T. Note that if you want multiple pieces of data in each node, you simply use a class type that has multiple instance variables and plug in this class for the type parameter T.

Display 15.8   A Generic Linked List Class (part 1 of 3)

```
1    public class LinkedList3<T>
2    {
3        private class Node<T>
4        {
5            private T data;
6            private Node<T> link;
7            public Node( )
8            {
9                data = null;
10               link = null;
11           }

12           public Node(T newData, Node<T> linkValue)
13           {
14               data = newData;
15               link = linkValue;
16           }
17       }//End of Node<T> inner class

18       private Node<T> head;

19       public LinkedList3( )
20       {
21           head = null;
22       }

23       /**
24        Adds a node at the start of the list with the specified data.
25        The added node will be the first node in the list.
26       */
27       public void addToStart(T itemData)
28       {
29           head = new Node<T>(itemData, head);
30       }
31       /**
32        Removes the head node and returns true if the list contained at least
33        one node. Returns false if the list was empty.
34       */
35       public boolean deleteHeadNode( )
36       {
37           if (head != null)
38           {
39               head = head.link;
40               return true;
41           }
42           else
43               return false;
44       }
```

This linked list holds objects of type T. The type T should have well-defined **equals** *and* **toString** *methods.*

Display 15.8   A Generic Linked List Class (part 2 of 3)

```
45        /**
46         Returns the number of nodes in the list.
47        */
48        public int size( )
49        {
50            int count = 0;
51            Node<T> position = head;
52            while (position != null)
53            {
54                count++;
55                position = position.link;
56            }
57            return count;
58        }

59        public boolean contains(T item)
60        {
61            return (find(item) != null);
62        }
63        /**
64         Finds the first node containing the target item, and returns a
65         reference to that node. If target is not in the list, null is returned.
66        */
67        private Node<T> find(T target)
68        {
69            Node<T> position = head;
70            T itemAtPosition;
71            while (position != null)
72            {
73                itemAtPosition = position.data;
74                if (itemAtPosition.equals(target))
75                    return position;
76                position = position.link;
77            }
78            return null; //target was not found
79        }

80        /**
81         Finds the first node containing the target and returns a reference
82          to the data in that node. If target is not in the list, null is returned.
83        */
84        public T findData(T target)
85        {
86            return find(target).data;
87        }
```

Type **T** *must have well-defined* **equals** *for this method to work.*

(continued)

Display 15.8   A Generic Linked List Class (part 3 of 4)

```
88      public void outputList( )              Type T must have well-defined toString
89      {                                      methods for this to work.
90          Node<T> position = head;
91          while (position != null)
92          {
93              System.out.println(position.data);
94              position = position.link;
95          }
96      }

97      public boolean isEmpty( )
98      {
99          return (head == null);
100     }

101     public void clear( )
102     {
103         head = null;
104     }
105     /*
106      For two lists to be equal they must contain the same data items in
107      the same order. The equals method of T is used to compare data items.
108     */
109     public boolean equals(Object otherObject)
110     {
111         if (otherObject == null)
112             return false;
113         else if (getClass( ) != otherObject.getClass( ))
114             return false;
115         else
116         {
117             LinkedList3<T> otherList = (LinkedList3<T>)otherObject;
118             if (size( ) != otherList.size( ))
119                 return false;
120             Node<T> position = head;
121             Node<T> otherPosition = otherList.head;
122             while (position != null)
123             {
124                 if (!(position.data.equals(otherPosition.data)))
125                     return false;
126                 position = position.link;
127                 otherPosition = otherPosition.link;
128             }
129             return true; //no mismatch was not found
130         }
131     }
132 }
```

Display 15.9   A Sample Class for the Data in a Generic Linked List

```java
1   public class Entry
2   {
3       private String item;
4       private int count;

5       public Entry(String itemData, int countData)
6       {
7           item = itemData;
8           count = countData;
9       }

10      public String toString( )
11      {
12          return (item + " " + count);
13      }

14      public boolean equals(Object otherObject)
15      {
16          if (otherObject == null)
17              return false;
18          else if (getClass( ) != otherObject.getClass( ))
19              return false;
20          else
21          {
22              Entry otherEntry = (Entry)otherObject;
23              return (item.equals(otherEntry.item)
24                          && (count == otherEntry.count));
25          }
26      }
```

\<There should be other constructors and methods, including accessor and
mutator methods, but we do not use them in this demonstration.\>

```java
27  }
```

Display 15.10 A Generic Linked List Demonstration

```
1    public class GenericLinkedListDemo
2    {
3        public static void main(String[] args)
4        {
5            LinkedList3<Entry> list = new LinkedList3<Entry>( );
6
7            Entry entry1 = new Entry("Apples", 1);
8            list.addToStart(entry1);
9            Entry entry2 = new Entry("Bananas", 2);
10           list.addToStart(entry2);
11           Entry entry3 = new Entry("Cantaloupe", 3);
12           list.addToStart(entry3);
13           System.out.println("List has " + list.size( )
14                               + " nodes.");
15           list.outputList( );
16           System.out.println("End of list.");
17       }
18   }
```

Sample Dialogue

```
List has 3 nodes.
Cantaloupe 3
Bananas 2
Apples 1
End of list.
```

 PITFALL: Using Node Instead of Node<T>

This pitfall is explained by example, using the LinkedList3<T> class in Display 15.8. However, the lesson applies to any generic linked structure with a node inner class. The type parameter need not be T and the node class name need not be Node, but for simplicity, we will use T and Node.

When defining the LinkedList3<T> class in Display 15.8, the type for a node is Node<T>; it is not Node. However, it is easy to forget the type specification <T> and write Node instead of Node<T>. If you omit the <T>, you may or may not get a compiler error message, depending on other details of your code. If you do get a compiler error message, it is likely to seem bewilderingly strange. The problem is that Node actually means something. (We do not have time to stop and explain what Node means, but it means something similar to a node with data type Object, rather than data type T.) Your only defense against this pitfall is to be very careful, and if you do get a bewildering compiler error message, look for a missing <T>.

PITFALL: (continued)

Sometimes a compiler warning message can be helpful when you make this mistake. If you get a warning that mentions a type cast from Node to Node<T>, look for an omitted <T>.

Finally, we should note that sometimes your code will compile and even run correctly if you omit the <T> from Node<T>. ∎

The equals Method for Linked Lists

The linked lists we presented in Displays 15.3 and 15.7 did not have an equals method. We did that to keep the examples simple and not detract from the main message. However, a linked list class should normally have an equals method.

equals

There is more than one approach to defining a reasonable equals method for a linked list. The two most obvious are the following:

1. Two linked lists are equal if they contain the same data entries (possibly ordered differently).
2. Two linked lists are equal if they contain the same data entries in the same order; that is, the data in the first node of the calling object equals the data in the first node of the other linked list, the data in the two second nodes are equal, and so forth.

It is not true that one of these is the correct approach to defining an equals method and the other is incorrect. In different situations, you might want different definitions of equals. However, the most common way to define equals for a linked list is approach 2. A definition of equals that follows approach 2 and that can be added to the class LinkedList2 in Display 15.7 is given in Display 15.11. The generic linked list in Display 15.8 also contains an equals method that follows approach 2.

Note that when we define equals for our linked list with type parameter T, we are trusting the programmer who wrote the definition for the type plugged in for T. We are assuming the programmer has redefined the equals method so that it provides a reasonable test for equality. Situations like this are the reason it is so important to always include an equals method in the classes you define.

Display 15.11 **An equals Method for the Linked List in Display 15.7** (part 1 of 2)

```
 1    /*
 2     For two lists to be equal they must contain the same data items in
 3     the same order.
 4    */
 5    public boolean equals(Object otherObject)
 6    {
 7        if (otherObject == null)
 8            return false;
 9        else if (getClass( ) != otherObject.getClass( ))
10            return false;
```

(continued)

Display 15.11   An **equals** Method for the Linked List in Display 15.7 (part 2 of 2)

```
11          else
12          {
13              LinkedList2 otherList = (LinkedList2)otherObject;
14              if (size( ) != otherList.size( ))
15                  return false;
16              Node position = head;
17              Node otherPosition = otherList.head;
18              while (position != null)
19              {
20                  if ( (!(position.item.equals(otherPosition.item))))
21                      return false;
22                  position = position.link;
23                  otherPosition = otherPosition.link;
24              }
25              return true; //A mismatch was not found
26          }
27      }
```

15.2 Copy Constructors and the **clone** Method ★

There are three ways to do anything:

The right way,

the wrong way,

and the army way.

Advice reputedly given to new army recruits

The way Java handles cloning, and object copying in general, is complicated and can be both subtle and difficult. Some authorities think that the clone method was done so poorly in Java that they prefer to ignore it completely and define their own methods for copying objects. I have some sympathy for that view, but before you dismiss Java's approach to cloning, it might be a good idea to see what the approach entails. Linked data structures, such as linked lists, are an excellent setting for discussing cloning because they are an excellent setting for discussing deep versus shallow copying.

This section first presents a relatively simple way to define copy constructors and the clone method, but this approach unfortunately produces only shallow copies. We then go on to present one way to produce a deep copy clone method and to do so within the official prescribed rules of the Java documentation.

Readers with very little programming experience may be better off skipping this entire section until they become more comfortable with Java. Other readers may prefer to read only the first subsection and possibly the immediately following Pitfall subsection.

Simple Copy Constructors and clone Methods ★

Display 15.12 contains a copy constructor and clone method definitions that could be added to the definition of the generic linked list class in Display 15.8. The real work is done by the private helping method copyOf, so our discussion focuses on the method copyOf.

The private method copyOf takes an argument that is a reference to the head node of a linked list and returns a reference to the head node of a copy of that linked list. The easiest way to do this would be to simply return the argument. This would, however, simply produce another name for the argument list. We do not want another name; we want another list. So, the method goes down the argument list one node at a time (with position) and makes a copy of each node. The linked list of the calling object is built up node by node by adding these new nodes to its linked list. However, there is a complication. We cannot simply add the new nodes at the head (start) end of the list being built. If we did, then the nodes would end up in the reverse of the desired order. So, the new nodes are added to the end of the linked list being built. The variable end of type Node<T> is kept positioned at the last node so that it is possible to add nodes at the end of the linked list being built. In this way a copy of the list in the calling object is created so that the order of the nodes is preserved.

The copy constructor is defined by using the private helping method copyOf to create a copy of the list of nodes. Other details of the copy constructor and the clone method are done in the standard way.

Although the copy constructor and the clone method each produce a new linked list with all new nodes, the new list is not truly independent because the data objects are not cloned. See the next Pitfall section for a discussion of this point. One way to fix this shortcoming is discussed in the Programming Tip subsection entitled "Use a Type Parameter Bound for a Better clone."

Exceptions ★

A generic data structure, such as the class LinkedList in Display 15.12, is likely to have methods that throw exceptions. Situations such as a null argument to the copy constructor might be handled differently in different situations, so it is best to throw a NullPointerException if this happens and let the programmer who is using the linked list handle the exception. This is what we did with the copy constructor in Display 15.12. A NullPointerException is an unchecked exception, which means that it need not be caught or declared in a throws clause. When thrown by a method of a linked list class, it can be treated simply as a run-time error message. The exception can instead be caught in a catch block if there is some suitable action that can be taken.

Display 15.12 **A Copy Constructor and clone Method for a Generic Linked List (part 1 of 2)**

```
1    public class LinkedList3<T> implements Cloneable
2    {
3        private class Node<T>
4        {
5            private T data;
6            private Node<T> link;

7            public Node( )
8            {
9                data = null;
10               link = null;
11           }

12           public Node(T newData, Node<T> linkValue)
13           {
14               data = newData;
15               link = linkValue;
16           }
17       }//End of Node<T> inner class

18       private Node<T> head;
```

This copy constructor and this clone method do not make deep copies. We discuss one way to make a deep copy in the Programming Tip subsection "Use a Type Parameter Bound for a Better clone."

<All the methods from Display 15.8 are in the class definition, but they are not repeated in this display.>

```
19       /**
20        Produces a new linked list, but it is not a true deep copy.
21        Throws a NullPointerException if other is null.
22       */
23       public LinkedList3(LinkedList3<T> otherList)
24       {
25           if (otherList == null)
26               throw new NullPointerException( );
27           if (otherList.head == null)
28               head = null;
29           else
30               head = copyOf(otherList.head);
31       }
32
33
```

Display 15.12   A Copy Constructor and **clone** Method for a Generic Linked List (part 2 of 2)

```
34      public LinkedList3<T> clone( )
35      {
36          try
37          {
38              LinkedList3<T> copy =
39                              (LinkedList3<T>)super.clone( );
40              if (head == null)
41                  copy.head = null;
42              else
43                  copy.head = copyOf(head);
44              return copy;
45          }
46          catch(CloneNotSupportedException e)
47          {//This should not happen.
48              return null; //To keep the compiler happy.
49          }
50      }

51      /*
52        Precondition: otherHead != null
53        Returns a reference to the head of a copy of the list
54        headed by otherHead. Does not return a true deep copy.
55      */
56      private Node<T> copyOf(Node<T> otherHead)
57      {
58          Node<T> position = otherHead;//moves down other's list.
59          Node<T> newHead; //will point to head of the copy list.
60          Node<T> end = null; //positioned at end of new growing list.
```

*Invoking **clone** with **position.data** would be illegal.*

```
61          //Create first node:
62          newHead =
63                  new Node<T>(position.data, null);
64          end = newHead;
65          position = position.link;

66          while (position != null)
67          {//copy node at position to end of new list.
68              end.link =
69                  new Node<T>(position.data, null);
70              end = end.link;
71              position = position.link;
72          }
```

*Invoking **clone** with **position.data** would be illegal.*

```
73          return newHead;
74      }
75  }
```

PITFALL: The `clone` Method Is Protected in `Object` ★

When defining the copy constructor and `clone` method for our generic linked list (Display 15.12), we would have liked to have cloned the data in the list being copied. We would have liked to change the code in the helping method `copyOf` by adding invocations of the `clone` method as follows:

```
newHead =
      new Node((T)(position.data).clone( ), null);
end = newHead;
position = position.link;

while (position != null)
 {//copy node at position to end of new list.
    end.link =
        new Node((T)(position.data).clone( ), null);
    end = end.link;
    position = position.link;
}
```

This code is identical to code in `copyOf` except for the addition of the invocations of `clone` shown in red and the type casts shown in red. (The type casts are needed because Java thinks `clone` returns a value of type `Object`.)

If this modified code (with the `clone` method) would compile (and if the type plugged in for T has a well-defined `clone` method that makes a deep copy), then this modified code would produce a truly independent linked list with no references in common with the list being copied. Unfortunately, this code will not compile.

If you try to compile this code, you will get an error message saying that the method `clone` is protected in the class `Object`. True, we used the type T, not the type `Object`, but any class can be plugged in for T. So when the generic linked list is compiled, all Java knows about the type T is that it is a descendent class of `Object`. Since the designers of the `Object` class chose to make the method `clone` protected, you simply cannot use the `clone` method in the definition of methods such as `copyOf`.

Why was the `clone` method labeled `protected` in `Object`? Apparently for security reasons. If a class could use the `clone` method unchanged from `Object`, then that would open the possibility of copying sections of memory unchanged and unchecked and so might give unauthorized memory access. The problem is made more serious by the fact that Java is used to run programs on other machines across the Internet.

The way Java defines the `clone` method in `Object` and the way it specifies how `clone` should be defined in other classes is controversial. Do not be surprised if some future version of Java handles the `clone` method differently. But for now, you are stuck with these `clone` problems.

In many situations, the version of `copyOf` in Display 15.12 (without the use of `clone`) is good enough, but there is a way to get a true deep copy. One way to get a deep copy is to somehow restrict the type T to classes that do have a public `clone` method that makes a deep copy. Something like this can be done and is discussed in the Programming Tip "Use a Type Parameter Bound for a Better `clone`." ∎

TIP: Use a Type Parameter Bound for a Better `clone` ★

One way to overcome the problem discussed in the previous Pitfall section is to place a bound on the type parameter T (in Display 15.12) so that it must satisfy some suitable interface. There is no standard interface that does the job, but it is very easy to define such an interface. The interface `PubliclyCloneable` given in Display 15.13 is just the interface we need. This short, simple interface guarantees all that we need to define generic linked lists whose clone method returns a deep copy.

Note that any class that implements the `PubliclyCloneable` interface has the following three properties:

1. The class implements the `Cloneable` interface. (This happens automatically because `PubliclyCloneable` extends `Cloneable`.)

2. The class has a public `clone` method.

3. The `clone` method for the class makes a deep copy (in the officially sanctioned way).

Condition 3 is not enforced by the Java compiler or run-time software, but like all interface semantics, it is the responsibility of the programmer defining the class to ensure that condition 3 is satisfied.

It is now easy to define our generic linked list whose `clone` method produces a deep copy. The definition is given in Display 15.14. We have already discussed the main points involved in this definition. The following Programming Example subsection discusses some of the minor, but possibly unclear, details of the definition.[1] ■

Display 15.13   The `PubliclyCloneable` Interface

```
1   /*
2     The programmer who defines a class implementing this interface
3     has the responsibility to define clone so it makes a deep copy
4     (in the officially sectioned way.)
5   */

6   public interface PubliclyCloneable extends Cloneable
7   {
8       public Object clone( );
9   }
```

Any class that implements `PubliclyCloneable` *must have a public* `clone` *method.*

Any class that implements `PubliclyCloneable` *automatically implements* `Cloneable`.

---

[1] You might wonder whether we could use a type parameter in the `PubliclyCloneable` interface and so avoid some type casts in the definition `copyOf`. We could do that, but that may be more trouble than it is worth and, at this introductory level of presentation, would be an unnecessary distraction.

Display 15.14 A Generic Linked List with a Deep Copy **clone** Method (part 1 of 3)

```
1    public class LinkedList<T extends PubliclyCloneable>
2                                          implements PubliclyCloneable
3    {
4        private class Node<T>
5        {
6            private T data;
7            private Node<T> link;

8            public Node( )
9            {
10               data = null;
11               link = null;
12           }

13           public Node(T newData, Node<T> linkValue)
14           {
15               data = newData;
16               link = linkValue;
17           }
18       }//End of Node<T> inner class

19       private Node<T> head;

20       public LinkedList( )
21       {
22           head = null;
23       }
24       /**
25        Produces a new linked list, but it is not a true deep copy.
26        Throws a NullPointerException if other is null.
27       */
28       public LinkedList(LinkedList<T> otherList)
29       {
30           if (otherList == null)
31               throw new NullPointerException( );
32           if (otherList.head == null)
33               head = null;
34           else
35               head = copyOf(otherList.head);
36       }

37
38       public LinkedList<T> clone( )
39       {
40           try
41           {
42               LinkedList<T> copy =
43                               (LinkedList<T>)super.clone( );
```

Display 15.14   A Generic Linked List with a Deep Copy **clone** Method (part 2 of 3)

```
44              if (head == null)
45                  copy.head = null;
46              else
47                  copy.head = copyOf(head);
48              return copy;
49          }
50          catch(CloneNotSupportedException e)
51          {//This should not happen.
52              return null; //To keep the compiler happy.
53          }
54      }

                                              This definition of copyOf gives
                                              a deep copy of the linked list.
55      /*
56       Precondition: otherHead != null
57       Returns a reference to the head of a copy of the list
58       headed by otherHead. Returns a true deep copy.
59      */
60      private Node<T> copyOf(Node<T> otherHead)
61      {
62          Node<T> position = otherHead; //moves down other's list.
63          Node<T> newHead; //will point to head of the copy list.
64          Node<T> end = null; //positioned at end of new growing list.

65          //Create first node:
66          newHead =
67              new Node<T>((T)(position.data).clone( ), null);
68              end = newHead;
69          position = position.link;
70          while (position != null)
71          {//copy node at position to end of new list.
72              end.link =
73                  new Node<T>((T)(position.data).clone( ), null);
74              end = end.link;
75              position = position.link;
76          }

77          return newHead;
78      }
79
80      public boolean equals(Object otherObject)
81      {
82          if (otherObject == null)
83              return false;
84          else if (getClass( ) != otherObject.getClass( ))
85              return false;
86          else
87          {
88              LinkedList<T> otherList = (LinkedList<T>)otherObject;
```

(continued)

Display 15.14 A Generic Linked List with a Deep Copy **clone** Method (part 3 of 3)

> <The rest of the definition is the same as in Display 15.8. The only difference between this definition of equals and the one in Display 15.8 is that we have replaced the class name LinkedList3<T> with LinkedList<T>.>

```
89          }

      <All the other methods from Display 15.8 are in the class definition,
      but are not repeated in this display. >

90          public String toString( )
91          {
92              Node<T> position = head;
93              String theString = "";
94              while (position != null)
95              {
96                  theString = theString + position.data + "\n";
97                  position = position.link;
98              }
99              return theString;
100         }
101     }
```

We added a toString method so LinkedList<T> would have all the properties we want T to have.

EXAMPLE: A Linked List with a Deep Copy **clone** Method ★

We have already discussed how and why the clone method of the generic linked list class in Display 15.14 returns a deep copy. Let's now look at some of the other details and see an example of using this linked list class.

Note the definition of the clone method. Why did we not simplify it to the following?

```
public LinkedList<T> clone( )
{
    return new LinkedList<T>(this);
}
```

This simple, alternative definition would still return a deep copy of the linked list and would work fine in most situations. It is likely that you would not notice any difference if you used this definition of clone in place of the one given in Display 15.14.

The only reason for all the other detail in the clone method definition given in Display 15.14 is to define the clone method as specified in the Java documentation. The reason that the Java documentation asks for those details has to do with security issues. (Some might say that there are three ways to define a clone method: the right way, the wrong way, and the Java way. This extra detail is the Java way.)

EXAMPLE: (continued)

If you look only quickly at Display 15.14 you might think the following at the start of the definition is an unimportant detail:

```
implements PubliclyCloneable
```

However, it ensures that the linked list class implements the Cloneable interface. In order for a class to have a Java-approved clone method, it must implement the Cloneable interface. It also allows you to make linked lists of linked lists and have a deep copy clone method in the linked list of linked lists.

A sample class that implements the PubliclyCloneable interface is given in Display 15.15. Display 15.16 shows a demonstration program that makes a deep copy clone of a linked list of objects of this sample class.

Display 15.15 **A PubliclyCloneable Class** (part 1 of 2)

```
1    public class StockItem implements PubliclyCloneable
2    {
3        private String name;
4        private int number;

5        public StockItem( )
6        {
7            name = null;
8            number = 0;
9        }

10       public StockItem(String nameData, int numberData)
11       {
12           name = nameData;
13           number = numberData;
14       }

15       public void setNumber(int newNumber)
16       {
17           number = newNumber;
18       }
```

(continued)

Display 15.15   **A PubliclyCloneable Class** (part 2 of 2)

```
19       public void setName(String newName)
20       {
21           name = newName;
22       }

23       public String toString( )
24       {
25           return (name + " " + number);
26       }

27       public Object clone( )
28       {
29         try
30         {
31            return super.clone( );
32         }
33         catch(CloneNotSupportedException e)
34         {//This should not happen.
35            return null; //To keep compiler happy.
36         }
37       }

38

39       public boolean equals(Object otherObject)
40       {
41           if (otherObject == null)
42               return false;
43           else if (getClass( ) != otherObject.getClass( ))
44               return false;
45           else
46           {
47               StockItem otherItem = (StockItem) otherObject;
48               return (name.equalsIgnoreCase(otherItem.name)
49                       && number == otherItem.number);
50           }
51       }
52   }
```

Display 15.16 Demonstration of Deep Copy **clone**

```
1    public class DeepDemo
2    {
3        public static void main(String[] args)
4        {
5            LinkedList<StockItem> originalList =
6                                  new LinkedList<StockItem>( );
7            originalList.addToStart(new StockItem("red dress", 1));
8            originalList.addToStart(new StockItem("black shoe", 2));

9            LinkedList<StockItem> copyList = originalList.clone( );
10           if (originalList.equals(copyList))
11               System.out.println("OK, Lists are equal.");

12           System.out.println("Now we change copyList.");
13           StockItem dataEntry =
14                       copyList.findData(new StockItem("red dress", 1));
15           dataEntry.setName("orange pants");

16           System.out.println("originalList:");
17           originalList.outputList( );

18           System.out.println("copyList:");
19           copyList.outputList( );
20
21           System.out.println("Only one list is changed.");
22       }
23   }
```

Sample Dialogue

```
OK, Lists are equal.
Now we change copyList.
originalList:
black shoe 2
red dress 1
copyList:
black shoe 2
orange pants 1
Only one list is changed.
```

TIP: Cloning Is an "All or Nothing" Affair

If you define a clone method, then you should do so following the official Java guidelines, as we did in Display 15.14. In particular, you should always have the class implement the Cloneable interface. If you define a clone method in any other way, you may encounter problems in some situations. If you want to have a method for producing copies of objects but do not want to follow the official guidelines on how to define a clone method, then use some other name for your "clone-like" method, such as copier, or make do with just a copy constructor. ■

Self-Test Exercises

9. In the definition of copyOf in Display 15.14, can we replace

```
newHead =
        new Node<T>((T)(position.data).clone( ), null);
```

with the following, which uses the copy constructor of T instead of the clone method of T?

```
newHead =
        new Node<T>(new T(position.data), null);
```

10. The definition of the clone method in Display 15.14 returns a value of type LinkedList<T>. But the class being defined implements the PubliclyCloneable interface, and that interface says the value returned must be of type Object. Is something wrong?

15.3 Iterators

Play it again, Sam.

Attributed (incorrectly) to the movie *Casablanca,* which contains similar lines.[2]

When you have a collection of objects, such as the nodes of a linked list, you often need to step through all the objects in the collection one at a time and perform some action on each object, such as writing it out to the screen or in some way editing the data in each object. An **iterator** is any object that allows you to step through the list in this way.

iterator

---

[2] There is a Woody Allen movie with this title, but it is based on the misquote from *Casablanca,* which was in common use before the movie came out.

Defining an Iterator Class

In Display 15.17, we have rewritten the class LinkedList2 from Display 15.7 so that it has an inner class for iterators and a method iterator( ) that returns an iterator for its calling object. We have made the inner class List2Iterator public so that we can have variables of type List2Iterator outside the class LinkedList2, but we do not otherwise plan to use the inner class List2Iterator outside of the outer class LinkedList2.

Use of iterators for the class LinkedList2 is illustrated by the program in Display 15.18. Note that, given a linked list named list, an iterator for list is produced by the method iterator as follows:

```
LinkedList2.List2Iterator i = list.iterator( );
```

The iterator i produced in this way can only be used with the linked list named list. Be sure to notice that outside of the class, the type name for the inner class iterator must include the name of the outer class as well as the inner iterator class. The class name for one of these iterators is

```
LinkedList2.List2Iterator
```

Display 15.17   A Linked List with an Iterator (part 1 of 3)

```
1    import java.util.NoSuchElementException;

2    public class LinkedList2          This is the same as the class in Displays 15.7 and
3    {                                  15.11 except that the List2Iterator inner class
4        private class Node             and the iterator( ) method have been added.
5        {
6            private String item;
7            private Node link;
```

<The rest of the definition of the Node inner class is given in Display 15.7.>

```
8        }//End of Node inner class

9        /**
10        If the list is altered any iterators should invoke restart or
11        the iterator's behavior may not be as desired.
12        */
13        public class List2Iterator      ◄──── An inner class for iterators for
14        {                                      LinkedList2.
15            private Node position;
16            private Node previous; //previous value of position
```

(continued)

Display 15.17   **A Linked List with an Iterator** (part 2 of 3)

```
17              public List2Iterator( )
18              {
19                  position = head; //Instance variable head of outer class.
20                  previous = null;
21              }

22              public void restart( )
23              {
24                  position = head; //Instance variable head of outer class.
25                  previous = null;
26              }

27              public String next( )
28              {
29                  if (!hasNext( ))
30                      throw new NoSuchElementException( );

31                  String toReturn = position.item;
32                  previous = position;
33                  position = position.link;
34                  return toReturn;
35              }

36              public boolean hasNext( )
37              {
38                  return (position != null);
39              }
40              /**
41               Returns the next value to be returned by next( ).
42               Throws an IllegalStateExpression if hasNext( ) is false.
43              */
44              public String peek( )
45              {
46                  if (!hasNext( ))
47                      throw new IllegalStateException( );
48                  return position.item;
49              }

50              /**
51               Adds a node before the node at location position.
52               previous is placed at the new node. If hasNext( ) is
53               false, then the node is added to the end of the list.
54               If the list is empty, inserts node as the only node.
55              */
56              public void addHere(String newData)
57              {
58                  if (position == null && previous != null)
59                      // at end of the list, add to end
60                          previous.link = new Node(newData, null);
```

Display 15.17   A Linked List with an Iterator (part 3 of 3)

```
61                  else if (position == null || previous == null)
62                          // list is empty or position is head node
63                          LinkedList2.this.addtoStart(newData);
64                  else
65                  {  // previous and position are consecutive nodes
66                          Node temp = new Node(newData, position)
67                          previous.link = temp;
68                          previous = temp;
69                  }
70          }
71          /**
72           Changes the String in the node at location position.
73           Throws an IllegalStateException if position is not at a node,
74           */
75          public void changeHere(String newData)
```

<The rest of the method **changeHere** is Self-Test Exercise 13.>

```
76          /**
77           Deletes the node at location position and
78           moves position to the "next" node.
79           Throws an IllegalStateException if the list is empty.
80           */
81          public void delete( )
82          {
83              if (position == null)
84                      throw new IllegalStateException( );
85              else if (previous == null)
86              {       // remove node at head
87                      head = head.link;
88                      position = head;
89              }
90              else // previous and position are consecutive nodes
91              {
92                      previous.link = position.link;
93                      position = position.link;
94              }
95          }
96      private Node head;
```

```
97      public List2Iterator iterator( )
98      {
99          return new List2Iterator( );
100      }
```

If **list** *is an object of the class* **LinkedList2***, then* **list.iterator( )** *returns an iterator for list.*

<The other methods and constructors are identical to those in Displays 15.7 and 15.11.>

```
101  }
```

Display 15.18   Using an Iterator (part 1 of 2)

```
1    public class IteratorDemo
2    {
3        public static void main(String[] args)
4        {
5            LinkedList2 list = new LinkedList2( );
6            LinkedList2.List2Iterator i = list.iterator( );

7            list.addToStart("shoes");
8            list.addToStart("orange juice");
9            list.addToStart("coat");

10           System.out.println("List contains:");
11           i.restart( );
12           while(i.hasNext( ))
13               System.out.println(i.next( ));
14           System.out.println( );

15           i.restart( );
16           i.next( );
17           System.out.println("Will delete the node for " + i.peek( ));
18           i.delete( );

19           System.out.println("List now contains:");
20           i.restart( );
21           while(i.hasNext( ))
22               System.out.println(i.next( ));
23           System.out.println( );

24           i.restart( );
25           i.next( );
26           System.out.println("Will add one node before " + i.peek( ));
27           i.addHere("socks");
28           System.out.println("List now contains:");
29           i.restart( );
30           while(i.hasNext( ))
31               System.out.println(i.next( ));
32           System.out.println( );
33           System.out.println("Changing all items to credit card.");
34           i.restart( );
35           while(i.hasNext( ))
36           {
37               i.changeHere("credit card");
38               i.next( );
39           }
40           System.out.println( );
```

Display 15.18   **Using an Iterator** (part 2 of 2)

```
41              System.out.println("List now contains:");
42              i.restart( );
43              while(i.hasNext( ))
44                  System.out.println(i.next( ));
45              System.out.println( );
46      }
47  }
```

Sample Dialogue

```
List contains:
coat
orange juice
shoes

Will delete the node for orange juice
List now contains:
coat
shoes

Will add one node before shoes
List now contains:
coat
socks
shoes

Changing all items to credit card.

List now contains:
credit card
credit card
credit card
```

The basic method for cycling through the elements in the linked list using an iterator is illustrated by the following code from the demonstration program:

```
System.out.println("List now contains:");
i.restart( );
while(i.hasNext( ))
    System.out.println(i.next( ));
```

The iterator is named i in this code. The iterator i is reset to the beginning of the list with the method invocation i.restart( ), and each execution of i.next( ) produces the next data item in the linked list. After all the data items in all the nodes have been returned by i.next( ), the Boolean i.hasNext( ) becomes false and the while loop ends.

Internally, the local variable `position` references the current node in the linked list, whereas the local variable `previous` references the node linking to the current node. The purpose of the `previous` variable will be seen when adding and deleting nodes. In the constructor and the `restart( )` method, `position` is set to `head` and `previous` is set to `null`.

To determine if the end of the list has been reached, `hasNext( )` returns whether or not `position` is `null`:

```
return (position != null);
```

To step through the list, the `next( )` method first throws an exception if we have reached the end of the list:

```
if (!hasNext( ))
    throw new NoSuchElementException( );
```

Otherwise, the method retrieves the string value of the iterator referenced by `position` in the variable `toReturn`, advances `previous` to reference the current position, advances `position` to the next node in the list, and returns the string:

```
String toReturn = position.item;
previous = position;
position = position.link;
return toReturn;
```

The definition of the method `changeHere` is left as a Self-Test Exercise. (If necessary you can look up the definition in the answer to the Self-Test Exercise.) The techniques for adding and deleting nodes are discussed in the next subsection.

The Java `Iterator` Interface

Java has an interface named `Iterator` that specifies how Java would like an iterator to behave. It is in the package `java.util` (and so requires that you import this package). Our iterators do not quite satisfy this interface, but they are in the same general spirit as that interface and could be easily redefined to satisfy the `Iterator` interface.

The `Iterator` interface is discussed in Chapter 16.

Adding and Deleting Nodes

To add or delete a node in a linked list, you normally use an iterator and add or delete a node at the (approximate) location of the iterator. Since deleting is a little easier than adding a node, we will discuss deleting first.

Display 15.19 shows the technique for deleting a node. The linked list is an object of the class `LinkedList2` (Display 15.17). The variables `position` and `previous` are the instance variables of an iterator for the linked list object. These variables each hold a reference to a node, indicated with an arrow. Each time `next( )` is invoked, `previous` and `position` reference subsequent nodes in the list. As indicated in Display 15.19, the node at location `position` is deleted by the following two lines of code:

```
previous.link = position.link;
position = position.link;
```

In Display 15.19, `next( )` has been invoked twice, so `position` is referencing the node with `"shoes"` and `previous` is referencing the node with `"socks"`.

To delete the node referenced by `position`, the link from the `previous` node is set to `position`s link. As shown in Display 15.19, this removes the linked list's reference to that node. The variable `position` is then set to the next node in the list to remove any references to the deleted node. As far as the linked list is concerned, the old node is no longer on the linked list. But the node is still in the computer's memory. If there are no longer any references to the deleted node, then the storage that it occupies should be made available for other uses. In many programming languages, you, the programmer, must keep track of items such as deleted nodes and must give explicit commands to return their memory for recycling. This is called **garbage collecting** or **explicit memory management**. In Java, this is done for you automatically, or, as it is ordinarily phrased, Java has automatic garbage collection.

garbage collecting

explicit memory management

Note that there are special cases that must be handled for deletion. First, if the list is empty, then nothing can be deleted and the `delete( )` method throws an exception. Second, if the node to delete is the head of the list, then there is no previous node to update. Instead, `head` is set to `head.link` to bypass the first node in the list and set a new head node.

Display 15.20 shows the technique for adding a node. We want to add a new node between the nodes named by `previous` and `position`. In Display 15.20, `previous` and `position` are variables of type `Node`, and each contains a reference to a node indicated with an arrow. Thus, the new node goes between the two nodes referenced by `previous` and `position`. In Display 15.20, the method `next( )` has been invoked twice to advance `previous` to `"orange juice"` and `position` to `"shoes"`.

A constructor for the class `Node` does a lot of the work for us: It creates the new node, adds the data, and sets the link field of the new node to reference the node named by `position`. All this is done with the following:

```
new Node(newData, position)
```

So that we can recognize the node with `newData` in it when we study Display 15.20, let's assume that `newData` holds the string `"socks"`. The following gets us from the first to the second picture:

```
temp = new Node(newData, position);
```

To finish the job, all we need to do is link the previous node to the new node. We want to move the arrow to the node named by `temp`. The following finishes our job:

```
previous.link = temp;
```

The new node is inserted in the desired place, but the picture is not too clear. The fourth picture is the same as the third one; we have simply redrawn it to make it neater.

Display 15.19 Deleting a Node

1. Existing list with the iterator positioned at "shoes"

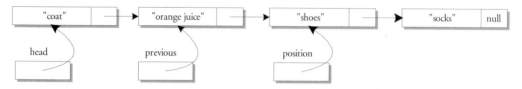

2. Bypass the node at `position` from `previous`

`previous.link = position.link;`

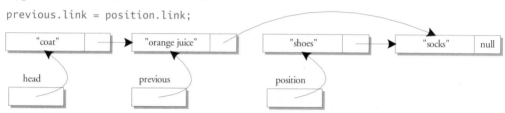

3. Update `position` to reference the next node

`position = position.link;`

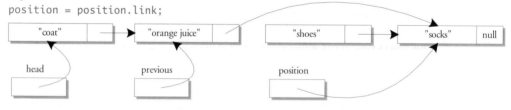

Since no variable references the node "shoes" Java will automatically recycle the memory allocated for it.

4. Same picture with deleted node not shown

To summarize, the following two lines insert a new node with `newData` as its data. The new node is inserted between the nodes named by `previous` and `position`.

```
temp = new Node(newData, position);
previous.link = temp;
```

`previous`, `position`, and `temp` are all variables of type `Node`. (When we use this code, `previous` and `position` will be instance variables of an iterator and `temp` will be a local variable.)

Just like deletion, special cases exist for insertion that must be handled. If the list is empty, then addition is done by adding to the front of the list. If the `position` variable is `null`, then the new node should be added to the end of the list.

Self-Test Exercises

11. Consider a variant of the class in Display 15.17 with no `previous` local variable. In other words, there is no reference kept to the node that links to the current node position. How could we modify the `delete` method to delete the `position` node and still maintain a correct list? The solution is less efficient than the version that uses `previous`.

12. Consider a variant of the class in Display 15.17 with no `previous` local variable. In other words, there is no reference kept to the node that links to the current node `position`. Write a method `addAfterHere(String newData)` that adds a new node after the node in `position`.

13. Complete the definition of the method `changeHere` in the inner class `List2Iterator` in Display 15.17.

14. Given an iterator pointing somewhere in a linked list, does `i.next( )` return the value that `i` is referencing prior to the invocation of `i.next( )` or does it return the value of the next node in the list?

15.4 **Variations on a Linked List**

I have called this principle, by which each slight variation, if useful, is preserved, by the term Natural Selection.

CHARLES DARWIN, The Origin of Species

In this section, we discuss some variations on linked lists, including the two data structures known as stacks and queues. Stacks and queues need not involve linked lists, but one common way to implement a stack or a queue is to use a linked list.

Display 15.20 Adding a Node between Two Nodes

1. Existing list with the iterator positioned at "shoes"

2. Create new Node with "socks" linked to "shoes"

```
temp = new Node (newData, position); // newData is "socks"
```

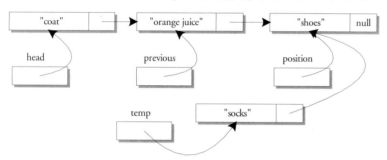

Local variable of type Node

3. Make previous link to the Node temp

```
previous. link = temp;
```

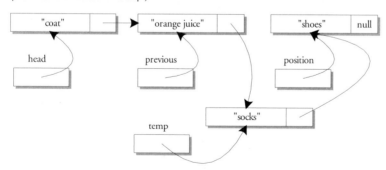

4. Picture redrawn for clarity, but structurally identical to picture 3

Doubly Linked List

An ordinary linked list allows you to move down the list in only one direction (following the links). A **doubly linked list** has one link that has a reference to the next node and one that has a reference to the previous node. In some cases the link to the previous node can simplify our code. For example, we will no longer need to have a `previous` instance variable to remember the node that links to the current position. Diagrammatically, a doubly linked list looks like the sample list in Display 15.21.

> **doubly linked list**

The node class for a doubly linked list can begin as follows:

```
private class TwoWayNode
{
    private String item;
    private TwoWayNode previous;
    private TwoWayNode next;

    ...
```

Display 15.21   A Doubly Linked List

The constructors and some of the methods in the doubly linked list class will require changes (from the singly linked case) in their definitions to accommodate the extra link. The major changes are to the methods that add and delete nodes. To make our code a little cleaner, we can add a new constructor that sets the previous and next nodes:

```
public TwoWayNode(String newItem, TwoWayNode previousNode, TwoWayNode nextNode)
    {
        item = newItem;
        next = nextNode;
        previous = previousNode;
    }
```

To add a new TwoWayNode to the front of the list requires setting links on two nodes instead of one. The general process is shown in Display 15.22. In the addToStart method we first create a new TwoWayNode. Because the new node will go on the front of the list, we set the previous link to null and the next link to the current head:

```
TwoWayNode newHead = new TwoWayNode(itemName, null, head);
```

Next we must set the previous link on the old head node to reference the new head. We can do this by setting head.previous = newHead, but we must take care to ensure that head is not null (i.e., the list is not empty). Finally, we can set head to newHead.

```
if (head != null)
{
        head.previous = newHead;
}
head = newHead;
```

To delete a node from the doubly linked list also requires updating the references on both sides of the node to delete. Thanks to the backward link there is no need for an instance variable to keep track of the previous node in the list, as was required for the singly linked list. The general process of deleting a node referenced by position is shown in Display 15.23. Note that some cases must be handled separately, such as deleting a node from the beginning or the end of the list.

The process of inserting a new node into the doubly linked list is shown in Display 15.24. In this case we will insert the new node in front of the iterator referenced by position. Note that there are also special cases for the insert routine when inserting to the front or adding to the end of the list. Only the general case of inserting between two existing nodes is shown in Display 15.24.

A complete example of a doubly linked list is shown in Display 15.25. The code in Display 15.25 is modified from the code in Display 15.17. Use of the doubly linked list is virtually identical to use of a singly linked list. Display 15.26 demonstrates addition, deletion, and insertion into the doubly linked list.

Display 15.22   Adding a Node to the Front of a Doubly Linked List

1. Existing list.

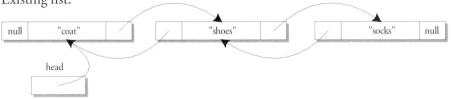

2. Create new TwoWayNode linked to "coat"

```
TwoWayNode newHead = new TwoWayNode (itemName, null, head) // itemName = "shirt"
```

3. Set backward link and set new head

```
head. previous = newHead;
head = newHead;
```

Display 15.23 Deleting a Node from a Doubly Linked List

1. Existing list with an iterator referencing "shoes"

2. Bypass the "shoes" node from the next link of the previous node

```
position.previous.next = position.next;
```

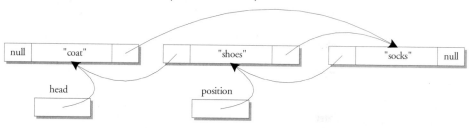

3. Bypass the "shoes" node from the previous link of the next node and move position off the deleted node

```
position. next.previous = position.previous;
position = position.next;
```

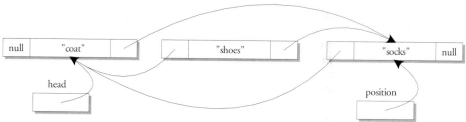

4. Picture redrawn for clarity with the "shoes" node removed since there are no longer references pointing to this node.

Display 15.24 Inserting a Node into a Doubly Linked List

1. Existing list with an iterator referencing "shoes"

2. Create new TwoWayNode with previous linked to "coat" and next to "shoes"

```
TwoWayNode temp = newTwoWayNode (newData, position.previous, position);
// newData = "shirt"
```

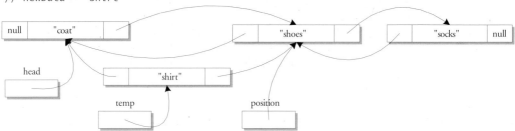

3. Set next link from "coat" to the new node of "shirt"

```
position.previous.next = temp;
```

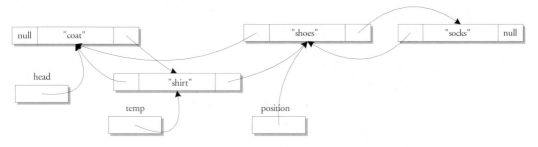

4. Set previous link from "shoes" to the new node of "shirt"

```
position.previous = temp;
```

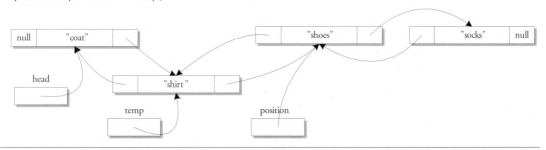

Display 15.25 **A Doubly Linked List with an Iterator** (part 1 of 3)

```java
1   import java.util.NoSuchElementException;

2   public class DoublyLinkedList
3   {
4       private class TwoWayNode
5       {
6           private String item;
7           private TwoWayNode previous;
8           private TwoWayNode next;

9           public TwoWayNode( )
10          {
11               item = null;
12               next = null;
13               previous = null;
14          }
15          public TwoWayNode(String newItem, TwoWayNode previousNode, TwoWayNode nextNode)
16          {
17               item = newItem;
18               next = nextNode;
19               previous = previousNode;
20          }
21      }//End of TwoWayNode inner class

22      public class DoublyLinkedIterator
23      {
24              // We do not need a previous node when using a doubly linked list
25              private TwoWayNode position = null;

26              public DoublyLinkedIterator( )
27              {
28                      position = head;
29              }
30              public void restart( )
31              {
32                      position = head;
33              }
34              public String next( )
35              {
36                      if (!hasNext( ))
37                              throw new IllegalStateException( );
38                      String toReturn = position.item;
39                      position = position.next;
40                      return toReturn;
41              }
```

Display 15.25   A Doubly Linked List with an Iterator (part 2 of 3)

```
42                public void insertHere(String newData)
43                {
44                    if (position == null && head != null)
45                    {
46                        // Add to end.  First move a temp
47                        // pointer to the end of the list
48                        TwoWayNode temp = head;
49                        while (temp.next != null)
50                            temp = temp.next;
51                        temp.next = new TwoWayNode(newData, temp, null);
52                    }
53                    else if (head == null || position.previous == null)
54                        // at head of list
55                        DoublyLinkedList.this.addToStart (newData);
56                    else
57                    {
58                        // Insert before the current position
59                        TwoWayNode temp = new TwoWayNode(newData,
60                                position.previous, position);
                            position.previous.next = temp;
61                        position.previous = temp;
62                    }
63                }

64                public void delete( )
65                {
66                    if (position == null)
67                        throw new IllegalStateException( );
68                    else if (position.previous == null)
69                    { // Deleting first node
70                        head = head.next;
71                        position = head;
72                    }
73                    else if (position.next == null)
74                    { // Deleting last node
75                        position.previous.next = null;
76                        position = null;
77                    }
78                    else
79                    {
80                        position.previous.next = position.next;
81                        position.next.previous = position.previous;
82                        position = position.next;
83                    }
84                }
85        }       // DoublyLinkedIterator
```

(continued)

Display 15.25   A Doubly Linked List with an Iterator (part 3 of 3)

```
86        private TwoWayNode head;

87        public DoublyLinkedIterator iterator( )
88        {
89            return new DoublyLinkedIterator( );
90        }

91        public DoublyLinkedList( )
92        {
93            head = null;
94        }

95        /**
96         The added node will be the first node in the list.
97        */
98        public void addToStart(String itemName)
99        {
100           TwoWayNode newHead = new TwoWayNode(itemName, null, head);
101           if (head != null)
102           {
103               head.previous = newHead;
104           }
105           head = newHead;
106       }
```
    <The methods hasNext, peek, clear, and isEmpty are identical
    to those in Display 15.17. Other methods would also normally
    be defined here, such as deleteHeadNode, size, outputList,
    equals, clone, find, or contains. They have been left off to
    simplify the example.>
```
107  }     // DoublyLinkedList
```

Display 15.26   Using a Doubly Linked List with an Iterator (part 1 of 2)

```
1    public class DoublyLinkedListDemo
2    {
3        public static void main(String[] args)
4        {
5            DoublyLinkedList list = new DoublyLinkedList( );
6            DoublyLinkedList.DoublyLinkedIterator i = list.iterator( );

7            list.addToStart("shoes");
8            list.addToStart("orange juice");
9            list.addToStart("coat");
```

Display 15.26   Using a Doubly Linked List with an Iterator (part 2 of 2)

```
10              System.out.println("List contains:");
11              i.restart( );
12              while (i.hasNext( ))
13                      System.out.println(i.next( ));
14              System.out.println( );

15              i.restart( );
16              i.next( );
17              i.next( );
18              System.out.println("Delete " + i.peek( ));
19              i.delete( );

20              System.out.println("List now contains:");
21              i.restart( );
22              while (i.hasNext( ))
23                      System.out.println(i.next( ));
24              System.out.println( );

25              i.restart( );
26              i.next( );
27              System.out.println("Inserting socks before " + i.peek( ));
28              i.insertHere("socks");

29              i.restart( );
30              System.out.println("List now contains:");
31              while (i.hasNext( ))
32                      System.out.println(i.next( ));
33              System.out.println( );
34          }
35   }
```

Sample Dialogue

```
List contains:
coat
orange juice
shoes

Delete shoes
List now contains:
Coat
Orange juice

Inserting socks before orange juice
List now contains:
coat
socks
orange juice
```

Self-Test Exercises

15. What operations are easier to implement with a doubly linked list compared with a singly linked list? What operations are more difficult?

16. If the `addToStart` method from Display 15.25 were removed, how could we still add a new node to the head of the list?

The Stack Data Structure

stack

A **stack** is not necessarily a linked data structure, but it can be implemented as a linked list. A stack is a data structure that removes items in the reverse of the order in which they were inserted. So if you insert "one", then "two", and then "three" into a stack and then remove them, they will come out in the order "three", then "two", and finally "one". Stacks are discussed in more detail in Chapter 11. A linked list that inserts and deletes only at the head of the list (such as the one in Display 15.3 or in Display 15.8) is, in fact, a stack.

push and pop

You can imagine the stack data structure like a stack of trays in a cafeteria. You can **push** a new tray on top of the stack to make a taller stack. Alternately, you can **pop** the topmost tray off the stack until there are no more trays to remove. A definition of a `Stack` class is shown in Display 15.27 that is based on the linked list from Display 15.3. A short demonstration program is shown in Display 15.28. The `addToStart` method has been renamed to `push` to use stack terminology. Similarly, the `deleteHeadNode` method has been renamed to `pop` and returns the `String` from the top of the stack. Although not shown here to keep the definition simple, it would be appropriate to add other methods such as `peek`, `clone`, or `equals` or to convert the class to use a generic data type.

Stacks

A *stack* is a last-in/first-out data structure; that is, the data items are retrieved in the opposite order to which they were placed in the stack.

Display 15.27 **A Stack Class** (part 1 of 2)

```
1    import java.util.NoSuchElementException;

2    public class Stack
3    {
4        private class Node
5        {
6            private String item;
7            private Node link;
```

Display 15.27   **A Stack Class** (part 2 of 2)

```
 8              public Node( )
 9              {
10                  item = null;
11                  link = null;
12              }
13              public Node(String newItem, Node linkValue)
14              {
15                  item = newItem;
16                  link = linkValue;
17              }
18      }//End of Node inner class

19      private Node head;

20      public Stack( )
21      {
22          head = null;
23      }


24      /**
25          This method replaces addToStart
26      */
27      public void push(String itemName)
28      {
29          head = new Node(itemName, head);
30      }
31      /**
32          This method replaces deleteHeadNode and
33          also returns the value popped from the list
34      */
35      public String pop( )
36      {
37          if (head == null)
38              throw  new IllegalStateException( );
39          else
40          {
41              String returnItem = head.item;
42              head = head.link;
43              return returnItem;
44          }
45      }
46      public boolean isEmpty( )
47      {
48          return (head == null);
49      }
50  }
```

Display 15.28 **Stack Demonstration Program**

```
1   public class StackExample
2   {
3        public static void main(String[] args)
4        {
5             Stack stack = new Stack( );
6             stack.push("Billy Rubin");
7             stack.push("Lou Pole");
8             stack.push("Polly Ester");

9             while (!stack.isEmpty( ))
10            {
11                 String s = stack.pop( );
12                 System.out.println(s);
13            }
14       }
15  }
```

Items come out of the stack in the reverse order that they were added.

Sample Dialogue

```
Polly Ester
Lou Pole
Billy Rubin
```

Self-Test Exercise

17. Display 15.27 does not contain a peek( ) method. Normally this method would return the data on the top of the stack without popping it off. How could a user of the Stack class get the same functionally as peek( ) even though it is not defined?

The Queue Data Structure

queue

A stack is a last-in/first-out data structure. Another common data structure is a **queue**, which handles data in a first-in/first-out fashion. A queue is like a line at the bank. Customers add themselves to the back of the line and are served from the front of the line. A queue can be implemented with a linked list. However, a queue needs a pointer at **tail** both the head of the list and at the **tail** (that is, the other end) of the linked list, because action takes place in both locations. It is easier to remove a node from the head of a linked list than from the tail of the linked list. So, a simple implementation will remove **front** nodes from the head of the list (which we will now call the **front** of the list) and we will **back** add nodes to the tail end of the list, which we will now call the **back** of the list (or the back of the queue).

The definition of a simple Queue class that is based on a linked list is given in Display 15.29. A short demonstration program is given in Display 15.30. We have not made our queue a generic queue to keep the definition simple, but it would be routine to replace the data type String with a type parameter.

Queue

A *queue* is a first-in/first-out data structure; that is, the data items are removed from the queue in the same order that they were added to the queue.

Self-Test Exercise

18. Complete the definition of the method addToBack in Display 15.29.

Display 15.29   **A Queue** Class (part 1 of 2)

```
1    public class Queue
2    {
3        private class Node
4        {
5            private String item;
6            private Node link;

7            public Node( )
8            {
9                item = null;
10               link = null;
11           }

12           public Node(String newItem, Node linkValue)
13           {
14               item = newItem;
15               link = linkValue;
16           }
17       }//End of Node inner class

18       private Node front;
19       private Node back;

20       public Queue( )
21       {
22           front = null;
23           back = null;
24       }
```

(continued)

Display 15.29 **A Queue Class** (part 2 of 2)

```
25        /**
26         Adds a String to the back of the queue.
27         */
28        public void addToBack(String itemName)
          <The definition of this method is Self-Test Exercise 18.>

29        public boolean isEmpty( )
30        {
31            return (front == null);
32        }

33        public void clear( )
34        {
35            front = null;
36            back = null;
37        }
38        /**
39         Returns the String in the front of the queue.
40         Returns null if queue is empty.
41         */
42        public String whoIsNext( )
43        {
44            if (front == null)
45                return null;
46            else
47                return front.item;
48        }
49
50        /**
51         Removes a String from the front of the queue.
52         Returns false if the list is empty.
53         */
54        public boolean removeFront( )
55        {
56            if (front != null)
57            {
58                front = front.link;
59                return true;
60            }
61            else
62                return false;
63        }
64  }
```

Display 15.30 Demonstration of the **Queue** Class

```
1    public class QueueDemo
2    {
3        public static void main(String[] args)
4        {
5            Queue q = new Queue( );

6            q.addToBack("Tom");
7            q.addToBack("Dick");
8            q.addToBack("Harriet");
9            while(!q.isEmpty( ))
10           {
11               System.out.println(q.whoIsNext( ));
12               q.removeFront( );
13           }
14           System.out.println("The queue is empty.");
15       }
16   }
```

Items come out of the queue in the same order that they went into the queue.

Sample Dialogue

```
Tom
Dick
Harriet
The queue is empty.
```

Items come out of the queue in the same order that they went into the queue.

In order to have some terminology to discuss the efficiency of our Queue class and linked list algorithms, we first present some background on how the efficiency of algorithms is usually measured.

Running Times and Big-*O* Notation

If you ask a programmer how fast his or her program is, you might expect an answer like "two seconds." However, the speed of a program cannot be given by a single number. A program will typically take a longer amount of time on larger inputs than it will on smaller inputs. You would expect that a program for sorting numbers would take less time to sort ten numbers than it would to sort one thousand numbers. Perhaps it takes two seconds to sort ten numbers, but ten seconds to sort one thousand numbers. How, then, should the programmer answer the question "How fast is your program?" The programmer would have to give a table of values showing how long the program took for different sizes of input. For example, the table might be as shown in Display 15.31. This table does not give a single time, but instead gives different times for a variety of different input sizes.

Display 15.31 Some Values of a Running Time Function

Input Size	Running Time
10 numbers	2 seconds
100 numbers	2.1 seconds
1,000 numbers	10 seconds
10,000 numbers	2.5 minutes

function

The table is a description of what is called a **function** in mathematics. Just as a (non-void) Java method takes an argument and returns a value, so too does this function take an argument, which is an input size, and returns a number, which is the time the program takes on an input of that size. If we call this function T, then $T(10)$ is 2 seconds, $T(100)$ is 2.1 seconds, $T(1,000)$ is 10 seconds, and $T(10,000)$ is 2.5 minutes. The table is just a sample of some of the values of this function T. The program will take some amount of time on inputs of every size. So although they are not shown in the table, there are also values for $T(1)$, $T(2)$, ..., $T(101)$, $T(102)$, and so forth. For any positive integer N, $T(N)$ is the amount of time it takes for the program to sort N numbers. The function T is called the **running time** of the program.

running time

So far we have been assuming that this sorting program will take the same amount of time on any list of N numbers. That need not be true. Perhaps it takes much less time if the list is already sorted or almost sorted. In that case, $T(N)$ is defined to be the time taken by the "hardest" list, that is, the time taken on that list of N numbers that makes the program run the longest. This is called the **worst-case running time**. In this chapter we will always mean worst-case running time when we give a running time for an algorithm or for some code.

worst-case running time

The time taken by a program or algorithm is often given by a formula, such as $4N + 3$, $5N + 4$, or N^2. If the running time $T(N)$ is $5N + 5$, then on inputs of size N the program will run for $5N + 5$ time units.

Below is some code to search an array a with N elements to determine whether a particular value target is in the array:

```java
int i = 0;
boolean found = false;
while (( i < N) && !(found))
{
    if (a[i] == target)
        found = true;
    else
        i++;
}
```

We want to compute some estimate of how long it will take a computer to execute this code. We would like an estimate that does not depend on which computer we use, either because we do not know which computer we will use or because we might use several different computers to run the program at different times.

One possibility is to count the number of "steps," but it is not easy to decide what a step is. In this situation the normal thing to do is count the number of **operations**. The term *operations* is almost as vague as the term *step*, but there is at least some agreement in practice about what qualifies as an operation. Let us say that, for this Java code, each application of any of the following will count as an operation: =, <, &&, !, [], ==, and ++. The computer must do other things besides carry out these operations, but these seem to be the main things that it is doing, and we will assume that they account for the bulk of the time needed to run this code. In fact, our analysis of time will assume that everything else takes no time at all and that the total time for our program to run is equal to the time needed to perform these operations. Although this is an idealization that clearly is not completely true, it turns out that this simplifying assumption works well in practice, and so it is often made when analyzing a program or algorithm.

Even with our simplifying assumption, we still must consider two cases: Either the value `target` is in the array or it is not. Let us first consider the case when `target` is not in the array. The number of operations performed will depend on the number of array elements searched. The operation = is performed two times before the loop is executed. Since we are assuming that `target` is not in the array, the loop will be executed N times, one for each element of the array. Each time the loop is executed, the following operations are performed: <, &&, !, [], ==, and ++. This adds five operations for each of N loop iterations. Finally, after N iterations, the Boolean expression is again checked and found to be `false`. This adds a final three operations (<, &&, !).[3] If we tally all these operations, we get a total of $6N + 5$ operations when the target is not in the array. We will leave it as an exercise for the reader to confirm that if the target is in the array, then the number of operations will be $6N + 5$ *or less*. Thus, the worst-case running time is $T(N) = 6N + 5$ operations for any array of N elements and any value of `target`.

We just determined that the worst-case running time for our search code is $6N + 5$ operations. But an operation is not a traditional unit of time, like a nanosecond, second, or minute. If we want to know how long the algorithm will take on some particular computer, we must know how long it takes that computer to perform one operation. If an operation can be performed in one nanosecond, then the time will be $6N + 5$ nanoseconds. If an operation can be performed in one second, the time will be $6N + 5$ seconds. If we use a slow computer that takes ten seconds to perform an operation, the time will be $60N + 50$ seconds. In general, if it takes the computer c nanoseconds to perform one operation, then the actual running time will be approximately

---

[3] Because of short-circuit evaluation, `!(found)` is not evaluated, so we actually get two, not three, operations. However, the important thing is to obtain a good upper bound. If we add in one extra operation, that is not significant.

$c\,(6N + 5)$ nanoseconds. (We said *approximately* because we are making some simplifying assumptions and therefore the result may not be the absolutely exact running time.) This means that our running time of $6N + 5$ is a very crude estimate. To get the running time expressed in nanoseconds, you must multiply by some constant that depends on the particular computer you are using. Our estimate of $6N + 5$ is only accurate to within a constant multiple.

big-O
notation

Estimates on running time, such as the one we just went through, are normally expressed in something called **big-O notation**. (The O is the letter "Oh," not the digit zero.) Suppose we estimate the running time to be, say, $6N + 5$ operations, and suppose we know that no matter what the exact running time of each different operation may turn out to be, there will always be some constant factor c such that the real running time is less than or equal to $c\,(6N + 5)$. Under these circumstances, we say that the code (or program or algorithm) runs in time $O(6N + 5)$. This is usually read as "big-O of $6N + 5$." We need not know what the constant c will be. In fact, it will undoubtedly be different for different computers, but we must know that there is one such c for any reasonable computer system. If the computer is very fast, the c might be less than 1—say, 0.001. If the computer is very slow, the c might be very large—say, 1,000. Moreover, since changing the units (say from nanosecond to second) only involves a constant multiple, there is no need to give any units of time.

Be sure to notice that a big-O estimate is an upper-bound estimate. We always approximate by taking numbers on the high side rather than the low side of the true count. Also notice that when performing a big-O estimate, we need not determine an exact count of the number of operations performed. We only need an estimate that is correct up to a constant multiple. If our estimate is twice as large as the true number, that is good enough.

An order-of-magnitude estimate, such as the previous $6N + 5$, contains a parameter for the size of the task solved by the algorithm (or program or piece of code). In our sample case, this parameter N was the number of array elements to be searched. Not surprisingly, it takes longer to search a larger number of array elements than it does to search a smaller number of array elements. Big-O running-time estimates are always expressed as a function of the size of the problem. In this chapter, all our algorithms will involve a range of values in some container. In all cases N will be the number of elements in that range.

The following is an alternative, pragmatic way to think about big-O estimates:

> *Only look at the term with the highest exponent and
> do not pay attention to constant multiples.*

For example, all of the following are $O(N^2)$:

$$N^2 + 2N + 1, \quad 3N^2 + 7, \quad 100N^2 + N$$

All of the following are $O(N^3)$:

$$N^3 + 5N^2 + N + 1, \quad 8N^3 + 7, \quad 100N^3 + 4N + 1$$

These big-O running-time estimates are admittedly crude, but they do contain some information. They will not distinguish between a running time of $5N + 5$ and a running time of $100N$, but they do let us distinguish between some running times and so determine that some algorithms are faster than others. Look at the graphs in Display 15.32 and notice that all the graphs for functions that are $O(N)$ eventually fall below the graph for the function $0.5N^2$. The result is inevitable: An $O(N)$ algorithm will always run faster than any $O(N^2)$ algorithm, provided we use large enough values of N. Although an $O(N^2)$ algorithm could be faster than an $O(N)$ algorithm for the problem size you are handling, programmers have found that, in practice, $O(N)$ algorithms perform better than $O(N)$ algorithms for most practical applications that are intuitively "large." Similar remarks apply to any other two different big-O running times.

Display 15.32   **Comparison of Running Times**

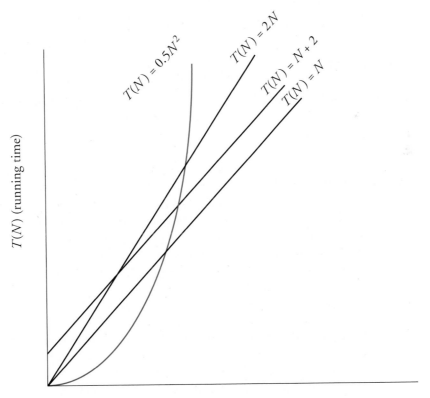

$T(N) = 0.5N^2$

$T(N) = 2N$

$T(N) = N + 2$

$T(N) = N$

$T(N)$ (running time)

N (problem size)

Some terminology will help with our descriptions of generic algorithm running times. **Linear running time** means a running time of $T(N) = aN + b$. A linear running time is always an $O(N)$ running time. **Quadratic running time** means a running time with a highest term of N^2. A quadratic running time is always an $O(N^2)$ running time. We will also occasionally have logarithms in running-time formulas. Those normally are given without any base, since changing the base is just a constant multiple. If you see log N, think log base 2 of N, but it would not be wrong to think log base 10 of N. Logarithms are very slow growing functions. So, an $O(\log N)$ running time is very fast.

In many cases, our running-time estimates will be better than big-O estimates. In particular, when we specify a linear running time, that is a tight upper bound and you can think of the running time as being exactly $T(N) = cN$, although the c is still not specified.

Self-Test Exercises

19. Show that a running time $T(N) = aN + b$ is an $O(N)$ running time. (*Hint:* The only issue is the plus b. Assume N is always at least 1.)

20. Show that for any two bases a and b for logarithms, if a and b are both greater than 1, then there is a constant c such that $\log_a N \le c(\log_b N)$. Thus, there is no need to specify a base in $O(\log N)$. That is, $O(\log_a N)$ and $O(\log_b N)$ mean the same thing.

Efficiency of Linked Lists

Now that we know about big-O notation, we can express the efficiency of various methods for our linked data structures. As an example of analyzing the run-time efficiency of an algorithm, consider the find method for the linked list class in Display 15.3. This method starts at the head of the list and sequentially iterates through each node to see whether it matches the target. If the linked list contains many nodes, then we might get lucky if the target is found at the head of the list. In this case the computer only had to execute one step: Check the head of the list for the target. In the worst case the compute might have to search through all n nodes before finding (or not finding) the target. In this case the computer had to execute n steps. The worst case will obviously take longer to execute than the best case. On average we might expect to search through about half of the list before finding the target. This would require $n/2$ steps. In our big-O notation, the find operation is $O(n)$. However, the addToStart method requires only linking a new node to the head of the list. This runs in $O(1)$ steps (that is, a constant upper bound on the running time that is independent of the size of the input).

Next we shall briefly examine more elaborate data structures that are capable of performing find operations in fewer steps. However, a detailed treatment of these more advanced data structures is beyond the scope of this chapter. The goal of this chapter is to teach you the basic techniques for constructing and manipulating data structures based on nodes and links (that is, nodes and references). The linked lists served as good examples for our discussion.

15.5 Hash Tables with Chaining

Seek, and ye shall find.

MATTHEW 7:7

hash table
hash map

A **hash table** or **hash map** is a data structure that efficiently stores and retrieves data from memory. There are many ways to construct a hash table; in this section we will use an array in combination with singly linked lists. In the previous section we saw that a linked list generally requires linear, or $O(n)$, steps to determine if a target is in the list. In contrast, a hash table has the potential to execute a fixed number of steps to look up a target, regardless of the size of n. We saw that a constant-time lookup is written $O(1)$. However, the hash table we will present may still require n steps, but such a case is unlikely.

An object is stored in a hash table by associating it with a *key*. Given the key, we can retrieve the object. Ideally, the key is unique to each object. If the object has no intrinsically unique key, then we can use a **hash function** to compute one. In most cases the hash function computes a number.

hash function

For example, let's use a hash table to store a dictionary of words. Such a hash table might be useful to make a spell checker—words missing from the hash table might not be spelled correctly. We will construct the hash table with a fixed array in which each array element references a linked list. The key computed by the hash function will map to the index of the array. The actual data will be stored in a linked list at the hash value's index. Display 15.33 illustrates the idea with a fixed array of ten entries. Initially each entry of the array hashArray contains a reference to an empty singly linked list. First we add the word "cat", which has been assigned the key or hash value of 2 (we'll show how this was computed shortly). Next we add "dog" and "bird", which are assigned hash values of 4 and 7, respectively. Each of these strings is inserted as the head of the linked list using the hash value as the index in the array. Finally, we add "turtle", which also has a hash of 2. Since "cat" is already stored at index 2, we now have a **collision**. Both "turtle" and "cat" map to the same index in the array. When this occurs in a hash table with **chaining**, we simply insert the new node onto the existing linked list. In our example there are now two nodes at index 2: "turtle" and "cat".

collision
chaining

To retrieve a value from the hash table, we first compute the hash value of the target. Next we search the linked list that is stored at hashArray[hashValue] for the target, using an iterator to sequentially search the linked list. If the target is not found in this linked list, then the target is not stored in the hash table. If the size of the linked list is small then the retrieval process will be quick.

Display 15.33 **Constructing a Hash Table**

1. Existing hash table initialized with ten empty linked lists

```
hashArray = new LinkedList 3[SIZE]; // SIZE = 10
```

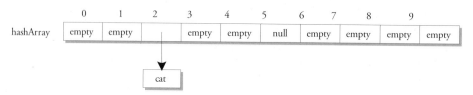

2. After adding "cat" with hash of 2

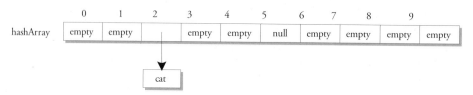

3. After adding "dog" with hash of 4 and "bird" with hash of 7

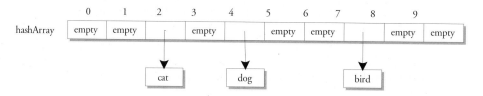

4. After adding "turtle" with hash of 2 – collision and chained to linked list with "cat"

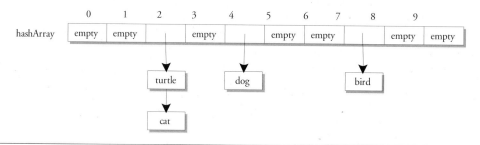

A Hash Function for Strings

A simple way to compute a numeric hash value for a string is to sum the ASCII value of every character in the string and then compute the modulus of the sum using the size of the fixed array. A subset of ASCII codes is given in Appendix 3. Code to compute the hash value is shown below:

```
private int computeHash(String s)
{
    int hash = 0;
    for (int i = 0; i < s.length( ); i++)
    {
        hash += s.charAt(i);
    }
    return hash % SIZE;// SIZE = 10 in example
}
```

For example, the ASCII codes for the string "dog" are as follows:

```
d       -> 100
o       -> 111
g       -> 103
```

The hash function is computed as follows:

```
Sum             =   100 + 111 + 103       = 314
Hash = Sum % 10 =   314 % 10              = 4
```

In this example we first compute an unbounded value, the sum of the ASCII values in the string. However, the array was defined to only hold a finite number of elements. To scale the sum to the size of the array, we compute the modulus of the sum with respect to the size of the array, which is 10 in the example. In practice the size of the array is generally a prime number larger than the number of items that will be put into the hash table.[4] The computed hash value of 4 serves like a fingerprint for the string "dog". However, different strings may map to the same value. We can verify that "cat" maps to $(99 + 97 + 116)$ % $10 = 2$ and also that "turtle" maps to $(116 + 117 + 114 + 116 + 108 + 101)$ % $10 = 2$.

A complete code listing for a hash table class is given in Display 15.34, and a demonstration is provided in Display 15.35. The hash table definition in Display 15.34 uses an array in which each element is a LinkedList2 class defined in Display 15.7.

Display 15.34   **A Hash Table Class** (part 1 of 2)

```
1    public class HashTable
2    {
3        // Uses the generic LinkedList2 class from Display 15.7
4        private LinkedList2[] hashArray;
5        private static final int SIZE = 10;

6        public HashTable( )
7        {
8            hashArray = new LinkedList2[SIZE];
```

(continued)

---

[4] A prime number avoids common divisors after modulus that can lead to collisions.

Display 15.34   A Hash Table Class (part 2 of 2)

```
9              for (int i=0; i < SIZE; i++)
10                     hashArray[i] = new LinkedList2( );
11         }

12         private int computeHash(String s)
13         {
14             int hash = 0;
15             for (int i = 0; i < s.length( ); i++)
16             {
17                 hash += s.charAt(i);
18             }
19             return hash % SIZE;
20         }

21         /**
22          Returns true if the target is in the hash table,
23          false if it is not.
24         */
25         public boolean containsString(String target)
26         {
27             int hash = computeHash(target);
28             LinkedList2 list = hashArray[hash];
29             if (list.contains(target))
30                     return true;
31             return false;
32         }
33         /**
34          Stores or puts string s into the hash table
35         */
36         public void put(String s)
37         {
38             int hash = computeHash(s);// Get hash value
39             LinkedList2 list = hashArray[hash];
40             if (!list.contains(s))
41             {
42                 // Only add the target if it's not already
43                 // on the list.
44                 hashArray[hash].addToStart(s);
45             }
46         }
47     } // End HashTable class
```

Display 15.35 Hash Table Demonstration

```java
1   public class HashTableDemo
2   {
3        public static void main(String[] args)
4        {
5             HashTable h = new HashTable( );

6             System.out.println("Adding dog, cat, turtle, bird");
7             h.put("dog");
8             h.put("cat");
9             h.put("turtle");
10            h.put("bird");
11            System.out.println("Contains dog? " +
12                      h.containsString("dog"));
13            System.out.println("Contains cat? " +
14                   h.containsString("cat"));
15            System.out.println("Contains turtle? " +
16                   h.containsString("turtle"));
17            System.out.println("Contains bird? " +
18                   h.containsString("bird"));

19            System.out.println("Contains fish? " +
20                   h.containsString("fish"));
21            System.out.println("Contains cow? " +
22                   h.containsString("cow"));
23        }
24   }
```

Sample Dialogue

```
Adding dog, cat, turtle, bird
Contains dog? true
Contains cat? true
Contains turtle? true
Contains bird? true
Contains fish? false
Contains cow? False
```

Efficiency of Hash Tables

The efficiency of our hash table depends on several factors. First, let's examine some extreme cases. The worst-case run-time performance occurs if every item inserted into the table has the same hash key. Everything will then be stored in a single linked list. With n items, the find operation will require $O(n)$ steps. Fortunately, if the items that we insert are somewhat random, the probability that all of them will hash to the same key is highly unlikely. In contrast, the best-case run-time performance occurs if every item inserted into the table has a different hash key. This means that there will be no collisions, so the find operation will require constant, or $O(1)$, steps because the target will always be the first node in the linked list.

We can decrease the chance of collisions by using a better hash function. For example, the simple hash function that sums each letter of a string ignores the ordering of the letters. The words "rat" and "tar" would hash to the same value. A better hash function for a string s is to multiply each letter by an increasing weight depending upon the position in the word. For example:

```
int hash = 0;
for (int i = 0; i < s.length( ); i++)
{
    hash = 31 * hash + s.charAt(i);
}
```

Another way to decrease the chance of collisions is by making the hash table bigger. For example, if the hash table array stored 10,000 entries but we are only inserting 1,000 items, then the probability of a collision is much smaller than if the hash table array stored only 1,000 entries. However, a drawback to creating an extremely large hash table array is wasted memory. If only 1,000 items are inserted into the 10,000-entry hash table then at least 9,000 memory locations will go unused. This illustrates the **time-space tradeoff**. It is usually possible to increase run-time performance at the expense of memory space, and vice versa.

time-space tradeoff

Self-Test Exercises

21. Suppose that every student in your university is assigned a unique nine-digit ID number. You would like to create a hash table that indexes ID numbers to an object representing a student. The hash table has a size of N, where N has less than nine digits. Describe a simple hash function that you can use to map from ID number to a hash index.

22. Write an outputHashTable( ) method for the HashTable class that outputs every item stored in the hash table.

15.6 Sets

There are two classes in good society in England. The equestrian classes and the neurotic classes.

GEORGE BERNARD SHAW, *Heartbreak House*

A set is a collection of elements in which order and multiplicity are ignored. Many problems in computer science can be solved with the aid of a set data structure. A variation on linked lists is a straightforward way to implement a set. In this implementation the items in each set are stored using a singly linked list. The `data` variable contains a reference to an object we wish to store in the set, whereas the `link` variable refers to the next `Node<T>` in the list (which in turn contains a reference to the next object to store in the set). The node class for a generic set of objects can begin as follows:

```
private class Node<T>
{
    private T data;
    private Node<T> link;

    ...
```

A complete listing is provided in Display 15.37. The `Node` class is a private inner class, similar to how we constructed the generic `LinkedList3<T>` class in Display 15.8. In fact, the set operations of `add`, `contains`, `output`, `clear`, `size`, and `isEmpty` are virtually identical to those from Display 15.8. The `add` method (which was `addToStart`) has been slightly changed to prevent duplicate items from being added into the set. Display 15.36 illustrates two sample sets stored using this data structure. The set `round` contains `"peas"`, `"ball"`, and `"pie"`, whereas the set `green` contains `"peas"` and `"grass"`. Since the linked list is storing a reference to each object in the set, it is possible to place an item in multiple sets by referencing it from multiple linked lists. In Display 15.36, `"peas"` is in both sets since it is round and green.

Fundamental Set Operations

The fundamental operations that our set class should support are as follows:

- Add Element. Add a new item into a set.
- Contains. Determine if a target item is a member of the set.
- Union. Return a set that is the union of two sets.
- Intersection. Return a set that is the intersection of two sets.

We should also make an iterator so that every element can be retrieved from a set. This is left as a programming project for the reader. Other useful set operations include methods to retrieve the cardinality of the set and to remove items from the set.

Display 15.36 Sets Using Linked Lists

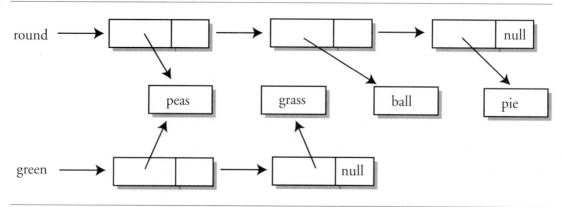

Code to implement sets is provided in Display 15.37. The add method is similar to adding a node to the front of a linked list. The head variable always references the first node in the list. The contains method is identical to the find method for a singly linked list. We simply loop through every item in the list looking for the target.

The union method combines the elements in the calling object's set with the elements from the set of the input argument, otherSet. To union these sets we first create a new empty Set<T> object. Next, we iterate through both the calling object's set and otherSet's set. All elements are added (which creates new references to the items in the set) to the new set. The add method enforces uniqueness, so we don't have to check for duplicate elements in the union method.

The intersection method is similar to the union method in that it also creates a new empty Set<T> object. In this case we populate the set with items that are common to both the calling object's set and otherSet's set. This is accomplished by iterating through every item in the calling object's set. For each item, we invoke the contains method for otherSet. If contains returns true, then the item is in both sets and can be added to the new set.

A short demonstration program is shown in Display 15.38.

Display 15.37 Set<T> Class (part 1 of 4)

```
1    // Uses a linked list as the internal data structure
2    // to store items in a set.
3    public class Set<T>
4    {
5        private class Node<T>
6        {
7            private T data;
8            private Node<T> link;
```

Display 15.37   **Set\<T\> Class** (part 2 of 4)

```
 9            public Node( )
10            {
11                data = null;
12                link = null;
13            }
14            public Node(T newData, Node<T> linkValue)
15            {
16                data = newData;
17                link = linkValue;
18            }
19        }//End of Node<T> inner class

20      private Node<T> head;

21        public Set( )
22        {
23                head = null;
24        }
25        /**
26         Add a new item to the set. If the item
27         is already in the set, false is returned;
28         otherwise, true is returned.
29        */
30        public boolean add(T newItem)
31        {
32                if (!contains(newItem))
33                {
34                        head = new Node<T>(newItem, head);
35                        return true;
36                }
37                return false;
38        }

39      public boolean contains(T item)
40      {
41          Node<T> position = head;
42          T itemAtPosition;
43          while (position != null)
44          {
45              itemAtPosition = position.data;
46              if (itemAtPosition.equals(item))
47                  return true;
48              position = position.link;
49          }
50          return false; //target was not found
51      }
```

(continued)

Display 15.37 **Set<T> Class** (part 3 of 4)

```
52        public void output( )
53        {
54            Node position = head;
55            while (position != null)
56        {
57                System.out.print(position.data.toString( ) + " ");
58                position = position.link;
59            }
60            System.out.println( );
61        }
62
63        /**
64         Returns a new set that is the union
65         of this set and the input set.
66         */
67        public Set<T> union(Set<T> otherSet)
68        {
69            Set<T> unionSet = new Set<T>( );
70            // Copy this set to unionSet.
71            Node<T> position = head;
72            while (position != null)
73            {
74                unionSet.add(position.data);
75                position = position.link;
76            }
77            // Copy otherSet items to unionSet.
78            // The add method eliminates any duplicates.
79            position = otherSet.head;
80            while (position != null)
81            {
82                unionSet.add(position.data);
83                position = position.link;
84            }
85            return unionSet;
86        }
87
88        /**
89         Returns a new set that is the intersection
90         of this set and the input set.
91         */
92        public Set<T> intersection(Set<T> otherSet)
93        {
94            Set<T> interSet = new Set<T>( );
95            // Copy only items in both sets.
96            Node<T> position = head;
97            while (position != null)
98            {
99                if (otherSet.contains(position.data))
```

Display 15.37   **Set<T> Class** (part 4 of 4)

```
98                            interSet.add(position.data);
99                    position = position.link;
100            }
101            return interSet;        The clear, size, and isEmpty methods are identical
102        }                            to those in Display 15.8 for the LinkedList3 class.
103    }
```

Display 15.38   **Set Class Demo** (part 1 of 2)

```
1    class SetDemo
2    {
3        public class static void main(String[] args)
4        {
5                // Round things
6                Set round = new Set<String>( );
7                // Green things
8                Set green = new Set<String>( );

9                // Add some data to both sets
10                round.add("peas");
11                round.add("ball");
12                round.add("pie");
13                round.add("grapes");

14                green.add("peas");
15                green.add("grapes");
16                green.add("garden hose");
17                green.add("grass");

18                System.out.println("Contents of set round: ");
19                round.output( );
20                System.out.println("Contents of set green: ");
21                green.output( );
22                System.out.println( );

23                System.out.println("ball in set round? " +
24                        round.contains("ball"));
25                System.out.println("ball in set green? " +
26                        green.contains("ball"));
```

(continued)

Display 15.38   Set Class Demo (part 2 of 2)

```
27              System.out.println("ball and peas in same set? " +
28                      ((round.contains("ball") &&
29                       (round.contains("peas"))) ||
30                      (green.contains("ball") &&
31                       (green.contains("peas")))));

32              System.out.println("pie and grass in same set? " +
33                      ((round.contains("pie") &&
34                       (round.contains("grass"))) ||
35                      (green.contains("pie") &&
36                       (green.contains("grass")))));

37              System.out.print("Union of green and round: ");
38              round.union(green).output( );
39              System.out.print("Intersection of green and round: ");
40              round.intersection(green).output( );
41          }
42  }
```

Sample Dialogue

```
Contents of set round:
grapes pie ball peas
Contents of set green:
Grass garden hose grapes peas

ball in set round?  true
ball in set green?  false
ball and peas in same set? true
pie and grass in same set? false
Union of green and round: garden hose grass peas ball pie grapes
Intersection of green and round: peas grapes
```

Efficiency of Sets Using Linked Lists

We can analyze the efficiency of our set data structure in terms of the fundamental set operations. Adding an item to the set always inserts a new node on the front of the list. This requires constant, or $O(1)$, steps. The contains method iterates through the entire set looking for the target, which requires $O(n)$ steps. When we invoke the union method for sets A and B, it iterates through both sets and adds each item into a new set. If there are n items in set A and m items in set B, then $n + m$ add methods are invoked. However, there is a hidden cost because the add method searches through its entire list for any duplicates before a new item is added. Although beyond the scope of this text, the additional cost results in $O(m + n)^2$ steps. Finally, the intersection method applied to sets A and B invokes the contains method of set B for each item in set *A*. Since the `contains` method requires $O(m)$ steps for each item in set *A*, then this requires $O(m) \times O(n)$ steps, or $O(mn)$ steps. These are inefficient methods in our implementation of sets. A different approach to represent the set—for example, one that used hash tables instead of a linked list—could result in an `intersection` method that runs in $O(n + m)$ steps. Nevertheless, our linked list implementation would probably be fine for an application that uses small sets or for an application that does not frequently invoke the `intersection` method, and we have the benefit of relatively simple code that is easy to understand.

If we really needed the efficiency, then we could maintain the same interface to the `Set<T>` class but replace our linked list implementation with something else. If we used the hash table implementation from Section 15.5, then the `contains` method could run in $O(1)$ steps instead of $O(n)$ steps. It might seem like the `intersection` method will now run in $O(n)$ steps, but by switching to a hash table it becomes more difficult to iterate through the set of items. Instead of traversing a single linked list to retrieve every item in the set, the hash table version must now iterate through the hash table array and then for each index in the array iterate through the linked list at that index. If the array is size *N* and the number of items in the hash table is *n*, then the iteration time becomes $O(N + n)$. In practice, we would expect *N* to be larger than *n*. So although we have decreased the number of steps it takes to look up an item, we have increased the number of steps it takes to iterate over every item. If this was troublesome, you could overcome this problem with an implementation of `Set<T>` that used both a linked list (to facilitate iteration) and a hash table (for fast lookup). However, the complexity of the code is significantly increased using such an approach. You are asked to explore the hash table implementation in Programming Project 10.

Self-Test Exercises

23. Write a method named `difference` that returns the difference between two sets. The method should return a new set that has items from the first set that are not in the second set. For example, if `setA` contains {1, 2, 3, 4} and `setB` contains {2, 4, 5}, then `setA.difference(setB)` should return the set {1, 3}.

24. What is the run time of the `difference` method for the previous question? Give your answer using big-*O* notation.

15.7 Trees

I think that I shall never see a data structure as useful as a tree.

ANONYMOUS

The tree data structure is an example of a more complicated data structure made with links. Moreover, trees are a very important and widely used data structure. So, we will briefly outline the general techniques used to construct and manipulate trees. This section is only a very brief introduction to trees to give you the flavor of the subject.

This section uses recursion, which is covered in Chapter 11.

Tree Properties

A tree is a data structure that is structured as shown in Display 15.39. In particular, in a tree you can reach any node from the top (root) node by some path that follows the links. Note that there are no cycles in a tree. If you follow the links, you eventually get to an "end." A definition for a tree class for this sort of tree of ints is outlined in Display 15.39. Note that each node has two references to other nodes (two links) coming from it. This sort of tree is called a **binary tree**, because each node has exactly two link instance variables. There are other kinds of trees with different numbers of link instance variables, but the binary tree is the most common case.

The instance variable named root serves a purpose similar to that of the instance variable head in a linked list (Display 15.3). The node whose reference is in the root instance variable is called the **root node**. Any node in the tree can be reached from the root node by following the links.

The term *tree* may seem like a misnomer. The root is at the top of the tree, and the branching structure looks more like a root branching structure than a tree branching structure. The secret to the terminology is to turn the picture (Display 15.39) upside down. The picture then does resemble the branching structure of a tree, and the root node is where the tree's root would begin. The nodes at the ends of the branches with both link instance variables set to null are known as **leaf nodes**, a terminology that may now make some sense. By analogy to an empty linked list, an **empty tree** is denoted by setting the link variable root equal to null.

Note that a tree has a recursive structure. Each tree has, in effect, two subtrees whose root nodes are the nodes pointed to by the leftLink and rightLink of the root node. These two subtrees are circled in Display 15.39. This natural recursive structure makes trees particularly amenable to recursive algorithms. For example, consider the task of searching the tree in such a way that you visit each node and do something with the data in the node (such as writing it out to the screen). There is a general plan of attack that goes as follows:

Preorder Processing

1. Process the data in the root node.
2. Process the left subtree.
3. Process the right subtree.

(margin notes:) binary tree · root node · leaf node · empty tree

Display 15.39   **A Binary Tree**

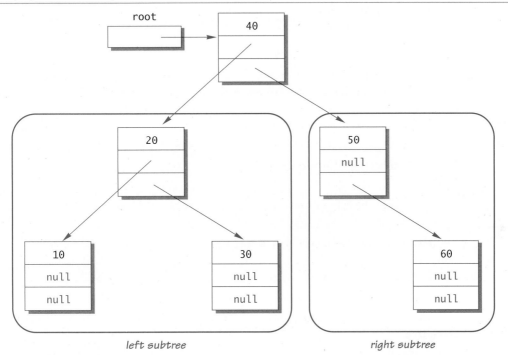

1   `public class IntTree`
2   `{`
3   `public class IntTreeNode`
4   `{`
5   `private int data;`
6   `private IntTreeNode leftLink;`
7   `private IntTreeNode rightLink;`
8   `} //End of IntTreeNode inner class`

9   `private IntTreeNode root;`
     `<The methods and other inner classes are not shown.>`

10 `}`

You obtain a number of variants on this search process by varying the order of these three steps. Two more versions follow:

inorder   **Inorder Processing**

1. Process the left subtree.

2. Process the data in the root node.

3. Process the right subtree.

Postorder Processing

1. Process the left subtree.

2. Process the right subtree.

3. Process the data in the root node.

Binary Search Tree Storage Rule

The tree in Display 15.39 has numbers that were stored in the tree in a special way known as the **Binary Search Tree Storage Rule**. The rule is summarized in the following box.

Binary Search Tree Storage Rule

1. All the values in the left subtree are less than the value in the root node.
2. All the values in the right subtree are greater than or equal to the value in the root node.
3. This rule applies recursively to each of the two subtrees.

(The base case for the recursion is an empty tree, which is always considered to satisfy the rule.)

---

binary search tree

A tree that satisfies the Binary Search Tree Storage Rule is referred to as a **binary search tree**.

Note that if a tree satisfies the Binary Search Tree Storage Rule and you output the values using the Inorder Processing method, then the numbers will be output in order from smallest to largest.

For trees that follow the Binary Search Tree Storage Rule and that are short and fat rather than tall and thin, values can be very quickly retrieved from the tree using a binary search algorithm that is similar in spirit to the binary search algorithm we presented in Display 11.6. The topic of searching and maintaining a binary storage tree to realize this efficiency is a large topic that goes beyond what we have room for here. However, we give one example of a class for trees that satisfy the Binary Search Tree Storage Rule.

EXAMPLE: A Binary Search Tree Class ★

Display 15.40 contains the definition of a class for a binary search tree that satisfies the Binary Search Tree Storage Rule. For simplicity, this tree stores integers, but a routine modification can produce a similar tree class that stores objects of any class that implements the Comparable interface. Display 15.41 demonstrates the use of this tree class. Note that no matter in which order the integers are inserted into the tree, the output, which uses inorder traversal, outputs the integers in sorted order.

(continued on page 868)

Display 15.40   **A Binary Search Tree for Integers** (part 1 of 2)

```
1    /**
2     Class invariant: The tree satisfies the binary search tree storage rule.
3     */
4    public class IntTree
5    {
6        private static class IntTreeNode
7        {
8            private int data;
9            private IntTreeNode leftLink;
10           private IntTreeNode rightLink;
11
12           public IntTreeNode(int newData, IntTreeNode newLeftLink,
13                                          IntTreeNode newRightLink)
14           {
15               data = newData;
16               leftLink = newLeftLink;
17               rightLink = newRightLink;
18           }
19       } //End of IntTreeNode inner class
20
21       private IntTreeNode root;
22
23       public IntTree( )
24       {
25           root = null;
26       }
27
28       public void add(int item)
29       {
30           root = insertInSubtree(item, root);
31       }
32
33       public boolean contains(int item)
34       {
35           return isInSubtree(item, root);
36       }
```

*The only reason this inner class is static is that it is used in the **static** methods insertInSubtree, isInSubtree, and showElementsInSubtree*

This class should have more methods. This is just a sample of possible methods

```
    public void showElements( )
    {
        showElementsInSubtree(root);
    }
```

(Note: The line numbering in the original has the following mapping:)

```
20       private IntTreeNode root;

21       public IntTree( )
22       {
23           root = null;
24       }

25       public void add(int item)
26       {
27           root = insertInSubtree(item, root);
28       }

29       public boolean contains(int item)
30       {
31           return isInSubtree(item, root);
32       }

33       public void showElements( )
34       {
35           showElementsInSubtree(root);
36       }
```

(continued)

Display 15.40 A Binary Search Tree for Integers (part 2 of 2)

```
37        /**
38         Returns the root node of a tree that is the tree with root node
39         subTreeRoot, but with a new node added that contains item.
40        */
41        private static IntTreeNode insertInSubtree(int item,
42                                                    IntTreeNode subTreeRoot)
43        {
44            if (subTreeRoot == null)
45                return new IntTreeNode(item, null, null);
46            else if (item < subTreeRoot.data)
47            {
48                subTreeRoot.leftLink = insertInSubtree(item, subTreeRoot.leftLink);
49                return subTreeRoot;
50            }
51            else //item >= subTreeRoot.data
52            {
53                subTreeRoot.rightLink = insertInSubtree(item, subTreeRoot.rightLink);
54                return subTreeRoot;
55            }
56        }

57        private static boolean isInSubtree(int item, IntTreeNode subTreeRoot)
58        {
59            if (subTreeRoot == null)
60                return false;
61            else if (subTreeRoot.data == item)
62                return true;
63            else if (item < subTreeRoot.data)
64                return isInSubtree(item, subTreeRoot.leftLink);
65            else //item >= link.data
66                return isInSubtree(item, subTreeRoot.rightLink);
67        }

68        private static void showElementsInSubtree(IntTreeNode subTreeRoot)
69        { //Uses inorder traversal.
70            if (subTreeRoot != null)
71            {
72                showElementsInSubtree(subTreeRoot.leftLink);
73                System.out.print(subTreeRoot.data + " ");
74                showElementsInSubtree(subTreeRoot.rightLink);
75            } //else do nothing. Empty tree has nothing to display.
76        }
77    }
```

Display 15.41   Demonstration Program for the Binary Search Tree

```
1   import java.util.Scanner;

2   public class BinarySearchTreeDemo
3   {
4       public static void main(String[] args)
5       {
6           Scanner keyboard = new Scanner(System.in);
7           IntTree tree = new IntTree( );

8           System.out.println("Enter a list of nonnegative integers.");
9           System.out.println("Place a negative integer at the end.");
10          int next = keyboard.nextInt( );
11          while (next >= 0)
12          {
13              tree.add(next);
14              next = keyboard.nextInt( );
15          }

16          System.out.println("In sorted order:");
17          tree.showElements( );
18      }
19  }
```

Sample Dialogue

```
Enter a list of nonnegative integers.
Place a negative integer at the end.
40
30
20
10
11
22
33
44
-1
In sorted order:
10 11 20 22 30 33 40 44
```

EXAMPLE: (continued)

The methods in this class make extensive use of the recursive nature of binary trees. If aNode is a reference to any node in the tree (including possibly the root node), then the entire tree with root aNode can be decomposed into three parts:

1. The node aNode.
2. The left subtree with root node aNode.leftLink.
3. The right subtree with root node aNode.rightLink.

The left and right subtrees do themselves satisfy the Binary Search Tree Storage Rule, so it is natural to use recursion to process the entire tree by doing the following:

1. Processing the left subtree with root node aNode.leftLink
2. Processing the node aNode
3. Processing the right subtree with root node aNode.rightLink

Note that we processed the root node after the left subtree (inorder traversal). This guarantees that the numbers in the tree are output in the order smallest to largest. The method showElementsInSubtree uses a very straightforward implementation of this technique.

Other methods are a bit more subtle in that only one of the two subtrees needs to be processed. For example, consider the method isInSubtree, which returns true or false depending on whether or not the parameter item is in the tree with root node subTreeRoot. To see if the item is anyplace in the tree, you set subTreeRoot equal to the root of the entire tree, as we did in the method contains. However, to express our recursive algorithm for isInSubtree, we need to allow for the possibility of subtrees other than the entire tree.

The algorithm for isInSubtree expressed in pseudocode is as follows:

```
if (The root node subTreeRoot is empty.)
    return false;
else if (The node subTreeRoot contains item.)
    return true;
else if (item < subTreeRoot.data)
    return (The result of searching the tree with
                              root node subTreeRoot.leftLink);
    return (The result of searching the tree with  else //item > link.data
                              root node subTreeRoot.rightLink);
```

The reason this algorithm gives the correct result is that the tree satisfies the Binary Search Tree Storage Rule, so we know that if

```
item < subTreeRoot.data
```

EXAMPLE: (continued)

then `item` is in the left subtree (if it is anywhere in the tree), and if

    item > subTreeRoot.data

then `item` is in the right subtree (if it is anywhere in the tree).

The method with the following heading uses techniques very much like those used in `isInSubtree`:

```
private IntTreeNode insertInSubtree(
                 int item, IntTreeNode subTreeRoot)
```

However, there is something new here. We want the method `insertInSubtree` to insert a new node with the data `item` into the tree with root node `subTreeRoot`. But in this case we want to deal with `subTreeRoot` as a variable and not use it only as the value of the variable `subTreeRoot`. For example, if `subTreeRoot` contains `null`, then we want to change the value of `subTreeRoot` to a reference to a new node containing `item`. However, Java parameters cannot change the value of a variable given as an argument. (Review the discussion of parameters in Chapter 5 if this sounds unfamiliar.) So, we must do something a little different. To change the value of the variable `subTreeRoot`, we return a reference to what we want the new value to be, and we invoke the method `subTreeRoot` as follows:

    subTreeRoot = insertInSubtree(item, subTreeRoot);

That explains why the method `insertInSubtree` returns a reference to a tree node, but we still have to explain why we know it returns a reference to the desired (modified) subtree.

Note that the method `insertInSubtree` searches the tree just as the method `isInSubtree` does, but it does not stop if it finds `item`; instead, it searches until it reaches a leaf node—that is, a node containing `null`. This `null` is where the item belongs in the tree, so it replaces `null` with a new subtree containing a single node that contains `item`. You may need to think about the method `insertInSubtree` a bit to see that it works correctly; allow yourself some time to study the method `insertInSubtree` and be sure you are convinced that after the addition, like so,

    subTreeRoot = insertInSubtree(item, subTreeRoot);

the tree with root node `subTreeRoot` still satisfies the Binary Search Tree Storage Rule. The rest of the definition of the class `IntTree` is routine.

Efficiency of Binary Search Trees

When searching a tree that is as short as possible (all paths from root to a leaf differ by at most one node), the search method isInSubtree, and hence also the method contains, is about as efficient as the binary search on a sorted array (Display 11.6). This should not be a surprise since the two algorithms are in fact very similar. In big-O notation, the worst-case running time is $O(\log n)$, where n is the number of nodes in the tree. That means that searching a short, fat binary tree is very efficient. To obtain this efficiency, the tree does not need to be as short as possible so long as it comes close to being as short as possible. As the tree becomes less short and fat and more tall and thin, the efficiency falls off until, in the extreme case, the efficiency is the same as that of searching a linked list with the same number of nodes.

Maintaining a tree so that it remains short and fat as nodes are added is a topic that is beyond the scope of what we have room for in this book. (The technical term for short and fat is *balanced*.) We will only note that if the numbers that are stored in the tree arrive in random order, then with very high probability the tree will be short and fat enough to realize the efficiency discussed in the previous paragraph.

Self-Test Exercises

25. Suppose that the code for the method showElementsInSubtree in Display 15.40 were changed so that

    ```
    showElementsInSubtree(subTreeRoot.leftLink);
    System.out.print(subTreeRoot.data + " ");
    showElementsInSubtree(subTreeRoot.rightLink);
    ```

    were changed to

    ```
    System.out.print(subTreeRoot.data + " ");
    showElementsInSubtree(subTreeRoot.leftLink);
    showElementsInSubtree(subTreeRoot.rightLink);
    ```

    Will the numbers still be output in ascending order?

26. How can you change the code for the method showElementsInSubtree in Display 15.40 so that the numbers are output from largest to smallest instead of from smallest to largest?

Chapter Summary

- A linked list is a data structure consisting of objects known as nodes, such that each node contains data and also a reference to one other node so that the nodes link together to form a list.

- Setting a link instance variable to `null` indicates the end of a linked list (or other linked data structure). `null` is also used to indicate an empty linked list (or other empty linked data structure).

- You can make a linked list (or other linked data structure) self-contained by making the node class an inner class of the linked list class.

- In many situations, a `clone` method or copy constructor is best defined so that it makes a deep copy.

- You can use an iterator to step through the elements of a collection, such as the elements in a linked list.

- Nodes in a doubly linked list have two links—one to the previous node in the list and one to the next node. This makes some operations such as insertion and deletion slightly easier.

- A stack is a data structure in which elements are removed in the reverse of the order they were added to the stack. A queue is a data structure in which elements are removed in the same order that they were added to the queue.

- Big-O notation specifies an upper bound for how many steps or how long a program will take to run based on the size of the input to the program. This can be used to analyze the efficiency of an algorithm.

- A hash table is a data structure that is used to store objects and retrieve them efficiently. A hash function is used to map an object to a value that can then be used to index the object.

- Linked lists can be used to implement sets, including common operations such as union, intersection, and set membership.

- A binary tree is a branching linked data structure consisting of nodes that each have two link instance variables. A tree has a special node called the root node. Every node in the tree can be reached from the root node by following links.

- If values are stored in a binary tree in such a way that the Binary Search Tree Storage Rule is followed, then there are efficient algorithms for reaching values stored in the tree.

Answers to Self-Test Exercises

1. ```
   mustard 1
   hot dogs 12
   apple pie 1
   ```

2. This method has been added to the class `LinkedList1` on the accompanying CD.

   ```java
   public boolean isEmpty( )
   {
       return (head == null);
   }
   ```

3. This method has been added to the class `LinkedList1` on the accompanying CD.

   ```java
   public void clear( )
   {
       head = null;
   }
   ```

   If you defined your method to remove all nodes using the `deleteHeadNode` method, your method is doing wasted work.

4. Yes. If we make the inner class `Node` a public inner class, it could be used outside the definition of `LinkedList2`, whereas leaving it as private means it cannot be used outside the definition of `LinkedList2`.

5. It would make no difference. Within the definition of an outer class there is full access to the members of an inner class whatever the inner class member's access modifier is. To put it another way, inside the private inner class `Node`, the modifiers `private` and `package access` are equivalent to `public`.

6. Because the outer class has direct access to the instance variables of the inner class `Node`, no access or mutator methods are needed for `Node`.

7. It would be legal, but it would be pretty much a useless method, because you cannot use the type `Node` outside of the class `LinkedList2`. For example, outside of the class `LinkedList2`, the following is illegal (`listObject` is of type `LinkedList2`):

   ```java
   Node v = listObject.startNode( ); //Illegal
   ```

   whereas the following would be legal outside of the class `LinkedList2` (although it's hard to think of anyplace you might use it):

   ```java
   Object v = listObject.startNode( );
   ```
   ```

```
8.  public class LinkedList2
    {
        public class Entry
        {
          private String item;
          private int count;

          public Entry( )
          {
              item = null;
              count = 0;
          }

          public Entry(String itemData, int countData)
          {
              item = itemData;
              count = countData;
          }

          public void setItem(String itemData )
          {
              item = itemData;
          }

          public void setCount(int countData)
          {
              count = countData;
          }

          public String getItem( )
          {
              return item;
          }

          public int getCount(  )
          {
              return count;
          }
        } // End of Entry inner class

        private class Node
        {
            private Entry item;
            private Node link;

            public Node( )
            {
                item = null;
                link = null;
            }
```

```
        public Node(Entry newItem, Node linkValue)
        {
            item = newItem;
            link = linkValue;
        }
    } //End of Node inner class

    private Node head;

    <Other definitions from LinkedList2 go here>

} // End of LinkedList2 class
```

The rest of the definition of LinkedList2 is essentially the same as in Display 15.7, but with the type String replaced by Entry. A complete definition is given in the subdirectory named "Exercise 8" on the CD that accompanies this text.

9. No, T is not guaranteed to have a copy constructor. Even if T has a copy constructor, it is illegal to use T with new like this.

10. No, you can use any descendent class of Object (which means any class type) as the returned type, because the value returned will still be of type Object.

11. The delete method must now search through the list to find the previous node and then change the link to bypass the current position. This is less efficient than the code in Display 15.17 since the reference to the previous node is already set.

```
public void delete( )
{
    if (position == null)
    {
        throw new IllegalStateException( );
    }
    else
    {
        Node current = head;
        Node previous = null;
        while (current != null)
        {
            if (current == position)
            {
                // Found the node to delete
                // Check if we're at the head
                if (previous == null)
                {
                    head = head.link;
                    position = head;
                }
                else// Delete in middle of list
                {
```

```
                    previous.link = position.link;
                    position = position.link;
                }
                return;
            }
            previous = current;   // Advance references
            current = current.link;
        }
    }
}
```

12. One problem with adding after the iterator's position is that there is no way to
    add to the front of the list. It would be possible to make a special case in which
    the new node were added to the front (e.g., if position is null, add the new data
    to the head) if desired.

    ```
    public void addAfterHere(String newData)
    {
        if (position == null && head != null)
        {
            // At end of list; can't add here
            throw new IllegalStateException( );
        }
        else if (head == null)
            // at head of empty list, add to front
            LinkedList2Iter.this.addToStart(newData);
        else
        {
            // Add after current position
            Node temp = new Node(newData, position.link);
            position.link = temp;
        }
    }
    ```

13. ```
    public void changeHere(String newData)
    {
        if (position == null)
            throw new IllegalStateException( );
        else
            position.item = newData;
    }
    ```

14. When invoking i.next( ), the value of the node that i is referencing is copied
    to a local variable, the iterator moves to the next node in the link, and then the
    value of the local variable is returned. Therefore, the value that i is referencing
    prior to the invocation is returned.

15. Insertion and deletion is slightly easier with the doubly linked list because we no
    longer need a separate instance variable to keep track of the previous node due to
    the previous link. However, all operations require updating more links (e.g.,
    both the next and previous instead of just the previous).
    ```

16. Use the iterator:

```
DoublyLinkedList.DoublyLinkedIterator i = list.iterator( );
i.restart( );
i.insertHere("Element At Front");
```

17. Pop the top of the stack and then push it back on:

```
String s = stack.pop( );
Stack.push(s);
// s contains the string on the top of the stack
```

18.
```
public void addToBack(String itemName)
{
    Node newEntry =
        new Node(itemName, null);
    if (front == null) //empty queue
    {
        back = newEntry;
        front = back;
    }
    else
    {
        back.link = newEntry;
        back = back.link;
    }
}
```

19. Just note that $aN + b \leq (a + b)N$, as long as $1 \leq N$.

20. This is mathematics, not Java. So, = will mean *equals*, not assignment.

    First note that $\log_a N = (\log_a b)(\log_b N)$.

    To see this first identity, just note that if you raise a to the power $\log_a N$, you get N, and if you raise a to the power $(\log_a b)(\log_b N)$ you also get N.

    If you set $c = (\log_a b)$, you get $\log_a N = c\ (\log_b N)$.

21. The simplest hash function is to map the ID number to the range of the hash table using the modulus operator:

```
hash = ID % N;      // N is the hash table size
```

22.
```
public void outputHashTable( )
{
  for (int i=0; i< SIZE; i++)
  {
    if (hashArray[i].size( ) > 0)
        hashArray[i].outputList( );
  }
}
```

23. This code is similar to `intersection`, but adds elements if they are not in `otherSet`:

```
public Set<T> difference(Set<T> otherSet)
{
  Set<T> diffSet = new Set<T>( );
  // Copy only items in this set but not otherSet
  Node<T> position = head;
  while (position != null)
  {
    if (!otherSet.contains(position.data))
        diffSet.add(position.data);
    position = position.link;
  }
  return diffSet;
}
```

24. As implemented above the complexity is identical to the `intersection` method. For every element in the set, we invoke the `contains` method of `otherSet`. This requires $O(nm)$ steps, where n is the number of items in the calling object's set and m is the number of items in `otherSet`'s set.

25. No.

26. Change

```
showElementsInSubtree(subTreeRoot.leftLink);
System.out.print(subTreeRoot.data + " ");
showElementsInSubtree(subTreeRoot.rightLink);
```

to

```
showElementsInSubtree(subTreeRoot.rightLink);
System.out.print(subTreeRoot.data + " ");
showElementsInSubtree(subTreeRoot.leftLink);
```

Programming Projects

 Many of these Programming Projects can be solved using AW's MyCodeMate. To access these please go to: www.mycodemate.com.

1. In an ancient land, the beautiful princess Eve had many suitors. She decided on the following procedure to determine which suitor she would marry. First, all of the suitors would be lined up one after the other and assigned numbers. The first suitor would be number 1, the second number 2, and so on up to the last suitor, number n. Starting at the suitor in the first position, she would then count three suitors down the line (because of the three letters in her name), and the third suitor would be eliminated from winning her hand and removed from the line.

Eve would then continue, counting three more suitors, and eliminate every third suitor. When she reached the end of the line, she would continue counting from the beginning.

For example, if there were six suitors, the elimination process would proceed as follows:

123456	Initial list of suitors; start counting from 1.
12456	Suitor 3 eliminated; continue counting from 4.
1245	Suitor 6 eliminated; continue counting from 1.
125	Suitor 4 eliminated; continue counting from 5.
15	Suitor 2 eliminated; continue counting from 5.
1	Suitor 5 eliminated; 1 is the lucky winner.

Write a program that creates a circular linked list of nodes to determine which position you should stand in to marry the princess if there are *n* suitors. Your program should simulate the elimination process by deleting the node that corresponds to the suitor that is eliminated for each step in the process.

 2. Although the `long` data type can store large integers, it can't store extremely large values such as an integer with 200 digits. Create a `HugeNumber` class that uses a linked list of digits to represent integers of arbitrary length. The class should have a method to add a new most significant digit to the existing number so that longer and longer numbers can be created. Also add methods to reset the number and to return the value of the huge integer as a `String` along with appropriate constructor or accessor methods. Write code to test your class.

Note: Use of a doubly linked list will make the next problem easier to implement.

3. Add a copy constructor to the `HugeNumber` class described in the previous problem that makes a deep copy of the input `HugeNumber`. Also create an `add` method that adds an input `HugeNumber` to the instance's `HugeNumber` value and returns a new `HugeNumber` that is set to the sum of the two values. Write code to test the additions to your class.

 4. Give the definition of a generic class that uses a doubly linked list of data items. Include a copy constructor, an `equals` method, a `clone` method, a `toString` method, a method to produce an iterator, and any other methods that would normally be expected. Write a suitable test program.

5. Complete the definition of the binary search tree class `IntTree` in Display 15.39 by adding the following: Make `IntTree` implement the `Cloneable` interface, including the definition of a `clone` method; add a copy constructor; add an `equals` method; add a method named `sameContents` as described later in this project; add a `toString` method; and add a method to produce an iterator. Define `equals` so that two trees are equal if (and only if) the two trees have the exact same shape and have the same numbers in corresponding nodes. The `clone` method and the copy con-

structor should each produce a deep copy that is equal to the original list according to the equals method. The boolean valued method sameContents has one parameter of type IntTree and returns true if the calling object and the argument tree contain exactly the same numbers, and returns false otherwise. Note that equals and sameContents are not the same. Also, write a suitable test program.

6. Write an addSorted method for the generic linked list from Display 15.8 such that the method adds a new node in the correct location so that the list remains in sorted order. Note that this will require that the type parameter T extend the Comparable interface. Write a suitable test program.

7. Add a remove method and an iterator for the Set class in Display 15.37. Write a suitable test program.

8. The hash table from Display 15.34 hashed a string to an integer and stored the same string in the hash table. Modify the program so that instead of storing strings it stores Employee objects as defined in Display 7.2. Use the name instance variable as the input to the hash function. The modification will require changes to the linked list, since the LinkedList2 class only created linked lists of strings. For the most generality, modify the hash table so that it uses the generic LinkedList3 class defined in Display 15.8. You will also need to add a get method that returns the Employee object stored in the hash table that corresponds to the input name. Test your program by adding and retrieving several names, including names that hash to the same slot in the hash table.

9. Display 15.34 and 15.35 provide the beginnings of a spell checker. Refine the program to make it more useful. The modified program should read in a text file, parse each word, see if it is in the hash table, and, if not, output the line number and word of the potentially misspelled word. Discard any punctuation in the original text file. Use the words.txt file as the basis for the hash table dictionary. This file can be found on the CD accompanying the textbook and also on the book's website. The file contains 45,407 common words and names in the English language. Note that some words are capitalized. Test your spell checker on a short text document.

10. Change the Set<T> class of Display 15.37 so that internally it uses a hash table to store its data instead of a linked list. The headers of the public methods should remain the same so that a program such as the demonstration in Display 15.38 should still work without requiring any changes. Add a constructor that allows the user of the new Set<T> class to specify the size of the hash table array.

For an additional challenge, implement the set using both a hash table and a linked list. Items added to the set should be stored using both data structures. Any operation requiring lookup of an item should use the hash table, and any operation requiring iteration through the items should use the linked list.

16

Collections, Maps and Iterators

Science is built up with facts, as a house is with stones. But a collection of facts is no more science than a heap of stones is a house.

JULES HENRI POINCARÈ, Quoted by Bertrand Russell in the preface to
Science and Method

Introduction

collection

iterator

A **collection** is a data structure for holding elements. For example, an `ArrayList<T>` object is a collection. Java has a repertoire of interfaces and classes that give a uniform treatment of collections. An **iterator** is an object that cycles through all the elements in a collection. In this chapter we discuss collections and iterators.

Prerequisites

Sections 16.1 to 16.3 can be considered one single large topic. These three sections require Chapters 1 through 9, Section 13.1 of Chapter 13, which covers interfaces, Chapter 14 on generics and the `ArrayList<T>` class, and Chapter 15 on linked data structures. The material on inner classes in Chapter 13 (Sections 13.2 and 13.3) is not needed except for a brief reference in the Programming Tip entitled "Defining Your Own Iterator Classes," which requires Section 13.2 (but not 13.3).

None of the material in this chapter is needed for the material on Swing and GUIs. So, you may skip this chapter and go directly to Chapter 17 if you prefer to cover Swing GUIs before considering the material of this chapter.

16.1 Collections

*Put all your eggs in one basket and
—WATCH THAT BASKET.*

MARK TWAIN, Pudd'nhead Wilson

A Java collection is a class that holds objects. This concept is made precise by the `Collection<T>` interface. A Java collection is any class that implements the `Collection<T>` interface. As we shall see, many of these classes can be used as predefined data structures similar to those we defined ourselves in Chapter 15. One example of a Java collection class, which you saw in Chapter 14, is the `ArrayList<T>` class. The `Collection<T>` interface allows you to write code that applies to all Java collections so that you do not have to rewrite the code for each specific collection type. There are other interfaces and abstract classes that are in some sense or another produced from the `Collection<T>`

interface. Some of these are shown in Display 16.1. In this section, we give you an introduction to this Java collection framework. The topic is too large to treat exhaustively in this book, so this can only be an introductory treatment.

Collections are used along with *iterators*, which are discussed in Section 16.3. Separating collections and iterators into two sections turns out to be a handy way of organizing the material, but the two topics of collections and iterators are intimately intertwined. In practice, you normally use them together.

Display 16.1   **The Collection Landscape**

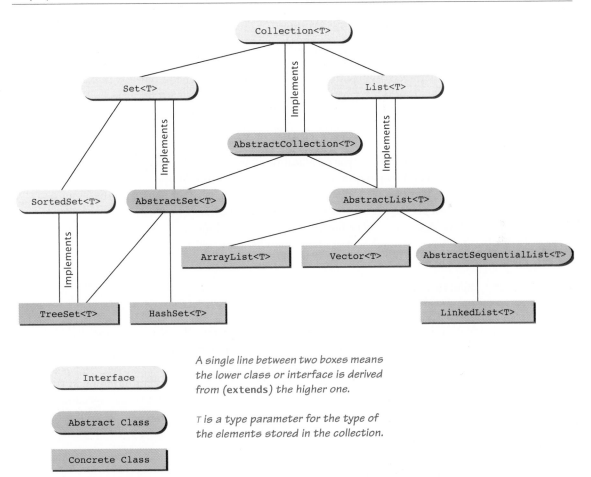

Before we discuss the Collection<T> interface, we need a brief detour to learn a bit more about parameter type specifications.

Wildcards

Classes and interfaces in the collection framework use some parameter type specifications that we have not seen before. For example, they allow you to say things such as, "The argument must be a ArrayList<T> but it can have any base type." More generally these new parameter type specifications use generic classes but do not fully specify the type plugged in for the type parameter. Because they specify a wide range of argument types, they are known as **wildcards**.

wildcard <?>   The easiest wildcard to understand is <?>, which says that you can use any type in place of the type parameter. For example,

```
public void sampleMethod(String arg1, ArrayList<?> arg2)
```

is invoked with two arguments. The first argument must be of type String. The second argument can be a ArrayList<T> with any base type.

Note that ArrayList<?> is different from ArrayList<Object>. For example, if the type specification is ArrayList<?>, then you can plug in an argument of type ArrayList<String> (as well as other types); you cannot plug in an argument of type ArrayList<String> if the type specification is ArrayList<Object>.

You can place a bound on a wildcard saying the type used in place of the wildcard must be an ancestor type or a descendent type of some class or interface. For example,

extends   <? extends String> says that the argument plugged in can be an object of any descendent class of the class String. The notation, restrictions, and meaning are the same as what we described for type bounds such as <T extends String>, which we discussed in Chapter 14.

For example,

```
public void
        anotherMethod(String arg1, ArrayList<? extends String> arg2)
```

is invoked with two arguments. The first argument must be of type String, but the second argument can be of any ArrayList<T> object provided the base type of the ArrayList<T> is a descendent type of String.

super   To specify that the wildcard type be an ancestor type of some class or interface, you use super rather than extends. For example, ArrayList<? super String> specifies an ArrayList<T> whose base type can be any ancestor class of the class String. As it turns out, we will have no occasion to use wildcard types involving super.

The Collection Framework

The Collection<T> interface is the highest level of Java's framework for collection classes. The Collection<T> interface describes the basic operations that all collection classes should implement. A summary of these operations (method headings) for the Collection<T> interface are given in Display 16.2. A more complete description can be found in Appendix 5. Because an interface is a type, you can define methods with a parameter of type Collection<T>. That parameter can be filled in with an argument that is an object of any class in the collection framework (that is, any class that implements the Collection<T> interface). This turns out to be a very powerful tool. Let's explore the possibilities. So far, we have seen one class that implements the Collection<T> interface, namely the class ArrayList<T>. In addition to the methods given in Chapter 14 for the ArrayList<T> class, the ArrayList<T> class also implements all the methods given in Display 16.2. There are a number of different predefined classes that implement the Collection<T> interface, and you can define your own classes that implement the Collection<T> interface. If you write a method to manipulate a parameter of type Collection<T>, it will work for all of these classes. Also, the methods in the Collection<T> interface ensure that you can intermix the use of different collection classes. For example, consider the method

```
public boolean containsAll(Collection<?> collectionOfTargets)
```

You can use this with two ArrayList<T> objects (one the calling object and one the argument) to see if one contains all the elements of the other. The two ArrayList<T> objects do not even have to have the same base type. Moreover, you can also use it with an ArrayList<T> object and an object of any other class that implements the Collection<T> interface to compare the elements in these two different kinds of Collection<T> objects.

Display 16.2 Method Headings in the **Collection<T>** Interface (part 1 of 3)

The Collection<T> interface is in the **java.util** package.

CONSTRUCTORS

Although not officially required by the interface, any class that implements the Collection<T> interface should have at least two constructors: a no-argument constructor that creates an empty Collection<T> object, and a constructor with one parameter of type Collection<? extends T> that creates a Collection<T> object with the same elements as the constructor argument. The interface does not specify whether the copy produced by the one-argument constructor is a shallow copy or a deep copy of its argument.

METHODS

```
boolean isEmpty( )
```
Returns **true** if the calling object is empty; otherwise returns **false**.

```
public boolean contains(Object target)
```
Returns **true** if the calling object contains at least one instance of **target**. Uses **target.equals** to determine if **target** is in the calling object.

(continued)

Display 16.2 Method Headings in the `Collection<T>` Interface (part 2 of 3)

```
public boolean containsAll(Collection<?> collectionOfTargets)
```

Returns **true** if the calling object contains all of the elements in `collectionOfTargets`. For an element in `collectionOfTargets`, this method uses `element.equals` to determine if `element` is in the calling object.

```
public boolean equals(Object other)
```

This is the **equals** of the collection, not the **equals** of the elements in the collection. Overrides the inherited method **equals**. Although there are no official constraints on **equals** for a collection, it should be defined as we have described in Chapter 7 and also to satisfy the intuitive notion of collections being equal.

```
public int size( )
```

Returns the number of elements in the calling object. If the calling object contains more than `Integer.MAX_VALUE` elements, returns `Integer.MAX_VALUE`.

```
Iterator<T> iterator( )
```

Returns an iterator for the calling object. (Iterators are discussed in Section 16.3.)

```
public Object[ ] toArray( )
```

Returns an array containing all of the elements in the calling object. If the calling object makes any guarantees as to what order its elements are returned by its iterator, this method must return the elements in the same order.

The array returned should be a new array so that the calling object has no references to the returned array. (You might also want the elements in the array to be clones of the elements in the collection. However, this is apparently not required by the interface, since library classes, such as `Vector<T>`, return arrays that contain references to the elements in the collection.)

```
public <E> E[ ] toArray(E[ ] a)
```

Note that the type parameter E is not the same as T. So, E can be any reference type; it need not be the type T in `Collection<T>`. For example, E might be an ancestor type of T.

Returns an array containing all of the elements in the calling object. The argument *a* is used primarily to specify the type of the array returned. The exact details are as follows:

The type of the returned array is that of *a*. If the elements in the calling object fit in the array *a*, then *a* is used to hold the elements of the returned array; otherwise a new array is created with the same type as *a*.

If *a* has more elements than the calling object, the element in *a* immediately following the end of the copied elements is set to `null`.

If the calling object makes any guarantees as to what order its elements are returned by its iterator, this method must return the elements in the same order. (Iterators are discussed in Section 16.3.)

```
public int hashCode( )
```

Returns the hash code value for the calling object.

Display 16.2   Method Headings in the **Collection<T>** Interface (part 3 of 3)

OPTIONAL METHODS

The following methods are optional, which means they still must be implemented, but the implementation can simply throw an **UnsupportedOperationException** if, for some reason, you do not want to give them a "real" implementation. An **UnsupportedOperationException** is a **RunTimeException** and so is not required to be caught or declared in a **throws** clause.

public boolean add(T element) *(Optional)*

Ensures that the calling object contains the specified **element**. Returns **true** if the calling object changed as a result of the call. Returns **false** if the calling object does not permit duplicates and already contains **element**; also returns **false** if the calling object does not change for any other reason.

public boolean addAll(Collection<? extends T> collectionToAdd) *(Optional)*

Ensures that the calling object contains all the elements in **collectionToAdd**. Returns **true** if the calling object changed as a result of the call; returns **false** otherwise.

public boolean remove(Object element) *(Optional)*

Removes a single instance of the element from the calling object, if it is present. Returns **true** if the calling object contained the element; returns **false** otherwise.

public boolean removeAll(Collection<?> collectionToRemove) *(Optional)*

Removes all the calling object's elements that are also contained in **collectionToRemove**. Returns **true** if the calling object was changed; otherwise returns **false**.

public void clear( ) *(Optional)*

Removes all the elements from the calling object.

public boolean retainAll(Collection<?> saveElements) *(Optional)*

Retains only the elements in the calling object that are also contained in the collection **saveElements**. In other words, removes from the calling object all of its elements that are not contained in the collection **saveElements**. Returns **true** if the calling object was changed; otherwise returns **false**.

Packages

All the collection classes and interfaces discussed in this chapter are in the **java.util** package.

The relationships between some of the classes and interfaces that implement or extend the **Collection<T>** interface are given in Display 16.1. There are two main interfaces that extend the **Collection<T>** interface: the **Set<T>** interface and the **List<T>** interface. Classes that implement the **Set<T>** interface do not allow an element

Set<T> List
interfaces

in the class to occur more than once. Classes that implement the List<T> interface have their elements ordered on a list, so there is a zeroth element, a first element, a second element, and so forth. A class that implements the List<T> interface allows elements to occur more than once. The ArrayList<T> class implements the List<T> interface.

The Set<T> interface has the same method headings as the Collection<T> interface, but in some cases the semantics (intended meanings) are different. For example, the semantics of adding new elements to the set do not allow duplicates. The add methods are described in Display 16.3. A complete list of the Set<T> interface is given in Appendix 5.

Display 16.3 Adding Elements in the Set<T> Interface

The Set<T> interface is in the `java.util` package.

The Set<T> interface extends the Collection<T> interface and has all the same method headings given in Display 16.2. However, the semantics of the add methods vary as described below.

```
public boolean add(T element) (Optional)
```

If element is not already in the calling object, element is added to the calling object and **true** is returned. If element is in the calling object, the calling object is unchanged and **false** is returned.

```
public boolean addAll(Collection<? extends T> collectionToAdd) (Optional)
```

Ensures that the calling object contains all the elements in `collectionToAdd`. Returns **true** if the calling object changed as a result of the call; returns **false** otherwise. Thus, if `collectionToAdd` is a Set<T>, then the calling object is changed to the union of itself with `collectionToAdd`.

The List<T> interface has more method headings than the Collection<T> interface, and some of the methods inherited from the Collection<T> interface receive somewhat different semantics. For example, the semantics of adding new elements to the set allow duplicates, and rules must be made about which element should be removed when there are duplicates. These methods, along with new method definitions, are described in Display 16.4. A complete list of the List<T> interface is given in Appendix 5.

Display 16.4 Selected Methods in the List<T> Interface (part 1 of 3)

The List<T> interface is in the `java.util` package.

The List<T> interface extends the Collection<T> interface.

ADDING AND REMOVING ELEMENTS

```
public boolean add(T element) (Optional)
```

Adds element to the end of the calling object's list. Normally returns **true**. Returns **false** if the operation failed, but if the operation failed, something is seriously wrong and you will probably get a run-time error anyway.

Display 16.4 **Selected Methods in the List<T> Interface** (part 2 of 3)

```
public boolean addAll(Collection<? extends T> collectionToAdd) (Optional)
```

Adds all of the elements in collectionToAdd to the end of the calling object's list. The elements are added in the order they are produced by an iterator for collectionToAdd.

```
public boolean remove(Object element) (Optional)
```

Removes the first occurrence of element from the calling object's list, if it is present. Returns true if the calling object contained the element; returns false otherwise.

```
public boolean removeAll(Collection<?> collectionToRemove) (Optional)
```

Removes all the calling object's elements that are also in collectionToRemove. Returns true if the calling object was changed; otherwise returns false.

NEW METHOD HEADINGS

The following methods are in the List<T> interface but were not in the Collection<T> interface. Those that are optional are noted.

```
public void add(int index, T newElement) (Optional)
```

Inserts newElement in the calling object's list at location index. The old elements at location index and higher are moved to higher indices.

```
public boolean addAll(int index,
                      Collection<? extends T> collectionToAdd) (Optional)
```

Inserts all of the elements in collectionToAdd to the calling object's list starting at location index. The old elements at location index and higher are moved to higher indices. The elements are added in the order they are produced by an iterator for collectionToAdd.

```
public T get(int index)
```

Returns the object at position index.

```
public T set(int index, T newElement) (Optional)
```

Sets the element at the specified index to newElement. The element previously at that position is returned.

```
public T remove(int index) (Optional)
```

Removes the element at position index in the calling object. Shifts any subsequent elements to the left (subtracts one from their indices). Returns the element that was removed from the calling object.

```
public int indexOf(Object target)
```

Returns the index of the first element that is equal to target. Uses the method equals of the object target to test for equality. Returns 1 if target is not found.

(continued)

Display 16.4   Selected Methods in the **List<T>** Interface (part 3 of 3)

`public int lastIndexOf(Object target)`

Returns the index of the last element that is equal to **target**. Uses the method **equals** of the object **target** to test for equality. Returns 1 if target is not found.

`public List<T> subList(int fromIndex, int toIndex)`

Returns a *view* of the elements at locations **fromIndex** to **toIndex** of the calling object; the object at **fromIndex** is included; the object, if any, at **toIndex** is not included. The *view* uses references into the calling object; so, changing the *view* can change the calling object. The returned object will be of type **List<T>** but need not be of the same type as the calling object. Returns an empty **List<T>** if **fromIndex** equals **toIndex**.

`ListIterator<T> listIterator( )`

Returns a list iterator for the calling object. (Iterators are discussed in Section 16.3.)

`ListIterator<T> listIterator(int index)`

Returns a list iterator for the calling object starting at **index**. The first element to be returned by the iterator is the one at **index**. (Iterators are discussed in Section 16.3.)

Collection Interfaces

The primary interfaces for collection classes are the **Collection<T>**, **Set<T>**, and **List<T>** interfaces. Both the **Set<T>** and the **List<T>** interfaces are derived from the **Collection<T>** interface. The **Set<T>** interface is for collections that do not allow repetition of elements and do not impose an order on their elements. The **List<T>** interface is for collections that do allow repetition of elements and do impose an order on their elements.

For-Each Loops

You can use a for-each loop with any of the collections discussed in this chapter.

PITFALL: Optional Operations

What is the point of an optional method heading in an interface? The whole point of an interface is to specify what methods can be used with an object of the interface type so that you can write code for an arbitrary object of the interface type. The reasoning behind these optional methods is that they normally would be implemented, but in unusual situations a programmer may leave them "unsupported." (The alternative would be to have two interfaces, one with and one without the optional operations. Uncharacteristically, Java designers opted for a smaller number of interfaces.) But there is still more to the story.

PITFALL: (continued)

The optional methods are not, strictly speaking, optional. Like the other methods in an interface, the optional methods must have a method body so that the optional method heading is converted to a complete method definition. So, what's optional? The "optional" refers to the semantics of the method. If the method is optional, then you may give it a trivial implementation and you will not have shirked your responsibility to follow the (unenforced) semantics for the interface.

To keep these optional methods from producing unexplained failures, the interface semantics say that if you do not give an optional method a "real" implementation, then you should have the method body throw an `UnsupportedOperationException`. For example, the `add` method of the `Collection<T>` interface is optional and so can be implemented as follows (provided you have good reason for this):

```java
public boolean add(T element)
{
    throw new UnsupportedOperationException( );
}
```

The `UnsupportedOperationException` class is a derived class of the `RunTimeException` class, so an `UnsupportedOperationException` is an unchecked exception, meaning it need not be caught in a `catch` block or declared in a `throws` clause.

The intention is that the code for a class that implements an interface with optional methods would be written and used in such a way that this `UnsupportedOperation` `Exception` would only be thrown during debugging. These rules on optional methods are part of the semantics of the interface, and like all other parts of the semantics of an interface, they depend entirely on the good will and responsibility of the programmer defining the class that implements the interface. ■

Optional Methods

When an interface lists a method as "optional," you still need to implement it when defining a class that implements the interface. However, if you do not want to give it a "real" definition, you can simply have the method body throw an `UnsupportedOperationException`.

TIP: Dealing with All Those Exceptions

If you examine the `Collection<T>`, `Set<T>`, and `List<T>` interfaces in Appendix 5 you will see that many of the methods are liberally sprinkled with statements that certain exceptions are thrown. All these exception classes are unchecked exceptions, meaning that they need not be caught in a `catch` block and need not be declared in a `throws` clause. They are there primarily for debugging. If you are using an existing collection class, you can view them as run-time error messages. If you are defining a class as a derived class of some other collection class, then most or all of the exception throwing

(continued)

TIP: (continued)

will be inherited, so you need not worry too much about it. If you are defining a collection class from scratch and want your class to implement one of the collection interfaces, then you do need to throw suitable exceptions as specified for the interface.

With one exception (no pun intended), all the exception classes mentioned in this chapter are in the package java.lang and so do not require any import statement. The one exception is the NoSuchElementException, which is used with iterators in Section 16.3. The NoSuchElementException is in the java.util package, which requires an import statement if your code mentions the NoSuchElementException class. ■

Self-Test Exercises

1. Give the definition of a boolean valued static generic method named inSome. The method inSome has two parameters of type Collection<T> and one parameter of type T. The method returns true if the parameter of type T is in either (or both) collections; it returns false otherwise.

2. Give the definition of a static generic method named getFirst that has one parameter of type List<T> and a return type of T. The method returns the first element in the list or null if the list is empty.

3. Give the definition of a static boolean valued method named noNull. The method noNull has one parameter of type Set<?> and removes null from the set if null is in the set; otherwise it leaves the set unchanged. The method returns true if the set is changed and false if it is not changed.

Concrete Collection Classes

Abstract-Set<T>
Abstract-List<T>

The abstract classes AbstractSet<T> and AbstractList<T> are there for convenience when implementing the Set<T> and List<T> interfaces, respectively. They have almost no methods beyond those in the interfaces they implement. Although these two abstract classes have only a few abstract methods, the other (nonabstract) methods have fairly useless implementations that must be overridden. When defining a derived class of either AbstractSet<T> or AbstractList<T>, you need to define not just the abstract methods but also all the methods you intend to use. It usually makes more sense to simply use (or define derived classes of) the HashSet<T>, ArrayList<T>, or Vector<T> classes, which are derived classes of AbstractSet<T> and AbstractList<T> and are full implementations of the Set<T> and List<T> interfaces.

Abstract-Collection<T>

The abstract class AbstractCollection<T> is a skeleton class for the Collection<T> interface. Although it is perfectly legal, you seldom, if ever, need to define a derived class of the AbstractCollection<T> class. Instead, you normally define a derived class of one of the descendent classes of the AbstractCollection<T> class.

HashSet<T>

If you want a class that implements the Set<T> interface and do not need any methods beyond those in the Set<T> interface, you can use the concrete class HashSet<T>. So, after all is said and done, if all you need is a collection class that does not allow elements to occur more than once, then you can use the HashSet<T> class and need not worry about all the other classes and interfaces in Display 16.1. The word "Hash" refers to the fact that the HashSet<T> class is implemented using a hash table, which was introduced in Chapter 15. The HashSet<T>, of course, implements all the methods in the Set<T> interface and adds no other methods beyond constructors. A summary of the Hash-Set<T> constructors and other methods is given in Display 16.5. If you want to define your own class that implements the Set<T> interface, you would probably be better off using the HashSet<T> class rather than the AbstractSet<T> class as a base class.

Display 16.5   Methods in the HashSet<T> Class

The HashSet<T> class is in the java.util package.

The HashSet<T> class extends the AbstractSet<T> class and implements the Set<T> interface.

The HashSet<T> class implements all of the methods in the Set<T> interface (Display 16.3). The only other methods in the HashSet<T> class are the constructors. The three constructors that do not involve concepts beyond the scope of this book are given below.

All the exception classes mentioned are the kind that are not required to be caught in a **catch** block or declared in a **throws** clause.

All the exception classes mentioned are in the package java.lang and so do not require any import statement.

```
public HashSet( )
```
Creates a new, empty set.

```
public HashSet(Collection<? extends T> c )
```
Creates a new set that contains all the elements of c. Throws a NullPointerException if c is null.

```
public HashSet(int initialCapacity)
```
Creates a new, empty set with the specified capacity.

Throws an IllegalArgumentException if initialCapacity is less than zero.

The methods are the same as those described for the Set<T> interface (Display 16.3.)

Display 16.6 shows a sample program that uses the HashSet<T> class. This program is conceptually similar to the program in Display 15.38, in which sets containing strings of round things and green things were manipulated in various ways using our own Set<T> class implemented with linked lists. However, the code listing in Display 16.6 uses the HashSet<T> class in place of our custom Set<T> class. Nevertheless, most of the code is identical because the Set<T> class was designed to have an interface similar to the HashSet<T> class. Both have add and contains methods. Functionality similar to our union and intersection methods can be achieved by using the HashSet<T> add-All and removeAll methods. To output the items in a HashSet<T> object we define an outputSet method. This method uses iterators, which are not discussed until Section 16.3, so for now you can ignore the details of how outputSet works.

In general, it is recommended that you use the collection classes unless they do not provide the functionality you need for your program. For example, say that you want every item added to the set to have a reference to the set that contains it. This could be useful if you want to determine whether two items are in the same set—you could just follow the reference to the containing set for each item and see whether they were the same. Without such a reference you would have to invoke the contains method for every set to learn whether the items were in the same set. If this were an important feature for your program, you might want to develop your own class instead of using one of the collection classes. If the collection classes were sufficient, the result would be shorter code that is generally easier to develop and maintain. Moreover, the collection classes like HashSet<T> have been designed with efficiency and scalability in mind.

Display 16.6 **HashSet<T> Class Demo** (part 1 of 3)

```
1    import java.util.HashSet;
2    import java.util.Iterator;
3    public class HashSetDemo
4    {
5        private static void outputSet(HashSet<String> set)
6        {
7            Iterator<String> i = set.iterator( );
8            while (i.hasNext( ))
9                System.out.print(i.next( ) + " ");
10           System.out.println( );
11       }
12
13       public static void main(String[] args)
14       {
15           HashSet<String> round = new HashSet<String>( );
16           HashSet<String> green = new HashSet<String>( );
17
18           // Add some data to each set
19           round.add("peas");
20           round.add("ball");
21           round.add("pie");
22           round.add("grapes");
23
24           green.add("peas");
25           green.add("grapes");
26           green.add("garden hose");
27           green.add("grass");
```

The outputSet method uses an iterator to print the contents of a HashSet<T> object. Iterators are described in Section 16.3.

Display 16.6   **HashSet<T> Class Demo** (part 2 of 3)

```
25              System.out.println("Contents of set round: ");
26              outputSet(round);
27              System.out.println("\nContents of set green: ");
28              outputSet(green);

29              System.out.println("\nball in set 'round'? " +
30                      round.contains("ball"));
31              System.out.println("ball in set 'green'? " +
32                      green.contains("ball"));

33              System.out.println("\nball and peas in same set? " +
34                      ((round.contains("ball") &&
35                       (round.contains("peas"))) ||
36                      (green.contains("ball") &&
37                       (green.contains("peas")))));
38              System.out.println("pie and grass in same set? " +
39                      ((round.contains("pie") &&
40                       (round.contains("grass"))) ||
41                      (green.contains("pie") &&
42                       (green.contains("grass")))));

43              // To union two sets we use the addAll method.
44              HashSet<String> setUnion = new HashSet<String>(round);
45              round.addAll(green);
46              System.out.println("\nUnion of green and round:");
47              outputSet(setUnion);

48              // To intersect two sets we use the removeAll method.
49              HashSet<String> setInter = new HashSet<String>(round);
50              setInter.removeAll(green);
51              System.out.println("\nIntersection of green and round:");
52              outputSet(setInter);
53              System.out.println( );
54      }
55  }
```

Sample Dialogue

```
Contents of set round:
grapes pie ball peas

Contents of set green:
grass garden hose grapes peas
```

(continued)

Display 16.6   **HashSet<T>** Class Demo (part 3 of 3)

```
ball in set round?   true
ball in set green?   false

ball and peas in same set? true
pie and grass in same set? false

Union of green and round:
garden hose grass peas ball pie grapes

Intersection of green and round:
peas grapes
```

Vector<T>

If you want a class that implements the List<T> interface and do not need any methods beyond those in the List<T> interface, you can use the ArrayList<T> or Vector<T> class. So, after all is said and done, if all you need is a collection class that allows elements to occur more than once, or you need a collection that orders its elements as on a list (that is, as in an array), or you need a class that has both of these properties, then you can use the ArrayList<T> or Vector<T> class and need not worry about all the other classes and interfaces in Display 16.1. The ArrayList<T> and Vector<T> classes implement all the methods in the List<T> interface. A table of methods for the ArrayList<T> class was given in Chapter 14 and a more complete table is given in Display 16.7. A table of methods for the Vector<T> class is also given in Display 16.7. A more complete list of the methods in these classes is given in Appendix 5. If you want to define your own class that implements the List<T> interface, you would probably be better off using either the ArrayList<T> or the Vector<T> class rather than the AbstractList<T> class as a base class.

Abstract–
Sequential–
List<T>

Linked–
List<T>

The abstract class AbstractSequentialList<T> is derived from the AbstractList<T> class. Although it does override some methods inherited from the class AbstractList<T>, it adds no completely new methods. The point of the AbstractSequentialList<T> class is to provide for efficient implementation of sequentially moving through the list at the expense of having inefficient implementation of random access to elements (that is, inefficient implementation of the get method). The LinkedList<T> class is a concrete derived class of the abstract class AbstractSequentialList<T>. (The implementation of the LinkedList<T> class is similar to that of the linked list classes we discussed in Chapter 15.) If you need a List<T> with efficient random access to elements (that is, efficient implementation of the get method), then use the ArrayList<T> or Vector<T> class or a class derived from one of these two classes. If you do not need efficient random access but need to efficiently move sequentially through the list, then use the LinkedList<T> class or a class derived from the LinkedList<T> class.

SortedSet<T>

TreeSet<T>

The interface SortedSet<T> and the concrete class TreeSet<T> are designed for implementations of the Set<T> interface that provide for rapid retrieval of elements (efficient implementation of the contains and similar methods). The implementation of the class is similar to the binary tree class discussed in Chapter 15 but with more sophisticated ways to do inserting that keep the tree balanced. We will not discuss the SortedSet<T> interface or the TreeSet<T> class in this text, but you should be aware of their existence so you know what to look for in the Java documentation should you need them.

Display 16.7 Methods in the Classes `ArrayList<T>` and `Vector<T>` (part 1 of 4)

The `ArrayList<T>` and `Vector<T>` classes and the `Iterator<T>` and `ListIterator<T>` interfaces are in the `java.util` package.

All the exception classes mentioned are unchecked exceptions, which means they are not required to be caught in a `catch` block or declared in a `throws` clause. (If you have not yet studied exceptions, you can consider the exceptions to be run-time error messages.)

`NoSuchElementException` is in the `java.util` package, which requires an import statement if your code mentions the `NoSuchElementException` class. All the other exception classes mentioned are in the package `java.lang` and so do not require any import statement.

CONSTRUCTORS

```
public ArrayList(int initialCapacity)
```

Creates an empty `ArrayList<T>` with the specified initial capacity. When the `ArrayList<T>` needs to increase its capacity, the capacity doubles.

```
public ArrayList( )
```

Creates an empty `ArrayList<T>` with an initial capacity of 10. When the `ArrayList<T>` needs to increase its capacity, the capacity doubles.

```
public ArrayList(Collection<? extends T> c)
```

Creates a `ArrayList<T>` that contains all the elements of the collection `c`, in the same order. In other words, the elements have the same index in the `ArrayList<T>` created as they do in `c`. This is not quite a **true** copy constructor because it does not preserve capacity. The capacity of the created list will be `c.size( )`, not `c.capacity`.

The `ArrayList<T>` created is only a shallow copy of the collection argument. The `ArrayList<T>` created contains references to the elements in `c` (not references to clones of the elements in `c`).

```
public Vector(int initialCapacity)
```

Creates an empty vector with the specified initial capacity. When the vector needs to increase its capacity, the capacity doubles.

```
public Vector( )
```

Creates an empty vector with an initial capacity of 10. When the vector needs to increase its capacity, the capacity doubles.

```
public Vector(Collection<? extends T> c)
```

Creates a vector that contains all the elements of the collection `c`, in the same order. In other words, the elements have the same index in the vector created as they do in `c`. This is not quite a **true** copy constructor because it does not preserve capacity. The capacity of the created vector will be `c.size( )`, not `c.capacity`.

The vector created is only a shallow copy of the collection argument. The vector created contains references to the elements in `c` (not references to clones of the elements in `c`).

(continued)

Display 16.7   Methods in the Classes `ArrayList<T>` and `Vector<T>` (part 2 of 4)

public Vector(int initialCapacity, int capacityIncrement)

Constructs an empty vector with the specified initial capacity and capacity increment. When the vector needs to grow, it will add room for **capacityIncrement** more items.
    (`ArrayList<T>` does not have a corresponding constructor.)

ARRAYLIKE METHODS FOR BOTH `ArrayList<T>` AND `Vector<T>`

public T set(int index, T newElement)

Sets the element at the specified **index** to **newElement**. The element previously at that position is returned. If you draw an analogy to an array *a*, this is analogous to setting a[index] to the value **newElement**. The **index** must be a value greater than or equal to zero and strictly less than the current size of the list.

public T get(int index)

Returns the element at the specified index. This is analogous to returning a[index] for an array *a*. The index must be a value greater than or equal to 0 and less than the current size of the calling object.

METHODS TO ADD ELEMENTS FOR BOTH `ArrayList<T>` AND `Vector<T>`

public boolean add(T newElement)

Adds **newElement** to the end of the calling object's list and increases its size by one. The capacity of the calling object is increased if that is required. Returns **true** if the add was successful. This method is often used as if it were a **void** method.

public void add(int index, T newElement)

Inserts **newElement** as an element in the calling object at the specified index and increases the size of the calling object by one. Each element in the calling object with an index greater than or equal to index is shifted upward to have an index that is one greater than the value it had previously.

The index must be a value greater than or equal to zero and less than or equal to the size of the calling object (before this addition).

Note that you can use this method to add an element after the last current element. The capacity of the calling object is increased if that is required.

public boolean addAll(Collection<? extends T> c)

Appends all the elements in **c** to the end of the elements in the calling object in the order that they are enumerated by a **c** iterator. The behavior of this method is not guaranteed if the collection **c** is the calling object or any collection including the calling object either directly or indirectly.

public boolean addAll(int index, Collection<? extends T> c)

Inserts all the elements in **c** into the calling object starting at position **index**. Elements are inserted in the order that they are enumerated by a **c** iterator. Elements previously at positions **index** or higher are shifted to higher numbered positions.

Display 16.7   Methods in the Classes `ArrayList<T>` and `Vector<T>` (part 3 of 4)

METHODS TO REMOVE ELEMENTS FOR BOTH `ArrayList<T>` AND `Vector<T>`

```
public T remove(int index)
```

Deletes the element at the specified index and returns the element deleted. The size of the calling object is decreased by one. The capacity of the calling object is not changed. Each element in the calling object with an index greater than or equal to `index` is decreased to have an index that is one less than the value it had previously.

The `index` must be a value greater than or equal to zero and less than the size of the calling object (before this removal).

```
public boolean remove(Object theElement)
```

Removes the first occurrence of `theElement` from the calling object. If `theElement` is found in the calling object, then each element in the calling object with an index greater than or equal to `theElement`'s index is decreased to have an index that is one less than the value it had previously. Returns `true` if `theElement` was found (and removed). Returns `false` if `theElement` was not found in the calling object. If the element was removed, the size is decreased by one. The capacity is not changed.

```
protected void removeRange(int fromIndex, int toIndex)
```

Removes all elements with index greater than or equal to `fromIndex` and strictly less than `toIndex`. Be sure to note that this method is **protected**, not **public**.

```
public void clear( )
```

Removes all elements from the calling object and sets its size to zero.

SEARCH METHODS FOR BOTH `ArrayList<T>` AND `Vector<T>`

```
public boolean isEmpty( )
```

Returns `true` if the calling object is empty (that is, has size 0); otherwise returns `false`.

```
public boolean contains(Object target)
```

Returns `true` if `target` is an element of the calling object; otherwise returns `false`. Uses the method `equals` of the object `target` to test for equality.

```
public int indexOf(Object target)
```

Returns the index of the first element that is equal to `target`. Uses the method `equals` of the object `target` to test for equality. Returns 1 if `target` is not found.

```
public int lastIndexOf(Object target)
```

Returns the index of the last element that is **equal** to `target`. Uses the method `equals` of the object `target` to test for equality. Returns 1 if `target` is not found.

ITERATORS FOR BOTH `ArrayList<T>` AND `Vector<T>`

```
public Iterator<T> iterator( )
```

Returns an iterator for the calling object. Iterators are discussed in Section 16.3.

(continued)

Display 16.7 Methods in the Classes `ArrayList<T>` and `Vector<T>` (part 4 of 4)

```
public ListIterator<T> listIterator( )
```

Returns a `ListIterator<T>` for the calling object. `ListIterator<T>` is discussed in Section 16.3.

```
ListIterator<T> listIterator(int index)
```

Returns a list iterator for the calling object starting at `index`. The first element to be returned by the iterator is the one at `index`. (Iterators are discussed in Section 16.3.)

CONVERTING TO AN ARRAY FOR BOTH `ArrayList<T>` AND `Vector<T>`

```
public Object[ ] toArray( )
```

Returns an array containing all of the elements in the calling object. The elements of the array are indexed the same as in the calling object.

```
public <E> E[ ] toArray(E[ ] a)
```

Note that the type parameter E is not the same as T. So, E can be any reference type; it need not be the type T in `Collection<T>`. For example, E might be an ancestor type of T.

Returns an array containing all of the elements in the calling object. The elements of the array are indexed the same as in the calling object.

The argument *a* is used primarily to specify the type of the array returned. The exact details are as follows:

The type of the returned array is that of *a*. If the collection fits in the array *a*, then *a* is used to hold the elements of the returned array; otherwise a new array is created with the same type as *a*.

If *a* has more elements than the calling object, then the element in *a* immediately following the end of the elements copied from the calling object is set to `null`.

MEMORY MANAGEMENT FOR BOTH `ArrayList<T>` AND `Vector<T>`

```
public int size( )
```

Returns the number of elements in the calling object.

```
public int capacity( )
```

Returns the current capacity of the calling object.

```
public void ensureCapacity(int newCapacity)
```

Increases the capacity of the calling object to ensure that it can hold at least `newCapacity` elements. Using `ensureCapacity` can sometimes increase efficiency, but it is not needed for any other reason.

```
public void trimToSize( )
```

Trims the capacity of the calling object to be the calling object's current size. This is used to save storage.

MAKE A COPY FOR BOTH `ArrayList<T>` AND `Vector<T>`

```
public Object clone( )
```

Returns a shallow copy of the calling object.

Self-Test Exercises

4. Can an object that instantiates the HashSet<T> class contain multiple copies of some element?

5. Suppose you want to define a class that orders its elements like a List<T> but does not allow multiple occurrences of an element like a Set<T>. Would it be better to make it a derived class of the ArrayList<T> class or a derived class of the HashSet<T> class?

Differences Between ArrayList<T> and Vector<T>

For most purposes, ArrayList<T> and Vector<T> are equivalent. There are only minor differences between the classes. The methods that are in both classes are given in Display 16.7. The class Vector<T> has more methods that ArrayList<T> does not have and that are not given in Display 16.7. However, most of the extra methods are little more than alternate names for methods that are in both ArrayList<T> and Vector<T>. None of the methods in Vector<T> do anything that cannot easily be done with an ArrayList<T>. The class ArrayList<T> is reputed to be more efficient than Vector<T>. The biggest difference between these two classes is that ArrayList<T> is newer than Vector<T> and was created as part of the Java collection framework, whereas Vector<T> is an older class that was retrofitted with extra method names to make it fit into the collection framework. You are encouraged to use ArrayList<T> rather than Vector<T>. However, a lot of existing code uses Vector<T>, so you should be familiar with Vector<T>.[1]

Nonparameterized Version of the Collection Framework ★

Before version 5.0, Java did not have type parameters. So, the collection framework consisted of ordinary classes and interfaces, such as Collection, List, ArrayList, and so forth, all of which had no type parameters. Although this older collection framework has been supplanted by the new, generic version, the old version's classes and interfaces, without type parameters, are still in the standard libraries and in a lot of older code. There is no longer any need for the older classes and interfaces that do not have type parameters. They can sometimes be harder to use and are less versatile than the new, generic classes with type parameters. You should not use the older classes and interfaces without type parameters. However, you will often see them used in older code. When reading older code, you will not go too far wrong in thinking of Collection as meaning Collection<Object>, ArrayList as meaning ArrayList<Object>, and so forth. This is not, strictly speaking, correct. For example, the classes ArrayList and ArrayList<Object> are not the same, but they are very similar.

---

[1] The biggest difference between Vector<T> and ArrayList<T> classes is that Vector<T> objects are *synchronized* while ArrayList<T> objects are not. However, synchronization is a topic that we do not cover and that is not relevant to the kinds of programming we are doing.

PITFALL: Omitting the <T>

If you omit `<T>` or a corresponding class name, such as using `ArrayList` instead of `ArrayList<String>`, then you may get a compiler error message. If you do get a compiler error message, it is likely to seem bewilderingly strange. The problem is that `ArrayList` and other class and interface names with `<T>` omitted actually mean something. (We do not have time to stop and explain what they mean, but a hint of what they mean is given in the starred subsection "Nonparameterized Version of the Collection Framework.") Your only defense against this pitfall is to be very careful, and if you do get a bewildering compiler error message, look for a missing `<T>` or a missing `<Class_Name>`.

Sometimes a compiler warning message can be helpful when you make this mistake. If you get a warning that mentions a type case from a class name without a `<T>` to a class name with a `<T>` or with a `<Class_Name>`, look for an omitted `<T>` or omitted `<Class_Name>`.

Finally, we should note that sometimes your code will compile and even run correctly if you omit the `<T>` from a class name in the collection framework. ■

16.2 Maps

A man has but one mother. But, a mother may have any number of sons.

Saying on a Wall Sampler

map

The Java **map** framework is similar in character to the collection framework, except that it deals with collections of ordered pairs. Objects in the map framework can implement mathematical functions and relations and so can be used to construct database classes. Think of the pair as consisting of a key K (to search for) and an associated value V. For example, the key might be a student ID number and the value might be an object storing information about the student (such as the name, major, address, or phone number) associated with that ID number. Commonly used interfaces and classes in this framework are shown in Display 16.8. In this chapter we will focus on the Map<K,V> interface, the AbstractMap<K,V> class, and the HashMap<K,V> class.

AbstractMap
<K,V>
HashMap<K,V>
Map<K,V>
interface

Since the map interface will map a key to a value, we must now specify two types of parameters instead of one as we did with collections. The Map<K,V> interface specifies the basic operations that all map classes should implement. A summary of these operations is given in Display 16.9. A more detailed description is in Appendix 5. Note that there are many similarities to the Collection<T> interface.

Display 16.8   **The Map Landscape**

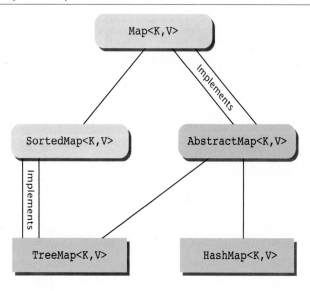

Interface

Abstract Class

Concrete Class

A single line between two boxes means
the lower class or interface is derived
from (extends) the higher one.

K and V are type parameters for the type of
the keys and elements stored in the map.

Display 16.9   **Method Headings in the Map<K,V> Interface** (part 1 of 3)

The Map<K,V> interface is in the `java.util` package.

CONSTRUCTORS

Although not officially required by the interface, any class that implements the Map<K,V> interface
should have at least two constructors: a no-argument constructor that creates an empty Map<K,V>
object, and a constructor with one Map<K,V> parameter that creates a Map<K,V> object with the
same elements as the constructor argument. The interface does not specify whether the copy produced by the one-argument constructor is a shallow copy or a deep copy of its argument.

(continued)

Display 16.9 Method Headings in the `Map<K,V>` Interface (part 2 of 3)

METHODS

`boolean isEmpty( )`

Returns **true** if the calling object is empty; otherwise returns **false**.

`public boolean containsValue(Object value)`

Returns **true** if the calling object contains at least one or more keys that map to an instance of **value**.

`public boolean containsKey(Object key)`

Returns **true** if the calling object contains **key** as one of its keys.

`public boolean equals(Object other)`

This is the **equals** of the map, not the **equals** of the elements in the map. Overrides the inherited method **equals**.

`public int size( )`

Returns the number of (key, value) mappings in the calling object.

`public int hashCode( )`

Returns the hash code value for the calling object.

`public Set<Map.Entry<K,V>> entrySet( )`

Returns a set *view* consisting of (key, value) mappings for all entries in the map. Changes to the map are reflected in the set and vice-versa.

`public Collection<V> values( )`

Returns a collection *view* consisting of all values in the map. Changes to the map are reflected in the collection and vice-versa.

`public V get(Object key)`

Returns the value to which the calling object maps **key**. If **key** is not in the map, then **null** is returned. Note that this does not always mean that the key is not in the map since it is possible to map a key to **null**. The **containsKey** method can be used to distinguish the two cases.

OPTIONAL METHODS

The following methods are optional, which means they still must be implemented, but the implementation can simply throw an **UnsupportedOperationException** if, for some reason, you do not want to give the methods a "real" implementation. An **UnsupportedOperationException** is a **RunTimeException** and so is not required to be caught or declared in a **throws** clause.

`public V put(K key, V value)` *(Optional)*

Associates **key** to **value** in the map. If **key** was associated with an existing value then the old value is overwritten and returned. Otherwise **null** is returned.

```
    public void putAll(Map<? extends K,? extends V> mapToAdd) (Optional)
```
Adds all mappings of **mapToAdd** into the calling object's map.

```
    public V remove(Object key) (Optional)
```
Removes the mapping for the specified key. If the key is not found in the map then **null** is returned; otherwise the previous value for the key is returned.

Concrete Map Classes

The abstract class `AbstractMap<K,V>` is convenient for implementing the `Map<K,V>` interface, just as the `AbstractSet<T>` class served the same purpose for the `Set<T>` interface. When defining a derived class of `AbstractMap<K,V>` you need to define not just the abstract methods but also all the methods you intend to use. It usually makes more sense to use (or define derived classes of) the `HashMap<K,V>` or `TreeMap<K,V>` classes, which are derived classes of `AbstractMap<K,V>` and are full implementations of the `Map<K,V>` interfaces. However, if you wish to implement your own map with your own data structures, then it would be appropriate to derive classes from `AbstractMap<K,V>`.

In this chapter we will focus only on the `HashMap<K,V>` class, which is a concrete implementation of the `Map<K,V>` interface. Internally, the class uses a hash table similar to what we discussed in Chapter 15. Note that this class does not make any guarantee as to the order of elements placed in the map. If you require order, then you should use the `TreeMap<K,V>` class (which internally uses a tree to store its elements) or the `LinkedHashMap<K,V>` class, which uses a doubly linked list to maintain order inside a `HashMap<K,V>` object. The `LinkedHashMap<K,V>` class is derived from the `HashMap<K,V>` class.

Knowing how hash tables operate is helpful in optimizing a program that uses a `HashMap`. When we created a hash table in Chapter 15, we used a fixed-sized array where each array entry referenced a linked list. A hash function mapped an input value, like a String, to an index in the array. If the size of the array is much smaller than the number of elements added, then there will be lots of collisions and execution performance will be low. On the other hand, if the size of the array is much larger than the number of elements added, then memory will be wasted. A similar tradeoff exists with the `HashMap<K,V>` class. One of the constructors allows us to specify an **initial capacity** and a **load factor**. The initial capacity specifies how many "buckets" exist in the hash table. This would be analogous to the size of the array of the hash table. The load factor is a number between 0 and 1. This variable specifies a percentage such that if the number of elements added to the hash table exceeds the load factor, then the capacity of the hash table will automatically increase. The default load factor is 0.75 and the default initial capacity is 16. This means that the capacity will be increased (by roughly double) once 12 elements are added to the map. This process is called **rehashing** and can be time consuming if you have a large number of elements in the map.

initial
capacity
load factor

rehashing

Although the capacity will automatically increase when necessary, your program will run more efficiently if the capacity is initially set to the number of elements you expect will be added to the map.

The HashMap<K,V>, of course, implements all the methods in the Map<K,V> interface and adds no other methods beyond constructors and an implementation of the clone( ) method. A summary of the HashMap<K,V> constructors and clone( ) is given in Display 16.10.

Display 16.10   Methods in the **HashMap<K,V>** Class

The HashMap<K,V> class is in the java.util package.

The HashMap<K,V> class extends the AbstractMap<K,V> class and implements the Map<K,V> interface.

The HashMap<K,V> class implements all of the methods in the Map<K,V> interface (Display 16.9). The only other methods in the HashMap<K,V> class are the constructors.

All the exception classes mentioned are the kind that are not required to be caught in a catch block or declared in a throws clause.

All the exception classes mentioned are in the package java.lang and so do not require any import statement.

public HashMap( )

Creates a new, empty map with a default initial capacity of 16 and load factor of 0.75.

public HashMap(int initialCapacity)

Creates a new, empty map with a default capacity of initialCapacity and load factor of 0.75.

Throws a IllegalArgumentException if initialCapacity is negative.

public HashMap(int initialCapacity, float loadFactor)

Creates a new, empty map with the specified capacity and load factor.

Throws a IllegalArgumentException if initialCapacity is negative or loadFactor nonpositive.

public HashMap(Map<? extends K,? extends V> m)

Creates a new map with the same mappings as m. The initialCapacity is set to the same size as m and the loadFactor to 0.75.

Throws a NullPointerException if m is null.

public Object clone( )

Creates a shallow copy of this instance and returns it. The keys and values are not cloned.

The remainder of the methods are the same as those described for the Map<K,V> interface (Display 16.9.)

A program that demonstrates the HashMap<K,V> class is given in Display 16.11. This is a variant of Programming Project 8 from Chapter 15. In this example the program uses the name instance variable as the key to map to an Employee object as defined in Display 7.2. Several sample Employee objects are created and added to the map using the first name as the key. The user is given the opportunity to type in names until enter is pressed on a blank line. Any name that exists in the map is retrieved and its information is output to the screen.

Display 16.11 **HashMap<K,V> Class Demo** (part 1 of 2)

```
1   // This class uses the Employee class defined in Chapter 7.
2   import java.util.HashMap;
3   import java.util.Scanner;
4   public class HashMapDemo
5   {
6       public static void main(String[] args)
7       {
8           // First create a hashmap with an initial size of 10 and
9           // the default load factor
10          HashMap<String,Employee> employees =
11              new HashMap<String,Employee>(10);

12          // Add several employees objects to the map using
13          // their name as the key
14          employees.put("Joe",
15              new Employee("Joe",new Date("September", 15, 1970)));
16          employees.put("Andy",
17              new Employee("Andy",new Date("August", 22, 1971)));
18          employees.put("Greg",
19              new Employee("Greg",new Date("March", 9, 1972)));
20          employees.put("Kiki",
21              new Employee("Kiki",new Date("October", 8, 1970)));
22          employees.put("Antoinette",
23              new Employee("Antoinette",new Date("May", 2, 1959)));
24          System.out.print("Added Joe, Andy, Greg, Kiki, ");
25          System.out.println("and Antoinette to the map.");

26          // Ask the user to type a name. If found in the map,
27          // print it out.
28          Scanner keyboard = new Scanner(System.in);
29          String name = "";
30          do
31          {
32              System.out.print("\nEnter a name to look up in the map. ");
33              System.out.println("Press enter to quit.");
```

(continued)

Display 16.11 **HashMap<K,V> Class Demo** (part 2 of 2)

```
34                    name = keyboard.nextLine( );
35                    if (employees.containsKey(name))
36                    {
37                        Employee e = employees.get(name);
38                        System.out.println("Name found: " + e.toString( ));
39                    }
40                    else if (!name.equals(""))
41                    {
42                        System.out.println("Name not found.");
43                    }
44              } while (!name.equals(""));
45         }
46   }
```

Sample Dialogue

```
Added Joe, Andy, Greg, Kiki, and Antoinette to the map.

Enter a name to look up in the map. Press enter to quit.
Joe
Name found: Joe September 15, 1970

Enter a name to look up in the map. Press enter to quit.
Andy
Name found: Andy August 22, 1971

Enter a name to look up in the map. Press enter to quit.
Kiki
Name found: Kiki October 8, 1970

Enter a name to look up in the map. Press enter to quit.
Myla
Name not found.
```

Self-Test Exercises

6. Can an object that instantiates the HashMap<K,V> class contain multiple copies of some element as a key? How about multiple copies of some element as a value?

7. Suppose that you want a HashMap<K,V> that maps a unique employee ID number to an Employee object. Give the definition for a HashMap<K,V> variable that defines and allocates the HashMap. You expect to have 100 employees in your organization. If the employee ID number is an integer between 0 and 100, is a map a good choice for a data structure to store this information?

16.3 **Iterators**

The White Rabbit put on his spectacles. "Where shall I begin, please your Majesty?" he asked.
"Begin at the beginning," the King said, very gravely, "And go on till you come to the end: then stop."

LEWIS CARROLL, *Alice in Wonderland*

iterator   An **iterator** is an object that is used with a collection to provide sequential access to the elements in the collection. In this section, we discuss iterators in general and iterators in the Java collection framework in particular.

The Iterator Concept

In the next subsection, we will discuss the Java Iterator interface, but before that, let's consider the intuitive idea of an iterator. An iterator is something that allows you to examine and possibly modify the elements in a collection in some sequential order. So, an iterator imposes an order on the elements of a collection even if the collection, such as the class HashSet<T>, does not impose any order on the elements it contains.

Something that is not an object—and thus not, strictly speaking, a Java Iterator—but that satisfies the intuitive idea of an iterator is an int variable i used with an array a. This iterator i can be made to start out at the first array as follows:

```
i = 0;
```

The iterator can give you the current element; the current element is simply a[i]. The iterator can go to the next element and give you the next element as follows:

```
i++;
"Gives you a[i]"
```

The concept of an iterator is simple but powerful enough to be used frequently.

The Iterator<T> Interface

Iterator<T>   Java formalizes the concept of an iterator with the Iterator<T> generic interface. Any
interface   object of any class that satisfies the Iterator<T> interface is an Iterator<T>. So, an array index is not a Java Iterator<T>. However, the index could be an instance variable in an object of an Iterator<T> class.

An Iterator<T> object does not stand on its own. It must be associated with some collection object. How is the association accomplished? In Java, any class that satisfies the Collection<T> interface must have a method, named iterator( ), that returns an Iterator<T>. For example, let's say c is an instance of the HashSet<T> collection class with some class plugged in for T. To make things concrete, let's plug in String for T; so c is an instance of the HashSet<String> collection class. You can obtain an iterator for c as follows:

```
Iterator<String> iteratorForC = c.iterator( );
```

You may not know what class the iteratorForC is an instance of, but you do know it satisfies the Iterator<String> interface, and so you know it has the methods in the Iterator<T> interface. These methods are given in Display 16.12.

Display 16.13 contains a simple demonstration of using an iterator with a Hash-Set<T> object. A HashSet<T> object imposes no order on the elements in the Hash-Set<T> object, but the iterator imposes an order on the elements, namely the order in which they are produced by next( ). There are no requirements on this ordering. If you run the program in Display 16.13 twice, the order of the elements' output will almost certainly be the same each time. However, it would not be an error if they were output in a different order each time the program ran.

If the collection used with an Iterator<T> imposes an order on its elements, such as an ArrayList<T> does, then the Iterator<T> will output the elements in that order. If you require an order with a HashSet<T> object then you may use the LinkedHashSet<T> class, which uses an internal doubly linked list to store the items in the order that they are added.

Display 16.12 Methods in the Iterator<T> Interface

The Iterator<T> interface is in the **java.util** package.

All the exception classes mentioned are the kind that are not required to be caught in a **catch** block or declared in a **throws** clause.

NoSuchElementException is in the **java.util** package, which requires an import statement if your code mentions the **NoSuchElementException** class. All the other exception classes mentioned are in the package **java.lang** and so do not require any import statement.

```
public T next( )
```

Returns the next element of the collection that produced the iterator.

Throws a NoSuchElementException if there is no next element.

```
public boolean hasNext( )
```

Returns **true** if next( ) has not yet returned all the elements in the collection; returns **false** otherwise.

```
public void remove( ) (Optional)
```

Removes from the collection the last element returned by **next**.

This method can be called only once per call to **next**. If the collection is changed in any way, other than by using **remove**, the behavior of the iterator is not specified (and thus should be considered unpredictable).

Throws IllegalStateException if the **next** method has not yet been called, or if the **remove** method has already been called after the last call to the **next** method.

Throws an UnsupportedOperationException if the **remove** operation is not supported by this Iterator<T>.

Display 16.13   **An Iterator**

```
1    import java.util.HashSet;
2    import java.util.Iterator;

3    public class HashSetIteratorDemo
4    {
5        public static void main(String[] args)
6        {
7            HashSet<String> s = new HashSet<String>( );

8            s.add("health");
9            s.add("love");
10           s.add("money");

11           System.out.println("The set contains:");

12
13
14

15

16           System.out.println( );
17           System.out.println("The set now contains:");

18
19
20

21           System.out.println("End of program.");
22       }
23   }
```

You cannot "reset" an iterator "to the beginning." To do a second iteration, you create another iterator.

Sample Dialogue

```
The set contains:
money
love
health

The set now contains:
money
love
End of program.
```

The **HashSet<T>** object does not order the elements it contains, but the iterator imposes an order on the elements.

> ### Iterators
>
> An iterator is something that allows you to examine and possibly modify the elements in a collection in some sequential order. Java formalizes this concept with the two interfaces `Iterator<T>` and `ListIterator<T>`.

TIP: For-Each Loops as Iterators

A for-each loop is not strictly speaking an iterator (because, among other things, it is not an object), but a for-each loop serves the same purpose as an iterator: it lets you cycle through the elements in a collection. When dealing with collections, you can often use a for-each loop in place of an iterator, and the for-each loop is usually simpler and easier to use than an iterator. For example, in Display 16.14 we have rewritten the program in Display 16.13 using for-each loops in place of iterators. Note that we needed to do some extra programming with the variable `last` in order to simulate `i.remove( )`. Sometimes an iterator works best, and sometimes a for-each loop works best. Many authorities would say that our code would be better if we had not replaced the first iterator loop in Display 16.13 with a for-each loop. ∎

Display 16.14 For-Each Loops as Iterators (part 1 of 2)

```
1   import java.util.HashSet;
2   import java.util.Iterator;

3   public class ForEachDemo
4   {
5       public static void main(String[] args)
6       {
7           HashSet<String> s = new HashSet<String>( );

8           s.add("health");
9           s.add("love");
10          s.add("money");

11          System.out.println("The set contains:");

12          String last = null;
13          for (String e : s)
14          {
15              last = e;
16              System.out.println(e);
17          }
```

```
18              s.remove(last);

19              System.out.println( );
20              System.out.println("The set now contains:");

21              for (String e : s)
22                  System.out.println(e);

23              System.out.println("End of program.");
24          }
25      }                                    The output is the same as in Display 16.13.
```

List Iterators

**ListIterator
\<T\>**

The collection framework has two iterator interfaces: the Iterator\<T\> interface, which
you have already seen and that works with any collection class that implements the
Collection\<T\> interface, and the ListIterator\<T\> interface, which is designed to work
with collections that implement the List\<T\> interface. The ListIterator\<T\> interface extends the Iterator\<T\> interface. A ListIterator\<T\> has all the methods
that an Iterator\<T\> has, plus more methods that provide two new abilities: a
ListIterator\<T\> can move in either direction along the list of elements in the collection, and a ListIterator\<T\> has methods, such as set and add, that can be used to change
the elements in the collection. The methods for the ListIterator\<T\> interface are
given in Display 16.15. See Appendix 5 for a more detailed description that includes
all exceptions thrown.

The map framework does not directly support the iterable interface, but you can
use the map's keySet( ), values( ), or entrySet( ) methods, which return iterable
sets containing the keys, values, or (key, value) mappings of the map.

The ListIterator \<T\> interface is in the java.util package.

The *cursor position* is explained in the text and in Display 16.16.

All the exception classes mentioned are the kind that are not required to be caught in a **catch**
block or declared in a **throws** clause.

NoSuchElementException is in the java.util package, which requires an import statement if
your code mentions the NoSuchElementException class. All the other exception classes mentioned are in the package java.lang and so do not require any import statement.

    public T next( )

Returns the next element of the list that produced the iterator. More specifically, returns the element immediately after the cursor position.

Throws a NoSuchElementException if there is no next element.

(continued)

Display 16.15 Methods in the **ListIterator\<T>** Interface (part 2 of 2)

`public T previous( )`

Returns the previous element of the list that produced the iterator. More specifically, returns the element immediately before the cursor position.

Throws a `NoSuchElementException` if there is no previous element.

`public boolean hasNext( )`

Returns **true** if there is a suitable element for **next( )** to return; returns **false** otherwise.

`public boolean hasPrevious( )`

Returns **true** if there is a suitable element for **previous( )** to return; returns **false** otherwise.

`public int nextIndex( )`

Returns the index of the element that would be returned by a call to **next( )**. Returns the list size if the cursor position is at the end of the list.

`public int previousIndex( )`

Returns the index that would be returned by a call to **previous( )**. Returns 1 if the cursor position is at the beginning of the list.

`public void add(T newElement)` *(Optional)*

Inserts **newElement** at the location of the iterator cursor (that is, before the value, if any, that would be returned by **next( )** and after the value, if any, that would be returned by **previous( )**).

Cannot be used if there has been a call to **add** or **remove** since the last call to **next( )** or **previous( )**.

Throws `IllegalStateException` if neither **next( )** nor **previous( )** has been called, or if the **add** or **remove** method has already been called after the last call to **next( )** or **previous( )**.

`public void remove( )` *(Optional)*

Removes from the collection the last element returned by **next( )** or **previous( )**.

This method can be called only once per call to **next( )** or **previous( )**.

Cannot be used if there has been a call to **add** or **remove** since the last call to **next( )** or **previous( )**.

Throws `IllegalStateException` if neither **next( )** nor **previous( )** has been called, or if the **add** or **remove** method has already been called after the last call to **next( )** or **previous( )**.

`public void set( T newElement)` *(Optional)*

Replaces the last element returned by **next( )** or **previous( )** with **newElement**.

Cannot be used if there has been a call to **add** or **remove** since the last call to **next( )** or **previous( )**.

Throws `IllegalStateException` if neither **next( )** nor **previous( )** has been called, or if the **add** or **remove** method has been called since the last call to **next( )** or **previous( )**.

The general idea of *next* and *previous* is clear, but we need to make it precise if you are to understand the next( ) and previous( ) methods of the ListIterator<T> interface. Every ListIterator<T> has a position marker in the list known as the **cursor**. If the list has *n* elements, they are numbered by indices 0 through *n*–1, but there are *n*+1 cursor positions, as indicated in Display 16.16. When next( ) is invoked, the element immediately following the cursor position is returned and the cursor is moved to the next cursor position. When previous( ) is invoked, the element immediately before the cursor position is returned, and the cursor is moved back to the preceding cursor position.

cursor

The ListIterator<T> Interface

The ListIterator<T> interface extends the Iterator<T> interface. The ListIterator<T> interface differs from the Iterator<T> interface by adding the following abilities: a ListIterator<T> can move in either direction along the list of elements in the collection, and a ListIterator<T> has methods, such as **set** and **add**, that can be used to change the elements in the collection.

Display 16.16 **ListIterator<T>** Cursor Positions

The default initial cursor position is the leftmost one.

 PITFALL: next Can Return a Reference

If i is an iterator, then i.next( ) returns an element of the collection that created i, but there are two senses of "return an element."

1. The invocation i.next( ) could return a copy of the element in the collection (for example, using a copy constructor or a clone method).

2. Alternatively, i.next( ) could return a reference to the element in the collection.

In case (1), modifying i.next( ) *will not* change the element in the collection (provided the copy was a deep copy). In case (2), modifying i.next( ) *will* change the element in the collection. The APIs for both the Iterator<T> and ListIterator<T> interfaces are vague on whether you should follow policy (1) or (2), but the iterators

(continued)

PITFALL: (continued)

for the standard predefined collection classes, such as `ArrayList<T>` and `HashSet<T>`, return references. So, you can modify the elements in the collection by using mutator methods on `i.next( )`. This is illustrated in Display 16.17. The comments we made about `i.next( )` also apply to `i.previous( )`.

The fact that `next` and `previous` return references to elements in the collection is not necessarily bad news. It means you must be careful, but it also means you can cycle through all the elements in the collection and perform some processing that might modify the elements. For example, if the elements in the collection are records of some sort, you can use mutator methods to update the records.

If you read the APIs for the `Iterator<T>` and `ListIterator<T>` interfaces, they say that a `ListIterator<T>` can change the collection, but presumably, a plain old `Iterator<T>` cannot. These API comments do not refer to whether or not a reference is returned by `i.next( )`. They simply refer to the fact that the `ListIterator<T>` interface has a set method, whereas the `Iterator<T>` interface does not have a set method. Do not confuse this with the point discussed in the previous paragraph. ■

Display 16.17 An Iterator Returns a Reference (part 1 of 2)

```
1   import java.util.ArrayList;            The class Date is defined in Display 4.13,
2   import java.util.Iterator;            but you can easily guess all you need to
                                          know about Date for this example.
3   public class IteratorReferenceDemo
4   {
5       public static void main(String[] args)
6       {
7           ArrayList<Date> birthdays = new ArrayList<Date>( );

8           birthdays.add(new Date(1, 1, 1990));
9           birthdays.add(new Date(2, 2, 1990));
10          birthdays.add(new Date(3, 3, 1990));

11          System.out.println("The list contains:");

12          Iterator<Date> i = birthdays.iterator( );
13          while (i.hasNext( ))
14              System.out.println(i.next( ));

15          i = birthdays.iterator( );
16          Date d = null; //To keep the compiler happy.
17          System.out.println("Changing the references.");
```

Display 16.17   **An Iterator Returns a Reference** (part 2 of 2)

```
18              while (i.hasNext( ))
19              {
20
21
22              }

23              System.out.println("The list now contains:");

24              i = birthdays.iterator( );
25              while (i.hasNext( ))
26                  System.out.println(i.next( ));

27              System.out.println("April fool!");
28          }
29  }
```

Sample Dialogue

```
The list contains:
January 1, 1990
February 2, 1990
March 3, 1990
Changing the references.
The list now contains:
April 1, 1990
April 1, 1990
April 1, 1990
April fool!
```

TIP: Defining Your Own Iterator Classes

There really is little need to define your own `Iterator<T>` or `ListIterator<T>` classes. The most common and easiest way to define a collection class is to make it a derived class of one of the library collection classes, such as `ArrayList<T>` or `HashSet<T>`. When you do that, you automatically get the method `iterator( )`, and if need be, the method `listIterator( )`, which takes care of iterators. However, if you should need to define a collection class in some other way, then the best way to define your iterator class or classes is to define them as inner classes of your collection class. ■

Self-Test Exercises

8. Does a HashSet<T> object have a method to produce a ListIterator<T>? Does an ArrayList<T> object have a method to produce a ListIterator<T>?

9. Suppose i is a ListIterator<T>. Will an invocation of i.next( ) followed by i.previous( ) return the same element for each of the two invocations or might they return two different elements? What about i.previous( ) followed by i.next( )?

Chapter Summary

- The main collection interfaces are Collection<T>, Set<T>, and List<T>. The Set<T> and List<T> interfaces extend the Collection<T> interface. The library classes that are standard to use and that implement these interfaces are Hash-Set<T>, which implements the Set<T> interface, and ArrayList<T>, which implements the List<T> interface.

- A Set<T> does not allow repeated elements and does not order its elements. A List<T> allows repeated elements and orders its elements.

- The Map<K,V> interface is used to store a mapping between a key K and a value V. It is commonly used to store databases in memory. The HashMap<K,V> class is a standard library class that implements a map.

- An iterator is something that allows you to examine and possibly modify the elements in a collection in some sequential order. Java formalizes this concept with the two interfaces Iterator<T> and ListIterator<T>.

- An Iterator<T> (with only the required methods implemented) goes through the elements of the collection in only one direction, from the beginning to the end. A ListIterator<T> can move through the collection list in both directions, forward and back. A ListIterator<T> has a set method; the Iterator<T> interface does not require a set method.

Answers to Self-Test Exercises

1.
```
public static <T> boolean inSome(T target,
                             Collection<T> c1, Collection<T> c2)

{
        return (c1.contains(target) || c2.contains(target));
}
```

2.
```
public static <T> T getFirst(List<T> aList)

{
     if (aList.isEmpty( ))
         return null;
     else
```

```
                return aList.get(0);
        }

3.   public static boolean noNull(Set<?> s)
     {
             return (s.remove(null));
     }
```

4.   No.

5.   It would make more sense to make it a derived class of the `ArrayList<T>` class. Then the elements are ordered. You can ensure against repeated elements by redefining all methods that add elements so that the methods check to see if the element is already in the class before entering it. A derived class of the `HashSet<T>` class would automatically ensure that no element is repeated, but it would seem to take a good deal of work to maintain the elements in order.

6.   Multiple copies of some element are not allowed as a key, but are allowed as values.

7.   The variable would be defined as:

     `HashMap<Integer,Employee> employeeMap = new HashMap<Integer,Employee>(100);`

     If the ID numbers are between 0 and 100 then the map will work, but a simple array or `ArrayList` might be a more appropriate data structure.

8.   A `HashSet<T>` does not. An `ArrayList<T>` does.

9.   The answer to both questions is the same: They will return the same element.

Programming Projects

 Many of these Programming Projects can be solved using AW's MyCodeMate. To access these please go to: www.mycodemate.com.

1.   Redo Programming Project 8 in Chapter 6, but this time do it for a vector of strings to be sorted into lexicographic order.

2.   The Sieve of Erastothenes is an ancient algorithm that generates prime numbers. Consider the list of numbers from 2 to 10 below:

2	3	4	5	6	7	8	9	10

     The algorithm starts with the first prime number in the list, which is 2, and then iterates through the remainder of the list, removing any number that is a multiple of 2 (in this case, 4, 6, 8, and 10), leaving:

2	3	5	7	9

     We then repeat the process with the second prime number in the list, which is 3, and then iterate through the remainder of the list removing any number that is a multiple of 3 (in this case 9), leaving:

2	3	5	7

We then repeat starting with each successive prime number but no elements are removed since there are no multiples of 5 or 7 (a more efficient implementation of the algorithm would stop without examining 5 or 7). The numbers that remain in the list are all prime numbers.

Implement this algorithm using an `ArrayList` of Integers that is initialized to the values from 2 to 100. Your program can iterate numerically through the `ArrayList` from index 0 to index `size( )-1` to get the current prime number, but should use an `Iterator` to scan through the remainder of the list to eliminate the multiples. You can use the `listIterator` method to retrieve the iterator starting at a specified index into the `ArrayList`. Output all remaining prime numbers to the console.

3. The birthday paradox is that there is a surprisingly high probability that two or more people in the same room happen to share the same birthday. By birthday, we mean the same day of the year (ignoring leap years), but not the exact birthday that includes the birth year or time of day. Write a program that approximates the probability that two or more people in the same room have the same birthday, for 2 to 50 people in the room.

The program should use simulation to approximate the answer. Over many trials (say, 5000), randomly assign birthdays (i.e., the number 1-365) to everyone in the room. Use a `HashSet` to store the birthdays. As the birthdays are randomly generated use the `contains` method of a `HashSet` to see if someone with the same birthday is already in the room. If so, increment a counter that tracks how many times at least two people have the same birthday and then move on to the next trial. After the trials are over divide the counter by the number of trials to get an estimated probability that two or more people share the same birthday for a given room size.

Your output should look something like the following. It won't be exactly the same due to the random numbers:

```
For 2 people, the probability of two birthdays is about 0.002
For 3 people, the probability of two birthdays is about 0.0082
For 4 people, the probability of two birthdays is about 0.0163
...

For 49 people, the probability of two birthdays is about 0.9654
For 50 people, the probability of two birthdays is about 0.969
```

Note: To generate a random number x, where $0 \leq x < 1$, use x = Math.random( );. This generates a random number between 0 and 1.

4. The textfiles `boynames.txt` and `girlnames.txt`, which are included in the source code for this book, contain lists of the 1000 most popular boy and girl names in the United States for the year 2005, as compiled by the Social Security Administration.

These are blank-delimited files where the most popular name is listed first, the second most popular name is listed second, and so on to the 1000th most popular name, which is listed last. Each line consists of the first name followed by a blank space followed by the number of registered births in the year using that name. For example the `girlnames.txt` file begins with:

```
Emily 25494
Emma 22532
```

This indicates that Emily is the most popular name with 25,494 registered namings, Emma is the second most popular with 22,532, and so on.

Write a program that determines how many names are on both the boys' and the girls' list. Use the following algorithm:

- Read each girl name as a String, ignoring the number of namings, and add it to a HashSet object.

- Read each boy name as a String, ignoring the number of namings, and add it to the same HashSet object. If the name is already in the HashSet, then the add method will return false. If you count the number of false returns, then this gives you the number of common namings.

- Add each common name to an ArrayList and output all of the common names from this list before the program exits.

5. Repeat the previous problem except create your own class, Name, that is added to a HashMap instead of a HashSet. The Name class should have three private variables, a String to store the name, an integer to store the number of namings for girls, and an integer to store the number of namings for boys. Use the first name as the key to the HashMap. The value to store is the Name object. Instead of ignoring the number of namings, as in the previous project, store the number in the Name class. Make the ArrayList a list of Name objects; each time you find a common name, add the entire Name object to the list. Your program should then iterate through the ArrayList and output each common name, along with the number of boy and girl namings.

6. In an ancient land, the beautiful princess Eve had many suitors. She decided on the following procedure to determine which suitor she would marry. First, all of the suitors would be lined up one after the other and assigned numbers. The first suitor would be number 1, the second number 2, and so on up to the last suitor, number *n*. Starting at the first suitor she would then count three suitors down the line (because of the three letters in her name) and the third suitor would be eliminated from winning her hand and removed from the line. Eve would then continue, counting three more suitors, and eliminating every third suitor. When she reached the end of the line she would reverse direction and work her way back to the beginning. Similarly, on reaching the first person in line, she would reverse direction and make her way to the end of the line.

For example, if there were 5 suitors then the elimination process would proceed as follows:

12345	initial list of suitors, start counting from 1
1245	suitor 3 eliminated, continue counting from 4, bounce from end back to 4
125	suitor 4 eliminated, continue counting back from 2, bounce from front back to 2
15	suitor 2 eliminated, continue counting forward from 5
1	suitor 5 eliminated, 1 is the lucky winner

Write a program that uses an ArrayList or Vector to determine which position you should stand in to marry the princess if there are *n* suitors. Your program should use the ListIterator interface to traverse the list of suitors and remove a suitor. Be careful that your iterator references the proper object upon reversing direction at the beginning or end of the list. The suitor at the beginning or end of the list should only be counted once when the princess reverses the count.

7. In "social networking" websites people link to their friends to form a social network. Write a program that uses HashMaps to store the data for such a network. Your program should read from a file that specifies the network connections for different user names. The file should have the following format to specify a link:

source_usernamefriend_username

There should be an entry for each link, one per line. Here is a sample file for five usernames:

```
iba           java_guru
iba           crisha
iba           ducky
crisha        java_guru
crisha        iba
ducky         java_guru
ducky         iba
java_guru     iba
java_guru     crisha
java_guru     ducky
wittless      java_guru
```

In this network everyone links to java_guru as a friend. iba is friends with java_guru, crisha, and ducky. Note that links are not bidirectional; wittless links with java_guru but java_guru does not link with wittless.

First, create a User class that has an instance variable to store the user's name and another instance variable that is of type HashSet<User>. The HashSet<User> variable should contain references to the User objects that the current user links to. For example, for the user iba there would be three entries, one for java_guru, crisha, and ducky. Second, create a HashMap<String,User> instance variable in your main class that is used to map from a username to the corresponding User object. Your program should:

- Upon startup read the data file and populate the HashMap and HashSet data structures according to the links specified in the file.

- Allow the user to enter a name.

- If the name exists in the map then output all usernames that are one link away from the user entered.

- If the name exists in the map then output all usernames that are two links away from the user entered. To accomplish this in a general way you might consider writing a recursive subroutine.

17

Swing I

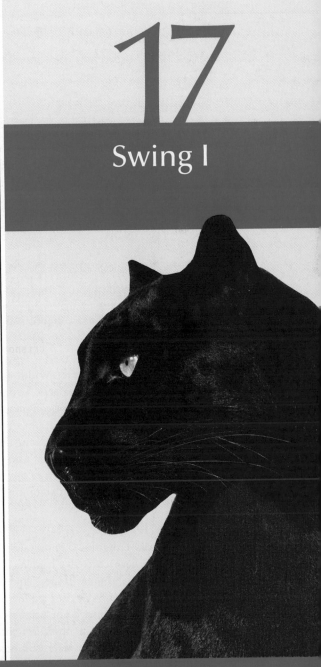

17 Swing I

> *"It Don't Mean a Thing If It Ain't Got That Swing"*
>
> SONG TITLE, *Duke Ellington*

Introduction

Swing
GUI

This is the first of three chapters that present the basic classes in the **Swing** package and teach the basic techniques for using these classes to define *GUIs*. **GUIs** are windowing interfaces that handle user input and output. *GUI* is pronounced "gooey" and stands for **graphical user interface**. Entire books have been written on Swing, so we will not have room to give you a complete description of Swing in three chapters. However, we will teach you enough to allow you to write a variety of windowing interfaces.

GUI

Windowing systems that interact with the user are often called **GUIs**. *GUI* is pronounced "gooey" and stands for **graphical user interface**.

AWT

The **AWT** (**Abstract Window Toolkit**) package is an older package designed for doing windowing interfaces. Swing can be viewed as an improved version of the AWT. However, Swing did not completely replace the AWT package. Some AWT classes are replaced by Swing classes, but other AWT classes are needed when using Swing. We will use classes from both Swing and the AWT.

Swing GUIs are designed using a particular form of object-oriented programming that is known as *event-driven programming*. Our first section begins with a brief overview of event-driven programming.

Prerequisites

Before covering this chapter (and the two chapters on applets[1] and more Swing), you need to have covered Chapters 1 through 5, Chapters 7 (inheritance), Chapter 13 (interfaces and inner classes), and Section 8.2 of Chapter 8 (abstract classes). (Section 8.2 of Chapter 8 does not require Section 8.1.) Except for one subsection at the end of this chapter, you need not have read any of the other chapters that precede this chapter.

To cover the last subsection entitled "A Swing Calculator," you need to first read Chapter 9, which covers exceptions. If you have not yet read Chapter 9, you can skip that last section.

---

[1] The chapter on applets is on the CD that accompanies this book.

17.1 Event-Driven Programming

My duty is to obey orders.

THOMAS JONATHAN (STONEWALL) JACKSON

event-driven programming

Event-driven programming is a programming style that uses a signal-and-response approach to programming. Signals to objects are things called *events,* a concept we explain in this section.

Events and Listeners

event
listener
firing an event

Swing programs use events and event handlers. An **event** is an object that acts as a signal to another object known as a **listener**. The sending of the event is called **firing the event**. The object that fires the event is often a GUI component, such as a button. The button fires the event in response to being clicked. The listener object performs some action in response to the event. For example, the listener might place a message on the screen in response to a particular button being clicked. A given component may have any number of listeners, from zero to several listeners. Each listener might respond to a different kind of event, or multiple listeners might respond to the same events.

If you have read Chapter 9 on exception handling, then you have already seen one specialized example of event-driven programming.[2] An exception object is an event. The throwing of an exception is an example of firing an event (in this case firing the exception event). The listener is the `catch` block that catches the event.

In Swing GUIs an event often represents some action such as clicking a mouse, dragging the mouse, pressing a key on the keyboard, clicking the close-window button on a window, or any other action that is expected to elicit a response. A listener object has methods that specify what will happen when events of various kinds are received

event handler

by the listener. These methods that handle events are called **event handlers**. You the programmer will define (or redefine) these event-handler methods. The relationship between an event-firing object, such as a button, and its event-handling listener is shown diagrammatically in Display 17.1.

Event-driven programming is very different from most programming you've seen before now. All our previous programs consisted of a list of statements executed in order. There were loops that repeat statements and branches that choose one of a list of statements to execute next. However, at some level, each run of a program consists of a list of statements performed by one agent (the computer) that executes the statements one after the other in order.

Event-driven programming is a very different game. In event-driven programming, you create objects that can fire events, and you create listener objects to react to the events. For the most part, your program does not determine the order in which things happen. The events determine that order. When an event-driven program is running,

---

[2] If you have not yet covered Chapter 9 on exceptions, you can safely ignore this paragraph.

Display 17.1 Event Firing and an Event Listener

The component (for example, a button) fires an event.

component — event → listener

This listener object invokes an event handler method with the **event** as an argument.

the next thing that happens depends on the next event. It's as though the listeners were robots that interact with other objects (possibly other robots) in response to events (signals) from these other objects. You program the robots, but the environment and other robots determine what any particular robot will actually end up doing.

If you have never done event-driven programming before, one aspect of it may seem strange to you: *You will be writing definitions for methods that you will never invoke in any program.* This will likely feel a bit strange at first, because a method is of no value unless it is invoked. So, somebody or something other than you, the programmer, must be invoking these methods. That is exactly what does happen. The Swing system automatically invokes certain methods when an event signals that the method needs to be called.

Event-driven programming with the Swing library makes extensive use of inheritance. The classes you define will be derived classes of some basic Swing library classes. These derived classes will inherit methods from their base class. For many of these inherited methods, library software will determine when these methods are invoked, but you will override the definition of the inherited method to determine what will happen when the method is invoked.

17.2 Buttons, Events, and Other Swing Basics

One button click is worth a thousand key strokes.

ANONYMOUS

In this section we present enough about Swing to allow you to do some simple GUI programs.

EXAMPLE: A Simple Window

Display 17.2 contains a Swing program that produces a simple window. The window contains nothing but a button on which is written "Click to end program." If the user follows the instructions and clicks the button with his or her mouse, the program ends.

The import statements give the names of the classes used and which package they are in. What we and others call the *Swing library* is the package named javax.swing. The *AWT library* is the package java.awt. Note that one package name contains an "x" and one does not.

This program is a simple class definition with only a main method. The first line in the main method creates an object of the class JFrame. That line is reproduced below:

```java
JFrame firstWindow = new JFrame();
```

This is an ordinary declaration of a variable named firstWindow and an invocation of the no-argument constructor for the class JFrame. A JFrame object is a basic window. A JFrame object includes a border and the usual three buttons for minimizing the window down to an icon, changing the size of the window, and closing the window. These buttons are shown in the upper-right corner of the window, which is typical, but if your operating system normally places these buttons someplace else, that is where they will likely be located in a JFrame on your computer.

The initial size of the JFrame window is set using the JFrame method setSize, as follows:

```java
firstWindow.setSize(WIDTH, HEIGHT);
```

In this case WIDTH and HEIGHT are defined int constants. The units of measure are pixels, so the window produced is 300 pixels by 200 pixels. (The term *pixel* is defined in the box entitled "Pixel.") As with other windows, you can change the size of a JFrame by using your mouse to drag a corner of the JFrame window.

The buttons for minimizing the window down to an icon and for changing the size of the window behave as they do in any of the other windows you have used. The minimization button shrinks the window down to an icon. (To restore the window, you click the icon.) The second button changes the size of the window back and forth from full screen to a smaller size. The close-window button can behave in different ways depending on how it is set by your program.

The behavior of the close-window button is set with the JFrame method setDefault-CloseOperation. The line of the program that sets the behavior of the close-window button is reproduced below:

```java
firstWindow.setDefaultCloseOperation(
                JFrame.DO_NOTHING_ON_CLOSE);
```

(continued)

EXAMPLE: (continued)

In this case the argument `JFrame.DO_NOTHING_ON_CLOSE` is a defined constant named `DO_NOTHING_ON_CLOSE`, which is defined in the `JFrame` class. This sets the close-window button so that when it is clicked nothing happens (unless we programmed something to happen, which we have not done). Other possible arguments are given in Display 17.3.

The method `setDefaultCloseOperation` takes a single `int` argument, and each of the constants described in Display 17.3 is an `int` constant. However, do not think of them as `int` values. Think of them as policies for what happens when the user clicks the close-window button. It was convenient to name these policies by `int` values. However, they could just as well have been named by `char` values or `String` values or something else. The fact that they are `int` values is an incidental detail of no real importance.

Descriptions of some of the most important methods in the class `JFrame` are given in Display 17.3. Some of these methods will not be explained until later in this chapter. A more complete list of methods for the class `JFrame` is given in Appendix 5.

A `JFrame` can have components added, such as buttons, menus, and text labels. For example, the following line from Display 17.2 adds the `JButton` object named end-Button to the `JFrame` named `firstWindow`:

```
firstWindow.add(endButton);
```

The description of how the `JButton` named `endButton` is created and programmed will be given in the two subsections entitled "Buttons" and "Action Listeners and Action Events" a little later in this section.

We end this subsection by jumping ahead to the last line of the program, which is

```
firstWindow.setVisible(true);
```

This makes the `JFrame` window visible on the screen. At first glance this may seem strange. Why not have windows automatically become visible? Why would you create a window if you did not want it to be visible? The answer is that you may not want it to be visible at all times. You have certainly experienced windows that disappear and reappear. To hide the window, which is not desirable in this example, you would replace the argument `true` with `false`.

JFrame

An object of the class `JFrame` is what you think of as a window. It automatically has a border and some basic buttons for minimizing the window and similar actions. As you will see, a `JFrame` object can have buttons and many other components added to the window and pro-grammed for action.

Display 17.2   **A First Swing Demonstration Program** (part 1 of 2)

```
1    import javax.swing.JFrame;
2    import javax.swing.JButton;                      This program is not typical of the
                                                       style we will use in Swing
3    public class FirstSwingDemo                       programs.
4    {
5        public static final int WIDTH = 300;
6        public static final int HEIGHT = 200;

7        public static void main(String[] args)
8        {
9            JFrame firstWindow = new JFrame();
10           firstWindow.setSize(WIDTH, HEIGHT);

11           firstWindow.setDefaultCloseOperation(
12                               JFrame.DO_NOTHING_ON_CLOSE);

13           JButton endButton = new JButton("Click to end program.");
14           EndingListener buttonEar = new EndingListener();
15           endButton.addActionListener(buttonEar);
16           firstWindow.add(endButton);

17           firstWindow.setVisible(true);
18       }
19   }
```
                        This is the file **FirstSwingDemo.java**.

```
1    import java.awt.event.ActionListener;
2    import java.awt.event.ActionEvent;    This is the file EndingListener.java.

3    public class EndingListener implements ActionListener
4    {
5        public void actionPerformed(ActionEvent e)
6        {
7            System.exit(0);
8        }
9    }
```

(continued)

Display 17.2 A First Swing Demonstration Program (part 2 of 2)

RESULTING GUI

Minimize (iconify)

Change window size to full screen.

Click to end program.

Close-window button

---

pixel

Pixel

A **pixel** is the smallest unit of space on which your screen can write. With Swing, both the size and the position of objects on the screen are measured in pixels. The more pixels you have on a screen, the greater the screen resolution.

Resolution's Relationship to Object Size

The relationship between resolution and size can seem confusing at first. A high-resolution screen is a screen of better quality than a low-resolution screen, so why does an object look smaller on a high-resolution screen and larger on a low-resolution screen? Consider a very simple case, namely a one-pixel "dot." For a screen of fixed size, if there are very many pixels (high resolution), then the one-pixel dot will be very small. If there are fewer pixels (low resolution) for the same size screen, then each pixel must be larger since the smaller number of pixels cover the same screen. So, if there are fewer pixels, the one-pixel dot will be larger. Similarly, a two-pixel figure or a figure of any number of pixels will look larger on a low-resolution (fewer pixels) screen.

Display 17.3 Some Methods in the Class `JFrame` (part 1 of 2)

The class `JFrame` is in the `javax.swing` package.

```
public JFrame()
```
Constructor that creates an object of the class `JFrame`.

Display 17.3   **Some Methods in the Class** `JFrame` (part 2 of 2)

---

   public `JFrame(String title)`

Constructor that creates an object of the class `JFrame` with the title given as the argument.

   public void `setDefaultCloseOperation(int operation)`

Sets the action that will happen by default when the user clicks the close-window button. The argument should be one of the following defined constants:

`JFrame.DO_NOTHING_ON_CLOSE`: Do nothing. The `JFrame` does nothing, but if there are any registered window listeners, they are invoked. (Window listeners are explained in Chapter 19.)

`JFrame.HIDE_ON_CLOSE`: Hide the frame after invoking any registered `WindowListener` objects.

`JFrame.DISPOSE_ON_CLOSE`: Hide and *dispose* the frame after invoking any registered window listeners. When a window is **disposed** it is eliminated but the program does not end. To end the program, you use the next constant as an argument to `setDefaultCloseOperation`.

`JFrame.EXIT_ON_CLOSE`: Exit the application using the `System exit` method. (Do not use this for frames in applets. Applets are discussed in Chapter 20 on the CD.)

If no action is specified using the method `setDefaultCloseOperation`, then the default action taken is `JFrame.HIDE_ON_CLOSE`.

Throws an `IllegalArgumentException` if the argument is not one of the values listed above.[3]

Throws a `SecurityException` if the argument is `JFrame.EXIT_ON_CLOSE` and the Security Manager will not allow the caller to invoke `System.exit`. (You are not likely to encounter this case.)

   public void `setSize(int width, int height)`

Sets the size of the calling frame so that it has the `width` and `height` specified. Pixels are the units of length used.

   public void `setTitle(String title)`

Sets the title for this frame to the argument string.

   public void `add(Component componentAdded)`

Adds a component to the `JFrame`.

   public void `setLayout(LayoutManager manager)`

Sets the layout manager. Layout managers are discussed later in this chapter.

   public void `setJMenuBar(JMenuBar menubar)`

Sets the menubar for the calling frame. (Menus and menu bars are discussed later in this chapter.)

   public void `dispose()`

Eliminates the calling frame and all its subcomponents. Any memory they use is released for reuse. If there are items left (items other than the calling frame and its subcomponents), then this does not end the program. (The method `dispose` is discussed in Chapter 19.)

---

[3] If you have not yet covered Chapter 9 on exceptions, you can safely ignore all references to "throwing exceptions."

The setVisible Method

Many classes of Swing objects have a `setVisible` method. The `setVisible` method takes one argument of type **boolean**. If w is an object, such as a `JFrame` window, that can be displayed on the screen, then the call

```
w.setVisible(true);
```

will make w visible. The call

```
w.setVisible(false);
```

will hide w.

SYNTAX

Object_For_Screen.setVisible(*Boolean_Expression*);

EXAMPLE (FROM DISPLAY 17.2)

```
public static void main(String[] args)
{
    JFrame firstWindow = new JFrame();
        .
        .
        .
    firstWindow.setVisible(true);
}
```

PITFALL: Forgetting to Program the Close-Window Button

The following lines from Display 17.2 ensure that when the user clicks the close-window button, nothing happens:

```
firstWindow.setDefaultCloseOperation(
                        JFrame.DO_NOTHING_ON_CLOSE);
```

If you forget to program the close-window button, then the default action is as if you had set it the following way:

```
firstWindow.setDefaultCloseOperation(
                        JFrame.HIDE_ON_CLOSE);
```

PITFALL: (continued)

In the program in Display 17.2 this would mean that if the user clicks the close-window button, the window will hide (become invisible and inaccessible), but the program will not end, which is a pretty bad situation. Since the window would be hidden, there would be no way to click the `"Click to end program."` button. You would need to use some operating system command that forces the program to end. That is an operating system topic, not a Java topic, and the exact command depends on which operating system you are using. ■

Self-Test Exercises

1. What Swing class do you normally use to define a window? Any window class that you define would normally be an object of this class.

2. What units of measure are used in the following call to `setSize` that appeared in the `main` method of the program in Display 17.2? In other words, 300 what? Inches? Centimeters? Light years? And similarly, 200 what?

   ```
   firstWindow.setSize(WIDTH, HEIGHT);
   ```

   which is equivalent to

   ```
   firstWindow.setSize(300, 200);
   ```

3. What is the method call to set the close-window button of the `JFrame` `someWindow` so that nothing happens when the user clicks the close-window button in `someWindow`?

4. What is the method call to set the close-window button of the `JFrame` `someWindow` so that the program ends when the user clicks the close-window button in `someWindow`?

5. What happens when you click the minimizing button of the `JFrame` shown in Display 17.2?

6. Suppose `someWindow` is a `JFrame` and `n` is an `int` variable with some value. Give a Java statement that will make `someWindow` visible if `n` is positive and hide `someWindow` otherwise.

Buttons

JButton

A button object is created in the same way that any other object is created, but you use the class `JButton`. For example, the following example from Display 17.2 creates a button:

```
JButton endButton = new JButton("Click to end program.");
```

The argument to the construct, in this case `"Click to end program."`, is a string that will be written on the button when the button is displayed. If you look at the picture of the GUI in Display 17.2, you will see that the button is labeled `"Click to end program."`

adding a button

We have already discussed adding components, such as buttons, to a JFrame. The button is added to the JFrame by the following line from Display 17.2:

```
firstWindow.add(endButton);
```

In the next subsection we explain the lines from Display 17.2 involving the method addActionListener.

The JButton Class

An object of the class JButton is displayed in a GUI as a component that looks like a button. You click the button with your mouse to simulate pushing it. When creating an object of the class JButton using **new**, you can give a string argument to the constructor and the string will be displayed on the button.

You can add a JButton object to a JFrame by using the method **add** with the JFrame as the calling object and the JButton object as the argument. You will later see that you can also add buttons to other GUI objects (known as "containers") in a similar way.

A button's action is programmed by registering a listener with the button using the method addActionListener.

EXAMPLE

```
JButton niceButton = new JButton("Click here");
niceButton.addActionListener(new SomeActionListenerClass());
someJFrame.add(niceButton);
```

The Close-Window Button Is Not in the Class JButton

The buttons that you add to a GUI are all objects of the class JButton. The close-window button and the other two accompanying buttons on a JFrame are not objects of the class JButton. They are part of the JFrame object.

Action Listeners and Action Events

Clicking a button with your mouse (or activating certain other items in a GUI) creates an object known as an event and sends the event object to another object (or objects) known as the listener(s). This is called firing the event. The listener then performs some action. When we say that the event is "sent" to the listener object, what we really mean is that some method in the listener object is invoked with the event object as the argument. This invocation happens automatically. Your Swing GUI class definition will not normally contain an invocation of this method. However, your Swing GUI class definition does need to do two things:

registering a listener

First, for each button, it needs to specify what objects are listeners that will respond to events fired by that button; this is called **registering** the listener.

Second, it must define the methods that will be invoked when the event is sent to the listener. Note that these methods will be defined by you, but in normal circumstances, you will never write an invocation of these methods. The invocations will take place automatically.

addAction-
Listener

The following lines from Display 17.2 create an `EndingListener` object named `buttonEar` and register `buttonEar` as a listener to receive events from the button named `endButton`:

```
EndingListener buttonEar = new EndingListener();
endButton.addActionListener(buttonEar);
```

The second line says that `buttonEar` is registered as a listener to `endButton`, which means `buttonEar` will receive all events fired by `endButton`.

action event
action
listener

Different kinds of components require different kinds of listener classes to handle the events they fire. A button fires events known as **action events**, which are handled by listeners known as **action listeners**.

Action-
Listener

An action listener is an object whose class implements the `ActionListener` interface. For example, the class `EndingListener` in Display 17.2 implements the `Action-Listener` interface. The `ActionListener` interface has only one method heading that must be implemented, namely the following:

action-
Performed

```
public void actionPerformed(ActionEvent e)
```

In the class `EndingListener` in Display 17.2, the `actionPerformed` method is defined as follows:

```
public void actionPerformed(ActionEvent e)
{
    System.exit(0);
}
```

If the user clicks the button `endButton`, that sends an action event to the action listener for that button. But `buttonEar` is the action listener for the button `endButton`, so the action event goes to `buttonEar`. When an action listener receives an action event, the event is automatically passed as an argument to the method `actionPer-formed` and the method `actionPerformed` is invoked. If the event is called e, then the following invocation takes place in response to `endButton` firing e:

```
buttonEar.actionPerformed(e);
```

In this case the parameter e is ignored by the method `actionPerformed`. The method `actionPerformed` simply invokes `System.exit` and thereby ends the program. So, if the user clicks `endButton` (the one labeled `"Click to end program."`), the net effect is to end the program and so the window goes away.

Note that you never write any code that says

```
buttonEar.actionPerformed(e);
```

This action does happen, but the code for this is embedded in some class definition inside the Swing and/or AWT libraries. Somewhere the code says something like

```
bla.actionPerformed(e);
```

and somehow `buttonEar` gets plugged in for the parameter `bla` and this invocation of `actionPerformed` is executed. But, all this is done for you. All you do is define the method `actionPerformed` and register `buttonEar` as a listener for `endButton`.

Note that the method `actionPerformed` must have a parameter of type `ActionEvent`, even if your definition of `actionPerformed` does not use this parameter. This is because the invocations of `actionPerformed` were already programmed for you and so must allow the possibility of using the `ActionEvent` parameter e. As you will see, in other Swing GUIs the method `actionPerformed` does often use the event e to determine which button was clicked. This first example is a special, simple case because there is only one button. Later in this chapter we will say more about defining the `actionPerformed` method in more complicated situations.

PITFALL: Changing the Heading for `actionPerformed`

When you define the method `actionPerformed` in an action listener, you are implementing the method heading for `actionPerformed` that is specified in the `Action-Listener` interface. Thus, the header for the method `actionPerformed` is determined for you, and you cannot change the heading. It must have exactly one parameter, and that parameter must be of type `ActionEvent`, as in the following:

```
public void actionPerformed(ActionEvent e)
```

If you change the type of the parameter or if you add (or subtract) a parameter, you will not have given a correct definition of an action listener.[4] The only thing you can change is the name of the parameter e, since it is just a placeholder. So the following change is acceptable:

```
public void actionPerformed(ActionEvent theEvent)
```

Of course, if you make this change, then inside the body of the method `actionPerformed`, you will use the identifier `theEvent` in place of the identifier e.

You also cannot add a `throws` clause to the method `actionPerformed`.[5] If a checked exception is thrown in the definition of `actionPerformed`, then it must be caught in the method `actionPerformed`. (Recall that a checked exception is one that must be either caught in a `catch` block or declared in a `throws` clause.) ∎

---

[4] Although it would be rather questionable style, you can overload the method named `actionPerformed` so that you have multiple versions of the method `actionPerformed`, each with a different parameter list. But only the version of `actionPerformed` shown above has anything to do with making a class into an action listener.

[5] If you have not yet covered exception handling (Chapter 9), you can safely ignore this paragraph.

TIP: Ending a Swing Program

A GUI program is normally based on a kind of infinite loop. There may not be a Java loop statement in a GUI program, but nonetheless the GUI program need not ever end. The windowing system normally stays on the screen until the user indicates that it should go away (for example, by clicking the "Click to end program." button in Display 17.2). If the user never asks the windowing system to go away, it will never go away. When you write a Swing GUI program, you need to use `System.exit` to end the program when the user (or something else) says it is time to end the program. Unlike the kinds of programs we saw before this chapter, a Swing program will not end after it has executed all the code in the program. A Swing program does not end until it executes a `System.exit`. (In some cases, the `System.exit` may be in some library code and need not be explicitly given in your code.) ∎

`System.exit`

Self-Test Exercises

7. What kind of event is fired when you click a `JButton`?

8. What method heading must be implemented in a class that implements the `ActionListener` interface?

9. Change the program in Display 17.2 so that the window displayed has the title "My First Window". *Hint:* Consult the description of constructors in Display 17.3.

EXAMPLE: A Better Version of Our First Swing GUI

Display 17.4 is a rewriting of the demonstration program in Display 17.2 that includes a few added features. This new version produces a window that is similar to the one produced by the program in Display 17.2. However, this new version is done in the style you should follow in writing your own GUIs. Notice that the window is produced by defining a class (`FirstWindow`) whose objects are windows of the kind we want. The window is then displayed by a program (`DemoWindow`) that uses the class `FirstWindow`.

Observe that `FirstWindow` is a derived class of the class `JFrame`. This is the normal way to define a windowing interface. The base class `JFrame` gives some basic window facilities, and then the derived class adds whatever additional features you want in your window interface.

Note that the constructor in Display 17.4 starts by calling the constructor for the parent class `JFrame` with the line

```
super();
```

(continued)

EXAMPLE: (continued)

As we noted in Chapter 7, this ensures that any initialization that is normally done for all objects of type JFrame will in fact be done. If the base class constructor you call has no arguments, then it will be called automatically, so we could have omitted the invocation of super() in Display 17.4. However, if the base class constructor needs an argument, as it may in some other situations, then you must include a call to the base class constructor, super.

Note that almost all the initializing for the window FirstWindow in Display 17.4 is placed in the constructor for the class. That is as it should be. The initialization, such as setting the initial window size, should be part of the class definition and not actions performed by objects of the class (as they were in Display 17.2). All the initializing methods, such as setSize and setDefaultCloseOperation, are inherited from the class JFrame. Because they are invoked in the constructor for the window, the window itself is the calling object. In other words, a method invocation such as

```
setSize(WIDTH, HEIGHT);
```

is equivalent to

```
this.setSize(WIDTH, HEIGHT);
```

Similarly, the method invocations

```
setDefaultCloseOperation(
          JFrame.DO_NOTHING_ON_CLOSE);
```

and

```
add(endButton);
```

are equivalent to

```
this.setDefaultCloseOperation(
          JFrame.DO_NOTHING_ON_CLOSE);
```

and

```
this.add(endButton);
```

In the class FirstWindow (Display 17.4) we added the title "First Window Class" to the window as follows:

```
setTitle("First Window Class");
```

You can see where the title is displayed in a JFrame by looking at the picture of the GUI given in Display 17.4.

EXAMPLE: (continued)

One thing we did differently in Display 17.4 than in Display 17.2 is to use an anonymous object in the following line:

```
endButton.addActionListener(new EndingListener());
```

The same action was performed by the following lines in Display 17.2:

```
EndingListener buttonEar = new EndingListener();
endButton.addActionListener(buttonEar);
```

In Display 17.2 we were trying to be extra clear and so we used these two steps. However, it makes more sense to use the anonymous object new EndingListener() since this listener object is never referenced again and so does not need a name.

The program DemoWindow in Display 17.4 simply displays an object of the class FirstWindow on the screen.

Almost all of the initialization details for the window in Display 17.4 have been moved to the constructor for the class FirstWindow. However, we have placed the invocations of the method setVisible in the application program that uses the window class FirstWindow. We could have placed an invocation of setVisible in the constructor for FirstWindow and omitted the invocation of setVisible from the application program DemoWindow (Display 17.4). If we had done so, we would have produced the same results when we ran the application program. However, in normal situations, the application program knows when the window should be displayed, so it is normal to put the invocation of the method setVisible in the application program. The programmer writing the class FirstWindow cannot anticipate when a programmer who uses the window will want to make it visible (or hide it).

Display 17.4 **The Normal Way to Define a JFrame** (part 1 of 2)

```
1    import javax.swing.JFrame;
2    import javax.swing.JButton;


3    public class FirstWindow extends JFrame
4    {
5        public static final int WIDTH = 300;
6        public static final int HEIGHT = 200;

7        public FirstWindow()
8        {
9            super();
10           setSize(WIDTH, HEIGHT);

11           setTitle("First Window Class");
```

(continued)

Display 17.4 The Normal Way to Define a **JFrame** (part 2 of 2)

```
12              setDefaultCloseOperation(
13                              JFrame.DO_NOTHING_ON_CLOSE);

14          JButton endButton = new JButton("Click to end program.");
15          endButton.addActionListener(new EndingListener());
16          add(endButton);
17      }
18  }
```

The class **EndingListener** *is defined in Display 17.2.*

This is the file **FirstWindow.java.**

This is the file **DemoWindow.java.**

```
1   public class DemoWindow
2   {
3       public static void main(String[] args)
4       {
5           FirstWindow w = new FirstWindow();
6           w.setVisible(true);
7       }
8   }
```

RESULTING GUI

JFrame Classes

When we say that a class is a **JFrame class** we mean the class is a descendent class of the class `JFrame`. For example, the class `FirstWindow` in Display 17.4 is a `JFrame` class. When we say an object is a **JFrame**, we mean that it is an object of some `JFrame` class.

Self-Test Exercises

10. Change the program in Display 17.4 so that the title of the `JFrame` is not set by the method `setTitle` but is instead set by the call to the base class constructor. *Hint:* Recall Self-Test Exercise 9.

11. Change the program in Display 17.4 so that there are two ways to end the GUI program: The program can be ended by either clicking the `"Click to end program."` button or clicking the close-window button.

Labels

label
JLabel

We have seen how to add a button to a `JFrame`. If you want to add some text to your `JFrame`, use a label instead of a button. A **label** is an object of the class `JLabel`. A label is little more than a line of text. The text for the label is given as an argument to the `JLabel` constructor as follows:

```
JLabel greeting = new JLabel("Hello");
```

The label `greeting` can then be added to a `JFrame` just as a button is added. For example, the following might appear in a constructor for a derived class of `JFrame`:

```
JLabel greeting = new JLabel("Hello");
add(greeting);
```

The next Programming Example includes a label in a `JFrame` GUI.

The JLabel Class

An object of the class `JLabel` is little more than one line of text that can be added to a `JFrame` (or, as we will see, added to certain other objects).

EXAMPLE (INSIDE A CONSTRUCTOR FOR A DERIVED CLASS OF JFrame)

```
JLabel myLabel = new JLabel("Hi Mom!");
add(myLabel);
```

Color

You can set the color of a JFrame (or other GUI object). To set the background color of a JFrame, you use

```
getContentPane().setBackground(Color);
```

For example, the following will set the color of the JFrame named someFrame to blue:

```
someFrame.getContentPane().setBackground(Color.BLUE);
```

Alternatively, if you set the color in the constructor for the JFrame, the invocation takes the form

```
getContentPane().setBackground(Color.BLUE);
```

which is equivalent to

```
this.getContentPane().setBackground(Color.BLUE);
```

The next Programming Example shows a JFrame object (in fact, two of them) with color. The method invocation getContentPane() returns something called the **content pane** of the JFrame. So,

```
getContentPane().setBackground(Color.BLUE);
```

actually sets the color of the content pane to blue. The content pane is the "inside" of the JFrame, so coloring the content pane has the effect of coloring the inside of the JFrame. However, you can think of

```
getContentPane().setBackground(Color);
```

as a peculiarly spelled method invocation that sets the color of the JFrame. (In this book, we will not be referring to the content pane of a JFrame except when we want to color the JFrame, so we will explain the content pane no further.)

You use getContentPane only when you give color to a JFrame. As you will see, to set the color of some component in a JFrame, such as a button, you simply use the method setBackground with the button or other component as the calling object. You will see examples of adding color to components in Section 17.3.

What kind of thing is a **color** when used in a Java Swing class? Like everything else in Java, a color is an object—in this case, an object that is an instance of the class Color. The class Color is in the java.awt package. (Note that the package name is java.awt, not javax.awt.)

In a later chapter, you will see how you can define your own colors, but for now we will use the colors that are already defined for you, such as Color.BLUE, which is a constant named BLUE that is defined in the class Color. The constant, of course, represents the color blue. If you set the background of a JFrame to Color.BLUE, then the JFrame will have a blue background. The type of the constant Color.BLUE and other such constants is Color. The list of color constants that are defined for you are given in Display 17.5. The next Programming Example has an example of a constructor with one parameter of type Color.

Display 17.5   **The Color Constants**

`Color.BLACK`	`Color.MAGENTA`
`Color.BLUE`	`Color.ORANGE`
`Color.CYAN`	`Color.PINK`
`Color.DARK_GRAY`	`Color.RED`
`Color.GRAY`	`Color.WHITE`
`Color.GREEN`	`Color.YELLOW`
`Color.LIGHT_GRAY`	

The class `Color` is in the `java.awt` package.

EXAMPLE: A GUI with a Label and Color

Display 17.6 shows a class for GUIs with a label and a background color. We have already discussed the use of color for this window. The label is used to display the text string `"Close-window button works."` The label is created as follows:

```java
JLabel aLabel = new JLabel("Close-window button works.");
```

The label is added to the `JFrame` with the method `add` as shown in the following line from Display 17.6:

```java
add(aLabel);
```

The GUI class `ColoredWindow` in Display 17.6 programs the close-window button as follows:

```java
setDefaultCloseOperation(JFrame.EXIT_ON_CLOSE);
```

This way, when the user clicks the close-window button, the program ends. Note that if the program has more than one window, as it does in Display 17.6, and the user clicks the close-window button in any one window of the class `ColoredWindow`, then the entire program ends and all windows go away.

Note that we set the title of the `JFrame` by making it an argument to `super` rather than an argument to `setTitle`. This is another common way to set the title of a `JFrame`.

If you run the program `DemoColoredWindow` in Display 17.6, then the two windows will be placed one on top of the other. To see both windows, you need to use your mouse to move the top window.

Setting the Title of a `JFrame`

The two most common ways to set the title of a `JFrame` are to use the method `setTitle`, as illustrated in Display 17.4, or to give the title as an argument to the base class constructor `super`, as illustrated in Display 17.6.

Self-Test Exercises

12. How would you modify the class definition in Display 17.6 so that the window produced by the no-argument constructor is magenta instead of pink?

13. Rewrite the following two lines from Display 17.6 so that the label does not have the name aLabel or any other name. *Hint:* Use an anonymous object.

    ```java
    JLabel aLabel = new JLabel("Close-window button works.");
    add(aLabel);
    ```

Display 17.6 A `JFrame` with Color (part 1 of 2)

```java
1   import javax.swing.JFrame;
2   import javax.swing.JLabel;
3   import java.awt.Color;

4   public class ColoredWindow extends JFrame
5   {
6       public static final int WIDTH = 300;
7       public static final int HEIGHT = 200;

8       public ColoredWindow(Color theColor)
9       {
10          super("No Charge for Color");
11          setSize(WIDTH, HEIGHT);
12          setDefaultCloseOperation(JFrame.EXIT_ON_CLOSE);

13          getContentPane().setBackground(theColor);

14          JLabel aLabel = new JLabel("Close-window button works.");
15          add(aLabel);
16      }
17      public ColoredWindow()
18      {
19          this(Color.GREEN);
20      }
21  }
```

This is an invocation of the other constructor.

This is the file `ColoredWindow.java`.

Display 17.6   A **JFrame** with Color (part 2 of 2)

```
1    import java.awt.Color;                          This is the file ColoredWindow.java.

2    public class DemoColoredWindow
3    {
4        public static void main(String[] args)
5        {
6            ColoredWindow w1 = new ColoredWindow();
7            w1.setVisible(true);

8            ColoredWindow w2 = new ColoredWindow(Color.GRAY);
9            w2.setVisible(true);
10       }
11   }
```

RESULTING GUI

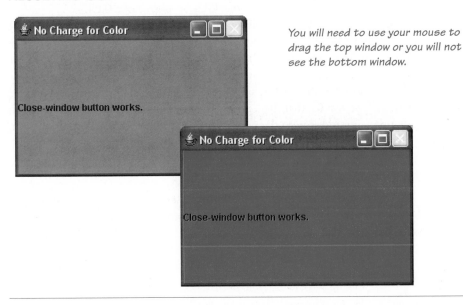

You will need to use your mouse to drag the top window or you will not see the bottom window.

17.3 Containers and Layout Managers

Don't put all your eggs in one basket.

PROVERB

There are two main ways to create new classes from old classes. One way is to use inheritance; this is known as the *Is-A relationship*. For example, an object of the class ColoredWindow in Display 17.6 *is a* JFrame because ColoredWindow is a derived class of the class JFrame. The second way to create a new class from an existing class (or classes) is to have instance variables of an already existing class type; this is known as *composition* or the *Has-A relationship*. The Swing library has already set things up so you can easily use composition. The actual code for declaring instance variables is in the Swing library classes, such as the class JFrame. Rather than declaring instance variables, you add components to a JFrame using the add method. This does ultimately set some instance variables, but that is done automatically when you use the add method. In this section, we discuss adding and arranging components in a GUI or subpart of a GUI.

Thus far, we have only added one component, either a button or a label, to a JFrame. You can add more than one component to a JFrame. To do so, you use the add method multiple times, but the add method simply tells which components are added to the JFrame; it does not say how they are arranged, such as side by side or one above the other. To describe how the components are arranged, you need to use a **layout manager**.

layout manager

In this section, we will see that there are other classes of objects besides JFrames that can have components added with the add method and arranged by a layout manager. All these classes are known as **container classes**.

container class

Border Layout Managers

Display 17.7 contains an example of a GUI that uses a layout manager to arrange three labels in a JFrame. The labels are arranged one below the other on three lines.

A layout manager is added to the JFrame class in Display 17.7 with the following line:

setLayout

```
setLayout(new BorderLayout());
```

Border-Layout

BorderLayout is a layout manager class, so new BorderLayout() produces a new anonymous object of the class BorderLayout. This BorderLayout object is given the task of arranging components (in this case, labels) that are added to the JFrame.

It may help to note that the above invocation of setLayout is equivalent to the following:

```
BorderLayout manager = new BorderLayout();
setLayout(manager);
```

Display 17.7   The **BorderLayout** Manager (part 1 of 2)

```
1   import javax.swing.JFrame;
2   import javax.swing.JLabel;
3   import java.awt.BorderLayout;

4   public class BorderLayoutJFrame extends JFrame
5   {
6       public static final int WIDTH = 500;
7       public static final int HEIGHT = 400;

8       public BorderLayoutJFrame()
9       {
10          super("BorderLayout Demonstration");
11          setSize(WIDTH, HEIGHT);
12          setDefaultCloseOperation(JFrame.EXIT_ON_CLOSE);

13          setLayout(new BorderLayout());

14          JLabel label1 = new JLabel("First label");
15          add(label1, BorderLayout.NORTH);

16          JLabel label2 = new JLabel("Second label");
17          add(label2, BorderLayout.SOUTH);

18          JLabel label3 = new JLabel("Third label");
19          add(label3, BorderLayout.CENTER);
20      }
21  }
```
                    This is the file **BorderLayoutJFrame.java.**

This is the file **BorderLayoutDemo.java.**

```
1   public class BorderLayoutDemo
2   {
3       public static void main(String[] args)
4       {
5           BorderLayoutJFrame gui = new BorderLayoutJFrame();
6           gui.setVisible(true);
7       }
8   }
```

(continued)

Display 17.7   The **BorderLayout** Manager (part 2 of 2)

Resulting GUI

A BorderLayout manager places labels (or other components) into the five regions BorderLayout.NORTH, BorderLayout.SOUTH, BorderLayout.EAST, BorderLayout.WEST, and BorderLayout.CENTER. These five regions are arranged as shown in Display 17.8. The outside box represents the JFrame (or other container to which you will add things). None of the lines in the diagram will be visible unless you do something to make them visible. We drew them in to show you where each region is located.

Display 17.8   **BorderLayout** Regions

BorderLayout.NORTH		
BorderLayout. WEST	BorderLayout.CENTER	BorderLayout. EAST
BorderLayout.SOUTH		

In Display 17.7, we added labels as follows:

```
JLabel label1 = new JLabel("First label");
add(label1, BorderLayout.NORTH);

JLabel label2 = new JLabel("Second label");
add(label2, BorderLayout.SOUTH);

JLabel label3 = new JLabel("Third label");
add(label3, BorderLayout.CENTER);
```

When you use a `BorderLayout` manager, you give the location of the component added as a second argument to the method `add`, as in the following:

```
add(label1, BorderLayout.NORTH);
```

The labels (or other components to be added) need not be added in any particular order, because the second argument completely specifies where the label is placed.

`BorderLayout.NORTH`, `BorderLayout.SOUTH`, `BorderLayout.EAST`, `BorderLayout.WEST`, and `BorderLayout.CENTER` are five string constants defined in the class `Border-Layout`. The values of these constants are `"North"`, `"South"`, `"East"`, `"West"`, and `"Center"`. Although you can use a quoted string such as `"North"` as the second argument to `add`, it is more consistent with our general style rules to use a defined constant like `BorderLayout.NORTH`.

You need not use all five regions. For example, in Display 17.7 we did not use the regions `BorderLayout.EAST` and `BorderLayout.WEST`. If some regions are not used, any extra space is given to the `BorderLayout.CENTER` region, which is the largest region.

(The space is divided between regions as follows: Regions are allocated space in the order first north and south, second east and west, and last center. So, in particular, if there is nothing in the north region, then the east and west regions will extend to the top of the space.)

From this discussion, it sounds as though you can place only one item in each region, but later in this chapter, when we discuss *panels,* you will see that there is a way to group items so that more than one item can (in effect) be placed in each region.

There are some standard layout managers defined for you in the `java.awt` package, and you can also define your own layout managers. However, for most purposes, the layout managers defined in the standard libraries are all that you need, and we will not discuss how you can create your own layout manager classes.

Flow Layout Managers

The `FlowLayout` **manager** is the simplest layout manager. It arranges components one after the other, going from left to right, in the order in which you add them to the `JFrame` (or other container class) using the method `add`. For example, if the class

---

Layout Managers

The components that you add to a container class are arranged by an object known as a **layout manager**. You add a layout manager with the method `setLayout`, which is a method of every container class, such as a `JFrame` or an object of any of the other container classes that we will introduce later in this chapter. If you do not add a layout manager, a default layout manager will be provided for you.

SYNTAX

Container_Object.`setLayout`(new *Layout_Manager_Class*());

EXAMPLE (WITHIN A CONSTRUCTOR FOR A CLASS CALLED `BorderLayoutJFrame`)

```
public BorderLayoutJFrame()
{
    ...
    setLayout(new BorderLayout());

    JLabel label1 = new JLabel("First label");
    add(label1, BorderLayout.NORTH);

    JLabel label2 = new JLabel("Second label");
    add(label2, BorderLayout.SOUTH);
    ...
}
```

---

in Display 17.7 had used the `FlowLayout` manager instead of the `BorderLayout` manager, it would have used the following code:

```
setLayout(new FlowLayout());

JLabel label1 = new JLabel("First label");
add(label1);

JLabel label2 = new JLabel("Second label");
add(label2);

JLabel label3 = new JLabel("Third label");
add(label3);
```

Note that if we had used the `FlowLayout` manager, as in the preceding code, then the add method would have only one argument. With a `FlowLayout` manager, the items are displayed in the order they are added, so that the labels above would be displayed all on one line as follows:

```
First label Second label Third label
```

extra
code on
CD

The full program is in the files FlowLayoutJFrame.java and FlowLayoutDemo.java on the accompanying CD. You will see a number of examples of GUIs that use the Flow-Layout manager class later in this chapter.

Grid Layout Managers

GridLayout

A **GridLayout manager** arranges components in a two-dimensional grid with some number of rows and columns. With a GridLayout manager, each entry is the same size. For example, the following says to use a GridLayout manager with aContainer, which can be a JFrame or other container:

```
aContainer.setLayout(new GridLayout(2, 3));
```

The two numbers given as arguments to the constructor GridLayout specify the number of rows and columns. This would produce the following sort of layout:

The lines will not be visible unless you do something special to make them visible. They are just included here to show you the region boundaries.

When using a GridLayout manager, each component is stretched so that it completely fills its grid position.

Although you specify a number of rows and columns, the rules for the number of rows and columns is more complicated than what we have said so far. If the values for the number of rows and the number of columns are both nonzero, then the number of columns will be ignored. For example, if the specification is new GridLayout(2, 3), then some sample sizes are as follows: If you add six items, the grid will be as shown. If you add seven or eight items, a fourth column is automatically added, and so forth. If you add fewer than six components, there will be two rows and a reduced number of columns.

There is another way to specify that the number of columns is to be ignored. You can specify that the number of columns is to be ignored by setting the number of columns to zero, which will allow any number of columns. So a specification of (2, 0) is equivalent to (2, 3), and in fact is equivalent to (2, n) for any nonnegative value of n. Similarly, you can specify that the number of rows is to be ignored by setting the number of rows to zero, which will allow any number of rows.

When using the GridLayout class, the method add has only one argument. The items are placed in the grid from left to right, first filling the top row, then the second row, and so forth. You are not allowed to skip any grid position (although you will later see that you can add something that does not show and so gives the illusion of skipping a grid position).

A sample use of the GridLayout class is given in Display 17.9.

Display 17.9 **The GridLayout** Manager (part 1 of 2)

```java
1   import javax.swing.JFrame;
2   import javax.swing.JLabel;
3   import java.awt.GridLayout;

4   public class GridLayoutJFrame extends JFrame
5   {
6       public static final int WIDTH = 500;
7       public static final int HEIGHT = 400;

8       public static void main(String[] args)
9       {
10          GridLayoutJFrame gui = new GridLayoutJFrame(2, 3);
11          gui.setVisible(true);
12      }

13      public GridLayoutJFrame(int rows, int columns )
14      {
15          super();
16          setSize(WIDTH, HEIGHT);
17          setTitle("GridLayout Demonstration");
18          setDefaultCloseOperation(JFrame.EXIT_ON_CLOSE);
19          setLayout(new GridLayout(rows, columns ));

20          JLabel label1 = new JLabel("First label");
21          add(label1);

22          JLabel label2 = new JLabel("Second label");
23          add(label2);

24          JLabel label3 = new JLabel("Third label");
25          add(label3);

26          JLabel label4 = new JLabel("Fourth label");
27          add(label4);

28          JLabel label5 = new JLabel("Fifth label");
29          add(label5);
30      }
31  }
```

Display 17.9   The **GridLayout** Manager (part 2 of 2)

Resulting GUI

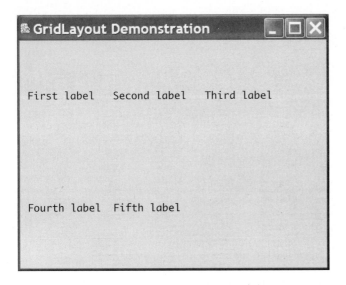

Note that we have placed a demonstration main method in the class definition in Display 17.9. This is handy, but is not typical. Normally, a Swing GUI is created and displayed in a main method (or other method) in some class other than the class that defines the GUI. However, it is perfectly legal and sometimes convenient to place a main method in the GUI class definition so that it is easy to display a sample of the GUI. Note that the main method that is given in the class itself is written in the same way as a main method that is in some other class. In particular, you need to construct an object of the class, as in the following line from the main method in Display 17.9:

```
GridLayoutJFrame gui = new GridLayoutJFrame(2, 3);
```

The three layout managers we have discussed are summarized in Display 17.10.

Next we will discuss *panels,* which will let you realize the full potential of layout managers.

Display 17.10 Some Layout Managers

LAYOUT MANAGER	DESCRIPTION
These layout manager classes are in the `java.awt` package.	
`FlowLayout`	Displays components from left to right in the order in which they are added to the container.
`BorderLayout`	Displays the components in five areas: north, south, east, west, and center. You specify the area a component goes into in a second argument of the **add** method.
`GridLayout`	Lays out components in a grid, with each component stretched to fill its box in the grid.

Self-Test Exercises

14. In Display 17.7, would it be legal to replace

```
JLabel label1 = new JLabel("First label");
add(label1, BorderLayout.NORTH);
JLabel label2 = new JLabel("Second label");
add(label2, BorderLayout.SOUTH);
JLabel label3 = new JLabel("Third label");
add(label3, BorderLayout.CENTER);
```

with the following?

```
JLabel aLabel = new JLabel("First label");
add(aLabel, BorderLayout.NORTH);
aLabel = new JLabel("Second label");
add(aLabel, BorderLayout.SOUTH);
aLabel = new JLabel("Third label");
add(aLabel, BorderLayout.CENTER);
```

In other words, can we reuse the variable aLabel or must each label have its own variable name?

15. How would you modify the class definition in Display 17.7 so that the three labels are displayed as follows?

```
First label
Second label
Third label
```

(There may be space between each pair of lines.)

16. How would you modify the class definition in Display 17.7 so that the three labels are displayed as follows?

```
First label
                          Second label
Third label
```

(There may be space between each pair of lines.)

17. Suppose you are defining a windowing GUI class in the usual way, as a derived class of the class JFrame, and suppose you want to specify a layout manager for the JFrame so as to produce the following sort of layout (that is, a one-row layout, typically having three columns):

What should the argument to setLayout be?

18. Suppose the situation is as described in Self-Test Exercise 17, except that you want the following sort of layout (that is, a one-column layout, typically having three rows):

What should the argument to setLayout be?

Panels

panel

A GUI is often organized in a hierarchical fashion, with window-like containers, known as *panels,* inside of other window-like containers. A **panel** is an object of the class JPanel, which is a very simple container class that does little more than group objects. It is one of the simplest container classes, but an extremely useful one. A JPanel object is analogous to the braces used to combine a number of simpler Java statements into a single larger Java statement. It groups smaller objects, such as buttons and labels, into a larger component (the JPanel). You can then put the JPanel object in a JFrame. Thus, one of the main functions of JPanel objects is to subdivide a JFrame (or other container) into different areas.

For example, when you use a BorderLayout manager, you can place components in each of the five locations BorderLayout.NORTH, BorderLayout.SOUTH, Border-Layout.EAST, BorderLayout.WEST, and BorderLayout.CENTER. But what if you want to put two components at the bottom of the screen in the BorderLayout.SOUTH position?

To do this, you would put the two components in a panel and then place the panel in the BorderLayout.SOUTH position.

You can give different layout managers to a JFrame and to each panel in the JFrame. Because you can add panels to other panels and each panel can have its own layout manager, this enables you to produce almost any kind of overall layout of the items in your GUI.

For example, if you want to place two buttons at the bottom of your JFrame GUI, you might add the following to the constructor of your JFrame GUI:

```
setLayout(new BorderLayout());

JPanel buttonPanel = new JPanel();
buttonPanel.setLayout(new FlowLayout());

JButton firstButton = new JButton("One");
buttonPanel.add(firstButton);

JButton secondButton = new JButton("Two");
buttonPanel.add(secondButton);

add(buttonPanel, BorderLayout.SOUTH);
```

The next Programming Example makes use of panels within panels.

EXAMPLE: A Tricolor Built with Panels

When first run, the GUI defined in Display 17.11 looks as shown in the first view. The entire background is light gray, and there are three buttons at the bottom of the GUI labeled "Green", "White", and "Gray". If you click any one of the buttons, a vertical stripe with the color written on the button appears. You can click the buttons in any order. In the last three views in Display 17.11 we show what happens if you click the buttons in left-to-right order.

The green, white, and gray stripes are the JPanels named greenPanel, whitePanel, and grayPanel. At first the panels are not visible because they are all light gray, so no borders are visible. When you click a button, the corresponding panel changes color and so is clearly visible.

Notice how the action listeners are set up. Each button registers the this parameter as a listener, as in the following line:

```
redButton.addActionListener(this);
```

Because this line appears inside of the constructor for the class PanelDemo, the this parameter refers to PanelDemo, which is the entire GUI. Thus, the entire JFrame (the entire GUI) is the listener, not the JPanel. So when you click one of the buttons, it is the actionPerformed method in PanelDemo that is executed.

EXAMPLE: (continued)

When a button is clicked, the `actionPerformed` method is invoked with the action event fired as the argument to `actionPerformed`. The method `actionPerformed` recovers the string written on the button with the following line:

```
String buttonString = e.getActionCommand();
```

The method `actionPerformed` then uses a multiway `if-else` statement to determine if `buttonString` is `"Green"`, `"White"`, or `"Gray"` and changes the color of the corresponding panel accordingly. It is common for an `actionPerformed` method to be based on such a multiway `if-else` statement, although we will see another approach in the subsection entitled "Listeners as Inner Classes" later in this chapter.

Display 17.11 also introduces one other small but new technique. We gave each button a color. We did this with the method `setBackground`, using basically the same technique that we used in previous examples. You can give a button or almost any other item a color using `setBackground`. Note that you do not use `getContentPane` when adding color to any component other than a `JFrame`.

Display 17.11   Using Panels (part 1 of 4)

```
1   import javax.swing.JFrame;
2   import javax.swing.JPanel;
3   import java.awt.BorderLayout;
4   import java.awt.GridLayout;
5   import java.awt.FlowLayout;
6   import java.awt.Color;
7   import javax.swing.JButton;
8   import java.awt.event.ActionListener;
9   import java.awt.event.ActionEvent;

10  public class PanelDemo extends JFrame implements ActionListener
11  {
12      public static final int WIDTH = 300;
13      public static final int HEIGHT = 200;

14      private JPanel greenPanel;
15      private JPanel whitePanel;
16      private JPanel grayPanel;

17      public static void main(String[] args)
18      {
19          PanelDemo gui = new PanelDemo();
20          gui.setVisible(true);
21      }
```

In addition to being the GUI class, the class **PanelDemo** *is the action listener class. An object of the class* **PanelDemo** *is the action listener for the buttons in that object.*

We made these instance variables because we want to refer to them in both the constructor and the method **actionPerformed**.

(continued)

Display 17.11   **Using Panels** (part 2 of 4)

```
22      public PanelDemo()
23      {
24          super("Panel Demonstration");
25          setSize(WIDTH, HEIGHT);
26          setDefaultCloseOperation(JFrame.EXIT_ON_CLOSE);
27          setLayout(new BorderLayout());

28          JPanel biggerPanel = new JPanel();
29          biggerPanel.setLayout(new GridLayout(1, 3));

30          greenPanel = new JPanel();
31          greenPanel.setBackground(Color.LIGHT_GRAY);
32          biggerPanel.add(greenPanel);

33          whitePanel = new JPanel();
34          whitePanel.setBackground(Color.LIGHT_GRAY);
35          biggerPanel.add(whitePanel);
36          grayPanel = new JPanel();
37          grayPanel.setBackground(Color.LIGHT_GRAY);
38          biggerPanel.add(grayPanel);

39          add(biggerPanel, BorderLayout.CENTER);

40          JPanel buttonPanel = new JPanel();
41          buttonPanel.setBackground(Color.LIGHT_GRAY);
42          buttonPanel.setLayout(new FlowLayout());

43          JButton greenButton = new JButton("Green");
44          greenButton.setBackground(Color.GREEN);
45          greenButton.addActionListener(this);
46          buttonPanel.add(greenButton);

47          JButton whiteButton = new JButton("White");
48          whiteButton.setBackground(Color.WHITE);
49          whiteButton.addActionListener(this);
50          buttonPanel.add(whiteButton);

51          JButton grayButton = new JButton("Gray");
52          grayButton.setBackground(Color.GRAY);
53          grayButton.addActionListener(this);
54          buttonPanel.add(grayButton);

55          add(buttonPanel, BorderLayout.SOUTH);
56      }
```

An object of the class **PanelDemo** *is the action listener for the buttons in that object.*

Display 17.11   Using Panels (part 3 of 4)

```
57      public void actionPerformed(ActionEvent e)
58      {
59          String buttonString = e.getActionCommand();

60          if (buttonString.equals("Green"))
61              greenPanel.setBackground(Color.GREEN);
62          else if (buttonString.equals("White"))
63              whitePanel.setBackground(Color.WHITE);
64          else if (buttonString.equals("Gray"))
65              grayPanel.setBackground(Color.GRAY);
66          else
67              System.out.println("Unexpected error.");
68      }
69  }
```

RESULTING GUI (When first run)

RESULTING GUI (After clicking Green button)

RESULTING GUI (After clicking White button)

(continued)

Display 17.11 Using Panels (part 4 of 4)

Resulting GUI (After clicking Gray button)

Adding Color

You color a JFrame as follows:

> *JFrame_Object*.getContentPane().setBackground(*Color*);

If this is inside a constructor for the JFrame, then the expression simplifies to

> getContentPane().setBackground(*Color*);

or the equivalent

> this.getContentPane().setBackground(*Color*);

You color a button, label, or any other component (which is not a JFrame) as follows:

> *Component_Object*.setBackground(*Color*);

Note that **getContentPane()** is only used with a JFrame.

EXAMPLE (INSIDE A CONSTRUCTOR FOR A DERIVED CLASS OF JFrame)

```
getContentPane().setBackground(Color.WHITE);
JButton redButton = new JButton("Red");
redButton.setBackground(Color.RED);
```

The Container Class

Container   The class called Container is in the java.awt package. Any descendent class of the class Container can have components added to it (or, more precisely, can have components added to objects of the class). The class JFrame is a descendent class of the class

Container, so any descendent class of the class JFrame can serve as a container to hold labels, buttons, panels, or other components.

Similarly, the class JPanel is a descendent of the class Container, and any object of the class JPanel can serve as a container to hold labels, buttons, other panels, or other components. Display 17.12 shows a portion of the hierarchy of Swing and AWT classes. Note that the Container class is in the AWT library and not in the Swing library. This is not a major issue, but it does mean that the import statement for the Container class is

```
import java.awt.Container;
```

container class

component

A **container class** is any descendent class of the class Container. The class JComponent serves a similar roll for components. Any descendent class of the class JComponent is called a JComponent or sometimes simply a **component**. You can add any JComponent object to any container class object.

The class JComponent is derived from the class Container, so you can add a JComponent to another JComponent. Often, this will turn out to be a viable option; occasionally it is something to avoid.[6]

The classes Component, Frame, and Window shown in Display 17.12 are AWT classes that some readers may have heard of. We include them for reference value, but we will have no need for these classes. We will eventually discuss all the other classes shown in Display 17.12.

When you are dealing with a Swing container class, you have three kinds of objects to deal with:

1. The container itself, probably some sort of panel or window-like object

2. The components you add to the container, like labels, buttons, and panels

3. A layout manager, which positions the components inside the container

You have seen examples of these three kinds of objects in almost every JFrame class we have defined. Almost every complete GUI you build, and many subparts of the GUIs you build, will be made up of these three kinds of objects.

Self-Test Exercises

19. What standard Java package contains the layout manager classes discussed in this chapter?

20. Is an object of the class JPanel a container class? Is it a component class?

21. With a GridLayout manager, you cannot leave any grid element empty, but you can do something that will make a grid element look empty to the user. What can you do?

---

[6] In particular, it is legitimate and sometimes useful to add JComponents to a JButton. We do not have space in this book to develop techniques for doing this effectively, but you may want to give it a try. You have had enough material to do it.

Display 17.12 **Hierarchy of Swing and AWT Classes**

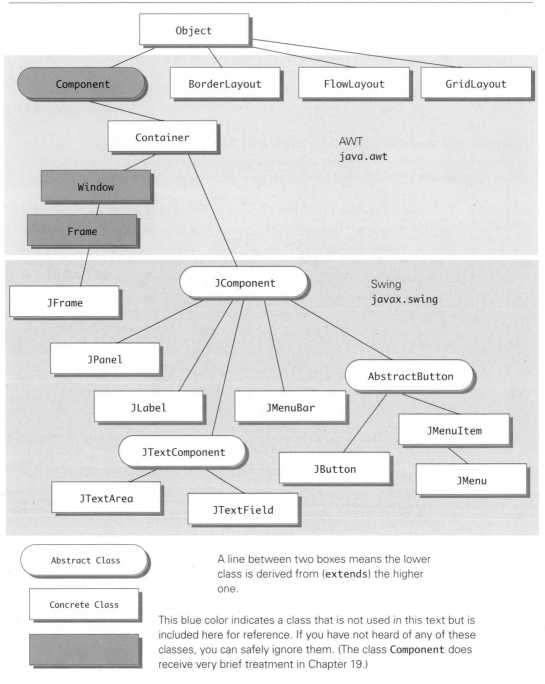

A line between two boxes means the lower class is derived from (**extends**) the higher one.

This blue color indicates a class that is not used in this text but is included here for reference. If you have not heard of any of these classes, you can safely ignore them. (The class **Component** does receive very brief treatment in Chapter 19.)

22. You are used to defining derived classes of the Swing class JFrame. You can also define derived classes of other Swing classes. Define a derived class of the class JPanel that is called PinkJPanel. An object of the class PinkJPanel can be used just as we used objects of the class JPanel, but an object of the class PinkJPanel is pink in color (unless you explicitly change its color). The class PinkJPanel will have only one constructor, namely the no-argument constructor. (*Hint:* This is very easy.)

TIP: Code a GUI's Look and Actions Separately

You can divide the task of designing a Swing GUI into two main subtasks: (1) Designing and coding the appearance of the GUI on the screen; (2) Designing and coding the actions performed in response to button clicks and other user actions. This dividing of one big task into two simpler tasks makes the big task easier and less error prone.

For example, consider the program in Display 17.11. Your first version of this program might use the following definition of the method actionPerformed:

```
public void actionPerformed(ActionEvent e)
{}
```

This version of the method actionPerformed does nothing, but your program will run and will display a window on the screen, just as shown in Display 17.11. If you click any of the buttons, nothing will happen, but you can use this version of your GUI to adjust details, such as the order and location of buttons.

After you get the GUI to look the way you want it to look, you can define the action parts of the GUI, typically the method actionPerformed.

If you include the phrase implements ActionListener at the start of your JFrame definition, then you must include some definition of the method actionPerformed. A method definition, such as

```
public void actionPerformed(ActionEvent e)
{}
```

stub   which does nothing (or does very little) is called a **stub**. Using stubs is a good programming technique in many contexts, not just in Swing programs.

Alternatively, when writing your first version of a Swing GUI like the one in Display 17.11, you could omit the definition of the method actionPerformed completely, *provided you also omit the phrase* implements ActionListener *and omit the invocations of* addActionListener. ■

The Model-View-Controller Pattern ★

Model-View-Controller

The technique we advocated in the previous Programming Tip is an example of a general technique known as the **Model-View-Controller** pattern. Display 17.13 gives a diagram of this pattern. The Model part of the pattern performs the heart of the application. The View part is the output part; it displays a picture of the Model's state. The Controller is the input part; it relays commands from the user to the Model. Each of the three interacting parts is realized as an object with responsibility for its own tasks. In a simple task such as the JFrame in Display 17.11, you can have a single object with different methods to realize each of the roles Model, View, and Controller.

To simplify the discussion, we have presented the Model-View-Controller pattern as if the user interacts directly with the Controller. The Controller need not be under the direct control of the user, but could be controlled by some other software or hardware component. In a Swing GUI, the View and Controller parts might be separate classes or separate methods combined into one larger class that displays a single window for all user interactions.

Self-Test Exercises

23. Suppose you omitted the method actionPerformed from the class in Display 17.11 and made no other changes. Would the class compile? If it compiles, will it run with no error messages?

24. Suppose you omitted the method actionPerformed and the phrase implements ActionListener from the class in Display 17.11 and made no other changes. Would the class compile? If it compiles, will it run with no error messages?

Display 17.13   The Model-View-Controller Pattern

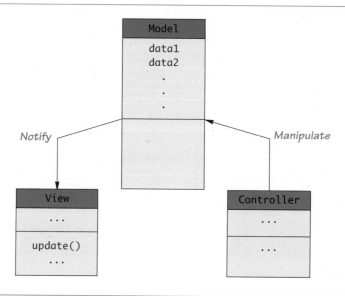

17.4   **Menus and Buttons**

For hours and location press 1.

For a recorded message describing services press 2.

For instructions on using our website press 3.

To use our automated information system press 4.

To speak to an operator between 8 am and noon Monday through

Thursdays press 7.

PHONE ANSWERING MACHINE

In this section we describe the basics of Swing menus. Swing menu items (menu choices) behave essentially the same as Swing buttons. They generate action events that are handled by action listeners, just as buttons do.

EXAMPLE: A GUI with a Menu

Display 17.14 contains a program that is essentially the same as the GUI in Display 17.11 except that this GUI uses a menu instead of buttons. This GUI has a menu bar at the top of the window. The menu bar lists the names of all the pull-down menus. This GUI has only one pull-down menu, which is named "Add Colors". However, there could be more pull-down menus in the same menu bar.

The user can pull down a menu by clicking its name in the menu bar. Display 17.14 contains three pictures of the GUI. The first is what you see when the GUI first appears. In that picture, the menu name "Add Colors" can be seen in the menu bar, but you cannot see the menu. If you click the words "Add Colors" with your mouse, the menu drops down, as shown in the second picture of the GUI. If you click "Green", "White", or "Gray" on the menu, then a vertical strip of the named color appears in the GUI.

In the next subsection, we go over the details of the program in Display 17.14.

Menu Bars, Menus, and Menu Items

When adding menus as we did in Display 17.14, you use the three Swing classes JMenuItem, JMenu, and JMenuBar. Entries on a menu are objects of the class JMenuItem. These JMenuItems are placed in JMenus, and then the JMenus are typically placed in a JMenuBar. Let's look at the details.

menu

menu item

A **menu** is an object of the class JMenu. A choice on a menu is called a **menu item** and is an object of the class JMenuItem. A menu item is identified by the string that labels it, such as "Green", "White", or "Gray" in the menu in Display 17.14. You can add as many JMenuItems as you wish to a menu. The menu lists the items in the order

Display 17.14   **A GUI with a Menu** (part 1 of 3)

```
1    import javax.swing.JFrame;
2    import javax.swing.JPanel;
3    import java.awt.GridLayout;
4    import java.awt.Color;
5    import javax.swing.JMenu;
6    import javax.swing.JMenuItem;
7    import javax.swing.JMenuBar;
8    import java.awt.event.ActionListener;
9    import java.awt.event.ActionEvent;

10   public class MenuDemo extends JFrame implements ActionListener
11   {
12       public static final int WIDTH = 300;
13       public static final int HEIGHT = 200;

14       private JPanel greenPanel;
15       private JPanel whitePanel;
16       private JPanel grayPanel;

17       public static void main(String[] args)
18       {
19           MenuDemo gui = new MenuDemo();
20           gui.setVisible(true);
21       }

22       public MenuDemo()
23       {
24           super("Menu Demonstration");
25           setSize(WIDTH, HEIGHT);
26           setDefaultCloseOperation(JFrame.EXIT_ON_CLOSE);
27           setLayout(new GridLayout(1, 3));

28           greenPanel = new JPanel();
29           greenPanel.setBackground(Color.LIGHT_GRAY);
30           add(greenPanel);

31           whitePanel = new JPanel();
32           whitePanel.setBackground(Color.LIGHT_GRAY);
33           add(whitePanel);
```

Display 17.14 A GUI with a Menu (part 2 of 3)

```
34          grayPanel = new JPanel();
35          grayPanel.setBackground(Color.LIGHT_GRAY);
36          add(grayPanel);

37          JMenu colorMenu = new JMenu("Add Colors");

38          JMenuItem greenChoice = new JMenuItem("Green");
39          greenChoice.addActionListener(this);
40          colorMenu.add(greenChoice);

41          JMenuItem whiteChoice = new JMenuItem("White");
42          whiteChoice.addActionListener(this);
43          colorMenu.add(whiteChoice);

44          JMenuItem grayChoice = new JMenuItem("Gray");
45          grayChoice.addActionListener(this);
46          colorMenu.add(grayChoice);

47          JMenuBar bar = new JMenuBar();
48          bar.add(colorMenu);
49          setJMenuBar(bar);
50      }
```

The definition of **actionPerformed** *is identical to the definition given in Display 17.11 for a similar GUI using buttons instead of menu items.*

```
51      public void actionPerformed(ActionEvent e)
52      {
53          String buttonString = e.getActionCommand();

54          if (buttonString.equals("Green"))
55              greenPanel.setBackground(Color.GREEN);
56          else if (buttonString.equals("White"))
57              whitePanel.setBackground(Color.WHITE);
58          else if (buttonString.equals("Gray"))
59              grayPanel.setBackground(Color.GRAY);
60          else
61              System.out.println("Unexpected error.");
62      }
63  }
```

(continued)

Display 17.14   A GUI with a Menu (part 3 of 3)

RESULTING GUI

RESULTING GUI (after clicking Add Colors in the menu bar)

RESULTING GUI (after choosing Green and White on the menu)

RESULTING GUI (after choosing all the colors on the menu)

in which they are added. The following code, taken from the constructor in Display 17.14, creates a new JMenu object named colorMenu and then adds a JMenuItem labeled "Red". Other menu items are added in a similar way.

```
JMenu colorMenu = new JMenu("Add Colors");

JMenuItem greenChoice = new JMenuItem("Green");
greenChoice.addActionListener(this);
colorMenu.add(greenChoice);
```

listeners

Note that, just as we did for buttons in Display 17.11, in Display 17.14 we have registered the this parameter as an action listener for each menu item. Defining action listeners and registering listeners for menu items are done in the exact same way as for buttons. In fact, the syntax is even the same. If you compare Display 17.14 and Display 17.11, you will see that the definition of the method actionPerformed is the same in both classes.

You add a JMenuItem to an object of the class JMenu using the method add in exactly the same way that you add a component, such as a button, to a container object. Moreover, if you look at the preceding code, you will see that you specify a string for a JMenuItem in the same way that you specify a string to appear on a button.

menu bar

A **menu bar** is a container for menus, typically placed near the top of a windowing interface. You add a menu to a menu bar using the method add in the same way that you add menu items to a menu. The following code from the constructor in Display 17.14 creates a new menu bar named bar and then adds the menu named colorMenu to this menu bar:

```
JMenuBar bar = new JMenuBar();
bar.add(colorMenu);
```

There are two different ways to add a menu bar to a JFrame. You can use the method setJMenuBar, as shown in the following code from the constructor in Display 17.14:

```
setJMenuBar(bar);
```

This sets an instance variable of type JMenuBar so that it names the menu bar named bar. Saying it less formally, this adds the menu bar named bar to the JFrame and places the menu bar at the top of the JFrame.

extra code on CD

Alternatively, you can use the add method to add a menu bar to a JFrame (or to any other container). You do so in the same way that you add any other component, such as a label or a button. An example of using add to add a JMenuBar to a JFrame is given in the file MenuAdd.java on the accompanying CD.

Menus

A menu is an object of the class `JMenu`. A choice on a menu is an object of the class `JMenu-Item`. Menus are collected together in a menu bar (or menu bars). A menu bar is an object of the class `JMenuBar`.

Events and listeners for menu items are handled in exactly the same way as they are for buttons.

Nested Menus ★

As shown in Display 17.12, the class `JMenu` is a descendent of the `JMenuItem` class. So, every `JMenu` object is also a `JMenuItem` object. Thus, a `JMenu` can be a menu item in another menu. This means that you can nest menus. For example, the outer menu might give you a list of menus. You can display one of the menus on that list by clicking the name of the desired menu. You can then choose an item from that menu by using your mouse again. There is nothing new you need to know to create these nested menus. You simply add menus to menus just as you add other menu items. There is an example of nested menus in the file `NestedMenus.java` on the accompanying CD.

extra code on CD

The `AbstractButton` Class

As shown in Display 17.12, the classes `JButton` and `JMenuItem` are derived classes of the abstract class named `AbstractButton`. All of the basic properties and methods of the classes `JButton` and `JMenuItem` are inherited from the class `AbstractButton`. That is why objects of the class `JButton` and objects of the class `JMenuItem` are so similar. Some of the methods for the class `AbstractButton` are listed in Display 17.15. All these methods are inherited by both the class `JButton` and the class `JMenuItem`. (Some of these methods were inherited by the class `AbstractButton` from the class `JComponent`, so you may sometimes see some of the methods listed as "inherited from `JComponent`.")

Adding Menus to a `JFrame`

In the following, we assume that all code is inside a constructor for a (derived class of a) `JFrame`. To see the following examples put together to produce a complete GUI, see the constructor in Display 17.14.

Creating Menu Items

A menu item is an object of the class `JMenuItem`. You create a new menu item in the usual way, as illustrated by the following example. The string in the argument position is the displayed text for the menu item.

```
JMenuItem redChoice = new JMenuItem("Red");
```

Adding Menu Item Listeners

Events and listeners for menu items are handled in the exact same way as they are for buttons: Menu items fire action events that are received by objects of the class `ActionListener`.

SYNTAX

```
JMenu_Item_Name.addActionListener(Action_Listener);
```

EXAMPLE

```
redChoice.addActionListener(this);
```

Creating a Menu

A menu is an object of the class `JMenu`. You create a new menu in the usual way, as illustrated by the following example. The string argument is the displayed text that identifies the menu.

```
JMenu colorMenu = new JMenu("Add Colors");
```

Adding Menu Items to a Menu

You use the method *add* to add menu items to a menu.

SYNTAX

```
JMenu_Name.add(JMenu_Item);
```

EXAMPLE (colorMenu IS AN OBJECT OF THE CLASS JMenu)

```
colorMenu.add(redChoice);
```

Creating a Menu Bar

A menu bar is an object of the class `JMenuBar`. You create a new menu bar in the usual way, as illustrated by the following example:

```
JMenuBar bar = new JMenuBar();
```

Adding a Menu to a Menu Bar

You add a menu to a menu bar using the method *add* as follows:

SYNTAX

```
JMenu_Bar_Name.add(JMenu_Name);
```

EXAMPLE (bar IS AN OBJECT OF THE CLASS JMenuBar)

```
bar.add(colorMenu);
```

(continued)

Adding a Menu Bar to a Frame

There are two different ways to add a menu bar to a JFrame. You can use the method add to add the menu bar to a JFrame (or to any other container). Another common way of adding a menu bar to a JFrame is to use the method setJMenuBar as follows:

SYNTAX

```
setJMenuBar(JMenu_Bar_Name);
```

EXAMPLE

```
setJMenuBar(bar);
```

Display 17.15 Some Methods in the Class AbstractButton (part 1 of 2)

The abstract class **AbstractButton** is in the **javax.swing** package.

All of these methods are inherited by both of the classes **JButton** and **JMenuItem**.

```
public void setBackground(Color theColor)
```

Sets the background color of this component.

```
public void addActionListener(ActionListener listener)
```

Adds an **ActionListener**.

```
public void removeActionListener(ActionListener listener)
```

Removes an **ActionListener**.

```
public void setActionCommand(String actionCommand)
```

Sets the action command.

```
public String getActionCommand()
```

Returns the action command for this component.

```
public void setText(String text)
```

Makes text the only text on this component.

```
public String getText()
```

Returns the text written on the component, such as the text on a button or the string for a menu item.

```
public void setPreferredSize(Dimension preferredSize)
```

Sets the preferred size of the button or label. Note that this is only a suggestion to the layout manager. The layout manager is not required to use the preferred size. The following special case will work for most simple situations. The **int** values give the width and height in pixels.

```
public void setPreferredSize(
                        new Dimension(int width, int height))
```

Display 17.15   Some Methods in the Class `AbstractButton` (part 2 of 2)

```
    public void setMaximumSize(Dimension maximumSize)
```

Sets the maximum size of the button or label. Note that this is only a suggestion to the layout manager. The layout manager is not required to respect this maximum size. The following special case will work for most simple situations. The `int` values give the width and height in pixels.

```
    public void setMaximumSize(
                    new Dimension(int width, int height))
```

```
    public void setMinimumSize(Dimension minimumSize)
```

Sets the minimum size of the button or label. Note that this is only a suggestion to the layout manager. The layout manager is not required to respect this minimum size.

Although we do not discuss the `Dimension` class, the following special case is intuitively clear and will work for most simple situations. The `int` values give the width and height in pixels.

```
    public void setMinimumSize(
                    new Dimension(int width, int height))
```

The Dimension Class

Objects of the class `Dimension` are used with buttons, menu items, and other objects to specify a size. The `Dimension` class is in the package `java.awt`. The parameters in the following constructor are pixels.

Constructor

```
    Dimension(int width, int height)
```

EXAMPLE

```
    aButton.setPreferredSize(new Dimension(30, 50));
```

The `setActionCommand` Method

When the user clicks a button or menu item, that fires an action event that normally goes to one or more action listeners where it becomes an argument to an `action-Performed` method. This action event includes a `String` instance variable that is known as the **action command** for the button or menu item and that is retrieved with the accessor method `getActionCommand`. The action command in the event is copied from an instance variable in the button or menu item object. If you do nothing to change it, the action command is the string written on the button or the menu item. The method `setActionCommand` given in Display 17.15 for the class `AbstractButton`

action
command

can be used with any `JButton` or `JMenuItem` to change the action command for that component. Among other things, this will allow you to have different action commands for two buttons, two menu items, or a button and menu item even though they have the same string written on them.

setAction-
Command
The method `setActionCommand` takes a `String` argument that becomes the new action command for the calling button or menu item. For example, consider the following code:

```
JButton nextButton = new JButton("Next");
nextButton.setActionCommand("Next Button");
JMenuItem chooseNext = new JMenuItem("Next");
chooseNext.setActionCommand("Next Menu Item");
```

If we had not used `setActionCommand` in the preceding code, then the button `nextButton` and the menu item `chooseNext` would both have the action command `"Next"` and so we would have no way to tell which of the two components `nextButton` and `chooseNext` an action event `"Next"` came from. However, using the method `setActionCommand`, we can give them the different action commands `"Next Button"` and `"Next Menu Item"`.

The action command for a `JButton` or `JMenuItem` is kept as the value of a private instance variable for the `JButton` or `JMenuItem`. The method `setActionCommand` is simply an ordinary mutator method that changes the value of this instance variable.

---

setActionCommand and getActionCommand

Every button and every menu item has a string associated with it that is known as the **action command** for that button or menu item. When the button or menu item is clicked, it fires an action event **e**. The following invocation returns the action command for the button or menu item that fired **e**:

```
e.getActionCommand()
```

The method `actionPerformed` typically uses this action command string to decide which button or menu item was clicked.

The default action command for a button or menu item is the string written on it, but if you want, you can change the action command with an invocation of the method `setActionCommand`. For example, the menu item `chooseNext` created by the following code will display the string `"Next"` when it is a menu choice, but will have the string `"Next Menu Item"` as its action command.

EXAMPLE
```
JMenuItem chooseNext = new JMenuItem("Next");
chooseNext.setActionCommand("Next Menu Item");
```

An alternate approach to defining action listeners is given in the next subsection. That technique is, among other things, another way to deal with multiple buttons or menu items that have the same thing written on them.

Listeners as Inner Classes ★

In all of our previous examples, our GUIs had only one action listener object to deal with all action events from all buttons and menus in the GUI. The opposite extreme also has much to recommend it. You can have a separate `ActionListener` class for each button or menu item, so that each button or menu item has its own unique action listener. There is then no need for a multiway `if-else` statement. The listener knows which button or menu item was clicked because it listens to only one button or menu item.

The approach outlined in the previous paragraph does have one down side: You typically need to give a lot of definitions of `ActionListener` classes. Rather than putting each of these classes in a separate file, it is much cleaner to make them private inner classes. This has the added advantage of allowing the `ActionListener` classes to have access to private instance variables and methods of the outer class.

In Display 17.16 we have redone the GUI in Display 17.14 using the techniques of this subsection.

Display 17.16 **Listeners as Inner Classes** (part 1 of 3)

<Import statements are the same as in Display 17.14.>

```java
1   public class InnerListenersDemo extends JFrame
2   {
3       public static final int WIDTH = 300;
4       public static final int HEIGHT = 200;

5       private JPanel greenPanel;
6       private JPanel whitePanel;
7       private JPanel grayPanel;

8       private class greenListener implements ActionListener
9       {
10          public void actionPerformed(ActionEvent e)
11          {
12              greenPanel.setBackground(Color.GREEN);
13          }
14      } //End of greenListener inner class

15      private class WhiteListener implements ActionListener
16      {
17          public void actionPerformed(ActionEvent e)
18          {
19              whitePanel.setBackground(Color.WHITE);
20          }
21      } //End of WhiteListener inner class
```

(continued)

Display 17.16   Listeners as Inner Classes (part 2 of 3)

```
22      private class grayListener implements ActionListener
23      {
24          public void actionPerformed(ActionEvent e)
25          {
26              grayPanel.setBackground(Color.GRAY);
27          }
28      } //End of grayListener inner class

29      public static void main(String[] args)
30      {
31          InnerListenersDemo gui = new InnerListenersDemo();
32          gui.setVisible(true);
33      }

34      public InnerListenersDemo()                      The resulting GUI is the same as in
35      {                                                Display 17.14.
36          super("Menu Demonstration");
37          setSize(WIDTH, HEIGHT);
38          setDefaultCloseOperation(JFrame.EXIT_ON_CLOSE);
39          setLayout(new GridLayout(1, 3));

40          greenPanel = new JPanel();
41          greenPanel.setBackground(Color.LIGHT_GRAY);
42          add(greenPanel);

43          whitePanel = new JPanel();
44          whitePanel.setBackground(Color.LIGHT_GRAY);
45          add(whitePanel);

46          grayPanel = new JPanel();
47          grayPanel.setBackground(Color.LIGHT_GRAY);
48          add(grayPanel);

49          JMenu colorMenu = new JMenu("Add Colors");

50          JMenuItem greenChoice = new JMenuItem("Green");
51          greenChoice.addActionListener(new greenListener());
52          colorMenu.add(greenChoice);

53          JMenuItem whiteChoice = new JMenuItem("White");
54          whiteChoice.addActionListener(new WhiteListener());
55          colorMenu.add(whiteChoice);
```

Display 17.16   Listeners as Inner Classes (part 3 of 3)

```
56              JMenuItem grayChoice = new JMenuItem("Gray");
57              grayChoice.addActionListener(new grayListener());
58              colorMenu.add(grayChoice);

59              JMenuBar bar = new JMenuBar();
60              bar.add(colorMenu);
61              setJMenuBar(bar);
62          }

63      }
```

Self-Test Exercises

25. What type of event is fired when you click a JMenuItem? How does it differ from the type of event fired when you click a JButton?

26. Write code to create a JButton with "Hello" written on it but with "Bye" as its action command.

27. Write code to create a JMenuItem with "Hello" as its displayed text (when it is a choice in a menu) but with "Bye" as its action command.

28. If you want to change the action command for a JButton, you use the method setActionCommand. What method do you use to change the action command for a JMenuItem?

29. Is the following legal in Java?

```
JMenu aMenu = new JMenu();
    ...
JMenu aSubMenu = new JMenu();
    ...
aMenu.add(aSubMenu);
```

30. How many JMenuBar objects can you have in a JFrame?

31. A JFrame has a private instance variable of type JMenuBar. What is the name of the mutator method to change the value of this instance variable?

32. Write code to create a new menu item named aChoice that has the label "Exit".

33. Suppose you are defining a class called MenuGUI that is a derived class of the class JFrame. Write code to add the menu item mItem to the menu m. Then add m to the menu bar mBar, and then add the menu bar to the JFrame MenuGUI. Assume that this all takes place inside a constructor for MenuGUI. Also assume that everything has already been constructed with new, and that all necessary listeners are registered. You just need to do the adding of things.

34. ★ How can you modify the program in Display 17.16 so that when the Blue menu item is clicked, all three colors are shown? The Red and White choices remain the same. (Remember the menu items may be clicked in any order, so the Blue menu item can be the first or second item clicked.)

35. ★ Rewrite the Swing GUI in Display 17.16 so that there is only one action listener inner class. The inner class constructor will have two parameters, one for a panel and one for a color.

17.5 Text Fields and Text Areas

Write your answers in the spaces provided.

COMMON INSTRUCTION FOR AN EXAMINATION

You have undoubtedly interacted with windowing systems that provide spaces for you to enter text information such as your name, address, and credit card number. In this section, we show you how to add these fields for text input and text output to your Swing GUIs.

Text Areas and Text Fields

text field
JText-Field

A **text field** is an object of the class JTextField and is displayed as a field that allows the user to enter a single line of text. In Display 17.17 the following creates a text field named name in which the user will be asked to enter his or her name:

```
private JTextField name;
    ...
name = new JTextField(NUMBER_OF_CHAR);
```

In Display 17.17 the variable name is a private instance variable. The creation of the JTextField in the last of the previous lines takes place inside the class constructor. The number NUMBER_OF_CHAR that is given as an argument to the JTextField constructor specifies that the text field will have room for at least NUMBER_OF_CHAR characters to be visible. The defined constant NUMBER_OF_CHAR is 30, so the text field is guaranteed to have room for at least 30 characters. You can type any number of characters into a text field but only a limited number will be visible; in this case, you know that at least 30 characters will be visible.

A Swing GUI can read the text in a text field and so receive text input, and if that is desired, can produce output by causing text to appear in the text field. The method getText returns the text written in the text field. For example, the following will set a variable named inputString to whatever string is in the text field name at the time that the getText method is invoked:

```
String inputString = name.getText();
```

Display 17.17   **A Text Field** (part 1 of 2)

```
1    import javax.swing.JFrame;
2    import javax.swing.JTextField;
3    import javax.swing.JPanel;
4    import javax.swing.JLabel;
5    import javax.swing.JButton;
6    import java.awt.GridLayout;
7    import java.awt.BorderLayout;
8    import java.awt.FlowLayout;
9    import java.awt.Color;
10   import java.awt.event.ActionListener;
11   import java.awt.event.ActionEvent;

12   public class TextFieldDemo extends JFrame
13                             implements ActionListener
14   {
15       public static final int WIDTH = 400;
16       public static final int HEIGHT = 200;
17       public static final int NUMBER_OF_CHAR = 30;

18       private JTextField name;

19       public static void main(String[] args)
20       {
21           TextFieldDemo gui = new TextFieldDemo();
22           gui.setVisible(true);
23       }

24       public TextFieldDemo()
25       {
26           super("Text Field Demo");
27           setSize(WIDTH, HEIGHT);
28           setDefaultCloseOperation(JFrame.EXIT_ON_CLOSE);
29           setLayout(new GridLayout(2, 1));

30           JPanel namePanel = new JPanel();
31           namePanel.setLayout(new BorderLayout());
32           namePanel.setBackground(Color.WHITE);

33           name = new JTextField(NUMBER_OF_CHAR);
34           namePanel.add(name, BorderLayout.SOUTH);
35           JLabel nameLabel = new JLabel("Enter your name here:");
36           namePanel.add(nameLabel, BorderLayout.CENTER);

37           add(namePanel);
```

(continued)

Display 17.17   A Text Field (part 2 of 2)

```
38            JPanel buttonPanel = new JPanel();
39            buttonPanel.setLayout(new FlowLayout());
40            buttonPanel.setBackground(Color.GREEN);
41            JButton actionButton = new JButton("Click me");
42            actionButton.addActionListener(this);
43            buttonPanel.add(actionButton);

44            JButton clearButton = new JButton("Clear");
45            clearButton.addActionListener(this);
46            buttonPanel.add(clearButton);

47            add(buttonPanel);
48        }

49    public void actionPerformed(ActionEvent e)
50        {
51            String actionCommand = e.getActionCommand();

52            if (actionCommand.equals("Click me"))
53                name.setText("Hello " + name.getText());
54            else if (actionCommand.equals("Clear"))
55                name.setText("");
56            else
57                name.setText("Unexpected error.");
58        }

59    }
```

This sets the text field equal to the empty string, which makes it blank.

RESULTING GUI (When program is started and a name entered)

RESULTING GUI (After clicking the "Click me" button)

The method `getText` is an input method, and the method `setText` is an output method. The method `setText` can be used to display a new text string in a text field. For example, the following will cause the text field `name` to change the text it displays to the string `"This is some output"`:

```
name.setText("This is some output");
```

The following line from the method `actionPerformed` in Display 17.17 uses both `getText` and `setText`:

```
name.setText("Hello " + name.getText());
```

This line changes the string in the text field `name` to `"Hello "` followed by the old string value in the text field. The net effect is to insert the string `"Hello "` in front of the string displayed in the text field.

---

getText and setText

The classes `JTextField` and `JTextArea` both contain methods called `getText` and `set-Text`. The method `getText` can be used to retrieve the text written in the text field or text area. The method `setText` can be used to change the text written in the text field or text area.

SYNTAX

Name_of_Text_Component.`getText()` returns the text currently displayed in the text field or text area.
Name_of_Text_Component.`setText(`*New_String_To_Display*`)`;

EXAMPLES

```
String inputString = ioComponent.getText();
ioComponent.setText("Hello out there!");
```

`ioComponent` may be an instance of either of the classes `JTextField` or `JTextArea`.

---

text area
JTextArea

A **text area** is an object of the class `JTextArea`. A text area is the same as a text field except that it allows multiple lines. Two parameters to the constructor for `JTextArea` specify the minimum number of lines and the minimum number of characters per line that are guaranteed to be visible. You can enter any amount of text in a text area, but only a limited number of lines and a limited number of characters per line will be visible. For example, the following creates a `JTextArea` named `theText` that will have at least 5 lines and at least 20 characters per line visible:

```
JTextArea theText = new JTextArea(5, 20);
```

There is also a constructor with one additional `String` parameter for the string initially displayed in the text area. For example:

```
JTextArea theText = new JTextArea("Enter\ntext here.", 5, 20);
```

Note that a string value can be multiple lines because it can contain the new-line character '\n'.

A `JTextField` has a similar constructor with a `String` parameter, as in the following example:

```
JTextField ioField =
            new JTextField("Enter numbers here.", 30);
```

If you look at Display 17.12, you will see that both `JTextField` and `JTextArea` are derived classes of the abstract class `JTextComponent`. Most of the methods for `JTextField` and `JTextArea` are inherited from `JTextComponent` and so `JTextField` and `JTextArea` have mostly the same methods with the same meanings except for minor redefinitions to account for having just one line or multiple lines. Display 17.18 describes some methods in the class `JTextComponent`. All of these methods are inherited and have the described meaning in both `JTextField` and `JTextArea`.

setLineWrap

You can set the line-wrapping policy for a `JTextArea` using the method `setLineWrap`. The method takes one argument of type `boolean`. If the argument is `true`, then at the end of a line, any additional characters for that line will appear on the following line of the text area. If the argument is `false`, the extra characters will be on the same line and will not be visible. For example, the following sets the line wrap policy for the `JTextArea` object named `theText` so that at the end of a line, any additional characters for that line will appear on the following line:

```
theText.setLineWrap(true);
```

output-only

setEditable

You can specify that a `JTextField` or `JTextArea` cannot be written in by the user. To do so, use the method `setEditable`, which is a method in both the `JTextField` and `JTextArea` classes. If `theText` names an object in either of the classes `JTextField` or `JTextArea`, then the following

```
theText.setEditable(false);
```

will set `theText` so that only your GUI program can change the text in the text component `theText`; the user cannot change the text. After this invocation of `setEditable`, if the user clicks the mouse in the text component named `theText` and then types at the keyboard, the text in the text component will not change.

To reverse things and make `theText` so that the user can change the text in the text component, use `true` in place of `false`, as follows:

```
theText.setEditable(true);
```

If no invocation of `setEditable` is made, then the default state allows the user to change the text in the text component.

Display 17.18   Some Methods in the Class **JTextComponent**

All these methods are inherited by the classes **JTextField** and **JTextArea**.

The abstract class **JTextComponent** is in the package **javax.swing.text**. The classes **JTextField** and **JTextArea** are in the package **javax.swing**.

```
public String getText()
```
Returns the text that is displayed by this text component.

```
public boolean isEditable()
```
Returns **true** if the user can write in this text component. Returns **false** if the user is not allowed to write in this text component.

```
public void setBackground(Color theColor)
```
Sets the background color of this text component.

```
public void setEditable(boolean argument)
```
If **argument** is **true**, then the user is allowed to write in the text component. If **argument** is **false**, then the user is not allowed to write in the text component.

```
public void setText(String text)
```
Sets the text that is displayed by this text component to be the specified **text**.

The Classes **JTextField** and **JTextArea**

The classes **JTextField** and **JTextArea** can be used to add areas for changeable text to a GUI. An object of the class **JTextField** has one line that displays some specified number of characters. An object of the class **JTextArea** has a size consisting of a specified number of lines and a specified number of characters per line. More text can be typed into a **JText-Field** or **JTextArea** than is specified in its size, but the extra text may not be visible.

The number of characters per line and the number of lines are a guaranteed minimum. More lines and especially more characters per line may be visible. (The space per line is actually guaranteed to be *Characters_Per_Line* times the space for one uppercase letter M.)

SYNTAX

```
JTextField Name_of_Text_Field = new JTextField(Characters_Per_Line);
JTextArea Name_of_Text_Area =
              new JTextArea(Number_of_Lines, Characters_Per_Line);
```

EXAMPLES

```
JTextField name = new JTextField(30);
JTextArea someText = new JTextArea(10, 30);
```

(continued)

There are also constructors that take an additional **String** argument that specifies an initial string to display in the text component.

SYNTAX

```
JTextField Name_of_Text_Field =
            new JTextField(Initial_String, Characters_Per_Line);
JTextArea Name_of_Text_Area =
     new JTextArea(Initial_String, Number_of_Lines, Characters_Per_Line);
```

EXAMPLES

```
JTextField name = new JTextField("Enter name here.", 30);
JTextArea someText =
   new JTextArea("Enter story here.\nClick button.", 10, 30);
```

Number of Characters per Line

The number of characters per line (given as an argument to constructors for **JTextField** or **JTextArea**) is not the number of just any characters. The number gives the number of em spaces in the line. An **em space** is the space needed to hold one uppercase letter M, which is the widest letter in the alphabet. So a line that is specified to hold 20 characters will always be able to hold at least 20 characters and will almost always hold more than 20 characters.

Scroll Bars

Scroll bars for text areas and text fields are discussed in Chapter 18. They are a nice touch, but until you reach Chapter 18, your GUI programs will work fine without them.

TIP: Labeling a Text Field

Sometimes you want to label a text field. For example, suppose the GUI asks for a name and a credit card number and expects the user to enter these in two text fields. In this case, the GUI needs to label the two text fields so that the user knows in which field to type the name and in which field to type the credit card number. You can use an object of the class **JLabel** to label a text field or any other component in a Swing GUI. Simply place the label and text field in a **JPanel** and treat the **JPanel** as a single component. For example, we did this with the text field **name** in Display 17.17. ∎

Self-Test Exercises

36. What is the difference between an object of the class JTextArea and an object of the class JTextField?

37. What would happen if when running the GUI in Display 17.17 you were to enter your name and click the "Click me" button three times?

38. Rewrite the program in Display 17.17 so that it uses a text area in place of a text field. Change the label "Enter your name here:" to "Enter your story here:". When the user clicks the "Click me" button, your GUI should change the string displayed in the text area to "Your story is " + lineCount + " lines long.". The variable lineCount is a variable of type int that your program sets equal to the number of lines currently displayed in the text area. Use a BorderLayout manager and place your text area in the region BorderLayout.CENTER so that there is room for it. You can assume the user enters at least one line before clicking the "Click me" button. The last line in the text area will have no '\n' and so you may need to add one if you are counting the number of occurrences of '\n'. Blank lines are counted.

TIP: Inputting and Outputting Numbers

When you want to input numbers using a Swing GUI, your GUI must convert input text to numbers. For example, when you input the number 42 in a JTextField, your program will receive the string "42", not the number 42. Your program must convert the input string value "42" to the integer value 42. When you want to output numbers using a GUI constructed with Swing, you must convert the numbers to a string and then output that string. For example, if you want to output the number 40, your program would convert the integer value 40 to the string value "40". With Swing, all input typed by the user is string input and all displayed output is string output. The techniques for converting back and forth between strings and numbers were given in Chapter 5 in the subsecton entitled "Static Methods in Wrapper Classes" and the Programming Example entitled "Another Approach to Keyboard Input." A simple example of a Swing GUI with numeric input and output is given in the next subsection. ∎

A Swing Calculator

Designing a realistic Swing calculator is one of the Programming Projects. In this programming example, we will develop a simplified calculator to get you started on that Programming Project. Display 17.19 contains a GUI for a calculator that keeps a running total of numbers. The user enters a number in the text field and then clicks either the + or – button. The number in the text field is then added into or subtracted from a running total that is kept in the instance variable result, and then the new total, the new value of `result`, is given in the text field. If the user clicks the "Reset" button, then the running total, that is, the value of `result`, is set to zero. When the GUI is first run, the running total, that is, the value of `result`, is set to zero.

Most of the details are similar to things you have already seen, but one new element is the use of exception handling. If the user enters a number in an incorrect format, such as placing a comma in a number, then one of the methods throws a `NumberFormatException`. If the user enters a number in an incorrect format, such as `2,000` with a comma instead of `2000`, the method `assumingCorrectNumberFormats` invokes the method `stringToDouble` with the alleged number string `"2,000"` as an argument. Then `stringToDouble` calls `Double.parseDouble`, but `Double.parseDouble` throws a `NumberFormatException` because no Java number string can contain a comma. Since the invocation of `Double.parseDouble` takes place within an invocation of the method `stringToDouble`, `stringToDouble` in turn throws a `NumberFormatException`. The invocation of `stringToDouble` takes place inside the invocation of `assuming-CorrectNumberFormats`, so `assumingCorrectNumberFormats` throws the `NumberFormat-Exception` that it received from the invocation of `stringToDouble`. However, the invocation of `assumingCorrectNumberFormats` is inside a `try` block. The exception is caught in the following `catch` block. At that point, the `JTextField` (named `ioField`) is set to the error message `"Error: Reenter Number."`.

Notice that if a `NumberFormatException` is thrown, the value of the instance variable `result` is not changed. A `NumberFormatException` can be thrown by an invocation of `stringToDouble` in either of the following lines of code from the method `assumingCorrectNumberFormats`:

```
result = result + stringToDouble(ioField.getText());
```

or

```
result = result − stringToDouble(ioField.getText());
```

If the exception is thrown, execution of the method `stringToDouble` ends immediately and control passes to the `catch` block. Thus, control passes to the `catch` block before the previous addition or subtraction is performed. So `result` is unchanged, and the user can reenter the last number and proceed with the GUI as if that incorrect number were never entered.

Uncaught Exceptions

In a Swing program, throwing an uncaught exception does not end the GUI, but it may leave it in an unpredictable state. It is best to always catch any exception that is thrown even if all that the **catch** block does is output an instruction to redo something, such as reentering some input, or just outputs an error message.

Display 17.19   A Simple Calculator   (part 1 of 4)

```
1    import javax.swing.JFrame;
2    import javax.swing.JTextField;
3    import javax.swing.JPanel;
4    import javax.swing.JLabel;
5    import javax.swing.JButton;
6    import java.awt.BorderLayout;
7    import java.awt.FlowLayout;
8    import java.awt.Color;
9    import java.awt.event.ActionListener;
10   import java.awt.event.ActionEvent;

11   /**
12    A simplified calculator.
13    The only operations are addition and subtraction.
14   */
15   public class Calculator extends JFrame
16                           implements ActionListener
17   {
18       public static final int WIDTH = 400;
19       public static final int HEIGHT = 200;
20       public static final int NUMBER_OF_DIGITS = 30;

21       private JTextField ioField;
22       private double result = 0.0;

23       public static void main(String[] args)
24       {
25           Calculator aCalculator = new Calculator();
26           aCalculator.setVisible(true);
27       }

28       public Calculator()
29       {
30           setTitle("Simplified Calculator");
31           setDefaultCloseOperation(JFrame.EXIT_ON_CLOSE);
32           setSize(WIDTH, HEIGHT);
33           setLayout(new BorderLayout());

34           JPanel textPanel = new JPanel();
35           textPanel.setLayout(new FlowLayout());
36           ioField =
37               new JTextField("Enter numbers here.", NUMBER_OF_DIGITS);
38           ioField.setBackground(Color.WHITE);
39           textPanel.add(ioField);
40           add(textPanel, BorderLayout.NORTH);
```

(continued)

Display 17.19   A Simple Calculator (part 2 of 4)

```
41          JPanel buttonPanel = new JPanel();
42          buttonPanel.setBackground(Color.GRAY);
43          buttonPanel.setLayout(new FlowLayout());

44          JButton addButton = new JButton("+");
45          addButton.addActionListener(this);
46          buttonPanel.add(addButton);
47          JButton subtractButton = new JButton("-");
48          subtractButton.addActionListener(this);
49          buttonPanel.add(subtractButton);
50          JButton resetButton = new JButton("Reset");
51          resetButton.addActionListener(this);
52          buttonPanel.add(resetButton);

53       add(buttonPanel, BorderLayout.CENTER);
54    }

55    public void actionPerformed(ActionEvent e)
56    {
57          try
58          {
59              assumingCorrectNumberFormats(e);
60          }
61          catch (NumberFormatException e2)
62          {
63              ioField.setText("Error: Reenter Number.");
64          }
65    }
```

A NumberFormatException does not need to be declared or caught in a catch block.

```
66    //Throws NumberFormatException.
67    public void assumingCorrectNumberFormats(ActionEvent e)
68    {
69          String actionCommand = e.getActionCommand();

70          if (actionCommand.equals("+"))
71          {
72              result = result + stringToDouble(ioField.getText());
73              ioField.setText(Double.toString(result));
74          }
75          else if (actionCommand.equals("-"))
76          {
77              result = result - stringToDouble(ioField.getText());
78              ioField.setText(Double.toString(result));
```

Display 17.19 A Simple Calculator (part 3 of 4)

```
79              }
80          else if (actionCommand.equals("Reset"))
81          {
82              result = 0.0;
83              ioField.setText("0.0");
84          }
85          else
86              ioField.setText("Unexpected error.");
87      }


88      //Throws NumberFormatException.
89      private static double stringToDouble(String stringObject)
90      {
91          return Double.parseDouble(stringObject.trim());
92      }

93  }
```

RESULTING GUI (When started)

RESULTING GUI (After entering 2,000)

(continued)

Display 17.19   **A Simple Calculator** (part 4 of 4)

RESULTING GUI (After clicking +)

RESULTING GUI (After entering 2000.0 and clicking +)

RESULTING GUI (After entering 42)

RESULTING GUI (After clicking +)

Self-Test Exercises

39. In the GUI in Display 17.19, why did we make the text field `ioField` an instance variable but did not make instance variables of any of the buttons `addButton`, `subtractButton`, or `resetButton`?

40. What would happen if the user running the GUI in Display 17.19 were to run the GUI and simply click the addition button without typing anything into the text field?

41. What would happen if the user running the GUI in Display 17.19 were to type the number 10 into the text field and then click the addition button three times? Explain your answer.

42. Suppose you change the `main` method in Display 17.19 to the following:

```java
public static void main(String[] args)
{
    Calculator calculator1 = new Calculator();
    calculator1.setVisible(true);

    Calculator calculator2 = new Calculator();
    calculator2.setVisible(true);
}
```

This will cause two calculator windows to be displayed. (If one is on top of the other, you can use your mouse to move the top one.) If you add numbers in one of these calculators, will anything change in the other calculator?

43. Suppose you change the `main` method in Display 17.19 as we described in Self-Test Exercise 42. This will cause two calculator windows to be displayed. If you click the close-window button in one of the windows, will one window go away or will both windows go away?

Chapter Summary

- Swing GUIs (graphical user interfaces) are programmed using event-driven programming. In event-driven programming, a user action, like a button click, generates an event, and that event is automatically passed to an event-handling method that performs the appropriate action.

- There are two main techniques for designing a Swing GUI class. You can use inheritance to create a derived class of one of the library classes such as `JFrame` or you can build a GUI by adding components to a container class. You normally use both of these techniques when defining a Swing GUI class.

- A windowing GUI is usually defined as a derived class of the class `JFrame`.

- A button is an object of the class JButton. Clicking a button fires an action event that is handled by an action listener. An action listener is any class that implements the ActionListener interface.

- A label is an object of the class JLabel. You can use a label to add text to a GUI.

- When adding components to an object of a container class, such as adding a button to a panel or JFrame, you use the method add. The components in a container are arranged by an object called a layout manager.

- A panel is a container object that is used to group components inside of a larger container. Panels are objects in the class JPanel.

- A menu item is a choice on a menu. A menu item is realized in your code as an object of the class JMenuItem. A menu is an object of the class JMenu. A menu item is added to a JMenu with the method add. A menu bar is an object of the class JMenuBar. A menu is added to a JMenuBar with the method add.

- A JMenuBar can be added to a JFrame with the method setJMenuBar. It can also be added using the method add, just as any other component can be added.

- Both buttons and menu items fire action events and so normally have one or more action listeners registered with them to respond to the events.

Answers to Self-Test Exercises

1. The JFrame class.

2. Sizes in Swing are measured in pixels.

3. ```
   someWindow.setDefaultCloseOperation(
                       JFrame.DO_NOTHING_ON_CLOSE);
   ```

4. ```
   someWindow.setDefaultCloseOperation(JFrame.EXIT_ON_CLOSE);
   ```

5. When you click the minimizing button, the JFrame is reduced to an icon, usually at the bottom of your monitor screen.

6. ```
   someWindow.setVisible(n > 0);
   ```

   The following also works but is not good style:

   ```
   if (n > 0)
       someWindow.setVisible(true);
   else
       someWindow.setVisible(false);
   ```

7. An action event.

8. ```
   public void actionPerformed(ActionEvent e)
   ```

9. Change

   ```
   JFrame firstWindow = new JFrame();
   ```

to

```
JFrame firstWindow = new JFrame("My First Window");
```

Alternatively, you can add the following:

```
firstWindow.setTitle("My First Window");
```

10. Delete

```
setTitle("First Window Class");
```

and replace

```
super();
```

with

```
super("First Window Class");
```

11. Change

```
setDefaultCloseOperation(
                    JFrame.DO_NOTHING_ON_CLOSE);
```

to

```
setDefaultCloseOperation(
                    JFrame.EXIT_ON_CLOSE);
```

12. Change the following line in the no-argument constructor in Display 17.6 from

```
this(Color.PINK);
```

to

```
this(Color.MAGENTA);
```

13. `add(new JLabel("Close-window button works."));`

14. Yes, it is legal. It is OK to reuse a variable name such as aLabel.

15. You need to change the add statements, as in the following rewritten section of code:

```
JLabel label1 = new JLabel("First label");
add(label1, BorderLayout.NORTH);

JLabel label2 = new JLabel("Second label");
add(label2, BorderLayout.CENTER);

JLabel label3 = new JLabel("Third label");
add(label3, BorderLayout.SOUTH);
```

16. You need to change the add statements, as in the following rewritten section of code:

```
JLabel label1 = new JLabel("First label");
add(label1, BorderLayout.NORTH);

JLabel label2 = new JLabel("Second label");
add(label2, BorderLayout.EAST);

JLabel label3 = new JLabel("Third label");
add(label3, BorderLayout.SOUTH);
```

17. The argument should be new GridLayout(1, 3). So, the entire method invocation is

```
setLayout(new GridLayout(1, 3));
```

Alternatively, you could use new GridLayout(1, 0). It is also possible to do something similar with a BorderLayout manager or a FlowLayout manager, but a GridLayout manager will work nicer here.

18. The argument should be new GridLayout(0, 1). So, the entire method invocation is

```
setLayout(new GridLayout(0, 1));
```

Alternatively, you could use new GridLayout(3, 1), if you know there will be at most three components added, but if more than three components are added, then a second column will be added. It is also possible to do something similar with a BorderLayout manager, but a GridLayout manager will work nicer here.

19. java.awt

20. An object of the class JPanel is both a container class and a component class.

21. To make it look as though you have an empty grid element, add an empty panel to the grid element.

22.
```
import javax.swing.JPanel;
import java.awt.Color;

public class PinkJPanel extends JPanel
{
    public PinkJPanel()
    {
        setBackground(Color.PINK);
    }
}
```

**extra code
on CD**

The class PinkJPanel is on the CD that accompanies this text.

23. It will not compile, but will give a compiler error message saying that action-Performed is not defined (since it claims to implement the ActionListener interface).

24. It will not compile, but will give compiler error messages saying that, in effect, the invocations of addActionListener such as

    ```
    redButton.addActionListener(this);
    ```

    have arguments of an incorrect type.

25. Clicking a JMenuItem fires an action event (that is, an object of the class Action-Event). This is the same as with a JButton.

26. ```
    JButton b = new JButton("Hello");
    b.setActionCommand("Bye");
    ```

27. ```
    JMenuItem m = new JMenuItem("Hello");
    m.setActionCommand("Bye");
    ```

28. To change the action command for a JMenuItem, you use the method set-ActionCommand, just as you would for a JButton.

29. Yes, it is legal.

30. As many as you want. Only one can be added with the method setJMenuBar, but any number of others can be added to using the add method.

31. setJMenuBar

32. ```
    JMenuItem aChoice = new JMenuItem("Exit");
    ```

33. ```
    m.add(mItem);
    mBar.add(m);
    setJMenuBar(mBar);
    ```

    You could use the following instead of using setJMenuBar:

    ```
    add(mBar);
    ```

    This will all take place inside a constructor named MenuGUI.

34. Register all three types of listeners with blueChoice, as follows:

    ```
    blueChoice.addActionListener(new RedListener());
    blueChoice.addActionListener(new WhiteListener());
    blueChoice.addActionListener(new BlueListener());
    ```

35. Replace the three inner classes with the following inner class:

    ```
    private class ColorListener implements ActionListener
    {
        private JPanel thePanel;
        private Color theColor;

        public ColorListener(Color c, JPanel p)
        {
    ```

```
            theColor = c;
            thePanel = p;
        }

        public void actionPerformed(ActionEvent e)
        {
            thePanel.setBackground(theColor);
        }
} //End of ColorListener inner class
```

Replace

```
redChoice.addActionListener(new RedListener());
```

with

```
redChoice.addActionListener(
                    new ColorListener(Color.RED, redPanel));
```

Also make similar changes to the menu items whiteChoice and blueChoice, with the obvious changes to colors and panels.

extra code
on CD

This is not really preferable to what we did in Display 17.16, but it is a good exercise. The complete program done this way is on the accompanying CD in the file named InnerListenersDemo2.java.

36. A JTextField object displays only a single line. A JTextArea object can display more than one line of text.

37. The contents of the text field would change to "Hello Hello Hello " followed by your name.

extra code
on CD

38. This program is on the CD that accompanies this text.

```
import javax.swing.JFrame;
import javax.swing.JTextArea;
import javax.swing.JPanel;
import javax.swing.JLabel;
import javax.swing.JButton;
import java.awt.GridLayout;
import java.awt.BorderLayout;
import java.awt.FlowLayout;
import java.awt.Color;
import java.awt.event.ActionListener;
import java.awt.event.ActionEvent;

public class TextAreaDemo extends JFrame
                            implements ActionListener
{
    public static final int WIDTH = 400;
    public static final int HEIGHT = 200;
    public static final int NUMBER_OF_LINES = 10;
```

```java
public static final int NUMBER_OF_CHAR = 30;

private JTextArea story;

public static void main(String[] args)
{
    TextAreaDemo gui = new TextAreaDemo();
    gui.setVisible(true);
}

public TextAreaDemo( )
{
    setTitle("Text Area Demo");
    setSize(WIDTH, HEIGHT);
    setDefaultCloseOperation(JFrame.EXIT_ON_CLOSE);
    setLayout(new GridLayout(2, 1));
    JPanel storyPanel = new JPanel( );
    storyPanel.setLayout(new BorderLayout( ));
    storyPanel.setBackground(Color.WHITE);

    story = new JTextArea(NUMBER_OF_LINES, NUMBER_OF_CHAR);

    storyPanel.add(story, BorderLayout.CENTER);
    JLabel storyLabel = new JLabel("Enter your story here:");
    storyPanel.add(storyLabel, BorderLayout.NORTH);

    add(storyPanel);

    JPanel buttonPanel = new JPanel( );
    buttonPanel.setLayout(new FlowLayout( ));
    buttonPanel.setBackground(Color.PINK);
    JButton actionButton = new JButton("Click me");
    actionButton.addActionListener(this);
    buttonPanel.add(actionButton);

    JButton clearButton = new JButton("Clear");
    clearButton.addActionListener(this);
    buttonPanel.add(clearButton);

    add(buttonPanel);
}

public void actionPerformed(ActionEvent e)
{
    String actionCommand = e.getActionCommand( );

  if (actionCommand.equals("Click me"))
  {
        int lineCount = getLineCount();
        story.setText("Your story is "
                            + lineCount + " lines long.");
```

```
        }
        else if (actionCommand.equals("Clear"))
            story.setText("");
        else
            story.setText("Unexpected error.");
    }

    private int getLineCount()
    {
        String storyString = story.getText();
        int count = 0;

        for (int i = 0; i < storyString.length(); i++)
            if (storyString.charAt(i) == '\n')
                count++;

        return count + 1;//The last line has no '\n'.
    }
}
```

39. We made the text field an instance variable because we needed to refer to it in the definition of the method `actionPerformed`. On the other hand, the only direct reference we had to the buttons was in the constructor. So, we need names for the buttons only in the constructor definition.

40. The GUI would try to add the string "Enter numbers here." as if it were a string for a number. This will cause a `NumberFormatException` to be thrown and the string "Error: Reenter Number." would be displayed in the text field.

41. Every time the user clicks the addition button, the following assignment is executed:

```
result = result + stringToDouble(ioField.getText());
```

So, the number in the text field is added to the total as many times as the user clicks the addition button. But, the value in the text field is the running total, so the running total is added to itself. Thus, the running total is added to the total as many times as the user clicks the addition button.

Let's say that the user starts the GUI, types in 10, and clicks the addition button. That adds 10 to `result`, so the value of `result` is then 0 plus 10, which is 10, and 10 is displayed. Now the user clicks the addition button a second time. That adds 10 to `result` again, so the value of `result` is 10 plus 10, which is 20, and 20 is displayed. Next the user clicks the addition button a third time. This time, 20 is in the text field, and so it is added to `result`, which is also 20. Thus, the value of `result` is now 40, and 40 is displayed. Note that it is always the number in the text field that is added in.

42. The two calculator windows are completely independent. Each has its own instance variable `result`, which has no effect on the other's instance variable `result`.

43. If you click the close-window button in either calculator window, the entire program ends because that causes an invocation of `System.exit`. There is no invocation of

System.exit in Display 17.19, but the following ensures that a System.exit that is in some library class will be invoked:

```
setDefaultCloseOperation(JFrame.EXIT_ON_CLOSE);
```

Programming Projects

Many of these Programming Projects can be solved using AW's MyCodeMate. To access these please go to: www.mycodemate.com.

1. Design and code a Swing GUI to translate text that is input in English into Pig Latin. You can assume that the sentence contains no punctuation. The rules for Pig Latin are as follows:

    a. For words that begin with consonants, move the leading consonant to the end of the word and add "ay." Thus, "ball" becomes "allbay"; "button" becomes "uttonbay"; and so forth.

    b. For words that begin with vowels, add "way" to the end of the word. Thus, "all" becomes "allway"; "one" becomes "oneway"; and so forth.

    Use a FlowLayout with a JTextArea for the source text and a separate JTextArea for the translated text. Add a JButton with an event to perform the translation. A sample application is shown below with the text translated to Pig Latin.

    To parse the source text, note that you can use the Scanner class on a String. For example the following code:

    ```
    Scanner scan = new Scanner("foo bar zot");
    while (scan.hasNext())
    {
        System.out.println(scan.next());
    }
    ```

    will output

    ```
    foo
    bar
    zot
    ```

2. Design and code a Swing GUI for a two-player tic-tac-toe (noughts and crosses) game on a 3 by 3 game board. The JFrame should use a BorderLayout with a JLabel in the NORTH region to display messages (e.g., who won the game), and a JPanel in the CENTER region to display the game board. For the game board in the JPanel, use a GridLayout manager with a 3 by 3 layout of JButton's in each cell to display the game board. The button labels should initially be blank. When a player clicks on an empty button an appropriate "X" or "O" should be placed in the label field of the button. If there is a winner (three in a row) then the program should display the winner in the JLabel located at the top of the window. If all nine cells have been filled without a winner the program should indicate that there was a tie.

3. Design and code a Swing GUI calculator. You can use Display 17.19 as a starting point, but your calculator will be more sophisticated. Your calculator will have two text fields that the user cannot change: One labeled "Result" will contain the result of performing the operation, and the other labeled "Operand" will be for the user to enter a number to be added, subtracted, and so forth from the result. The user enters the number for the "Operand" text field by clicking buttons labeled with the digits 0 through 9 and a decimal point, just as in a real calculator. Allow the operations of addition, subtraction, multiplication, and division. Use a GridLayout manager to produce a button pad that looks similar to the keyboard on a real calculator.

   When the user clicks a button for an operation: the operation is performed, the "Result" text field is updated, and the "Operand" text field is cleared. Include a button labeled "Reset" that resets the "Result" to 0.0. Also include a button labeled "Clear" that resets the "Operand" text field so it is blank.

   Hint: Define an exception class named DivisonByZeroException. Have your code throw and catch a DivisonByZeroException if the user attempts to "divide by zero." Your code will catch the DivisonByZeroException and output a suitable message to the "Operand" text field. The user may then enter a new substitute number in the "Operand" text field. Since values of type double are, in effect, approximate values, it makes no sense to test for equality with 0.0. Consider an operand to be "equal to zero" if it is in the range −1.0e−10 to +1.0e−10.

4. (The Swing part of this project is pretty easy, but to do this programming project you need to know how to convert numbers from one base to another.) Write a program that converts integers from base ten (ordinary decimal) notation to base two notation. Use Swing to perform input and output via a window interface. The user enters a base ten numeral in one text field and clicks a button with "Convert" written on it; the equivalent base two numeral then appears in another text field. Be sure to label the two text fields. Include a "Clear" button that clears both text fields when clicked. (*Hint:* Include a private method that converts the string for a base ten numeral to the string for the equivalent base two numeral.)

18

Swing II

Window listeners?
I thought windows were for looking not for listening.

Student answer on an exam

Introduction

Although this is the third chapter on Swing, we have entitled it "Swing II" because Chapter 17, entitled "Swing I," and this chapter are really one unit. This chapter is a continuation of Chapter 17, presenting more details about designing regular Swing GUIs. Chapter 18 on applets is a side issue that may be read after this chapter if you prefer.

Prerequisites

This chapter uses material from Chapter 17 (and its prerequisites).

Section 18.2 on icons and scroll bars is not used in subsequent sections and so may be skipped or postponed.

18.1 Window Listeners

A man may see how this world goes with no eyes.
Look with thine ears. . . .

WILLIAM SHAKESPEARE, *King Lear*

In Chapter 17 we used the method `setDefaultCloseOperation` to program the close-window button in a `JFrame`. This allows for only a limited number of possibilities for what happens when the close-window button is clicked. When the user clicks the close-window button (or either of the two accompanying buttons), the `JFrame` fires an event known as a **window event**. A `JFrame` can use the method `setWindowListener` to register a **window listener** to respond to such window events. A window listener can be programmed to respond to a window event in any way you wish. Window events are objects of the class `WindowEvent`. A window listener is any class that satisfies the `WindowListener` interface.

window event
window listener

WindowEvent
WindowListener

The method headings in the `WindowListener` interface are given in Display 18.1. If a class implements the `WindowListener` interface, it must have definitions for all seven of these method headings. If you do not need all of these methods, then you can define the ones you do not need to have empty bodies, like this:

```
public void windowDeiconified(WindowEvent e)
{}.
```

Display 18.1   Methods in the `WindowListener` Interface

The `WindowListener` interface and the `WindowEvent` class are in the package `java.awt.event`.

`public void` **`windowOpened(WindowEvent e)`**

Invoked when a window has been opened.

`public void` **`windowClosing(WindowEvent e)`**

Invoked when a window is in the process of being closed. Clicking the close-window button causes an invocation of this method.

`public void` **`windowClosed(WindowEvent e)`**

Invoked when a window has been closed.

`public void` **`windowIconified(WindowEvent e)`**

Invoked when a window is iconified. When you click the minimize button in a `JFrame`, it is iconified.

`public void` **`windowDeiconified(WindowEvent e)`**

Invoked when a window is deiconified. When you activate a minimized window, it is deiconified.

`public void` **`windowActivated(WindowEvent e)`**

Invoked when a window is activated. When you click in a window, it becomes the activated window. Other actions can also activate a window.

`public void` **`windowDeactivated(WindowEvent e)`**

Invoked when a window is deactivated. When a window is activated, all other windows are deactivated. Other actions can also deactivate a window.

The `WindowListener` Interface

When the user clicks any of the three standard `JFrame` buttons (for closing the window, minimizing the window, and resizing the window), that generates a window event. Window events are sent to window listeners. In order to be a window listener, a class must implement the `WindowListener` interface. The method headings for the `WindowListener` interface are given in Display 18.1.

EXAMPLE: A Window Listener Inner Class

Display 18.2 gives an example of a `JFrame` class with a window listener class that is an inner class. The window listener inner class is named `CheckOnExit`. A window listener class need not be an inner class, but it is frequently convenient to make a window listener class (or other kind of listener class) an inner class.

The main `JFrame` in Display 18.2 simply displays a message. What is interesting is how the window listener programs the close-window button. You can apply the window listener used in this `JFrame` to any `JFrame`. When the close-window button is clicked, a second, smaller window appears and asks: `"Are you sure you want to exit?"` If the user clicks the `"Yes"` button, the entire program ends and so both windows go away. If the user clicks the `"No"` button, only the smaller window disappears; the program and the main window continue. Let's look at the programming details.

When the close-window button in the main window is clicked, that fires a window event. The only registered window listener is the anonymous object that is the argument to `addWindowListener`. Below we repeat the relevant line of code, which is in the constructor for `WindowListenerDemo`:

```
addWindowListener(new CheckOnExit());
```

This anonymous window listener object receives the window event fired when the close-window button is clicked and then invokes the method `windowClosing`. The method `windowClosing` creates and displays a window object of the class `ConfirmWindow`, which contains the message `"Are you sure you want to exit?"` as well as the two buttons labeled `"Yes"` and `"No"`.

If the user clicks the `"Yes"` button, the action event fired by that button goes to the `actionPerformed` method, which ends the program with a call to `System.exit`. If the user clicks the `"No"` button, then the `actionPerformed` method invokes the method `dispose`. The method `dispose`, discussed in the next subsection, makes its calling object go away but does not end the program. The calling object for `dispose` is the smaller window (which is an object of the class `ConfirmWindow`), so this smaller window goes away but the main window remains.

Notice that even though we have registered a window listener, which says what should happen when the close-window button is clicked, we still need to invoke the method `setDefaultCloseOperation`. When the close-window button is clicked, the policy set by `setDefaultCloseOperation` is always carried out in addition to any action by window listeners. If we do not include any invocation of `setDefaultCloseOperation`, then the default action is to make the window go away (but not to end the program). We do not want our main window to go away, so we set the policy as follows:

```
setDefaultCloseOperation(JFrame.DO_NOTHING_ON_CLOSE);
```

This means that clicking the close-window button causes no action other than the actions of any window listeners. If you are using a window listener to set the action of the close-window button, you invariably want an invocation of `setDefaultCloseOperation` with the argument `JFrame.DO_NOTHING_ON_CLOSE`.

Display 18.2 A Window Listener (part 1 of 3)

```
1    import javax.swing.JFrame;
2    import javax.swing.JPanel;
3    import java.awt.BorderLayout;
4    import java.awt.FlowLayout;
5    import java.awt.Color;
6    import javax.swing.JLabel;
7    import javax.swing.JButton;
8    import java.awt.event.ActionListener;
9    import java.awt.event.ActionEvent;
10   import java.awt.event.WindowListener;
11   import java.awt.event.WindowEvent;

12   public class WindowListenerDemo extends JFrame
13   {
14       public static final int WIDTH = 300; //for main window
15       public static final int HEIGHT = 200; //for main window
16       public static final int SMALL_WIDTH = 200; //for confirm window
17       public static final int SMALL_HEIGHT = 100;//for confirm window

18       private class CheckOnExit implements WindowListener
19       {
20           public void windowOpened(WindowEvent e)
21           {}

22           public void windowClosing(WindowEvent e)
23           {
24               ConfirmWindow checkers = new ConfirmWindow();
25               checkers.setVisible(true);
26           }

27           public void windowClosed(WindowEvent e)
28           {}

29           public void windowIconified(WindowEvent e)
30           {}

31           public void windowDeiconified(WindowEvent e)
32           {}

33           public void windowActivated(WindowEvent e)
34           {}
```

This `WindowListener` *class is an inner class.*

A window listener must define all the method headings in the `WindowListener` *interface, even if some are trivial implementations.*

(continued)

Display 18.2   A Window Listener (part 2 of 3)

```
35            public void windowDeactivated(WindowEvent e)
36            {}
37      } //End of inner class CheckOnExit

38      private class ConfirmWindow extends JFrame implements ActionListener
39      {
40            public ConfirmWindow()
41            {
42                setSize(SMALL_WIDTH, SMALL_HEIGHT);
43                getContentPane().setBackground(Color.YELLOW);
44                setLayout(new BorderLayout());

45                JLabel confirmLabel = new JLabel(
46                            "Are you sure you want to exit?");
47                add(confirmLabel, BorderLayout.CENTER);

48                JPanel buttonPanel = new JPanel();
49                buttonPanel.setBackground(Color.ORANGE);
50                buttonPanel.setLayout(new FlowLayout());

51                JButton exitButton = new JButton("Yes");
52                exitButton.addActionListener(this);
53                buttonPanel.add(exitButton);

54                JButton cancelButton = new JButton("No");
55                cancelButton.addActionListener(this);
56                buttonPanel.add(cancelButton);

57                add(buttonPanel, BorderLayout.SOUTH);
58            }

59            public void actionPerformed(ActionEvent e)
60            {
61                String actionCommand = e.getActionCommand();

62                if (actionCommand.equals("Yes"))
63                    System.exit(0);
64                else if (actionCommand.equals("No"))
65                    dispose();//Destroys only the ConfirmWindow.
66                else
67                    System.out.println("Unexpected Error in Confirm Window.");
68            }
69      } //End of inner class ConfirmWindow
```

Another inner class.

Display 18.2   **A Window Listener** (part 3 of 3)

```
70
71        public static void main(String[] args)
72        {
73            WindowListenerDemo demoWindow = new WindowListenerDemo();
74            demoWindow.setVisible(true);
75        }
76
77        public WindowListenerDemo()
78        {
79            setSize(WIDTH, HEIGHT);
80            setTitle("Window Listener Demonstration");
81
82            setDefaultCloseOperation(JFrame.DO_NOTHING_ON_CLOSE);
83            addWindowListener(new CheckOnExit());
84
85            getContentPane().setBackground(Color.LIGHT_GRAY);
86            JLabel aLabel = new JLabel("I like to be sure you are sincere.");
87            add(aLabel);
88        }
89    }
```

Even if you have a window listener, you normally must still invoke `setDefaultCloseOperation`.

RESULTING GUI

This window is an object of the class `ConfirmWindow`.

When you click this close-window button, the second window appears.

The `dispose` Method

dispose The method `dispose` is a method in the class `JFrame` that releases any resources used by the `JFrame` or any of its components. So, a call to `dispose` eliminates the `JFrame` and its components, but if the program has items that are not components of the `JFrame`, then the program does not end. For example, in Display 18.2 the smaller window of the class `ConfirmWindow` invokes `dispose` (if the user clicks the "No" button). That causes that smaller window to go away, but the larger window remains.

The dispose Method

The class `JFrame` has a method named **dispose** that will eliminate the invoking `JFrame` without ending the program. When **dispose** is invoked, the resources consumed by the `JFrame` and its components are returned for reuse, so the `JFrame` is gone, but the program does not end (unless **dispose** eliminates all elements in the program, as in a one-window program). The method **dispose** is often used in a program with multiple windows to eliminate one window without ending the program.

SYNTAX

```
JFrame_Object.dispose();
```

The *JFrame_Object* is often an implicit **this**. A complete example of using **dispose** can be seen in Display 18.2.

PITFALL: Forgetting to Invoke `setDefaultCloseOperation`

If you register a window listener to respond to window events from a `JFrame`, you should also include an invocation of the method `setDefaultCloseOperation`, typically in the `JFrame` constructor. This is because the default or other behavior set by `setDefaultCloseOperation` takes place even if there is a window listener. If you do not want any actions other than those provided by the window listener(s), you should include the following in the `JFrame` constructor:

```
setDefaultCloseOperation(JFrame.DO_NOTHING_ON_CLOSE);
```

If you do not include any invocation of `setDefaultCloseOperation`, the default action is the same as if you had included the following invocation

```
setDefaultCloseOperation(JFrame.HIDE_ON_CLOSE);
```

which hides the `JFrame` when the close-window button is clicked. (The actions of any registered window listener are also performed.) ■

The WindowAdapter Class

In Display 18.2 we gave empty bodies to most of the method headings in the WindowListener interface. The abstract class WindowAdapter is a way to avoid all those empty method bodies. The class WindowAdapter does little more than provide trivial implementations of the method headings in the WindowListener interface. So, if you make a window listener a derived class of the class WindowAdapter, then you only need to define the method headings in the WindowListener interface that you need. The other method headings inherit trivial implementations from WindowAdapter. (WindowAdapter is unusual in that it is an abstract class with no abstract methods.)

For example, in Display 18.3 we have rewritten the inner class CheckOnExit from Display 18.2, but this time we made it a derived class of the WindowAdapter class. This definition of CheckOnExit is much shorter and cleaner than the one in Display 18.2, but the two implementations of CheckOnExit are equivalent. Thus, you can replace the definition of CheckOnExit in Display 18.2 with the shorter one in Display 18.3. The file WindowListenerDemo2 on the accompanying CD contains a version of Display 18.2 with this shorter definition of CheckOnExit.

extra code on CD

The class WindowAdapter is in the java.awt.event package and so requires an import statement such as the following:

```
import java.awt.event.WindowAdapter;
```

You cannot always define your window listeners as derived classes of Windowdapter. For example, suppose you want a JFrame class to be its own window listener. To accomplish that, the class must be a derived class of JFrame and so cannot be a derived class of any other class such as WindowAdapter. In such cases, you make the class a derived class of JFrame and have it implement the WindowListener interface. See Self-Test Exercise 4 for an example.

Display 18.3   Using WindowAdapter

This requires the following import statements:

```
import java.awt.event.WindowAdapter;
import java.awt.event.WindowEvent;
```

```
1    private class CheckOnExit extends WindowAdapter
2    {
3        public void windowClosing(WindowEvent e)
4        {
5            ConfirmWindow checkers = new ConfirmWindow();
6            checkers.setVisible(true);
7        }
8    } //End of inner class CheckOnExit
```

*If the definition of the inner class **CheckOnExit** in Display 18.2 were replaced with this definition of **CheckOnExit**, there would be no difference in how the outer class or any class behaves.*

Self-Test Exercises

1. When you define a class and make it implement the `WindowListener` interface, what methods must you define? What do you do if there is no particular action that you want one of these methods to take?

2. The GUI in Display 18.2 has a main window. When the user clicks the close-window button in the main window, a smaller window appears that says "`Are you sure you want to exit?`" What happens if the user clicks the close-window button in this smaller window? Explain your answer.

3. If you want a Swing program to end completely, you can invoke the method `System.exit`. What if you want a `JFrame` window to go away, but you do not want the program to end? What method can you have the `JFrame` invoke?

4. Rewrite the class in Display 18.2 so that the class is its own window listener. *Hint:* The constructor will contain

   ```
   addWindowListener(this);
   ```

18.2 Icons and Scroll Bars

> I ♥ ICONS.
>
> Bumper sticker

Icons

icon

ImageIcon

`JLabel`s, `JButton`s, and `JMenuItem`s can have icons. An **icon** is simply a small picture, although it is not required to be small. The label, button, or menu item may have just a string displayed on it, just an icon, or both (or it can have nothing at all on it). An icon is an instance of the `ImageIcon` class and is based on a digital picture file. The picture file can be in almost any standard format, such as `.gif`, `.jpg`, or `.tiff`.

The class `ImageIcon` is used to convert a picture file to a Swing icon. For example, if you have a picture in a file named `duke_waving.gif`, the following will produce an icon named `dukeWavingIcon` for the picture `duke_waving.gif`:

```
ImageIcon dukeIcon = new ImageIcon("duke_waving.gif");
```

The file `duke_waving.gif` should be in the same directory as the class in which this code appears. Alternatively, you can use a complete or relative path name to specify the picture file. Note that the picture file is given as a value of type `String` that names the picture file. The file `duke_waving.gif` and other picture files we will use in this chapter are all provided on the CD that accompanies this text.

setIcon   You can add an icon to a label with the method setIcon, as follows:

```
JLabel dukeLabel = new JLabel("Mood check");
dukeLabel.setIcon(dukeIcon);
```

Alternatively, you give the icon as an argument to the JLabel constructor, as follows:

```
JLabel dukeLabel = new JLabel(dukeIcon);
```

You can leave the label as created and it will have an icon but no text, or you can add
setText   text with the method setText, as follows:

```
dukeLabel.setText("Mood check");
```

Icons and text may be added to JButtons and JMenuItems in the same way as they are added to a JLabel. For example, the following is taken from Display 18.4, which is a demonstration of the use of icons:

```
JButton happyButton = new JButton("Happy");
ImageIcon happyIcon = new ImageIcon("smiley.gif");
happyButton.setIcon(happyIcon);
```

Display 18.4 **Using Icons** (part 1 of 3)

```
1    import javax.swing.JFrame;
2    import javax.swing.JPanel;
3    import javax.swing.JTextField;
4    import javax.swing.ImageIcon;
5    import java.awt.BorderLayout;
6    import java.awt.FlowLayout;
7    import java.awt.Color;
8    import javax.swing.JLabel;
9    import javax.swing.JButton;
10   import java.awt.event.ActionListener;
11   import java.awt.event.ActionEvent;


12   public class IconDemo extends JFrame implements ActionListener
13   {
14       public static final int WIDTH = 500;
15       public static final int HEIGHT = 200;
16       public static final int TEXT_FIELD_SIZE = 30;

17       private JTextField message;
```

(continued)

Display 18.4 **Using Icons** (part 2 of 3)

```
18      public static void main(String[] args)
19      {
20          IconDemo iconGui = new IconDemo();
21          iconGui.setVisible(true);
22      }


23      public IconDemo()
24      {
25          super("Icon Demonstration");
26          setSize(WIDTH, HEIGHT);
27          setDefaultCloseOperation(JFrame.EXIT_ON_CLOSE);

28          setBackground(Color.WHITE);
29          setLayout(new BorderLayout());

30          JLabel dukeLabel = new JLabel("Mood check");
31          ImageIcon dukeIcon = new ImageIcon("duke_waving.gif");
32          dukeLabel.setIcon(dukeIcon);
33          add(dukeLabel, BorderLayout.NORTH);

34          JPanel buttonPanel = new JPanel();
35          buttonPanel.setLayout(new FlowLayout());
36          JButton happyButton = new JButton("Happy");
37          ImageIcon happyIcon = new ImageIcon("smiley.gif");
38          happyButton.setIcon(happyIcon);
39          happyButton.addActionListener(this);
40          buttonPanel.add(happyButton);
41          JButton sadButton = new JButton("Sad");
42          ImageIcon sadIcon = new ImageIcon("sad.gif");
43          sadButton.setIcon(sadIcon);
44          sadButton.addActionListener(this);
45          buttonPanel.add(sadButton);
46          add(buttonPanel, BorderLayout.SOUTH);

47          message = new JTextField(TEXT_FIELD_SIZE);
48          add(message, BorderLayout.CENTER);
49      }


50      public void actionPerformed(ActionEvent e)
51      {
52          String actionCommand = e.getActionCommand();
```

Display 18.4   Using Icons (part 3 of 3)

```
53          if (actionCommand.equals("Happy"))
54              message.setText(
55                      "Smile and the world smiles with you!");
56          else if (actionCommand.equals("Sad"))
57              message.setText(
58                      "Cheer up. It can't be that bad.");
59          else
60              message.setText("Unexpected Error.");
61      }
62  }
```

RESULTING GUI [1]

View after clicking the "Sad" button.

**button with
only an icon**

You can produce a button or menu item with (just) an icon on it by giving the
ImageIcon object as an argument to the JButton or JMenuItem constructor. For example:

```
ImageIcon happyIcon = new ImageIcon("smiley.gif");
JButton smileButton = new JButton(happyIcon);
JMenuItem happyChoice = new JMenuItem(happyIcon);
```

If you create a button or menu item in this way and do not add text with the method
setText, you should use setActionCommand to explicitly give the button or menu item
an action command, since there is no string on the button or menu item.

All of the classes JButton, JMenuItem, and JLabel have constructors that let you
specify text and an icon to appear on the button, menu item, or label. The constructor
can specify no text or icon, text only, an icon only, or both text and an icon. When you
specify both text and an icon, the text is the first argument and the icon is the second

---

[1] Java, Duke, and all Java-based trademarks and logos are trademarks or registered trademarks of Sun
Microsystems, Inc. in the United States and other countries.

Icons and the Class `ImageIcon`

An **icon** is simply a small picture, although it is not really required to be small. The class `ImageIcon` is used to convert a picture file to a Swing icon.

SYNTAX

```
ImageIcon Name_Of_ImageIcon =
        new ImageIcon(Picture_File_Name);
```

The *Picture_File_Name* is a string giving either a relative or absolute path name to the picture file. (So if the picture file is in the same directory as your program, you need give only the name of the picture file.)

EXAMPLE

```
ImageIcon happyIcon =
        new ImageIcon("smiley.gif");
```

---

argument; also, the constructor for a `JLabel` requires a third argument, as described in Display 18.5. If you omit either text or an icon (or both) from the constructor, you can add them later with the methods `setText` and `setIcon`. Some of these methods for the classes `JButton`, `JMenuItem`, and `Jlabel` are given in Display 18.5.

Display 18.5   Some Methods in the Classes `JButton`, `JMenuItem`, and `JLabel` (part 1 of 2)

```
public JButton()
public JMenuItem()
public JLabel()
```

Creates a button, menu item, or label with no text or icon on it. (Typically, you will later use **setText** and/or **setIcon** with the button, menu item, or label.)

```
public JButton(String text)
public JMenuItem(String text)
public JLabel(String text)
```

Creates a button, menu item, or label with the **text** on it.

```
public JButton(ImageIcon picture)
public JMenuItem(ImageIcon picture)
public JLabel(ImageIcon picture)
```

Creates a button, menu item, or label with the icon **picture** on it and no text.

Display 18.5 Some Methods in the Classes `JButton`, `JMenuItem`, and `JLabel` (part 2 of 2)

```
public JButton(String text, ImageIcon picture)
public JMenuItem(String text, ImageIcon picture)
public JLabel(
        String text, ImageIcon picture, int horizontalAlignment)
```

Creates a button, menu item, or label with both the **text** and the icon **picture** on it.
`horizontalAlignment` is one of the constants `SwingConstants.LEFT`, `SwingConstants.CENTER`,
`SwingConstants.RIGHT`, `SwingConstants.LEADING`, or `SwingConstants.TRAILING`.
The interface `SwingConstants` is in the `javax.swing` package.

```
public void setText(String text)
```

Makes **text** the only text on the button, menu item, or label.

```
public void setIcon(ImageIcon picture)
```

Makes **picture** the only icon on the button, menu item, or label.

```
public void setMargin(Insets margin)
```

`JButton` and `JMenuItem` have the method `setMargin`, but `JLabel` does not.
The method **setMargin** sets the size of the margin around the text and icon in the button or menu
item. The following special case will work for most simple situations. The **int** values give the number
of pixels from the edge of the button or menu item to the text and/or icon.

```
public void setMargin(new Insets(
                    int top, int left, int bottom, int right))
```

The class `Insets` is in the `java.awt` package. (We will not be discussing any other uses for the class
`Insets`.)

```
public void setVerticalTextPosition(int textPosition)
```

Sets the vertical position of the text relative to the icon. The **textPosition** should be one of the
constants `SwingConstants.TOP`, `SwingConstants.CENTER` (the default position), or
`SwingConstants.BOTTOM`.
The interface `SwingConstants` is in the `javax.swing` package.

```
public void setHorizontalTextPosition(int textPosition)
```

Sets the horizontal position of the text relative to the icon. The **textPosition** should be one of the
constants `SwingConstants.RIGHT`, `SwingConstants.LEFT`, `SwingConstants.CENTER`,
`SwingConstants.LEADING`, or `SwingConstants.TRAILING`.
The interface `SwingConstants` is in the `javax.swing` package.

The Insets Class

Objects of the class `Insets` are used to specify the size of the margin in a button or menu item. The `Insets` class is in the package **java.awt**. The parameters in the following constructors are in pixels.

Constructor

```
public Insets(int top, int left, int bottom, int right)
```

EXAMPLES

```
aButton.setMargin(new Insets(10, 20, 10, 20));
```

setIcon and setText

The method **setIcon** can be used to add an icon to a `JButton`, `JMenuItem`, or `JLabel`. The argument to **setIcon** must be an `ImageIcon` object.

SYNTAX

Component.setIcon(*ImageIcon_Object*);

The *Component* can be a `JButton`, `JMenuItem`, or `JLabel`.

EXAMPLE

```
JLabel helloLabel = new JLabel("Hello");
ImageIcon dukeIcon = new ImageIcon("duke_waving.gif");
helloLabel.setIcon(dukeIcon);
```

The method **setText** can be used to add text to a `JButton`, `JMenuItem`, or `JLabel`.

SYNTAX

Component.setText(*Text_String*);

The *Component* can be a `JButton`, `JMenuItem`, or `JLabel`.

EXAMPLE

```
ImageIcon dukeIcon = new ImageIcon("duke_waving.gif");
JLabel helloLabel = new JLabel(dukeIcon);
helloLabel.setText("Hello");
```

The two examples are equivalent.

Self-Test Exercises

5. Write code to create a button that has on it both the text "Magic Button" and the picture in the file wizard.gif.

6. Write code to add the picture in the file wizard.gif to the JPanel named picturePanel. Assume that picturePanel has a FlowLayout manager.

7. Suppose you want to create a button that has the picture in the file wizard.gif on it and no text. Suppose further that you want the button to have the action command "Kazam". How would you create the button and set up the action command?

Scroll Bars

When you create a text area, you specify the number of lines that are visible and the number of characters per line, as in the following example:

```
JTextArea memoDisplay = new JTextArea(15, 30);
```

The text area memoDisplay will have room for 15 lines of text, and each line will have room for at least 30 characters. The user can enter more text, but only a limited amount of text will be visible. It would be better not to have a firm limit on the number of lines or the number of characters per line that the user can see in some convenient way. The way to accomplish this is to add scroll bars to the text area, although, as you will see, the Java code looks more like adding the text area to the scroll bars rather than the other way around.

view port   When using scroll bars, the text is viewed through a **view port** that shows only part of the text at a time. You can view a different part of the text by using the scroll bars that are placed along the side and bottom of the view port. It is as if the text were written on an unbounded sheet of paper, but the paper is covered by another piece of paper with a rectangular cutout that lets you see only a portion of the text. The cutout is the view port. This is illustrated in Display 18.6. You use the scroll bars to move the view port so that different portions of the text can be seen through the cutout view port. (You may prefer to think of the view port as fixed and the text as moving. These two ways of thinking are equivalent.) Swing allows you to add scroll bars to your text areas by using the class JScrollPane.

JScrollPane   An object of the class JScrollPane is essentially a view port with scroll bars. When you create a JScrollPane, you give the text area as an argument to the JScrollPane constructor. For example, if memoDisplay is an object of the class JTextArea (as created in the line of code at the start of this subsection), you can place memoDisplay in a JScrollPane as follows:

```
JScrollPane scrolledText = new JScrollPane(memoDisplay);
```

Display 18.6 View Port for a Text Area

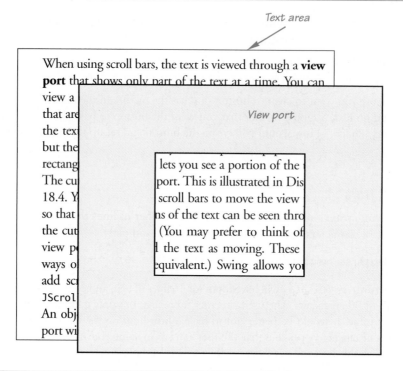

Text area

When using scroll bars, the text is viewed through a **view port** that shows only part of the text at a time. You can view a ~~~~~~~~~~~~~~~~~~~~ that are ~~~~~~~~~~~~~~~~~~~~ the text ~~~~~~~~~~~~~~~~~~~~ but the ~~~~~~~~~~~~~~~~~~~~ rectang ~~~~~~~~~~~~~~~~~~~~ The cu ~~~~~~~~~~~~~~~~~~~~ 18.4. Y ~~~~~~~~~~~~~~~~~~~~ so that ~~~~~~~~~~~~~~~~~~~~ the cut ~~~~~~~~~~~~~~~~~~~~ view p ~~~~~~~~~~~~~~~~~~~~ ways o ~~~~~~~~~~~~~~~~~~~~ add sc ~~~~~~~~~~~~~~~~~~~~ JScrol ~~~~~~~~~~~~~~~~~~~~ An obj ~~~~~~~~~~~~~~~~~~~~ port wi ~~~~~~~~~~~~~~~~~~~~

View port

lets you see a portion of the port. This is illustrated in Dis scroll bars to move the view ns of the text can be seen thro (You may prefer to think of l the text as moving. These equivalent.) Swing allows yo

---

Display 18.7 Some Methods in the Class `JScrollPane` (part 1 of 2)

The `JScrollPane` class is in the `javax.swing` package.

`public JScrollPane(Component objectToBeScrolled)`

Creates a new `JScrollPane` for the `objectToBeScrolled`. Note that the `objectToBeScrolled` need not be a `JTextArea`, although that is the only type of argument considered in this book.

`public void setHorizontalScrollBarPolicy(int policy)`

Sets the policy for showing the horizontal scroll bar. The `policy` should be one of

```
JScrollPane.HORIZONTAL_SCROLLBAR_ALWAYS
JScrollPane.HORIZONTAL_SCROLLBAR_NEVER
JScrollPane.HORIZONTAL_SCROLLBAR_AS_NEEDED
```

The phrase `AS_NEEDED` means the scroll bar is shown only when it is needed. This is explained more fully in the text. The meanings of the other policy constants are obvious from their names.
 (As indicated, these constants are defined in the class `JScrollPane`. You should not need to even be aware of the fact that they have `int` values. Think of them as policies, not as `int` values.)

Display 18.7   Some Methods in the Class `JScrollPane` (part 2 of 2)

```
public void setVerticalScrollBarPolicy(int policy)
```

Sets the policy for showing the vertical scroll bar. The `policy` should be one of

```
JScrollPane.VERTICAL_SCROLLBAR_ALWAYS
JScrollPane.VERTICAL_SCROLLBAR_NEVER
JScrollPane.VERTICAL_SCROLLBAR_AS_NEEDED
```

The phrase **AS_NEEDED** means the scroll bar is shown only when it is needed. This is explained more fully in the text. The meanings of the other policy constants are obvious from their names.
(As indicated, these constants are defined in the class `JScrollPane`. You should not need to even be aware of the fact that they have `int` values. Think of them as policies, not as `int` values.)

The `JScrollPane` can then be added to a container, such as a `JPanel` or `JFrame`, as follows:

```
textPanel.add(scrolledText);
```

This is illustrated by the program in Display 18.8.

Note the following two lines in the constructor definition in Display 18.8:

setting scroll bar policies

```
scrolledText.setHorizontalScrollBarPolicy(
                JScrollPane.HORIZONTAL_SCROLLBAR_ALWAYS);
scrolledText.setVerticalScrollBarPolicy(
                JScrollPane.VERTICAL_SCROLLBAR_ALWAYS);
```

Despite the imposing length of these two method invocations, they perform a very simple task. The first merely specifies that the horizontal scroll bar will always be present. The second specifies that the vertical scroll bar will always be present.

If you omit the invocation of the two methods `setHorizontalScrollBarPolicy` and `setVerticalScrollBarPolicy`, the scroll bars will be visible only when you need them. In other words, if you omit these two method invocations and all the text fits in the view port, then no scroll bars will be visible. When you add enough text to need scroll bars, the needed scroll bars will appear automatically.

Display 18.7 summarizes what we have said about the class `JScrollPane`. We are interested in using `JScrollPane` only with text areas. However, as we note in Display 18.7, `JScrollPane` can be used with almost any sort of component.

Display 18.8 A Text Area with Scroll Bars (part 1 of 3)

```
1    import javax.swing.JFrame;
2    import javax.swing.JTextArea;
3    import javax.swing.JPanel;
4    import javax.swing.JLabel;
5    import javax.swing.JButton;
6    import javax.swing.JScrollPane;
7    import java.awt.BorderLayout;
8    import java.awt.FlowLayout;
9    import java.awt.Color;
10   import java.awt.event.ActionListener;
11   import java.awt.event.ActionEvent;


12   public class ScrollBarDemo extends JFrame
13                         implements ActionListener
14   {
15       public static final int WIDTH = 600;
16       public static final int HEIGHT = 400;
17       public static final int LINES = 15;
18       public static final int CHAR_PER_LINE = 30;


19       private JTextArea memoDisplay;
20       private String memo1;
21       private String memo2;


22       public static void main(String[] args)
23       {
24           ScrollBarDemo gui = new ScrollBarDemo();
25           gui.setVisible(true);
26       }


27       public ScrollBarDemo()
28       {
29           super("Scroll Bars Demo");
30           setSize(WIDTH, HEIGHT);
31           setDefaultCloseOperation(JFrame.EXIT_ON_CLOSE);
```

Display 18.8 A Text Area with Scroll Bars (part 2 of 3)

```
32          JPanel buttonPanel = new JPanel();
33          buttonPanel.setBackground(Color.LIGHT_GRAY);
34          buttonPanel.setLayout(new FlowLayout());
35          JButton memo1Button = new JButton("Save Memo 1");
36          memo1Button.addActionListener(this);
37          buttonPanel.add(memo1Button);

38          JButton memo2Button = new JButton("Save Memo 2");
39          memo2Button.addActionListener(this);
40          buttonPanel.add(memo2Button);

41          JButton clearButton = new JButton("Clear");
42          clearButton.addActionListener(this);
43          buttonPanel.add(clearButton);

44          JButton get1Button = new JButton("Get Memo 1");
45          get1Button.addActionListener(this);
46          buttonPanel.add(get1Button);

47          JButton get2Button = new JButton("Get Memo 2");
48          get2Button.addActionListener(this);
49          buttonPanel.add(get2Button);

50          add(buttonPanel, BorderLayout.SOUTH);

51          JPanel textPanel = new JPanel();
52          textPanel.setBackground(Color.BLUE);

53          memoDisplay = new JTextArea(LINES, CHAR_PER_LINE);
54          memoDisplay.setBackground(Color.WHITE);

55          JScrollPane scrolledText = new JScrollPane(memoDisplay);
56          scrolledText.setHorizontalScrollBarPolicy(
57                      JScrollPane.HORIZONTAL_SCROLLBAR_ALWAYS);
58          scrolledText.setVerticalScrollBarPolicy(
59                      JScrollPane.VERTICAL_SCROLLBAR_ALWAYS);

60          textPanel.add(scrolledText);

61          add(textPanel, BorderLayout.CENTER);
62      }
```

(continued)

Display 18.8   A Text Area with Scroll Bars (part 3 of 3)

```
63        public void actionPerformed(ActionEvent e)
64        {
65            String actionCommand = e.getActionCommand();


66            if (actionCommand.equals("Save Memo 1"))
67                memo1 = memoDisplay.getText();
68            else if (actionCommand.equals("Save Memo 2"))
69                memo2 = memoDisplay.getText();
70            else if (actionCommand.equals("Clear"))
71                memoDisplay.setText("");
72            else if (actionCommand.equals("Get Memo 1"))
73                memoDisplay.setText(memo1);
74            else if (actionCommand.equals("Get Memo 2"))
75                memoDisplay.setText(memo2);
76            else
77                memoDisplay.setText("Error in memo interface");
78        }
79  }
```

RESULTING GUI

Scroll Bars

The class `JScrollPane` is used to add scroll bars to a `JTextArea` (and certain other components). The `JTextArea` object is given as an argument to the constructor that creates the `JScrollPane`. The `JScrollPane` class is in the `javax.swing` package.

SYNTAX

```
JScrollPane Identifier = new JScrollPane(Text_Area_Object);
```

EXAMPLES

```
JTextArea memoDisplay = new JTextArea(LINES, CHAR_PER_LINE);
JScrollPane scrolledText = new JScrollPane(memoDisplay);
textPanel.add(scrolledText);
```

Self-Test Exercises

8. When setting up a `JScrollPane`, do you have to invoke both of the methods `setHorizontalScrollBarPolicy` and `setVerticalScrollBarPolicy`?

9. In Display 18.7, we listed the constructor for `JScrollPane` as follows:

   ```
   public JScrollPane(Component objectToBeScrolled)
   ```

   This indicates that the argument to the constructor must be of type `Component`. But we used the constructor with an argument of type `JTextArea`. Isn't this some sort of type violation?

EXAMPLE: Components with Changing Visibility

The GUI in Display 18.9 has labels that change from visible to invisible and back again. Since the labels contain nothing but an icon each, it appears as if the icons change roles from visible to invisible and back again. When the GUI is first run, the label with Duke not waving is shown. When the `"Wave"` button is clicked, the label with Duke not waving disappears and the label with Duke waving appears. When the button labeled `"Stop"` is clicked, the label with Duke waving disappears and the label with Duke not waving returns. Note that you can make a component invisible without making the entire GUI invisible.

(continued)

EXAMPLE: (continued)

In this GUI, a label becomes visible or invisible when a button is clicked. For example, the following code from the method `actionPerformed` in Display 18.9 determines what happens when the button with the text `"Wave"` on it is clicked:

```
if (actionCommand.equals("Wave"))
{
    wavingLabel.setVisible(true);
    standingLabel.setVisible(false);
}
```

We used the `setVisible` method on the labels containing the icons rather than directly on the icons because the class `ImageIcon` does not have the `setVisible` method.

The two statements

```
wavingLabel.setVisible(true);
standingLabel.setVisible(false);
```

make `wavingLabel` visible and `standingLabel` invisible.

Display 18.9 Labels with Changing Visibility (part 1 of 3)

```
1   import javax.swing.JFrame;
2   import javax.swing.ImageIcon;
3   import javax.swing.JPanel;
4   import javax.swing.JLabel;
5   import javax.swing.JButton;
6   import java.awt.BorderLayout;
7   import java.awt.FlowLayout;
8   import java.awt.Color;
9   import java.awt.event.ActionListener;
10  import java.awt.event.ActionEvent;

11  public class VisibilityDemo extends JFrame
12                              implements ActionListener
13  {
14      public static final int WIDTH = 300;
15      public static final int HEIGHT = 200;
16      private JLabel wavingLabel;
17      private JLabel standingLabel;
18      public static void main(String[] args)
19          {
```

```
20              VisibilityDemo demoGui = new VisibilityDemo();
21              demoGui.setVisible(true);
22          }

23      public VisibilityDemo()
24      {
25              setSize(WIDTH, HEIGHT);
26              setDefaultCloseOperation(JFrame.EXIT_ON_CLOSE);
27              setTitle("Visibility Demonstration");

28              setLayout(new BorderLayout());

29              JPanel picturePanel = new JPanel();
30              picturePanel.setBackground(Color.WHITE);
31              picturePanel.setLayout(new FlowLayout());

32              ImageIcon dukeStandingIcon =
33                      new ImageIcon("duke_standing.gif");
34              standingLabel = new JLabel(dukeStandingIcon);
35              standingLabel.setVisible(true);
36              picturePanel.add(standingLabel);

37              ImageIcon dukeWavingIcon = new ImageIcon("duke_waving.gif");
38              wavingLabel = new JLabel(dukeWavingIcon);
39              wavingLabel.setVisible(false);
40              picturePanel.add(wavingLabel);

41              add(picturePanel, BorderLayout.CENTER);

42              JPanel buttonPanel = new JPanel();
43              buttonPanel.setBackground(Color.LIGHT_GRAY);
44              buttonPanel.setLayout(new FlowLayout());

45              JButton waveButton = new JButton("Wave");
46              waveButton.addActionListener(this);
47              buttonPanel.add(waveButton);

48              JButton stopButton = new JButton("Stop");
49              stopButton.addActionListener(this);
50              buttonPanel.add(stopButton);
51              add(buttonPanel, BorderLayout.SOUTH);
52          }
53      public void actionPerformed(ActionEvent e)
54      {
55              String actionCommand = e.getActionCommand();
```

(continued)

Display 18.9 Labels with Changing Visibility (part 3 of 3)

```
56          if (actionCommand.equals("Wave"))
57          {
58              wavingLabel.setVisible(true);
59              standingLabel.setVisible(false);
60          }
61          else if (actionCommand.equals("Stop"))
62          {
63              standingLabel.setVisible(true);
64              wavingLabel.setVisible(false);
65          }
66          else
67              System.out.println("Unanticipated error.");
68      }
69  }
```

RESULTING GUI (After clicking Stop button)

RESULTING GUI (After clicking Wave button)

18.3 The Graphics Class

Drawing is my life!

The Graphics class

In this section we show you how to produce drawing for your GUIs using the Graphics class.

Coordinate System for Graphics Objects

origin

(x, y)

When drawing objects on the screen, Java uses the coordinate system shown in Display 18.10. The **origin** point (0, 0) is the upper-left corner of the screen area used for drawing (usually a JFrame or JPanel). The *x*-coordinate, or horizontal coordinate, is positive and increasing to the right. The *y*-coordinate, or vertical coordinate, is positive and increasing in the downward direction. The point (*x*, *y*) is located *x* pixels in from the left edge of the screen and down *y* pixels from the top of the screen. All coordinates are normally positive. Units as well as sizes of figures are in pixels. When placing a rectangle on the screen, Java often uses a coordinate like (200, 150) to specify where the rectangle is located.

Note that, when specifying the location of a rectangle or other figure, the coordinates do not indicate the center of the rectangle, but instead indicate the location of the upper-left corner of the rectangle. In Display 18.10, the X marks the location of the point (200, 150) and the rectangle shown is at location (200, 150).

bounding box

When placing a figure other than a rectangle on the screen, Java encloses the figure in an imaginary tightly fitting rectangle, sometimes called a **bounding box**, and positions the upper-left corner of the imaginary rectangle. For example, in Display 18.10, the oval displayed is located at point (200, 150).

The Method paint and the Class Graphics

paint

Almost all Swing and Swing-related components and containers have a method named paint. The method paint draws the component or container on the screen. Up until now, we have had no need to redefine the method paint or to even mention it. The method paint is defined for you and is called automatically when the figure is displayed on the screen. However, to draw geometric figures, like circles and boxes, you need to redefine the method paint. It is the method paint that draws the figures.

Display 18.10   Screen Coordinate System

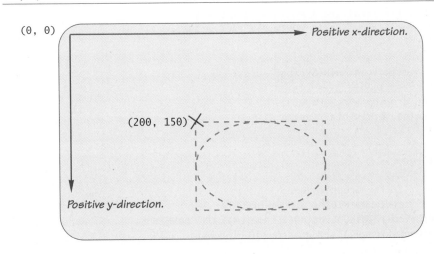

Display 18.11 shows a GUI program that displays a JFrame with a rather primitive face drawn inside of it. The mouth and eyes are just straight line segments. We will soon see how to get round eyes and a smile (and more), but the basic technique can be seen more clearly in this simple figure. The code for drawing the face is given in the method paint.

Display 18.11   Drawing a Very Simple Face (part 1 of 2)

```
1    import javax.swing.JFrame;
2    import java.awt.Graphics;
3    import java.awt.Color;

4    public class Face extends JFrame
5    {
6        public static final int WINDOW_WIDTH = 400;
7        public static final int WINDOW_HEIGHT = 400;

8        public static final int FACE_DIAMETER = 200;
9        public static final int X_FACE = 100;
10       public static final int Y_FACE = 100;

11       public static final int EYE_WIDTH = 20;
12       public static final int X_RIGHT_EYE = X_FACE + 55;
13       public static final int Y_RIGHT_EYE = Y_FACE + 60;
14       public static final int X_LEFT_EYE = X_FACE + 130;
15       public static final int Y_LEFT_EYE = Y_FACE + 60;

16       public static final int MOUTH_WIDTH = 100;
17       public static final int X_MOUTH = X_FACE + 50;
18       public static final int Y_MOUTH = Y_FACE + 150;

19       public static void main(String[] args)
20       {
21           Face drawing = new Face();
22           drawing.setVisible(true);
23       }

24       public Face()
25       {
26           super("First Graphics Demo");
27           setSize(WINDOW_WIDTH, WINDOW_HEIGHT);
28           setDefaultCloseOperation(JFrame.EXIT_ON_CLOSE);
29           getContentPane().setBackground(Color.white);
30       }
```

Display 18.11   **Drawing a Very Simple Face** (part 2 of 2)

```
31        public void paint(Graphics g)
32        {
33            super.paint(g);
34            g.drawOval(X_FACE, Y_FACE, FACE_DIAMETER, FACE_DIAMETER);
35            //Draw Eyes:
36            g.drawLine(X_RIGHT_EYE, Y_RIGHT_EYE,
37                                    X_RIGHT_EYE + EYE_WIDTH,Y_RIGHT_EYE);
38            g.drawLine(X_LEFT_EYE, Y_LEFT_EYE,
39                                    X_LEFT_EYE + EYE_WIDTH, Y_LEFT_EYE);
40            //Draw Mouth:
41            g.drawLine(X_MOUTH, Y_MOUTH, X_MOUTH + MOUTH_WIDTH, Y_MOUTH);
42        }
43    }
```

RESULTING **GUI**

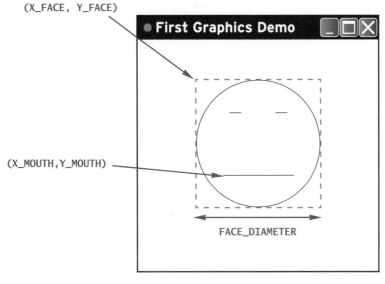

(X_FACE, Y_FACE)

First Graphics Demo

The red box is not shown on the screen. It is there to help you understand the relationship between the **paint** method code and the resulting drawing.

(X_MOUTH,Y_MOUTH)

FACE_DIAMETER

The method paint is called automatically, and you normally should not invoke it in your code. If you do not redefine it, the method paint for a JFrame object simply draws a frame border, title, and other standard features, and then asks the components to all invoke their paint methods. If we did not redefine the method paint, then the JFrame would have a border and title but would contain nothing. The code in the redefinition of paint explains how to draw the face. Let's look at the details.

Graphics   Notice that the method paint has a parameter g of type Graphics. Graphics is an abstract class in the java.awt package. Every container and component that can be drawn on the screen has an associated Graphics object. (To be precise, every JComponent has an associated Graphics object.) This associated Graphics object has data specifying what area of the screen the component or container covers. In particular, the Graphics object for a JFrame specifies that the drawing takes place inside the borders of the JFrame object. (Since Graphics is an abstract class, every Graphics object is an instance of some concrete descendent class of the Graphics class, but we usually do not care about which descendent class. All we normally need to know is that it is of type Graphics.)

The Graphics class, and so any Graphics object g, has all the methods that we will use to draw figures, such as circles, lines, and boxes, on the screen. Almost the entire definition of the paint method in Display 18.11 consists of invocations of various drawing methods with the parameter g as the calling object.

When the paint method in Display 18.11 is (automatically) invoked, the parameter g will be replaced by the Graphics object associated with the JFrame, so the figures drawn will be inside the JFrame. Let's look at the code in this method paint.

Notice the first line in the definition of paint in Display 18.11:

```
super.paint(g);
```

Recall that super is a name for the parent class of a derived class. The class in Display 18.11 is derived from the class JFrame, so super.paint is the paint method for the class JFrame. Whenever you redefine the method paint, you should start with this invocation of super.paint. This ensures that your definition of paint will do all the things the standard paint method does, such as draw the title and border for the JFrame. (This lesson applies even if the class is derived from some class other than JFrame.)

drawOval   The following invocation from the method paint draws the circle forming the head:

```
g.drawOval(X_FACE, Y_FACE, FACE_DIAMETER, FACE_DIAMETER);
```

The last two arguments give the width and height of the enclosing rectangle, shown in red. The fact that these two arguments are equal is what makes it a circle instead of a typical oval. The first two arguments give x- and y-coordinates for the position of the circle. Note that a figure is positioned by giving the position of the upper-left corner of an enclosing rectangle.

drawLine   The only other drawing statements in the method paint are invocations of g.drawLine. The method g.drawLine draws a straight line between two points with x- and y-coordinates (x_1, y_1) and (x_2, y_2), where the argument positions for the four coordinate numbers are indicated below:

```
g.drawLine(x₁, y₁, x₂, y₂)
```

For example, the invocation that draws the mouth is as follows:

```
g.drawLine(X_MOUTH, Y_MOUTH, X_MOUTH + MOUTH_WIDTH, Y_MOUTH);
```

Since both *y*-coordinates (Y_MOUTH) are the same, the line is horizontal. The line for the mouth begins at coordinates (X_MOUTH, Y_MOUTH) and extends to the right for MOUTH_WIDTH pixels.

The Graphics Class

Every container and component that can be drawn on the screen has an associated Graphics object. This associated Graphics object has data specifying what area of the screen the component or container covers. In particular, the Graphics object for a JFrame specifies that the drawing takes place inside the borders of the JFrame object.

When an object g of the class Graphics is used as the calling object for a drawing method, the drawing takes place inside the area of the screen specified by g. For example, if g is the Graphics object for a JFrame, the drawing takes place inside the borders of the JFrame object.

Some of the commonly used methods of the class Graphics are given in Display 18.12.

Graphics is an abstract class in the java.awt package.

Some of the commonly used methods of the class Graphics are given in Display 18.12. Note that most methods come in pairs, one whose name starts with draw and one whose name starts with fill, such as drawOval and fillOval. The one that starts with draw will draw the outline of the specified figure. The one that starts with fill will draw a solid figure obtained by filling the inside of the specified figure. In the next few subsections we discuss some of these methods.

Display 18.12 **Some Methods in the Class Graphics** (part 1 of 3)

Graphics is an abstract class in the **java.awt** package.
Although many of these methods are abstract, we always use them with objects of a concrete descendent class of **Graphics**, even though we usually do not know the name of that concrete class.

```
public abstract void drawLine(int x1, int y1, int x2, int y2)
```
Draws a line between points (x1, y1) and (x2, y2).

```
public abstract void drawRect(int x, int y,
                              int width, int height)
```
Draws the outline of the specified rectangle. (x, y) is the location of the upper-left corner of the rectangle.

```
public abstract void fillRect(int x, int y,
                              int width, int height)
```
Fills the specified rectangle. (x, y) is the location of the upper-left corner of the rectangle.

Display 18.12 Some Methods in the Class **Graphics** (part 2 of 3)

```
public void draw3DRect(int x, int y, int width,
                                  int height, boolean raised)
```

Draws the outline of the specified rectangle. (x, y) is the location of the upper-left corner. The rectangle is highlighted to look like it has thickness. If **raised** is **true**, the highlight makes the rectangle appear to stand out from the background. If **raised** is **false**, the highlight makes the rectangle appear to be sunken into the background.

```
public void fill3DRect(int x, int y, int width,
                                  int height, boolean raised)
```

Fills the rectangle specified by

```
draw3DRec(x, y, width, height, raised)
```

```
public abstract void drawRoundRect(int x, int y,
          int width, int height, int arcWidth, int arcHeight)
```

Draws the outline of the specified round-cornered rectangle. (x, y) is the location of the upper-left corner of the enclosing regular rectangle. **arcWidth** and **arcHeight** specify the shape of the round corners. See the text for details.

```
public abstract void fillRoundRect(int x, int y,
          int width, int height, int arcWidth, int arcHeight)
```

Fills the rounded rectangle specified by

```
drawRoundRec(x, y, width, height, arcWidth, arcHeight)
```

```
public abstract void drawOval(int x, int y,
                                  int width, int height)
```

Draws the outline of the oval with the smallest enclosing rectangle that has the specified width and height. The (imagined) rectangle has its upper-left corner located at (x, y).

```
public abstract void fillOval(int x, int y,
                                  int width, int height)
```

Fills the oval specified by

```
drawOval(x, y, width, height)
```

```
public abstract void drawArc(int x, int y,
                        int width, int height,
                        int startAngle, int arcSweep)
```

Draws part of an oval that just fits into an invisible rectangle described by the first four arguments. The portion of the oval drawn is given by the last two arguments. See the text for details.

```
public abstract void fillArc(int x, int y,
                             int width, int height,
                             int startAngle, int arcSweep)
```

Fills the partial oval specified by

```
drawArc(x, y, width, height, startAngle, arcSweep)
```

Drawing Ovals

drawOval

An oval is drawn by the method drawOval. The arguments specify the location, width, and height of the smallest rectangle that encloses the oval. For example, the following line draws an oval:

```
g.drawOval(100, 50, 300, 200);
```

This draws an oval that just fits into an invisible rectangle whose upper-left corner is at coordinates (100, 50) and that has a width of 300 pixels and a height of 200 pixels. Note that the point that is used to place the oval on the screen is not the center of the oval or anything like the center, but is something like the upper-left corner of the oval.

Note that a circle is a special case of an oval in which the width and height of the rectangle are equal. For example, the following line from the definition of paint in Display 18.11 draws a circle for the outline of the face:

```
g.drawOval(X_FACE, Y_FACE, FACE_DIAMETER, FACE_DIAMETER);
```

Since the enclosing rectangle has the same width and height, this produces a circle.

Some of the methods you can use to draw simple figures are shown in Display 18.12. A similar table is given in Appendix 5.

Drawing Arcs

Arcs, such as the smile on the happy face in Display 18.13, are described by giving an oval and then specifying what portion of the oval will be used for the arc. For example, the following statement from Display 18.13 draws the smile on the happy face:

drawArc

```
g.drawArc(X_MOUTH, Y_MOUTH, MOUTH_WIDTH, MOUTH_HEIGHT,
          MOUTH_START_ANGLE, MOUTH_ARC_SWEEP);
```

which is equivalent to

```
g.drawArc(X_MOUTH, Y_MOUTH, MOUTH_WIDTH, MOUTH_HEIGHT, 180, 180);
```

The arguments MOUTH_WIDTH and MOUTH_HEIGHT determine the size of an invisible rectangle. The arguments X_MOUTH and Y_MOUTH determine the location of the rectangle. The upper-left corner of the rectangle is located at the point (X_MOUTH, Y_MOUTH). Inside this invisible rectangle, envision an invisible oval that just fits inside the invisible rectangle. The last two arguments specify the portion of this invisible oval that is made visible.

Display 18.14 illustrates how these last two arguments specify an arc of the invisible oval to be made visible. The next-to-last argument specifies a start angle in degrees. The last argument specifies how many degrees of the oval's arc will be made visible. If the last argument is 360 (degrees), then the full oval is made visible.

Display 18.13 **Drawing a Happy Face** (part 1 of 2)

```
1   import javax.swing.JFrame;
2   import java.awt.Graphics;
3   import java.awt.Color;


4   public class HappyFace extends JFrame
5   {
6       public static final int WINDOW_WIDTH = 400;
7       public static final int WINDOW_HEIGHT = 400;


8       public static final int FACE_DIAMETER = 200;
9       public static final int X_FACE = 100;
10      public static final int Y_FACE = 100;


11      public static final int EYE_WIDTH = 20;
12      public static final int EYE_HEIGHT = 10;
13      public static final int X_RIGHT_EYE = X_FACE + 55;
14      public static final int Y_RIGHT_EYE = Y_FACE + 60;
15      public static final int X_LEFT_EYE = X_FACE + 130;
16      public static final int Y_LEFT_EYE = Y_FACE + 60;


17      public static final int MOUTH_WIDTH = 100;
18      public static final int MOUTH_HEIGHT = 50;
19      public static final int X_MOUTH = X_FACE + 50;
20      public static final int Y_MOUTH = Y_FACE + 100;
21      public static final int MOUTH_START_ANGLE = 180;
22      public static final int MOUTH_ARC_SWEEP = 180;
```

Display 18.13   **Drawing a Happy Face** (part 2 of 2)

```
23          public static void main(String[] args)
24      {
25          HappyFace drawing = new HappyFace();
26          drawing.setVisible(true);
27      }

28      public HappyFace()
29      {
30          super("Graphics Demonstration 2");
31          setSize(WINDOW_WIDTH, WINDOW_HEIGHT);
32          setDefaultCloseOperation(JFrame.EXIT_ON_CLOSE);
33          getContentPane().setBackground(Color.white);
34      }
35      public void paint(Graphics g)
36      {
37          super.paint(g);
38          g.drawOval(X_FACE, Y_FACE, FACE_DIAMETER, FACE_DIAMETER);
39          //Draw Eyes:
40          g.fillOval(X_RIGHT_EYE, Y_RIGHT_EYE, EYE_WIDTH, EYE_HEIGHT);
41          g.fillOval(X_LEFT_EYE, Y_LEFT_EYE, EYE_WIDTH, EYE_HEIGHT);
42          //Draw Mouth:
43          g.drawArc(X_MOUTH, Y_MOUTH, MOUTH_WIDTH, MOUTH_HEIGHT,
44                  MOUTH_START_ANGLE, MOUTH_ARC_SWEEP);
45      }
46  }
```

RESULTING GUI

Display 18.14 Specifying an Arc

```
g.drawArc(x, y, width, height, 0, 90);
```

```
g.drawArc(x, y, width, height, 0, -90);
```

```
g.drawArc(x, y, width, height, 0, 360);
```

```
g.drawArc(x, y, width, height, 180, 90);
```

The angles are numbered with zero degrees, as shown in Display 18.14. In the first figure, the start angle is zero degrees. The counterclockwise direction is positive. So a start angle of 90 degrees would start at the top of the oval. A start angle of –90 degrees would start at the bottom of the oval. For example, the smile on the happy face in Display 18.13 has a start angle of 180 degrees, so it starts on the left end of the invisible oval. The last argument is also 180, so the arc is made visible through a counterclockwise direction of 180 degrees, or halfway around the oval in the counterclockwise direction.

Self-Test Exercises

10. Give an invocation of a method to draw a horizontal line from point (30, 40) to point (100, 60). The calling object of type Graphics is named g.

11. Give an invocation of a method to draw a horizontal line of length 100 starting at position (30, 40) and extending to the right. The calling object of type Graphics is named g.

12. Give an invocation of a method that draws a vertical line of length 100 starting at position (30, 40) and extending downward. Use graphicsObject (of type Graphic) as the calling object.

13. Give an invocation of a method to draw a solid rectangle of width 100 and height 50 with the upper-left corner at position (20, 30). The calling object of type Graphics is named graphicsObject.

14. Give an invocation of a method to draw a solid rectangle of width 100 and height 50 with the upper-right corner at position (200, 300). The calling object of type Graphics is named g.

15. Give an invocation of a method to draw a circle of diameter 100 with the center at position (300, 400). The calling object of type Graphics is named g.

16. Give an invocation of a method to draw a circle of radius 100 with the center at position (300, 400). The calling object of type Graphics is named g.

Rounded Rectangles ★

rounded
rectangle

A **rounded rectangle** is a rectangle whose corners have been replaced by arcs so that the corners are rounded. For example, suppose g is of type Graphics and consider what would be drawn by the following:

```
g.drawRoundRect(x, y, width, height, arcWidth, arcHeight)
```

The arguments x, y, width, and height determine a regular rectangle in the usual way. The upper-left corner is at the point (x, y). The rectangle has the specified width and height. The last two arguments, arcWidth and arcHeight, specify the arcs that will be used for the corners so as to produce a rounded rectangle. Each corner is replaced with a quarter of an oval that is arcWidth pixels wide and arcHeight pixels high. This is illustrated in Display 18.15. To obtain corners that are arcs of circles just make arcWidth and arcHeight equal.

paintComponent for Panels

You can draw figures on a JPanel and place the JPanel in a JFrame. When defining a JPanel class that contains a graphics drawing, you use the method paintComponent instead of the method paint, but otherwise the details are similar to what we have seen for JFrames. JFrames use the method paint. However, JPanels—and in fact all JComponents—use the method paintComponent. A very simple example of using paintComponent with a JPanel is given in Display 18.16.

If you look back at Display 17.12 in Chapter 17, you will see that a JPanel is a JComponent, but a JFrame is not a JComponent. A JFrame is only a Component. That is why they use different methods to paint the screen.

Action Drawings and repaint

The program in Display 18.17 is similar to the program in Display 18.13. It draws a happy face similar to the happy face given in Display 18.13, but with one difference: There is a button at the bottom of the GUI that says Click for a Wink. When you click that button, the left eye winks. (Remember the left eye is on your right.) Let's see the details.

Display 18.15 A Rounded Rectangle

```
g.drawRoundRect(x, y, width, height, arcWidth, arcHeight);
```
produces:

Display 18.16 **paintComponent** Demonstration (part 1 of 2)

```java
1  import javax.swing.JFrame;
2  import javax.swing.JPanel;
3  import java.awt.GridLayout;
4  import java.awt.Graphics;
5  import java.awt.Color;

6  public class PaintComponentDemo extends JFrame
7  {
8      public static final int FRAME_WIDTH = 400;
9      public static final int FRAME_HEIGHT = 400;

10     private class FancyPanel extends JPanel
11     {
12         public void paintComponent(Graphics g)
13         {
14             super.paintComponent(g);
15             setBackground(Color.YELLOW);
16             g.drawOval(FRAME_WIDTH/4, FRAME_HEIGHT/8,
17                        FRAME_WIDTH/2, FRAME_HEIGHT/6);
18         }
19     }

20     public static void main(String[] args)
21     {
22         PaintComponentDemo w = new PaintComponentDemo();
23         w.setVisible(true);
24     }
25     public PaintComponentDemo()
26     {
27         setSize(FRAME_WIDTH, FRAME_HEIGHT);
28         setDefaultCloseOperation(JFrame.EXIT_ON_CLOSE);
29         setTitle("The Oval Is in a Panel");
30         setLayout(new GridLayout(2, 1));
31         FancyPanel p = new FancyPanel();
32         add(p);
33         JPanel whitePanel = new JPanel();
34         whitePanel.setBackground(Color.WHITE);
35         add(whitePanel);
36     }
37 }
```

(continued)

Display 18.16   `paintComponent` Demonstration (part 2 of 2)

RESULTING GUI

The program in Display 18.17 has a private instance variable wink of type boolean. When the value of wink is false, the paint method draws an ordinary happy face. When the value of wink is true, the paint method draws the face the same except that the left eye is just a straight line, which looks like the eye is closed. The variable wink is initialized to false.

When the button labeled Click for a Wink is clicked, this sends an action event to the method actionPerformed. The method actionPerformed then changes the value of the variable wink to true and invokes the method repaint. This use of the method repaint is new, so let's discuss it a bit.

repaint   Every JFrame (in fact, every Component and every Container) has a method named repaint. The method repaint will repaint the screen so that any changes to the graphics being displayed will show on the screen. If you omit the invocation of repaint from the method actionPerformed, then the variable wink will change to true, but the screen will not change. Without an invocation of repaint, the face will not change, because the method paint must be called again with the new value of wink before the change takes effect. The method repaint does a few standard things and, most importantly, will also invoke the method paint, which redraws the screen. Be sure to note that you should invoke repaint and not paint.

Now we explain why, when wink has the value true, the method paint draws the face with the left eye changed. The relevant part of the code is the following, which draws the left eye:

```
if (wink)
    g.drawLine(X_LEFT_EYE, Y_LEFT_EYE,
                         X_LEFT_EYE + EYE_WIDTH, Y_LEFT_EYE);
else
    g.fillOval(X_LEFT_EYE, Y_LEFT_EYE, EYE_WIDTH, EYE_HEIGHT);
```

Display 18.17   An Action Drawing (part 1 of 3)

```
1    import javax.swing.JFrame;
2    import javax.swing.JButton;
3    import java.awt.event.ActionListener;
4    import java.awt.event.ActionEvent;
5    import java.awt.BorderLayout;
6    import java.awt.Graphics;
7    import java.awt.Color;

8    public class ActionFace extends JFrame
9    {
10       public static final int WINDOW_WIDTH = 400;
11       public static final int WINDOW_HEIGHT = 400;

12       public static final int FACE_DIAMETER = 200;
13       public static final int X_FACE = 100;
14       public static final int Y_FACE = 100;

15       public static final int EYE_WIDTH = 20;
16       public static final int EYE_HEIGHT = 10;
17       public static final int X_RIGHT_EYE = X_FACE + 55;
18       public static final int Y_RIGHT_EYE = Y_FACE + 60;
19       public static final int X_LEFT_EYE = X_FACE + 130;
20       public static final int Y_LEFT_EYE = Y_FACE + 60;

21       public static final int MOUTH_WIDTH = 100;
22       public static final int MOUTH_HEIGHT = 50;
23       public static final int X_MOUTH = X_FACE + 50;
24       public static final int Y_MOUTH = Y_FACE + 100;
25       public static final int MOUTH_START_ANGLE = 180;
26       public static final int MOUTH_ARC_SWEEP = 180;

27       private boolean wink;

28       private class WinkAction implements ActionListener
29       {
30           public void actionPerformed(ActionEvent e)
31           {
32               wink = true;
33               repaint();
34           }
35       } // End of WinkAction inner class
```

(continued)

Display 18.17 **An Action Drawing** (part 2 of 3)

```
36        public static void main(String[] args)
37        {
38            ActionFace drawing = new ActionFace();
39            drawing.setVisible(true);
40        }

41        public ActionFace()
42        {
43            setSize(WINDOW_WIDTH, WINDOW_HEIGHT);
44            setDefaultCloseOperation(JFrame.EXIT_ON_CLOSE);
45            setTitle("Hello There!");
46            setLayout(new BorderLayout());
47            getContentPane().setBackground(Color.white);

48            JButton winkButton = new JButton("Click for a Wink.");
49            winkButton.addActionListener(new WinkAction());
50            add(winkButton, BorderLayout.SOUTH);
51            wink = false;
52        }

53        public void paint(Graphics g)
54        {
55            super.paint(g);
56            g.drawOval(X_FACE, Y_FACE, FACE_DIAMETER, FACE_DIAMETER);
57            //Draw Right Eye:
58            g.fillOval(X_RIGHT_EYE, Y_RIGHT_EYE, EYE_WIDTH, EYE_HEIGHT);
59            //Draw Left Eye:
60            if (wink)
61                g.drawLine(X_LEFT_EYE, Y_LEFT_EYE,
62                                   X_LEFT_EYE + EYE_WIDTH, Y_LEFT_EYE);
63            else
64                g.fillOval(X_LEFT_EYE, Y_LEFT_EYE, EYE_WIDTH, EYE_HEIGHT);
65            //Draw Mouth:
66            g.drawArc(X_MOUTH, Y_MOUTH, MOUTH_WIDTH, MOUTH_HEIGHT,
67                          MOUTH_START_ANGLE, MOUTH_ARC_SWEEP);
68        }

69    }
```

Display 18.17   **An Action Drawing** (part 3 of 3)

RESULTING GUI (When started)

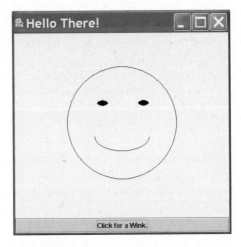

RESULTING GUI (After clicking the button)

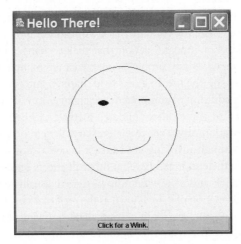

If wink has the value true, then the eye is drawn as a line, which looks like a closed eye. If wink has the value false, then the eye is drawn as an oval, which looks like an open eye.

The repaint and paint Methods

When you change the graphic's contents in a window and want to update the window so that the new contents show on the screen, do not call `paint`; call `repaint`. The `repaint` method takes care of some overhead and then calls the `paint` method. Normally, you do not define `repaint`. As long as you define the `paint` method correctly, the `repaint` method should work correctly. Note that you often define `paint`, but you normally do not call `paint`. On the other hand, normally you do not define `repaint`, but you do sometimes call `repaint`.

Some More Details on Updating a GUI ★

Most of the changes to a GUI windowing system that we have seen are updated automatically so that they are visible on the screen. This is done by an object known as the **repaint manager**. The repaint manager works automatically, and you need not even be aware of its presence. However, there are a few updates that the repaint manager will not do for you. You have already learned that you need an invocation of `repaint` when your GUI changes the figure drawn in the JFrame as in Display 18.17.

repaint manager

Two other updating methods that you will often see when looking at Swing code are `validate` and `pack`.

Every container class has the method `validate`, which has no arguments. An invocation of `validate` causes the container to lay out its components again. An invocation of `validate` is a kind of "update" action that makes changes in the components actually happen on the screen. Many simple changes that are made to a Swing GUI, like changing color or changing the text in a text field, happen automatically. Other changes, such as some kinds of addition of components or changes in visibility, may require an invocation of `validate` or some other "update" method. Sometimes it is difficult to decide whether an invocation of `validate` is necessary. When in doubt, include an invocation of `validate`. Although invoking `validate` when it is not needed can make your program a little less efficient, it will have no other ill effects on your GUI.

validate

The method `pack` causes the window to be resized, usually to a smaller size, but more precisely to an approximation of a size known as the *preferred size*. (Yes, you can change the preferred size, but we do not have room to cover all of the Swing library in these few chapters.)

pack

We do not have room in this book to go into all the details of how a GUI is updated on the screen, but these few remarks may make some code you find in more advanced books a little less puzzling.

18.4 Colors

One colored picture is worth a thousand black and white pictures.

Variation on a Chinese proverb

In this section we tell you how to specify colors for the figures you draw with the graphics methods. We also show you how to define your own colors using the class Color.

Specifying a Drawing Color

setColor

When drawing figures with methods such as drawLine inside of the definition of the paint method, you can think of your drawing as being done with a pen that can change colors. The method setColor will change the color of the pen.

For example, consider the happy face that is drawn by the GUI in Display 18.13. If you change the definition of the paint method to the version shown in Display 18.18, the eyes will be blue and the mouth will be red. (The file HappyFaceColor.java on the accompanying CD contains a version of the changed program. It consists of the program in Display 18.13 with the definition of the paint method replaced by the one in Display 18.18 and with the class name changed from HappyFace to HappyFaceColor.)

extra code on CD

The setColor Method

When you are doing drawings with an object of the class **Graphics**, you can set the color of the drawing with an invocation of **setColor**. The color specified can later be changed with another invocation of **setColor**, so a single drawing can have multiple colors.

SYNTAX

Graphics_Object.setColor(*Color_Object*);

EXAMPLE

g.setColor(Color.BLUE);

Display 18.18 Adding Color

```
1     public void paint(Graphics g)
2     {
3         super.paint(g);
4         //Default is equivalent to: g.setColor(Color.black);
5         g.drawOval(X_FACE, Y_FACE, FACE_DIAMETER, FACE_DIAMETER);
6         //Draw Eyes:
7         g.setColor(Color.BLUE);
8         g.fillOval(X_RIGHT_EYE, Y_RIGHT_EYE, EYE_WIDTH, EYE_HEIGHT);
9         g.fillOval(X_LEFT_EYE, Y_LEFT_EYE, EYE_WIDTH, EYE_HEIGHT);
10        //Draw Mouth:
11        g.setColor(Color.RED);
12        g.drawArc(X_MOUTH, Y_MOUTH, MOUTH_WIDTH, MOUTH_HEIGHT,
13                  MOUTH_START_ANGLE, MOUTH_ARC_SWEEP);
14    }
```

*If you replace the method **paint** in Display 18.13 with this version of
paint, then the happy face will have blue eyes and red lips.*

Defining Colors

Display 17.5 in Chapter 17 lists the standard colors in the class `Color`, which are defined for you. If that table does not have the colors you want, you can use the class `Color` to define your own colors. To understand how this is done, you need to first know a few basic facts about colors. By mixing red, green, and blue light in varying amounts, the human eye can be given the sensation of seeing any color the eye is capable of seeing. This is what an ordinary television set does to produce all the colors it displays. The television mixes red, green, and blue light and shines these lights on the screen in differing amounts. This is often called the **RGB color system**, for obvious reasons. Since a computer monitor is basically the same thing as a television set, colors for computer monitors can be produced in the same way. The Java `Color` class mixes amounts of red, green, and blue to produce any new color you might want.

RGB color system

When specifying the amount of each of the colors red, green, and blue, you can use either integers in the range 0 to 255 (inclusive) or `float` values in the range 0.0 to 1.0 (inclusive). For example, brown is formed by mixing red and green. So, the following defines a color called `brown` that will look like a shade of brown:

Color constructors

```
Color brown = new Color(200, 150, 0);
```

This color `brown` will have a 200.0/255 fraction of the maximum amount of red possible, a 150.0/255 fraction of the maximum amount of green possible, and no blue. If you want to use fractions to express the color, you can. The following is an equivalent way of defining the same color `brown`:

```
Color brown =
new Color((float)(200.0/255), (float)(150.0/255), (float)0.0);
```

You need the type casts `(float)` because the constructors for the class `Color` only accept arguments of type `int` or `float`, and numbers like 200.0/255 and 0.0 are considered to be of type `double`, not of type `float`.

Some constructors for the class `Color` and some of the commonly used methods for the class `Color` are summarized in Display 18.19.

RGB Colors

The class `Color` uses the RGB method of creating colors. That means that every color is a combination of the three colors red, green, and blue.

Display 18.19 **Some Methods in the Class `Color`** (part 1 of 2)

The class `Color` is in the `java.awt` package.

```
public Color(int r, int g, int b)
```

Constructor that creates a new `Color` with the specified RGB values. The parameters r, g, and b must each be in the range 0 to 255 (inclusive).

Display 18.19   Some Methods in the Class **Color** (part 2 of 2)

```
public Color(float r, float g, float b)
```
Constructor that creates a new **Color** with the specified RGB values. The parameters r, g, and b must each be in the range **0.0** to **1.0** (inclusive).

```
public int getRed()
```
Returns the red component of the calling object. The returned value is in the range **0** to **255** (inclusive).

```
public int getGreen()
```
Returns the green component of the calling object. The returned value is in the range **0** to **255** (inclusive).

```
public int getBlue()
```
Returns the blue component of the calling object. The returned value is in the range **0** to **255** (inclusive).

```
public Color brighter()
```
Returns a brighter version of the calling object color.

```
public Color darker()
```
Returns a darker version of the calling object color.

```
public boolean equals(Object c)
```
Returns **true** if c is equal to the calling object color; otherwise, returns **false**.

PITFALL: Using doubles to Define a Color

Suppose you want to make a color that is made of half the possible amount of red, half the possible amount of blue, and no green. The following seems reasonable:

```
Color purple = new Color(0.5, 0.0, 0.5);
```

However, this will produce a compiler error. The numbers 0.5 and 0.0 are considered to be of type double, and this constructor requires arguments of type float (or of type int). So, an explicit type cast is required, as follows:

```
Color purple = new Color((float)0.5, (float)0.0, (float)0.5);
```

Java does allow the following method of specifying that a number is of type float, and this can be simpler than the previous line of code:

```
Color purple = new Color(0.5f, 0.0f, 0.5f);
```

An even easier way to avoid these problems is to simply use int arguments, as in the following:

```
Color purple = new Color(127, 0, 127);
```

(continued)

(You may feel that the values of 127 should be replaced by 128, but that is a minor point. You are not likely to even notice the difference in color between, say, 127 red and 128 red.)

In any final code produced, these `float` numbers should normally be replaced by defined constants, such as

```
public static final float RED_VALUE = (float)0.5;
public static final float GREEN_VALUE = (float)0.0;
public static final float BLUE_VALUE = (float)0.5;
```

Note that even though the defined constants are specified to be of type `float`, you still need a type cast. ■

The `JColorChooser` Dialog Window

The class `JColorChooser` can be used to produce a dialog window that allows you to choose a color by looking at color samples or by choosing RGB values. The static method `showDialog` in the class `JColorChooser` produces a window that allows the user to choose a color. A sample program using this method is given in Display 18.20. The statement that launches the `JColorChooser` dialog window is the following:

```
sampleColor =
    JColorChooser.showDialog(this, "JColorChooser", sampleColor);
```

When this statement is executed, the window shown in the second GUI picture in Display 18.20 is displayed for the user to choose a color. Once the user has chosen a color and clicked the OK button, the window goes away and the chosen color is returned as the value of the `JColorChooser.showDialog` method invocation. So, in this example, the `Color` object returned is assigned to the variable `sampleColor`. If the user clicks the Cancel button, then the method invocation returns `null` rather than a color.

The method `JColorChooser.showDialog` takes three arguments. The first argument is the parent component, which is the component from which it was launched. In most simple cases, it is likely to be `this`, as it is in our example. The second argument is a title for the color chooser window. The third argument is the initial color for the color chooser window. The window shows the user samples of what the color he or she chooses will look like. The user can choose colors repeatedly, and each will be displayed in turn until the user clicks the OK button. The color displayed when the color chooser window first appears is that third argument.

The color chooser window has three tabs at the top labeled Swatches, HSB, and RGB. This gives the user three different ways to choose colors. If the Swatches tab is clicked, the window displays color samples for the user to choose from. This is the way the

Display 18.20   **JColorChooser** Dialog (part 1 of 2)

```
1    import javax.swing.JFrame;
2    import javax.swing.JPanel;
3    import javax.swing.JButton;
4    import javax.swing.JColorChooser;
5    import java.awt.event.ActionListener;
6    import java.awt.event.ActionEvent;
7    import java.awt.BorderLayout;
8    import java.awt.FlowLayout;
9    import java.awt.Color;


10   public class JColorChooserDemo extends JFrame
11                                    implements ActionListener
12   {
13       public static final int WIDTH = 400;
14       public static final int HEIGHT = 200;

15       private Color sampleColor = Color.LIGHT_GRAY;


16       public static void main(String[] args)
17       {
18           JColorChooserDemo gui = new JColorChooserDemo();
19           gui.setVisible(true);
20       }

21       public JColorChooserDemo()
22       {
23           setDefaultCloseOperation(JFrame.EXIT_ON_CLOSE);
24           getContentPane().setBackground(sampleColor);
25           setLayout(new BorderLayout());
26           setTitle("JColorChooser Demo");
27           setSize(WIDTH, HEIGHT);
28           JPanel buttonPanel = new JPanel();
29           buttonPanel.setBackground(Color.WHITE);
30           buttonPanel.setLayout(new FlowLayout());
31           JButton chooseButton = new JButton("Choose a Color");
32           chooseButton.addActionListener(this);
33           buttonPanel.add(chooseButton);
34           add(buttonPanel, BorderLayout.SOUTH);
35       }
```

(continued)

Display 18.20   **JColorChooser** Dialog (part 2 of 2)

```
36        public void actionPerformed(ActionEvent e)
37        {
38            if (e.getActionCommand().equals("Choose a Color"))
39            {
40                sampleColor =
41                    JColorChooser.showDialog(this, "JColorChooser", sampleColor);
42                if (sampleColor != null)//If a color was chosen
43                    getContentPane().setBackground(sampleColor);
44            }
45            else
46                System.out.println("Unanticipated Error");
47        }
48    }
```

RESULTING GUI (Three views of one GUI)

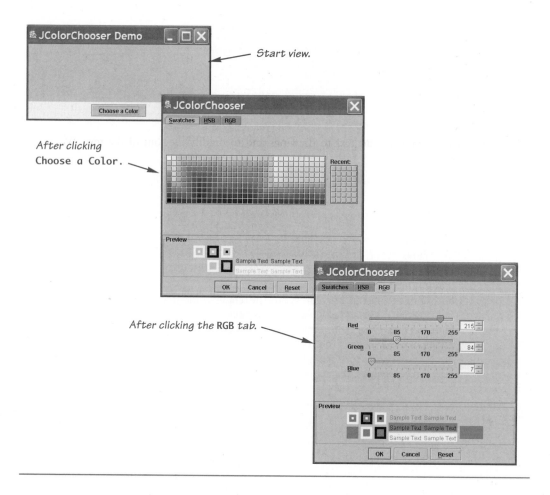

Start view.

After clicking
Choose a Color.

After clicking the RGB tab.

window first comes up. So, if the user clicks no tab, it is the same as clicking the Swatches tab. The RGB tab allows the user to choose a color by specifying the red, green, and blue values. The HSB tab gives the user a chance to choose colors in a way we will not discuss. To really understand the JColorChooser dialog window, you need to run the program in Display 18.20 to see it in action.

Self-Test Exercises

17. How would you change the method paint in Display 18.18 so that the happy face has one blue eye (the right eye) and one green eye (the left eye)?

18. How would you change the method paint in Display 18.18 so that the happy face not only has blue eyes and a red mouth, but also has brown skin?

18.5   Fonts and the drawString Method

It is not of so much consequence what you say,

as how you say it.

ALEXANDER SMITH, *Dreamthorp. On the Writing of Essays*

Java has facilities to add text to drawings and to modify the font of the text. We will show you enough to allow you to do most things you might want to do with text and fonts.

The drawString Method

Display 18.21 contains a demonstration program for the method drawString. When the program is run, the GUI displays the text "Push the button." When the user clicks the button, the string is changed to "Thank you. I needed that." The text is written with the method drawString.

The method drawString is similar to the drawing methods in the class Graphics, but it displays text rather than a drawing. For example, the following line from Display 18.21 writes the string stored in the variable theText starting at the *x*- and *y*-coordinates X_START and Y_START:

```
g.drawString(theText, X_START, Y_START);
```

The string is written in the current font. A default font is used if no font is specified. The details about fonts are discussed in the next subsection.

Display 18.21 Using **drawString** (part 1 of 3)

```
1   import javax.swing.JFrame;
2   import javax.swing.JPanel;
3   import javax.swing.JButton;
4   import java.awt.event.ActionListener;
5   import java.awt.event.ActionEvent;
6   import java.awt.BorderLayout;
7   import java.awt.Graphics;
8   import java.awt.Color;
9   import java.awt.Font;

10  public class DrawStringDemo extends JFrame
11                              implements ActionListener
12  {
13      public static final int WIDTH = 350;
14      public static final int HEIGHT = 200;
15      public static final int X_START = 20;
16      public static final int Y_START = 100;
17      public static final int POINT_SIZE = 24;

18      private String theText = "Push the button.";
19      private Color penColor = Color.BLACK;
20      private Font fontObject =
21                      new Font("SansSerif", Font.PLAIN, POINT_SIZE);

22      public static void main(String[] args)
23      {
24          DrawStringDemo gui = new DrawStringDemo();
25          gui.setVisible(true);
26      }


27      public DrawStringDemo()
28      {
29          setSize(WIDTH, HEIGHT);
30          setDefaultCloseOperation(JFrame.EXIT_ON_CLOSE);
31          setTitle("drawString Demonstration");

32          getContentPane().setBackground(Color.WHITE);
33          setLayout(new BorderLayout());

34          JPanel buttonPanel = new JPanel();
35          buttonPanel.setBackground(Color.GRAY);
36          buttonPanel.setLayout(new BorderLayout());
```

Display 18.21   Using **drawString** (part 2 of 3)

```
37            JButton theButton = new JButton("The Button");
38            theButton.addActionListener(this);


39            buttonPanel.add(theButton, BorderLayout.CENTER);


40        add(buttonPanel, BorderLayout.SOUTH);
41    }


42    public void paint(Graphics g)
43    {
44        super.paint(g);
45        g.setFont(fontObject);
46        g.setColor(penColor);
47        g.drawString(theText, X_START, Y_START);
48    }


49    public void actionPerformed(ActionEvent e)
50    {
51        penColor = Color.RED;
52        fontObject =
53            new Font("Serif", Font.BOLD|Font.ITALIC, POINT_SIZE);
54        theText = "Thank you. I needed that.";


55        repaint();
56    }
57  }
```

RESULTING GUI (Start view)

Display 18.21 Using **drawString** (part 3 of 3)

RESULTING GUI (After clicking the button)

Fonts

The program in Display 18.21 illustrates how the font for the method drawString is set. That program sets the font with the following line in the definition of the method paint:

setFont

```
g.setFont(fontObject);
```

In that program fontObject is a private instance variable of type Font. Font is a class in the java.awt package. Objects of the class Font represent fonts.

In Display 18.21 the variable fontObject is set using a constructor for the class Font. The initial font is set as part of the instance variable declaration in the following lines taken from Display 18.21:

```
private Font fontObject =
                new Font("SansSerif", Font.PLAIN, POINT_SIZE);
```

Font

The constructor for the class Font creates a font in a given style and size. The first argument, in this case "SansSerif", is a string that gives the name of the font (that is, the basic style). Some typical font names are "Times", "Courier", and "Helvetica". You may use any font currently available on your system. Java guarantees that you will have at least the three fonts "Monospaced", "SansSerif", and "Serif". To see what these fonts look like on your system, run the program FontDisplay.java on the accompanying CD. It will produce the window shown in Display 18.22.

extra code on CD

Most font names have no real meaning. The names just sounded right to the creator. However, the terms "Serif," "Sans Serif," and "Monospaced" do mean something, which may help you keep the names of the three guaranteed fonts clear in your mind. **Serifs** are those small lines that sometimes finish off the ends of the lines in letters. For example, S has serifs (at the two ends of the curved line), but S does not have serifs. The "Serif" font will always have these decorative little lines. *Sans* means without, so

Display 18.22 **Result of Running FontDisplay.java**

Fonts may look somewhat different on your system.

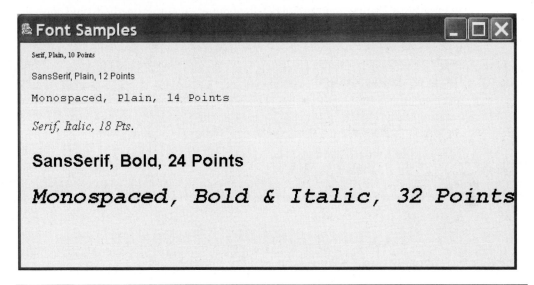

the "SansSerif" font will not have these decorative little lines. As you might guess, "Monospaced" means that all the characters have equal width.

Fonts can be given style modifiers, such as bold or italic, and they can come in different sizes. The second and third arguments to the constructor for Font specify the style modifications and size for the font, as in the following, which occurs in the actionPerformed method in Display 18.21:

```
new Font("Serif", Font.BOLD|Font.ITALIC, POINT_SIZE);
```

The second argument specifies style modifications. Note that you can specify multiple style modifications by connecting them with the symbol | as in Font.BOLD|Font.ITALIC.[2] The last argument specifies the size of the letters in the version of the font created.

point size Character sizes are specified in units known as *points*, so the size of a particular version of a font is called a **point size**. One **point** is 1/72 of an inch, but measurements of font sizes are not as precise as might be ideal; two different fonts of the same point size may be slightly different in size.

The method setFont sets the font for the Graphics object, which is named g in Display 18.21. The font remains in effect until it is changed. If you do not specify any font, then a default font is used.

---

[2] The symbol | produces a "bitwise or of the numbers," but that detail need not concern you. You need not even know what is meant by a "bitwise or of the numbers." Just think of | as a special way to connect style specifications.

There is no simple way to change the properties of the current font, such as making it italic. Every change in a font normally requires that you define a new Font object and use it as an argument to setFont.

Display 18.23 gives some useful details about constructors, methods, and constants that are members of, or are related to, the class Font.

The drawString Method

The drawString method writes the text given by the *String* at the point (*X, Y*) of the *Graphics_Object*. The text is written in the current font, color, and font size.

SYNTAX

Graphics_Object.drawString(*String, X, Y*);

EXAMPLE

g.drawString("I love you madly.", X_START, Y_START);

Display 18.23   Some Methods and Constants for the Class **Font** (part 1 of 2)

The class **Font** is in the `java.awt` package.

CONSTRUCTOR FOR THE CLASS Font

public Font(String fontName, int styleModifications, int size)

Constructor that creates a version of the font named by **fontName** with the specified **styleModifications** and **size**.

CONSTANTS IN THE CLASS Font

Font.BOLD

Specifies bold style.

Font.ITALIC

Specifies italic style.

Font.PLAIN

Specifies plain style—that is, not bold and not italic.

NAMES OF FONTS (These three are guaranteed by Java. Your system will probably have others as well as these.)

"Monospaced"

See Display 18.22 for a sample.

"SansSerif"

See Display 18.22 for a sample.

Display 18.23   Some Methods and Constants for the Class **Font** (part 2 of 2)

```
"Serif"
```

See Display 18.22 for a sample.

METHOD THAT USES Font

```
public abstract void setFont(Font fontObject)
```

This method is in the class `Graphics`. Sets the current font of the calling `Graphics` object to `fontObject`.

Self-Test Exercises

19. Suppose g is an object of type `Graphics`. Write a line of code that will set the font for g to Sans Serif bold of size 14 points.

20. Suppose g is an object of type `Graphics`. Write a line of code that will set the font for g to Sans Serif bold and italic of size 14 points.

Chapter Summary

- You can define a window listener class by having it implement the `WindowListener` interface.

- An icon is an object of the class `ImageIcon` and is created from a digital picture. You can add icons to `JButtons`, `JLabels`, and `JMenuItems`.

- You can use the class `JScrollPane` to add scroll bars to a text area.

- You can draw figures such as lines, ovals, and rectangles using methods in the class `Graphics`.

- You can use the method `setColor` to specify the color of each figure or text drawn with the method of the class `Graphics`.

- You can define your own colors using the class `Color`.

- Colors are defined using the RGB (red/green/blue) system.

- You can use the method `drawString` of the class `Graphics` to add text to a `JFrame` or `JPanel`.

- You can use the method `setFont` to set the font, style modifiers, and point size for text written with the `drawString` method of the `Graphics` class.

Answers to Self-Test Exercises

1. All the methods in Display 18.1. If there is no particular action that you want the method to perform, you can give the method an empty body.

2. The smaller window goes away but the larger window stays. This is the default action for the close-window button and we did not change it for the smaller window.

3. `dispose`

4. The import statements are the same as in Display 18.2. The rest of the definition follows. This definition is in the file `WindowListenerDemo3` on the accompanying CD.

extra code on CD

```java
public class WindowListenerDemo3 extends JFrame
                                 implements WindowListener
{
    public static final int WIDTH = 300; //for main window
    public static final int HEIGHT = 200; //for main window
    public static final int SMALL_WIDTH = 200; //for confirm window
    public static final int SMALL_HEIGHT = 100;//for confirm window

    private class ConfirmWindow extends JFrame
                                implements ActionListener
    {
        public ConfirmWindow()
        {
            setSize(SMALL_WIDTH, SMALL_HEIGHT);
            getContentPane().setBackground(Color.YELLOW);
            setLayout(new BorderLayout());

            JLabel confirmLabel = new JLabel(
                        "Are you sure you want to exit?");
            add(confirmLabel, BorderLayout.CENTER);

            JPanel buttonPanel = new JPanel();
            buttonPanel.setBackground(Color.ORANGE);
            buttonPanel.setLayout(new FlowLayout());

            JButton exitButton = new JButton("Yes");
            exitButton.addActionListener(this);
            buttonPanel.add(exitButton);

            JButton cancelButton = new JButton("No");
            cancelButton.addActionListener(this);
            buttonPanel.add(cancelButton);

            add(buttonPanel, BorderLayout.SOUTH);
        }

        public void actionPerformed(ActionEvent e)
        {
```

```
            String actionCommand = e.getActionCommand();

            if (actionCommand.equals("Yes"))
                System.exit(0);
            else if (actionCommand.equals("No"))
                dispose();//Destroys only the ConfirmWindow.
            else
                System.out.println(
                        "Unexpected Error in Confirm Window.");
        }
} //End of inner class ConfirmWindow

public static void main(String[] args)
{
    WindowListenerDemo3 demoWindow =
                        new WindowListenerDemo3();
    demoWindow.setVisible(true);
}

public WindowListenerDemo3()
{
    setSize(WIDTH, HEIGHT);
    setTitle("Window Listener Demonstration");

    setDefaultCloseOperation(
                JFrame.DO_NOTHING_ON_CLOSE);
    addWindowListener(this);

    getContentPane().setBackground(Color.LIGHT_GRAY);
    JLabel aLabel =
            new JLabel("I like to be sure you are sincere.");
    add(aLabel);
}

//The following are now methods of the class WindowListenerDemo3:
public void windowOpened(WindowEvent e)
{}

public void windowClosing(WindowEvent e)
{
    ConfirmWindow checkers = new ConfirmWindow();
    checkers.setVisible(true);
}

public void windowClosed(WindowEvent e)
{}

public void windowIconified(WindowEvent e)
{}
```

```
        public void windowDeiconified(WindowEvent e)
        {}

        public void windowActivated(WindowEvent e)
        {}

        public void windowDeactivated(WindowEvent e)
        {}
    }
```

5. ```
   JButton magicButton = new JButton("Magic Button");
   ImageIcon wizardIcon = new ImageIcon("wizard.gif");
   magicButton.setIcon(wizardIcon);
   ```

   There are a number of other ways to accomplish the same thing. Below are two of a number of valid alternatives:

   ```
   JButton magicButton = new JButton("Magic Button");
   magicButton.setIcon(new ImageIcon("wizard.gif"));
   ```

   ```
   ImageIcon wizardIcon = new ImageIcon("wizard.gif");
   JButton magicButton =
                   new JButton("Magic Button", wizardIcon);
   ```

6. ```
   ImageIcon wizardIcon = new ImageIcon("wizard.gif");
   JLabel wizardPicture = new JLabel(wizardIcon);
   picturePanel.add(wizardPicture);
   ```

   There are a number of other ways to accomplish the same thing. Below is one valid alternative:

   ```
   picturePanel.add(new JLabel(
                       new ImageIcon("wizard.gif")));
   ```

7. ```
   ImageIcon wizardIcon = new ImageIcon("wizard.gif");
   JButton magicButton = new JButton(wizardIcon);
   magicButton.setActionCommand("Kazam");
   ```

   There are a number of other ways to accomplish the same thing. Below is one valid alternative:

   ```
   JButton magicButton =
               new JButton(new ImageIcon("wizard.gif"));
   magicButton.setActionCommand("Kazam");
   ```

8. No. You can invoke none, one, or both methods.

9. No. The class JTextArea is a descendent class of the class Component. So, every JTextArea is also a Component.
   ```

10. `g.drawLine(30, 40, 100, 60);`

11. `g.drawLine(30, 40, 130, 40);`

12. `graphicsObject.drawLine(30, 40, 30, 140);`

13. `graphicsObject.fillRect(20, 30, 100, 50);`

14. `g.fillRect(200, 300, 100, 50);`

15. `g.drawOval(250, 350, 100, 100);`

16. `g.drawOval(200, 300, 200, 200);`

17. Insert `g.setColor(Color.GREEN)` as indicated below:

```
//Draw Eyes:
g.setColor(Color.BLUE);
g.fillOval(X_RIGHT_EYE, Y_RIGHT_EYE, EYE_WIDTH, EYE_HEIGHT);
g.setColor(Color.GREEN);
g.fillOval(X_LEFT_EYE, Y_LEFT_EYE, EYE_WIDTH, EYE_HEIGHT);
```

18. Replace the following line in the paint method:

```
g.drawOval(X_FACE, Y_FACE, FACE_DIAMETER, FACE_DIAMETER);
```

with

```
Color brown =
        new Color(200, 150, 0);
g.setColor(brown);
g.fillOval(X_FACE, Y_FACE, FACE_DIAMETER, FACE_DIAMETER);
```

Note that there is no predefined color constant `Color.BROWN`, so you need to define a color for brown. You may prefer some other arguments instead of (200, 150, 0) so that you get a shade of brown that is more to your liking.

19. `g.setFont(new Font("SansSerif", Font.BOLD, 14));`

20. `g.setFont(new Font("SansSerif",`
    `                   Font.BOLD|Font.ITALIC, 14));`

Programming Projects

myCodeMate *Many of these Programming Projects can be solved using AW's MyCodeMate. To access these please go to:* www.mycodemate.com.

1. Write a program that draws a Sierpinski gasket. A Sierpinski gasket or triangle is a type of fractal. It is an example of how an orderly structure can be created as a result of random, chaotic behavior.

   The creation of a Sierpinski gasket is fairly simple. There are three points that form the corners of a triangle. In the figure below, they are labeled as A, B, and C.

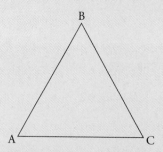

To draw the Sierpinski gasket follow the algorithm:

1. Randomly pick one of the three corners. Call this the current point. (Alternatively, you could also randomly select any point inside the triangle).

2. Randomly pick one of the three corners. Call this the target point.

3. Calculate the midpoint between the current point and the target point.

4. Draw a single pixel at the midpoint.

5. Set the current point to the midpoint.

6. Go back to step 2 and repeat many times (e.g., 50,000 iterations).

It would seem like you should get a random mess of dots since the algorithm randomly picks a target corner each time. Instead, if this process is repeated many times, you will get a very orderly picture with a repeating structure:

To draw a single pixel at coordinate (X,Y) use the `drawLine` method where the start and endpoints are both (X,Y).

To generate a random number x, where $0 \le x < 1$, use $x =$ Math.random();. For example, multiplying by 3 and converting to an integer results in an integer that is from 0 to 2.

2. The file named "humphrey-img.txt" contained with the code for this book holds raw image data[3] of a Martian rock called "Humphrey" that was taken by the Mars Exploration Rover Spirit. The format of this text file is as follows:

First line: single number indicating the height and width of the image (in this case, 461).

Lines 2–462: A row of 461 numbers each separated by a space. Each number represents a pixel in grayscale and ranges from 0 to 255 where 0 is black and 255 is white.

For example, the following data describes a 3 by 3 square where every pixel is white except for a black line along the diagonal from the upper-left corner to the bottom-right corner:

```
3
0 255 255
255 0 255
255 255 0
```

a. Write a program to read in the data from the file and display it in a JFrame window. To draw a single pixel at coordinate (X,Y) use the drawLine method where the start and endpoints are both (X,Y). For speed, the contents of the file should be read into an array once and the array data used in the paint() method to draw the image. The final image should appear similar to the following picture:

Image Credit: NASA/JPL

---

[3] The original raw image data has been cropped and converted to a textual format for purposes of this project.

b. In this particular image, only about 2/3 of the shades of gray are used. For example, if the image consisted entirely of shades in the range from 150–160 then the entire image would appear to be almost the same shade of gray. One method to enhance such an image is to scale the shade of each pixel to the entire range from 0 to 255. Pixels that were originally at value 150 would be drawn with the value 0, pixels that were originally 151 would be drawn with the value 25, and so on up to pixels of the shade 160, which would be drawn with the value 255. This technique spaces out the shading so the details are easier to see.

To compute the new shade for a pixel at coordinate (i,j) :

$$NewShade(i,j) = \frac{255 \times (OriginalShade(i,j) - MinOriginalShade)}{(MaxOriginalShade - MinOriginalShade)}$$

MinOriginalShade is the smallest scale of gray in the original image and MaxOriginalShade is the largest scale of gray in the original image.

Modify your program so that the image is drawn using the scaling technique described above. The brightness and details in the resulting image should be a little bit easier to distinguish.

3. Write a GUI program that uses the methods in the Graphics class to draw a smiley face when the window is activated, and a frowny face when the window is deactivated. This will require use of a WindowListener to detect the activation or deactivation events.

4. Write a "skeleton" GUI program that implements the WindowListener interface. Write code for each of the methods in Display 18.1 that simply prints out a message identifying which event occurred. Print the message out in a text field. Note that your program will not end when the close-window button is clicked (but will instead simply send a message to the text field saying that the windowClosing method has been invoked). Include a button labeled Exit that the user can click to end the program.

5. Enhance the face drawing in Display 18.17 in all of the following ways: Add color so the eyes are blue and the mouth is red. When the face winks, the line that represents a closed eye is black not blue. Add a nose and a brown handlebar mustache. Add buttons labeled "Smile" and "Frown". When the "Frown" button is clicked, the face shows a frown (upside down smile); when the "Smile" button is clicked, the face shows a smile. When the user clicks the close-window button, a window pops up to ask if the user is sure he or she wants to exit, as in Display 18.2.

6. Write a GUI program to sample different fonts. The user enters a line of text in a text field. The user then selects a font from a font menu. Offer the three guaranteed fonts and at least two other fonts. The user also selects any desired style modifiers (bold and/or italic) from a style menu, and selects point size from a point size menu that offers the following choices: 9, 10, 12, 14, 16, 24, and 32. There is also a "Display" button. When the "Display" button is clicked, the text is displayed in the font, style, and point size chosen.

19

Java Never Ends

And thick and fast they came at last,
And more, and more, and more—

LEWIS CARROLL, *Through the Looking-Glass*

Introduction

Of course there is only a finite amount of Java, but when you consider all the standard libraries and other accompanying software, the amount of power and the amount to learn seem to be endless. In this chapter we give you a brief introduction to four topics to give you a flavor of some of the directions you can take in extending your knowledge of Java. The four topics are multithreading, networking with stream sockets, JavaBeans, and the interaction of Java with database systems.

Prerequisites

You really should cover most of the book before covering this chapter. However, Section 19.1 requires only Chapters 17 and 18 and their prerequisites. Section 19.2 requires Chapters 1 through 5, 9, and 10. Sections 19.3 and 19.4 require only Chapters 1 through 6. Aside from references to Section 19.1 in Section 19.2, all sections are independent of each other and may be read in any order.

19.1 Multithreading

"Can you do two things at once?"
"I have trouble doing one thing at once."

Part of a job interview

thread A **thread** is a separate computation process. In Java, you can have programs with multiple threads. You can think of the threads as computations that execute in parallel. On a computer with enough processors, the threads might indeed execute in parallel. In most normal computing situations, the threads do not really execute in parallel. Instead, the computer switches resources between threads so that each thread in turn does a little bit of computing. To the user this looks like the processes are executing in parallel.

You have already experienced threads. Modern operating systems allow you to run more than one program at the same time. For example, rather than waiting for your virus scanning program to finish its computation, you can go on to, say, read your e-mail while the virus scanning program is still executing. The operating system is using threads to make this happen. There may or may not be some work being done in parallel depending on your computer and operating system. Most likely the two computation threads are simply sharing computer resources so that they take turns using the computer's resources. When reading your e-mail, you may or may not notice that response is slower because resources are being shared with the virus scanning program. Your e-mail reading program is indeed slowed down, but since humans are so much slower than computers, any apparent slowdown is likely to be unnoticed.

EXAMPLE: A Nonresponsive GUI

Display 19.1 contains a very simple action GUI. When the "Start" button is clicked, the GUI draws circles one after the other until a large portion of the window is filled with circles. There is 1/10 of a second pause between the drawing of each circle. So, you can see the circles appear one after the other. If you're interested in Java programming, this can be pretty exciting for the first few circles, but it quickly becomes boring. You are likely to want to end the program early, but if you click the close-window button, nothing will happen until the program is finished drawing all its little circles. We will use threads to fix this problem, but first let's understand this program, which does not really use threads in any essential way, despite the occurrence of the word Thread in the program. We explain this Swing program in the next few subsections.

Thread.sleep

In Display 19.1 the following method invocation produces a 1/10 of a second pause after drawing each of the circles:

```
doNothing(PAUSE);
```

which is equivalent to

```
doNothing(100);
```

The method doNothing is a private helping method that does nothing except call the method Thread.sleep and take care of catching any thrown exception. So, the pause is really created by the method invocation

Thread.sleep
```
Thread.sleep(100);
```

This is a static method in the class Thread that pauses whatever thread includes the invocation. It pauses for the number of milliseconds (thousandths of a second) given as an argument. So, this pauses the computation of the program in Display 19.1 for 100 milliseconds or 1/10 of a second.

"Wait a minute," you may think, "the program in Display 19.1 was not supposed to use threads in any essential way." That is basically true, but every Java program uses threads in some way. If there is only one stream of computation, as in Display 19.1, then that is treated as a single thread by Java. So, threads are always used by Java, but not in an interesting way until more than one thread is used.

You can safely think of the invocation of

```
Thread.sleep(milliseconds);
```

as a pause in the computation that lasts (approximately) the number of milliseconds given as the argument. (If this invocation is in a thread of a multithreaded program, then the pause, like anything else in the thread, applies only to the thread in which it occurs.)

Display 19.1 Nonresponsive GUI (part 1 of 3)

```
1    import javax.swing.JFrame;
2    import javax.swing.JPanel;
3    import javax.swing.JButton;
4    import java.awt.BorderLayout;
5    import java.awt.FlowLayout;
6    import java.awt.Graphics;
7    import java.awt.event.ActionListener;
8    import java.awt.event.ActionEvent;

9    /**
10   Packs a section of the frame window with circles, one at a time.
11   */
12   public class FillDemo extends JFrame implements ActionListener
13   {
14       public static final int WIDTH = 300;
15       public static final int HEIGHT = 200;
16       public static final int FILL_WIDTH = 300;
17       public static final int FILL_HEIGHT = 100;
18       public static final int CIRCLE_SIZE = 10;
19       public static final int PAUSE = 100; //milliseconds

20       private JPanel box;

21       public static void main(String[] args)
22       {
23           FillDemo gui = new FillDemo();
24           gui.setVisible(true);
25       }

26       public FillDemo()
27       {
28           setSize(WIDTH, HEIGHT);
29           setTitle("FillDemo");
30           setDefaultCloseOperation(JFrame.EXIT_ON_CLOSE);
```

Display 19.1   Nonresponsive GUI (part 2 of 3)

```
31              setLayout(new BorderLayout());
32              box = new JPanel();
33              add(box, "Center");

34              JPanel buttonPanel = new JPanel();
35              buttonPanel.setLayout(new FlowLayout());
36              JButton startButton = new JButton("Start");
37              startButton.addActionListener(this);
38              buttonPanel.add(startButton);
39              add(buttonPanel, "South");
40          }

41      public void actionPerformed(ActionEvent e)
42      {
43          fill( );
44      }

45      public void fill()
46      {
47          Graphics g = box.getGraphics();

48          for (int y = 0; y < FILL_HEIGHT; y = y + CIRCLE_SIZE)
49              for (int x = 0; x < FILL_WIDTH; x = x + CIRCLE_SIZE)
50              {
51                  g.fillOval(x, y, CIRCLE_SIZE, CIRCLE_SIZE);
52                  doNothing(PAUSE);
53              }
54      }

55      public void doNothing(int milliseconds)
56      {
57          try
58          {
59              Thread.sleep(milliseconds);
60          }
61          catch(InterruptedException e)
62          {
63              System.out.println("Unexpected interrupt");
64              System.exit(0);
65          }
66      }
67  }
```

Nothing else can happen until actionPerformed *returns, which does not happen until* fill *returns.*

Everything stops for 100 milliseconds (1/10 of a second).

(continued)

Display 19.1 **Nonresponsive GUI** (part 3 of 3)

Resulting GUI (When started)

Resulting GUI (While drawing circles)

If you click the close-window button while the circles are being drawn, the window will not close until all the circles are drawn.

Resulting GUI (After all circles are drawn)

The method Thread.sleep can sometimes be handy even if you do not do any multithreaded programming. The class Thread is in the package java.lang and so requires no import statement.

The method Thread.sleep can throw an InterruptedException, which is a checked exception—that is, it must be either caught in a catch block or declared in a throws clause. We do not discuss InterruptedException in this book, leaving it for more advanced books on multithreaded programming, but it has to do with one thread interrupting another thread. We will simply note that an InterruptedException may be thrown by `Thread.sleep` and so must be accounted for, in our case by a simple catch block. The class `InterruptedException` is in the `java.lang` package and so requires no import statement.

Thread.sleep

`Thread.sleep` is a static method in the class `Thread` that pauses the thread that includes the invocation. It pauses for the number of milliseconds (thousandths of a second) given as an argument.

The method `Thread.sleep` may throw an `InterruptedException`, which is a checked exception and so must be either caught in a `catch` block or declared in a `throws` clause. The classes `Thread` and `InterruptedException` are both in the package `java.lang`, so neither requires any import statement.

Note that `Thread.sleep` can be invoked in an ordinary (single thread) program of the kind we have seen before this chapter. It will insert a pause in the single thread of that program.

SYNTAX

```
Thread.sleep(Number_Of_Milliseconds);
```

EXAMPLE

```
try
{
    Thread.sleep(100); //Pause of 1/10 of a second
}
catch(InterruptedException e)
{
    System.out.println("Unexpected interrupt");
}
```

The getGraphics Method

The other new method in Display 19.1 is the `getGraphics` method, which is used in the following line from the method `fill`:

getGraphics

```
Graphics g = box.getGraphics( );
```

The `getGraphics` method is almost self-explanatory. As we already noted in Chapter 18, almost every item displayed on the screen (more precisely, every `JComponent`) has an associated `Graphics` object. The method `getGraphics` is an accessor method that returns the associated `Graphics` object (of the calling object for `getGraphics`), in this case, the `Graphics` object associated with the panel box. This gives us a `Graphics` object that can draw circles (or anything else) in the panel box.

We still need to say a bit more about why the program in Display 19.1 makes you wait before it will respond to the close-window button, but otherwise this concludes our explanation of Display 19.1. The rest of the code consists of standard things we have seen before.

---

getGraphics

Every `JComponent` has an associated `Graphics` object. The method `getGraphics` is an accessor method that returns the associated `Graphics` object of its calling object.

SYNTAX

```
Component.getGraphics( );
```

EXAMPLE (see Display 19.1 for context)

```
Graphics g = box.getGraphics( );
```

Fixing a Nonresponsive Program Using Threads

Now that we have explained the new items in the program in Display 19.1, we are ready to explain why it is nonresponsive and to show you how to use threads to write a responsive version of that program.

Recall that when you run the program in Display 19.1, it draws circles one after the other to fill a portion of the frame. Although there is only a 1/10 of a second pause between drawing each circle, it can still seem like it takes a long time to finish. So, you are likely to want to abort the program and close the window early. But, if you click the close-window button, the window will not close until the GUI is finished drawing all the circles.

Here is why the close-window button is nonresponsive: The method fill, which draws the circles, is invoked in the body of the method `actionPerformed`. So, the method `actionPerformed` does not end until after the method fill ends. And, until the method `actionPerformed` ends, the GUI cannot go on to do the next thing, which is probably to respond to the close-window button.

Here is how we fixed the problem: We have the method `actionPerformed` create a new (independent) thread to draw the circles. Once `actionPerformed` has created this new thread, the new thread is an independent process that proceeds on its own. The method `actionPerformed` has nothing more to do with this new thread; the work of `actionPerformed` is ended. So, the main thread (the one with `actionPerformed`) is ready to move on to the next thing, which will probably be to respond promptly to a click of the close-window button. At the same time, the new thread draws the circles. So, the circles are drawn, but at the same time a click of the close-window button will end the program. The program that implements this multithreaded solution is given in the next Programming Example.

EXAMPLE: A Multithreaded Program

Display 19.2 contains a program that uses a main thread and a second thread to implement the technique discussed in the previous subsection. The general approach was outlined in the previous subsection, but we need to explain the Java code details. We do that in the next few subsections.

The Class Thread

Thread

In Java, a thread is an object of the class Thread. The normal way to program a thread is to define a class that is a derived class of the class Thread. An object of this derived class will be a thread that follows the programming given in the definition of the derived (thread) class.

run()

Where do you do the programming of a thread? The class Thread has a method named run. The definition of the method run is the code for the thread. When the thread is executed, the method run is executed. Of course, the method defined in the class Thread and inherited by any derived class of Thread does not do what you want your thread to do. So, when you define a derived class of Thread, you override the definition of the method run to do what you want the thread to do.

In Display 19.2 the inner class Packer is a derived class of the class Thread. The method run for the class Packer is defined to be exactly the same as the method fill in our previous, unresponsive GUI (Display 19.1). So, an object of the class Packer is a thread that will do what fill does, namely draw the circles to fill up a portion of the window.

start()

The method actionPerformed in Display 19.2 differs from the method actionPerformed in our older, nonresponsive program (Display 19.1) in that the invocation of the method fill is replaced with the following:

```
Packer packerThread = new Packer( );
packerThread.start( );
```

This creates a new, independent thread named packerThread and starts it processing. Whatever packerThread does, it does as an independent thread. The main thread can then allow actionPerformed to end and the main thread will be ready to respond to any click of the close-window button.

Display 19.2   Threaded Version of **FillDemo** (part 1 of 3)

```
1    import javax.swing.JFrame;
2    import javax.swing.JPanel;
3    import javax.swing.JButton;
4    import java.awt.BorderLayout;
5    import java.awt.FlowLayout;
6    import java.awt.Graphics;
7    import java.awt.event.ActionListener;
8    import java.awt.event.ActionEvent;

9    public class ThreadedFillDemo extends JFrame implements ActionListener
10   {
11       public static final int WIDTH = 300;
12       public static final int HEIGHT = 200;
13       public static final int FILL_WIDTH = 300;
14       public static final int FILL_HEIGHT = 100;
15       public static final int CIRCLE_SIZE = 10;
16       public static final int PAUSE = 100; //milliseconds
```

The GUI produced is identical to the GUI produced by Display 19.1 except that in this version the close-window button works even while the circles are being drawn, so you can end the GUI early if you get bored.

(continued)

Display 19.2 **Threaded Version of FillDemo** (part 2 of 3)

```
17          private JPanel box;

18          public static void main(String[] args)
19          {
20              ThreadedFillDemo gui = new ThreadedFillDemo();
21              gui.setVisible(true);
22          }

23          public ThreadedFillDemo()
24          {
25              setSize(WIDTH, HEIGHT);
26              setTitle("Threaded Fill Demo");
27              setDefaultCloseOperation(JFrame.EXIT_ON_CLOSE);

28              setLayout(new BorderLayout());

29              box = new JPanel();
30              add(box, "Center");

31              JPanel buttonPanel = new JPanel();
32              buttonPanel.setLayout(new FlowLayout());
33              JButton startButton = new JButton("Start");
34              startButton.addActionListener(this);
35              buttonPanel.add(startButton);
36              add(buttonPanel, "South");
37          }

38          public void actionPerformed(ActionEvent e)
39          {
40              Packer packerThread = new Packer();
41              packerThread.start();
42          }

43          private class Packer extends Thread
44          {
45              public void run()
46              {
47                  Graphics g = box.getGraphics();
48                  for (int y = 0; y < FILL_HEIGHT; y = y + CIRCLE_SIZE)
49                      for (int x = 0; x < FILL_WIDTH; x = x + CIRCLE_SIZE)
50                      {
51                          g.fillOval(x, y, CIRCLE_SIZE, CIRCLE_SIZE);
52                          doNothing(PAUSE);
53                      }
54              }
```

You need a thread object, even if there are no instance variables in the class definition of Packer.

start "starts" the thread and calls run.

run is inherited from Thread *but needs to be overridden. This definition of* run *is identical to that of* fill *in Display 19.1.*

Display 19.2 Threaded Version of `FillDemo` (part 3 of 3)

```
55              public void doNothing(int milliseconds)
56              {
57                  try
58                  {
59                      Thread.sleep(milliseconds);
60                  }
61                  catch(InterruptedException e)
62                  {
63                      System.out.println("Unexpected interrupt");
64                      System.exit(0);
65                  }
66              }
67      } //End Packer inner class

68  }
```

run()

We only need to explain the method `start` and we will be through with our explanation. The method `start` initiates the computation (process) of the calling thread. It performs some overhead associated with starting a thread and then it invokes the run method for the thread. As we have already seen, the run method of the class `Packer` in Display 19.2 draws the circles we want, so the invocation

```
packerThread.start( );
```

does draw the circles we want, because it calls run. Note that you do not invoke run directly. Instead, you invoke `start`, which does some other needed things and then invokes run.

This ends our explanation of the multithreaded program in Display 19.2, but there is still one, perhaps puzzling, thing about the class `Packer` that we should explain. The definition of the class `Packer` includes no instance variables. So, why do we need to bother with an object of the class `Packer`? Why not simply make all the methods static and call them with the class name `Packer`? The answer is that the only way to get a new thread is to create a new `Thread` object. The things inherited from the class `Thread` are what the object needs to be a thread. Static methods do not a thread make. In fact, not only will static methods not work, the compiler will not even allow you to define run to be static. This is because run is inherited from `Thread` as a nonstatic method and that cannot be changed to static when overriding a method definition. The compiler will not let you even try to do this without creating an object of the class `Packer`.

The Thread Class

A thread is an object of the class **Thread**. The normal way to program a thread is to define a class that is a derived class of the class **Thread**. An object of this derived class will be a thread that follows the programming given in the definition of the derived (thread) class's method named **run**.

Any thread class inherits the method start from the class **Thread**. An invocation of **start** by an object of a thread class will start the thread and invoke the method **run** for that thread.

See Display 19.2 for an example.

The Runnable Interface ★

There are times when you would rather not make a thread class a derived class of the class Thread. The alternative to making your class a derived class of the class Thread is to have your class instead implement the Runnable interface. The Runnable interface has only one method heading:

```
public void run()
```

A class that implements the Runnable interface must still be run from an instance of the class Thread. This is usually done by passing the Runnable object as an argument to the thread constructor. The following is an outline of one way to do this:

```
public class ClassToRun extends SomeClass implements Runnable
{
    ....
    public void run()
    {
        //Fill this just as you would if ClassToRun
        //were derived from Thread.
    }
    ....
    public void startThread()
    {
        Thread theThread = new Thread(this);
        theThread.run();
    }
    ....
}
```

The above method startThread is not compulsory, but it is one way to produce a thread that will in turn run the run method of an object of the class ClassToRun. In Display 19.3 we have rewritten the program in Display 19.2 using the Runnable interface. The program behaves exactly the same as the one in Display 19.2.

Display 19.3 The **Runnable** Interface (part 1 of 2)

```
1    import javax.swing.JFrame;
2    import javax.swing.JPanel;
3    import javax.swing.JButton;
4    import java.awt.BorderLayout;
5    import java.awt.FlowLayout;
6    import java.awt.Graphics;
7    import java.awt.event.ActionListener;
8    import java.awt.event.ActionEvent;

9    public class ThreadedFillDemo2 extends JFrame
10                                  implements ActionListener, Runnable
11   {
12       public static final int WIDTH = 300;
13       public static final int HEIGHT = 200;
14       public static final int FILL_WIDTH = 300;
15       public static final int FILL_HEIGHT = 100;
16       public static final int CIRCLE_SIZE = 10;
17       public static final int PAUSE = 100; //milliseconds
18       private JPanel box;

19       public static void main(String[] args)
20       {
21           ThreadedFillDemo2 gui = new ThreadedFillDemo2();
22           gui.setVisible(true);
23       }

24       public ThreadedFillDemo2()
25       {
26           setSize(WIDTH, HEIGHT);
27           setTitle("Threaded Fill Demo");
28           setDefaultCloseOperation(JFrame.EXIT_ON_CLOSE);

29           setLayout(new BorderLayout());

30           box = new JPanel();
31           add(box, "Center");

32           JPanel buttonPanel = new JPanel();
33           buttonPanel.setLayout(new FlowLayout());

34           JButton startButton = new JButton("Start");
35           startButton.addActionListener(this);
36           buttonPanel.add(startButton);
37           add(buttonPanel, "South");
38       }
```

(continued)

Display 19.3 The **Runnable** Interface (part 2 of 2)

```
39      public void actionPerformed(ActionEvent e)
40      {
41          startThread();
42      }

43      public void run()
44      {
45          Graphics g = box.getGraphics();
46          for (int y = 0; y < FILL_HEIGHT; y = y + CIRCLE_SIZE)
47            for (int x = 0; x < FILL_WIDTH; x = x + CIRCLE_SIZE)
48            {
49                g.fillOval(x, y, CIRCLE_SIZE, CIRCLE_SIZE);
50                doNothing(PAUSE);
51            }
52      }

53      public void startThread()
54      {
55          Thread theThread = new Thread(this);
56          theThread.start();
57      }

58      public void doNothing(int milliseconds)
59      {
60          try
61          {
62              Thread.sleep(milliseconds);
63          }
64          catch(InterruptedException e)
65          {
66              System.out.println("Unexpected interrupt");
67              System.exit(0);
68          }
69      }
70  }
```

Self-Test Exercises

1. Since sleep is a static method, how can it possibly know what thread it needs to pause?

2. Where was polymorphism used in the program in Display 19.2? (*Hint:* We are looking for an answer involving the class Packer.)

19.2 **Networking with Stream Sockets**

Since in order to speak, one must first listen, learn to speak by listening.

MEVLANA RUMI

When computers want to communicate with each other over a network, each computer must speak the same "language." In other words, the computers need to communicate using the same *protocol*. One of the most common protocols today is **TCP**, or the **Transmission Control Protocol**. For example, the HTTP protocol used to transmit web pages is based on TCP. TCP is a stream-based protocol in which a stream of data is transmitted from the sender to the receiver. TCP is considered a reliable protocol because it guarantees that data from the sender is received in the same order in which it was sent. An analogy to TCP is the telephone system. A connection is made when the phone is dialed and the participants communicate by speaking back and forth. In TCP, the receiver must first be listening for a connection, the sender initiates the connection, and then the sender and receiver can transmit data. The program that is waiting for a connection is called the **server** and the program that initiates the connection is called the **client**.

An alternate protocol is **UDP**, or the **User Datagram Protocol**. In UDP, packets of data are transmitted but no guarantee is made regarding the order in which the packets are received. An analogy to UDP is the postal system. Letters that are sent might be received in an unpredictable order, or lost entirely with no notification. Although Java provides support for UDP, we will only introduce TCP in this section.

Sidebar terms (left margin):
TCP
Transmission Control Protocol

server
client
UDP
User Datagram Protocol

Sockets

Network programming is implemented in Java using **sockets**. A socket describes one end of a connection between two programs over the network. A socket consists of an address that identifies the remote computer and a **port** for both the local and remote computer. The port is assigned an integer value between 0 and 65,535 that is used to identify which program should handle data received from the network. Two applications may not bind to the same port. Typically, ports 0 to 1,024 are reserved for use by well-known services implemented by your operating system.

The process of client/server communication is shown in Display 19.4. First, the server waits for a connection by listening on a specific port. When a client connects to this port, a new socket is created that identifies the remote computer, the remote port, and the local port. A similar socket is created on the client. Once the sockets are created on both the client and the server, data can be transmitted using streams in a manner very similar to the way we implemented File I/O in Chapter 10.

Display 19.5 shows how to create a simple server that listens on port 7654 for a connection. Once it receives a connection a new socket is returned by the `accept( )` method. From this socket we create a `BufferedReader`, just as if we were reading from a text file described in Chapter 10. Data is transmitted to the socket using a `DataOutputStream`, which is similar to a `FileOutputStream`. The `ServerSocket` and `Socket` classes are in

Sidebar terms (left margin):
sockets

port

Display 19.4 Client/Server Network Communication through Sockets

1. The server listens and waits for a connection on port 7654.

2. The client connects to the server on port 7654. It uses a local port that is assigned automatically, in this case, port 20314.

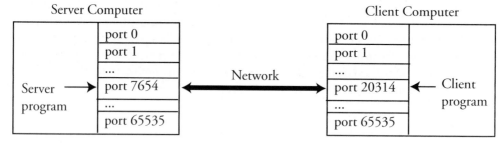

The server program can now communicate over a socket bound locally to port 7654 and remotely to the client's address at port 20314.

The client program can now communicate over a socket bound locally to port 20314 and remotely to the server's address at port 7654.

the java.net package, while the BufferedReader and DataOutputStream classes are in the java.io package. Once the streams are created, the server expects the client to send a name. The server waits for the name with a call to readLine( ) on the BufferedReader object and then sends back the name concatenated with the current date and time. Finally, the server closes the streams and sockets.

Display 19.6 shows how to create a client that connects to our date and time server. First, we create a socket with the name of the computer running the server along with the corresponding port of 7654. If the server program and client program are running on the same computer then you can use **localhost** as the name of the machine. Otherwise, the hostname should be set to the name of the computer (e.g., my.server.com). After a connection is made, the client creates stream objects, sends its name, waits for a reply, and prints the reply.

localhost

Note that the socket and stream objects throw checked exceptions. This means that their exceptions must be caught or declared in a throws block.

Display 19.5 Date and Time Server (part 1 of 2)

```java
1   import java.util.Date;
2   import java.net.ServerSocket;
3   import java.net.Socket;
4   import java.io.DataOutputStream;
5   import java.io.BufferedReader;
6   import java.io.InputStreamReader;
7   import java.io.IOException;

8   public class DateServer
9   {
10     public static void main(String[] args)
11     {
12         Date now = new Date();

13         try
14         {
15           System.out.println("Waiting for a connection on port 7654.");
16           ServerSocket serverSock = new ServerSocket(7654);
17           Socket connectionSock = serverSock.accept();

18           BufferedReader clientInput = new BufferedReader(
19               new InputStreamReader(connectionSock.getInputStream()));
20           DataOutputStream clientOutput = new DataOutputStream(
21               connectionSock.getOutputStream());

22           System.out.println("Connection made, waiting for client " +
23               "to send their name.");
24           String clientText = clientInput.readLine();
25           String replyText = "Welcome, " + clientText +
26               ", Today is " + now.toString() + "\n";
27           clientOutput.writeBytes(replyText);
28           System.out.println("Sent: " + replyText);

29           clientOutput.close();
30           clientInput.close();
31           connectionSock.close();
32           serverSock.close();
33         }
34         catch (IOException e)
35         {
36           System.out.println(e.getMessage());
37         }
38     }
39   }
```

(continued)

Display 19.5 Date and Time Server (part 2 of 2)

Sample Dialogue *Output when the client program in Display 19.6 connects to the server program.*

```
Waiting for a connection on port 7654.
Connection made, waiting for client to send their name.
Sent: Welcome, Dusty Rhodes, Today is Fri Oct 13 03:03:21 AKDT 2006
```

Display 19.6 Date and Time Client (part 1 of 2)

```java
1   import java.net.Socket;
2   import java.io.DataOutputStream;
3   import java.io.BufferedReader;
4   import java.io.InputStreamReader;
5   import java.io.IOException;

6   public class DateClient
7   {
8     public static void main(String[] args)
9     {
10        try
11        {
12          String hostname = "localhost";
13          int port = 7654;

14          System.out.println("Connecting to server on port " + port);
15          Socket connectionSock = new Socket(hostname, port);

16          BufferedReader serverInput = new BufferedReader(
17              new InputStreamReader(connectionSock.getInputStream()));
18          DataOutputStream serverOutput = new DataOutputStream(
19              connectionSock.getOutputStream());

20          System.out.println("Connection made, sending name.");
21          serverOutput.writeBytes("Dusty Rhodes\n");

22          System.out.println("Waiting for reply.");
23          String serverData = serverInput.readLine();
24          System.out.println("Received: " + serverData);

25          serverOutput.close();
26          serverInput.close();
27          connectionSock.close();
28        }
```

localhost refers to the same, or local, machine that the client is running on. Change this string to the appropriate hostname (e.g., my.server.com) if the server is running on a remote machine.

```
29          catch (IOException e)
30          {
31             System.out.println(e.getMessage());
32          }
33    }
34  }
```

Sample Dialogue   *Output when client program connects to the server program in Display 19.5.*

```
Connecting to server on port 7654
Connection made, sending name.
Waiting for reply.
Received: Welcome, Dusty Rhodes, Today is Fri Oct 13 03:03:21 AKDT 2006
```

Sockets and Threading

blocking

If you run the program in Display 19.5 then you will notice that the server waits, or **blocks**, at the serverSock.accept( ) call until a client connects to it. Both the client and server also block at the readLine( ) call if data from the socket is not yet available. In a client with a GUI you would notice this as a nonresponsive program while it is waiting for data. For the server, this behavior makes it difficult to handle connections with more than one client. After a connection is made with the first client, the server will become nonresponsive to the client's requests while it waits for a second client.

The solution to this problem is to use threads. One thread will listen for new connections while another thread handles an existing connection. Section 19.1 describes how to create threads and make a GUI program responsive. For the server the accept( ) call is typically placed in a loop and a new thread is created to handle each client connection:

```
while (true)
{
   Socket connectionSock = serverSock.accept( );
   ClientHandler handler = new ClientHandler(connectionSock);
   Thread theThread = new Thread(handler);
   theThread.start( );
}
```

In this code ClientHandler is a class that implements Runnable. The constructor keeps a reference to the socket in an instance variable, and the run( ) method would handle all communications. A complete implementation of a threaded server is left as Programming Project 7 and 8.

Self-Test Exercises

3. What is the purpose of a port in the context of a socket?

4. Consider a threaded server that is expected to have up to 100 clients connected to it at one time. Why might this server require a large amount of resources such as memory, disk space, or processor time?

19.3 JavaBeans

Insert tab A into slot B.

Common assembly instruction

JavaBeans

JavaBeans refers to a framework that facilitates software building by connecting software components from diverse sources. Some of the components might be standard existing pieces of software. Some might be designed for the particular application. Typically, the various components were designed and coded by different teams. If the components are all designed within the JavaBeans framework, that simplifies the process of integrating the components and means that the components produced can more easily be reused for future software projects. JavaBeans have been widely used. For example, the AWT and Swing packages were built within the JavaBeans framework.

The Component Model

You are most likely to have heard the word "component" when shopping for a home entertainment system. The individual pieces, such as a receiver/amplifier, DVD player, speakers, and so forth, are called "components." You connect the components to produce a working system, but you do not connect them in just any way. You must connect them following the interface rules for each component. The speaker wire must connect to the correct plug, and there better be a plug for it to connect to. You may think it is obvious that a receiver/amplifier needs to have connections for speakers; it is obvious if the receiver/amplifier design is going to be used to make many identical units for use by many different people. However, if you were only making one receiver/amplifier for one home entertainment system, you might just "open the box" and connect the wire inside. Software systems, unfortunately, are often constructed using the "open the box" approach. The component model says that components should always have well-defined connections for other components, which in our case will be other software components, not speakers, but the idea is the same.

The JavaBeans Model

A component model specifies how components interact with one another. In the case of JavaBeans, the software components (classes) are required to provide at least the following interface services or abilities:

1. **Rules to Ensure Consistency in Writing Interfaces:**
   For example, the rules say, among other things, that the name of an accessor method must begin with get and that the name of a mutator method must start with set. This same rule has always been a style rule for us in this book, but it was a "should do." In the JavaBeans framework it becomes a "must do." Of course, there are other rules as well. This is just a sample rule.

event handling

2. **An Event Handling Model:**
   This is essentially the event-handling model we presented for the AWT and Swing. (Remember the AWT and Swing were done within the JavaBeans framework.)

persistence

3. **Persistence:**
   Persistence means that an object has an identity that extends beyond one session. For example, a JFrame of the kind we have seen so far may be used, and when you are finished using it, it goes away. The next time you use it, it starts out completely new, born again just as it started before. Persistence means the JFrame or other component can retain information about its former use; its state is saved, for example, in a database someplace.

introspection

4. **Introspection:**
   Introspection is an enhancement of simple accessor and mutator methods. It includes facilities to find out what access to a component is available as well as providing access.

5. **Builder Support:**
   These are primarily IDEs (Integrated Development Environments) designed to connect JavaBean components to produce a final application. Some examples are Sun's Bean Builder, Symantec's Visual Cafe, and Borland's JBuilder.

What Is a JavaBean?

A **JavaBean** (often called a *JavaBean* component or simply a *Bean*) is a reusable software component (Java class or classes) that satisfies the requirements of the JavaBeans framework and that can be manipulated in an IDE designed for building applications out of Beans.

What Are Enterprise JavaBeans?

The **Enterprise JavaBean** framework extends the JavaBeans framework to more readily accommodate business applications.

Self-Test Exercises

5. What is meant by *persistence*?

6. What event-handling model is used with JavaBeans?

19.4 Java and Database Connections

It is a capital mistake to theorize before one has data.

SIR ARTHUR CONAN DOYLE (*Sherlock Holmes*), *Scandal in Bohemia*

As an example of how Java has been extended to interact with other software systems, in this section, we will briefly describe how Java interacts with database management systems. This is not a complete enough introduction to allow you to immediately start writing Java code for database manipulations. The intent of this section is to let you know what kinds of things are available to you for database programming in Java.

SQL

SQL SQL is a standard for database access that has been adopted by virtually all database vendors. The initials SQL stand for Structured Query Language. SQL is pronounced either by saying the letters or by saying the word "sequel." SQL is a language for formulating queries for a relational database. SQL is not part of Java, but Java does have a library (and accompanying implementation software) known as JDBC that allows you to embed SQL commands in your Java code.

SQL works with relational databases. Most commercially available database management systems are relational databases. A relational database can be thought of as a collection of named tables with rows and columns, such as those shown in Display 19.7. In this brief introduction we will not go into the details of the constraints on tables, but to see that there are some constraints, note that in the three tables in Display 19.7, no relationship is repeated. For example, if we had one entry for each book with all the information—title, author, ISBN number[1], and author's URL—then there would be two entries giving Dan Simmons' URL, since he has two books in our database.

The following is a sample SQL command:

```
SELECT Titles.Title, Titles.ISBN, BooksAuthors.Author_ID
FROM Titles, BooksAuthors
WHERE Titles.ISBN = BooksAuthors.ISBN
```

This will produce the table shown in Display 19.8. That table contains all titles with matching ISBN number and author ID, given in Display 19.8. The ISBN number is the bridge that connects the tables Titles and BooksAuthors.

---

[1] The ISBN number is a unique identification number assigned to (almost) every book published.)

JDBC

According to most authorities, JDBC stands for "Java Database Connectivity." It allows you to insert SQL commands in your Java code. In order to use Java's JDBC you need to have JDBC and a database system compatible with JDBC installed. JDBC is available from Sun. Various Microsoft and Oracle database systems are among the many commercially available database systems that are compatible with JDBC. Typically, you need to download and install a JDBC driver for your database system.

Conceptually JDBC is simple: You establish a connection to a database system (either on your computer or over the Internet) and execute SQL commands, and you do this all within your Java code. The details are not trivial, but hopefully you now know enough about JDBC to know whether you wish to study it further.

Display 19.7   Relational Database Tables

Names

AUTHOR	AUTHOR_ID	URL
Adams, Douglas	1	http:// ...
Simmons, Dan	2	http:// ...
Stephenson, Neal	3	http:// ...

Titles

TITLE	ISBN
Snow Crash	0-553-38095-8
Endymion	0-553-57294-6
The Hitchhiker's Guide to the Galaxy	0-671-46149-4
The Rise of Endymion	0-553-57298-9

BooksAuthors

ISBN	AUTHOR_ID
0-553-38095-8	3
0-553-57294-6	2
0-671-46149-4	1
0-553-57298-9	2

Display 19.8 Result of SQL Command in Text

Result

TITLE	ISBN	AUTHOR_ID
Snow Crash	0-553-38095-8	3
Endymion	0-553-57294-6	2
The Hitchhiker's Guide to the Galaxy	0-671-46149-4	1
The Rise of Endymion	0-553-57298-9	2

Self-Test Exercises

7. Give an SQL command to produce a table of book titles with corresponding author and author ID from the table `Result` in Display 19.8 and one of the tables in Display 19.7. Follow the example of an SQL command given in the text.

Chapter Summary

- A thread is a separate computation process. A Java program can have multiple threads.

- You use the class `Thread` to produce multiple threads.

- The static method `Thread.sleep` inserts a pause into the thread in which it is invoked.

- A socket refers to an endpoint that connects two programs over a network.

- TCP refers to a reliable, streaming protocol for network communication. It ensures that data is received in the same order it was sent.

- JavaBeans refers to a framework for producing Java components that are easy to combine with other JavaBean components to produce new applications.

- JDBC allows you to insert SQL commands into your code to access and manipulate databases.

- Using JDBC, you can insert SQL database commands in your Java code.

Answers to Self-Test Exercises

1. The invocation of `Thread.sleep` takes place inside a thread. Every action in Java takes place inside some thread. Any action performed by a method invocation in a specific thread takes place in that thread. Even if it does not know where it is, a method's action takes place where the method invocation is; if you were lost and yelled out, you might not know where you are but the yell would still be wherever it is you are.

2. The class `Packer` inherits the method `start` from the base class `Thread` and it is not overridden. The method `start` invokes the method `run`, but when `start` is invoked by an object of the class `Packer`, it is the definition of `run` that is given in the class `Packer` that is used, not the definition of `run` given in the definition of `Thread`. That is exactly what is meant by late binding or polymorphism.

3. A port is used to identify which program should receive data from the network. Only one program may be bound to a specific port.

4. Each client connection may run in its own thread, requiring a large amount of memory, disk space, or processor time.

5. *Persistence* means that a component's state can be saved so that the next time it is used it remembers what state it was in.

6. The same one that is used for Swing and AWT.

7.
```
SELECT Result.Title, Names.Author, Result.Author_ID
FROM Result, Names
WHERE Result.Author_ID = Names.Author_ID
```

Programming Projects

 Many of these Programming Projects can be solved using AW's MyCodeMate. To access these please go to: www.mycodemate.com.

 1. Write a GUI program that uses the methods in the `Graphics` class together with threads to draw a smiley face, wait two seconds, draw a frowny face, wait two seconds, and repeat starting with the smiley face. A separate thread should be started to implement the two-second timer. The application should be responsive and exit immediately if the user decides to close the window.

2. Create a class named `TimerAlarm` that extends Thread and implements a timer. Don't use the built-in Timer class for this exercise. Your class constructor should take as input an integer named t representing time in milliseconds and an interface object named `obj` that defines a method named `alarmAction( )`. You will need to define this interface. Every t milliseconds the class should invoke method `obj.alarmAction( )`. Add `pause( )` and `play( )` methods that disable and enable the invocation of `alarmAction( )`. Test your class with code that increments and prints out a counter.

3. Write a GUI program that animates a four-colored "beach ball" in place by rotating the colors. The beach ball can be drawn as a solid circle with four different colors in each of the four quadrants of the circle. Use a thread to rotate the colors every quarter second.

4. Modify the GUI in Display 19.2 so that the circles are alternately red, white, and blue, and so that they fill the area from bottom to top instead of top to bottom.

5. Produce a GUI similar to the one in Display 19.2 except that instead of filling an area with circles, it launches a ball (which is just a circle) and the ball bounces around inside a rectangle. You can create the illusion of a moving ball by repeatedly erasing the ball and redrawing it at a location a little farther along its path. Look up the method setXORMode in the class Graphics. It will take care of the erasing.

6. This project shows how to create a simple Web server. Create a server program that listens on port 8000. When a client connects to the server the program should send the following data to the client:

```
"HTTP/1.0 200 OK\n\n" + body
```

Where body is the String "<HTML><TITLE>Java Server</TITLE>This web page was sent by our simple <B>Java Server</B></HTML>". If you know HTML, feel free to insert your own content. The header line identifies the message as part of the HTTP protocol that is used to transmit web pages.

When the server is running you should be able to start a web browser and navigate to your machine on port 8000 and view the message. For example, if the server is running on your local machine, you could point your web browser to http://localhost:8000 and the message in body should be displayed.

7. Modify the server from Programming Project 6 so that the content for body is read from a file on the local hard drive instead of hard-coded into the program. This file should contain the HTML string from Programming Project 6. In addition, modify the server so that a new thread is created for each connection. Test the server by starting up two or more web browsers and navigate to your site. Each browser should display the message.

8. Create a threaded chat server and a corresponding chat client. Using the port of your choice, create a server that starts a new thread for every client that connects to it. Every message that the server receives from a client should be broadcast back to all other clients. The chat client should allow the user to type in a string of text and have it sent to the server upon pressing enter. Use threads on the client so messages can be retrieved from the server and displayed even while the user is typing. Test your server by connecting to it with multiple clients and verifying that messages are transmitted by back and forth.

abstract	final	public
assert*	finally	return
boolean	float	short
break	for	static
byte	goto	strictfp
case	if	super
catch	implements	switch
char	import	synchronized
class	instanceof	this
const	int	throw
continue	interface	throws
default	long	transient
do	native	true*
double	new	try
else	null*	void
enum	package	volatile
extends	private	while
false*	protected	

* These are not listed as keywords in the Sun documentation. However, some authorities list them as keywords. Preferring to err on the side of more safety, this book treats them as keywords.

Precedence and Associativity Rules 2

PRECEDENCE	ASSOCIATIVITY
From highest at top to lowest at bottom. Operators in the same group have equal precedence.	
Dot operator, array indexing, and method invocation: ., [ ], ()	Left to right
++ (postfix, as in x++), −− (postfix)	Right to left
The unary operators: +, −, ++ (prefix, as in ++x), −− (prefix), !, ~ (bitwise complement)[a]	Right to left
new and type casts (*Type*)	Right to left
The binary operators *, /, %	Left to right
The binary operators +, −	Left to right
The binary operators <<, >>, >>> (shift operators)[1]	Left to right
The binary operators <, >, <=, >=, instanceof	Left to right
The binary operators ==, !=	Left to right
The binary operator &	Left to right
The binary operator ^ (exclusive or)[a]	Left to right
The binary operator |	Left to right
The binary operator &&	Left to right
The binary operator ||	Left to right
The ternary operator (conditional operator) ?:	Right to left
The assignment operators =, *=, /=, %=, +=, −=, &=, |=, ^=, <<=, >>=, >>>=	Right to left

a.Not discussed in this book.

The characters shown here form the ASCII character set, which is the subset of the Unicode character set that is commonly used by English speakers. The numbering is the same whether the characters are considered to be members of the Unicode character set or of the ASCII character set. Character number 32 is the blank. Only printable characters are shown.

32		56	8	80	P	104	h
33	!	57	9	81	Q	105	i
34	"	58	:	82	R	106	j
35	#	59	;	83	S	107	k
36	$	60	<	84	T	108	l
37	%	61	=	85	U	109	m
38	&	62	>	86	V	110	n
39	'	63	?	87	W	111	o
40	(	64	@	88	X	112	p
41	)	65	A	89	Y	113	q
42	*	66	B	90	Z	114	r
43	+	67	C	91	[	115	s
44	,	68	D	92	\	116	t
45	–	69	E	93	]	117	u
46	.	70	F	94	^	118	v
47	/	71	G	95	_	119	w
48	0	72	H	96	'	120	x
49	1	73	I	97	a	121	y
50	2	74	J	98	b	122	z
51	3	75	K	99	c	123	{
52	4	76	L	100	d	124	|
53	5	77	M	101	e	125	}
54	6	78	N	102	f	126	~
55	7	79	O	103	g		

SYNTAX

System.out.printf(*Format_String*, *Output_1*, *Output_2*, ..., *Output_Last*);

Format_String is a string including one format specifier for each *Output* argument. *Format_String* is output with each format specifier replaced by its corresponding *Output* argument in the format given by the *Output* argument's format specifier.

Display A4.1   Format Specifiers for `System.out.printf`

CONVERSION CHARACTER	TYPE OF OUTPUT.	EXAMPLES
d	Decimal (ordinary) integer.	%5d %d
f	Fixed-point (everyday notation) floating-point.	%6.2f %f
e	E-notation floating-point.	%8.3e %e
g	General floating-point. (Java decides whether to use E-notation or not.)	%8.3g %g
s	String.	%12s %s
c	Character.	%2c %c
b	Boolean. The corresponding *Output* argument is a Boolean expression. Outputs **true** or **false**.	%6b %b
n	Denotes a line break. This does not correspond to an *Output* argument. It is approximately equivalent to \n.	%n

A number of the form $N.M$ in a format specifier specifies a field width of N spaces with M digits after the decimal point. If only one number N is given, it specifies a field width, and if there is a decimal point in the output, then the number of digits after the decimal point is determined by Java.

When the value output does not fill the field width specified, then blanks are added in front of the value output. The output is then said to be *right justified*. If you add a hyphen (–) after the %, then any extra blank space is placed after the value output and the output is said to be *left justified*. For example, `%8.2f` is right justified and `%-8.2f` is left justified.

This appendix summarizes most of the library classes used in this book. This appendix includes some methods, and even some classes, that are not discussed in the text. The lists of class methods and other class members contain the most commonly used members and the members used in this book, but they are not complete lists of methods for the classes given here.

If a class or interface is derived from another class or interface, respectively, then in some cases, the table for the derived class or interface lists only new methods and does not list all the inherited methods.

Abstract Button

Package: `javax.swing`
The classes `JButton` and `JMenuItem` are also in this package.
All these methods are inherited by the classes `JButton` and `JMenuItem`.
`AbstractButton` is an abstract class.
Ancestor classes:

```
Object
   |
   +--Component
          |
          +--Container
                 |
                 +--JComponent
                        |
                        +--AbstractButton
                              |           \
                              +--JButton   +--JMenuItem
```

`public void addActionListener(ActionListener listener)`

Adds an `ActionListener`.

`public String getActionCommand()`

Returns the action command for this component.

`public String getText()`

Returns the text written on the component, such as the text on a button or the string for a menu item.

`public void removeActionListener(ActionListener listener)`

Removes an `ActionListener`.

`public void setActionCommand(String actionCommand)`

Sets the action command.

```
public void setBackground(Color theColor)
```
Sets the background color of this component.

```
public void setMaximumSize(Dimension maximumSize)
```
Sets the maximum size of the button or label. Note that this is only a suggestion to the layout manager. The layout manager is not required to respect this maximum size. The following special case will work for most simple situations. The `int` values give the width and height in pixels.

```
public void setMaximumSize(
                    new Dimension(int width, int height))
```

```
public void setMinimumSize(Dimension minimumSize)
```
Sets the minimum size of the button or label. Note that this is only a suggestion to the layout manager. The layout manager is not required to respect this minimum size.
Although we do not discuss the `Dimension` class, the following special case is intuitively clear and will work for most simple situations. The `int` values give the width and height in pixels.

```
public void setMinimumSize(
                    new Dimension(int width, int height))
```

```
public void setPreferredSize(Dimension preferredSize)
```
Sets the preferred size of the button or label. Note that this is only a suggestion to the layout manager. The layout manager is not required to use the preferred size. The following special case will work for most simple situations. The `int` values give the width and height in pixels.

```
public void setPreferredSize(
                    new Dimension(int width, int height))
```

```
public void setText(String text)
```
Makes text the only text on this component.

ArrayList<T>

Package: `java.util`

Ancestor classes:

```
Object
   |
   +--AbstractCollection<T>
            |
            +--AbstractList<T>
                     |
                     +--ArrayList<T>
```

All the exception classes mentioned are unchecked exceptions, which means they are not required to be caught in a `catch` block or declared in a `throws` clause.
`NoSuchElementException` is in the `java.util` package, which requires an import statement if your code mentions the `NoSuchElementException` class. All the other exception classes mentioned are in the package `java.lang` and so do not require any import statement.

CONSTRUCTORS

`public ArrayList(int initialCapacity)`

Creates an empty `ArrayList<T>` with the specified initial capacity. When the `ArrayList<T>` needs to increase its capacity, the capacity doubles.
Throws an `IllegalArgumentException` if `initialCapacity` is negative.

`public ArrayList()`

Creates an empty `ArrayList<T>` with an initial capacity of **10**. When the `ArrayList<T>` needs to increase its capacity, the capacity doubles.

`public ArrayList(Collection<? extends T> c)`

Creates a `ArrayList<T>` that contains all the elements of the collection `c` in the same order as they have in `c`. In other words, the elements have the same index in the `ArrayList<T>` created as they do in `c`. This is not quite a true copy constructor because it does not preserve capacity. The capacity of the created `ArrayList<T>` will be `c.size()`, not `c.capacity`.
The `ArrayList<T>` created is only a shallow copy of the collection argument. The `ArrayList<T>` created contains references to the elements in `c` (not references to clones of the elements in `c`).

Throws:
`NullPointerException` if `c` is `null`.

ARRAYLIKE METHODS

```
public T set(int index, T newElement)
```

Sets the element at the specified `index` to `newElement`. The element previously at that position is returned. If you draw an analogy to an array `a`, this is analogous to setting `a[index]` to the value `newElement`. The `index` must be a value greater than or equal to `0` and strictly less than the current size of the list.

Throws:

`IndexOutOfBoundsException` if the `index` is not in this range.

```
public T get(int index)
```

Returns the element at the specified index. This is analogous to returning `a[index]` for an array `a`. The `index` must be a value greater than or equal to `0` and less than the current size of the calling object.

Throws:

`IndexOutOfBoundsException` if the `index` is not in the required range.

METHODS TO ADD ELEMENTS

```
public boolean add(T newElement)
```

Adds `newElement` to the end of the calling object's list and increases its size by 1. The capacity of the calling object is increased if that is required. Returns **true** if the add was successful. This method is often used as if it were a **void** method.

```
public void add(int index, T newElement)
```

Inserts `newElement` as an element in the calling object at the specified index and increases the size of the calling object by 1. Each element in the calling object with an index greater than or equal to `index` is shifted upward to have an index that is 1 greater than it had previously.
The `index` must be a value greater than or equal to `0` and less than *or equal to* the size of the calling object (before this addition).
Note that you can use this method to add an element after the last current element. The capacity of the calling object is increased if that is required.

Throws:

`IndexOutOfBoundsException` if the index is not in the prescribed range.

```
public boolean addAll(Collection<? extends T> c)
```

Appends all the elements in `c` to the end of the elements in the calling object in the order that they are enumerated by a `c` iterator. The behavior of this method is not guaranteed if the collection `c` is the calling object or any collection including the calling object either directly or indirectly.

Throws:

`NullPointerException` if `c` is `null`.

> public boolean addAll(int index, Collection<? extends T> c)

Inserts all the elements in c into the calling object starting at position index. Elements are inserted in the order that they are enumerated by a c iterator. Elements previously at positions index or higher are shifted to higher numbered positions.

Throws:

IndexOutOfBoundsException if index is not both greater than or equal to zero and less than size().
NullPointerException if c is null.

METHODS TO REMOVE ELEMENTS

> public T remove(int index)

Deletes the element at the specified index and returns the element deleted. The size of the calling object is decreased by 1. The capacity of the calling object is not changed. Each element in the calling object with an index greater than or equal to index is decreased to have an index that is 1 less than the value it had previously.
The index must be a value greater than or equal to 0 and less than the size of the calling object (before this removal).

Throws:

IndexOutOfBoundsException if the index is not in the prescribed range.

> public boolean remove(Object theElement)

Removes the first occurrence of theElement from the calling object. If theElement is found in the calling object, then each element in the calling object with an index greater than or equal to theElement's index is decreased to have an index that is 1 less than the value it had previously. Returns true if theElement was found (and removed). Returns false if theElement was not found in the calling object. If the element was removed, the size is decreased by 1. The capacity is not changed.

> protected void removeRange(int fromIndex, int toIndex)

Removes all elements with index greater than or equal to fromIndex and strictly less than toIndex. Be sure to note that this method is protected, not public.

> public void clear()

Removes all elements from the calling object and sets its size to zero.

SEARCH METHODS

> public boolean isEmpty()

Returns true if the calling object is empty (that is, has size 0); otherwise returns false.

> public boolean contains(Object target)

Returns true if target is an element of the calling object; otherwise returns false. Uses the method equals of the object target to test for equality.

```
public int indexOf(Object target)
```

Returns the index of the first element that is equal to **target**. Uses the method **equals** of the object **target** to test for equality. Returns −1 if **target** is not found.

```
public int lastIndexOf(Object target)
```

Returns the index of the last element that is equal to **target**. Uses the method **equals** of the object **target** to test for equality. Returns −1 if **target** is not found.

ITERATORS

```
public Iterator<T> iterator()
```

Returns an iterator for the calling object. Iterators are discussed in Section 16.3.

```
public ListIterator<T> listIterator()
```

Returns a **ListIterator<T>** for the calling object. **ListIterator<T>** is discussed in Section 16.3.

```
ListIterator<T> listIterator(int index)
```

Returns a list iterator for the calling object starting at **index**. The first element to be returned by the iterator is the one at **index**. (Iterators are discussed in Section 16.3.)

Throws:

IndexOutOfBoundsException if **index** does not satisfy:
`0 <= index <= size()`

CONVERTING TO AN ARRAY

```
public Object[] toArray()
```

Returns an array containing all of the elements in the calling object. The elements of the array are indexed the same as in the calling object.

```
public <E> E[] toArray(E[] a)
```

Note that the type parameter E is not the same as T. So, E can be any reference type; it need not be the type T in **Collection<T>**. For example, E might be an ancestor type of T.
Returns an array containing all of the elements in the calling object. The elements of the array are indexed the same as in the calling object.
The argument *a* is used primarily to specify the type of the array returned. The exact details are as follows:
The type of the returned array is that of *a*. If the collection fits in the array *a*, then *a* is used to hold the elements of the returned array; otherwise a new array is created with the same type as *a*.
If *a* has more elements than the calling object, then the element in *a* immediately following the end of the elements copied from the calling object are set to **null**.

Throws:

ArrayStoreException if the type of *a* is not an ancestor type of the type of every element in the calling object.
NullPointerException if *a* is **null**.

MEMORY MANAGEMENT

`public int size()`

Returns the number of elements in the calling object.

`public int capacity()`

Returns the current capacity of the calling object.

`public void ensureCapacity(int newCapacity)`

Increases the capacity of the calling object to ensure that it can hold at least `newCapacity` elements. Using `ensureCapacity` can sometimes increase efficiency, but its use is not needed for any other reason.

`public void trimToSize()`

Trims the capacity of the calling object to be the calling object's current size. This is used to save storage.

MAKE A COPY

`public Object clone()`

Returns a shallow copy of the calling object.

Boolean

See Section 5.1 in Chapter 5.

BufferedReader

Package: `java.io`
The `FileReader` class is also in this package.
Ancestor classes:

```
Object
    |
    +--Reader
          |
          +--BufferedReader
```

`public BufferedReader(Reader readerObject)`

This is the only constructor you are likely to need. There is no constructor that accepts a file name as an argument. If you want to create a stream using a file name, you use

`new BufferedReader(new FileReader(File_Name))`

When used in this way, the `FileReader` constructor, and thus the `BufferedReader` constructor invocation, can throw a `FileNotFoundException`, which is a kind of `IOException`.
If you want to create a stream using an object of the class `File`, you use

`new BufferedReader(new FileReader(File_Object))`

When used in this way, the `FileReader` constructor, and thus the `BufferedReader` constructor invocation, can throw a `FileNotFoundException`, which is a kind of `IOException`.

```
public void close() throws IOException
```
Closes the stream's connection to a file.

```
public int read() throws IOException
```
Reads a single character from the input stream and returns that character as an **int** value. If the read goes beyond the end of the file, then −1 is returned. Note that the value is returned as an **int**. To obtain a **char**, you must perform a type cast on the value returned. The end of a file is signaled by returning −1. (All of the "real" characters return a positive integer.)

```
public String readLine() throws IOException
```
Reads a line of input from the input stream and returns that line. If the read goes beyond the end of the file, **null** is returned. (Note that an **EOFException** is not thrown at the end of a file. The end of a file is signaled by returning **null**.)

```
public long skip(long n) throws IOException
```
Skips **n** characters.

Byte

See Section 5.2 in Chapter 5.

Character

Package: `java.lang`
Ancestor classes:

```
        Object
           |
        +--Character
```

Implemented interfaces: `Comparable, Serializable`
The **Character** class is marked **final**, which means it cannot be used as a base class to derive other classes.

```
public static boolean isDigit(char argument)
```
Returns **true** if its **argument** is a digit; otherwise returns **false**.

EXAMPLES

Character.isDigit('5') returns true. Character.isDigit('A') and Character.isDigit('%') both return false.

```
public static boolean isLetter(char argument)
```
Returns **true** if its **argument** is a letter; otherwise returns **false**.

EXAMPLES

Character.isLetter('A') returns true. Character.isLetter('%') and Character.isLetter('5') both return false.

```
public static boolean isLetterOrDigit(char argument)
```

Returns **true** if its **argument** is a letter or a digit; otherwise returns **false**.

EXAMPLES

`Character.isLetterOrDigit('A')` and `Character.isLetterOrDigit('5')` both return **true**. `Character.isLetterOrDigit('&')` returns **false**.

```
public static boolean isLowerCase(char argument)
```

Returns **true** if its **argument** is a lowercase letter; otherwise returns **false**.

EXAMPLES

`Character.isLowerCase('a')` returns **true**. `Character.isLowerCase('A')` and `Character.isLowerCase('%')` both return **false**.

```
public static boolean isUpperCase(char argument)
```

Returns **true** if its **argument** is an uppercase letter; otherwise returns **false**.

EXAMPLES

`Character.isUpperCase('A')` returns **true**. `Character.isUpperCase('a')` and `Character.isUpperCase('%')` both return **false**.

```
public static boolean isWhitespace(char argument)
```

Returns **true** if its **argument** is a whitespace character; otherwise returns **false**. Whitespace characters are those that print as whitespace, such as the space character (blank character), the tab character (`'\t'`), and the new-line character (`'\n'`).

EXAMPLES

`Character.isWhitespace(' ')` returns **true**. `Character.isWhitespace('A')` returns **false**.

```
public static char toLowerCase(char argument)
```

Returns the lowercase version of its **argument**. If the **argument** is not a letter, it is returned unchanged.

EXAMPLE

`Character.toLowerCase('a')` and `Character.toLowerCase('A')` both return `'a'`.

```
public static char toUpperCase(char argument)
```

Returns the uppercase version of its **argument**. If the **argument** is not a letter, it is returned unchanged.

EXAMPLE

`Character.toUpperCase('a')` and `Character.toUpperCase('A')` both return `'A'`.

Collection<T> Interface

Package: `java.util`
Ancestor interfaces: None
All the exception classes mentioned are unchecked exceptions, which means they are not required to be caught in a `catch` block or declared in a `throws` clause.
All the exception classes mentioned are in the package `java.lang` and so do not require any `import` statement.

CONSTRUCTORS

Although not officially required by the interface, any class that implements the `Collection<T>` interface should have at least two constructors: a no-argument constructor that creates an empty `Collection<T>` object, and a constructor with one parameter of type `Collection<? extends T>` that creates a `Collection<T>` object with the same elements as the constructor argument. The interface does not specify whether the copy produced by the one-argument constructor is a shallow copy or a deep copy of its argument.

```
public boolean contains(Object target)
```

Returns `true` if the calling object contains at least one instance of `target`. Uses `target.equals` to determine if `target` is in the calling object.

Throws:

`ClassCastException` if the type of `target` is incompatible with the calling object (optional).
`NullPointerException` if `target` is `null` and the calling object does not support `null` elements (optional).

```
public boolean containsAll(Collection<?> collectionOfTargets)
```

Returns `true` if the calling object contains all of the elements in `collectionOfTargets`. For `element` in `collectionOfTargets`, this method uses `element.equals` to determine if `element` is in the calling object.

Throws:

`ClassCastException` if the types of one or more elements in `collectionOfTargets` are incompatible with the calling object (optional).
`NullPointerException` if `collectionOfTargets` contains one or more `null` elements and the calling object does not support `null` elements (optional).
`NullPointerException` if `collectionOfTargets` is `null`.

```
public boolean equals(Object other)
```

This is the `equals` of the collection, not the `equals` of the elements in the collection. Overrides the inherited method `equals`. Although there are no official constraints on `equals` for a collection, it should be defined as we have described in Chapter 7 and also to satisfy the intuitive notion of collections being equal.

```
public int hashCode()
```

Returns the hash code value for the calling object. Neither hash codes nor this method are discussed in this book. This entry is only here to make the definition of the `Collection<T>` interface complete. You can safely ignore this entry until you go on to study hash codes in a more advanced book. In the meantime, if you need to implement this method, have the method throw an `UnsupportedOperationException`.

```
public boolean isEmpty()
```

Returns `true` if the calling object is empty; otherwise returns `false`.

```
Iterator<T> iterator()
```

Returns an iterator for the calling object. (Iterators are discussed in Section 16.3.)

```
public Object[] toArray()
```

Returns an array containing all of the elements in the calling object. If the calling object makes any guarantees as to what order its elements are returned by its iterator, this method must return the elements in the same order.

The array returned should be a new array so that the calling object has no references to the returned array. (You might also want the elements in the array to be clones of the elements in the collection. However, this is apparently not required by the interface, since library classes, such as `Vector<T>`, return arrays that contain references to the elements in the collection.)

```
public <E> E[] toArray(E[] a)
```

Note that the type parameter E is not the same as T. So, E can be any reference type; it need not be the type T in `Collection<T>`. For example, E might be an ancestor type of T.

Returns an array containing all of the elements in the calling object. The argument *a* is used primarily to specify the type of the array returned. The exact details are as follows:

The type of the returned array is that of *a*. If the elements in the calling object fit in the array *a*, then *a* is used to hold the elements of the returned array; otherwise a new array is created with the same type as *a*.

If *a* has more elements than the calling object, the element in *a* immediately following the end of the copied elements is set to `null`.

If the calling object makes any guarantees as to what order its elements are returned by its iterator, this method must return the elements in the same order. (Iterators are discussed in Section 16.3.)

Throws:

`ArrayStoreException` if the type of *a* is not an ancestor type of the type of every element in the calling object.
`NullPointerException` if *a* is `null`.

```
public int size()
```

Returns the number of elements in the calling object. If the calling object contains more than `Integer.MAX_VALUE` elements, returns `Integer.MAX_VALUE`.

OPTIONAL METHODS

The following methods are optional, which means they still must be implemented, but the implementation can simply throw an `UnsupportedOperationException` if for some reason you do not want to give them a "real" implementation. An `UnsupportedOperationException` is a `RunTimeException` and so is not required to be caught or declared in a `throws` clause.

`public boolean` **add(T element)** *(Optional)*

Ensures that the calling object contains the specified **element**. Returns **true** if the calling object changed as a result of the call. Returns **false** if the calling object does not permit duplicates and already contains **element**; also returns **false** if the calling object does not change for any other reason.

Throws:

UnsupportedOperationException if this method is not supported by the class that implements this interface.
ClassCastException if the class of **element** prevents it from being added to the calling object.
NullPointerException if **element** is **null** and the calling object does not support **null** elements.
IllegalArgumentException if some other aspect of **element** prevents it from being added to the calling object.

`public boolean` **addAll(Collection<? extends T> collectionToAdd)** *(Optional)*

Ensures that the calling object contains all the elements in **collectionToAdd**. Returns **true** if the calling object changed as a result of the call; returns **false** otherwise. If the calling object changes during this operation, its behavior is unspecified; in particular, it behavior is unspecified if **collectionToAdd** is the calling object.

Throws:

UnsupportedOperationException if this method is not supported by the class that implements this interface.
ClassCastException if the class of an element of **collectionToAdd** prevents it from being added to the calling object.
NullPointerException if **collectionToAdd** contains one or more **null** elements and the calling object does not support **null** elements, or if **collectionToAdd** is **null**.
IllegalArgumentException if some aspect of an element of **collectionToAdd** prevents it from being added to the calling object.

`public void` **clear()** *(Optional)*

Removes all the elements from the calling object.

Throws:

UnsupportedOperationException if this method is not supported by the class that implements this interface.

`public boolean` **remove(Object element)** *(Optional)*

Removes a single instance of **element** from the calling object, if it is present. Returns **true** if the calling object contained **element**; returns **false** otherwise.

Throws:

UnsupportedOperationException if this method is not supported by the class that implements this interface.
ClassCastException if the type of **element** is incompatible with the calling object (optional).
NullPointerException if **element** is **null** and the calling object does not support **null** elements (optional).

```
    public boolean removeAll(Collection<?> collectionToRemove) (Optional)
```

Removes all the calling object's elements that are also contained in **collectionToRemove**. Returns **true** if the calling object was changed; otherwise returns **false**.

Throws:

UnsupportedOperationException if this method is not supported by the class that implements this interface.
ClassCastException if the types of one or more elements in **collectionToRemove** are incompatible with the calling collection (optional).
NullPointerException if **collectionToRemove** contains one or more **null** elements and the calling object does not support **null** elements (optional).
NullPointerException if **collectionToRemove** is **null**.

```
    public boolean retainAll(Collection<?> saveElements) (Optional)
```

Retains only the elements in the calling object that are also contained in the collection **saveElements**. In other words, removes from the calling object all of its elements that are not contained in the collection **saveElements**. Returns **true** if the calling object was changed; otherwise returns **false**.

Throws:

ClassCastException if the types of one or more elements in **saveElements** are incompatible with the calling object (optional).
NullPointerException if **saveElements** contains one or more **null** elements and the calling object does not support **null** elements (optional).
NullPointerException if **saveElements** is **null**.

Color

Package: **java.awt**
Ancestor classes:

```
        Object
          |
        +--Color
```

CONSTRUCTORS

```
    public Color(float r, float g, float b)
```

Constructor that creates a new **Color** with the specified RGB values. The parameters r, g, and b must each be in the range **0.0** to **1.0** (inclusive).

```
    public Color(int r, int g, int b)
```

Constructor that creates a new **Color** with the specified RGB values. The parameters r, g, and b must each be in the range **0** to **255** (inclusive).

METHODS

public **Color brighter()**

Returns a brighter version of the calling object color.

public **Color darker()**

Returns a darker version of the calling object color.

public boolean **equals(Object c)**

Returns **true** if **c** is equal to the calling object color; otherwise returns **false**.

public int **getBlue()**

Returns the blue component of the calling object. The returned value is in the range **0** to **255** (inclusive).

public int **getGreen()**

Returns the green component of the calling object. The returned value is in the range **0** to **255** (inclusive).

public int **getRed()**

Returns the red component of the calling object. The returned value is in the range **0** to **255** (inclusive).

CONSTANTS

Color.BLACK	Color.MAGENTA
Color.BLUE	Color.ORANGE
Color.CYAN	Color.PINK
Color.DARK_GRAY	Color.RED
Color.GRAY	Color.WHITE
Color.GREEN	Color.YELLOW
Color.LIGHT_GRAY	

Comparable **Interface**

Package: `java.lang`
Ancestor interfaces: none
The **Comparable** interface has only one method heading that must be implemented.

public int **compareTo(Object other)**

The method **compareTo** should return
a negative number if the calling object "comes before" the parameter **other**,
a zero if the calling object "equals" the parameter **other**,
and a positive number if the calling object "comes after" the parameter **other**.
The "comes before" ordering that underlies **compareTo** should be a total ordering. Most normal ordering, such as less-than on numbers and lexicographic ordering on strings, are total orderings.

Double

See Section 5.1 in Chapter 5.

File

Package: `java.io`
Ancestor classes:

```
Object
  |
  +--File
```

Many of these methods throw a `SecurityException` if a security manager exists and is unhappy with the method invocation. This is not likely to be a concern for readers of this book and we have not noted this in the method descriptions.

The class `SecurityException` is an unchecked exception class, which means you need not catch it or declare it in a `throws` clause.

public `File(String fileName)`

Constructor. `fileName` can be either a full or a relative path name (which includes the case of a simple file name). `fileName` is referred to as the **abstract path name**.

Throws:

`NullPointerException` if the path name `fileName` is `null`.

public boolean `canRead()`

Tests whether the program can read from the file. Returns `true` if the file named by the abstract path name exists and is readable by the program; otherwise returns `false`.

public boolean `canWrite()`

Tests whether the program can write to the file. Returns `true` if the file named by the abstract path name exists and is writable by the program; otherwise returns `false`.

public boolean `createNewFile()`

Creates a new empty file named by the abstract path name, provided that a file of that name does not already exist. Returns `true` if successful; returns `false` otherwise.

Throws:

`IOException` if an I/O error occurs.

public boolean `delete()`

Tries to delete the file or directory named by the abstract path name. A directory must be empty to be removed. Returns `true` if it was able to delete the file or directory. Returns `false` if it was unable to delete the file or directory.

public boolean `exists()`

Tests whether there is a file with the abstract path name.

public `String getName()`

Returns the last name in the abstract path name (that is, the simple file name). Returns the empty string if the abstract path name is the empty string.

```
public String getPath()
```
Returns the abstract path name as a `String` value.

```
public boolean isDirectory()
```
Returns `true` if a directory (folder) exists that is named by the abstract path name; otherwise returns `false`.

```
public boolean isFile()
```
Returns `true` if a file exists that is named by the abstract path name and the file is a normal file; otherwise returns `false`. The meaning of *normal* is system dependent. Any file created by a Java program is guaranteed to be normal.

```
public long length()
```
Returns the length in bytes of the file named by the abstract path name. If the file does not exist or the abstract path name names a directory, then the value returned is not specified and may be anything.

```
public boolean mkdir()
```
Makes a directory named by the abstract path name. Will not create parent directories. See `mkdirs`. Returns `true` if successful; otherwise returns `false`.

```
public boolean mkdirs()
```
Makes a directory named by the abstract path name. Will create any necessary but nonexistent parent directories. Returns `true` if successful; otherwise returns `false`. Note that if it fails, then some of the parent directories may have been created.

```
public boolean renameTo(File newName)
```
Renames the file represented by the abstract path name to `newName`. Returns `true` if successful; otherwise returns `false`. `newName` can be a relative or absolute path name. This may require moving the file. Whether or not the file can be moved is system dependent.

Throws:

`NullPointerException` if parameter `newName` is null.

```
public boolean setReadOnly()
```
Sets the file represented by the abstract path name to be read only. Returns `true` if successful; otherwise returns `false`.

Float
See Section 5.1 in Chapter 5.

Font

Graphics

Package: `java.awt`
Ancestor classes:

```
        Object
           |
        +--Font
```

CONSTRUCTOR

`public Font(String fontName, int styleModifications, int size)`

Constructor that creates a version of the font named by **fontName** with the specified **styleModifications** and **size**.

CONSTANTS

`Font.BOLD`

Specifies bold style.

`Font.ITALIC`

Specifies italic style.

`Font.PLAIN`

Specifies plain style—that is, not bold and not italic.

NAMES OF Fonts
(These three are guaranteed by Java. Your system will probably have others as well as these.)

`"Monospaced"`

See Chapter 19 for a sample.

`"SansSerif"`

See Chapter 19 for a sample.

`"Serif"`

See Chapter 19 for a sample.

METHOD THAT USES Font

`public abstract void setFont(Font fontObject)`

This method is in the class **Graphics**. Sets the current font of the calling **Graphics** object to **fontObject**.

HashMap<K,V> Class

Package: `java.awt`
Ancestor classes:

```
        Object
          |
        +--Graphics
```

`Graphics` is an abstract class.

Although many of these methods are abstract, we always use them with objects of a concrete descendent class of `Graphics`, even though we usually do not know the name of that concrete class.

```
public abstract void drawRect(int x, int y,
                                int width, int height)
```

Draws the outline of the specified rectangle. (x, y) is the location of the upper-left corner of the rectangle.

```
public abstract void fillRect(int x, int y,
                                int width, int height)
```

Fills the specified rectangle. (x, y) is the location of the upper-left corner of the rectangle.

```
public void draw3DRect(int x, int y, int width,
                                int height, boolean raised)
```

Draws the outline of the specified rectangle. (x, y) is the location of the upper-left corner. The rectangle is highlighted to look like it has thickness. If `raised` is `true`, the highlight makes the rectangle appear to stand out from the background. If `raised` is `false`, the highlight makes the rectangle appear to be sunken into the background.

```
public void fill3DRect(int x, int y, int width,
                                int height, boolean raised)
```

Fills the rectangle specified by

```
draw3DRec(x, y, width, height, raised)
```

```
public abstract void drawArc(int x, int y,
                          int width, int height,
                          int startAngle, int arcSweep)
```

Draws part of an oval that just fits into an invisible rectangle described by the first four arguments. The portion of the oval drawn is given by the last two arguments. See Chapter 19 for details.

```
public abstract void drawLine(int x1, int y1, int x2, int y2)
```

Draws a line between points (x1, y1) and (x2, y2).

```
public abstract void drawOval(int x, int y,
                                int width, int height)
```

Draws the outline of the oval with the smallest enclosing rectangle that has the specified width and height. The (imagined) rectangle has its upper-left corner located at (x, y).

```
    public void drawPolygon(int[] x, int[] y, int points)
```

Draws a polygon through the point
(x[0], y[0]), (x[1], y[1]), ..., (x[points − 1], y[points − 1]).
Always draws a closed polygon. If the first and last points are not equal, it draws a line from the last
to the first point.

```
    public void drawPolyline(int[] x, int[] y, int points)
```

Draws a polygon through the point
(x[0], y[0]), (x[1], y[1]), ..., (x[points − 1], y[points − 1]).
If the first and last points are not equal, the polygon will not be closed.

```
    public abstract void drawRoundRect(int x, int y,
                int width, int height, int arcWidth, int arcHeight)
```

Draws the outline of the specified round-cornered rectangle. (x, y) is the location of the upper-left
corner of the enclosing regular rectangle. arcWidth and arcHeight specify the shape of the round
corners. See the text for details.

```
    public abstract void drawString(String text, int x, int y)
```

Draws the **text** given by the specified string, using this graphics object's current font and color. The
baseline of the leftmost character is at position (x, y) in this graphics object's coordinate system.

```
    public abstract void fillArc(int x, int y,
                        int width, int height,
                        int startAngle, int arcSweep)
```

Fills the partial oval specified by

```
    drawArc(x, y, width, height, startAngle, arcSweep)
```

```
    public abstract void fillOval(int x, int y,
                                    int width, int height)
```

Fills the oval specified by

```
    drawOval(x, y, width, height)
```

```
    public void fillPolygon(int[] x, int[] y, int points)
```

Fills (with color) the polygon specified by

```
    drawPolygon(x,y,points).
```

```
    public abstract void fillRoundRect(int x, int y,
                int width, int height, int arcWidth, int arcHeight)
```

Fills the round rectangle specified by

```
    drawRoundRec(x, y, width, height, arcWidth, arcHeight)
```

```
    public abstract void setFont(Font fontObject)
```

Sets the current font of the calling **Graphics** object to **fontObject**.

Package: `java.util`
Ancestor classes:

```
Object
  |
  +--AbstractMap<K,V>
         |
         +--HashMap<K,V>
```

Implements interfaces: `Map<K,V>`, `Cloneable`, `Serializable`

The `HashMap<K,V>` class implements all of the methods in the `Map<K,V>` interface. The only other methods in the `HashMap<K,V>` class are the constructors.

All the exception classes mentioned are the kind that are not required to be caught in a catch block or declared in a throws clause. All the exception classes mentioned are in the package `java.lang` and so do not require any import statement.

`public HashMap( )`

Creates a new, empty map with a default initial capacity of 16 and load factor of 0.75. The capacity is the number of slots in the hash table. The load factor is the percentage of capacity before the size of the table is automatically increased.

`public HashMap(int initialCapacity)`

Creates a new, empty map with a default capacity of `initialCapacity` and load factor of 0.75.

Throws:

`IllegalArgumentException` if the initial capacity is negative.

`public HashMap(int initialCapacity, float loadFactor)`

Creates a new, empty map with the specified capacity and load factor.

Throws:

`IllegalArgumentException` if the initial capacity or the load factor is negative.

`public HashMap(Map<? extends K,? extends V> m)`

Creates a new map with the same mappings as m. The `initialCapacity` is set to the same size as m and the `loadFactor` to 0.75.

Throws:

`NullPointerException` if m is null.

`public Object clone( )`

Creates a shallow copy of this instance and returns it. The keys and values are not cloned.

The remainder of the methods are the same as those described for the `Map<K,V>` interface.
New background shade

HashSet<T>

Package: `java.util`
Ancestor classes:

```
Object
  |
  +--AbstractCollection<T>
       |
       +--AbstractSet<T>
            |
            +--HashSet<T>
```

Implements interfaces: `Cloneable, Collection<T>, Serializable, Set<T>`
The `HashSet<T>` class implements all of the methods in the `Set<T>` interface. The only other methods in the `HashSet<T>` class are the constructors. The two constructors that do not involve concepts beyond the scope of this book are given below.
All the exception classes mentioned are the kind that are not required to be caught in a **catch** block or declared in a **throws** clause.
All the exception classes mentioned are in the package `java.lang` and so do not require any import statement.

`public HashSet()`

Creates a new, empty set.

`public HashSet(Collection<? extends T> c)`

Creates a new set that contains all the elements of `c`.

Throws:
`NullPointerException` if `c` is `null`.

`public HashSet(int initialCapacity)`

Creates a new, empty set with the specified capacity.

Throws:
`IllegalArgumentException` if `initialCapacity` is less than zero.

The methods are the same as those described for the `Set<T>` interface.

Integer
See Section 5.1 in Chapter 5.

Iterator<T> Interface

Package: `java.util`

Ancestor interfaces: none

All the exception classes mentioned are the kind that are not required to be caught in a `catch` block or declared in a `throws` clause.

`NoSuchElementException` is in the `java.util` package, which requires an `import` statement if your code mentions the `NoSuchElementException` class. All the other exception classes mentioned are in the package `java.lang` and so do not require any `import` statements.

`public boolean hasNext()`

Returns `true` if `next()` has not yet returned all the elements in the collection; returns `false` otherwise.

`public T next()`

Returns the next element of the collection that produced the iterator.

Throws:

`NoSuchElementException` if there is no next element.

`public void remove()` *(Optional)*

Removes from the collection the last element returned by `next`.
This method can be called only once per call to `next`.

Throws:

`IllegalStateException` if the `next` method has not yet been called, or the `remove` method has already been called after the last call to the `next` method.
`UnsupportedOperationException` if the `remove` operation is not supported by this `Iterator`.

JButton

See `AbstractButton`.

JFrame

Package: `javax.swing`

Ancestor classes:

```
Object
  |
  +--Component
        |
        +--Container
              |
              +--Window
                    |
                    +--Frame
                          |
                          +--JFrame
```

```
public JFrame()
```

Constructor that creates an object of the class `JFrame`.

```
public JFrame(String title)
```

Constructor that creates an object of the class `JFrame` with the title given as the argument.

```
public Component add(Component componentAdded)
```

Adds **componentAdded** to the `JFrame`. Typically used as a **void** method.

```
public Container getContentPane()
```

Returns the content pane of the calling `JFrame` object. `Container` is a class in the package `java.awt`.

To set the color of a `JFrame` use

```
getContentPane().setBackground(Color c)
```

If you use **setBackground** without the **getContentPane()**, you will not get any error messages, but you will probably not see the color.

```
public void setDefaultCloseOperation(int operation)
```

Sets the action that will happen by default when the user clicks the close-window button. The argument should be one of the following defined constants:

`JFrame.DO_NOTHING_ON_CLOSE`: Do nothing. The `JFrame` does nothing, but if there are any registered window listeners, they are invoked. (Window listeners are explained in Chapter 17.)
`JFrame.HIDE_ON_CLOSE`: Hide the frame after invoking any registered `WindowListener` objects.
`JFrame.DISPOSE_ON_CLOSE`: Hide and *dispose* the frame after invoking any registered window listeners. When a window is **disposed** it is eliminated but the program does not end. To end the programs, you use the next constant as an argument to `setDefaultCloseOperation`.
`JFrame.EXIT_ON_CLOSE`: Exit the application using the `System exit` method. (Do not use this for frames in applets. Applets are discussed on the accompanying DVD.)

If no action is specified using the method `setDefaultCloseOperation`, then the default action taken is `JFrame.HIDE_ON_CLOSE`.

Throws:

`IllegalArgumentException` if the argument is not one of the values listed above.
`SecurityException` if the argument is `JFrame.EXIT_ON_CLOSE` and the Security Manager will not allow the caller to invoke `System.exit`. (You are not likely to encounter this case.)

```
public void setLayout(LayoutManager manager)
```

Makes **manager** the layout manager for the `JFrame`.

```
public void setSize(int width, int height)
```

Sets the size of the calling frame so that it has the **width** and **height** specified. Pixels are the units of length used.

> **public void setTitle(String title)**
>
> Sets the title for this frame to the argument string.

> **public void dispose()**
>
> Eliminates the calling frame and all its subcomponents. Any memory they use is released for reuse. If there are items left (items other than the calling frame and its subcomponents), then this does not end the program. (The method **dispose** is discussed in Chapter 17.)

> **public void setJMenuBar(JMenuBar menubar)**
>
> Sets the menu bar for the calling frame.

JMenuItem

See AbstractButton.

JPanel

Package: `javax.swing`
Ancestor classes:

```
         Object
            |
         +--Component
               |
            +--Container
                  |
               +--JComponent
                     |
                  +--JPanel
```

> **public JPanel()**
>
> Constructor that creates an object of the class JPanel.

> **public JPanel(LayoutManager manager)**
>
> Constructor that creates an object of the class JPanel with the given layout manager.

> **public Component add(Component componentAdded)**
>
> Adds **componentAdded** to the JPanel. Typically used as a **void** method.

> **public void setBackground(Color c)**
>
> Sets the color of the JPanel.

> **public void setLayout(LayoutManager manager)**
>
> Makes **manager** the layout manager for the JPanel.

JScrollPane

Package: `javax.swing`
Ancestor classes:

```
Object
  |
  +--Component
        |
        +--Container
              |
              +--JComponent
                    |
                    +--JScrollPane
```

public JScrollPane(Component objectToBeScrolled)

Creates a new `JScrollPane` for the `objectToBeScrolled`. Note that the `objectToBeScrolled` need not be a `JTextArea`, although that is the only type of argument considered in this book.

public void setHorizontalScrollBarPolicy(int policy)

Sets the policy for showing the horizontal scroll bar. The `policy` should be one of
```
JScrollPane.HORIZONTAL_SCROLLBAR_ALWAYS
JScrollPane.HORIZONTAL_SCROLLBAR_NEVER
JScrollPane.HORIZONTAL_SCROLLBAR_AS_NEEDED
```
The phrase `AS_NEEDED` means the scroll bar is shown only when it is needed. This is explained more fully in Chapter 17. The meanings of the other policy constants are obvious from their names. (As indicated, these constants are defined in the class `JScrollPane`. You should not need to even be aware of the fact that they have `int` values. Think of them as policies, not as `int` values.)

public void setVerticalScrollBarPolicy(int policy)

Sets the policy for showing the vertical scroll bar. The `policy` should be one of
```
JScrollPane.VERTICAL_SCROLLBAR_ALWAYS
JScrollPane.VERTICAL_SCROLLBAR_NEVER
JScrollPane.VERTICAL_SCROLLBAR_AS_NEEDED
```
The phrase `AS_NEEDED` means the scroll bar is shown only when it is needed. This is explained more fully in Chapter 17. The meanings of the other policy constants are obvious from their names. (As indicated, these constants are defined in the class `JScrollPane`. You should not need to even be aware of the fact that they have `int` values. Think of them as policies, not as `int` values.)

JTextArea

See `JTextComponent`.

JTextComponent

Package: `javax.swing.text`
The classes `JTextField` and `JTextArea` are in the package `javax.swing`.
All these methods are inherited by the classes `JTextField` and `JTextArea`.
Ancestor classes:

```
Object
    |
    +--Component
          |
          +--Container
                |
                +--JComponent
                      |
                      +--JTextComponent
                      |               \
                      +--JTextField   +--JTextArea
```

public **String getText()**

Returns the text that is displayed by this text component.

public boolean **isEditable()**

Returns **true** if the user can write in this text component. Returns **false** if the user is not allowed to write in this text component.

public void **setBackground(Color theColor)**

Sets the background color of this text component.

public void **setEditable(**boolean **argument)**

If **argument** is **true**, then the user is allowed to write in the text component. If **argument** is **false**, then the user is not allowed to write in the text component.

public void **setText(String text)**

Sets the text that is displayed by this text component to be the specified **text**.

JTextField
See JTextComponent.

List<T> **Interface**

Package: `java.util`
Ancestor interfaces: `Collection<T>, Iterable<T>`
All the exception classes mentioned are the kind that are not required to be caught in a `catch` block or declared in a `throws` clause.
All the exception classes mentioned are in the package `java.lang` and so do not require any `import` statement.

CONSTRUCTORS

Although not officially required by the interface, any class that implements the `List<T>` interface should have at least two constructors: a no-argument constructor that creates an empty `List<T>` object, and a constructor with one parameter of type `Collection<? extends T>` that creates a `List<T>` object with the same elements as the constructor argument. If the argument imposes an ordering on its elements, then the `List<T>` created should preserve this ordering.

public boolean contains(Object target)

Returns `true` if the calling object contains at least one instance of `target`. Uses `target.equals` to determine if `target` is in the calling object.

Throws:

`ClassCastException` if the type of `target` is incompatible with the calling object (optional).
`NullPointerException` if `target` is `null` and the calling object does not support `null` elements (optional).

public boolean containsAll(Collection<?> collectionOfTargets)

Returns `true` if the calling object contains all of the elements in `collectionOfTargets`. For `element` in `collectionOfTargets`, uses `element.equals` to determine if `element` is in the calling object. The elements need not be in the same order or have the same multiplicity in `collectionOfTargets` and in the calling object.

public boolean equals(Object other)

If the argument is a `List`, returns `true` if the calling object and the argument contain exactly the same elements in exactly the same order; otherwise returns `false`. If the argument is not a `List`, `false` is returned.

public int hashCode()

Returns the hash code value for the calling object. Neither hash codes nor this method is discussed in this book. This entry is only here to make the definition of the `List` interface complete. You can safely ignore this entry until you go on to study hash codes in a more advanced book. In the meantime, if you need to implement this method, have it throw an `UnsupportedOperationException`.

boolean isEmpty()

Returns `true` if the calling object is empty; otherwise returns `false`.

`Iterator<T> iterator()`

Returns an iterator for the calling object. (Iterators are discussed in Section 16.3.)

`public Object[] toArray()`

Returns an array containing all of the elements in the calling object. The elements in the returned array are in the same order as in the calling object. A new array must be returned so that the calling object has no references to the returned array.

`public <E> E[] toArray(E[] a)`

Note that the type parameter E is not the same as T. So, E can be any reference type; it need not be the type T in `Collection<T>`. For example, E might be an ancestor type of T.
Returns an array containing all of the elements in the calling object. The elements in the returned array are in the same order as in the calling object. The argument a is used primarily to specify the type of the array returned. The exact details are described in the table for the `Collection<T>` interface.

Throws:

`ArrayStoreException` if the type of a is not an ancestor type of the type of every element in the calling object.
`NullPointerException` if a is null.

`public int size()`

Returns the number of elements in the calling object. If the calling object contains more than `Integer.MAX_VALUE` elements, returns `Integer.MAX_VALUE`.

OPTIONAL METHODS

As with the `Collection<T>` interface, the following methods are optional, which means they still must be implemented, but the implementation can simply throw an `UnsupportedOperationException` if for some reason you do not want to give them a "real" implementation. An `UnsupportedOperation-Exception` is a `RunTimeException` and so is not required to be caught or declared in a `throws` clause.

`public boolean add(T element)` *(Optional)*

Adds `element` to the end of the calling object's list. Normally returns `true`. Returns `false` if the operation failed, but if the operation failed, something is seriously wrong and you will probably get a run-time error anyway.

Throws:

`UnsupportedOperationException` if the `add` method is not supported by the calling object.
`ClassCastException` if the class of `element` prevents it from being added to the calling object.
`NullPointerException` if `element` is null and the calling object does not support `null` elements.
`IllegalArgumentException` if some aspect of `element` prevents it from being added to the calling object.

```
public boolean addAll(Collection<? extends T> collectionToAdd)
```
(Optional)

Adds all of the elements in `collectionToAdd` to the end of the calling object's list. The elements are added in the order they are produced by an iterator for `collectionToAdd`.

Throws:

`UnsupportedOperationException` if the `addAll` method is not supported by the calling object.
`ClassCastException` if the class of an element in `collectionToAdd` prevents it from being added to the calling object.
`NullPointerException` if `collectionToAdd` contains one or more `null` elements and the calling object does not support `null` elements, or if `collectionToAdd` is `null`.
`IllegalArgumentException` if some aspect of an element in `collectionToAdd` prevents it from being added to the calling object.

```
public void clear()
```
(Optional)

Removes all the elements from the calling object.

Throws:

`UnsupportedOperationException` if the `clear` method is not supported by the calling object.

```
public boolean remove(Object element)
```
(Optional)

Removes the first occurrence of `element` from the calling object's list, if it is present. Returns `true` if the calling object contained the `element`; returns `false` otherwise.

Throws:

`ClassCastException` if the type of `element` is incompatible with the calling object (optional).
`NullPointerException` if `element` is `null` and the calling object does not support `null` elements (optional).
`UnsupportedOperationException` if the `remove` method is not supported by the calling object.

```
public boolean removeAll(Collection<?> collectionToRemove)
```
(Optional)

Removes all the calling object's elements that are also in `collectionToRemove`. Returns `true` if the calling object was changed; otherwise returns `false`.

Throws:

`UnsupportedOperationException` if the `removeAll` method is not supported by the calling object.
`ClassCastException` if the types of one or more elements in the calling object are incompatible with `collectionToRemove` (optional).
`NullPointerException` if the calling object contains one or more `null` elements and `collection-ToRemove` does not support `null` elements (optional).
`NullPointerException` if `collectionToRemove` is `null`.

```
public boolean retainAll(Collection<?> saveElements) (Optional)
```

Retains only the elements in the calling object that are also in the collection `saveElements`. In other words, removes from the calling object all of its elements that are not contained in the collection `saveElements`. Returns `true` if the calling object was changed; otherwise returns `false`.

Throws:

`UnsupportedOperationException` if the `retainAll` method is not supported by the calling object.
`ClassCastException` if the types of one or more elements in the calling object are incompatible with `saveElements` (optional).
`NullPointerException` if the calling object contains one or more `null` elements and `saveElements` does not support `null` elements (optional).
`NullPointerException` if the collection `saveElements` is `null`.

NEW METHOD HEADINGS

The following methods are in the `List<T>` interface but were not in the `Collection<T>` interface. Those that are optional are noted.

```
public void add(int index, T newElement) (Optional)
```

Inserts `newElement` in the calling object's list at location `index`. The old elements at location `index` and higher are moved to higher indices.

Throws:

`IndexOutOfBoundsException` if the `index` is not in the range:
`0 <= index <= size()`.
`UnsupportedOperationException` if this `add` method is not supported by the calling object.
`ClassCastException` if the class of `newElement` prevents it from being added to the calling object.
`NullPointerException` if `newElement` is `null` and the calling object does not support `null` elements.
`IllegalArgumentException` if some aspect of `newElement` prevents it from being added to the calling object.

```
public boolean addAll(int index,
             Collection<? extends T> collectionToAdd) (Optional)
```

Inserts all of the elements in `collectionToAdd` to the calling object's list starting at location `index`. The old elements at location `index` and higher are moved to higher indices. The elements are added in the order they are produced by an iterator for `collectionToAdd`. Returns `true` if successful; otherwise returns `false`.

Throws:

`IndexOutOfBoundsException` if the `index` is not in the range:
`0 <= index <= size()`.
`UnsupportedOperationException` if the `addAll` method is not supported by the calling object.
`ClassCastException` if the class of one of the elements of `collectionToAdd` prevents it from being added to the calling object.
`NullPointerException` if `collectionToAdd` contains one or more `null` elements and the calling object does not support `null` elements, or if `collectionToAdd` is `null`.
`IllegalArgumentException` if some aspect of one of the elements of `collectionToAdd` prevents it from being added to the calling object.

```
public int indexOf(Object target)
```

Returns the index of the first element that is equal to **target**. Uses the method **equals** of the object **target** to test for equality. Returns −1 if **target** is not found.

Throws:

ClassCastException if the type of **target** is incompatible with the calling object (optional). **NullPointerException** if **target** is **null** and the calling object does not support **null** elements (optional).

```
public int lastIndexOf(Object target)
```

Returns the index of the last element that is equal to **target**. Uses the method **equals** of the object **target** to test for equality. Returns −1 if **target** is not found.

Throws:

ClassCastException if the type of **target** is incompatible with the calling object (optional). **NullPointerException** if **target** is **null** and the calling object does not support **null** elements (optional).

```
public List<T> subList(int fromIndex, int toIndex)
```

Returns a *view* of the elements at locations **fromIndex** to **toIndex** of the calling object; the object at **fromIndex** is included; the object, if any, at **toIndex** is not included. The *view* uses references into the calling object; so, changing the view can change the calling object. The returned object will be of type **List<T>** but need not be of the same type as the calling object. Returns an empty **List<T>** if **fromIndex** equals **toIndex**.

Throws:

IndexOutOfBoundsException if **fromIndex** and **toIndex** do not satisfy: 0 <= fromIndex <= toIndex <= size().

```
ListIterator<T> listIterator()
```

Returns a list iterator for the calling object. (Iterators are discussed in Section 16.3.)

```
ListIterator<T> listIterator(int index)
```

Returns a list iterator for the calling object starting at **index**. The first element to be returned by the iterator is the one at **index**. (Iterators are discussed in Section 16.3.)

Throws:

IndexOutOfBoundsException if **index** does not satisfy: 0 <= index <= size()

```
public T get(int index)
```

Returns the object at position **index**.
Throws an **IndexOutOfBoundsException** if the **index** is not in the range: 0 <= index < size().

`public T remove(int index)` *(Optional)*

Removes the element at position `index` in the calling object. Shifts any subsequent elements to the left (subtracts one from their indices). Returns the element that was removed from the calling object.

Throws:

`UnsupportedOperationException` if the `remove` method is not supported by the calling object.
`IndexOutOfBoundsException` if index does not satisfy:
`0 <= index < size()`

`public T set(int index, T newElement)` *(Optional)*

Sets the element at the specified `index` to `newElement`. The element previously at that position is returned.

Throws:

`IndexOutOfBoundsException` if the `index` is not in the range:
`0 <= index < size()`.
`UnsupportedOperationException` if the `set` method is not supported by the calling object.
`ClassCastException` if the class of `newElement` prevents it from being added to the calling object.
`NullPointerException` if `newElement` is `null` and the calling object does not support `null` elements.
`IllegalArgumentException` if some aspect of `newElement` prevents it from being added to the calling object.

`ListIterator<T>` Interface

Package: `java.util`
Ancestor interfaces: `Iterator<T>`
The *cursor position* is explained in Chapter 16.
All the exception classes mentioned are the kind that are not required to be caught in a `catch` block or declared in a `throws` clause.
`NoSuchElementException` is in the `java.util` package, which requires an `import` statement if your code mentions the `NoSuchElementException` class. All the other exception classes mentioned are in the package `java.lang` and so do not require any `import` statements.

`public void add(T newElement)` *(Optional)*

Inserts `newElement` at the location of the iterator cursor (that is, before the value, if any, that would be returned by `next()` and after the value, if any, that would be returned by `previous()`). Cannot be used if there has been a call to `add` or `remove` since the last call to `next()` or `previous()`.

Throws:

`IllegalStateException` if neither `next()` nor `previous()` has been called, or the `add` or `remove` method has already been called after the last call to `next()` or `previous()`.
`UnsupportedOperationException` if the `remove` operation is not supported by this `Iterator`.
`ClassCastException` if the class of `newElement` prevents it from being added.
`IllegalArgumentException` if some property other than the class of `newElement` prevents it from being added.

`public boolean hasNext()`

Returns **true** if there is a suitable element for **next()** to return; returns **false** otherwise.

`public boolean hasPrevious()`

Returns **true** if there is a suitable element for **previous()** to return; returns **false** otherwise.

`public int nextIndex()`

Returns the index of the element that would be returned by a call to **next()**. Returns the list size if the cursor position is at the end of the list.

`public T next()`

Returns the next element of the list that produced the iterator. More specifically, returns the element immediately after the cursor position.

Throws:

NoSuchElementException if there is no next element.

`public T previous()`

Returns the previous element of the list that produced the iterator. More specifically, returns the element immediately before the cursor position.

Throws:

NoSuchElementException if there is no previous element.

`public int previousIndex()`

Returns the index that would be returned by a call to **previous()**. Returns −1 if the cursor position is at the beginning of the list.

`public void remove()` *(Optional)*

Removes from the collection the last element returned by **next()** or **previous()**.
This method can be called only once per call to **next()** or **previous()**.
Cannot be used if there has been a call to **add** or **remove** since the last call to **next()** or **previous()**.

Throws:

IllegalStateException if neither **next()** nor **previous()** has been called, or the **add** or **remove** method has already been called after the last call to **next()** or **previous()**.
UnsupportedOperationException if the **remove** operation is not supported by this **Iterator**.

```
public void set(T newElement) (Optional)
```

Replaces the last element returned by `next()` or `previous()` with `newElement`.
Cannot be used if there has been a call to **add** or **remove** since the last call to `next()` or `previous()`.

Throws:

`UnsupportedOperationException` if the **set** operation is not supported by this `Iterator`.
`IllegalStateException` if neither `next()` nor `previous()` has been called, or the **add** or **remove** method has been called since the last call to `next()` or `previous()`.
`ClassCastException` if the class of **newElement** prevents it from being added.
`IllegalArgumentException` if some property other than the class of **newElement** prevents it from being added.

Long

See Section 5.1 in Chapter 5.

Math

Package: `java.lang`

```
        Object
          |
        +--Math
```

The `Math` class is marked `final`, which means it cannot be used as a base class to derive other classes.

```
public static double abs(double argument)

public static float abs(float argument)

public static long abs(long argument)

public static int abs(int argument)
```

Returns the absolute value of the **argument**. (The method name **abs** is overloaded to produce four similar methods.)

EXAMPLES

`Math.abs(-6)` and `Math.abs(6)` both return 6. `Math.abs(-5.5)` and `Math.abs(5.5)` both return 5.5.

```
public static double ceil(double argument)
```

Returns the smallest whole number greater than or equal to the **argument**.

EXAMPLE

`Math.ceil(3.2)` and `Math.ceil(3.9)` both return 4.0.

```
    public static double floor(double argument)
```
Returns the largest whole number less than or equal to the `argument`.

EXAMPLE

`Math.floor(3.2)` and `Math.floor(3.9)` both return `3.0`.

```
    public static double max(double n1, double n2)
  , public static float max(float n1, float n2)
    public static long max(long n1, long n2)
    public static int max(int n1, int n2)
```
Returns the maximum of the arguments `n1` and `n2`. (The method name `max` is overloaded to produce four similar methods.)

EXAMPLE

`Math.max(3, 2)` returns `3`.

```
    public static double min(double n1, double n2)
    public static float min(float n1, float n2)
    public static long min(long n1, long n2)
    public static int min(int n1, int n2)
```
Returns the minimum of the arguments `n1` and `n2`. (The method name `min` is overloaded to produce four similar methods.)

EXAMPLE

`Math.min(3, 2)` returns `2`.

```
    public static double pow(double base, double exponent)
```
Returns `base` to the power `exponent`.

EXAMPLE

`Math.pow(2.0,3.0)` returns `8.0`.

```
    public static long round(double argument)
    public static int round(float argument)
```
Rounds its `argument`.

EXAMPLES

`Math.round(3.2)` returns `3`. `Math.round(3.6)` returns `4`.

```
    public static double sqrt(double argument)
```
Returns the square root of its `argument`.

EXAMPLE

`Math.sqrt(4)` returns `2.0`.

Map<K,V> Interface

Package: `java.util`
Ancestor interfaces: None
All the exception classes mentioned are unchecked exceptions, which means they are not required to be caught in a **catch** block or declared in a **throws** clause. No **import** statement is required since these exception classes are in the package `java.lang`.

CONSTRUCTORS

Although not officially required by the interface, any class that implements the Map<K,V> interface should have at least two constructors: a no-argument constructor that creates an empty Map<K,V> object, and a constructor with one Map<K,V> parameter that creates a Map<K,V> object with the same elements as the constructor argument. The interface does not specify whether the copy produced by the one-argument constructor is a shallow copy or a deep copy of its argument.

METHODS

```
public boolean containsKey(Object key)
```

Returns **true** if the calling object contains **key** as one of its keys.

Throws:

`ClassCastException` if the type of **key** is incompatible with the type for this map (optional).
`NullPointerException` if the key is **null** and this map does not permit **null** keys (optional).

```
public boolean containsValue(Object value)
```

Returns **true** if the calling object contains one or more keys that map to an instance of **value**.

Throws:

`ClassCastException` if the type of **value** is incompatible with the type for this map (optional).
`NullPointerException` if the value is **null** and this map does not permit **null** values (optional).

```
public Set<Map.Entry<K,V>> entrySet( )
```

Returns a set view consisting of (key, value) mappings for all entries in the map. Changes to the map are reflected in the set and vice-versa.

```
public boolean equals(Object other)
```

This is the **equals** of the map, not the **equals** of the elements in the map. Overrides the inherited method **equals**.

```
public V get(Object key)
```

Returns the value onto which the calling object maps **key**. If **key** is not in the map then **null** is returned. Note that this does not always mean that the key is not in the map, since it is possible to map a key to **null**. The **containsKey** method can be used to distinguish the two cases.

Throws:

`ClassCastException` if the type of **key** is incompatible with the type for this map (optional).

`NullPointerException` if the key is **null** and this map does not permit **null** keys (optional).

> ### public int hashCode( )

Returns the hash code value for the calling object. The hash code of a map is defined to be the sum of the hashCodes of each entry in the map's entrySet view.

> ### public boolean isEmpty( )

Returns true if the calling object is empty; otherwise returns `false`.

> ### public int size( )

Returns the number of (key, value) mappings in the calling object.

> ### public Collection<V> values( )

Returns a collection view consisting of all values in the map. Changes to the map are reflected in the collection and vice-versa.

OPTIONAL METHODS

The following methods are optional, which means they still must be implemented, but the implementation can simply throw an `UnsupportedOperationException` if, for some reason, you do not want to give them a "real" implementation. An `UnsupportedOperationException` is a `RunTimeException` and so is not required to be caught or declared in a `throws` clause.

> ### public V put(K key, V value) *(Optional)*

Associates **key** to **value** in the map. If **key** was associated with an existing value then the old value is overwritten and returned. Otherwise `null` is returned.

Throws:

`ClassCastException` if the type of **key** or **value** is incompatible with the type for this map (optional).
`NullPointerException` if the key or value is `null` and this map does not permit `null` keys or values (optional).
`IllegalArgumentException` if some aspect of the key or value prevents it from being stored in this map (optional).
`UnsupportedOperationException` if the put operation is not supported by this map (optional).

> ### public void putAll(Map<? extends K,? extends V> mapToAdd) *(Optional)*

Adds all mappings of **mapToAdd** into the calling object's map.

Throws:

`ClassCastException` if any type of **key** or **value** of **mapToAdd** is incompatible with the type for this map (optional).
`NullPointerException` if **mapToAdd** is `null` or any key or value of **mapToAdd** is null and this map does not permit null keys or values (optional).
`IllegalArgumentException` if some aspect of the key or value from **mapToAdd** prevents it from being stored in this map (optional).
`UnsupportedOperationException` if the **putAll** operation is not supported by this map (optional).

```
    public V remove(Object key) (Optional)
```

Removes the mapping for the specified key. If the key is not found in the map then **null** is returned, otherwise the previous value for the key is returned.

Throws:

ClassCastException if the type of **key** is incompatible with the type for this map (optional).
NullPointerException if the key is **null** and this map does not permit **null** keys (optional).
UnsupportedOperationException if the remove operation is not supported by this map (optional).

ObjectInputStream

Package: **java.io**
The **FileInputStream** class is also in this package.
Ancestor classes:

```
        Object
          |
        +--InputStream
              |
            +--ObjectInputStream
```

```
    public ObjectInputStream(InputStream streamObject)
```

There is no constructor that takes a file name as an argument. If you want to create a stream using a file name, you use

```
    new ObjectInputStream(new FileInputStream(File_Name))
```

Alternatively, you can use an object of the class **File** in place of the *File_Name*, as follows:

```
    new ObjectInputStream(new FileInputStream(File_Object))
```

The constructor for **FileInputStream** may throw a **FileNotFoundException**, which is a kind of **IOException**. If the **FileInputStream** constructor succeeds, then the constructor for **ObjectInputStream** may throw a different **IOException**.

```
    public void close() throws IOException
```

Closes the stream's connection to a file.

```
    public boolean readBoolean() throws IOException
```

Reads a **boolean** value from the input stream and returns that **boolean** value. If **readBoolean** tries to read a value from the file and that value was not written using the method **writeBoolean** of the class **ObjectOutputStream** (or written in some equivalent way), then problems will occur.

If an attempt is made to read beyond the end of the file, an **EOFException** is thrown.

```
public char readChar() throws IOException
```

Reads a **char** value from the input stream and returns that **char** value. If **readChar** tries to read a value from the file and that value was not written using the method **writeChar** of the class **ObjectOutputStream** (or written in some equivalent way), then problems will occur.

If an attempt is made to read beyond the end of the file, an **EOFException** is thrown.

```
public double readDouble() throws IOException
```

Reads a **double** value from the input stream and returns that **double** value. If **readDouble** tries to read a value from the file and that value was not written using the method **writeDouble** of the class **ObjectOutputStream** (or written in some equivalent way), then problems will occur.

If an attempt is made to read beyond the end of the file, an **EOFException** is thrown.

```
public float readFloat() throws IOException
```

Reads a **float** value from the input stream and returns that **float** value. If **readFloat** tries to read a value from the file and that value was not written using the method **writeFloat** of the class **ObjectOutputStream** (or written in some equivalent way), then problems will occur.

If an attempt is made to read beyond the end of the file, an **EOFException** is thrown.

```
public int readInt() throws IOException
```

Reads an **int** value from the input stream and returns that **int** value. If **readInt** tries to read a value from the file and that value was not written using the method **writeInt** of the class **ObjectOutput-Stream** (or written in some equivalent way), then problems will occur.

If an attempt is made to read beyond the end of the file, an **EOFException** is thrown.

```
public long readLong() throws IOException
```

Reads a **long** value from the input stream and returns that **long** value. If **readLong** tries to read a value from the file and that value was not written using the method **writeLong** of the class **ObjectOutputStream** (or written in some equivalent way), then problems will occur.

If an attempt is made to read beyond the end of the file, an **EOFException** is thrown.

```
Object readObject( ) throws ClassNotFoundException, IOException
```

Reads an object from the input stream. The object read should have been written using **writeObject** of the class **ObjectOutputStream**.

Throws:

ClassNotFoundException if the class of a serialized object cannot be found.
If an attempt is made to read beyond the end of the file, an **EOFException** is thrown. May throw various other **IOException**s.

```
public int readShort() throws IOException
```

Reads a **short** value from the input stream and returns that **short** value. If **readInt** tries to read a value from the file and that value was not written using the method **writeShort** of the class **ObjectOutputStream** (or written in some equivalent way), then problems will occur.

If an attempt is made to read beyond the end of the file, an **EOFException** is thrown.

```
public String readUTF() throws IOException
```

Reads a **String** value from the input stream and returns that **String** value. If **readUTF** tries to read a value from the file and that value was not written using the method **writeUTF** of the class **ObjectOutputStream** (or written in some equivalent way), then problems will occur.

If an attempt is made to read beyond the end of the file, an **EOFException** is thrown.

```
public int skipBytes(int n) throws IOException
```

Skips **n** bytes.

ObjectOutputStream

Package: **java.io**
The **FileOutputStream** class is also in this package.
Ancestor classes:

```
Object
  |
  +--OutputStream
        |
        +--ObjectOutputStream
```

```
public ObjectOutputStream(OutputStream streamObject)
```

There is no constructor that takes a file name as an argument. If you want to create a stream using a file name, you use

```
new ObjectOutputStream(new FileOutputStream(File_Name))
```

This creates a blank file. If there already is a file named *File_Name*, then the old contents of the file are lost.
If you want to create a stream using an object of the class **File**, you use

```
new ObjectOutputStream(new FileOutputStream(File_Object))
```

The constructor for **FileOutputStream** may throw a **FileNotFoundException**, which is a kind of **IOException**. If the **FileOutputStream** constructor succeeds, then the constructor for **ObjectOutputStream** may throw a different **IOException**.

```
public void close() throws IOException
```

Closes the stream's connection to a file. This method calls **flush** before closing the file.

```
public void flush() throws IOException
```

Flushes the output stream. This forces an actual physical write to the file of any data that has been buffered and not yet physically written to the file. Normally, you should not need to invoke `flush`.

```
public void writeBoolean(boolean b) throws IOException
```

Writes the `boolean` value **b** to the output stream.

```
public void writeChar(int n) throws IOException
```

Writes the `char` value n to the output stream. Note that it expects its argument to be an `int` value. However, if you simply use the `char` value, then Java will automatically type cast it to an `int` value. The following are equivalent:

```
outputStream.writeChar((int)'A');
```

and

```
outputStream.writeChar('A');
```

```
public void writeDouble(double x) throws IOException
```

Writes the `double` value **x** to the output stream.

```
public void writeFloat(float x) throws IOException
```

Writes the `float` value **x** to the output stream.

```
public void writeInt(int n) throws IOException
```

Writes the `int` value **n** to the output stream.

```
public void writeLong(long n) throws IOException
```

Writes the `long` value **n** to the output stream.

```
public void writeObject(Object anObject) throws IOException
```

Writes its argument to the output stream. The object argument should be an object of a serializable class, a concept discussed in Chapter 10.

Throws:

Various `IOExceptions`.

```
public void writeShort(short n) throws IOException
```

Writes the `short` value **n** to the output stream.

```
public void writeUTF(String aString) throws IOException
```

Writes the `String` value **aString** to the output stream. UTF refers to a particular method of encoding the string. To read the string back from the file, you should use the method **readUTF** of the class `ObjectInputStream`.

PrintWriter

Package: `java.io`
The `FileOutputStream` class is also in this package.
Ancestor classes:

```
        Object
          |
          +--Writer
                |
                +--PrintWriter
```

public PrintWriter(OutputStream streamObject)

This is the only constructor you are likely to need. There is no constructor that accepts a file name as an argument. If you want to create a stream using a file name, you use

```
new PrintWriter(new FileOutputStream(File_Name))
```

When the constructor is used in this way, a blank file is created. If there already was a file named *File_Name*, then the old contents of the file are lost. If you want instead to append new text to the end of the old file contents, use

```
new PrintWriter(new FileOutputStream(File_Name, true))
```

(For an explanation of the argument `true`, see Chapter 10.)
When used in either of these ways, the `FileOutputStream` constructor, and so the `PrintWriter` constructor invocation, can throw a `FileNotFoundException`, which is a kind of `IOException`. If you want to create a stream using an object of the class `File`, you can use a `File` object in place of the *File_Name*.

public void close()

Closes the stream's connection to a file. This method calls `flush` before closing the file.

public void flush()

Flushes the output stream. This forces an actual physical write to the file of any data that has been buffered and not yet physically written to the file. Normally, you should not need to invoke `flush`.

public final void print(*Argument*)

Same as `println`, except that this method does not end the line, and so the next output will be on the same line.

public final void println(*Argument*)

The *Argument* can be a string, character, integer, floating-point number, boolean value, or any combination of these, connected with + signs. The *Argument* can also be any object, although it will not work as desired unless the object has a properly defined `toString()` method. The *Argument* is output to the file connected to the stream. After the *Argument* has been output, the line ends, and so the next output is sent to the next line.

RandomAccessFile

Package: `java.io`

```
Object
  |
  +--RandomAccessFile
```

public **RandomAccessFile**(String fileName, String mode)

public **RandomAccessFile**(File fileObject, String mode)

Opens the file, does not delete data already in the file, but does position the file pointer at the first (zeroth) location.
The **mode** must be one of the following:
"r" Open for reading only.
"rw" Open for reading and writing.
"rws" Same as **"rw"**, and also requires that every update to the file's content or metadata be written synchronously to the underlying storage device.
"rwd" Same as **"rw"**, and also requires that every update to the file's content be written synchronously to the underlying storage device.
"rws" and **"rwd"** are not covered in this book.

public void **close**() throws IOException

Closes the stream's connection to a file.

public void **setLength**(long newLength) throws IOException

Sets the length of this file.
If the present length of the file as returned by the **length** method is greater than the **newLength** argument, then the file will be truncated. In this case, if the file pointer location as returned by the **getFilePointer** method is greater than **newLength**, then after this method returns, the file pointer location will be equal to **newLength**.
If the present length of the file as returned by the **length** method is smaller than **newLength**, then the file will be extended. In this case, the contents of the extended portion of the file are not defined.

public long **getFilePointer**() throws IOException

Returns the current location of the file pointer. Locations are numbered starting with 0.

public long **length**() throws IOException

Returns the length of the file.

public int **read**() throws IOException

Reads a byte of data from the file and returns it as an integer in the range 0 to 255.

```
public int read(byte[] a) throws IOException
```

Reads up to `a.length` bytes of data from the file into the array of bytes. Returns the total number of bytes read or -1 if the end of the file is reached.

```
public final boolean readBoolean() throws IOException
```

Reads a `boolean` value from the file and returns that value.

If an attempt is made to read beyond the end of the file, an `EOFException` is thrown.

```
public final byte readByte() throws IOException
```

Reads a `byte` value from the file and returns that value.

If an attempt is made to read beyond the end of the file, an `EOFException` is thrown.

```
public final char readChar() throws IOException
```

Reads a `char` value from the file and returns that value.

If an attempt is made to read beyond the end of the file, an `EOFException` is thrown.

```
public final double readDouble() throws IOException
```

Reads a `double` value from the file and returns that value.

If an attempt is made to read beyond the end of the file, an `EOFException` is thrown.

```
public final float readFloat() throws IOException
```

Reads a `float` value from the file and returns that value.

If an attempt is made to read beyond the end of the file, an `EOFException` is thrown.

```
public final int readInt() throws IOException
```

Reads an `int` value from the file and returns that value.

If an attempt is made to read beyond the end of the file, an `EOFException` is thrown.

```
public final long readLong() throws IOException
```

Reads a `long` value from the file and returns that value.

If an attempt is made to read beyond the end of the file, an `EOFException` is thrown.

```
public final short readShort() throws IOException
```

Reads a `short` value from the file and returns that value.

If an attempt is made to read beyond the end of the file, an `EOFException` is thrown.

```
public final String readUTF() throws IOException
```
Reads a String value from the file and returns that value.

If an attempt is made to read beyond the end of the file, an EOFException is thrown.

```
public void seek(long location) throws IOException
```
Moves the file pointer to the specified location.

```
public void write(byte[] a) throws IOException
```
Writes a.length bytes from the specified byte array to the file.

```
public void write(int b) throws IOException
```
Writes the specified byte to the file.

```
public final void writeBoolean(boolean b) throws IOException
```
Writes the boolean b to the file.

```
public final void writeByte(byte b) throws IOException
```
Writes the byte b to the file.

```
public final void writeChar(char c) throws IOException
```
Writes the char c to the file.

```
public final void writeDouble(double d) throws IOException
```
Writes the double d to the file.

```
public final void writeFloat(float f) throws IOException
```
Writes the float f to the file.

```
public final void writeInt(int n) throws IOException
```
Writes the int n to the file.

```
public final void writeLong(long n) throws IOException
```
Writes the long n to the file.

```
public final void writeShort(short n) throws IOException
```
Writes the short n to the file.

```
public final void writeUTF(String s) throws IOException
```
Writes the String s to the file.

Scanner

Package: `java.util`
Ancestor classes:

```
Object
   |
   +--Scanner
```

The `Scanner` class can be used to obtain input from files as well as from the keyboard. Values to be read should be separated by whitespace characters, such as blanks and/or new lines. When reading values, these whitespace characters are skipped. (It is possible to change the separators from whitespace to something else, but white-space is the default.)

`public Scanner(InputStream streamObject)`

There is no constructor that accepts a file name as an argument. If you want to create a stream using a file name, you can use

`new Scanner(new FileInputStream(File_Name))`

When used in this way, the `FileInputStream` constructor, and thus the `Scanner` constructor invocation, can throw a `FileNotFoundException`, which is a kind of `IOException`.
To create a stream connected to the keyboard use

`new Scanner(System.in)`

`public Scanner(File fileObject)`

If you want to create a stream using a file name, you can use

`new Scanner(new File(File_Name))`

`public int nextInt()`

Returns the next token as an `int`, provided the next token is a well-formed string representation of an `int`.

Throws:

`NoSuchElementException` if there are no more tokens.

`InputMismatchException` if the next token is not a well-formed string representation of an `int`.

`IllegalStateException` if the `Scanner` stream is closed.

`public boolean hasNextInt()`

Returns `true` if the next token is a well-formed string representation of an `int`; otherwise returns `false`.

Throws:

`IllegalStateException` if the `Scanner` stream is closed.

```
public long nextLong()
```

Returns the next token as a **long**, provided the next token is a well-formed string representation of a **long**.

Throws:

NoSuchElementException if there are no more tokens.

InputMismatchException if the next token is not a well-formed string representation of a **long**.

IllegalStateException if the **Scanner** stream is closed.

```
public boolean hasNextLong()
```

Returns **true** if the next token is a well-formed string representation of a **long**; otherwise returns **false**.

Throws:

IllegalStateException if the **Scanner** stream is closed.

```
public byte nextByte()
```

Returns the next token as a **byte**, provided the next token is a well-formed string representation of a **byte**.

Throws:

NoSuchElementException if there are no more tokens.

InputMismatchException if the next token is not a well-formed string representation of a **byte**.

IllegalStateException if the **Scanner** stream is closed.

```
public boolean hasNextByte()
```

Returns **true** if the next token is a well-formed string representation of a **byte**; otherwise returns **false**.

Throws:

IllegalStateException if the **Scanner** stream is closed.

```
public short nextShort()
```

Returns the next token as a **short**, provided the next token is a well-formed string representation of a **short**.

Throws:

NoSuchElementException if there are no more tokens.

InputMismatchException if the next token is not a well-formed string representation of a **short**.

IllegalStateException if the **Scanner** stream is closed.

```
public boolean hasNextShort()
```

Returns **true** if the next token is a well-formed string representation of a **short**; otherwise returns **false**.

Throws:

IllegalStateException if the **Scanner** stream is closed.

```
public double nextDouble()
```

Returns the next token as a **double**, provided the next token is a well-formed string representation of a **double**.

Throws:

NoSuchElementException if there are no more tokens.

InputMismatchException if the next token is not a well-formed string representation of a **double**.

IllegalStateException if the **Scanner** stream is closed.

```
public boolean hasNextDouble()
```

Returns **true** if the next token is a well-formed string representation of a **double**; otherwise returns **false**.

Throws:

IllegalStateException if the **Scanner** stream is closed.

```
public float nextFloat()
```

Returns the next token as a **float**, provided the next token is a well-formed string representation of a **float**.

Throws:

NoSuchElementException if there are no more tokens.

InputMismatchException if the next token is not a well-formed string representation of a **float**.

IllegalStateException if the **Scanner** stream is closed.

```
public boolean hasNextFloat()
```

Returns **true** if the next token is a well-formed string representation of a **float**; otherwise returns **false**.

Throws:

IllegalStateException if the **Scanner** stream is closed.

```
public String next()
```

Returns the **next token**.

Throws:

NoSuchElementException if there are no more tokens.

IllegalStateException if the **Scanner** stream is closed.

```
public boolean hasNext()
```

Returns **true** if there is another token. May wait for a next token to enter the stream.

Throws:

IllegalStateException if the Scanner stream is closed.

```
public boolean nextBoolean()
```

Returns the next token as a **boolean** value, provided the next token is a well-formed string representation of a **boolean**.

Throws:

NoSuchElementException if there are no more tokens.

InputMismatchException if the next token is not a well-formed string representation of a **boolean** value.

IllegalStateException if the Scanner stream is closed.

```
public boolean hasNextBoolean()
```

Returns **true** if the next token is a well-formed string representation of a **boolean** value; otherwise returns **false**.

Throws:

IllegalStateException if the Scanner stream is closed.

```
public String nextLine()
```

Returns the rest of the current input line. Note that the line terminator '\n' is read and discarded; it is not included in the string returned.

Throws:

NoSuchElementException if there are no more lines.

IllegalStateException if the Scanner stream is closed.

```
public boolean hasNextLine()
```

Returns **true** if there is a next line. May wait for a next line to enter the stream.

Throws:

IllegalStateException if the Scanner stream is closed.

```
public Scanner useDelimiter(String newDelimiter);
```

Changes the delimiter for input so that **newDelimiter** will be the only delimiter that separates words or numbers. See the subsection "Other Input Delimiters" in Chapter 2 for the details. (You can use this method to set the delimiters to a more complex pattern than just a single string, but we are not covering that.)

Returns the calling object, but we have always used it as a **void** method.

Serializable Interface

See Section 10.4 in Chapter 10.

Set<T> Interface

Package: `java.util`
Ancestor interfaces: `Collection<T>`
All the exception classes mentioned are the kind that are not required to be caught in a `catch` block or declared in a `throws` clause.
All the exception classes mentioned are in the package `java.lang` and so do not require any `import` statement.

CONSTRUCTORS

Although not officially required by the interface, any class that implements the `Set<T>` interface should have at least two constructors: a no-argument constructor that creates an empty `Set<T>` object, and a constructor with one parameter of type `Collection<? extends T>` that creates a `Set<T>` object with the same elements as the constructor argument.

```
public boolean contains(Object target)
```

Returns `true` if the calling object contains at least one instance of `target`. Uses `target.equals` to determine if `target` is in the calling object.

Throws:

`ClassCastException` if the type of `target` is incompatible with the calling object (optional).
`NullPointerException` if `target` is `null` and the calling object does not support `null` elements (optional).

```
public boolean containsAll(Collection<?> collectionOfTargets)
```

Returns `true` if the calling object contains all of the elements in `collectionOfTargets`. For `element` in `collectionOfTargets`, this method uses `element.equals` to determine if `element` is in the calling object. If `collectionOfTargets` is itself a `Set<T>`, this is a test to see if `collectionOfTargets` is a subset of the calling object.

Throws:

`ClassCastException` if the types of one or more elements in `collectionOfTargets` are incompatible with the calling object (optional).
`NullPointerException` if `collectionOfTargets` contains one or more `null` elements and the calling object does not support `null` elements (optional).
`NullPointerException` if `collectionOfTargets` is `null`.

```
public boolean equals(Object other)
```

If the argument is a `Set<T>`, returns `true` if the calling object and the argument contain exactly the same elements; otherwise returns `false`. If the argument is not a `Set<T>`, `false` is returned.

```
public int hashCode()
```

Returns the hash code value for the calling object. Neither hash codes nor this method is discussed in this book. This entry is only here to make the definition of the **Set<T>** interface complete. You can safely ignore this entry until you go on to study hash codes in a more advanced book. In the meantime, if you need to implement this method, have it throw an **UnsupportedOperationException**.

```
public boolean isEmpty()
```

Returns **true** if the calling object is empty; otherwise returns **false**.

```
Iterator<T> iterator()
```

Returns an iterator for the calling object. (Iterators are discussed in Section 16.2.)

```
public Object[] toArray()
```

Returns an array containing all of the elements in the calling object. A new array should be returned so that the calling object has no references to the returned array.

```
public <E> E[] toArray(E[] a)
```

Note that the type parameter E is not the same as T. So, E can be any reference type; it need not be the type T in **Collection<T>**. For example, E might be an ancestor type of T.
Returns an array containing all of the elements in the calling object. The argument *a* is used primarily to specify the type of the array returned. The exact details are described in the table for the **Collection<T>** interface.

Throws:

ArrayStoreException if the type of *a* is not an ancestor type of the type of every element in the calling object.
NullPointerException if *a* is **null**.

```
public int size()
```

Returns the number of elements in the calling object. If the calling object contains more than **Integer.MAX_VALUE** elements, returns **Integer.MAX_VALUE**.

ADDING AND REMOVING ELEMENTS

Although many are optional, the following methods are almost always implemented for classes that implement the **Set<T>** interface.

```
public boolean add(T element) (Optional)
```

If **element** is not already in the calling object, **element** is added to the calling object and **true** is returned. If **element** is in the calling object, the calling object is unchanged and **false** is returned.

Throws:

UnsupportedOperationException if the **add** method is not supported by the set.
ClassCastException if the class of **element** prevents it from being added to the set.
NullPointerException if **element** is **null** and the set does not support **null** elements.
IllegalArgumentException if some other aspect of **element** prevents it from being added to this set.

`public boolean` **addAll(Collection<?** `extends` **T> collectionToAdd)** *(Optional)*

Ensures that the calling object contains all the elements in `collectionToAdd`. Returns `true` if the calling object changed as a result of the call; returns `false` otherwise. Thus, if `collectionToAdd` is a `Set<T>`, then the calling object is changed to the union of itself with `collectionToAdd`.

Throws:

`UnsupportedOperationException` if the `addAll` method is not supported by the set.
`ClassCastException` if the class of some element of `collectionToAdd` prevents it from being added to the calling object.
`NullPointerException` if `collectionToAdd` contains one or more `null` elements and the calling object does not support `null` elements, or if `collectionToAdd` is `null`.
`IllegalArgumentException` if some aspect of some element of `collectionToAdd` prevents it from being added to the calling object.

`public void` **clear()**

Removes all the elements from the calling object.

Throws:

`UnsupportedOperationException` if the `clear` method is not supported by the calling object.

`public boolean` **remove(Object element)**

Removes the `element` from the calling object, if it is present. Returns `true` if the calling object contained the `element`; returns `false` otherwise.

Throws:

`ClassCastException` if the type of `element` is incompatible with the calling object (optional).
`NullPointerException` if `element` is `null` and the calling object does not support `null` elements (optional).
`UnsupportedOperationException` if the `remove` method is not supported by the calling object.

`public boolean` **removeAll(Collection<?> collectionToRemove)** *(Optional)*

Removes all the calling object's elements that are also contained in `collectionToRemove`. Returns `true` if the calling object was changed; otherwise returns `false`.

Throws:

`UnsupportedOperationException` if the `removeAll` method is not supported by the calling object.
`ClassCastException` if the types of one or more elements in `collectionToRemove` are incompatible with the calling object (optional).
`NullPointerException` if the calling object contains a `null` element and `collectionToRemove` does not support `null` elements (optional).
`NullPointerException` if `collectionToRemove` is `null`.

`public boolean retainAll(Collection<?> saveElements)` *(Optional)*

Retains only the elements in the calling object that are also contained in the collection `saveElements`. In other words, removes from the calling object all of its elements that are not contained in the collection `saveElements`. Returns `true` if the calling object was changed; otherwise returns `false`. If the argument is itself a `Set<T>`, this changes the calling object to the intersection of itself with the argument.

Throws:

`UnsupportedOperationException` if the `retainAll` method is not supported by the calling object.
`ClassCastException` if the types of one or more elements in the calling object are incompatible with `saveElements` (optional).
`NullPointerException` if `saveElements` contains a `null` element and the calling object does not support `null` elements (optional).
`NullPointerException` if `saveElements` is `null`.

Short

See Section 5.1 in Chapter 5.

String

Package: `java.lang`
`String` is marked `final` and so you cannot use it as a base class to derive another class.
Implements interfaces: `CharSequence`, `Comparable`, `Serializable`
Ancestor classes:

```
        Object
          |
        +--String
```

CONSTRUCTORS

`public String()`

Creates a `String` object that represents an empty character sequence. Note that this is a pretty useless constructor since `String` objects are immutable.

`public String(BufferedString buffer)`

Creates a new `String` object that contains the same sequence of characters that is currently contained in the `BufferedString` argument. This is a deep copy; subsequent modification of the `BufferedString` object does not affect the newly created string.

Throws:

`NullPointerException` if `buffer` is `null`.

```
public String(char[] value, int offset, int count)
```

Creates a new `String` that contains characters from a subarray of the character array argument. The `offset` argument is the index of the first character of the subarray, and the `count` argument specifies the length of the subarray. The contents of the subarray are copied. This is a deep copy; subsequent modifications of the character array do not affect the newly created string.

Throws:

`IndexOutOfBoundsException` if the elements specified by `offset` and `count` are not all within the bounds of the `value` array.
`NullPointerException` if `value` is null.

```
public String(String original)
```

Creates a new `String` object so that it represents the same sequence of characters as the argument. Unless an explicit copy of `original` is needed, use of this constructor is unnecessary since `String` objects are immutable.

Throws:

`NullPointerException` if `original` is null.

METHODS

```
public char charAt(int position)
```

Returns the character in the calling object string at the `position`. Positions are counted 0, 1, 2, etc.

EXAMPLE

After program executes `String greeting = "Hello!";`
`greeting.charAt(0)` returns `'H'`, and
`greeting.charAt(1)` returns `'e'`.

Throws:

`IndexOutOfBoundsException` if `position` is negative or not less than the length of the calling object string.

```
public int compareTo(String aString)
```

Compares the calling object string and the string argument to see which comes first in the lexicographic ordering. Lexicographic order is the same as alphabetical order but with the characters ordered as in Appendix 3. Note that in Appendix 3 all the uppercase letters are in regular alphabetical order and all the lowercase letters are in alphabetical order, but all the uppercase letters precede all the lowercase letters. So, lexicographic ordering is the same as alphabetical ordering when either both strings are all uppercase letters or both strings are all lowercase letters. If the calling string is first, it returns a negative value. If the two strings are equal, it returns zero. If the argument is first, it returns a positive number.

EXAMPLE

After program executes `String entry = "adventure";`
`entry.compareTo("zoo")` returns a negative number,
`entry.compareTo("adventure")` returns 0, and
`entry.compareTo("above")` returns a positive number.

Throws:

`NullPointerException` if `aString` is null.

```
public int compareToIgnoreCase(String aString)
```

Compares the calling object string and the string argument to see which comes first in the lexico-graphic ordering, treating uppercase and lowercase letters as being the same. (To be precise, all uppercase letters are treated as if they were their lowercase versions in doing the comparison.) Thus, if both strings consist entirely of letters, the comparison is for ordinary alphabetical order. If the calling string is first, it returns a negative value. If the two strings are equal, ignoring cases, it returns zero. If the argument is first, it returns a positive number.

EXAMPLE

After program executes `String entry = "adventure";`
`entry.compareToIgnoreCase("Zoo")` returns a negative number,
`entry.compareToIgnoreCase("Adventure")` returns `0`, and
`"Zoo".compareToIgnoreCase(entry)` returns a positive number.

Throws:

`NullPointerException` if `aString` is `null`.

```
public boolean contentEquals(StringBuffer stringBufferObject)
```

Returns `true` if and only if this `String` represents the same sequence of characters as the `String-Buffer` argument.

Throws:

`NullPointerException` if `stringBufferObject` is `null`.

```
public boolean equals(String otherString)
```

Returns `true` if the calling object string and the `otherString` are equal. Otherwise returns `false`.

EXAMPLE

After program executes `String greeting = "Hello";`
`greeting.equals("Hello")` returns `true`
`greeting.equals("Good-Bye")` returns `false`
`greeting.equals("hello")` returns `false`
Note that case matters: `"Hello"` and `"hello"` are not equal because one starts with an uppercase letter and the other starts with a lowercase letter.

```
public boolean equalsIgnoreCase(String otherString)
```

Returns `true` if the calling object string and the `otherString` are equal, considering uppercase and lowercase versions of a letter to be the same. Otherwise returns `false`.

EXAMPLE

After program executes `String name = "mary";`
`name.equalsIgnoreCase("Mary")` returns `true`

```
public int indexOf(String aString)
```

Returns the index (position) of the first occurrence of the string **aString** in the calling object string. Positions are counted 0, 1, 2, etc. Returns −1 if **aString** is not found.

EXAMPLE

After program executes `String greeting = "Hi Mary!";`
`greeting.indexOf("Mary")` returns 3, and
`greeting.indexOf("Sally")` returns −1.

Throws:

`NullPointerException` if **aString** is null.

```
public int indexOf(String aString, int start)
```

Returns the index (position) of the first occurrence of the string **aString** in the calling object string that occurs at or after position **start**. Positions are counted 0, 1, 2, etc. Returns −1 if **aString** is not found.

EXAMPLE

After program executes `String name = "Mary, Mary quite contrary";`
`name.indexOf("Mary", 1)` returns 6.
The same value is returned if 1 is replaced by any number up to and including 6.
`name.indexOf("Mary", 0)` returns 0.
`name.indexOf("Mary", 8)` returns −1.

Throws:

`NullPointerException` if **aString** is null.

```
public int lastIndexOf(String aString)
```

Returns the index (position) of the last occurrence of the string **aString** in the calling object string. Positions are counted 0, 1, 2, etc. Returns −1 if **aString** is not found.

EXAMPLE

After program executes `String name = "Mary, Mary, Mary quite so";`
`greeting.indexOf("Mary")` returns 0, and
`name.lastIndexOf("Mary")` returns 12.

Throws:

`NullPointerException` if **aString** is null.

```
public int length()
```

Returns the length of the calling object (which is a string) as a value of type **int**.

EXAMPLE

After program executes `String greeting = "Hello!";`
`greeting.length()` returns 6.

```
    public String substring(int start)
```

Returns the substring of the calling object string starting from `start` through to the end of the calling object. Positions are counted 0, 1, 2, etc. Be sure to notice that the character at position `start` is included in the value returned.

EXAMPLE

After program executes `String sample = "AbcdefG";`
`sample.substring(2)` returns `"cdefG"`.

Throws:

`IndexOutOfBoundsException` if `start` is negative or larger than the length of the calling object.

```
    public String substring(int start, int end)
```

Returns the substring of the calling object string starting from position `start` through, but not including, position `end` of the calling object. Positions are counted 0, 1, 2, etc. Be sure to notice that the character at position `start` is included in the value returned, but the character at position `end` is not included.

EXAMPLE

After program executes `String sample = "AbcdefG";`
`sample.substring(2, 5)` returns `"cde"`.

Throws:

`IndexOutOfBoundsException` if the `start` is negative, or `end` is larger than the length of this `String` object, or `start` is larger than `end`.

```
    public String toLowerCase()
```

Returns a string with the same characters as the calling object string, but with all letter characters converted to lowercase.

EXAMPLE

After program executes `String greeting = "Hi Mary!";`
`greeting.toLowerCase()` returns `"hi mary!"`.

```
    public String toUpperCase()
```

Returns a string with the same characters as the calling object string, but with all letter characters converted to uppercase.

EXAMPLE

After program executes `String greeting = "Hi Mary!";`
`greeting.toUpperCase()` returns `"HI MARY!"`.

```
    public String trim()
```

Returns a string with the same characters as the calling object string, but with leading and trailing whitespace removed. Whitespace characters are the characters that print as whit space on paper, such as the blank (space) character, the tab character, and the new-line character `'\n'`.

EXAMPLE

After program executes `String pause = "    Hmm    ";`
`pause.trim()` returns `"Hmm"`.

StringBuffer

Package: `java.lang`
StringBuffer is marked **final** and so you cannot use it as a base class to derive another class. Ancestor classes:

```
Object
   |
   +--StringBuffer
```

CONSTRUCTORS

   `public StringBuffer()`

Creates a **StringBuffer** object with no characters in it and an initial capacity of 16 characters.

   `public StringBuffer(int capacity)`

Constructs a **StringBuffer** object with no characters in it and an initial capacity specified by the argument.

Throws:

NegativeArraySizeException if **length** is less than 0. **NegativeArraySizeException** is a derived class of **RuntimeException**, and so is an unchecked exception, which means it is not required to be caught or declared in a **throws** clause.

   `public StringBuffer(String ordinaryString)`

Constructs a string buffer so that it represents the same sequence of characters as the **ordinaryString** argument; in other words, the initial content of the string buffer is a copy of **ordinaryString**. The initial capacity of the string buffer is 16 plus the length of **ordinaryString**.

Throws:

NullPointerException if **ordinaryString** is **null**.

METHODS

   `public StringBuffer append(char[] charArray,`
                              `int offset, int length)`

Appends the string representation of the characters in **charArray** starting at **charArray[offset]** and extending for a total of **length** characters. Note that the calling object is changed and a reference to the changed calling object is returned.

Throws:

ArrayIndexOutOfBoundsException if **offset** and **length** are not consistent with the range of **charArray**.

   `public StringBuffer append(char c)`

Appends the character argument to the **StringBuffer** calling object and returns this longer string.

```
public StringBuffer append(char[] charArray)
```

Appends the string representation of the **char** array argument to this string buffer. Note that the calling object is changed and a reference to the changed calling object is returned.

```
public StringBuffer append(double d)
```

Appends the string representation of the **double** argument to the **StringBuffer** calling object and returns this longer string.

```
public StringBuffer append(float d)
```

Appends the string representation of the **float** argument to the **StringBuffer** calling object and returns this longer string.

```
public StringBuffer append(int n)
```

Appends the string representation of the **int** argument to the **StringBuffer** calling object and returns this longer string.

```
public StringBuffer append(long n)
```

Appends the string representation of the **long** argument to the **StringBuffer** calling object and returns this longer string.

```
public StringBuffer append(String ordinaryString)
```

Appends the **String** argument to the **StringBuffer** calling object and returns this longer string. If **ordinaryString** is **null**, then the four characters **"null"** are appended to this string buffer. Note that the calling object is changed and a reference to the changed calling object is returned.

```
public StringBuffer append(StringBuffer bufferedString)
```

Appends the **StringBuffer** argument to the **StringBuffer** calling object and returns this longer string.
If **bufferedString** is **null**, then the four characters **"null"** are appended to this string buffer. Note that the calling object is changed and a reference to the changed calling object is returned.

```
public int capacity()
```

Returns the current capacity of the calling object. The capacity is the amount of storage currently available for characters. The capacity will automatically be increased if necessary.

```
public char charAt(int position)
```

Returns the character in the calling object string at **position**. Positions are counted 0, 1, 2, etc.

Throws:

IndexOutOfBoundsException if **position** is negative or not less than the length of the calling object.

```
contentEquals
```

There is no such method for the class **StringBuffer**, but see the method **contentEquals** for the class **String**.

```
public StringBuffer delete(int start, int end)
```

Removes the characters in a substring of the calling object. The substring to remove begins at the specified start and extends to the character at index end − 1 or to the end of the calling object if no such character exists. If start is equal to end, no changes are made. Note that the calling object is changed and a reference to the changed calling object is returned.

Throws:

StringIndexOutOfBoundsException if start is negative, greater than length(), or greater than end. StringIndexOutOfBoundsException is a derived class of RuntimeException, and so is an unchecked exception, which means it is not required to be caught or declared in a throws clause.

```
public void ensureCapacity(int minimumCapacity)
```

Ensures that the capacity of the calling object is at least equal to minimumCapacity. If the current capacity of the calling object is less than minimumCapacity, then the capacity is increased. The new capacity is the larger of: minimumCapacity and twice the old capacity, plus 2.
If the minimumCapacity is nonpositive, this method takes no action and simply returns.

```
Start public boolean equals(Object otherObject)
```

Warning: This is the method inherited from Object. It is not overridden for the class StringBuffer and does not work as you might expect. Normally, it should not be used.

```
public int indexOf(String aString)
```

Returns the index (position) of the first occurrence of the string aString in the calling object. Positions are counted 0, 1, 2, etc. Returns −1 if aString is not found. Note that the argument is of type String, not StringBuffer.

Throws:

NullPointerException if aString is null.

```
public int indexOf(String aString, int start)
```

Returns the index (position) of the first occurrence of the string aString in the calling object that occurs at or after position start. Positions are counted 0, 1, 2, etc. Returns −1 if aString is not found. Note that the argument is of type String, not StringBuffer.

Throws:

NullPointerException if aString is null.

```
public int lastIndexOf(String aString)
```

Returns the index (position) of the last occurrence of the string aString in the calling object string. Positions are counted 0, 1, 2, etc. Returns −1 if aString is not found. Note that the argument is of type String, not StringBuffer.

Throws:

NullPointerException if aString is null.

```
public int length()
```

Returns the length of the calling object as a value of type `int`.

```
public StringBuffer replace(int start,
                    int end, String ordinaryString)
```

Replaces the characters in a substring of the calling object with characters in the `ordinaryString`. The substring begins at the specified `start` and extends to the character at index `end` −1 or to the end of the calling object if no such character exists. First the characters in the substring are removed and then the specified `ordinaryString` is inserted at `start`. (The calling object will be lengthened to accommodate the `ordinaryString` if necessary.) Note that the calling object is changed and a reference to the changed calling object is returned.

Throws:

`StringIndexOutOfBoundsException` if `start` is negative, greater than `length()`, or greater than `end`. `StringIndexOutOfBoundsException` is a derived class of `RuntimeException`, and so is an unchecked exception, which means it is not required to be caught or declared in a `throws` clause.

```
public void setLength(int newLength)
```

Sets the length of the calling object. The calling object is altered to represent a new character sequence whose length is specified by the argument. For every nonnegative index k less than `newLength`, the character at index k in the new character sequence is the same as the character at index k in the old sequence. If the `newLength` argument is less than the current length of the string buffer, the string buffer is truncated to contain exactly the number of characters given by the `newLength` argument.
If the `newLength` argument is greater than the current length, sufficient null characters (`'\u0000'`) are appended to the string buffer so that length becomes the `newLength` argument.

Throws:

`IndexOutOfBoundsException` if `newLength` is negative.

```
public String substring(int start)
```

Returns the substring of the calling object starting from `start` through to the end of the calling object. Positions are counted 0, 1, 2, etc. Be sure to notice that the character at position `start` is included in the value returned. Note that the substring is returned as a value of type `String`, not `StringBuffer`.

Throws:

`StringIndexOutOfBoundsException` if `start` is negative or larger than the length of the calling object. `StringIndexOutOfBoundsException` is a derived class of `RuntimeException`, and so is an unchecked exception, which means it is not required to be caught or declared in a `throws` clause.

> `public String substring(int start, int end)`

Returns the substring of the calling object starting from position **start** through, but not including, position **end** of the calling object. Positions are counted 0, 1, 2, etc. Be sure to notice that the character at position **start** is included in the value returned, but the character at position **end** is not included. Also note that the substring is returned as a value of type **String**, not **StringBuffer**.

Throws:

StringIndexOutOfBoundsException if **start** is negative, or **end** is larger than the length of this calling object, or **start** is larger than **end**. **StringIndexOutOfBoundsException** is a derived class of **RuntimeException**, and so is an unchecked exception, which means it is not required to be caught or declared in a **throws** clause.

> `public String toString()`

Creates a new **String** object that contains the same character sequence calling object and returns that **String** object. Subsequent changes to the calling object do not affect the contents of the **String** returned.

StringTokenizer

Package: `java.util`.
Ancestor classes:

```
        Object
          |
          +--StringTokenizer
```

> `public StringTokenizer(String theString)`

Constructor for a tokenizer that will use whitespace characters as separators when finding tokens in **theString**.

> `public StringTokenizer(String theString, String delimiters)`

Constructor for a tokenizer that will use the characters in the string **delimiters** as separators when finding tokens in **theString**.

> `public StringTokenizer(String theString, String delimiters,`
> `                       boolean returnDelimiters)`

Creates a tokenizer similar to **StringTokenizer(String theString, String delimiters)**, but with the following differences: If **returnDelimiters** is **true**, the delimiters are also returned by **nextToken**; each delimiter is returned as a one-character **String**. If **returnDelimiters** is **false**, the deliminters are not returned by **nextToken**. Thus, if **returnDelimiters** is **false**, the tokenizer created is the same as with **StringTokenizer(String theString, String delimiters)**.

> `public int countTokens()`

Returns the number of tokens remaining to be returned by **nextToken**.

```
    public boolean hasMoreElements()
```
Same as **hasMoreTokens**.

```
    public boolean hasMoreTokens()
```
Tests whether there are more tokens available from this tokenizer's string. When used in conjunction with **nextToken**, it returns **true** as long as **nextToken** has not yet returned all the tokens in the string; returns **false** otherwise.

```
    public String nextToken()
```
Returns the next token from this tokenizer's string.

Throws:

NoSuchElementException if there are no more tokens to return. **NoSuchElementException** is one of the exceptions that need not be declared in a **throws** clause or caught in a **catch** block.

Vector<T>

Package: **java.util**
Ancestor classes:

```
        Object
          |
        +--AbstractCollection<T>
              |
            +--AbstractList<T>
                  |
                +--Vector<T>
```

CONSTRUCTORS

```
    public Vector()
```
Creates an empty vector with an initial capacity of **10**. When the vector needs to increase its capacity, the capacity doubles.

```
    public Vector(Collection<? extends T> c)
```
Creates a vector that contains all the elements of the collection **c** in the same order as they have in **c**. If **c** is a vector, the capacity of the created vector will be **c.size()**, not **c.capacity**.

Throws:
NullPointerException if **c** is **null**.

```
    public Vector(int initialCapacity)
```
Creates an empty vector with the specified initial capacity. When the vector needs to increase its capacity, the capacity doubles.

```
public Vector(int initialCapacity, int capacityIncrement)
```

Constructs an empty vector with the specified initial capacity and capacity increment. When the vector needs to grow, it will add room for **capacityIncrement** more items.

ARRAYLIKE METHODS

```
public T get(int index)
```

Returns the element at the specified index. This is analogous to returning a[index] for an array a.

Throws:

ArrayIndexOutOfBoundsException if the **index** is not greater than or equal to 0 and less than the current size of the vector.

```
public T set(int index, T newElement)
```

Sets the element at the specified **index** to **newElement**. The element previously at that position is returned. If you draw an analogy between the vector and an array a, this is analogous to setting a[index] to the value **newElement**.

Throws:

ArrayIndexOutOfBoundsException if the **index** is not greater than or equal to 0 and strictly less than the current size of the vector.

METHODS TO ADD ELEMENTS

```
public void add(int index, T newElement)
```

Inserts **newElement** as an element in the calling vector at the specified index. Each element in the vector with an index greater or equal to **index** is shifted upward to have an index that is 1 greater than the value it had previously.

Note that you can use this method to add an element after the last current element. The capacity of the vector is increased if that is required.

Throws:

ArrayIndexOutOfBoundsException if the index is not greater than or equal to 0 and less than *or equal to* the current size of the vector.

```
public boolean add(T newElement)
```

Adds **newElement** to the end of the calling vector and increases its size by 1. The capacity of the vector is increased if that is required. Returns **true** if successful. Normally used as a **void** method.

METHODS TO REMOVE ELEMENTS

```
public void clear()
```

Removes all elements from the calling vector and sets its size to zero.

```
public T remove(int index)
```

Deletes the element at the specified index and returns the element deleted. Each element in the vector with an index greater than or equal to `index` is decreased to have an index that is 1 less than the value it had previously.

Throws:

`ArrayIndexOutOfBoundsException` if the `index` is not greater than or equal to 0 and less than the current size of the vector.

```
public boolean remove(Object theElement)
```

Removes the first occurrence of `theElement` from the calling vector. If `theElement` is found in the vector, then each element in the vector with an index greater than or equal to `theElement`'s index is decreased to have an index that is 1 less than the value it had previously. Returns `true` if `theElement` was found (and removed). Returns `false` if `theElement` was not found in the calling vector.

SEARCH METHODS

```
public boolean contains(Object target)
```

Returns `true` if `target` is an element of the calling vector; otherwise returns `false`.

```
public int indexOf(Object target)
```

Returns the index of the first element that is equal to `target`. Uses the method `equals` of the object `target` to test for equality. Returns −1 if `target` is not found.

```
public int indexOf(Object target, int startIndex)
```

Returns the index of the first element that is equal to `target`, but only considers indices that are greater than or equal to `startIndex`. Uses the method `equals` of the object `target` to test for equality. Returns −1 if `target` is not found.

```
public boolean isEmpty()
```

Returns `true` if the calling vector is empty (that is, has size 0); otherwise returns `false`.

```
public int lastIndexOf(Object target)
```

Returns the index of the last element that is equal to `target`. Uses the method `equals` of the object `target` to test for equality. Returns −1 if `target` is not found.

```
public T firstElement()
```

Returns the first element of the calling vector.

Throws:

`NoSuchElementException` if the vector is empty.

```
public T lastElement()
```

Returns the last element of the calling vector.

Throws:

NoSuchElementException if the vector is empty.

ITERATORS

```
public Iterator<T> iterator()
```

Returns an iterator for the calling vector. (Iterators are discussed in Chapter 16.)

```
ListIterator<T> listIterator()
```

Returns a list iterator for the calling vector. (Iterators are discussed in Chapter 16.)

```
ListIterator<T> listIterator(int index)
```

Returns a list iterator for the calling vector starting at index. The first element to be returned by the iterator is the one at index. (Iterators are discussed in Chapter 16.)

CONVERTING TO AN ARRAY

```
public Object[] toArray()
```

Returns an array containing all of the elements in the vector. The elements of the array are indexed the same as in the vector.

```
public <E> E[] toArray(E[] a)
```

Note that the type parameter E is not the same as T. So, E can be any reference type; it need not be the type T in Collection<T>. For example, E might be an ancestor type of T.
Returns an array containing all of the elements in the calling object. The elements in the returned array are in the same order as in the calling object. The argument a is used primarily to specify the type of the array returned. The exact details are described in the table for the Collection<T>.

Throws:

ArrayStoreException if the base type of a is not an ancestor class of all the elements in the vector. NullPointerException if a is null.

MEMORY MANAGEMENT

```
public int capacity()
```

Returns the current capacity of the calling vector.

```
public void ensureCapacity(int newCapacity)
```

Increases the capacity of the calling vector to ensure that it can hold at least newCapacity elements. Using ensureCapacity can sometimes increase efficiency, but its use is not needed for any other reason.

```
public void setSize(int newSize)
```

Sets the size of the calling vector to `newSize`. If `newSize` is greater than the current size, the new elements receive the value `null`. If `newSize` is less than the current size, all elements at index `newSize` and greater are discarded.

Throws:

`ArrayIndexOutOfBoundsException` if `newSize` is negative.

```
public int size()
```

Returns the number of elements in the calling vector.

```
public void trimToSize()
```

Trims the capacity of the calling vector to be the vector's current size. This is used to save storage.

MAKE A COPY

```
public Object clone()
```

Returns a clone of the calling vector. The clone is an identical copy of the calling vector.

OLDER METHODS

These are methods that are not part of the newer collection framework, but are retained for backward compatibility. You should use the above newer methods instead. But, you may find these used in older code.

```
public void addElement(T newElement)
```

Same as `add`.

```
public void insertElementAt(T newElement, int index)
```

Same as `add`.

```
public T elementAt(int index)
```

Same as `get`.

```
public void removeAllElements()
```

Same as `clear`.

```
public boolean removeElement(Object theElement)
```

Same as `remove`.

```
public void removeElementAt(int index)
```

Same as `remove` but does not return the element removed.

```
public void setElementAt(T newElement, int index)
```

Same as `set` with the arguments reversed but does not return the element replaced.

`WindowListener` Interface

Package: `java.awt.event`
The `WindowEvent` class is also in this package.
Extends the `EventListener` interface.

`public void windowActivated(WindowEvent e)`

Invoked when a window is activated. When you click in a window, it becomes the activated window. Other actions can also activate a window.

`public void windowClosed(WindowEvent e)`

Invoked when a window has been closed.

`public void windowClosing(WindowEvent e)`

Invoked when a window is in the process of being closed. Clicking the close-window button causes an invocation of this method.

`public void windowDeactivated(WindowEvent e)`

Invoked when a window is deactivated. When a window is activated, all other windows are deactivated. Other actions can also deactivate a window.

`public void windowDeiconified(WindowEvent e)`

Invoked when a window is deiconified. When you activate a minimized window, it is deiconified.

`public void windowIconified(WindowEvent e)`

Invoked when a window is iconified. When you click the minimize button in a `JFrame`, it is iconified.

`public void windowOpened(WindowEvent e)`

Invoked when a window has been opened.

Index

Symbols

\# (sharp), 663
%n (line breaks), 65
% (remainder) operators, 26
&& (and) operator, 113
' (quotes), 23
() (parentheses), 24–26, 95
* (conditional) operators, 106–107
+ (concatenation) operator, 34
++ (increment) operators, 30–33
+ (plus) operator, 195
, (commas) in `for` statements, 135–139
-- (decrement) operators, 30–33
... (ellipsis), 370, 663
. (dots), 7
; (semicolons) in `for` statements, 137
? wildcard, 884
= (assignment) statements, 7, 16
  arrays, 348–350
  class type variables, 278–279, 283
== (equality) operators, 108
  arrays, 348–350
= (equal sign), 7
@ tag, 319
[] (square brackets), 335–336
\n (new lines), 64
{} (braces), 177
  placing of, 97
|| (or) operator, 113
~ (tilde), 663

A

`AbstractButton` class, 970–973
abstract classes, 494–500
  interfaces, 697
`AbstractCollection<T>` class, 892
abstract data types. *See* ADTs
abstraction, 197
`AbstractList<T>` class, 892
`AbstractMap<K, V>` class, 902
abstract methods, 494, 497
abstract names, 595
`AbstractSequentialList<T>` class, 896

`AbstractSet<T>` class, 892
Abstract Window Toolkit (AWT), 924
access
  arrays, 335–340
  default, 442
  friendly, 442
  indexes, `ArrayList` class, 743
  inner/outer classes, 717
  packages, 440–446
  permissions, modifying, 426–430
  private members, 205
  random access to binary files, 618–624
  to redefined base methods, 447–449
  static variables, 256
accessor methods, 200–206
  arrays, 364
  automatic unboxing, 267
  leaking, 303
action command, 973
action drawings, 1038–1044
action events, 934–941
`ActionListener` interface, 935
action listeners, 934–941
`actionPerformed` method, 935
actions, programming, 963
activation records, 645
actual parameters, 185.
    See arguments
Adapter patterns, 667–668
`addActionListener` object, 935
adding
  to `ArrayList` class, 746–747
  colors, 960, 1045
  listeners to menus, 971–972
  `main` method, 252
  menus, `JFrame` class, 970
  nodes, 792, 824–827, 828
`add` method, 744
addresses, 273
ADTs (abstract data types), 197
algorithms
  binary searches, 654–662
  loops, 128–132
  sorting, 669
alphabetical ordering, 110–111

ancestor classes, 424
and (&&) operator, 113
anonymous classes, 728–731
anonymous objects, 286–291
APIs (application programming interfaces), 197
appending text files, 571–574
applets, 4–5
application programming interfaces. *See* APIs
applications, 4. *See also* programs
  examples of, 5–8
applying
  `ArrayList` class, 742–747
  `Comparable` interfaces, 702, 704
  constructors, 223–224
  `drawString` method, 1052–1054
  exceptions, 543–545
  `File` class, 695–596
  icons, 1011–1013
  inner classes, 730–731
  iterators, 822–823
  linked lists, 790–795
  panels, 957–960
  references, 291–310
  `WindowAdapter` class, 1009
arcs
  drawing, 1033–1037
  specifying, 1036
areas (text), 978–985
  scroll bars, 1020–1022
  view ports, 1018
arguments, 7
  arrays, 351, 391
  constructors, 222
  copy constructors, 301–307
  correspondence, 182
  length of arrays, 348
  `main` methods, 354–355
  no-argument constructors, 225–226
  null constants to methods, 297
  output, formatting, 63–64
  parameters, 179
  `String` class, 36
  terminology, 185
  variables, indexes, 346
  wrapper classes, 271